I A

USSR

Zahony

BORSOD-ABAÚJ-ZEMPLÉN

◎Miskolc

SZABOLCS-SZATMÁR

◉Nyíregyháza

Bükk Mts.

arjan

Matra Mts.

Eger

HEVES

Tisa

Hatvan

Debrecen◎

HAJDU-BIHAR

rzsébet

SZOLNOK

●Szolnok

emet

BÉKÉS

Békéscsaba

●Szentes

CSONGRÁD

◉Hodmezövasarhely

ROMANIA

◎Szeged

Tisa

⊛ Capital, 1,750,00
◎ Over 100,00
◉ 75–100,00
● 25–75,000

EXPLOSION

EXPLOSION
The Hungarian Revolution of 1956

John P. C. Matthews

HIPPOCRENE BOOKS
New York

Cataloging-in-Publication data for this book is available from the Library of Congress.

ISBN: 978-0-7818-1174-3
ISBN-10: 0-7818-1174-0

Published 2007 by Hippocrene Books, Inc.

For information, contact:
Hippocrene Books, Inc.
171 Madison Avenue
New York, NY 10016

Printed in the United States of America

*This book is dedicated
to the nameless and all-but-forgotten children of Budapest,
whose selfless feats of incredible bravery astonished the Russians
and inspired their elders to carry on the fight to victory,
when that prospect seemed least likely*

CONTENTS

Acknowledgements

THE LONGER I WORKED ON THE BOOK the more I realized that I was just part of a gigantic team effort. Hundreds of people had already played key roles in obtaining, collecting and providing information. I mean, of course, the scores of journalists, writers, diplomats, memoirists and scholars on whose output I have drawn so heavily. To name just a few there are the wire service journalists Ronald Farquhar (Reuters), Endre Márton (Associated Press), Ilona Nyilás and Russell Jones (United Press) and Katherine Clark (International News Service). Then there are the foreign correspondents like Noel Barber (*Daily Mail*), Sefton Delmer (*Daily Express*), Peter Fryer (*Daily Worker*), Gordon Shepherd (*Daily Telegraph*), Victor Zorza (*Manchester Guardian*), Americans John MacCormac and Homer Bigert (*New York Times*), and Barrett McGurn (*New York Herald Tribune*), Fritz Molden of Vienna's *Die Presse* and Ernst Halperin of Munich's *Münchner Merkur*, and magazine correspondents like John Sadovy (*LIFE*) and Jean-Pierre Pedrazzini (*Paris-Match*). Then there are all those RFE correspondents in Austria and for a while in Hungary, largely unkown to the public, of whom Collins, Gedye, Hier, Koch, Leason, Michie, Napier, Palásthy and Tormay are worth mentioning. Also there are memoirs by such participants as Sándor Kopácsi, Béla Kiraly, Endre Márton Tibor Meray, Gergely Pongrátz and the two young Freedom Fighters writing under the fictitious names of "László Beke" and "Tamás Szabó." Absolutely indispensable are the informed, on-the-spot dispatches of British and American diplomats Sir Leslie Fry and A. Spencer Barnes. But equally valuable are two anthologies assembled forty-five years apart: Melvin Lasky's *A White Book, The Hungarian Revolution ...as recorded in Documents, Dispatches, Eye-Witness Accounts and Worldwide Reactions*, 1957 and *The Hungarian Revolution of 1956: A*

History in Documents, 2002, assembled by Hungarian and American scholars Csaba Békés, Malcolm Byrne and János Rainer.

And, of course, there are books by scholars such as Tamás Aczél, Tibor Filep, Charles Gati, Johanna Granville, Jenö Györkei and Miklós Horváth, András B. Hegedüs, Bennett Kovrig, Sergei N. Khrushchev, György Litván, Zsuzsánna Körösi and Adrienne Molnár, Béla Száz, Strobe Talbott, William Taubman, George Urban and many, many others.

Many of the above-mentioned were no longer with us by the time I began work on the book, so I was unable to mine anything but their written works. I do feel greatly indebted to all of them.

But it is my interaction with and help from living persons which brought home to me what a team endeavor I was embarked upon.

In Hungary, first and foremost, Dr. Csaba Békés of the Institute for the History of the 1956 Revolution gave me invaluable advice and help and found me collaborators without whom I would have been at a crippling disadvantage. Among these are the late András B. Hegedüs, László Eörsi, György Litván, Adrienne Molnár at the Institute, Balázs Szalontai with whom I spent many hours in the Széchényi Library, and Dan Tura who acted as my guide and interpreter around Budapest and Csepel and accompanied me to Tatabánya, Györ, Mosonmagyaróvár and Sópron and even to the Staatsarchiv in Vienna, then helped in selecting for translation appropriate interviews conducted earlier by the Institute. Friends of many years, Erika Laszlo and Eva Veress gave me repectively advice and a letter which had been in the latter's attic for over 40 years. Two Hungarians I have yet to meet, but without whose help this book could never have been published, are András Bocz of the English Department of Pécs University, who did a great amount of excellent translating of Hungarian documents and portions of books for me and then proceeded to translate the entire book back into Hungarian and act as my agent in Hungary, and last, but certainly not least, Áttila Szakolczai of the Institute for the Study of the Hungarian Revolution of 1956, who read the entire uncut manuscript and found literally hundreds of errors, large and small, thus preventing a virtual catastrophe and greatly improving the accuracy of the book's contents. In addition he gave me much valuable information which I was able to incorporate into my text. Finally he wrote a letter highly recommending its publication in Hungary. To all of these Hungarian colleagues I am profoundly grateful.

In the United States the greatest support has come from my wife, Verna, who not only solved innumerable computer crises into which I got myself and copy-read and corrected every day's output, but willingly sacrificed most of her normal social life to my seven-days-a-week (and frequently to 10:30 p.m.) writing schedule. I should add that my computer-wise son, Kai, came to my rescue when I inadvertently, but permanently, wiped out 26,000 words from my computer. He brought back more than half of it by scanning some rough hard copy I had fortunately made.

Next, I am greatly indebted to Margery Cuyler, who volunteered to act as my editor, chapter by chapter, turning opaque prose into readable English.

Equally essential to the enterprise was my old friend and school and college roommate, Ralph C. Woodward, who cheered me on from the beginning, then stepped in as my agent when finding a publisher became all-important.

Advice and information from two friends of almost as long-standing—colleagues from Radio Free Europe's Central Newsroom days—Bernard V. Leason and Leslie H. Whitten, Jr., were more than welcome, the latter convincing me to drop one chapter which he clearly saw did not fit.

Two old friends from academia, distinguished Professor of European History emeritus of Columbia University István Deák and Professor of Politics Charles Gati of Johns Hopkins University's School of Advanced International Studies in Washington, D.C. kindly agreed to read portions of the MS offering corrections and advice, which I gladly took.

Dr. August Molnár, President of the American Hungarian Foundation in New Brunswick, New Jersey, told me of the existence of the files from the UN Committee on the Problem of Hungary which the UN had turned over to the Foundation when it could no longer house them. He generously allowed me full use of this archive. I was ably assisted there by his staff members Margaret Papai and Patricia Fazekás. I am also grateful for the courteous and efficient service of the following curators and archivists: Ellen Scaruffi and Tanya Chebotarev at the Rare Book and Manuscript Library of Columbia University; David Haight, Michelle Kopfer and Chalsea Millner at the Dwight D. Eisenhower Library in Abilene, Kansas; and Elena Davidson, Anatole Shmeleve and A. Ross Johnson at the Hoover Institution on War, Revolution and Peace at Stanford University.

A few documents and the letter from Pál Veress had already been translated by Rita di Fiore, but I would have been lost without the translation services of Judit Hajnal Ward, Foreign Title Specialist at Rutgers University

EXPLOSION

Libraries, and the team of translators she assembled and headed: Andrea Kicsák, Áttila Köszeghy, Ábel Meszáros, and Judit Meszáros Ward.

While ninety-five percent of the book is based on written documentation, the presence in this country of two participants, one from the very beginning, the other a major player at the very end (1988 and on), plus the son of the major Soviet leader of that time, was too important to pass up. I am most grateful for the interviews granted me by Stephen (Istvan) Lakatos, formerly of Szeged University, Ivan Berend, author of the famous Berend report reversing thirty years' contention that the revolution was a "fascist counter-revolution," now a professor of history at UCLA, and Sergei N. Khrushchev, now a professor of international affairs at Brown University.

There are countless others who contributed in one way or another, but I will mention only the following: Greta Cuyler, Ambassador William Harrop, Paul Henze, Professor Mark Kramer, Kati Márton, Professor Károly Nagy, Dr. Áttila Pók, Margery Perkins, András Pongrátz, William S. R. Rogers and Richard Stibolt.

It has been a humbling experience to work with so many people whose minds and writing skills are so far superior to mine. It has also been fun.

Some of the Main Actors in This Book*

Andropov, Yuri Vladimirovich (1914–1984) A Soviet Communist Party careerist, from July 1954 to March 1957 Soviet Ambassador to Hungary, between 1967 and 1982 head of the Soviet KGB (secret police) and from May 1982 to his death in November 1984, Premier of the Soviet Union.

Barnes, A. Spencer, Chargé d'Affaires of the U.S. Budapest Legation from August 1956 until the arrival of the new Minister, Edward T. Wailes, in the middle of the Revolution. He resumed this position after Wailes was recalled in early 1957 until replaced by Garret G. Ackerman, Jr.

Beam, Jacob D. (1908–1993) Deputy Assistant Secretary of State for European Affairs from October 1955 to June 1957.

"Beke, László" A married student at the Fine Arts Faculty in Pest who fought in the Revolution and fled with his wife before the second intervention, emigrating to Canada where he wrote his memoir, *A Student's Diary*, on which portions of this book are based. It was written under a pseudonym to protect his parents and friends, still in Hungary, and was published in 1958.

Bibó, István (1911–1979) University Lecturer in Szeged, Minister of State for the Petöfi Party in the Nagy Government and the only government minister to remain at his post in the Parliament building when the Russians

---

*Excluding such world figures as Eisenhower, Dulles, Nagy and Khrushchev

invaded on November 4, 1956. He was sentenced to life imprisonment in 1958 but freed in the general amnesty of 1963.

Bulganin, Nikolai A. (1895–1975) Chairman of the Soviet Council of Ministers (i.e., Premier) at the time of the Revolution, but basically a mouthpiece for Khrushchev.

Dobi, István (1898–1968) Originally a Smallholders politician, but basically a stooge for the Communist Party, he was chairman of the Hungarian Presidential Council (i.e. President), largely a figurehead position, from 1952 to 1967.

Donáth, Ferenc (1913–1986) A supporter of Imre Nagy who was arrested in 1951 and sentenced to fifteen years in prison by the Rákosi government, later rehabilitated and a member of the Nagy government, he was sentenced to 12 years imprisonment in 1958, but amnestied in 1960.

Dudás, József (1912–1957) A Communist partisan during World War II, he was dismissed from the Party in 1945 and joined the Smallholders. During the Revolution he headed a fighting group called the Hungarian National Revolutionary Committee, which acted as though it were the new, emerging revolutionary government. He was arrested, tried and executed in January 1957.

Erdei, Ferenc (1910–1971) General Secretary of the National Peasant Party, he was made a Minister in Imre Nagy's government and was taken prisoner with Maléter at Tököl the night of November 3, 1956, but released shortly thereafter.

Farquhar, Ronald A Scot who was one of Reuters most experienced correspondents in East Central Europe, he came down from his permanent posting in Prague to cover the Revolution after the first few days and ended by being the last western correspondent still reporting from Budapest well into 1957.

Fry, Sir Leslie British Minister in Budapest before, during and after the Revolution.

Gerö, Ernö (1898–1980) A leading Communist politician who returned to Hungary with the Soviet Army in 1944. He was in the Central Leadership serving as head of various ministries until 1952 when he became Rákosi's deputy as Deputy Prime Minister. He was promoted to Prime Minister in July 1956 when Rákosi was forced out. It was his hard-line speech on the evening of October 23 which triggered the Revolution. On October 28 he fled to the Soviet Union, where he stayed until 1960 but was allowed to join the new Hungarian Communist Party. He was expelled from this in 1962, ending his career.

Gomulka, Wladislaw (1905–1982) A Polish Communist who escaped Stalin's purges by being in the Polish Underground instead of in Moscow, he was expelled in 1949, imprisoned from 1951 to 1954, then placed under house arrest. In 1956 he was readmitted to the Party and in October, four days before the outbreak of the Revolution in Hungary, elected to the Polish Central Committee and made First Party Secretary, contrary to Soviet wishes.

Grebennyik, Kuzmin Y. With the rank of Brigadier General, he was the Soviet Union's Budapest City Commander from November 4th on under the direction of KGB General Ivan A. Serov.

Griffith, William E. (1920–1998) Radio Free Europe's Political Advisor in Munich before, during and after the Revolution.

Hayter, Sir William G. (1905–1995) British Ambassador to Moscow from 1953 to 1957.

Hoover, Herbert C. Jr. (1903–1969) Under Secretary of State under John Foster Dulles and chairman of the Operations Coordinating Board from October 1954 to February 1957.

Horváth, Imre (1901–1958) His whole career was in the Hungarian foreign and diplomatic service. In July 1956 he was appointed Foreign Minister by Ernö Gerö, then fired by Nagy when he came to power and later reinstated by János Kádár.

Horváth, Márton (1906–1987) Editor-in-chief of *Szabad Nép* from 1954 to

November 1956. Was not allowed to join the new Communist Party (Hungarian Socialist Workers' Party) due to his support of the Revolution, but was never prosecuted.

Iván-Kovács, László (1930–1957) First organizer and commander of the Corvin Passage group and appointed to the Revolutionary Armed Forces Committee of the National Guard, he was arrested on March 12, 1957, tried, sentenced to death and executed on December 30, 1957.

Jackson, C. D. (1902–1964) Special assistant to President Eisenhower for psychological warfare operations from February 1953 to March 1954.

Kádár, János (1912–1989) Hungarian Minister of the Interior from 1948 to 1950, imprisoned by Rákosi from 1951 to 1954, a district party secretary from July 1956, elected on Oct. 25, 1956 to First Party Secretary, a Minister of State in the Nagy government, deserted on November 1 and appointed by the Russians to head their totally controlled regime from November 4 on. Premier of the Hungarian Socialist Workers' state from that date until April 1958 and First Party Secretary from Nov. 4, 1956 to May 1988.

Kéthly, Anna (1896–1976) Chairperson of the newly constituted Social Democratic Party in October 1956, named Minister of State in the Nagy government, chaired the Hungarian Revolutionary Council in exile in Strasbourg, France from 1957 on.

Király, Béla (1912–) A career Army officer who had reached the rank of General by 1952, he was condemned in a show trial in that year to life in prison; released for reasons of health in September 1956, he was appointed by Nagy to be Commander of the National Guard (Revolutionary Armed Forced Committee), resisted capture and fought in a long retreat to the Austrian border, established the World Federation of Hungarian Freedom Fighters in early 1957, took his Ph.D. at Columbia University and became a professor of history, and returned to Hungary in June 1989. Promoted to Colonel General in 1990, ran successfully for Parliament and served as a member from 1990 to 1994.

Kopácsi, Sándor (1922–2001) A colonel and Chief of Police for Budapest in the fall of 1956, he was appointed by Imre Nagy to be deputy commander of the National Guard under General Király. Part of the Nagy trial in 1958, he was sentenced to life in prison, but amnestied under the general amnesty in 1963 and emigrated to Canada.

Kovács, Béla (1908–1959) Chairman of the Smallholders' Party from 1945–1947, when he was arrested and sentenced to 20 years in prison in the USSR. He was released in 1956, again headed the Smallholders' Party and was made a Minister of State in the Imre Nagy government. Arrested in 1957 and held briefly, he was never prosecuted.

Loszonczy, Géza (1917–1957) Sentenced to 25 years in prison in a 1951 show trial, he was released in 1954 when Imre Nagy came to power, and became editor of *Magyar Nemzet* (Hungarian Nation) during 1956. Named a Minister of State in the Nagy government, he fled with Nagy to the Yugoslav Embassy, was interned with Nagy in Romania, was to be tried with Nagy but died in prison while on a hunger strike before the trial.

Malenkov, Georgii M. (1901–1988) Member of the Soviet Central Committee from 1937 to 1957, Chairman of the Council of Ministers (Presidium) (in effect Prime Minister) from March 1953 to February 1955, deputy Prime Minister from February 1955 to June 1957, at which time he was demoted to director of a power station in central Siberia.

Márton, Endre (1910–2005) During the Revolution Chief Associated Press correspondent in Budapest, while his wife, Ilona Nýilas, worked for United Press. As Hungarian citizens, both were jailed in January 1955. He was not freed until August 1956. Both covered the entire Revolution and aftermath, only leaving the country with their two small daughters in mid-January 1957, at which point they emigrated to the U.S.

Mikoyan, Anastas I. (1895–1978) Member of the Soviet Presidium from 1935 to 1966, he was First Deputy Chairman from 1955 to 1957 and again from 1957 to 1964. As the Politburo's expert on Hungary he traveled frequently to Hungary before, during and after the Revolution.

Mindszenty, Cardinal József (1892–1975) Primate of Hungary, he was arrested late in 1948, tortured, and finally tried and sentenced in February 1949 to life imprisonment. Freed during the Revolution, he was given refuge in the U.S Legation in Budapest on Nov. 4, 1956, where he remained until September 1971, at which time he was allowed, actually forced, to leave for the West under an agreement between the Vatican and the Kadar government.

Münnich, Ferenc (1886–1967) Hungarian Ambassador to the USSR under Rakosi, September 1954 to August 1956, Ambassador to Yugoslavia under Gerö from August 1956 to October 25, 1956, Member of the Central Committee, the Military Committee and Presidium during the Revolution, he was made Minister of the Interior in the Nagy government, then deserted with Kadar on November 1st and headed both the Interior and Defense Ministries under Kádár until promoted to Prime Minister in April 1958, in which capacity he served until 1961.

Piros, László (1917–2006) Minister of the Interior, July 1954 to October 26, 1956, fled to the USSR with Gero and Hegedüs on October 28, but returned November 3 to participate in the arrest of General Maléter and his delegation at Tököl. Went back to USSR on November 10, 1956 and only returned to Hungary in 1958.

Pongrátz, Gergely (1932–2005) One of the commanders of the Corvin Passage group until November 1, 1956, when he was elected top commander, he, with his brothers, managed to evade the Russians escape to the West and emigrate to the U.S. where he later wrote, in Hungarian, *Corvin Circle 1956*.

Pongrátz, Ödön (1923–) Eldest of six Pongrátz brothers who all fought in the Revolution, he, having served as an officer in the Hungarian Army, was one of the earliest commanders of the Corvin Passage group. He was appointed to the Revolutionary Armed Forced Committee on November 1, 1956 as the chief representative of the civilian Freedom Fighters on that body. Escaped with his brothers and emigrated to the U.S.

Ráczá, Sándor (1933–) At twenty-three he became a member of his local factory workers' council; after the second Soviet intervention he was elected to the Central Workers' Council of Greater Budapest. On November 14, after eloquently criticizing the performance of the Council's chairman in negotiation with Kádár and calling for a vote of no confidence, he was surprisingly elected Chairman himself and began to negotiate with some success directly with the Soviet High command. But on December 11 he was arrested at the Parliament building when he arrived to negotiate with Kádár. Sentenced to life imprisonment in 1958, he was freed under the general amnesty of 1963.

Rajk, László (1909–1949) Minister of the Interior, then Foreign Minister, he was the first major figure in Eastern Europe to be arrested on charges of "Titoism" and being a spy for the West. Sentenced to death and quickly executed after this show trial in 1949, he was declared innocent and rehabilitated in 1956 and reburied along with three others similarly tried and executed in a ceremony on October 6, 1956, which attracted a crowd of 200,000 people and was a precursor to the Revolution.

Rákosi, Mátyás (1892–1971) Known to his compatriots as "the Little Stalin," he was First Secretary of the Hungarian Communist Party from 1945 until July 18, 1956, when he was replaced by Ernö Gerö. Flown to the Soviet Union three days later, he made repeated attempts to play a role in Hungarian affairs from his exile in the USSR or simply to return to his native land to die there—all of them unsuccessful.

Révai, József (1898–1959) An ideologue and one of the four most powerful Stalinists in Hungary, he was Minister of Education from 1945 to 1953 and a member of the Party Politburo (Presidium) until he was dropped on October 24, 1956 and fled Moscow. He did not dare return to Hungary until April 1957, at which time he became a member of the new Communist Party's Central Committee.

Serov, A. Ivan (1905–1991) Head of the KGB from 1953 to 1958, he gained his reputation during the Second World War by carrying out mass deportations from the Baltic States. Sent to Hungary at the very beginning of the Revolution to Command the Soviet and Hungarian State Security forces up through December 1956, he was in overall charge, outranking the Soviet military commanders, in fact, if not officially.

Suslov, Mikhail A. (1902–1982) A member of the Soviet Presidium from 1955 to 1982, he accompanied Mikoyan in his trips to Hungary during the

Revolution and took part in the Politburo session on the night of October 28–29, 1956.

Szábo, János (1897–1957) A fifty-nine year old truck driver, he became known as "Uncle Szabo" during the Revolution as he organized and commanded armed groups made up largely of teenagers at Széna Square. Captured in the Pilisi hills in December, he was one of the first to be tried and his execution was announced by Radio Budapest on February 5, 1957.

"Szábo, Tamás," (1941–) Pseudonym of a 15-year-old boy who fought in the Revolution and then escaped to the West, settling in Paris. His book, *Boy on a Rooftop*, on which parts of this book are based, was first published in French in 1957 and in English in 1958.

Szigethy, Attila (1912–1957) A leader of the National Peasant Party, he was considered acceptable to the Communists in that he was elected to represent the city of Györ in Parliament from 1947 to 1957. Active in the Revolution, he was elected chairman of the Györ National Council and the Transdanubian National Council. Arrested, he managed to commit suicide before he could be tried.

Szilágyi, Jozsef (1912–1958) A close friend of Nagy, he headed Nagy's secretariat during the Revolution and was tried with him and executed in June 1958.

Tildy, Zoltán (1889–1961) Founding member of the Smallholders' Party and President of Hungary from 1946 to 1948, he was kept under house arrest from then until the Revolution in 1956. He was a Minister of State in Nagy's government; tried and sentenced to six years in prison in 1958, he was released in an early amnesty the following year.

Voroshilov, Klementi E. (1881–1969) Chairman of the Allied Control Commission in Hungary from 1945 to 1946, Deputy Chairman of the USSR Council of Ministers from 1946 to 1953, chairman of the Council of Ministers (in effect, President of the Soviet Union) from 1953 to 1960.

Wailes, Edward T. U. S. Minister to Budapest from the fall of 1956 to the spring of 1957, he arrived in the middle of the Revolution and was never able to present his credentials to the Nagy government and declined to do so to the Kadar government, so Washington was forced to recall him in early 1957.

Zhukov, Georgii K. (1896–1974) Soviet military hero in the Second World War, he served as Soviet Minister of Defense from 1955 to 1957. He was the senior commander of the Soviet Army during the second Soviet intervention.

Preface

THE HUNGARIAN REVOLUTION OF 1956 is one of the great historical events of the twentieth century. It was an unplanned, leaderless, spontaneous explosion brought on by a confluence of fateful errors. In late October and early November of 1956 the world's attention was riveted on the uprising in Budapest and the revolution which quickly enveloped the whole country; even more so when it was all brutally crushed by the Soviet Union in what seemed like just a few days. The editors of *Time* magazine jettisoned their candidates for "Man of the Year" at the last minute to put a painting of a composite "Hungarian Freedom Fighter" on the cover as "Man of the Year."

But in less than a year, the Revolution was overshadowed by *Sputnik*. That startling event, which seemed to imply that the Soviet Union was ahead of the United States scientifically and thus at least its equal as the world's second superpower, spurred the United States into a frenzy of government support for beefing up U.S. scientific education as well as its space program. The Cold War, meanwhile, began to shift from its stalemate in Europe to Africa and Latin America, where the Soviet Union was expanding its influence. While Khrushchev visited the U.S. in 1959, President Eisenhower's return visit to Moscow was cancelled after an American U-2 spy plane was shot down over Sverdlovsk. Fidel Castro's Cuba soon went Communist and within a few years the two superpowers found themselves on the brink of World War III in what came to be known as "the Cuban missile crisis." Not long after Kennedy was assassinated, Khrushchev was ousted in Russia and the United States became mired in the long Vietnam War.

As American attention concentrated on Southeast Asia, cracks began to appear in the ossified Soviet empire after the Prague Spring of 1968. This was followed by bloody "police riots" on the Polish Baltic coast in 1970, more Polish disturbances in 1976, the foundation of "Charter '77" in Prague the next year, and finally, the birth of Solidarity in Poland in 1980. To prevent a Soviet invasion of Poland, Polish Premier General Jaruzelski declared war on his own people in December 1981. Solidarity was too strong to be crushed, however, and, after operating underground for some years, emerged intact. Then came that extraordinary year of 1989. Mikhail Gorbachev, concerned with all the serious problems in the Soviet Union which the Brezhnev regime had for too long ignored, realized that he could accomplish nothing at home if the Soviet Union were to become involved in suppressing a revolt in Eastern Europe. Being a forthright man, when he was asked would the Soviet Union try to prevent any of the Satellites from leaving the bloc if it decided to do, so he said "no." At first no one believed him, so he had to repeat it several times before people realized he was serious. Beginning with Solidarity's forcing free elections in Poland, which the Communists lost, the whole Communist system in Eastern Europe began to collapse like a house of cards, with Hungarians letting "vacationing" East Germans flee to freedom across their border into Austria, the "Velvet Revolution" in Prague, the fall of the Berlin Wall and bloody overthrow of Ceauşescu in Romania, all in the space of a few months.

No wonder the Hungarian Revolution of 1956 is barely remembered, if at all. Yet, had it not taken place when it did, it is doubtful that any of the above-mentioned events would have occurred.

It is to put the Hungarian Revolution back into its proper historical perspective that this book has been written.

This book, however, is *not* a history of the Hungarian Revolution. The Revolution still awaits its Hugh Thomas,* its professional historian, who will some day do it justice. I hope that that historian may find this book useful when he or she undertakes to write a definitive history. What I have attempted to do here is recreate, from contemporary documentation—mostly journalistic reports and memoirs written soon after—a picture of what it was like, day by day, to live through that exhilarating and tragic time. To do so I have included as many viewpoints, including my own, as my research—

*Author of *The Spanish Civil War, Cuba, the Pursuit of Freedom* and *A History of the World* most often based on the research of countless others—could uncover. I am not writing "history," but rather what I call "historical journalism." Thus, many of my sources are journalists reporting events as they unfolded. To give it the immediacy of their on-the-spot reports I have, throughout much of the book, resorted to the historical present tense. While only some of the passages are direct quotations, the entire book is based on the observations of others. Where there are errors of fact, these can usually be traced to the original sources, which I was not able to check. Where there are errors of judgment, these are entirely mine. Naturally my own biases and blind spots cannot help but skew this telling of the Revolution. Someone else working with all the same sources might have used different passages and emerged with a picture different from mine. But I have tried to use so many sources that my own voice may be muted, or sometimes even counteracted, and the reader's own judgment can come into play. Only in one case have I been forced to resort to fictitious names. Columbia University's oral history project conducted in early 1957 with Hungarian refugees who came to this country wisely kept the names of those interviewed secret, to prevent the possibility of reprisals back in Hungary. Someone was given access to that list a decade or so later who promised never to reveal any names. That promise was broken and the keepers of the list vowed never again to let anyone see it. Today, with the Communist regime in Hungary long gone, there would be no point in holding back the names. But long searching on both sides of the Atlantic has convinced me that the list was either destroyed or that those who own it refuse to acknowledge its existence. Thus I have been forced to make up names for these very real and valuable eyewitnesses, many of whom are doubtless still alive today.

The Revolution did not take place in a vacuum. It was the result of past Communist actions in Hungary and, like other minor explosions which preceded it in Poland and Hungary and even Czechoslovakia,* was triggered by Nikita Khrushchev's secret speech denouncing Stalin at the Soviet Twentieth Party Congress in February 1956. People tend to forget that Poland, too, was in revolt at that time. Indeed, the Polish defiance of Moscow had much to do with touching off the student demonstrations in Hungary. The Soviets were much more worried about Poland with its twenty-

*For a full account of those minor explosions see my own *Tinderbox: East-Central Europe in the Spring, Summer and Early Fall of 1956,* Fenestra Books, Tucson, Arizona, 2003.

eight million people and a history of beating Russians armies (giving the Red Army its only defeat ever in 1920, for instance) than it was about Hungary with its population of nine million. The Poles were prepared to fight, but only if they had to. Gomułka, their leader and a staunch Communist, did everything he could to prevent any Polish action that might provoke a Russian attack. The Poles had a reputation for headstrong, hopeless revolts, the last being the Warsaw Uprising of 1944. But when the Hungarians began fighting the Russian occupiers, the Poles held back and the Czechs and Slovaks ostensibly backed the Russians.

In America, where people were focused on the general election campaign, the Gallup Poll two weeks before the election had Adlai Stevenson's percentage so close to President Eisenhower's that it was too close for a clear prediction. Yet when the election was held two weeks later, Eisenhower won in a landslide. The difference can be wholly accounted for by the twin crises overseas, Hungary and Suez. Those undecided and "probably for Stevenson" did what voters did in the 1944 election between Roosevelt and Dewey: they followed the old Western adage "Don't change horses in the middle of the stream." In 1944 the stream had been World War II, still very much in progress; in 1956 it was the twin overseas crises that few understood, but all feared might lead to war. Ironically, as the reader will discover, the one man alive at the time who had the most to do with causing those two crises was none other than Eisenhower's Secretary of State, John Foster Dulles. Though he may never have realized it, Eisenhower had the blunders of his own Secretary of State to thank for his decisive re-election.

This book has been long in gestation. Indeed, much of the documentation on which it is based was collected while the Hungarian Revolution was taking place. As a staff member of Free Europe Press in Munich I had a ringside seat, as it were, to what was happening in Hungary. Sensing that what I was collecting might some day be of historical value and that I, myself, might some day make use of it, I saved almost every item which came out of Radio Free Europe's Central News Room, where I had previously been an editor for two years. When I returned to the U.S. in 1959 I brought with me a trunkful of documentation. It then sat in my cellar for decades gathering dust while I virtually forgot about it. After retirement, I thought, I would have time to make use of these materials to write something authoritative about that painful but all-important Cold War landmark.

Like many, I had grown to think of the Iron Curtain and the division of

Europe as an almost permanent condition. When the Iron Curtain abruptly fell in 1989, some years before I retired, I assumed that that would be the end of my retirement project, for so many actual participants would now be writing about the Revolution from their intimate involvement in it that there would be no room for an outsider like me. Hundreds of such eyewitness accounts *were* published, mostly in Hungary and most of them never translated. But by the time I retired I found that oddly, while academic authors had written several excellent summaries, and much documentation had been published, no one so far had attempted to give a complete treatment of the Revolution and its aftermath. I decided that it would be wrong to sit on all that documentation and not try to make use of it. I decided, in other words, to proceed with my original project.

Before I had done much work, however, I discovered that no one had written an adequate account of the build-up to the Revolution—the remarkable series of smaller explosions which occurred in both Poland and Hungary and even Czechoslovakia prior to the outbreak of the Revolution in Hungary—so I spent seven years researching and writing a book on that as a prequel to the present book.

Until the Revolution occurred, Hungary, for me, was just another East European country about which I knew practically nothing. But the Revolution engaged me as nothing has before or since. Hungary, I decided, had something distinctive about it and I was determined to find out more. In the course of the intervening years I confess to having become something of a Magyarphile. How could one not be impressed with a people, just fifteen million in the whole world, who produced such world-famous scientists as John von Neumann, father of the modern computer, Edward Teller, Leó Szilárd, Eugene Wigner, and Albert Szentgyörgyi (the latter two Nobel Prize winners) or such orchestra conductors as Eugene Ormándy, George Széll, Georg Solti, Antal Doráti, and Nicholas von Dohnányi? How many Americans remember that Hungary placed third in the world at the 1952 Olympics, behind the USA and USSR, or know that the mother of the great African-American concert pianist, Andre Watts, is Hungarian? Hungarians, I found, might disagree profoundly, might even despise each other, but they seldom undertake a profession or a project without a strong will to excel.

There is a more personal reason for my writing this book; it goes beyond my predilection for things Hungarian.

When I joined Radio Free Europe as an idealistic twenty-two-year-old, I did so with the hope that I might make a small contribution toward righting the wrong that our President, an aging and sick Franklin Delano Roosevelt, had inadvertently done to the people of Eastern Europe at Yalta. One of my motives for writing this book is not dissimilar. This time, however, the wrong is closer to home and I feel personally involved.

No one likes being fooled, or made a fool of. No one likes discovering that he has spent more than five years of his life devoted to an elaborate hoax, a hoax, moreover, that contributed to the deaths of thousands of people and unbelievable suffering to many thousands of others. No matter that others above me and without my knowledge perpetrated the hoax; I was part of it.

None of us in the Free Europe organization doubted that the United States government sincerely wanted to see the countries of Eastern Europe achieve their freedom and would do everything short of war to help that come about. Even those of us who had not been told that government money was supporting us were certain that it must be; and why else would they be spending so much for almost around-the-clock broadcasts to Eastern Europe and elaborate and costly balloon-leaflet operations to reach the people of Eastern Europe? None of us knew for sure what the "actions short of war" would be, but we never doubted that they existed and we could imagine what some of them might be.

It took total inaction on the part of the U.S. government—in fact, stubborn refusal to act—for us at Free Europe to realize that "Liberation" and "Rollback" were just slogans of propaganda, gimmicks for domestic political consumption, which had no real policy behind them, and that Free Europe was just an elaborate front to hide the fact that there never was any policy for bringing freedom to the East European satellites at all.

Other than show my revulsion at such an appalling state of affairs by resigning in disgust, there was nothing else I could do.

Now, fifty years later, if this book can help to set the record straight, perhaps it can serve as my amends for having been part of that disastrous hoax.

Prologue

IT IS THE LATE SUMMER OF 1956, the height of vacation time. All over the United States and Europe people are returning to their workday lives tanned and refreshed, while others go off for their turn of annual escape, relaxation and pleasure. In New York the Dodgers are still in Brooklyn, the Giants still at the Polo Grounds in Manhattan, and while Bobby Thompson's series winning grand slam on a two and three count with two outs in the bottom of the ninth is only a memory, there is still a good chance of another "subway series." Red Sox fans are wondering: "Will this be the year?" And this is an election year. General Eisenhower will be running for re-election and the Democrats will again be running Adlai Stevenson. Only this time they think they have a chance. People are disappointed, even disillusioned with the General's performance in the White House. Mistakes have been made, his health has been uncertain, and there is a general malaise over his inattention to his job and lack of follow-through.

On the international front there is unsettling news. The British and French are so alarmed over Egypt's Gamal Nasser's seizing the Suez Canal in late July that they are mobilizing their military reserves. Behind the Iron Curtain in that half of Europe that has been cut off from the West now for twelve years, a bloody uprising had taken place in Poznań, Poland, in late June, and western correspondents are reporting strikes and demonstrations, though seldom mentioned in the local press. For the average citizen in Eastern Europe, returning refreshed from the Baltic, Black Sea or Lake Balaton, life seems to be looking up. Fantastic changes have been occurring since Khrushchev's secret denunciation of Stalin at the Twentieth Party

1

Congress in late February. Though it was meant strictly for the party faithful, the revelation was so shocking that news of it had quickly leaked. Now party members no longer have to rely on watered down versions being read to them by their superiors, for the Americans have gotten their hands on the full text and the Voice of America, BBC and Radio Free Europe have broadcast it in full. A few lucky Poles, Czechoslovaks and Hungarians have even found the printed text in their own language lying in a field or wood, courtesy of Free Europe's balloon-leaflet campaign.

In Hungary, the tiny land-locked country occupying the center of Europe's Carpathian Basin, surrounded almost entirely by Slavic countries, the changes have been breathtaking. First there was the admission by Mátyás Rákosi, the country's Stalinist leader, that the trial and execution of his potential rival, László Rajk, seven years ago had been a completely bogus affair. Rajk, it seems, was completely innocent. Rákosi blamed it all on the then head of the secret police, Gabor Péter, whom he had since had arrested and incarcerated so that Péter could not reveal that it had all been done at Rakosi's behest. His admission and his insistence on staying in power had so infuriated the intellectuals in the party that a wide rift in the leadership had developed. This made it necessary for the Kremlin's expert on Hungarian affairs, Anastas Mikoyan, to fly to Budapest and "persuade" him to resign and retire to the Soviet Union. That was in July. And just before that in late June there had been the tumultuous eight-hour meeting of the Petőfi Circle, a discussion group organized by the communist youth organization, DISZ. This heated, standing-room-only debate had involved six thousand intellectuals, mostly party members. Overnight it became the talk of Budapest and brought on an attempted crackdown by Rákosi and his hardliners. Never mind that the man Mikoyan has picked to replace Rákosi, Ernő Gerő, is almost as bad, having been his chief deputy for years. The daily press and radio are now much livelier than before, even sometimes truthful. The Communists appear to be in considerable disarray.

* * *

It is now early October. Everyone is back at his or her place of work and the political campaigns in the United States have been in full swing since Labor Day. The reservists in England and France are beginning to champ at the bit, having been on the alert since August. In Budapest the big upcoming event is the state re-burial of László Rajk and his fellow victims. Until it comes, no one has any idea how big it will be. Júlia Rajk, his widow, has not

2

only insisted that a public re-burial take place, but that it is with full honors and on a Saturday afternoon so that the workers can attend. She picks October Sixth, a former national holiday of mourning over the execution of thirteen Hungarian generals by the Austrians in 1849 following the crushing of the Hungarian Revolution of 1848. The government, which would have much preferred a private re-burial, is divided over who will represent them. In the end, the country's figurehead President and other Central Committee members attend; First Secretary Gerő is conveniently in the Crimea consulting with Khrushchev and Tito while János Kádár and others who were involved in the prosecution of Rajk stay away. One key politician, Imre Nagy, who had been forced to resign from the Premiership of the country by Rákosi in early 1955 and even been kicked out of the Party, is conspicuously present. Just two days ago word of his readmission to the Party has swept Budapest. On his arrival he greets Júlia Rajk with a kiss on both cheeks and a warm embrace. Words pass between them, but the wind is too strong for anyone else to overhear. Not only is it extremely blustery, it is cold and wet, not the sort of day one would expect many people to turn up. And yet hours before the official ceremonies at 4:00 p.m., hordes of people begin to arrive and file past the four biers placed on one side of the massive mausoleum built for Lajos (Louis) Kossuth, leader of the Hungarian Revolution of 1848. Budapest has not seen anything like it in years, not since the communists came to full power nine years ago. Estimates agree that when the crowd is fully assembled it numbers at least two hundred thousand. Rajk had friends, but not two hundred thousand. As Minister of the Interior and thus in nominal charge of the dreaded ÁVO (State Security, which included the secret police) he was not exactly beloved by the people. No, as everyone realizes— party officials in particular—this is massive proof that the people are fed up with communist brutality, lies and show trials, that things are going to have to change. All of the government speeches, though couched in communist jargon, reflect this. But it is the one non-government speaker, Béla Szász, who best sums it up. Júlia Rajk has insisted that he, as one of her husband's fellow accused, be allowed to speak.

"Trumped up charges," he shouts into the microphone, "the gallows, threw László Rajk into an unmarked grave for seven years but today his death looms like a warning symbol before the Hungarian people and the world. For when thousands upon thousands pass before these coffins, it is not only to pay the victims the last honors; it is their…irrevocable resolution to bury an epoch; to bury, forever, lawlessness, tyranny, the Hungarian disciples of iron-fisted rule; the moral dead of the shameful years…"[*]

Such a stir sweeps through the crowd that, were this not a funeral, thunderous applause would surely have erupted. Only the somberness of the occasion and the bitter cold wind restrains them.

[*]György Litván, a young member of Imre Nagy's entourage on that day, told the author on October 30, 1999: "I'm not sure whether it would not have been better for the Revolution to have started on that day."

CHAPTER I

Demonstrations

Győr (pronounced Dyur), ***Hungary, Tuesday, October 16, 1956***

GYŐR, HUNGARY'S LARGEST WESTERN CITY (population 70,000), lies on the curve of a meandering southern branch of the Danube, miles from the main channel of that famous river, and some sixty-five miles west and slightly to the north of Budapest. Capital of its county, Győr-Sopron, it has become in the twentieth century a manufacturing center of heavy vehicles. But it is also an educational and cultural center for the region.

Today, in the Jókai Cinema Theatre, nearly a thousand people gather to hear one of the country's most popular writer/poets, Gyula Hay. Though a Communist Party member, Hay is a liberal and it is of the reform movement that is sweeping Hungary that he speaks today.

The local press will refer to this meeting as the "first entirely free, public and outspoken debate since the year of change" (i.e. when the Communists took over).

People in the question period speak out vigorously against current Stalinist practices, call for the abolition of Soviet military bases and the return of Cardinal Mindszenty as the Primate of Hungary.

Hay admits, in answer to a question, that the Hungarian press is not free but "directed," but says the "directing" is "functioning badly" and that things will be better after the big meeting of Hungarian journalists due to take place on October 28.[1]

Szeged (pronounced SEG-ed), ***Tuesday, October 16, 1956***

Szeged, a city of around 170,000, lies on a plain some 120 miles south-east of Budapest, not more than fifteen miles from the Yugoslav border. It straddles one of Hungary's main rivers, the Tisza, just west of where a smaller river, the Maros, merges into it. Ever since the disastrous floods of 1879, a protective dike has encircled the city. Once considered the economic center of a region known as the Bánát, it lost this distinction in 1920 when two-thirds of Hungary was ceded to neighboring countries after the First World War. A year later, the University of Kolozsvár (capital of Transylvania and then known as Cluj, Romania) was moved to Szeged, thus establishing it as a university town. In 1951 it split into two sister institutions: the University of Szeged and the Medical University, with their buildings in separate parts of the old city.

For over a week now, almost since the university students returned for the fall semester, there has been talk of withdrawing from the Communist youth organization, DISZ (Union of Working Youth), and re-establishing a student organization which existed before the communists came to power, MEFESZ (Federation of Hungarian University and College Students). DISZ is a Communist organization covering all young people in the country. When MEFESZ was abolished, the students were forced to join DISZ even though that organization had never been oriented toward students and has little interest in them. Naturally the university chapter of DISZ consists entirely of students. The Communist DISZ leadership has called a meeting for this afternoon in an effort to head off this growing sentiment.[2]

When the hour comes the Auditorium Maximum quickly fills, for students from the School of Medicine have come over from their location at Rákóczi Square some twelve blocks away. A group of reform-minded students, led by András Lejtényi, is in a room nearby discussing with the DISZ committee members points to be brought up in the debate. Lejtényi, realizing they are just wasting time with no possibility of agreement, suddenly cuts off discussion. "Let's go," he exclaims, "a mass of students is waiting for us." As soon as they enter the auditorium, Lejtényi and his colleagues occupy the area around the microphone. The DISZ leadership finds itself outnumbered. Lejtényi starts to read the student requests and outlines his plan for the formation of a new MEFESZ. There are frequent expressions of total agreement. But there are also diehards present who speak in violent opposition, especially against the formation of a new, independent student organization. They are always shouted down. The great majority of students seem determined to leave the DISZ. When the final vote is taken the result turns out to be overwhelming. Cheers erupt. Students can scarcely wait to rush out and spread the news. Before they do, the new leadership announces that the first university-wide meeting of the new Szeged chapter of MEFESZ will be held here next Saturday, October 20 at 4:00 p.m.

There is no precedent in the Communist world for an action such as this.

No organization is allowed to exist beyond party control, even such non-political entities as sports or stamp-collecting clubs. Any organization that can make decisions totally outside the party's control is a dangerous threat. ÁVO (secret police) spies who were in the audience quickly get the word out to their superiors. Before the day is out the Ministry of Defense in Budapest has ordered its military reservists to report immediately for at least a week of active duty.[3]

The Soviet Special Army Corps, headquartered in Székesfehérvár, some forty miles southwest of Budapest, but with units all over Hungary, also goes on the alert. As early as mid-July its commander, Lt. General Piotr N. Lashchenko, had been ordered to prepare a plan so that Soviet troops could "maintain, defend and, in certain cases, restore socialist social order" in Hungary. The plan has the code name "Volna" ("Wave"). Now the early stage of that plan goes into effect.[4]

Budapest, Wednesday, October 17, 1956

Budapest is one of the world's most beautiful cities; some think the most beautiful in Europe. Home to 1,850,000 inhabitants in 1956, it contains one-fifth of the population of Hungary and much of its industry, though being mostly in the suburbs and not visible to tourists, except on the clearest of days. Tourists gaze enthralled from two superb vantage points. Both of these are in Buda: Gellért Hill and the Fisherman's Bastion on Castle Hill. From each, one can view most of the city and the wide Danube curving through the metropolis. The only vistas in Pest are of Buda, and those only from the river's edge, for Pest is as flat as Buda is hilly. They were two cities until the last century, when they were united by one of Europe's first suspension bridges, the Széchényi Chain Bridge, built by Adam Clark, an English engineer. For its first decade as a united metropolis it was known as Pest-Buda. Actually the city has incorporated a third city, the oldest of the three, Óbuda, which is just south of an old Roman settlement known as Aquincum on the Buda side of the Danube. From the top of Gellért Hill not only can all of Pest and much of Buda be seen, but all seven main bridges connecting the two parts of the city. Today the southernmost, Lágymányos, crosses just above the split in the river around the twenty-mile-long Csepel Island, where the bulk of the city's factories are located; but there was no bridge there in 1956. Looking north, one can just make out Árpád Bridge (Stalin Bridge in 1956) crossing the northern tip of Margaret Island. This island is one vast beautiful park with sports facilities and a single hotel, the Grand, on it. At the near end is the Margit (Margaret) Bridge making a slight "V" as it crosses the southern tip of the island. Only from an airplane, however, can the broad avenues of Pest be seen radiating out from the center with curving boulevards connecting them like strands of a spider's web which conveniently end up in each case at a bridge across the Danube. The streets of Buda, on the other hand, must fit in with the topography. Many are squiggles going every which way. Only those in the flat sections or at the base of the hills are straight.

Today, not long after dawn has broken over the capital city, twenty-four-year-old László Beke,[5] a student at the School of Fine Arts in Pest, quietly leaves his apartment in a level section of Buda and walks to a local post office on Béla Bartók Avenue. He asks the phone clerk to get him a certain number in Szeged. He is calling his cousin Ferenc.

"Is that you, Feri?"

"Hello! László? Hello!"

"Feri," shouts László, "did you change your old suit for a new one?" Even at this hour and over a public phone he dares not speak too openly, for nearly all phone calls are monitored.

There is a short pause. Then "Yes," crackles Feri's distorted voice over the bad connection, "I did! We all did!"

So it is true! The students of Szeged have stood up to the Communists and formed their own non-Communist organization. The news had reached Budapest last night, but László Beke wanted to be sure. Now he is. A rush of adrenaline surges through him. "Now it's our turn," he thinks.

After informing his wife, Éva, László contacts his five closest friends. Later in the day they meet in a tiny, cold room in his city district of Kelenföld. "We've got to do something here in Budapest," says Károly Imre, one of his student friends. "The best way to begin is to ask that the Stalinist professors be removed from our respective faculties."

"Let's get rid of *all* the Communist professors," chimes in another.

All have their grudges against specific professors. These are invariably well-known Communists among faculties that are predominantly non-Communist. They decide to skip the day's lectures and reach as many of their friends around the city as they can. By midnight a plan is in place.

Students are not the only young people affected by the profound discontent sweeping the country. While László Beke and his friends are working out their plans, a conclave of young workers is meeting in the Red Star

Tractor Works in Kispest under the auspices of DISZ to complain of the many economic grievances in their lives. A resolution concerning these is adopted and sent to Party headquarters.[6]

Budapest, Thursday, October 18

At 7:00 a.m. László Beke and his five fellow students fan out across Budapest to catch particular friends they have not yet reached by phone before they disappear into lectures and classes. Beke finds one in the College of Drama and another in his Fine Arts College. In this way they and other students who have heard the news from Szeged try to get the word to all of Budapest's ten thousand university students.

Younger faculty members, at least those who are not party members, seem to know what is going on. One approaches László and whispers, "I know you guys are up to something. You can count on my help." Some of them even volunteer to put in a good word for the students' demands at faculty council meetings. But what Beke and his friends at the Collage of Fine Arts are planning goes far beyond what these well-meaning faculty realize. They are planning on confronting the Communist faculty members themselves—directly.

It is too late for written invitations, so everything is done by phone. They invite professors and members of the press, even though they know the press is under Party control, to a meeting in the College's main auditorium at four o'clock that very afternoon. In all some twenty-five of these guests are invited—including representatives of the main party paper *Szabad Nép* (*Free People*), *Szabad Ifjúság* (*Free Youth*) and *Csillag* (*Star*), as well as several section heads from the education department and two party secretaries. Some have prior commitments, but many accept.

Before the invitees walk in, some three hundred students from the College of Arts and about twenty-five students representing other colleges and universities around Budapest have already packed the small auditorium. The university officials know they are walking into a highly charged atmosphere, but they are, after all, the authorities and have handled unruly students before.

Beke's friend, Károly Imre, leads off. He speaks first of the Szeged action and the significance of this apparent rebellion. Then he introduces the subject of Stalinism among the professors at the college. While he is speaking, students near the doors quietly get up and lock them.

EXPLOSION

One by one the students step up to the microphone and unload their grievances. László complains of the suppression of free opinion and the fact that
the works of Western artists cannot be studied, nor any Western languages.
He ends by demanding the dismissal of the three most avowed Stalinists at
the College. Some of the "guests" stand up and protest, but without the
microphone their efforts are not effective.

There is no interruption from the floor, but more and more students ask
to speak and inevitably there is more and more repetition of charges. Several
reporters and professors get up to leave, but find they are trapped and must
resume their seats. It is well into the evening before the meeting comes to a
close.

Budapest, Friday, October 19, 1956

Official reaction to the confrontation at the School of Fine Arts is immediate. László and his friends and even his wife are called in one by one before
the school's discipline board and told they are being dismissed. "Your
behavior has been under surveillance for some time now," László is told.
"We know you have been carrying on anti-state activities! You are not worthy of the university's trust in you! You have failed a university supported
by the People's Democracy. And as for the scholarship you have been
given—you've simply stolen money that belongs to the people!"

Their fellow students at the School of Fine Arts react to these dismissals
with the announcement that they will boycott all classes and lectures and
vow to stay away until the Stalinist professors are fired.

Already one of the student demands is conceded by the government.
Minister of Education, Albert Kónya, announces on Radio Budapest certain
changes as a result of student agitation. Among these is the promise to abol-
ish the compulsory teaching of Russian in schools and colleges.[7]

Pécs (pronounced PAITCH)

In Pécs, a mining town on the southern edge of the Mecsek Mountains
and ninety-five miles southwest of Budapest, the university students respond
at once to Minister Kónya's announcement by demanding that the local DISZ
convene a student parliament to discuss these reforms and the solution of
certain problems pertaining strictly to Pécs.[8]

And those who read today's Szabad Ifjúság (Free Youth) find a two-page
feature entitled "University Students want to voice their Opinion" in which

10

the newspaper backs up many of their demands but adds that in some cases the students are going too far. "We cannot agree with some...demands," it writes. "These were probably born by the revolutionary current now rushing high through our universities."[9]

Budapest, Saturday, October 20, 1956

During the night a warm, humid breeze has swept through the city. The sudden change brings misty weather and early morning ground fog. Before dawn László Beke and three of his expelled colleagues head off to a pre-arranged meeting point on the Hill of Three Borders in Buda. All potential meeting places in the university are now out of the question; they fear ÁVO* informers are now looking for all of them.

Each college and university is supposed to send five delegates. They converge through the mist from all parts of the city, some from as far away as fifteen miles. But all leave their well-lit streetcars at least a mile before their destination to go the rest of the way to the meeting point on foot through side roads and fields. They do not want to call attention to themselves. All told, forty-three representatives show up. They have already designated themselves the Free Students' Council of Budapest. Now, as they sit on their coats in a circle like signers of a modern Magna Carta, they vote to leave the old DISZ and set up their own branches of the new MEFESZ. The planning goes quickly. They know that if they do not act with dispatch the ÁVO can crush the whole movement with sudden arrests.

Their resolve is stiffened by the extraordinary news they hear on Radio Free Europe—cursorily confirmed by Radio Budapest—that Gomulka has been elected First Party Secretary in Poland and a delegation of Soviet Politburo members, led by Khrushchev himself, has been rebuffed by the Poles and returned empty-handed to Moscow. All the Western radios, in fact, are full of news from Poland, and it does not matter whether Hungarians listen to the BBC, VOA, RFE, Radio Diffusion Française, Vatican Radio or Radio Madrid; all give extensive reporting on the events of Poland.

---

*During the "New Course," a period of reform in Hungary between 1953 and 1955, the ÁVO changed its name from Division of State Security (Hungarian Acronym: ÁVO) to Office of State Security (Hungarian acronym: ÁVH). Since neither the personnel nor the practices of the organization changed one iota, the people went on calling it ÁVO, as they did throughout the Revolution. For this reason, and also because it is easier to pronounce, the term "ÁVO" will be used throughout this book, rather than the technically correct ÁVH.

EXPLOSION

Szeged, Saturday, October 20, 1956

The students of Szeged are overjoyed at the news from Poland. It confirms that the tide of events is with them. The first meeting of their new organization MEFESZ, decreed four days ago, gets under way in the Auditorium Maximum at precisely 4:00 p.m. Not only students are present, but also the Rector of the University, Dr. Dezső Baróti, his swept-back silver hair standing out among all the young heads, and the Dean of the Law School, József Perbíró, handsome, despite his thick, dark-framed glasses. Both are front and center. Neither has much of an inkling as to what will occur, but they respect their students and admire their audacity. The Dean sits behind a table with a lectern on it, acting at the behest of Baróti as official convener, facing the audience. The Rector, with other distinguished faculty members, sits in the front row. To the left, before a single microphone, András Lejtényi and Tamás Kiss, leaders of the new organization, clutch their notes and gesticulate in nervous excitement, as they bring the meeting to order.[10] Others, such as twenty-three-year old Assistant Professor István (Stephen) Lakatos—even though they are not students—feel totally involved. They stand at the sides, in the back and even behind the speakers in the front to witness this historic occasion. Two thousand people are packed into a space designed for far fewer.

The meeting begins with supportive remarks from Professor Perbíró. Next, András Lejtényi, a second year law student, outlines the operational structure of the new MEFESZ that he and his fellow law students Tamás Kiss and Imre Tóth have worked out. The points are accepted enthusiastically without much debate.

It soon becomes clear that it is not simply things that are wrong with academia that concern them, but everything that they think is wrong in Hungary today. They are acutely conscious of their own history and how similar the situation is today to what it was in 1848 when the revolutionary youth of that time produced a twelve-point Manifesto called "Demands of the Hungarian Nation." In the end they decide to formalize their complaints as a series of "demands" for changes, to be addressed, eventually, to the only sources of power in the nation, the government and the party. While they want to make it twelve, they find they are unable to keep it that low and end up with fourteen.

The list begins with matters close to their daily lives at the university but expands in no time to national and even international matters. The final list includes a call for a public reprimand of political leaders for the crimes they had committed and the terror they had caused, including the return of Rákosi to the country to stand trial, a call for Imre Nagy to head a new government, a complete purging of the Rákosi holdovers in the current government, a public trial of Mihály Farkas, former head of the secret police, return to use of the Kossuth emblem, return to March 15 and October 6 being national holidays, multi-party elections, freedom of the press and other matters anathema to the Communist regime. Not all are expressed as "demands." Some are affirmations, like the last point, a pledge of solidarity with the students of Poland.

The heated atmosphere is punctuated with shouting and applause and occasionally debate is suspended while a congratulatory or supportive telegram from some other university is read aloud.

Having hammered together their program and list of demands, the Szeged MEFESZ decides to publicize them. They know they cannot rely on the official media so they elect to do it themselves. Small delegations of two or three are appointed to carry the document, by train, car or motorcycle, to universities and colleges all over the country. These delegates are to urge the establishment of MEFESZ in each locality and ask for these new organizations to select delegates to attend a national organizing meeting of MEFESZ in Budapest a week from today, October 27.

Budapest

Back in Budapest the students of the Technical University of Building and Commerce are already convening their own emergency meeting from which they issue their own demands. These include:

–We demand the moral and material appreciation of engineers. The starting salary should be between 1,500 and 1,600 forints…
–A university degree and professional qualifications should be…essential for leading positions.
–The autonomy of universities should be restored.
–We demand a public trial…of Farkas and his associates.
–In the event of non-compliance (of these demands)…we will show our dissatisfaction by demonstrating.

In response to this, the Rector of the Commerce section of the university, Dr. László Gillemot, calls an extraordinary meeting of the Board and issues a statement saying:

"The University Board supports the students in their rightful claims and wishes to co-operate…. The natural condition of this is a guarantee of order and discipline within the University."

When a report of this appears in *Szabad Ifjúság* (*Free Youth*), the editor adds the editorial comment that "demonstrations on the street…we feel cannot have any good results…."[11]

Moscow

First Secretary of the Soviet Communist Party Nikita Khrushchev calls a meeting of the Presidium of the Central Committee to discuss the situation in Poland from which he, Mikoyan, Molotov, Kaganovich and Marshal Zhukov have just returned, following a nearly sleepless one night visit to Warsaw. They are irritable and weary, but the situation in Poland calls for decisions. They have failed to prevent the election of Gomułka to head the Polish Communist Party, and there is also a distinct possibility that Marshal Rokossovsky, a Soviet citizen of Polish extraction, whom Stalin appointed as Polish Minister of Defense, will lose his position on the Polish Politburo before the day is over. If he does not, Presidium members agree, a decision on Poland can be postponed. If he does, new military maneuvers may have to be ordered in preparation for a "military solution" in Poland.

Before the meeting breaks up, the subject of events in Hungary must be discussed. Ambassador Andropov's reports concerning the continuing unrest are quite alarming. Perhaps it would be well for Mikoyan to go there for an on-the-spot survey and then write a report that can be sent to inform the fraternal (i.e. other satellite) parties.[12]

Budapest, Sunday, October 21, 1956

Budapest is enshrouded in fog. Only around noon as it burns off does the pale disc of a sun become visible. The art student László Beke stays in his small room all day working on posters. Éva, his wife, who has just discovered she is pregnant, ventures out several times to meet with their friends and bring back the latest news. She is as excited as he. All over the city students are preparing for meetings that have been called for tomorrow.

But most of the citizens of Budapest are quite unaware of this activity.

Today, being Sunday, much of the populace is out for a stroll on this gray, yet mild, autumn day, enjoying the scores of parks, particularly in the hills of Buda, walking their dogs along tree-lined streets or the Corso along the Pest side of the Danube where people go to see and be seen.

One individual, thirty-four-year-old Pál Jónás, the first National Chairman of the original MEFESZ, receives a telegram delivered to his home address. By discipline he is an economist, but since his release in 1954 after six years in Communist jails and prison camps he has been forced to become a common laborer. Currently he works in a motorcycle factory, called the Iron and Utensils Company, though as an intellectual he has been active in founding the Petőfi Circle in 1955. The telegram is from the students of Szeged University and bears yesterday's date. They wish to inform him that his former organization has been re-established and that they aim to spread it to other universities. Moreover, after other chapters of MEFESZ have been established and officers elected by secret ballot, they intend to hold a national meeting of delegates from these new chapters on Saturday, October 27 in Budapest and would be more than pleased if he would agree to attend.[13]

Meanwhile at Communist Party headquarters, Central Committee member Károly Kiss, attending a twentieth anniversary meeting of members of the International Brigades in Spain, warns that "chauvinism, and anti-Soviet slander and anti-Semitism have increased in our country" and that "those who think they can abuse…our militant Party as much as they want are very much mistaken." The Party cannot "tolerate such symptoms without taking action."[14]

Because nearly all of the leading Communists, Rákosi, Gerő, Révai, though not Nagy, are Jewish, as was Béla Kun, leader of the Communist government which briefly existed in 1919, any increase in anti-Communism tends to bring with it an increase in latent anti-Semitism among the Hungarian populace.

Budapest, Monday, October 22, 1956

Another foggy morning. The Budapest MEFESZ Council, established two days ago at the pre-dawn meeting on Three Borders Hill, has called for a second early morning meeting at the College of Fine Arts on Stalin Avenue (formerly Andrássy Ave.) in Pest. They figure that the heavy traffic will make the gathering students less conspicuous there. They select the largest empty room they can find and close the doors. They have a copy of the Szeged MEFESZ manifesto, and using that as a base, they begin to compose their own. All their ideals and dreams are invested in the enterprise, and in their excitement it is impossible to keep their voices down.[15] Hearing the ruckus, people in the vicinity open the doors to see what is going on. Intrigued, they enter without closing the doors behind them. As a result, more and more people drift in. The MEFESZ members are too involved to notice until some of the newcomers begin to speak up. Some of these are obviously not students. Two, in fact, are members of the Central Committee of the Hungarian Workers (Communist) Party. But they seem to be caught up in the fervor of the moment and one, Ágnes Kenyeres, is particularly passionate in her remarks supporting the students. This startles Sándor Ék, a loyal Communist, who has also wandered in. He will later testify against her.[16]

When the manifesto is completed, the students feel immense pride in what they have done. Once the document is properly typed up, a five-member delegation is appointed to take it straight to the government to ask that it be given full publicity. Beke, and the others not on the delegation, wait nervously for several hours for their return.

At the Parliament building a Deputy Prime Minister finally agrees to see the delegation. He glances at the demands with a disdainful air, then spots one point that galls him. "You have no right," he shouts, "to declare your sympathies with Poland. The Central Committee has not yet come to a decision on the subject!"[17]

Shortly after 11 a.m., the delegation returns to the College of Fine Arts. Béla Kós, the leader, states that a Deputy Minister claims the government will be willing to discuss the petition in two weeks' time, but until then no publicity is to be given these demands. The students burst into derisive curses at this blatant evasion. They swear that they will get their demands heard and that they will also demonstrate to show their fellow citizens that they are in complete sympathy and solidarity with the students and people of Poland.[18]

*　　*　　*　　*

Not far away on Bajza Street members of the Hungarian Writers Association, excited by the news from Poland, have just sent messages of greeting and congratulation to Polish writers and journalists in Warsaw. Now they are planning a small ceremony to show their solidarity with the Poles.

The Polish Embassy is not happy with the idea of their doing it in front of their embassy, so the Association decides to shift it to the Josef Bem statue in Buda tomorrow at 4:00 p.m. Bem was the Polish General who in 1848 joined the armed forces of Louis Kossuth and defeated the Austrians many times in Transylvania before being overcome by the Czarist armies.

The Petőfi Circle, that group of liberal Communist intellectuals which has been sparking reform, is also in session, composing its own list of demands. These stress that the government should rescind a number of out- dated statutes as well as deprive Rákosi, though he is no longer in the coun- try, of his party membership, lest he attempt to return to the scene. And a new organization, "March 15 Circle," made up of students from Eötvös Lóránd University's College of Arts and Sciences, is meeting to plan a stu- dent demonstration tomorrow at the Petőfi memorial statue a few blocks away from their campus in Pest.[19]

Debrecen (pronounced DEBretsen)

Debrecen, Hungary's eastern-most city, which lies about 140 miles to the east of Budapest and twenty miles west of the Romanian border, has a pop- ulation of 120,000. It is the capital of Hajdú-Bihar County, probably the rich- est agricultural region of Hungary. Through the more recent centuries its protection has come from its citizens' ability to make peace and compromise with foreign invaders. Known not only as the bastion of the Calvinist Church in Hungary, Debrecen used to be referred to as "the Calvinist Rome" throughout all Eastern Europe. Its famous "Great Church" was both the site of Louis Kossuth's proclamation of Hungarian independence from Austria in 1849 and the site of the first meeting of the provisional government of Hungary in 1944 during the country's "Liberation" by the Red Army. The University, which bears the name of Kossuth, has three colleges: natural sci- ences, medicine and agriculture. Built largely in the 1920s, its architecture, though on a properly grand scale, is less ornate and massive than most Hungarian university buildings, which were constructed in the days of the Austro-Hungarian Empire. Located on the southern edge of the city, it has been literally carved into what is left of the Great Forest. With its lushness in trees and vegetation it resembles a beautiful, spread-out American univer- sity campus. Through this campus loops the end of the primary streetcar line that runs up the length of Debrecen's main street bisecting the city all the way to the railroad station on Petőfi Square. So while the students in their sylvan setting are quite isolated from the city, thanks to the streetcar line, they can be at Market Street in the center of the old town in fifteen minutes and at the railway station in another five.

Today they are all on campus, but despite attendance at lectures and classes, it is no usual Monday. Copies of the Szeged MEFESZ manifesto have been circulating, and meetings of the existing student DISZ leadership have been taking place at all three colleges. At one meeting, the students decide to summon the student body from all three colleges for a joint conference tomorrow at 3:00 p.m. They also concoct a list of twenty-nine points, which they try to persuade the editor of the local party paper, *Néplap*, to print in tomorrow's edition of the newspaper. They are in close touch by phone with students at the Technical University in Budapest.

* * * *

Not far to the north on the Tisza River near the town of Vásárosnamény, the Soviet Army begins building a pontoon bridge and units of the Red Army from Carpatho-Ukraine prepare to cross as part of "Operation Volna."[20]

Miskolc (pronounced MISHkolts) *(same day)*

The second largest industrial city (after Budapest) in Hungary, Miskolc, with its population of 140,000, lies partially in the Szinva Valley 113 miles northeast of Budapest. Closely linked with the town of Diósgyőr further up the valley, it has long been known as a producer of iron and steel—the coal and iron being obtained from local sources—and heavy industrial equipment. Today the students of Miskolc Technical University, acting on the initiative of the Szeged students, but still meeting under the aegis of the old DISZ, establish their own MEFESZ, disbanding the old DISZ. They draw up their own list of demands. It is even more radical. Among them are: the withdrawal of Soviet troops, Hungary's disengagement from the Warsaw Pact and an announcement of the nation's neutral status. Towards the end of the meeting their DISZ representative arrives from Budapest and announces that there will indeed be a national meeting of students in Budapest on October 27. The gathering immediately elects delegates to attend that meeting, but dismisses their local leaders before doing so.[21]

In the nearby Hungarian State Rolling Stock and Machine Factory, Miskolc's and Diósgyőr's industrial giant, politically motivated workers, but party members in good standing, decide to initiate an "open Party day," to be held October 25. At this meeting workers will be allowed to seek solutions to certain urgent social problems that have been neglected. A petition is circulated with signature sheets, but these soon run out and new ones need to be handed out.[22]

Budapest (same day)

The Agricultural Section of the Party's Central Committee is meeting in the Agricultural Ministry on Parliament Square with the secretaries of County Party Committees and agricultural department heads. The consensus is that the cooperative farm movement is not only at a standstill, but the tendency to withdraw has become very strong in the past few days. Cooperatives should be given independence. The rigid limitations of copying the Soviet model have simply impoverished the peasants. It is important to try to keep the cooperatives, but those peasants who wish to leave should be allowed to do so without any punishment.[23]

Soviet Corps chief of staff, Colonel Malashenko, who left his headquarters at Székesfehérvár this morning, arrives at the Soviet Embassy on Stalin Avenue in Pest where he learns from Ambassador Andropov of the student demonstrations that are planned for tomorrow.[24]

Over in Buda in the massive buildings of the Technical University of Building and Commerce, which dominate that portion of the Danube's right bank, there is a beehive of activity. The local leaders of the university's DISZ have convened a meeting in the great hall for two o'clock. They know of the efforts of local students to re-establish the former MEFESZ and they aim to head it off while they still have the power. Many faculty object to any meeting taking place, but they are outvoted by their colleagues in a hastily called meeting just after 1:00 p.m. The rectors of both schools of the dual university, Dr. László Gillemot and Dr. Tibor Cholnoky, agree to attend.

Around two o'clock the great hall, or "aula" as it is known, begins to fill. This is a huge auditorium with a skylight ceiling some twenty-five meters from the level floor. The space is made bigger by the fact that wide corridors on all four sides are connected by massive square arches, which exist on two floor levels. While the room itself seats two thousand, three thousand more can sit in the balconies or stand in the corridors. A raised platform and dais have been erected and the two rectors, the Communist Party Secretary, lesser Party officials, the numerous young DISZ officials and various faculty and administrative officials begin to find their places. The DISZ student officials, all wearing blue jackets, red ties and white shirts, are grouped on one side of the platform. They wear the uniform of the Union of Working Youth (DISZ). Looking down at their bodies, shortened by the angle, Béla Lipták, a twenty-year-old engineer in his fourth year, suddenly sees them as penguins or booby birds. He laughs to himself and then pokes his friend and classmate Attila Ménes to see if he doesn't agree. Attila sees the similarity and laughs his approval out loud. They are fellow engineers and fellow athletes. Béla is a six-foot-two high-jumper, and Attila, his teammate, is nearly six-foot-four. Unlike László Beke, they have no particular interest in politics. They are here simply because of curiosity. They do not expect much to happen.

And until nearly 3:00 p.m. when formal speeches begin, nothing much does. Even then it seems to be the same old thing. With at least two thousand students in the hall there is a constant murmur. The two rectors, various Communist officials and the Youth leaders talk *at* the students; the students' only defense against this is not to listen. And it is not easy to tune out the speeches, for loudspeakers have been rigged on all six pillars and there is no shortage of speakers.[25] The DISZ officials talk of special train passes, cheaper textbooks, better food and housing. None of the students give the slightest reaction. They never do. They've heard it all before. It is the authorities' show, so the students let them do all the talking.[26]

Suddenly Béla, who has been busy polishing his "gold" ring, gets an elbow in his ribs. Attila is calling his attention to some commotion down below on the speakers' platform. Others notice, too, and the murmur in the aula begins to subside. It is about 3:30. No one is actually at the microphone, but excited voices emanating from some sort of struggle are nonetheless amplified by it. The students' murmur abruptly stops. Then, through the confusion of sounds comes a high-pitched voice: "I represent the MEFESZ of Szeged! I want to speak!" The room becomes tense. No one knows who has spoken, but it is an unprecedented interruption. Then Béla and Attila see the "penguins" shoving a small person away from the microphone. He is shouting and gesticulating, but they can hear nothing and the blue-coated DISZ officers push him all the way to the wall.

The university's Party Secretary, Mrs. Orbán, strides to the microphone and begins to admonish the students. "You have only one duty! Your duty is to study!" she shouts. "You don't want the MEFESZ of Szeged!" As she rants on Béla wonders who the little fellow is who wants to speak. Is he out of his mind? Doesn't he know he'll be kicked out of his university? Not only that but they will beat the shit out of him and throw him in jail, thinks Béla.

Demonstrations

Members of the Military Department move toward the speakers' platform. As cadet officers, they are allowed to carry weapons, so the other students give way. All eyes are on them. Suddenly, from the back of the room a voice booms out "Let him speak!" It is Jancsi Danner, a six-foot-four fifth year architect whose size commands respect. Again the room is silent. Danner's ears are red and his mouth quivering, but he stands his ground defiantly. Then László Zsindely, a few rows in front of Béla and Attila, begins to clap. A few next to him and then the whole section of balcony begins to clap as well. Soon the whole aula is ringing with thunderous applause. It is like a miracle. The applauding students begin to rise from their seats and the noise becomes even louder. The Party officials around the microphone grow nervous. They are furious, but also uncertain as to what to do. The applause goes on and on as the students realize they are participating in a spontaneous demonstration of opposition that, as long as it continues, the authorities can do nothing about.

Now there is total chaos on the platform. The Party Secretary runs to the telephone. The "penguins'" faces are as white as sheets. Once more through the pandemonium comes the high-pitched voice: "I represent the MEFESZ of Szeged. Please allow me to speak!"

Béla and Attila can stand it no more. They leave their seats and bound down the stairs to the main floor. Others similar in size are already starting to move forward through the applauding students toward the small Szeged student surrounded by the terrified DISZ officers. It is entirely spontaneous and they do it in spite of the fact that the cadet officers now on the platform can be seen to be fingering their revolvers. As the self-selected large students, led by Danner, get closer, the circle of DISZ officers gets thinner. The students begin to push the whole group toward the microphone, elbowing the smaller "penguins" away as they do. As they approach it Danner's long arm reaches out and pulls the microphone up to his mouth. "I ask the representative of the students of Szeged to speak!" A deafening ovation greets this announcement. As it subsides, Danner lowers the mike to his waist for the diminutive Szeged student and he, Béla, Attila, and a dozen others form a protective circle around him. None of them, and practically no one else in the room, realizes that the Szeged student is none other than András Lejtényi, leader of the Szeged students.

"Fellow students! Hungarians!" he begins as tears well up in Béla's eyes. "Once again, the wind of freedom is blowing in from Poland. The Polish

21

exchange students at our university are asking for our support. Russian troops are surrounding Warsaw, but the Polish Army is also encircling the Russians."

Flash bulbs begin to pop from all over the hall and strangers begin to rush off to telephones.

"We students of Szeged have decided to follow the Poles in establishing our independent student organization, the MEFESZ." Lejtényi then tells them what they have done in Szeged. He ends up with a passionate plea: "Please join with us. Do not believe the lies being spoken here today. Please form your own MEFESZ!"

At this point the speaker pauses and seems confused, for his short speech has not elicited the applause he expects. His voice falters and without starting on a particular note he begins to mumble the words of the forbidden national anthem. Somebody joins in on the proper pitch and soon the hymn most hated by the communists is filling the auditorium. It has not been heard in public, except in Churches at the end of each mass, since the communists took over ten years ago, but nearly everyone knows it. It is an anthem that can only be sung while standing at attention. The great chandelier of the aula trembles as the volume soars. By the time they finish nearly all the students are in tears. Something has happened. They are no longer scared of the authorities. And having lost their fear, they feel gloriously free.

With Danner and his colleagues surrounding the microphone the floor is theirs. Immediately about twenty hands go up requesting to speak.

Everyone gets his or her chance. Finally, around five o'clock a motion is made that the assemblage vote to leave the DISZ and establish a MEFESZ branch at the Technical University. The DISZ officers do everything they can to prevent a vote, but while they are allowed to speak, they do not control the microphone. The motion carries by acclamation and another long round of applause ensues. Several of the communist faculty members and DISZ officers leave in disgust, but the Building School Rector, Tibor Cholnoky, and other faculty remain.

Among the first speakers to address the new organization is a student who gives a detailed report on what has been going on in Poland. Gomułka and his backers, he says, had to confront the opposition of the most important members of the Soviet politburo only last Friday and he let them know to their faces that he was completely informed of their Army's maneuvers to surround the Polish capital, but was not going to negotiate with a gun to his head. When someone asks the speaker from where he gets his information, for there is nothing like that in the Hungarian press, he replies that he heard it in a Russian language broadcast from Poland.

Shouts of "Long Live Gomułka!" and "Long live our Polish sister nation!" break out from the crowd and soon the room is rocking with three thousand voices chanting these slogans.

A fourth-year architecture student asks for the floor to give his analysis of today's predicament. "In the Soviet Union," he says, "the leadership has embarked on the liquidation of the Stalinist inheritance. Eight months ago, during the Twentieth Party Congress of the Soviet Communist Party, Comrade Khrushchev revealed Stalin's crimes. The disclosure was followed by all kinds of reforms in the Soviet Union, in agriculture, industry, legislation, party organization. I do not deny that during the eighteen months when Imre Nagy was premier things advanced considerably in Hungary....But Rákosi turned Nagy out of office in order to push us back into a 'second Stalinism.' In July of this year we finally got rid of Rákosi. We are not unaware of the part played by our Soviet comrades in the expulsion of 'our little Stalin.' We are grateful to them for it. At the same time we hoped for a quick improvement in our position. Nothing of the kind followed. Here we are at the end of October without having seen any true reform, any democratic change; things are still being dragged out indefinitely. The present leaders still seem to be dominated by the shadows of Rákosi and Stalin. See how the Polish comrades take their country's destiny into their own hands! ...Once the surprise and apprehension of the beginning have vanished, the Soviet comrades themselves will approve them in the end. Why shouldn't we Hungarians follow their example? Why shouldn't we profit now by the changes that have taken place in Poland?"

"Long live Imre Nagy!" someone interrupts. "Long live the Hungarian Gomułka!"

"Exactly, long live Imre Nagy," answers the speaker. "But it's not just a question of changing personnel: we need a new program. An overall program, but one that points new roads for us, with precision. It's up to us to state the major demands of our nation. Just like one hundred and eight years ago, we are charged with defining *what the Hungarian Nation demands.*"

An intoxicating thrill runs through the audience at these words. "Right, the nation's demands!" "Come on, let's put them into writing!" "Right, let's get down to work right away," is shouted from the crowd.[27]

EXPLOSION

A student with a shock of black hair proposes that each Department nominate delegates to a general committee that would write up all the demands voiced so far into a proper document. This is quickly accomplished and the newly elected committee members retire to a classroom while the speeches, and, in many cases sloganeering, goes on.[28]

Not all the speakers are young. One, who introduces himself as József Szilágyi, an adult night student who is also a close friend of Imre Nagy, says with authority: "What you are doing is not illegal! The Hungarian Constitution gives you the right to free speech and the right to petition your government. And it is the duty of the government to respond to your concerns!" And the writer, Péter Kuczka, tells them "Your Party Secretary is lying to you. Your duty is not to return to your studies but to support the Polish workers and the people who are fighting for all of us."[29]

The Committee has come up with twelve demands. Cheers go up as each one is read out. But soon people are calling out for others to be added.

Around 7:00 p.m. one shy student when he reaches the microphone stutters "Wh-wh-why are the Ru-Ru-Russians still here? C-c-could th-th-the R-Russians l-l-leave?" A deathly silence pervades the room. Then, all of a sudden, applause breaks out and all the students are on their feet clapping and shouting "Yes!" Then mixed with the applause a chant begins to develop, at first quite faint but soon deafening: "Russkies Go Home! Russkies Go Home!" Everyone is astonished. The Party members, DISZ officers and Rector Cholnoky are dismayed that it has come to this. As the chant begins to fade Party Secretary Orbán strides over the microphone and says as ominously as she can, but with a quavering voice: "This meeting is over, it is closed. Anyone who remains will be participating in an illegal gathering the penalty for which is expulsion!" With that she abruptly marches out, followed by the DISZ officers and Party officials. Representatives of the press also leave, though one, a redheaded young man from *Szabad Ifjúság*, elects to stay.

To everyone's surprise, the rector, officers of the Military Department and a few professors remain.[30] So do five thousand students, for whom, at this point, threats of expulsion are quite meaningless. The twelve demands soon become fourteen, with the complete withdrawal of Russian troops becoming number four.

A new speaker at the microphone suggests taking these demands to the Radio so that the citizens of Budapest can hear them in their nightly news.

István Jankovich, an assistant professor, offers to take a delegation with the manifesto in his tiny Fiat Topolino. A few appropriately small students go off with him. It is now just after eight o'clock.

Zoltán Zelk, representing the Association of Hungarian Writers, asks for the floor. He is popular with the students, but his speech leaves them dissatisfied; it is too cautious. He announces that the Writers' Association is holding a ceremony in solidarity with the Poles tomorrow at 4:00 p.m. at the Bem memorial statue in Buda. There will be the laying of a wreath and some speeches, but definitely no demonstration.

"Fine!" yells someone in the audience. "We students of the Technical University will provide the demonstration!" This brings on such a sustained roar of approval that Zelk, though he tries, is unable to continue and has to leave the rostrum.

When the noise dies down a professor who has asked to speak says that while he approves of the demonstration he urges them to "be careful." He is assured that they will be. All they want is a calm, silent, peaceful demonstration that will impress everyone that they mean business.[31]

Across the Danube on the opposite bank of the river a similar meeting of about two thousand students is taking place in the auditorium of Karl Marx University of Economics. It has been under way for an hour. Following a report by two student members of the Petőfi Circle on its meeting the previous evening, the debate has been heated. The Dean of the university, Tibor Kardos, has done his best to put brakes on the proceedings. Now, while he grants that the students have a right to hold a silent demonstration at the Petőfi Monument tomorrow afternoon, he says the teachers must not join them. But Prof. Imre Tóth, head of the History Department and a non-communist, is so eloquent in his praise of the students that the Dean falls under his spell. Suspecting that the ÁVO has already been alerted about their plans, Prof. Tóth says that he, personally, thinks demonstrating, even silently, is neither safe nor wise. On the other hand, if the students decide they must march, then the teachers and the university party organizations should back them up and go with them. His arguments carry weight, but no final decisions are made. All agree to resume the meeting at nine tomorrow morning.[32]

*   *   *   *

Not far away Prof. Jankovich in his Fiat Topolino is delivering four students from the Technical University at the main gate of the radio station in

Sándor Bródy Street. One of them, an engineer named Mihály Sámson, has been playing a passive role all evening scribbling notes for his diary. Now he takes an active part in trying to get the manifesto of fourteen points broadcast. A guard accompanies them to the editor-in-chief of the news broadcasts, a tired-looking little blond man who seems sympathetic. After quickly running through the text he looks up and says "you know, my young friends, that we cannot broadcast such demands over Budapest Radio."

"Is what we have said so terrible?" Sámson inquires.

The editor wipes his forehead and calls to one of his associates. "Here," he says, "take this resolution and write a short bulletin with these young comrades about the meeting they have been having this afternoon and evening....Above all, nothing derogatory. Let me have your copy in ten minutes."

Three quarters of an hour later the delegation, still at the station, hears the "short, not derogatory bulletin" broadcast. The report speaks of the afternoon meeting and hastily mentions "student demands" without listing any, then adds, "Certain provocations were noted, but the majority of the young audience would have nothing to do with them."

Sámson and his fellow delegates are furious. They are all too familiar with this system of political fakery. They hasten back to the meeting to report that the radio, in effect, has refused to air their manifesto. It is now past nine o'clock.

When they make this brief report the noisy meeting turns even more so. "More censorship!" yells someone in the audience. Their anger is somewhat assuaged when the red-haired reporter from *Szabad Ifjúság* tells the assemblage that he approves of their demands and will have them printed in his paper, but he strongly advises them to delete the passage dealing with the withdrawal of Russian troops. "That would have a disastrous effect," he adds.

But the next speaker gets unanimous support when he says, "We refuse any censorship. We would rather find a way on our own to publicize our resolution."

Someone else calls out, "They refused a delegation of four. Let's see what they do with a delegation of four thousand!" Such a roar of acclamation greets this remark that there is scarcely any need for debate. People, in fact, begin to gather up their belongings in anticipation of a spontaneous move on the radio station. But now, Colonel István Marián, the commander of the military department, and his men quickly move to the microphone. Most people have forgotten that the military has also stayed behind after the official "closing" of the meeting.

Col. Marián is a short man, a farmer's son from Transylvania. Béla Lipták lowers the microphone and silently prays that he will not address the assembly with the greeting: "Comrades." Anything but "comrades."

"My sons!" says Marián. Never mind that half of us are female, thinks Lipták, at least he didn't say "comrades."

"My life is not more valuable than yours. I, too, am first a Hungarian and then everything else comes after that. But I am older and know this regime better than you do. I will not allow you to walk into an ÁVO trap in the dark of the night. No, we will march in daylight tomorrow and we will march only after obtaining the proper permits. We will not break any laws. And if we do a good job tonight, tomorrow the whole capital will march with us. And then I will be happy to march at the head of your demonstration."

This, says Béla to himself, is what I have been waiting for: someone who knows what he is doing and will be able to provide the leadership we need. At that moment he and many others decide they will stick with Colonel Marián.[33]

Other sober voices agree with the Colonel and the room settles back into a give and take discussion of tomorrow's action. The writer Péter Kuczka wants to speak a second time but the students, knowing his long association with Rákosi, prevent him and bodily remove him from the platform. The head of the Faculty of Marxist Studies also tries to speak, but the students refuse to hear him.[34]

It is now about 11 o'clock. Danner, Lipták and their fellow guards are no longer needed around the microphone and decide the meeting can continue without them. They ask Bandi Nemcsik to take the list of demands to Iván Sándor, editor of the school's in-house newspaper, *A Jövő Mernök (The Future Engineer)*. They know he has both the guts and ability to get the four-teen demands printed by tomorrow morning. Then they ask their Rector, Tibor Cholnoky, if they may have his permission to reproduce the manifesto on the university stencil duplicators. He hesitates, gives some excuses and finally refuses. He does not dare take responsibility for something that might cost him his job.

Not far away a young and quite beautiful blond assistant professor named Katalin Nemes overhears the exchange. She approaches the students and says: "Listen, I can show you where the stencil room is, and if you can force the door I will teach you how to operate it. I use those copiers to reproduce my homework and tests."

They had known Kati as young and beautiful; now they know her as brave. For the rest of their acquaintance she becomes "Blondie" whenever they refer to her. No more than two minutes are required to break the lock and soon Béla Lipták, Jancsi Danner, Ede Némethy and a few others have stenciled and are running off the fourteen demands. By midnight the demands and the notices of tomorrow's demonstration have been printed.

The meeting is still in session; there are many details about tomorrow's demonstration that still need to be worked out, but the numbers of those in attendance begin to drop for many have far to go to their beds.

At long last the meeting breaks up. It takes another hour before the little clots of excited students, rehashing that unbelievably long session, dissolve and disappear into the night. But not Mihály Sámson. He still has his diary to write and while he has many notes, he is afraid that if goes to sleep now, his memory will be too bleary for him to get it right. As an engineer, getting it precisely right has been his whole life. He sits down to begin. For a minute he is not sure whether to date it October 22 or October 23, for it is already two hours into the new day. But it all began on October 22, so that is the date he uses. Three hours later his diary, full of quotation marks around much of what he records as precisely as he can remember it, is complete. With light already showing in the eastern sky, he, too, goes home to bed.[35]

Budapest, Tuesday, October 23, 1956

Pest is all in blue shadow when the sun's first hazy rays light up the peak of Freedom Hill with its radio tower and Gellért Hill with its giant (sixty feet tall) black Peace Statue, a woman, holding a palm frond high above her head.* The monument was actually completed in 1944 before the Soviets took Budapest. It was intended to honor Horthy's son, killed during the war, but the wily old sculptor offered it instead to Marshal Voroshilov, first Russian Governor of "liberated" Hungary, as a monument to that Soviet hero.[36] Prominent by day as it towers over the city, this gigantic statue is even more noticeable by night, lit as it is by the intersecting beams of thirty

---

*Because the frond closely resembles a fish—and also because the statue was actually dedicated to "the Soviet Hero"—the people of Budapest disparagingly refer to her as "the fishmonger."

28

powerful searchlights. Soon the tops of other hills in Buda come into light. The foliage is mostly yellow with splotches of crimson and brown, for this year "Indian Summer"—or as the Hungarians say "Old Women's Summer"—has come unusually late and lasted longer than it normally does. Now the Palace, the Matthias Church, and the chalky white gash nearby with its conical turrets known to the world as "The Fisherman's Bastion," all atop Castle Hill, are bathed in sunlight. Across the Danube in Pest church towers, especially the two, as well as the dome, of St. Stephen's Cathedral, become highlighted by the sun, as does the ornate rooftop of the Parliament building sitting on the Pest Danube embankment. Its spires and particularly the giant red star perched on the spike of its dome shine in the new light. The star, lit from the inside as it has been all night long, takes on an orange hue as the golden rays reflect off its red glass.

It is not yet 7:00 a.m., yet scores of yellow and white streetcars, their lights piercing the still dark streets, are already gliding and clacking through both halves of the city taking hundreds of thousands of people to work. Budapest will not have a modern subway system for another two decades. Of course, there is the Földalatti (Underground) built for the Millennium celebrations in 1896. Budapesters have always been proud of the fact that they had the first underground railway on the continent of Europe, just a few years younger than the London Underground. But the Földalatti is a single line going from Vörösmarty Square in the center of the city, through Deák Square and then under the length of Andrássy Avenue (now Stalin Avenue) to Heroes' Square (now Stalin Square). Only if one is going to the opera or a concert or taking children to the zoo in City Park just past Heroes' Square (the last stop) does one use it. It is quite useless for going to and from work for most people.

* * * *

At the great West Railroad Station on Marx Square in Pest the overnight train from Belgrade is disgorging a group of very important people. First Secretary of the Hungarian Workers' (Communist) Party, Ernő Gerő, Premier of Government, András Hegedűs, Politburo Members János Kádár, Antal Apró, István Kovács, and other high officials are just returning from nine days of important negotiations with Yugoslavia, a country from which Hungary has been estranged since 1948. Gerő, in fact, has been outside the country, except for a few days just prior to the Yugoslav trip, since early September.[37] They are aware that they are returning none too soon to a crisis of growing proportions, but none seems aware of just how far things have gone until each is greeted with a copy of the Students' Sixteen Demands and notice of the afternoon demonstration on his desk. Phone calls home, reports from underlings, and reading back issues of *Szabad Nép*, even listening to the foreign broadcasts of Radio Budapest, have not really kept them abreast of developments. They are so in tune with their own media, which is heavily censored and slanted, that they do not always strive to read between the lines, as do the non-communist majority of readers. A meeting of the Political Committee (Politburo) has been called for ten o'clock. Now, while Gerő heads straight for Party Headquarters, large black limousines take the rest of them to their homes on Rózsadomb in Buda for a shower, shave and change of clothes.

*   *   *   *

Béla Lipták, who has had only three hours' sleep, finds himself surrounded by tired, mostly sleeping blue-collar workers on tram line 49. It is already seven by the time he arrives at gate four of the university to find six-foot-four Jancsi Danner already there. "The government has issued a permit for our demonstration," he announces. Then he slaps Lipták on the back and hands him a tricolor armband. Lipták stares at it, red, white and green, the Hungarian colors. For years now it has been forbidden for private citizens to display these colors in public. "Go to gate number two," says Danner, "and check the identity cards of all who enter. Only students and those who belong here. No strangers. None." Then he turns to Iván Szabó and says "Iván, could you get ahold of a bullhorn? We may need one later."

Lipták bounds off to gate four. He feels ten feet tall. With his tricolor armband he is now marked as a Hungarian patriot forever! The first person he checks is none other than Kati "Blondie." She is clearly impressed with his armband and with great formality takes out her identity card. Béla notices that her blue eyes have gone misty.

Though he is not aware of it, during his duty on the gate Radio Budapest announces that the student demonstration in solidarity with Poland will take place this afternoon, though the report seems more oriented toward the Writers Association than students and it erroneously states it will be in front of the Polish Embassy, not the Bem Memorial.[38]

While Béla is checking identities, one of his fellow mimeographers of last night, Antal Nógrádi, is busy sending stencils of the fourteen demands out into the countryside via motorcycle, particularly the mining districts such as Tatabánya. Taxi drivers are given copies of the demands and told to distribute them to all of their clients and fellow taxi drivers.[39]

An hour later when there are four gatekeepers on hand Béla figures he is no longer needed and decides to attend his mechanics class. His professor, Prof. Mutnyánszky, is a remnant of the old school and beloved of all his students. He has taught generations of engineers, including some Nobel Prize winners. World famous men like Theodor von Kármán, John (János) von Neumann, Edward (Ede) Teller, Eugene (Ödön) Wigner and Leó Szilárd have each sat in this same well and stared at these same ancient sliding blackboards. But today Prof. Mutnyánszky is not himself. He keeps losing his train of thought. At length he puts down the chalk, wipes his hands, walks slowly back to his desk and turns to face the class. For a moment he fiddles with his glasses. He looks around the room as though studying each face. Then, his voice choked with emotion, he says, "Go my young friends, go! This is not a day for mechanics. You have a higher duty today. Make this a proud day in the history of our much-suffering, poor nation."[40]

Béla leaves the classroom to join his classmates in practicing their marching formation in front of the Chemistry Building. On his way he spots Iván Sándor, editor of *The Future Engineer*, with a large bundle of the just printed copies. The demands are featured on the front page, but mysteriously they have become sixteen during the night. (For a complete list of the sixteen demands, see the Appendix to this Chapter.)

Some last minute additions were voted after Béla and his friends were stenciling their copy but had reached the newspaper in time for inclusion. Sándor offers a batch to Béla, who decides to take them to the universities in Pest. As he jumps on a streetcar with his tricolor armband and newspapers still smelling of drying ink, all eyes are on him. An elderly woman gets up and comes to stand next to him as if to prevent any ÁVO agent from seeing his armband. A mailman comes over and whispers, "I heard it from my daughter. I know everything. Be careful!"

* * * *

While the report of yesterday's meetings in the Party newspaper, *Szabad Nép*, are extensive, they are not entirely truthful. Nevertheless, those students who read the editorial feel encouraged. It reads in part:

> Thus far the voice of our youth has been gagged both in matters of national importance and in its own concerns. In recent years our young people have

nourished deep resentments, in many respects justified. So let us not be surprised if they raise their voices today. Those who call on them to express their views with caution are ignorant of the development of these young people and do not understand their real intentions…

Out on the streets the Fourteen Points from last night have been posted on trees, billboards and walls all over the city. People stop to read them, for the most part in silence, afraid to speak aloud those bold words that so many have thought in private. But here and there people do read them aloud to others, evoking cries of "About time!" and "Go on boys, go to it!"[41]

At the Marxism-Leninism University the DISZ "penguins" are still in control so Béla does not leave many there. The reception is far better at The Academy of Dramatic Arts, where someone pins a Polish insignia to his lapel. On his way to Lóránd Eötvös University a woman stops him on the street, hugs him, kisses the Polish insignia and unleashes a barrage of excited Polish. Béla points to his armband and not knowing how else to communicate, hands her a copy of *The Future Engineer*.

*   *   *   *

It is ten o'clock. At 17 Ákademia Street, headquarters of the Hungarian Communist Party not far from the Parliament Building, First Secretary Ernő Gerő is waiting for the meeting of the Politburo to begin. He has, like all other members, found a copy of the students' Sixteen Demands sitting atop his pile of mail in his office. He was so furious with this impudent document that he did not bother to read it through and swiped it to the floor. He knows what has to be done. He knows exactly how much his Party's power is based on fraud at the polling stations, on the power of its secret police and the Russian army units based in Hungary. In the July Plenum, before he was chosen to replace Rákosi, he had publicly been described by others, who hoped to prevent his elevation to party leader, as "impatient," "very austere in his relations with people," and "does not tolerate criticism, does not follow advice of comrades…and does not love the people." In turn, few people love him, for he was Rákosi's closest disciple and always strove to be as ruthless as his master.[42] This humorless, chain-smoking ascetic earned his reputation for ruthlessness in the Spanish Civil War where, instead of fighting the fascists, he devoted himself to "liquidating" communists suspected of being disloyal to Stalin. Afterward, having fled to Russia, he became a

Soviet citizen. The writer Pál Ignotus once referred to him as "a soulless Stalinist technocrat, a cross between an Inquisitor and a computer."[43]

Shortly after the meeting begins, Interior Minister László Piros is called forward and asked to give an explanation of why he had issued a permit for the student demonstration. As he stutters out his reasons, Gerő interrupts him with a string of curses. After others have heaped abuse on him, Piros admits that he may have made the wrong decision. Put to a vote, the Political Committee overwhelmingly recommends the permit be rescinded. Piros is ordered to draft a short statement and have it broadcast on the radio immediately.

* * * *

Meanwhile the meeting of students at Marxism-Leninism University has resumed. The main theme is not whether there should be a demonstration, but whether or not it should be silent. András Kiss, just returned from his obligatory military service to begin his third term as a foreign trade student, not only argues that it should, but that the red flags of the DISZ organization should be carried and prominently displayed. This, he argues, is to show that the demonstration is approved by and led by the party, and to insure against accusations of "counter-revolution." Just before the meeting breaks up the President of the university comes to address them. He gives his approval of the demonstration and their demands, with one exception: he objects to their demanding that the Russians leave Hungary. The time is not right for such a demand and he insists that they withdraw it. A cloudburst of boos erupts upon the President and he is forced to leave the hall in dismay.[44]

* * * *

Far to the east in Debrecen students, who had established a MEFESZ branch the night before at Louis Kossuth University, are feverishly summoning fellow students to a meeting in the great square in front of the main building.[45]

Last night representatives of the three colleges had laid down a joint program in twenty-nine points. The editor of the main party newspaper, *Néplap*, had promised to print them today, but a party county secretary, Ferenc Kulcsár, has made him renege on his promise. Around 10:30 Ágoston Székelyhidi, a fourth year student, reads out the twenty points that all three colleges have agreed upon. With minor alterations they are basically the same as the Szeged and Budapest versions. Only sections on Hungarian minorities abroad and a Central European Confederation have been added.

EXPLOSION

The two thousand students gathered in the square applaud after the reading of each point and are even more enthusiastic about the suggestion that they all march into town, where they will demand that this program gets published today in a special edition of *Néplap* in thirty-five thousand copies. Students rush to the basement of the main building to construct placards and various photos and even banners to take on their march.

Around 11:00 they start off holding hands in rows of eight and head for the Great Forest (Nagyerdő) Boulevard, which will take them to Simonyi Street leading directly to the center of the city. Three students representing the three colleges and József Kozák, a well-known athlete, carrying the national flag without the communist emblem in its center, head the procession. They are ahead of the Budapest demonstration by more than two hours.[46]

Shortly after this the First Secretary of the County Party Committee, Comrade Zoltán Komócsin, phones the local Army Commander, Major Imre Garab. He is allowed to issue the Major orders, because in emergencies it is legal for the highest party official to take over control of the Army.

"Comrade Major," he says. "The students are starting a demonstration and we expect there will be some turmoil this afternoon which may turn to mob violence by evening. You must prevent this demonstration by all means."

"Comrade Komócsin, I haven't a clue as to what you mean. How am I supposed to prevent this demonstration?"

"Very simple, Comrade Major, command your troops to be out there and, if necessary, have them use their weapons."

"Comrade Komócsin, we are a training unit. This is not in our profile. Moreover, I am not a butcher who breaks up a crowd and shoots unarmed people."

There is a brief silence. Then in a voice of controlled fury: "Comrade Major, I order you to report to me at Party headquarters at once!"

When Garab gets there he finds that the ÁVO regiment commander, Major Simon, is also there. Komócsin dresses Garab down in front of him and then the ÁVO chief piles on, saying the only way to put an end to this trouble is with arms, it is the only way to assure the power of the party. Garab erupts: "Listen, so far as I am concerned power that needs the support of bayonets isn't worth shit! I am not going to interfere in these events. I

34

haven't been ordered by my superior commander; I and my troops will stay in our barracks."

Major Garab then returns to his headquarters, calls in his officers and says all troops will be confined to barracks and no weapons are to be handed out.[47]

*   *   *   *

In Miskolc there are no plans for a demonstration, but the workers of the Hungarian State Rolling Stock and Machine Factory, who yesterday came up with their own seventeen points, mostly concerning labor conditions and wages, adhere to the suggestion of one worker. He advocates taking on four further points, all of them radical, from the students of the local technical school. These include: withdrawal of Soviet troops, disengagement from the Warsaw Pact, neutrality and a new government. The party members present approve the document with all twenty-one points and agree to have an "open party day" on the twenty-fifth.

*   *   *   *

Back in the capital over in Pest just off Deák Square, Sándor Kopácsi, chief of police for the city of Budapest, is just arriving in his office. He is a short, wiry man, with a dark beard, even though clean-shaven. He comes from a proletarian background; like his father he was a metal worker from the north. As a teenager he fought with the partisans against the Nazis, joined the party early and through sheer ability has reached this position of power in his early 30s. His deputy has been impatiently waiting for him. "The phones are ringing off the hooks!" he exclaims. "Everyone is looking for you. Comrade Márton Horváth [editor of the Party daily newspaper] wants you to call the minute you get in." This is not exactly the reception Kopácsi was expecting to get on the first day back from vacation. He calls Horváth, who is in his office at *Szabad Nép* (Free People).

"I've been trying to reach you since dawn," yells Horváth. "Why, in the face of so grave a situation, are the police getting their kicks by provoking the crowd?"

Kopácsi is completely taken aback. What grave situation? What provocation? Like everyone he is aware of the student demands which this morning they have plastered on lampposts all over Budapest along with announcements of their demonstration this afternoon. But what's this about a provocation? He asks Horváth to explain.

It seems that members of the newspaper staff had reported the presence of "large mounted police units" in the streets of Budapest. Since Kopácsi knows he has no mounted police units, large or small, he is stumped. "Comrade Horváth," he says, "I have just returned from holidays. I'll find out what is going on and call you right back." When he reaches him by phone, Tibor Pőcze, Deputy Minister of Interior, is also flummoxed. "What's this all about?" A pause, then "Shit! The National School of Mounted Police! We're going to be giving you some mounted police in a few months' time. In their training, they have to get both the students and horses accustomed to city traffic. The teachers take them on a little excursion every Tuesday morning." Pőcze promises he will have them return to their school immediately, at a gallop. But while he has him on the phone Pőcze tells Kopácsi that the Minister of the Interior, László Piros, wants to see him in his office, *now*. Then he advises him "not to appear in civilian clothes, like last time. They hate that here."

On his way to the Ministry of the Interior, Kopácsi learns that at 12:53 this afternoon Radio Budapest had broadcast the following bulletin: "In order to assure public order, the Minister of the Interior is not permitting any public meetings and demonstrations until further notice."

Kopácsi finds Interior Minister Piros in a nasty mood. He has no great love for this son of a butcher who is barely his elder. And Piros' first words are: "Kopácsi, this is a nice damned mess your friends have arranged for me!" (The reference to "friends" means "Imre Nagy," of whom Kopácsi is known to be a great admirer.)

"You are speaking of the demonstration, Comrade Minister? From my reports these are communist students who are planning to demonstrate."

"You tell that to some of the other comrades," says Piros, opening the door to the conference room. Kopácsi notices that the seat next to the five under secretaries usually occupied by the Soviet advisor, Comrade Yemelyanov, is vacant. He whispers a query to Pőcze: "Dismissed; left for Moscow" is the quiet response.

Minister Piros enters, accompanied by an obvious, by the ill-fitting cut of his civilian suit, Russian. He is a crafty looking little blond-headed man with shifty blue eyes and an air of great self-importance. He reminds Kopácsi of certain Nazi officers he has seen during the war. Piros says by way of introduction: "Comrades, please meet the new comrade counselor just arrived from Moscow." No name is mentioned and it is only days later that Kopácsi discovers that this, in fact, is the famous Ivan Serov, chief of the Soviet KGB.

The Hungarians greet him politely. Serov returns the greetings with a cold blink of his eyes.

"I invited Comrade Kopácsi, our police chief," Piros begins, "to reveal his plans for this afternoon. As you know, earlier today I forbade the demonstration."

All eyes turn to Kopácsi as he rises to answer. "I would like to begin with a question, Comrades. What should we do, if, despite the ban, the students carry on their demonstration regardless?"

There is a silence around the table until Piros explodes: "You are here, Comrade, precisely to respond to that question."

"Fine. To prevent a demonstration I have to be properly equipped. Horthy's police had billy sticks; we don't. Horthy's police had mounted police with sabers that could strike a flat blow, but which rarely killed anybody. We don't. Our firemen are not trained in crowd control, as were theirs. The only weapons at our disposal are dangerous ones, rifles and machine-guns."

"A rifle has a butt, doesn't it?" asks Piros.

"Suppose rifle butts don't do the job. Suppose they resist or even counterattack. Who will take responsibility, Comrade Minister, for having shot at an unarmed crowd and possibly caused dozens of deaths?"

Kopácsi then explains that it is wrong to reduce a political problem to a police problem. And he adds that he completely disagrees with Piros' order banning the demonstration.

To everyone's surprise the Soviet Comrade Counselor rises without even asking to speak. He pushes back his unruly hair and signals the interpreter. Then, spitting out each syllable, he says: "The fascists and imperialists send their shock troops into the streets of Budapest and there are still comrades of your armed forces who hesitate to use arms!" It is an accusation, not a question. Serov goes on speaking of capitalists disguised as students, and landowners' representatives and the "need to teach the fascist underworld a lesson."

The senior ÁVO officers present are no democrats, but they think such language has gone out of style. Their amazement encourages Kopácsi to respond.

"If you'll permit me just a word, Comrade Minister. Clearly the comrade counselor from Moscow has not had time to inform himself of the situation in our country. He should know that it is not fascists and other imperialists

37

who are planning this demonstration. These are university students, sons and daughters of workers and peasants, very carefully chosen, the pride of our intelligentsia who want to show their solidarity with their Polish comrades."

His face beet red, the little counselor speaks softly to Piros. But when Kopácsi's words are translated he flies into a rage. The deputy ministers all counsel Piros to seek higher authority, passing the responsibility up the line. Piros reaches for the red phone. Everyone waits silently, the little Russian staring daggers at Kopácsi.

Piros is talking into the red phone. Suddenly the rasping voice of Gerő can be heard.

"Yes, Comrade Gerő, I agree, Comrade Gerő, your orders will be executed, Comrade Gerő."

The Politburo has decided to lift the ban. The news is soon carried by Radio Budapest.[48]

* * * *

But the broadcast comes at 2:23, only after Kopácsi and the Deputy Minister of the Interior, Fekete, have already reached the Technical University where the students are due to begin their march at 2:30. They are directed through the crowded corridors to the main amphitheater of the Engineering School building, where several thousand students are packed in, listening to last minute instructions from their leaders. The speaker notices the entrance of uniformed police and ad libs: "I will profit from the presence of police officers in the room to tell them that the students of Budapest have decided to do without your authorization. The demonstrations will take place anyway. We will shout in the face of the leadership that we want change."

Everyone turns toward Kopácsi and starts to boo.

Kopácsi spots an old peasant friend, Jóska, seated on the rostrum. He pushes through the crowd and reaching Jóska says, "Tell them not to get worked up. The ban is lifted." Then he adds that "we would like to announce it ourselves," and signals to Deputy Minister Fekete. There is a deathly silence as Fekete climbs up on the rostrum. Fekete pulls out the order from his pocket and reads to the crowd:

"The ban is lifted, but the students, mindful of the cause of socialism, are begged to expel all agitators from their ranks etc." He finishes with the words, "The Party...declares itself entirely in agreement with the students' noble determination for renewal. It has asked me to offer its message of solidarity to you."

The ovation that follows is like an exploding bomb.[49]

Outside, while it is only sixty-one degrees Fahrenheit, the sun is shining brightly, giving the impression of a warm day. Students have been standing around for several hours, but few are idle. They are making armbands and cockades so that every marcher will bear Hungarian colors. Some have been making banners identifying specific marching groups, others with slogans, for the pledge to silence does not mean that they cannot display their opinions. Placards are written, and some of these placards are quite intentionally provocative. Among the more prominent are: "Student grants students can live on!" "No more compulsory Russian!" "Democratize the Party!" "We Want Imre Nagy!" and "Russians Go Back to Russia!"[50]

When word had come on the radio that Interior Minister Piros had forbidden the march, there had been consternation and a near riot among the milling students until Colonel Marián appeared on the roof of the Machinery Laboratory and using a bullhorn asked: "Will you obey the Minister's orders?" As if on cue a resounding "NO" rose from the crowd. Jancsi Danner, heading a small delegation with Imre Majoros at the wheel, went speeding off in a university-owned Škoda to confront the Minister. During the long wait Béla Lipták notices that a great many more men in trench coats are accumulating outside the university gates. They are taking a lot of photographs and making phone calls.

*   *   *   *

In Pest another delegation, not of students, but highly ranked party journalists, had also rushed off to try to counter Minister Piros' order banning the demonstration. But they know better than to go to the Ministry of the Interior, so they go straight to Party headquarters. Lead by *Szabad Nép's* managing editor, Márton Horváth, the delegation is received by Gerő, Révai, the Stalinist ideologue, Kádár and Marosán, both of whom had been imprisoned by Rákosi. "I am very vexed with you," blurts out Gerő before Horváth can say a word. But Horváth is too full of what he wants to say to be put off by Gerő's remark. The masses must not be taken lightly, says Horváth; the government can delay no longer, things have reached their ultimate point and it is time to act.

"You have lost your mind!" shouts Gerő. "You understand nothing! You underestimate the strength of our proletarian power!" (Even Horváth does not realize that by "proletarian power" Gerő means exclusively: "political security police.")

"Comrade Gerő, what will happen if the young men and women of the universities decide to ignore the ban and carry on their silent demonstration everywhere?"

"There will be shooting," Gerő replies without hesitation. "The troops will know how to use their weapons."

"Fire on them! Fire on them!" chimes in the ideologue Révai almost hysterically.

When one of the younger journalists, Pál Locsei, has the audacity to ask Gerő a provocative question, Marosán turns on him and yells, "You are nothing but a filthy, mangy dog! I'm going to call the orderlies at once and have you thrown out!"

This proves unnecessary as the young man feels he has no choice but to leave the room. Only Kádár remains silent. But Gerő, for all of his brusque bravado, is clearly shaken as he realizes what mayhem would result with so many students being fired on.

As all the participants leave the room after the session, the young banished journalist takes Kádár aside and whispers, "What about you, Comrade Kádár? Don't you hold any position? By avoiding any decision you are making the same mistake that already brought you down and sent you to prison after the Rajk affair." "Shut up!" hisses Kádár, giving him a cold stare. "Things are not so simple as you seem to think."[51]

All this took place about two o'clock.

*   *   *   *

Now it is half an hour later. At the Technical University on the same rooftop where Colonel Marián had stood, the unmistakable figure of Jancsi Danner appears. With him is a small man in police uniform. "My name is Sándor Kopácsi, the police chief of Budapest," he shouts through the bullhorn. "I bring you good news. Your march has been permitted." He tries to say something else but his voice is swallowed up in the cheers that greet this news.[52] Following this announcement, more students begin to flow down the broad steps of the main building from the aula where they had congregated and begin to form up by school and by class in front of the main entrance. The boulevard between the university complex and the Danube embankment is wide enough for large groups to maneuver.

With the announcement of the ban's revocation the general mood swings from anger to optimism bordering on triumph. The government and Party made a bad decision, then vacillated and reversed the decision in the face of the student's determination. The students now feel more confident than before.[53]

In Fő (Main) Street in Buda ÁVO Captain János Mester and Lieutenant Mihály Varga leave ÁVO headquarters to investigate a report that employees of the main Radio Station at Sándor Bródy Street in Pest are about to organize a strike. They are to report back to headquarters by phone at regular intervals.[54]

Back at the Technical University, Col. Marián once again takes over the bullhorn. "Our silent solidarity march will start at gate number two. We will march north, up to Gen. Bem's Square on the west bank of the Danube. There we will take part in a commemoration of Polish-Hungarian friendship directed by the Writers' Union. The march will start immediately."

László Gabányi raises an enormous Hungarian flag, no emblem in its middle. Gate two is opened and row upon row of students, arms linked, shoulder to shoulder, pour out in the direction of Gellért Square. Béla Lipták figures there must be at least ten thousand people, maybe more, assembled for the march. He and his fellow engineers are near the front. They are all silent now; only the tramp of hundreds of feet can be heard scraping the cobblestones. It is like a dream, thinks Lipták, a miracle. As they flow into Gellért Square all traffic comes to an abrupt halt. Pedestrians freeze in place, wide-eyed in astonishment. A sanitation worker drops her twig broom, then kneels and crosses herself as the national flag passes before her. A tall man with a sweeping moustache removes his hat and stands at rigid attention. Lipták notices a young traffic policeman reach for his cap to remove it in a sign of respect, then quickly pretending he is just wiping sweat from his brow, he replaces it.

As the procession flows through the square it begins to draw like a magnet people on both sides of the street. They follow along on the sidewalks so that soon those on the sidewalks equal the number of students in the middle.[55]

Across the Danube students from Marxism-Leninism University and Lóránd Eötvös University, who are lined up along the east embankment, see the great national flag slowly leading the Technical University students and raise their own flags to begin a march to the Petőfi Statue just north of where the Erzsébet (Elizabeth) Bridge, destroyed in the war and not yet rebuilt, used to join Pest. It is an extraordinary sight to see these two great colorful masses of people inching north on either side of the great river, which flows in the opposite direction at three times the speed.

Lipták and his fellow engineers are headed straight up the left embankment to Bem Square. But certain sections of the parade well behind them after passing the Gellért Hotel on Gellért Square turn right onto Szabadság (Freedom) Bridge to cross over to Pest. Not only do they want to join with the students of other universities, they want to take the long way to the Bem memorial so that they can pass through the center of Pest and be seen by a maximum number of Budapest's citizens.

Even though the students carefully keep to the right-hand side of the road going over the bridge, their crossing the bridge proves to be a problem for Chief of Police Kopácsi who, with a police motorcycle escort, is slowly following the lead sections of the parade. He notices a huge black limousine halted near the bridge. Its windows are curtained and by its license plate Kopácsi knows that it is from the Soviet Embassy. A young man gets out of the limousine and hurries over to the police car. "Comrade Kopácsi," he says in good Hungarian. "I am Comrade Andropov's interpreter. I recognized your car. Would you be kind enough to help us get across the bridge? We are rather pressed for time."

"Of course, with pleasure." Kopácsi has his driver, George, put on his white gloves and grab the white disc on a stick policemen use for directing traffic. George gets out and stops the procession. Meantime, Kopácsi, seeing the limousine door still open and Andropov beckoning to him, strides quickly over to the Soviet Ambassador's car. "Comrade Kopácsi, the ambassador thanks you," translates the interpreter. "Not at all. That's the least I could do." Andropov continues in Russian. While Kopácsi speaks Russian, his comprehension is not all that good, so he waits for the interpreter. "Comrade Andropov asks whether, in your opinion, things are not going a bit too far. Some of the banners are insulting to the Soviet Union."

Kopácsi turns crimson. He knows precisely which banners the Ambassador means. He tries to explain that these are young students and they are under the supervision of the DISZ organization. Just as he is doing this some loud voices come from the procession that is halted not more than three meters away. There are unfriendly remarks about Kopácsi's police uniform and the Soviet pennant on the limousine, which Kopácsi notices for the first time. Ambassador Andropov gives him a cold look, thanks him again in

Russian and pulls the door shut, and the limousine glides across the bridge under the hostile stare of several thousand young Hungarians.[56]

When it reaches the Pest side of Freedom Bridge Ambassador Andropov's limousine is again ensnared in a tide of demonstrating students. His driver is obliged to turn right rather than left, to get out of and around the mass of students flowing toward the Petőfi statue.

At the Petőfi Statue

At the Petőfi statue itself the modestly sized Plaza appears to be already full, yet streams of students, many led by their faculty, continue to flow into it from Váci Street and Kossuth Ave. as well as the Belgrade Quay. This inflow compacts more tightly the thousands already there; ten thousand would be a good guess. Banners, signs and flags can be seen held above the throng, but nobody is speaking. They are keeping their pledge of a silent demonstration. One flag waving above peoples' heads draws angry attention. It has the communist insignia in its middle. People quietly demand it be lowered and before its owner can do anything about it dozens of hands pull the four corners taut and someone with a large pocket knife carves the hated symbol out of it. As the flag with a gaping hole in its middle is raised a cheer of approval from nearby participants breaks out. Then silence descends again.

In the midst of the dark mass of people the green copper statue of the poet Petőfi stands out on its high pedestal in the afternoon sun, right arm raised dramatically to the sky, fingers in an aristocratic pose. It is three times life size and even from a distance one can see that Petőfi was an exceedingly handsome man, with refined features, his pointed moustaches, pointed beard and carefully coiffured yet wind-swept hair. He is wearing a cape and has a scroll in his left hand, presumably the famous poem he wrote on the eve of March 15, 1848. This national poem is so stirring that it sparked the uprising that lead to that revolution more than a century ago. Ever since, Hungarian schoolchildren have willingly committed it to memory.

Several speeches are made and the students' sixteen points are read out to great acclaim. Then a well-known actor from the National Theatre, Imre Sinkovits, pushes his way through the crowd and takes his stance on the first step of the monument facing the crowd. He calls out for silence. As a hush falls across the multitude he raises his right arm in exact imitation of the statue above him and begins to recite in dramatic tones the Petőfi National Poem. This famous work has not been heard in public now for over a decade.

"Talpra Magyar!…
"On your feet Hungarians! Your Country calls you!
"Now is the time, now or never!
"Shall we freemen be, or slaves? That's the question!
"We swear! We swear by the God of the Magyars
"That we will never more be slaves!

(There are many other verses, but each ends with the refrain: "We will never more be slaves!")

No one wants to upstage this famous actor, but since all know the poem by heart, everyone now begins to mouth the words in unison with his delivery, while joining in loudly at each refrain. When he finishes there is an outpouring of applause and even before this dies down Sinkovits is declaiming another patriotic poem. Again there is applause as he finishes, only this time, the silence having been broken, there are cries from the audience calling for this or that poem. Before Sinkovits can begin again, a group near the front begins to sing the national anthem. As with the students at the Technical University the night before, people in the crowd have not heard it in public, except for church, for over a decade and until Sinkovits hears and decides to join in, it almost doesn't catch on. But gradually it spreads and, despite the considerable breeze, an ocean of voices in remarkable unison soon soars over the plaza. By the time the last note sounds there is not a dry eye in the crowd, yet faces are glowing and smiles are broad. No one has ever felt such pride, such unity, such elation before.

But over near the Lenin Institute banner a scuffle breaks out. Someone objects vocally to the red flags and says "these people are not wanted here." Before the dispute can come to blows someone starts the crowd singing the Marseillaise, after which comes the Internationale. By the time this anthem is over the controversy is forgotten.[57]

As silence returns the student marshals announce the beginning of the march to General Bem's statue in Buda some two and a half miles away. The edge of the crowd nearest the Váci Street and Kossuth Ave. begins to move out and the mass of people expands without seeming to diminish in the slightest. It is now about 3:30.

ÁVO Captain Mester, now at the Radio Station, is just finishing his telephone report to his boss, Major Mézes, when the latter says: "Wait a minute, Captain, have you been out in the street?" "No, but the two sentries say that noise can be heard outside…Far away for the moment. From the direction of the Danube…"

"What kind of noise?"

"Shouts of 'Hurrah!' and songs…"

"All right. We know about that. That's at the Petőfi statue. It was expected. But it's essential to examine the street outside the radio station. Go do this yourself."

"As things stand now it might not be advisable for me to be in the street in the uniform of an ÁVO Captain."

"You're right. I order you to take off your uniform and put on civilian clothes."

In less than half an hour a battalion of ÁVO troops will arrive at the radio station. Whether this is to protect First Secretary Gerő, who is expected to record his speech later in the day, or to defend the radio from a possible assault is not clear.[58]

While the demonstration streaming from the Petőfi plaza can no longer be considered "silent," people for the most part are still observing the prohibition. Indeed, it is far more impressive to see young people walking in silence than not, and silence attracts attention to their banners and signs.

As they flow along Kossuth Avenue police are out in force, but are not spread out in lines, which would make each individual officer too vulnerable, but only in small groups along the way. They herd the demonstrators wherever they can back onto the sidewalks. But there are not enough of them and so the marchers inevitably flow back onto the street once they have passed these clots of funneling police.

When the processors reach the Astoria Hotel on the right and turn left onto the Grand Boulevard, they find large crowds have assembled to watch. Curious streetcar passengers getting on and off trams pause to see what is going on. Here at the crossing of the Grand Boulevard the marchers are joined by the students not only of the several humanities universities but high school students as well, led by their teachers. Emboldened by their unity, growing numbers and greater number of onlookers, some of the students cannot keep themselves from shouting a few slogans.

"Rákosi should be returned and tried!" "Down with Gerő!" "No more Hungarian Uranium for the Soviet Union!" "Imre Nagy for Premier!"

"Restore the Kossuth Crest!" "No more compulsory Russian!" But the cry of "Russians Go Home!" is not yet heard.

The shouting is occasional and not mechanical and not every slogan catches the enthusiasm of the crowd so that it gets repeated rhythmically. But by the time the procession has passed through Deák Square and headed for Bajcsy-Zsilinszky Avenue the slogans have become a regular part of the otherwise silent march.

The students are all bareheaded. Now occasional fedoras and caps, even military caps on fully uniformed soldiers, begin to prove that the marchers are no longer exclusively students. As they pass the beginning of Stalin (formerly Andrássy) Avenue the marchers can see that every lamppost has the fourteen demands plastered on it. One shouted slogan, for those who sympathize, is difficult to ignore: "Whoever is Hungarian, come with us!"

Along the way, particularly on the long Bajcsy-Zsilinszky Avenue, every window is open, packed with people, some practically hanging out. A young woman stands perilously close to the edge of a ledge with no rail on the second storey of the insurance company where she works. She rapturously waves a Hungarian flag on a long pole slowly back and forth. While most of the students sport their own cockade of red-white-and-green, most of the newcomers have nothing. They are rewarded by women in a ribbon factory several stories above the street who shower the parade with long red, white and green ribbons. The shoe and sweets stores below have been shut for the occasion, their owners standing on the sidewalk waving to the passing thousands. They now stoop to pick up the ribbons and hand them to those passing by. Students from the Lenin Institute proudly carry their banner, but the crowd derides their red flags. One group of women yells for them to burn them. The students pretend they have not heard, but one by one the flags are furled and kept out of sight.

It is nearing four o'clock, the time set by the Writer's Association for the ceremonies at General Bem's memorial to begin.

Over in Buda, Béla Lipták and his fellow marchers from the Technical University have reached the Bem Quay, long since having passed through Adam Clark Circle with the Széchényi Chain bridge on the right and the great tunnel under Castle Hill on the left. They, too, have picked up a great many new participants along the way.

The long shadow of the steep and rocky Gellért Hill is already extending across the river into Pest, but Castle Hill above them, being set further back from the river, does not yet block the sun. Lipták is still in a dream. He imagines that it is not just him and his fellow students marching but all the famous Hungarians he has read about as a schoolboy: St. Stephen, founder of the nation, Matthias Corvinus, the great renaissance King who brought so much Italian and other Western culture to the country, Prince Rákóczi with his rugged kuruc soldiers and even Louis Kossuth himself with his bloodied but unbowed redcaps. Soon he conjures up poets, playwrights and musicians. He feels the collective soul of Hungary is sweeping along with them. When he sees a lady in a white smock at Döbrentei Square waving a Hungarian flag with a ragged hole in the middle, he realizes that that mutilated flag is now the symbol of their cause.

At the Bem Memorial

As they arrive at Bem Square almost on the dot of 4:00 p.m. they see that several hundred people already surround the statue with flowers heaped around its base. Also prominently displayed are, on its front, a giant Kossuth Crest and on the side a large Polish flag with its distinctive double-headed eagle. And someone has even dug up an old Kossuth flag from 1848 to complete the decoration. The statue is striking in that it is painted black, and General Bem, five to six times life-size, seems to be both striding forward and pointing with his left arm. A sword juts out under his great coat, but most notable is his large hat with an enormous feather arching back over it. He resembles neither a Pole nor a general, yet doubtless this depiction is historically accurate.

The Square is open to the Danube on the east, though some distance from the Bem Quay and the tram tracks, which run along the river embankment. It has the Ministry of Foreign Affairs on the south, and the Pálffy Barracks of the Zrínyi Military Academy on the west. To the north are several six-storey buildings with a street between them. The statue is perched on a knoll and both that fact and its size make it much more prominent than the Petőfi memorial. The square, which is also much bigger, is filling with people from all directions, but the main part of the march through Pest has yet to cross the Margaret Bridge to join it.

Just at this time, down in Szeged, the city where it all started a week ago, students from the two universities, having gathered in the Cathedral Square with their flags and banners, now set off through Árpád Square to the City Hall on Széchényi Square. They are in a happy mood chanting slogans and singing songs as they go first to the Kossuth Statue on Klauzál Square and then to the Rókus section of the city, where they are joined by thousands of workers just finishing their work shifts.[59]

* * * *

Far to the east in Debrecen, the student march, which began before noon, has long since reached Red Army Avenue in the city's center. Around one o'clock a delegation of thirty students had entered the Party Committee building and been greeted by a grinning Party Secretary, Zoltán Komócsin, standing on the staircase. Negotiations in a small conference room had quickly produced the "compromise" that *Néplap* can immediately print all the students' demands, save the one about withdrawing Soviet troops. The chanted slogans could be clearly heard in the conference room. Outside, where someone has put the national flag with the Kossuth coat-of-arms out of a window of the Déry Museum, the delegation announces the results of the negotiation in an attempt to quiet the ever-more-noisy crowd. Nevertheless, the demonstrators want more results and march off in the direction of the Golden Bull Hotel. Here they split into three groups, the largest turning onto Kossuth Street to go to the MÁV railroad wagon factory to persuade its three thousand workers to join the demonstration, the next going to the Hungarian Roller Bearing factory and the third to the printing plant of *Néplap*. When they are refused entry at the MÁV plant, the students simply climb over the fence. Now these workers and those from Debrecen's other factories become part of a greatly enlarged crowd.[60] The third group of students have forced the newspaper, *Néplap*, to evacuate its printing shop, claiming it "in the name of the people," while they set and run off all twenty of their demands, ignoring Komócsin's entreaty to drop the demand for the withdrawal of Soviet troops.

The city began the day awash in red flags left over from yesterday's celebration of the twelfth anniversary of its liberation by the Red Army. Now it finds itself in a massive and thorough purging of these flags wherever the students penetrate the city shouting "Down with the Red Flags!" "Russkies Go Home!" The university students are joined enthusiastically in this enterprise by high school students, one of whom, Pál Madocsi,[61] is a seventeen-year-old apprentice in the food industry. Madocsi, who spends half his time in class and half working as a part-time employee of a restaurant in the center of town, has been ordered by his boss to close and shutter the establishment lest the crowd turn too boisterous and windows get broken. Rather than return to his dormitory, Madocsi joins a group of teenagers who not only help to remove all the red flags, they go after the red stars as well, after people shout that they, too, should be removed.

* * * *

On St. Stephen's Boulevard in Pest at this time the long march through the city is about to cross Mari Jászai Square as it approaches the Margaret Bridge. It has already passed through Marx Square that has the West Station with its impressive (for the year in which it was built) all-glass front, on the right.

The students' reception by the populace, a large number of whom have decided to join them, has been spectacular. And their numbers have been greatly swelled by thousands of workers, mostly young, pouring out of West Station and off the trams in Marx Square. They have been on their way home, but this is too much to pass up. They are about to experience in practice what the textbooks of Marxism so insistently emphasized: direct revolutionary alliance between the workers and the students.[62] Budapest has not seen so many Hungarian flags, retrieved from closets and attics—even some with the old Kossuth crest on them—since the end of the War.

Among the new marchers, most of whom have never seen each other before, there is considerable discipline, yet a sense of gaiety. People find themselves discussing the events of the day and pouring out their anti-regime feelings to utter strangers and laughing as these strangers, in turn, confide in them. Dora Scarlett, a fortyish British communist with prematurely white hair who works in the foreign department of Radio Budapest, has never seen Budapest so happy. The most exciting thing is the sound of laughter—people laughing out loud.[63] No communist parade or demonstration was ever like this!

Now, as the procession moves onto the wide Margit (Margaret) Bridge, the leading groups of students link arms again and move to the right side so that streetcars can pass without hindrance. László and Éva Beke, who joined the march as it turned onto the Grand Boulevard nearly three quarters of an hour ago, are near the middle. As they reach the tip of Margaret Island where the bridge angles a few degrees south in a very slight "v," they look ahead and then back. László is astounded. Not only is the bridge entirely full, he cannot even see the end in Pest. His quick calculation is that there are anywhere from fifty to eighty thousand people taking part. He has been fearful of the possible effect of the long walk on Éva's pregnancy, but Éva would not have missed this for the world.[64]

As the main part of the march begins to flow into Bem Square somewhat after 4:00 p.m. the leaders find that the ceremonies are already under way. The wreath from the Writers' Association has been laid at the base of General Bem's statue. The Petőfi Circle has provided a sound truck. After some introductory remarks, including praise for their Polish brothers, the Petőfi Circle representative hands the microphone over to a student from the Technical University. He, in turn, praises the Polish students for their recent action and then proceeds to read their sixteen points.

By now people are packed around the monument even more tightly than at the Petőfi memorial gathering. The side streets become so full that no one can enter the square. Close to one hundred thousand people are there and more keep coming. On the west side cadets hang out of every window of their barracks, legs dangling, waving and shouting to the crowd. They have been forbidden to take part (in fact have been locked in their barracks), but when the crowd shouts for flags they soon display them in abundance.[65] Police Chief Sándor Kopácsi cannot believe his eyes when he sees them from afar. "The Army's future commanders!" he thinks to himself, then spots the huge Hungarian flag flying over the barracks with a ragged hole where the Rákosi-designed communist crest belongs. Just then a mighty roar comes up from the crowd. Kopácsi realizes for the first time that real trouble is coming and orders George to drive him back to headquarters at once.[66]

Around this time, Col. Miklós Orbán, commander of the ÁVO's interior law-enforcement troops, leads two platoons in trucks from the guard battalion headquarters at Fő Street in Buda to the Radio Station in Pest. The second platoon is equipped with machine guns and masses of ammunition as well as rifles and pistols. There are already some 270 soldiers from the guard and special battalion at the radio in preparation for its defense.[67]

Péter Veres, President of the Hungarian Writers' Association, is a famous poet and former Peasant Party leader who has cooperated rather too much with the communists. He begins to speak into the microphone, which students hold up to his face, but somehow the amplification from the sound truck parked on the street below does not carry across the mass of people. When he reads the Writers' Association's newly crafted Seven Points, they are such a watered-down version of what the students have just presented that everyone loses interest. He drones on, and his speech is subject to increasing catcalls and insults as the audience grows restless. People, particularly on this day, are tired of platitudes and jargon.

Some in the crowd notice that the Communist Hungarian flag is still flying over the Foreign Ministry. Demands for its replacement are soon being voiced. After some delay, someone in the Ministry complies.

Veres finishes his oration to light applause and some catcalls and then other speakers attempt to get the crowd's attention. But the Petőfi Circle sound truck, brought there to reach hundreds, not the hundred thousand now on hand, only reaches the people in the center. Ferenc Bessenyei takes the microphone to declaim the National Poem, "Szozat" by Mihály Vörösmarty.

Meantime, as individuals mill around the edges, more and more people continue to arrive, particularly workers who have been getting word-of-mouth reports all day at their places of work and now want to see for themselves what is going on. Just above the sea of heads, like steam rising off a hot surface, wisps of smoke swirl up here and there and then disappear. A good smoke helps to relieve a dull, half-heard speech. Those in the middle, with their arms virtually pinned to their sides, regret that they lack this option.

It is now past five o'clock and there are still speakers to be heard from. The writer Tibor Déry climbs onto the top of the sound truck and with an electric megaphone in hand he suggests that "we all go to Parliament Square where microphones and amplifiers have been rigged up and everybody will be able to hear."[68] This strikes everyone as eminently sensible and the crowd begins slowly to expand back toward Margaret Bridge, but in a disciplined manner, as if this were all part of a pre-arranged program. Not everyone decides to go, however. Most of Béla Lipták's fellow engineers and others from the Technical University decide they have made their demonstration and are not interested in more speeches. In orderly groups they form up and return to the Technical University or, in some cases, simply go home. Assistant Professor Jankovich in his Fiat is influential in advising this action. He has become alarmed at the roars of the crowd and senses that what started out as a silent, peaceful demonstration may turn into something quite ugly.[69]

Radio Budapest in its 5:30 broadcast in Hungarian to Western Europe declares: "National flags, young people with rosettes of the national colors singing the Kossuth song, the Marseillaise and the Internationale—this is how we can describe Budapest today bathed in October sunshine [as it] celebrates a new Ides of March. This afternoon a vast youth demonstration took place in our capital....At first there were only thousands, but they were joined by young workers, passersby, soldiers, old people, secondary-school students and motorists. The vast crowd grew to tens of thousands. The streets resounded with these slogans: 'People of Kossuth, march forward hand in hand,' 'We want a new leadership,' 'We trust Imre Nagy,' 'Long live the People's Army'...The streets of Budapest are filled with a new wind of greater freedom...'[70]

The staff members at the radio station have been waiting all afternoon for First Secretary Ernő Gerő to show up and record his speech for broadcast tonight. By now, however, going to the station is out of the question and recording equipment and technicians are sent to the Secretary's offices in Akadémia Street.[71]

* * * *

The students are now definitely in a minority. Moreover, this trip back across the Margaret Bridge, has not been planned, so there are no student marchers giving directions. Instead of keeping to one side so that the trams can go by in the middle, the host fills the whole bridge with anywhere from thirty to forty people marching abreast. Who cares about trams at this point? The crowd, now in a purposeful, boisterous mood as it willingly re-crosses the river to Parliament Square, begins shouting new slogans: "Into the Danube with Rakosi!" "Into the Government with Imre Nagy!" Rendered in Hungarian these slogans, like most shouted this day, are in rhyme and quickly catch on.[72]

As the shadows from the Buda hills, particularly Gellért and Castle Hills, stretch over Pest, the lights on the bridge go on before the last marcher has set foot in Mari Jászai Square. Once again the procession passes the Ministry of the Interior. On the way to Buda people had noticed a number of guns and faces in every window, alien, worried faces. Some in the parade ranks had shaken fists and yelled insults at them. Now, excited by their increase in numbers, some of the demonstrators begin chanting "Down with the ÁVO!"[73] László Beke and his friends, thinking of the thousands upon thousands of good Hungarians who have been tortured and murdered in this building, whistle and curse and shake their fists as they pass it a second time.[74]

Word has gotten out of the shift to Parliament Square and people now converge from all directions, not just the Margaret Bridge. The Square, which is technically Kossuth Square, is popularly known as Parliament

Square because it is dominated by the magnificent Parliament building. This imposing edifice, constructed between 1884 and 1904, is, but for its pointed dome and spires, modeled on the British Houses of Parliament. As city squares go, Parliament Square is huge. Not only does it run the length of the parliament building, it goes beyond it at both ends. New York's Rockefeller Center would easily fit into it. No one knows its full capacity, but already now in early dusk there are at least two hundred thousand people in it with more arriving all the time.

In Debrecen, where the student march into the city began before noon, a second demonstration, largely of workers and townspeople, has been going on in the center of the city all afternoon. On the principle of "if you can't beat them, join them," Comrade Komócsin and other members of the party secretariat lead one section of the parade past city hall half-heartedly joining in on some of the milder slogans. But his attempt to commandeer the demonstration is doomed to failure. Already in several sections of the city, not only have the red flags all disappeared, most of the red stars on building tops have been torn off and gleefully destroyed by young patriots. Soon City Hall is invaded, its red flag torn to shreds and communist coat of arms torn from the entrance hall wall, along with the "honor bulletin board" listing the names of "Hero Stachanovite Workers."[75] Comrade Komócsin and his colleagues retreat to party headquarters where they appeal to the ÁVO to break up the demonstration.[76]

Meanwhile, the more activist members of the crowd in front of City Hall cry out "Let's go to Police Headquarters to free the political prisoners!" This now becomes the goal of the crowd as though it had been the raison d'être of the demonstration all along. The main doors, of course, are locked, but guards with submachine guns can be seen through the windows on either side. Demands that the political prisoners be released and the red flag removed are ignored by the police. Someone yells that he knows very well where the cells and torture chambers are in the back, and leads part of the growing crowd to the rear. Now the building is surrounded. Soon the demands to free these innocent prisoners become powerful unison chants; but still there is no reaction from inside. This infuriates the crowd even more and some of the wilder members pick up stones and begin to break windows.

Suddenly the front doors fly open and ÁVO security police rush out with rifles that they fire noisily into the air. After several more volleys over their heads they succeed in momentarily stunning the crowd. The ÁVO now advance in close order, pushing and beating people with their rifle butts. Some take out long clubs and begin beating those in the front. Many fall to the ground, but those behind do not budge. "You bums!" "You traitors!" "You scum of the earth," people yell at them. Others shout, "Why don't you join us?" But as the beating grows wilder the curses of the people grow more indignant and coarse.

Seeing the crowd will not be broken up, someone gives the order to fire. A volley rips into the mass of people. Three or four are killed outright and a dozen fall wounded. "You rotten bastards!" "You murderers!" "You've sold yourselves to the Russians!" people yell back in outrage. But rather than the people retreating, it is the ÁVO policemen who do, for the enraged crowd seizes several of them, wrenches their rifles from them and beats and stomps on them, some say to death, though this is never confirmed.[77]

It is just past 7:00 p. m.

But most people, hearing the use of firearms and seeing ÁVO soldiers on trucks with machine guns, retreat back to side streets. János Ménes, President of the City Council (i.e. mayor), almost gets himself lynched when he gets into an argument with the enraged demonstrators who have seen the shooting. Searchlights are sweeping the sky and shots are fired aimlessly for a long time. Eventually electric wires are damaged and the main street plunged into total darkness.[78]

In Szeged at this time the demonstrators, now grown to over two thousand, are marching with torches from the Kossuth Statue to the plaza in front of the main theatre. Here they stop to sing the national anthem while a few enter the theatre to persuade those inside to join them. With the play, which happens to be Shaw's *Saint Joan*, interrupted, those in the audience decide to exit the theatre. The cast members also file out still in their costumes. Since it is the trial scene, one of the actors is dressed as the Bishop. The sight of him in the lamplight quiets the crowd and he offers to render the Petőfi National Poem. Though the demonstrators have heard it several times today, they are happy to hear it done even better by this professional actor, so he climbs to the outside balcony on the front of the theatre and recites it dramatically to a sea of torches below.[79]

From here the demonstrators head out on the Louis Kossuth Avenue to the Szeged Hemp Factory where workers on the night shift decide to quit work and join them. Great shouts of "long live worker-student unity" are taken up as they head back to the Kossuth statue in the center of the city. It is well after midnight when the crowd breaks up and goes home. Nobody is aware that the city's party leadership will soon begin to distribute submachine guns to "trustworthy comrades," and that by dawn Soviet tanks from Romania will be rumbling through Szeged on their way to Budapest.[80]

In Parliament Square in Pest between two and three hundred thousand people are pressing up against the parliament building straining to hear speeches that when they can hear them, do not impress them. Apparently the authorities have decided not to provide the "much better" sound system Tibor Déry had promised. It appears to be an effort to calm down and possibly disperse the crowd. Calls of "shut up" or "We want Imre Nagy!" are frequently louder than the voice of the speaker.

Minister Ferenc Erdei, former member of the Peasant Party, tries to address the crowd from a balcony. Few can hear him, but since his first word is "Comrades," he is booed and whistled at so that he is unable to carry on. His parting words are "Imre Nagy is on the way!"

Now streetlights go on around the rim of the square, but near to the Parliament building it is getting darker, for few, if any lights are on in the building itself. Suddenly the gigantic red star on the dome's spire is lit, spewing an atmospheric halo of red around it. A gasp goes up from the crowd, which takes it as a deliberate affront. "Turn off that damned star! Turn it off!" yell individuals and soon the protest is taken up as a roaring chant. An ad hoc delegation of cooler heads manages to gain entrance into the Parliament building with the aim of explaining to the authorities why the crowd considers the lighting of the red star such a provocation. Some time passes without the return of the self-appointed delegation. At length the red star is switched off. A cheer of triumph rises from the square, tapering off into a babble of voices.

In Moscow it is already past 10:00 p.m. and the Presidium of the Central Committee is in session. The meeting was called for other reasons but the crisis in Hungary soon becomes central. As a result of this meeting Marshal Georgii Zhukov issues orders for the mobilization of five Soviet divisions.[81]

In Budapest, Chief of Police Kopácsi is back in his office frantically answering phone calls from police stations all over the city. Twenty-one precincts have called requesting orders. The most pressing is from a small station on the edge of City Park, a Lieutenant Kiss, whom Kopácsi knows well. Its seems a huge crowd has gathered in Heroes Square (now Stalin's Square), well over a mile from Parliament Square, and they are attempting to pull down the giant Stalin statue (one of the sixteen student demands). The statue does not so much concern Kopácsi, who knows the city council has already scheduled it for removal. What appalls him is the size of the crowd which Kiss insists is anywhere from one hundred thousand to two hundred thousand.

"How many are you at the precinct?"

"Twenty-five, Comrade Colonel."

"Do you think you are going to break up a crowd of one hundred thousand with twenty-five policemen?"

Kiss waits a few seconds. "We have forty rifles, Comrade Colonel," he says finally. Kopácsi realizes that if he were to say, "Fine, use them," Lieutenant Kiss would do just that. So he relieves Kiss of any duty to control or coerce the crowd and suggests that he send people in plain clothes to find out who all these people are. In half an hour Kiss calls back to say most of them are young workers, and they are trying to pull the statue down with ropes attached to trucks but so far these ropes have busted.[82]

Back in Kossuth (Parliament) Square

All daylight has now faded from the sky and the crowd in Parliament Square has only the streetlights, often scores of meters away, to see by. People sense that most of the government is somewhere in the Parliament building, even though very few windows are lit. The Radio has already announced that Gerő will speak on the radio to the nation at 7:00 p.m. This quickly was changed to 8:00 p.m. But not many in the crowd are aware of this. They want to see live bodies here in front of them, people they can talk back to.

Then, without the slightest warning, the entire square is plunged into darkness. Not just the streetlights, but all the buildings surrounding the square, including the Parliament building.

This less-than-subtle hint by the authorities that "everybody should go home now" is greeted with curses and shouts of "How stupid do they think we are?" But there is no panic and no movement. Within a few seconds someone takes out his copy of *Szabad Nép*, rolls it up into a cone and sets fire to it with his cigarette lighter. In no time others nearby have done the same, for everyone has a copy of today's *Szabad Nép*—it has the full text of Gomułka's speech defying the Stalinists, a virtual collector's item—even if they don't have fire. Moreover, special one page editions with the students' sixteen demands were handed out to those entering the square only a short while ago.

Within a few minutes the square is aglow with tens of thousands of flickering torches. Government bureaucrats hovering in the darkened Parliament building are awestruck at the sight. Some speculate on what will happen when the crowd runs out of paper to burn. "Let's put the lights back on," says Erdei nervously. "I will talk to the crowd." "It's no use," says a colleague, "you won't change anything." "It's worth a try," retorts Erdei.

Outside someone starts up the national anthem and soon the square is filled with a window-rattling rendition of it. While the paper torches continue to burn, another favorite, Kossuth's famous song, thunders through the plaza.

> Louis Kossuth sent the message
> That his army is a wreckage
> If he needs us, we are coming
> The enemy can start packing.
> Long Live Hungary!

As the notes of that song die away the lights in the square are suddenly switched back on.

They have won again. This time the roar of victory, sweet victory, goes on and on. There are now at least three hundred thousand people—some, including Kopácsi's police, estimate a half a million—standing in the square.[83]

About this time Police Chief Kopácsi receives a call from a policewoman in their child protection unit, which sends shivers down his spine. She is reporting from Parliament Square. "Comrade Kopácsi," she almost whispers, "There are people on the roofs." It is not difficult to know what she means by "people." Kopácsi realizes that the Interior Ministry, without informing him, has stationed armed security police on the roofs around the square. If ever they were to open up with machine guns the slaughter would be unimaginable.[84] Indeed, one person who does imagine such a scene figures that the dead would not fall, they would be packed in so tight; it would be like unloading the gas chambers at Auschwitz.[85] Now the crowd takes up a popular love song, which takes on special meaning for this occasion: "Overnight We'll Turn the Whole World Upside Down!"[86] In the midst of this song, the elegant, solemn profile of Minister Ferenc Erdei, former mem-

EXPLOSION

ber of the Peasant Party—a man who threw in his lot with the Communists years ago—appears on the balcony. He has barely time to clear his throat before cries of "Get out!" "We don't want you!" "It's Imre Nagy we want to hear," compel him to silence.

* * * *

Imre Nagy is still at his home on Orsó Street in Buda. He arrived back from his holiday at the Balaton only this afternoon, and he is still somewhat out-of-touch, despite all the attempts of his friends Géza Losonczy and Miklós Vásárhelyi to bring him up-to-date. They are somewhat hampered in this by the fact that they, too, having witnessed only some of the demonstration are not certain about what is now transpiring. They know there is a crowd in Parliament Square and that they are clamoring for him, but that is all.

About 7:30 p.m. Tamás Aczél, one of only two Hungarian writers to have received the Stalin Prize, arrives. He listens to their discussion and then Nagy, looking harassed and anxious, asks Aczél what is going on.

"The crowd keeps asking for you without a break. Don't wait any longer, Uncle Imre: you must come to prevent a tragedy," says Aczél urgently.

"If it isn't already too late," adds Vásárhelyi a forty-year-old journalist who had been a party member for twenty years until he had been expelled last year for being too close to the fallen Nagy. "We are all late!" he continues "…the nation is advancing with giant steps and you, the leader, stay here wondering what you ought to do! I find that monstrous!"[87]

But Nagy's dilemma is not so simple. He is a loyal communist and always has been. He believes strongly in Party discipline. He has only been let back into the Party two weeks ago. He is not a member of the government or the Party's Central Committee. He has no power. Moreover, all the disturbances now going on have been caused by the stupidity and pigheadedness of his rival, Gerő. He, Nagy has been on vacation. Why should he go down to Pest to pull Gerő's chestnuts out of the fire? But, in fact, he does not really comprehend the situation. Despite his having been Premier of the State for two years, he is not, and never has been, a true leader. Moreover, he has always been convinced that liberalization must come from the top, from the Party. The idea that it could bubble up from the bottom without party leadership is entirely alien to him. Eventually he gives in to his friends' pleadings and goes upstairs to write out a short speech.

58

Gerő's Speech

While Nagy is writing his speech, Ernő Gerő's voice is heard on Radio Budapest at precisely 8:00 p.m. The speech that the Radio had been promised would be pre-recorded and last approximately forty-five minutes is being broadcast live from Gerő's office, for he had been revising it up to the last minute.

Gerő's voice is unpleasant, querulous and high-pitched. Due to his many years in the Soviet Union his accent has a slightly foreign ring to it. Nevertheless, everyone listens with bated breath for now, surely now, there will be some clear indication that the government is beginning to heed their wishes.

> Dear Comrades! Dear Friends! Working People of Hungary!...It is our res-
> olute and unalterable intention to develop, widen and deepen democracy in
> our country...but of course we want a socialist democracy, not a bourgeois
> democracy. We will defend the development of our people's democracy in
> all circumstances and against any threat, wherever it may come from. The
> main purpose of our enemies today is to undermine the power of the work-
> ing class, to shake the people's faith in their Party...to loosen the close and
> friendly ties between our country...and the other countries building social-
> ism, particularly between our country and the Soviet Union...
>
> They heap slanders on the Soviet Union; they assert the trade relations
> with the Soviet Union are one-sided and that our independence has to be
> defended, not against the imperialists, but against the Soviet Union. All this
> is a barefaced lie, hostile slanders without a grain of truth. The truth is that
> the Soviet Union not only liberated our country from the yoke of Horthy fas-
> cism and German imperialism...it concluded a treaty with us on a basis of
> total equality. And it is this same policy that it pursues today....We condemn
> those who are striving to sow the poison of chauvinism among our youth and
> who employ the democratic freedom that our state has given to the workers
> for the organization of nationalist demonstrations. Such demonstrations will
> not succeed in shaking our Party in its determination to follow the road that
> it has carved out for itself in order to create a Socialist Democracy.... We are
> patriots, but we are also proletarian internationalists.[88]

A totally Stalinist speech! Devoid of any hint that the students might have any right on their side. Not at all what people expected. Doubtless Gerő was imagining how it would look tomorrow on the front page of *Pravda*, not how the Hungarian people would take it. Nearly everyone who hears it is in a state of shock. For one thing, the speech is only twelve minutes long. When it abruptly ends there is a long silence before a voice finally comes on saying "The speech by Ernő Gerő has concluded." The technicians at the Radio are furious; they had made space for forty-five minutes, and now they must improvise and quickly get some music on the air.

The students who have congregated back in the aula at the Technical University are more than furious; they are outraged. "He called us fascist rabble!" someone yells, and this epithet spreads like wildfire. In point of fact, the phrase was not used by Gerő, but both the words "rabble" and "fascist" were, so he might just as well have.

In Parliament Square, however, virtually no one hears the speech. Transistor radios have not been invented and battery-powered portable radios are rare. Only a few on the edge of the crowd even hear about it from passersby. They are still waiting for Imre Nagy who, they are frequently assured, is on his way.

Meantime, an officer of a Hungarian armored division comes into the crowd shouting excitedly, "They are shooting the crowd in front of the radio building. Come there quickly!" Nobody believes him and he is almost beaten up. "They are just trying to break us up!" "Don't believe him, it's a trick." "Stick together! Stick together," various people call out. Later a truck arrives with young people on it. They show empty shells from teargas guns trying to convince the crowd. Again there are cries of "Don't believe them. They are only trying to get us to disperse."

"Stick together! Stick together!" So only a few decide to leave for the radio.[89]

At Nagy's home on Orsó Street Aczél and the others are beside themselves by the time Nagy slowly descends the staircase and puts on his overcoat. Needless to say Aczél has never driven with such abandon around the twisting roads of Buda, despite his precious cargo. As they cross over to Pest, Nagy notices a Hungarian flag with a hole in the middle. Then after a few seconds he says, "But, ...all the flags are the same...What's going on, then?" No one answers but he begins to sweat in spite of the coolness of the evening and takes out his handkerchief to mop his face.

Aczél manages to find an unlocked door and they plunge into the semi-dark corridors of the Parliament building. He takes stairs two a time, then looks back at his old colleague struggling to keep up with Vásárhelyi at his side. At length they find the office of József Mekis, one of the vice premiers.

"You shouldn't have come here," he says, startled to see Nagy. "The Central Committee is supposed to meet next week and your case will be on the agenda."

Vásárhelyi grabs Mekis by the shoulders. "Have you gone mad?" he shouts. "You talk about next week when the whole population of Budapest is waiting at the door. We must act, and fast. Imre Nagy must be made premier without delay. Don't you understand what's coming? It's revolution!"

Mekis' face turns ashen. With no one talking the noise of the crowd outside is frightening in its intensity. Then in an instant the room fills with students, journalists, writers and radio reporters who have all learned of Nagy's presence. Now they all stop talking, hoping Nagy will say something.

But, without a word to anyone and a contemptuous glance at Mekis, Nagy turns toward the French doors leading to the balcony, thrusts aside the curtains and walks outside.[90]

At first no one in the crowd recognizes him. The light is dim and he is now surrounded by a number of people who have followed him out. He waves to the crowd, but no one recognizes him. People have said that "Nagy is coming" so many times from that balcony without his appearing that few now expect him to appear. Someone finds a portable searchlight and turns it on him. Still, it takes several minutes for the crowd to realize it is him. Slowly the groundswell starts: "Éljen!" "Long Live!"

Nagy opens his lips to speak but does not until the crowd is completely silent, for he has been warned that the much-vaunted public address system is not working. Then in his strongest voice he calls out "Comrades!" Those who can hear him can scarcely believe it. Boos and whistles erupt immediately. "We're not comrades, we're Hungarians!" someone shouts. But Nagy, confused and startled as he is by this reception, determinedly reads out his prepared speech. At one point he stops reading his text, looks out over the crowd and says: "You called me here to give my opinion and I'm giving it."[91] He calls for calm and for negotiations with the Party. He has no power right now. He has to be readmitted to the highest echelons of the Party and then the country will return to the June 1953 program and the country put back on the right track. But everyone must be patient. He promises that all their demands will be discussed in the Parliament. The best thing they all can do right now is go home. Hungarian blood is precious and must not be spilled needlessly.[92]

There is little applause when he finishes. Surprised and a bit crestfallen, he is about the leave the balcony, since he can no longer conceal his feelings, when he thinks better of it. Usually such meetings end with a singing of the Internationale. This time, in his deep baritone, he sings the first lines of the Hungarian National Anthem: "God Bless our Hungarian People..." The crowd takes this as the true feeling of the man they have waited so long to hear, and immediately take up the anthem and sing it with feeling.[93]

* * * *

For many it has been a tumultuous day and they are inclined to take Nagy's advice and go home. It would be wrong, however, to assume that all of Budapest is in that square, or that all of Budapest is even aware of what has been going on. Budapest is a great city of nearly two million souls. Life goes on in spite of great events. Before the day is over the record will show that there have been fifty-nine marriages, one hundred twenty births and sixty-three natural deaths involving thousands of citizens who are not yet aware of what has been happening in the streets.[94]

One of those who takes Nagy's advice is the niece of József Kővágó, former mayor of Budapest who had been freed from jail only days before. His family is celebrating his return with a grand dinner at his home in Buda when she bursts in with red-white-green rosettes on her blouse and shouts at the top of her voice:

"Uncle Misi, it was just wonderful! It was tremendous! We stood in front of the parliament and lit some newspapers, carrying them as torches, and sang together, 'We are not comrades, we are not comrades.' We also sang the national anthem and the national prayer. It was just wonderful! I'll never forget it. It is a wonderful feeling to be a Hungarian!"

"Of course, Judy, it is a wonderful thing to be a Hungarian," replies Kővágó, as he kisses her cheek, "but I am afraid it will be a long time before we can become Hungarian. The Russians are still very much with us.[95]

The Sixteen Demands of the Students of the Budapest Technical University

October 22, 1956

(Below is a composite listing of "The Sixteen Demands." The original is not available to the author. This list is made up from three lists: one which was given to a Budapest construction company on October 24, listed as document Number 24 in *The 1956 Hungarian Revolution: A History in Documents*, another which is taken from the list reported by John McCormac in the *New York Times*, also on October 24, and the third taken from Tibor Méray's book, *That Day in Budapest*, pp. 59–60. I have listed them as nearly as possible in their original order. The demand for the withdrawal of Russian troops, for instance, is listed first in two of the above-mentioned lists. This is because the intervention on the twenty-fourth by Russian troops suddenly made it the most important of the demands. As originally written, however, it was listed fourth, so that is where it is listed here. In several cases more than one demand is listed under one number and in a few cases the demands are more affirmations or announcements of intent than actual demands.)

1. We demand new local, secret elections of the Hungarian Workers (Communist) Party so that a new Party Congress can be convoked in the shortest possible time and a new Central Committee elected.

2. We demand the immediate dismissal of all guilty leaders of the Stalinist-Rákosi era and a re-shuffling of the government under the leadership of Imre Nagy.

3. We demand that Mihály Farkas and his accomplices be tried in open court and that Matyas Rakosi be returned from abroad to stand trial before the people's tribunal.

4. We demand the withdrawal of Soviet troops from Hungary in consonance with the provisions of the peace treaty with Hungary.

5. We demand general, impartial and secret elections in Hungary with the participation of several political parties to elect a new National Assembly.

6. We demand reconsideration and revision of Hungarian-Soviet and Hungarian-Yugoslav political, economic and cultural relations on the basis of total political and economic equality and non-interference in one another's internal affairs.

7. We demand that Hungary's foreign trade contracts be published and that straightforward information about Hungary's uranium ore resources, exploitation and Russian concessions be made public.

8. We demand a reorganization by experts of the entire Hungarian economy based on her actual natural resources, making use of uranium deposits in the national interest and revising the centralization of the economy.

9. We demand a total revision of industrial norms and production quotas set for workers in all industry, settlement of wage demands, the establishment of a minimum wage and recognition of the workers' right to strike.

10. We demand a revision in the system of compulsory deliveries of farm produce and equal rights for individual farmers and members of cooperatives.

11. We demand that all political and economic cases be retried in independent courts, that the innocent be released and rehabilitated. We demand that all prisoners of war and civilians deported to the Soviet Union be immediately returned to Hungary.

12. We demand freedom of opinion, speech, press and radio and that personal files [held by the Security Police] be made public and eventually destroyed.

13. We demand that the statue of Stalin be immediately removed and replaced by a monument honoring the heroes and martyrs of the 1848–9 war for independence.

14. We demand the restoration of the Kossuth coat-of-arms and new uniforms for our national army worthy of national traditions. We demand that March 15 and October 6 be declared national holidays.

15. We declare our solidarity with the workers and students of Warsaw.

16. We are determined to set up immediately local organizations of MEFESZ and to convoke a Youth Parliament in Budapest on Saturday, October 27. Tomorrow, at 2:30 we will gather in front of the Technical University and other institutions of higher learning, then march to Bem Square to express our solidarity with the Polish freedom movement. Factory workers are free to join the march.

CHAPTER II

Hungary, Its Origins and History[*]

JUST WHAT *does* it mean to be a Hungarian?

Well, it means you can dance the Csárdás, eat food with a lot of paprika on it, sing ancient folksongs that sound different from most Western folksongs because they are based on the pentatonic scale, and learn other languages easily because your own is so complex.

But why is this? Aren't Hungarians like other Europeans?

Well, yes and no. It is true that being in the heart of Europe they are European. But unlike a majority of European countries, Hungary's origins are not European, but central Asiatic. Surrounded by people who speak German, a Slavic or Romance language, which are all considered European, Hungarians speak a non-Indo-European language that has its origins on the far side of the Urals in Central Asia. Only Finnish and Estonian are related to it, but the relationship goes back so many thousands of years that Finns and Hungarians today cannot understand one another.

Of course today's Hungarians are a mixture not only of the Asiatic clans who made the longer journey over the centuries, mixing with Turkic people along the way, but all of their German, Slav and Romance neighbors with whom they have fought and intermarried during the more than eleven centuries they have been in Europe. But it is the Hungarian language and culture that bind them together. A Hungarian today, be he or she ninety percent eth-

---

[*]Most of this chapter is taken from C.A. Macartney's *Hungary,* Aldine Publishing Company, Chicago, 1962 and William P. Juhász's essay *A Thousand Year Old Nation, in Imre Kovács' Facts about Hungary: The Fight for Freedom* (Hungarian Committee, New York, 1966)

nically German or Slovak, is heir to the Magyar culture. Because these individuals speak and think in Hungarian—assuming that is their first language—they view the world quite differently than do Slovaks or Germans.

Unless the reader is of Hungarian origin, or is already familiar with Hungarian history, it may be profitable to take this short excursion—in this and the following chapter—before rejoining the action in Budapest on October 23, 1956. For those of Hungarian background, these two chapters may well be skipped.

Origins, Real and False

Hungarians are not Huns, any more than Germans are. The Germans got stuck with that epithet in World War I by the British, who wanted to barbarize them. Attila the Hun, who was the scourge of Europe at the time of the disintegration of the Roman Empire, died in 453, four and a half centuries before the Hungarians came to Europe. He may well have been related, for Attila is a popular name in Hungary today, but the Huns were just one of many peoples from whom the Hungarians are descended. Hungarians call themselves Magyars [pronounced MAWDyars], and Hungary is to them Magyarország, or Magyarland.

Many thousands of years ago people known as Uralic and Altaic, after their home in the Ural Altai mountains, split into Uralic and Altaic branches and from the latter came the Finno-Ugrians who settled in the middle Volga region of what is now Russia. About 3,500 years ago, Aryans penetrating from the south pushed one branch, the Finns, northwestward into what is today Finland. The Ugrians were pushed back beyond the Urals to the sparse forests along the Ob, Tobol, Ishim and Irtish rivers. After a while they expanded out into an area known today as the Kirghiz Steppe, which was in the path of the great migration of peoples. Here they began to give up their lives of hunting, fishing, and gleaning for stock-breeding. This transformed their whole political, economic and social structure. They became nomads, living their lives mostly in the saddle and often engaging in warfare. Meat, mare's milk, and fish supplanted their earlier diet from gleanings and agriculture.

Migration to the Carpathian Basin

In the ninth century they moved again, settling between the Don and Dnieper rivers and then further west to between the Dnieper and Dniester rivers. By then the Magyars consisted of seven tribes made up of 108 clans and numbered at least half a million. Having decided to migrate, they elected as their ruler the most powerful of the seven chieftains, Árpád. With much oath-taking and drinking of intermingled blood, they agreed to accept in perpetuity the first of his male issue as kings of the nation. They had just suffered defeat from the Petchenegs, a nation newly arrived from the east, and had lost their grazing land. Árpád now led his people west to the edge of the Carpathian Mountains. While they considered where to go next, the Emperor Arnulf enlisted a contingent of them to help him subjugate his rebellious vassal, Sviatopluk, on the other side of the Carpathians. Seeing how empty and weak was the land, the contingent of Magyars decided to come back and raid it, which they did in the year 894. This led to the decision for the entire nation to go there and in the autumn of 895 and spring of 896 they crossed through the passes of the Carpathians with their enormous herds of cattle and horses and spread out into the Alföld, the steppe-like area east of the Danube River.

Even when viewed from the moon, the Carpathian or Danubian Basin can be seen as a distinctly enclosed space, with the Alps to the west, Tatras to the north and the Carpathians curving like a sickle along the east and southern borders. When the Magyars flowed into their "promised land," it was accomplished in a matter of months. No European nation ever had so precise a date for its founding. One thousand years later, in 1896, they were able to celebrate their millennium without the slightest historical dispute.

Of course, there were some indigenous peoples: Moravian Slavs in the northwest, Slovenes in the section west of the Danube (an area called Panonnia by the Romans but soon dubbed Dunántúl—Beyond the Danube— by the Hungarians), some other Slav settlements in the Alföld between the Tisza and the Danube, and some nomads from Asia like themselves: the Székelys. But there was room for all. These locals were quickly conquered, became servants of the wealthier clan and tribal chiefs, and in time were absorbed and became Magyars.

Though the locals were agricultural, the Magyars stuck with their nomad ways of grazing cattle and waging war on horseback with bow and arrows. Soon their chieftains were leading lightning attacks into Western Europe with as many as six thousand horsemen. Europe became fearful until they learned the ways of these new marauders and employed superior feudal war techniques. Near Augsburg in today's Bavaria the Magyars met with crushing defeat in 955 at the hand of Otto the Great and never again ventured so far into the West.

Géza and King Stephen

The Magyars now began to fight among themselves, some by seeking to ally themselves with Byzantium. It was during this period that they were exposed to Christianity, both from Rome and Byzantium, and some tribal chiefs elected to convert. One tribe rejected both forms of Christianity and elected to convert to Judaism. For some time, at least, Jews in Hungary were not necessarily ethnically so. The intertribal rivalry ended with the victory of a Prince Géza, who established good relations with the Christian Emperor, Otto the Great. Géza was married to a Christian. His son, Vajk, was raised as a Christian, and baptized with the Christian name, Stephen [István].

When Géza died in 997, István should have inherited the throne, but a certain elder member of the family, Koppány, claimed the succession. István, whose commitment to Christianity had already been sealed by his marriage to the Christian Princess Gisella, daughter of the Bavarian King Henry III, was only able to prevail with his father-in-law's and wife's heavy cavalry from Bavaria. Then, in the year 1000 he applied to Rome for recognition as king. Pope Sylvester II sent back the gifts of a crown and an apostolic cross, tokens not only of the Pope's approval but also of his understanding that Stephen would Christianize all of Hungary. Stephen then crowned himself on Christmas Day 1000 A.D. He then set about converting his countrymen, by a process known throughout the Christian world of that time. This sometimes involved offering to shorten by a head those who declined to convert. The nation was flooded with priests from Bavaria and other western principalities. Sometimes the proselytizing was a bit too vigorous. Gellért Hill in Buda gets its name from an overzealous Bavarian monk who was found to be so obnoxious that he was stuffed into a barrel and thrown off the top, thus assuring his martyrdom.

Stephen's coronation transformed his relationship to his people. As King he was allowed virtually unlimited powers. Fortunately for his subjects he exercised them with justice and mercy, and the country flourished under him for thirty-eight years. The institution of slavery existed in Hungary at that time and he did not interfere with it. He did, however, free his own slaves as an example to others. He was proclaimed a saint in 1083 and has been celebrated ever since on August 20 as the father of Christian Hungary.

Land ownership soon fell into three categories: those lands owned by the clans (about half of the whole), those lands given to the Church, and the land retained by the king. This last was divided up into counties (forty-two in Stephen's day), each of which had its representative of the crown in his own *vár* (fortress).

After Stephen

After Stephen, Hungary suffered a long period of fluctuating fortunes: fights over the crown due to no direct male descendants, offering the crown to foreign princes, and much foreign alignment and intrigue through arranged marriages with foreign royalty. Some of this involved the acquisition of additional land. Croatia, for instance, was a dynastic acquisition, and for a while the royal title was "King of Hungary and Croatia." But Croatia was never treated as an integral part of Hungary and was administered by a *bán* (viceroy) through its own institutions. Transylvania, on the other hand, while it had the complexity of many independently minded Székelys and later Saxons and later still Schwab people (both of the latter from Germany) who kept to themselves in well-developed towns, was considered part of the Kingdom of Hungary.

Renaissance and the Golden Bull

Because of the influence of so many foreign monks, mostly German, but Italian and French as well, Hungary began to look westward in spite of its basically eastern culture. In the countryside Magyar encampments gave way to villages and then small cities. A network of bishops' sees and cloisters arose alongside the royal administrative seats. Foreigners from Western Europe, particularly artisans, architects, and artists, were welcomed into the land, and while the resulting buildings were western, a certain eastern influence frequently crept in. While Gregorian chant and western harmonies predominated in Church and secular music, Magyar folk music based on the pentatonic scale survived and flourished in the villages as it does to this day.

As the hereditary lines kept dying out, the kings of Hungary were now chosen by a conclave of freeholders, high nobility, prelates, and lesser nobles; this group also acted as the King's Council. Many of these men were foreign born, and while loyal to the Crown of St. Stephen, were not always respectful of the man wearing it. King Endre II's follies and extravagances became too much for the Council, and in 1222, just six years after the signing of the Magna Carta in England, Endre was forced to sign the famous "Golden Bull" which put certain restrictions on him and gave a firmer status, in public law, to the landed nobility.

Invasions from the East

Once the scourge of Western Europe, Hungary now became a bulwark against, but sometimes victim of, incursions of pagan nomad horsemen from the East, namely Petchenegs and Cumanians. But in 1241, several hundred thousand Mongol, or Tartar, horsemen of Great Khan Ogotai, third son and heir of Genghis Khan, easily overwhelmed the frontier posts and poured into Hungary. All summer long and into that autumn the Tartars ravished central Hungary. Then, when the Danube froze over, they crossed into Dunántúl on Christmas Day and did the same there. King Béla IV, pursued by their light cavalry, ingloriously fled to an island off the Dalmatian coast. Hungary was saved from complete destruction only by the death of the Great Khan Ogotai in far off Karakorum. Batu Khan, who had led the army into Hungary, needed to get back to take part in the contest for succession. In March 1242 the Tartars left Hungary as suddenly as they had entered it.

Those who survived the Tartar onslaught did so only by escaping to forests and marshes. Plague and starvation followed the destruction, and that year Hungary lost close to half of its population. Only in the northwest and in the Székely areas of Transylvania did people escape the devastation.

King Béla completely revised the country's defensive system. He built chains of fortresses, called in great numbers of colonists from foreign lands to repopulate the land, and saw to it that Hungary was surrounded by a ring of client states or "bánáts" to act as a cushion against foreign invasion.

Religious Divisions

Most Christians in Hungary looked to Rome; that is to say, their local church belonged to the Roman Catholic hierarchy. Yet Hungary was one of the first countries in Europe to be exposed to Protestantism when hordes of Hussites broke into northern Hungary from Moravia. While directed mostly at the Roman clergy and nobles, their assault did not spare the common people. The movement was beaten back, but it left a strong influence in Hungary in the fifteenth and sixteenth centuries and the first Bible ever translated into Hungarian was the Hussite Bible. It also paved the way for later incursions of Protestantism, by the Lutherans and Calvinists and Unitarians. Hungary never witnessed a counter-reformation, except in the western part that remained under the Hapsburgs, due to the nearly two-hundred-year occupation of Hungary by the Osman Turks; these tolerated all religions but no religious disturbances. Debrecen, in the east, became the great center of Protestantism and remains so to this day, while the west is solidly Catholic.

János Hunyadi

The Osman Turks, who had crossed over into Europe in 1352, had been advancing across the Balkan Peninsula ever since. Sultan Marad was preparing for a major attack on Hungary. Hungary's King Sigismund died just at this time, leaving a daughter but no heir, only a pregnant wife. Even when it turned out to be a boy, the royal council did not feel Hungary could afford a long regency, so elected the young King of Poland, Wladislaw III, to be the new King of Hungary.

It happened that a Czech warlord was threatening northwestern Hungary and the Turks, advancing from the south. At this most critical time, a remarkable leader named János Hunyadi saved Hungary. Hunyadi came from rather humble origins but his genius had catapulted him into positions of great authority. By the time the young Polish king, whom the Hungarians referred to as "Ulászló," came on the scene, Hunyadi was Bán of Szörény in Transylvania. The new king immediately made him Captain General of Belgrade (Hungarian: Nándorfehérvár) and Voivode of Transylvania. In 1442 he brilliantly defeated the Turkish Army in Transylvania. He then persuaded the young king to let him undertake a campaign in the Balkans to put the Turks on the defensive. He was so successful that the Sultan agreed to a peace surrendering all of Serbia.

Unfortunately, the Papal Legate, who was organizing a crusade, persuaded Hunyadi that a Christian's word given to an infidel need not be kept. The next year, together with the young king, he launched a drive into Bulgaria. An enraged Sultan met them outside Varna and defeated them disastrously. The young king was killed, and Hunyadi was lucky to escape with his life. Hunyadi had other setbacks, but in 1456 he so heavily routed the Turkish army at Belgrade that the Turks did not restart their advance into Europe for another seventy years. The Pope ordered church bells throughout Europe to be rung daily at noon, but Hunyadi never learned of this, for he died a few weeks later of a fever. One of the most powerful personalities in Hungarian history, Hunyadi established a national unity and order which transcended privileges and special interests and succeeded in raising Hungary to the status of a great power.

Matthias Corvinus

His son Matthias (Mátyás), who took the name Corvinus, almost did not make it. After his father's death, his older brother was murdered and he, at the age of sixteen, was taken off to Prague and thrown into prison. So great was the name of Hunyadi, however, that when the throne became vacant a huge multitude of common nobles met on the ice of the frozen Danube on January 24, 1458, and proclaimed Matthias king. Emissaries had to fetch him from Prague, and when brought back to Buda, he was enthroned amid great rejoicing.

Matthias Corvinus turned out to be a true Renaissance Prince. A first-class soldier, skilled administrator, speaking half a dozen languages with equal fluency, he was a learned astrologer, connoisseur, and patron of the arts. His library, "Corvina," was world-famous and some of it survives to this day. The first book printed in Buda antedates the English painter Caxton by some years. He had sumptuous buildings built in Buda and Kolozsvár (today Cluj-Napoca, Romania), where he was born. While the Turks later destroyed most of these, still standing is the magnificent coronation church in Buda, built in the late nineteenth century in neo-Gothic style, set on the foundation of a church he had built. It bears his name today, and next to it proudly stands an equestrian statue of him.

Because he took as his second wife Beatrix of Aragon, daughter of the King of Naples, the early Italian Renaissance had a strong influence in his court.

Still, he was not without Magyar pride. When his father-in-law decided to send him a Spanish horse-master, he responded, "For centuries we have been famed for our skill in horsemanship, so that the Magyar has no need to have his horses dance with crossed legs, Spanish fashion." When he died at a ripe age, the people mourned him, saying: "King Matthias is dead, justice is departed."

Despite two wives, Matthias left no legitimate male heirs, so the jockeying for power among the court cliques began all over again.

Hungary Split into Three Parts

The winner turned out to be another Pole, whom the Bohemians had earlier chosen as their King. The Hungarians called him Ulászló II, and he was so passive, agreeing so readily to anything proposed, that he earned the nick-name "King O.K." Things went from bad to worse under him and the Hungarian nobles swore they would never again pick a foreigner.

Meanwhile Turkish power had reached its zenith, vanquishing the north-ern Balkans, then taking Belgrade and Pétervárad. In the catastrophic battle of Mohács in southern Hungary in 1526, a great majority of the Hungarian nobles and senior clergy perished. Hungary now lay open to the Turks. Hungarians were made even more vulnerable by the fact that they were unable to persuade any allies in the West to join them in defending their country.

For nearly two centuries, Hungary was plunged into its most miserable period. The Turks held the central part of the country, including the city of Buda; the Austrians controlled a small section in the northwest; and only in Transylvania, which paid tribute to the Turks but was not occupied, did any-thing like true independence exist. This did, however, contribute to the sur-vival of Hungarian spiritual freedom. But by accepting protection for west-ern Hungary from the Austrian Emperor, Hungary gave up its control of national defense. And by insisting on its existence as a separate kingdom, it forfeited the right to be represented in the Emperor's court council and had to accept decisions that it had no part in making.

This problem of occupation by two foreign powers was aggravated by the religious rift. The worldliness and slack morals of many of the Catholic cler-gy, the attempt by powerful nobles to seize ecclesiastical estates, and the unpopularity of the Hapsburg power on the one hand versus the relative Turkish tolerance of the Protestant churches in the large middle section of Hungary on the other led to a conversion of most Hungarians there from Roman Catholicism to Protestantism. After the Turks left Hungary, many of these converts reverted to Catholicism, particularly with the proselytizing of the new Jesuit order, but the Catholic Church never again achieved prepon-derance over the combined Reformed, Lutheran and Unitarian churches. Perhaps one good outcome of the long Turkish occupation is that, unlike most of the West European countries, Hungary never experienced any reli-gious wars.

Turkish Retreat and Freedom Fights

Toward the end of the seventeenth century, the Ottoman Empire began its slow disintegration. In 1683, the Turkish forces, already in sharp decline, made a last desperate attempt to take Vienna, which they had been besieging for months. A coalition of forces under the Polish King Jan Sobieski routed the Sultan's forces. This gave heart to several European countries, which resolved to help the Hungarians drive the Turks out of Hungary. In 1686, they freed Hungary's ancient capital of Buda. Liberating armies retook all but the southernmost part of the country, and eventually Louis of Baden took that as well. The Hapsburgs drove into the Balkans and soon all of Hungary was reunited, and it, plus Croatia, became part of the Hapsburg Empire. In 1691, Transylvania also lost its autonomy and came under nominal Hapsburg control.

At the beginning of the eighteenth century, the first full-scale national revolt against foreign oppressors broke out, sparked by a mass rising of peasants in Northeast Hungary. The movement took on a nationwide aspect when one of Hungary's most distinguished and wealthy aristocrats, Ferenc Rákóczi II, after an inner struggle, assumed its leadership. This was extraordinary, because Rákóczi was so wealthy that he owned a large part of Hungary. Raised by Austrian Jesuits at the Viennese Court, he was a devout Catholic. Nevertheless, he was a Hungarian patriot. Louis the XIV of France promised much, but delivered very little. The Russian Czar, Peter the Great, promised much and delivered nothing. Actually, the French were involved in fighting the forces of a Hapsburg-Dutch-English coalition and so were not in a position to help, but they wanted Rákóczi to harass and distract the Hapsburgs. They persuaded a parliament of the insurgents to dethrone the Hapsburg Emperor, who also carried the title King of Hungary, and choose Rákóczi as their new monarch. Hungary now became a battlefield for nearly a decade. Drained of their strength, the Kuruc forces finally surrendered in 1711. Rákóczi and his entourage fled to Poland. He then became an émigré in France and eventually died in Turkey.

But while he had failed to gain Hungary's independence, he had so inspired the nation that within a few years it brought about an amazing national renaissance, a reconciliation between classes, and a flourishing of art, music and poetry. Though still oppressed, things were not as bad as before, and Hungarians had given proof that the nation was still very much alive.

Life under Maria Theresa and Joseph II

With Austria now firmly in control, by virtue of the fact that the Austrian

Emperor or Empress was also the King or Queen of Hungary, and political matters more relaxed after Rákóczi's long struggle, Hungarians now took a more prominent role in the affairs of the Austrian empire, particularly in the military. Maria Theresa practiced absolutism, but it was a humane absolutism, and during her forty years on the throne (1740–1780) she became well liked in Hungary. She, in turn, had a special Hungarian bodyguard of noble youths who brought the ideas of the French enlightenment to Hungary. New laws were decreed, particularly in education, which until then had been entirely in the hands of the churches, and economic exploitation was eased. The Viennese court refused to let Hungary industrialize, since she was looked upon as the source the Empire's food and raw materials. Bohemia and Moravia, the Czech lands, where industry was already well-established, got all the new industry.

Her son, Joseph II (1780–1790), modeled himself on Frederick II of Prussia as an enlightened absolutist. He tried, against the wishes of the privileged orders, to alleviate the lot of the peasants and managed to stir up the Romanian peasants in Transylvania to the point where they felt he was trying to destroy the Hungarian landowners. This developed into a very destructive peasant revolt, which did not endear the two nationalities to one another but did stir Romanian national culture and consciousness.

Though a devout Catholic, Joseph II promoted tolerance towards Protestants and riled Hungarian Catholic prelates by making the German language obligatory for all administrative matters. Latin had been the language of the Church and the law, and Joseph was forced to rescind this rule, though German later did become the language not only of the military and government officials, but also of most of society.

Resentment against this German language decree on the part of students and writers helped to spark a flourishing Hungarian literature which helped produce such great poets as Mihály Vörösmarty and Dániel Berzsenyi and such novelists as Mór Jókai and József Eötvös; these writers played leading roles in the formation of Hungarian cultural life. Literature in Eastern Europe, and particularly poetry, has always played a political role, on a scale quite unknown in Western Europe or the English-speaking world, and this was the time when János Arany and Sándor Petőfi began to have such an influence on Hungarian public life. This was the time, also, when Count István Széchényi, an aristocrat of many parts, founded the Hungarian Academy of Sciences and the Széchényi National Library. He was responsible for the construction of the Széchényi chain bridge, the first suspension bridge in Europe and the first to link Buda and Pest, by the English engineer Adam Clark.

The linking of Pest to Buda and the inclusion of Óbuda into the new city of Budapest made it the largest metropolitan conglomeration in the country, but the total population of the combined cities was only 150,000. Ninety-six percent of all of Hungarians at this time lived in villages and towns no bigger than 20,000.[1]

The Revolution of 1848

Eighteen forty-eight, like 1968, was a year of student risings. Unlike 1968, however, 1848 was not confined to students but had a profound effect on political life, toppling governments all over Europe in a way that changed the face of Europe. The old order, established by Metternich at the Congress of Vienna in 1815, came crashing down, and while some governments were re-established with many of the old faces, nothing was quite the same again.

The uprisings started in Paris and quickly spread to Vienna and Berlin and, of course, to Hungary. The capital of Hungary at that time was not Buda or Pest, but Pozsony (today's Bratislava, capital of Slovakia). But the student demonstrations on March 15, where Petőfi declaimed his famous National Song calling on Hungarians to rise up and never more be slaves, took place in Pest and the government in Pozsony was only informed of it the next day.

Reform had been in the air for some time, discussed in periodicals, at county assemblages and even in the National Assembly. There were basically five areas of concern: freedom for the serfs, together with gifts of land, assurances of the rights of man, popular representation with free elections, abolition of special privileges and unequal taxation, and social and economic reform, including prisons and the abolition of the old guilds.

The twelve student demands were more specific, like freedom of the press and assembly, equality before the law, equal taxes, and abolition of serfdom. About the only thing that differed from the demands of the students in 1956 was the demand for union with Transylvania (then governed separately to keep Hungarians divided).

Before the student uprising in March, the reform movement was split between two positions, gradual and radical. The leader of the gradual reforms was Count István Széchényi; the leader of radical reform was a fiery orator in the National Assembly named Louis Kossuth, who was idolized by

Hungarian youth. Defying censorship, Kossuth issued reports on what was going on in Parliament and at county meetings. For this he was thrown into prison, where he read all of Shakespeare and gained so fluent a command of English that he later addressed English and American audiences in Shakespearean cadences. Kossuth wanted freedom first for independence and democracy, and then all else, such as land and other reforms, would follow.

The student demands were reflected in laws passed by the National Assembly in April. These in turn were approved by the Court in Vienna, which itself had undergone something of a transformation, or at least pretended it had. A new Hungarian cabinet was formed and Kossuth became the soul of the freedom movement. Széchényi was crushed at the thought of all the destruction he was sure the revolution would bring, and he retired to an Austrian sanitarium where, in 1860, he committed suicide.

By summer, it was open warfare between the Viennese Court and Hungary. Since no successor government to Minister-President Count Lajos Batthyány had been named after his resignation, Kossuth now became the *de facto* dictator of Hungary. Led by a young genius of a general, Artúr Görgey, Hungarian armies repeatedly defeated the Austrians. In December Emperor Ferdinand abdicated in favor of his nephew, Franz Joseph. Kossuth saw that this was directed against Hungary, since the new Emperor had not, like his predecessor, sworn to uphold Hungary's "April Laws."

Austrian armies now marched on Budapest, reaching Pest in two weeks. The General in charge, Windischgraetz, announced "final victory." At this point an Imperial manifesto announced the dissolution of the Austrian Constitutional Assembly and the constitution of the entire monarchy as an indivisible and indissoluble constitutional Austrian Empire. Hungary was to be partitioned into five units. The Kossuth government, which had fled to the east of the country, met in the Calvinist Church in Debrecen on April 14, 1849 and proclaimed the dethroning of the House of Hapsburg and Hungarian emancipation from Austria; they pronounced Kossuth as leader of the newly independent country. At this point Czar Nicholas I, who was concerned that revolution might spread to Russian-occupied Poland, indicated his readiness to Franz Joseph to send Russian forces to Austria to put down Hungary.

In June, two Russian armies entered Hungarian territory, bringing combined Austrian-Russian forces up to 370,000 men versus a Hungarian Army of only 152,000. For a while, General Josef Bem, hero of the Polish rising of 1831, who had offered his services to Hungary, managed to defeat the Russian armies in Transylvania. It was here that the young poet, Sándor Petőfi, was slain, though his body was never recovered from the battlefield.

But it was an unequal struggle. On August 11, Kossuth handed over his powers to György and fled with a few supporters to Turkey. Though he later toured England and the U.S. in a vain attempt to drum up support for Hungary, he never returned to Hungary and died in exile.

Austrian Retribution

Austrian retribution was swift and brutal. Most of the military and political leaders of the revolt were executed, including thirteen generals. Others escaped abroad. General Bem also fled to Turkey and here began his third campaign of fighting the Russians on behalf of his Polish homeland.

Hungary was put under a military dictatorship headed by Austrian General Haynau, who boasted the he would "see to it that there should be no more revolutions in Hungary for a hundred years."

Two years later, a civilian regime replaced the military one. While the administration was no longer brutal, it was calculated to eliminate all traces of independence. Almost every class and every nationality in Hungary soon was chafing against this authoritarian regime. The country began to split into those who wanted full independence, which Kossuth in exile was still calling for, and reformers who wanted a compromise with the Austrians, provided it did justice to Hungary's historic rights and needs. This second group found its leader in Ferenc Deák, a quiet, sensible, upstanding man who had been the leader of the reformers in Parliament before Kossuth became a member. He held that the "April laws" were still valid and that any laws since then which modified them were not. But he also recognized that laws concerning Hungary's relationship with the rest of the Monarchy were imperfect and needed adjustment.

The "Ausgleich" (Compromise)

Austria's loss of its Italian provinces in 1859 convinced the Emperor Franz Josef that the centralist forces in the Monarchy were not strong enough to hold down all the elements of national and social opposition within the Empire. Sharing some of this with its most troublesome, yet most powerful and able nationality, Hungary, made sense. Over the next eight years Ferenc

Deák was able to negotiate the famous "Ausgleich" (Compromise) of 1867, setting up the Austro-Hungarian Empire. This "dual monarchy" was to work remarkably well, considering its complexity, until it was destroyed by the First World War.

With relative independence and Vienna no longer trying to manage the Hungarian economy, foreign capital poured into Hungary, railroads were built with remarkable speed and industrialization expanded on a much larger scale. These were boom years for Hungary and the years when most of Budapest was built, culminating in the building frenzy that preceded the celebration of the Millennium in 1896.

One of the social phenomena which accompanied this great economic expansion was the rise and integration of Hungarian Jews into fuller participation in the nation's life. Many laws restricting Jews were struck down, and professions to which they had previously been barred were opened to them. Until the 1840s, Jews were not even allowed to live in counties where mining was important and were often prohibited from owning real estate.[2] Christians, mostly Germans, dominated all the town and city institutions at mid-century, Hungarian Christians preferring to remain in the countryside, dealing with agricultural matters. During the Ausgleich, particularly the latter half, all of this changed.

Even before the Compromise, Jews had always been in commerce and banking and had come to dominate these fields.[3] Now they began to become captains of industry and run for public office. Jews were encouraged to Magyarize their names and those who became prominent in Hungarian society even sought ennoblement from the crown. This, of course, came at a monetary price, and Prime Minister Kálmán Tisza, who had taken up the defense of Jews against an emerging anti-Semitic wing of the opposition Independence Party, is believed to have solved some of his financial problems and get re-elected by obtaining ennoblements for several prominent Jewish families. In any case, beginning in 1882 there was a boom of Jewish ennoblements in Hungary.[4] All of this meant that Jews toward the end of the nineteenth century were far more prominent and integrated into Hungarian life than they were in other East European countries. Many were among the more prominent citizens of the nation.

This elevation and integration unfortunately was followed by a rise of anti-Semitism, which peaked in the first decade of the twentieth century. By that time half of Budapest's lawyers, half of its doctors and seventy percent of its journalists were Jewish.[5] But as in Germany, they felt themselves to be Hungarians first and Jews second, if they bothered to think of it at all. Jews were spread out all along the political spectrum, with impoverished intellectuals, like impoverished intellectuals everywhere, tending toward the extremes of right and left.

Restless Nationalities, Empire's Collapse and Hungary Dismembered

All during this time of growth and prosperity, the nationalities in the Hungarian part of the dual empire were getting more restless and affirmative. Just as Hungarians had rankled under Austrian suzerainty, so Romanians, Serbs, Croats, Ruthenians, Slovaks and others clamored for more autonomy, if not complete independence from Hungary. The outbreak of the First World War (triggered by the assassination of the archduke Ferdinand in hostile Serbia) put all of this on hold, but with the collapse of the Austro-Hungarian Empire in 1918, these nationalities all erupted at once.

The collapse brought more turmoil to Hungary than Austria, for while Austria was bereft of its Slavic holdings—Bohemia, Moravia, Slovenia and the Hungarian portion of the empire—and thus became totally Germanic, Hungary had fewer Hungarians than Slavs and Romanians within its borders, all of them clamoring for freedom. When the Treaty of Trianon was signed in June 1920, Hungary was deprived of 71.4 percent of its pre-war territory and 63.5 percent of her population.[6] Hungary's pre-war population of over twenty million was reduced to seven and a half million, leaving 3,200,000 ethnic Hungarians outside its borders. These Hungarians now became citizens of Romanian Transylvania, Czechoslovakian Ruthenia, the Slovak portion of the new state of Czechoslovakia, and the Croatian, Slovenian, and Serbian portions of the new state of Yugoslavia and the Burgenland portion of Austria.

A Communist Interlude

Most of this had occurred long before the Treaty of Trianon (part of the Versailles Treaty) was signed. Hungary could not have prevented it in any case, for, with the collapse of the Monarchy, and the collapse of a left-leaning republic headed by Mihály Károlyi, who had taken Hungary out of the war, a small group of Communists under the leadership of Béla Kun had seized power and established, for four bloody months from March 21 to

August 1, 1919, a Soviet Hungarian Republic or Commune. The Communists had sweetened the pill of their coup d'etat with the promise that the Soviet Russian Army, then advancing on Poland, would help restore much of the territory Hungary was losing at the Peace Treaty in Paris. Only the invasion and occupation by Romanian and other troops brought this Communist experiment to an abrupt end.

There followed a period of fierce persecution of the Communists. This purge quickly became known as the "White Terror" to distinguish it from the "Red Terror" which had taken place under the Béla Kun regime. A strong streak of anti-Semitism emerged in the midst of this persecution. While anti-Semitism in Hungary had been on the rise for three decades, it achieved particular virulence at this time for the simple reason that a majority in the government of Béla Kun, including Kun himself, had been Jewish.

Admiral Horthy Takes Charge

The "summary" justice of the Hungarian Communists had been almost as brutal as that which had been occurring in the newly established Union of Soviet Socialist Republics, in former Czarist Russia, but the "White Terror" which followed under the regent, Admiral Miklós Horthy, was even more ruthless, for it went on far longer and was thus more thorough. Those Communists who did not slip out to Vienna and later move on to Moscow faced execution or long jail terms.

Under the authoritarian regime of the regent, Admiral Horthy—regent of a non-existent monarch and admiral in a no-longer-existing Navy—the Communists were outlawed and thus had no seats in Parliament. Consequently they had no real influence in the country and would not emerge again until they arrived, after long years of exile in Moscow, in 1944 with the Red Army.

The history of Horthyite Hungary is that of a strong, authoritarian leader who kept switching his prime ministers to suit the changing times but was finally overcome by outside powers he could no longer control. His first important prime minister, Count István Bethlen, was an aristocrat who believed in holding the lower classes in their place. Under his predecessor, Count Pál Teleki, there had been much-needed land reform passed involving only 7.5 percent of the arable land in the country. The understanding was that this was the first of several land reform laws to be undertaken. When it came time for the great estates to give up this land to the landless peasants, they

EXPLOSION

naturally parted with the least fertile and most inaccessible corners of their estates, with the result that less than half of the land was actually handed over. Bethlen saw to it that there were no more land reform bills. He was equally strict in dealing with labor unrest and deft in neutralizing the considerable opposition he faced in parliament. Had it not been for the worldwide Depression, the prosperity he had begun might well have continued. He resigned in August 1931.

His successor, Count Gyula Károlyi, another aristocrat of unbending conservatism, reaped the whirlwind of strikes, a revolt of small farmers crushed by debt, jobless university graduates, and a revived Right Radicalism directed especially against the Jews who were the creditors. He threw in the towel in September 1932.

Bending with the wind, Horthy appointed the leader of the Right Radicals, Captain Gyula Gömbös.

Gömbös was a fascist slightly before his time. It was he who came up with the term "axis." Only the Axis he imagined was to contain Italy, Hungary and a Germany he hoped would be led by Hitler, who had not yet been elected. Gömbös died in 1936 and his successors were all overshadowed by events in Germany.

Fending Off Nazi Germany

With the growth of Nazi Germany's power under Hitler, Horthy had to face realities, particularly when the Third Reich absorbed Austria. If Czechoslovakia was to be carved up, Hungary should get back its lands. In fact, it did get back a sliver of southern Slovakia, where most Hungarians lived, as well as Ruthenia. In February 1939, Horthy appointed Count Pál Teleki, who was determined not to let Hungary become involved in a conflict with the West. Nonetheless, he soon found himself agreeing that in case of a major war, Hungary "would take up her position beside the Axis powers," except that she would never attack Poland.

When Hitler demanded that Hungary join in attacking Yugoslavia, which contained former Hungarian lands and over half a million Hungarians, Horthy refused, but he did not feel he could refuse access through Hungary. Britain had threatened to declare war on Hungary if she joined Hitler in the attack. This was too much for Count Teleki and on April 2 he took his own life.

Hungary had not been in Hitler's plans to attack Russia in June 1941, but the Hungarian generals were eager to get in on the spoils of a war not expected to last more than a few weeks. The following January Britain did declare war on Hungary and a few days later Hungary declared war on the United States.

Though his country was now allied with the Axis powers, Horthy still believed that the West would win in the end. But he also believed that the West did not want bolshevism in Europe and that Hungary could regain its favor while continuing to fight the Russians. While he had agreed to a law limiting Jews to twenty percent of the professions and even to its later being cut to six percent, he was affording the Jews of Hungary protection unparalleled in Europe. He even opened secret conversations with the West in August 1943. Hitler decided in March 1944 that he could no longer allow a regime he did not trust to be across his vital communications with the Eastern front. He summoned Horthy and gave him the choice of full cooperation or undisguised occupation as an enemy country. Horthy naturally chose the former, but it required disbanding all but the pro-Nazi parties and letting the Germans do what they wanted. This, of course, meant rounding up the Jews. Some 450,000 Jews outside of Budapest were sent to Auschwitz, of whom not more than 120,000 survived.

Germans and Arrow Cross Take Over as Soviets Advance

Horthy managed to stop the Jewish deportations before they began in Budapest. On October 15 he announced on the wireless that he was opening negotiations with Moscow for a "preliminary armistice." The Germans at once seized him and forced him to abdicate, allowing Szálasi, the leader of the local Nazi party, The Arrow Cross Party, to take over the administration of the country. To the Arrow Crossists this meant primarily the slaughtering of the Jews; whether this was accomplished by deportation or right there in Budapest seemed to make little difference.

Soviet forces had already crossed into Hungary and by January Budapest was under siege. The last retreating German troops crossed into Austria on April 4, 1945, with a host of civilian sympathizers. With them, someone had taken the symbol of Hungarian sovereignty, the crown of St. Stephen. This precious item, after being handed over to the American Army, was to spend the next twenty-eight years in the vaults of Fort Knox, Kentucky, before being returned to Hungary by President Jimmy Carter in 1977.

CHAPTER III

Hungary under Communism

1944–1945

ON DECEMBER 21, 1944, a provisional National Assembly for a new government met in the Protestant Great Church in Debrecen, the same church from which Kossuth had proclaimed independence from Austria in 1849. A National Front had been proclaimed three weeks earlier in Szeged. The Front's program—heavily influenced by the Communists—was issued a few days before the Assembly met. This naturally called for a clear break with the Arrow Cross Party, still in power in Budapest where the Nazis had placed them in October, and included land reform and nationalization of mines, and the oil and electrical generating industries, as well as state supervision of large industries and banking.

It was during the National Assembly meeting in newly liberated Debrecen that the Communists reemerged as a major political entity. Even though their numbers were tiny—five thousand in the whole country—they were to grow quickly. The reasons for this rapid growth were no different from the sudden expansion of Communist Party membership in each of the nearby countries overrun by the Soviet armies: idealism, the experience of Nazi barbarism (particularly against the Jews), the belief that Communism was the wave of the future, the need for a sharp break with the past and, in a few cases, the fact that food (provided by the Russians) was handed out free at Communist Party headquarters. The Party soon began to attract opportunists, even small fry who had recently served the fascist Arrow Cross Party or the Horthy government. Nearly all were welcome.

Under the influence of the Soviet army of occupation, party membership grew to 150,000 in just five months, to five hundred thousand by October 1945 and to nearly nine hundred thousand by mid-1948.[1]

In the government that emerged from the Debrecen assembly in December 1944, Communists gained only three portfolios out of a possible twelve. But in November 1945 they were to gain two key portfolios to their strategy: interior and agriculture. Everybody but the fleeing nobility was in favor of agricultural reform—though not necessarily the Communist version—and those who controlled the Interior Ministry controlled the police.

Land reform was universally popular because Hungary, alone among the countries of Europe in 1945, was still essentially a country of vast estates, several million landed peasants and at least as many landless peasants. The Minister of Agriculture, who was to carry out the land reform, was a Communist by the name of Imre Nagy, and it was this national exposure in carrying out what everyone felt was so necessary that gained Nagy, a Muscovite,* the fame and popularity which brought him to power in 1953 and again in 1956.

On January 20, 1945, an armistice agreement was signed in Moscow. From this an Allied Control Commission evolved which was to operate in all of the occupied countries. But in those countries where the Soviet Union was the sole occupying power, the Western Allies soon found themselves outmaneuvered and gradually gave up doing more than protest Soviet actions they considered totally illegal.

One of these was supervising democratic elections. The Hungarians soon came to see that "international" supervision of their elections meant "Soviet" supervision.

One of the first things the coalition government did was clean Arrow Crossists, Nazi sympathizers and Horthyites out of government positions. The Communists promoted "people's courts" in place of the old judicial courts, which were considered tainted. The government was compelled to legalize these courts, and by April 1945 they had rendered judgment over nearly ten thousand Arrow Cross and other political "criminals."[3]

By the fall of 1945, the Communists felt they were ready for open elections. They knew they could not get a majority, but had cobbled together a left-wing "united front" which they were certain would outperform the country's largest political party, the Smallholders. In the heat of the campaign the

---

*One who had spent his exile years in Moscow and not in jail or underground in Hungary.

Communists resorted to violent disruption of other parties' meetings until a truce was called on September 26. The Communists were confident that since the main strength of the Smallholders was in the countryside, winning municipal elections would affect the later nation-wide elections.

To their amazement, the Smallholders eked out a plurality of 50.4 percent of the votes in the municipal elections, while the left-wing "United Front" polled a combined total of only 42.76 percent. Marshal Voroshilov, the Soviet commander of the occupation forces, was so furious he reportedly slapped Rákosi across the face when the latter tried to explain.

On October 16, Voroshilov convoked the leaders of all parties and recommended a single-list electoral alliance to predetermine their shares in the National Assembly. He proposed forty percent for the Smallholders and made wild threats of increasing the occupying army,.and starving the country if they did not comply. He even upped the Smallholders' percentage to 47.5, but even this the Smallholders rejected. In the end Voroshilov tentatively agreed to abide by the election outcome and keep a coalition government.

The Smallholders handed Voroshilov and the Communists a crushing disappointment by winning fifty-seven percent of the national vote. The Communists polled only seventeen percent, exactly the same as did the Social Democrats. Voroshilov agreed to have the leader of the Smallholders, Béla Kovács, named Minister of Agriculture, but he refused to let the Smallholders hold any more than fifty percent of the ministerial positions.[4]

1946–1948

On February 1, a republic was proclaimed, but it was already something of a misnomer when the leading political party was unable to exercise the power it should have been allowed. The Hungarian Communist Party was boring from within in every sector with obvious help from the Soviet authorities. Rival parties were infiltrated and spied on. Leaders met with mysterious "accidents" which the police seemed never able to solve, false accusations were leveled at government people whom the Communists wanted to get rid of, and the Communist press kept repeating these charges *ad infinitum.*

The leadership of the Hungarian Communist Party was in the hands of four men: Mátyás Rákosi, Ernő Gerő, Mihály Farkas and József Révai. All were Muscovites and all Jewish. The leader, whom Stalin had carefully selected, was Mátyás Rákosi, who was well aware of Stalin's anti-Semitism.

In intellect and willpower Rákosi was far superior to the other three. Clever, divisive, fluent in many foreign languages, Rákosi, despite his short, stocky build and bald, bullet-shaped head with little pig eyes, could be smooth, quite cultivated, and charming when he needed to be. Seeing that the Party had a long way to go before it would be ready to take over the country, he developed what he later boasted were "salami tactics."

Hungary, even though it entered the Second World War late, suffered catastrophic losses. Roughly forty percent of its national wealth had been removed or destroyed by the Germans. In addition, over six hundred thousand Hungarians had been killed on the battlefields or lost their lives in German concentration camps. The massive looting by the Red Army in 1945 did not hold a candle to the organized pillage of the Soviet occupation which requisitioned seventy-five percent of Hungary's industrial power for military and reconstruction purposes, sending much of it to the Soviet Union, never to be seen again. Granted, Hungary was a defeated enemy country, but nothing of this sort had been agreed to at Potsdam.[5]

Hungary's Peace Treaty, signed in Moscow on February 10, 1947, was a tremendous disappointment to all Hungarians. Not only did they lose all of Transylvania to Romania, and the territory Hitler had allowed them from Slovakia, but the Russian troops, which should have left the country, were allowed to stay on as the Russians had argued they needed them to keep communication lines open to their occupying forces in Austria. If and when an Austrian Peace Treaty was signed and Soviet troops left Austria, then they would quit Hungary as well.

By 1947, when Communists were forced out of the French and Italian governments in which they had participated since the war's end, just the reverse was happening in Eastern Europe. Hungary's non-Communist Prime Minister, Ferenc Nagy, was quite aware of Rákosi's "salami tactics" but felt increasingly powerless to prevent them. When Nagy was invited to participate in a world congress of Socialists in Switzerland, he gladly seized the opportunity both for some respite from the pressure the Communists were putting on him and some advice from fellow socialists. Rákosi, operating from his preferred position of Vice Premier, had been orchestrating a campaign of slander, through the Interior Ministry, against Nagy. While he was in Switzerland, Rákosi informed Nagy by phone that should he decide to return to Hungary, his life would be in danger. When the thoroughly demoralized and intimidated Nagy decided to heed Rákosi's threat by remaining in

Switzerland, Rákosi used Nagy's failure to return as proof of the truth of the trumped up charges against him. On May 30, when the Soviet-dominated Allied Control Commission renewed charges against him, Nagy, still in Switzerland, announced his resignation.

Now Rákosi's salami tactics moved into high gear. Content to remain only deputy prime minister (he did not assume the Prime Ministership until 1952), Rákosi prepared for new elections at the end of August 1947. This time the elections were thoroughly rigged. But even with a maximum amount of help from the occupation forces, the Communists garnered only twenty-two percent of the vote. Rákosi, however, was not disappointed. The leftist bloc, led by the Communists, got 60.8 percent. The Communists were now totally in charge. Rákosi, however, was careful to keep up the pretense of a coalition government with non-Communict "fellow travelers" as pure window-dressing.

The last goal before proclaiming the country a "people's democracy" was the destruction of the Social Democratic Party and the absorption of its remnants into the Communist Party, an essential element in the march to power of every Communist Party. As long as the representatives of real socialism were around, the bogus Soviet version called "dictatorship of the proletariat" was in danger of being exposed. The methods were many, working on the most left-wing members, defaming and physically threatening the leaders right up to actual jailings and even assassinations. In Hungary the official merger of the two parties was accomplished on June 12, 1948, and the combined Party was renamed the Hungarian Workers Party, partly to mask the fact that it was now completely Communist.

It was no accident that these forced mergers occurred after the establishment of the new Cominform in 1947, which took the place of the Comintern (Communist International, which had been disbanded in the middle of the war), and Stalin's forcing Yugoslavia out of the Cominform in 1948.

Now Sovietization proceeded apace. The Hungarian flag was seldom seen in public, but lots of Soviet flags were; everything Soviet was extolled and copied, from Soviet-type collectivization of the farms—a brutal process in many cases—to Soviet industrialization, including emphasis on heavy industry. The new steel works established at Dunaújváros or Dunapentele, soon to be renamed Sztálinváros, made no economic sense whatsoever in that Hungary, while the bauxite center of Europe, contains almost no iron ore and only enough coal for domestic needs, both of which now had to be imported. Collectivization totally alienated the peasantry, and yields dropped. As a result of this the standard of living plummeted and many peasants actually went hungry. The promised equality of abundance turned out to be equality of paucity and misery.

This did not go unnoticed in the West, where East European exiles were calling attention to it, but there seemed to be little, save ineffectual diplomatic protests, that could be done about it. Western Europe was struggling to control the damage of strikes and sabotage being done, on Stalin's orders, by the Western Communist Parties and trying to rebuild Western Europe with the help of the Marshall Plan. American policy was almost exclusively focused on this effort.

In Hungary the Communist Party was succeeding in subverting the Protestant Churches, or at least rendering them harmless, but was having difficulty with the Catholic Church. Cardinal Mindszenty had pulled his support of various splinter Catholic parties in 1947, urging Catholics instead to vote for the Smallholders. Possessing an impeccable anti-Nazi record and great popularity for his forthright, if inflexible, stands, Mindszenty had become a major thorn in the Communists' side. He was also fighting attempts by the Communists to insert bogus "peace priests" into the Church. When he was arrested the day after Christmas, 1948, and tried, obviously tortured, convicted, and given a life sentence the following February, the news caused consternation and major protests in the West. Even more alarming than that, however, was the Communist coup d'etat in Prague some days later, slipping Czechoslovakia, the last East-Central European state which had maintained a semblance of freedom, behind the Iron Curtain. This proved to be a major wake-up call, and within months the North Atlantic Treaty Organization (NATO) had been established.

1949–1953

While America began to remobilize, after its precipitous disarmament in 1945 and 1946 (it would accelerate this remobilization after the outbreak of war in Korea in 1950) leading figures both in and outside of government pondered what could be done about Eastern Europe. The result was a private organization made up of American leaders, many of whom had held leading positions in the U.S. government, known as the National Committee for a Free Europe. Conceived and organized in 1949, it began operations in 1950 and by 1951 had launched the organization for which it was most famous:

Radio Free Europe. By this time it was secretly receiving funds from the U.S. government through the CIA, a fact that was not revealed to the public until the late 1960s, but suspected by the Communists all along.

By now the Cold War was fully engaged. The Iron Curtain completely sealed off Eastern Europe and the Soviet Union from the rest of the world. A paranoid Stalin was acting as though he owned all of Eastern Europe and was preparing to absorb these countries into the Soviet Union just as he had the three Baltic republics in 1940. Everything Stalin did was mimicked in the satellite countries; there was no better mimic than Mátyás Rákosi, who prided himself on his nickname, "Stalin's best pupil."

When Stalin attacked Tito, all of the satellites attacked Tito and Titoism became a sort of disease to be rooted out. It was also time to purge all the unreliable elements out of the bloated East European Communist Parties that the Soviet Union itself had fostered. In each country, but especially in Hungary, this provided Stalin, and his henchmen, like Rákosi, a chance to get rid of Communist leaders whom he did not feel he could trust, particularly any Communists who had not been trained in Moscow, but had spent the war underground or in jail. This coincided in Hungary with Rákosi's rivalry with the most famous and popular Hungarian Communist, László Rajk. Until the Gestapo caught him, Rajk had run the wartime Communist underground in Hungary, and when he returned from Germany in 1945, he was not only better known, but also preferred by local Party cadres to the Muscovites who arrived on the backs of the Red Army. Rákosi maneuvered Rajk into a position where he could be accused of cooperating with Tito, had him arrested in May 1949 and, after a summer of torturing, tried in September. Rajk was a tough nut who would not crack. At length Rákosi persuaded János Kádár to tell Rajk that the Party needed a scapegoat, that as a loyal Communist he should confess to all the crimes they were asking him to. After his conviction they would pretend to execute him, but in reality send him off to retirement in the Soviet Union. Rajk, a fanatical Communist, agreed and memorized his confession, which sounded rote and most unconvincing. But instead of going off to retirement in the Soviet Union, he was executed by hanging on October 15. Similar trials were carried out in the other satellites, but Rajk's was the first.

After Rajk's trial more and more arrests and deportations followed, mostly former Social Democrats, but also many Communists. This was combined with frenzied exhortations to increase industrial output and speed collectivization of the farms, all at the behest of Soviet "advisors" with whom the country was now flooded.

Anyone who was not a Communist or kowtowing to them could be considered "an enemy of the people." Under this rubric between the years 1945 and 1953, an estimated 350,000 to 400,000 families, or well over a million people, belonging to the former upper or middle classes were deported to the countryside or forced to move into relatively tiny living quarters. Their former abodes were handed over to Party officials or persons being rewarded by the Communists.[6] At the same time some seventy thousand peasants were branded "kulaks" (a Russian word meaning "wealthy peasant") and had their homes and lands confiscated.[7]

As he was nearing a mirror image of Stalin, Rákosi decided in 1952 to become the Prime Minister of the country as well as Party Chief. It was a meaningless self-promotion, but psychologically it increased his dictatorial powers. He was now not just the source of all terror but also the object of obsequious servility and obscene adulation, as was Stalin at this time in Russia. People began to refer to him as "the little Stalin." Hungary was a nation of cowed citizens.[8]

Hungarian broadcasts from abroad which counteracted this oppressive regime, when they suddenly began in 1951, were exceedingly welcome. Radio Free Europe began with short news broadcasts and music, but in 1952 the Voice of Free Hungary began a full spectrum of programs and hourly news broadcasts. The Communists began at once to "jam" the broadcasts as they were already doing with the BBC and VOA. Jamming is achieved by broadcasting on the same wavelength an irritating, high-pitched wa-oo-wa-oo sound so fast that it sounds like rapid bubbles. This completely obliterates the incoming broadcast. It has to be done fairly close to the receiving radio sets, however, to be effective. Since most radio sets are in cities, the Communists built their jamming stations around cities. The result was that most people living in cities could not properly hear the broadcasts, whereas people in the countryside could hear them quite clearly. This, of course, provided an additional incentive for city-dwellers to visit the countryside on weekends. RFE countered the jamming by shifting to different frequencies, and by broadcasting on several frequencies at the same time. When news was really important, the voltage was upped so that it practically blew the tubes out of the poor listener's radio set. It also gave away the fact that he had been clandestinely listening to RFE, which was, of course, illegal, and if he were discovered, he would be swiftly punished with fines or prison.

The regime media soon began to attack RFE. This accomplished two things: it advertised the fact of RFE broadcasts and it frequently gave away information that had been in the RFE broadcasts that Hungarians not listening would not have otherwise heard. It also afforded the Hungarian population some entertainment, for it was gratifying to see one's oppressor stung by the broadcasts and see to what lengths the regime would go to disprove them. It also reminded Hungarians that they were not entirely alone. Others knew of their plight and were trying to do something about it.

Toward the end of 1952 hopes were also lifted when Americans elected General Dwight D. Eisenhower President. Both Eisenhower and his Secretary of State throughout the campaign had called for a "rollback of the Iron Curtain" and for a policy of "liberation" from Communism to supplant that of mere "containment" of Communism.

1953–1955

The most important Cold War event in 1953 was the death of Stalin on March 5. It led to great fear and apprehension on the part of all the Communist leaders and to the sudden birth of "collective leadership" in the Kremlin. Within months the Communist world was shaken by such explosions as the revolt of inmates in the Siberian labor camp of Vorkuta, the riots in Plzeň, Czechoslovakia, over a currency reform, and a nationwide uprising in the Soviet Zone of Germany, referred to by the Communists as the German Democratic Republic. This last was begun by construction workers in East Berlin complaining of the regime's duplicity regarding their work norms and wages, but spread overnight to the entire zone and entailed a brutal suppression by the Soviets with twenty-six on-the-spot executions and up to fifty thousand arrests.[9]

Due to the Soviet leaders' fear of Stalin's secret police head, Lavrenty Beria, and using as a pretext the East German uprising, with which he had only some connection, Beria was tricked into capture by elements of the Red Army in late June and incarcerated for later trial and execution in December.

This removed Rákosi's chief backer and further sealed the fate of Gabor Péter, the Hungarian secret police chief who had already been arrested in 1952. The Soviet comrades had heard disturbing things about Hungary where it looked as though Rákosi's brutal ways were about to create an explosion. Rákosi was summoned to Moscow, but along with him he was ordered to bring not only his cronies Farkas and Gerő, and the powerless puppet President, István Dobi, but also, ominously, Imre Nagy.

In May the comrades had ordered Rákosi to give up the Premiership and find someone else for that position. Rákosi, while searching for a candidate who would be acceptable to him *and* the Russians, procrastinated, which had further annoyed Moscow. Now he faced the reprobation of the entire Presidium. One after another they attacked him for his "cult of personality," his constant use of terror, the disastrous economic results of his forced collectivization. Beria, who had not yet been arrested, accused him of trying to become "the Jewish King of Hungary." Khrushchev, Malenkov and Molotov then told him he was to give up the premiership to Imre Nagy, reconstruct the Party leadership and draft a new economic and political program. The obvious reasons for their choice were that Nagy was the other end of the political spectrum from Rákosi, popular with the Hungarian people, not only for his having accomplished the land reform but the fact that he was not Jewish, and last, a Muscovite whom they knew and felt they could trust.[10]

There had never been any love lost between Nagy and Rákosi, so it was with some relish that Nagy, with a program called "The New Course" and later referred to as the June Resolutions, proceeded to undo many of the worst acts of Rákosi. He relaxed the collectivization, allowing some farmers to leave the collectives, curbed the secret police (ÁVH, but still called ÁVO by the people), closed the infamous Recsk detention camp, freed many of the political prisoners Rákosi had put in prison on trumped up, or even no, charges, and, because Rákosi still delayed on a new economic program, introduced his own, which drastically cut back investment in Rákosi's pet economic dinosaurs, like the steel plant at Sztálinváros, and shifted investments to light industry to produce more consumer goods for the people.

Because of his long service and his promises to reform, Rákosi, who had always been "their man in Hungary," was able to persuade the Soviet Presidium into making the mistake of allowing him to retain his position as First Party Secretary. As Stalin had already proved and Khrushchev was later to prove, this is by far the most important post in any Communist-run country. Rákosi was not about to take Nagy's changes lying down.

While many Hungarians, particularly Party liberals, thought that salvation in the form of Nagy had come, within months Rákosi began to undermine and sabotage Nagy's program almost before it could get off the ground.

At the Third Party Congress held in May 1954, just ten months after Nagy had assumed the premiership, Rákosi, while paying lip service to the June Resolutions in the major address, made it appear that all the mistakes of the past had now been remedied. In fact, Nagy's program was only beginning or completely stalled due to Rákosi's sabotaging. While there had been a spurt in the standard of living when the "New Course" had been introduced, the country was in such financial trouble with foreign debt that many of the new programs had to be delayed. As people's standard of living stagnated, many people became somewhat disillusioned with Nagy. Moscow had blessed Hungary's new "collective leadership" as a proper mirror image of what had evolved in the Kremlin, but in fact the collective leadership in Hungary was made up of Rákosi and the entire Party apparatus on one side, and Nagy and just a few liberals on the other.

Still, things Nagy had called for, like secret Party elections and greater democratization within the Party, had paid off. As a consequence, only fifty-five percent of the delegates were re-elected, incompetence being held as the reason why forty-five percent did not make it. In spite of Rákosi's opposition, the New Course had reversed nearly every trend of Rákosi's Stalinist policy.[11]

As 1954 wore on, Nagy found he had more than Rákosi to contend with. While Radio Free Europe had somewhat muffled its criticisms when Nagy so drastically changed the course of Hungary, he was still, so far as the Hungarian editors at RFE were concerned, a Communist, and therefore fair game. Personal attacks were sometimes aired, which Nagy thought completely uncalled for, and he became sensitive to what the Voice of Free Hungary was saying about him.

In the fall the Radio unleashed a campaign designed to influence local elections in Hungary, this time with a major difference. The broadcasts were accompanied by leaflets dropping from the skies; written in Hungarian, these leaflets said essentially the same thing as the broadcasts. The leaflets were borne by hydrogen-filled polyurethene balloons, which were supposed to collapse, spilling their hydrogen as they did, but a few reached the ground intact with some hydrogen still in them. Although they only appeared on certain days when the winds were right and not many were seen either descending or on the ground, the Radio kept referring to them. When they were found, the regime made such a fuss about collecting and destroying them that soon everyone in Hungary knew about them.

The balloons were launched by an offshoot of the Radio, called Free Europe Press, which hitherto had only published magazines. They were launched from sites in West Germany near the Czechoslovak and Austrian frontiers at night and frequently were over their target areas before daylight. This was possible because above eighteen thousand to twenty thousand feet the rotation of the earth causes the winds to go invariably from west to east. When surface winds blow in different directions, however, the balloons can be taken so far off course that by the time they have reached twenty-five thousand to thirty thousand feet, a straight line of drift at that height will either not take them over the target area or it will take so long that the dry ice in the timing device evaporates too soon. Czechoslovakia, just across the border, was almost impossible to miss, but balloons with Hungarian leaflets had to traverse most of Austria. So flights to Czechoslovakia were frequent, to Hungary less frequent and to Poland infrequent and not begun until 1955.

On October 15, not long after the first leaflets were dropped, the Nagy regime sent a strong diplomatic protest to the United States saying this was a gross violation of Hungarian sovereignty and calling the leaflets "inciting," "slanderous" and "seditious."

The U.S. took its time in replying, but when it did on December 20, 1954, it observed that Free Europe was a private organization, and while this was an "unusual" method of communication, "this is due solely to the actions of the Hungarian Government and to those…responsible for the policy of erecting barriers against normal intercourse among peoples." As to the contents of the leaflets, the State Department did not feel any were "inciting" or "seditious" and that certain Hungarian government officials share these beliefs "as in recent months they publicly criticized present conditions in Hungary including references to flagrant abuses of police power and judicial processes…."[12]

"Operation Focus," which is what Free Europe called its campaign, was in the form of "twelve demands" and purported to be from the National Resistance Movement whose initials in Hungarian spelled "NEM," which is also the Hungarian word for "no." Most of the leaflets appear to have fallen over the western part of the country and as far south as Pécs and the Mecsek Mountains, where "the balloons caused much excitement. People hid the leaflets and later on secretly passed them from hand to hand."[13] In one village in Dunántúl people were very happy, saying over and over, "The Americans are coming!" while the ÁVO mobilized units to pick them up from the ground. One miner in Tatabánya saw some of them on the roof of his house and crept through the opening of the attic to retrieve them. There were many lying in the street, but he did not dare pick those up.[14] In Szombathely from one of the loudspeakers in Republic Square people heard the announcement at noon, repeated many times: "If somebody finds a leaflet he should immediately hand it in to the police, as this is his patriotic duty."[15] "One of the good results," reported a peasant boy who escaped to Austria in February 1955, "is that it adds to the work of the Communists." In Dunaföldvár, a few days after they landed, an anonymous sender mailed several dozen leaflets in closed envelopes to local Communist officials. The police were then sent anonymously a list of the recipients, all "known to be in possession" of these forbidden leaflets. Those Communists who did not deliver the leaflets within a few days had their houses searched, setting up a major controversy between the police and local Communist officials.[16]

"Threatened with long prison sentences," said one informant who had escaped from Sopron to Austria, "it may be that some unfortunates will have to suffer on account of the leaflets. People, however, have learned to be cautious. It is a pity that this disgusting system has turned the straight-forward, outspoken Hungarians into suspicious, taciturn and unsociable men."[17]

In September and October the leaflets caused such a sensation that people in Budapest were willing to pay ten and twelve forints for one, but as they changed from the "twelve demands" to issues of a mini-newspaper called *Free Hungary*, the novelty wore off. People thought them "a very good idea" and "were glad to get them," but a number found the texts disappointing."[18] The focus campaign was not found specific enough to each local community to be effective and the little newspapers were too bland. Many thought the texts should be "more savage," and that the Communists only understood violent language.[19] At one point Radio Budapest actually broadcast the text of the "Twelve Demands" and one young woman from a good family, when she reached Austria, said, "I must say I was shocked to note how leftist this text was."[20]

But as one informant observed, "the leaflets did not influence the elections in the smallest degree, since the election results were prepared in advance."[21]

From the many reports of the action that came to RFE from escapees, emigrants, travelers and other sources, it was not too difficult to get an idea of the mood of the Hungarian people. Following are some verbatim accounts.

> "In my modest opinion the balloon action was started at just the right moment, when the horrible experiences of ten years were beginning to kill the hope for a better future. The greater part of Hungarians have been waiting for liberation since 1945. Their resistance has been lessened by the relaxation of the conspiracies and cruelties of the police and those of the occupation troops…. The national resistance, very strong at the beginning, has lost much of its unity and is limited now to individual actions…."[22]

Confidential source: "Budapest intellectuals…felt that the contents of the leaflets were disappointing. This is the American 'June Road' [New Course] they said. Why did the leaflets not take a strong line, instead of merely asking for fulfillment of the 'June Road' promises? Hungarians did not want the June Road to succeed. They wanted the regime to be swept away. They did not care about making the local councils the 'servants of the people,' they wanted the local councils to be abolished."[23]

A sixty-three-year-old woman: "As far as I know they intend to overthrow the regime and not only to cause resistance. No half-way work can be tolerated here."[24]

A sixty-four-year-old Jewish emigrant to Israel: "The leaflets certainly are helpful: they encourage people to resist the regime and give them hope in spite of their long waiting…."[25]

Approval of the leaflet action was by no means uniform. One young man from Budapest said that in addition to endangering those who are caught with the leaflets, the "operation has contributed to the false assumption that RFE is trying to organize active resistance leading to a revolution, which would be doomed to failure. Therefore, he charged, 'RFE is being irresponsible.'"[26]

A number of high officials in the U.S. Department of State agreed with this young man's assessment, but they could only advise and were powerless to control what was strictly a CIA operation.

One of the Americans in charge, William E. Griffith, RFE's Political Advisor, wrote a "personal and strictly confidential" letter to Eisenhower's advisor on psychological warfare, C.D. Jackson, on October 20:

> I could send you reams of material which seem to me to prove that…Focus [is] successful, but Sam [referring to Sam Walker, the head of Free Europe

Press—ed.] can give this to you much better.... I think that...FOCUS represent[s] the most significant and successful development in U.S. political warfare since FEC began operations....The [State] Department Foreign Service Officers did their best to sabotage FOCUS in every way.... I now feel that the FSOs on the desks are...actually sabotaging the Administration's foreign policy.... It appears that the desk officers do not believe it is possible to create an internal mass opposition in Eastern Europe.... I have always thought it both possible and desirable. Now I believe we are...off to a good start in Hungary.[27]

At this time Imre Nagy finally had his program approved by the Central Committee, and it looked as though Rákosi might be on his way out. But it was a pyrrhic victory, for Rákosi, who had been secretly shuttling back and forth to Moscow, now began a whispering campaign in the Party that "a hostile, right-wing wave was sweeping the country."[28] In Moscow, meantime, Khrushchev had finally outmaneuvered Malenkov, Nagy's main protector, by getting him ousted from the Premiership. He had also succumbed to Rákosi's criticisms of Nagy. The chief trouble with Nagy's plan for reconverting from heavy to light industry was that it was going to cost a lot of money. When Moscow declined to provide it and even declined Nagy's suggestion of greater trade between the two countries as a solution, Nagy proposed increasing trade with the West. Trading outside the bloc seemed tantamount to treason in the minds of many of the Soviet comrades and Rákosi was encouraged to attack the suspect Nagy and his program, which he did at the December meeting of the Central Committee. The Hungarian leaders were then called to Moscow in January 1955, where Khrushchev forced the deposed Malenkov to lead off in attacking Nagy.

On their return from Moscow, Rákosi proceeded to engineer Nagy's downfall. While the latter lay ill in bed with what he was told was a serious heart condition, Rákosi condemned Nagy's program as "rightist deviation" at a March meeting of the Central Committee. Nagy, however, refused to admit that there was anything wrong with his popular program and refused to resign. He wanted an opportunity to defend his program as soon as he was well enough. Rákosi, however, called on Moscow to help. Suslov was dispatched, and when he found he could not get Nagy to change his mind, he helped prepare a final prosecution brief against Nagy. Nagy was removed from the Premiership as well as the Politburo on April 14. The following

November he was deprived of his Party membership. Only his popularity kept him from arrest.

Rákosi was back, but his victory far from total. Moscow would not let him resume the premiership; that went to a nonentity, András Hegedűs. It made little difference since Hegedűs was completely under his control. Wholesale terror, however, did not resume, no new collectivization drive got under way and the policy of rehabilitation was not rescinded. Now hundreds of persons whom he had put in prison were in circulation and were eager to get back at him.

Two important international events of great importance to Hungary now occurred. A four-power Peace Treaty was signed on May 15, ending the allied occupation of Austria. Soviet troops, along with French, British and American troops all left Austria, which was now pledged to perpetual neutrality. At first Hungarians were overjoyed, for it meant that Soviet troops would soon leave Hungary as well, as their sole reason for being in Hungary had now been removed. The day before, however, the Soviet Union and other nations of the Eastern bloc had signed a treaty in Warsaw, the long-delayed reaction to the establishment of NATO. In this Treaty was a clause stating that Soviet troops were to be stationed in Hungary indefinitely, or as long as NATO existed. Thus, while the Hungarians were happy for their neighbors, they were bitterly disappointed for themselves.

Internationally, Rákosi had to pull in his horns, for just eleven days later Khrushchev made his journey to Belgrade to ask, as it were, Tito's forgiveness for the nasty treatment by Stalin and the rest of the bloc in keeping him out of the Cominform. This dramatic, modern journey to Canossa appeared to imply that the Soviet Union now recognized the legitimacy of more than one road to socialism. It was a move that also gave John Foster Dulles pause, wondering whether he should continue aid, especially military aid, to Tito if he was going to rejoin the Communist bloc.

In the fall of 1955, the Hungarian Writer's Association experienced a minor revolt. This brought a sharp condemnation from the Central Committee and the expulsion of several popular writers. But putting the lid back on only made the controversy simmer.

Another diplomatic protest to the United States in December over the balloon program, which had grown in size and frequency, met with the same American response as before.

Then in February 1956, Rákosi and other high Party officials journeyed to Moscow to attend the Twentieth Soviet Party Congress. None of the foreign comrades were allowed to hear Khrushchev's dramatic secret speech, but they were nonetheless told about it in some detail. For the man who had prided himself on the nickname "Stalin's best pupil," it must have been a traumatic moment. Indeed, he did not come home with the delegation, but lingered a few more days in Moscow. "You can't act in this way," he told Ambassador Andropov, who had also remained in Moscow. "You shouldn't have hurried. What you have done at your Congress is a disaster. I don't know what will come of it, either in your country or in mine."[29]

From Rákosi's first few public appearances and speeches in Budapest, no one could have told that anything much had happened in Moscow. Even when he made the offhand announcement on March 27 in the provincial town of Eger that Rajk was innocent, his trial a complete travesty, the blame was quickly put on Gabor Péter, the ex Áv6 chief, and his deputy Farkas, now conveniently in jail. This meant, of course, that all of the others who were either executed with Rajk or given long jail terms were equally innocent and those still alive were now rehabilitated, freed, and offered monetary compensation. Since everyone knew that Rákosi was behind Rajk's trial and execution, people were amazed that Rákosi made not the slightest confession of guilt nor offered to resign.

The Soviets, meanwhile, just to show the Hungarians how fully they backed Rákosi, published his article on Leninist principles on the front page of *Pravda* on May 2, which meant it had to be reprinted the next day on the front page of *Szabad Nép*. A week later, just to make sure that the restless Hungarians understood how fully the Soviets backed him, President Voroshilov sent Rákosi greetings calling him "dear friend," which was another way of saying "Stop criticizing our man."

The day after Voroshilov's "dear friend" greeting, Rákosi gave a speech so harsh and so Stalinist that American Minister Ravndal said its tone and content "has disappointed locals harboring even the most cautious hopes."[30] Somewhat later the *Times* of London commented that Rákosi is "still apparently firmly in the saddle and has used the unrest to drive further nails into the political coffin of Mr. Nagy."[31]

But the unrest was not just among the writers but among musicians, students, young Party intellectuals, and even the workers. The Hungarian Musicians' Federation, at a May 19 conference, proposed a lifting of censorship and complained in an article signed by their President, Zoltán Kodály, that "our musical life in recent years shows not only stagnation but sure signs of retrogression."[32]

Liberal Party members, in an attempt to win back the disaffected and those intellectuals who had once been fellow travelers, sanctioned a discussion group that had been functioning within DISZ, the official Communist youth organization, called the Petőfi Circle. The idea was also to provide a safety valve for all the anger that was building up within the Party. The evening discussions of this group, which were always centered on a single topic, grew more and more outspoken, and thus increasingly popular and each had to be held in a bigger place than the last. By June they were meeting in the old Officers Club off Váci Street, which could easily accommodate eight hundred seated persons, but many more on steps and standing, if need be. On the evening of June 19, some two thousand former partisans met to hear a discussion of "The Old Illegal Communists and the Young Intellectuals of the Day." Like many other old Communists, László Rajk had fought on the Loyalist side in the Spanish Civil War. Júlia Rajk, his widow, decided to attend. When it came time for questions she stood up and spoke the following:

> Comrades, there are no words with which to tell you what I feel facing you after cruel years in jail, without a word, a crumb of food, a letter, or a sign of life reaching me from the outside, living in despair and hopelessness. When they took me away I was nursing my five-month-old infant. For five years I had no word of my baby.

Then turning to face the white-faced functionaries on the rostrum she shouted, "You not only killed my husband, but you killed all decency in our country. You destroyed Hungary's political, economic and moral life. Murderers cannot be rehabilitated; they must be punished!"

Then turning back to the audience she asked, "Where were all the members of the Party while these things were happening? How could they allow such degeneration to take place without rising in wrath against the guilty?"

Choking with emotion she cried out, "The nadir of our Party's immorality was reached when László Rajk was executed. I demand a Party housecleaning. Comrades, stand by me in this fight!"

There was a shocked silence for a few seconds, then applause, building to a crescendo as the audience rose to their feet and even the men on the rostrum followed their lead. News of this address was all over Budapest the next day.[33]

The Party media had studiously ignored the Petőfi Circle, but now felt obliged to mention it, particularly since the role of the press was to be the subject of the next meeting. On June 24 *Szabad Nép* called the Circle "a shaft of sunlight" and urged more Party members and government officials to attend the meetings. Whether it was this call or Mrs. Rajk's speech, some six thousand people showed up for the June 27 discussion of the media; loud-speakers had to be set up in the courtyard and street for the overflow that could not manage to pack into the auditorium. The discussion, which frequently was out of control of the organizers, went from 6:30 p.m. until 2:00 a.m. Throughout the meeting there were cries of "Down with Rákosi!" and "We want Nagy!" This time news of the meeting was not just all over Budapest, all of Budapest was talking about it the next day.

The next day was memorable for another event: the Poznań, Poland, workers' uprising, which took several days to put down. Suddenly the Party was galvanized. Worried by the news from Poland and stung by all the criticism at the Petőfi Circle meeting, it called a Central Committee meeting on June 30. Rákosi and his henchmen rammed through a resolution calling the Petőfi Circle "counter-revolutionary...full of fascists, imperialists, and paid agents of the Americans" and charging that it was all organized mainly by "a certain group around Imre Nagy." The full text of this appeared in *Szabad Nép* the next day, as did the notice that two of the speakers, the writers Tibor Déry and Tibor Tardos, had been expelled from the Party.

The Petőfi Circle was forced to draw in its horns, suspend operations for the summer and agree to smaller, by-invitation-only meetings in the fall. Its fame was now such, however, that Petőfi Circles proliferated in the provinces during the rest of the summer.

The Kremlin, worried about reports from Ambassador Andropov, decided to send Mikhail Suslov to Budapest. Rákosi convinced Suslov that he was their only option, but Khrushchev, after a talk with the Yugoslav Ambassador in Moscow, doubted Suslov's report and decided to send Anastas Mikoyan, who knew Hungary better, for a more sophisticated reading. Mikoyan was sent ostensibly to attend the July 17 meeting of the Central Committee, but when he heard Rákosi unveil his plan for the immediate arrest of four hundred high Party and formerly high (like Nagy) officials, he realized he had to act. Mikoyan allowed him to finish before confronting him. Gerő tried to save the situation by suggesting to Rákosi that mass arrests were not "reconcilable with our new brand of socialist legality."[34] Seeing Mikoyan's firm opposition to Rákosi, the Hungarian comrades began to shift. Eventually Rákosi was not only voted down but out, with Gerő voted into his place. Rákosi was secretly flown to the Soviet Union on July 21, whence he never returned.

Unfortunately, Gerő was simply a colorless carbon copy of Rákosi. While pressure built up, he continued to drag his feet on all suggested reforms. When he was not postponing decisions in Budapest, he was in the Soviet Union consulting with Khrushchev or in Yugoslavia negotiating with Tito. In Hungary manifold problems abounded. A few weeks earlier the Hungarian government had been forced to cancel six hundred trains in the country due to lack of coal, and only on October 5 could forty of the most important passenger trains be restored to service, the rest having to wait until October 25.[35] And earlier still, it had been announced that due to unfavorable weather, the harvest was much worse than the previous year, between sixteen and eighteen percent less.[36]

While Nagy was waiting to be readmitted to the Party, non-Communist political leaders from the past began to emerge. Zoltán Tildy, the Calvinist minister who had been incommunicado since 1948 but once led the Smallholders Party, began making statements obviously meant to ingratiate himself with the liberal wing of the Hungarian Communist Party. Rumors reached the American Legation, where A. Spencer Barnes, now the Chargé d'Affaires in the absence of a Minister, reported to Washington that both the regime and representatives of Nagy had approached the Smallholder leader Béla Kovács, who appeared to be backing Nagy.[37]

In Washington a top secret summary of cables circulating around the State Department on September 21 quoted Spencer Barnes in Budapest as saying, "the Soviets now realize Hungary has entered on a course from which return will be increasingly difficult as long as the general Soviet posture in international affairs remains unchanged, and that in the absence of a severe crackdown in Hungary, mere 'braking action' will not be enough to forestall demands for increasing freedom in one field after another."[38]

The Rajk reburial took place on October 6 (see Prologue). The Hungarian Supreme Court quashed the sentence of imprisonment passed in 1948 on Bishop Lajos Ordas of the Evangelical Church on October 10 and had him reinstated to his former position. *Szabad Nép* (*Free People*) wrote on the fifteenth that Soviet laws should not be taken as an example in every case, that those responsible for the Rajk trial should now be put in the dock and that every Hungarian over eighteen should be able to get a passport since "a free state should have free citizens."[39]

Also on October 15, Spencer Barnes, noting Nagy's rising star, sent a cable to Washington saying that when Nagy had been premier he "reacted openly and violently to attacks on his regime by the VOA and RFE, and the Legation feels that we should do all we can to forestall such an occurrence once more."[40]

English foreign correspondent Sefton Delmer of the *Daily Mail*, sensing there was something brewing, flew to Budapest to investigate. After a few days he cabled his newspaper: "Hungary is on the verge of revolution. Everything points to an imminent explosion."[41]

CHAPTER IV

Explosion

Budapest, October 23, 1956, 6:30 p.m.

WHEN THE MAIN BODY OF DEMONSTRATORS left Bem Square in Buda for Parliament Square in Pest, several hundred students decide to break off and go instead to the Radio Station in Sándor Bródy Street. They want to see whether they can get their sixteen demands broadcast to the nation now that the power of their demonstrations has been shown.

Like the Party headquarters in Akadémia Street, the Radio Station has spilled out over the years into a number of neighboring buildings so that it now covers an entire block. It runs back from Sándor Bródy Street between two parallel streets, Puskin [Pushkin] and Szentkirályi streets with garage entrances on Krúdy Street in the rear. The National Museum, fronting on Museum [Múzeum] Boulevard, stands to the east with its garden separating it from the Radio. The main entrance, however, is in Sándor Bródy Street. Over its massive oaken doors it has an arched portico supported by two columns. Above this is a narrow balcony reached by French doors.[1]

The guards outside the main entrance, unlike twenty-four hours ago, will not allow any of them into the building. When harsh words are hurled at the guards, they merely call for reinforcements. For some time this stalemate goes on; but all the while more and more people keep filling the street, among them young workers and students who are only too eager to find a situation where they can vent their rage.

"Open up the door!" they yell. "We want a truthful radio!" "Display the Hungarian flag!" This last demand gets an instant response from young workers inside the radio building who are in full sympathy with the crowd.

109

They rush around trying to find a flag they can hoist to show their approval. There *is* a flag, they know, but it is locked in the warehouse and the key is in the superintendent's office and nobody knows where the key to *his* office is. At length the young staff members' shoulders force the warehouse door open and the flag is brought out in triumph. But the crowd, meantime, has grown impatient.

An amazingly agile youth manages to scale the wall clutching only at tiny crevices with his fingers. When he reaches the second storey balcony he unfurls a small red-white-green flag that he ties to the balustrade. A cheer goes up from the crowd as he completes this remarkable feat.[2]

While this is going on, several hundred ÁVO reinforcements arrive in trucks driving up Museum Boulevard. Seeing that Sándor Bródy Street is blocked, they drive around to the back where the troops enter through the garages, an access to the building complex no one in the crowd is aware of.[3]

A while later a white ambulance with large red crosses on its sides drives along Museum Boulevard and starts to turn into Sándor Bródy Street. Seeing it is an ambulance, people begin to give way so it can pass through the crowd. But one youth jumps up on the running board. Within seconds he spots ÁVO uniforms under the white coats. "Hey," he yells. "These guys are ÁVO!" In no time the crowd surges forward, closing the gap. The two men in the ambulance are rudely pulled from the vehicle, their white coats torn off as they are thrown to the ground. Somehow in the hubbub they disappear into the crowd. The crowd now forces the rear doors open. There among the bandages are submachine guns. Cries of anger ring out as these are removed from the "ambulance." In a sudden fury the crowd topples the ambulance onto its side. Later it will be burned.[4]

*   *   *   *

Over in the offices of the Party newspaper, *Szabad Nép*, editors are gathered in the editor-in-chief's office discussing how the paper should report the events of the day. Editor-in-Chief Márton Horváth, a man grown obese by high living, is sitting behind his magnificent desk. He considers himself a liberal Communist. He has stuck his neck out by having the paper praise the Petőfi Circle just before he took part in its volatile June 27 meeting. Then, a few days later, when the Central Committee condemned it, he was forced to retract it. During the discussion several reports come that First Secretary Gerő is preparing to give an "adamant" speech condemning the demonstrations. The junior editors are distressed at this news. "But Comrade Horváth," they say, "that must be prevented at all costs! In the climate that prevails now, a 'hard' line by Gerő would certainly mean a catastrophe!"

Horváth is inclined to agree and finally is persuaded to call Gerő directly to dissuade him from taking this course. As his editors watch in silence, Horváth reaches out for the red phone that will connect him directly to Gerő's office. But he has already been summarily rejected by Gerő that very morning. Three times his shaking hand reaches out for the phone. Finally he grabs it. But after speaking only a few words he puts it down in obvious relief. Gerő's secretary has told him curtly: "Until he has made his speech, Comrade Gerő refuses to have any telephone contact with you or anyone else." At least this is unambiguous.[5]

7:23 p.m. A bulletin on Radio Budapest announces that the previous bulletin at 4:30 stating that the next meeting of the Central Committee would be held on October 31 is "erroneous." The correct information is that it will meet "in a few days."

At the Radio

The radio's roving recording van, which has been at the Bem memorial demonstration to record the speeches, now tries to return to its home base in the station's courtyard. It is an old Dodge, somewhat beaten up, but very reliable and also very large by European standards. At first it cannot make its way through the tightly packed crowd. But people are quickly led to believe that this van has the "microphone-in-the-street" for which they had been asking the Radio, so gradually space is made until the van is backed right up against the building.

A power cable is drawn through a window on the ground floor and technicians begin to hook up a microphone. The press of people around the vehicle is so great that there is nowhere to mount it but on the roof of the van. By this action the authorities are saying: "You students want to broadcast your demands to the nation? OK, here is your opportunity."

A female student in her early twenties is helped up onto the roof of the van where a young woman announcer is already standing next to the microphone. The announcer switches it on and begins, with professional calm and poise, the usual introduction: "This is Radio Budapest. You are about to hear etc." Meanwhile, the student has pulled a document out of her handbag and begins to read. She reads it out in a slow, dramatic, but tremulous voice, loud enough for those around the van to hear.

Few, if any, in the crowd know anything about the workings of radio. Those few who do realize that very seldom are recordings which are made in the street or even in a studio put directly live onto the air. Editing—and in communist countries, censoring—must first take place. But most people think that if she is speaking into the mike, then it must be coming out on the radio. They urge people watching from ground-floor apartments to put their radios on the windowsills so people can verify that the demands are being broadcast. But, instead of her voice, nothing but gypsy music is coming out of the radios.

"They've tricked us again!" "They are making fools of us!" people cry out in rage and humiliation. "It's a fraud!" "Those bastards!"

"It will be broadcast later, be patient!" yells the announcer.

"Be patient? Yet again? You people can't make fools of us forever!"

Sensing the rising hostility of the crowd as this new "evidence of treachery" is passed from mouth to mouth, the announcer and driver decide to slip into the crowd as unobtrusively as they can, abandoning the van. The van is soon broken into and found to be empty.[6]

*   *   *   *

In her second floor office on the Sándor Bródi side of the inner courtyard Comrade Valéria Benke, Director of the station, decides she must confront the crowd. A single woman in her 40s, dressed plainly with no make up and no-nonsense straight dark hair, she is an ex-Director of the Party Academy and a member of the Central Committee. With the radio's flag now hanging from the balcony alongside the small one, she goes out onto the balcony and shouts "Comrades!" But her voice is hopelessly weak against the cacophony of voices from below. "Comrades!" she tries again with no result. Her third and strongest "Comrades!" is loud enough to be heard and the noise abates. Then from below comes the reply: "There are no comrades here!" A journalist in an even louder voice roars "We are all Hungarians!" This is heard by most of the crowd and those nearest the speaker cheer loudly. Miss Benke realizes that without a loudspeaker it is useless to try to reason with this mob and she retreats through the French doors and back to her office.[7]

Then, she implores Péter Erdős, a writer who is active in the Petőfi Circle and an employee of the radio, to see whether he cannot calm them down. He is not unknown to the public and is basically on their side, so he agrees to try. Furthermore, technicians have now rigged up a microphone and loudspeaker on the balcony. Erdős begins: "Hungarians! It is I, Péter Erdős, a

112

delegate of the Petőfi Circle who is speaking to you!" The shouting subsides, but so does his amplification, for a rock thrown from below puts it out of commission. The din returns and he cannot make himself heard. In desperation he draws a document from his pocket and throws it down to his audience as he cries out proudly: "My mandate from the Petőfi Circle." It is picked up and passed from hand to hand, but it only affects those few who read it. The gesture is soon swallowed up in the rising roar of the crowd. Erdős, genuinely perplexed, retreats back through the net curtains of the French doors.[8]

It is almost 8:00 p.m. Valéria Benke reminds some colleagues in her office that Gerő is about to speak. Someone switches on a radio in a corner of the room. The volume needs to be turned up high to overcome the noise from the street, even though the windows look out onto the inner courtyard.

Outside, while people put radios in their windows, few in the noisy crowd hear more than a few phrases of the speech. But they hear the tone of Gerő's angry voice and the old, hackneyed communist clichés and before long word passes through the mass of people that Gerő had called them "a fascist mob." The phrase goes through crowd like wildfire and the curses and catcalls directed at Gerő suddenly increase.

"We had started the day," think some of the students, "in a euphoric mood spreading our sixteen demands as far as we could. But now, many hours later, not a single demand has been realized. The government not only refuses to take us seriously or give our demands any publicity, it now even calls us, many of whom are long-standing communists, a 'fascist mob'! It is an outrage! Such a government must go. How can we give up and go home now? If we do, we will never get back our momentum."

So the growing mass of people, now jamming the entire length of Sándor Bródy Street, grows even more volatile.

Everyone in Valéria Benke's office sits motionless during the talk. Some find the speech quite conciliatory; others think it a disaster. All are shocked by its brevity. They had been told it would last forty-five minutes and the studio's schedule had been re-arranged to accommodate that bloc of time. There is a most unprofessional gap of silence before the announcer says what few can quite believe: "The speech by Ernő Gerő has concluded." Then comes another long gap before the voice announces: "And now for some dance music" and the sounds of a gypsy violin begins to waft through the room, until the radio is snapped off.

EXPLOSION

A Hungarian mechanized Army unit from Piliscsaba now arrives in trucks along the Museum Boulevard. They do not know about the rear entrance through the garages, so their commanding officer has them disembark at the corner of Sándor Bródy Street. But there is still a solid mass of people between them and the Radio entrance. Rather than further disturb what he can see is an already-worked-up crowd, the officer decides to deploy his men outside in the Museum Garden behind the wall. Here they form two lines, one with rifles pointed out toward the street, the second with rifles pointed toward the ground.

The crowd soon begins to taunt them. "Hey! I'm a Hungarian!" yells one man baring his chest. "Shoot me here!"

Most of the soldiers are conscripts, not long off the farm. They insist they would never shoot fellow Hungarians. Then one of them, in his discomfort, lets the cat out of the bag. "We don't even have ammunition," he confesses. This information spreads quickly through the crowd and the taunting stops. But people, no longer feeling intimidated, decide to overturn the two trucks in which they had come, dislodging the drivers in a firm but friendly manner before they do. After this they begin to fraternize with the soldiers.[9]

Valéria Benke decides at last to admit the delegation of students, who have been patiently waiting now for several hours outside the main entrance. When György Kovács, a foreign correspondent for the radio, offers to go down to open the door and escort them up to her office, she looks at him in utter surprise. "You must be crazy!" she gasps. "Once you open those doors the whole street will come in!" Instead, she sends Kovács out onto the balcony to announce her decision.

It takes some while for him to make himself understood. But he has help. Two demonstrators have already been on the balcony for some time. One is a thin-faced man in a black coat who has been acting like a hoarse muezzin—except that he has been leading the crowd in slogans, not Muslim prayers—and the other a thick-set bearded man in heavy boots. It is he who manages to quiet the people below, so that Kovács can make his announcement.

"Comrade Benke is willing to talk to a delegation of not more than 25; but they cannot come through the main door." This is greeted with jeers, for how else are they to get in? But others lose no time in getting their friends to hoist them up from the roof of the radio van to where they can grab ahold of a bit of balustrade and clamber over onto the balcony. As they dust them-

114

selves off and smooth back their hair, Kovács leads them to Benke's office. The delegation that had waited so long is let in a side entrance. They tell their colleagues "If we are not back in an hour, consider us captives." As they enter Benke's office Kovács finds them a "quaint mixture of bravado and apprehension."[10]

The Director's office is handsomely furnished with an antique desk at the far end and the obligatory, standard issue pictures of Lenin and Stalin on the wall, which grace every government office. Once the salon in a millionaire's flat, it is a huge room with lace curtains on the French doors. The room is purposely divided into two sections, the private one at the far end and the public end dominated by a large conference table seating at least two dozen, with blotting pads, paper and pencils at each setting.

They take their seats around this table at the head of which Valéria Benke and the writer Péter Erdős are already sitting. Radio staff members who happen to be on duty sit in chairs along the walls. Not all the members of the delegation are in their early 20s; one is at least in his 30s. There is also one young woman and one man in the uniform of the Beszkart Tram Company.

"What do you want of Radio Budapest?" asks Benke.

There is a pause of unease as they glance around the table, for there is no chosen leader in the group. Then one youth jumps up and cries: "We want Radio Budapest to belong to the people; we shall not move an inch until it belongs to the people!"

"What do you mean by saying that Radio Budapest should belong to the people?" asks Benke, who had earlier sneered to an associate "*They* are not the people!" as she peered down at the crowd through the curtains.

"And just how do you envisage this transfer of the radio to the service of the people?" she adds.

"Bring the microphone down to the street so that whoever wants can express his opinion!"

Péter Erdős intervenes: "What use will it be to us to bring the microphone down to the street? You yourselves cannot vouch for everyone on the street. How do you know what someone may shout into the microphone?"

The same youth jumps up and shouts, "We have had enough of this claptrap, empty phrases, demagoguery. We are not leaving. You can't feed us that any longer!"

Erdős, who was jailed under Rákosi, turns livid with indignation.

"How dare you call me a demagogue? That is the same name they used when the ÁVO locked me up in jail!"

Other members of the delegation succeed in calming their companion down while another says quietly: "We demand the reading of our sixteen points. Interrupt the broadcast and we will read it."

"These are young people," thinks Benke to herself, "who scarcely remember the Second World War. They don't seem to realize that radio programs are only interrupted for extraordinary events like declarations of war, air raids or signings of peace agreements. No way am I going to interrupt any broadcast."

"Will you read the sixteen points?" the students persist.

"We are actually in agreement with a majority of the points," replies Benke with some sincerity, "and we might be able to agree with the others if they were more suitably worded."

Now what appears to be a genuine negotiation begins to take place, interrupted occasionally by phone calls and disturbances in the street. At one point Benke leaves the table to go make a telephone call at her desk. Kovács, sitting not far away, overhears her quietly order the manager of the main transmitting station at Lakihegy, ten miles' distant, "If you hear any unusual voices or programs, cut off all transmissions." She then returns angrily to the table and tells the deputation that there must be a temporary adjournment. They all have to file out into the hallway. Benke and her cohorts are in no rush to conclude an agreement and, as a result, it is now more than an hour since the group was admitted to the station building. Out in the street, in fact, rumors of their arrest are rife and calls for their liberation from the clutches of the ÁVO come from every quarter. The crowd is beginning to turn ugly.[11]

László Beke, the art student who had learned of the Szeged University students' action via an early morning phone call to his cousin Feri a week ago, is back in action. Having seen his wife, Éva, home to their apartment after the long march, he has joined his friends Imre, Peti and Géza in Parliament Square and from there they have headed toward the Radio. Hearing the commotion as they approach, they spot a construction site around the corner from Sándor Bródy Street. They decide to pile the bricks onto small carts used to move mortar around, and wheel them to in front of the Radio building. As they get there they hear that the delegation inside has been killed by the ÁVO.[12]

*　*　*　*

116

Realizing that more than an hour has gone by since they were admitted to the building, the students in the deputation decide they should reassure their colleagues outside that all is OK with them and that the Radio is going to broadcast most, if not all, of their demands. Several thus go out onto the balcony. They are not prepared for the fevered pitch to which the crowd has risen nor the fact that bricks and cobblestones are now being lofted toward the building with some regularity.

The two from the crowd who have been on the balcony for some time immediately recognize the delegates. The bearded one shouts at the top of his voice: "Hungarians, these are your men!" Then the delegates yell: "Listen to us. We are your men. We've been negotiating with the management of the Radio." The noise under the balcony subsides for a few seconds. Then some one with a particularly powerful voice yells: "Interrupt the broadcast!" As the delegates try to explain that they are making progress, some one else shouts "Traitors!" This is followed by a fusillade of broken bricks, one of which smashes a French door behind them. The delegates hastily retreat to safety.[13]

It is not quite nine o'clock. In the square outside the National Theatre and the *Szabad Nép* building many people have gathered after the Gerő speech to show their anger in front of the Party newspaper. One old-time journalist, Ferenc Oltai (not his real name), who had been fired from the paper after Rákosi's return to power in 1955, finds himself in their midst. Suddenly he notices the crowd beginning to run across the square in all directions. Next he hears sudden explosions as "bullets thick as hail sweep over the area." In panic he joins the others, shouting and shoving as they flee to the shelter of the theatre's arcade. Then, as quickly as it had begun, the shooting stops. People wait, but it is over and gingerly, one by one, people come back out into the open. Everyone agrees the firing came from rooftops on the opposite side. There are bullet pockmarks everywhere and, as Oltai goes back to the *Szabad Nép* offices from which he had come, he notices several wounded and dead still lying in the street.[14]

About this time Chief of Police Sándor Kopácsi receives a call in his office from the police station on Lujza Blaha Square opposite the *Szabad Nép* Party newspaper building and the National Theatre.

"Comrade Kopácsi, it's started!"

"What's started?"

"They are shooting."

EXPLOSION

An hour earlier this same lieutenant had called to say that a detachment
of ÁVO troops had positioned themselves on the roof of the building in
which his police branch station is located. Kopácsi had called Piros, Minister
of the Interior and head of the ÁVO, and Piros had denied they were there,
just as the ÁVO always does whenever a top-secret operation is underway.

"Was anyone injured?"

"No, as soon as the shooting started, people ran for cover under the theatre arcades."

"Could the ÁVO have been using blanks?"

"Absolutely not….I saw the bullets ricocheting off the asphalt. We went
out to see the marks and they were there."

But the lieutenant is wrong. At least three people are hit and one
unshaven youth in a leather coat is killed. His body will lie in its blood on
the steps of the National Theatre until morning.[15]

Over in Parliament Square many of the three hundred thousand people
gathered there are refusing to budge. They have just heard their hero, Imre
Nagy, address them as "comrades," as though nothing had taken place today
to make that word obsolete. And while they are deeply disappointed in his
speech, they were happy to see him lead them in a non-communist patriotic
Hungarian song. He may still end up leading the government like Gomułka
in Poland. If they disperse and go home, when will they ever again share
such emotional unity they have achieved tonight? Many of the younger ones,
however, go off to join the more than a hundred thousand in Stalin Square to
help in toppling his gigantic statue. A few are enticed to go to the radio
where the ÁVO is said to be giving people a hard time. But most are wary
of these adventures knowing what the ÁVO is capable of. They should go
home…but not yet.

Inside the Parliament building, a disconsolate Imre Nagy is still trying to
comprehend the boos and whistles his speech has caused, when he is told
that a delegation from the newly formed MEFESZ is waiting to see him.
Now, for the first time, he hears from their own mouths what the students are
demanding not just from the government, but specifically from him. They
don't seem to realize that he is powerless, that all power lies with the Central
Leadership and right now he is nothing. His belief in Party discipline is total
and unbending. But, he assures them, he will do his best if he is given a
chance.

118

Back at the Radio

Valéria Benke had requested fire engines earlier in the evening, but these had been stopped by the crowds a long way short of the Radio complex and had had to return to their stations. In its place the ÁVO troops roll out an ancient fire hose and some garden hoses they find in the cellar. The suddenly opened windows and jets of water take the crowd by surprise. Those nearby, when hit by the force of the stream from the fire hose, are bowled over, but the garden hoses only succeed in wetting the crowd. Still, much of Sándor Bródy Street near the entrance is cleared. Emboldened by their success, the ÁVO men rush out the main entrance with the hose in an attempt to have the stream reach farther. Unfortunately for them, the hose not only begins to spring leaks, it becomes the victim of bold individuals in the crowd who now attack it with knives. In no time it is useless. The ÁVO men are lucky to get back into the building before getting caught. The crowd, now wet but angrier, surges back in even greater mass than before. People seize the abandoned radio van and manage with slow heaves to turn it around so that it is facing the oaken doors that no amount of pounding or pushing has yet budged. With this improvised battering ram they begin methodically to pound the doors. With each crash the sound of wood splitting increases. But it is a slow and exhausting process.

Inside the Radio there is near panic at the sound. Though there are now close to five hundred troops fully armed inside the complex, no one wishes to fire on unarmed people, and no such order has been given. Morale is poor for there is a difference in attitude between the two groups of soldiers inside the building complex: the ÁVO and the regular Army. The highest-ranking officer is Army Colonel Ferenc Konok, who by all rights should be in command. But having talked extensively with people in the street, he has told Ms. Benke that he has no intention of opening fire on them. Both she and Major Fehér, the ÁVO's highest-ranking officer on the scene, feel differently. She feels "this little game" has been going on long enough and only a few deaths by gunfire will put an end to it.

Rebellious staff members have been locked in editorial offices in the interior. In the courtyard troops are now hurriedly prying open wooden cases of tear gas grenades. These are quickly distributed to troops, who take them to the upper floors along with the guns to shoot them. At a given signal, windows all along the Radio side of Sándor Bródy Street are opened and tear gas grenades come shooting out.[16]

"It is a terrible thing to be tear gassed," thinks Károly Szabolcsi, a forty-three-year-old office worker who had joined the demonstration only because he works a few blocks away. He came out after work to see what was going on. Now he is one of many who suffer. His eyes sting and water so that he cannot see, his nose and mouth start running and the acrid taste makes him want to vomit. Fortunately, the grenade has only exploded near him.[17] Anna Gábor, a twenty-two-year-old secretary, sees a teenager standing nearby hit on the head by an exploding canister. One minute there is a face, the next none. His death must have been instantaneous. But the most terrible thing, she notes, is that this body without a face remains standing for what seems like a full minute before the tightly packed crowd moves enough for it to fall.[18]

There are shrieks and panic in the crowd, yet no one is trampled under, for there is little movement, the mass of people is so tightly packed. Moreover, nearly all are temporarily blinded with tears. Before any gas has reached her Anna Gábor looks up for one split second and sees two ÁVO soldiers at a window pointing down and laughing. It is a sight she will never forget. Moans give way to mutterings against the secret police. Within a few minutes these curses and mutterings have gathered into one great chant: "Death to the ÁVO!"

Slowly the edges of the crowd back away and the compression is lessened. People holding handkerchiefs and scarves to their eyes and noses begin to stagger out of the multitude to somewhere where they can sit down or lean on a wall to recover. Others help carry out the writhing, screaming wounded. The crowd begins to thin. People in buildings opposite the radio who have been watching from open windows decide to close them.

Fortunately, only so many tear-gas canisters can be lobbed out of the windows at one time. This gives those who have not yet been overcome some time to react. And there are quite a few present who have served in the army and know how to cover the canisters with fabric—in this case coats—before they explode, so that their effect is greatly lessened. Some youths even throw the unexploded ones back. And people inside the radio also begin to feel the effects as the gas drifts back through the broken windows.

Then, again without warning, the upper storey windows open and smoke flares are tossed down into the street. Few actually hit people, for the street is rapidly clearing, but they bounce ominously along the cobblestones spewing green sparks and acrid smoke. Some daring youngsters pick them up and toss them back at the Radio building. It is not too difficult to get a few inside. Several fires are started in rooms on the ground floor.

9:23: Radio Budapest says: "Dear Listeners, you now hear a special announcement: the Politburo…has called on the Central Committee to meet immediately in order to discuss the present situation and the tasks to be carried out."[19]

Stalin's Statue

It is now about 9:30 p.m. Two miles away on the section of György Dózsa Avenue known as Stalin Square (formerly Heroes' Square), another crowd, estimated by the police to be over one hundred thousand, is nearing the climax of its task: toppling the giant statue of Stalin.* The removal of this statue is one of the students' demands.

For three hours the multitude has labored to bring the twenty-four-foot bronze statue to the ground. The fact that it stands on a massive red limestone pedestal equally high complicates the task. Before any serious work begins some wag climbs the statue and hangs a sign across Stalin's chest. The sign, which is a parody of a well-known Hungarian song, says:

> Russians when you start to flee,
> I beg of you, forget not me!

It gets many a belly laugh when people first see it.

A medical student in a white shirt next climbs up and places ropes around the neck. With several ten-ton trucks "borrowed" from the Beszkart Tram

*The Communists tore down the beloved Church of Regnum Marianum in 1951 in order to erect this statue. In 1945 when the Soviet Army completed the "liberation" of Hungary—which everyone knows included the raping of hundreds of thousands of women and young girls—the most famous sentence a Russian soldier addressed to a Hungarian was "Hand over your watch!" Most Soviet soldiers had never seen a wrist or pocket watch before and collecting them became all the rage in the Red Army. As American soldiers in Germany well remember, a Mickey Mouse watch, in Soviet eyes, was worth ten times the best Swiss watch that money could buy. The Stalin statue in Budapest was facing a clock tower on the other side of the square and Stalin's right arm was extended as though he were about to shake someone's hand. Shortly after the statue was erected, some wag, in the dead of night, painted an inscription on its base: "Hand over your watch!" The inscription was not there for more than a few hours, but that was long enough for all of Budapest to hear and laugh about it.

Company revving their engines, the ropes are pulled taut. Three times the engines strain and three times the ropes snap, with an audible sigh of disappointment from the crowd each time. Finally people fetch a 150-foot steel cable and this, too, is placed around the neck. As the cable tightens and the truck engine roars there is a sudden high screeching of tires on the cobblestones. People nearby are nauseated by the stench of burning rubber.

But still the statue does not budge.

Dániel Szegő, an engineer who has been watching, realizes what is wanted. He goes off to his factory and returns with an oxy-acetylene torch and welder's gloves and mask. A small scaffolding is built for him so he can reach the area of the statue just above the boots, which he reckons to be the most vulnerable section of the bronze. All this takes some time and the crowd, determined to stay until the figure is toppled, amuse themselves with singing and creating new slogans.

But now the acetylene torch's blue flame is making the bronze glow red. A hush comes over the crowd as Szegő makes first one hole and then another in a row at the back of Stalin's knees. When he is finished he signals people on the ground and quickly descends. The truck engines roar again. The tires whine on the cobblestones. Then slowly the hated dictator's form pitches forward about twenty-five degrees. A cheer goes up from the crowd and instinctively they back away. The engines roar again and this time the statue crashes into the street with a giant "bong." The ecstatic roar from the multitude is so great that it can be heard by the thousands in Parliament Square two miles away. It is now about 9:40 p.m.

The prostrate statue, still hitched up with the steel cables to the trucks, is then dragged slowly along the street. Off it clatters along the György Dózsa Avenue, then down to Rakoczi Út, scattering white sparks so bright they literally light up the street signs as they go along. It is then dragged to Lujza Blaha Square, where it is deposited in front of a pharmacy between the Party newspaper building and the National Theatre.

The next morning people paint graffiti on it, including a large "W.C." on the side of Stalin's face to induce the less inhibited to relieve themselves there. Then scores of people set about with hammers, iron pipes and various other tools to cut and break it up. But first the great head is severed from the body and dragged to the center of the square where someone places a stop sign in the hole where the nose once was. Then people begin breaking off small pieces of the infamous statue to take home as souvenirs. It is a process that will go on for several days.[20]

Back in the Parliament building Imre Nagy is informed that he is wanted in Communist Party headquarters two blocks away. He says quick good-byes to the MEFESZ students, who are encouraged by this interruption, and goes on foot the short distance to 17 Akadémia Street. He is accompanied by his son-in-law, Ferenc Jánosi, Géza Losonczy, one of the brightest of the young liberal communist leaders, Ferenc Donáth and several others who had all gone with him to the Parliament building.

As they enter the party building they find it is alive with armed ÁVO officers rushing around. Two of these officers step up, one on either side of Nagy, as he mounts the red-carpeted stairs to Gerő's office. Jánosi has the feeling that they are there less to protect than "to prevent any of us from escaping." The group is shown to a waiting room. Here an American correspondent of Hungarian extraction, Leslie Bain, representing the North American Newspaper Alliance, appears also to be waiting to see Gerő. Recognizing Nagy and realizing his extreme importance at the moment, Bain comes over to Jánosi and asks if he may speak to Nagy. Nagy looks up and shakes his head. Jánosi whispers to Bain that although Nagy is not under arrest, he is not allowed to speak to anyone.[21]

Gerő keeps Nagy waiting; but not for long. When he is admitted he is told that his entourage must wait outside.

Gerő is not alone. András Hegedűs, the young, balding Prime Minister, is also there. Gerő does not ask Nagy to sit down. It is a confrontation of two totally different types of men who heartily despise each other. The only thing they have in common is forty years of Party membership and the fact that both had been trained in Moscow and spent long years in the Soviet Union. Gerő is tall, sallow, stiff, humorless and crafty; Nagy is roly-poly, warm and folksy, with flowing moustaches. Gerő speaks in a cold, clipped voice; Nagy, despite all those years in the Soviet Union, still speaks in the rich, rolling accent of the town he was born in, Kaposvár, some fifty-seven years ago. Moreover, he loves the arts: painting and music, the opera, theatre as well as good food and wine.

Instead of a communist greeting, both insincerely mumble "szervusz," an old German-Latin greeting meaning "at your service" used mostly by students or close friends, which these two most certainly are not.

"Well!" Gerő explodes.

"Well, what?" Nagy fires back.

"See what you have brought on!"

"Come now, I've just gotten back from vacation. If this is why you sent for me, I may as well leave now."

Gerő leaps up from behind his desk. "*You,* yes exactly!" he yells. "It was *you* who cooked up this dish and now you can just stew in its juice! You have instigated the riots!"

"I have instigated nothing, and you know it!" yells back Nagy, losing his composure. "It's your fault, Gerő, and yours too, Hegedűs. As well as your Rákosi's."

"What do you mean to insinuate by that?" counters Gerő.

"I am merely pointing out to you," says Nagy, returning to his usual tone of voice, "that I have warned the party and government on a number of occasions that they were playing with fire."

"A fire set by Imre Nagy," puts in Hegedűs sarcastically.

"You have no position, no authority," says Gerő, "so how did you dare go to Parliament and incite the crowds by speaking from the balcony?"

Nagy, who has spent the day quietly with his friends largely unaware of what was happening in the streets and who has only reluctantly agreed to go to Parliament at the incessant urging of his friends, finds the word "incite" so totally the opposite of what has just taken place that he can find no adequate words to reply.

"Well," says Gerő, scornfully, "if you are such a good Party member, why *did* you go to Parliament Square?"

Nagy still feels it hopeless to try to explain. All he says is: "Everything that is happening now could have been prevented if you had handled the situation better during the day."

Then he adds with conviction: "You have been—and still are—following a worthless, slapdash policy of half-measures and insults."

"Well," says Gerő with sarcasm, "'Mister Nagy,' who had his vanity wounded because he did not get everything he wanted from the Central Committee, is organizing a fascist riot….I'll drown it in blood, this riot of yours!" Gerő is now trembling with anger.

Nagy, genuinely shocked, looks him in the eyes. "You don't know what you're saying…. Blood….But who is it that's out in the street? It's the young, the people…. "

"It's counterrevolutionaries," says Gerő stubbornly. "I'll give orders to fire on them."

"Ordering troops to fire on the people has always been your specialty," says Nagy, referring to Gerő's bloody role in Spain of having fellow communists shot. "I, on the other hand, have always tried to reconcile the people's and the party's views."

At this point Hegedűs, sensing that this confrontation is getting them nowhere, has already gone on too long, and may lose them the backing of Nagy, which they need, steps in and announces: "The Central Committee is soon to go into session. Comrade Gerő and I are supposed to attend. Please be patient with us a little longer and go wait for us with your friends."

Nagy makes no protest at this. It appears the party needs him, but formalities must be observed, so he was willing to bow to them, however humiliating.[22] Earlier in the day, Gerő had summoned the Soviet military attaché and asked him to notify Soviet Lt. General Lashchenko, commander of the Special Army Corps in Hungary, that it was time to unleash operation "Volna" (code name of the plan for the Soviet Special Army Corps in Hungary to "restore socialist social order" in Hungary). Gerő was playing his ace in the hole without notifying any member of the Central Committee. Now he receives a phone call from Soviet Ambassador Yuri Andropov himself, obviously annoyed that Gerő had not spoken directly to him. Andropov has been on the phone with the general and it seems that the general will not take orders, even from a Soviet ambassador.* It must come from his military superior, and that means getting the Kremlin to order Marshal Zhukov to do it. Andropov adds that the request cannot come from him, but must come from the Hungarian government.

Back to the Radio

Dora Scarlett, the British Communist who works for the English language section of the Radio, is walking back from Parliament Square where she has heard Imre Nagy. She tries to telephone the station, but gets no answer. Coming out of the telephone booth on Vörösmarty Square, she hears

---

*Soviet Ambassadors in the Satellite countries of Eastern Europe, unlike Soviet Ambassadors in the rest of the world, were not diplomats in any sense of the word; they were strictly communist party appointees and had ties directly to the Politburo, often completely bypassing their own Ministry of Foreign Affairs, to which they owed only nominal allegiance.

what sounds like a short salvo of guns. A minute later as she proceeds down Váci Street she hears a second salvo. (What she hears is actually the tear-gas guns and detonations of the canisters in Sándor Bródy Street.) As she reaches Museum Boulevard, just past the Astoria Hotel, she finds the street black with people, many shouting slogans. An overturned armored car is burning, the stench of its thick, black smoke coming off its brightly burning tires, filling the street. When she questions a passerby he answers nonchalantly: "It's an ÁVO car." Near the Museum Garden gates and all along Pushkin Street she sees Hungarian Army trucks loaded with soldiers. All are surrounded by people vehemently arguing with the soldiers. The street is wet and there is still enough tear-gas in the air to make her eyes smart.

Despite the water, tear-gas and smoke flares, the ÁVO troops inside the Radio see that the people are not going away. If they come back in force and begin again to use the Dodge van as a battering ram they may well gain entry to the Radio. So the decision is made to clear the street with force. A platoon of soldiers with fixed bayonets rushes out the door and takes a stand in front of the radio. The bayonets are intimidating enough, but suddenly they raise their rifles and fire into the air. Within a few minutes they have cleared the street from Pushkin Street to Szentkirályi Street and set up barriers at the intersections.[23]

The platoon then goes back into the Radio assuming their job of intimidation is successful. In fact, it is short-lived. Their delegation of twenty-five is inside the Radio still captive, if they haven't all been shot. Their colleagues are determined to rescue them. The old Dodge is still near the entrance. Many hands maneuver it back into place and start battering the wooden doors with it rhythmically. Inside the ÁVO troops, still with fixed bayonets, are waiting for them in the courtyard.

Around this time Lt. Col. Solymosy returns to the scene. He brings with him several caissons of ammunition that is distributed quietly to the troops under his command. With this distribution come fresh orders: troops are not to use their weapons unless actually fired upon. If, however, anyone does fire on them, they must fire back.[24]

Also about this time several Hungarian tanks, their turrets open and crews waving to people on the sidewalks, clank up Museum Boulevard and stop at the corner of Sándor Bródy Street. As soon as people see that they are Hungarian, they climb up on them and decorate them with Hungarian flags yelling to their fellows, "The Army is with us! The Army is with us!" One tank moves up to the Radio entrance, where those using the Dodge van as a battering ram stop to see what will happen. Out of the tank steps Lt. Col. István Zaleczky. He grabs the Hungarian flag that someone has stuck onto the tank and steps up onto the turret. As he turns to face them the crowd grows suddenly silent. Against the guttural throbbing of his tank's engine he shouts: "Do not be afraid! We are not here to shoot anyone. The Army is fully aware of the people's grievances and wishes to see them resolved...peacefully."

Before he can shout another sentence, gunfire cuts him down. People can see smoking rifles being withdrawn from upper windows in the Radio. ÁVO Captain J.M., seeing the Army officer with the Hungarian flag in his hand addressing the crowd, figures he has joined the mob and orders the soldiers under him to shoot him down.[25]

People are aghast. The tank with the body of its commander collapsed on its top drives off in sudden panic. The crowd begins an ominous drone that gradually evolves into one big roar of "Death to the ÁVO!"

Now those with the Dodge van return to their labor with renewed vigor. At last the ancient wooden doors give way with an earsplitting wrench. The Dodge van is pulled back. György Kovács, the Radio's foreign correspondent in the V.I.P. glass waiting room at the far end of the courtyard, sees "a huge tide of human beings clamber over the smashed doors." He retreats further into the Radio.[26] The ÁVO, however, wait until about eighty of the intruders are through the gate and into the courtyard before they launch their counterattack. Those who are not immediately butchered are taken prisoner. No one can escape, for the entrance is now full of security troops pouring out into the street. Once in the street they line up and fire a salvo into the air. Startled, people freeze in their tracks. Then they begin to move again. But the troops have no intention of waiting for the storm of rocks and bricks that may follow. They level their rifles and shoot at the feet of, or directly into, the crowd.

The crowd is stunned. Shrieks of pain and fury fill the air. These are followed by curses of outrage as the dead and wounded, some streaming blood, are dragged out of the line of fire. Few believed that even the ÁVO—who are, after all, Hungarians—would fire on an unarmed civilian crowd of their countrymen. Now from the back, where the bullets have not penetrated, bricks and rocks inevitably begin to arc through the air, taking several ÁVO men down with anguished cries of pain. Rather than take any more casualties, the Security troops withdraw back through the shattered entrance carrying their wounded comrades with them. But others appear in the windows and begin to shoot randomly.

With guns on only one side, the fight is outrageously uneven. What the patriots need now are weapons with which to return the ÁVO's fire. And some of these are not far away. Several submachine guns were taken from the ÁVO "ambulance"; but this is not enough. There are many regular Army trucks parked nearby full of soldiers with rifles. They are under orders not to use them, but once they learn the ÁVO is shooting defenseless civilians, they may be more willing to hand them over, especially if the patriots plead for them.

László Beke is in the crowd. As he runs to get out of the line of fire he notices two people fall near him. He soon learns that they are his fellow students from the School of Fine Arts, Géza Julis and Jenő Borhy. Confusion, screaming of the wounded, and bitter fury of the defenseless fill the dimly lit street. One thing is certain: the rock-throwing stage is over; it is now impossible to venture into the street without being mowed down by the ÁVO machine guns.[27]

Béla Lipták is also in the crowd, though not so near to the Radio entrance as Beke. He notes that when the bullets hit the pavement they make a high-pitched *phing* sound, but when a bullet hits flesh it makes a much deeper *thud* sound.

One thought fills everyone's mind: where to get weapons to return the ÁVO's fire. This has already occurred to many young workers, especially those who work in places like the United Lamp factory, where small arms are clandestinely manufactured in great quantities. As Lipták reaches Museum Avenue he notices a large truck with a crowd around it. "What's happening?" he asks.

"The truck is from the Soroksári Street arms factory, you know, the United Lamp Factory. They brought rifles and ammunition," says the man next to him. Lipták immediately begins to push his way through the crowd to get a rifle. The one he is given is covered with grease and his first reaction is that he will soil his new corduroy jacket. He finds a garbage can with newspaper in it and starts rubbing off the grease. By the time he finishes this job another truck appears on the scene. A young man calls out: This truck is from Újpest (an industrial area of Pest) and we are on our way to the Károlyi

Barracks in Budaörs (a town on the western edge of Buda) to get more arms. If you want to help, get on."

Lipták climbs in back and finds three young men and two young women sitting opposite him. By their dress he soon realizes he is the only student on the truck; the others all seem to be factory workers. They are all holding onto the same grimy rifles as Béla.

When the truck turns onto Üllői Avenue, the driver, seeing no traffic ahead, steps on the gas. When he reaches about sixty m.p.h. there is a sudden bump—possibly a brick in the road—and all the rifles that had been laid on the floor jump into the air. As they fall back, one of them goes off. The boy next to Béla falls forward, blood streaming from his right ear. Béla grabs him as the truck screeches to a halt. Because he is wearing a tricolor armband and is a student, the others all expect him to decide what to do. Knowing that the Haynal Clinic is only a few hundred yards away, Béla directs the driver to it. The night watchman opens the door and emergency help is called. In a few minutes the boy is being carted off on a stretcher and they are back on the road. But the right side of Béla's new jacket is now smeared with blood.[28]

László Beke and his friends also go after guns. His friend Peti Lorenc leads a group to Csepel Island where the largest of all Hungary's arms factories is located. Imre and Géza run to military barracks nearby. But László commandeers several trucks and takes a large group of Technical University students to the city Police Station on Ferenc Vigyázó Street well over a mile away.

Two armed guards at the police station are obviously impressed with the size and discipline of the group. The guards' friendly demeanor seems to indicate approval, so Beke brushes by them as Feri Kovács pins tricolor ribbons on both. The officer in charge, a major, has about a hundred men under him. When Beke encounters him his face reminds Beke of one of his university professors.

"In the name of the Students' Revolutionary Council, surrender your arms!" says László, surprised at the tone and volume of his own voice. His heart is pounding as he stares at the police major in front of him. Without arms, he and his fellow students are defenseless and could all be arrested there and then.

After what seems an eternity the forty-five-year-old officer steps toward them, salutes László and says with a weak smile: "All right boys. They're yours." László cannot help rushing forward to hug him.

They are lucky. Only minutes later orders go out from Colonel Kopácsi to all police stations that they are not to surrender *any* arms and if it looks as though this cannot be done without violence, they are to surrender them, but only after removing bolts and rendering them useless.

Not a mile away in the Duna Hotel near the Danube, British foreign correspondent Sefton Delmer is phoning his newspaper, the *Daily Express*, in London. He has what is known as an "exclusive," for he is the only British correspondent in Budapest and he has experienced nearly all of the day's events.

"I have been a witness today," he dictates, "of one of the great events of history. I have seen the people of Budapest catch the fire of Poznań and Warsaw and come out in open and bitter rebellion against their Soviet overlords."

"I have marched with these rebels and almost wept for joy with them as the Soviet emblems in the Hungarian flags were torn out by the angry exulted crowds..."

"As I telephone this dispatch I can hear the roar of ten thousand-strong delirious crowds made up of boy and girl students, of Hungarian soldiers still wearing their Russian-type uniforms and overalled factory workers, marching and shouting defiance against Russia."

"At 9:30 p.m. (GMT) the firing started...I can hear their guns as I phone...."

"Another crowd in an ecstasy of patriotic fervor has overturned a statue of Stalin...."

"Thousands more...are yelling themselves hoarse for their hero Imre Nagy...."

"Like Gomułka, Nagy is now making his comeback...."

On the second floor of the *Daily Express* building in London James Nicol, Deputy Foreign Editor, scurries across the newsroom to the Managing Editor, Edward Pickering. "We're all right," he says. "We've got Tom Delmer on the blower and he's started dictating his stuff." But back at his desk Nicol suddenly screams, "Good God, have you been cut off?"

"No, Mr. Delmer said to phone him back."

"Telephone him back! Hold the line open! Tell him we're holding the front page!"

But phoning Delmer back turns out to be a problem. Desperate calls to western capitals establish the fact that all lines to Hungary are now cut off. Their correspondent in Vienna had dined with Delmer last night, but failed to get this phone number. Then Nicol remembers his friend, the American *New York Times* correspondent, Sydney Gruson, in Prague. He is not available, but his wife, Flora Lewis, suggests a man there in Prague who works for Press-Wireless, called Francis Polak. Polak is glad to oblige, for the phone lines from Prague to Budapest are open, and for the next several hours Delmer's copy is dictated to him and thence to London.[29]

Other western correspondents—Austrian, German, French, American (John MacCormac of the *New York Times)*, and correspondents for the wire services—file their stories before the lines are cut off.

In Moscow, where the local time is already 12:45 a.m., the Soviet Presidium is once more in session. While Poland is still a major worry, the situation in Hungary quickly becomes the main item of discussion. Reports from Ambassador Andropov are most worrisome and he is urging the intervention of Soviet forces. Khrushchev and all but one of the other members of the Presidium are for immediate military intervention. The sole member who opposes this action is Anastas Mikoyan, the one person on the Presidium who is considered the Hungarian expert, for he has been there many times and knows the situation well. Without Nagy's help he believes that the "movement" now in progress cannot be taken into hand. "This will be the cheapest way for us....Let the Hungarians restore order. If our troops go in, we will ruin things for ourselves. If we leave them alone," he insists, "the Hungarians themselves will restore order....We should try political measures, and only then send in troops." But the others, who are still smarting from the defeat they have received at the hands of Poland's Wladyslaw Gomułka just a few days ago, are not about to get into another dubious undertaking when military might will quickly solve the problem. The vote to intervene is taken.

The Presidium also decides to send Mikoyan and Suslov, as well as KGB Chief Serov, back to Budapest to provide on-the-scene reports.

The orders which Marshal Georgii K. Zhukov and Marshal Vassily Sokolovsky give do not involve just the Special Corps stationed in Hungary, but a Soviet Mechanized division based in Romania and two divisions (one mechanized, one rifle) from the Transcarpathian Military District based in the Ukraine. All three of these divisions have been put on alert more than an

EXPLOSION

hour earlier, that is to say, before 8:00 p.m. Budapest time. The division from Romania is to control southern Hungary and occupy the towns of Szeged and Kecskemét, and the divisions from the Ukraine are to control eastern Hungary and occupy the towns of Debrecen, Nyíregyháza, Jászberény and Szolnok, while the Special Corps is to occupy Budapest, other cities in the west and cut off the western border. All told this involves 31,500 soldiers and 1,130 tanks and self-propelled guns.[30]

Back in Budapest, Tamás Szabó, a dark-haired fifteen-year-old whose six-foot height makes him look much older than he is, has persuaded his best friend, Feri, to join him in observing the day's events. An only child, he and his parents have no love for the communists. They have only recently been allowed to return to Budapest from the countryside to which the regime had deported them without explanation over three years ago. For Tamás, a naturally cheerful boy, having to part with his friends had been a misery. Yesterday, as he was walking with his father down Museum Boulevard, a girl had thrust a leaflet with the student demands into his hand. He had decided then and there that he would take part—without telling his parents. He has used the excuse of going to buy flowers for his mother's birthday.

Tamás and Feri, joined by Feri's sister and her girl friend, have watched the Stalin statue come down and have followed it to its resting place in front of the National Theatre. When they get fairly near Stalin's head Tamás notices that a small fire is burning next to it and people are taking things out of their pocket and throwing them onto the fire. "What are they burning?" he asks a worker in front of him. The worker takes a small booklet out of his pocket. It is his communist party card. "That's what they're burning," he says, brandishing it in front of the group and then stepping forward and heaving it into the fire. Tamás and Feri wish they had party cards to add to the conflagration. Then suddenly they remember: they have DISZ cards, all young people must have them. With relish they dig these out of their pockets and push their way through the crowd to throw them into the flames. "At last we've found a good use for these papers," says Feri in a voice for all to hear.[31]

Not far away in one of the university's big lecture theatres known as the "Gólyavár," a scheduled meeting of the Petőfi Circle is in progress. Ever since the huge, long meeting of June 27 the Circle has been forced by the government to hold its meetings by invitation only. But they have continued to discuss a single topic each time. Tonight it is medicine and the past role

132

of doctors which is being debated. Professor Antal Babics, the famous urologist, is admitting that Gábor Péter, the hated secret police chief, had been his friend and had, in fact, been arrested in his apartment. Professor István Rusznyák is admitting that it was he who had signed the medical certificate enabling the Politburo to get rid of Nagy in April of 1955. Suddenly the door bursts open and some young students come running in. The outraged chairman wants to know the meaning for this rude intrusion. "The ÁVO is shooting demonstrators! The revolution, it's begun!" they shout, almost in unison. "Listen...you can hear the gunfire!" The audience can indeed hear the gunfire, but they really resent the interruption of this highly important meeting. They are in complete agreement with their chairman, who bids the young men: "Please leave this room at once and close the door behind you." The Petőfi Circle, which had served as the intellectual womb of the revolution, has now become irrelevant. History is passing it by.[32]

*   *   *   *

A few moments later the red telephone rings in Police Chief Sándor Kopácsi's office. It is his major general army friend.

"Sándor, we've got trouble."

"I know. Your men are handing out weapons in the streets"

"That's the first problem. The crowd is returning the ÁVO's fire. But there's an even bigger problem...Our best units are out of control!"

"What do you mean?"

" I sent two motorized units to control the carnage. Instead of cleaning up the streets they've started taking shots at the ÁVO. The ÁVO is a band of assholes and animals. They started this; but if we stay on the sidelines we'll watch the Army crumble away. Before long this could turn into a civil war."

"What do you suggest?" asks Kopácsi.

"We have to confine the blaze. Your men are not compromised in the eyes of the crowd. Send a detachment to relieve the Radio. There's a good chance the people will let them pass while they are busy burning the cars the ÁVO had the asinine idea of disguising as ambulances. We've got to put a stop to it, Sándor...."

Kopácsi sees he is right and immediately calls the Mosonyi barracks where he has a commando unit of one hundred officers armed with submachine guns and grenades, all of whom are especially trained for street combat.

"No problem, Comrade Colonel," is the commanding officer's answer.

"When can I tell the people at the radio you will be there?"

"If all goes well, inside of thirty minutes."

Kopácsi calls Valéria Benke and tells her "Help is on the way, Comrade Benke, stand firm."

"Kopácsi, come quickly, or we'll all be done for!" She sounds so terrified, he hardly recognizes her voice.

But the commando unit never reaches the Radio. The people are quite willing to let them through, but the ÁVO, who have seen the Army soldiers giving guns to the people, now trust no one. As soon as members of the police unit show themselves in the street the ÁVO open fire.

The unit commander, calling from a private apartment near Sándor Bródy Street, tells Kopácsi, "I've got two men seriously wounded and we can't advance a centimeter. The moment the ÁVO see us they spray us with bullets. The defenders are like maniacs."

Kopácsi asks whether the crowd is armed and his subordinate says he cannot tell, but that they are friendly toward him and his men.

"Send your wounded to the nearest hospital and return the unit immediately to its barracks," orders Kopácsi.[33]

First Party Secretary Gerő has doubts about his fellow Central Committee member Marton Horváth, editor-in-chief of the party paper *Szabad Nép*, so he sends József Révai, the staunch Stalinist ideologue who was one of the three most powerful men under Rákosi, over to the newspaper. Oszkár Betlen, one of the hardliners on the editorial staff, threatens: "Not a line to the composing staff until he gets here!"

Outside on the street a crowd gathers with other thoughts in mind. Like the crowd in front of the radio which wants the student demands to be read over the airwaves, these want to see them printed in the newspaper. As in the case of the radio, security guards are posted at all entrances and these have been reinforced during the day. Only persons with passes are admitted.

Ferenc Oltai, the former journalist who had earlier been admitted with friends, finds himself on the fourth floor being blocked outside Horváth's closed door by Révai's "gorillas" who have accompanied him to the paper. He decides to join his former colleagues in a large room on the same floor where he finds them all in a very anxious, animated state. Most of them, though loyal party members, can no longer hold back their disgust and hatred of Révai and Gerő.

Before Révai emerges from Horváth's office, there is a terrible crashing sound from downstairs that freezes everyone's blood. The demonstrators outside, unable to restrain their frustration and anger at not being able to send a delegation in to the paper, have begun to throw rocks through the windows. It is only the prelude to an assault.

This comes about a half an hour later when armed insurgents, who have been at the Radio, appear on the scene and begin to fire on the guards. The guards take cover inside the building and return the fire, but, unlike the Radio where there are hundreds of defenders, here at the newspaper there are only a dozen of them. After a few fatalities, they quickly surrender.

Led by persons who know the inside of the building, the demonstrators are soon outside the heavy, locked doors to the composing room just off the stairs of the second and third stories. Oltai and his friends can clearly hear the shouted conversation between the intruders and the compositors behind the locked doors.

Eventually the iron doors are opened and the printers allow the crowd into the composing room, but they refuse to set type for the student demands. Printers at *Szabad Nép* have been sent to prison for the most trivial indiscretion. This request is way too risky. So, the sixteen points are not going to be printed, but then neither is *Szabad Nép*. The people are taking over the building. As they begin to come up the stairs to the fourth floor those staff members still there, along with Oltai, decide to disappear down the back stairs. Office doors are left open so that they will not be smashed.

The demonstrators search desperately for documents that will incriminate the paper but find nothing but mimeographed sheets and news agency dispatches. These they grab and hurl out of the windows. People on the ground gather them up and add them to the conflagration of books and propaganda materials which have been torn out of the *Szabad Nép*/Soviet ground floor book store and set afire some minutes before. In the library they find collections of old copies of *Szabad Nép*, which they also hurl out of the window. But nothing of value is stolen or broken.

As Oltai and his colleagues go out a side door they spot József Révai tottering down the stairs shouting, "Shoot them! shoot them!" His "gorillas" have obviously deserted him and Miklós Gimes and Pál Lőcsei, former employees like Oltai, half carry him through the inconspicuous side door to his armor-plated car, which is waiting to carry him safely home to his villa in Rózsadomb.[34]

The Central Committee Meets

The Central Committee is now meeting at Party headquarters at 17 Akadémia Street (that is, those members who have been able to get into the center of the city). The great majority of members give servile support to Gerő. But certain members present, like Imre Mező, a sincere advocate of liberalization, Kálmán Pongrácz, the former-worker Mayor of Budapest, István Kovács and József Köböl speak in favor of re-admitting Nagy to the Central Committee. At first this makes little impression on the majority. But as reports of fighting around the radio, the toppling of the Stalin statue, and the looting of the offices of *Szabad Nép* filter in, they are more and more inclined to bring Nagy aboard.

The meeting is temporarily interrupted when Gerő must take a call from Moscow. The Presidium of the Soviet Central Committee is also in session, though it is two hours further into the night in Moscow, and Khrushchev is on the phone. He is calling a meeting of all party secretaries of the Eastern bloc, save Poland, for tomorrow and asks Gerő to come to the Soviet Union tomorrow. Gerő replies that this is simply not possible. "The crisis here in Budapest is far too dangerous!" But, having been caught off guard by Khrushchev's call, he fails to ask him to have Zhukov order Soviet troops to intervene.

Gerő now realizes that he was wrong to try to bring the Soviet Army in by himself. He must get approval from the Central Committee for his scheme to bring in the Soviets at this time. The debate on Nagy's admission is temporarily suspended while the pros and cons of calling in the Soviet Army are debated. Since the reports coming in—including one from Lt. General Hegyi who arrives breathless from the Radio—are so dire, panic begins to overwhelm the Committee. With little debate it approves Gerő's suggestion. Before they can phone the Kremlin, however, Khrushchev himself calls to say that Andropov has called him and relayed Gerő's request and the Soviets will gladly respond but—nightmare of nightmares—he insists that they can do nothing until they have the request in writing. Gerő is beside himself. There are almost no government ministers present. "Then have the President of the Council of Ministers sign it," replies Khrushchev.[35]

The Soviet officials are simply covering their tails. Zhukov, in fact, had given the order several hours ago and the Soviet Special Army Corps in

Hungary, put on high alert twenty-four hours ago, is already on its way to Budapest.

The written request for Soviet intervention will be drafted not by the Hungarians, but by Andropov several days from now. It will be predated to October 24, and will be signed by András Hegedűs, who will, by the time he signs it, have ceased to be Prime Minister for four days. Andropov will then send it via ciphered telegram to Moscow on October 28.[36]

*   *   *   *

Back at the Radio still more Army trucks are arriving and, because of the crowds, are forced to park several blocks away from the Radio.

Now the crowd's arguments and pleadings with the soldiers—most of whom are of peasant stock like the workers and many of the students—are backed up with bloody evidence in the form of wounded men and women. It does not take much persuasion to convince soldiers that they are doing the right thing in handing over their weapons. And they see no harm in instructing the recipients in how to use them.

András Molnár, a twenty-year-old student of the Karl Marx University of Economics, is one of those who boards a truck headed for Csepel. The truck only gets as far as the Grand Boulevard (Nagykörút) before it runs into a great commotion. It seems an ÁVO officer in an apartment building has fired into a crowd and killed a woman and wounded two other people. Enraged members of the crowd had stormed into the building, found the culprit and pulled him out into the street where the crowd had beaten him to death. His car, recognized by local people, had been overturned and burned.

This episode convinces the driver of the truck not to go on to Csepel, but return to the Radio. Here Molnár is given a submachine gun that, to his relief, he knows how to operate, having just spent a month of compulsory military training during this past summer.[37]

Many of those searching for weapons simply walk to a nearby Army barracks. One of these is Pál Kabelács, a nineteen-year-old worker whose buddies had urged him to go to the Radio. His first reaction had been "Not me, I'm not gonna get shot." But he *had* come anyway and when asked "Who wants a gun?" was so eager that he pushed aside many to get there. He received a drum magazine machine gun.

He goes straight to an attic and pushes a couple of terracotta tiles out of the way to give him a space to shoot through. But he finds that eight others have already beaten him to this attic. After he fires a few rounds, a "kid" comes up and tells him only to shoot where he sees the flash of one of the ÁVO guns since these are so precise and clearly seen in the dark. The only trouble with this is that the ÁVO can see the patriots' gun flashes, too. At one point the return fire gets so heavy that they decide to stop firing for about an hour.[38]

It is almost midnight before any substantial return of the ÁVO's fire begins around the Radio, but when it does, it comes in great volume and from may directions.

Inside the Radio Valéria Benke and the few staff who have remained feel much more under siege now than when it was just rocks flying through the windows. A number of security soldiers have been killed outright. But it is the sight of bloody heads—for it is largely head wounds the security troops are sustaining—which is driving her close to hysteria. Most of the staff, including Péter Erdős, and all of the visitors have long since deserted the doomed building, escaping through the garages and leaving her to "hold the fort." She keeps telephoning Party headquarters for help, but the big shots are all to busy, and the promises of help never materialize.

At the Party building on Akadémia Street the Central Committee has just voted to re-admit Nagy to the Central Committee and to appoint him Prime Minister in Hegedűs' place. But then they make Hegedűs his deputy. The members had voted earlier to call the uprising "the work of counterrevolutionary, fascist forces." Two delegates leave the conference room and go down to tell Nagy, who is waiting with his friends. Nagy expresses reservations. First of all, he wants his rival Gerő removed from the position of Party Secretary and second, he does not want to have certain members now on the Central Committee retained. The delegates return to the conference room with this news.

Gerő blows his stack. A stream of curses emanates from his distorted face and he suggests withdrawing the offer to Nagy. But the vote recommending Nagy be premier has been taken and others have already made up their minds that Nagy must be brought aboard. Nagy is now allowed to join the group but says he will agree to be premier only if Kádár is willing to become Party Secretary replacing Gerő. Kádár, however, declines, meaning that Gerő must remain Party Secretary. Nagy now bows to the will of the Party, but he insists that Piros, Révai and several others be removed from the Central Committee and that his friends Géza Losonczy and Ferenc Donáth be elected to it. Within minutes the Central Committee votes his wishes. The resolution, however, only instructs the Political Committee to make these appointments in the future, it does not carry them out then and there. So Nagy goes to his cot for some sleep knowing that he will be appointed premier, but not yet. He will learn of his actual appointment from others, and only much later.

It is now well into Wednesday, October 24. All of the Central Committee's resolutions are given this date.[39]

At Budapest Police headquarters off Deák Square Police Chief Kopácsi is at his wits end. All evening he has tried to reach his ultimate boss, Interior Minister Piros, to get new orders, always being told "Comrade Piros is busy. He will call you back when he can."

Finally the red telephone rings. It is Minister Piros sounding quite inebriated. "Kopácsi what do you want from me?" he says in a voice betraying not just drinking, but exhaustion.

"The situation is critical. I've received no orders from anybody."

"Orders? You've got it easy. You're not being attacked like my men. Concentrate your forces at Police Headquarters. I'll let you know when I need them."

Kopácsi then makes the mistake of mentioning the emergency plan, Plan "M," he has just opened.

"Are you crazy? You ask for supplies when all my vehicles are under attack and my drivers are being slaughtered? Be happy you're not wearing an ÁVO uniform!" Then after a long pause, "Do your best. Report from time to time."

About a half an hour later, about 2 a.m., an officer comes into his office to say he has his wife on the line and she says she must speak with Kopácsi urgently. When he picks up the phone a high female voice says excitedly: "Excuse me, I live in the southwest side of Buda and there's a terrible racket; a huge armored division is coming into the city."

"Have you heard this noise for long?"

"For the past ten minutes."

"Have you seen any tanks?"

"Yes. They're moving along the base of the hill. They're huge with a very long cannon. At least a hundred must have passed."

* * * *

Béla Lipták's truck is again going down Üllői Avenue. They have been prevented from crossing the Petőfi Bridge by a long line of Soviet tanks approaching. They turn left onto Hungária Boulevard and soon run into another big crowd at the HÉV railroad station near Baross Square. It seems that the director of the Ruggyanta rubber factory refuses to take part in the proposed general strike called for today, the twenty-fourth, and refuses to shut down the plant. Béla has the driver take them to the main gate where he asks in an officious voice for the emergency loud speaker. The confused gatekeeper eyes Béla's tricolor armband and his bloody coat and, without hesitation, flips the switch and points to the microphone. "A General Strike has been declared in Budapest. This factory will shut down immediately!" To make it sound more authentic Béla repeats this announcement twice more. As they leave, the porter says apologetically: "The shut-down procedure takes some time, you know. These are chemical processes."[40]

*   *   *   *

Tamás Szabó and his friend Feri have long since sent the girls home. Now they join a group going to the Barracks on Szentkirályi Street not far from the Radio. Here they find soldiers passing guns out through the ground floor windows and each of them gets a Tommy gun. Being fifteen-year-olds, neither knows how they work. "Come on," says Feri, "let's ask that scar-faced man how they work." The scar-faced man is glad to oblige. Then he says, "Follow me, my young friends" and people part respectfully as they move forward. The racket of rifle fire in Sándor Bródy Street is horrendous and the smoke so thick that little can be seen. "Frightened?" asks Feri. "No" says Tamás, his heart beating 130 times a minute.

"Keep close to the wall and follow me slowly," says scar-face not just to Tamás and Feri but to some twenty others he has recruited. He enters a passage in a building opposite the Radio, obtains an attic key from the superintendent and then shows them how to force openings in the roof tiles. They fire at the Radio entrance and doubt they hit anyone. At length a young girl appears and offers them cigarettes. Later they are told if anyone wants anything to eat or drink just knock on any door in the apartment building. All the women and children are in the cellar, but there is someone still in each apartment.[41]

László Beke, after obtaining arms from the police station in Ferenc Vigyázó Street, has returned to the Radio and is now on a rooftop looking down on the battleground. He sees about thirty bodies in front of the Radio and in the dim light cannot make out how many, if any, are ÁVO. One of those bodies may well be Mihály Simon, the diary-writing engineer who, with the small group of students from the Technical University, had carried the demands into the radio a little over twenty-four hours ago and argued with the editors. He will do no more writing in his diary. At precisely 2:10 a.m. a bullet shot from the Radio entered his skull. His diary will be found by a friend who, when he escapes and emigrates to Canada, decides to take it with him. Like the diary of Anne Frank, it will be unknown until the friend, in answer to an ad in *Irodalmi Újság*, sends it to Tibor Méray, who then will publish portions of it in 1969 in his book *"I Was in Budapest That Day."*[42]

Beke is one of those who will make the first penetration of the Radio building around 3 a.m.

András Molnár notes that the ÁVO troops are firing not just from the Radio Building but also from the rooftops of several nearby buildings including some *across* Sándor Bródy Street from the Radio. He is with a group firing from behind the same stone wall in the Museum Garden that the Army troops had been deployed behind. Around 3 a.m. four Soviet tanks appear on Sándor Bródy Street and stop in front of the Radio entrance. One tank aims its cannon directly at the group behind the wall. Molnár jumps up and starts to run for better cover when he feels a sharp pain in his forehead and loses consciousness. Late the next afternoon he finds himself in a private home near the Museum Garden being nursed by a young woman he has never seen before. She assures him that he is safe, no ÁVO people live in the building, and that later in the afternoon he will be taken to the Surgery Clinic of the Budapest University School of Medicine.[43]

For a few moments the Soviet tanks, their engines roaring, dominate the street and the insurgents hold their fire, as do the ÁVO soldiers. But the tank commanders have assigned places throughout the city to which they are supposed to go: ministries, the parliament building, bridges and major intersections. Soon they move off and intermittent firing resumes.

During a lull in the shooting, a group of armed patriots makes a rush for the ten-foot wide shattered entrance. Some shots come from high up, but the attackers meet no resistance on the ground floor. It has been abandoned by the defending ÁVO, who leave several of their dead comrades behind. More insurgents make the crossing and soon there is a pitched battle within the Radio building.

The defenders find their situation precarious. They are running low on ammunition as well as able-bodied men. Scores have been killed (Months later the official report of the Kádár regime will list only twenty—ed.) and more than twice that number wounded severely enough to be unable to fight. Few of the Army soldiers have taken any part; many have simply disappeared. Major Fehér is told repeatedly by his subordinates that without reinforcements they cannot hold out much longer. By the time intense fire sweeps the control room, the Radio's transmissions have been shifted to a studio in the Parliament building which is already hooked up to the Lakihegy transmission station. While programming may not be quite what it was scheduled to be, it is continuous and still completely in the hands of the Party.[44]

2:30 a.m. "This is Radio Budapest. Dear listeners, we read you an announcement:

"Fascist, reactionary elements have launched an armed attack against public buildings and our armed forces. For the sake of restoring order and until further measures are taken, all gatherings, meetings and demonstrations are banned...signed: The Council of Ministers of the Hungarian People's Republic."[45]

*   *   *   *

The sky is turning light, though stars can still be seen. The temperature has dropped to a seasonal fifty-four degrees Fahrenheit. Béla Lipták, who like most of his colleagues has been up all night, is walking back across Freedom (Szabadság) Bridge to Gellért Square where the demonstration had begun. He finds the scene surreal. People, some fully dressed, others in their nightgowns or pajamas, are in the process of building barricades. They have heard, and some seen, the Soviet tanks as they roared in columns into the city. Some are carrying old bedsprings, others bricks or chairs. One group is digging up cobblestones with crowbars, others with less likely garden tools. They intend to blockade the bridge so that the Soviet tanks, which they think are only on the Pest side, cannot come across to Buda. A policeman twice Béla's age looks at him with his tricolor band and bloodied coat and asks humbly: "What do we do now?" Without thinking Béla answers automatically: "Push them out of the city." He sees two elderly ladies in their dressing gowns—probably spinster sisters, he thinks—struggling with a heavy cobblestone and quickly gives them a hand lifting it into a truck. "Just in case you might need it, you know," says one of them. A few minutes later Béla, now on one of the trucks, looks back; he sees that everyone has come to a standstill. They are watching the trucks, which they have just loaded, drive across the bridge.

Halfway across the Russian tanks on the Pest bridgehead begin to fire point blank at them. The first truck is hit and bursts into flame. Béla's driver tries to make a quick U-turn, but rams into a pole. The cobblestones fly forward, people fall and jump off. It is chaos. Everyone runs back towards Buda. Nobody makes it to the Pest side.

When Béla gets back to the Technical University and hears his heavy footsteps echo in the empty hall of the aula, he sees the door of the DISZ office open. It is Jancsi Danner with a machine gun slung over his shoulder looking just as dirty and tired as Béla. "We must be the first ones back," he observes.[46]

It is now fully daylight and while Soviet tanks are stationed all over Budapest, so are the insurgents at roadblocks and in side streets checking every vehicle which comes their way. A number of ÁVO cars in various sections of the city have been stopped, the occupants disarmed and arrested or beaten and the car overturned and burned.

The fight to capture the Radio is still raging, though two-thirds of it is now in the hands of the insurgents, who are attacking not only from all sides, but from above and below.

Lieutenant Tamás Havasi of the ÁVO finds himself in a narrow corridor way inside the building with civilians and wounded security troops going back and forth getting in each other's way, irritating one another. By chance he enters one of the offices, where he sees soldiers sprawled on chairs and a wounded radio clerk, his head bandaged, lying on a desk. He also sees two telephones on the desk. He picks up one; no dial tone. He picks up the other which is a special "direct line" phone. Still no dial tone. He jiggles and shakes it and is about to slam it down in disgust, when suddenly there is a dial tone.

The highest officer present leaps at the phone, snatching it out of Havasi's hands. A second later a bullet zooms through the room and everyone hits the floor.

"Hello! Is this Comrade Gerő's secretariat?....I want to talk to Comrade Gerő!....From the radio station....You hear them shooting at us from every direction and you want to know where I'm calling from?"

The officer turns crimson. "Put him on the wire!" he shouts. "This is an order!" He adds, "Well, call him if he isn't there!....There can't be any business more important than this! Don't try to tell me how to behave! This is a matter of life and death!"

The admirably trained secretariat cannot be moved. No one dares disturb the first Party Secretary. Nevertheless, the call does get transferred.

"Give us Gerő on the phone!" yells the officer. There is a long silence.

"Is this Comrade Gerő? This is the radio station calling." The officer gives his name and rank and tries to describe the circumstances with bullets whizzing through the room.

"We have no more ammunition! We can no longer defend the station! Send us help!....We've been hearing the same thing since midnight! No outfit has come to help us....You'll have to understand the responsibility is yours. The strength of our resistance and fine behavior are beside the point. We don't need praise, we need reinforcements! Comrade Gerő, you must understand: it's not only our lives that are at stake, it is the fate of the radio, of the whole country, of our world!....Oh, all right; we'll try to hold out. But try to understand that we have only ammunition for a few minutes more. After that, we're finished."

Gerő has more important things to worry about. He is fighting for his own life, to maintain his position. Only hours ago he was almost voted out of office and now he has the Soviet Army in Budapest to deal with. Besides, if the radio is overwhelmed by the counterrevolutionaries with martyrs being created into the bargain, he will have a good excuse for having called in the Russians.[47]

At Party headquarters the new premier of the country, Imre Nagy, is still being "protected" by guards from the security service (ÁVO), though he has been allowed to get some sleep on a cot, in a room set aside for this purpose. Ernő Gerő, still the Party First Secretary, is desperately trying to figure out how to contain his rival Nagy. The only way he can do this, he figures, is if he can somehow cut into Nagy's overwhelming popularity with the people. At length a scheme comes to him. He calls in his aides and they begin to work on two statements that they will have broadcast on the radio. If possible they will get Nagy to sign the second statement, though it is not entirely necessary, because there will be time to persuade him to sign it after the fact. But they will tell him nothing about the first. The first will announce the government's request for Soviet troops. The second will call for martial law. The two statements will be run so closely that it will give the listener the impression that Nagy is behind both statements.

But first there must be the announcement of the new government and the appointment of Nagy as Prime Minister of a new government.

Explosion

This comes at 6:13 with the dry, factual "At its meeting on October 24, 1956, the Central Committee of the Hungarian Workers' Party elected as members: Comrades Ferenc Donáth, Géza Losonczy, György Lukács, Ferenc Münnich, Imre Nagy. Members of the new Politburo are:" (and then its lists them in alphabetical order so that Nagy is next to last out of twelve. Then come alternate Politburo members). "The Central Committee reaffirmed and strengthened the position of Comrade Gerő as First Party Secretary." (Then follows a list of Central Committee Secretaries. Then comes the statement: "The Central Committee moved that the Presidium [i.e. Politburo] of the People's Republic elect Comrade Imre Nagy Chairman of the Council of Ministers [Prime Minister], and Comrade András Hegedűs First Deputy Chairman. The Central Committee instructed the Politburo to draft a resolution for the solution of the problems confronting the Party and the country." This is the end of the official announcement, but the announcer is so excited by the news that he adds "Attention! Attention! We repeat the announcement. Imre Nagy has become the new Premier and András Hegedűs his First Deputy."

Now at 7:00 a.m. comes the first announcement that Nagy knows nothing about.

"Attention! Attention! The dastardly armed attack of counterrevolutionary gangs during the night has created an extremely serious situation. The bandits have penetrated into factories and public buildings and have murdered many civilians, members of the national defense forces, and fighters of the State security organs. The government was unprepared for these bloody, dastardly attacks and therefore applied for help, in accordance with the terms of the Warsaw Agreement, to the Soviet formations stationed in Hungary. The Soviet formations, in compliance with the government's request, are taking part in the restoration of order..."

Twenty minutes later at 7:20 a. m. comes the announcement of summary jurisdiction with the name of Imre Nagy at the end of it as though the action emanated from him.

Hungarians who are up at this hour and hear the two announcements are confused. How could their hero, Imre Nagy, call in Soviet troops and then declare martial law? Yet...is that not what they heard on the radio? Yet the Radio lies, as does the government, so people are inclined to withhold judgment until they learn more. Still, they are shaken by the news.

*   *   *   *

145

EXPLOSION

By 9:30, with the insurgents occupying the second floor and now coming down from the fifth floor Ms. Benke and the station's artistic director, Comrade Szécsi, decide to surrender. Informing the defenders and attackers that the radio station is surrendering, however, takes several frustrating minutes.

In the brief lull between the decision and the actual announcement of surrender, many ÁVO men and officers burst into the cloak room where most of the civilians, women and even children, who had been trapped in the station's nursery, had sought refuge. They demand and quickly are given civilian clothes while they strip off their uniforms.

Various groups that had been huddling in interior rooms are now flushed out, disarmed and herded downstairs by the insurgents.

Army Captain Ernő Zágon finds himself cut off from his men, students at the Petőfi Military Academy, who had been among the defenders. He is mistakenly put with a group of twenty ÁVO officers and men. This group is taken to the library on the ground floor, where they are ordered to remove their coats and caps and strip off their shoulder tabs. Everyone fears the worst when they are taken from the library to a coal bin in the cellar and the light is switched off. The Petőfi Military Academy students, meanwhile, are lined up in the courtyard and have the sixteen points read to them. After this they are free to go.

Likewise all of the civilian men and women are allowed out the door. This includes a number of the ÁVO, now in civilian clothes, including Comrade Benke herself, who has commandeered a hat from one of the women to cover her giveaway Russian haircut.

Those awaiting execution in the cellar are the last to be dealt with. After one and a half hours in the dark the door opens and a student enters. "Gentlemen," he says, "you are free to go." He then passes out cigarettes and gives bread to anyone who says he is hungry.[48]

Those insurgents who had remained at their positions across the street from the Radio in order to see that no ÁVO escaped, now come down into the street to see the havoc they have wrought. They stare at the Radio building with its shattered, glassless window frames, its smashed entrance and pockmarked balcony. For every bullet that struck a human victim, at least a hundred must have been fired. And it is no wonder. Very few, if any, of the insurgents had ever been in a battle before and the young ÁVO troops, many of whom were recent recruits, have been trained for just about everything *but* a pitched battle.

Radio Free Europe

Outside the little hamlet of Schleissheim just north of Munich in Bavaria, West Germany, is a forest of radio antennas. They are not for sending but receiving, and they are receiving twenty-four hours a day, seven days a week. They belong to Radio Free Europe, a supposedly private organization that most Americans, few Europeans and no one in the communist world believe for a minute is private. The antennas are picking up radio signals not just from Europe, but from all over the world. They are relaying to RFE in Munich the output of the news agencies Reuters and International News Service, which RFE pays for. But they are also relaying output from a lot of other western news agencies like the Associated Press, United Press, Agence France Press and Deutsche Presse Agentur, which they are stealing out of the airwaves (quite illegally), and for which they do not pay a cent. And of course they steal all of the communist news agency transmissions in English and French to their Embassies in the West. They transmit radio teletype versions of all of the major TASS (Russian) and all of the MTI (Hungarian) news stories to the editors of RFE, long before most Soviet or Hungarian citizens get out of bed in the morning. The same goes for all of the other East European countries, including Yugoslavia and even Albania. They even steal, and occasionally make use of, the transmissions from New China News Agency in Peking.

Radio Free Europe is, in fact, the most comprehensive and up-to-date news and information gathering center in the world.

Naturally, this means that the editors at RFE are just as up-to-date on what the official media is saying in these countries as the people in these countries themselves. In the case of the Hungarian Desk, it also means that the editors get to read the entire Hungarian press only a couple of days after it appears in Hungary, for these newspapers and magazines come very quickly through Vienna.

So the Hungarian editors and the Americans in the Political Advisor's Office, for whom much of this regime media output is quickly translated into English, know a great deal about what is going on in Hungary—at least as much as is possible from official communist sources. But they also have western sources: travelers, correspondents who go through or are permanently stationed in Eastern Europe, and even, clandestinely, secret reports from the U.S. Legation in Budapest. All summer long they have followed the political ferment building in Hungary, marveled at the accounts of the Petőfi Circle meetings and the vast throng that turned out for László Rajk's reburial on October 6.

But for all of this massive flow of information, the exile editors at Radio Free Europe cannot take an objective view. They reject most of the regime-generated information out-of-hand as suspect, if not totally mendacious. For one reason or another each exile is strongly anti-communist. That is why they are here. Radio Free Europe is an anti-communist radio. Beyond their anti-communism that unites them, they have extremely varied backgrounds and experiences both in Hungary before they left (at different times and for different reasons) and since becoming exiles. Very few of them were journalists or radio broadcasters before they came to RFE and this lack of journalistic experience tends to show up in their scripts and even news broadcasts. Some are right-wing to the point that they would prefer to see a prewar, pre-land reform Hungary come back into existence. On the other side of the spectrum are a few who are sufficiently realistic to realize that many of the changes wrought by the communists are not all bad and would probably have to be retained, at least for a time, in any Hungary liberated from communism. And there are many who fall between these two extremes. Meantime, it is their job to make contact with their compatriots at home, inform them as to what is really going on in the outside world, as well as in Hungary, give them hope that their present afflictions will not last forever and that they have not been forgotten.

While RFE does not broadcast around the clock, several of the radios, the Hungarian among them, broadcast as much as sixteen hours a day on a variety of different kilocycles, and at varying kilowatt volumes in an attempt to beat the regime's jamming.

Each country "desk" has a morning meeting of its editors that is attended by American political advisors, to discuss the latest news, how it is to be played, as well as what programs are to be aired that day. These meetings are conducted in English for the benefit of the Americans, but also for the observers from the other desks who may well not know the language of the country in question. So that the main Political Adviser, William E. Griffith, and his deputies can attend each of these meetings, they are held at hourly intervals, the Hungarian one each morning at 10:00.

Representatives of the various central supportive departments and from each of the other country desks are allowed to attend these daily country desk meetings with one rule: they are there as observers only and may not take part in any of the discussions or even speak, unless asked a specific question.

On this particular morning the observers almost outnumber the Hungarians and the Political Advisor and his staff and are forced to stand along the walls. Though the news is only a few hours old, everyone has heard that there has been some sort of uprising in Budapest and that Imre Nagy is now Premier and in charge.

Political Advisor William E. Griffith, a thirty-six-year-old American, fluent in German and French, who had, until his appointment, been part of the American Occupation's administration, opens the meeting in his high nasal voice by asking the head of the Hungarian Desk, Andor Gellért, to summarize the situation. Gellért, who has served in the American OSS, and has been Hungarian Desk Head since September 1954, only recently returned from sick leave.[49]

Before he responds, Gellért, a sallow, almost sickly complexioned man in his 50s with long yellowish-silver hair slicked back off his sloping forehead, Konrad Adenauer style, takes out his glasses and reads in his deep, slow and heavily accented English the texts of the two announcements from Radio Budapest which had been picked up by the monitors in Schleissheim, just hours before. There is a pause after he finishes.

"Well?" says Griffith impatiently.

"It means," replies Gellért ponderously, "that Imre Nagy is finished! No Hungarian who has called in the Soviet troops can retain the respect of the Hungarian people. No one who has declared martial law can retain his popularity. Nagy, scarcely before he has begun, is finished!

"There is now only one man in Hungary whom every Hungarian respects...and that man is Cardinal Mindszenty!"

There is a sudden stirring and murmuring in the room.

"You think Nagy called in the Russians?" rasps Griffith in his high-pitched voice. "His voice was not on the radio, was it?"

"No," replies Gellért, "there was no broadcast of Nagy's voice, but the regime would never broadcast that Nagy was now Prime Minister if it were not so and the announcement of martial law was said to be his. So obviously, he is in charge and must have at least agreed to the Soviet intervention

EXPLOSION

even if he did not initiate it. By this action Nagy has cooked his own goose, Nagy is finished."

(When Gerő conceived his scheme he was thinking primarily of his own skin. To have the Hungarian Desk at RFE now fall into his trap, to have them buy what he is trying to sell to Nagy's followers in Hungary, to have RFE swallow it hook, line and sinker is, for him, an unanticipated extra dividend.)

"Well," says Griffith, "you may be right, but there is still no proof that Nagy called in the troops. Certainly it was in Gerő's interests to do so. But you are right, Nagy has been badly compromised."

The discussion which follows concerns not only the treatment of Imre Nagy and a new build-up of support for Cardinal Mindszenty, but what new programs are being devised to take advantage of the situation.

As the meeting breaks up one young American observer,* who has been biting his tongue to remain silent, rushes up to Griffith's Deputy, Paul Henze, and asks him "What makes Gellért and the rest of you guys so certain it was Nagy who called in the troops? Maybe it was just done in his name! Maybe he's a captive. Maybe he even has a gun to his head!" Henze turns on the young man and says with a superior smile: "And what makes you think you know more than Mr. Gellért?"

Later in the day in an analysis sent around to all desks for use in broadcasts, Griffith will end his summary by writing: "Nagy begins his Prime Ministership already incriminated by Soviet troop intervention and martial law. This will probably seriously lower his present popularity and make his survival more doubtful."[50]

But the anti-communist editors of the Hungarian Desk are already taking their cue from Gellért's "Nagy is finished!," not the Political Advisor's somewhat more cautious approach. They feel relieved and vindicated. True communists eventually show their true colors, and now Nagy has shown his. Those editors who had resented having to mute their anti-communism when the popular Nagy had been in power between 1953 and 1955 can now unleash their contempt upon him. They lose no time in calling him a "traitor" who has "Hungarian blood on his hands" for calling in the Soviet troops and just about every vile name they can think of. This will go on for many days during the unfolding revolution. The Americans at RFE are largely unaware of this denigration and name-calling. William Rademaekers, the

*The author

150

only American in the Political Advisor's Office fluent in Hungarian—in fact, the only American in the whole of RFE who understands and speaks Hungarian—has his hands too full of reading and analyzing what is coming in from Hungary to monitor what "the Voice of Free Hungary" is saying.

Unfortunately, all those non-communists in Hungary who prefer to get their news from RFE or the BBC rather than from their own communist-controlled radio are inclined to believe RFE. What Gerő would have had difficulty in accomplishing—the task of denigrating Nagy's reputation and people's trust in him—is now greatly enhanced by RFE's vicious Hungarian broadcasts.

CHAPTER V

Revolution

FROM THE BEGINNING *of the demonstrations, those who were taking part in these actions were conscious of doing something both exciting and revolutionary. Yet no one thought it possible or even desirable to bring about a genuine revolution. All ultimate power in the form of police and guns was in the hands of the government. The students' only desire was to force that government to make certain changes. No one hoped for, dreamed of, or even wanted the impossible. Nor were any of them trying to get rid of socialism. Socialism was a given which they all accepted, indeed, had grown up under. What they hoped for and were determined to get was changes in the government position. When they did not get even the slightest change, their frustration turned to fury and violence. But that violence did not include intentionally hurting people: rocks through windows and pulling down a hated statue were not intended to do bodily harm to anyone, though rocks surely could. It was only when the regime, and specifically the ÁVO, began to do bodily harm by shooting unarmed men and women that the thought of actually killing their tormentors, the ÁVO, occurred to people on the scene. That moment was when the revolution was physically born. All the demonstrations and colorful action that preceded it might, after all, have led to slight changes and these to a subsequent peaceful solution, had there been any flexibility on the regime's part. And what gave birth to that moment was Gerő's hard-line speech in which he gave a flat "no" to all of the people's aspirations for change. For revolutions are born not because the pot has been brought to a boil—as Khrushchev's denunciation of Stalin and the ensuing changes promising a better future had done—but when the lid is*

153

suddenly put back on, as Gerő did with his speech. While no one particularly wanted or expected a revolution, nearly everyone was quick to realize that it was *a revolution when it happened.*

For all those boys and girls under the age of twenty life up to then had been dull, regimented, and full of compulsion, usually on a mass scale. It was also full of fear, fear of getting into trouble with the authorities, whether at school or in the street, fear of neighbors who might report you to the authorities. It was too dangerous to have more than a very few close friends. Only in the home could you even begin to say what you felt like saying. "They," whether in the form of a local Communist Party member, policeman or teacher (who was also usually a Party member), kept you from doing things you wanted to do and forced you to lead a double life, one in the outside world, another in the home.

In the home you learned gradually about your native land, Hungary, in bits and pieces. In school you learned about the great Soviet Union, its heroes and wonderful accomplishments. Hungarian children also learned about the Great October Revolution, the civil war and guerilla warfare, since this last had played so crucial a role in the Great Patriotic War (i.e. Second World War). These Soviet events, in the form of stories and movies, as well, of course, as football matches and other sporting events, were the most exciting things to which these children were exposed.

So when the Revolution began, they each had a lifetime of boredom to make up for, a lifetime of fear to escape from and a lifetime of narrowly confined relationships to break out of.

No wonder there was such an explosion of youthful energy, of immediate bonding with those of other classes or backgrounds, of patriotism that had been bottled up in all those kitchens. For the first time in their short lives they were doing something important on their own, something so important it became worth dying for.

They took pride, first, in calling themselves "Hungarians," which soon became a ruse to force other Hungarians to join them by implying that "they," the communists, were not true Hungarians. Then they thought of themselves as patriots. When the fighting began, Western news reporters immediately referred to them as rebels or insurgents. But they did not think of themselves as such. When Soviet tanks arrived and began killing them and it quickly became a patriotic war between Hungarians and the Soviet Army, they were still patriots. No one had thought of, or used the term, "Freedom

Fighters." Indeed, that term appears to have been used by some Western news correspondent and then picked up by Western radios. It did not become known in Hungary for several days and was never to have the currency in Hungary that it did in the West. The more common word was "Felkelők" (Uprisers).

Budapest, Wednesday, October 24, 1956
Soviet Tanks Move into Budapest

At approximately 2 a.m. a column of over one hundred Soviet tanks from Székesfehérvár, forty miles southeast of the city, rolled into the outskirts of Budapest. The roar of engines and clanking treads was so great that no one along the way could sleep through it. Because of heavy ground fog it had taken them two hours, but once in the city the fog dissipated and the lead tanks knew exactly which main streets to take to reach their appointed goals. There was little or no traffic to impede them; all streetcar operations had ceased hours before, and only some trucks with young insurgents were occasionally encountered along the way. Passing through Zsigmond Móricz Square each Soviet T-34 tank made a screeching sound as it came off Fehérvári Ave. and made its jerky turn, skidding on the cobblestones, to enter Béla Bartók Avenue. Other columns would later follow this same route.

At the same time other mechanized units of the Soviet Special Army Corps entered the city from different directions, some passing through Moscow Square and Széna Square in Buda, others coming up from the south through the suburb of Soroksár on the Pest side of the city. By daylight, 290 tanks, 120 armored vehicles, 156 cannons and 6,000 Soviet troops manning them were in Budapest.[1] No infantry units were thought necessary.

Ambassador Yuri Andropov had had a major hand in the planning of "Volna," the Soviet Army operation to restore civil order in Hungary, now in progress. Before taking up his post in Budapest he had witnessed firsthand the East German uprising of June 1953 and had seen how effective the massive use of Soviet tanks had been in putting down that sudden, nation-wide revolt. Swift, ruthless action by Soviet tanks, he was certain, would quickly intimidate the "counter-revolutionaries."[2]

It is now 5:00 a.m. The sight and sound of all those Soviet tanks rumbling around their city is indeed intimidating. But it is also infuriating. Just as the revolution is beginning to take hold with only the ÁVO to prevent its consummation—since both the Army and regular police have been neutral or even helpful so far—the Russians have to put their noses into what is strictly a Hungarian affair. So now it is not just the ÁVO that the patriots must fight, but the whole Soviet Army. Had the Soviets just come in peacefully and occupied the city it might have been possible to explain the situation to them and have them leave without a shot being fired. But no, having reached and placed guarding vehicles at such points as the Soviet Embassy, Parliament building and the Party headquarters, as well as bridges and key intersections, the rest of the T-34 tanks are now racing around the city, their hatches closed, shooting at anything that moves or any building with a light in it, on the assumption that anyone up this early in the morning is up to no good.

Even the central headquarters of the Budapest municipal police is not immune. Since it was not on their list of buildings to guard and the thicket of antennas on its roof is not visible in the early dawn light, the tanks see only a building with lots of lights in it. One Soviet tank stops in the middle of Tanács Boulevard to take care of the situation.

A number of people in police headquarters are looking out of their windows watching the tanks go by. When they notice the turret on the stationary tank pivot in their direction, several scream, "Lights out!" Before the lights can be cut off at the central switch a long spray of machine-gun fire sweeps the facade of the building leaving bullets embedded in the wall. "Hey," thinks Sándor Kopácsi, "we're supposed to be friends." But his next thought is genuine fear of being killed by "friendly fire."

The telephones start ringing as though set off by the machine-gun burst. Stations are calling in complaints of other buildings being shot at by tanks. One building on Engels Square, which has police observers on its roof, is badly shot up because of its lights and even one of the policemen on the roof is wounded.

Some minutes later a third armored column passes along Tanács Boulevard. The last tank, which is towing an artillery piece, stops in the middle of the street. The hatch opens and a soldier climbs out. Despite the throbbing tank engine one can hear his heavy boots hit the cobblestones. The towing rope apparently needs adjusting.

From a window in Anker Passage a rifle shot fells the Soviet tankman. Only seconds later bottles filled with gasoline arc out of several windows from the higher floors of buildings on Anker Passage. Explosions suddenly illuminate the buildings on both sides of the Boulevard. One of the bottles falls right into the open turret and ignites inside of the tank. Of the five or six crewmen, only two manage to escape through the burning hatchway. One hides under an archway, the other makes a break for it across the Boulevard, as if trying to reach Police Headquarters. Just as he reaches the bank of flowers in the middle divider, a rain of bullets cuts him down. A young man in a Basque beret leans out of a window in Anker Passage and aims his machine gun. One, two, three bursts and the body of the fallen Russian jumps with each.[3]

Over in Buda at Zsigmond Móricz Square the young students and workers, who had congregated there in hopes of intercepting the incoming Soviet tank columns, are losing their enthusiasm. They had held up a column of tanks by spilling a drum of gasoline in the roadway and then setting it afire. But the tanks had simply let the fire burn out and then had driven on. The patriots had not opened fire, not wanting to start something when the Russians themselves had not fired on them. They were too late to set up a proper barricade. Now the barricades they have since built look hopelessly haphazard. They feel discouraged. There has been no action at all to compare with the Radio, from which a number of them had originally come. They are dead tired from having been up all night and feel humiliated that after so short a period their revolution is being crushed by the Soviet Army. Most of them decide to hide their weapons, and go home to bed. A few, however, drawn by the sounds of explosions in Pest, decide to go back across the river. The Kilián Barracks on Üllői Avenue, they hear, is the place to be.[4]

A while later, these patriots from Zsigmond Móricz Square find that, in defiance of Budapest Radio's announcement of a curfew until 9:00 a. m., there are more and more insurgents walking the streets of Pest.[5] It is now around 6:30 a.m. There is a particularly large gathering of people in front of the Kilián Barracks. The Radio has yet to announce the government's "request" to the Soviet Army, or the brief announcement of summary justice (i.e. martial law) minutes later in the name of Imre Nagy.

Tanks are now noisily patrolling all of the main streets of Budapest. Still, the Radio remains silent on the subject, as though nothing were happening.

The soldiers at the Kilián Barracks have very few arms. Moreover, they are in a minority in the barracks, which is also occupied by some 1,500 conscripted workers, youths who because of their parental background are considered unreliable and not fit for the Army, but needed for various State projects, like road building. It is many of these, rather than the soldiers, who will become Kilián Barracks Freedom Fighters.

The Insurgents Begin to Organize

Not far away in the large amphitheater of the Corvin Cinema fifteen-year-old Tamás Szabó and his friend Feri are sitting among many soldiers and armed civilians who took part in the siege of the Radio. They are being addressed by a Captain Kiss who is organizing a defense of this round, thick-walled facility. Tamás notices that the Captain has taken the braid from his shoulder and stitched it onto his collar, like the old Hungarian uniforms.

"Citizens, comrades," says Captain Kiss, "we are now going to form the Corvin battalion. If the Soviet troops intervene in our Hungarian Revolution, the Corvin battalion will fight them. But first let us sing our national anthem." They all rise. For Tamás and Feri and many others in the audience, it is the first time they have ever sung it in public. Never have the words applied so exactly to the present situation. They are deeply moved by the volume and unity of the singing and are surprised, though not ashamed, to be crying before it is over.

"I need five officers to command the five companies. I will read out the names I have selected and I ask them to come up onto the stage as I read them."

Tamás sees that one of the five is "scar-face," the man who had recruited them. It turns out his name is János Kovács, an ex-colonel in the police. He will be taking over the fifth company and will be known as Captain Kovács. Tamás and Feri decide to join his company.

Everyone is asked to return to his or her home and recruit as many people as possible, then return in a few hours. But first, those who were in the fighting at the Radio are asked to form into groups. Each group should consist of twenty to thirty persons and choose its own leader. Tamás walks up the slanting auditorium floor to the back of the hall to see whom he knows. Soon he spots a group of his schoolmates gesticulating wildly at him. He goes over and is at once asked to be the leader of the group, inasmuch as he is the only one who has already taken part in the fighting. They are all fifteen or sixteen years old. Tamás finds that, at thirty-eight persons, they are the largest group.

Then comes the announcement that all those under the age of sixteen are too young to take part and must go home at once. The group protests vociferously and Captain Kovács comes over to assure them that they are exempted; he authorizes them to stay.

The headquarters of the fifth company is established not in the theatre building, but in a neighboring school on Prater Street that is reached via an enclosed concourse, or arcade, through a five-story apartment building. The school is a three-storey building with a modern kitchen on the ground floor, which will be used to prepare food for all the fighters in the Corvin Theatre and Corvin Passage area.

Tamás's group is assigned a classroom. They pile the benches in a corner and some of the boys immediately lie down to catch up on their sleep.[6]

At the battered radio station on Sándor Bródy Street the insurgents are finding that the victory they have won is probably a pyrrhic one. Nearly all of the equipment in the broadcasting studios has been destroyed in the fight or later by the ÁVO. Moreover, the signal on the one frequency still available barely reaches the outskirts of Budapest. They will not be able to broadcast their demands to the nation after all.[7]

Around 11:00 a.m. Tamás Szabó's group, assigned to fire on Soviet tanks coming from Rákóczi Street along the Grand Boulevard section know as József Boulevard, has its baptism of fire. They are placed in third storey apartments, believing the Soviet guns are too close to the buildings to aim that high. As luck has it, two Soviet armored cars packed with soldiers stop right under their positions. The boys try to throw their few hand grenades right onto them, but lacking practice, they miss. The Russians immediately realize where the grenades came from and spray the windows with machine-gun fire. The angle puts most of the bullets into the ceilings and no one is hit, but then a machine gun on the roof of a building on the other side of the Boulevard shoots down on them. "Must be those ÁVO guys," thinks Tamás. He and another colleague rush upstairs, shooting off a lock to gain entrance to the attic. They fire their guns at the machine gun and its two operators, whom they can clearly see, but miss. The machine gun now aims at them. Someone downstairs takes advantage of their preoccupation with Tamás and his pal to fire his own machine gun. One of the ÁVO men slumps forward. But simultaneously the gun on the third floor falls silent. Finding his companion dead, the second ÁVO officer disappears, only to emerge on the street a minute later in street clothes. Before he has a chance to identify himself to the Russians he is taken to be one of the insurgents and is quickly gunned down.[8]

EXPLOSION

Further along Ferenc József Boulevard in front of the Corvin Theater passage, a battle is raging. Eight Soviet tanks and as many armored cars keep driving by the passage, firing as they go. The tanks seem immune to the patriot's fire and all attempts to put square cobblestones in their treads fail to break a single tread. But machine-gun fire shreds the tires of the last armored car and it is forced to stop. The crew of the car fire point-blank into a crowd of onlookers down the street. Withering fire from windows on both sides of the Boulevard kills two Russians, while two more escape through the smoke.

A young boy of about twelve runs up with a vinegar bottle full of gasoline and smashes it against the armored vehicle. Unseen by the Russians, he scampers back and hides behind a tree. The gasoline is all over the car but there are no tracer bullets to ignite it. An old bearded man of about seventy in ragged clothes with matches in his hands walks as briskly as he can right up to the car, drops a lighted match on the gasoline, which immediately flares up, and walks away to safety. The crowd watching cheer and shout "Long Live Hungarian Freedom!" Now other Molotov cocktails rain down on the car, adding to the flames. Two more crew members try to escape through the fire but are shot before they can get clear. The people who have been watching from hiding places now rush into the street and cheer their patriot heroes.[9]

Over on Bajcsy-Zsilinszky Ave. about this time a young Soviet Army major at the head of a stationary armored column emerges from his tank, ostensibly to stretch his legs and have a smoke. He lights up. Suddenly he takes to his heels and runs under the porte-cochere of a large apartment building. When he spots two tenants of the building just standing there he tears the insignia off his shoulders and asks them for asylum, explaining in halting German that he refuses to fight against an unarmed civilian population. The two Hungarians quickly close the entrance gate and are surprised that the tanks do not open fire on it, but instead drive off. Major Akopyan, of Armenian extraction, will join the Freedom Fighters in making propaganda among the Soviet troops. Only during the second Soviet intervention will he realize he can no longer stay in Hungary, and must escape to the West. He will be killed by Soviet troops in the woods of Buda in his attempt.[10]

At 11:44 the Radio reports that a group of "counterrevolutionaries" have surrendered in front of the Chain Bridge (Lánchíd). No figure is given. Throughout the day such announcements are made to give the impression that resistance among the insurgents is crumbling, while, in fact, the very opposite is occurring.[11]

Around noon Russian T-34 tanks come rushing down Rákóczi Avenue shooting indiscriminately right and left. Two shells crash into the Astoria Hotel, throwing German businessmen occupants to the floor on the other side of the building. Two gaping, smoldering holes expose bedrooms that fortunately were not occupied. Most of the hotel's inhabitants, if not cowering in the lobby, have heeded the management's call for them to proceed to the cellar.[12]

Nagy Addresses the Nation

At ten minutes past noon Imre Nagy makes his first radio address to the nation. He says in part:

> People of Budapest, I inform you that all those who…lay down their arms and cease fighting by 2:00 p.m. today will be exempted from prosecution. At the same time I state that…we will realize as soon as possible the systematic democratization of our country in every field of Party, State, political and economic life. Heed our appeal, stop fighting and secure the restoration of calm and order in the interest of the future of our country.

Nagy goes on to promise the development of "Socialism" in a manner "corresponding to our own national characteristics," and the "radical improvement of the workers' living conditions" He excoriates "hostile elements" who "joined the ranks of peacefully-demonstrating Hungarian youth," and "turned against the People's Democracy…" He reiterates the amnesty offer, the call for order, asks workers to "defend the factories and machines," and says "Our future is at stake. The great road of progress of our national existence lies before us.…Line up behind the Party, line up behind the government!"

The speech is immediately followed by a scratchy recording of the National Anthem.

*   *   *   *

In the early morning ground fog prevents a plane from Moscow from landing at Ferihegy Airport outside of Budapest, forcing it to land ninety kilometers to the west at Veszprem. Anastas Mikoyan and Michael Suslov, Presidium members, and Ivan Serov, KGB chief, are on board. They are met by General Mikhail S. Malinin and set out for the city in armored personnel carriers accompanied by tanks. They note that in contrast to Buda, where things are calm, there is continuous shooting in Pest, though "single shots from counter-revolutionaries" are met with salvos from the Soviet forces. They go first to the Ministry of Defense and then to the Party building to converse with Gerő, Nagy and others and there they remain for the day. In the late afternoon they send a ciphered cable back to the Kremlin that says in part:

> We had the impression that Gerő especially, but other comrades as well, are exaggerating the opponent's strength and underestimating their own strength. At two o'clock [this afternoon] the situation in the city was as follows:
>
> "All the hotbeds of insurgency have been crushed; liquidation of the main hotbed, at the radio station, where about four thousand people are concentrated, is still going on. They raised a white flag, but when representatives of the Hungarian authorities appeared [the insurgents] presented the removal of Gerő from his post as a condition of surrender, which of course was rejected. Our command is setting for itself the task of liquidating this hotbed tonight. It is significant that the Hungarian colleagues here, above all the state security personnel, put up violent resistance to the insurgents and tolerated defeat here only because ammunition was exhausted and a fresh battalion of Hungarian troops mutinied and attacked them.
>
> "The comrades express the opinion that the Hungarian Army conducted itself poorly, although the Debrecen division performed well....
>
> "Because a turning point in the events has occurred, it has been decided to use Hungarian units more boldly for patrolling, for detaining suspicious elements and people violating the introduction of a state of emergency, and for guarding important installations....
>
> "The Hungarian comrades, especially Imre Nagy, approved the use of more Hungarian military units, militia, and state security units to lighten the burden on Soviet troops and to emphasize the role of Hungarians themselves in liquidating the riots...
>
> "Today, not a single newspaper was published, only a bulletin. It has been arranged to have at least one newspaper published tomorrow...."[13]

News Spreads to the Provinces

Word of the demonstrations, the toppling of the Stalin statue and the armed assault on the radio station reaches all of Hungary's provincial cities long before dawn, thanks to the perfectly operating telephone system within the country and the fact that the students have been in touch on a regular basis for some days now.

In the northern industrial city of Miskolc something quite similar to the outbreak of violence in Debrecen occurs, but on the twenty-fifth, not the twenty-fourth. Two groups of young workers and some high school students—all between the ages of fifteen and eighteen—commandeered two trucks and set off for Budapest. They were immediately pursued by ÁVO trucks, overtaken, caught and brought back to the city, where they were placed in a centrally located ÁVO prison. News of the arrest of these youths quickly spread and by 11:00 p.m. a large crowd had gathered outside the prison demanding their release. Alarmed at the size of the crowd, the ÁVO secretly released the youths via the back door. Some of the freed youths even came around and mingled with the crowd without anyone in the latter realizing it.

Around 4:00 a.m. on the twenty-sixth people began to throw stones through the building's windows. Then, around 6:00 a.m. when it was getting light, the ÁVO commander, Col. Gyula Gati, fired his pistol into the air. It was the signal for the ÁVO troops to toss hand grenades down into the crowd. Twenty-six people were killed, including a number of children, the oldest of whom was a miner's daughter aged fifteen.

News of this massacre spreads not only around the town, but also to the mines. The miners, who had already organized themselves into workers' councils on the Yugoslav model two weeks ago at the behest of the government, drop work at once. They disarm the mine's guards, arm themselves with rifles and sticks of dynamite and march three thousand strong into the town. They surround the ÁVO building and begin to toss sticks of dynamite through the already broken windows. After a few explosions the miners pour into the building and pull out some fifteen terrified secret policemen. The great majority, they discover later, escaped through the backdoor. Among the captured are Col. Gati and his pregnant wife, who had been spotted earlier firing a machine gun from an upper window. They are tied to the back of trucks and dragged to the monument for Soviet soldiers fallen in the Second World War. Here the Colonel and five others are lynched on the monument itself. Only at the last minute are some students able to save the pregnant Mrs. Gati from the same fate. Though picked up a few days later, she is never prosecuted.[14]

In Szeged, where no one has any access to firearms, the populace gathers along the streets where Russian tanks are moving to jeer and indicate that Russians are not wanted. The students hold a silent march with the young women students in the front rows. This does not deter the ÁVO police from breaking up the march with rifle butts and taking many of the students, including the young women, into custody. After they have them out of sight in ÁVO headquarters, the security police slap the faces of the women and beat the male students before releasing them.

The professors, together with Rector Baróti, announce that there will be no further classes until the Russians have left. Nonetheless, by nightfall Russian tanks are parked at all the major street corners and there are almost as many ÁVO patrols in the streets as people.[15]

In Székesfehérvár, where the Soviet Special Corps for Hungary is head-quartered and nearly forty percent of the officers are billeted with Hungarian families, violence comes about in a different way. When a large crowd gathers around the Interior Ministry's Main Department to protest the ÁVO's bloody role in Budapest, Hungarian Army and Police are in such fear of losing control of the crowd that they decide to fire salvos into the air. A nearby Soviet armored vehicle suddenly thinks *it* is being fired on and shoots in the direction of the shots. Seven people are killed and thirteen wounded, including several policemen.[16]

On Thursday, in the southern mining town of Pécs, when it comes time for the afternoon shift of miners to go down into the shafts, many refuse. This is quite unprecedented, for strict discipline is always maintained among miners. Many of the workers in the local factories also stop work. By evening people are told to stay in their homes and a state of siege is declared.[17]

In the western city of Győr on the road to Vienna, Thursday the twenty-fifth starts out quietly. Those not otherwise engaged are glued to their radios. Imre Nagy's speech at midday does not contain much to their liking, but one thing he says catches their attention: "Let's put our national flags on our houses." Within an hour flags without the communist insignia are being raised not only over houses but shops and other commercial enterprises.

Over in the big railroad car factory on the same day a number of workers leave their jobs and march to the main office, which carries a large neon sign saying "Wilhelm Pieck* Car and Engine Factory." Some workers climb up

---

*Wilhelm Pieck, an old East German communist, is the Premier of the German Democratic Republic.

and dismantle the tubes saying "Wilhelm Pieck," while others bring paint and paint in the word "Magyar" (Hungarian). There is also a large red star to come down. After this is accomplished they all sing the national anthem and then head for the main gate, as the morning shift is over.

Meanwhile in town young Gábor Földes, communist director of the local theatre, leads a group of about thirty carrying a national flag. They are marching to the county offices of the Communist party shouting "We want Freedom! Long Live the Communist Party!" Local high school students and young apprentices join them along the way so that a sizeable crowd has assembled by the time they reach the offices. Földes then delivers an eloquent speech declaring that the students and workers fighting in Budapest are not fascists and counter-revolutionaries but honorable Hungarians fighting for "our freedom."

Sections of the crowd now begin to remove all of the red stars in sight and also to demolish the central Soviet war memorial. Later, in the early evening, another group of demonstrators breaks into the local jail, disarming the local commander and releasing political prisoners. At this point trucks of ÁVO reinforcements arrive and a conflict ensues in which they shoot into the crowd, killing four people and wounding several others. They also arrest a number of students.[18]

Veszprém, an ancient trading center west of Székesfehérvár and north of Lake Balaton, is a college town. All day Thursday the professors endeavor to keep the students occupied in small groups of twenty to thirty to keep them separated and out of trouble. Yesterday the students took over the DISZ offices and mimeographed leaflets that have already been distributed in the city. Because of their telephone contact with students in Budapest and their better reception of foreign radios than other parts of Hungary, they are much better informed as to the situation both in Budapest and around the country than are the local ÁVO, who do not dare listen to foreign radios. At one point the ÁVO actually phone them to ask for information.

Inside the college buildings there is something of an uproar. The students have been ordered to stay in their respective buildings and not leave campus, but they have been rigging up amplifiers everywhere so that everyone can hear what the foreign radios are saying. When the ÁVO attempt to enter the buildings to "quiet" the students, the faculty will have none of it and tell them to go away.

EXPLOSION

Expecting leadership from the students, the townspeople are disappointed and wonder where they are. The crowd has staged a big demonstration earlier in the day, marched to the Soviet monument and torn the red star off its top. Now this sizeable gathering marches to the college. Outside the closed iron gates of the college they yell anti-regime slogans and taunt the students to come out. The students feel badly about their situation, but their most popular professors are begging them not to get involved with the crowd. Eventually they are told to turn out all the lights and leave the buildings via rear windows and coal chutes. When the assemblage finally realizes that there is no one left in the buildings, it breaks up and goes home.[19]

Radio Budapest at 1:23 p.m. repeats the amnesty offer due soon to expire, but this time adds that the offer includes "members of the armed forces." Then it goes on to say: "Several listeners…have turned to us for explanation of the…arrival of Soviet troops in Budapest.…These Soviet units are stationed in Hungary in accordance with the Warsaw Pact." Hungarians in Eastern Hungary who are watching Soviet units pouring in from Romania and the Ukraine marvel at this statement. "The Hungarian government… asked that Soviet troops help to control the murderous attacks of counterrevolutionary bands. These Soviet soldiers are risking their lives in order to defend…the capital's peaceful population and the peace of our nation. After order is restored the Soviet troops will return to their bases. Workers of Budapest, welcome with affection our friends and allies!" (This announcement is made some nine hours after Soviet tanks began firing on scores of buildings in Budapest and have already killed dozens of Hungarian citizens, most of them non-combatants.)

Only minutes after the passing of the 2:00 p.m. deadline the radio announces that the deadline has been extended to 6:00 p.m. They follow this with the announcement—premature as it turns out—that "armed forces" (for some reason they forget to use the term "counterrevolutionaries") which had penetrated the radio building have now announced that they are ready to surrender.

Reports of surrender are usually based upon a modicum of truth. Many more weapons have been given out than there are youths who know how to use them, and many of the insurgents, particularly the students, are discouraged enough to give up without a fight. The Hungarian Army sends out units in three separate waves to "recapture" certain sites said to be held by the rebels and a total of 6,500 men are used in these operations. But it is easy to judge their effectiveness when, at the end of the day, they reported that 360 people were captured, but only eighty-seven of them were armed at the time of capture.[20]

In Moscow, where it is just turning night, the meeting to which Khrushchev had invited Gerő now takes place. The conference was originally conceived as one in which Khrushchev would report to top party officials of the other East bloc countries on the recent changes in Poland and what the Soviet Union was doing about it. Events have overtaken him, however, and he finds he must spend even more time explaining the situation in Hungary. Only the Czechoslovak, East German and Bulgarian comrades are present; the Hungarian and Romanian comrades are absent. The Poles, of course, were not invited.

After explaining what has happened in Poland and the Soviet analysis of it, Khrushchev turns to Hungary. He gives a forthright account of how the Soviet intervention came about, citing the roles of Gerő, Andropov and himself. He states factually the changes in the Hungarian Central Committee and the fact that Imre Nagy has not only been re-elected to the Central Committee but also given the government post as President of the Council of Ministers (i.e. Premier). He also states that the Hungarians have set up an "Action Group" of five to suppress the uprising, namely Bata, Piros, Kovács, Emmerich and Vas, pointing out, however, that all five failed to get re-elected to the Central Committee.

Then, to reassure the foreign comrades that all is going well, he gives the following report, as reported by Jan Svoboda, Prime Minister of Czechoslovakia.

"There are no longer any demonstrations in Budapest on the evening of October 24. Near the Danube there are several groups of bandits. These consist of groups of fifteen to twenty people armed with pistols and weapons seized from soldiers. Resistance is still occurring on certain street corners, roofs and balconies. On several streets there are barricades. The bandits temporarily occupied two railway stations and one of the two radio stations. The bandits wanted to tear down the statue of Stalin. When they were unsuccessful in this task, they seized a welder's torch and cut the statue to pieces, and then disposed of the whole thing.

"The Hungarian internal security forces performed very well, but suffered most of the casualties from among the twenty-five dead and fifty wounded. Also, one Soviet officer was killed and twelve soldiers were wounded. The unrest has been confined to Budapest so far. Everywhere else, in cities and in villages, there is calm. The workers from Csepel factory [sic] defended themselves with bare hands against the armed bandits."[21]

Before the end of the working day, Gusztáv Gogolyák, Director of "Post Office No. 118," which is code for the covert radio jamming operation in Budapest, orders radio technicians all over the country to close down all facilities immediately, shred their documents and lock the doors of their stations. Suddenly, with no more of the pulsing wa-wa-wa sound coming out of their radios, people throughout the land jump up to turn down the volume on their sets. The western radio station they are tuned to is now coming through as clear as Radio Kossuth (Radio Budapest). The psychological message, "we are still here and the jamming is now gone," has a profound impact on all listeners.[22]

Reports Reach the West

Initial news reports of the demonstrations, the outbreak of fighting and the appearance of Soviet tanks are carried on the front pages of all the major newspapers in Western Europe and the United States. There is very little detail, however, about what is now actually happening, as all telephone and teletype (telex) contact to the West has been cut off by the Hungarian government. As a consequence, editorial opinion is sparse. The *New York Times*, however, does have this to say:

> ...to paraphrase the Communist Manifesto, a spectre is haunting the communist despots—the spectre of freedom. This revolution is already shaking the empire that Stalin built. It makes a mockery of Soviet professions of respect for national sovereignty and non-interference in other people's internal affairs.

The first eyewitness accounts of the fighting and destruction, on this first day of the revolution, come from German and Austrian businessmen as they cross into Austria this afternoon. Some of these reports make it sound as though full-scale war, possibly even the Third World War, has broken out, though the businessmen had no trouble reaching the border, once they had managed to exit Budapest.

The United States Legation on Freedom Square has no Minister, only a Chargé d'Affaires, Spencer Barnes, a sensitive man in his fifties. Barnes and his staff, particularly the Hungarian members, have been all over the city and have managed to report with great precision what has been happening up until the legation's telex was cut off last night. At 3:00 p.m. he tries to send the following message, in typical cablese, to Washington:

Legation considers earliest and highest level statement by US government urgently required by present situation in Hungary, and suggests text along following lines:

> The United States considers the fight in Hungary as renewed expression intense desire freedom long held by Hungarian people. This fight is new incidence their willingness give their lives this end, as on other famous occasion Hungary's fight for liberty against Russian troops.
>
> The demands reportedly made by students and populace clearly fall within the framework of those human rights to which every free people entitled.
>
> US considers intervention Soviet forces and ruthless killing unarmed Hungarians as yet another example of continuing occupation Hungary by alien and enemy force for their own purposes. Employment these troops to shoot down Hungarian people breaks every moral law and demonstrates that Hungary is to Soviet Russia merely a colonial possession, the demand of whose people for democratic liberty warrants the use of naked force.
>
> What has happened in Hungary amounts to armed aggression by army of one power against people of another. United States and world await outcome with intense interest.

Barnes goes on to recommend a diplomatic protest to Soviet and Hungarian governments within a matter of a day or two on continuing presence of Soviet troops, not on legal grounds, but on the brazen occupation nature of Soviet troops stationing in Hungary both before and after the Austrian Peace Treaty's signing and the Warsaw Pact. He points out that scores of Hungarians in the past twenty-four hours have demanded "give us arms," "give us diplomatic assistance," "what is America going to do for us in this hour?"[23]

Because he is unable to send this message via telex he asks the assistance of the British Legation, which has radio contact with London. Sir Leslie Fry, the British Minister, agrees, but it is several hours before the text can be transmitted by courier through the embattled one-mile interval between the two legations.

Fry radios the Foreign Office:

My United States colleague would be grateful if the message (in American cypher) in my immediately following telegram could be passed at once to his government as his telegram No. 157.[24]

The record shows, unfortunately, that Telegram Number 157 only reaches the Department of State at 8:36 a.m. on Thursday, October 25, almost twenty-four hours after Barnes had drafted it. While a statement from President Eisenhower is forthcoming, and Barnes' draft will be the base of it, it will not sound as decisive.

Exile groups in America are quick to react. Without waiting for any more details than what they have read in the *New York Times, Washington Post* and other major U.S. papers, they send telegrams to the U.S. Department of State. Monsignor Béla Varga, President of the Hungarian National Council, advises John Foster Dulles that "intervention by the United States is legally and strongly supported by Article 34, of the United Nations Charter and by the continuous violation of the war-time and postwar agreements assuring the now captive nations the right of self-determination through free and unfettered elections....We beg you, Mr., Secretary, to request urgently the Security Council of the United Nations to take energetic action primarily aimed at stopping the massacre...."[25] Later in the day a whole group of prominent exiles visit Dulles.

In Munich, Germany, the U.S. Director of the Munich Center of International Broadcasting (i.e. "Voice of America," or VOA) cables his boss in Washington:

Believe that broadcasts of 'Americana' to Hungary during people's rebellion and description of same as 'riots' counterproductive and should be immediately reexamined. Staff members here could not understand how VOA in Hungarian from Washington last night could tell Hungarians about *Globemaster* landing on Arctic ice shelf, activities of Soviet observers of American election and cancer research could only cause dismay and resentment. Effect further aggravated by fact that BBC Hungarian [service] which followed immediately after the VOA broadcast, carried two sharp commentaries on the situation, strongly condemning the use of Soviet forces to put down the uprising...

In reference to your request for guidance suggestions: during the current phase when Hungarian uprisings seem still to be continuing, would suggest heavy cross-reporting of Hungarian and Polish events plus world-wide expression of solidarity and sympathy for the Hungarian people....[26]

Meanwhile, back in Budapest British Minister Fry cables his government "It is now dark and at the moment the firing has diminished. Machine-gun fire from a Russian tank has struck Her Majesty's Legation, fortunately causing little damage. All staff will stay for night, and the rest remain in their homes..."[27]

Budapest, Thursday, October 25, 1956

At 5:00 a. m. early risers hear Radio Budapest claim that "the attackers are laying down their arms and surrendering *en masse*...only a few groups are still putting up resistance in Budapest, in Rákóczi Street near the Palace Hotel, in Magdolna Street, and near the Ferencváros Railroad Station....The fighting at the Radio Station has not yet completely ended. A small number of those on the premises have not yet complied with demands for surrender. There is shooting going on. The operations to clear the broadcasting station will start after daybreak. There are still small groups composed of a few people who wander about the street or take up positions in doorways. They are firing, taking advantage of the darkness of night and the dim light of dawn."[28] No mention is made of the Corvin Cinema area on József Boulevard where the greatest number of revolutionaries is gathered.

Early morning fog, caused by the dropping temperature, surrounds the city. It will only dissipate when a strong wind from the west comes up at mid-morning. The shooting has died down and Buda, at least, is abnormally quiet for this hour. Few of the streetcars are operating and the Soviet tanks, except those operating in Pest, especially near the Kilián Barracks, are stationary. Last night the insurgents decided it was useless to hold the radio station any longer, since, in its badly damaged state, it was of so little value to them. Most of them slip away before the Soviet assault begins. Radio Budapest's report is out-of-date.

Austrian journalist Jenő Pogány, who has been in Budapest since the twenty-third, notices that the gunfire during the night diminishes. He and his fellow western journalists at the Duna hotel all assume that the revolution has been beaten down and all are prepared to write their reports to that effect.[29] The government, which had called for a curfew, now decides it must lift it if things are ever to get back to normal. In an appeal broadcast at six o'clock it asks "people to start traffic—streetcars, trolleybuses and buses—wherever possible. Workers must resume work. Let factories produce and offices and enterprises operate," says the Central Committee as though it were waving a magic wand. "On the other hand, all educational establishments" (which the government obviously feels are the source of its troubles)...will remain closed until further notice."

A report a short while later claims the "counter-revolutionary gangs have set fire to several public buildings, dwellings and department stores in Budapest....At present there is a tremendous struggle to extinguish a serious fire at the National Museum."[30] The "counterrevolutionary gangs" which have set these fires, as much of the populace has witnessed, are the Soviet T-34 tanks indiscriminately shelling buildings.

The Minister of Defense, General István Bata, having included individual Hungarian soldiers in the promise of amnesty, now declares "I instruct those members of the Army who, for one reason or another, have been separated from their units to report to their commanding officers immediately." Thirty-five minutes later, at 9:15, he says to this not-exactly-unified army: "I order that...the soldiers of our People's Army completely eliminate by midday the counterrevolutionary forces still to be found in Budapest."[31] (The record will later show that thirty-one soldiers died, thirty-four were wounded—though it does not indicate on whose side they were fighting—and 175 disappeared by the end of Thursday, October 25.)[32]

Yesterday around 5:00 p.m. Lt. Col. Horváth, Commander of the Kilián Barracks, phoned Col. Pál Maléter to say that armed insurgents and some of his own soldiers had thrown him out around noon because of his refusal to bring his soldiers out onto the street where they could choose whether or not to join the revolution. Today, Maléter, under orders from his superior, leads a group of five tanks through the city to take charge of the barracks. Unfortunately, he has his driver go too fast and the last two tanks, driven by country boys who do not know Budapest, fall far behind, get hopelessly lost and sheepishly find their way back to the base. Maléter, seeing his unit reduced, places one tank at either end of the gigantic building and then attempts to enter through the central door of the barracks. Surprise; it doesn't fit. Nor, being so tightly wedged, can the tank back up. He pulls his broad shoulders and six-foot-two frame up out of the turret, orders the driver to turn the turret around so that the gun is facing the Corvin Passage, on which it later fires, and goes into the building to take charge.

There has always been great confusion about the Kilián (formerly Maria Theresia) Barracks. First of all, it is an enormously long building. It has three sections of nearly equal size and it is only the middle section that is used as an Army Barracks. The sections on either side are used to house labor battalions, freshly conscripted troops or for storage, but it is only the central part that Maléter is taking over, though he attempts to control what transpires in the other two sections. The labor conscripts quickly join the revolution and invite Corvinists, students and others to join them, over the strenuous objections of Col. Maléter, who was sent to protect the facility and all the people in it. This turns out to include scores of old people, women and children taking shelter in the multi-level cellars under the building. Maléter has no sympathy for the revolutionists, whom he considers undisciplined rabble. He is shocked by all the children running around with guns. Though he gets into a number of fire-fights with the revolutionaries across the street in the Corvin Complex, he never orders his men to fire at the Russians or their tanks. Having once trained with the Russians, he has high regard for them and does not regard them as "the enemy."[33]

As the citizens of Budapest venture out after the cancellation of the curfew, they can see for themselves what lies the radio had been fostering. Most of the destruction has been caused, and is still being caused, by Soviet tanks. The "armed bandits" have not been liquidated; they can be seen with their armbands and submachine guns over their shoulders, all over the city, some of them manning checkpoints, others on missions to ferret out ÁVO agents. There has been no looting; on the contrary, wherever store windows have been smashed all of the merchandise is still sitting untouched in the display cases. In some there are notes warning people not to take anything, as this would sully the purity of the revolution. In the vicinity of the Kilián Barracks and the Corvin Cinema the hulks of twelve burnt-out Soviet tanks can be seen.

* * * *

Soviet tanks are no longer racing around. They have stopped shooting. Since nearly all have radios, they are in constant touch with each other. It seems as though some sort of cease-fire order has been given. Some think it is the influence of Imre Nagy. Those tanks in guarding positions have their hatches open and they have even hoisted white flags. This sight is too much for the Hungarian populace to resist. Almost all have some Russian; the young ones have been forced to study it. Some yell insults at the invaders, but most try to engage them in conversation. And since these troops have been in Hungary now for more than a year, a few of them know some Hungarian. Moreover, the students have printed up many leaflets in Russian and some of these are passed up to the leather-helmeted tankman. One such leaflet reads:

> Russian Friends! Do not shoot!
> They have tricked you. You are fighting not against counterrevolutionaries, but against revolutionaries. We fighting Hungarians want an independent, democratic Hungary.
> Your fight is pointless: you are not shooting at fascists but at workers, peasants and university students.
> Stop the fight!
> Revolutionary Youth.[34]

A Peaceful Demonstration Heads for Parliament Square

A peaceful demonstration has been called for later this morning in Parliament Square in which no one is to carry any weapons. As word of this is spread, groups of people begin to form in various parts of the city with the intention of joining the demonstration.

The first large group of about five hundred forms in Lujza Blaha Square in front of the battle-scarred *Szabad Nép* building. As it moves down Rákóczi Avenue with a whole forest of fluttering flags, people begin to chant demands for the removal of Gerő and the withdrawal of the Soviet troops. When they arrive at the Astoria Hotel with its gaping shell holes, they notice sixteen Soviet tanks in various positions in front of the hotel, as this is a major nerve center from which orders are issued to Soviet armor in the city. All of the hatches are open and many of the crews are even out of their tanks. A thirty-nine-year-old textile worker, who has spent several years in a Russian prison and become fairly fluent in the language, teams up with a woman friend, also fluent in Russian, and they do their best to explain the situation to these tank crews.

Then the quite unexpected happens. Young Hungarians, both men and women, jump up onto the tanks offering cigarettes to the crews and pinning Hungarian flags to the tank aerials. The Soviet tank commander is furious, but helpless to do anything about it. Seeing the textile worker and his friend conversing in Russian, the organizers of the march ask them to persuade the commander to have the tanks, now covered with Hungarian flags, to lead the procession to Parliament Square. The commander says adamantly he has no orders to do so and therefore cannot. The two "interpreters" then decide to work on the individual tank commanders. They succeed in two cases and while the top commander is completely opposed to this, he promises he will not open fire on these two tanks.[35]

"Let's go to Parliament Square!" people shout. "Good Russki. Show us what a good cabbie you are!"[36] Several of the Hungarians are even invited into the tanks to act as navigators, while dozens of demonstrators cover the outsides waving their flags and calling out to each other gleefully. The two are followed by an armored car and then a third tank, manned by Hungarian veterans, who know very well how to operate it. There is a great ovation as they all start off.

Word of this strange procession spreads quickly around Pest. "This is a peaceful demonstration!" the demonstrators call out to bystanders. "The radio is telling lies!" "We want to be free!" With the obvious cease-fire and the friendliness of the Russians, who, embarrassed at being kissed by the women and children riding on their tanks, nonetheless smile and wave at the crowds, a mood of euphoria takes over. Maybe the revolution is over. At least the fighting is. Again and again people break into the national anthem and the Kossuth recruiting song and more and more people join the march. The Soviet soldiers yell out from time to time that they have no intention of fighting the Hungarian people.[37] At one point Hungarian Army trucks drive up and words are exchanged with the middle-aged leader who is holding the national flag in his hand. Some people think the soldiers are warning them they are armed. Others think that they are offering them arms. The leader's reply rings out loud and clear: "No! Our only weapon is the flag!" and he holds it aloft.[38]

As they reach Szabadságtér (Freedom Square) from Bajcsy-Zsilinszky Avenue, about two thousand demonstrators branch off to the American legation, which stands at the far end, just off the main route of the march down the center of the Freedom Square. From here they have not more than a block to go to Kossuth tér (known to most Westerners as "Parliament Square"). They pause, sing the national anthem and call out to those inside "Why don't you help us?" They can see faces in the windows, and clearly do not want to budge until someone has come out to talk to them.[39]

At length, Spencer Barnes, the American Chargé d'Affaires, emerges onto a balcony and reads in American-accented Hungarian from a paper he holds in his hand:

> We understand the situation and it has been reported to our government as fully as we are able. You will understand that we ourselves can take no decision; this is a matter for our government and the United Nations. We have been in Hungary for many years and we think we understand the situation.[40]

The crowd acknowledges his statement with subdued applause, salutes the American flag and then moves on toward Parliament Square, taking up once again the chants of "Down with Gerő!" and "Russians Go Home!"

When the main body of the crowd comes down Vécsey Street into Parliament Square, they pass the Ministry of Agriculture building on the right-hand corner. It is a two-hundred-year-old massive structure four storeys tall. But as they enter the Square their backs are to the building's façade, so they do not notice the many open windows with Blue Police (ÁVO), guns at the ready, watching them.

The various groups now converge on the Parliament building across the Square, where several dozen Soviet tanks are guarding Gates VI and IX. These are used as entrances and exits for traffic going into and out of the huge gothic Parliament, which so dominates the Square. Some demonstrators go up to the Main Gate as well, while a few hang back near the Rákóczi statue, which, being on a slight rise, provides a better view. All told the crowd now numbers between twenty and twenty-five thousand.

No sooner do the lead tanks reach the fence around the Parliament than they wheel around and face the crowd. The crowd is in a festive mood and seeing all of those other Soviet tanks, many with their hatches open and tankmen standing in them, they take flowers and flags to decorate them as well. When the students cannot find a tankman in the open hatch to whom they can hand their Russian language leaflets, they shove them into the tanks' eye slits, like mail into mail boxes.[41]

The leaders, who think Prime Minister Nagy is in the Parliament building, attempt to persuade the guards to let them through with their message. Meanwhile, the happy crowd once again breaks into the national anthem. In this setting and with this many people, it sounds much better than it did while they were marching. It is around 11:00 a.m.

A few blocks away at 17 Akadémia Street the Central Committee is meeting, with Mikoyan, Suslov and KGB head Serov taking part. Serov has heard disturbing reports of Soviet soldiers fraternizing with the Hungarian demonstrators. He goes outside to see for himself, comes back in a fury and gives the order for the Soviet tanks guarding the party building to proceed to the Parliament Square and "liquidate" the demonstration. The record does not show whether he has planned or is even aware of the ÁVO trap.

The Massacre Begins

Suddenly, without any warning, heavy machine gun fire opens up from the upper windows and roof of the Agriculture building. People begin to fall. The singing abruptly stops. When people begin to realize what is happening they start to flee, but many more fall before they do. Anguished cries from persons who have seen their families and little ones cut down and screams of the wounded fill the air between the bursts of gunfire. Fire is being directed at the people on the tanks and a number, including a Soviet officer and several soldiers, are killed. The Soviets, as surprised as the crowd, respond automatically. Jumping into their tanks and noting exactly where the firing is coming from they fire their heavy machine guns back at the windows and roof of the Agriculture Ministry. Plaster flies as they rake the windows and rooftop. Within five minutes they manage to silence all of the ÁVO guns. "If they had not, thousands would have died," says an eyewitness, Béla Kocsis, later.[42] But the Russians do not realize they are ÁVO; they assume it is rebels they have vanquished. Then they realize—or at least think—that they have been led into a trap. All that friendly fraternization was simply designed to bring them here to get killed. They turn their guns on the fleeing crowd, many of whom have recently been on the tanks, and increase the slaughter.

Other Soviet tanks acting on Serov's orders now come down Akadémia Street and open fire, but with shells, not just machine guns. The massacre is unbelievable.[43]

From the first opening burst of the ÁVO to the last explosion of a tank shell, the shooting—interrupted briefly when ambulances came to pick up wounded—has lasted less than twenty minutes, though many claim it lasted much longer. Many wounded might have made it had they not been mercilessly mowed down as they tried to stand up or make their escape. A great many, however, do manage to escape, especially those who were close to the Agriculture building and other buildings with arcades. Some, such as Péter Bíró, a porcelain painter, miraculously escape from where the firing is heaviest. He manages to dive under one of the Soviet armored cars and then make his way to an arcade, before he gets hit in the thigh from a shell fired from Akadémia Street. Before being wounded, he notices one shell burst on the Parliament building itself.[44]

One nurse, who later will tell her story when she escapes to Vienna, believes that around six hundred people were killed; she personally handled sixty dead bodies. One particular body she cannot get out of her mind: a woman who had her head and arms shot away was lying in her blood-drenched fur coat, while her three children, miraculously alive, were crying piteously.[45] Another eyewitness sees many old people and children among the dead.[46] One witness, János Bartolmy, sees a stack of bodies piled by the Rákóczi statue which he estimates to be at least two hundred. The wounded he sees carried away number at least five hundred.[47]

Other estimates of the number of dead will range from three hundred to eight hundred based on the testimony of dozens of eyewitnesses before the United Nations. A member of the British Legation counts twelve truckloads of dead being removed from the Square several hours after the massacre.[48] No one will ever know the true number, because instead of their being given a proper burial, the bodies are dumped into tributaries of the Danube. Later in the afternoon river fleet sailors will fish twenty-five bodies out of the river.[49]

From windows of nearby apartment buildings, towels, sheets, shirts—anything that will do for bandages—are tossed down.[50]

Ambulances, the first of which is fired on and virtually destroyed, soon arrive to remove the wounded and trucks soon after to remove the dead. Later still, fire trucks will hose down the bloody cobblestones; but evidence of blood will be visible for weeks. All of Hungary will soon come to know this day as "Bloody Thursday."

A sizeable group of demonstrators who escaped the onslaught reappear in front of the U.S. Legation, this time shouting in fury and brandishing several bloody flags. "This is a peaceful demonstration right here in front of you. You have seen how they massacred people like cattle. It was cold-blooded murder!" An American diplomat appears eventually and reads the same statement read earlier by Barnes. Seeing they can get no further satisfaction from the Americans, the demonstrators proceed to the British Legation just off Vörösmarty Square where Minister Fry eventually allows fifty of them into the Legation, where he greets them. Speakers urge him to tell the world that an "entirely peaceful demonstration" had resulted in unbelievable bloodshed because of the "unjustifiable shooting...by the secret police." Fry assures them that he is being a "faithful reporter" to Her Majesty's Government of all that is going on.[51]

* * * *

Inside the U.S. Legation the telex room on the ground floor is full of people. Since six o'clock this morning the line has been open to Washington and they cannot believe their good fortune. "It appears we have friends in the telegraph office," types the operator to his counterpart in Washington. "Very unusual." "Seems the crowd has left from in front of the Legation and things again seem rather quiet." He is crouched typing with the telex machine on the floor because when he began early this morning there was a gun battle going on in Freedom Square that made sitting or standing up perilous.

"Still there State Department?"

"Yes, will stay with you until you advise."

"Budapest Radio has just announced Gerő has been relieved of Party position and has been replaced by Kádár who is to speak over the radio shortly."

Over in the British Legation, Minister Fry is cabling the Foreign Office. His mind is on the big picture.

> The Hungarian Tricolors without the Communist emblem, now flying on many public and other buildings throughout this city, while orderly crowds carrying their flags and singing patriotic songs are moving about at will....
>
> But casualties have been very severe, even amongst the women and children, and the populace are terrified of massive reprisals. The success of this revolt against Communism is clearly in the balance and, as I see it, we have a magnificent opportunity to tip the scales. Is there not justification for placing the situation at once before the United Nations, giving the widest possible publicity to our action? The mere fact of our application would be beneficial.

Nagy and Kádár Speak on the Radio

The time is 3:18 p.m. Radio Budapest announces: "Now Comrades János Kádár and Imre Nagy will address you." Since these are pre-recorded messages neither seems aware of the massacre that has just taken place. Kádár comes first. He explains the complexity of the situation and then says that "after order has been restored, the government should conduct talks with the Soviet government in the spirit of complete equality between Hungary and the Soviet Union,...for the equitable and just settlement of questions pending between the two Socialist countries." He ends with the usual communist flourish "Workers, Communist comrades be unflinching and firm. Defend the order of the people's power...etc"

Nagy sounds quite different. He does not begin with "Comrades" but rather "Working people of Hungary."

> During the past few days our country has lived through tragic events. A small group of counter-revolutionary provocateurs launched an armed attack against the order of our People's Republic, an attack that has been support-ed by part of the workers of Budapest because of their bitterness over the sit-uation of the country. This bitterness has been aggravated by the political and economic mistakes of the past....The new Party leadership and government under my direction are resolved to draw the fullest lessons from the tragic events. Soon after the restoration of order the National Assembly will be called. At that session I will submit an all-embracing and basic program of reform....
>
> For the realization of this program it is absolutely necessary to stop the fighting immediately, to restore order and peace, and to continue produc-tion...the Hungarian government will begin talks with the Soviet Union con-cerning the relations between the Hungarian People's Republic and the Soviet Union, and, among other things, concerning the withdrawal of Soviet forces stationed in Hungary....
>
> The withdrawal of Soviet forces...will take place without delay after the restoration of peace and order...

Nagy follows this announcement with an assurance that for all those who took up arms *without* the intent of overthrowing the government there will be a spirit of "reconciliation and understanding and to them martial law will not apply."

He ends by saying,

> I am filled with profound grief over every drop of blood shed during these tragic days...let this tragic fight, this useless shedding of blood, be ended. Hungarians, friends, comrades, let us set out under the leadership of the Party along the road of peaceful and creative work, building a better, more beauti-ful Socialist future for our people.

The announcement of Soviet troop withdrawal is a courageous, possibly foolhardy, move, for, while it was discussed, it was *not* technically approved by a vote either of the Political Committee or by Mikoyan and Suslov. After the broadcast, in fact, as soon as it is translated for Mikoyan he goes to Nagy and says, "Why did you promise to negotiate with the Soviet Union about the removal of Soviet troops from Hungary when the majority of the Politburo rejected this proposal?" Nagy's reply is that before the broadcast the Central leadership *had* debated this and "taking into account the working masses, especially the biggest workers' centers, indeed a series of party organiza-tions...in order to be masters of the situation once more and preserve [our] practical influence on the workers, they [including Gerő, Kádár and Hegedűs] were compelled to agree with this—in their opinion slight, and not categorical—demand to withdraw troops." It is only after this that Suslov and Mikoyan announce that they see this statement of Nagy's "as the gravest mistake" since Soviet withdrawal would mean the "inevitable entry of American troops."[52]

Nonetheless, the rather naive and jingoistic ending of Nagy's radio address indicates how out-of-touch he is with the situation in the country. He has been a "prisoner" in the Party building now for over forty hours, not in the sense of being under guard, but restricted as to movement and informa-tion. He knows only what the radio and Party people around him have told him. He is also a prisoner of forty years of Party discipline and jargon that makes him accept all too compliantly what he is told. He had heard the shooting in Parliament Square; it was too loud and too long not to have been heard. But he was told no details. Had he actually seen what was happening, it is doubtful he would have allowed this speech to go on the air.

Shortly after this Mikoyan and Suslov send a coded cable back to the Kremlin through the Soviet Embassy. This, in part, is what it says:

> Apart from this, Comrade Serov saw shooting start between our tanks and a Hungarian [border, i.e. "green" ÁVO] company in front of the Party center building itself, which had been sent there to reinforce the defense of the Party headquarters. Our tanks thought that the soldiers were insurgents. Ten of the Hungarian company lost their lives in this exchange of fire, and one of their men was seriously hurt. This all happened as the Hungarian Comrades were sitting in Party headquarters. Meanwhile, one of our tanks' gunners fired a round from a large-caliber two-barreled gun at the windows of the chamber. Inside the plaster started to fall, creating panic among the leading party func-tionaries. As a result, they filed into the cellar, but it was not properly equipped, so they went up again and continued working. The heavy fire increased the tension in the capital. In the afternoon peaceful protesters took to the streets everywhere with national and black flags...

The report goes on to note the suggestion of the Hungarian Politburo member, József Köböl that "in the interest of calm the Hungarian government should ask the Soviet government to withdraw Soviet troops from Hungary after order had been restored."

We announced," the report continues, "that in no case should the question of Soviet troop withdrawal from Hungary be raised, as this would mean the entry of American troops. We said that it could be announced that the Soviet troops returned to their former barracks after law and order had been returned to Budapest. The other members of the Political Committee did not support Köböl.[53]

* * * *

The British and American legations are as confused about Nagy's status as are the Hungarians.

"We could criticize Mr. Nagy," says a British Guidance for News Department, "for calling the Russians in and for suppressing the riots with such brutality. But it may be to our interest to have Mr. Nagy in power. At the moment he seems to offer the best prospects for a more liberal Communist regime in Hungary. It is a bitter irony that he should have to begin with bloodshed....Legation had many telephone calls asking for armed British intervention....I recommend that we should say as little as possible..."[54]

"Our impression yesterday," says U.S. Chargé d'Affaires Barnes in a telex to Washington, "was that in view of Nagy being blamed for calling in Soviet troops, that he lost a great deal of popularity; where he stands today and how the people would view a further retreat from Kádár to Nagy, we do not, (repeat not) know. We presume Nagy is to all intents and purposes Premier. Should the blame for the calling of Soviet troops now be placed on Gerő and he be made the scapegoat for all this which is going on now, and if he [Nagy] made further concessions, he might have a chance..."[55]

News of the Massacre Spreads

Just as the news of the apparent cease-fire had spread through Budapest and even to a few outlying towns, so news of the Parliament Square massacre spread and, thanks to the foreign radios, not just to the population of Budapest, but to the whole of Hungary. Workers who had been prepared to go back to work—a distinct minority—now vow not to go back until every last Soviet soldier has left the country. People know the ÁVO was involved in the massacre they expected as much and the ÁVO is already hated. But there has been no nationwide hatred of the Russians who have been living among them and have been dependent upon them for food and, in the cases of many officers, lodging. Now the ancient hatred is revived. Now the memory of Russia's treachery in 1849, kept alive in schoolbooks, is rekindled.

Radio Budapest goes through a great pretense that there is rejoicing in the streets at the news of Gerő's fall. Indeed, in some places there is genuine rejoicing. But something far more serious than the Party head's losing his job has taken place and the mood of the city has turned somber, as the hundreds of black flags carried by the crowds and hanging from the windows attest.

The fighting, re-ignited by the ÁVO and KGB General Serov in Parliament Square, takes on a grim and relentless character—for those who have the stomach for it. Many of the Soviets do not. Some individual soldiers defect, and those wounded and in Hungarian hospitals are terrified of being handed back for they fear Siberia, if not execution, on grounds of desertion. One wounded Russian soldier confesses to the twenty-two-year-old volunteer nurse who is tending him that his own officer had shot him when he refused to fight against the Hungarians.[56]

Károly Szabolcsi, who had been tear-gassed in front of the Radio, later wounded seriously enough to go to the hospital, is now "playing hooky" from that hospital. Having retrieved his rifle from its hiding place, he is on Lenin Square where he sees five Russian tanks, each flying a Hungarian flag. His fellow freedom fighters suspect a trick and fire a few shots at the tanks to see whether they will return the fire. They do not. Instead the hatches open and white handkerchiefs are waved. Their commander, a young lieutenant, says to some Russian-speaking civilians that they do not want to fight. "Kill them, kill them!" cry some in the crowd, but it is soon made clear to them that these Russians not only do not want to fight the Hungarians, they want the Hungarians to come to the Soviet Union and help them liberate their own people. Then and there they hand over the tanks to the crowd, which fortunately has enough individuals with military experience to operate them, and off they drive.[57]

Near the Kilián Barracks where Üllői Road meets the Ferenc József section of the Grand Boulevard (Nagykörút), two tram cars are jammed together. A Russian tank, which met its fate earlier this morning, is now part of the barricade. Imre Vizi, known to everyone there as "Railroad Worker"

(Vasutas), discovers a gasoline pump nearby and organizes the filling of empty bottles, which are taken from a neighborhood convenience store they break into for this purpose. Whether coming from Rákóczi Avenue, Üllői Road or up from Boráros Square on the river, every tank must slow down to no more than thirty-five kilometers an hour to navigate around this barrier. This means that very few vehicles can get by without being hit by one of the hundreds of "molotov cocktails" the insurgents have in store for them.[58]

On the opposite side of the river at Móricz Zsigmond Circle, some sixty students have devised a plan to trap fifteen Soviet tanks they know are headed their way. Empty cars and buses are positioned so that once the tanks are in the circle area they can quickly be pushed into position and overturned. The sixty students are joined by eighty more, summoned by radio, so there is sufficient manpower by the time the tanks arrive. The fourth and last barricade is only partially complete when the Soviets, now partially in the trap, catch on to what is going on. They let loose an ear-splitting volley of shells at this fourth obstacle, killing many of the students who are there. Now young boys rush out with buckets of soapy water that they deftly dump behind the lead tanks. The next tanks coming up on those in front, which have stopped to open fire, are unable to stop. Their treads skid and slip, causing them to crash into the stationary tanks. The tanks swing their turrets wildly, trying to get at the youngsters in the soap brigade, but these duck down and most of them escape. Now comes the barrage of molotov cocktails. The lead tanks shoot their way through the already damaged fourth barricade and those in the rear manage to back up and avoid the soapy cobblestones. Still, while many of the young freedom fighters are killed, three Soviet tanks are totally disabled and two more go off with flames burning on them.[59]

* * * *

Radio Budapest is still doing its best to convince the Freedom Fighters that stopping the fighting is the only sane course of action. It enlists the popular writer Gyula Hay, who only two weeks ago in Győr had helped to spark the revolution with his speech in the Jókai Theatre. Hay starts off by reminding his listeners that "I was among you, marching along with you on the streets of Budapest." Then he points out that "Radical changes are going on in state and party leadership. Our most important demands are being put into effect. Imre Nagy is our man, his program our program....You do not have to fear retaliation, yet there is no time to waste. We have to revert to peaceful means at the earliest possible moment, fighting should stop immediately. Not even quiet manifestations are suitable measures now because they can be misinterpreted." Hay does not say who will misinterpret them, but it is obvious that he fears the Soviets, ÁVO and hard-liners in the government are the ones who will choose to.[60]

The southern industrial area of Budapest known as Csepel has already provided many young worker/freedom fighters and many guns to the cause. The main business of today, since production has stopped, is the election of workers' councils. There are nearly forty thousand workers in eighteen different enterprises in Csepel, so the method of election is not always the same. Some members are elected in absentia, others find that as soon as they are elected they are bodily removed by other armed workers and taken to police stations to be put into custody. These latter usually turn out to be hard-line party members whom the Party, through Trade Union representatives, is trying to place on these new workers' councils so as to be able to control or at least hamper them. Once the basic shop councils have been elected, factory-wide councils must be elected from these. These, in turn, must elect a central Csepel workers' council. It is a process that will consume several days.[61] The first workers' council is founded on October 26.

The revolution comes late to the mining town of Pécs. Only this morning have the university students held a meeting in which they threw out the DISZ organization and established a chapter of MEFESZ. The new organization quickly decides to organize a mass meeting in the center of the town this afternoon.[62]

At the mineheads outside of town the miners call a meeting of the entire workforce. The Party secretary and the Director of the mines, however, decide to take advantage of this gathering. They insist that they be allowed to speak first. Knowing what they are going to say, the miners allow them. Sure enough, they call on the miners' patriotism and urge them to go back to work. But the miners are incensed over the massacre in Budapest. One burly fellow jumps up onto the podium and roughly pushes the Director aside. "We're not going down again into the mines until the Russian troops leave Hungary!" he shouts into the microphone. The miners roar their approval. Kálmán Hajnal,[63] a miner with communication responsibilities, rushes to the nearest phone and rings up all his friends in the different shafts around Pécs. Within a quarter of an hour all coal production has ceased in the entire Pécs coal basin. Thanks to the Russians and their continuing occupation, the strike will go on, not for days, or even weeks, but for months.[64]

The miners now go into town to attend a meeting called by the students. Though they are by far the largest contingent, together with the students, townspeople and some soldiers, their number comes to 40,000. Pécs has seen nothing like it since the end of the war. From this large and disorganized gathering they manage to elect a provisional revolutionary committee to run the town. Many of the town officials have disappeared or are keeping a low profile by staying home. Their work needs to be done.

But electing a Provisional Revolutionary Committee is not enough for this excited mass of people. They want action. A number of red stars begin to come crashing down off official buildings. This brings the arrival of an ÁVO detachment which tries to disperse the crowd by firing into the air. When this has little effect, they shoot into the crowd, killing four and wounding ten. The crowd is about to erupt, but before it has a chance to attack the ÁVO with bare hands, Col. Bradács, who is in charge, grabs the microphone and shouts that he wants to avoid any more bloodshed; that he, too, is in favor of the revolution. To prove this, he takes off his cap and rips the red star off it. All of his troops quickly follow his example. This quiets the crowd which then, all-too-naively, agrees to disperse.[65]

The citizens of Nyíregyháza near the Soviet Ukrainian border are beside themselves in frustration. People in other parts of the country are calling for a withdrawal of Soviet troops and all *they* see all day long is more troops pouring in from the Ukraine traversing their small city. An afternoon gathering of several hundred people in the town's center, through which the tanks and trucks are streaming, decides it is time they blocked the way of this insolent traffic. But when they put themselves across the road holding hands, the Soviet tanks simply shoot just above their heads and show no signs of stopping. There are, as yet, no freedom fighters in the area.[66]

The city of Sopron, even further to the west than Nyíregyháza is to the east, is a city surrounded on three sides by Austria, to whom—after the Treaty of Trianon—it briefly belonged, until its citizens voted to have it return to Hungary. As a consequence, reception of Western radios is better than in most parts of Hungary and the people are therefore well informed. Most of the local ÁVO are the Green Police border guards and there are no Russians near the town. Sopron, with its fifteenth century center intact, is famous for its school of forestry. There is considerable esprit de corps in this college of forestry, situated on the southwest edge of town in a beautiful forest-like campus, enclosed by walls and fences. The students threw out the DISZ some days ago and the MEFESZ is very active. But because the college is isolated from the town, and the faculty close to the student body, they have managed to keep the lid on while making the revolutionary transition with very little bloodshed. Though almost outside the territory of Hungary, Sopron succeeds in becoming something of a communications center in the days ahead.

The revolution's impact beyond the borders of Hungary, especially in those areas heavily populated by Hungarians, such as Slovakia, Transylvania (in Romania), Carpathian Ruthenia (then in the USSR) and the Voivodina (Vajdaság) and Banat in Yugoslavia, is considerable. Closest to Budapest is Slovakia.

While the Czechoslovak radio and press refer to events in Budapest only in the most cursory form, using the Soviet line that the "counterrevolution-aries" are being easily put down with the help of Soviet forces, there are numerous references to party meetings, pledges of loyalty taking place all around Czechoslovakia. There are also veiled threats that the regime is prepared to deal forcefully with any similar attempts in Czechoslovakia.

At Nickelsdorf on the Austro-Hungarian border a convoy of six Austrian cars loaded with Austrian, Dutch, Belgian, German and Swiss businessmen and tourists reaches the border. They are full of vivid descriptions of Budapest and the sights they have subsequently seen on the way to the border. Dozens of eager foreign journalists who have stationed themselves there now interview them. Werner Henne, a Swiss citizen from Berne, tells a reporter from the Vienna *Bildtelgraf* that he has seen with his own eyes the bodies of twenty insurgents strung up on flagpoles along the famous Corso and that when the radio station was finally retaken today some of the "Rioters" who were captured inside the building were hurled from the fourth floor windows.[67] One new detail is the sighting of many Soviet jet aircraft in the air.[68]

In Washington, D.C., after hours of consultation and editing by Secretary of State John Foster Dulles, President Eisenhower issues a statement on the situation in Hungary. In Budapest it is close to midnight, so few Hungarians learn of it until Friday, October 26. Much is what Barnes had written, though words like "fight in Hungary" are reduced to "development in Hungary." Then, in place of Barnes's "ruthless killing of unarmed Hungarians" passage, the statement reads: "The U.S. deplores the intervention of Soviet forces which under the treaty of peace should have been withdrawn, and the presence of which in Hungary is now demonstrated is not to protect Hungary against armed aggression from without, but rather to continue an occupation of Hungary by forces of an alien government for its own purposes." Eisenhower then adds "The heart of America goes out to the people of Hungary."[69]

About this time RFE monitors pick up a weak signal from northern Hungary which appears to come from Miskolc. The signal is very close to Radio Kossuth (Radio Budapest) and actually breaks in on top of a radio Budapest broadcast. A voice demands "put an end to the butchery...in Budapest....Soviet troops should be withdrawn" and "all those persons who were involved in the personality cult" should be "eliminated." Most of the broadcast is in the form of a series of demands.

The intermittent, fading voice calls for "a new government in the spirit of Béla Kun and László Rajk."

After less than an hour of broadcasting, the mysterious voice goes off the air, but before it does it identifies itself as the Miskolc studio of the Hungarian Radio broadcasting on the two-hundred-twenty-four-meter band."[70]

In Washington and New York, where it is still within diplomatic working hours, diplomats are taken up with the Hungarian situation. At 6:07 p.m. Secretary Dulles gets on the phone with the U.S. Ambassador to the UN, Henry Cabot Lodge, Jr. He tells him that the Department is thinking of bringing the Hungarian matter up before the Security Council. He is worried that people will say that these were great moments and these fellows were ready to stand up and die and we were caught napping and doing nothing.[71]

Around 7:00 p.m. Eastern Standard Time Secretary Dulles cables his ambassador in London:

> Please advise Selwyn Lloyd personally from me that developments in Hungary up to moment increasingly suggest desirability of inscription of matter on Security Council agenda...we should promptly focus UN attention on their situation and at the same time obtain an opportunity of informal talk with the Soviet Permanent Representative which might lead to an alleviation of the situation which is beginning to assume major dangerous implications. Would appreciate if possible a reply by 10:00 a.m. our time Saturday (October 27) as I am meeting with the President on this matter at 11:00.[72]

Revolution

About the same time in New York Ambassador Henry Cabot Lodge, Jr. is reacting to several possible scenarios suggested by the Department. In an early evening telex to Walter Walmsley in the Department of State he says:

> UN action would provide psychological benefits beyond what could be expected from unilateral U.S. action in support of Hungary because it is an expression of sympathy by many nations. Even if final action is blocked by a Soviet veto, the initiative would, in addition to increasing U.S. prestige, add to the prestige of the UN in the eyes of the satellite peoples, who now hold the organization in low esteem, because of its past failure to note their plight....

In Moscow, Nikita Khrushchev summons the Yugoslav Ambassador, Veljko Mićunović, despite the late hour. Hungary is virtually the only topic of conversation. Mićunović thinks that Khrushchev looks worried, to put it mildly. The Soviet leader says that blood has been shed in Hungary and accuses the West. Anti-Soviet elements have taken up arms against the socialist "camp" and the Soviet Union. He says the West is seeking revisions of the results of World War II and has started in Hungary. They will go on to crush each socialist state in Eastern Europe one by one. But the West, he says, has miscalculated. Will Mićunović please send a message to Tito about this situation and the Soviet Union's readiness to answer force with force? Khrushchev assures Mićunović that the whole Presidium feels this way. Though the Yugoslav feels this may be an exaggeration, he realizes that he is nonetheless to pass this on to Tito. Then Khrushchev adds that the Soviet Union will, of course, support a political solution in Hungary—if such is still possible. But it is clear to Mićunović that the Soviet leader has little faith in such a solution.[73]

* * * *

British journalist Noel Barber, who writes for the *London Daily Mail,* has been on his way to Budapest all day. A car had met him at the Vienna airport and driven him straight to the foggy border, which he crossed at 8:30 p.m. On his way to the capital he is stopped and searched eleven times, once so thoroughly that he has difficulty explaining to the Soviet officer, who speaks good German, why his suitcase has tiny animals, a bib and tiny dressing gown. He had left in such a rush he had forgotten to remove these items for his newborn baby.

Fatherhood is something new to Barber, a swashbuckling British foreign correspondent in the most flamboyant tradition. With eyes as wide as Orson Welles, without Welles' pop-eyed look, Barber's pugilistic features and stocky build attest to his attraction to action and danger.

As he enters the outskirts of Buda his headlights shine on wet, foggy streets with the stark evidence of war—broken windows, burnt out cars and trucks, electric poles torn down. In no time he finds his car enmeshed in a curtain of electric streetcar wires which his car is trailing along. Meant to ensnare Soviet tanks, they are even more effective in ensnaring the wheels and fenders of Barber's car. As he nears Adam Clark Square on the Buda side of the Chain Bridge his car gets stuck in a hole where Freedom fighters had removed cobblestones to make barricades. He switches off his lights to get out and try to free the car. As he does so he notices that in the square, which is actually a circle, three burned-out tram cars make a barricade behind which men could take cover and fire. Half a dozen large trees have been dropped across the road as another barricade and electric cables are strewn everywhere.

After freeing his car, Barber tries driving without lights. This is not a success. He soon hits what turns out to be a tree trunk, which dents his fender. He switches on his lights and inches forward until the Chain Bridge, enveloped in mist, is in view. There is a sudden crack of automatic fire from behind half a dozen barricades, followed quickly by an enormous roar from a tank halfway across the bridge. The shell whistles overhead and explodes on the hill behind. The Soviets have seen his lights.

Barber switches off the lights and ignition and dives behind his car. A barrage of machine-gun fire erupts from the nearby barricades in answer to the Soviet tank. After crouching there for a few minutes, Barber spots a small figure running across the square. It dives down next to him. The figure turns out to be a young woman in a dirty green raincoat with an automatic slung over her shoulder. In poor German she asks who he is.

When he answers "British," she whispers in heavily accented English: "You are hurt?"

"No, I'm fine."

"They fire on you, the Russkies. They always fire on automobile lights."

After the firing dies down she persuades him to get back into the car while she guides him, without lights, across the square and onto a side street where she has him park the car. Then she leads him down the side street to the Square. On impulse he stops to shake her hand and thank her. Her name is Ilona, twenty-two and already divorced. Later he discovers she has large gray eyes and tight black curls. She wears a cheap scarf knotted at her throat and slacks under her raincoat. Through the grime on her face he could see fine bone structure. Then he joins her walking across a carpet of broken glass to one of the barricades. Before they get there all hell breaks loose with an enormous clap. The Soviets have started firing again.

The two flop to the ground and then crawl the rest of the way to the barricade where, counting Ilona, there are nine Freedom Fighters, seven of whom are under twenty. One girl has a leg wound with blood seeping through the bandage. One boy, János, is only fifteen.

By 2:00 a.m. the moon becomes visible as the fog begins to thin. For the first time Barber can see some of the faces. One man, the only one besides Ilona not under twenty, turns out to speak excellent English. He is an economist, very neat with rimless glasses. His name is Dénes and Barber will later persuade him to become his guide and interpreter. Fifteen-year-old János, Barber discovers, has a freckled face and an infectious grin.

The group is spread out over three overturned trolley coaches. Most are in the center coach, but two, including János, are now in the right-hand one.

There is a terrifying roar, whistle and crash as a shell tears into the right-hand coach. The freedom fighters answer with their machine guns, but all the Russians are now inside their tanks. Ilona clutches Barber's arms. She is so apprehensive she can't move. Could he check on the two in the shattered coach?

He does and first finds a body without a head. Then he hears moaning and tears away at wreckage to get to it. János is still alive, but only just.

Barber lifts him up as gingerly as he can. János is trying to smile. "Ruszkik haza!" he gasps. Barber pillows his head and shoulders into his right arm and gives him a drink from his metal flask. Then he lights a cigarette and lets János take a few puffs. János clings to his gun and tries to grin. Barber, trying to hold back his tears, strokes the boy's hair until he finally slumps lifeless in the crook of his arm. It is 5:30 a.m. and the dawn of a new day.[74]

Budapest, Friday, October 26, 1956

The resumption of fighting, caused by the deliberate massacre in Parliament Square, has spread to all parts of the city. An enflamed, embittered populace now feels in total sympathy with the young fighters. As a gray, wet dawn seeps through the foggy metropolis, centers of resistance, where more or less constant fighting is in progress, become clearly apparent. In Pest there are not just the Corvin Cinema and Passage and the Kilián Barracks, where thousands of freedom fighters are congregated, but the nearby fighting groups of Tompa Street, under János Bárány, and the Tűzoltó Street under István Angyal, with less than a hundred Freedom Fighters each. In Buda the fighting groups are not only at Széna Square, where some two hundred teenagers serve under "Uncle Szabó," but groups on the Vár (Castle) Hill and at Móricz Zsigmond Square. Teenage girls and young women are in all of these groups, though more often as nurses and cooks than as fighters.

There are still many bodies in the streets. The bodies of Soviet soldiers are likely to have had lime strewn over them, whereas most of the Hungarian bodies are under national flags.

But wherever there are Soviet tanks—and they are at almost every major intersection and bridge—fighting is likely to break out at any minute. Moreover, hundreds of freedom fighters operating in small bands are fanning out across the city with slips of paper in their hands containing the addresses of specific ÁVO officers they are hunting down. Most of these Freedom Fighters are responsible in that they wish only to disarm and intern these men. They wish to see them given a fair trial so that they can get the justice they deserve. But there are some among them who secretly hope their prey will put up resistance, so that they can legitimately be killed.

And this morning there is a new, quite terrifying sound: the crump and crash of Soviet mortars on Gellért Hill and down in Csepel where they land. There is also an occasional thunderous barrage of Soviet light artillery and tank guns which shakes the ground both near the firing and where the shells hit, as often as not on buildings not even targeted. In such a warlike setting and with a constant drizzle of fine rain, it is astonishing to see how many people there are out on the streets. At 5:00 this morning the Radio announced that the "gradual restoration of order makes it possible for the people of Budapest to buy their most necessary goods between 9:00 a.m. and 2:00 p.m."[75] Now huge bread lines, peopled largely by old women, are forming in all parts of the city.

Noel Barber, after forty minutes of deep sleep in Ilona's apartment and a cup of steaming tea, has managed to reach the Duna Hotel by detouring way up to the Stalin Bridge, not yet controlled by the Soviets. Dénes is with him and they set out for a tour of the inner city. Barber is amazed at the number of burned out cars, the amount of broken glass and torn-up cobblestones that he is forced to maneuver around. The radio has talked of some looting, so at one corner, when Dénes spots two kids trying to force open a shop window, he says "Stop the car! I have to give those boys a good thrashing." But it seems they are not trying to loot at all. Both are under ten. One holds some black bread crusts, the other a cigarette tin full of water. They are trying to feed a puppy trapped in the closed shop.

In the next street Barber counts the bodies of fifteen teenagers strewn around three burned-out Soviet tanks. And just around the corner: a long bread line. Later in the day as they are walking back to the hotel from the British Legation they see a small car being stopped by a group of men, some with guns. Suddenly the cry goes up "Death to the ÁVO!" They swoop in on the car, pull the man out. In no time the group has swollen to over 100. Someone fires a pistol shot into the gas tank and the car bursts into flames. Then the crowd sets on the man, who tries to run, but is easily caught and quickly beaten to death. He is left, a twisted heap on a mound of broken glass.[76]

*   *   *   *

Szabad Nép is publishing again. Radio Budapest broadcasts excerpts of its lead article entitled "Order and Peace are Needed." "Enough bloodshed!" it begins. "…the premiership of Imre Nagy, the replacement of Ernő Gerő, the first declarations of Imre Nagy and János Kádár, and the expected reform of the government show that we have at last begun to take the right measures." But instead of spelling out what the right measures are, the Party newspaper falls back on the usual communist euphemisms and jargon.[77]

Over in Buda, the last train allowed into Budapest pulls into the South Station. All other trains for the next few days are stopped by the Soviets at the outskirts and the passengers forced to walk into the city. Railway employees help the Freedom Fighters in the area to decouple three of its cars—a Pullman, a modified sleeping car and a mail car—and push them onto tracks leading into the streetcar lines. From here it is an easy task to push them downhill through Moscow Square to Széna Square where they crash into a disabled Soviet tank. They become not only a barricade, but an obstacle which stops or slows Soviet tanks for the rest of the Revolution. On the far side is a temporary building at a subway construction site where the Freedom Fighters set up a machine gun. Using buildings around the square, they are able to shoot from three directions at anything approaching the square.[78]

At the Kilián Barracks on Üllői Ave and the nearby Corvin Cinema and Passage on Ferenc and József Boulevard there is almost constant gunfire. The use of molotov cocktails has become so deadly that Soviet tanks no longer try to rush through with their guns blazing, but are keeping their distance and firing only when they see something move. Since the Freedom Fighters do not yet have full underground passages through the area—many cellar walls still need to have holes knocked through them—movement above ground is occasionally necessary.

At the Corvin Passage

The Corvin Passage fighters have captured a seventy-six-millimeter field gun that they use as an anti-tank gun. They have no armor-piercing shells, but they can disable a tank by blowing off its treads. The problem is, Soviet machine guns take a heavy toll of the crew while they are trying to aim the gun. One of the reasons for Gergely Pongrátz's rapid rise to leadership is his quick solutions for problems. In this case his solution is: the gun to be aimed at exactly where a tank first comes into view, and long rope lanyard to be pulled from a secure position behind a wall, and a lookout on the second floor with the same sightline as the gun. He calls "Fire," the lanyard is pulled and almost every time a tank is crippled. Molotov cocktails finish the job.[79]

But the large number of tanks that attack is discouraging; they just keep coming. After a while there are so many crippled hulks of burning tanks that the new tanks cannot get near. Still the shelling from those tanks in the distance causes tremendous damage to the buildings and dust and smoke envelop the broad streets for hours at a time. Casualties, too, are heavy, for there are freedom fighters in or near almost every window. Despite these losses, morale is high.

There are intervals between attacks when the freedom fighters cheer and come out into the street to retrieve what booty they can. But soon there is another assault and they must scurry back to their posts. It is late afternoon when the last attack comes. Compared to the others, it seems mercifully brief.

The fact that the Russians are taking such heavy losses after three full days of fighting and without any real progress is a thorn in the side of the Soviet military. It has obvious career implications for the senior officers.

Yet, without infantry, or totally destroying the area with shells and bombs—which they do not want to have to do—the Soviets are beginning to understand, they will never be able to conquer the area. Only the Hungarian Army has the necessary infantry on hand. So Soviet General Mikhail Malinin finds it necessary to involve his Hungarian counterpart, Major General István Kovács. Planning begins today for a final assault on the area.

*   *   *   *

In three days of fighting an extraordinary rapport has sprung up between members of the individual "battalions" of fighters. Even smaller units have a remarkable variety of people in them. One "Corvinist" recalls the tragic betrayal of a group of four youths who were on guard duty in their hideout near Soroksár when one close range burst of Russian machine gun fire killed them all. When their bodies were recovered for burial it was found that one was a worker, one was a student, one a peasant boy and the fourth a humble gypsy worker. Here is the revolution encapsulated.[80] No one knows or cares about another's background, religion or politics. No one knows his friends' real names. Everyone goes by nicknames made up on the spot, which stick to them so that they even introduce themselves to newcomers as: "Conductor," "Spectacles," "Cloth Cap," "Stump Hand," "Tall Man," "Frog Face," "Railroad" or "Moustache," the last being Gergely Pongrátz's nickname.[81] All of this will be a boon later when they are able to deny truthfully in trials that they never knew so-and-so and cannot have real names tortured out of them. But now it is a mark of camaraderie and a clean break with the past.

During a lull in the fighting Ödön Pongrátz, a Corvin commander with a heavily lined face and full moustache who is a natural leader, sends over thirty Freedom Fighters to the Kilián Barracks to take up positions there. (Pongrátz is the oldest of six brothers, all of whom are taking part in the revolution. His twenty-four-year-old brother, Gergely, known as "Moustache" because of his larger, drooping moustache, is also a natural leader. Both are numbered among the commanders of the Corvin Passage.) Ödön Pongrátz is astounded when Col. Maléter has their arms taken from them and sends them back with the explanation that only soldiers can fight at the barracks, no civilians. Pongrátz, who has twice been in the Army, and thus knows the importance of military discipline, is nonetheless offended. He is particularly bitter, too, because it was he, long before Maléter arrived, who persuaded many of the recruits to join the revolution.

Both Pongrátz and Maléter find it necessary to discipline some of their youngest volunteers. Pongrátz later today catches a young boy who has stolen a pair of shoes from a nearby apartment. He confiscates the shoes and the boy's rifle and demotes him from "fighter" to gasoline bottle filler. He explains to the boy and his companions that if he is interested in new shoes or any other property he makes two mistakes: first, he takes someone else's property and second, he is diverted from the main task of defending his country and its freedom, in which one has a choice of whether or not to seize things. He then has the boys vote on who should get the shoes, and they soon decide on one of their number whose shoes are falling apart.[82]

In Maléter's case the disciplining comes only later, after Nagy and he have accepted the revolution on October 28 and begin to appreciate the contribution that these incredibly brave young volunteers are making. Only after the fighting are they welcomed back into the barracks. When Maléter hears or suspects any of the young boys of looting he makes a speech about it. When they appear to object to his attitude he seizes the most obvious culprits, empties their pockets of jewelry and valuables, slaps their faces and says: "You have no business being here! This is not allowed here! Get out!"[83]

The Mosonmagyaróvár Massacre

Out in the countryside, except for the immediate area around Budapest and a few cities occupied by the Soviets, the revolution is proceeding apace. Manifestations, which took place in the larger towns several days ago, are now taking place in the villages. There are basically three reactions: where there is little unrest and the party is so well entrenched that any manifestation is quickly snuffed out; where the Party leadership simply gives way peacefully to the rebels who take over; and third, areas where the Party and the ÁVO try, but fail, to suppress the revolution and conflict erupts before the local insurgents triumph.

Western travelers have the impression that most of the western section of Hungary, known as Dunántúl, or by its Roman name, Pannonia, is now in the hands of the Freedom Fighters. If one judges by the flags, destroyed Soviet memorials and partisan roadblocks, this is true. But the Hungarian Army, which is still largely neutral, is still intact, and the ÁVO, though most of its members have changed into regular police uniforms, has not yet disappeared.

Revolution

In the small town of Mosonmagyaróvár (population 22,000) just eighteen kilometers from the Austrian border, workers from the local bauxite factories and students from the local agricultural college have already held a silent demonstration last night. The Petőfi National Song was recited and the national anthem sung. Now, at 9:30 a.m. a large group of workers, on strike for the past three days, visit the agricultural college to get the students to join them in a demonstration in the center of town. From there they will march to the Level Street Security Police barracks on the edge of town, where they propose to take down the red star and replace it with a green-white-red national flag. Professor K. Papp, head of the Marxism-Leninism Department, tries to dissuade the students, but he has little influence on them. While he dislikes her intensely, he nevertheless enlists the services of Prof. Katalin Gieber, a twenty-six-year-old unmarried teacher, who is one of the faculty members most popular with the students. When she hears where they are headed she tells them she doesn't think it's a good idea. For two days she has chased away machine-gun bearing ÁVO soldiers who have tried to enter the college to prevent the students from listening to the radio. She wants nothing more to do with them. Professor Gieber finally agrees to go with the demonstration on one condition: that anyone, including the young workers, who has a weapon discard it now.

This done, the students march solemnly down through the gates of the modern part of the campus, joining the workers in the road. Flags are carried, but there is no shouting of slogans; this is also to be a silent demonstration. The roadway is wet from an early morning drizzle. There is no particular ceremony in front of the town hall; it is merely a meeting point. The crowd by now is well over a thousand. It is joined by many townspeople along the way, old people, mothers with children, people of all ages, so that it soon doubles in size. They are walking on a main road and bus route passing many houses. The barracks is a good three kilometers from the town center. People are talking quietly with people next to them and Professor Gieber keeps muttering that "this doesn't sound good, guys. Let's go back." "Are you scared Professor?" asks one of the students, and of course she replies that she isn't. Then one of the old bauxite workers, who has heard her, turns and says, "My dear, why are you afraid? My son is a soldier here, too. He won't shoot at his own father."

Not far from the barracks Prof. Gieber notices her colleagues, Prof. Papp and Assistant Prof. Indics, coming back against the flow of the crowd. She

197

tells her students she doesn't "like the look of this, they seem to know something we don't."

As the barracks comes into view around the curve of the road an ÁVO officer can be seen standing in front of the building obviously expecting them. Three or four of the leaders of the march go up to the gate and the officer, hands held over his head, comes out to greet them. Words are exchanged and then several embraces. The officer is a resident of the town. He joins in singing the national anthem. Then he listens while the leaders read the sixteen-point demands from Budapest. Then suddenly, he pulls the leaders aside, and as the marchers press forward he pulls out his pistol and shoots into the air.

Within a split second thirty ÁVO soldiers and officers open fire with machine guns. They fire from shallow trenches in front of the building and from the windows of the barracks. It is like shooting fish in a barrel, for the area in which the front portion of the crowd is contained, between houses on one side and the fence on the other, is no more than fifteen meters in diameter. With the marchers pushing up from behind, escape to the rear is impossible. Soon after the first burst of gunfire doubles up those in the front and sends the rest to the ground in desperation, hand grenades are tossed into the seething mass of humanity. In a series of horrible detonations the exploding grenades sever limbs and hands and mutilate bodies already spouting blood. After a brief pause in which those who can try to get up to run or crawl away, another blast of machine gun fire cuts them all down. Bits of human flesh are strewn around as the bullets tear into their innocent victims.

A British journalist intent on getting his reports and pictures out of Hungary happens to be passing Mosonmagyaróvár, on his way to the Austrian border, when he hears the guns fire and sees a flock of frightened crows suddenly wheel into the sky. He swings the car around and in five minutes is on the scene. What he sees makes him vomit. A whole field of moving, dying bodies, their limbs wriggling. He is reminded of freshly caught fish flopping in the bottom of a boat. Some ÁVO men are nonchalantly carrying their two machine guns from the trenches back into the barracks.

Katalin Gieber is one of the first to be hit. Some students see blood coming out of her mouth and help her to a covered bus stand some five or six meters away. An exploding bullet has mutilated one hand, her other arm is so badly hit that only an artery connects the upper and lower halves. But worst of all, a whole clip of bullets has penetrated her chest, piercing at least one lung. Fortunately, she is among the first dragged to safety, for she would never have survived the second withering blast of machine gun fire.

Though there must be an ambulance in a town this size, none comes. Instead she is removed with others by truck to the town hospital. There she will receive appallingly bad care with one doctor, Dr. Ágoston Munka, instead of consoling his patients, telling them he ought to slap their faces instead of tending their wounds, for getting into such a predicament. The only care she receives is to have her wounds sutured—repeatedly—when infection makes reopening mandatory. Dr. Munka refuses to send her to the much better hospital in Győr, to which he sends many less badly wounded than she. When, in his absence, another doctor sneaks her off to Győr for her tenth operation, pieces of her coat are removed from her main wound.

Survivors of the massacre phone for help from the nearest city, Győr. Attila Szigethy, head of the revolutionary National Council there, dispatches six small scout cars with armed Freedom Fighters under the command of Gábor Földes and Árpad Tihanyi. Together with townspeople who have just been given guns from the local Army garrison, they lay siege to the barracks. The confrontation is brief. The ÁVO know they are badly outnumbered and there is no escape. Some twenty surrender and are taken into custody. Of the four officers, one has been killed, and the commandant, Captain Dudás, who had given the signal for the massacre, has somehow managed to escape. He tore off his tunic and other insignia which might identify him as ÁVO and ran to an ambulance that was just coming up. He pushed the driver into the street and raced into town as though headed for the hospital. He sped on, stopping only when he reached the border of Czechoslovakia. Others say he escaped in his own car.

A third quite badly wounded ÁVO officer, Lieutenant Stefko, is found hiding in the cellar, and the fourth, Lieutenant Gyenes, is caught in an office on the third floor. He shows fear, but not the slightest regret over what has happened. Suddenly he lunges for the window and plunges out. Whether to commit suicide or attempt to escape makes little difference, for his groaning body is quickly stomped on by a hundred boots. Later a picture, taken through the window from which he had jumped, shows a muddy, bloody body sprawled on its back on a wet, muddy pavement, its rubber overcoat hunched up around the shoulders baring a white belly. The body is encircled by several score of Basque berets and workman's caps looking down at it. The picture will become known around the world.

The wounded ÁVO officer is taken with the rest of the wounded to the small hospital and kept isolated from the rest for his own safety.

A total of eighty-two people, including small children and one eighteen-month-old baby, have been slaughtered. Another two hundred have been wounded, twelve so seriously that they die within twenty-four hours, bringing the total killed to ninety-four. The call to neighboring cities goes out, for no rural hospital could ever be prepared for such a disaster. The call soon reaches neighboring Austria and within hours the Austrian Red Cross has put out an emergency call for Austrians to donate blood. In the meantime, serum, bandages and morphine are dispatched to the town as quickly as possible.

In the U.S. many hours later, Ellsworth Bunker, President of the American Red Cross, will announce that he is authorizing the International League of the Red Cross to spend up to $25,000 as an initial American contribution for emergency supplies for the Hungarian injured.[84]

When Western correspondents arrive the next day they find piles of limbs, bodies laid out in the local church, bodies stacked up in the local morgue and nearly all of them with their dried blood not yet washed off. The weeping and anguish of their families is indescribable.

News of this latest ÁVO brutality travels quickly around the country. By evening even Radio Free Europe is telling what it has learned of the massacre. In Budapest the news has the effect of switching the Freedom Fighters' fury back onto the Secret Police, intensifying the hunt already in progress.

At Party Headquarters on Akadémia Street the Central Leadership, or Political Committee, of the Party Central Committee is in session. The comrades seem hopelessly divided.

After many hours of acerbic and, what seems at times, surreal debate, Nagy and his colleagues succeed in getting the committee to approve a statement which is broadcast by Radio Budapest at 3:45 in the afternoon. That statement says in part:

1. The Central Committee...suggests...to the Presidential Council that it formulate propositions with the view to the election of a new national government...this latter...will create an independent, free, democratic and socialist country...

2. This new government will start conversations with the Soviet government in order to establish relations between the two countries on the basis of complete equality of rights and non-interference in internal affairs...

3. The Central Committee approves the elections of workers' councils in the factories with the cooperation of the trade union organizations....It is necessary before all to adjust the lowest pay.

4. The government grants amnesty to all who took part in the armed struggle. (The statement then adds that this applies only to those who lay down their arms by 10:00 p.m. tonight.)

5. The Central Committee and government...express their firm resolve to defend the conquests of our popular democracy and not to deviate from the cause of socialism."[85]

In Washington

In far off Washington, where it is still morning, the 301st meeting of the National Security Council has been hearing Allen W. Dulles, Director of the Central Intelligence Agency (and also younger brother of John Foster Dulles), explain about what has taken place in Poland and Hungary. "The Hungarian revolt," says Dulles, "may demonstrate the inability of a moderate national Communist regime to survive in any of the satellites. What has happened would seem to indicate only two alternatives: One, either to return to a hard Stalinist regime, or two, to permit developments in the direction of genuine democracy....The Revolt in Budapest has early taken a far more serious turn than that in Warsaw. Indeed, I believe that the revolt in Hungary constitutes the most serious threat yet to be posed to continued Soviet control of the satellites. It confronts Moscow with a very harsh dilemma: Either to revert to a harsh Stalinist policy, or to permit democratization to develop in the satellites to a point which risks the complete loss of Soviet control..."

The President inquires whether Dulles has had any information about Czech reaction to these events. Dulles replies:

"I have had very little on this point. In any event, practically all the potential Gomułkas have been pretty well slaughtered..."

Governor Harold Stassen, President Eisenhower's assistant for disarmament, asks: "In view of the great significance of what is taking place in Hungary and Poland, would it not be advisable for you, Mr. President, to call a special meeting of the National Security Council to discuss the whole problem of Hungary and Poland?"

"I'm not sure," President Eisenhower replies, "that discussion in the National Security Council is the best initial step. I do believe that the responsible departments and agencies should proceed at once to formulate the clearest possible analysis of what has happened in these two countries. Such an analysis can then be presented to the National Security Council. I think such a procedure would be better than plunging right into discussion of these difficult subjects."

Governor Stassen points out that "the basic decisions will have to be taken presently by the Soviet Union. They will either have to revert to the old harsh policy of Stalin...or else they will have to let things go on as they are going."

"If the Soviets do revert to Stalin's policies," replies Eisenhower, "they would stand bankrupt before the whole world." Then he turns to a slightly different topic. "I have a memorandum on my desk about another question which concerns me which is being posed by the Soviet Union. In view of the serious deterioration of their position in the satellites, might they not be tempted to resort to very extreme measures and even precipitate a global war?...After all, Hitler had known well from the first of February 1945 that he was licked. Yet he carried on to the very last and pulled down Europe with him in his defeat. The Soviets might even develop some desperate mood such as this."

"Well," replies Stassen, "wouldn't it be prudent to get some message to Marshal Zhukov indicating that the achievement of freedom in the Soviet Satellites should not be considered as posing any real threat to the national security of the USSR?"

"No," replies Eisenhower, after some reflection, "I don't believe such a move would be worthwhile. I doubt the Soviet leaders genuinely fear an invasion by the Western powers." Eisenhower will change his mind on this after Stassen does some more lobbying and convinces the Secretary of State of its efficacy.[86]

Back in Budapest, Marian Bielicki, reporting for the Polish student magazine *Po Prostu*, is accompanying the first shipment of blood plasma and medicines from Warsaw to Budapest. As the Polish plane lands he can make out a group of people near a blue bus, with white flags and red crosses. He writes:

In the distance we hear machineguns. A heavy tank drives in; from the other side an armored car; soldiers with red-starred helmets jump out and surround our plane. Light machineguns are pointed at us. The soldiers faces are covered with dirt; they are unshaven and sweating. My heart beats. Why are they pointing their weapons at me? An officer in a leather coat leaps out from the tank and explains that they have come to insure the security of the plane...I look at the faces of the Soviet soldiers. I see not only tiredness on their faces, not only the burden of days spent in fighting and under fire, but their eyes express insecurity, something uncomfortable, something which suggests how ill at ease they feel in their present role. It is not only my impression; my friend R. feels it too: the Russian uncertainty, and the stiff, silent hatred of a group of Hungarians...

We had left Warsaw convinced that Hungary had become peaceful, and here before reaching Budapest, we hear about the war, about "front lines." We hear shooting. E. takes me aside towards a young woman in a dark blue coat over a white nurse's uniform. The woman speaks slowly, but with obvious emotion: "You are a journalist—you simply don't have the right to lie! It is a lie that fascist and counter-revolutionaries are fighting in the city. We are fighting, our nation is fighting, for *real* democracy, for real socialism, for freedom and independence! You will be convinced about this yourself. Our aims are the same as your own nation put forward..." The woman (a surgeon, as I learned later) goes off to the Red Cross bus. A big, black motorcar of our Polish Embassy is waiting for us; we follow the bus. There is deadly silence in our car.

In front of us is the road to Budapest. At the Soviet post, heavy weapons, several nests of machineguns. All the soldiers are in position, with their fingers on the trigger. An officer with a small machinegun and several soldiers come forward, their guns pointing at us: "From the Polish Embassy?" He takes a rapid look at the passengers. We can proceed. Two kilometers further, at a crossroad, we are stopped again. Another armed checkpoint: "Lengyel? [Pole?]" Friendly, smiling faces. "Poles are friends. Poles are brothers." This happens again and again before our car enters the streets of a workers' suburb.

Long walls of empty factories. Little houses in front of which a few people hover, ready to hide. Something uncanny in the air. An atmosphere that I cannot yet divine. Is it horror, fear, hatred or despair? Behind the iron gates of one of the industrial works, a group of armed people. They explain they are workers who are defending their factories....At one of the insurgent posts, we are advised to take a longer road because on Üllői Ave. there is heavy fighting going on between Hungarian soldiers defending their barracks, and Soviet tanks…From windows and balconies, heavy wet flags are drooping, green-white-red, and also black colors of mourning. The symbol of freedom and the symbol of death, the price of freedom….

One thing emerges from all the chaotic information—the whole nation is on the side of the insurgents. The division is clear: the nation on one side, and on the other, the Stalinist faction of the government and the ÁVO. There are thousands of communists among the insurgents. The Hungarian Army is either neutral or takes the side of the revolution. The workers have occupied their own plants. The whole working class and youth and students are on the barricades…[87]

*　*　*　*

All western radios by now have carried President Eisenhower's statement so that few Hungarians are unaware of it, even if few know quite what he said. In Strasbourg the Council of Europe passes a resolution, part of which concerns East-West relations which, while not specifically mentioning Hungary, calls on European nations "to examine as a matter of urgency" what is now going on.[88] In Paris, French Foreign Minister Christian Pineau, in answer to a reporter's question, says yes, Britain, France and the United States may soon take the matter of Soviet intervention in Hungary to the United Nations.[89] In Rome, Italian Foreign Minister Gaetano Martino says in the Italian parliament that "the Warsaw Pact can in no way justify the intervention of Russian troops" in Hungary. Italy does not wish to "interfere in the internal affairs of another country" but "has the right and duty to voice its concern, and its solidarity with the victims of the brutal slaughter which has occurred….Foreign intervention in Hungary" has produced "one of the most tragic repressions in history."[90] Without consulting any other member of the United Nations, Franco's Spanish cabinet announces that it will put the matter of Soviet actions in Poland and Hungary before the UN.[91]

In neutral Austria, which had seen the Soviet occupation troops leave only a year and a half ago, the respected newspaper *Die Presse* declares rather audaciously: "The weakness of communism was never more evident than it is now in Budapest, where the Prime Minister receives counter-revolutionaries and accepts their terms, where the Defense Minister has to set a deadline for his troops to quell the revolt, and where the Communist Party Central Committee has to fire the Party boss under popular pressure while fighting is still going on. This should serve as a lesson for Moscow…"[92] In

West Berlin, the *Morgenpost* writes that "the intervention of Soviet forces in Poland and Hungary reveals the real purpose of the Warsaw Pact." The *New York Times*, meantime, in comparing the situations in Poland and Hungary, repeats what has become (partially due to RFE's faulty appraisal) the American belief that Nagy called in the Russians when it states: "The difference is that Nagy and Kádár have had to call out Russian tanks and Russian troops to kill patriotic Hungarians in the streets of Budapest. They come to power with hands stained with the blood of their people, acting not as men who defy Moscow, but as men who have admitted that their survival in power is made possible only by the occupying Russian forces. The difference is a major one....It cannot fail to...influence our own people's attitude toward the two regimes installed this week." For the Hungarian exiles at RFE such an editorial is grist for their mill, and they give it extensive play on the air.

* * * *

After a day of heavy fighting at the complex of Freedom Fighter strong points around the Corvin Cinema and the Kilián Barracks, internal troubles develop. Fifteen-year-old Tamás Szabó has had enough harrowing experiences today to last a lifetime. These include being trapped by and then killing, in a desperate shoot-out, the ÁVO man who had been involved in his deportation, being captured and held with others in the East Station and then being liberated and able to return to his base. Now he recognizes a man trying to get into the stronghold, but who does not know the password, as one of his captors at the East Station. When the man pulls a gun the guards kill him. Captain János-Kovács, who comes to see what has happened, finds an incriminating piece of paper in the man's jacket pocket. He calls his company into the Prater School gymnasium. There he announces:

"Comrades, we have a traitor among us. I have just learnt this from a paper found on the man you just shot. Lock the doors, and tell me what should be done with a traitor."

"Death," they reply almost in unison.

The Captain raises his hand and asks for silence. Then he takes the paper from his pocket and reads the name of a person he seems not to know. At the same time a scuffle breaks out near one of the exits. He calls again for silence, but those in the scuffle do not hear him, so he takes out his revolver and fires it twice into the ceiling. But it is too late for the unfortunate traitor, who has been hideously mutilated by those who had caught him trying to escape. "You should not have done that," says Ivan Kovács, "even if he deserved it. Take his body away."[93]

Later, as night comes onto Budapest there is a flare-up at the Kilián Barracks. But no Soviets are involved. Col. Pál Maléter, who took over command at the Kilián Barracks yesterday, takes a dim view of most of the so-called Freedom Fighters.

A tall, slender military man, of ramrod straight bearing, Maléter had been a Horthyite officer who had fought alongside Hitler's Armies in Russia and been wounded and captured by the Russians. After some time in prison camp he threw in his lot with the Soviets and was trained to parachute into Transylvania to lead the partisans already fighting there. His skill was legendary, for not only had he won many small battles, he had not lost a single soldier by the end of the war. Known for his ambition, he volunteered for, or was given, jobs others avoided. On October 25 Major General Tóth sent him, now a thirty-six-year-old Colonel, to the Kilián Barracks where some eight hundred soldiers, recruited only three weeks ago and basically unarmed, were billeted. Their officers had deserted them on the twenty-fourth when some of them had gone over to the insurgents. Maléter's orders were to get rid of any fraternizing insurgents, take command and defend the barracks from the revolutionaries.

When he arrived with his three tanks and fellow officers on October 25, two burnt-out Soviet tanks blocked his way. He was disgusted at the carnage he saw, bodies not of fascists, but mostly children strewn around the battle scarred Üllői Road. Inside the two end sections he found not just the labor conscripts, but a number of students and a few young workers, as well. These had persuaded many of the recruits to join the insurgents. Maléter was faced with a stark choice: risk a lot of bloodshed in getting rid of the insurgents and their soldier sympathizers, or work out some compromise to get rid of them. The Soviets seemed to be observing an unofficial truce at this point, so he was able to sit down and talk. He could not convince them that their cause was hopeless and that they should lay down their arms, but he could discourage many of them from using the barracks as a fortress against the Soviets. In the end he agreed to let them stay if it was clearly understood that he was in command and it was to be a strictly military installation. Anyone who had prior military training was free to stay, all others should clear out and all "these children" should be sent home.

Now, two days later in the early evening, some of those serving under him take his disdain for the scruffy, neighboring Freedom Fighters a bit too far by firing on two boys from Corvin who are approaching the barracks without prior notification. One is killed and the other badly wounded. Ödön Pongrátz is incensed and orders his men to return the fire. He then sends an ultimatum to Maléter to hold his men's fire or else Pongrátz will turn their two captured anti-tank guns on the barracks. When this does not appear to have had any response, Pongrátz has one shot fired at the barracks. It makes quite a hole in one of the walls. That brings on a quick, though uneasy, truce between the two strongholds.[94]

His brother Gergely has a different version, or possibly a different incident, which he claims happens on the same evening.

Whatever the truth of these incidents, there is obvious bad blood between the Corvin Freedom Fighters and Maléter.[95]

Mikoyan Reports

Anastas Mikoyan, in his report to the Soviet Central Committee today, states the following alternatives in his reaction to demands to change the Hungarian government:

> Two possible routes lie ahead of us: one is to reject these demands, not to change the composition of the government and to continue the struggle relying on the Soviet army. If we do so, we will lose the trust of the peaceful population—workers, university students—and there will be further victims, which will further enlarge the chasm between the government and the population. If we go down this road, we will lose.
>
> That is why the Hungarian comrades feel that the other road is acceptable: to bring a few democrats into the government, believers in people's democracy, from former petit-bourgeois parties, from intellectual, student and workers' circles—five or six people in a government of twenty to twenty-two members.
>
> In reply to our warning that the inclusion of bourgeois democrats is a slippery slope, that we must be careful lest they fall and lose the respect of the masses, Nagy said that this step is being taken at its very minimum, as a last resort. So that the leadership will not fall from our hands....
>
> We have already informed you of the Soviet troop withdrawal. We were not informed of the changes in the government by the leadership—it seems they only inform us once they have made a decision. We have asked Comrade Nagy, and he has promised that they will avoid making any deci-

sion on this issue before we arrive [at the Hungarian leadership meeting understood].

Then Mikoyan, doubtless because he has been deliberately misinformed by the Soviet military, which does not wish to admit the difficulties it is encountering, puts on rose-colored glasses to report to his Soviet colleagues:

> The military opposition has been successfully liquidated. The troops have no direct military targets, only small, dispersed conflicts, shots fired from roofs at various points in the city. There are small partisan actions and small bands of counter-revolutionary bands hiding in houses and the disarming of the population has fallen to the police and civic organizations. This is the job of local organizations, not the troops, who can at most just help.[96]

In the U.S. Embassy in Moscow, Ambassador Charles ("Chip") Bohlen cables the U.S. State Department: "It appears more likely the Soviet Government has decided to cut its losses in the forlorn hope that Nagy, by placing himself at the head of a popular revolution, may be able to prevent the complete collapse of the regime. They (the Soviets) can hardly have much confidence in this possibility, but in the circumstances they may well have to come to the conclusion that it is preferable to a total military occupation of Hungary."[97]

Hungarian Exiles Take Action

Hungarians in the Western world are doing all they can to bring aid to their country. Monsignor Béla Varga, President of the Hungarian National Council in the U.S. and former President of the Hungarian Parliament, again writes to Secretary John Foster Dulles. "It is the fourth* day of the waging of regular warfare by the Soviet Red Army against the Hungarian nation," he begins. The Council is asking Dulles to "1. Take action with the United Nations Security Council in order to prevent further bloodshed in Hungary...." and 2. "insist with the United Nations that the Hungarian civilians and armed forces, which are fighting for the restoration of national independence and human freedom, be declared to be a regular national force and not individual criminals to be convicted on the basis of the Hungarian penal code..."

In Paris, where he happens to be attending a congress of the International Peasant Union, Ferenc Nagy, the last freely elected Premier of Hungary, sug-

---

* Actually, it is the third.

gests that the U.S. should take a direct approach to the Soviet Union in order to get a cease-fire. Unfortunately, like most former heads of state, he cannot conceive of any plan that does not involve himself playing a key role. If the U.S. will approach the Soviets directly, he tells American Ambassador Douglas Dillon, then he will agree to broadcast to Hungary over VOA and RFE appealing to both Hungarian sides to lay down their arms. He is confident that his old friend Béla Kovács would consent to a request from himself to serve as mediator between the two opposing Hungarian sides. He feels that if the two Hungarian sides can be brought together, they can present a united front to the Soviets. Dillon passes this information on to Washington for what it is worth, in hopes of getting a response he can give to Ferenc Nagy.[98]

In Hungary, members of the Hungarian Central Committee, particularly the Stalinist members, are as out-of-touch with what is transpiring in their country as the exile Ferenc Nagy, but with less excuse; they at least live in Hungary. As members of an elite which considers reality to be what the Party says it is, they have no conception of what their compatriots have suffered over the past ten years. And most importantly, they are confined to the communist controlled media for their information. Even when they can see that little of what their media says is true, they dare not listen to Western radios nor read non-communist periodicals, lest they be found out and accused of anti-party actions, which could lead to serious consequences.

The general population is not so hampered. Though they have difficulty hearing the Voice of America and Radio Free Europe and the BBC, because of the jamming, they have learned where reliable information can be gotten. The people, through word of mouth, the telephone and letters, talk to one another, at least close friends and family. And news from the West, especially news about what is happening in Hungary, travels quickly. Thus it is not via Radio Budapest that the provinces learn of what has been happening in Budapest these past few days. Tamás Szabó now finds this out for himself when a friend sharing guard duty with him tells him, "Somebody told me that the situation is the same in all the big towns as it is in Budapest. A chap living in this block—I had a few words with him on the way down to the cellars—even said the whole of western Hungary would soon be in the hands of the revolutionaries."

"How can he possibly know if he's never been out of his cellar?" asks Tamás.

"They've got a radio set and they listen to 'Free Europe' programs. It was announced on that. It was also reported that a lot of Russian soldiers were fighting on the side of the Revolutionaries."

"I haven't seen a single one doing that," says Tamás. " I can't believe it."

"Don't be silly. They're not all bad, even here, in the Kilián Barracks. Apparently Maléter has specified in his armistice conditions that these Russian soldiers must be given the right to seek asylum in Hungary."[99]

At RFE in Munich, staff members are reading the latest account of the day's events in Hungary and current analysis of the situation written by William E. Griffith, Political Advisor. The "situationer" begins: "Telephone, telegram and telex communications again cut off since late last night; no information available except from Radio Budapest and MTI (Hungarian Press Agency)." There follows, however, a most astute compilation of everything which can be gleaned from official sources, including a number of suppositions that can be made from things *not* mentioned. At the end of his analysis Griffith begins by saying, "Indications still so fragmentary that it is most difficult to judge situation." But he goes on to say:

> Still assume Soviets will crush armed rebellion, since alternative for them would presumably be relatively rapid loss of all satellites, but continuation fighting suggests Soviets wish to confine their intervention to minimum number of troops and desirous or at least willing to have Hungarian regime continue political attempts end rising by concessions. However, by now rising so clearly anti-communist as well as anti-Soviet that doubtful that any political concession regime is prepared to make will have much effect.

Back in Budapest Police Chief Sándor Kopácsi has been haunted by phone calls from a mysterious voice trying to win him over to the side of the insurgents. Now he receives another but this time he says "next to me I have the Pongrátz brothers and István Angyal." The revolution is only a few days old, but already these names are well known to Kopácsi.

This is the beginning of negotiations between the revolutionaries and the government that will continue as long as the fighting lasts.[100]

* * * *

Pál Veress, a young artist who is not allowed to show his art and who has been forced by the regime to become an economist, is sitting in his apartment in Buda. His children are in bed, but his wife, Éva, has been in the hospital with a strange stomach ailment since Tuesday, and he is writing her a long letter. It is not so much to assure her that things are going well on the home front, as to let her know what he knows about, what is going on in Hungary.

My Dearest Éva:

.... All radio stations around the world are broadcasting about us. "Being called a Hungarian is an honor again" (A quote from Petőfi's national song). Everyone is amazed by the courage of the revolutionaries. The "Parliament of Europe" in Strasbourg has sent a message to commend the brave Hungarian students. Even President Eisenhower said that we are doing a good job, and that it was not fair that we were not granted our right to autonomy, even though it was declared in the peace treaty. About two thousand students marched to the building of the Hungarian Embassy in Warsaw. They were cheering our revolution until Polish security police dressed as civilians ran out of the building and beat them with sticks. There was a tremendous mess, but fortunately, no other weapons were used but sticks and tear gas.

Budapest must still be in turmoil tonight. There were a couple of pleas on the radio; other than that there has been no news. They are rejecting the accusations of executing some of the protesters. They stopped calling them teenaged gangs. The President of the People's Front even called the fighters "patriots." If anyone deserves this title, they indeed do. Their victory is tremendous. Even if the revolution gets crushed a hundred times, the Russians will be forced out of Hungary sooner or later...

The ten o'clock news on the radio today was cancelled [unlike yesterday]. They only read a few messages. (Just like this: The following people want to let their families know that they are fine. And then they read the names.) Then they announced that they are not able to broadcast more messages, so they do not want any more calls at the given number. The quality of the broadcasting is getting worse and worse. Our telephone did not work at all before. Around nine o'clock there was a soft buzzing tone, then after 10, there was nothing again....

Imre Nagy has promised the delegates from Borsod County to grant all their demands. (But the radio did not have the nerve to announce what the demands were.) He is pleading with them to abandon their strike. He has promised to form a People's Front government, and he will honor choices of the public in selecting his cabinet.

It is forty-five minutes past midnight. The radio has stopped broadcasting. I drank tea I made for myself. (I wonder who these barbarians are shooting at with heavy artillery. My windows are shaking.)

My dear love, please be a good patient, so you will not have to stay in the hospital for a long time. Please find comfort in the fact that the world where our kids can have an honorable and dignified future has only begun yesterday. This is worth even more then the Széchényi Library itself, and it was worth the sacrifice of those poor boys, too, who voluntarily went there...

I have just heard on the Voice of America that their listeners had heard the voice of a rebel station. They say this is the first time the world can hear from the rebels. Unfortunately, I was not able to find it on the radio. They said the messages were requests for more strikes.

Tomorrow I will draw something nice for you.

Good night, speedy recovery, and I love you one thousand times,

Your loving husband

Pál[101]

Budapest, Saturday, October 27, 1956

Dawn comes with an overcast sky and a strong wind from the west which brings slightly warmer air and rain later in the day.

Inside the Hungarian government two factions pulling in quite different directions will become more obvious before nightfall. Nagy is nominally in charge of his government, but he still has little real influence on measures being carried out. Soviet comrades Mikoyan and Suslov are in on every decision, or at least try to be, and their reading of what is taking place naturally has a strong influence on how the Presidium in the Kremlin will react next.

Nagy's main concern is to get a cease-fire so that he will no longer be on the other side of the barricades from the great mass of his countrymen. The Stalinists and the Soviet military have one goal: the crushing of what they believe to be an uprising of young "bandits" under foreign influence. These wholly divergent views of the situation lead not only to confusion within the government, but confusion in the minds of the Hungarian populace and the outside world as to what the Hungarian government stands for.

Yesterday, according to Mikoyan and Suslov's report to the Soviet Presidium, both Nagy and Kádár promised they would not include Soviet troop withdrawal in any of their public proclamations; yet Nagy had. He had also not felt it necessary to have a curfew and to prohibit demonstrations in order to have military force work. Mikoyan and Suslov are emphatic that "a really strict curfew must be imposed, not only at night but during the day, too, to prevent all demonstrations."

They are equally emphatic that "the majority of the members of the Central Leadership and the Directorate are firmly for the suppression of the counter-revolution." But then in the same breath they state that they consider it necessary and acceptable for the sake of wider public support that "a certain number of influential petit-bourgeois politicians" enter the government. They also state that István Bata, who heads the Defense Ministry, does not have "the necessary knowledge and experience" and should be replaced by Ferenc Münnich. Then they quote Kádár as saying: "We must differentiate between the counterrevolutionaries who want to destroy the people's democratic system, who must be fought to the bitter end" and the masses, who had to be separated from them and brought over to the communists' side. Then they quote Nagy as saying: "We have decided that alongside the armed suppression of the uprising, we must continue a policy to win over the intellectuals and the masses, we must go to meet the people's movement and national feelings so that we can stand firm at the head of the people's movement, and by doing so beat the counterrevolutionaries and preserve the people's democratic system." The other route, says Nagy, would mean the masses remain opposed to the leadership, which would be forced to rely on Soviet forces and thus be isolated from the nation.[102]

*   *   *   *

Confirmation that Defense Minister István Bata lacks "knowledge and experience" comes just after 6:00 a.m. when he has the following announcement made by Radio Budapest: "Attention! Attention! The curfew applying to the territory of Budapest, issued by the Armed Forces' High Command, remains valid until revoked. We call upon the people of Budapest to remain in their homes today, October 27, and not to expose themselves to danger....In cases of absolute necessity persons moving about individually may leave their homes until 9:00 a.m. but the military are forced to use their arms against groups of three or more."[103]

In fact, people pay no more attention to these "orders" than do the soldiers "forced" to fire on groups of "three or more." There are many people in the streets by this time, including groups far larger than three, and many of the soldiers to whom these orders are supposedly issued are already fighting at the side of the patriots.

Radio Budapest itself is hardly more realistic. When a "new government" is announced at 11:12 in the morning the Radio commentator waxes ecstatically about it as though night had been turned into day. "A new government has been formed and took the oath with Comrade Imre Nagy at its head, pledging to lead the country out of the tragic situation…Will this government be able to cope with the tasks it faces?…This government is not only willing; it is capable of realizing its objectives….The composition of the new government proves that several Hungarian politicians have come back to the places they deserved to occupy after having been neglected for years…those persons now heading the government enjoy the confidence of all of us…" What has happened is that two non-communist politicians—one, Zoltán Tildy, a former member of the Smallholders' Party, and former President of the Republic, but known to have been a fellow traveler, the other, Béla Kovács, also a former member of the Smallholders' Party—have been named to a new government, but as individuals, not representing their former party. Moreover, they have not been sworn in. Kovács is in a hospital in Pécs. He has only agreed to be considered and will not actually come to Budapest until November 1. He had only been phoned by President Dobi and told that Nagy would like to include him in his cabinet. When, still in Pécs, he reads the published list, he is very much "surprised" to find several "die-hard communists" on it. The next day he drafts his letter of resignation. True, there are some other new names, but they are all communists, many holdovers from previous governments, which means they served under Rákosi. In spite of Nagy's good intentions, real power, to the extent that the government *has* any power, is still concentrated in the hands of two dozen heavily compromised Communists.[104]

The people are not stupid. Yes, the new government is better than the previous one, but it is still loaded with communists. Tildy and Kovács are regarded as window dressing. And the government's program is utterly vague in comparison to the specific demands that all segments of Hungarian society have put before it. So Radio Budapest's commentator, for all his forced enthusiasm, is simply whistling in the dark.

The Party newspaper *Szabad Nép*, now publishing again, is siding with the patriots. It takes sharp issue with yesterday's *Pravda* editorial which alleged that the people's action, the insurrection, "had been unleashed through the underground work of Anglo-American imperialists."

"We calmly state that this assertion by *Pravda* is an insult to the one and a half million people of Budapest."

"The five-day long bloody, tragic and yet magnificent fight has been unleashed...by...our own mistakes and crimes, which one has to name the first and foremost the fact that we failed to keep alive the sacred flame of national independence, that heritage of our great ancestors."[105]

*   *   *   *

Another British journalist is on his way to Budapest. He has been in Hungary before; last July, in fact. It had been the first foreign country he ever visited and he loved it. Now he was back again "and felt safe among friends," not just because of his love for Hungary but because he is in a country "where 'we' are in power." Peter Fryer is a communist and a correspondent for the London *Daily Worker*. Perhaps he is more journalist than communist, for once he gets over his shock of not being whisked to Budapest in an official car as he was last time, he uses his wits in getting transportation. A German Red Cross official and a German journalist are in a car full of food and medical supplies. They are dropping some off at a town called Mosonmagyaróvár and then will proceed to Budapest and are willing to take him along.

In Mosonmagyaróvár the streets are packed. People addressing them in French, German and English immediately surround the car. Fryer notes tremendous tension in the air, like the feeling in a British mining town when some disaster draws crowds to the pithead. He soon finds out why and notes that there is black crepe with every national flag. The medicines must be handed over to the authorities in the Town Hall. These authorities turn out to be brand new, a revolutionary committee set up yesterday after the massacre. The party secretary was a bully, they say, but not a criminal, so we just told him to go home and stay there for a while. There are quite a few communists on the revolutionary committee, but workers, not Party officials. Fryer is impressed with how well they work together. Most are working class. A majority are former Social Democrats, whose desire to build socialism was stifled, once their party was forced to merge with the communists. The communists had never made use of them or anyone else. The Party bosses ran the town by issuing orders.

Mosonmagyaróvár is a poor town. The people had been promised a better life and were perfectly willing to work for it. Instead life grew worse instead of better. The old Socialists on the committee are vehement in their denunciation of the communist form of "socialism." "It has been eight years of hell," they tell Fryer. By yesterday the whole town was in ferment and peo-

215

ple poured out of their houses to join the worker-student demonstration. Five thousand people had taken part, including old men and women and children.

Fryer is told that one of the ÁVO officers, Lt. Stefko, is still in the hospital. He and the Germans are then taken in a slow, silent procession along the avenue of plane trees to the little chapel and mortuary in the town cemetery. Hundreds go with them and they meet hundreds coming back who have identified family members, sweethearts or friends, workmates or fellow students. Many are weeping and Fryer himself finds it impossible to hold back the tears. The mourners make way for Fryer and his German colleagues and gently push them to the very front. The bodies are in rows, dried blood still on their clothes. A few have bunches of flowers on their breasts. There are girls of sixteen and one tiny coffin with an eighteen-month-old baby. "After eleven years of 'people's democracy,'" thinks Fryer, "it has come to this: that the security police is so remote from the people, so alien to them, so vicious and so brutal that it turns its weapons on a defenseless crowd and murders the people who were supposed to be masters of their own country."

Back in the town he thinks "if the Americans are guilty of seeking to foster counter-revolution…surely the Rákosis and the Gerős are a hundred times more guilty for providing the soil in which seeds sown by the Americans can grow."

Then he notices a general movement in the direction of the hospital where an immense crowd has gathered. They are clamoring ever more insistently for Lt. Stefko to be handed over to them. A delegation is now inside insisting that the Hospital Director hand Stefko over to them. The Director does all he can to deflect them, but soon Fryer and his German colleagues see a stretcher carried by four men with Stefko on it. He has on a blue shirt and is carried so close to Fryer that he might have reached out and touched him. The man is fully conscious and knows quite well what awaits him. His head jerks back and forth and there is spittle on his lips. As the crowd catches sight of the stretcher a howl of derision, hatred and anger erupts. People climb the wire fence to spit on him and curse him. They push with all their might against the iron gates. Their sheer weight soon bursts them open and the crowd surges in. The kicking and stomping is quickly over. The body is taken to Lenin Street and hanged upside down on a sycamore tree.

After returning to England in November with time to reflect, Fryer will write in his book *Hungarian Tragedy*:

This was no counter-revolution organized by fascists and reactionaries. It was the upsurge of a whole people, in which rank-and-file communists took part, against a police dictatorship dressed up as a Socialist society—a police dictatorship backed up by Soviet armed might.

I am the first Communist journalist from abroad to visit Hungary since the revolution started. And I have no hesitation placing the blame for these terrible events on the shoulders of those who led the Hungarian Communist Party for eleven years—up to and including Ernő Gerő. They turned what could have been the outstanding example of people's democracy in Europe into a grisly caricature of Socialism.[106]

Needless to say, none of his dispatches are printed as written in the *Daily Worker*. When he returns to Britain and discovers this, he will resign in furious protest and, eventually, resign from the British Communist Party.

Back in Pest there is a lull in fighting around the Corvin Passage. As a consequence, small groups of enterprising Corvinists go out "hunting" Soviet tanks, not to destroy, but to capture them. This they do by jumping on the tank from behind, blocking its means of vision with rags and then, when the hatch pops open, offering to throw hand grenades inside if they do not go where they are bidden. By the morning's end half a dozen T-34 tanks are lined up next to the Corvin Cinema with their captured crews, including one major, imprisoned in the Prater Street School.[107]

In Nyíregyháza, close to the Soviet Ukrainian border, the unarmed citizenry are still frustrated by their inability even to slow the Soviet military traffic pouring, from time to time, through their city. But they have heard of the events, not only in Budapest but other parts of the country, such as in Mosonmagyaróvár. And their blood is beginning to boil. Eight thousand defy orders against free assembly to mass in the city square, from which some climb the Korona Hotel to tear off its red star, while they shout the usual slogans. Others surge into Bessenyei Square and pull down all the stars on the government buildings. The crowd persuades the police to rip the Communist insignia off their uniforms, and march with them around the city waving flags and singing the national anthem. The ÁVO, seeing the size of the crowd, appear to melt away. By the time the first Soviet armored units of the day begin their drive through town, the crowd is so worked up that it surrounds and overturns the first two trucks. Then it assaults the stalled Soviet tank column with rocks and stones, hurting several of the surprised soldiers who emerge to find out what is causing all the noise in their tanks. The lead armored car is not stalled, but, as it makes it way through the crowd two thirteen-year-old boys, who have seized a machine gun from one of the overturned trucks, open fire. A Soviet major is killed and several of the soldiers in the car are wounded. Now the Russian tanks begin firing their machine guns, first into the air, then into the crowd. A man with a flag in his hands and three more are killed instantly; nine others are severely wounded. Four tanks ram into the crowd, forcing people back into side streets. For the remainder of the day tanks will block all the side streets, as the armored columns continue to move through the town. The Revolution and war against the Soviet Union has finally come to Nyíregyháza.[108]

As the Revolution spreads across the land, new revolutionary committees take over not only the civil government but also the local radio stations. Today, for the first time, these stations begin to broadcast extensively and every one of them designates that it is "free," to distinguish it from the former, communist-controlled radios. Most have a range not much beyond the county in which they are located, but some are quite powerful.

Radio Free Europe's monitors in Schleissheim first picked up Radio Free Győr, late yesterday evening.

Later today Radio Free Győr boasts that they have been joined by Radio Free Mosonmagyaróvár and the "powerful Szombathely radio station" which has agreed to broadcast Radio Free Győr's programs so that "we can tell our listeners this evening that Radio Free Győr is transmitting, so to speak, to almost the entire Dunántúl" (Western Hungary). RFE is quick to broadcast the fact of these new radios to the whole of Hungary so that people in Debrecen soon learn of what is going on in Western Hungary. After a few days of these reports RFE makes the editorial decision to broadcast some of these local transmissions exactly as recorded, to be a sort of amplifying sounding board for these radios, carefully identifying them before and after each broadcast. It is, perhaps, the greatest service RFE can provide the Hungarian people, and greatly speeds up the progress and consolidation of the Revolution in the countryside.

A few hours later Radio Free Miskolc is picked up saying:

> The Hungarian people have lost confidence in some men in Imre Nagy's government…
>
> Hungarians, patriots, in the past few days something has been born which did not exist before…freedom has not been lost. Today Imre Nagy has the

people's confidence. But is this enough? Guns are still shooting in Budapest. Can it be our wish that Soviet troops should take the arms from our freedom fighters? Hungarians do not want this to happen. The new government should not lean on foreign arms; rather it should lean on the people. There is no need for foreign weapons.

Hungarians do not want to kill Hungarians. The people have spoken their judgment with arms. Soviet troops should be sent home and no more Hungarian blood shed in Budapest. Imre Nagy should have the courage to get rid of those politicians who can only lean on weapons used for the suppression of the people..."[109]

Hungarians do not want to kill Hungarians, but Hungarians also do not want to be killed *by* other Hungarians, as can be seen in the attack this afternoon on the Kilián Barracks. The Soviets, who have lost a great many tanks to molotov cocktails in the Corvin Cinema area along the Grand Boulevard (Nagykörút), are convinced that it is the Kilián Barracks with its extra thick walls which is the strongest holdout. They plan to move sub units of Soviet tanks from the Népliget (People's Park) in an attack on the barracks. These are special tanks with short barrels especially designed to blast through reinforced concrete. A secondary objective is to free three of their tanks which have been trapped nearby, but not yet destroyed. Lacking infantry, the Soviets have enlisted the help of the Hungarian Army in the form of a company of fifty artillery cadets with small arms. The Hungarian commander, Col. Vilmos Koltai, orders his men to lie on the tanks Soviet-style, as that will get them into the combat area faster than if they were to walk or run behind the tanks. Several officers object, saying this would be certain death, and could only end in great loss of life and failure of this irresponsible operation. Col. Koltai, knowing his orders come from the Soviet High Command, insists on their being carried out. Reluctantly the Hungarian troops lie on the tanks. Hardly have they gotten as far as Nagyvárad Square when withering fire opens up from the Freedom Fighters. At this point Lt. Babják jumps down and orders his men to do the same. They refuse to go further. Without the infantry, the attack will be no better than any previous foray. In effect, the operation has failed.[110]

Yet the twenty Soviet tanks still have their orders and they need to free those three trapped tanks. They move within close range and then lay down a heavy barrage, penetrating large sections of the wall and causing many casualties. After several hours of battle, however, they fail to rescue the three stranded tanks, which, in the meantime, are destroyed. They also lose half a dozen of their own tanks. What the Soviet High Command does not realize is that it is not just the molotov cocktails which are doing the damage, but nitroglycerine. The chemical engineers from the Technical University have set up a chemistry laboratory within the Kilián Barracks and are manufacturing nitroglycerine. It is this high explosive which lifts fifty-five-ton Stalin tanks a full meter into the air while blowing them into pieces.[111]

* * * *

Readers of the *New York Times* in the United States learn that there is some conflict between the President and the Secretary of State about the legality of the presence of Soviet troops in Hungary. Secretary Dulles feels that there is little doubt that Soviet troops have the legal right to be there, but a question might be raised about the legitimacy of their use to put down an internal rebellion. And even this raises a problem for the hand-wringing diplomats of "Foggy Bottom," for the Soviet intervention is at the request of the Hungarian government. If, they say for example, there were to be a communist rebellion in Italy and the Italian government were to ask for the aid of the American troops currently stationed in Italy, there is no doubt that they would be used to crush such a rebellion. British troops had done just that in Greece in 1945.

There is some consideration of what might confront the United States in the case the rebels should succeed in setting up a government of their own. This would present the U.S. with a major dilemma. The United States would be sympathetic to a free government in Hungary. But officials in Washington do not want to offer a major provocation to the Soviet Union through the recognition of a Hungarian government unfriendly to Moscow. Such a provocation, it is felt by the highest officials in Washington, could possibly lead to war.[112]

U.S. Legation Reports

Earlier in the day U.S. Chargé d'Affaires Spencer Barnes fires off a long cable to Washington explaining not only the current situation but also the three-part dilemma the insurgents face, in view of the regime's statements that it will engage in ruthless suppression if the insurgents do not surrender. The insurgents can: A. Fight to the end and die, causing great suffering to the unarmed population; B. Fight and die in the hope of holding out long enough for some outside intervention or pressure to modify the regime and/or its

capability of ruthless suppression; or C. Accept that the government is acting in good faith in its promised concessions and surrender.

These "evil choices facing the insurgents," writes Barnes,

> seem to pose a most critical and moral problem for the U.S. Government.
> The U.S. cannot by complete inaction condone the Soviet Union while it
> exercises its military capabilities in suppressing this struggle. This leads log-
> ically to the question of what the U.S. government can do to increase the
> chances of the second alternative being realized...
>
> The Legation's impression is that France has taken the initiative in this
> move. The Legation strongly believes, both from a practical standpoint of
> maintaining stature and influence among the captive peoples and because of
> moral responsibility to stand behind past official statements implying sup-
> port for the captive peoples, that the U.S. Government should lead and vig-
> orously press the Hungarian case in the UN and use all of its influence to
> mobilize world opinion against this ruthless suppression of the Hungarian
> insurgents by Soviet power....
>
> The Legation does not have a clear view of the possible alternatives open
> to the U.S. Government between the extremes of a "legalistic case" before
> the UN and material support. *But alternatives between these two extremes
> must exist* [emphasis added], and for some the alternative risk attached might
> not be too great. The Legation believes it to be in the United States' interest,
> in view of the violent and widespread reaction against communist rule by the
> Hungarian people, that careful consideration be given to the means of sup-
> porting the insurgent population and that some risk is warranted by the emer-
> gence of this tremendous revulsion against Soviet domination.[113]

Because it must go through the British Legation and Foreign Office in
London, the above urgent and crucial telegram, sent on October 26 at 11:00
a.m. Budapest time, does not reach the Department of State until 10:09 p.m.
Washington time on October 29, more than two days later. It is not called to
the attention of the responsible diplomat, Robert M. McKisson, until 1:10
a.m. on October 30.[114]

Barnes' reference to the British government opinion is a result of a
twenty-minute conference he has with Minister Sir Leslie Fry prior to Fry's
forwarding this telegram.

Barnes is impressed with Sir Leslie's calm and dignified demeanor. Sir
Leslie could easily be some Duke from the house of Windsor, "crow's feet"
at the corner of his Windsor eyes and typically long upper lip. His neat dress,

thinning hair slicked back from a high forehead and erect bearing all beto-ken "upper-class Englishman." He has already had a distinguished career in India and despite his aloof appearance has been long enough in Hungary to become totally immersed in its affairs. His looks belie a warm regard for the Hungarian people.

Fry, in fact, forwards another follow-up telegram for Barnes in which the latter says: "Legation greatly concerned over the news of troop movements into Hungary and believes that the Soviets will shortly have involved them-selves so deeply that any compromise will be impossible..."

Sir Leslie has already urged the Foreign Office that "we must do nothing to encourage the idea that military support might be forthcoming; and any-thing we do must be done at once..." His suggestion for immediate action is a large, well-publicized convoy of food and medicine from the Western pow-ers, which, even if prevented from entering Hungary by the Soviets, will force them to make a similar gesture.

He is relieved, he says in another message to London, to learn that taking the issue to the UN is being considered and suggests that "to avoid a charge of 'interference in domestic affairs'" the report to the Security Council could stress "that Hungary has in fact been invaded anew and is again being reduced to subjection by a foreign power."[115]

In a third message he tells London "I do not know whether it would be possible to accord recognition to any group, however large, within a country other than its *de jure* or *de facto* Government. But quite apart from such con-siderations, the first essential seems to be to obtain United Nations interven-tion in some form or other. While we talked among ourselves about the com-promise that the West would regard as acceptable, the people would be crushed: and when they were, our chance of helping them would presumably be very greatly diminished."[116]

Shortly thereafter, Fry receives a message from London that the State Department is "becoming increasingly concerned over the absence of news of their mission in Budapest" and asks that "we pass to them as soon as pos-sible any information we may receive."[117]

British good sense and restraint is reflected in its BBC broadcasts in most languages to Europe today: "We must not scare the Russians," it says, "by giving the impression that we are exploiting these troubles to carry Western powers to the Soviet border. We must do nothing which would make it a matter of prestige for the Red Army to go on to the bitter end."[118]

In Paris, meantime, Lord Ismay calls a special private meeting of the NATO Council to discuss the situation in Hungary.[119] Lord Ismay has already received a paper from the Foreign Office entitled "Possibilities for [NATO] Action on Hungary." This paper, in addition to suggested appeals to the Soviet government and the UN Security Council, suggests that NATO representative M. Spaak, now in Moscow, be asked to speak directly to top Soviet officials, adding, "we might suggest a guarantee on the Austrian model of Hungary's neutrality, perhaps of her demilitarization."[120]

Dulles in Action

In Washington, Secretary of State John Foster Dulles is sending a blizzard of cables to allies, nations currently serving on the UN Security Council, states which signed the Hungarian Peace Treaty and even states whom he feels may be influenced by the events in Hungary which would otherwise have no interest in a "Cold War" matter. He wants the strongest consensus he can build before going to the United Nations. He has not received Barnes' views on the urgency of concrete Western action—it is not clear that he ever will see those cables, for the situation will be very different three days hence. He is, in any case, operating on a very different wavelength. As a lifelong lawyer, he is seeking to employ as many legal precedents, such as treaties and charters, as he can in making a case against the Soviet Union.

On this he runs into trouble. Henry Cabot Lodge, Jr., American Ambassador to the United Nations, cables him from New York that "The U.K. and the French objected to first paragraph of Department's draft letter to Security Council President on ground that reference to the UN Charter rights and freedoms might embarrass them in Cyprus and Algeria."[121] Then, in a second cable, Lodge informs him: "Both French and UK indicated objection to any Commission of Inquiry, fearing precedent this might set in their own problems as colonial powers." Lodge also says in this cable that "The tone [of the debate] should not prevent a favorable development of the present situation [in Hungary]....Any move for a cease-fire should be avoided in order not to allow the Russian and Hungarian Communist regime to consolidate [their] positions."[122]

Sir Pierson Dixon, UN Ambassador for the United Kingdom, meanwhile cables the Foreign Office: "Mr. Lodge suggested that we should confine tomorrow's meeting to debating the agenda and putting our case in such a way as not to commit ourselves to asking for a particular line of action from the Council. He thought we might consider the terms of a draft resolution early next week in the light of the views expressed in the Council, particularly those of the Soviet representative....Mr. Lodge said he was thinking of giving a straightforward narrative of events with as little 'cold war' coloring as possible. He said we should try to avoid giving any impression that we were trying to provoke a veto [from the Soviet Union]."[123]

*   *   *   *

In Vienna, the Austrian News Agency reports that "a thousand Hungarian civilians today crossed the border into Austria at the Mogersdorf-Jenersdorf district." But there are reports of Soviet forces being observed in Western Hungary today, particularly around the Szombathely area. A senior official of the Austrian Ministry of the Interior believes they are there to prevent any of the rebel leaders from escaping. There is considerable reinforcement of the Austrian Army and Gendarmerie on the Austrian side of the border in preparation for disarming any refugees and moving them quickly away from the border area.[124]

In Munich, RFE's Political Advisor, William E. Griffith, is still taking a gloomy view. He points out that the government changes will have little or no effect on the insurgents, that the Soviet Army is rapidly becoming "the one effective instrument of control" and he continues to assume it will "crush the insurgents." While "tomorrow is the forbidden October 28 National Holiday in Czechoslovakia," he feels it "unlikely" that something might flare up.[125]

*   *   *   *

Work on the final assault on the Kilián Barracks/Corvin Passage, begun two days ago, but delayed because of possible truce negotiations which are not panning out to the military's satisfaction, now resumes in the Ministry of Defense. On the twenty-sixth Imre Nagy had gotten word of the attack and infuriated the Russian General Malinin by trying to cancel his plans to begin with a major artillery barrage of the area. "Do not shoot [with heavy artillery] at the apartment blocks," Nagy had told Major General István Kovács over the phone, "as it would create a very difficult situation. Please do not carry the plan out this way; avoid mass bloodshed. I'm afraid of the consequences...I will resign...." When Major General István Gábor translated this into Russian for General Malinyin, the Soviet General's reply to Nagy was: "Artillery preparations will not begin without a separate order.

But I will bring reinforcements in, including heavy weaponry. Please take into account the answer which they [the insurgents] gave when summoned to capitulate. They refused to peacefully give up the fight unless the state security forces were disarmed and the Hungarian Army restores order. They demanded a provisional government, elections by December 31 and a general amnesty. Unless your government restores order soon, I will take the military path."

The Soviets ask Major General Kovács to draw up the plan of attack. But as neither general knows the exact positions of the insurgents, they call upon a "Corvinist" from the Ministry's cellar prison to sketch this for them. A plan to plant huge explosive mines under the buildings comes to naught when they cannot locate an accurate map of the area's sewers. Likewise a plan to bomb the Cinema from a helicopter is abandoned. In the end, the Hungarian contribution is to be 350 infantrymen reinforcing the infantry under Lt. Colonel Zoltán Tóth, commander of the 12th Kecskemét mechanized regiment. Tóth reports to his superior, Col. András Márton, commander of the Miklós Zrínyi Military Academy. Contact is to be made with the Soviet division near the Szabadság (Freedom) Bridge at three o'clock tomorrow morning and the attack to be launched one hour later. The Soviet Division stationed at Dimitrov Square will provide the tanks.[126]

But over at Party Headquarters the leading members of the Central Committee are arguing over whether or not to seek a cease-fire. János Kádár emphasizes that a cease-fire should not involve branding the participants as "counterrevolutionaries." If, on the other hand "anyone after the declaration should still rise against our People's Republic, then measures [should] be taken against them to the point of their surrender or execution."

Kádár goes on to say that a big problem is the division between the Central Committee and the newly appointed, six-person Directorate, consisting of himself as President and Antal Apró, Károly Kiss, Ferenc Münnich, Imre Nagy and Zoltán Szántó.

Mikoyan responds that he does not agree that there is any division between the Central Committee and the new Directorate. The Directorate is needed "if we are to be resolute" and not be swayed by all the demands. "If we want to head the workers movement, then we must call upon it to cease the struggle. We must not negotiate in the crossfire using street microphones, but we must hold meetings, factory meetings. The comrades must show resolution. If they make a new set of concessions tomorrow, then it will not be possible to stop it…if we let the trade union leadership out of our hands, then a parallel center will form and we play into the enemy's hands."

András Hegedűs, who has been excluded from the Directorate, counters with "I support a cease-fire, but not against bandits and looters…." Nagy puts in impatiently: "A cease-fire has to be declared as quickly as possible. There was absolute uncertainty even this morning when they wanted to start a military operation at 6:00 a.m." Then he fumes at Hegedűs: "Comrade Hegedűs has a lot to do with the fact that there's serious fluctuation within the leadership. Yesterday morning he agreed with us and now he again contemplates new military operations."

Nagy is uneasy. He knows that members of his own Political Committee have secretly plotted new military operations in the past and may well do so again. It is imperative that the Committee vote for a cease-fire. The discussion drags on. He eventually gets his vote, but it is well into the new day, Sunday, October 28, before he does.[127]

Sunday, October 28, 1956

While it is only a couple of hours past midnight in Budapest, in the United States it is still Saturday the twenty-seventh. In Dallas, Texas, where U.S. Secretary of State John Foster Dulles is about to address the Dallas Council on World Affairs, it is only 7:00 p.m. Dulles is making a political speech, for the United States is in the midst of a presidential election campaign. The speech has long been on the docket; it was scheduled weeks before anything began to happen in Poland and Hungary. But, of course, there is a passage on the "captive peoples" of Eastern Europe in the earliest draft. There always is this element in a Dulles speech, for it always produces a warm response from Americans of East European heritage, many of whom formerly voted Democratic. Because of recent events he has to change the passage somewhat, and has gotten the President's approval earlier today for these changes.

"In Eastern Europe," he says,

> …the spirit of patriotism, and the longing of individuals for freedom of thought and conscience and the right to mold their own lives, are forces which erode and finally break the iron bonds of servitude.
>
> Today we see dramatic evidence of this truth. The Polish people now loosen the Soviet grip upon the land they love. And the heroic people of

226

Hungary challenge the murderous fire of Red Army tanks. These patriots value human liberty more than life itself. And all who peacefully enjoy liberty have a solemn duty to seek, by all truly helpful means, that those who now die for freedom will not have died in vain. It is in this spirit that the United States and others have today acted to bring the situation in Hungary to the United Nations Security Council.

The weakness of Soviet imperialism is being made manifest...It is weak because it seeks to sustain an unnatural tyranny by suppressing human aspirations which cannot indefinitely be suppressed and by concealing truths which cannot indefinitely be hidden....

Today our nation continues its historic role. The captive peoples should never have reason to doubt that they have in us a sincere and dedicated friend who shares their aspirations. They must know that they can draw upon our abundance to tide them over the period of economic adjustment...Nor do we condition economic ties between us upon the adoption by these countries of any particular form of society." The Poles have a right to be skeptical of this statement, for unbeknownst to the public and, indeed, to most of Washington, Dulles, only a few weeks ago, had turned down flat their secret request for a loan of $500,000,000 for just such a purpose.

And let me make this clear, beyond a possibility of doubt: The United States has no ulterior purpose in desiring the independence of the satellite countries. Our unadulterated wish is that these peoples, from whom so much of our own national life derives, should have sovereignty restored to them and that they should have governments of their own free choosing. We do not look upon these nations as potential military allies. We see them as friends and as part of a new and friendly and no longer divided Europe...[128]

*   *   *   *

In Hungary, shortly after 4:00 a.m., the Pongrátz's mother calls her sons at the Corvin complex from their home in Soroksár. Their twelve-year-old sister has just counted two tanks and thirty trucks full of Russian soldiers assembled in the town square and headed for Budapest. The Pongrátz brothers know every inch of the road from Soroksár to Budapest and immediately they know just where to set up an ambush: the terminal of the electric railway at Közvágóhíd where the road passes under two railway bridges about three hundred meters apart. But there is no time to be lost. A full truckload of revolutionaries is armed with four machine guns, two for each bridge, a submachine gun for each boy and half a dozen hand grenades each. When they arrive it is still dark, but there are high streetlights spaced at sufficient intervals for most of the highway to be clearly seen. They quickly deploy on and around the two bridges.

The Soviet convoy is led by the two tanks, followed by the trucks almost a kilometer behind. The patriots let the tanks go, but as soon as all the trucks are between the two bridges they open fire. It is all over in ten minutes. A few trucks get away, but most are put out of action, are exploding or burning, and the road is strewn with dead Soviet soldiers. They have lost a whole infantry unit, while the revolutionaries have only one wounded. By the time the tanks return, the insurgents have vanished into the night.[129]

*   *   *   *

The military is still working at cross-purposes with the government, which has just voted for a cease-fire. As planned, a column of Soviet armored troop carriers—known as "open coffins" because, while armored, they have no roof—bearing 360 Hungarian assault infantry and accompanied by eighteen Soviet tanks has been moved from the Népliget [People's Park] down to Boráros Square on the river. From here they are to split and attack the Corvin complex from two different directions: one from Nagyvárad Square down Üllői Avenue, the other from Calvin Square. There are six storm groups of twenty men each and 240 men in reserve. Each group has two or more tanks. These are both the T-34s, with the vulnerable spare gas tanks strapped to their back topsides and the much heavier, more powerful T-54 (Stalin) tanks.

Diverging somewhat from the plan, three T-34s clank down Üllői Ave. to survey the Corvin Cinema and its environs, even though it is still quite dark. Cannons and other explosions are soon heard, but then nothing. When, after a reasonable time, these tanks do not return, three Stalin tanks are sent after them. Again the roar of cannons and more explosions. Two of the Stalin tanks return, one badly damaged. The Soviet officers then withdraw to confer. No order is given to the Hungarian sub-units.

Col. Márton, the top Hungarian commander, goes back to the divisional staff and finds that the Soviets are still continuing their supplementary survey. Only many hours later does he discover that Imre Nagy had gotten wind of the attack, had phoned Defense Minister Janza at dawn in a fury and strictly forbidden the operation. Nevertheless, the orders to hold off do not reach the military in the field in time and the Soviets attack again, but without the Hungarian infantry support, losing not only more tanks but a great number of Soviet soldiers, some of whom had been seen to surrender to the rebels. Their superior officers are later warned by Lt. General Lashchenko himself that if any of their troops surrender, lay down their arms or give them to the enemy, they, the officers, will be removed from their posts.[130]

From the viewpoint of the Corvin/Kilián Barracks complex, the attack, though intense, is no great threat. Even under the dimmest of streetlights Soviet tanks can be seen and their diesel engines roar so loudly that they advertise their coming a good half mile away. The Freedom Fighters have been putting Soviet tanks out of commission now for four days and have been getting better and better at it. And to blow up the Stalin tanks, which do not carry vulnerable gasoline tanks on them like the T-34s, they now have nitroglycerine. Most of the Russian prisoners are given over to the care of Col. Maléter and his men in the Kilián Barracks, who see that the wounded ones are taken to a hospital.

Gen. Béla Király Engaged

In a centrally located military hospital, an ex-Major General is visited by three young friends. He is only a few weeks out of prison, where his health suffered. The revolution, they tell him, is a success so far, but they need professional leadership. People in the government are willing to appoint him to the highest command if he will only come. Ex-Major General Béla Király, a forty-four-year-old veteran of Horthy's and the communist army, is not so sick that he cannot get dressed and slip unnoticed out of the hospital. Two cars are waiting, one filled with youths with automatic weapons, the second with a place reserved for him and a policeman standing beside it. The face of the policeman almost makes Király turn and run. He had been a fellow prisoner, but not just an ordinary one: an ÁVO informer. Király suspects he is walking into a trap. He spots an old friend in a car across the street and quickly goes over to him. "Do me a favor, Jancsi. Follow the second car and see where they take me. If I do not phone you within twenty-four hours then you'll know I've been betrayed."

As they drive off, Király, who has been hospitalized since before the twenty-third, is astounded at the wreckage of Budapest, some of the buildings still smoldering. He is taken to Police Headquarters on Deák Square where the Freedom Fighters have a sort of office. It is not a trap. They begin planning at once.[131]

"In order to stop further bloodshed and ensure peaceful progress, the government of the Hungarian People's Republic has ordered a general and immediate cease-fire. It instructs the armed forces to fire only if attacked." This announcement is made, and made repeatedly, over Radio Budapest beginning at 11:05 in the morning.[132]

There is no dramatic cessation of combat, for little is in progress. The battle at the Corvin/Kilián Barracks complex has been over for several hours and only occasional rifle fire can be heard. But the Soviet tanks soon go back to their staging or guarding areas and no more machine-gun fire is heard.

*   *   *   *

Homer Bigert, of the *New York Times*, is one of the ones who have no difficulty crossing the border at Nickelsdorf this morning and he heads straight for Mosonmagyaróvár. He finds the town calm. Thousands of people are milling around the small chapel at the cemetery where coffins are stacked up both inside and outside the building awaiting burial. The rain has stopped but there is a chill wind whipping across the leaden sky. A little band of musicians, blue-lipped and shivering, escort each coffin from the threshold of the chapel to the individual graves, playing a funeral dirge.

*   *   *   *

From Vienna U.S. Ambassador Lewellyn Thompson cables the Department: "We are encountering among our Austrian friends a strong tendency to blame the U.S. for the present predicament of the Hungarian patriots. Reference is frequently made to RFE and our balloon operations as having incited the Hungarians to action and our failure to do anything effective for them now that they have risen against their Communist oppressors. When asked what we could do, they have nothing to suggest."[133]

Noel Barber, of the *Daily Mail,* who *is* getting his dispatches out by racing each day to the Austrian border, writes:

> This morning I tried to cross the Margaret Bridge to Széna Square where rebels had fought desperately for twelve hours yesterday. No sooner had my car—with a Union Jack on one side and a white flag on the other—moved onto the bridge than the Russians opened fire on me. I backed, and then walked halfway across on foot, the flag in one of my upheld arms. They stopped me half way across, and I soon saw why.
>
> In the middle was a three-ton lorry, and around it—like icing on a wedding cake—the road was covered with flour. Two bodies lay by its side—the

driver and his mate. Ostensibly they had been bringing flour into the city. But the Russians found a cache of arms hidden and shot them out of hand.

Lined up by the bridge were fifteen Soviet trucks. I could not pass, so I went back to the car and drove along the river—despite the curfew—to Stalin Bridge. Here I managed to get across, helped by packets of American cigarettes....I made my way back through the back streets [of Buda] to Széna Square, where a scene of such desolation lay before me, that I just can't describe it....Behind the barricade hundreds of [teenage] fighters waited in the pouring rain. The whole square was literally torn to pieces. Every stone that could be taken from the road and pavements had been pick axed to use for shelter walls...

Everywhere people ask me one thing: "When is help coming?"

"Please, anything...even one gun," a girl begged me.

"Can't the British help? We are fighting for the world," said another.

It makes me ill, unable to reply.

What makes the situation so difficult is that, though the government has agreed to most of the demands of the fighters, there is no leader with whom authority can deal. Government speakers can only plead on the radio. But each group of fighters fights separately. The Russians have deliberately and calculatingly kept the fight alive, and now—unless pressure comes from outside—they must reduce the country.[134]

Nagy Addresses the People

"People of Hungary!" says Imre Nagy over Budapest Radio,

...The government rejects the view that sees the present formidable popular movement as a counterrevolution. Undoubtedly, as in all great uprisings, unsavory elements have used the past days to commit crimes. It is also true that reactionary, counter-revolutionary elements have joined in and are attempting to use events to overthrow the people's democratic regime.

But it is also indisputable that in this movement a great national and democratic movement, embracing and unifying all of our people, has unfolded itself with elementary force....

The grave crimes of the preceding era released this great movement. The situation was aggravated even further by the fact that up to the very last the leadership was unwilling to break...with its old and criminal policy. This, above all, led to the tragic fratricidal fight in which so many people are dying on both sides.

In the midst of the fighting was born a government of democratic national unity, independence and socialism...

231

The government wants to rely, first of all, on the militant Hungarian working class, but naturally, it wants to rely also on the entire Hungarian working people....

New armed forces will be formed from units of the Army, of the police, and of the armed workers and youth groups.

The Hungarian government has come to an agreement with the Soviet government whereby Soviet forces shall withdraw immediately from Budapest and, simultaneously with the formation of our new Army, shall evacuate the city. The Hungarian government has started negotiations to settle relations between the Hungarian People's Republic and the Soviet Union with regard to the withdrawal of Soviet forces stationed in Hungary....

After the re-establishment of order we shall organize a new and single State police and we shall dissolve the organs of State security. No one who took part in the fighting need fear reprisals....

Nagy adds that there will be a full amnesty, the introduction of the Kossuth coat of arms, the declaration of March 15 as a national holiday, a general pay raise, price and norms balances, and the end of compulsion in the agricultural cooperatives.[135]

People's reaction to the speech can be gauged by Radio Free Miskolc's broadcast a few hours later. "We listened to the speech of Imre Nagy attentively, we immediately wondered...: *How could there have been patriots on both sides?* The people of Miskolc think that the true Hungarian patriots were in the ranks of the peacefully demonstrating students and workers and *not* among the ÁVO bandits who shot at a defenseless crowd....The working people of Borsod County do not only want withdrawal of Soviet troops from Budapest, but desire that they withdraw completely from Hungary and go home. We are very sorry that Imre Nagy...only mentioned Budapest. [We] will take Imre Nagy's speech this evening with a grain of salt..."[136]

During the Cease-Fire

At the Corvin Cinema, Gergely Pongrátz is returning from Boráros Square where he has just handed over a large group of Russian prisoners during the cease-fire. He finds that two of their student patriots have come with a letter from Colonel Mikhail Y. Kuzminov, Commander of Soviet forces in Budapest, addressed to the "Budapest Headquarters of the Resistance Movement." Kuzminov promises a full amnesty and free passage and assures them the Revolution has accomplished its goal because Imre Nagy has been appointed Prime Minister and will fulfill their goals. He asks that they acknowledge that there is no further reason for bloodshed and that they thus lay down their arms. The tone of the letter is not threatening and written very persuasively. All ten of the revolutionary "Commanders," including the original organizer of the Corvin group, László Iván-Kovács, gather now to discuss how to answer this letter. Their whole future appears to depend on the answer. After a while, one of the commanders, "Cannonball" Gyurka, suggests they consult Col. Pál Maléter. After all, about 2:00 p.m. he had hung out a white flag and sent an emissary over to say that there would be no more firing from the Kilián Barracks, so long as there was no firing at them, and this had been strictly observed. Ödön Pongrátz is selected to take him the letter.[137]

As expected, his weapons are taken from him at the door and he has to wait quite some time before being ushered into a cellar room where the Colonel is lying on his cot. "What do you want?" he demands, not even looking up at Pongrátz.

But Maléter sits up in bed, takes the letter and reads it. "Well, what do you want?" he asks upon finishing it. "You are fighting with little guns against tanks, of which there are many hundred more outside this city. Be pleased that you are getting an amnesty. Go home and sleep!" He tosses the letter on the floor. "Very well," says a furious Pongrátz, bending down to retrieve the letter, "we will write our own answer to Col. Kuzminov and your advice will be recorded in history."[138]

The Corvin Commanders are neither diplomats nor writers. They put together, nonetheless, a document which quite eloquently sums up their demands. They are not aware of Nagy's statement of today and still feel he is somehow responsible for the country's predicament, so say as their tenth and last point:

> We do not recognize the present provisional government and we demand that Péter Veres [the peasant poet who had spoken rather unsuccessfully at the Bem memorial on October 23] be entrusted with forming the new provisional government.

In the final paragraph they state:

> If you do not accept our demands, and we do not expect that you will,…the fight for freedom of a suffering nation and its rights will continue to the final victory.

Long live independent, free Hungary!
Budapest, October 28, 1956 Supreme Command of the Hungarian
Resistance Movement.[139]

Whether Maléter has second thoughts about his treatment of Pongrátz or is merely reacting to Nagy's announcement that the government accepts that the revolution is genuine and its demands accepted, he sends his Sergeant-Major over to Corvin to ask Pongrátz to come see him. Pongrátz has no intention of going back to the Kilián Barracks and sends someone to suggest that Maléter come to him. Maléter realizes the only way he can have any influence over Pongrátz is to go to him, so he decides to pay him a visit.

The meeting is not a pleasant one; they talk past one another, but since Maléter is on the revolutionaries' turf he must hear them out. They talk about themselves, who they are and what they are fighting for. For the first time Maléter realizes they are not at all the "fascist rabble" the radio has made them out to be and has himself believed. Though he dare not show it, he is deeply moved. By the time he returns to the barracks he is a changed man.[140]

* * * *

In Western Europe and North America press comment has been voluminous. But today even such a faraway place as Brazil takes note of the massacre last Thursday with the São Paulo newspaper *Correioda Manha* running a front page headline: "Russian Troops Impose Reign of Terror on Budapest" and a sub headline: "Russian soldiers open fire on Hungarian people—Thousands wounded." The lead editorial is titled "Active and Bloody Colonialism."[141]

In the Communist world the revolution, when mentioned at all—except for Poland and Yugoslavia—is played down and inevitably called a "counterrevolution." The East German government, which was briefly overthrown by a nationwide revolt in June 1953, is taking no chances. Premier Otto Grotewohl tells a radio and television audience this evening, "We are not going to change the government because it is the fashionable thing to do. We do not want any fashionable illnesses." Dissolution of the government, he says, "would lead to such a situation as in Hungary." East Germany's 270,000 troops and security police have been on an emergency alert for over a week.[142]

As a result of yesterday morning's meeting at Police Headquarters, the Corvin group and the Tűzoltó Street group both receive informal visits from high-ranking government delegations this evening. Brigadier General Lorinc Kana calls on Angyal and Brigadier General Gyula Váradi and other high-ranking officers call on the Pongrátz brothers and their fellow commanders. The latter, thinking a workers' hostel not suitable for receiving such a delegation, hastily take over the apartment of a certain Dr. Kramolin on the second floor overlooking the cinema theatre. With the doctor more than busy in his hospital, this soon becomes the Commanders' Office. The government officials have come to find out under what conditions the insurgents will give up their arms. The revolutionaries say that only after the Russians have left will they give up their arms, but admit they might be willing to surrender them to the Army or a new Army loyal to Nagy. Váradi cannot help noticing all of the tanks outside in the courtyard. He is told of their capture and the captive crews with the officers allowed to keep their unloaded pistols. He keeps shaking his head and repeating "unbelievable, unimaginable."[143]

Spencer Barnes in the U.S. Legation has had no answers to his many cables. Today he tries to explain his actions in regards to contact with the revolutionaries. But his cable sounds as though he were talking to himself. At the end he says:

> It now appears certain that the Soviets are moving troops based in other satellite areas, perhaps in the Soviet Union itself....They can, by progressive use of force, maintain control of Pest and get control of Buda, and clear up the provinces. However, the mounting wave of pro-Hungarian feeling in the West makes it possible that the Soviets also might be willing to extricate themselves from the present situation through an armistice, followed by negotiations....Legation feels that any approaches from the insurgents, handled delicately are perhaps best kept alive so that a better chance may exist for the Hungarian government to have some one to negotiate with.... Legation requests advice as soon as possible.[144]

This telegram, delayed like all the others, takes twenty-three hours to reach the Department.

Sir Leslie Fry, over in the British Legation, assures Whitehall that the business of getting families and non-essential personnel and other British subjects out of Budapest has been at the back of his mind for some time, "but this prolonged resistance to the Russians could hardly have been foreseen." Many of the scattered British community in Budapest are elderly women with whom it is hard to maintain contact at present. He is worried about the fighting spreading to Buda where most of them are. "There are increasing reports of indiscriminate Russian firing everywhere. It seems possible that the Russians are trying, or will try to force matters to a conclusion before the Security Council proceedings can get far."

As to the Legation itself, "The building is solid, we have provisions here and in the basement....Morale—which I do not need to say is high—will be sustained by our all being under one roof. It might be preferable, when the convoy comes about, to route it through the Czech frontiers at Szob. Evacuation by air seems too iffy etc."

On a third matter Sir Leslie tells the Foreign office, "There are now so many British journalists in Budapest that I propose to stop sending detailed reports on matters which they can as well cover."[145]

*   *   *   *

Two hours after the answer to Col. Kuzminov's letter is delivered to Soviet headquarters, the revolutionaries at Corvin Passage are invited to send a delegation to Communist Party headquarters. When they get there they find leaders from nine or ten other resistance groups have been similarly summoned. The conference is moved to ÁVO headquarters, where they are joined by four Army colonels and the atomic scientist Ferenc Jánosi, Imre Nagy's son-in-law who, along with Dr. Imre Molnár, Minister of Justice, is representing the Party.

Even before any of the revolutionaries can speak they are verbally abused by the Party people present, who shout, "You mean to pretend that you are Freedom Fighters?!" The Colonels want to know where the real leaders are and who the strategist is who has organized such successful resistance. They do not believe the answers: that they are mostly workers and students, that there is no single leadership, they are all leaders. It takes a while for them to convince the government officials that since they have been successful in withstanding the Soviet attacks, "surrendering" arms is out of the question. Once the Soviets are gone, they will gladly hand their weapons over to a government agency which fulfills their demands. It then turns on what this new government agency, now being referred to as the National Guard, will consist of. The Freedom Fighters are reluctant to have the ratio be one-third Army, one-third Police and one-third them. They feel strongly that at least half of the new National Guard should be made up from volunteers from their ranks. Agreement is almost reached when one of the Revolutionaries says that the government's contention that the Russians are leaving is only that, a claim. They cannot guarantee a Russian withdrawal, only the Russians can do that. This brings the negotiations to a standstill. They have been going on now for six hours and it is already early morning.

*   *   *   *

Among the scores of Western correspondents at the Hegyeshalom-Nickelsdorf border crossing point today who have been vacuuming all transients for news is one Frederick ("Fritz") Hier, correspondent for Radio Free Europe. He is impressed with the crowds of Austrians who, despite the inclement weather, have come out to help. Druggists have emptied their shelves, Red Cross officials and priests direct truck after truck to the border where they are reloaded into Hungarian vehicles. Farmers bring paper sacks of apples or potatoes. It is chaotic, but everything does somehow get through.[146]

Not far away in Győr two Italian journalists, who are putting up overnight at a hotel there, report that they have seen with their own eyes Soviet tanks go over to the side of the insurgents and fire on their own tanks.

There are no Russians in Győr. They abandoned their barracks a few days ago in an effort to avoid conflicts and are camping in tents with their wives and children in a nearby wood. The townspeople are so gratified that they have been taking them fresh eggs and milk and the "National Revolutionary Committee" has invited them to return to their barracks.

Out in the main square in front of City Hall a vociferous crowd of 1,200 people is heckling a speaker from the balcony. Attila Szigeti is a stout, florid man with sweeping blond moustaches. He is well known to the public since he has been a city official and represented Győr in the Parliament in Budapest. Despite his Communist Party affiliation and personal friendship with Imre Nagy, he has been one of the main leaders of the Revolution in Győr and he has gotten himself elected President of the Revolutionary Council. But there are few, if any, communists in the crowd below him, and they refuse to be mollified by his reassuring words. People are saying that having Szigeti on the Committee constitutes a "stab in the back" for all those in the revolution who are fighting communism.

Suddenly Father Irén, a Benedictine monk, hoists himself up onto one of the Town Hall pillars. With his black cassock billowing in the wind he shouts: "I am not speaking as a priest, but as a Hungarian. Communism must go! We must purge this Committee!" Within seconds someone in the crowd shouts: "Hang Szigethy!" The poor man hurriedly vanishes from the balcony.

In Moscow, Ambassador Charles Bohlen cables the State Department that the Soviets' attempt to justify "armed intervention in Hungary by reference to the Warsaw Pact, far from 'legalizing' Soviet action is in effect an indictment of the Warsaw Pact itself, and I assume will be used in the Security Council debate to full effect, particularly in light of constant repetition of the charge in Soviet propaganda about the aggressive nature of NATO....The Soviets may realize the dangers of attempting to justify their action under the Warsaw Pact and therefore may not, in the Security Council debate, emphasize this point."

Then, in reply to a State Department round-up on the Hungarian situation sent to all diplomatic posts—a message which had complained of little information from the U.S. Legation in Budapest—Bohlen says "the British Ambassador here has shown me in confidence a series of telegrams from the British Legation in Budapest which, having its own radio transmitter, has been giving a running and most informative account of events there, including some points of considerable interest not in circular telegrams [i.e. from the Department of State] under reference. I assume Department has had access to these messages, particularly in view of the breakdown of communication with our Legation there." Bohlen obviously suspects that the State Department has *not* been asking the Foreign Office to see their messages, otherwise reference would surely have been made in the circular he refers to.[147]

Barber Wounded

British journalist Noel Barber over a drink with his old friend Tom (Sefton) Delmer hears the rumor that the Russians are leaving Budapest. When Dénes confirms with a friend in the government that the Russians are indeed supposed to be leaving, Barber and Delmer decide that the three of them should cruise around in his car to see whether this is, in fact, true.

They quickly find it is not. On the Margaret Bridge the soldiers at a Soviet checkpoint are alert for any movement. As they turn the corner a burst of machine-gun fire is let loose on them. Barber backs the car faster than he ever has before, screeches his tires and turns down the main street, but slowly. There are downed cables to be avoided and he doesn't want to run into another trigger-happy guard at a checkpoint. They are flying a Union Jack on one side and a white flag on the other. A hundred yards further along the lights pick up a single Russia soldier with a tommy gun. Barber dims his lights and waits for an order to halt. None comes. Unafraid, he drives slowly past the soldier. He sees that the little swine is grinning. Then the Russian opens up point blank. Six bullets rip into the side of the car; one smashes a wheel, another blows off the tailpipe. Then two or three bullets smash windows on the left-hand side and the windshield. Barber knows he's been hit. He jams on the brakes and slumps against Delmer. Tom Delmer jumps out of the car and runs to rave at the little Russian in what little Russian he possesses, explaining they are British journalists. The Russian, gawking at his handiwork, replies, but Delmer does not understand him. Barber, meanwhile, who can feel the blood oozing out of his chest and sticking to his shirt, manages to stagger out of the car. He nearly collapses while urging hoarsely: "Tom, Tom, get me to a doctor!" Delmer and their Hungarian interpreter bind up Barber's head with their handkerchiefs and bundle him back into the car.

Delmer has no idea where to find a doctor, but he knows where the British Legation is and drives them there, clanking along on three and a half wheels.

Barber is quickly bedded down and smothered in blankets and hot water bottles. "See that the office gets the story," Barber keeps gasping. "God what a headache I've got!" But it takes an hour for the doctor to reach the Legation and by then Barber, having lost so much blood, is white as a sheet. The doctor's first words: "He needs a transfusion—even before the operation."

An ambulance drives him to the nearest hospital. Even with lights ablaze and a Red Cross flag flying on an obvious ambulance, the Russians open fire on them twice. After the transfusion, Barber is operated on for over an hour. Two head wounds take fifty stitches, but by some miracle the bullet which has penetrated his skull behind his left ear had not touched his brain.[148]

*   *   *   *

In the Kremlin the Soviet Presidium has been meeting all day. In the morning Voroshilov and Molotov have been mounting an attack on Comrades Suslov and Mikoyan. At one point Voroshilov even says "American secret services are more active in Hungary than Comrades Suslov and Mikoyan are." But Khrushchev and Bulganin and many others reproach Voroshilov for his remarks. When news comes of Nagy's announcement earlier today that the recent events had been a "national, democratic uprising" and not a "counter-revolution," consternation breaks out and the attacks on Mikoyan and Suslov are renewed.

Voroshilov suggests "working out a line of our own" and then making "a group of Hungarians" join it. Bulganin goes even further, concluding that at some point "we may have to appoint a government ourselves."

Earlier Bulganin has agreed with Khrushchev that a political solution is preferable, "otherwise we have to resort to occupation. That would make us adventurists." Khrushchev, at this point, brings in a new argument for a peaceful, political solution being preferable when he observes "the British and French are just beginning to make trouble in Egypt. Let us not end up in the same company."

Now it is late evening and Suslov's latest report is presented orally to the Presidium. Voroshilov and Molotov refrain from their earlier criticism. The situation is more complex than they had imagined and an inconclusive discussion goes well into the next day, October 29.[149]

At the UN

At the United Nations in New York the Security Council is being called into an emergency Sunday session for the first time since June 1950 when the North Koreans invaded South Korea. At that time the Soviet Union was boycotting the Security Council in a dispute over rotation so it was not present when the Security Council passed the "uniting for peace" resolution enabling the UN to take immediate action against the communist invasion. The Soviet Union learned its lesson. Never again will the communist bloc be found without the Soviet veto, and that is something which France, Great Britain and the U.S., who have called this meeting, are trying to avoid. The letter to the current Council President, M. Cornut-Gentille of France, is couched in delicate terms, the revolution in Hungary being referred to as the "situation in Hungary," and the USSR is not identified as "a party to the dispute" lest it erupt from the very beginning and try to block any discussion at all by wild countercharges. Some, familiar with the UN Charter, find this rather strange, for if a country is named "a party to the dispute" it is automatically forbidden to vote in any debate about it. But John Foster Dulles is sensitive to the charge, already being heard in the West, that it is his policies of "liberation" and "rollback" which have caused the uprising—and he would rather not give the Soviets a chance to get into that.

It is midnight in Budapest, but only four in the afternoon in New York. Dulles, who has been at his desk practically since he returned from Dallas, is in constant touch by phone and teletype with his Ambassador to the UN,

Henry Cabot Lodge, Jr. The two have been working all weekend, both on the letter requesting the emergency meeting and on a draft resolution which they will put before the Council. But in addition, Dulles has been cabling nearly the entire roster of U.S diplomatic posts around the world in an effort to build a strong majority of support before going to the UN.

It is not an easy task to mobilize the entire free world over a weekend. Dulles has personally passed on every cable, and re-written many of them before scrawling his last name in giant letters at the bottom. U.S. Ambassadors and Chiefs of Mission have had to abandon their weekend plans at the last minute in order to corral Foreign Ministers or heads of state, who are themselves engaged in private weekend activities. Many agree to back the tripartite effort wholeheartedly, but many are caught off guard, need to confer with their president, etc. so it is a mixed bag of responses. Nonetheless, considering that all this activity has taken place on a Saturday and Sunday morning, to have reached so many with a positive result is quite a remarkable achievement.

Just as the tripartite powers expect, Soviet representative Arkady A. Sobolev wastes no time in launching into every argument he can think of to dismiss a discussion of "the situation in Hungary" by accusing the Western powers of causing the uprising in the first place, of trying to cover up for their colonial problems in Algeria and Cyprus, of using the trouble in Hungary to gain votes in the U.S. election and trying to stir up more trouble in Hungary by giving the Hungarians the impression that the UN is going to do something. Everything that he throws out calls for an answer from some delegate, even if not the authors of the letter.

At one point the President of the Council, M. Cornut-Gentille, rebukes Sobolev, saying: "So far, however, there is every reason to believe that the foreign intervention was spontaneous and that it occurred before any appeal was made by the Hungarian government. Moreover, that appeal was not made until after the night of October 23–24, when the Soviet troops intervened. There was, therefore no justification in the Warsaw Treaty for their intervention, for according to article four of that Treaty its members are allied against foreign aggression only; it could certainly be invoked by the Hungarians against the Russians, but not by the Hungarians against the Hungarians…"

For some reason neither Lodge, nor anyone else, picks up on this argument. They are all too busy answering Sobolev's numerous charges. "It is

clear that we are not going to try to reach a vote today on anything of substance, so that there can be no sound reason for the delay." (Lodge and
Dulles are convinced that the longer they can delay a vote, the more progress
will be made by the revolutionaries, so that when a cease-fire comes the
Soviet position will be less tenable. Time, they think, is on their side.)[150]

After the Security Council Session, Lodge telegrams Washington the latest draft of a resolution which, if it passes, will be the only UN "action" at
this time. After the usual "whereas" clauses it says:

> Considering the events which have taken place in Hungary and the direct
> intervention of Soviet troops...
> Desiring to see respected the independence and sovereignty of Hungary...
> Invites the USSR to cease immediately all intervention in internal affairs
> in Hungary.[151]

The lion, after all of the diplomatic commotion around the world, seems
poised to give birth to a mouse.

CHAPTER VI

Revolution Triumphant (Part 1)

TO SAY THAT THE REVOLUTION *by October 29, 1956 was "triumphant," when there is still considerable fighting ahead and many government changes have not yet occurred, may seem unduly arbitrary or even premature. But here are some irrefutable facts that tend to justify the epithet. First, what occurred in Budapest—a physical confrontation with the authorities— occurred almost simultaneously in the provincial cities across Hungary. Second, with the exception of Budapest, the municipal governments and party apparatus, even the ÁVO, in all of these towns had disappeared and had been replaced by revolutionary councils. Third, a cease-fire had been called for by a national government which was only barely in control of Budapest at the time. Fourth, Nagy had publicly announced that Soviet troops would soon be leaving Budapest, and on the twenty-ninth that "soon" became "now." Fifth, by the twenty-ninth not only was there a mostly free press, every radio in the country, save Radio Kossuth in Budapest, was call-ing itself "free radio such-and-such." Sixth, all the main demands made of the government were unanimous and the first of these was that Russian troops should leave Hungary. By the twenty-ninth, there was nothing the communist party, the security police or the Soviets could have done to reverse any of these facts. The Revolution had triumphed.*

But here on the twenty-ninth of October 1956 is also a good time to pause and recognize a fact which most historians have ignored because few names or dates can be attached to it. That fact, or phenomenon, which astounded Hungarians at the time as much as it did the outside world, was the behav-ior of the children of Budapest. For it was the kids, schoolboys and school-

girls, and in many cases street urchins considered the riff-raff of society, who did the most to defeat the thought-to-be invincible Soviet Army. It was only a battle, not a war, but the Freedom Fighters won it, and they could not have without the heroic sacrificial feats of these children. In not being able to come close to defeating the insurgents, those hundreds of Soviet tanks, which will rumble out of Budapest on the thirtieth and thirty-first, have themselves been defeated.

There are existing accounts of some of these children's feats. Here are just a few:

Endre Márton, Hungarian chief Budapest correspondent for the Associated Press, who himself was arrested and jailed from January 1955 to August 1956 just prior to the Revolution, wrote on October 30: "Misi is a hero...at thirteem. Thanks to training in the Communist Youth Movement he knew how to shoot a gun...Wounded in the leg by a grenade, he is recovering in the children's ward of a Budapest hospital. I found him playing with the other children in the ward, a model airplane their toy."

An Austrian doctor, just back from Budapest on the twenty-eighth of October, told the Reuters correspondent in Vienna, "I saw Hungarian children taking part in the battle against the Russians. I saw young girls push burning rags into Soviet vehicles and a nine-year-old boy sabotage a Russian armored car. He was cutting the tires with a cramp iron. While a Russian soldier fixed it with a spare wheel, he crept under the armored car and bored a hole into its gas tank. Then he held a match to the escaping gasoline. I couldn't see whether he escaped or was burned with the car."

Another Austrian told the Neue Kurier *of Vienna on October 26 that "he had seen a thirteen-year-old girl marching with a group of 120 workers pointing rifles at a Soviet tank. When a few bursts of machine-gun fire felled a number of them, one of whom was carrying a Hungarian flag, the girl picked up the flag and marched on until she, too, was shot down. The doctors discovered on her a letter written to her mother saying that her brother had been killed and she had to replace him."*

Russell Jones of the United Press wrote of "a fourteen-year-old girl, who turned herself into a human torch to set fire to three Russian trucks and the guns they towed. She died with a half dozen Russian soldiers caught in the flames. I saw the charred remains of her body...covered with a Hungarian flag and a pathetic bunch of artificial flowers.

"An elderly man wept as he translated a note pinned to the flag: 'Here

lies a Hungarian girl of fourteen years. She died for her country. All Hungary mourns her.'"

Gordon Shepherd reported to his paper The Daily Telegraph *on October 29 that he "had seen a boy aged eight or nine climb onto a Soviet tank and pour a little bottle of gasoline into its eye slits in an attempt to start a blaze."*

Noel Barber, in his book Seven Days of Freedom, *wrote that when Eugene-Géza Pogány, a Vienna newspaper correspondent, toured the Kilián Barracks, he saw a small, pitiful figure with blond hair, his face deathly white, in a hospital bed. He inquired whether he was wounded.*

"'Not at all,' replied the Army doctor. 'The boy's totally exhausted. With a machinegun he defended an important street intersection virtually alone for three days and nights.'

"The boy's name was Jancsi (Johnny). He was thirteen."

Doubtless Jancsi recovered and returned to the fight. Less certain is whether he survived.

So it was not just the university students—though they were in combat by the hundreds and scores of them died heroic deaths; and it was not just the young workers—though thousands of them were in combat and hundreds died heroic deaths. Without the children, they could never have destroyed all those tanks. And the kids themselves could never have done it had they not possessed incredible courage and willingness, even eagerness, to sacrifice themselves.

Where did this come from?

Since most of them perished, we shall never know the real answer to that question. But we can at least attempt to divine an answer by looking at what they had already experienced in their short lives. Their entire remembered lives had been lived under Communism. They had been taught from kindergarten up that Socialism (Communism) was the highest calling of mankind, and that they, and everyone in the Soviet world, must make sacrifices for the common good. They were taught that because of Socialism (Communism), they were living in a happy, prosperous time and that things would only get better and better. They had this drummed into them day in and day out.

But when they went home they heard their parents talk of higher wages, shorter working hours and much greater happiness in the days of "capitalist exploitation." What they saw and experienced in their day-to-day lives— broken down transportation, houses with peeling paint, potholes in their muddy streets, shortages of shoes, clothes, even sometimes food, long lines with the people in them grumbling and snapping at each other—was in such sharp contrast to, almost the exact opposite of, what they were being told in school and on the radio, that they soon began to associate Socialism (Communism) with lies and lying. Many of the children, certainly, came from basically Christian homes and had been taught right from wrong. But the regime so oppressed the Church and individual believers, and fear was so pervasive in this period, that this was not always the case. More likely it was something deep in the human personality that yearns for justice and decency over evil and degeneracy. The children began to think of communists as "them," and they did not want to be like "them." Being open, just, and decent was what they craved, and when the time came they embraced these to the full.

On a more personal level, each child had a friend whose parents or relative had been fined, or put in jail or been deported to the countryside, or whose older brother or brother's friend had been picked up by the ÁVO and been grilled and tortured before being released. And all these bad things were done by "them," the Communists. On a still more personal level, they had come home from school to find their father or mother in silent tears at the kitchen table, their father possibly drunk in his misery, and not willing to talk about it. Maybe it was a lost job, a denunciation by a neighbor, demotion or fine. Maybe the reason was even having to agree to spy on the neighbors for the ÁVO, in return for enough money to pay overdo rent and avoid eviction. Whatever the unacknowledged cause of their tears, the children knew it had something to do with "them."

So without realizing it, each filled up a personal well of undying hatred for "them," the cause of everyone's misery. Any way they could find to cheat, lie to, or obstruct "them," whether in or out of school, the kids considered a victory. It became a major source of enjoyment in their daily life of "play."

When the Revolution burst all of their bonds, all this came out into the open. Children their age who had been regarded as secret or potential colleagues, now became real friends in no time. And, as in all friendships, rivalry to outdo the other in the great game of destroying Soviet tanks played its part. So, too, did loyalty in these new friendships. If you had a good friend whom "they" had killed in front of your eyes, getting back at them for killing your friend became your strongest motive.

All this, of course, is speculation, for we do not know what went on in

246

their minds. They are gone. They are part of what Timothy Garten Ash calls the "evaporation of history." What we do know—and what the people of Budapest and the Russians knew at the time—is that they performed with such daring, such incredible bravery and persistence, that they outshone their elders. The Revolution was in danger of sputtering out. The Russians, to all intents and purposes, were gaining full control. Yet it was the children's incredible acts of bravery which inspired their elders to keep the Revolution going. Their extraordinary behavior remains a unique phenomenon in the history of the twentieth century.

Budapest, Monday, October 29, 1956

A cold north wind has brought winter overnight. Snow is sticking in the Mátra mountains; in Budapest it is a mixture of snow and rain sweeping down the Danube and gusting around the corners of buildings. It simply returns yesterday's wind-dried city to a new wetness.

The sixth day of the Hungarian Revolution dawns with Soviet soldiers still in the streets and tanks at every major intersection. The first street-sweepers are at work clearing, with tinkle and crash, the endless mounds of brick and splintered glass. Occasional gunfire is heard, but no major battles are in progress. Soviet troops are uncomfortably on the defensive. Many have told Russian-speaking Hungarians that their orders, before entering Budapest, were that they would be fighting fascists backed by American troops. In fact one Soviet officer says he was told "the place is full of American troops."[1] The facts that a) this is obviously not so, and that b) the Hungarian people now hate them for the havoc they have wrought, must have penetrated even the thickest of skulls. The wild, trigger-happy phase is over. Except when trying to exterminate the freedom fighters, they are now on their best behavior.

The solidarity and moral discipline of the city's population have been astounding. There is an unwritten law that no plundering is to take place and wherever a few criminal elements, released mistakenly when political prisoners where freed, break this law, it is quickly corrected and compensated for. People take a fierce pride in disproving the lies of Radio Budapest, which said the capital was "prey to looters and rioters." And many of the freedom fighters do their best to prevent the lynching of hated ÁVO officers. Four of them today will prevent the lynching of an ÁVO major. They will agree with the crowd that the mere fact that he is a major in the ÁVO means that he deserves to die, but if the crowd does put him to death without a trial, it will only be used by the government to blacken the nature of their "cause." They strip him of his uniform and let him go.[2]

The big question hanging over the city is: can the Nagy government get the Russians out of Budapest, and once that is accomplished, can they get them out of Hungary? Will the Soviets ever agree to relinquish their control over Hungarian uranium? Nagy has promised they will leave Budapest, but he still faces two big obstacles: Rákosi holdovers in his government who bitterly oppose any form of coalition government and the Soviet Union which does not want to abandon its military grip on all of Eastern Europe. Until Hungary can secede from the Warsaw Pact, there is little hope of this.

The leaders of all the revolutionary groups are still meeting with government officials. Having earlier been invited over to the Ministry of Defense, they all now traipse through the cold blustery dawn to that building. They are met by Brigadier General Gyula Váradi, who has them sit down in the lobby. After it becomes obvious that Váradi is to be their sole contact at the Defense Ministry, some of these leaders become indignant and insist that the group be received by the Minister himself, who has been seen arriving at the building. So finally they are taken to meet the Minister Lt. General Károly Janza and his superior, General István Kovács.

After about half an hour of reviewing the negotiations General Janza picks up the telephone to tell Imre Nagy that he is negotiating the "surrender" of the revolutionaries' arms. Several leaders jump to their feet as Ödön Pongrátz shouts "By no means! We are ready to hand over our arms only to those in whose hands we see the accomplishments of our glorious revolution secure!" Nagy at this point says he wants to receive the group. They all head over to the Parliament building. It is 9:45 a.m.

In the course of discussions with Nagy, Janza argues that an armored division cannot be withdrawn in such a short time, and he begins to list all the technical difficulties. This is too much for Ödön Pongrátz and some of his follow leaders. He jumps up and pounds on the table saying: "If they were able to appear on the scene in three hours, they can certainly leave in six!" Shouts of "Yes! Yes!" and other loud comments follow and nearly all of them stand up and start arguing. First Minister Janza stands up and tries to calm the group and then Nagy tries. Even though he succeeds in getting them back into their seats, Nagy, despite his moral prestige as a national figure, is too passive to take charge. The arguing seems to lead nowhere. Janza insists that as soon as the Russians withdraw people will start killing all the Communists. Finally, after two hours of heated discussion the revolutionaries agree that they will hand over their weapons to the Hungarian Army, since they are convinced by now that the Army will never fight against them.[3]

News that the United Nations Security Council has adjourned without even adopting a resolution about Hungary comes as a shock to those who hear it this morning on their radios. For days the revolutionaries have voiced their dismay over the failure of the West, and particularly the United States, to give them any real help. "You know," one English-speaking Hungarian tells John MacCormac of the *New York Times*, "we have been rather disappointed that you have not helped us." When MacCormac asks him if he wants World War III, the man replies: "Not that, but tell me, if China could send volunteers to Korea, why could not the United States send us some help?"

The revolutionaries with whom MacCormac talks seem utterly objective and clear-headed. They deplore the fact that they have "no organization and therefore no leaders." While they would like to see the fighting end, they are skeptical about Nagy's promises and will never surrender their arms before the Soviets leave. They are also skeptical about the dissolution of the ÁVO.

Indeed, they have every right to be. While the Minister of the Interior later today will announce their dissolution, in fact all the ÁVO will do is remove their Blue Police uniforms and put on fresh uniforms of the regular Police, which each man has in his closet along with civilian clothes for times when they do not want it known that they are ÁVO.[4]

Szabad Nép *Reappears*

For the first time in a week, *Szabad Nép* is published, but with a difference. In place of the communist symbol at the top left-hand side of the front page it now has the Kossuth coat of arms. Its tone and tune have also changed. Under the headline "We Salute the Victorious Dawn..." the lead article makes it sound as though they have been with and for the patriots all along—they just were not able to say so.

But praise for the young is unstinting: "This splendid victory of Hungarian youth is also a triumph in the country's struggle...this youth has proved that it is capable of heroic acts, that they loved the homeland more than their lives...they proved that they truly represent the interests of the nation and the broad masses of the people..."

Of course, we must be wary of "counterrevolutionary groups and looters" which "could inflict much damage, shed much blood, commit atrocities...and may well stain the actions of our revolutionary youth..."

In another article Miklós Molnár counters the dispatch from Budapest printed in *Pravda* yesterday under the title "The Collapse of the Anti-Popular Adventure in Hungary." "The events in Hungary," he writes, "were neither anti-popular, nor an adventure: nor was there a collapse....Something did collapse: that was the rule of the anti-popular Rákosi-Gerő clique."[5]

Marian Bielicki, the Polish correspondent from *Po Prostu* in Warsaw, is a witness to just how the population of Budapest receives this new, pro-Revolution edition of *Szabad Nép*. He sees two soldiers throw out bundles of newspapers from an armored car. But nobody picks them up until the car has driven away. Then only a few people respond. One young man gathers up several copies, shouts something in Hungarian which Bielicki does not understand and then tears them to bits. At this point many people snatch at the bundles and without reading a word, tear the individual newspapers to bits and put them in a trashcan. This is torture for Bielicki, who has recently had sincere discussions with many of the writers of this newspaper.

"Don't read this slop!'" shouts the young man who first approached one of the bundles. "Whatever the Communists print serves the Russians and not the Hungarians. That's why their soldiers are distributing communist newspapers. The Kossuth symbol is just a pretext..."

"But why don't you even read it?" asks Bielicki almost desperately.

Somebody answers: "Even if it is the truth, it comes too late. When you have lied too much, nobody will believe you."[6]

But there are new newspapers out on the streets today. One called *Egyetemi Ifjúság* (University Youth) examines the problem of Imre Nagy in gaining the trust of the nation. "Tuesday evening...the entire Hungarian people trusted Imre Nagy as a man who would represent its interests. Since then this confidence has weakened day-by-day...people feel disappointed in him. This disappointment was caused by mistakes, just as it was a mistake when Radio Free Europe broadcast that it was Imre Nagy who had called in the Soviet troops. Soviet troops were called in by András Hegedűs on Tuesday night. He said so himself to the Writers' delegation, of which László Benjámin was a member. Imre Nagy was fooled and outwitted by the treacherous Gerő clique, which issued orders in his name and behind his back. He was cut off from the people. Then when he learned the truth and discovered what was going on in the street, he was isolated and not permitted to act. On Wednesday morning at six o'clock, the Writers Association phoned Imre Nagy to ask him what measures he intended to take. It was only then that Imre Nagy learned that he was Prime Minister! By then, Soviet troops had already arrived in Budapest....Yesterday, in the first speech he made freely, he announced among other things that the Soviet troops would immediately be withdrawn from Budapest. If he continues to act in this spirit, then we were right when we said that Imre Nagy is a true Hungarian, a man of our revolution..."[7]

Radio Free Győr is the first of the free radios to announce that the Soviet troops are, in fact, beginning to leave Budapest. At 11:15 a.m. they say, "We have learned that...Soviet troops have started to withdraw from the capital. Troops leaving Budapest have already passed through Székesfehérvár." This announcement is repeated at 12:15 and again at 4:00 p.m.[8]

Since peace has come to Borsod County, Radio Free Miskolc broadcasts the announcement that the "Workers' Council of Borsod County calls on all persons who possess weapons and who are not members of the National Guard to report to Miskolc Bocskay Military Establishment and to enlist. Those who do not want to participate...must turn in their weapons."[9]

Some troops withdraw from Budapest

Two British correspondents, A. J. Cavendish of the United Press and Geoffrey Blyth of the London *Daily Mail*, who both arrive in Budapest today, have conflicting versions of the Soviet pullout. Blyth, who found a ring of steel surrounding Budapest when he arrived, sees no sign of movement at all by evening, whereas Cavendish, who arrives via an entirely different route, encounters the pullout even before he has reached the city limits.

The piece he files to London begins:

> Soviet tanks and troops crunched out of this war-battered capital today carrying their dead with them. They left a wrecked city where the stench of death already rises from the smoking ruins to mingle with the chill fog from the Danube River. I arrived here from Warsaw by plane, car and foot, walking the last five miles...

EXPLOSION

No sooner were we on the road north to Budapest than we ran into a massive southbound Soviet convoy headed by two armored cars. Ten T-54 tanks, their red stars still visible through the grime of gunpowder, oil and blood, waddled behind....Then came numerous motorcycles and trucks. On the back of one tank lay the corpse of a Soviet soldier, his eyes staring vacantly back at the Hungarian capital. Other bodies were in the trucks. The Russian tankmen in their black crash helmets looked tired and grim. They were retreating for the first time since they steamrollered into central Europe during World War II...

As Cavendish's car enters the city he sees huge holes where cannon shells have punctured workers' houses and shattered windows on all sides. Telephone and high tension wires loop crazily like wet spaghetti and overturned railroad cars which have been used as barricades look as though a giant sewing machine had stitched bullet holes back and forth.

Now he sees convoys of Hungarian trucks serving as ambulances flying Red Cross flags. The doctors' once-white aprons are so blood-spattered they look like butchers. His car windows are open and he thinks he can hear the moaning of wounded inside. One truck has a large white sign saying "Dead Bodies." The stench is overpowering and soon mingles with the acrid smell of cordite as they enter a devastated area where a battle must have been fought.

Now, well into the suburbs, they see another convoy of Soviet tanks, lumbering along like circus elephants, one behind the other. He counts at least 60. They twitch from side to side as their steel treads slip on wet debris or oil slicks. Bursts of machine-gun fire can be heard in the distance and a Soviet tankman standing in the wide road waves them to a detour. A tank gun coughs in the distance and a split second later there is the muffled concussion felt in the eardrums as the shell explodes. The crack of rifle fire can now be heard, as well.

At length the street becomes so littered that Cavendish decides to abandon the car and walk the rest of the way. Some minutes later, when he has reached Rákóczi Ave., a Soviet tank, not lumbering but roaring along, causes him to jump into a nearby doorway. He feels a twinge of shame, for Hungarian women walking along scarcely take any notice of it. But he can see hatred in their faces. He doubts whether the Soviets have ever churned up such hatred, anywhere, anytime.[10]

Negotiations

It is 2:00 p.m. and a high-level government delegation consisting of Brigadier General Gyula Váradi and Colonels Pál Maléter, Lajos Tóth and András Márton and several others are gathered in Dr. Kramolin's apartment, now the Corvin headquarters. As the Corvin delegation is introduced to them the name "Pongrátz" comes up five times. General Váradi, half in jest, asks whether there are any more Pongrátz brothers. "Yes," comes the answer. "He just went home to see whether our mother and sister are alright."

Col. Maléter leads off by saying:

"Comrades, the Revolution is victorious. The Soviet troops have begun to withdraw from Budapest; therefore, without further wrangling, lay down your arms. The Army will take care of the restoration of law and order and it will take the place of the withdrawing Soviet troops..."

Before he can go further he is interrupted by Ödön Pongrátz: "...It is not possible to talk of laying down arms for the precise reason that the Revolution is victorious. We insist you honor the agreement made at the Ministry of Defense! We agreed on a new armed force which will be made up 50% by the Revolutionaries..."

Maléter wants to reply, but General Váradi cuts him off.

"Theoretically an agreement was reached, but the actual percentage in the National Guard were not agreed upon. We still feel there should be equal representation between the Army, Police and Revolutionaries. I think, too, that it would be of major importance to limit the age to those twenty or older. Those under twenty should be disarmed and the four hundred officers of the Zrínyi Academy should take their place in commanding positions. They can organize the revolutionary groups into Army regiments and they can start their training immediately."

"You can't mean that!" cry several Corvinists. "Eighty percent of our fighters are under the age of twenty. We can thank these youngsters that the Russians are moving out of Budapest and the Revolution has been won. These young people did not take into account the superior power ranged against them; they valued freedom more than their own lives. Almost half of these boys and girls are already national heroes and martyrs. The other half, who still live and have weapons in their hands, must be assured that their comrades did not die in vain."

This causes a lively discussion and the eventual compromise that the youngsters under eighteen will only have their weapons taken from them after the Soviets have left. Another compromise is that the Army officers will be assigned posts alongside the current leaders as advisors, not as commanders. Then discussion turns to the Corvin National Guard unit, which will be set up within the overall National Guard. In the end the Army officers even accept the 50% figure for revolutionary membership in the New National Guard. It is early evening when the meeting breaks up.[11]

The better part of three Soviet mechanized divisions are still in the heart of Budapest, however, and the concentration is so great that Western diplomats and correspondents—excepting Cavendish and those he may have talked to—report no movement whatsoever and even express doubt about whether a Soviet withdrawal will, in fact, take place. Only the free radios are reporting the start of the withdrawal and these cannot be heard in Budapest. Radio Free Europe, which is monitoring the free radios, is reluctant to pass on any such report until it is corroborated by Western journalists or diplomats.

Formation of the National Guard

Ex-Major General Béla Király, after his meeting with Kopácsi and others at police headquarters on October 28, visits Imre Nagy in the Parliament late in the evening of the next day.

Király shows him the proposal he and Kopácsi have come up with for a National Guard made up of Army members loyal to Nagy, freedom fighters and students. Nagy sits down in an armchair and Zoltán Tildy, soon to be Minister of State, sits on one arm and reads over Nagy's shoulder. A few word changes are suggested and then Nagy agrees to sign the document.

Király and his colleagues march proudly out of the great hall with official authority to supervise two ministries, and set up a National Guard to keep order in the country.

It is nearly dawn on the thirtieth when the group gets back to Police Headquarters. Király finds he has been summoned by the Army's Revolutionary Committee to the Defense Ministry. Despite Nagy's signature, Király is still an ex-General under sentence of life for allegedly having spied on his country. In the main meeting room of the Defense Ministry the Committee is in the process of firing Generals Tóth, Szabó, Hazai and Hidvégi, who are considered Rákosi-Stalinists. Király is known to most of the men in the room. When his six-foot-four, ramrod straight frame appears in the doorway, a cheer goes up.

As soon as the ovation dies down the chairman of the meeting proposes that Király be immediately appointed chairman of the Revolutionary Military Committee. But General Váradi rises from the audience and says, "I was one of the judges who condemned Király. I cannot vote for his chairmanship before he answers one question: During his trial he confessed that he was a conspirator and saboteur, so I naturally was convinced he had committed these crimes. Now I cannot decide what to do."

Király responds that it is beneath his dignity to respond to security police charges, but that no, he was never a spy.

The chairman then announces that Király will be their new chairman and instructs the attorney general of the Army to review Király's sentence so that it can be legally quashed and he can be restored to his former rank within the next twenty-four hours. Organizing the new National Guard begins with opening the Army's arsenal for the arming of some twenty-six thousand Freedom Fighters.

This morning Király visits Defense Minister General Károly Janza and tells him he will accept the appointment of Budapest Commander on two conditions: that he have his own staff and that some forty generals whom Rákosi had kicked out of the Army be reinstated. Janza agrees to both.[12]

The Soviet Line

In Moscow, *Pravda* is cleaving to the original Soviet line on Hungary. "Events in Hungary," it writes, "made it crystal clear that a reactionary counterrevolutionary underground, well-armed and thoroughly prepared for decisive action against the people's government, had been organized with outside help. This is borne out by the fact that the rebels acted according to a plan laid out in advance and were led by people experienced in military affairs, namely by officers of the Horthy regime....Bourgeois propaganda is now trying to present the working people as the pioneers of the armed rising..."[13]

Two diplomatic receptions are held here this afternoon and evening, one at the Afghanistan Embassy for the visiting Afghan Prime Minister and the other at the Turkish Embassy in celebration of the Turkish national holiday. British Ambassador Sir William Hayter and American Ambassador Charles Bohlen, despite efforts to avoid more than normal courtesies, find themselves being sought out at both receptions by Prime Minister Bulganin and Party Secretary Khrushchev, who are more than usually effusive. The Soviet leadership in general, most of which is present, seem to be in considerably better spirits than on the last two occasions when they were seen in public.

The fact that the two Soviet leaders are so eager to be seen chatting with the two top Western diplomats makes Bohlen feel that some clear decision has been made about Hungary. Hayter has noted that there was a stream of black cars entering the Kremlin yesterday, indicating that a meeting of the Presidium was taking place, a rare occasion for a Sunday. Bohlen feels, and Hayter tends to agree, that the decision to back Nagy and be guided by him in the use of Soviet troops in Hungary has been made by the Presidium. Foreign Minister Shepilov answers questions put to him by Western journalists.

Soviet troops in Hungary have already stopped firing, he says, and if the insurgents cease-fire and if there is no danger, Soviet troops will withdraw from Budapest. Asked about the causes of the events in Hungary, he replies that there are circles who wish to improve the work of the state administration and also the welfare of the people. There were "bureaucratic manifestations" in the past and one must satisfy the demands of workers, peasants and intellectuals for the improvement of the situation. (This, the journalists note, is quite a different line from this morning's *Pravda*.) Asked about Nagy's statement that he would demand that Soviet troops definitely withdraw from all of Hungary, Shepilov cuts the conversation off with "I have said all I have to say about that."

Marshal Zhukov is only present at the Turkish reception, so when Zhukov deliberately approaches him, U.S. Ambassador Bohlen is pleased to have an extended conversation, narrowing his focus to Hungary and Poland. Zhukov sticks straight to the Party line with a mixture of outright lies, half-truths and "possibly some elements of real fact." Asked about the Nagy statement about total withdrawal, Zhukov maintains that the statement had not referred to "immediate" withdrawal from Budapest, that Soviet troops, there by invitation, would not leave until asked to or "until order is restored." On the general withdrawal: this was a matter which must be considered by all of the members of the Warsaw Pact. Zhukov then makes the following statements: 1. No Soviet forces had been sent to Hungary "recently" (i.e. within sixty-four hours). 2. Soviet troops had only opened fire *after* some of their officers had been killed by the insurgents, 3. Soviet troops in Hungary are not under his command, but under the command of the Hungarian Minister of Defense, 4. Soviet troops had only been in action in Budapest and had taken no action against "new" local authorities in the rest of Hungary, 5. Not a single Soviet soldier has defected to the rebels, and 6. Soviet losses in Budapest, contrary to Western news reports, have not been heavy.

Zhukov insists he is not a politician and that the sole function of the Army is to carry out orders given to it.[14]

American Policy Approaches

Back in Budapest, U.S. Chargé d'Affaires Spencer Barnes is trying to give his government his best suggestions as to what the U.S. should do.

In the morning, after giving his assessment of the local situation he says that "the Legation considers that the number one problem for the U.S. in the Security Council is to demonstrate that what has developed here is a war between the Hungarian people on the one hand and the USSR and a small group of strategically-located Quislings* on the other."[15]

In the evening he speculates that the Soviet Presidium, from current signs, may be fairly evenly divided between those who want to crush the revolution and those who want to solve the problem with Nagy and without further military action. "If this is a good guess," he cables Washington, "and if the reaction in the West is weak-kneed," that fact would appear to tip the scale "in favor of the iron fist school. The Legation would recommend that pressure on the Soviets be heavy and in any possible form that appears compatible with Washington's assessments of the risks."[16]

An hour later he adds that the "Nationalistic groups desperately need (A) high level support from the Western powers which probably involves the offer of an international commission to represent the nationalistic cause in negotiating a settlement...and (B) Western military material support to give a better bargaining strength and fighting potential [to the nationalists] if the conflict is to be kept alive."[17]

Meanwhile in Washington, Secretary of State John Foster Dulles is at the White House talking to President Eisenhower. He has no idea what the cur-

---

*Quisling was the Norwegian collaborator whom the Nazis made Prime Minister of Norway during World War II. Because Norway was among the first European countries conquered by the Nazis, the name Quisling quickly became synonymous with "traitor/collaborator" and has remained so ever since.

rent situation on the ground in Hungary is, nor is he particularly concerned with it. The important thing right now is to avoid any situation which might flare up into World War III. He wonders if it might not be desirable to try to find an occasion for Ambassador Bohlen to bring to the attention of the Soviet leaders the statement he had made in his Dallas speech assuring the Soviets that the U.S. has no "ulterior motives." It would be stressed that he had made this statement "with the full approval of the President." Eisenhower agrees, but then adds that it might be good to draw Nehru into it. He then reads a letter addressed to Dulles, which he has dictated just a few minutes before, on the subject of involving Nehru. Dulles, who cannot stand Nehru, says yes, he has been thinking along the same lines, and then reads Eisenhower a statement *he* has written on the plane back from Dallas addressed not to Nehru, but the Soviet leaders about his Dallas statement.

The President observes that the Soviets might be willing to talk sense now, more than at any time since his administration has been in power. The way he might approach it would be to say to them that things are not going the way any of us want and we had better have a meeting to recognize these points. Would Shepilov be the right person to approach? Dulles replies that Shepilov is pretty far down the ladder. Undoubtedly, he adds, there is a battle going on in the Presidium—some obviously want to go back to Stalin's ways—but it is too late, now, for that. He adds that they are "up against a tough problem." Yes, replies Eisenhower, we need to take advantage of that. Now is the time to talk about reducing tensions in the world. Dulles agrees, but without much enthusiasm. We would have to be very careful not to do anything which might make it look to the satellite world that we were selling them out, he concludes.

Of course, says the President, nothing much can be accomplished until things are settled down. Then he goes back to his idea of involving Nehru as a third party, but this elicits no response from the Secretary.[18]

Dulles then hurries back to the State Department, where he cables the Embassy in Moscow:

> Personal for Ambassador from Secretary. I call your attention to the following language from my Saturday night speech at Dallas.
>
> "The U.S. has no ulterior purpose in desiring the independence of the satellite countries....We do not look upon these nations as potential military allies..."

We would like this to come to the attention of the highest Soviet authorities, including Zhukov...Dulles[19]

Among the many messages deposited into his "In" box this afternoon is a priority telegram which was sent at 7:00 a.m. today from U.S. Ambassador Henry Cabot Lodge in New York. It reads:

Re Hungary in the United Nations Security Council:

following is the plan of action:

1. The U. S. Mission to the UN will negotiate a draft resolution with other Security Council members, seeking a nine-power sponsorship, which will call for withdrawal of all Soviet Armored forces, political police and para-military forces and seek to verify the withdrawal by UN observation of a "neutral" and "objective" kind.

2. The resolution will be introduced at a Security Council meeting on Thursday, November 1

3. Possibly [could] interrogate the Hungarian [delegate] at the Council Table.

4. We will adjourn the meeting without seeking a vote.

For the above plan we will need at the earliest possible moment the State Department's ideas on the maximum and minimum contents of the draft resolution.

Lodge

British Policy Approaches

In London, the Foreign Office receives a morning telegram from their Ambassador at the United Nations in New York, Sir Pierson Dixon, stating that "the Italian Government were apparently themselves about to request a meeting of the Council when it was learned that the tripartite action had already been taken." Their "draft went a good deal further than our own letter in suggesting that the Council should urgently apply 'the measures provided for by the Charter,' and, first of all, make an investigation in Hungary of the grave situation there. We suggested that it would be unwise to use such language when we none of us yet knew what action the Council might usefully take. This suggestion was well taken and my Italian colleague has agreed to amend his letter....The Americans are encouraging other delegations to express their concern by writing to the President [of the Council] and not ask to participate in the Council proceedings."[20]

Not long afterwards the Foreign Office receives a short burst of a message from Sir Leslie Fry in Budapest: "The Hungarians are doing what the Yugoslavs did in 1948," he cables. "The only difference is that the Hungarians, with far greater cause, have rejected not merely Russian domination but communism also. Should we not say this bluntly and publicly?"

The record shows no Foreign Office reply to this outburst, but one Peter Matthews, a high official in the Northern Department, which includes Hungary, is distressed at the Legation's suggestion that it discontinue sending factual reports since there are now so many British journalists in Budapest. "It is difficult to exaggerate the importance of Mr. Fry's factual telegrams, which have been almost the only source of news from Budapest. Without them the Budapest Radio would have had matters entirely their own way.

"If the Russians do withdraw their troops, this will have been, to a substantial extent, because world opinion has been able to observe their performance in Budapest. But for Mr. Fry's telegrams, this would not have been possible.

"The BBC have made a strong request that they may not be cut off from this source of information."[21]

This internal memo has almost immediate results, for at 7:10 GMT Foreign Minister Selwyn Lloyd himself telegraphs to Fry: "Today's experience shows press communications remain uncertain and that your reports are irreplaceable. Please therefore telegraph as often and as fully as you can...I may have to make statements in the House from time to time and I must rely on your reports to put events in correct perspective. I cannot rely on press messages."[22]

In the House of Commons this evening Foreign Secretary Selwyn Lloyd, in fact, gives a speech on Hungary. In the course of it he explains what Britain is doing in concert with others in the UN and announces that "As a practical gesture of sympathy, Her Majesty's government have ordered the dispatch by Royal Air Force aircraft of 15,000-pounds worth of medical supplies and 10,000-pounds worth of food from British Army stores in Germany to Vienna for relief work in Hungary."[23]

Reactions in the East

In the communist countries media reaction to events in Hungary follow closely the Soviet line, with the exception of Yugoslavia and Poland. In Belgrade the Communist Party daily, *Borba*, says that the Nagy government "is still in time" in the sense that a "realistic possibility exists to prevent the worst." The new government, with its "positive program," possesses a "real chance—provided it starts carrying the program out in a decisive way—to prevent the outbreak of civil war, re-establish peace, and make possible the further development of socialism" (read "communism"). It goes on to point out that "state affairs cannot be improved until the Rákosi-Gerő elements (Hegedűs, for example) who are responsible for the present crisis are removed." Tanjug, the Yugoslav press agency, publishes the text of a letter this evening sent by Tito earlier today to the Hungarian Workers (Communist) Party. "The significance of these events," he points out, "far surpasses Hungary's frontiers because they directly concern the interests of the international socialist development in general." Tito is clearly worried about the effect of the revolution on the vast majority of Yugoslav people who are almost as fed up with communism as the Hungarians.[24]

In Bucharest, *New York Times* correspondent Welles Hangen hears rumors all day of numerous arrests of Magyar student leaders of demonstrations in cities throughout Transylvania, particularly Cluj (Hungarian: Kolozsvár) and Timişoara (Hungarian: Temesvár), but as the Romanian authorities have forbidden any Western journalists to travel outside of Bucharest, he is unable to obtain any hard facts.

In Warsaw, students mount an honor guard in front of the Polish-Hungarian Institute. A Hungarian national flag, with an inscription, "In Tribute to the Hungarian Nation," flies over the building. Numerous candles have been lit in front of the Institute and a box, overflowing with Polish zlotys, sits among them to collect donations for drugs and medicines for Hungary.[25]

Reactions in the West

Media reaction in the West continues to glow with astonishment and praise for what now are known universally as the Hungarian Freedom Fighters. Even left-wing newspapers which have muted their criticism of the USSR in the past, like the Norwegian *Arbeiderblat*, do not spare the rhetoric.

"We are following a struggle which seems hopeless," writes the socialist paper, "but which has been carried forward by an invincible force we have seldom seen...it is as if the torrent of history is passing through us, which

261

happens only rarely in a lifetime….It looks as though we may even hope for what is least probable: a victory.

"We remember once before we had this feeling that the history of the world…was opening its gates to a new period of happiness for mankind. That was thirty-nine years ago: the Russian Revolution…

"One thing we will say now…because circumstances have already spoken unmistakably: Communism is finished…."[26]

In Paris, U.S. Ambassador Douglas Dillon reports on the first session of the Fifth Congress of the International Peasant Union, just concluded, where tension over Hungary was evident in every speech. The resolution, which was adopted unanimously, greets the Hungarian freedom fighters, calls on all Hungarians around the world to aid their countrymen against the Soviets, and appeals to the UN Security Council to send a special commission immediately to Budapest to organize an armistice. The resolution also appeals for volunteers to go fight in Hungary.

Reaction in Denmark has been particularly active. All Danish newspapers today are soliciting help for Hungary following the example of two Danish businessmen, the Tholstrup brothers, who on the first day of the revolution personally equipped two trucks with medicine and food and drove them to the Austro-Hungarian border. A big protest meeting is taking place today in K. B-Hallen where the former Minister of Foreign Affairs, Ole Bjorn-Kraft, and Frode Jacobsen, former Minister and member of the Danish Liberty Council, are the featured speakers. While police are guarding the Soviet Embassy from the wrath of the Danish people, someone last night did manage to explode a bomb nearby, fortunately with no injuries.[27]

Yesterday the Finnish Red Cross launched a nationwide appeal for blood and medicines for Hungary, and today all of Helsinki's non-communist papers are featuring the appeal, with no reference, of course, to the Soviet Union. By yesterday evening the Finns had dispatched by air, via Frankfurt and Vienna, 436 flasks of blood plasma complete with transfusion apparatus.[28]

Demonstrations of support and pleas for aid have been particularly vociferous and numerous among the Hungarian emigrants in the West. In Canada, where there are sixty thousand Hungarian émigrés, demonstrations have taken place in all the major cities, particularly in Vancouver and Toronto, under the sponsorship of the Canadian Hungarian Federation. Today the President of the Federation, Gábor Temesváry, leads a six-man delegation to ask Canada's External Affairs Minister, Lester Pearson, to denounce Soviet brutality and give all possible food and medical aid to the insurgents. Minister Pearson tells the delegation that an RCAF plane has been furnished to fly five tons of Red Cross medical supplies to Hungary. The Federation is also sponsoring a new organization called "The Legion of Freedom," to be composed of volunteers to go fight in Hungary "should the need arise." A retired Hungarian General, Jenő Tömöry, will head the legion.

Many churches are raising funds and the Hungarian Jewish Association of Toronto is holding a fund-raising meeting today.

A large poster, made by the Canadian Hungarian Federation and reprinted in a number of newspapers, reads:

Why don't you HELP HUNGARY![29]

In Washington, where Hungarian Americans yesterday demonstrated outside of the White House, one of those demonstrators is now in the Department of State seeing Mr. Robert Murphy, Deputy Under Secretary of State, and Ambassador Jacob Beam. The record lists her as Mrs. Donald Dawson, but she is known to the world as the famous and beautiful movie star Ilona Massey of Hungarian origin. She urges action, not words, and pleads that medicine, ammunition and other supplies be sent to the Freedom Fighters soon because any delays will mean that it will be too late. Mr. Murphy tries to placate her by pointing out what steps have been taken to send medicine and relief supplies and then proudly mentions the action taken by the U.S. in the UN yesterday. Ms. Massey expresses appreciation for the latter, but thinks it is no substitute for sending supplies and ammunition now, before it is too late.[30]

In Munich, West Germany, Imre Pongrácz, principal Munich representative of the exile Hungarian National Council, made up of several dozen émigré organizations and churches both protestant and catholic in Germany and Austria, hands an appeal to the American Consul, Edward Page, Jr. In addition to pointing out that the peace treaty calls for the Soviet Army to leave Hungary at the same time that it left Austria, the appeal states the Soviet Army is there to fight aggression from outside, not to make war on the Hungarian people. The appeal ends with a plea that the United States do all that it can to prevent unjustified reprisals.[31]

RFE to the Rescue

Back in Hungary a dramatic call for help from the hospital in Debrecen earlier today has produced results. At approximately noon Radio Free Miskolc gives the following announcement:

"Attention, Attention, hello, hello, Attention!

"An appeal from the Debrecen hospital:

"We ask you in the interest of saving lives...of private citizens and soldiers who were wounded in the fight for freedom, to send immediately to our hospital a complete iron lung because the one here has been damaged. We await your help...."

Two hours later Radio Free Europe replies:

"Attention! Attention!"

"We heard the urgent message concerning the iron lung. We are doing everything possible to rush the iron lung today to Debrecen. One reason for the delay is that there are no iron lungs available in Munich."

At 10:10 p.m. Radio Miskolc says "This is the Borsod Workers Council. We request that the Hajdúszoboszló Airport illuminate their airfield... because the iron lungs [sic] are on their way."

Four minutes later the same radio says, "We call upon all amateurs to assist in the landing of the airplane, get into contact with the machine and direct it toward Hajdúszoboszló, where a lighted field is awaiting it, descend vertically twenty-five grade and on the horizontally lighted landing."

"Hello! Hello! Attention! The airplane is at present above Debrecen. It is above Debrecen!"

Finally at 11:54 Radio Free Miskolc says: "Attention! Radio stations Ferihegy (the main Budapest airport), Debrecen and all other Hungarian airport radio stations and the German radio station (i.e. RFE) which is directing the plane.

"Attention! You must direct the plane to Miskolc. We are awaiting it. It can land at the Miskolc airport. We shall then forward the iron lung to its place of destination."[32]

Aid from the West

Trucks carrying medical supplies from the Austro-Hungarian border to Budapest are being stopped by Russian troops and not allowed to proceed. This is learned from a British citizen just returned to Vienna from Sopron who talked to many of the drivers earlier today. The Soviets claim that weapons may be concealed in the shipments, so each truck is forced to unload for a thorough inspection. When no weapons are found, the reloaded trucks are still prevented from going to Budapest, pending instructions from Soviet headquarters. This seems to corroborate the U.S. Legation's information that medical supplies that reach the Austro-Hungarian border are not arriving in Budapest.[33]

End of the Day

Close to midnight, two Hungarian tanks with National Guardsmen riding on them issue an ultimatum to the ÁVO who are holed up in their headquarters/barracks on Maros St. in Buda: Surrender by 2 a.m. or the whole building will be destroyed by shelling. Shortly before the deadline, the ÁVO give up without a fight. The ordinary recruits are let go, but it takes three trucks provided by "Uncle Szabó" from Széna Square to cart off all of the officers and non-commissioned officers to the Police Academy in Böszörményi Road. It is easy to tell the guilty ones; they have all changed into fresh civilian clothes, whereas those who know themselves to be guilty of no crimes remain in their uniforms. Inside the building the National Guardsmen discover all the latest type of guns and food and ammunition sufficient enough for them to have held out for five days. Tomorrow, "Uncle Szabó" will shift his headquarters to this building.[34]

Radio Free Győr toward the end of its broadcasting day strives to keep the record straight when it says, "Contrary to what was announced by Radio Budapest, we state that the population of Budapest is still fighting with arms-in-hand for its freedom. Therefore, the Workers' Councils of Pécs, Dorog, Tokod, Tatabánya, Tata, Miskolc and others have adopted a resolution that the immediate departure of the Russians can be attained with one weapon only: the strike. The Workers Councils of Pécs, Dorog and Tata took a pledge that they will not produce coal until the last Russian division is withdrawn from Hungary."[35]

Some Hungarians listening to foreign broadcasts tonight hear a new item few of them pay much attention to. It seems that an Israeli military force today has thrust deep into the Sinai peninsula occupied by Egypt and driven seventy miles before stopping to dig in some twenty miles short of the Suez Canal. The Israelis claim that they have launched the operation in order to diminish the fedayeen bases in the Sinai. The Egyptians deny any official connection with the fedayeen and claim they are throwing the Israeli forces back.[36]

Tuesday, October 30, 1956

On this date so many major, revolutionary events occurred in Hungary that it might easily be considered the most important day of the whole revolution. Premier Nagy declared a new government, dropping the Rákosi holdovers and adding non-communists, thereby announcing the end of one-party rule. Kádár hinted at the end of the Hungarian Workers (Communist) Party, which had, in any case, disintegrated, and that a new party would be formed in its place. The Hungarian Delegate to the UN, Kós, was recalled, the Soviet Army officially began to evacuate Budapest, while unannounced fresh Soviet troops and armor poured into the country from the Ukraine. Radio Budapest became "Radio Free Kossuth" with new employees. A bloody assault by the freedom fighters on the Municipal Party Headquarters at Republic Square ended in summary executions and some lynchings of ÁVO police. A new National Guard under General Király and Col. Kopácsi was designated by Nagy. And Cardinal Mindszenty was liberated and brought to Budapest by a Hungarian Army unit. Yet two things which occurred outside Hungary on the very same day eclipsed all of these significant events. First of all, in Moscow the Russians issued a Declaration greatly altering their foreign policy toward the rest of the Socialist world and particularly the Soviet Union's relations with the satellite countries of Eastern Europe. This new policy appears to place the cap of approval on the major changes that have occurred in Hungary. Second, Britain and France issued a joint ultimatum to Israel and Egypt to pull back their forces, an ultimatum which was a thinly disguised cover for their invasion of Egypt to take back the Suez Canal which Nasser had seized in the early summer. Though totally unrelated to the Hungarian situation, it had the effect of pulling the rug out from under the Revolution by immobilizing the West just when it might have been able to take full advantage of the newly declared Soviet foreign policy, and thus shore up and make permanent Hungary's astounding self-liberation. While the two moves soon became interrelated, no prior knowledge by the Soviets on one side, or the British and French on the other, at least as to the timing of the other's actions, existed. It was a disastrous accident of history that they occurred on the same day.

266

Revolution Triumphant (Part 1)

The Situation in Budapest

The weather has suddenly turned mild. From the freezing temperatures of yesterday it has now warmed up to the mid-50s Fahrenheit and the inhabitants of Budapest this morning enjoy mild sunshine as they walk about shattered sections of their city. All vehicles seem to carry Hungarian tricolor flags, but black flags can be seen on many buildings and white, homemade crosses tilt over shallow graves in parks near to where the fighting was fiercest. One change has been noted on the pedestal of the Petőfi statue, which, aside from the great poet's name carved into its base, has the date, "March 15, 1848." Overnight someone has painted on the back, "October 23, 1956."[37]

Very few Soviet armored vehicles go roaring by; the rest are still stationed at bridges and street corners. The streets are full of pedestrians. Everyone carries at least one newspaper, often two, for the freedom to print without censorship is sprouting journals like mushrooms. Some shop windows are riddled or smashed, but the goods remain untouched. The people Radio Budapest has called "plunderers" caught some people stealing this morning and marched them off to the police station with signs held over them: "We are thieves and brigands."

There is, in fact, a reigning sense of euphoria from the liberating influence of the Revolution's success which brings out goodwill and humor in everyone. After the Russian troops looted the largest delicatessen in Budapest, people quickly erected a sign on its entrance: "This operation was bravely carried out by our glorious Russian allies. We shall not forget their heroic deed."[38]

Westerners, spotted by their clothes, are barraged with questions. "Well, what is happening outside?" comes a question in German. Or "What are Britain and America doing?" comes another in English. "Will they send us some bazookas*?"[39]

Radio Budapest, though it cannot avoid broadcasting major events of the rapidly changing scene, is still trying to influence the populace by stretching the truth. Thus in the early morning it claims: "the withdrawal of Soviet troops from Budapest...is in progress" when in fact the official withdrawal will not begin until three o'clock this afternoon. "At 9:00 a.m. all fighting

*Handheld tubes for firing anti-tank missiles developed by the Americans for use in World War II.

267

must cease and armed groups still resisting shall then participate in restoring peace and order" it announces as though saying this will make it so. On the other hand, such facts as the firing of István Kovács from his post of First Secretary of the Budapest Party Committee and the election of the dissident Central Committee member, József Köböl, to take his place are factually reported. And the official declarations of the Hungarian Writers Association and the Hungarian Actors and Film Actors Guild extolling the revolution are read on the air by their respective presidents, Péter Veress and Ferenc Bessenyei.[40]

More effective with the Nagy government than any of these broadcast demands are the visits of delegations from all over the country to Nagy himself. Typical of these is one which occurs late tonight when some workers from Csepel present him with a sixteen-point resolution. In conversation with him they get confirmation of Nagy's previous statements about the troop evacuation from Budapest, the dissolution of the Security (Secret) Police and preparations for free elections. They in turn ask him for education for their children according to religious and moral principles, freedom for private craftsmen and, most important, abolition of the Communist Party committees in industrial plants.[41]

At Ferihegy, Budapest's municipal airport, airplanes from Britain, Poland, Czechoslovakia, East Germany and Romania arrive at various points throughout the day bearing medicine and food.[42]

Young Communists István Angyal and Per Olaf Csongóvai, leaders of the Tüzoltó Street Freedom Fighter group, have been trying to entice the new Party leader, János Kádár, to visit their headquarters to see for himself how dedicated the Freedom Fighters are to the cause of Socialism. Today, during the cease-fire, they visit him in the Parliament building with three others representing the Tompa Street and Corvin Passage groups. Interior Minister Ferenc Münnich and Antal Ápro sit in on the meeting, which takes place around the same time that József Dudás, leader of a Freedom Fighter group in Buda, is meeting with Imre Nagy and the Corvin Passage people are meeting with Col. Pál Maléter.

Kádár says he was convinced, when so many important buildings were being attacked on the first day of the Revolution, that it was well planned. Only later, when he saw the spontaneous rise of workers and revolutionary councils all across the country, did he realize it was a nationwide people's movement. "If we are counterrevolutionaries," they cut in, "what would we be doing with these?" And those who have them slap down their party cards on the table.

"The best way for the Party to save itself," says Angyal, "is if it changes sides. Then the Party could take over the leadership of the Revolution. But it must first take up the demands of the Revolution."

"That is an interesting suggestion," Kádár replies. "But first of all you have to protect all of the Party centers."

"Our offer is not for the Revolution to join the Party," Csongovai explodes. "It is for the Party to join the Revolution!"

"Well, we'll consider this," replies Kádár. "We might find some way for this to happen."

A document of agreement is then drafted. When a typed version comes back, the revolutionaries find it greatly altered. Every reference, for instance, to "Socialism" has been dropped. The next day, when the "agreement" is published in *Szabad Nép*, and the revolutionaries see that almost none of the things Kádár agreed to in the typed text are included, they realize they have been badly cheated.[43]

Situation in the Countryside

An early morning broadcast from Radio Free Győr carries an appeal from the Győr County National Council stating that the general strike does *not* apply to electricity, water and gas workers, nor to workers in the food industries or industries directly connected to consumer goods.[44]

A new center of political power is emerging in Győr today as four hundred delegates from the National Councils recently established in Transdanubia (Dunántúl) converge from all over Western Hungary for a meeting which will last up to midnight tonight. To a Western reporter, Barrett McGurn of the *New York Herald Tribune*, who is observing the scene but does not understand Hungarian, it is proof "that the Hungarian patriots have no organization of any sort." In the course of the meeting, Attila Szigethy, Chairman of the Győr National Council, argues against any steps which might threaten the achievements of the Revolution, particularly setting up a "Counter Government" opposing the Nagy regime in Budapest and continuing the armed struggle when so much has already been won. Nevertheless, the assembly decides it will open negotiations with the Nagy government on the basis of six demands which, given the weakness of the Nagy regime and its obvious inability to achieve them, can certainly be considered unreasonable. It ends its message to the Nagy government with the threat that it will not give it recognition until these six demands have been satisfied. In effect, the western part of the country is declaring its defiance of the government in Budapest.[45]

But it is not only in the countryside that the government is defied. József Dudás, a former communist in his 40s, who had been expelled from the Party in 1946 for being a member of the minority Demény faction and spent eight years in a forced labor camp, has emerged as one of the leaders of the freedom fighters in Buda with some three hundred heavily armed fighters under his command. He calls himself the chairman or president of the Hungarian Revolutionary Committee and acts as though the whole country were behind him. He is the *enfant terrible* of the Revolution and clearly considers himself Nagy's equal. Dudás had left Buda for Pest yesterday and now is ensconced in the *Szabad Nép* building where so many new newspapers are being produced, in addition to *Szabad Nép*. Not only does he issue demands of the Nagy government in the name of his Committee, he aspires to deal on an international level as well. His wishful thinking, which is something he shares with many of his fellow countrymen, is combined with his utter ignorance of the United Nations and how it operates. Thus after declaring that his Committee repudiates the Warsaw Pact as violating both the UN Charter and the Hungarian Peace Treaty, he declares his (the Committee's) intention to place Hungary under the protection of the UN Security Council and wires an appeal directly to the Security Council to this end.

A Cacophony of Freedom Radios

The airwaves in Hungary today are filled with new voices on newly established "free" radios. In addition to the powerful stations at Győr and Miskolc, RFE monitors now pick up steady broadcasts from Szombathely, Debrecen, Nyíregyháza, Szeged, Pécs and the transmission station at Balatonszabadi.

Radio Free Győr, speaking for the County Vas, says the general strike will continue "until the mad and ignominious bloodshed ends." It also quotes a resolution from teachers and students in Szombathely "demanding that all books written in the Stalinist and Rákosi's spirit…should be immediately discarded from the library of the school."

The Lovászi oil-miners declare over Radio Free Győr that they will not deliver one drop of oil into the pipeline which might be used for Soviet tanks, until the government, preferably Imre Nagy himself, states over the radio who is to get the oil they are producing.[46]

The most lively and outspoken of the free radios is Radio Free Miskolc. It carries appeals from teacher groups for textbook revision, elimination of compulsory Russian, and inclusion of other languages in the curriculum, as well as observations on international affairs. It suggests, for instance, that the Hungarian UN delegate, Péter Kós, be recalled and that Hungary be represented by a neutral state of the UN's designation. It also appeals to fellow Hungarians in neighboring countries, though they are addressed as "fellow Slovaks" and "fellow Romanians."

The broadcasts are interrupted by frequent waves of jamming, which, since all jamming in Hungary ceased several days ago, can only be coming from Czechoslovakia, a mere fifty kilometers away.

The station also carries commentaries countering the Soviet propaganda line. In one the commentator argues that "Lenin taught—and this argument of his is still valid—that revolution cannot be exported, nor, respectively can it be imported. In accordance with this, we cannot call the present revolution an imported counterrevolution. This is not a counterrevolution; this has been the dynamic explosion of a people suppressed, longing for freedom."[47]

Radio Free Europe, which is in more and more contact with the freedom radios, also gets direct appeals, such as for the iron lung yesterday. At 11:00 p.m. tonight a resistance fighter from the Széna Square group headed by "Uncle Szabó" appears at the RFE office in Vienna with a request that RFE publicize a meeting in Budapest at 10:00 a.m. tomorrow.

At the very end of the day the Borsod County (Miskolc) Radio repeats news it has heard from Debrecen which, in turn, reports an announcement from the town of Kisvárda that "Many thousands of tanks with light and heavy arms are pouring into the country. Motorized infantry is advancing towards Nyíregyháza. New Russian units! Marshal Zhukov do you know this? You must know!"[48]

Soviet Actions

If the reader is confused about the Soviet troop withdrawal, so were the Hungarians. The free radios reported troops leaving Budapest and passing through Székesfehérvár as early as mid-morning on the twenty-ninth. Indeed, the British reporter, Cavendish, filed a long description of the retreat confirming what these radios reported. But this was not the formal pullout from Budapest. These units were sections of the two divisions which had been stationed in Hungary for several years. Not only had they been badly mauled by the freedom fighters, losing as many as a hundred tanks destroyed or put out of action in a few days, they had not fought particularly well, becoming quickly aware that the "fascists" they had been called upon to fight were, in fact, students, young workers and even children of a populace they had been living among. They had become demoralized to the point of ineffectiveness. There had been defections and some tanks had even been surrendered to the insurgents. Indeed, some tanks had even become involved in skirmishes against the incoming Soviet units which had come to replace them. Zhukov and company had ordered them home, and in some disgrace. Fresh units, including a number of Mongolian troops, which had already been brought in during the first two days of the uprising, had already replaced them in Budapest before they began their pullout on the twenty-ninth.

Hungarian Major General István Kovács on Sunday had designated Col. László Zólomy, who had headed the regular Army contingent at the radio station on the night of October 23, to plan, together with his Soviet counterparts, the Soviet withdrawal from Budapest. He suggested to the Soviets that those areas where there had been no fighting should be the first to be evacuated. This proposal was rejected by the Soviets on the twenty-ninth and they decided to do the exact opposite. But Hungarian General Gyula Váradi's negotiations at the Corvin Cinema to get the patriots to hand over their weapons were not successful. Thus they reverted to the plan of emptying the city of all Soviet troops except for the Fifth District, where all the government buildings are. This first phase would last from 3:00 p.m. today until midnight, and the second from midnight until 5:00 a.m. tomorrow, October 31. The evacuation does begin on time, and the second phase will take most of tomorrow. Instead of heading home to the Soviet Union, however, they will settle in a ring about ten to fifteen kilometers from the city and dig in.[49]

Defense Minister Janza says over Radio Budapest that the Soviets have "agreed" to his "request" that they withdraw. In Miscolc, a Hungarian Army Commander puts it somewhat differently. "Marshal Zhukov," he states over Radio Free Miskolc, "has given the order for the withdrawal of Soviet troops." "In Záhony [a Hungarian town near the Soviet border—ed.] the orderly withdrawal of the Soviet troops is being organized," another broadcast announces. "It will be carried out by railroad and car transportation. We ask the population...to keep discipline and to help in the smooth withdrawal of Soviet troops."

But further to the east the free Radio of the Szabolcs-Szatmár Worker's Council gives a solemn warning. "After the cease-fire," it says, "foreign [i.e. Soviet] troops were still advancing for two whole days. For two days they did not stop the tanks...The cease-fire was not sincere!...We should not be drunk with the present news. The tanks are still here! But those Russians troops which were nearest to the frontier have turned back; they have departed..."[50]

Hungarian Railway men, who have their own radio communication system, are telling Westerners that Soviet transport units are taking over all rail communications between Budapest and Romania.[51]

Soviet jamming of Western radios during most of 1956 has diminished, particularly on BBC which, at times, has ceased altogether. Today the London *Times* notes that jamming "has returned with a vengeance."[52]

Back in Budapest, Major General Béla Király has called an organizational meeting at 11:00 a. m. for the new National Guard, which he will command. He selects the Kilián Barracks as a symbolic setting for the meeting, even though he is aware that Col. Pál Maléter's reputation as hero of the Revolution is not just overblown, but quite mistaken. He is unaware, however, of how much bad blood exists between Maléter and the Corvin group until he hears that the newly elected Commander, twenty-four-year-old Gergely ("Moustache") Pongrátz, flatly refuses to attend the meeting. Király apologizes to him, but says it is too late to change the location and urges his attendance. Pongrátz wrestles with his conscience and finally decides to attend, but arrives after every one of the other three hundred attendees—freedom fighters and workers' council members—is in place. Király, who is meeting Gergely Pongrátz for the first time, greets him at the door and propels him up to the head table and plunks him down next to himself. Pongrátz notes that the seat on the other side of Király is unoccupied. After some chitchat, Pongrátz asks Király if they cannot begin the meeting, implying that his time is worth more than others in the room. Király replies that they cannot begin until the host, Col. Maléter, arrives and opens the meeting. Pongrátz would like to walk out, but cannot in front of all those people. Moreover, he wants to confront Maléter at his first opportunity.

A minute or so later Maléter strides in and begins a gracious, if somewhat stiff, welcome to the assemblage. Hardly has he begun when Pongrátz in a loud voice rudely asks Király if this is what he promised him on the phone. Maléter looks over nervously, but continues. Király, in a much lower voice, says that he had been unable to find Maléter when he phoned him, "but since he is the host please let him finish speaking."

At the end of Maléter's brief speech a soldier summons him to the phone and Király gets up to speak in his place. Before he can get a word out someone stands up and yells: "Long Live Maléter, the hero of Budapest!" In the roar of applause which follows Gergely Pongrátz loses his self-control. He jumps up, telling Király he has to speak. Király tries to calm him down, saying "later, later," but Pongrátz impetuously yells, "I won't wait, I'm going to speak now," and seizes the microphone.

His first words are "I hope that the man who just shouted 'Long Live Maléter, Hero of Budapest' is not from the ÁVO, but just misinformed."

He then proceeds to unload all his grievances, telling each incident he knows that will reveal Maléter's unheroic behavior in the Kilián Barracks.

In the midst of his harangue, Maléter strides back into the room, so Gergely says he is not one to say things behind another's back and so says it all over again, including the part of his shooting two boys.

Maléter's answer is brief. "Yes, it is true that I smacked two boys across the face. Even now I would slap anyone that I find with a gold watch or jewelry in his pocket. We are not fighting the Revolution so that these robbers could soil the image of the Revolution. The Revolution was successful and we have to look ahead, not back. We will have time to settle our differences when the Russians leave Hungary. Until then, we need unity. We are the true comrades-in-arms and brothers of Moustache and the Corvinists, and, in the interests of the Revolution, we have to overlook each other's mistakes and forgive each other. Anyone who does not do this is a traitor to the Revolution. Comradeship and friendliness rule and nothing can take that away." With that Maléter leans back and, projecting his great arm behind Király's head, seizes the much smaller Pongrátz by the neck and pulls him over and embraces him.

A storm of applause breaks out. While there are a few shouts of "Traitor!" and "He has no business among us!" from the Corvinists, these are overwhelmed and swallowed up in the long ovation. Maléter has won the day.

The meeting now goes on to discuss the establishment of the National Guard with Király as its head and Kopácsi as his deputy and with Tamás

Csáti, Vilmos Oláh, Ödön Pongrátz and one other as members of the Revolutionary Armed Forces Committee. Király then closes the meeting by reading Nagy's declaration establishing the National Guard.[53]

In Moscow the Presidium of the Central Committee is in session again for almost the entire day and well into the evening. Due to reassuring reports received from Mikoyan and Suslov over the past several days, and discussion of a policy paper calling for a major shift of Soviet policy toward its East European satellites, which has long been in the works, the whole tenor of the discussion takes a surprising turn. All the members, including the hardliners Molotov and Voroshilov, reach a consensus—ephemeral though it may be—that the Soviet Union should forego large-scale military intervention in Hungary. Marshal Zhukov himself concedes that the Soviet Union has to be ready, if necessary, to withdraw troops, not just from Budapest, but all of Hungary. "This has been a military-political lesson for us," he adds with resignation.[54]

Today's last report from Mikoyan and Suslov arrives too late for any of the Presidium members to read it before the unanimous vote is taken. Ironically, it is very different from the previous reports on which much of the consensus of the vote has been based. It reads:

> The political situation…is not getting better; it is getting worse. The party organizations are in the process of collapse. Hooligan elements have become more insolent, seizing district party committees, killing communists….The factories are stalled. The people are sitting at home. The railroads are not working. Hooligan students and other resistance elements have changed their tactics and are displaying greater activity….Almost not shooting at all…[they] instead are seizing institutions…last night the central party's printing office was seized.
>
> [The group of fighters sent last night by the new Defense Minister to quell some insurgents] did not open fire" because the Central Committee advised them not to spill blood….Imre Nagy was sleeping in his apartment, and they, apparently, did not want complications with Nagy, fearing that opening fire without his knowledge would be an occasion for weakening the leadership.
>
> They occupied the regional telephone station. The radio station is working, but it does not reflect the opinion of the Central Committee, since, in fact, it is in foreign hands.

The anti-revolutionary newspaper [he means "anti-counterrevolution-ary"] did not come out because there were counterrevolutionary articles in it...

...as of the present moment the weapons have not been surrendered, except for a few hundred rifles. The insurgents declare that they will not give them up peacefully until Soviet troops leave Budapest, and some even say until Soviet troops leave Hungary. Thus peacefully liquidating this hotbed is impossible....The Hungarian Army has occupied a wait-and-see position. Our military advisors say that relations between Hungarian officers and generals and Soviet officers have deteriorated....There is no trust as there was earlier...

Last night Andropov was summoned. Nagy asked him: is it true that new Soviet military units are continuing to enter Hungary from the USSR? If yes, then what is their goal? We did not negotiate [sic] this.

We intend to state to Imre Nagy today that the troop movements were in accordance with our agreement, that from now on we do not intend to bring any more troops on account of the fact that the Nagy government is dealing with the situation in Hungary.

We propose...to cease sending troops into Hungary, continuing to concentrate them on Soviet territory...[55]

A New Hungarian Government

Mikoyan's gloomy assessment of the situation is well hidden from the Hungarian comrades when he bids goodbye to them in the Parliament building around midday, before the governmental changes are announced. General Béla Király, whom Nagy wants to make commander of the new National Guard with Police Chief Sándor Kopácsi as his deputy, is sitting in an antechamber waiting to see Nagy. He grabs Kopácsi by the arm and whispers, "I know who is with Nagy; it's Mikoyan. I saw him go in a while ago. A lot depends on what's going on in there." When the door opens and the small Armenian comes out, overcoat draped over one arm of his blue suit, he leans back and says something in Russian to the man walking behind. It is Nagy, and they continue conversing in Russian until Nagy notices Király and Kopácsi and beckons them over.

"Tovarishch Mikoyan, here are two of the future leaders of the Hungarian Armed Forces."

Mikoyan shakes their hands and says in Russian, "Now we have to leave your country. Do all you can to help comrade Nagy." Then he turns to Nagy, extending his hand, and says: "Comrade Nagy, save what you can."

The two men embrace and Kopácsi thinks he detects tears in Mikoyan's eyes as he turns around. Then he leaves with his two bodyguards and János Kádár sees him down to his tank.

"This may be the turning point," says Nagy to his two next visitors. Mikoyan and Suslov, it seems, have accepted everything. When Kádár returns he sweeps into the room and says "Imre, have we done it?"

"We've done it, János!" Nagy replies, beaming.[56]

Only minutes later in the early afternoon Premier Nagy addresses the nation over the radio and announces not just a new government, but the end to one-party rule.

"Hungarian workers, peasants, intellectuals. As a result of the revolution…and the mighty movement of democratic forces our nation has reached the crossroads.…In the interests of further democratization…the Cabinet has abolished the one-party system and has decided we should return to a system of government based on the democratic cooperation of the coalition parties as they existed in 1945. In accordance with this decision, a new Cabinet has been set up within the national government. Its members are: Imre Nagy, Zoltán Tildy (Smallholders), Béla Kovács (former leader of the Smallholders), Ferenc Erdei (former Peasant Party, but a Communist Party toady), János Kádár (who had been jailed under Rakosi), and Géza Losonczy (an anti-Rákosi Communist).

"The national government appeals to the headquarters of the Soviet command to begin immediate withdrawal of Soviet troops from Budapest. At the same time…we are going to request the Soviet Union to withdraw all Soviet troops from Hungary.

"…We recognize all the autonomous democratic authorities which were formed during the revolution.…We rely on them and want their support. To safeguard the achievements of the revolution we must first of all establish order. Fratricidal war must stop immediately. Avoid all disturbances!"[57]

Nagy is followed by new non-communist Minister of State Zoltán Tildy, who apologizes for his disjointed delivery, but he has not had time to write anything down. After praising the freedom fighters as having surpassed the youth of March 15, 1848 and promising that "the national government will bury the heroes of the revolution with military honors and will take generous care of the wounded and the families of those heroes who fell in battle," he

EXPLOSION

declares that "the least the nation can do is to declare the day on which the struggle began a national holiday…"

He asks that the "fighting university youth" send delegates to him in the Parliament building so they can help in the "formation of a National Guard Battalion to help restore order."[58]

He also announces that "Péter Kós, 'former representative' of Hungary at the UN, has been recalled and that a new UN delegation will be appointed…." (Later in the day Kós will be denounced by the Revolutionary Committee of the Ministry of Foreign Affairs and his statements in the UN repudiated. Kós, it is later discovered, is not a Hungarian at all, but a Hungarian-speaking Russian with Soviet citizenship whose real name is Leo Konduktorov.)[59]

"I am convinced," Tildy continues, "that the people and leaders of the Soviet Union will see, once they negotiate with a free and not humiliated nation, how different our relationship is, how much greater the mutual understanding, respect and love."

He ends his brief talk with an appeal to members of his own party to begin reorganization both in Budapest and the provinces. Before the day is out a provisional executive committee of the Smallholders' Party is formed in Budapest, which includes József Kővágó, former Mayor of Budapest. Kővágó is being asked to serve as Mayor again.

Now János Kádár steps to the microphone as the new communist Minister of State. "I want you to know," he begins, "that all the resolutions passed today by the Council of Ministers have been fully approved by the Presidium of the Hungarian Workers' (Communist) Party and I want to add that I fully approve of all that was said by the speakers before me—Imre Nagy, Zoltán Tildy….I speak to Communists…Comrades, owing to the leadership of the past years our Party has been cast under a grave shadow. We must rid our party of this burden. The ranks of the Party will shake, but I am sure that no…honest, sincere Communist will leave the Party. Those who joined us for selfish reasons…will be the ones to leave."

While Kádár knows the Party is in a shambles and that they are going to have to start a new party with a new name, he stops just short of making this announcement.[60]

Imre Nagy later today has discussions with former Social Democrats Anna Kéthly, Gyula Kelemen and a man named Kőműves concerning the possibility of a reborn Social Democratic Party joining a coalition government. During the talks it is agreed that the Party shall be reconstituted (and the 1948 merger with the Communists thus liquidated). The Party will also be given back its old headquarters, editorial office and newspaper, *Népszava*. Miss Kéthly and her colleagues say they will consider the offer. Miss Kéthly may leave soon for Vienna to get the advice of Western Socialists.[61]

The Assault on the Municipal Party Headquarters on Republic Square

As is so often the case, the bloodiest, most senseless battles are often fought after the war has, to all intents and purposes, been won. Such is the case with the assault today on the Municipal Party Headquarters on Republic Square in Pest. It begins quite innocently about nine a.m. when many housewives are queuing up at a food store, for despite the generosity of Hungary's farmers, food shortages have developed in certain sections of the city. Some of them notice a truck pull up to the supposedly empty Party Municipal Headquarters on the edge of Republic Square and unload huge quantities of bacon and sausages. When a patrol of armed freedom fighters comes by a few minutes later, the queuing women tell them about what they have seen. The patrol decides to investigate. A small group of unarmed boys is sent into the building.

When the boys do not come out, members of the patrol of Freedom Fighters enter the building. One of the first two people they meet, both of whom are dressed in brand new clothes, cannot come up with any identification, or any good reason for having none. As they are talking, four hand grenades tied together come hurtling down the staircase. Fortunately they explode way below them at the bottom of the stairwell, but shooting quickly breaks out. The patrol, rather than get trapped in the building, run for their lives. The building, it seems, is full of ÁVO. They have been stocking up for several days on food and ammunition and are prepared to hold the building under whatever siege may come.

As soon as the twenty-four man patrol begins to shoot from positions behind trees in the park, the ÁVO open up with murderous and quite indiscriminate fire, killing civilians in the food queues as well as anyone they can spot in the broad park. Republic Square park is some two hundred-by-two hundred meters square. Its dozens of trees spaced well apart, with bare bushes, paths and concrete benches, afford little protection.

As the patriots have nothing heavier than light machine guns and the

EXPLOSION

ÁVO have a perfect view of the park from their four storey building the battle, which now rages on for several hours, results in heavy casualties on the part of the freedom fighters, but no apparent progress toward capturing the building. Two Western news photographers, attracted by the din of gunfire, are soon on the scene: John Sadovy for *LIFE* magazine and Jean-Pierre Pedrazinni for *Paris Match*. (Both men will be wounded, Sadovy just on the hand, but Pedrazinni, before he can get many pictures, gets a machine gun burst in his stomach and leg. He will lie in a Budapest hospital for several days, then be flown back to Paris where he will die five days after being shot.) Col. Maléter in the Kilian Barracks is asked to send some tanks to shell the party building. While he is willing to oblige, four of his five tanks are under repair, so only one T-34 shows up. This immediately starts shelling the ground floor windows and destroys the front gate.

After about fifteen minutes of this, three more tanks show up from the direction of the Eastern Station all flying Hungarian flags. They have been sent by the Ministry of Defense to help defend the Party Municipal headquarters. But seeing one tank already firing on the building they decide to join in.

With such an array of armor against them the ÁVO do not have a chance, yet the battle rages on.

John Sadovy, the *LIFE* photographer, finds himself trapped behind a small tree when the fighting really flares up and people around him are dropping like flies. White-coated first-aid people, mostly women, are coming and going picking up the wounded and driving them to hospitals. Sadovy notices that the white coats make no difference to the ÁVO. These unarmed angels of mercy are shot down as well. Teenagers take over from some of the women who have fallen. Sadovy sees one stretcher-bearer, carrying the back end, get shot. Without looking back the first man does his best to drag the blood-drenched stretcher with its deadweight victim on it to safety before he, too, catches a bullet.

Eventually the shelling knocks out all resistance on the lower floors and the freedom fighters, of whom there are now several hundred, begin to enter the building from several sides. Shots still crack out from the upper floors, but only sporadically. As soon as the shooting ceases, ÁVO men begin to come out of the building with their hands in the air. The first to emerge is an officer, alone. It is the quickest killing Sadovy has ever seen. He came out laughing and the next thing Sadovy knew he was flat on the ground. Sadovy thought he had just fallen. Six young ÁVO men wearing police uniforms come out together, their shoulder boards torn off and their hands up. There is a quick argument. "We're not as bad as you think we are," shouts one, then muffled shots so close they can scarcely be heard, and the six crumple gracefully, like a scythe cutting through corn. Sadovy, who has seen three years of warfare, has seen "nothing to compare with the horror of this." One man gets as far as the park before he is cut down.

Freedom Fighters are uniformly against lynching. Infuriated mobs, however, are not easy to control and some in this crowd now have guns. Moreover, hundreds of people have seen the ÁVO shoot down innocent civilians standing in the food lines and women Red Cross workers trying to rescue the wounded in the park. One senior ÁVO officer is seized before he can be shot or taken into custody, stripped to his pants and furiously beaten to death. His bleeding body is hung upside down on a tree. Hundred forint notes, which are found in his pockets, are plastered to his bleeding body and a wad of bills is stuffed into his mouth. As women step up and spit at the body, the mob chants: "This is what you wanted and now you've got it! This is how you go to hell!"[62]

Then they bring out a little boy, carried on someone's shoulders. He is about five years old with a sweet face. There are shouts of "Don't kill him" from the crowd. He is the son of one of the ÁVO officers. Sadovy feels himself snapped back to reality. One most unfortunate non-ÁVO casualty is Comrade Imre Mező, Party Secretary for the city of Budapest. It is his building, after all, and he has every right to be there. Later today he will die of his wounds. To have such a high communist official killed at this late date in the revolution bodes ill for the future.[63]

Indeed, a number of potential lynchings are stopped by patriots before things get out of hand. In another part of the city on this same day an ÁVO man is caught who has markedly Jewish features. The mob has surrounded him and is about to cut his throat when the leader of those who had captured him stops the would-be executioners and turns to the man, yelling: "If you belonged to any other religion we would finish you off. But as it is, we are going to let you off. Go home, and if you want to live, get rid of that damned uniform as soon as you can!" Though there *are* some isolated acts of anti-Semitism, in this case being Jewish saves this man's life.[64]

The New Radio Budapest

"Dear Listeners, we are beginning a new chapter in the history of the

Hungarian radio," comes an early afternoon announcement, just after Kádár has spoken. "For many years the radio has been an instrument of lies: it merely carried out orders. It lied day and night; it lied on all wavelengths. Not even at the hour of our country's rebirth did it cease its campaign of lies. But the fight which won victory in the streets…has flared up within the walls of the radio, too. Those who spoke those lies are no longer among the staff of the Hungarian Radio, which will henceforth bear the name Kossuth and Petőfi. We who are now at the microphone are in the majority new men. We shall follow the words of the old oath: 'We shall tell the truth, the whole truth and nothing but the truth.'"[65]

With the muzzle now removed from Radio Budapest a much belated special announcement soon follows. It was not Nagy, says the broadcast, who has called in the Soviet troops, nor was he responsible for "the disgraceful imposition of summary jurisdiction." Nagy's signature is on neither authorizing document. Both are the work of "András Hegedűs and Ernő Gerő. They bear the full responsibility before the nation and history."

Further light is cast on this vital matter by the new newspaper *Igazság* (Truth), which writes that "even on Friday [October 26] the Gerő-Hegedűs clique wanted to force Imre Nagy to sign a pre-dated letter calling on Soviet troops to help crush the rebellion. Of course, Imre Nagy would not give his signature."[66]

Cardinal Mindszenty Is Liberated

József Cardinal Mindszenty was arrested on the day after Christmas 1948. After more than a month of starvation, sleep deprivation and torture he endured a three-day trial beginning on February 3, 1949 in a People's (Communist) Court. He was found guilty of totally bogus charges and sentenced to life in prison. Because of his popularity and perceived danger to the communist regime, he has been moved from one prison to another for nearly eight years to keep his whereabouts hidden from the public.

He is now being held prisoner at the small palace outside the northern town of Felsőpetény, but only a few people in the government know this.

In early October the Cardinal became aware of ferment among the intellectuals and students by listening to Radio Budapest on a small radio he was allowed. But on October 24 his radio was confiscated and he has been completely in the dark ever since. Nor have the guards answered any of his questions.

Today they break their silence. His chief guard tells him he has to be moved, his life is in danger. "But who would threaten me? he asks. "The mob" is all the ÁVO man says.

"I won't go," says the Cardinal stubbornly. "If it is the will of God that I should die here, here I will die. But I will not move."

The officers are puzzled and consult among themselves. Then one of them suggests to the Cardinal that he yield to "force" and that the "force" to be used would be simply taking his arm gently. "No," answers the Cardinal. At this they become anxious and grab at him to pull him off his chair. Mindszenty resists. They are still pulling when a guard rushes up the stairs to say a Russian type armored car is coming up the drive. This turns out to be János Horváth, head of the government's Office of Church Affairs. He comes rushing in saying, "Your Excellency, your life is not safe in this place. I have orders to move you!"

"I will not go," replies the Cardinal. "You have taken everything from me there is to take. You can take nothing else."

While Horváth goes off to telephone Budapest, townspeople from the village of Felsőpetény begin to appear in the driveway; first children, then several hundred adults. They had seen Horváth's armored car.

Horváth's telephone call, however, is intercepted by a Hungarian military unit at Rétság, just twenty kilometers away. The secret of the Cardinal's whereabouts is out. The entire unit piles into cars and trucks and heads for Felsőpetény. Meanwhile the villagers are surrounding the castle and shouting "Freedom for Mindszenty and bread for the Hungarian people!"

Not more than thirty minutes after Horváth's departure Mindszenty's guards approach the Cardinal with startling news: they have formed a "revolutionary council" and now, showing great respect for the man they have been treating like dirt, they apologize, say he has been kept illegally and is free to go. The Army unit from Rétság now arrives and helps him pack up his few belongings for the journey to his home in Buda.

At the ten o'clock news, Radio Free Kossuth announces the Cardinal's liberation and his departure for Buda, giving all credit to the Army unit.[67]

Reaction Outside Hungary

The Polish Communist Party, led by its new leader Władisław Gomułka, today appears to back the Hungarian demands for withdrawal of Soviet troops from Hungary. Couched in typical, but unmistakable, language, the official statement, addressed directly to Hungarians, concludes that "you and we are on the same side, the side of freedom and socialism."[68]

The Czechoslovak Central Committee sends an expression of "fraternal sympathy," but reminds the Hungarians that Czechoslovaks are "firmly linked with the people of your country by firm ties of friendship and cooperation [i.e. Communism] which have been successfully developing in the past twelve years." They want this friendship to continue "to grow and strengthen. We shall, especially now, do everything in our power to help bring this about." One of the first actions the Czechoslovaks take to bring about this "strengthening" of communist position is to begin jamming the free Hungarian radios as well as Western radios broadcasting into Hungary.[69]

There is no pronouncement on Hungary in the German Democratic Republic (East Germany) today, but there is considerable tension due to unannounced Soviet troop movements. The Soviets removed 33,500 soldiers from East Germany earlier this year with great fanfare as part of a general "peace offensive." Now they are all being returned surreptitiously, but their numbers are too great not to be noticed. Not only that, but today arms are being taken away from the members of the East German paramilitary organization "Sports and Technics," as they are considered unreliable in the present circumstances.[70]

In Romania the government today decrees a totally unexpected new increase in the minimum wage from 350 to 400 lei, effective November 1.

Unrest continues in the Hungarian sections of Transylvania. "We don't listen to Radio Free Europe anymore," says Tibor Karcsó of Marosvásárhely, "since Radio Kossuth is saying the same things." The Romanian Army, meanwhile, is seething over the recent confiscation by the Soviet Army of much of its artillery (presumably carted off to Hungary), leaving "two divisions armed only with sub-machine guns."[71]

In the Free World, developments in Hungary are front-page news in nearly every country around the globe and hundred of editorials continue to extol the bravery of the freedom fighters. To cite just a few examples of non-press reaction in Western Europe: In Norway today, students are giving a day's worth of labor to raise relief funds, the Hungarian Legation in Oslo is removing the red star from its building and someone has scrawled "Long Live a Free Hungary" on its wall. One thousand students paraded outside the Soviet Embassy last night and, the British Minister notes today, in connection with the arrival on the twenty-seventh of three Russian journalists for a month's visit, that they "could hardly have chosen a worse moment to try to make friends with the Norwegian Labour Party." In Oxford, England, an appeal for relief funds is being circulated to all twenty-eight colleges in the university and to every university in Britain. Two Oxford undergraduates, Jan Rankin and Robert Oakeshott, who left the university without permission and flew from London to Vienna with penicillin for Hungarian wounded, got as far into Hungary as Sopron with their precious cargo, whence it was taken to Budapest. They have already reported back by phone instances of Russian soldiers firing on ambulances and killing six Red Cross workers and trampling medical supplies into the mud. The students are certain to be disciplined on their return, but many dons unofficially applaud their initiative.

Closer to Hungary, a tug of war has been taking place between the former Premier of Hungary, Ferenc Nagy, and the Austrian and British governments. Nagy arrived at Schwechat Airport outside Vienna via Air France from Paris last night and was immediately "held" by Austrian authorities. Since there was a temporary R.A.F. operation going on at the airport, the Austrians appealed to the British to get him out of the country quickly on an RAF flight to Britain. As British Ambassador Sir Geoffrey Wallinger observed, "it would be completely inappropriate that Ferenc Nagy should be in or near Vienna at the present time. Apart from anything else, there could be no more striking support for the Soviet thesis that the Hungarian revolt had been engineered in the West." While the British managed to arrange everything in a matter of hours, and Nagy agreed to go quietly, in the end he preferred the midnight train to Zürich, rather than a free trip to the United Kingdom.[72]

U.S. and British Policies on Hungary Contrasted

It is interesting to note that on this date, a full week after Gerő had cleverly branded Nagy with responsibility for a) calling in the Soviet troops and b) declaring martial law, neither the U.S. nor the British Legations appear yet to be aware that Nagy was responsible for neither. In addition the two legations appear to be falling behind in the task of keeping up with what is happening in the Nagy government. The U.S. Legation, having given its policy recommendations yesterday, is busy today reporting everything going on in the street. The British Legation, having temporarily left reporting up to British journalists, is concentrating on the main task: how to rid Hungary of Soviet troops.

Sir Leslie Fry suggests to the Foreign Office that "the decisive factor influencing the Russians may be their prestige, rather than the fate of the Hungarian regime, which the Russians must now regard as impotent and unreliable. Our problem is to devise a face-saving formula that will permit Russian forces to withdraw, ostensibly at the request of the present Hungarian regime, without their appearing to have been turned out by the anti-communist Hungarian people."

"I cannot pretend to offer an answer to this problem....My purpose in raising it is simply to emphasize its importance. If we can get the Russians out, the Hungarians may safely be left to settle their own destiny; it will not be communism....Whatever negotiating position we adopt, the vital point to be secured is the withdrawal from Hungary of all Soviet armed forces."[73]

The British Foreign Office, in a long cable on the Hungarian situation sent to its delegation in Paris, reports on the current situation:

"The Nationalists, who appear to control large areas of the country out-side Budapest....have insisted on the withdrawal of Soviet troops from Hungary before they lay down their arms....It is doubtful whether Nagy is able, or can afford, to make this concession, as he was at least nominally responsible for calling in the Soviet troops, and in conversation with the United States Ambassador at Moscow Zhukov has said that the withdrawal of Soviet troops from Hungary is a matter for all members of the Warsaw Treaty....Briefly, the choice before the Soviet leaders is between long term repression on an unprecedented scale and concessions which could only weaken the Soviet position in the Satellites."[74]

But at the same time the Foreign Office, in a cable to its UN delegation in New York, takes all of the starch out of Minister Fry's suggestion about a quick announcement about seeking a UN observer team for Hungary when it cables:

The possible psychological advantage in Hungary of a proposal to establish a United Nations Commission of Observers might soon be lost if the Russians were to veto this proposal; whereas the proposal, once made, would remain an embarrassing precedent as regards Cyprus, etc.[75]

Britain, as the world is reminded elsewhere today, is still a colonial power.

John Foster Dulles has a very different perspective of the situation. The author of the "rollback" of the Iron Curtain and "liberation of the captive peoples" policies takes a much more distanced approach. In a long cable which he signs and sends around to all the major U.S. Embassies titled "the

State Department's assessment of recent events in Hungary" (i.e. as of October 30, 1956) he says:

> ...The dominant issue is the use of Soviet troops for the brutal repression of the Hungarian People. After inviting them to help restore order and after stressing that their presence in Hungary is legal under the Warsaw Pact, Nagy has reversed his position and has promised to have them withdrawn from Budapest, on condition that the fighting stops, and to negotiate their final departure from Hungary. The Soviets are justifying the use of their troops on the grounds that the rebellion in Hungary was incited by the United States and they stress the invitation of the Hungarian Government in this regard. The official organ of the Hungarian Workers (Commie) Party has categorically rejected this interpretation and attributes the uprisings (sic) to past policies of the Hungarian regime. Poland and Yugoslavia appear to follow the same line, while other East European Commie regime (sic) are supporting the Soviet version—thus creating a major ideological split on this issue in the Commie world.
>
> The question is whether the Soviets are willing to allow stabilization under the Nagy Government, which is committed to the withdrawal of their troops (with all that implies for the other satellite countries), or whether they must proceed to reestablish complete control over the country in the role of an alien occupier (which implies a huge military burden for the future and nullifies their present world posture).
>
> The U.S. objective at this stage is primarily to encourage cessation of the use of Soviet troops against the Hungarian people and to establish condition (sic) for their eventual withdrawal from Hungary. Our Security Council action is directed toward these ends. Meanwhile, in view of the delicate balance with regard to the Nagy regime and its pledge to rid the country of Soviet troops, the U.S. is refraining at this point from adopting any stand on Nagy. There is some evidence, however, that the regime is attempting a deception in order to break the resistance. The U.S. will aim to hold it (the Nagy Regime) to its promises.... DULLES[76]

Declaration by the Government of the USSR

Since March the Kremlin leaders have seen cracks emerge in their East European empire—cracks which most of them had no idea were there. The ferment catalyzed by the de-Stalinization *has* gone much further than intended—certainly much further and faster than within the Soviet Union itself. Not only does it have to be halted, but the origins of the strains must somehow be eliminated. The countries of Eastern Europe can no longer be treated as Stalin treated them. An entirely new basis of relations needs to be established if there is to be stability in the area.

To this end a special commission has been set up by the Central Committee to work out and draft a new policy, which, once approved by the Central Committee, can be announced to the world and implemented. Rumors that such a major policy shift is being formulated have been making the rounds of the Western diplomatic community in Moscow for some time. As early as June 4 Britain's Ambassador, Sir William Hayter, cabled Whitehall that the embassy "has indications that Moscow is preparing to make some special announcement about the satellites."[77] Various statements over the summer, some by Khrushchev himself, follow this rumor.[78] Yet, whenever the time seems ripe something comes up to delay the announcement.

Not until events get out of hand—a new, unwanted government in Poland which they can no longer control, and a full-scale insurrection in Hungary—does the Presidium of the Central Committee feel forced to make a decision on whether or not to implement the new policy. They spend the whole of today debating it, and while that does not seem a sufficient amount of time to consider such a major change in the country's policy, they feel they have no choice. Even Molotov and Voroshilov, the hardliners, and Zhukov, representing the military, agree that there is no other alternative. In the end the vote to announce and implement the new policy is unanimous.[79]

Presumably the original text of the document made no reference to specific countries, at least not in the context of today's twin crises. So before the session Khrushchev commissions Politburo members Brezhnev, Pospelov and Shepilov to bring the document up-to-date so that it relates more exactly to today's situation. This they are able to do in a few hours.*

---

*The notion that they wrote the entire document in this short time, as some seem to feel the record indicates, is preposterous on the face of it. The further notion, widely held in the United States and by many others in the West, that the document was an elaborate trick to lull the Hungarians into thinking they had won their freedom, while preparing to crush the revolution, is equally so. There is absolutely no precedent in Soviet history for announcing such a far-reaching policy, printed in full the next day in *Pravda*—which means it was printed in full in all of the Party papers in Eastern Europe the next day—just to fool the regime of one small country. The document was a genuine, major policy turnaround of historical significance: Many of its provisions were carried out, albeit not quite on the schedule originally envisaged, and references continued to be made to it as official policy for some years.

As with most Soviet documents, it is difficult to ascertain the real import of the contents from its ponderous title:

DECLARATION BY THE GOVERNMENT OF THE USSR ON THE PRINCIPLES OF DEVELOPMENT AND FURTHER STRENGTHENING OF FRIENDSHIP AND COOPERATION BETWEEN THE SOVIET UNION AND OTHER SOCIALIST STATES.

Indeed, it is difficult to understand quite what the communist jargon in the text means. In the few passages quoted below a translation is, thus, provided.

"The Soviet government is ready to discuss measures insuring...the strengthening of economic ties between socialist countries in order to remove any possibilities of violating the principles of national sovereignty, mutual advantage, and equality in economic relations..." (Translation: The Stalinist economic exploitation of the satellites will stop.)

"The Soviet Government is ready to examine...the question of Soviet troops stationed on the territory of [Warsaw Pact] countries." (Translation: We are prepared to negotiate the possible withdrawal of Soviet troops from Hungary and Romania, though not Poland and East Germany.)

"The Soviet Government has given instructions to its military command to withdraw its units from Budapest as soon as this is considered necessary by the Hungarian Government."*

"The Soviet Government is willing to enter into relevant negotiations with the Hungarian government and other participants of the Warsaw Pact on the question of the presence of Soviet troops in Hungary..." (Translation: We are willing to consider withdrawing troops from Hungary, since it is not, like East Germany and Poland, strategically vital to us.)

It has taken the Soviet leadership eight months to come to the full realization that the Stalinist hold on Eastern Europe cannot be maintained without Stalin and his methods. With Stalin repudiated, his methods must follow.

But the men who are making this courageous, albeit tardy, decision are not fully aware of how fast their position in Hungary is deteriorating. They have yet to read the latest report from Mikoyan and Suslov. Moreover, they are totally unaware of what the British and French are up to at this very hour. Thus at the very time that this momentous change in Soviet foreign policy is

---

*The revisers of the Declaration know perfectly well that this is already taking place, but they write it this way in order to save face.

proclaimed to the world—and Radio Moscow will carry it this night—its impact is trumped by the new events in the Middle East.

There is at least one Western leader who appreciates the significance of the document. When he reads of it tomorrow and of the Soviet pullout from Budapest, President Dwight Eisenhower, in a televised address to the nation tomorrow, will call it "the dawn of a new day." If carried out it would constitute "the greatest forward stride toward justice, trust and understanding among nations in our generation."[80] Eisenhower will maintain this attitude until Dulles tells him it may all be a trick. Then, on November 4, Eisenhower is forced to concede that Dulles must be correct.

Ambassador Sir William Hayter has this to say in a cable he will send the Foreign Office tomorrow:

"The declaration implies that the Soviet Government have decided that they cannot continue to use their armed forces to alter the course of the Hungarian Revolution. It means also that they cannot now use their armed forces for internal purposes in Poland or Romania.

"…They must, therefore, be prepared to see a non-communist regime set up in Hungary….

"The Soviet Government have, of course, made many theoretical statements about the independence of the People's Democracies. But the present declaration is much more important, since the Soviet Union now proposes to take practical and concrete steps to abandon its authority over these countries. The reason for this abandonment seems to be the Soviet Government's realization of two facts, that the regimes in these countries are very fragile, and that if they show signs of collapse the means hitherto available…for bolstering them up and suppression will not now work.

"The implications of this new policy for the Soviet Union are very serious. If Hungary throws off communism as well as Soviet domination, the infection seems almost certain to spread to other satellites, particularly to Poland, and more serious still, to East Germany.

"Fear of such developments in East Germany may incline the Soviet Government to make proposals to the German Federal Republic e.g. genuinely free elections and reunification in return for withdrawal from NATO and a guarantee of neutrality…

"The declaration is issued in the name of the Soviet Government; the Communist Party is nowhere mentioned. This may be in order to preserve the prestige of the Party from too close an association with a defect." (sic; defeat?)[81]

Britain and France Move on Suez

Britain and France tonight begin to move troop-carrying aircraft and landing craft south from Cyprus to Egypt, shortly after the expiration of their ultimatum for Israeli and Egyptian soldiers to cease-fire and pull back. The two allies appear to ignore President Eisenhower's plea for them to hold back, and the U.S. attempt in the Security Council to pass a resolution urging them to do so is blocked by the two European allies, causing an unprecedented split within NATO. Meanwhile the British Air Ministry is warning all aircraft without special clearance papers to keep clear of the Eastern Mediterranean and the Admiralty is doing the same for shipping. Five aircraft carriers, three British and two French, are in the midst of the largest naval flotilla seen in the Mediterranean since World War II. President Eisenhower is canceling plans for an election campaign trip to the southwest in order to stay in close touch, as the crisis in the Middle East develops.

The Suez Crisis

The Suez crisis and the Hungarian Revolution are forever linked. We know now, from the historical record, that neither caused the other—or rather, that it was not the Israeli-British-French action which caused the Russians to decide to intervene decisively to crush the Hungarian Revolution, as many suspected, or even wanted to believe, at the time. We also know, however, that the attack on Egypt had the effect of making the Soviet decision far more decisive than it might have been. Soviet reasoning, at least initially, was based more on fear of being thought weak than eagerness to take advantage of a golden opportunity. The decision to intervene in Hungary would have been made even had there been no Suez crisis, although it would probably not have been made as precipitously as it was. I know of no precedent in history of a major power making a major change in foreign policy and announcing it to the world, and then reversing it the very next day.

Nevertheless, because of the eternal linkage between the two crises, it is important for those whose primary concern is Hungary to understand how completely unrelated, until their fateful conjunction, the two crises were.

The Suez crisis was precipitated by John Foster Dulles' reneging on the

U.S. pledge—along with Britain, France and the World Bank—to provide loans to build the Aswan Dam. This dam was Nasser's great dream for restoring Egypt to its ancient state of historic grandeur. The reneging was done so abruptly that Nasser, within days, seized the Suez Canal eleven years before it was due by treaty to revert to Egypt. Nasser felt forced into this action as he desperately needed cash to begin building the dam to which he and his reputation were totally committed. The French and British regarded this seizure not only as retaliation for the West's having pulled the rug out from under him, but as a sign of Arab imperialism. Moreover, the Suez Canal was Europe's, but particularly Britain's, lifeline, with far more British ships passing through it yearly than those of any other nation. Leaving Nasser in charge meant giving him a chance to choke off shipping whenever he felt like it. The canal, they felt, had to be recovered.

Knowing the U.S. would disapprove of military action—though not necessarily the threat of it—Sir Anthony Eden and his allies purposely did not inform Dulles, hoping the canal would be quickly captured and the U.S. would be faced with a *fait accompli*. Many things went wrong, however, delaying the action, which did not begin until October 29, when Israeli forces invaded the Sinai peninsula. The French and British ultimatum to Egypt and Israel the next day, quickly followed by bombing, came on the same day on which the Soviet Union issued its Declaration on new relations with the satellites. The U.S. (read Dulles and Eisenhower), infuriated at not having been informed, immediately sought to halt the British and French invasion by taking it to the UN Security Council. When blocked by French and British vetoes, the U.S. took it to the General Assembly where the U.S. resolution condemning the action and demanding immediate withdrawal carried on November 2, with enthusiastic Soviet backing.

But while Americans thought that they had shown moral superiority to the world in halting the invasion of Egypt and rebuffing France and England, that was not the perception of the Arabs and much of the Third World. Three days after the vote and just one day after the Soviet Union moved to crush the Hungarian Revolution, Moscow threatened to bombard France and England with rocket-borne atomic bombs if they did not cease and pull back. The Anglo-French force had already ceased and had been pulling back for two days, but most Arabs and Third World people did not know that. The Kremlin claimed full credit for halting the Anglo-French adventure. Years later, many in the Arab and Third Worlds still believed that it was the Soviet

Union, not the U.S. in the UN, which had settled the crisis. Of course, the maneuver was also designed to cover up what they were doing in Hungary. And they even had the chutzpah to send a note to Washington proposing joint Soviet-U.S. military action against the Anglo-French forces. This, while they were making war on the Hungarian people!

Khrushchev, who, less than a week before had appeared helpless to come to the aid of a new ally on whom he had lavished valuable military hardware, was able, through feigned atomic blackmail, to take full credit at no cost to the Soviet Union and at the same time deflect the world's attention from what he was doing in Hungary.

CHAPTER VII

Revolution Triumphant (Part 2)

WHILE THE TRIUMPH *of the Hungarian Revolution continued to gather momentum on October 31, the world now knows that October 31 was also the date on which the fate of the Revolution was sealed. On that day the Presidium of the Soviet Central Committee decided that it had to reverse its policy, announced just the day before—at least insofar as Hungary was concerned—or risk losing not only Hungary, but the rest of its empire in Eastern Europe. Indeed, many feared a domino effect which might endanger the Communist Party's control over the USSR itself, for the infection was already showing signs of reaching into the Hungarian population living in the Western Ukraine.*

Oddly enough the Chinese communists played a decisive, if ambivalent, role in Khrushchev's decision. And we must make no mistake, while there was some free-wheeling discussion among the comrades on the Presidium, once the First Secretary had made up his mind, the others eventually fell in behind him. The Chinese had played a crucial role in convincing Khrushchev on the thirtieth that the Soviet Union should refrain from intervening militarily. The trouble was, as Khrushchev's son, Sergei, has written, "he simply could not make up his mind whether Moscow should intervene or should allow the Hungarians to solve their problems independently." [1] *Khrushchev, in his memoirs,* Khrushchev Remembers, *is careful not to mention his fear of the Revolution infecting his people, but to put it in terms of international power blocs: "If the counterrevolutionaries did succeed and NATO took root in the midst of the Socialist countries, it would pose a seri-*

ous threat to Czechoslovakia, Yugoslavia, and Rumania, not to mention the Soviet Union itself." [2]

A Chinese Party delegation, headed by Liu Shao-chi, second only to Mao Tse-Tung, was in Moscow at the time because Khrushchev had asked Mao to send him a delegation for consultations. The night before the Presidium's decision not to intervene militarily, Liu had persuaded Khrushchev that this was not the right course. Then, on the night of October 30–31, after the decision not to intervene had already been made by the Presidium and the Declaration of the change of Soviet policy had already been proclaimed to the world, the talks were continued. As Khrushchev describes it: "We sat up the whole night, weighing the pros and cons of whether or not we should apply armed force in Hungary, First Liu Shao-chi said it wasn't necessary: we should get out of Hungary, he said, and let the working class build itself up and deal with the counter-revolution on its own. We agreed.

"But then, after reaching this agreement, we started discussing the situation again, and someone warned of the danger that the working class might take a fancy to the counter-revolution. The youth in Hungary was especially susceptible.

"I don't know how many times we changed our minds back and forth about what to do. Liu Shao-chi would consult with Mao Tse-tung. It was not a problem....Mao is like an owl, he works all night long. Mao always approved whatever Liu recommended. We finally finished this all-night session with a decision not to apply military force in Hungary. Once we had agreed on that, I went home.

"When I climbed into bed that morning, I found I was still too preoccupied with the whole problem to rest. It was like a nail in my head.*

"Later in the morning the Presidium of the Central Committee met to hear my report on how our discussion with the Chinese delegation had gone. I told them how we had changed our position a number of times and how we had finally reached our decision to not apply military force in Hungary.

---

*There is good reason to believe that the "nail in his head" was caused by the harrowing pictures of the bloodied body of the ÁVO officer strung up by his heels in Republic Square and similar pictures which the Soviet Embassy had flown to Moscow and delivered to his doorstep in the early evening of October 30. (See *Nikita Khrushchev and the Creation of a Superpower* p. 192.) These—though scholars have not been able to confirm their existence—and the news that the Party Secretary of the City of Budapest, Imre Mezo, had been killed in the assault, must have kept reverberating in his mind.

*However, I then told the Presidium what the consequences might be if we
didn't lend a helping hand to the Hungarian working class...."*[3]

Wednesday, October 31, 1956
Moscow

Today's deliberation in the Presidium, by Khrushchev's own account, is
"long." The Presidium had, after all, come to a unanimous decision yesterday not to intervene militarily and, if necessary, pull its troops not only out
of Budapest, but also from all of Hungary. These leading Central Committee
members may have reached their exalted positions by observing strict party
discipline, but they are not sheep; they all have minds of their own. They
must be convinced of why a reversal is necessary and be given time to weigh
not only the alternatives, but also the consequences of the new action proposed.

"We should reexamine our assessment and should not withdraw our
troops from Hungary and Budapest," says Khrushchev. "Instead we should
take the initiative in restoring order in Hungary. If we depart from Hungary,
it will give a great boost to the Americans, English and French—the imperialists. They will perceive it as weakness on our part and will go onto the
offensive. We would then be exposing the weakness of our positions...."

"To Egypt they will then add Hungary.

"We have no other choice."

"After yesterday's session, this discussion is all pointless," objects
Deputy Prime Minister Saburov. "It will vindicate NATO!"

"Yesterday was only a compromise decision," puts in ex-Foreign
Minister Molotov.

Comrades Voroshilov, Bulganin and Zhukov all object to the term "reexamine," while Comrade Furtesova says, "We showed patience, but now
things have gone too far. We must assure that victory goes to our side."

"We should use the argument that we will not let socialism in Hungary
be strangled," says Comrade Pospelov.

Eventually there is only one member left still arguing against a change,
Deputy Prime Minister Saburov. When the final vote is taken, he, too, capit-
ulates and makes it appear to be unanimous. But it is not unanimous.[4]

Two votes, those of Suslov and Mikoyan, who have not yet returned from
Hungary, are missing.

Once the decision is made, discussion turns to how to implement it. They agree that they should create a "Provisional Revolutionary Government." Münnich, whom Rákosi and Khrushchev favor, seems to be the obvious choice to head it, but Kádár should be with him and if Nagy agrees to come on board, well and good, he can be a Deputy Premier.

Contact is then made with Marshal Konev, commander of the Warsaw Pact forces, to see how long preparations for launching a full-scale intervention in Hungary would take. "Three days, no longer" is his reply. He is then instructed to begin at once. Marshal Zhukov is then ordered to work out a plan of attack. In the course of this, Zhukov boasts that he will completely smash the counter-revolution in three days.[5]

While the all-day session of the Presidium is in progress, American Ambassador Charles Bohlen tells Washington in a mid-day cable:

> Soviet policy is reacting to fast-developing events outside its borders and depending on these events can, and indeed does, shift accordingly. It is thus more than possible that Soviet policy on the withdrawal of troops from Budapest made to me last night about seven o' clock by Zhukov and repeated in the Declaration, may be subject to change....If the Nagy government has completely lost control and what is termed in the Declaration as "black reaction and counterrevolution" has taken over, this position on troop withdrawal may well be reversed. However, the general line of the Declaration, which will be further analyzed in a subsequent message, certainly at the time of its issuance, would indicate that the Soviet Union is preparing to cut its losses in Hungary and accept a high degree, if not complete independence of the satellites in general.[6]

It is dark by the time the Presidium takes it "unanimous" vote. Now Khrushchev remembers that Liu Shao-chi and his delegation are due to leave for Peking this evening and Liu is leaving with the impression that no military intervention will take place. Rather than re-engage talks, Khrushchev phones Liu and asks that he arrive somewhat early at the airport where he can meet him and bring him up-to-date. Indeed, Khrushchev is so nervous about his apparent vacillation that he persuades the entire Presidium to journey to the airport as proof of Soviet resolve in the matter. The Chinese, as usual, are enigmatic. They show no alarm at this change, but Liu points out that there is not time now to inform Mao. "I can't get Mao Tse-Tung's consent at this moment, but I think he will support you. As soon as I arrive in Peking I will inform the Politburo...and we will relay back to you our formal decision. But you may assume that you have our backing." Outwardly, Khrushchev shows relief. He still feels himself junior to Mao.[7]

Budapest

All night long Soviet tanks have been rumbling and roaring out of Budapest, first from one sector, then another, but they are still very much in evidence in the center of the city and outside the Soviet Embassy along Stalin (Andrássy) Avenue. Only the empty Ministry of the Interior, once headquarters for the ÁVO, no longer has tanks surrounding it. It will be early afternoon before the last tank departs, well behind schedule.

Villagers about twenty kilometers southeast of the city, however, report a Russian unit of tanks, anti-tank guns and anti-aircraft guns, which had pulled out of Budapest, stopping and digging defensive trenches.[8]

For the first time in a week, however, there is no sound of guns anywhere in the city. And despite a slight drizzle for a few hours, nothing can dampen the spirits of the populace as they survey their shattered, but liberated, city and eagerly read the two dozen uncensored newspapers celebrating the nation's remarkable achievement.

American Chargé d'Affaires Spencer Barnes, who has been hearing the noise of departing Soviet armor all night, has lost his skepticism. In a telegram meant for his incoming superior, Minister Edward T. Wailes, who has now reached Vienna, he states:

> In a dramatic overnight change, it became virtually certain in Budapest this morning that this Hungarian Revolution is now a fact of history. Personal observations, newspaper stories, and radio content tend to confirm complete Soviet troop withdrawal from the city, apparently under Hungarian protection.
>
> Our initial view...is that it would be desirable for the President to make a statement in the very near future. This might indicate U.S. willingness to initiate some type of immediate economic aid, to be followed by broader political and economic discussions...[9]

Britain's Minister, Sir Leslie Fry, cables the Foreign Office after a tour of the city: "I was astonished by the extent of the many areas affected. It is nothing short of a miracle that the Hungarian people should have withstood and turned back this diabolical onslaught. They will neither forget nor forgive." He urges that rather than have British aid flown in on scheduled Sabena (Belgian) flights, that they be flown in on British aircraft. "Judging from the reception given everywhere to the British flag, it would be an immense tonic to the people of Budapest." In another telegram he suggests, "Neutrality on the Austrian pattern might perhaps suit this country (and us)."[10]

At the Kilián Barracks in Budapest's Ninth District, some 1,200 soldiers and civilian freedom fighters agree to leave the building around 8:00 a.m. One young man, with a five-day growth on his face and a filthy blood-soaked bandage on his head, tells English correspondent Gordon Shepherd "We have not surrendered. Our commander and headquarters are still in the Barracks and we are keeping our arms."

The National Guard, with Major General Béla Király as its chief and Col. Sándor Kopácsi of the police as his deputy, is established this morning at a meeting held in the Ministry of Defense. The meeting is attended by delegates from all of the major fighting units in the city, as well as students from their own organized militias. A representative of the Tűzoltó Street group, Per Olaf Csongovai, suggests that rather than accepting the participation of further groups, the existing groups should be strengthened. He does this so those groups which have recently acquired arms in order to be able to call themselves revolutionaries, but did not take part in any of the fighting, can be excluded. There is also considerable opposition to accepting members of the József Dudás group, as their members have consistently refused to obey warnings and undergo identity checks. National Guard identity cards, essential for avoiding chaos, are manufactured on the spot.

In Republic Square, now swarming with curious citizens viewing the severed trees and bloody patches of soil and pavement where so many died yesterday, as well as the shattered remains of the municipal party headquarters, a new activity begins. After the fighting yesterday, people swore they heard faint voices calling for help coming from the drains near the party building. Others were certain they heard them coming from the ground in the park. It is thought that during the war the Gestapo had plans for extensive underground cells and torture chambers. Frantic digging begins, but hand shovels prove frustratingly inadequate.

Meanwhile, over in Buda on Sváb Hill, five civilian freedom fighters from "Uncle Szabó's" Széna Square group are investigating a mysterious house next to the Normafa Restaurant. People tell them that large black cars keep appearing, only at night, and that no one in the neighborhood has ever seen the inside of the building. The freedom fighters discover a forty-five-year-old man inside who claims to be a retired electrician. A quick body search reveals that, in fact, he is an ÁVO non-commissioned officer, who has received decorations for his services to the People's Republic. They force him to open a secret cellar door where they find four prison cells behind heavy steel doors. Each cell has one small cot and two buckets. All cells are empty, but one has very fresh bloodstains in it. With the assistance of a rifle butt, the ÁVO man confesses that the bloodstains are from three students who were executed here last night. He refuses to reveal anything else. A further search of the building turns up Russian documents and Russian passports without photographs. They take their ÁVO prisoner and all the Russian documents back to their headquarters.[11]

The University Revolutionary Committee is issuing a challenge to Nagy which will be broadcast tonight on Free Radio Kossuth. "We consider the present political leadership a temporary solution," they say. "We support Imre Nagy so far as he and his government fulfill our demands. Therefore we use every means to free him from all Stalinist influence. We demand, therefore... that the old Stalinists Antal Apró, Erik Molnár, Ferenc Nezvál, János Csergő and Mrs. József Nagy should quit the government. We would like to see Mrs. Anna Kéthly, György Lukács and Gyula Illés in the government....We want neither Stalinism nor Capitalism. We want a Hungary, independent from every country; a truly democratic and truly socialist Hungary..."[12]

But Nagy, while not impervious to advice from the young, feels entitled to take some credit for what has already been achieved. And having read the text of the Soviet Declaration this morning, he is feeling ebullient. Noting that there are large crowds strolling through Parliament Square he decides to give an impromptu speech from the balcony outside his office. Loudspeakers are hooked up and his intention announced over them before he steps out.

Hungarian brothers, I am once again addressing you with great love.

The revolution of which you were the heroes has been won! These heroic days have brought about our National Government, which will now fight for the freedom and independence of our nation. We will tolerate no interference in Hungarian domestic affairs." *(There is applause. In fact, each of his sentences is followed by applause or shouts of "Yes.")*

We stand on the basis of equal rights, of national sovereignty and the equality of nations. We will build our policy firmly upon the will of the Hungarian people.

Dear friends, ...we have removed enormous obstacles from the way. We have chased away the Rákosi and Gerő gang! [Loud cheers] "They will answer for their crimes. They tried to defile me, too. They spread the lie that it was I who had called the Russian troops into the country. This is a base lie. On the contrary, it is I, Imre Nagy,...who fought that they be withdrawn." [Loud cheers and shouts of "Russki go home !"]

My dear friends, on this day we have started negotiations for the withdrawal of Soviet troops from the country and for the repudiation of the duties which fall to us in the Warsaw Pact. But we are asking you for patience. I think the results are such that you can give us that much confidence....Stand by us, support us in the patriotic work...have confidence in the government to create order and peace that we may carry out our broad democratic program.

Long live the independent, free and democratic Hungarian Republic!
Long live Hungary!

In the Countryside

In Pécs, the former leader of the Independent Smallholders Party, Béla Kovács, who is presumed to be a member of the present government, but who has never accepted, gives a speech in the Pécs County Hall to a gathering of local Smallholders party leaders in which he calls for a neutral Hungary. "It is necessary to establish relations, based on equal rights, with all nations, and one cannot tie the country's fate to one or another military bloc. *The Hungarian people demand a neutral Hungary.*[13]

As Russians continue to pour in from the East, Western correspondents and aid officials continue to pour into Hungary from the West. Even Radio Free Europe now has a correspondent in Győr, and today at Szentgotthárd, southwest of Győr, an RFE team is recording the demands of the local national committee for broadcast tonight to the whole country from Munich. New among these demands is one calling for free access to all of Hungary for journalists from the entire world, free travel and cultural exchange with all of the world and the prevention of "Senseless sabotage and all manifestations of personal revenge" against communists and the ÁVO.

"For years we have listened to RFE in this room," one of the committee members tells the RFE correspondents, "and we never believed that we would see the day when RFE representatives would actually be here, and we would be making a broadcast for RFE."[14]

Reaction in Eastern Europe

Open support of the Hungarian Revolution by Polish students and other citizens of Warsaw is manifested today by the thousands of Hungarian tri-color ribbons sprouting on caps and lapels. But in other satellite countries any indication of sympathy is dangerous. Waves of arrests and dismissals from jobs are occurring in Czechoslovakia and in East Germany the regime announces, in an attempt to nip any revolt in the bud, the arrest of seventy-three of its citizens whom it accuses of being "Western spies." In Romania, László Bányai, the Rector of Bolyai University in Cluj (Hungarian: Kolozsvár), assembles the entire student body and forbids them to go tomorrow, All Saints' Day, to Házsongárdi Cemetery, where many of the great contributors to Hungarian literature and thought lie buried. He had just been informed of a massive demonstration the students were secretly planning to hold there. Because many young ethnic Hungarian workers and students in Romania crossed the border to join the freedom fighters in the first days of the Revolution, the border is now tightly sealed.[15]

Reaction in the Free World

Hungarian legations in the West are now publicly declaring their loyalty to the Nagy regime and the Revolution. In Stockholm, Minister József Hajdú speaks not only for his staff in Stockholm, but also for the Hungarian diplomatic missions in Copenhagen and Oslo. In London the Hungarian press attaché telephones his message that "the Minister and every member of the Hungarian Legation...welcome from our hearts the victory of our Hungarian people and the new democratic and coalition government..."[16]

In Washington, the Planning Board of the National Security Council meets to update U.S. policy toward Poland and Hungary. By the end of their meeting they produce a reasonable document insofar as it goes, but it is obvious that not one of the board members has read the morning newspaper carrying news of the Soviet Declaration of its new policy toward the countries of Eastern Europe. This fact alone tends to make their conclusions and recommendations moot.

Courses of action which they propose include "discouraging and, if possible, preventing further Soviet armed intervention in Hungary," by mobilizing "all appropriate pressures, including UN action, on the USSR...(while reassuring the USSR that we do not look upon Hungary or the other satellites as potential allies).

EXPLOSION

"In line with this approach, [we should] consider whether it is advisable to make in the UN or elsewhere a proposal of Hungarian neutrality on the Austrian model."[17]

The Planning Board, however, makes no suggestion as to what the "appropriate pressures" on the Soviet Union, other than the UN, might be.

In Munich, where RFE Political Advisor William E. Griffith must be much more on top of the current situation than members of the Planning Board of the National Security Council, a new analysis for October 31 is circulated. Griffith finds the Soviet Declaration "mild in tone, less condemnatory of the Hungarian revolutionaries than before" and that its issuance "probably means that Khrushchev and other supporters of the liberalization course are maintaining their ascendancy; it is probable, barring a reversal in the present CPSU Presidium course, that Soviet troops will evacuate Hungary and probably Romania and leave only a line of communications troops in Poland."

As to Hungarian prospects, Griffith writes:

Assuming Soviet troops leave Hungary (and this now seems likely) I can see no indigenous forces which can likely be able to prevent the establishment of a western-style democracy, with Hungary either neutral, like Austria, or (at worst from our viewpoint) a Finnish-type situation. The Nagy "government" surely is more and more in the hands of the Revolutionary Council, which must have the real power in its hands by now. The Communist Party is completely disorganized, the reorganized Social Democratic Party will probably reduce it to a complete shell. I assume that the Cardinal has the most prestige of anyone. I presume that the Christian Democratic Party will be organized and play a major role.[18]

Now most of Eastern Europe is asleep and even Radio Free Europe is about to go off the air. In the U.S. tonight, President Eisenhower was to have made a political speech to the nation winding up his political campaign. Instead he speaks not as a candidate for office, but as the President, discussing foreign events which "have no connection whatsoever with matters of partisanship."

The main portion of his speech deals with the crisis in the Middle East with which he and his Secretary of State have been most concerned for the past two days. But he also speaks of events in Poland and Hungary and all of Eastern Europe.

"Today," he says "a new Hungary is rising from this struggle, a Hungary which we hope from our hearts will know full and free nationhood."

"Only yesterday the Soviet Union issued an important statement on its relations with all the countries of Eastern Europe. This statement recognized the need for review of Soviet policies, and the amendment of these policies, to meet the demands of the people for greater national independence...." After predicting the consequences of this Declaration and calling it, if enacted, "the greatest forward stride...among nations in our generation," the President tells how the U.S. is responding.

"The United States has made clear its readiness to assist economically the new and independent governments of these countries....We have also publicly declared that we do not demand of these governments their adoption of any particular form of society as a condition on our economic assistance....

"We have also...sought clearly to remove any false fears that we would look upon new governments in these Eastern European countries as potential military allies. We have no ulterior purpose...."[19]

Budapest

Radio Free Kossuth is playing Mozart's Requiem at the end of its broadcasting day in honor of all those who have fallen since October 23. Tomorrow, All Saint's Day, which is being recognized for the first time since the communists took over Hungary, will be a national holiday.

Moscow

It is not quite midnight in Moscow, and an exhausted Nikita S. Khrushchev has long since fallen asleep. Suddenly he is awakened by the ringing of his special telephone. In these nerve-wracking days it can mean just about anything.

Mikoyan is on the line. He and Suslov have just returned from Budapest and have learned of the Presidium's reversal in deciding to crush the revolution with the Red Army. Though events in Budapest have become worse and unpredictable, Anastas Ivanovich still has faith that Nagy can turn the corner and that things will soon be under control. Khrushchev is annoyed at being awakened for nothing new. He has heard all of Mikoyan's arguments before and the decision has been made. What is the point of continuing to talk into his valuable sleep time? Mikoyan senses that Khrushchev is about to cut him off and say goodnight. He begins to talk faster and becomes more and more emotional, his Armenian accent beginning to slur his Russian. He insists that it would be a terrible mistake, the action is premature, the decision can be called off, and at the very least there should be another meeting of the Presidium at which he and Suslov can argue their case.

"Suslov has not called me," interrupts Khrushchev, "and we've already decided."

Mikoyan continues to argue. "It's begun," thinks Khrushchev to himself. "I've been thinking how I must convince Gomułka tomorrow, and now I have to start here in Moscow with Mikoyan!" Fortunately for Khrushchev, his mind is made up. Mikoyan goes on as though he were terrified of stopping. Finally Khrushchev cuts in: "Anastas, we won't get anywhere now, it's late. If you want, let's meet before my departure for the airport. We'll talk then with clearer minds. In the meantime, calm down; think it over." Since Mikoyan lives in the house right next door, such a meeting is easy. What is not easy is getting back to sleep. For a long time Nikita Sergeyevich turns and tosses.

Thursday, November 1, 1956

It is still dark when he gets up. The usual breakfast is awaiting him, but he pushes it aside. He takes some sips of tea with lemon, but even this he does not finish. He gets up, strides into the next room and picks up a special telephone which connects him to the guard at his gate. "Tell Mikoyan that I'm coming outside," he tells the captain. Mikoyan does not keep him waiting and they greet each other, not coldly, but lacking the usual warmth of their long friendship. They decide to walk along a path by the wooden fence. Mikoyan speaks first, repeating much of what he had said last night. "All is not yet lost," he insists. "We should wait and see how events develop. But we must in no case send troops into the situation."

Khrushchev has always admired Mikoyan's intellect, particularly his wisdom and ability to negotiate. But it takes a person of a different mindset when it comes to taking action.

Time is running out and the rumble of the cumbersome ZIS-110 limousine entering the courtyard begins to drown out Mikoyan's words. It is time to go, but still Mikoyan continues to talk. Khrushchev finally reaches the limit of his patience: "So what are you trying to achieve, Anastas? They are hanging and killing communists in Budapest, and you want us to sit with our arms folded and wait until American tanks show up on our border? We have to help the Hungarian workers. They are our class brothers. History won't forgive us if we are timid and indecisive."

Mikoyan has no reply.

"Furthermore, the decision is already made," Khrushchev continues. "We discussed everything and could arrive at no other conclusion. Do you think it is any easier for me?" He sighs and adds, "We have to act; we have no other course."

Mikoyan grabs his sleeve and draws him back. "If there is bloodshed I don't know what I will do with myself!" he almost shouts into Khrushchev's face. Khrushchev looks at him in amazement. He has never seen Mikoyan like this.

After a pause he says as calmly as he can, "Anastas, you're a reasonable person. Think it over, take all the factors into consideration and you will see that we've made the only right decision. If there is bloodshed, it will spare us greater bloodshed later. Think it over and you'll understand that...." Khrushchev does not finish his sentence. He doesn't want to recount any of this conversation to Malenkov and Molotov, who are waiting for him at the airport. He doesn't want to "betray" his friend. But Mikoyan's last despairing words have shaken him and all the way to the airport and even on the plane they keep coming back to him. "He won't do anything," he keeps trying to reassure himself. Indeed, Anastas Mikoyan does not even attempt suicide.[20]

At an airport near Brest on the Polish-Soviet border the Soviet leaders meet with Gomułka and his Premier, Jozef Cyrankiewicz. They do not inform the Poles of the Presidium's decision. They describe the situation, and the Poles listen in silence. Then they ask the Poles what should be done, now that Imre Nagy is demanding that the USSR withdraw its forces.

"Don't withdraw them!" answers Gomułka.

"But what then?" asks Khrushchev. "Hungarian communists are being exterminated. They are being killed and hanged. Should our forces just look on? ...We have to consider carefully where this is going!"

"We still think that your forces should not be withdrawn, but neither should you order them to intervene," says Gomułka. "You have to leave time for the government, which is taking a counterrevolutionary position, to show its true colors. Then the Hungarian working class will rise up and overthrow it."

"But how much time should we leave?" asks Khrushchev, "How much time will pass before the [working class] has the strength to fight back? They are killing party activists who advocate the right policies. Destroying them physically!"

Unable to persuade the Poles that military intervention in Hungary was the way to go, the two delegations bid each other goodbye. While Molotov flies back to Moscow, Malenkov and Khrushchev fly on to Bucharest where they are to meet with the Bulgarian, Czechoslovak and Romanian government and party leaders. The East Germans, while members of the Warsaw Pact, are not included. The Russians still regard them with ambivalence. One moment they are a full-fledged member of the bloc, the next, simply an occupied part of Germany to be used as a bargaining chip in the East-West struggle.[21]

Budapest

The weather has turned much colder during the night, bringing freezing temperatures to most of the country, though parts of the city are bathed in bright sunlight this morning, before gray skies and light precipitation take over.

It is All Saints Day, celebrated as a national holiday legally for the first time in ten years. There has been no early morning news broadcast on the radio, only entertainment and classical music until 8:15.[22] People never stopped visiting the graves of deceased family members in the city's cemeteries on this day. Although some would furtively carry small bunches of flowers to the cemetery, most preferred to avoid the prying eyes of the secret police by buying them at the cemetery gate, despite the higher cost. But today everyone is out on the streets with flowers, for it is not only cemeteries that are being visited, but also countless graves all over the city. Wherever there are parks or just patches of green, temporary graves have been dug and makeshift crosses erected.

Most parents, by now, know where their children are, but those children who never came home may still be in a morgue or unknown grave and parents are still desperately searching for them. The cemeteries are alive with women bundled up and in kerchiefs, carrying flowers and flickering, glass-encased candles. Candles, often more than a few, are placed on the temporary graves in the city parks as well. And tonight they will be joined by hundreds of thousands in windows, from which black flags of mourning already hang.

People are drawn to the scenes of the greatest fighting. The Kilián Barracks with its four-foot-thick walls is still standing, but it is missing an entire corner where the walls and all four floors have been blasted away by Soviet shelling, leaving a great gash. Over at the unbelievably pockmarked radio building on Sándor Bródy Street a white banner has been tied to the wrought-iron balustrade of the damaged balcony. On the wall above, the bullet-ridden letters "Magyar Rádió" curve over the balcony. On the banner attached to the railing, with the same lettering, but with the Kossuth emblem in the middle, are the words Magyar (Hungarian) Szabad (Free) Rádió.

At three o'clock this afternoon, hundreds of thousands of people will heed yesterday's call for church bells to ring, sirens to be sounded and the entire population of Budapest to stop what they are doing and stand, bare-headed and at attention "in the streets and at workplaces" to pay homage to "our dead heroes," while "traffic also should stop during this minute."[23]

The mood of the populace is mixed, for the air of freedom is so intoxicating that, despite the destruction and tragic deaths, many feel giddy with delight. Instead of the five dull stereotyped newspapers, all saying essentially the same thing, two dozen sprightly presented newspapers, all saying something different, have burst upon the scene and are being snatched up, and even paid for, which the first issues had not been. Only *Szabad Nép* has not appeared. At the last minute it was discovered that several of the articles included for publication were written by "counterrevolutionaries," so the whole issue had to be cancelled.

Even though RFE, with jamming gone, now comes in clear as a bell, nobody bothers to listen to it, for the free radios inside the country are far more varied and up-to-date, even carrying news of what people abroad are saying about Hungary.

Public transportation has not yet been restored, but neat mounds of broken glass and downed electric wires with white paper attached to the loose ends indicate that a beginning is being made. Since almost no one is going to work, except to pick up information and pay packets, there are lots of volunteers for clean-up crews. And there are still sections of the city where unexploded mines or shells lie exposed in the streets as well as bodies of Soviet soldiers covered with lime.[24]

In Republic square, thousands watch a steam shovel dig up mounds of earth where yesterday only hand shovels had begun to seek the underground cells thought to contain prisoners of the ÁVO. Hope begins to wane as no more voices are detected. By day's end no cells have been found.

Others watch firemen clearing up still smoldering ashes of Soviet books burned in the streets and buildings set ablaze in the first onslaught.[25]

In the Parliament Building, Premier Imre Nagy meets his inner cabinet for the first time today. Discussion is lively, but with only four participants besides Nagy—János Kádár, Zoltán Tildy (Smallholders), Ferenc Erdei and Géza Losonczy—some sixteen decisions are made. Among the most important are:

1) That Zoltán Tildy should meet with Cardinal Mindszenty today to convince him to make a declaration in support of law and order and the government.

2) That the Cabinet fully agrees with Béla Kovács's statement in Pécs yesterday about Hungary's neutrality and measures must be taken immediately to get him up to Budapest today.

3) That radio broadcasts must continue to come from the Parliament building with increased control. The Cabinet appoints a commissioner to see and pass upon every political statement submitted before it goes on the air.

4) That Ambassador Andropov be summoned at once to explain why Soviet armed forces continue to enter Hungary and that an official protest will be presented to him.

5) That in the absence of the Foreign Minister, Imre Horváth, Imre Nagy will immediately take over the duties of Foreign Minister as well as retaining the position as President of the Council of Ministers.

6) That, after hearing reports from Generals Pál Maléter, István Kovács and Béla Király on the withdrawal, and on more Soviet forces continuously entering the country, the National Guard needs more financial and moral support.

7) That the country should declare, if Soviet troop movements do not stop, its neutrality, refraining, for the time being, from deciding which type of neutrality it will adopt, that of Switzerland, Austria or Yugoslavia.

8) That the Dudás group is such a threat to unity that it needs to be eliminated. Nagy will initiate negotiations, but if he fails to reach a satisfactory agreement with Dudás, Gen. Maléter will be authorized to arrest him.[26]

Ambassador Andropov is summoned as soon as the meeting is over and confronted with the facts. For a while Andropov dissembles. He has the temerity to tell Nagy to his face that he is misinformed: no new Soviet forces have entered Hungary. Nagy maintains his composure; he would like to believe Andropov, but he knows Andropov is lying. He delivers a formal protest to a grim-faced Andropov and invites him to bring his answer to the inner cabinet, which will meet again this afternoon.

Any Hungarian could do worse than remain glued to his radio set today. Not only are the free radios in the countryside broadcasting accurate stories of what is happening in their area, Free Radio Kossuth has one astounding announcement after another. Much of what has taken place in this morning's cabinet meeting is announced, but there are other news items and interviews worth listening to. Col. Pál Maléter, now promoted to Major General and serving as Deputy Minister of Defense, holds a press conference with foreign correspondents. Maléter's reputation as the hero of the Kilián Barracks and, in fact, the hero of the revolution has mushroomed within a couple of days. His Army colleagues and the populace in general cannot believe that the Soviets could have been defeated so thoroughly in front of the Kilián Barracks without a strong military commander in charge. When asked, Maléter has modestly spoken the truth that his soldiers only defended themselves, but he does not add that they were defending themselves from the revolutionaries, and that he only went over to their side on the twenty-eighth, after most of the fighting was finished. He had made an honest attempt to assure the Defense Ministry that he had *not* gone over to the insurgents, but this had purposely not been publicized and an article by Péter Komoly had appeared in *Igazság,* the very popular newspaper of "the revolutionary Hungarian Army and youth," extolling Maléter under the headline "In the heart of the revolution: the Kilián Barracks." Though he knew he was not the hero people thought him, Maléter, now totally committed to the Revolution, realizes he has a role to play which, were he too factually truthful, would undercut that role and harm the revolution.[27]

Cardinal Mindszenty, back at his Palace in Buda, tells the foreign press, radio and television correspondents, "After long imprisonment I greet all the sons of the Hungarian nation. I bear no hatred against anyone....The struggle being waged for [Hungarian] liberty is unparalleled in world history. Our young men deserve all the glory. They deserve our gratitude and...our prayers."

The situation in the country is very serious and all conditions for continuing normal life are absent. A way towards fruitful development must be found as soon as possible. I am collecting information and in two days I shall speak to the nation about ways towards a solution.[28]

An appeal by the National Writers' Association calls on everyone to guard the "purity of the revolution," and not to "pass judgment in the streets....Hand over the guilty unharmed either to the National Guard or Army patrols. Personal revenge is an act unworthy of us. The whole world is watching and recognizes the honor of our revolution....Do not besmirch it."[29]

Unfortunately, along with political prisoners released, there have been a number of common criminals inadvertently freed as well. These elements, when they join the ranks of the Freedom Fighters, *do* begin to besmirch the Revolution.

Continuing Reaction in the Communist World

In Romania, where there are several million Hungarians, demonstrations have taken place in Cluj (Hungarian: Kolozsvár), Bucharest, Oradea (Hungarian: Nagyvárad), Timisoira (Hungarian: Temesvár) and Târgu-Mureş (Hungarian: Marosvásárhely), where police have even fired on the demonstrators. Romanian Army units, armed with submachine guns and rifles, are now patrolling all of these towns. In Bucharest and all of the universities in Transylvania, student petitions demanding the release of students arrested during recent protest meetings have been circulating. The students arrested in Bucharest had been shouting for French language courses, instead of Russian. The Romanian government, meanwhile, has shut down all train travel to Belgrade and even Western diplomats who had permission to drive there in their own cars have had this permission withdrawn.[30]

In Yugoslavia, where less than a million Hungarians reside in Voivodina, reportage by Yugoslav communist correspondents from Hungary is markedly different today than in previous days. Rather than praise the revolutionaries, they write such lines as:

[One can] lament the collapse of communist power and authority in this country's northern neighbor....The next few days will decide the future of Hungary [i.e. of Hungarian Communism]....The Hungarian Communists are in fear of popular reprisals: they are passing through the most difficult days in the history of their party;...The Communist Party has lost its influence among the masses. It seems as though it no longer exists anymore.[31]

Politika, the Yugoslav Party daily, says that the Nagy government is no longer "master of the situation" and that contrary to earlier reports "that peace is prevailing in Budapest and all over Hungary,...disorder reigns everywhere."[32]

In Czechoslovakia, where the regime's reaction is similar to that in Romania, the lid is on so tight that no news of opposition or demonstrations is able to leak out, even to neighboring Hungary.

In East Germany, on the other hand, university students, led by those of Humboldt University in East Berlin, today verbally attack the Communist Youth organization (FDJ), demanding the abolition of the mandatory study of Russian and Marxism-Leninism, the end of paramilitary training and the establishment of free elections to student councils. Dr. Alfred Neuman, First Secretary of East Berlin's Socialistische Einheits Deutschland (Communist) Party, rejects the demands as an attempt to split the youth movement. But later in the day, Fritz Lange, Minister of Education, announces that English and French will replace the teaching of Russian in some secondary schools.[33]

In Warsaw, meantime, thousands of students meet at the Polytechnic Institute to adopt a resolution expressing "full support for the revolutionary forces" in Hungary and protesting the "participation of Soviet forces in suppressing the uprising." This is called an "irresponsible outburst" by the Party paper *Trybuna Ludu*. Students have to be dissuaded by the authorities from leading a protest march to the Soviet Embassy. On the sidewalk outside Warsaw University's Faculty of Fine Arts, students place a huge reproduction of a picture showing robots shooting down men, women and children. Beside it hangs a green-white-red banner of Hungary. Nearby the Picasso "Dove of Peace" is displayed with a large tear falling from one eye. [34]

Free World Reaction

In New York the *New York Times*, under the headline "Victory in Hungary," writes in its lead editorial this morning: "All signs point to a victory for freedom in Hungary. At the cost of the lives and blood of still uncounted martyrs, the communist despotism there has, at least temporarily, been overthrown." But in commenting on the Soviet Declaration of October 30, the *Times* notes that the involvement of the whole Warsaw Pact in the decision to pull its troops from Hungary is "an ominous loophole."

"There is still need for vigilance against Moscow's future moves. But Moscow has been forced to retreat, and in that fact lies the great victory won by the Hungarian youth, workers and peasants."

In Washington, the National Security Council is about to meet in the White House to discuss the situation in Hungary as well as the Middle East. Twenty minutes before, however, Secretary of State John Foster Dulles telephones President Eisenhower to tell him that the situation in Hungary has changed dramatically for the better, making it unnecessary to focus on that subject. The Council can concentrate, as the Secretary is doing, on the Middle East.

Thus, when the President enters the Cabinet room, he tells the assembled National Security Council that except insofar as it will be the subject for the Director of Central Intelligence, he does not wish the Council to take up the subject of the situation in the Soviet satellites, but rather to concentrate on the Middle East. As this is the day after the publication of the Soviet Union's Declaration on its future relations with the satellite countries, many on the Council are surprised by this announcement, though they feel the President must have a good reason. Nevertheless, Allen W. Dulles, Director of Central Intelligence, says he has a few remarks he wants to make on the situation in Hungary.

> In a sense what has occurred there is a miracle. Events have belied all of our past view that a popular revolt in the face of modern weapons is an utter impossibility. Nevertheless, the impossible has happened, and because of the power of public opinion, armed forced could not effectively be used. Our estimates are that approximately 80% of the Hungarian Army has defected to the rebels with arms. Soviet troops themselves have had no stomach for shooting down Hungarians, except in Budapest.

Allen Dulles then comments on the Soviet Declaration of October 30. "This statement," he says, "is one of the most important statements to come out of the USSR in the last decade." After summarizing it, but making no attempt to analyze it, Dulles turns back to Hungary and says:

> The main problem facing us today in Hungary is the lack of a strong guiding authority around which the rebels can rally. Nagy is failing to unite the rebels, and they are demanding that he quit. Somehow a rallying point must be found in order to prevent chaos inside Hungary, even if the Soviets do

withdraw from the country. In such a heavily Catholic nation as Hungary, Cardinal Mindszenty might prove to be such a leader and unifying force.[35]

At this point the President stops Dulles with the firm injunction that the main reason for the meeting is to discuss the Middle East and what he calls an act of unilateral belligerency by America's closest allies. His brother, Secretary of State, known to intimates as "Foster," now takes over the discussion of Britain and France's unwarranted, unilateral assault on Egypt.[36]

A few hours later the Department of State receives the following coded telegram from its Legation in Budapest:

> While we have no way of knowing the present Soviet attitude, it must be remembered that Soviet troops have not (repeat not) withdrawn very far from the city, and that continued anarchy or extreme right-wing developments here during the next few days could hardly be pleasant to the Soviets; if any consideration is being given by the Soviets to a second intervention, such developments would certainly increase its chances.
>
> *...the potentiality of U.S. influence in this period is tremendous.* [emphasis added—ed.] The attitude of the people on the streets has been touchingly pro-American, and our medical and economic aid are becoming known.
>
> We believe, therefore that the present situation indicates further U.S. statements as soon as possible. The effect of such a statement, of course, is the greatest if it comes from the President or Secretary, but the arrival of Minister Wailes may also prove an opportunity.

There follows a draft of such a statement by Barnes emphasizing the U.S. desire for the restoration of law and order and the peaceful processes of courts, plus the U.S. intention to open formal talks on economic aid with the present government, the results of which would be honored with any subsequent government.[37]

Budapest

At almost the exact time that the National Security Council is meeting in Washington, Imre Nagy is presiding over the second inner cabinet meeting of the day. This time Soviet Ambassador Andropov is present at the beginning. He has a cock-and-bull story from Moscow that the new troops are coming to secure the departure of Soviet citizens and to see that the withdrawal goes smoothly. General István Kovács, chief of the Hungarian General Staff, then reveals to the cabinet the full extent of the Soviet troop movements, new pontoon bridges, etc. with a series of aerial photographs taken since this morning. They clearly show Soviet forces entering Hungary and converging on Budapest. Andropov turns crimson. Without giving him a chance to recover and dissemble any further, Nagy tells him that as a consequence of Soviet perfidy in this matter, Hungary is immediately renouncing the Warsaw Pact, is declaring itself neutral and at the same time will seek recourse to the United Nations asking that the four great powers help in defending the country's new neutral status. Finally, Nagy tells Andropov that if Soviet troops evacuate Hungary in the shortest possible time for such a military operation, Hungary will annul its telegram to the United Nations.

With Andropov dismissed, the cabinet wastes no time in drafting the various messages announcing these measures. These announcements will go out to diplomatic missions in Budapest, to Secretary General Dag Hammarskjold at the United Nations and last of all to Klimenti Voroshilov, President of the Council of Ministers of the USSR. This last message will ask the Soviet head of state to fix a date and venue for negotiations both on withdrawal of Soviet troops from all of Hungary and for negotiations on Hungary's withdrawing from the Warsaw Pact.[38]

The Social Democrats have so far refused to join the government. They want to see the Soviets gone before they commit themselves. Their Party leader, Anna Kéthly, was to have flown to Vienna today to attend an international meeting of Socialists, but she had to stop halfway to Ferihegy because the Soviets had taken over the airport and ringed it with ninety tanks. A member of the Austrian Socialist Party had to drive to Budapest to fetch her in his car.[39]

Shortly after the embarrassment at turning the Socialist leader back from Budapest's airport, the Soviet Embassy makes the announcement that "Hungarian airfields are surrounded by Soviet tanks in order to insure the transportation by plane of members of families of Soviet troops stationed in Hungary and of those injured." While this excuse scarcely covers the real reason, it is not a total lie, for some six hundred families of Soviet officials and soldiers are removed from Hungary by the 177th Soviet bomber squadron between today and November 3.[40] The Hungarian government adds that while the Hungarian Air Force wanted to prevent this development, "the government, conscious of its responsibility, did not allow any shooting."[41]

Just a few minutes before 8:00 p.m. Imre Nagy goes on the air.

People of Hungary! The Hungarian National Government.. .declares the neutrality of the Hungarian People's Republic. The Hungarian people, on the basis of independence and equality and in accordance with the spirit of the UN Charter, wishes to live in true friendship with its neighbors, the Soviet Union and all the peoples of the world....The revolutionary struggle, fought by the Hungarian people, has at last carried the cause of freedom and independence to victory. This heroic struggle has made possible the enforcement, in our people's inter-State relations, of its fundamental national interest: neutrality. We appeal to our neighbors, countries near and far, to respect the unalterable decision of our people.[42]

But in the provinces, where many are not tuned in to Free Radio Kossuth, many people are still skeptical of Nagy, particularly in the western part of the country. In Sopron, for instance, the citizens there tell RFE reporter Bernard Leason, "the general strike is still the most powerful weapon we Hungarians hold against the Russians, and this weapon will be used until the Russian troops are out of the country. The general strike," they continue, "also weakens the position of Imre Nagy....Unless Nagy is able to fulfill his promise...if the withdrawal of troops is not fulfilled, the people will not agree to lay down their arms and stop resistance."[43]

Later, around nine o'clock, after Nagy's announcement of neutrality, Free Radio Kossuth carries a pre-recorded address by Kádár in which he announces the formation of a new party, the Hungarian Socialist Workers' Party.

But shortly before this broadcast is aired, János Kádár and Ferenc Münnich tell their associates in the Parliament building that they are going to dinner. Their driver takes them not to a restaurant, but straight to the Soviet Embassy. There another car with Soviet plates is waiting for them and they are whisked away to the Soviet headquarters at Tököl in the southern part of Csepel Island. There they will spend the night and then be flown in the early morning to Moscow. Their driver, when he returns to the Parliament, says it looks as though everything had been carefully arranged ahead of time.[44]

*　　*　　*　　*

Traveling in the opposite direction, but under very different circumstances, are Nikita Khrushchev and Georgii Malenkov. They are now in Bucharest. While they have had little difficulty convincing the Bulgarian, Romanian and Czechoslovak comrades of the necessity of intervening in

Hungary, there are a great many hands to shake, pleasantries to exchange and lavish Romanian hospitality to endure. It is nighttime before the talks are completed and all thought of flying on to their main, but secret, destination, Brioni, an island in the Adriatic where Tito has his favorite villa, must be put off until the morrow.

The United Nations, New York

Imre Nagy's message to Secretary General Dag Hammarskjold arrives in the UN teletype room around 12:25 p.m. New York time. It takes a minute or so to print. This, in part, is what it says:

> Reliable reports have reached the government of the Hungarian People's Republic that further Soviet units are entering into Hungary....The President...expressed his strongest protest....He demanded the instant and immediate withdrawal of these Soviet forces. He informed the Soviet Ambassador that the Hungarian Government immediately repudiates the Warsaw Treaty, and, at the same time, declares Hungary's neutrality. The Government of the Hungarian People's Republic made the declaration of neutrality on November 1, 1956. Therefore I request your Excellency promptly to put on the agenda of the forthcoming General Assembly of the United Nations the question of Hungary's neutrality by the four great powers.

> Imre Nagy, President of the Council of Ministers and Foreign Minister[45]

The teletype attendant recognizes this as something important and sends it by special messenger directly to the Secretary General's office, where it is delivered at precisely 12:35 p.m. There it creates little excitement. All attention in this office is on the Middle East. Moreover, it is the lunch hour and the office is virtually empty. Not only does the Secretary General's office make no announcement of its arrival to the various national delegations, it even denies [mistakenly], some hours later, that such a message has been received. News agencies, having heard in Budapest that the message had been sent, phone the UN for confirmation. Since no one in the Secretary General's office seems aware of it, the agencies are told "no, nothing of that sort has arrived."[46]

Finally the UN Press Chief, realizing that these inquiries are based on authentic information, goes in person to the Secretary General's office and, after some digging, finds the telegram. He calls a "flash" conference of UN correspondents and reads out the text. It is 2:00 p.m., nearly an hour and a half after the teleprinter had typed the urgent message out. By 2:30 the Nagy appeal has been mimeographed and distributed to all UN delegates. With no marks of urgency on it, however, it gets dumped into "IN" boxes with all of the other innumerable mimeographed notices that the Secretariat produces each day. Most delegates do not see it until several hours later, some not even until night. One of these is the Secretary General himself, who does not get around to acknowledging it until 1:05 a.m. on November 2. By this time the Soviets have cut the land lines and the acknowledgment has to be routed to Geneva for possible relay somehow on to Budapest.

Fortunately, not everyone in the UN is mesmerized by the Suez crisis, to the exclusion of what is going on in Hungary. There is a small, entirely informal group of delegates, mostly from South America and other Catholic countries, as well as a few members of the Secretariat staff, who follow closely what is happening in Eastern Europe. The most active in this group is Dr. Emilio Nunez-Portuondo of Cuba, who has been tirelessly speaking of Soviet oppression in Eastern Europe now for five years. As soon as he learns of the Nagy message he goes into action, buttonholing every delegate he knows and spreading the word to his informal group. Time after time he is told, in effect: "Look, there are only troop movements going on in Hungary, but there is actual shooting in Suez. Let's deal with the five-alarm fire first and then we'll deal with the one alarm fire in Hungary." This attitude is, in fact, an accurate reflection of the position taken by the U.S. delegation, which warns fellow delegates that if the Suez matter is not dealt with immediately it could well lead to World War III.

It is only a few hours before the special meeting of the General Assembly, dealing exclusively with the crisis on Suez. Nunez-Portuondo and his colleagues are running into three main obstacles. First parliamentary procedural nitpickers argue that since this emergency session of the Assembly has now been called exclusively to deal with Suez, it cannot deal with any other matter. Then there are those who say that since the Security Council is still "seized of" (bureaucratic jargon for "considering") the matter of Hungary, the Assembly cannot legally discuss it. Nunez-Portuondo has good rebuttals for both these arguments, but he is stymied by the third. Some delegates claim that it is unclear exactly what Nagy means when he speaks of "the forthcoming Assembly." The regular forthcoming Assembly is not due to begin until November 12. Surely this is what Nagy means, for it is not likely that he could have known of this emergency Assembly which has been called for only within the last twenty-four hours. Only tomorrow will Nunez-Portuondo discover what the UN Secretariat should have told him even before he began his lobbying campaign. A mere eighteen minutes after the first message was received from Nagy, a second message arrived on the same teletype machine, also addressed to Secretary General Hammarskjold and also signed by Nagy. It reads:

> I have the honor to inform you that Mr. János Szabó, First Secretary of the Permanent Mission, will represent the Hungarian People's Republic at the special session of the General Assembly of the United Nations to be convened on November 1, 1956 at New York.

Nagy knew perfectly well about the "special" session of the General Assembly, and that is the one to which he wanted the Hungarian item to be added.

But far and away the greatest obstacle faced by Nunez-Portuondo and his colleagues is that his efforts receive no backing whatsoever from members of the U.S. delegation. It is almost as though the delegation has orders to shun him. As one delegate says: "The United States, having decided not to go to war over Hungary, has therefore decided to do nothing at all."

Naturally the Department of State does not want it to *look* as though the U.S. is doing nothing. Yesterday, the thirty-first, Dulles had sent a two-page draft resolution to Lodge to be introduced in the Security Council with paragraphs beginning "Convinced," "Deploring," "Anxious to see," "Calls upon," "Expresses," "Affirms," and finally "Decides to establish a committee composed of [left blank] to determine facts regarding the situation in Hungary and to report results of its findings" and "to hold itself available to provide, at the request of the Government of Hungary, observers and other appropriate facilities which may be helpful in the present situation...."[47]

All of this slow and deliberate approach would be frustrating enough had it been prepared for debate in the emergency session of the General Assembly. But this resolution was to be introduced in the Security Council, where Dulles and Lodge knew full well that after hours, and possibly several days, of useless debate, it would be vetoed by the Soviet Union. It is an exercise in futility, but it looks good in the American press and to the Hungarian-Americans who will be voting in the general election in just a few days.

At 9:08 the U.S. Mission to the United Nations receives a message from Dulles in Washington. It is not even addressed to Ambassador Lodge, just the Mission. It is worth quoting in its entirety.

1. Understand Hungary has asked for United Nations General Assembly consideration of item entitled "The Question of Hungary's Neutrality and the Defense of This Neutrality by the Four Great Powers." We understand the Secretary General [is] seeking clarification [as to] whether Hungary wishes immediate consideration [at] special General Assembly.

2. Unless subsequent developments suggest otherwise, meanwhile we believe U.S. should seek early Security Council meeting to resume consideration of Hungarian item on basis of resolution along lines of DEPTEL 228 [the message with the draft resolution quoted above—ed.] reviewing idea of observation function for Committee on basis [of] Vienna's repeated USUN.
   DULLES[48]

The record shows no attempt on the part of Secretary General Hammarskjold to seek clarification from Nagy. The message the Secretary General sends early Friday morning is merely an acknowledgement.

Budapest, Friday, November 2, 1956

An uneasy calm prevails in the city on this cold, bright November morning. There are more people in the streets, for while some of the big factories like Ganz and Lang have started up again, most workers have not yet gone back to work. Workers from the Revolutionary Committee of Csepel have appealed this morning to workers all over Hungary to end the strike. The Revolutionary Council of the Hungarian State Railways makes an appeal over Free Radio Kossuth for railwaymen "to take up your service immediately to help the railway traffic get started." Some tramcars are running again and more soon will be as the overhead wires are restored and rubble cleared away. Later this afternoon the National Council of North and East Hungary will announce that the local workers' councils "have decided to discontinue the strike. The continuation of the strike," they add, "will not enable us to hinder the Soviet Army's stay in our country. We must hinder their stay...by not giving them food, not giving them fuel and accommodation...."[49]

Huge signs have been erected at major intersections all over Budapest saying:

"The purity of our revolution permits us to use this method of collection for the families of the martyrs."

It is signed "The Hungarian Writers' Association." Under each of the signs is a large empty ammunition box filling up with anywhere from ten to one hundred forint notes, lots of coins and even some Austrian schillings and English pounds. In just a few hours over 110,000 forints are collected this way.

Restaurants and espresso bars are open again and newspaper vendors delight in calling out the twenty different headlines of the uncensored press. But there is little in the press about what is on everyone's mind: that Budapest is ringed with Russian armor and more and more Soviet troops are said to be pouring into the country.[50]

Dr. István Katona, Medical Director of the Stephen Hospital (István Kórház), which serves all of southern Budapest, tells a Western reporter that for three days earlier this week the hospital was able to serve only a fraction of the nearby wounded and dying. "The Soviets burned twenty ambulances coming to the aid of the wounded. They killed or wounded half of our personnel. When we organized stretcher bearers to substitute for the destroyed ambulances, they killed nine and thirteen were wounded.

"Our chief surgeon, Dr. Aurél Guszics, suffered a nervous breakdown when he saw the streets littered with writhing wounded who could not be reached due to the murderous fire." Dr. György Kemény estimates that several hundred Hungarians may have bled to death in one night alone, due to the hospital's not being able to reach them. As he goes down one ward, the Western correspondent asks each person how he or she was wounded. Lívia Czudarhelyi, 19, had been shot by the secret police when she asked for a ride in their truck. Zsigmond Kruker stepped from the doorway of his home to pull his small daughter off the street. József Mikori, 17, was one of many crushed by a Soviet tank against a wall; he was one of the few survivors. Lajos Hajdú was one of twelve who had responded to a promise of amnesty by surrendering. All had been immediately shot. He is one of only four survivors. Wendel Márkus, a seventy-two-year-old janitor, beloved by his tenants, lies dying. He had helped a woman carry potatoes and bread through the gate of his building. Ferenc Burucz, a soldier, has just died. He had been shot by his own officer because he refused to fire on a milling crowd of his countrymen.[51]

Victor Zorza reports back to his paper, *Manchester Guardian* in England:

"Yesterday Mr. Nagy said that he had asked the Big Four to recognize Hungary's neutrality. Hungary is waiting anxiously for their reaction. The people here can understand why Moscow is delaying its reply. But why, it is asked, have Western governments not replied immediately that they acknowledge Hungary's neutrality? By delaying its reply, even for a day, the West is making things easier for Moscow. It is, in effect, countenancing the march of Soviet troops on Budapest...."[52]

Yesterday and today are days of discovery. The mysterious villa in a wooded area on Sváb Hill in Buda, which the Freedom Fighters from Széna Square had investigated yesterday, turns out indeed to have been a special ÁVO interrogation and torture facility. The villa is not more than a few minutes walk from Rózsadomb (Rose Hill), where all the villas of the Party leaders are located behind a large fence guarded by security police. The most interesting of these, which was briefly ransacked yesterday before the National Guard took over, is Mátyás Rákosi's. The partisans who visit it have never seen such luxury. Not just a swimming pool, large, ornate bathrooms and two grand pianos, but all the electronic equipment, cigars, wines, liquors, all products of the capitalist West, that no one else in Hungary has ever seen. Rákosi's salary had been forty thousand forints a month, and it is easy to see where much of it had gone.

The most interesting building is a summer house located in the midst of all of these villas. Concealed beneath it, people find a huge bunker, not unlike Hitler's under the Reichstag, also luxuriously equipped and stocked. Underground passages are discovered which lead from it to each of the villas.

Today is also a day of departures. Throughout the day cars from the Soviet Embassy, with military escorts, have been driving out to Ferihegy, Budapest's main airport, taking embassy employees and their dependents as well as Hungarian officials who have been closely associated with the Rákosi regime. Gerő and Hegedűs have already been evacuated this way; now it is the turn of other military and secret police officials who feel their lives are in danger. Many of these Hungarians have already spent much of their lives in the Soviet Union; a good many even have Soviet citizenship. But the fact that the Soviets are removing them with such security can mean only one of two things: they either know too much and need to be kept where they can be silenced, or the Soviets feel they will have need for them again.

Such treatment is not extended to most of the families of military and other Soviet personnel. They can be seen down at the docks along the

Danube, their personal possessions in suitcases and bundles tied round with ropes, looking like so many peddlers or peasants going to market. Russian officials, some still in uniform, mingle with Italians, East Germans, Indonesians and even a few families from Western legations, all waiting to go down the gangways to the river steamships tied up at the floating docks. These will take them up river to Bratislava, capital of the Slovak portion of Czechoslovakia. From there most of them will travel by train to Prague.

All along the embankment thousands of grinning Hungarians are watching. Every now and then they take up a cry, first heard more than a week ago: "Ruszkik Haza!" ("Russians Go Home!") It is repeated rhythmically until it reaches thunderous proportions. Then comes silence as the objects of their scorn shuffle in humiliation down onto the ships.

Early this morning Soviet helicopters were evacuating Russian families from Buda and parts of the city from where the evacuees found it difficult to get to the Soviet Embassy. By the end of the day only Ambassador Andropov and a few secretaries are left in the huge Embassy building in which the hallways are piled high with boxes and files.[53]

General Király has a difficult job. As he was later to write:

> It was not easy to get rid of the Muscovite elements of the army who were able, before nationalist control could take over, to issue orders to the troops and move them around, creating confusion and controversies which took considerable time to straighten out in the revolutionary upheaval and excitement and uncertainty of authority. [My] intention was to create a defense of depth in the city of Budapest to hold back the Russians in case of a renewal of their attack, at least for a few days, to give time to the new government to arouse the free world to intervene....But the pro-Soviet group in the Ministry sabotaged these preparations. This group was greatly assisted by new men sent by plane from Moscow. It was composed of members of the new group of the Soviet military academy, who, upon arrival in Budapest, became the chief saboteurs of the new military reorganization and the most active agents and spies of the Soviet High Command in preparing the second invasion.

These men will serve as the backbone of the post-Revolution Hungarian military.[54]

In the Countryside

Things are returning to normal in the countryside, where whatever fighting there has been ceased four or five days ago. Some communities are proud of how peacefully they made the transition; others, like the people of Somogy County, are proud that revenge for the wrongs of the past ten years has not taken over. This is not a time for "revenge or counter-revenge, but a time of calling to account," says a broadcast from Radio Rákóczi, Kaposvár. "In Somogy the majority of criminals is already awaiting the judgment of an independent Hungarian court in the place they deserve. We should be proud that the people of Somogy do not lose their sense of justice and that in Kaposvár the passion of revenge has not caused blood to flow...." [55]

Free Radio Kossuth reports that "5,416 detained persons have been freed in the course of recent revolutionary events. In Csolnok yesterday, the doors of the political internment camp were opened. It was a touching scene as six hundred political prisoners sang the national anthem before the national flag with the government delegates who had released them...the prisoners have all returned to their homes...."[56]

Remembering how quickly the iron lung had been produced by RFE for the hospital in Debrecen, the workers' council of Borsod County now broadcasts an appeal in German for Salk serum vaccine. In the last six weeks 150 cases of polio have been diagnosed in Borsod County and forty of those afflicted have already died.[57]

The same workers' council, whose chairman, József Kiss, flew to Budapest yesterday to urge Nagy to declare an Austrian-like neutrality, now warns the citizens of Miskolc that there are sufficient Soviet armed forces in the immediate area to take the town in four hours. All the city has in opposition is some heavy artillery, a few infantrymen and a lot of youngsters with rifles and submachine guns. The city hears more worrisome news when a traveler, who arrived from Czechoslovakia this morning, reports having seen heavy concentrations of Czechoslovak troops massed at the frontier, just miles from the city.[58]

In Eastern Hungary there has been so much activity by Soviet aircraft that Debrecen, Nyíregyháza and Szolnok have all called for precautionary blackouts for the past two nights, believing a new Soviet onslaught was beginning. A squadron of heavy bombers and jet fighters flies over Záhony this morning in the southwest direction of Békéscsaba, where a Russian motorized unit has just been stationed. In the west a Soviet bomber flies over Győr today dropping leaflets calling on the Freedom Fighters to lay down their arms or risk bombing. Throughout the country at airfields, now surrounded by Russian tanks, planes which are said to be there to evacuate wounded Soviet soldiers inevitably disgorge dozens of heavily armed Soviet soldiers upon arrival.[59]

In Kecskemét, south of Budapest, where Soviet soldiers recently stacked their arms and went into the town asking for food and offering money to pay for it, a Soviet officer tells the town's Revolutionary Committee that the reason Soviet reinforcements have been brought into Hungary is to prevent widespread mutiny among Soviet troops already here.[60]

In Sopron, one student who is a member of one of the fifteen groups sent out from the Revolutionary Student Council of Budapest to co-ordinate student groups throughout the country sits down for an interview with RFE reporter Barney Leason. The Sopron students are running the town from a ramshackle old building in the Mining and Engineering University. Everyone wears the tricolor armband and all are silent and serious. The student, who left Budapest only yesterday, says the demands are now basically down to three: complete Russian withdrawal, free and secret elections and neutrality on the Austrian pattern.

"There is no sense in compromising," he says, "since so many people have already died in the struggle. The students are quite willing to continue the struggle and, if necessary, to die fighting. It is stupid of the regime to speak of bloodshed since the number of people, Russians included, who have died in the revolution would total no more than ten percent of the number of people who have been killed or tortured by communist regimes since the end of the War.

"Regarding the current leadership of the revolutionary organizations," he says, "these men are not well known since any honest man was unknown in past years." The same, he feels, pertains to literature, where none of the known writers are better than mediocre and the really good ones not yet known. "And what of the future?" Leason asks, "assuming the Russians don't come in again."

The student, who is only twenty and brimming with idealism, says there will be five to seven parties participating in the general elections. "Should the Communists be allowed to participate?" "Of course, why not? Not allowing them to participate would be undemocratic. Kádár admitted three days ago that the Communists would not receive much support in these elections."

Then, when questioned about the students' own organizational efforts, he admits that people are sick of bureaucracy. He adds, "It will take time for the people to overcome their distrust of everyone who aspires to be a leader. Everyone is very cautious." He feels, however, that Hungary will develop a system somewhere between socialism and bourgeois democracy. Nationalized heavy industry and utilities should remain in government hands. Possibly the workers themselves will become the owners of some factories. These things have to be decided by the people involved in a democratic way. But as for central planning, that must go. The economy of any country is too complicated to be organized centrally as it has been in Hungary.

"The students," he concludes, "are not anxious to have, nor do they expect to have, a good life all at once. Everyone will have to do his best to raise living standards and it is important that there should be obvious results from work well done. Revolutionary enthusiasm will not decrease until the Russians are gone."[61]

But students and others in Sopron are not yet fully aware of the extent of Soviet troop movements around the country. New Soviet units are crossing pontoon bridges across the Tisza River all day, according to Free Radio Nyíregyháza, not far from the scene, and the better part of two mechanized Soviet divisions are now moving on Budapest from the east. The military Radio of Miskolc says Soviet troops were passing through the city all night. The radio also reports that Hungarian National Guard and police groups at the Miskolc railroad station were disarmed by the Soviets without a fight. Standing orders not to fire on any Soviet troops lest that be used as an excuse for the Soviets to commence hostilities puts the Hungarian Armed Forces at a distinct disadvantage. Conflicting orders deliberately issued by high Hungarian Army officers disloyal to the Nagy government are adding to the confusion. The Győr military radio meanwhile says that all direct contact been the Trans-Danubian Revolutionary Council and the government in Budapest has been severed and for this reason it is having to make independent decisions for the area.[62] The same radio reports that the Trans-Danubian Honvéd forces are refusing to carry out orders issued by Defense Minister Janza, demanding that he be removed and replaced by General Nádor.[63]

Back in Budapest the Nagy government delivers three diplomatic verbal notes during the day to the Soviet Embassy: the first simply reminding the Soviets of the government's request to begin negotiations, the second saying that the mixed Committee charged with preparing the Soviet withdrawal should begin today, November 2, and naming the Hungarian delegates to the mixed committee, and the third protesting further Soviet Army units entering Hungary.[64] Premier Nagy, having had no response from the West to his request for recognition of Hungary's declaration of neutrality, fires off another cable to Secretary General Dag Hammarskjold. He gives more explicit up-to-date information on the continuing invasion of Soviet armed forces, his government's actions with the Soviets in trying to get negotiations for withdrawal going, and finally he repeats his request that the "Great Powers recognize the neutrality of Hungary." He asks the Security Council to instruct the Soviet and Hungarian governments to start negotiations immediately and make known all of the above to the members of the Security Council.[65] This message, which cannot have arrived at the UN later than noon New York time and must have been available to delegations within the next several hours, is not forwarded to the State Department by the U.S. UN Mission in New York until ten minutes after midnight on November 3.[66]

*　　*　　*　　*

Nagy is still having trouble with József Dudás and his All-Hungarian National Committee. Today he learns that the Dudás group, not content to occupy just the *Szabad Nép* building in Pest, has made an assault on the Ministry of Foreign Affairs in Buda and taken possession of it. Since Nagy is not only the head of government but is now also his own Minister of Foreign Affairs, this is a double insult. Gen. Béla Király, with a detachment of the new National Guard, is sent over to re-take the building. This Király does without any loss of life. But Dudás is not there. It seems he is elsewhere, sick in bed, and it is the Buda section of the All Hungarian National Committee that has taken it into its collective head to capture the Foreign Ministry, thinking it was still full of Russian advisors.

Later, the same night, Király locates Dudás at his home and invites him to come as soon as possible to the Ministry of Defense. When Dudás arrives with his wife and several aides, Col. László Zólomy, who is acting as Király's private secretary, insists on collecting all arms before Király enters the room. Thus, while Király is negotiating with him, Dudás is, in effect, under arrest. Király comes to the conclusion, however, that Dudás is no longer a threat to the Revolution and holding him could cause more harm than it is worth. Dudás' men, back at the *Szabad Nép* building, had threatened physical attacks if Dudás was not out of the Defense Ministry building by a certain time.[67]

Cardinal Mindszenty is still preparing to speak to the nation, but today he holds a brief press conference for the foreign press in his residential palace in Buda. Looking a little less pale than when he arrived on Wednesday, the Cardinal answers all questions in slow but precise German. The room is a small one and all, including the Cardinal, must stand. He says "it was wonderful what started here on October 23. Our youth, our soldiers, our workers and very many Russian soldiers rose up against the regime. We have many heroes now, but there are thousands of wounded in our hospitals." When someone asks him to comment on reports of groups which would like to name him Premier, the Cardinal suddenly stiffens. In a voice shaking with anger he says firmly, "I am the Prince Primate of Hungary," and quickly walks out the door, abruptly ending the meeting.[68]

Changes are being made in the Hungarian foreign diplomatic service. Already the Hungarian Ambassadors to Moscow, Washington, East Berlin, New Delhi, Copenhagen, Vienna and Sofia have been relieved of their positions and new men will soon be sent to take their places. In Vienna, all the Hungarian communist diplomats and legation employees who have been relieved of their positions are leaving for Czechoslovakia this afternoon. Former Foreign Minister Imre Horváth, who was the Minister to Vienna, and his minister and commercial attaché fled earlier to Bratislava.[69]

Reaction Abroad

Eastern Europe

In Prague, people are doing what everybody does when there are rumors of war: they are lining up in front of food stores to lay up as many provisions as they can. News from the Middle East and rumors of unrest in the entire Eastern bloc seem to presage a major war.[70]

In East Berlin, where people are still trying to adjust to the Soviet Declaration of October 30—which did not mention the German Democratic Republic—the official party newspaper, *Neues Deutschland*, suggests that now is the time for both the North Atlantic Treaty Organization (NATO) and the Warsaw Pact to be dissolved so that both sides can pull back their troops. The idea has been floated before by the Soviets, so while such a development would be beneficial to East Germany, such a statement may well have been sanctioned by Moscow.[71]

In Poland the Central Committee puts out yet another statement pleading with the Polish people to refrain from "manifestations" and "demonstrations," as such actions are a "grave danger" at a time when "international tension has reached a tearing point." The statement baldly states that "the presence of Soviet troops in Poland is not only in the interests of the Soviet Union, but even more in the interest of an independent Poland."[72]

The West

The press in Paris today welcomes Hungary's decision for neutrality. "Hungary will become another link in the chain of neutral countries running from Scandinavia to Yugoslavia," writes the Socialist newspaper *Populaire de Paris*. But the more conservative paper *Aurore*, under the heading "Nagy's Great Hour," writes, "Moscow seems to be playing a monstrous double game. On the one hand she gives in to the claims of national independence, on the other hand she returns surreptitiously with all her might and intends to crush with an iron hand and in blood all those who committed the crime of demanding liberty and singing the Marseillaise."[73]

In London, *The Spectator*, publishes an article by Zoltán Szabó in which he quotes Denis Healey, during a debate in the House of Commons, commenting on Hungary that "a people without leaders defeated a ruling clique without followers."[74]

In New York, the *New York Post* writes that "Russia still has the military might to drown the revolt in blood. Only swift diplomatic action can forestall this danger. The United Nations is the proper vehicle for such action. It is time for America to take the lead in placing the issue on the agenda—even at the risk of jeopardizing our current alignment with the Russians in the Middle East upheaval."[75]

In Munich, RFE's Political Advisor, William E. Griffith, finds that "Nagy's position appears to have been substantially improved by his declaration of neutrality and appeal for departure of Soviet troops....His position is also improved by the fact that Béla Kovács is now in Budapest and has joined the government."[76]

Meeting of the Presidium in Moscow

Today the Soviet Presidium hears a direct, eyewitness account about the situation in Hungary from Hungarian participants. Comrades Kádár and Münnich have just been flown in this morning and are joined by István Bata, the ex-minister of Defense, whom the Soviets had brought from Hungary several days ago. Kádár does most of the talking. Because he was operating as a member of the Nagy government less than twenty-four hours ago, the Soviet Comrades pay close attention to what he has to say.

> We made a mistake in calling the demonstrations a counterrevolution. They were seeking the ouster of the Rákosi clique and making social demands and demands for more democratization. I took part in one meeting and no one wanted counterrevolution.
>
> I don't know how the counterrevolutionaries spread the demand for the withdrawal of Soviet troops, but I have to admit that everyone now demands it. The general strike is a demand for the withdrawal of troops and even I agree that this is necessary. We may starve, but the troops must be withdrawn. Yesterday the government was talking about the Soviet Declaration on relations with other socialist states and our declaration of neutrality. Your Declaration made a good impression, it was a reassuring gesture. Everyone was prepared to go back to work, but then people learned about the Soviet troops being redeployed—news spreads quickly—so many decided not to go back to work yet.
>
> Our party, the Hungarian Workers' Party, is the weakest link; it has ceased to exist. Some have been killed, others saved, but as an organization it doesn't function.
>
> The coalition parties don't want counterrevolution. Béla Kovács, who is recreating the Smallholders Party, is against the return of landowners and capitalists.

To the question: How did the decision about neutrality emerge? Kádár answers:

> The masses are very stirred up about the Soviet troop movements. When asked about them, Ambassador Andropov kept giving excuses which were quickly proven to be untrue. It is obvious that the troops are moving on Budapest and the government feels Budapest must be defended. In this atmosphere Zoltán Tildy suggested that we declare what many of the people have been demanding: neutrality. Everyone supported it. Even I supported and still support it. I voted for these two measures, withdrawal from the Warsaw Pact and neutrality. If Soviet troops withdraw our new party and the other coalition parties will be able to fight against the counterrevolutionaries.
>
> If you persist in using military force it will be destructive and lead to much bloodshed. What will happen then? The morale of Communists will be reduced to zero and the socialist countries will suffer losses.

Comrade Bata thinks the Nagy regime is laying the groundwork for a confrontation between Hungarian and Soviet troops. He feels order can only be restored through a military dictatorship.[77]

In another part of Moscow Sir William Hayter is telling the Foreign Office, "I find it hard to believe the Soviet government intend to go into reverse in Hungary. To do so would be to disavow their declaration of policy about the satellites...a declaration which is still being publicized extensively here and which the Chinese Government today endorses." The probable explanation for Soviet troop movements in Hungary is: a) so much confusion that it only seems like movement, or; b) "that the Russians are bringing in extra forces to cover their retreat." A brief while later he tells Whitehall, "There is *one* circumstance" in which what he had just said "might cease to be valid. If anarchy should prevail in Hungary...[the] Soviet Government might well be tempted to set up a Communist Government and 'accede to its request' for support in restoring order."

He adds that Khrushchev was not at any of the functions he would normally have attended today, "so may well be taking a personal look at the Hungarian scene."[78]

Much earlier in the day Nikita Khrushchev and Georgii Malenkov, having spent the night in Bucharest, are preparing to fly to their secret destination, Brioni Island in the Adriatic.

But today in the Balkans the weather has turned nasty. In fact, Khrushchev had been told by his pilot, Tsybin, that they could not fly. There are thunderstorms en route and they are going to have to fly through mountains. Khrushchev had asked him: "I hear the weather is bad? They don't want us to fly?"

"Quite right, we shouldn't fly," replies Tsybin, breaking into a grin.

"But if we have to?" Khrushchev inquires.

"If we have to, we fly, Nikita Sergeyevich," replies the pilot, grinning even more broadly. "Do you order us to get ready?"

"Let's go," Khrushchev answers. Tsybin is an excellent pilot and Khrushchev has full confidence in him. But poor Malenkov, "who gets carsick even on a good road," is petrified. As Khrushchev later describes it, "There were storm clouds all around us and lightning flashes. I couldn't sleep and just sat by the window. I have flown a lot during and after the war, but never in such terrible conditions....Malenkov turned as pale as a ghost from all the turbulence...."

Their successful landing near Dubrovnik does not bring an end to their journey. They must pile into a small launch. The sea is very rough. Malenkov lies down in the bottom and closes his eyes. Khrushchev now worries about two things: will they actually make it through these crashing waves to Brioni, and when and if they get there, will Malenkov be able to walk and talk?

Actually, he has a much bigger worry. For some time now he has seen the shadow of Tito behind Nagy. It is as though everything Nagy has done was first planned in Belgrade. If the Poles would not budge, how will it be with Tito?

Tito is waiting on the jetty for their arrival, though it is now totally dark. There are embraces and kisses despite the recently strained relations. Once they have settled in and freshened up, Khrushchev tells his host exactly why they have come. He does all the talking; Malenkov is still too nauseated to speak. Khrushchev starts off emotionally saying that Communists in Hungary are being murdered, butchered and hanged. He mentions Nagy's appeals to the United Nations and his withdrawal from the Warsaw Pact. Then he states an internal reason. There are people in the Soviet Union who will say that as long as Stalin was in command, everybody obeyed and there were no big shocks. But since these (unprintable word) came to power Russia has suffered defeat and the loss of Hungary. And then there is the British and French aggressive pressure on Egypt. It provides a favorable moment for a further intervention by Soviet troops. "They are bogged down there and we are stuck in Hungary."

Khrushchev gets the surprise of his life when Tito tells him "You are absolutely right. You should send your soldiers in as quickly as possible and crush the counterrevolution before it gets any further." This comes, of course, only after Khrushchev's long and tortured discourse, designed to wheedle Tito around to the Soviet position. So when Tito's answer comes, Khrushchev feels doubly relieved.[79]

"Well, we'd better get some rest now because we have to return to Moscow in the morning," says Khrushchev, longing for a good night's sleep. "No, don't go. Why don't you stay until the weather clears?" says their host. Khrushchev thanks him, but says they must get back to Moscow.

"Tell me," says Tito casually, trying to catch Khrushchev in an unguarded moment, "when are you planning to restore order in Budapest?" Khrushchev is not about to let Tito in on his exact plans. "Well," he says vaguely, "we haven't decided on any exact day, but it will be fairly soon."

He realizes that Tito well knows that an exact day and even hour has been set, but that Tito is not going to get any further information out of him. The Yugoslavs are taking no direct part and therefore have no need to know. But Tito is not about to lose this opportunity to plumb Khrushchev's mind and he insists that the two stay up talking; Khrushchev can sleep in the plane going home tomorrow. And indeed, they do talk until five in the morning. Only then, with the sky lightening in the east, is Nikita Sergeyevich able to join a prostrate Malenkov for a long nap before departure for Moscow.

One of the main topics of discussion is who should head up the new provisional Hungarian government, which the Soviets will set up. Khrushchev says it will be Ferenc Münnich. He has known Münnich for thirty years now, used to work with him in the Soviet Union, and he is dependable. Tito argues strongly for Kádár. Münnich, he says, is too inflexible and he was Rákosi's Ambassador to Moscow. He will not be able to win over the people. Kádár, on the other hand, was jailed by Rákosi and has much more of a following. He is flexible and careful. Khrushchev would rather stick with the person he knows best—he barely knows Kádár—but over the course of the night's discussion he realizes that Tito is right, Kádár will head the government and Münnich be his right-hand man. But in return for Khrushchev's choosing Kádár over Münnich, Khrushchev extracts a promise from Tito: he must try to persuade Nagy, after the Soviet intervention, to issue a statement announcing his own resignation, due to his inability to stop the violence, and his support for the Kádár regime, which he will be free to join if he wishes.[80]

Washington

The wheels of the Department of State move slowly, but now, three full days after the Soviet Union has announced its new policy on dealing with the satellites, the Department is ready to notify its posts around the world what its reaction is. The message will not go out until after 10:00 p.m. tonight, so will reach many of the posts four full days after the Soviet pronouncement. Here are some key passages:

> The Soviet October 30 declaration on withdrawal [withdrawal of troops was actually only a small part of it—ed.] appears to reflect a basic Soviet decision that it must now change the nature of its relationship with its East European satellites....

The Soviets appear to feel that nationalist and anti-Soviet feeling has reached a danger point where losses must be cut by accepting a high degree of independence in the satellites, but within a "socialist" framework...

...At present it is not clear whether the Sovs (sic) feel Hungarian developments threaten commie (sic) control of Eastern Europe to the point where the Hungarian rebellion must be crushed....

....The Sovs probably desire to continue to avoid a battle with the Hungarian Government; they may feel the Hungarian estimate of the hopelessness of their position will force that Government to take actions to reverse its major anti-communist decisions....

The possibility of Sov involvement in the Middle East, plus the situation in the other satellites are factors of still unknown magnitude, which may tend to influence Sovs to postpone a final decision....

Dulles [81]

Earlier in the day, State Department spokesman Lincoln White announces that the United States has received formal notification of Hungary's withdrawal from the Warsaw Pact and declaration of neutrality, via its Legation in Budapest. White declines to comment on these developments.

New York

The *New York Times*, on the other hand, feels it is its duty to comment. "Already it begins to look," it writes, "as if the Soviet concessions to Eastern Europe announced last Tuesday were too little and too late. That statement was obviously based on the assumption that by concessions, even at such a late date, Hungary might be kept in the Communist camp and the revolutionary virus in Eastern Europe might be kept from spreading beyond Poland and Hungary....It is ominous news indeed that Soviet tanks have placed a cordon of steel around Budapest and that more Soviet tanks are entering the country...."[82]

A few blocks to the east on New York's East River, the debate on the Anglo-French-Israeli attack on Egypt in the UN's special session of the General Assembly has been going on since five o'clock yesterday afternoon. John Foster Dulles gave his major address at seven last night, after which the Assembly adjourned for supper. Before he began, those in the unofficial group at the UN concerned with Hungary made sure that he had the latest news from Hungary before he went onto the Assembly floor. Dulles began by saying, "I doubt that any representative ever spoke from this rostrum with as heavy a heart as I have brought here tonight." He was speaking of the Suez situation, not Hungary, and the fact that the United States was going to have to vote against its allies Britain and France.[83]

Dulles spoke several more times as the debate went on into the evening and the early hours of today, but never once mentioned Hungary. Only Sir Pierson Dixon of Britain mentioned it in passing. "I cannot help contrasting [our action at Suez] with the armed actions of the Soviet Union aimed at perpetuating its domination of Hungary." But none of the delegates picked up on this.

The vote on the American resolution did not come until 3:30 this morning, November 2. It was considered a triumph to have gotten it passed in one sitting. At this point the Italian delegate, Vitteti, rose to speak on a point of order. He referred to Nagy's second appeal "which has just been circulated to us."* He stressed the urgency of events in Hungary and said, "I hope that the United Nations—and if necessary, this special emergency session—will take immediately whatever action is possible, with regard to this request of the Hungarian people." Then he sat down. He had risen on a point of order, not to make a motion. He had been advised against making a formal motion in order to avoid a protracted procedural argument with the Soviet Union's Sobolev.[84]

About 4:00 a.m. Secretary Dulles rises once again to speak on the Suez issue, which has already been decided. He looks drawn and haggard, though neither he nor anyone else is aware that tomorrow at this time he will be in a hospital on an operating table. As he comes to the conclusion of his comments he says, "I want to express my endorsement of the intervention made by the representative of Italy [on] the Hungarian situation....I hope that this matter, which is on the agenda of the Security Council, will be kept urgently before it, and we shall not be preoccupied with the Middle East to the exclusion of assisting the State of Hungary to regain its independence." Just minutes later the Assembly adjourns. Only minutes after these words are spoken VOA and RFE broadcast them to Hungary, where it is now 10:30 a.m. They bring an upsurge of needed hope. Hungarians, and even Americans and others around the world, think that Dulles is calling for quick action. He is not. He is well aware how the word "urgent" will play with the

---

*It had been circulated twelve hours before.

press and with the voters of Hungarian extraction who will be going to the polls in three days' time. But he is even more aware that "keeping" the Hungarian issue in the Security Council, where debate can go on for days and then end up with a Soviet veto, is the best way to avoid having to take any real action. The only real action the UN can take is through the General Assembly, which it had just done in regard to Suez.

While the delegates are falling into their beds, Sir Geoffrey Wallinger, Her Majesty's Ambassador to Vienna, is suggesting to the Foreign Office that if the Nagy government, in its appeal to the UN, could be persuaded to welcome, *inter alia,* an observer mission to Budapest, this might get around the Foreign Office's objection about precedents for such observer teams being set. There is no indication that his idea ever escapes the Foreign Office's gravitational field.[85]

After the General Assembly's nearly all-night session, today is understood to be a day off. But waking up to The *New York Times* headlines: SOVIET TANKS AGAIN RING BUDAPEST; NAGY DEFIANT, APPEALS TO UN makes it impossible for the U.S., British and French delegations, which had been working on the Hungarian issue for over a week, to ignore the obvious. By late morning they agree that a special Security Council session must be called after all. A letter is dispatched by special messenger to the current Security Council President, Mr. Entezam of Iran. For some reason it does not reach Mr. Entezam until 1:00 p.m. He is more concerned with Cairo than Budapest, but nonetheless decides he must call a special session for today. He feels he cannot get a quorum before 5:00 p.m., so calls it for that hour, which is 11:00 p.m. in Budapest. There news of the special meeting on Hungary causes another spurt of hope.

While Secretary Dulles is collapsed into a well-deserved sleep, his daily staff meeting meets in Washington at 9:15 under the leadership of the Under Secretary, Herbert Hoover, Jr. The main topics for discussion are the intelligence failure to predict any of the three crises, Suez, Poland, and Hungary, and the current situation in Hungary. Mr. Hoover feels that the Hungary situation is being lost and that we should demand a very prompt review of what actually has gone wrong. He also wants to know precisely what we *have* done so that adequate publicity can be focused on this. Ambassador Beam states that we still don't know what we can do until we know more about the Nagy government.[86]

At the UN the Americans, French and British agree to meet two hours before the scheduled 5:00 p.m. meeting of the Security Council to plan and agree on a strategy. They soon find there is a vast difference between the U.S. approach and that of the French and British. The latter both have substantive resolutions drafted, while the U.S. is not ready for a substantive resolution and has no authority to put one forward today. Both the British and French resolutions, after expressing concern "at the flagrant violation by the Soviet Union of the Independence and sovereignty of Hungary," call on all nations to "recognize and respect the neutrality of Hungary." Lodge confesses that the State Department does not yet know how to handle the Hungarian declaration of neutrality. He says that the immediate objective should be to question the Hungarian representative in the Council. It is obvious to the French and British that the Americans do not want to move the debate to the General Assembly where action might be taken. Lodge says, without much conviction, that more pressure can be put on the Soviets in the Security Council by keeping a substantive resolution hanging in suspense.

Ambassador Lodge then goes so far as to observe that his colleagues' eagerness to get the Hungarian matter to the General Assembly might be interpreted as a desire on their part to distract the Assembly's attention away from the Middle East. At this point the exchanges turn frigid.

Dixon says he cannot understand the American position. The developments in Eastern Europe are not less important than the Middle East. There seems a real prospect of Hungarian independence if the Russians can be induced to withdraw. Surely this is the best psychological moment to bring all possible pressure on the Russians. Dixon then observes acidly that the apparent reluctance of the Americans to harass the Russians on Hungary contrasts oddly with the alacrity with which they are pursuing their two closest allies. It seems to him this is deliberate procrastination to leave the decks free for Assembly "action against us."[87]

Lodge is somewhat taken aback, though he has initiated the exchange, and breaks off the talks to phone Washington. Secretary Dulles is up and back in his office. The following exchange ensues:

> *Lodge:* My British and French colleagues are next door in a very emotional condition—they say there will be bad impressions in their respective countries if we are in a hurry to put them on the dock and drag in Russia as well. I told them that was unjustified.

Dulles: They just want the limelight off them and want to have the three of us go in together on this. I think it is a mockery for them to come in, with bombs falling over Egypt, and denounce the Soviet Union for perhaps doing something that is not quite as bad.

Lodge: I agree.

Dulles: There should be no resolution introduced this evening. Just discuss the situation and suggest it would be useful to get a representative of the new Hungarian Government here as quickly as possible. I think one is more or less en route. We should watch the situation carefully and have this fellow get here fast.

Lodge: I don't think it's possible for us to agree on a resolution.

Dulles: We don't have any hard information as to what is going on in Hungary—no doubt because of Egypt. Anyway, keep it on the agenda.[88]

Dixon and de Guiringaud, the French delegate, are convinced that either of their similar resolutions will easily gather the seven votes in the Security Council necessary to move the matter to the General Assembly, where they claim they can get fifty-three votes. They figure that the U.S., however reluctantly, will have to vote for it. Still, in an attempt to preserve unity, Sir Pierson suggests that they *not* table their substantive motions today if the Americans will agree to calling for another session tomorrow, by which time they could work out a tripartite resolution. Lodge, evidently relieved at this suggestion, accepts at once.

As the Security Council session opens, observers are expecting the United States to put forward a hard-hitting substantive resolution, since both Britain and France are "in the dog house" over Suez. Instead, before Lodge can begin his statement Nationalist China raises the issue of the Hungarian representative's credentials. Lodge throws himself into this discussion with such force and alacrity that it is obvious the Americans have put China up to this opening ploy. A legalistic debate goes for an hour before an impatient delegate from Peru, Señor Belaunde, demands clarification from the Secretariat, so they can get into the substantive part of the meeting. Undersecretary General Protich, who is sitting in for Hammarskjold (who is busy with Suez matters), is asked whether the Secretariat feels that János Szabó is entitled to represent Hungary. Protich announces: "We have not officially received any particular information on any credentials from the

Hungarian government itself." An aide leans forward to whisper in Protich's ear. Protich's face turns red. He rises to make a correction: "I have just been informed by the Legal Office that a cable has been received from the Hungarian government appointing Dr. János Szabó at the emergency session of the General Assembly yesterday." The cable had arrived thirty hours ago.

Even this does not end the hair-splitting. "If he was appointed for yesterday's Assembly meeting, does this entitle him to attend today's Security Council meeting?" And so forth.

When Lodge finally launches into his prepared speech it is quite feeble in its references to the Russians and dwells on the obscurity of recent events in Hungary and the need for time to clarify them.

Several other delegates who follow seem well-informed on recent events in Hungary, castigate the Russians and read out portions of Nagy's second appeal to the UN to great effect and much applause from the gallery. Sobelov's replies are weak, betraying considerable embarrassment. The French and British speeches are equally forceful, bringing even more applause from the gallery, but true to their agreement with Lodge, neither mentions the substantive resolutions they have prepared.

During a recess for supper the Americans let it be known that they would be satisfied to give it a rest tomorrow, Saturday, November 3 and not meet again until Sunday. The President of the Council, Entezam of Iran, in answer to a question, even suggests the Council not meet again until Monday, November 5. The British and French are furious when they get wind of this and force Lodge to stick to their agreement for a meeting tomorrow. Dixon, in fact, asks Lodge whether he cannot get clearance from the Department tonight to negotiate a tripartite resolution. Lodge, who has no intention of getting the U.S. sullied by joining with the quarantined French and British in any tripartite resolution, assures them that he is confident they will be able to work out such a tripartite resolution tomorrow.[89]

He then telegrams a long report to the State Department. At the end he requests authority to introduce a substantive resolution tomorrow which would include a paragraph appointing a committee to investigate the Hungarian matter, but with the names of the states left blank, which would cause a vote to be delayed and a Soviet veto thus avoided. He warns, however, that this tactic risks giving the UK and France priority, since their resolutions are complete. In any case, he believes "resolutions should be introduced by the U.S. and not be tripartite."[90]

340

Only a few hours later, John Foster Dulles, the chief architect of U.S. foreign policy for the past four years, will be stricken and taken in great pain to Walter Reed Hospital in Washington, where he will be operated on ostensibly for appendicitis, but actually for intestinal cancer.

Saturday, November 3, 1956

Budapest

On this bitterly cold November day gray clouds sweep over the city from which dustings of snow fall from time to time, accumulating lightly in the hills of Buda. For the second day in a row there is neither crack of gunfire nor roar of tanks' diesel engines. The whole city is turning to the constructive tasks of cleaning up the debris and getting life back to normal. Gangs of workers begin clearing the formerly majestic avenues of mountains of rubble and broken glass, which are then carted away by large trucks.

Only a few trams are in service, but buses are back plying their routes through the city, packed from door to door, with even a few passengers clinging to running boards. Long queues can be seen at every stop. Scores of bullet-ridden tram cars lie on their sides where they had been used as barricades, often across tracks that might otherwise be used. Heavy trucks with winches begin towing them away, but it will be several days before they are all removed and probably several days more before all the electric wires and those holding them in place are up again.

With more and more people going back to work, the streets fill with streams of cars, trucks and motorcycles. Traffic policemen in blue-green uniforms appear at the main crossings and direct the ever-increasing flow.

As life revives, shutters on stores, particularly food stores, are going up and queues of hungry people quickly form in front of them, some as long as a city block with two hundred people in them. Official sources say that basic food such as bread, milk, flour, butter and lard are in sufficient supply, but only barely. The government has stopped all food exports and, in addition, has received large deliveries from the West.

A few shopkeepers try doubling prices and quickly regret it. One woman who doubles the price of her eggs gets immediate wrathful protests from her customers, attracting a small crowd. Her eggstand is destroyed, but not the eggs. These are confiscated by the police when they come to restore order.[91]

In Tűzoltó Street in Pest, one of the centers of the Freedom Fighters, there is great hustle and bustle. Cars are coming from the country bringing huge amounts of food. The dead who are not already lying in Ferenc Square are just being buried. The boys are putting together their schedule for night-time sentry duty; mothers are coming to visit their sons. The only disturbing thing to the leader, Istvan Angyal, is that groups of soldiers who have been in the nearby Kilián Barracks for a week have begun leaving today, saying they are being sent on leave.

Angyal gets together eight to ten boys and has them fill baskets with apples, butter, lemons, noodles, milk powder and sugar. Then he takes them to visit all the houses in the neighborhood, where they give food to families with children.[92]

Free Radio Kossuth reports that "members of the State Security Police (ÁVO) are appearing at the prosecutor's office *en masse* asking to be taken into custody. In the 13th (Angyalföld) District in Budapest early this morning, thirty former security policemen reported. The situation is said to be similar in other districts."[93]

Népszava today addresses those citizens who wish to continue the general strike. "For more than a week the whole country has been at a standstill: traffic is paralyzed, mines are quiet, and there is no life in the factories. Life, however, goes on. Children ask for food, shoes and clothes become shabby, fuel is consumed, and gas and electric power become less. There is no replacement and our reserves are nearly exhausted. Some irresponsible persons say: 'Never mind, the West will help!' We are sincerely grateful…for the speedy, considerable and touching shipments of drugs, blood plasma, food and clothing…We thank you again and are expecting the further assistance due a neutral land. But it would be naive to believe a country can be fed and clothed by other nations for a long period and that they build up the country instead of us….We cannot be our own enemies and, thus, we should not continue the strike."

In Csepel smoke is rising from the chimneys of all but one of the enterprises, as nearly 80 percent of the workers are back on their jobs. The one factory not yet working involves an open-hearth furnace which so far lacks the raw materials to begin.[94]

In the Countryside

In Vienna the Austrian Red Cross, responding to the pleas of Free Radio Miskolc for serum to fight the outbreak of polio in Borsod County, has collected a few liters of gamma globulin. But due to all the activity of Soviet tanks in Western Hungary they are not sending any transports into Hungary today. Fritz P. Molden, editor of Vienna's daily *Die Presse*, offers this morning to drive the gamma globulin in his car to Miskolc. He takes his Budapest correspondent, Hungarian-born Eugen Géza Pogány, with him as an interpreter. Pogány, who has witnessed the revolution from the first day, has just returned to Vienna.

Finding the border closed at Hegyeshalom, on the main Vienna-Budapest route, they drive south and cross into Sopron, where students at the Mining Academy tell them the road to Budapest is blocked. They head up to Győr, passing forty Soviet tanks going the other way, and find the town gloomy compared to the peaceful and cheerful atmosphere of two days ago when Molden had visited. They are surprised that the road to Budapest is almost deserted and only encounter Soviet howitzers dug in at the side of the road outside of the capital city. Hungarian soldiers at their checkpoints are delighted to see a Western car headed east. Having left Vienna in the early afternoon, it is early night by the time they enter Budapest, lit up again as a peaceful city with buses and a few streetcars moving about. They decide to put up overnight at the Duna hotel and drive on to Miskolc early tomorrow morning.[95]

In Dunapentele, still called Sztálinváros by the communists, a confrontation of sorts is taking place between the local Revolutionary Council and Soviet troops advancing on the city from the south. The city, which is known as a center for steel manufacturing, lies on the Danube directly south of Budapest. "Why had they come up from Romania?" the Hungarians want to know. "We have been informed that counter-revolutionary fascists led by German and Horthyite officers are carrying out a bloody counter-revolution to overthrow the government. We have been invited in by your government to put down this fascist counter-revolution," is the reply. It takes some time for the Hungarians to convince the Russians, if, indeed they do, that this is a vile invention, that Rákosi and his gang had ruined Hungary and the people have risen up to overthrow his regime in a great popular movement and that Hungary wants to live in peace with all its neighbors as a neutral country. The upshot, however, is that the Soviets agree that neither party will shoot at the other, nor will the Russian armored units enter the city, and that tomorrow, November 4, at 10:00 a.m., they will meet again in the barracks of the

Hungarian Military Command in Dunapentele to negotiate further for a compromise solution.[96]

In snowbound Sopron, which Soviet troops have yet to reach, RFE correspondent Bernard Leason is conducting one last interview with local students. Though there is no slackening in their idealism, they are aware that the little peninsula of Hungarian territory projecting into Austria on which their city sits is now cut off by Soviet troops. The students seem not the slightest bit concerned for themselves. "What worries them now is that all they have accomplished in these last two weeks may be so quickly torn down. The United Nations is their only hope and all of their optimism is now focused there. But even if the worst occurs, they are all convinced that what they have done is right, and will live for a long, long time."[97]

Soviet Troop Movements

Today there is scarcely a county in Hungary in which Soviet troops are not on the move. Yesterday two Soviet armored trains, ignoring a red light, crossed the Soviet border into Záhony. Today Soviet railroad workers are reported to be building a new rail line from Záhony to Nyíregyháza.[98]*

At Pápa Airport, south of Győr, Soviet troop transports arrive incessantly. As soon as one unit is fully formed up it heads west to the borderland.

In the south, where tanks are already surrounding the uranium mines at Pécs, which Hungarian soldiers are defending, Russian units are headed toward Kaposvár and Nagykanizsa. The Soviet commander tells the Workers' Council of Baranya County in Pécs, which has gone out to meet them, that they have no intention of interfering in the affairs of their city.

Soviet troops leaving Kaposvár, Imre Nagy's home town, attempt to take over the airport of Taszár. They meet with resistance from the Hungarian troops guarding the airport, however, and are driven back in a sharp exchange of fire.[99]

Six railroad trains loaded with Russian troops and ammunition, which began their journey at Záhony near the Soviet border at midnight, now arrive at the village of Szajol just west of Szolnok. The troops disembark, march

---

*Due to a wider gauge track in Russia, all trains going into and out of Russia must be lifted onto wider or narrower wheel carriages, a laborious process which takes from four to eight hours, depending on the size of the train. The fact that the Soviets are extending their wider gauge track well into Hungary is an indication of how long they expect to occupy the country.

across the Tisza River on a recently built pontoon bridge, and are loaded into trucks and cars which take them to trains waiting in Szolnok. These are now waiting to be dispatched toward Budapest.[100]

Viennese military circles estimate that there are now five new armored divisions in Hungary: three motorized divisions, two rifle divisions, plus two flying corps. This does not include the original two Special Corps Divisions, some units of which have already been pulled out of the country.[101]

Sealing Off the Austrian Frontier

Most of today's troop movements in Western Hungary are connected with the attempt to seal off the Austro-Hungarian border. While the border checkpoints are still manned by Hungarians, Soviet checkpoints complete with tanks are usually not more than ten kilometers back. Traffic on most roads in the border area is now reduced to local farmers.

All Western convoys going toward Austria are stopped. This includes the American five-car convoy of diplomatic dependents trying for the second day in a row to get to Vienna and a convoy of twenty-eight Western journalists.

Yesterday the American five-car convoy, draped in American flags for identification, was halted about ten miles from the Austrian border. When the American press attaché, the only Russian-speaking member of the group, began to protest and explain who they were, the Soviet officer in charge told him: "Polemics are useless. You will please turn back to Budapest!" A phone call to Budapest caused a cable to Washington, and in no time Under Secretary Robert Murphy was calling on Soviet Ambassador Zarubin, who said he would get through to his government immediately. So this morning the convoy set out again at 9:00 a.m. from Budapest, this time armed with a written guarantee in Russian from Ambassador Andropov.

Nevertheless, they are stopped again, this time by Russian soldiers at a railroad crossing within two hundred meters of the Austrian border. The soldiers yell, "Go back or we shoot!" They refuse even to look at the Russian language document, as does the local Soviet commander. "I have orders to deal only with the President of the local Hungarian National Council and the Swedish (sic) Red Cross," he keeps repeating stubbornly. Captain Thomas Gleason, the Assistant Military attaché, who today is in charge of the convoy, asks permission to go back to Mosonmagyaróvár where he can phone his Legation. This they are permitted and soon the whole sequence of transatlantic cables and calls and assurances is repeated with greater emphasis. The convoy, meantime, must spend the night in Mosonmagyaróvár.[102]

The convoy of twenty-eight journalists which is also stopped not far from Mosonmagyaróvár by Soviet tanks fare less well than the American convoy. Being individualists accustomed to fending for themselves, and with a number being able to express themselves in Russian, they give the Russians rather more vociferous objections than did the American convoy. As a consequence the Russians treat them rather roughly, driving their tanks into several of the cars and pushing them into the ditch before arresting their occupants. They even open warning fire on one car which refuses to stop, makes a U-turn and speeds away.

The occupants of this car have good reason not to stop. Sefton Delmer has learned that Nagy himself has been questioned by the Russians as to the whereabouts of Noel Barber. They do not like what he has been writing. On learning that he is a marked man, Barber, who is far from recovered from his head wound, decides that he must nevertheless leave his hospital and get out of the country as soon as possible. Before he leaves the hospital Barber has a last visit from his guide and friend, Dénes, who refuses to go with him. From Dénes he learns that Ilona, who had saved him that first night, has been killed, shot in a bread queue and then run over by the tank that had shot her.

Now Delmer, who is at the wheel of Barber's wreck-of-a-car, realizes that if he stops, they may be asked to get out and that arrest would surely follow, as, indeed, it does for his fellow journalists.

After back-tracking for a few miles, they decide they must try to cross the border illegally and take out across the fields. A Hungarian who offers to guide them says they must keep off the fields near the border for they are sown with mines. They must keep to the cart tracks. These, unfortunately, quickly turn to sticky mud and Delmer, with Barber now at the wheel, and the Hungarian guide must get out and push. This they do for the next four hours while the sky gets darker. Near the border two Hungarian border guards near a plowed strip are eager to help. In a minute the car lurches across and inadvertently knocks down a pole with an Austrian flag on it. They are thirteen miles from where they had tried to cross the frontier legally.

Barber cannot help looking back through his shattered rear window. He blows a kiss. As he will write a few days later: "It wasn't for Hungary, whose glory will never fade. No, it was for Dénes—alive, I hoped—and for that kid of fifteen; but most of all it was for that black-haired girl who had led my car to safety in smashed-up Buda. Somewhere Ilona lay, dead and smeared with blood. I huddled back in my filthy blankets and for the first time in my adult life I cried bitterly."[103]

To seal off Hungary from the West it must be done not only on the ground but also in the air. Every day Swiss and Austrian planes have been landing at Ferihegy outside of Budapest unloading cargoes of medical and food supplies. Today, when a Swiss Air plane is warned off, with anti-aircraft fire, no less, the plane is told by its owners not to land in Vienna, from which it had taken off, but to return to Zürich. From now on, aware that they will be refused landing rights, or worse, no more planes from the West attempt to fly in.[104]

While the Soviets seal their side of the border, Austrian Minister to Hungary, Walter Peinsipp, calls on Imre Nagy today to inform him officially that some days ago Austria had set up a "neutral zone" on its side of the border in which only locals, Austrian and Red Cross officials and journalists issued special permits are allowed to be. This is specifically designed to keep Hungarian émigrés and other unauthorized persons from trying to cross from Austria into Hungary. The Austrian Army, Peinsipp informs Nagy, is strictly patrolling this zone, which extends well back into Austrian territory for the entire length of the border. Nagy expresses his "satisfaction" at this news.[105]

Technical Talks on Soviet Military Withdrawal

At noon today thousands of Hungarians watch as the seven-member Soviet military delegation headed by Major General Malinin, resplendent in dress uniforms and glittering medals, enters the Parliament building to negotiate the terms of a Soviet troop withdrawal. General Malin is accompanied by Major General Shchelbanin, Lt. General Stepanov and four other officers. Newly promoted Major General Pál Maléter, now also the Minister of Defense, Major General István Kovács, Chief of Staff, Col. Miklós Szűcs and the required civilian member, Ferenc Erdei, are waiting to greet them. As they virtually march down the corridor along the long red carpet to their appointed conference room, Maléter towers above the Russians and his colleagues. The talks, which are conducted in great secrecy, last several hours.

It is difficult to discern how they are going when they break off, but at least the Hungarians do not look crestfallen. Though it does not get out, those close to Maléter find that the talks have gone extremely well. The Soviets seem to agree to everything accept the date of actual departure and on this they are only weeks apart. Restoration of Soviet monuments, departure ceremonies with bands, speeches and presentation of gifts and flowers and full military honors; these are the things which seem to concern the Soviet side. But no announcement, other than that the talks will resume at 10:00 p.m. tonight at Soviet headquarters, is made.

Imre Nagy, who is present at the opening of the talks, quickly steps out. He is working feverishly on the political side to head off the coming Soviet onslaught. He has made desperate advances through the Yugoslav Embassy to Tito, hoping he might serve as mediator. Now he is talking with Romanian Deputy Foreign Minister Aurel Malnasan, who flew in late last night from Bucharest at his behest, to see whether his boss, Gheorghiu-Dej, might have sufficient interest and influence in the Kremlin to stave off the "military solution."

Reaction in the Communist World

The Soviet Communist Party is preparing the Russian people for trouble in Hungary. From talks of "counterrevolutionary fascist gangs" in the early days to straight reports on workers' councils and mistakes of the Rákosi regime, it is now switching back, despite the Declaration made on October 30, to a hostile attitude. Readers of most Moscow newspapers this morning read in yesterday's TASS dispatch from Budapest:

> In Budapest, Miskolc, Győr, Debrecen and other Hungarian towns industrial enterprises, public transport, and government establishments continue to stand idle. Schools, theatres, museums, and stadiums have been closed.
> During the last few days in the capital and in the provinces outrages and disorder have been perpetrated by counterrevolutionary gangs. The premises of many public and party organizations have been smashed, and mass acts of violence and murder of public leaders have taken place.

Echoes of the Declaration on Relations with other Socialist States, however, can still be discerned. Both *Pravda* and *Izvestia* state that "the public in the People's Democracies stresses that alliance and friendship with the USSR on the basis of full equality and sovereignty are in line with the fundamental vital interests of the socialist states."[106]

Students in East Berlin have a quite different attitude. Today they distribute pamphlets with an ironical appeal for more military training and more para-military instruction. "The example of Hungary," says the pamphlet "shows we can use it!" Ulbricht, who is all too aware of these pamphlets, tells the Volkskammer that it is "a disgrace" that none of the students did anything to impede its distribution.[107]

While three more Polish planes with aid for Hungary take off from Warsaw airport this morning, panic buying, which began in Prague yesterday, today is taking over Warsaw and other Polish cities. After a huge run on the banks, it is not just food which is being purchased, but jewelry and valuables of every sort. The situation in Hungary and the war in the Middle East are not even the main causes of this buying spree. It is the large-scale movement of Soviet troops and armor across Poland to East Germany which began yesterday and is continuing today. This, to the Poles, seems to indicate a major war in the making.[108]

In Cluj (Hungarian: Kolozsvár), Romania, the Hungarian half of the university remains closed today after clashes between the Hungarian and Romanian students. There is a university-wide boycott against classes in Marxism-Leninism and Russian Language and even printed demands have appeared that these subjects be eliminated from the curriculum. There is strong pressure to evict all Westerners, except diplomats, from Romania, but even diplomats are being harassed.[109]

Yesterday's cancellation of the Yugoslav government's weekly news conference is an indication of the quandary Tito feels himself to be in. In principle he is against any intervention by foreign troops. Yet the danger which lurks in Imre Nagy's promise of free, multi-party elections is a direct threat to the Yugoslav regime. This demand was heard a few years ago in Yugoslavia and Tito had it immediately suppressed.

Some Reactions in the West

The West European press is daily extolling the courage and fortitude of Hungary, but none more so than that of little Denmark, half the size of Hungary in area and population. Today, Copenhagen's main newspaper, *Berlingske Tidene*, writes:

> Hungary's martyrdom touches us as nothing else has done for many years. We don't just read of it. It is about us....Suddenly, we find ourselves taken back to the time many years ago, when our own young people fought, fell and triumphed....
>
> There is not a man in Denmark who, so few years after our own fight for freedom, can read the freedom song from Budapest without pain....

We cannot consider ourselves quit of our obligation to "fighting Hungary" any more than gifts alone would at one time have wiped out the debt we felt towards Finland and Norway....[110]

In Washington, Monsignor Béla Varga, last speaker of the democratically elected Hungarian parliament and President of the Hungarian National Committee in the U.S., has either not seen reports of Cardinal Mindszenty's press conference yesterday, or chooses to ignore it. He tells the American press, which gives it wide publicity, that Cardinal Mindszenty may soon become premier of Hungary. "If the whole country wants him—if the peasants want him—I think the Cardinal will feel it is his duty, not only to Hungary, but to the whole world." It is yet another instance of how out-of-touch the emigration is from the reality of political life in Hungary today.[111]

From Bonn, the *New York Times* correspondent, Arthur Olsen, writes that the West German government is profoundly disturbed at signs of the United States' hesitation to provide forceful backing of Hungary's struggle to throw off the Soviet yoke. Neither Adenauer nor his top ministers advocate U.S. military intervention, but they have been hoping for the strongest possible U.S. political backing of the Hungarian rebels against what is seen from Bonn as a Soviet attempt to re-conquer the country. So far they don't see it.

Nagy Announces a New Government

Early this afternoon the radio announces that the Hungarian Presidium (in effect Nagy himself) has appointed a new government made up mostly of non-communist party members all of whom bear the title "Minister of State." These are: Anna Kéthly, (Socialist), Gyula Kelemen (Socialist), József Fischer (Socialist), István B. Szabó (Smallholder), István Bibó (Petőfi/Peasant) and Ferenc Farkas (Petőfi/Peasant). The appointment of Pál Maléter (Communist) to be Minister of Defense was announced earlier. Antal Apró, József Bognár and Ferenc Erdei, all Deputy Prime Ministers and Communists, have been removed from office. In addition eighteen heads of government ministries, all Communists, have also been removed. The deputy ministers will run all of these ministries until proper replacements are found. This means that only five Communists remain in the government: Nagy, Kádár and Münnich (neither of whom have been seen since November 1), and Losonczy and Maléter.[112] The government has at last caught up with the Hungarian people.

Cardinal Mindszenty's Address

In an address to the nation this evening Cardinal Mindszenty begins: "By the grace of God I am the same as I was before my imprisonment. I stand... just as I was eight years ago, although imprisonment has left its mark on me."

First he turns to the outside world, saying, "This is my first chance to thank [foreign countries] for what has been given us." He also thanks all those who prayed for him during his imprisonment and expresses his gratitude to "the world press and radio, whose electrical wave network is the only true Great Power in the air."

Speaking of Hungary, and quite forgetting, or possibly ignoring, Poland, he says, "There is one thing in which we are foremost. There is not a single nation which, in the course of its thousand years' history, has suffered more than we have. We had to keep fighting for our freedom, mostly in defense of the Western countries. This stopped the continuity of our development, we had to rise again by our own force. Now...Hungary is enjoying the sympathy of all civilized nations."

While the national anthem does ask God to protect each Hungarian "when he is fighting against his enemy," the fact is today "we hope we have no enemy! For we are not enemies of anyone. We desire to live in friendship with every people and every country." Old-fashioned nationalism "should never again be a source of fighting between countries." The feeling of nationalism should "flourish [only]...in the field of common culture."

Now Hungary's "entire position will be decided by what the two hundred million-person Russian Empire intends to do with the military force standing within our frontiers....We are neutral. We give the Russian Empire no cause for bloodshed. But has the idea not occurred to the leaders of the Russian Empire that we will respect the Russian people far more if it does not oppress us? It is only an enemy people which is attacked by another country. We have not attacked Russia and sincerely hope that the withdrawal...will soon occur.

"...The situation is also made critical by the fact that production has stopped....We are facing famine. It was a nation worn down to the bone, that fought for its liberty. And so work must be resumed. This is essential for the continuation of the nation's life....Let everyone in the whole world know that this fight was not a revolution, but a fight for freedom."[113]

EXPLOSION

Moscow

In Moscow, where the decision to crush the revolution has long been decided, the Presidium is meeting again with the participation of Kádár, Münnich and ex-foreign Minister Horváth. Kádár tries to explain to the Soviet comrades that it was due to their persistent mistakes that the situation developed in Hungary as it did. "You would only deal with three or four members of the Hungarian leadership, and for much of the time it was only Rákosi. This was the source of many mistakes. This monopolizing of relations with the Soviet Union meant that any criticism of Rákosi he made into a criticism of the Soviet Union. When it was clear from the Twentieth Party Congress that Rákosi should have left the leadership, your telegram congratulating him caused great confusion in the Hungarian Party. As for today, it is true they are killing communists,…and Nagy is providing a cover for this. I agree with you that the correct course of action at this point is to form a revolutionary government. But I would like…to emphasize one point: the whole nation is taking part in this movement. The nation does not want to liquidate the people's democratic order [i.e., Communism]. The withdrawal of Soviet troops from Hungary has great significance, great importance. If we strengthen the military relationship, we become weakened in the political relationship and Hungarian national sentiments will be offended.

"As to the new revolutionary government: it must not be puppet-like; there must be a base for its activities and support from the workers. It must be clear what sort of relationship we will have with the USSR….But if we are to declare that the Nagy government is counterrevolutionary, that will make all the parties counterrevolutionary."

At this point Khrushchev and Malenkov, back from Brioni, join the Presidium. Khrushchev declares that Kádár will be the head of the new government and Münnich his deputy, as Minister of Defense and Minister of the Interior.

Having heard of Kádár's criticisms of past Soviet policy, Khrushchev freely admits that "we were too late in requesting that [Rákosi] be replaced, and that it was his and Mikoyan's fault that Gerő was selected to replace him rather than Kádár. Gerő and Rákosi are "honorable communists, but they did many stupid things." The exclusion of Nagy from the Party was a mistake and a reflection on Rákosi's stupidity. "Some of the rebels," he admits, "are not enemies. They were antagonized by mistakes of the leadership. But now

352

we cannot regard Nagy as a communist. Dulles needs someone exactly like that. We are still for upholding our Declaration, but with Nagy that is not possible for Hungary. The traitors want to use Nagy as a screen. If he is not forced to resign, you can be certain that he will be working for the enemy."[114]

American Ambassador to Moscow Charles ("Chip") Bohlen strongly suspects the Soviets are about to take strong military action in Hungary. His reasons, which he sends via ciphered telegram to Washington, are: changes in the Soviet press, changes in Zhukov with whom he has talked at several diplomatic occasions—at the most recent "he had an air of satisfaction and even triumph"—and the Anglo-French invasion of Egypt. The military talks now going on in Hungary, he says, are little more than a device to gain time.[115]

Budapest

Only after she has listened to Cardinal Mindszenty on the radio does Mrs. Pál Maléter get a phone call from Maléter informing her that he is going to Tököl, the Soviet military headquarters south of Csepel, in a few minutes. She has scarcely seen him since it all began and now he is not only a Major General, but also the nation's Minister of Defense. She begs him not to go; she is all too aware of the dangers of Soviet Headquarters at ten o'clock at night with Budapest ringed with Soviet armor. He had told her about this entrenchment, which is why she is so frightened. As she continues to beg him, he gets a bit angry and finally rebukes her in a somewhat military tone: "Please understand that everything is going on according to diplomatic rules! This is where we will conclude the negotiations that started at noon. Although they accepted everything at noon, the signatures and some technical details are still missing." Then after a slight pause he adds: "Please understand; nothing counts here, no wife, no family, I just have to go out there even at the expense of my life, for the entire country is waiting for my assistance." At that point Mrs. Maléter realizes he fully knows what he is doing and she can no longer keep him from his higher duty.[116]

Captain Lajos Csibi, a senior officer in the Kilián Barracks before Maléter took over, now accosts Maléter in the Parliament Building from which he had just called his wife. Looking Maléter straight in the eyes he asks him, "Couldn't this invitation be a trap? Don't you think there's a danger the Russians will arrest you?" Maléter thinks for a moment, smiles and says, "I don't think the Russians would do such a thing. The talks have been frank and understanding."

An old friend of Maléter's, Márk Molnár, who had resigned his commission but then joined him in the Kilián Barracks as a civilian, has been acting as Maléter's aide de camp, albeit without uniform. Maléter had re-commissioned him a major, but had not bothered to get him a uniform. By rights he should accompany Maléter to Tököl, but an ADC without uniform is unthinkable. Whether because of this or because he wished to spare his friend what he suspected might happen to him, Maléter now stalks stiffly into Molnár's small office, takes a military stance in front of him and says coldly, "Major Molnár, I will not be requiring your services this evening. Report for duty tomorrow morning as usual." A confused Molnár salutes angrily. Maléter, who is not one with whom one argues, salutes back. Then Maléter suddenly steps completely out of character. He leans forward, holds out his enormous hand, grips Molnár's like a vice and says one word: "Goodbye!" before turning on his heel and leaving. Molnár, to whom he has never said "goodbye" when he expects to see him the next day, is suddenly overwhelmed with foreboding.[117]

General Béla Király and his deputy, Sándor Kopácsi, are present when Nagy sees Maléter and his colleagues in the delegation, Major General István Kovács and Col. Szűcs, off to Tököl.

"It'll turn out all right, you'll see," Maléter says assuringly. "General Malinin is a great guy and the other two generals, Shchelbanin and Stepanov, also seem fine. These military men are faithful and loyal negotiating partners. We've had to discuss delicate problems, dates, difficult formalities such as the military music and farewell speeches for the moment of departure. Don't laugh, comrades, the Soviet government insists on it as well as the restoration of their monuments. We had to discuss mass psychology among other things. Tonight we are to clear up the final details."

"Let's hope," sighs Nagy. He then orders Maléter to phone as soon as he gets there and then phone in a report each hour thereafter. "Good luck, my boys," he says. "I won't budge until you get back…"

Maléter dons his kepi, smiles, salutes and departs as Nagy gives him an encouraging wave. Then Nagy adjusts his pince nez glasses, looks up and says, "Jóska, send in everyone who has problems. We're not going to laze about, are we? The night is long."

Maléter calls in to say he has arrived safely. An hour later he calls to say the talks are going very well, "everything is in good order." Even his body-guards in an anteroom, who can hear the tone of the conversation if not the individual words, feel it is going well.

At midnight there is a dramatic interruption. A score of green-capped Soviet policemen burst through the ante-chamber and literally smash down the door of the conference room. They swarm inside, covering the Hungarian delegation with their submachine guns. They are followed by a blond man who saunters casually into the room. It is KGB chief Ivan Serov.

General Malinin, who is as startled and horrified as the Hungarians, bellows an oath, jumps to his feet and wants to know what is happening.

Maléter stands up slowly to his full height, "So that was it, was it?" he says to his Russian colleagues.

Malinin begins profound apologies, but Serov hurries over to him and whispers in his ear. A disgusted looking Malinin shakes his head, then looks over to Maléter with a shrug that says he knew nothing about this, it has nothing to do with the code of honor between army generals. Then, quite shattered by the experience, he quietly leaves the room followed by the other two Soviet generals.

"The Hungarian delegation is under arrest," announces Serov loudly once the Russians are gone. Out in the ante-chamber one of the Hungarians wants to go down fighting. "Stop it!" Maléter orders. "It is useless to resist."[118]

It is well past midnight. November 4 has begun.

But in the Parliament building when there is no third call from Maléter and all calls to Tököl get no response, Király asks Nagy for orders.

"Re-establish contact with the Hungarian government representatives by sending mediators to the site." Király sends a major in an army tank with a large white flag attached to its aerial with orders to radio in his progress as he goes. At Tököl he reports getting past the first gate and then being followed by two T-54s until he reaches the main gate. Here he says he is going to leave the tank for a moment to notify their commander. Some shouts in Russian are then heard and the sounds of a scuffle...then nothing. Nagy takes the news stoically and suggests Király and Kopácsi get a few hours of rest. Then he himself retires to his bed in the Parliament building.[119]

A Contrast of British and U.S. Diplomatic Concerns

Sir Leslie Fry and his staff at the British Legation have many pieces of information to forward to Whitehall today in addition to such news as the newly constituted Nagy government. Even that, he says, should be taken with some reserve until "I can obtain confirmation that personalities listed have in fact agreed to participate. Miss Kéthly, for example, is at the moment held up at the frontier on her way back from Vienna." Were there no Russians in the country, he is sure this new government would do a "good job." Fry is also trying to check out something he heard from a reliable source that Nagy is appealing today to the Secretary General of the United Nations himself to visit Hungary. To reinforce this Nagy is said to be thinking of flying to New York as soon as possible from an airfield still in Hungarian hands.

In another cable Fry reveals his annoyance at the Foreign Office's nit-picking about "neutrality" having to be based on "the passage of a constitutional law," rather than just being declared. "Clearly this could be arranged only after the withdrawal of Russian forces from Hungary, free elections and convening of a national assembly..."

"What seems necessary at the moment," he says pointedly, "is that as many countries as possible should proclaim themselves in favor of Hungarian neutrality."[120]

Other cables report in great detail on Soviet troop movements, state that Kádár appears to have gone over to the Russians and that the Russians may press him to take Nagy's job, that much of the satellite press is now referring to Nagy as a "traitor."[121]

By contrast, American cable traffic from the American Legation, while reporting major events of today, is concerned with supplying facts for Ambassador Lodge to use in answering Sobolev in the UN, relaying, among other things, that there is no decision yet about a Hungarian delegate to the UN (despite the fact that Nagy two days ago had authorized János Szabó to represent Hungary for the time being), asking for clarification of the Department cable saying Soviet Embassy in Washington claims Soviet Embassy in Budapest has settled the U.S. convoy problem, and asking for information on the purpose of the sixteen-man United Nations group rumored to be arriving in Budapest today. All the cables now bear Minister Edward T. Wailes signature, for he has finally arrived in Budapest.[122] Wailes, who resembles the Danish comedian Victor Borge, is a career officer and a quick study. He soon comes to absorb and appreciate what Barnes has been living through and to resent the parochialism of the State Department in Washington.

Ernő Gerő, who had been Mátayás Rákosi's right-hand man for many years, was appointed First Secretary of the Party in Rákosi's place when the Soviet politburo member Anastas Mikoyan persuaded Rákosi to resign and retire to Moscow. Gerő's subsequent footdragging concerning carrying out the expected reforms built up extreme discontent in the country. His harsh, brief radio speech on the evening of October 23, 1956, in which he tried to put the lid on the student demonstrations and call for reform, was the spark which set off the Revolution. (AP/Wide World Photos)

János Kádár, whose refusal to accept Nagy's offer that he replace Gerő as First Party Secretary kept Gerő in that all-important post, to the consternation of the Hungarian people, was appointed First Party Secretary when Gerő fled and was a minister in Imre Nagy's government. He secretly betrayed Nagy on November 1 and went over to the Russians, who made him the head of their puppet government when they invaded on November 4. Though he relinquished the premiership in the spring of 1958, Kádár remained First Party Secretary until the spring of 1988. (AP/Wide World Photos)

Imre Nagy, like most of the Communist leaders of Hungary, was known as a "Moscovite" in that he spent most of his exile years in Moscow, returning to Hungary behind the Soviet Red Army in 1944. Made minister of agriculture in the first post-war government, he brought about the sweeping land reform of 1945–46, which made him not just popular with the peasants but with much of the rest of the populace. The Soviets picked him as the obvious man to replace Rákosi when, after Stalin's death, they felt obliged to remove the "best of Stalin's pupils" lest his harsh measures in Hungary cause an explosion. Nagy's reform government, undoing most of the worst of Rákosi's work, lasted from June 1953 until spring of 1955, at which time Rákosi, who had remained party secretary, was able to get the Soviets to oust Nagy and have himself returned to power. Only after the Revolution had broken out was Nagy brought back as the only Communist who might be able to control the situation. Before he had a chance to achieve this the Soviets intervened a second time, and Nagy fled to the Yugoslav embassy. Through trickery the Soviets captured him, and shipped him to a prison in Budapest. He and his colleagues were secretly executed. Because he refused to admit to any of the accusations against him in his trial he quickly became a martyr and symbol of a Revolution he neither led nor was ever able to control. (AP/Wide World Photos)

Having failed to topple the giant statue of Stalin with ropes, which always broke, demonstrators are beginning to pull up a steel cable (lower right) to place around the statue's neck. Even with steel cables attached to a truck the statue did not give. Eventually an acetylene torch was used to make a row of holes just above the boots and behind the knees. Thus weakened, the statue gave way and the truck was able to pull it down. Note the man obscuring Stalin's face; he appears to be standing on the outstretched dictator's arm. (AP/Wide World Photos)

The entire statue, still attached by a steel cable to a truck, was pulled through the streets of Budapest until it came to rest in Luiza Square not far from the Szabad Nép building. Here the head was later severed from the body and dragged to the middle of the square with a stop sign placed in the hole where part of the face had been. (Getty)

A column of Soviet Stalin tanks drives into Budapest during the second intervention on November 4, 1956. This picture was taken surreptitiously from a window several floors above the street. (Getty)

The remains of several Soviet tanks in the street near the Kilián Barracks. Molotov cocktails, unless they happen to detonate ordnance inside a tank, seldom were able to cause such devastation, though they put many tanks out of commission. Much of the incredible destruction of heavy Soviet tanks was accomplished with nitro-glycerine, which chemistry students from the Technical University manufactured in a makeshift labratory they set up inside Kilián Barracks. (Getty)

The front entrance to the radio station on Sándor Bródy Street some days after the fighting. While insurgents captured the station at the beginning of the Revolution, it was retaken by the Soviets and not until October 30, 1956, did the patriots take over the running of the station. Only after that date was the banner on the balustrade, mimicking the typography of the sign on the building, put in place. Note that it says, "Magyar Szabad (Free) Rádió." (Getty)

A young boy Freedom Fighter, probably not more than twelve or thirteen. Over 80 percent of the Freedom Fighters in the first stages of the Revolution were twenty-years-old or younger, and a surprisingly large number of children from eight to fifteen were among them. (Getty)

A young girl Freedom Fighter, probably in her early to mid-teens. While most women acted as nurses, messengers or cooks, many, like this young girl, actually took part in the fighting and were killed. (Getty)

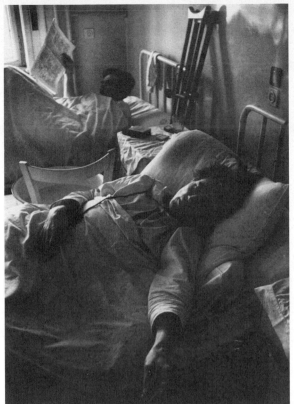

Wounded Freedom Fighters in a hospital. Most hospitals, including the 1,200-bed Péterfy Street Hospital, quickly ran out of beds and filled up the corridors with wounded—as they did the morgues with the dead. Many of the walking wounded among the Freedom Fighters insisted on going home, or even back to the fighting, in order to make room for the more seriously injured. (Getty)

Two dead Soviet soldiers killed during the first days of the fighting. Note that they have been lightly sprinkled with lime. While fallen Hungarians almost always had a national flag draped over them, aad often received a quick burial in a shallow grave in a nearby park, most of the Soviet soldiers lay for several days where they had fallen before the Soviets got around to picking them up. For sanitary reasons the Hungarians sprinkled them with lime. (AP/Wide World Photos)

Young ÁVO recruits in regular police uniforms, having just emerged with their hands up from the Party Municipal Building at Republic Square, were executed in cold blood by infuriated citizens. They had watched these same ÁVO men shoot indiscriminately into a crowded bread line of women, and seen them kill Red Cross workers in white coats, who were trying to rescue the wounded in the park. While all were shot, not all perished. (Getty)

A woman, doubtless related to the fallen Freedom Fighter lying here in the Republic Square under a national flag and bunches of flowers, prays as she pays her last respects. Note that two more bodies of fallen Freedom Fighters, not yet covered with national flags, are partially obscured behind the woman. (AP/Wide World Photos)

Crowds walking on a Sunday in late November 1956, or possibly early December, along a street, possibly Rakoczy Ut, shattered by the Soviet onslaught, which crushed the Revolution. It was many months before any rebuilding began. (AP/Wide World Photos)

Hundreds of coffins with as yet unidentified dead in them are lined up outside of Budapest's cemeteries for citizens to come identify their loved ones. For those whose sons or daughters were still among the missing, it was a harrowing and exhausting business. (AP/Wide World Photos)

Some soldiers and a Soviet tank hold up a peaceful march of women (center) on December 4, 1956, as they attempt to reach the Tomb of the Unknown Soldier in Heroes' Square (then, Stalin Square). The women, many mourning husbands or children killed in the recent onslaught, chose the first month's anniversary of the second Soviet intervention to hold their demonstration. They specifically asked that men stay off the streets, and that only women take part in the demonstration. (AP/Wide World Photos)

The women, whose persist-ence has won out over the Soviet authorities, have been given permission to place flowers on the Tomb of the Unknown Soldier in Heroes' Square. Note the white fur-hatted Soviet sol-dier (exact center) with his back to the camera, con-trolling the column of women with a flag, and the Soviet soldiers apart from the women on the left. (AP/Wide World Photos)

A baby being handed across a ditch near the Austrian border. It is most unlikely that either the officer or the person receiving the baby is any relation to the baby. Many small children in the early days of the mass exodus from Hungary were simply sent with tags on them asking, in Hungarian or German, that the recipient take good care of them. Since so many Austrians in Burgenland, near where the above scene took place, are of Hungarian extraction, and even had Magyar relatives on the other side of the border, they had no difficulty reading the messages in Hungarian. (AP/Wide World Photos)

Ilona Tóth, a twenty-five-year-old medical student who served as a volunteer nurse in the Sándor Péterfy Street Hospital, testifies at her trial for murdering an ÁVO patient by injecting gasoline into his vein. Beside her is one of her accomplices, Milos Gyöngyossi, twenty-eight, also a medical student. Neither denies the charges. They were sentenced to death and executed shortly after the trial. (AP/Wide World Photos)

József Kővagó (left), former mayor of Budapest and reappointed to that position during the Revolution, observes Anna Kéthly (middle), head of the Hungarian Social Democratic Party and minister in Imre Nagy's government, talking to Major General Béla Kiraly (right) before the three of them testify before the United Nations Special Committee on the "Problem of Hungary" in February 1957. Kéthly is the only member of Nagy's government who happened to be outside of Hungary. (AP/Wide World Photos)

Budapest Street scene in early 1957, and then the same scene one year later. In the right-hand photograph one building appears to have been repaired, but the taller building only has its windows repaired. Note the pile of bricks on the sidewalk still standing in front of it. (AP/Wide World Photos)

Distinguished guests observe a moment of silence at the Nagy reburial ceremony in Heroes' Square on June 16, 1988. Some of the figures in the front are, from left to right: Hungarian Lutheran bishop Gyula Nagy, cardinal and archbishop László Paski, and American ambassador Mark Palmer, wearing his signature bow tie. (AP/Wide World Photos)

Aside from the safety of the U.S. convoy, the Department's main concern is that the newly arrived Wailes gets his credentials accepted. (The day before in Vienna Wailes had received a cable advising *not* to present his credentials and if pressed by the Hungarian Foreign Ministry upon arrival to say he was "awaiting official instructions.") Today there is a long cable urging Wailes to present his credentials "at once" because of: 1) Soviet military movements; 2) Nagy's acceptance of peoples' demands; 3) Nagy's appeals to the UN, and 4) "Desirability that [he] enjoy proper formal access to Hungarian authorities..." The message then spells out exactly what he is to say when he comes before Imre Nagy:

> Mr. President: In presenting the Letter accrediting me as Minister...I express to your Excellency, on behalf of the Government and people of the United States, warmest greetings to the people of Hungary. In this momentous hour of their national life, the Hungarian people have shown highest courage, integrity of purpose, and unfaltering spirit. Their just struggle for freedom and independence commands the sympathy and the admiration of the entire world. My Government understands and supports these aspirations of the people of Hungary.
>
> In accordance with the clear purposes of my Government, I assure your Excellency that I shall devote myself earnestly and unceasingly to the promotion of good will and friendly understanding between Hungary and the United States and to the advancement of those ideas and principles, which inspire our two peoples, give rise to mutual interests and ensure the welfare of both countries. It is my sincere hope...etc. etc.[123]

At Radio Free Europe in Munich, William E. Griffith, who yesterday stated that Nagy's position is greatly strengthened, today calls the situation "most unclear." Sobelov's UN statement "that Nagy is misinformed about the return of the Soviet troops may indicate that the alleged reason for Soviet reconcentration (to guard the evacuation of families and the wounded) may have some basis. I personally think the Soviets may well yet not have decided what to do." As to what RFE's "line" should be from now on: "We should continue to stress national unity and avoid any criticism of Nagy or of the regime..."[124] After days of Hungarian broadcasts calling Nagy a traitor with Hungarian blood on his hands, this change of line, even if followed, is not likely to make much difference.

United Nations, New York

The main attention at the United Nations today is still on the Middle East. A climactic session of the General Assembly is due this evening during which it is expected that a special force of UN troops will be voted into existence which will replace the British and French troops now in Egypt. But due to Cuba's insistence yesterday, the Security Council meets this afternoon at 3:00 p.m. on Hungary. Everyone, including the French and the British, expects a tripartite resolution to be introduced. Instead it is only the United States which puts the resolution forward. Sir Pierson Dixon cables the Foreign Office: "When I saw Mr. Lodge this morning I learnt that he had been instructed to table a resolution immediately without further consultation with us and the French despite our agreement of yesterday and what he told me last night."[125]

When the text does arrive, Sir Pierson tells the Foreign Office he can vote for it without amending it, since there is no reference to sending any UN observers. He adds: "I think the omission of any mention of Hungary's declaration of neutrality is a genuine reflection of American uncertainty and desire not to commit themselves now to any guarantee."[126]

The draft in any case brings very little pressure on the Soviet Union in that it merely expresses "the earnest hope" that Soviet armed forces will withdraw from Hungary.

No sooner does the session open than the Yugoslav delegate moves to adjourn it on the grounds that negotiations between Hungary and the Soviet Union are in progress and the Security Council should not interfere, but wait to see how the negotiations work out.[127] Western delegates are astonished by this move and even further astonished when Ambassador Lodge eagerly supports it. "We believe," says Lodge, "that adjournment for a day or two would give a real opportunity to the Hungarian government to carry out its announced desire to arrange for an orderly and immediate evacuation of all Soviet troops."

No other Western delegate shares Lodge's optimism and apparent belief in the Soviet Union's good faith. Mr. Walker of Australia states: "Unfortunately, the world has had some experience of the course that 'negotiations' sometimes take in a country where the Soviet Union has been able to establish military supremacy." Monsieur de Guiringaud of France says flatly that "negotiations" are not possible if one of the parties is not free. Sir

Pierson Dixon says: "It would be quite misleading, and unfair to the Hungarians to take the comfortable view...that we can now leave the Hungarian question to settle itself." He urges immediate passage of the American resolution, concluding, "I do not frankly see how the Council can do less." The French delegate states with considerable clairvoyance: "We have not only the right but the duty to find out whether [these Russian troop movements] are not rather a re-grouping of Soviet forces so that they will be able to intervene with such suddenness to make possible the establishment of a regime to the liking of the Soviet Union."

Nevertheless, Lodge makes no further movement to bring his resolution to a vote and instead calls on the Soviet and Hungarian delegates to comment on the negotiations in progress. Neither delegate can do more than say that negotiations are in progress. When de Guiringaud asks why the resolution is not put to a vote, Lodge simply ignores him. The Council President, Entezam of Iran, says the Council must soon adjourn since the General Assembly is due to meet at 8:00 p.m. This raises a host of protests from all the Western delegates but Lodge. The two bodies can meet at the same time, they are willing to split their delegations. But when this gets no support from the U.S. delegate, the proposals for simultaneous meetings are dropped.

Again President Entezam moves that the Council adjourn until Monday, November 5. More protests erupt and Walker of Australia says things are so desperate in Hungary that the Council cannot meet any later than tomorrow, Sunday, November 4, at 5:00 p.m. Since it is in the form of a formal motion, Entezam feels he has to put it to a vote. Only he and Lodge vote against it, thus voting for further delay. But since there are three abstentions, Peru, Russia and Yugoslavia, the motion fails to get the necessary seven votes. With some satisfaction Entezam now announces the Council will adjourn until Monday. Thus, due to the deliberate tactics of the United States, November 3 comes to an end without even a vote on its purely symbolic resolution on Hungary.

CHAPTER VIII

The Second Intervention

Sunday, November 4, 1956

THE SOVIET ATTACK *began around 4:30 a.m. Imre Nagy, in his announce-*
ment, said it came at "daybreak"; journalists in their reports referred to it
as "dawn." It was neither. Those in Pest who were awakened by the first
shuddering explosions looked out and saw the night sky turn to multiple
flashes of red and crimson behind the dark silhouette of Buda's hills as the
thundering booms shook the earth and rattled windows. It was a surprise
many had feared, but a surprise nonetheless, for hadn't the bilateral talks
been about Soviet troop withdrawal? And isn't Sunday a day of rest? The
growing volume and intensity of the shelling, even though the shells were not
yet landing in the center of the city, were terrifying. Adding to the terror was
the familiar roar of tank engines, only this time instead of hundreds, there
were two thousand. And as the sky grew lighter, the noise became a swelling
background to the exploding shells. Heavy artillery, including the famous
Katyusha rockets from their multiple launchers, mortars and cannons from
the T-54 Stalin tanks, was the source of all this shelling.

With daylight the sky began to fill with Soviet bombers making bombing
runs over Hungarian Army positions and a few known strong points in the
city, and MIG-16s diving and screaming by at low altitudes strafing the same
targets. Dubbed by the Soviets as "Operation Whirlwind," this vengeful
blitzkrieg with the best that the Soviet Red Army had to offer was in return
for its humiliation of only a week ago.

Even before the shelling begins, the city is penetrated by Soviet scouts and even some tanks as communists loyal to Moscow in the Hungarian Army make it possible for them to slip through the Hungarian Army defenses. Sándor Kopácsi, Deputy Commander of the National Guard, is slumped over his desk in Police Headquarters, head on his arms, when he is aroused from his slumber by the sound of three Stalin tanks clattering by at a terrific speed headed for the Ministry of the Interior. He wakes his boss, General Béla Király, dozing nearby in an armchair. Király has been phoning in reports of Soviet troop activity to Nagy ever since it was clear that Maléter and his delegation were not coming back. He tried to convince Nagy that the Soviet Union was in the process of launching an attack on Budapest and that either he or Nagy must inform the troops that we are at war with the Soviet Union.

"This is a political affair," Nagy answered. "You must know that such a declaration is a thing for the government, not the military. I forbid you to make such a statement!"

"I am completely aware of this," Király replied. "That is why I propose that you...make the decision, or, if you prefer, I will do it with your consent."

"No," said Nagy firmly. "We will not issue such a declaration whatever the case....We cannot undertake war against the Soviet Union....Please continue to inform me of events."[1]

By now the guns have begun and Király realizes that the city is finally under attack. He stands up, asks for a weapon, which until then he had not carried, and tells Kopácsi he must phone Nagy once again.

Nagy is aware of the situation. When Király presses him to give orders to resist the invaders, Nagy quite firmly says, "I refuse to give the order to resist by arms." When Király asks him if he wants to issue orders for surrender, Nagy pauses and then says he will not give that either.

"As you wish, Comrade Nagy. Shall I continue to give you reports?"

"No, I do not wish any more reports. It is useless, my friend," says Nagy resignedly. "Thank you. Please thank everybody for me."[2]

Király puzzles over this for some time. He is not aware that Nagy is about to record his statement to the nation and is preparing to quit the Parliament building.

Meanwhile, over in the Ministry of Defense ex-minister of Defense Lt. General Károly Janza is giving orders right and left that Hungarian troops must show absolutely no resistance and should welcome the Soviet troops warmly. When Janza enters Col. Zólomy's office, Zólomy, who had refused to let his troops fire on the crowd at the Radio, now tells Janza that he is answerable only to Premier Nagy, that Janza no longer has authority. Janza then, in Zólomy's presence, rings up Király at the city's Police Headquarters. Király, like Zólomy, tells Janza that he is not a member of the government and not only will he not lay down his arms, but he is about to take up a battle position so that the Russians will not be able to capture him.

Király now decides to call the members of the Revolutionary Council for Public Safety together at the Deák Square Police Headquarters. Among those who attend is Col. István Marián, head of the military department of the Technical University who had been so forceful in the long meeting of October 22 and in the demonstration the following day. When he arrives he finds a sharp debate in progress. Király says the attack has come from all directions and Nagy refuses to give the order to open fire. While the debate continues, Marián slips out of the room and telephones the university, telling them not to take up the fight, but to leave the university, leaving behind only a guard to be provided by the fire service.

When he returns to the room Király asks him how many university students can be counted upon to fight. Marián tells him between three and four thousand.

Király then stands and announces he is leaving for Buda. "Well, Sándor," he says, looking down on Kopácsi and extending his long arm, "our paths are going to separate now. I'm going to lead a company up to the Belvedere on Mount János [Freedom Hill]. It's not forbidden to take up a position as 'observers.' After that…we'll see." It is clear to Kopácsi that Király has no intention of surrendering and, in fact, is going to fight. Col. Marián and Vilmos Oláh decide to accompany him to Buda. They first visit Castle Hill, where Marián passes on Király's orders for the liaison officers to come down to the Number 56 tram stop behind Castle Hill. Then they go to the Zugliget and from there to the border guard barracks, where Marián organizes a security blockade.

Col. Marián proposes going one by one to the Academy, but most are against that. Király says that each of them must "listen to their own conscience. If somebody tries to save something that is salvageable, that is laudable. If someone wants to fight, he should. If someone decides to take a road that leads straight to the West, that is also acceptable. I now ask those who want to join General Görgényi to leave immediately. Let's not stand on ceremony or be emotional." Col. Marián then leaves to join his student brigades.

Király will later write: "Even if it does not sound heroic I had to say that I did not keep the Supreme Command together in order to organize a guerilla war, or to prolong Hungarian suffering with stubborn warfare. My only aim was that if Imre Nagy did make some sort of acceptable compromise, there would be some sort of organization on which he could rely. That is why I strengthened the defense of Szabadság Hill, and this is why I was willing to fight on to keep the Supreme Command alive until such a moment arrived...."[3]

Minutes after his exchange with Király, Nagy steps into a recording booth in the Parliament radio station and records the statement he has been hastily scribbling. After he has made the recording, it is quickly translated into English, German, Russian and French and then recorded in those languages.

Nagy Broadcast

At 5:20 a.m. the announcer on Radio Free Kossuth calls out: "Attention! Attention! Premier Imre Nagy will address the Hungarian people."

Then comes a lower, calmer voice saying:

"This is Premier Imre Nagy speaking. Today at daybreak Soviet troops attacked our capital with the obvious intent of overthrowing the legal democratic Hungarian government. Our troops are in combat. The government is at its post. I notify the people of our country and the entire world of this fact."

A recording of the Hungarian national anthem follows and then the announcement is repeated again. After another rendition of the anthem the message is given in English, German, Russian and French, interspersed by the anthem. Only at 5:58 is there an interruption of this sequence and the announcement is given: "Imre Nagy, Premier of the national government, appeals to Pál Maléter, Defense Minister, István Kovács, Chief of Staff, and the other members who went to the Soviet Army Headquarters at ten o'clock last night and have not yet returned, to return at once and take charge of their respective offices."

Nagy Escapes

Nagy does not stay in the Parliament building, however. After a few phone calls (one of which is to his wife and daughter) he drives to the Yugoslav Embassy where, by secret pre-arrangement with the Yugoslav Ambassador, he and a few other close government officials and their families have been invited to seek shelter in just such an emergency. In his attempts to reach Tito, Nagy was informed by the Yugoslav Ambassador that the Soviets might intervene in force once again and he should avoid being taken prisoner. Tito, who regards Nagy as the most suitable Hungarian Communist from the Yugoslav standpoint, would prefer to have him in Yugoslav hands so that he may bargain with the Soviets and get him placed into the new puppet government which he knows the Soviets are about to install. If the Russians were to get Nagy, Tito reasons, Nagy, and all Tito's hopes for a Hungarian regime closer to his own, may simply disappear.

Cardinal Mindszenty Receives Asylum in the U.S. Embassy

Cardinal Mindszenty, who spoke last night from the Parliament building, had gotten to bed only at midnight. He is awakened by a telephone call from Minister Zoltán Tildy, asking him to return to the Parliament building, as the Russians had begun to attack the city and Nagy wants him with the government. As he spoke, the Cardinal could see the ghostly glare of the explosions filling the sky. After seeking shelter in the cellar for a few minutes, the Cardinal thinks better of it, calls his chauffeur and orders him to drive to Parliament.

Soviet tanks are already beginning to race through the city streets, but fortunately the Chain Bridge, which they use to cross over to Pest, has not yet been secured.

In the Parliament building, in addition to Tildy, he encounters Bishop Imre Szabó, István Bibó of the Peasant Party, and the Communist Zoltán Vas. The last tells him, "I will remain on the side of the Hungarian people."

But Mindszenty also finds growing chaos. With no top Army officials around to give orders to the four hundred Hungarian troops and forty tanks defending the building and Nagy nowhere to be found, Tildy decides he must take charge. The fight would be hopeless and hundreds of lives needlessly lost should they try to defend the Parliament. Moreover, the beautiful symbol of Hungarian nationhood would be destroyed. Tildy commands the senior officer to have the tanks hold their fire and prepare to return to their bases and his men put their guns on lock.

But the Cardinal can see no purpose in his presence and wants to return to his Palace to celebrate Sunday mass. By chance he runs into Dr. Egon Turchányi, who has offered to help him during the past several days. They find that the Cardinal's car has been forced away. Walking back to Buda is now impossible, as all bridges are blocked. He inquires which is the nearest foreign embassy. Somebody mentions the American Embassy over on Freedom Square. But how to get out of the building? All of the main entrances to Parliament are now sealed off by the Soviet troops. The Cardinal and Turchányi pull up their cassocks so that they will not be visible under their overcoats and, surrounded by a number of young Hungarians in the building, they slip out a small side entrance not yet under guard. The Square is full of Soviet soldiers, but it is not yet fully light and no one bothers with them.

Turchányi realizes they cannot risk even a momentary rejection by some low level official at the entrance to the U.S. Legation; there are too many Soviet soldiers around who could be attracted to such a scene. Instead of going directly to the Embassy when they enter Freedom Square, therefore, he spies the open lobby of the bank across from the Legation and has the Cardinal and his secretary hide there while he races off to a phone. While the Cardinal waits anxiously, Turchányi opens negotiations with the U.S. Legation on giving refuge to the Cardinal. Admitting foreign nationals to the U.S. Embassy at such a time is strictly against U.S. policy. "Won't he be separated from the Hungarian people?" argues the diplomat on the other end of the line. "No one can separate Cardinal Mindszenty from his people, not even the entire might of the Soviet Empire. In seeking temporary asylum he does so as a last desperate measure!" No one in the Legation, not even the newly arrived Minister, Edward T. Wailes, can make such a momentous decision. Washington must be consulted. Fortunately, the Secretary of State, now hospitalized, is not available to weigh the pros and cons of this decision. His Deputy, Herbert Hoover, Jr., prefers to consult the White House immediately. "Sure," says the President, and back in Budapest Turchányi gets the green light in less than an hour since his first call. An American Army officer now crosses the Square to accompany the Cardinal to his new residence and Minister Wailes welcomes the Cardinal cordially.[4]

Deputy Commander of the National Guard Sándor Kopácsi now arrives at Parliament with a detachment of fifty uniformed police. But he finds Tildy has already made the decision not to try to defend the Parliament. He will surrender the building without putting up armed resistance in return for the

Soviets allowing all of the civilians to leave unharmed. Kopácsi attends a gathering in Tildy's office, where he finds the old man in tears. Besides himself, Sándor Rónai, an old Rákosi supporter, István Dobi, long-time President (a largely symbolic post) of the country, who is well-known as a drunkard, and István Bibó, a former Peasant party member, who joined the government only yesterday, are the only government members still in the building. Rónai and Dobi say they are going to follow Tildy's example and quit the building. But Bibó, a tall, quiet man, who has been studiously typing a document in his small office before he was called to this meeting, declares, "As for me, all I want is that the whole world and all generations to come know what happened in Budapest in 1956. That is my sole task. If you can delay the invasion of Parliament," he adds, looking at Kopácsi, "so much the better. If not, I will continue in the presence of the occupiers."

As soon as the Hungarian troops see Kopácsi and the others emerging from the Parliament without their guns and carrying white flags they cry out in astonishment and rage. Tildy, visibly in tears, is called a coward and worse. "You're not going to make us surrender, are you?" call out soldiers as they throw back the hatches of their tanks. "You're crazy! We'll pass the Russkies through the mill!" But sharp orders are shouted back at them from their commander and as the full weight of it sinks in the soldiers, instead of stacking their arms neatly as they have been commanded, throw them down into a heap, weeping and cursing as they do. They do not wait around to be made captives like the civilians whom they feel have betrayed them. Many, before the end of the day, will find a unit of the Freedom Fighters, where they will offer their services and expertise.

Now the Soviet tanks enter Parliament Square. The lead tank rattles up to the main gate and its turret opens. Out hops a tankman, followed by a Soviet Colonel. With the help of an interpreter this officer finds out where the broadcast room is and goes there on the run. No need to blast the door down, it is open. They can hear Nagy's voice, so to make their entrance more dramatic, they kick the door down anyway. But it is not the head of the Hungarian government that they arrest, it is only his voice. After the Colonel recovers from his initial shock, he walks over and arrests the voice by unplugging the tape recorder. "Where is Imre Nagy?" Nobody knows. The Colonel then sends for the President, István Dobi. A minute later Dobi, red-faced and teetering, shows up. The colonel orders him to sign an act of surrender of the Hungarian Armed forces, which he pulls from his pocket all prepared in Russian and Hungarian. Dobi, pulling himself up and with all the dignity that he can muster, says, "If the representative of the Soviet Union wishes to speak with me, I will be at his disposal in my office." With that he turns on his heels and walks, as steadily as he can manage, out the door.[5]

A Message from Ferenc Münnich

Almost two hours earlier, before the barrage has startled the citizens of Budapest awake, a Soviet officer somewhere in the countryside switches on a recording made two or three days ago by Ferenc Münnich. It is broadcast on the wavelength frequency usually occupied by the Balatonszabadi transmitter, which normally broadcasts Hungary's foreign language programs, so few Hungarians hear it. The officer is just following orders. Nobody has told him that the head of the new Soviet-appointed government will be Kádár. He was told it was to be Münnich. So at 5:05 a.m. RFE monitors in Germany pick up the following:

> This is a statement by Ferenc Münnich:
> An open letter to the Hungarian working people: compatriots, our worker and peasant comrades, we the undersigned, Antal Apró, János Kádár, István Kossa and Ferenc Münnich, former Ministers in the Imre Nagy government, announce that on November 1, 1956 we broke our relations with this Government, left this government and took the initiative of forming the Hungarian Revolutionary Worker-Peasant Government....
> Respected champions of the working class movement have been murdered—Imre Mező...Comrade Kalmár...Sándor Sziklai. In addition many, many respected sons of the working class and peasantry have been exterminated.
> As members of the government we could no longer watch idly...while, under the cover of democracy, counter-revolutionary terrorists and bandits are bestially murdering our workers...and dragging our country into anarchy....We have decided to fight with all our strength against the threatening danger of Fascism and reaction....

Fifty-five minutes later, the broadcast which *was* supposed to announce to the world the new Russian-appointed government is made over Radio Szolnok:

> Attention! Attention! This is Comrade János Kádár speaking:
> The Hungarian Revolutionary Worker-Peasant Government has been formed....The composition of the government is the following: Premier,

János Kádár; Deputy Premier, Dr. Ferenc Münnich, [also] Minister of the Armed Forces and of Public Security; Minister of State, György Marosán; Minister of Finance. István Kossa; Foreign Minister, Imre Horváth; Minister of Agriculture, Imre Dögei; Minister of Industry, Antal Apró; Minister of Commerce, Sándor Rónai.

This will come as news to comrade Rónai, as he is at this moment in the Parliament building and still a member of the Nagy government.

There follows a long list of Rákosi era ills, which the new government aims to correct, most of which the Nagy government has already corrected, and then a list of fifteen points of the new government's program.

István Bibó's Press Conference

While the Soviet troops make a point of occupying the Duna Hotel hoping thereby to put a muzzle on the foreign journalists, most of whom are staying there, it will be many days before the Soviets manage to get control of the telephone system, which is still operating perfectly. Thus, István Bibó is able to get out the word that he is holding a press conference in the Parliament building for the foreign journalists at 10:30. Ambassador Andropov, whose press secretary is among those invited, strongly advises as many Western journalists as he can reach "not to attend."

Bibó knows exactly what he wants to tell the press. This tall, rather scholarly looking man, who only days ago was a professor at the University of Szeged, has it all typed out and copies are available to those who want them. As the only legal member of the Nagy government still in his place—and he will remain in the Parliament building until November sixth, when he finally goes home—Bibó has this to say to the world:

> In this situation I state that Hungary has no intention of following an anti-Soviet policy. I reject the slander that fascist or anti-Semitic actions have stained the glorious Hungarian Revolution. The entire Hungarian nation has participated in it, without class or religious discrimination.
>
> The attitude of the people who rose up was moving and wonderful. They turned only against the oppressing foreign army and against their gangs of henchmen.
>
> My orders to the Hungarian nation are not to consider the occupying army or the puppet government to be set up by this army as legal authorities and to use all weapons of passive resistance against them.

I am not in a position to give orders for armed resistance. I joined the government only one day ago and it would be irresponsible on my part to allow that the precious blood of the Hungarian youth should flow further. The people of Hungary have sacrificed enough blood to show the world their tenacious attachment to freedom and justice. Now it is the turn of the world powers.

It is my conviction that now when the liberation of East European countries has almost been realized, in this historical moment, the only means by which world peace can be insured is by taking the risk of a world war. On the other hand, deferring the decision endangers the policy of the free world and makes certain the outbreak of a world war at a later date, just as was the case in the past two instances when Western isolationist tendencies and the policy of appeasement towards the aggressor prevailed.

I appeal to the great powers of the world for a wise and courageous decision in the interest of my enslaved nation and of the liberty of all East European nations. God preserve Hungary....

The Soviet Blitzkrieg Appears to Take Budapest

There is no doubt that the Soviet invasion has caught everyone off guard. The majority of Hungarian Army units are surrounded and disarmed in their barracks. Those who attempt to fight are quickly overpowered. While those in entrenched positions in the outskirts put up a stiff fight, there is little they can do to answer the heavy bombardments from artillery, rockets and military aircraft. Sheer numbers of shells and enemy troops overwhelm them in a few hours of fighting in the suburbs of the city, though in a few places the Soviets pay a high price in losses.

There are other reasons why the Soviet attack goes so smoothly. Many soldiers, following the command of their officers even before the Soviet troops arrive, lay down their arms and simply go home. More devastating, treachery on the part of high military officials in the Hungarian Army has seen to it that just before most of their numerous artillery pieces are put in place at the head of major avenues they are rendered useless by having their breach blocks removed.[6]

Around 6:30 a.m., two hours after the bombardment had begun, the shelling suddenly stops. But the noise of tank treads rattling on cobblestones can be heard in most sections of the city, as can the dull explosions of tank cannons and rat-at-tatting of machine gun fire. More and more tanks converge on the center, where most of the important installations are located. By now all bridges are in Soviet hands, as are all government buildings, including now the Parliament building.

K.G.B. General K.Y. Grebennyik, in command of this new assault on the Hungarian capital—the third such Soviet assault in twelve years—has deliberately avoided attacking Freedom Fighter groups in Széna Square, the Castle, the Corvin Cinema Passage and Kilián Barracks so he can concentrate on obliterating the current government and taking full control of the city. He is convinced that once the Freedom Fighters see their cause is hopeless, it will only be a day or two before they, too, surrender. Meanwhile, "Operation Whirlwind" is going like clockwork.

At eight a.m. he issues an ultimatum to the Nagy Government. If the city of Budapest does not surrender in four hours, that is, at 12:00 noon, the city will be bombed.[7]

Fritz Molden, the Austrian editor who has driven from Vienna with gamma globulin for the polio victims in Miskolc, realizes he and Eugene-Géza Pogány can never make it there today, or possibly ever. He locates a delegate of the International Red Cross Mr. Povey, who is also staying at the Duna Hotel, and hands the gamma globulin to him; Mr. Povey says he will try to get it to Miskolc, but if he cannot, he will see that it is used in Budapest. Indeed, not only typhus, but also polio epidemics will break out in the capital later in the month.[8]

Aside from moving Soviet tanks, the streets are empty, and aside from occasional explosions in the distance or a rattle of small arms nearby, an oppressive silence begins to reign over the city. It is the lull before the storm.

One of the last government installations to fall is the MTI (Hungarian Telegraph Agency) building in Buda with some 225 people in it, fifty of whom are women. One teletype operator gets on the line to the Associated Press in Vienna, and from 5:30 until almost 11:00 a.m. when the line is cut, gives a running account of what he thinks is going on. Excerpts from the complete four-hour record will appear in the *London Times* and the *New York Times* tomorrow morning.

Shortly after 11:00, in a massive attack, the Russians take the building with a great loss of life among the defenders.

The re-occupation of Budapest may have gone like clockwork but now the lull is over. Fighting breaks out in nearly every sector of the city, for Freedom Fighters who had gone to spend Sunday at home have now had time, by whatever devious routes they had been forced to follow, to reach their assigned stations. And certain Hungarian Army units are still fighting. Around ten o'clock the 51st anti-aircraft artillery unit, for instance, firing from Juta Hill, breaks up a Soviet military column by destroying two tanks, two rocket launchers and a truck, killing eleven Soviet soldiers and three guides (former ÁVO officers) and wounding ten more in the process. The rest of the soldiers in the column abandon their vehicles and flee.[9] Mark Molnár, leading a group of twenty partisans on Castle Hill, notices that the Soviet columns are using the 390-yard tunnel under the hill to reach the Chain Bridge, to which it leads directly. Collecting all the hand grenades they can carry, they hide themselves just above the neo-classic archway with its Doric columns and simply drop grenade after grenade as the Soviet vehicles emerge from the tunnel one after the other. Eleven armed vehicles are destroyed in this manner before the Soviets see where the grenades are coming from and counter-attack.[10]

Attacks Around the Country

Békéscsaba in the southeast is taken in the early morning, although shots from the Revolutionary Council building kill a few Soviet soldiers.

The assault on Székesfehérvár comes even earlier than that on Budapest. The invading forces shoot up the Army command, the officer's mess and the town and county office buildings, as well as the post office. A wounded Freedom Fighter and a surrendering soldier are both executed with a shot to the head. Hungarian soldiers who line up to open fire are given the order not to do so, and Soviet tanks crush cannons captured earlier by civilians before they can be used.

In Szombathely, where the battle also started at 4.00 a.m., around a dozen Hungarians, mostly in the new National Guard, lost their lives, and members of the National Committee were quickly rounded up by Soviet soldiers with ex-ÁVO men directing them.

In Kaposvár, where seven Hungarians were killed, it took thirty-five Soviet tanks and many infantry to take over the prison and the former Party headquarters occupied by Freedom Fighters.

In Miskolc the few students in the National Guard who are on duty fire on Soviet troops as they take over the university in the pre-dawn invasion. Caught in a Soviet crossfire, two students are killed and three more wounded. Soviet troops meantime open fire without warning on the barracks of the second air defense unit, which has been neutral during the revolution, killing one soldier in his sleep.[11]

Western Legations

Both the British and American legations have managed to send their dependents out of Hungary via convoys of private cars, though the fate of the twice-stopped American convoy is still in doubt. The British wisely took the shorter route to Komárom on the Slovak border, avoiding the more trouble-some Austrian border, and thence to Bratislava and out to Vienna. Today the Austrian Minister Peinsipp cleverly turns the last Red Cross convoy from Austria, the Styrian—which arrived only last night with medicine and food—into an outgoing convoy to get his Austrian citizens and dependents out. The convoy departs only at 7:30, three hours after the Soviet onslaught begins. Still, they succeed in avoiding all Russians, thanks to those red cross-es and their Embassy guide, Herr Lipsch, who knows how to navigate all the small back roads through Buda and the suburbs. They manage to go via small country roads, and some fields, all the way to Komárom without being stopped. Herr Lipsch even manages to return to the Legation in the evening to tell his tale.[12]

Taking their place in the legations are journalists and other nationals who have not managed, or did not try, to get out. More arrive from hotels during lulls in the fighting today. The British, who have quite a few subjects who are permanent residents of Budapest, have done their best to bring these in, but many of the older ones prefer their apartments in Buda. The Americans do not have this problem. Both legations, however, have a strict policy about not allowing foreign nationals shelter, particularly locals, lest it lead to major complications. Today both legations turn down requests for shelter from many foreign journalists and not a few Hungarians by sticking to this poli-cy. The French and Italians are far more liberal.

Fritz Molden, staying with some fifty other Western journalists in the Duna Hotel, is advised by Austrian Minister Peinsipp that he and the twelve other Austrian journalists and chauffeurs should seek shelter in some other Western legation for the time being. When traffic across the bridges is again allowed, they should of course come over to the Austrian Legation. Michel Cordy, a French journalist, says that he feels staying at the Duna is soon going to become untenable; the Soviets are all around the hotel and there has been some fierce fighting nearby. He intends to go to the French Legation across Stalin (formerly Andrássy) Avenue near the Soviet Embassy at Bajza Street where there are lots of tanks and very little fighting. He invites his fellow Austrian, West German, and Dutch journalists to come with him. Then, when Austrian Socialist MP Peter Strasser turns up blustering that he has been turned away from both the U.S. and the British legations, even though he was caught in a firefight, he extends the invitation to him, as well.

Avoiding all the main streets, the convoy of journalists' cars makes its way past dozens of Soviet tanks and through some gunfire to Stalin Avenue, arriving at the French Legation on Lendvay Street unhindered about 11:00 a.m. Legation Counselor Quiock and Military Attaché de la Geneste are most gracious about letting all of these strangers in. As they do so, they politely let them know that there is no food. This, of course, is an exaggeration, but with all of these new mouths to feed, it will soon become a reality. Minister Jean Paul Boncour is stuck at his residence in Buda, but he knows of this foreign "invasion" of his legation.

Peter Strasser and Molden decide to take a walk in the early afternoon and are repeatedly stopped by heavily armed Hungarian patrols. These tell them that the fighting has been intense at the Corvin Passage and Kilián Barracks, where there are over four thousand Freedom Fighters dug in. They also hear that a large ammunition depot near the Western Station has been broken into and trucks are now carting arms off to the fighting areas. On Arena Ave. they see a steady procession of trucks filled with uniformed soldiers and armed Freedom Fighters all headed for the Ninth District, where the fighting is taking place. Some of the trucks, he is told, are actually headed for Buda across the Stalin Bridge, which the Soviets have not yet taken. It is obvious to the two Austrians that the area all around the French Embassy, even near the Soviet Embassy, is completely under the control of the Hungarians.

Soviet aircraft are still flying low overhead, but they are not dropping bombs but leaflets in Hungarian urging the Hungarians to surrender. Bombs, however, are falling on the citadel atop Gellért Hill in Buda, for while the Soviets, thanks to treachery in the Hungarian Army, had no trouble taking it this morning, it has been retaken by the Hungarians for its strategic importance.

In the American Legation on Freedom Square, only two blocks from the Parliament building, officials have very little idea of what is going on. One reason for this is that the shades have been pulled down and in the downstairs room where most people have congregated around the radio teletype machine, safes have been pushed up against the windows to prevent stray bullets from entering. Having had such extremely poor contact with the State Department throughout the Revolution, this new radio teletype is an exciting luxury and they keep the line open to Washington all day long.

An open line sometimes leads to trivial conversation, but from time to time Minister Wailes himself and Ambassador Beam and others of high rank are also conversing. About 6:00 a.m. Wailes tells the Department that they have sufficient reports of the Soviet attack to start the destruction of their priority material, that is, their secret documents, to prevent the Russians from capturing them.

There follows a conversation of sorts in which it is clear that the main concern of the legation is the fate of the American convoy of family dependents, whereas the Department is most interested is seeing that Wailes is properly accredited to the Nagy government. Ambassador Beam in Washington suggests Wailes present his credentials "immediately, if this is feasible and desirable." Wailes replies that "at the moment" he doubts "if I could find the gentleman on whom I should call, even if I could navigate the streets." As Wailes and others try to convey what they are going through—"a few jets just flew overhead, but no immediate street fighting"—the Department fills the Legation in with such exciting tidbits of news as that Lodge himself has been the one to break the news to the UN about the Soviet attack, and later that Lodge is calling a special meeting of the Security Council. At one point Wailes breaks off because "a Hungarian State Minister has just rung our doorbell" so goes off "to see what he has on his mind." A few minutes later Wailes is back, saying, "he is one of the ones appointed yesterday. Will give you his name in a few minutes." (The Minister, of course, is István Bibó, delivering in person a message he wants sent directly to President Eisenhower.) Wailes does not know what it says, since it is in Hungarian, but the message will be transmitted in "takes" as it gets translated. Here, in part, is what Bibó writes:

> Hungary...will be defeated if it does not receive help. In this moment the most necessary kind of help is political, not military. It is clear that the new phase of the USSR's intentions is related to the British intervention in Egypt....Both President Eisenhower and Secretary Dulles...in earlier speeches said that only by risking a world war can a sure way be found to

avert the outbreak of a new world war. Eisenhower [should] call on the Soviet Union to quickly withdraw its troops from Hungary....

We strongly emphasize that in this moment the fate of Eastern Europe and the entire world depends on the action of the President; the next few critical days will determine whether we enter on a path of peace and liberation or whether we shall increase the appetite of aggression and proceed to a certain world catastrophe.

The teletype conversation then resumes. Wailes promises to try to get for Lodge as much accurate information on the "Soviet build-up as possible," as though today were suddenly several days ago and not November 4 in the middle of the Soviet onslaught.

Messages about Cardinal Mindszenty's request for asylum are interspersed with operator chitchat and when the Cardinal is admitted the first thing the Department wants is for Wailes to get a "statement" from him. In due course they get it. The Cardinal is appropriately terse: "I protest against this aggression," he says, "and ask for the forceful and speedy defense of my country from the USA and other powers."

Having given asylum to Mindszenty, and later to Dr Turchányi, the Legation is faced with the demand from American journalists seeking shelter in the Legation that they be allowed to bring their interpreters and foreign assistants with them. At first the answer is "no," but then the Legation relents and says it is all right to bring foreign nationals so long as they are not Hungarian.

Then it appears that Béla Kovács, the Smallholder Minister of State, may be seeking asylum, and Deputy Under Secretary Murphy approves this, though it never occurs. Most difficult to decide is the case of the permanent AP correspondent, Endre Márton, who is a Hungarian not long out of a Rákosi jail, and his wife, Ilona, who is the UP stringer, which is to say a non-salaried, but fully accredited journalist, who may or may not have a retainer, and is paid by the article. Wailes is inclined to take in this couple and their two children and asks the Department to leave it up to his judgment, which they do.[13] They are an exceedingly attractive family: he has the looks of a matinée idol, she is young and beautiful and their two daughters, Julja (eight) and Kati,* (six) are charming. As it turns out, they stay only ten days before returning to their home in Buda.

*Today the famous American writer, Kati Marton.

Sir Leslie Fry, having managed to get his civilians and dependents out of the country, is concentrating on reporting to the Foreign Office what is going on. With many more Hungarian sources than the Americans have, he is able to report on the size and nature of the assault, what appears to be happening to the Nagy government, and the Soviet ultimatum shortly after it is announced. He also passes on that his Dutch counterpart has been watching, from his villa in Buda, Soviet bombers dropping bombs just west of the railroad station in Csepel. Sir Leslie will relent later on his policy of excluding foreign nationals from the legation. "I am taking…such Commonwealth citizens, families of Hungarian staff and members of our domestic staff as are presenting themselves. I shall also take any wounded who may appear," he tells the Foreign Office.[14]

United Nations, New York

About 1:13 a.m. New York time (7:13 a.m. Budapest time), Australian Representative Ronald Walker interrupts the General Assembly debate on Suez on a point of order and brings the first news of the Soviet attack by reading a Reuters news bulletin from Budapest. "…In view of this news," he says, "I am now asking the President of the Security Council to invite members…to meet with him within half an hour in his office…regarding the next steps…to be taken by the Security Council."

Some twenty minutes later, American Ambassador Lodge rises, also on a point of order, to repeat what Walker has said, only he quotes from an Associated Press dispatch. He adds that the American Legation in Budapest was under fire (not true) and the staff sheltering in the basement (an exaggeration). Lodge is pale and shaking with indignation. He is genuinely shocked at the news and feels a sense of humiliation at having been betrayed by the Soviet delegate, Sobolev, who had cynically talked of bloodshed in Egypt when he knew his country was about to shed a great deal more in Hungary. Playing to the gallery he now says, "I simply want to say in this great General Assembly of the United Nations how much our hearts go out to the people of Hungary, and with how much warmth and feeling we think of them, and wish for them a happy issue out of their trials, and a future of independence."

When the Assembly adjourns at 3:00 a.m. and the Security Council starts up just five minutes later, Lodge opens his speech with the dramatic words:

A few minutes ago, we received word of the appeal of the Prime Minister of

Hungary while his city was burning. Budapest, according to his own radio broadcast, is surrounded by a thousand Soviet tanks firing phosphorus shells to burn it out. We can hear the Hungarian National Anthem playing. It ends with the words: "Here is where you live….And here is where you die…." If ever there was a time when action in the United Nations could literally be a matter of life or death to a whole nation, this is clearly that time. If ever there was a situation which threatened the peace of the world, this is that situation.

Lodge now does what he could easily have done four or five days ago. He rams his resolution through the Security Council in only two hours. This time he welcomes the inevitable Soviet veto he had claimed it was so important to avoid before. But in his rush he quite forgets that the situation has greatly changed since he tabled his resolution. The Nationalist Chinese delegate is too diplomatic to point this out, but he suggests an amendment that refers to the actual Soviet aggression, which Lodge quickly accepts.

After a successful vote to move the matter to the General Assembly, Lodge declares, "We can truly say to the Hungarian people that by your heroic sacrifice you have given the United Nations a brief moment in which to mobilize the conscience of the world on your behalf. We are seizing that moment and we shall not fail you." This brings applause from the gallery. But to others, who understand the workings of the United Nations, and who realize that Lodge, by his delaying actions over the past week, has already failed Hungary miserably, these words ring hollow.

By the time Lodge puts forth a resolution in the 5:00 p.m. General Assembly's special meeting on Hungary, the resolution is entirely different from the one just passed in the Security Council. References are made to Nagy's radio appeal to the world earlier today, to his messages to the UN of November 1 and 2, to the Soviet Declaration of October 30, and to "the grave loss of life and widespread bloodshed among the Hungarian people" now being caused by Soviet forces.

Then, in addition to calling on the Soviet Union to "desist forthwith from all armed attack," it calls on the Secretary General "to investigate the situation by sending observers named by him as soon as possible"; calls upon the Soviet and Hungarian governments to "permit these observers…to enter the territory of Hungary"; and requests the Secretary General "to inquire, on an urgent basis, into the needs of the Hungarian people for food, medicine and other similar supplies and to report to the Security Council as soon as possible."

In this first-ever General Assembly session on Hungary, the American resolution condemning the Soviet Union and asking her to withdraw her troops at once passes, after only four hours of speeches, by a vote of fifty to eight, with fifteen countries abstaining.[15]

János Kádár, supposed Premier of the new five-man puppet government, is not even in Hungary; he is still in Uzhgorod (Hungarian: Ungvár) in the Soviet Ukraine. Yet a message is composed over his signature with today's date stating that "Imre Nagy's requests to the United Nations to have the Hungarian question discussed in the United Nations have no legal force and cannot be considered as requests emanating from Hungary as a state. The Revolutionary Workers and Peasants Government objects categorically to any discussion of the said question either by the Security Council or by the General Assembly...."[16] Because this message is only circulated at the UN on November 7, it probably was written and transmitted only on the sixth or seventh and thus was falsely pre-dated to the fourth. UN delegates tend to take it at face value as a regular government communication, particularly when circulated on UN stationary. They have no idea that the real authors of the note are Russians and that the Kádár "government" on November 4 consists of five Soviet puppets.

Battles around Budapest

From ten o'clock on, fighting breaks out around each of the three main railroad stations, at Széna Square and Zsigmond Móricz Square, the citadel on Gellért Hill and the Castle—all in Buda—and along the Grand Boulevard in Pest which curves around from Oktagon circle on Stalin Avenue all the way to Boráros Square on the river. This time, however, the patriots are up against the Red Army's elite units, far more disciplined and efficient than the occupation troops they faced in October, and far more ruthless. Many, in fact, are Mongolian troops who have been told that the Danube is the Suez Canal.[17]

Over the next few days as the fighting progresses the percentage of former criminals in the ranks of the Freedom Fighters becomes more pronounced. Knowing that if captured alive, long prison terms or even execution await them, many choose fighting until death as the preferable option.

By far the heaviest fighting, however, is where the eighth and ninth districts meet in Pest near the Corvin Cinema Passage off the Grand Boulevard and the Kilián Barracks on Üllői Ave. Here the fighting begins almost at dawn when a Soviet tank discovers that the Hungarian tank parked at the strategically important corner of Kisfaludy Street and Üllői Ave is unoccupied and pulls up next to it. One Hungarian leader blames another for sending the tank occupants to bed at 2:00 a.m. He, in turn, is blamed for having allowed so many to go home on Saturday, so that those who are left have to work doubly long shifts. Unfortunately for the Freedom Fighters, this corner gives a clear view down Üllői Ave to the Grand Boulevard, and also down Kisfaludy Street to the Prater Street School on the far side of Prater Street. All of the Corvin Passage reinforcements, mostly children under twenty, are billeted in the Prater Street School. In order to reach the Corvin Passage they must go above ground across the street. Now every time they try, the heavy machine gun on the tank mows them down, littering the street with dead and dying children. And the tank is out of range of molotov cocktails.

János Mesz, known as "Peg-Leg," a middle-aged criminal with a wooden leg, who is now beloved of his fellow fighters, tries his best to wheel his small anti-tank gun around between the tank's firings to knock it out. Instead the tank is too quick and shoots an all-too-accurate shell, smashing the gun with a frightful explosion. When the smoke drifts away "Peg-leg" and his two young companions are twisted motionless on the ground. "Peg-Leg," still breathing, is dragged out of the line of fire, but will die of his wounds in a hospital on November nineteenth. Several more attempts are made to cross over with the same devastating result. After about half an hour the Soviet tank suddenly bursts into flame. Someone has smashed through about ten attic walls to get to the tank and then finished it off with a shower of molotov cocktails. Now all the youngsters still left in the Prater Street School rush across the street, picking up their wounded as they do. Fourteen of their comrades lie dead. Of the original four hundred youngsters who gathered at the Prater School on October 24, only one hundred are left. Tamás Szabó, who had spent Saturday at home, is one of these. After Iván-Kovács has assigned them positions and told them not to leave them unless ordered to, he calls out, "Hold tight, boys! It is only a matter of hours before the UN troops arrive!"[18]

By now shells are crashing into all of the buildings in the area, the noise is earsplitting and acrid smoke obstructs almost everyone's view. This time it is not just tanks coming through the smoke, but platoons of disciplined Soviet infantry. The battle rages until two p.m. when the Soviet forces withdraw to regroup. The Corvin Passage fighters have sustained fifty-three dead and are sending twenty-three of their wounded to the hospital, but they have smashed and burned six Soviet tanks and killed or wounded a whole regiment of Soviet soldiers. In the Kilián Barracks, which, because of its size, has taken even more hits from artillery and tank shells, the statistics are similar.

At Tűzoltó Street, one block closer to the river from the Kilián Barracks, the Freedom Fighters are in buildings with much thinner walls. The artillery and tank barrage causes so much destruction that the fighters there decide to leave in pairs, with others firing at different positions along the street to distract attention from those escaping. They vow they will all meet up again at Tűzoltó Street tonight, but when the time comes, only a few manage to get back.[19]

The Tűzoltó Street fighters and those in Tompa Street next door do not fight from fixed positions, but move around a lot, quite like Uncle Szabó's group in Széna Square. They have smashed through cellar walls all the way from the Kilián Barracks to Nagyvárad Square, where Soviet tanks tend to congregate before an attack, a distance of over five hundred meters. They only have to come up at street intersections. They have also been training for this day ever since the fighting stopped on October 28.

By the end of the day Budapest is far from the subdued city it appeared to be at eight o'clock this morning, and the Soviets have taken far greater casualties in men and tanks than they expected. They are, however, once again in control of the citadel, and from the top of Gellért Hill they are able to lob heavy artillery shells into whatever section of the city they want to, something which they had not wished nor attempted to do during their first intervention.

A Message from Radio Free Europe

Radio Free Europe, while largely ignored during the days of freedom, has again acquired many more listeners as the situation grows grimmer. Today a great many people are listening, and, because there are only Czechoslovak jamming stations trying to jam the broadcasts and jamming has not yet restarted on Hungarian soil, people in Budapest and other cities can hear it quite clearly. Now they are treated to a short review of world press reaction to what is happening in Hungary.

Announcer: "We have already reported several times that Western radio stations interrupt their broadcasts in order to report about Hungarian events. In

London, Paris, Washington and everywhere in the free countries the news of the Soviet attack has caused immense indignation....The Italian papers *Il Tempo* and *Il Messagero* and the *British Evening Standard*, for example, had special editions. The three Paris radio stations publicize proclamations for help for the Hungarians. The French radios emphasize that all Europe is looking toward the UN with anxiety. The General Assembly will meet tonight in order to discuss the Hungarian situation. Radio Stockholm says that the General Assembly of the UN will have to use sanctions against the Soviet Union. This morning the *British Observer* publishes a report of its Washington correspondent. This situation report was written before the Soviet attack early this morning. In spite of this, the *Observer* correspondent writes that the Russians have probably decided to beat down the Hungarian Revolution with arms. The article goes on: "If the Soviet troops really attack Hungary, if this...should become true and the Hungarians hold out for three or four days, then the pressure upon the government of the U.S to send military help to the Freedom Fighters will become irresistible."

This is what the paper writes in today's number. The paper observes that the American Congress cannot vote for war as long as the presidential elections have not been held. The article continues:

"If the Hungarians continue to fight until Wednesday, we shall be closer to a world war than at any time since 1939...."

The apparent message of this broadcast—that if the Freedom Fighters can just hold out until Wednesday, the day after the American election, the West will surely come in to save them—ignites, like cooking gas, new hope in every Hungarian who hears of it, but especially the young people who know nothing of the outside world.[20]

Freedom Radios[21]

While Budapest has never had more Western newspaper correspondents in it, the Soviets, by cutting off the Austrian border and cutting the phone and teletype lines and even air traffic to the West, have managed to smother Hungary under a fog of silence. None of those seasoned members of the fourth estate are able to get a word of this dramatic story out to their readers. Hungarian radios, however, are still operating. Out of this fog the world has already heard the voice of Premier Imre Nagy telling exactly what was happening early this morning. For the rest of the day, Radio Free Europe and others broadcasting into Hungary glean the Hungarian airwaves as best they can and report these desperate messages addressed to the outside world. Some sample messages follow.

7:00 a.m. Trans-Danubian Free Military Radio

Announcement that the Soviet troops pushing into Budapest have imprisoned the Nagy government.

"…All Budapest bridges have been occupied by Soviet troops, Újpest has fallen. The Army units and Freedom Fighters at Csepel continue to hold out. Soviet light bombers continue to enter the southern area of Trans-Danubia. Soviet armored units and artillery assisted by the air force are heavily attacking the bridge at Dunaföldvár."

8:00 a.m. Reports that Soviet and Hungarian troops are fighting between Miskolc, and Helyőcsaba, and that the Soviet Air Force has started to use incendiary bombs.

"The revolutionary council of the Miskolc Garrison Troops has declared a state of siege for the city. A Hungarian air bomber unit has started a big attack against Soviet troops crossing the Tisza….The miners of Pécs have armed themselves and have joined the Army troops fighting the Soviets…."

8:30 a.m. Reports that Soviet paratroops have landed in the Almásfüzitő area and that Soviet paratroopers have occupied the industrial plants of Győr and the radio station at Balatonszabadi.

Radio Free Dunapentele

6:30 a.m. "…The situation is serious but not hopeless. Our anti-aircraft artillery has been put into action all along the line. The fight against the intruder is raging everywhere! Hungarians, do not let the Russian troops carry out a massacre in our beloved country! Take your arms and stand united for…the defense of our country….The Dunapentele garrison troops will hold out to the last man. Death to the Soviet occupiers!"

"…Doctors, nurses and hospital workers, report immediately to your places in the hospital. Soldiers and civilians who know how to handle guns should come immediately to the Béla Bartók House of Culture. Those under eighteen and over sixty-one should immediately return to their homes…."

Radio Free Győr

10:00 a.m. Reports that the miners of Tatabánya, aided by Hungarian Army units, are advancing between Tatabánya and Budapest and that the

Tatabánya-Budapest railroad line, used for Soviet reinforcements, has been broken through at two points near Szár.

Unidentified Free Radio (Location Unknown)

12:34 p.m. "Civilized people of the world, listen and come to our aid, not with declarations, but with force, with soldiers and arms. Do not forget that there is no stopping the wild onslaught of Bolshevism. Your turn will also come, once we perish. Save our souls! Save our souls!

"Peoples of Europe whom we helped for centuries to withstand the barbaric attacks from Asia, listen to the tolling of Hungarian bells warning against disaster….Civilized people of the world, we implore you to help us in the name of justice, of freedom, of the binding moral principle of active solidarity. Our ship is sinking. Light is failing, the shadows grow darker every hour over the soil of Hungary. Listen to the cry, civilized people of the world, and act; extend to us your fraternal hand.

"SOS, SOS—may God be with you."

Radio [Free] Rákóczi

1:35 p.m. "…This is the Hungarian Army radio called Radio Rákóczi."

"If you are receiving our broadcasts, acknowledge to Radio Rákóczi. We are breaking off for we are in immediate danger!"

"We ask urgently for immediate help!"

"Free Europe! Free Europe! Acknowledge broadcasts of Radio Rákóczi!"

Unidentified Free Radio (Location Unknown)

12:00 p.m. "We ask Radio Free Europe to indicate the wavelengths and frequencies of the other Hungarian radio stations without naming the place…."

Radio Free Vác

12:32 p.m. "Attention, Radio Free Europe, attention! We request immediate information. Is help coming from the West?"

Radio [Free] Csokonai

2:20 p.m. "We request Radio Free Europe to relay immediately the following message to the Secretary General of the UN:

"Appeal to the Secretary General of the UN…

"Since the only legal Hungarian government, that of Imre Nagy, has been imprisoned, and since that was the only organ which represented the official attitude of the Hungarian nation, in the name of our country we ask that the UN, by every possible means, pass a final resolution for the restitution and the protection of the liberty which we had already once won.

"We now address a message to the delegates of the UN member States:

"In the coming hours you will decide the life or the death of this nation. While your sons are at peace and happy, we sons of the Hungarian nation are falling under the cruel fire of Soviet tanks and bombers. We turn to you for you are the last citadel of hope.

"Exercise the opportunity which our nation has given you and save our country from destruction and slavery! We are asking for immediate and effective help....Show that the UN can carry out its will, and by its resolution make it possible for our country again to be free...."

All of the above broadcasts are in Hungarian. RFE's sole Hungarian-speaking American, Bill Rademaekers, has joined Hungarians on the RFE staff in attempting to monitor all of the Hungarian radio broadcasts, both those of the "free" stations and those now under control of the Soviets.

Rademaekers has been working night and day for two weeks and is at the point of exhaustion. He learned his Hungarian at the Army Language School at Monterey, California, a few years ago. Still in his twenties, he remains fluent. But it is not his native language and having listened steadily for twelve hours his head is reeling. Suddenly through the ether he hears a voice in clear American-accented English, "Four score and seven years ago our fathers brought forth upon this continent a new nation conceived in liberty and dedicated to the proposition that all men are created equal...." It is too much. As he listens Rademaekers begins to shake. Soon his shaking is uncontrollable and he breaks down, blubbering and cursing. He has reached the end of his tether. And yet the calm voice in his headphones goes on: "the brave men living and dead have consecrated it far beyond our poor power to add or detract...." Rademaekers tears off his headset and staggers out of the radio booth. He needs air; he needs to lie down so he can stop shaking.

President Eisenhower Secretly Decides
No UN Force for Hungary

In Washington, Acting Secretary of State Herbert Hoover Jr. rushes over to the White House for an emergency meeting with the President. When his aide, Joseph N. Greene, gets back to the State Department he dictates the following memorandum:

November 4, 1956
Hungary
a. A statement by the President was approved for release by Mr. Hagerty.
b. A letter from the President to Premier Bulganin was approved.
c. The text of a resolution to be introduced at the 4:00 p.m. session of the Special Session of the General Assembly was approved and telephoned to New York.
d. A Departmental text of a speech for Ambassador Lodge was also telephoned to New York.
e. It was decided there should be no UN force for Hungary.
Joseph N. Greene[22]

Later in the afternoon, the White House releases the text of a cable which President Eisenhower has just sent to Marshal Nikolai Bulganin, Chairman of the Council of Ministers, the senior government, as opposed to Party, position in the Soviet Union.

Referring to the Declaration of the Soviet Government of October 30, which he had so praised in his recent speech, Eisenhower says,

we have been inexpressibly shocked by the apparent reversal of this policy. It is especially shocking that this renewed application of force against the Hungarian Government and people took place while negotiations were going on between your representatives and those of the Hungarian Government for the withdrawal of Soviet forces....

I urge in the name of humanity and in the cause of peace that the Soviet Union take action to withdraw Soviet forces from Hungary immediately...

It is my hope that your representative [in the United Nations] will be in a position to announce at the Session today that the Soviet Union is preparing to withdraw its forces from that country and to allow the Hungarian people to enjoy the right to a government of their own choice.

The cable, though signed by the President, has been drafted by Herbert Hoover, Jr.[23]

Monday, November 5, 1956

In the United States the editorial writers, lacking firsthand reports from Western correspondents in Hungary, are already writing Hungary and its

Revolution off. "The day, at least, seems lost in Hungary," writes the *Washington Post*, "and the reimposition of the Communist terror there in full force may tend to deter independence movements in other parts of the Soviet satellite empire." "The anti-Communist rebellion, after a brief hour of victory, appears to have been destroyed by Russian steel," writes the *New York Telegram and Sun*, "leaving the Kremlin and a clique of Budapest puppets in full control of the country."

In reality the "clique of Budapest puppets," Kádár, Münnich and three others, are in control of nothing and are nowhere near Budapest, which they dare not attempt to enter for another three days. They are not even in control of their own radio, which is composed and managed from Moscow, though the broadcasts are coming from the town of Szolnok and the Balatonszabadi transmitter. Proof of this comes when the exact same news stories in both Hungarian and Russian are broadcast from Radio Moscow fifteen minutes before they appear on "Radio Kossuth." As for the Revolution being "destroyed by Russian steel," this would be news to all of the Soviet infantrymen who are dropping like flies on Üllői Avenue today, choosing to take their chances against withering fire from Hungarian patriots rather than be shot by their own officers, as they have seen happen.

The hour-and-a-half long artillery barrage, which begins from Soviet batteries atop Gellért Hill at 6:00 this morning, is even more intense and destructive than all of yesterday's shelling. Every main center of nationalist resistance around the city is hit, but the biggest concentration of fire is on the Corvin Passage and Kilián Barracks. Through captured Soviet officers the Freedom Fighters learn of this coming barrage in time to vacate most of the buildings. Most take shelter in the cellar of the Prater Street School and other cellars in the neighborhood. As soon as the shelling ceases, many take up positions on those portions of the buildings that are still standing, in preparation for the tank and infantry attack. The Soviets, confident that no one could survive such a heavy bombardment, are astounded to find such resistance and take heavy casualties in infantry and even lose some more tanks to molotov cocktails.

Back at the Kilián Barracks there are just too many Russians, and the attack is continuous. Soon those few Freedom Fighters and soldiers still in the barracks run out of ammunition. When they finally heed the calls for surrender, the Soviets wait until they are certain all have come out. Then they execute the lot in a burst of machine-gun fire.

EXPLOSION

The Corvin Passage fighters, who still have plenty of ammunition, leave during a lull to join other groups, but one group elects to stay to make things as costly as possible for the Soviets. This they do so well that the Corvin Passage is only taken in late afternoon. They die to the last man, for the Soviet troops have been told to take no prisoners, even wounded ones.[24]

Another area receiving continuous bombardment throughout the day from the howitzers on Gellért Hill is the industrial suburb of Csepel, or "Red Csepel" as it is known, since it has always been a stronghold of the Hungarian Communists. Here, thousands of armed workers have fought off every Soviet patrol that has tried to enter the area. Soviet Commander Grebennyik is reluctant to send his troops against workers, so is content to give them the message as to who is in charge via long-range artillery.

One of the technical miracles in Budapest, during the Revolution and the days of its suppression, is the operation of the telephone system. People cannot travel from one part of the city to the other, or often even venture out into the street, but they can telephone family and friends without difficulty to exchange news and rumors. Citizens even take advantage of this to phone foreign embassies and legations to inform them of things they feel they ought to know. The American Legation, though it can do very little about all the pleas for help, nonetheless takes notes of most of these calls. Here are a few recorded today:

11:40 "The Petőfi revolutionary group, fighting around the Radio Station, asks for news. They are under mortar fire. Will hold out as long as possible"

"Eighth and Ninth Districts appeal for help, under terrible fire."

13:00 "Military no longer able to fight. Only civilians fighting, have insufficient ammunition. Russians bombing city to pieces."

"Russians collecting revolutionaries in the streets and taking them to Russia by train."

14:00 "The Hungarian Freedom Fighters' Center in the mountains of Buda [Probably Király—ed] is in heavy fighting with the Russians. They ask for help. Asking immediate intervention from the part of the UN...."

15:50 "Ferenc Boulevard Four. Air raid shelter collapsed. Forty children trapped, salvage impossible as Russians keep house under fire. Appeal for aid."

"Clinics being fired on, many patients wounded by shell fire."

17:00 "Appeal from desperate father: Approximately fifty youths, who had no part in the fighting, but were recruited into the police forces [National Guard—ed.] are now retained in the Ministry of Interior as 'fascists.'"

"Appeal from hospital in Sándor Péterfy Street [a huge 1,200 bed hospital —ed.] Filled with wounded, more being brought in. Electric lighting failing. Operating Room partly out of order."[25]

The American Legation is not only getting appeals from Hungarians on the outside, but from the Cardinal himself. The Legation learns that the Soviets are planning to advance on the Kilián Barracks by smashing though the University Children's Clinic on Üllői Ave. If they go through with it, it seems certain two to three hundred additional children will be slaughtered. Cardinal Mindszenty appeals to Wailes to have Washington intervene with Moscow to prevent this.[26] Later, the Cardinal receives a telephone call from Freedom Fighters holding out in the main post office on Sándor Petőfi Street. They want his blessing before they die. He willingly gives it to them.[27]

The Legation also receives eyewitness reports from reliable informants such as the German reporter for *Der Spiegel*, Hans Germani, this morning near the Kilián Barracks. Before he is wounded, he reports seeing "hundreds of corpses" in that area, as well as five destroyed Soviet tanks. Other destroyed tanks are reported near the Astoria Hotel in the Harmincad area, and five burnt-out hulks are smoldering in front of the Vienna gate on Castle Hill. A number of ÁVO, back in their old uniforms, have been spotted helping the Soviet troops search houses and round up people.[28]

Sniper fire is so pervasive that Soviet plans to bring in more infantry are cancelled for the time being. Most Soviet shooting is done from tanks and MIG fighter planes. Unlike the Kilián Barracks and Corvin Cinema Passage, the small groups fighting at Széna and Móricz squares in Buda, though not as well organized, can hide their arms and vanish within minutes into the civil population. The Soviets, for instance, are surprised tonight when they find their armored column coming up Fehérvári Avenue into Zsigmond Móricz Square is ambushed with molotov cocktails and machine gun fire, losing five troop-carrying trucks. Though the accompanying tanks shoot up all the surrounding buildings, the Freedom Fighters, who quickly meld into the neighborhood as civilians, claim they killed or wounded at least one hundred Soviet soldiers, while sustaining twenty dead of their own.[29]

Soviet tanks are attacked today in many working class suburbs such as Kőbánya, Kispest and Zugló, where barricades have quickly been erected to trap or slow them down. The patriots are far from defeated at the end of the second full day of fighting.

Though the "best information available" is that Imre Nagy is a captive of the Soviets, only the Soviets and the Yugoslavs know that this is not true. The Soviets are furious that they did not capture him. Now they, and their puppet Kádár, are doing their best to persuade Nagy to join the new "government," for unless he does Kádár will have an almost impossible task of trying to win over the population. The Soviets have a document all ready for Nagy to sign and this is taken to him at the Yugoslav Embassy. Nagy waves this aside and writes his own declaration. He ignores Kádár, and refers to himself as "the responsible leader of the government," who has always been "loyal to my people and my country…" Kádár will have near apoplexy when he reads it and will have to be persuaded all over again that he really needs to have Nagy in his "government."

Since Soviet tanks are shooting up buildings all over Budapest, the report that a Soviet tank has accidentally machine gunned an upper window in the Yugoslav Embassy at 3:30 this afternoon and killed the Yugoslav Cultural Attaché, Milenko Milanov, and wounded several others is taken by Western journalists, when they finally learn of it, as not at all unlikely. The difficulty with this explanation, however, is that the Yugoslav Embassy is at the corner of Stalin Ave. and Stalin (Heroes) Square, not far from the Soviet Embassy, where, except for this morning's episode, no fighting is taking place. Moreover, the building is quite some distance from its neighbors. The Yugoslavs know very well that it was deliberate and launch a diplomatic protest immediately.

Less understandable is an eyewitness report of a Soviet Officer and five soldiers entering the unguarded Egyptian Embassy this afternoon and looting it completely, over the loud protests of the Egyptian Ambassador and his wife. Even their spare clothes are taken.[30]

Fighting in the Country

The military radio stations, which gave so much information yesterday, have fallen silent. Nevertheless, from the Communist controlled stations and the few Freedom stations still occasionally on the air it is possible to get a picture of fighting in the rest of the country. In almost every case, yesterday, Army units were surrounded, disarmed and sent home. Only bands of Freedom Fighters still resist. The exception, however, is in Dunapentele (formerly Sztálinváros), where the military, still very much intact and backed by worker and student Freedom Fighters, is defying the local Soviet forces' attempt to take the city. The radio there even suggests that the whole area around the city be declared a distribution place for the International Red Cross into which supplies could be parachuted.

In Miskolc, the patriots have broken through the Soviet lines and are now retreating to higher ground in the Garadna Valley. Groups of twenty to thirty have been harassing Soviet convoys. Groups of Freedom Fighters also break out of Gyöngyös and Eger and are heading for the woods. In Szeged, the entire Revolutionary Committee yesterday fled across the Yugoslav border fifteen miles to the south. Yugoslav soldiers refused to admit them until they had given up their arms. In Pécs, where patriots are guarding the uranium mines, the soldiers, who have already transported over seventy cannons into the mountains, today are disarmed and told to go home. This they pretend they are very glad to do. Instead, however, they remove their uniforms and head for their cannons in the mountains.

In Győr, Nyíregyháza, Debrecen and Miskolc, the Soviets declare that all weapons must be handed in by 4:00 this afternoon, a clear indication that armed patriots are still operating in these areas.

In Sopron lightly armed students trying to block the main highway were forced to surrender to heavily armed Soviet columns when they discovered that all of the anti-tank guns they had put into position had been rendered inoperable by the removal of their breach blocks. Hundreds of refugees and Hungarian Army troops, nevertheless, were able to flee to Austria. Today RFE reporter Leason learns that the idealistic student he had interviewed two days ago in Sopron was killed when the Soviets launched a brief attack on the students in the city.[31]

Radios

Excepting a few weak signals emanating from stations still in the hands of patriots, the bulk of broadcasting in Hungary today, when not dance music, is taken up with orders issued either by the Soviet military commander in Budapest, Lt. General Kuzmin Y. Grebennyik, or his counterparts in provincial Hungarian cities. There are also long harangues from Kádár, Münnich or other members of his clique, to which no one pays any attention. The news is about as truthful as Radio Moscow's announcement, interrupting a program at one p.m. yesterday, that "the Hungarian counterrevolution has been crushed." There is a sharp difference in tone between the "orders" of the occupier and the attempts at justification and promises of the Kádár group.

In Munich, RFE Monitoring circulates a memo to all language desks and departments:

> We should like to call to your attention the fact that radios Dunapentele and Vác, which are still broadcasting sporadically from pockets of resistance in Hungary, have specifically requested for their own protection that they be referred to as Radios Rákóczi and Csokonai respectively. Please bear this in mind in any publications or broadcast which you make.[32]

Actually, there are at least two other "free" radios still broadcasting after the circulation of this memo: Radio Rajk, which is controlled by Hungarian Communist idealists who despise Rákosi and Gerő and are opposing Kádár, and Radio Róka (Fox), whose location is unknown.

Early this morning Radio Rajk said, "János Kádár and his reorganized Party may attempt to fool the nation and the world, but the fact is that Russian guns are destroying democracy and Communism in Hungary. As convinced Communists, we must be the first to confess that it was not only Stalin who used Communism as a pretext to expand Russian imperialism and to suppress free peoples."

Late this afternoon a commentator on Radio Rajk says: "But we also want to speak of traitors…the János Kádárs, who play the dirty role of colonial governors.…We send them the message that we consider them all traitors to Communism.…These gangsters will continue Rákosi's work by falsifying historical events, not only of 1945, but those of yesterday and the day before.…"

In addition to frequent, pathetic pleas for help Radio Róka transmits quite accurate and detailed news of the fighting in Budapest.[33]

There is yet another freedom radio heard in Vienna which says it is in Budapest but gives no call name or number. A woman's voice gives a description of the harrowing end to the fighting at the Kilián Barracks and then breaks into sobs when she begins telling of all the women and children who have been killed. Then a man speaks: "Russian troops are searching every home and building for weapons. All Hungarian men are being rounded up and crowded near Budapest railroad stations for deportation under heavily armed guards."[34]

"When, at 5:00 p.m. [this afternoon]" writes Attis Jungstrom, a visiting

Swede, "Budapest Radio began to broadcast dance music, and gay songs were sung to convince the world that everything was in order in the city, to the accompaniment of artillery fire outside our windows, a primitive instinct in me arose to trample the wretched soundbox under my feet."[35]

World Reaction

A wave of indignation sweeps across Western Europe this morning as people who had not heard the radio or seen television news read about the brutal Soviet intervention in their morning newspapers. By noon all official government flags and many private ones are flying at half-mast to mourn what has happened.

In Paris an estimated fifty thousand youths, mostly students, march on the Soviet Embassy today chanting, "Russians are murderers!" "Get out of Hungary!" they shout, as gendarmes move in to prevent them from getting close enough to the Embassy to throw rocks. When the crowd swells with new recruits the police are forced to call in reinforcements of steel-helmeted gendarmes with carbine rifles to control the crowd. The demonstration is dispersed finally without violence.[36]

Meanwhile Paul Reynaud, former Prime Minister and one of the honorary Presidents of France's European Movement, states publicly, "Let us not forget that the Hungarian insurrection was staged by youth—this very same youth that had never known anything except Communist brain-washing. There could not have been any more magnificent rejection of Communism."[37]

In Italy, Socialist Party leader Pietro Nenni, who has cooperated with the Italian Communist Party so much that he is a winner of the Soviet Union's "Stalin Prize," recoils in anger. This Soviet action, he says, "creates a situation without precedent for the international workers movement, which cannot accept situations of force and the politics of power."[38]

The Liberal Party leader, Giovanni Malagodi, suggests that all the NATO countries should withdraw their ambassadors from Moscow.

In West Berlin, over one hundred thousand candle-carrying West Berliners tonight gather in front of City Hall emitting wildly anti-Soviet outbursts. The crowd roars, "Out with the Russians!" for minutes before the president of the West Berlin Senate, Willy Brandt, can make himself heard. A large section of the crowd demands that they march to the Brandenburg Gate, entrance to East Berlin and the Soviet Sector. They yell that they want revenge and shout that Smirnov, the Soviet Ambassador, should go back to Moscow. Those who try to read their speeches from notes are shouted down with the slogan, "Deeds, not words!" Several thousand students this afternoon try unsuccessfully to reach the Soviet Embassy with wreaths of green-red-white and a large banner which reads in Cyrillic, "Freedom for Berlin."[39]

In Britain, Foreign Secretary Selwyn Lloyd reminds people that "Hungary's brave struggle for freedom is still going on against heavy odds." Sefton Delmer phones his paper in Britain from Austria, where he arrived from Hungary only Saturday: "I feel like a man who has just learned that one of his best friends has been murdered."

In the United States, large demonstrations take place both in New York and Washington. In Washington, it is a stationary rally where government, labor and religious leaders and some former East European leaders speak out against Soviet perfidy and call upon the U.S. to lead a worldwide drive to aid Hungary.

In New York, reaction takes the form of a march of many Hungarian-American organizations up Fifth Avenue, followed by a service in St. Patrick's. There is also a large and rowdy demonstration in front of the Soviet UN delegation's headquarters with demands the U.S. break off all relations with the USSR until the latter takes its troops out of Hungary.

In Holland, over sixty thousand people hold a silent procession through Amsterdam, while many young people attack Communist organizations in the city, causing police to come out to protect the buildings and pick up the debris. In Rotterdam, Dutch longshoremen cease loading Soviet ships and say they will no longer touch anything going to or coming from the Soviet Union.[40]

In Denmark, which feels particularly close to Hungary, demonstrations were held all over the country yesterday, including one in front of the Soviet Embassy and one with thirty-eight thousand participants at the football match with Holland.

In Sweden, a beheaded dummy, smeared with catsup to portray blood, is thrown over the fence at the Soviet Embassy as a symbolic protest. Protests of one form or another take place in every country of Western Europe including Ireland and Iceland.

In most Communist countries, the Soviet line is copied slavishly, but in Poland, Gomułka argues for the long view. "Politics should not be conducted from the perspective of a few days....At the same time," he insists, "we must state that the Hungarian events cannot have any influence on our plans as devised by the Eighth Plenum" at which he, Gomułka was elected. Among the Polish people, Sydney Gruson of the *New York Times* reports, the first reaction is "livid anger," which is followed by "a sober realization that Poland walks a tightrope and that any emotional gesture might prove suicidal."

World Press Comment

Press comment runs from the emotional to the sober and rational, with rather less of the latter. The Hague's *Telegraaf* writes, "Such an abominable deed must not remain unpunished." And Italy's *Il Tempo* cries out "governments…should take steps to recall their ambassadors from that thing, stained with shame, called the Soviet Union….All honest nations should break off economic relations with the Moscow highwaymen. No honest person would consider welcoming into his home the accomplices of assassins and thieves. And thus all honest parliaments should cast from their midst the Communists, the lackeys paid by Russia."

Nearly every British paper speculates on whether, and to what degree, Britain and France's action in Egypt influenced Soviet action in Hungary. But several sense that an extraordinary turning point that will set things off in a new direction has been reached. *The News Chronicle* today writes:

> Should we leave these people to starve or die in the hands of the Communist invaders, thereby extinguishing all hope of resistance in Central Europe— perhaps for a generation?
>
> Or should we intervene and face the consequences? A recurring nightmare since 1945 is now transformed into reality.
>
> Decisions must now be taken which will either run the risk of a third world war, or else accept the moral surrender which will make Munich an act of glorious courage by comparison.

The *Manchester Guardian* does not see it as a dilemma. "There is tragically little that can be done," it says. But looking at the prospects for the Soviet Union's future it writes:

> So thorough is the collapse of Soviet Russia and her reliance on naked force that the aggression on Hungary has been given over to the most blatant lies. There is besides Hungary another victim. The whole fistful of attempts since Stalin's death to make Communist words fit Communist facts and to let the air of reason partly into the windowless room has gone under. Social

EXPLOSION

Democratic workers become once again "fascist gangs." Moscow's marionettes turn into "honest patriots" and "it goes without saying," asserts the Soviet delegate to the United Nations—that for anyone to interfere while the Soviet troops kill Hungarians "would be unlawful and contrary to the Charter."

Hungarians become Refugees

An estimated fifteen thousand Hungarians cross over into Austria today fleeing the reimposition of Soviet terror in their native land. Most are old people and children, but there are also young people who feel certain that they face arrest and imprisonment, if not execution, if they stay. Most come on foot, although some are in oxcarts and other farm vehicles, packed to the last inch of space. Some are pushing baby carriages filled with a bundled up child or their worldly goods, others carrying a single suitcase or bundle and frequently a small child as well. There are not many men.

Most are crossing in places where the landmines were recently removed, or places so swampy that no mines have ever been sown. There are heartbreaking partings at the border, for frequently the father or young man, having seen his family to the frontier, turns back to rejoin the fight or, in the case of some women, to tend a parent or child too sick to make the journey.

This tragic stream of humanity comes in clumps, whole families and, in some cases, larger groups from a single village. Out of the drizzle, which occasionally turns to snow, they suddenly materialize near Schattendorf and Andau in Burgenland, and further north at Nickelsdorf. Some are so weary from their long trek that they can scarcely stand and have to be supported by family and friends. There are no loud lamenting or nervous cries of distress. Those who can walk upright, do, silently and often with tears streaming down their faces. Some children have tags on them saying "Please take good care of my daughter" or "son. I must return to fight for my homeland," or "to take care of my sick father." It makes no difference whether the labels are written in German or Hungarian. The Burgenlanders who read them are mostly ethnic Hungarians. These people are their neighbors, in some cases, even relatives.

To make things easier for their neighbors, the Austrians have put up Austrian flags just inside the border every fifty meters so that the Hungarians can tell when they have reached their goal. The Austrian border patrols say that so far no Soviet soldier has crossed into Austria. Near Andau, on the

Hungarian side, there is a small footbridge across a small canal which many mistake for the border. From the bridge one can see some of the Austrian flags, though not the village of Andau. Nevertheless, this major route of flight will become known in the West as "the bridge at Andau."[41]

In Vienna, a group of Hungarian Freedom Fighters issues an appeal for United Nations observers to come to Hungary quickly before Soviet troops and the Security Police can take their revenge. "If the UN cannot save our freedom, at least it may be able to save our lives."[42]

The American Embassy in Vienna announces today that the American convoy, along with several other convoys of journalists and others totaling about one hundred persons, passed through Nickelsdorf on the border earlier today.

At Radio Free Europe the "line" as proposed by Griffith's Political Advisor's Office is: "news and press reviews only," "original commentaries on our part would at this moment be out of place."[43]

Bulganin Makes an Outrageous Proposal

This evening Premier Nikolai Bulganin sends a long message addressed to President Eisenhower which is released to the press even before it gets into the President's hands. After comparing armed forces of the two countries in the area, Bulganin proposes that the U.S. and Russia join in a military coalition to keep the peace in the Middle East. The message is full of mock urgency and bombast such as that if peace cannot be brought to the Middle East "the United Nations will lose all of its international prestige and will collapse."

White House Press Secretary James C. Hagerty points out that while the Soviets have released the message to the press, they only gave it to the U.S. Ambassador in Moscow, so that the President has not yet seen it. However, since there are only two matters before the UN right now and one of those is addressed to the Soviet Union, the Soviet Union has "an obligation before the world to carry out the resolution dealing with Hungary....That they have not done."[44]

Tuesday, November 6, 1956

Gunfire and tank noises have permeated the night. Now, under overcast skies and slightly less cold weather, a Soviet artillery barrage from Gellért Hill again opens up at 6:00 a.m. It is as intense or worse than yesterday's.

EXPLOSION

The targets are the same: Kilián Barracks and Corvin Passage, Széna Square the Vár (fortress on Castle Hill) and Csepel, which Soviet forces have still not penetrated. The smell of cordite from the smoke drifting through the city streets has become so familiar to the populace that they hardly notice it any more.

As dawn comes over the city Soviet tank commanders begin to spot a well-printed poster which has mysteriously appeared and been posted all over the city during the night. It is signed by the Commander of the Hungarian Armed Forces (unnamed), the Federation of Hungarian Writers, and the Revolutionary Committee of University Students. Its main points are:

1) Immediate withdrawal of all Soviet forces from Hungary

2) Immediate release of Imre Nagy and restitution of his rights

3) "Recognition of our heroes" as such, instead of their being branded "Fascist reactionaries and counter-revolutionaries"

4) Discussion between all Hungarian organizations, then discussions with the Soviet Union and finally discussions with the United Nations

5) Free, multi-party elections

6) An independent, neutral Hungary

Emphasis is placed on the fact that the revolution has been nationwide, that there is no intention of going back to an old order and that these facts have been completely misrepresented by the Russians and other members of the Eastern bloc.[45]

When translated into Russian, it is not exactly what the Soviets want to read over their morning coffee. Hungarians, however, gain a grim satisfaction on reading it and some spirit the posters away to show to others or keep as a private souvenir.

Soviet Commander's Order of the Day

For three days the Kádár puppet government has been issuing orders through strange announcers over the radio. Soviet Lt. Gen. Grebennyik cannot see that it has made the slightest difference in the behavior of the Hungarian populace. Since he is in charge, in any case, it is time for him to bring some order to this chaos. Today he issues his first "Order of the Day."

It is posted prominently all over town as well as printed in the regime press and broadcast on the radio. He gives the usual preamble as to why the Soviet forces are here and that their presence in Budapest is only a temporary measure. He then gives the following orders:

1) All arms must be laid down on November 9 at the latest by 5:00 p.m. Nobody who obeys this order will be punished, and those, who after this time will have weapons in their possession, will be strictly called to account for it.

2) Curfew obtains from 7:00 p.m. to 7:00 a.m., and the orders of Soviet patrols must be obeyed unconditionally.

3) The workers must resume their work. He who prevents the workers from doing so will be made responsible for it.

4) The local authorities will supply the shops with food and fuel, and the food shops will be open from 8:00 a.m. to 8:00 p.m.

Up until now food from all countries has been gratefully accepted and graciously acknowledged by private individuals and government agencies alike. This morning, however, before it mysteriously goes off the air again, Radio Kossuth announces that while it is most grateful for all of the aid promised by the Soviet Union, "our pride forbids us to accept any aid from capitalist countries." Radio Kossuth (Budapest) will remain off the air for most of today.[46]

Because the Soviets have blockaded the city for almost a week now, there is very little food left in the food stores and even less in people's larders. As soon as food stores open, huge lines form, even though there may be a Soviet tank shooting it out with patriots in the next block. Sir Leslie Fry reports that in spite of all the wild shooting in the streets, "women with babies in their arms are risking their lives to call at Her Majesty's Legation for milk."[47]

In neighboring Czechoslovakia, where reservists are being called back into the Armed Forces, people can read in their newspapers this morning that "Life in Hungary is being normalized."[48]

It is not just Hungarians who are suffering from hunger pangs. Soviet troops, who are used to the age-old practice of armies living off the land, are getting hungry. More and more reports come in to the Western legations of Soviet troops looting food stores. Someone from Csillaghegy reports that there are two hundred Soviet tanks on top of Rókahegy. This morning they waved a white flag as though surrendering, luring Hungarian civilians and revolutionaries up the hill. When they reached the top they were ordered to lay down their arms. There would be a truce until noon. Thereupon the Russians went down off the hill to loot the food stores below.

Food stores are not the only ones being broken into. Yesterday a large department store was broken into and Soviet soldiers were observed carting every type of merchandise out of it. But there were not enough soldiers to clear out the store. Today they return, only this time they round up as many Hungarians as they can find, lead them into the store and tell them they can take anything they want. Cameras then record these Hungarian civilians leaving the store, which has been clearly broken into, carrying merchandise in their arms. This will become part of a Soviet propaganda movie which will be shown again and again all over the world.[49]

As if artillery shells falling short or beyond their targets indiscriminately destroying apartment houses, churches and other public buildings of no military value were not enough, Soviet tanks continue to shoot randomly around the city. There is now scarcely a single hotel in the center of the city which has not yet been hit. The Austrian editor Fritz Molden, when telephoning the Duna Hotel, discovers that the hotel dining room and kitchen have been destroyed. More shocking still is that the room he and Mr. Pogány were staying in, number 307, no longer has a floor and the Danube can be seen through the gaping hole. Today the Indian, Czechoslovak and Polish Embassies and British and French legations are hit, though it seems clear these were random hits and not deliberate. The worst, however, is the deliberate shelling of hospitals. When U.S. Minister Edward T. Wailes, in an attempt to save the children's hospital on Üllői Ave. yesterday, phoned the Soviet Embassy, Andropov told him curtly, "There is nothing I can do about it" and hung up.

This morning Fritz Molden and a Dutch journalist, Hendrik Baljon, and Austrian Prof. Greiteman decide to take advantage of a lull in the fighting to visit the Szabolcs Street Hospital on the far side of the Western Railroad Station, a half mile from the French Legation. They want to find out what the hospital most needs from the West. A car belonging to the Social Democratic Party is just pulling up to unload wounded persons as they arrive. In the hallway are a number of wounded Freedom Fighters with bloody bandages waiting for treatment. A tired Chief Surgeon courteously receives the foreigners in German of World War I vintage. Only yesterday he has moved the operating room to the cellar because tanks had shelled the upper floors, as his visitors can clearly see. His hospital has received a fresh supply of drugs from the International Red Cross on Saturday, so is relatively well off. Other hospitals in the city are in much worse shape. His children's ward, however, has run out of baby food and there is no more milk or rich canned food. The shortage of surgeons is worst. So many have been gunned down by the Soviets while they were in transit. Ambulances appear to be a favorite target of the tanks. One young female doctor in his Surgical Department was trying to pick up wounded persons near the West Railroad Station yesterday and get them into ambulances when machine gun fire put three slugs in her chest and one in her spine. "We operated on her last night and so far she is pulling through. We sincerely hope that she will live. She is such a brave and dear young girl."

Back at the French Legation, while they are at lunch, a Soviet shell hits the villa next door precisely at 12:40. There is a shattering noise and splinters of glass land in everyone's soup. A Russian tank captain on Stalin Avenue thinks he has seen something suspicious in the attic of this villa and decided to remove the suspicion from his mind. There are a few moments of confusion in the dining room, then several journalists grab the small children present, saying, "boom, boom" in their ears as though this were a game, and carry them down to the cellar. Fighting actually does break out in the area a while later and all head for the cellar. The Military Attaché calls the Soviet Embassy to protest and request that the Soviet troops leave the area. Whether or not this has any influence, he is able to sound the all clear by 2:30 p.m. Later, when the Legation asks the Soviet Embassy whether they can post a guard in front of the Legation, Andropov has the chutzpah to reply: "That is the job of the Hungarians. And I would not wish to interfere in Hungarian affairs."[50]

While the delegation was visiting the Szabolcs Street Hospital around ten o'clock this morning, Budapest Radio, to the great relief of most of its listeners, suddenly went off the air. Only later do people learn the cause: Freedom Fighters have captured it. All strata of the population welcome this recess from provocative dance music, court-martial threats and amnesty promises. In the early evening, Radio Budapest comes back on the air, without explanations for the gap. Among the repulsive mix of waltzes and decrees is the announcement that the promise of amnesty is being extended another twenty-four hours. There is also an announcement designed to weaken the resistance of those who already feel weak with hunger: the Russians, who are the cause of people's hunger and the destruction of Budapest, are now promising to supply Hungary with food and building materials. Specifically the Soviets are promising fifty thousand tons of grain, three thousand tons of meat and two thousand tons of butter and fats. People can easily detect from its technically slipshod presentation that Radio Budapest is now broadcasting from a new, makeshift location.[51]

In the afternoon, during another lull, Molden and two Dutch colleagues attempt to walk all the way to the Duna Hotel on the Danube in search for food. They get as far as Izabella Street, six blocks from the legation, when they are suddenly caught in a cross-fire from which they are lucky to escape alive. It is the beginning of the battle of Izabella Street, a very bloody affair from which neither side can claim victory.

When Freedom Fighters who surrender are not immediately executed they are handed over to the resurgent Security Police, who give them the "concession" of being shot rather than hanged. But their bodies are then put on display. Already there are a number of bodies of patriotic Hungarians hanging on the bridges over the Danube. Those young people not found with weapons, but in apartment buildings or just on the street, are seized, have their hands tied behind them and are led off to railroad stations and put into train boxcars.[52]

Edward T. Wailes has been on the job for only four days, but already he has about had it with Washington. He fires off a midday telegram as follows:

I have heard radio reports periodically of statements in the UN [i.e. Dulles and Lodge] and of other commentary to the effect that the situation in Budapest and Hungary is unclear. The situation in Budapest, at least, is entirely clear. The Soviets have been systematically cleaning up the city; slaughter has been continuous, over the last three days, of men, women and children, with hospitals and clinics included among the targets, despite which resistance is evidently not (repeat NOT) yet entirely broken. I estimate that the heaviest shelling came a few hours after Radio Moscow was broadcasting that all resistance had been liquidated. These are facts, not (repeat NOT) rumors.

Soviet armor around the city...is totally preventing the supply of food from reaching the population...Soviet action in Budapest...is calculated to starve out the people and the Soviets cannot (repeat NOT) help but know it.[53]

In Washington, a meeting of the Special Committee on Soviet and Related Problems is taking place with Ambassador Jacob Beam in the chair.

The first measure, says Beam, is that RFE will broadcast appeals to the Russians troops in Russian urging them not to fire on Hungarians. The second is that the U.S plans to distribute relief in Hungary through the International Red Cross. The third is that the State Department is going to tighten up on issuing U.S. passports and the fourth is that administrative action is to be taken to make it easier for refugees from Eastern Europe to enter the U.S.

The question of Anna Kéthly, the Hungarian Social Democrat who is the only member of the Nagy government in the West and who has just arrived in New York, comes up. She is scheduled to make a major speech in New York on Thursday. "The United States," said chairman Beam, "should not take any initiative to get her before the UN, but we should not hold back our seconding support." Then, in connection with the coming U.S. Agricultural exhibit in Moscow, Cox (CIA) asks, "Will there be a resolution of condemnation [over Hungary]?" Beam: "Not yet. People might be put too much on the spot to go along with it."[54]

Hungary beyond Budapest

Western military intelligence estimates that there are now 4,600 tanks and 200,000 Soviet soldiers in Hungary. While between 1,500 and 2,000 of these tanks are concentrated in Budapest the majority are spread out across the countryside in and around every major city and town. A good many near Dunapentele, Vác and Pécs are still engaged in offensive action. And a few, if caught in any narrow streets of Miskolc, Győr or cities of this size, meet the same fate from local Freedom Fighters as do the ones in Budapest. The fact that the Kádár radio declares that there is "complete calm in Szeged, Cegléd and Kecskemét" leads listeners to the inevitable conclusion that the opposite is true for the rest of the country.[55]

The nationwide strike is still in force. In Mosonmagyaróvár the local Soviet commander asks the mayor of Moson, a local village, why the people are not working. "For what and for whom shall we start working?" replies the mayor. At this the Soviet officer loses his temper and offers to string him up on the nearest tree. "You can hang me if you want to," replies the mayor, "but it won't help you to get people starting to work again."[56]

EXPLOSION

Soviet/Kádár and Freedom Radios

All over the country local radios are announcing deadlines for surren-der—and extensions of these deadlines—as well as decrees about returning to work and pronouncements voiding laws passed by the Nagy government. Workers are told that special buses will be provided for workers who depend on public transportation, which, of course, is not working due to the nation-al strike. Nobody shows up to board them. Many of these announcements are made in what can only be referred to as "broken Hungarian," foreigners try-ing to speak Hungarian. Nobody pays the slightest attention.

Radio listeners do, on the other hand, twirl their dials searching for the few free radios which, from time to time, break through all the Communist garbage. One radio, starting just before midnight last night and continuing on into today, has a single message: "Do not believe Communist and Soviet radio stations! Do not surrender! Hungary is not lost!" Then, shifting wave-lengths it says "Clara calling Ibolya" and suddenly shifts into Morse code. Sometimes it identifies itself as the "Radio of the National Freedom Fighters." But it is not heard after today.[57]

A much louder signal comes from Radio [Free] Rákóczi, which says, "Do not surrender! We will receive help! Soviet troops shall be withdrawn! Hungary consists not only of Communists! The country's population refus-es to accept the Communist rule, for the Communists were elected by no one, but appointed exclusively by the Soviets. We call on everyone to refuse to accept Communist orders."[58]

Radio Rákóczi at one point addresses an appeal to the International Red Cross in Geneva: "…For the moment Dunapentele, the former Sztálinváros, seems to be the only place in Hungary where there are no Russian troops and the city is in the hands of the Hungarian Revolutionary Army. We appeal to you for the preservation of this city for the activities of the International Red Cross." At this point heavy jamming blots out the broadcast, but it is repeat-ed again a quarter of an hour later and then again in German.

Radio [Free] Róka, which appears to be located in Budapest, announces at 2:00 p.m., "Yesterday we recaptured the parliament building. We are holding the road to Székesfehérvár and to Kecskemét also. We are not allow-ing, nor should you, any more Soviet troops to enter the capital. We have wiped out the majority of Soviet troops who have entered before. We urgent-ly request food, medicine and armed help. This is Róka [Fox] speaking."

Whether anyone believes such extravagant claims is beside the point. They are on the air and they give desperate people much needed hope.

Radio Rákóczi in mid-afternoon says, "We desperately need guns, ammunition and food parachuted in around Dunapentele.... The Soviet troops called on us to lay down arms. We will not comply with this call.... The time for consideration we were granted will soon expire, after which they will attack. We are prepared, we expect the attack.... Please drop arms, ammunition, medicine, bandages and food for us by parachute."[59]

World Reaction

Spontaneous student and some organized demonstrations took place all over Western Europe yesterday, but they are only a prelude to what is happening today. In Paris, several thousand irate students last night stormed the Communist Party newspaper *L'Humanité*, hurling rocks through the windows and trying to set it afire. The large French Communist Party promises to avenge this and today the police are out in force. In the French Assembly a storm of applause greets Foreign Minister M. Christian Pineau's tribute to Hungary, despite the usual catcalls from the Communist deputies. The Assembly votes by 432 votes to 150 (all Communist) to debate the events in Hungary tomorrow, which has been proclaimed "Hungary Day." Meanwhile Jean Paul Sartre, Simone de Beauvoire and other prominent left-wing French intellectuals denounce Soviet repression of the Hungarian freedom movement, saying they have a right to protest, for they have never before expressed unfriendly sentiments to the Soviet Union.

Tiny Luxembourg, which has seldom seen a demonstration of any sort, exploded last night when students went on a rampage, stoning the Communist Party headquarters and newspaper and urging everyone who is invited to today's reception at the Russian Embassy in honor of tomorrow's Russian national holiday to boycott it. The holiday commemorates the "great October Revolution," which brought the Communists to power in Russia in 1917. This evening the students surge on the Embassy, a large villa on the edge of the city, just as guests are beginning to arrive for their caviar and vodka. Two thousand students and other demonstrators rip down railings and burst through police cordons to get at the Embassy, completely disrupting the reception and sending Ambassador Yvan Mielnik scurrying to the cellar, where the students promptly lock him in. Furniture is overturned and heaved out of the windows. Plates of canapés follow. Unopened champagne bottles are used as clubs to smash the chandeliers. A portrait of Mrs. Nikita Khrushchev is torn from the wall. Most of the few guests scatter, but two join the seventy-member staff in barricading themselves in the attic. Now, mattresses and personal clothing fly out of upper floor windows, fuel for bonfires being set on the lawn. Disregarding extraterritoriality, troops are called out and together with the police, order is restored by 8:00 p.m. and the crowd disperses by 11:00 p.m.[60]

In Goteborg, Sweden, thousands of Swedish workers march through the streets of this port city in a torch procession demonstrating against Soviet action in Hungary. Ten thousand people join a student demonstration in Stockholm taking a petition on Hungary to the Swedish Foreign Office. In Upsala, a protest demonstration is held against an upcoming Soviet state visit and in Gothenburg it is announced that the visit of Russian violinist David Oistrahk, scheduled for November 21, will not take place.

In West Berlin, students stone a Communist bus and clash with West Berlin police in a demonstration trying to desecrate the Soviet memorial, which stands just inside West Berlin. In Berne, police have to use teargas and dogs to break up a demonstration of over a thousand students trying to get at the Soviet Embassy. In Spain, the government announces that Spain is withdrawing from the Olympics rather than associate with Soviet athletes. Holland also announces its withdrawal from the Olympics, while young Dutchmen demonstrating outside Dutch Communist Party headquarters in Amsterdam seize and throw every person who makes a pro-Communist remark into the canal in front of the building. Dockworkers in both Antwerp and Rotterdam continue to refuse to handle or repair Soviet ships.[61] In neighboring Denmark, the Red Cross is dispatching supplies and a field kitchen to Austria to help the Hungarian refugees at a Danish hospital in Graz.

Even in far off Argentina, over two thousand women dressed in black march through Calle Florida after a mass for the fallen in Hungary is held in the Cathedral. They march in silence with Hungarian and Argentine flags festooned in black crepe. They stop for a few minutes of silence in front of the Soviet Embassy, then move on.[62]

World Press Comment

In Vienna, Oskar Pollak, writing in the Socialist *Arbeiter Zeitung*, says, "The Russians have smashed Hungary's freedom in order to prevent the Poles, Czechs, Romanians, and East Germans from becoming free." *Die*

Presse comments: "We are all in heavy debt. We have missed the opportunity and failed to take action which might have saved the Hungarian people."[63]

Stockholm Tidningen laments that "There is not much that we, a small country in a remote corner of the globe, can do....What we can do is marshal our resources and give support to the humanitarian relief action...."[64]

In the U.S., *The Washington Evening Star* writes that the men in the Kremlin are "afraid of freedom. They can *not* tolerate freedom in their own country or any of the captive lands." The *Chicago Tribune* observes woefully that "the events in Hungary offered the best hope of Communist dissolution the world had seen," and blames its failure on "the Suez action."[65]

In neutralist India, where the Communists have been making considerable inroads in the past few years, *The Times of India* in Bombay points out that "here we have again the classic pattern of lightning communist coup, accompanied by all the instruments of terror and/or oppression perfected by the Stalinist regime." The *Daily News of Colombo* writes, "This is clear proof that Russia, in spite of her deferent social and political system, is just as much an imperialist power as Britain and France."[66]

The Main News of the Day

Despite all that is happening in Hungary, very little news of it is reaching the outside world. Hungary is already "yesterday's news" and today the headlines in the evening newspapers concern a threat of World War III, for the Kremlin propagandists have done it again. Yesterday they startled Washington by offering their bloody hands for a great power alliance to "keep the peace in the Middle East." Today Bulganin sends notes to Tel Aviv, Paris and London. In the latter two he threatens to bombard France and Britain with long-range rockets, and, by implication, with atomic bombs. Coming three days after their brutal attack on Hungary, the next to final sentence, "We are fully determined to crush the aggressors by the use of force," sends a chill down everyone's spine. Never mind that the Soviets have never even tested a rocket with a warhead, people know they have long-range rockets and that they have tested atomic, even hydrogen, bombs. Government officials in France and Britain recognize that this is just an outrageous bluff, for why would they risk World War III for a situation that is (a) already being solved and (b) completely outside of their primary interests? The answer, of course, is that they are risking nothing. For the Kremlin it is a win-win situation. Any response from the West will imply that the threats are taken seriously and therefore *are* serious. And even if they receive no replies, the damage they intended has been done. Intimidation of the populace is what they are after. They well know that democracies are heavily influenced by popular opinion. An intimidated people is worth more than an intimidated government. Thus, before these notes are handed over to the Ambassadors of the respective countries TASS releases the texts to the world press and banner headlines are in the evening papers before the governments even know what is in the notes. With this brilliant propaganda coup, the Soviet Union is able to force Hungary to the inside pages of all Western newspapers.[67]

And then there is the other major news story of the day: the presidential election in America. That forces the world's attention on Hungary even further back in the newspapers.

Budapest

There are many Hungarians who are praying for General Eisenhower to win, for they feel once the election is over he will be able to turn his full attention to them.

Tamás Szabó, the six-foot fifteen-year-old who had taken part in the fighting at the Radio and then was selected leader of a group of twenty-eight sixteen-year-old Freedom Fighters at the Prater Street School, is still fighting. He has lost three of his best friends in three days, has a long leg wound that hurts and is not sure how much more he can take. What is left of his group has long since left the Prater St. School and has been operating out of a new base on Rákóczi Ave. His group has come under the command of a battalion leader known as "Uncle Jenő" and they have joined several other groups who are all assembling in buildings along Landler Street (István Ave. today) which runs into György Dózsa Ave, at the corner of the City Park (Városliget).

Yesterday, Tamás was told, "Tomorrow's election day for a new President of the United States. Radio Free Europe says we must hold out until it is finished." Today, Tamás and other group leaders are assembled in a large cellar room to hear "Uncle Jenő" give them a talk.

"The first thing, boys," he says, "is not to worry. We shall soon be getting help. One thing only we must do: hold tight. The world has its eyes on us. The newspapers of the West are talking of nothing else. Everywhere they're holding demonstrations in our favor, and public opinion is insisting that help should be sent to Hungary. The monstrous treachery of the Russians has shocked and scandalized the whole world. Millions and millions of people have heard over the radio of the killing and looting perpetrated by the Soviet Army. We haven't the right to lose heart, we haven't the right to retreat until we have obtained freedom and independence for our country. The West will help us, the West cannot stand aside and watch the Soviet Union oppress our country like this. Whatever the sacrifices asked of us, we must hold on until help arrives. There is no possibility of retreat for us. We must look ahead, and keep looking ahead."[68]

Later, when Tamás is with a smaller group of friends, "Uncle Jenő" comes up to them and says, "Radio Free Europe says that we must hold out for two more days. As soon as the new president assumes his responsibilities, the UN troops will certainly begin to arrive. At someone's house today I saw an illegal Hungarian newspaper which said that there would be masses of volunteers and regular troops at the Austrian frontier."

But "Uncle Jenő" has more on his mind than just sitting tight. He learns that a fresh company of mechanized Soviet troops is moving into the City Park (Városliget), preparing to dig in, for the Soviets much prefer wide open spaces, particularly for their tanks, so they cannot become vulnerable to molotov cocktails. He gathers youngsters like Tamás around him and asks them what they think they should do about the situation. Several, who have been inspired by his talk, think they should attack, and at night, tonight in fact, before the Russians have had a chance to dig in. Whether or not he has steered them to it, "Uncle Jenő" now lays out a plan of attack. There are several hundred youths available in the combined groups. And nearly all become involved.

While the Soviets are on the far side of the park, the only way the boys can get to the park is to cross Dózsa Avenue, which is very wide. This would not be so bad if it could be done in the dark. But there are huge, high street lights lighting up the avenue. They must run across in small groups very fast. This they accomplish without incident, but finding their way through the bushes and trees of the park in the dark becomes another hazard. They are supposed to attack all at once, but when one group stumbles into a Soviet patrol, a firefight ensues, tipping the enemy off. There is total confusion in the battle that follows, but surprise is on the side of the teenagers and most of the tanks and other vehicles turn and flee from the park to avoid capture.

Many of the infantry stay, however, and Soviet firepower and professional training begins to turn the surprise victory into a rout. Tamás is one of the lucky ones, but many are cut down as they try to cross back over Dózsa Avenue. No one knows how many are killed or wounded, but less than half make it back to the cellars of Landler Street. It is Tamás' last major battle. Once convinced that the ÁVO is after him and he cannot explain his wound, he will say goodbye to his parents and, with many close calls on the way, reach and cross the Austrian frontier.[69]

In the U.S., election night is still in its early stages. No one will ever read of the bloody night battle of the City Park where teenagers attacked the mighty Red Army and temporarily put it to rout, because no Western journalist—though some in the French Legation clearly heard it—will ever learn of it. When President Eisenhower accepts Adlai Stevenson's gracious concession and goes on to celebrate his re-election, Hungary is far from his mind.

Wednesday, November 7, 1956

Today is the fourth day of the Soviet attempt to crush the Hungarian Revolution, and despite Moscow's claims that it is all over, Marshal Zhukov's boast to do it in three days has already proved inaccurate. Heavy fighting continues in many parts of the city, even at places like the Kilián Barracks, where a surrender took place two days ago, and the Corvin Passage, which was also abandoned on the fifth. New groups take over these positions or the old ones return. The Russians are finding it increasingly difficult to consider specific areas pacified even if there is no fighting there for several days. There are still fixed positions like the Vár (Castle Hill) and Csepel, which they have still not penetrated, but more and more it is becoming a guerilla war. And the Soviets have adopted a new tactic. Whenever a tank draws sniper fire it stops to mark from where the fire came and then radios for help. Within a few minutes eight or ten tanks will show up. Then they fire at the ground floor of the building, and maybe the buildings on either side of it. They keep blasting away until the building falls into a heap in the street. The method is like killing a fly with a sledgehammer, but it is effective. After a while snipers learn that one or two shots can cause the destruction of a whole neighborhood, and it is the people who live in these buildings who have been supporting and feeding them, and whose homes, if not their lives, are being ruined.[70] One estimate is that some seven thousand people have died since

Sunday morning and another three thousand have been badly wounded. Civilian casualties from all this Soviet firepower are now believed to be as much or greater than those sustained by the revolutionaries.

Military intelligence officers in Vienna today revise their estimate of Soviet strength in Hungary downward from twenty to fifteen divisions, but put the tank figure at 5,700. The American Legation this morning gets a report that the Soviets are so frustrated by the unexpected opposition they have met, in spite of their lightning attacks throughout the country, that they have sent for ten infantry divisions which may arrive as early as tomorrow. The number of divisions may be an exaggeration, but the fact that they are due tomorrow is not. Snow-blocked mountain passes in the Carpathians, however, hold up this infantry. They will only arrive in Hungary on the eleventh.[71]

Western diplomats still cannot go out into the city, so they are entirely dependent upon the eyes and ears of those who visit them. One "reliable Western observer," who has managed to get through much of the city this morning, reports to Sir Leslie Fry that the largest concentrations of tanks are still along the Danube, around the Ministry of Defense and the Parliament Building and, of course, the Soviet Embassy. Heavy fighting is going on in the Vár area and throughout the length of the four main avenues in Pest, where barricades and destroyed Soviet tanks are impeding further Russian attacks.

The Military History Museum on Castle Hill, the Music Academy in Pest and the Palace and Imperial Hotels are in flames, as are a good many houses surrounding them. The informant also saw twelve-year-old boys carrying arms and Russian tanks looking very disorganized and firing wildly. In his report Sir Leslie also says the first detachment of infantry was spotted last night. He ends his report to the Foreign Office by writing, "Until there is a United Nations intervention or the Russians withdraw, fighting will undoubtedly continue. All accounts agree that the Hungarians are displaying suicidal bravery and are determined to resist to the end."[72]

At the French Legation, where life in the cellar is beginning to seem normal, a truck arrives from Petőfi Hospital in the Seventh District. The driver brings food supplies and asks for drugs in return. The accompanying physician says that the hospital is caring for over two thousand wounded persons, their ages ranging from thirteen to twenty-two years. "A whole generation is dying before having a chance to live," he observes. "The older generation is standing aside, watching." He says he cannot detain slightly wounded youths because they insist on going home, or back to their units, in order to make room for other wounded.

During the worst bombardments the Austrian Minister, Dr. Peinsipp, supplied several Budapest hospitals with food. Now physicians and Red Cross nurses and even, occasionally, starving children show up at the Austrian Legation asking for food.[73]

Hungary beyond Budapest

Quoting a local newspaper, Radio Pécs this morning says that order has been restored in Szeged, Cegléd, Kecskemét and Szolnok, leaving listeners to wonder about the several dozen other towns in Hungary outside the capital. The report then goes on to state, however, that on the outskirts of these four towns "fascist groups and bandits" are still fighting. There is continued fighting at Dunaföldvár south of Dunapentele and local radios indicate that there is fighting in Kalocsa, Kecskemét and Mohács.[74]

In Szentgotthárd, despite appeals and threats by the local Soviet Commander, no work has begun. Workers in the silk factory, where there is a possibility of returning tomorrow in four-hour as opposed to eight-hour shifts, state that they will only resume work if they receive a written guarantee that no reprisals will be taken against the resistance fighters remaining behind in the city. The scythe factory will not be able to resume work due to an extreme coal shortage. Refugees from Szentgotthárd tell fellow refugees this morning that they should not believe for a minute the regime radio's promises that if they return they will remain untouched, if they beg forgiveness for fleeing the country. "They are just waiting until we all return before they start their reign of terror." Youths who escaped from their village of Kondorfa to Szentgotthárd and thence to Austria last night say they had fled their village because the Soviets are rounding up all the young people and sending them somewhere.[75]

Workers' Councils' elections were held yesterday all over Western Hungary under strict democratic procedures. This was to replace all of the workers' council members who were arrested in the past few days, among them a number of Communists. All the old Communist leaders in the factories have returned and are trying to assert their former authority, but none were elected to the new workers' councils.

In Győr, the National Council for Trans-Danubia is drafting a more restrained list of demands which they are going to present to the Kádár regime, hoping thereby to secure the continued existence of the various revolutionary workers' councils.[76]

Today, the great Soviet Holiday, which has always been a big holiday in Hungary under the Communists, is declared a regular workday by the Kádár "government," due to the present circumstances in the country. Since virtually nobody is going to work in any case, the announcement has little effect other than giving citizens the gratification of not having to celebrate, for once, another country's major holiday.[77]

Hungarian Freedom Radios

Radio Rákóczi, broadcasting from Dunapentele through Communist jamming, is picked up by RFE monitors this morning saying:

...At three o'clock in the morning the attack against the town started from three directions. For the moment the noise of battle [has] ceased but...in the negotiations the town was called on to surrender....The talks...an artillery attack was the result of our military Command having said it would defend the town to the last man. Reports say [that there is fighting] in several parts in the country, thus in Budapest, in Pécs....In the name of all honest Hungarians we appeal to all honest men in the world!

...Do you love liberty? So do we.

Have you wives and children? So have we.

Have you....We, too, have wounded who have given their blood for the sacred cause of liberty, but we have no bandages for our wounded and we have no medicine to alleviate their suffering. And what shall we give our children who are asking for bread?....The last piece of bread has been consumed....

We ask you in the name of all that is dear to you, we ask you to help us! Do you not think that those who have died for liberty, our beloved ones who are now silent, are accusing all those who would have been able to help and who did not help?

...That the UN has the possibility to....

...Is this what you want? Your conscience...when we are fighting...for freedom of the whole world? This is our message today, when as far as we know the extraordinary session of the United Nations will meet.

This is our message to President Eisenhower on the day [after] his election, to which we add that [if] during his presidency he will stand by the oppressed and those who are fighting for freedom, a blessing shall fall on him.

413

EXPLOSION

We have received no answer to our yesterday's appeal that Dunapentele should be declared a center for the Red Cross in Hungary.

Answer us, did you receive our call which we will repeat today?

Radio Rákóczi Hungary! Radio Rákóczi Hungary! Free Europe, Munich! Free Europe, Munich! Repeat whether you have received our message at 8:35.[78]

Not only RFE monitors pick up the above, but listeners in Budapest, which is not that far distant from Dunapentele. The text, once translated into English and German, is immediately released by RFE to the Western press so that these words will appear in newspapers all over the world tomorrow, November 8.

At 10:12 Radio Rákóczi says:

Free Europe, Munich...attention. We ask you to repeat in Russian the following appeal to Soviet soldiers in Hungary:

Soldiers! Your State was created at the cost of bloody fighting so that you could have freedom. Today is the thirty-ninth anniversary of that revolution. Why do you want to crush our liberty? You can see that it is not factory proprietors, not landowners, and not the bourgeoisie who have taken up arms against you, but the Hungarian people, who are fighting desperately for the same rights you fought for in 1917.

Soviet soldiers! In Stalingrad you showed how you could defend your country against a foreign invader. Why are you surprised that [we are defending] our country....? (passage unintelligible)

Soldiers! Do not take up arms against the Hungarian nation!

About the same time RFE monitors pick up Radio [Free] Róka:

This is Radio Róka! This is Radio Róka! We are holding our own in the Eighth (Budapest) District. Soviet losses are great. The Soviets have received reinforcements from the direction of Rákospalota and Vecsés. Two buildings of the János* Hospital are in flames. We are holding our own in the Eighth District. Please forward to Free Europe.

In late morning Radio Rákóczi comes back on the air:

We are fighting against overwhelming odds.

Possibly our radio will soon be annihilated. We shall continue to fight a partisan war. We ask for urgent help, we ask for armed help for Hungary.

---

*Probably means István Hospital, which is near the 8th district. János Hospital is in Buda.

Attention! Attention! We ask you to forward the above call for help to President Eisenhower and to Anna Kéthly. We ask for immediate intervention, we ask for immediate intervention, we ask for immediate intervention.

Continue to listen to our broadcasts. As soon as we have time to come from the firing line...we will continue.

The announcer does have time a while later and broadcasts the exchange that had taken place between the Soviet Commander in Kecskemét and Dunapentele's National Committee and Military Command. This goes as follows:

Soviet Commander: "I call on the garrison forces of Dunapentele to lay down arms. All officers, NCOs and soldiers who lay down their arms will preserve their lives, their liberty and their political rights. If the garrison does not lay down its arms, the Soviet Command will take the city by force. After fighting is over—soldiers and civilians will be treated as POWs." The Dunapentele Military Command answers, "Dunapentele is the foremost Socialist town in Hungary. The majority of residents are workers and power is in their hands. After the victorious Revolution of October 23, the workers elected the National Committee....The Military Command is in close collaboration with the National Committee....The population of the town is armed....The houses were built by the workers themselves....The workers will defend the town from Fascist excesses...but also from Soviet troops. We are prepared to live in peace with the Soviets so long as they don't interfere in our internal affairs....The majority of factories and plants are working. There are no counter-revolutionaries in the town....

"We suggest further negotiations in a neutral zone ...."

Just before 1:00 p.m. Radio Rákóczi comes on again. "Soviet tanks and planes are attacking Dunapentele. The battle continues with unflagging violence."

It is the last time the station is heard from.

Reaction in the West

Paris is gripped by the Hungarian tragedy for a third day in a row. Last night there were demonstrations and counter-demonstrations between those protesting Soviet intervention in Hungary and French Communist Party members. Violence erupted at the Communist Party headquarters, which was invaded by demonstrators. Communists used furniture as clubs in a wild fight in which several rooms were set on fire. Not far away at the building of the Communist newspaper *L'Humanité*, another crowd with a Hungarian flag dug cobblestones out of the streets and hurled them through windows. Communist employees replied by throwing tin with bolts and scrap metal back at the demonstrators. The injured on both sides were given first aid treatment in nearby cafés. The Soviet Embassy was so thoroughly cordoned off by police that no one could get near it.

Today a crowd of some twenty-five thousand French men and women, led by five former Prime Ministers of France and the former Hungarian Minister to Paris, march up the Champs Elysées to register their protest. With traffic diverted, the demonstrators fill the wide avenue shouting slogans such as "Liberty for Hungary! Death to the Communists!" and "Damnation to the Soviet Union!" Linking arms and carrying French and Hungarian flags the demonstrators fill the huge circle of Étoile surrounding the Arc de Triumphe. Before they do, each group, as it arrives, lays a wreath at the tomb of the Unknown Soldier under the Arch. Then, after short speeches, they sing the Marseillaise and the Hungarian National Anthem.

Rather than tangle with the Paris Police guarding the Soviet Embassy, which is holding its November 7 reception, protesters, many of them workers from the Socialist Force Ouvriere, hold an anti-Soviet rally in a hall of the Rue de Grenelles almost directly opposite the Soviet Embassy.

Meanwhile, members of the Communist-run dockers union at St. Nazaire and Brest engage in a work stoppage tonight in protest over Hungary.[79]

In New York City, a surging, shouting crowd of three thousand fill the street in front of the Soviet Mission to the UN, as they battle hundreds of New York Police, some of whom are mounted on horses. Their chants reverberate off Manhattan's tall buildings as if amplified. Police manage to disperse the crowd after several hours, without making any arrests.[80]

Readers of the *New York Herald Tribune* learn that Christopher Emmet, Chairman of the American Friends of the Captive Nations, yesterday formally petitioned President Eisenhower to call an emergency session of the U.S. Congress today or tomorrow, to consider measures to be taken against the Soviet Union until it removes its armed forces from Hungary.

Mr. Emmet says that "if this crime is allowed to pass with condemnation in words alone, if we take no action to save the lives and restore the liberty of the Hungarian people which have earned their freedom as gloriously as any people in history, then hope will perish....

"Your administration is pledged not to use force, but there are measures short of war at our command which perhaps may still save or regain the liberty of the Hungarian people.

"The United States can take the lead in the imposition of stringent economic sanctions and in calling for a world-wide boycott of the Soviet Union until Hungary is set free....We respectfully urge you to call an emergency session of Congress...."[81]

The *New York Times* writes that Eisenhower's re-election "guarantees the continuity of American policy...and averts the usual paralysis...between the election and inauguration...by a change of administration.

"...The most haunting appeal to him comes from the embattled Hungarian patriots...."[82]

In Austria, the government charges the local Communist newspaper, *People's Voice* (*Volkstimme*), with "high treason" and begins formal legal proceedings against it. The paper has been printing scurrilous stories about how arms and agents have been sent in from Austria to the revolutionaries under the guise of aid shipments and the entire Communist press in the East has been re-printing them word for word as front page news. Confident the paper has been making these stories up out of whole cloth and that there is not a shred of evidence to support them, Foreign Minister Leopold Figl assures the nation that "Austria is fully conscious of her obligation as a neutral state." He also expresses his satisfaction with the U.S. statement yesterday, aimed at the Russians, that any violation of Austria's border would be considered "a grave threat to peace," a statement that is carried on all front pages in Austria today.[83]

In Naples a crowd of protesters burns copies of the Communist paper *L'Unita* in front of the local Communist Party headquarters. In Mexico City, the Hungarian National Council orders the Hungarian colony to observe the month of November as a period of national mourning to honor victims of the Revolution.[84]

For Communists, November 7 is *the* major holiday of the year. Even Communist Freedom Fighter István Angyal in Budapest today puts up a red flag. He wants the Russian soldiers they are fighting to see that while they made their revolution in 1917, which he, too, is celebrating, "we Hungarians have made our own in 1956."[85]

Every Soviet Embassy and Legation around the world has been stocked with caviar and vodka for today's annual celebration of "The Great October Revolution" of 1917. This event was not, in fact, a revolution but a coup d'etat which took place on this date. At the time, people in Russia were still using the old Orthodox Church's calendar and this date fell in October; hence its name. Today, in most cases, the food supply is much greater than the guests can handle as diplomats and other officials, even people who in the past have been friendly toward the Soviet Union, stay away in droves. In one case, Brussels, there is actually a scarcity of food. The local caterer decides that the food can be better used by Hungarian refugees and, at the last minute, donates it to aid organizations working in Austria.[86]

In Reykjavik, Iceland, a large crowd assembles to jeer at the few Icelanders who dare attend. Some protesters enter the Embassy grounds and cut down the Soviet flag. When a Soviet official attempts to re-hoist it he is abused and intimidated. Mud and rotten vegetables are thrown at the Embassy and windows broken.[87]

In Bonn, capital of West Germany, only two Foreign Ministry officials attend. They do so for one reason only, as a part of their intelligence-gathering activities. In the Soviet reception in East Berlin, the two top East German officials, Otto Grotewohl and Walter Ulbricht, are missing. Something important enough for the Soviets to forgive this breach of protocol must be keeping them away.[88]

In Moscow, the Soviet leaders make remarkably brief visits to the traditional gala ball. And when they leave, it is not through the front door where they can be observed, but through the back exit. None of the NATO Ambassadors attend, but Sir William Hayter learns from the Swedish Ambassador, who does, that he had a conversation with Khrushchev about Hungary and Khrushchev was very much on the defensive. Khrushchev maintains that the Soviet government was fully prepared to agree to neutrality for Hungary, and would still agree to it if the present government (i.e. Kádár, his puppet) were to propose it. But the Nagy government had been unable to stop at that point and Fascism was beginning. It is now, he maintains, simply not possible for the Soviet Army to withdraw in the face of Fascist snipers.

Obviously staged demonstrations by KGB employees in civilian clothes and Komsomol* members take place in front of the British and French Embassies during the traditional Red Square military parade. When no tanks appear in the parade and a Western military attaché makes this observation

*The Soviet Youth organization.

out loud, a Russian nearby jokingly remarks: "They must all be in Hungary." Westerners in Moscow note that there is a rise in listening to foreign radios, especially the BBC, among university students, despite the increase in jamming, not only of Russian language broadcasts but also of broadcasts in English.[89]

Moscow receives two official messages today: one of which it answers immediately, the other it ignores. The one it answers immediately is from India's Prime Minister Nehru, who wants to know precisely what Soviet intentions in Hungary are since its actions are so at variance with its Declaration of October 30. Bulganin replies today that the Soviet intervention had occurred only after "counterrevolutionary elements" had taken over the country and that Russia will negotiate with the Hungarian government on the withdrawal of its troops "when peace and order is [sic] restored" in Hungary. The message ignored is one from the International Committee of the Red Cross in Geneva. It comes in the form of an international broadcast on a wavelength exclusively reserved for the Red Cross in time of war or extreme emergency and is directed specifically to the Soviet government. The appeal is for a cease-fire in Budapest so that Red Cross workers can pick up the hundreds of wounded who are lying among the dead in the streets. The broadcast reminds the Soviets of the Geneva conventions that protect the rights of civilians during conflicts. They also remind the Soviets that there are still three teams of International Red Cross workers in Budapest as well as a dozen national Red Cross teams elsewhere in Hungary.[90]

* * * *

In Austria today, the Danish Red Cross Field Hospital has been getting the runaround from Soviet officials at the Austro-Hungarian border. The field hospital, consisting of 130 vehicles and 150 personnel, among these fifteen surgeons, is waiting to get the green light to go to Budapest, or, if not Budapest, somewhere in Western Hungary where they are needed.

The Soviet officials at the border are not competent to allow them in and must consult higher authorities. When they have no answer after an hour and a half, they are told that the Commanding Officer in Szentgotthárd is not competent and must consult his superior in Zalaegerszeg. Then the word comes back that he, too, is not competent, it must go to the Commander in Szombathely. Eventually they get an answer from the Commander in Szombathely that he cannot let them go to Budapest, he is only responsible for Western Hungary. In Western Hungary, he assures them, there has been no fighting, and therefore they are not needed. When the Danes finally get through to Budapest they get an answer, supposedly from the Kádár government, which is not even in Budapest, that the regime has "no desire to accept the offer." A Hungarian border guard delivers this news in tears. Before giving the answer he thanks the Danes profusely for what they are offering. After he tells them the answer he adds tearfully, "They cannot be blamed for refusing this help. It was not them, it is the decision of the Soviet Supreme Command."[91]

In a hospital five thousand miles away, Walter Reed in Washington, D.C. the President of the United States is visiting his Secretary of State, operated on last week for stomach cancer. He is accompanied by the acting Secretary, Herbert Hoover, Jr. Secretary Dulles, say the doctors, is making good progress in recovering from his surgery. The Secretary has been getting all of the overseas cables from the Department and is keeping abreast of fast changing events through newspapers, television and radio. The President's visit is kept to half an hour.[92]

The Special UN General Assembly on Hungary, which was to have met today at 3:00 p.m. (9:00 p.m. Budapest time), is being temporarily postponed to give all the speakers who have not yet spoken in the Middle Eastern debate time to do so. There is a possibility that the Assembly will be convened late tonight, but officials cannot predict how long the extended session on the Middle East will take. The Italians are prepared to press for a UN force to be sent to Hungary immediately. The U.S. delegation says it is "working on a statement." They say that the Italian initiative is being followed "with great interest."[93]

Thursday, November 8, 1956

Budapest

Much of Budapest looks like an abandoned city today, the fifth day of fighting. Much of the fighting will cease before sundown. With no help from the West, yesterday, the expected day, hopes are understandably flagging. It is mostly a lack of ammunition among the Hungarian fighters, however, which causes the fighting to peter out. There is still heavy fighting in the worker strongholds of Újpest, Kőbánya and Csepel, where the workers operating an anti-aircraft gun shot down an Ilyushin 28 bomber attacking them yesterday. But today the Kilián Barracks falls into Russian hands for the second time. All but twenty-seven Freedom Fighters, who escape through cellars, are killed or wounded by the time the ammunition runs out. One of the twenty-seven carries a letter signed by nine of the defenders shortly before they perished. "We will vanish," it says, "because we are only a small number, because we are poor and alone. However, we are determined to fight against Soviet slavery because it is impossible to live under it."

The Citadel on Gellért Hill was occupied by the Russians last night. Instead of facing executions, the survivors were disarmed and allowed to go home, possibly a tribute to their courage and consideration of their youth, though certainly it is completely out of character with what has been happening elsewhere.

Hunger is another factor. Everyone is hungry and tired. The Soviet soldiers today are taking advantage of this to try to win over the populace. All up and down the totally ruined Rákóczi Avenue this morning Soviet soldiers are taking loaves of bread and tins of meat to those who have survived the onslaught in their cellars. But the people, though glad to have some food, quickly notice that the meat tins are Hungarian and realize they are simply receiving looted food.[94]

Because fighting has moved to the suburbs, the Danube bridges are open today and Dr. Peinsipp, Austrian Minister, is able to deliver food to the French and British legations in a Hungarian Red Cross van. The American Legation, which is not in need, has a food shipment waiting at the Austrian border to come in as soon as it is permitted.[95]

The two Hungarian doctors and nurses who unload the food at the British Legation explain that the nationalists know that the amnesty terms of the Russians will not be observed; that is why few will ever surrender. They say that two "important Russians" arrived by air yesterday, though they do not know which two. They also say that a few days ago they encountered a Russian Captain commanding a detachment of tanks; he asked them where he might find a responsible nationalist commander to whom he and what was left of his unit of tanks might surrender. He explained to them that three small Hungarian boys had put three of his tanks out of action with bottles of lighted gasoline, in spite of the fact that all three were shot down in the act of doing it. This had convinced him that Hungarian resistance sprang from something so fundamental that he and his men did not want to go on fighting it. They also say that Red Cross Headquarters and several hospitals are badly damaged from the Soviet shelling. At the gates of one hospital a crowd of civilians seeking shelter was mowed down by machine guns from Russian tanks. Dr. Ole Lippman, a Danish Red Cross doctor who is working in another hospital, says that today more than a hundred wounded people were admitted to his hospital: every one of them victims of Soviet machine gun fire into a single food queue.[96]

So many Red Cross workers have been killed or wounded trying to rescue wounded in the streets that they have had to resort to throwing ropes to those still strong enough to grasp them, so they could be pulled out of the line of fire. Russian wounded, they say, are refusing to return to their units or even to go to hospitals now in Russian hands, since they know that they will be shot for having left their tanks. They are now under strict orders not to leave their tanks in any circumstances.[97]

The U.S. Legation is still receiving phone calls. One woman calls to express deep gratitude for what the Legation has done for the Budapest Fire Brigade. She goes on to tell of those firemen who have been taken to the cemetery and murdered, and of another group taken to the cellars of a restaurant in the East Station to remove people imprisoned there for the past five days without food or drink, in a state of near dementia. The massacre at the Kun Street Fire Station was caused by liberated prisoners, still in prison garb, who had foolishly shot at the Russians, who thereupon surrounded it with tanks and not only destroyed it, but the Social Insurance Hospital next door.

One long printed document headed "We Accuse" is a list of complaints addressed directly to the Russians and signed: For the IX District Armed Forces Revolutionary Youth, István Angyal, Commander." The style and tone is quite similar to that of printed posters which appear all over Budapest today chastising the Kádár government for calling the Freedom Fighters "fascists and counter-revolutionaries" when they "know very well that we are not."[98]

Another, complaining that Radio Free Europe reports that "only a few determined revolutionaries" are fighting in Budapest—obviously a broadcast of yesterday or the day before—wants the Legation to know the truth and then lists in extraordinary detail over a dozen places where fighting is taking place around Budapest, and listing also those installations which have been destroyed or damaged.

Early yesterday morning, several Soviet T-54 tanks pulled up in front of the Parliament building and disgorged a small group of civilians who quickly entered the building, though there was no gunfire in the vicinity. They were János Kádár and four of his colleagues, the alleged "new government" of Hungary. Ferenc Münnich has preceded them by a day. They have come from Szolnok where they have been since late November 4. Later this morning, Kádár will receive his first visitor, Ambassador Yuri Andropov.

Not far away in the British Legation, Sir Leslie Fry is writing another report to the Foreign Office. He ends it with the observation: "Present indications point unmistakably to a Soviet disposition to reimpose Stalinism in Hungary and to maintain it by the continued presence of their armed forces. The Hungarian people can thus expect ruthless retribution; and their only hope lies in the United Nations."[99]

Hungary Beyond Budapest

Some combat continues in the outskirts of Dunapentele where workers fighting alongside regular army units were overwhelmed by superior Soviet forces yesterday. Mainly they lacked sufficient anti-tank weaponry. They also had little defense against the bombs and strafing of the Soviet Air Force.

In the area near Győr in the west, the Soviets are attacking partisans with ten tanks and an estimated ten thousand troops in an offensive which began at dawn yesterday from the Szombathely-Pápa-Komárom railway line in an attempt to split off the northwest corner from the rest of Hungary. Fierce fighting continues outside of Pécs in the south, particularly in the Komló forest north of the city and parts of the Mecsek mountains around the uranium mineheads. There are four areas further along the Yugoslav border where small battles are being fought. Due to the thick underbrush and marshy areas it is not suitable for tanks to operate in this area, giving partisans a better chance of survival. But lack of sufficient ammunition is still the chief problem facing most of the Freedom Fighter units across the country. Nearly all shooting has ceased in the eastern part of the country.[100]

The forty Hungarian Border Guards who had been refusing to surrender at Hegyeshalom, vowing as recently as yesterday to fight to the death, cross over the border today and seek asylum in Austria, rather than face imprisonment and probable deportation.[101]

Over in Parliament Square, a large black limousine pulls up to the southern side entrance. Ambassador Yuri Andropov has come to welcome "the government" to Budapest, but also to make an assessment for the Kremlin as to how their puppet regime is performing.

Andropov is genuinely shocked that there seems to be no one in that gigantic building. Except for six Government Ministers and a few soldiers, there is nobody there—and this is not the lunch hour. Where are the deputy Ministers, where are the aides, where are the secretaries? He finds the scene quite eerie.

Though he has only been back in Budapest for a few hours and only seen it from the slit windows of a tank, Kádár maintains that "life is getting back to normal in Budapest." Admittedly "the government has hardly had any contact with the country and the large companies of Budapest. The majority of the workers would like to return to their work, but they are afraid of the revenge of the bandits." So far the fight against the "fascists" is being carried on exclusively by the Soviets. Would it not be a good idea, says Kádár, to involve more Hungarians in it? In a telephone conversation with Army Corps Commander Lashchenko yesterday the Soviet general seemed to have approved his idea, but has not yet given an official answer. Kádár suggests that two regiments of Hungarian soldiers be established as soon as possible made up of loyal Communists and former Security Police, but he seems to expect the Soviets to do this for him. He feels it will be of great political significance to have at least some Hungarians fighting.

Kádár expects to receive the Yugoslav Ambassador later today and the question of Imre Nagy will be discussed. Kádár believes Nagy must be pressured into signing the document prepared for him announcing his resignation. Kádár feels it is essential that Nagy and all the other people staying with him sign a statement agreeing that they would do no harm to Kádár's new government. Only once they have signed such a document can their fate be decided. Kádár then gives Andropov his personal opinion that Nagy and his entourage "should be allowed to go to Yugoslavia in order to avoid straining relations with the Yugoslav leadership, provided, of course, that they meet the above conditions. The Yugoslavs, he adds, are most likely making every effort to save Nagy, not because they need him, but because they are afraid certain things that are quite "undesirable for them" may result.

Andropov is rather taken aback by Kádár's two requests at their parting. Would it be possible, asks Kádár, for the Supreme Command of the Soviet Army to help him restore normal working conditions at the Hungarian Radio? (My God, thinks Andropov, if he cannot find Hungarians to provide security at the Radio, where is he going to find men for those two regiments of Hungarian troops?) The second request is even more pathetic. Could he have some help from the Supreme Command in setting up a printing press so they can print their new Party newspaper, *Népszabadság*?

As Andropov will explain in the special ciphered message he will send to Moscow later today, "While our Hungarian friends do not have their own newspaper, the rebels circulate in every street of the city their newspaper entitled *Igazság* (Truth) that publishes provocative material against our friends and the Soviet Army."[102]

The citizens of Budapest have sized up the political situation for what it is. Mimicking the regime radio they print up handbills and pass them out to their fellow citizens. The handbills read:

WANTED: Nine million fascist counter-revolutionaries, all former factory owners, bankers and Cardinals. Their main centers of aristocratic living are Csepel, Újpest and Kőbánya. Fortunately there are six honorable Hungarians to form a government and save the country."[103]

It gets a welcome laugh in such grim times.

In Moscow, Nikita Khrushchev is furious with Tito, thinking he has broken their agreement at Brioni over what to do about Nagy. Yesterday he sent Tito a long message arguing against Nagy "and his accomplices" taking refuge in Yugoslavia and saying, "the Presidium believes that the only correct solution would be to transfer Nagy and his group to the authority of the Hungarian government." Today Tito sends an equally long reply in which he demurs, "We believe that now it is irrelevant whether our Embassy in Budapest acted correctly or incorrectly; it is important that we resolve this problem jointly...." Then he explains why he cannot just hand Nagy over. It is "on the basis of what is stated in our Constitution about granting the right of asylum, and on the basis of international custom...we cannot violate our word and simply hand those people over...."[104]

Later today, Khrushchev finds himself dealing with another problem involving Hungary. The Students of Moscow State University have been paying too much attention to foreign radio broadcasts and to what foreign students in Moscow have been telling them about events in Hungary. They have been making critical remarks about their own government and the Red Army. He has the Komsomol call a meeting in the Sports Palace. Here he repeats the Soviet line on Hungary and reminds them, indirectly, but obviously, that they have no right to be studying at the expense of factory workers and peasants if they are critical of the government which put them there, and every one of them can easily be replaced.[105]

Freedom Radios

The Freedom Radios are all but snuffed out. Very early this morning when it is still night, Radio Róka (Fox) states that the revolutionaries will not give up, or lay down their arms and will fight as long as their ammunition lasts. And they plead for help from the West lest all the blood that has been shed proves to be in vain. The Soviets, they say, are using inhuman tactics, including incendiary bombs.

An hour later Radio Rákóczi at Dunapentele tries to broadcast. It is interspersed with Morse code signals and only one sentence is intelligible: "Do not give up your arms!" possibly instructions to groups breaking up. But the suburbs of Dunapentele will finally fall to the Soviets before the end of the day.

At daybreak, Radio Rajk gives its only transmission of the day. True to the ideals of Communism, the announcer says,

> Pay no attention to the promises...of the traitor, János Kádár. Do not believe...that Kádár's clique will insure sovereignty for Hungary at the very moment when a foreign army is engaged in mass slaughter in our unfortunate Fatherland, when the lofty tenets of Communism and sovereignty are [trampled underfoot?] in the most bloody and barbarous fashion. Who appointed János Kádár and his clique as the so-called government—the sovereign Hungarian nation, or the foreign occupier...? And even if the new Rákosi were truly inclined to carry out his obviously false promises, what guarantee is there the Soviet leadership would give him an opportunity to do so? Not the government of János Kádár, but the leadership of the Soviet Union is the absolute master in our homeland, which has again become degraded to the status of a colony....[106]

Reaction in the West

Shouting anti-Communist slogans demonstrators march across downtown Vienna this evening attacking Communist and East European offices in an orgy of destruction. Windows are smashed, fires set and more than fifty persons injured as police, swinging rubber truncheons, fail to halt the crowd.[107]

Paris endures rioting for the third night in a row, only this time it is five thousand irate Communists seeking revenge for the destruction wrought on their institutions last night. Police have banned the gathering, but it takes Republican Guards with tear gas and fixed bayonets to clear the crowd off the boulevard into side streets. Elsewhere in France, demonstrators surge into Communist Party offices in Strasbourg, Caen and Rennes, throwing furniture from windows, smashing windows and setting fire to documents and newspapers.[108]

Nearly three thousand University of London students wearing black armbands battle foot and mounted police as they try to hand in a petition at the Soviet Consulate condemning Russia's brutal behavior in Hungary. Elsewhere a concert planned for tonight to open "British-Soviet Friendship Month" is cancelled and the chief cartoonist of the *Daily Worker*, Gabriel, announces his resignation because he "profoundly disagrees" with the newspaper's policy over Hungary.[109]

In the U.S., George Meany, President of the fifteen-milion-strong AFL-CIO Labor Union, telegrams President Eisenhower calling on the government to "urge every country outside of the Iron Curtain to sever all cultural, scientific, technical and economic relations with the Soviet Union," and "energetically block every effort of Moscow to seat in the UN the puppet regime it has imposed by brute force on the Hungarian people."[110]

In Switzerland, resolutions demanding a break in economic and cultural relations with Russia are demanded as two leading Communist party members and Ulrich Kaegi, editor of the Swiss Communist publication *Vorwaerts*, resign from their Party membership. In Geneva, the International Labor Organization recommends that it work with the UN in sending observers to Hungary, while in Lausanne the Swiss Olympic Committee decides to boycott the Olympics if the Soviets take part. In Geneva, Denis de Rougemont, Director of the European Cultural Center, writes in today's *Journal de Geneve*, "We must put Communism under the ban of civilized humanity. And in practice that means: break off all relations, diplomatic or other, with Soviet Russia."[111]

Neutral Finland's Secretary General of the Finnish National Union of Students today informs the secretariat of the Communist-controlled International Union of Students in Prague that it is disaffiliating from the I.U.S.[112]

In Montevideo, Uruguay, a crowd carrying sticks and torches burns down the Russian Consulate before police can arrive on the scene. In far-off

Djakarta, Indonesia, the Foreign Ministry, which had played genial host to Khrushchev and Bulganin a year and a half ago, censures the use of Russian force in Hungary.[113]

In Washington, the American military is taking the Soviet rocket-attack threats to France and England more seriously than the Europeans, "American commanders around the world," writes the Associated Press, "have been alerted to tighten their defense readiness," according to the Joint Chiefs of Staff. Some naval maneuvers are cancelled and training activities of the Strategic Air Command have been reduced to keep it assembled for instant reaction. The *New York Herald Tribune*'s foreign correspondent Marguerite Higgins, who covers the Pentagon these days, writes today:

> The United States feels the Soviet moves would have any one of three purposes:
>
> 1. To create a gigantic bluff which has the deliberate aim of scaring the British and French out of the Middle East by making them fear military action of some kind against Europe, or even against themselves.
>
> 2. To prepare a new move to crush Władysław Gomułka.
>
> 3. To take advantage of the British and French preoccupation in the Middle East and the deployment of four hundred thousand French troops in Algeria to undertake a new aggression in Europe or Asia or even an all-out-attack on Europe.[114]

Several newspapers in New York, meanwhile, carry alarmist stories this morning about Soviet troop movements on the Polish frontier.

This heightened fear of war in Washington does not go unnoticed in the Kremlin.

Indeed, Bulganin's reply today to Eisenhower's long November 4 note of controlled outrage and sincere attempt to bring the Soviets to their senses is as belligerent and contemptuous as any note the President has ever received, saying, in effect, "mind your own business."

One of the President's reactions, somewhat conforming with Christopher Emmet's appeal of yesterday that he call an emergency session of Congress, is to call the Congressional leaders to the White House later today.[115]

The President also meets with his National Security Council. Oddly, despite the Hungarian crisis and Nagy's appeals to the UN, the Security Council has not met for a week. At its last meeting it did not even deal with

Hungary, since Secretary of State John Foster Dulles had assured the President that the Hungarian situation was essentially resolved, and the Council needed to concentrate on the much more serious problem of the Middle East.

Today Under-Secretary Hoover is in Foster Dulles' place and Allen Dulles, Director of the CIA, reviews the situation in Hungary, suggesting that Kádár may yet turn out to be a sort of Hungarian Gomułka, though not that he would put his trust in Kádár. While Soviet prestige in Western Europe has reached its lowest point in years, the rebellion in Hungary will be extinguished in a matter of days, if not hours. The Soviets will nevertheless be faced with a problem in Hungary for many, many years. "Our problem right now," says the Director, "is what more we can do?"

The President says this is indeed a bitter pill for us to swallow. The whole business is shocking to the point of being unbelievable. We say we are at the end of our patience, but what can we really do that is constructive? What good, for instance, would breaking off diplomatic relations do? The Soviets don't care. Somewhere Nehru (or was it possibly Foster Dulles, or Lodge) has said that what was really happening in Hungary was obscure. Could anything be blinder?

Vice President Nixon feels that the most important thing is to see that the rest of the world really understands what is happening in Hungary, particularly people in Asia. He also feels we should give the Congressional leaders a good stiff talk on Hungary. In this regard, Dulles feels discussion of Hungary should come first, rather than where it is now scheduled to come last, and others agree.

The President ends the meeting by saying that we must be careful in briefing the Congressional leaders not to place all the blame for what has happened in Hungary on Great Britain and France. We should instead put the Near East situation in its true perspective, and indicate clearly the ultimate Communist responsibility for what has occurred in the Middle East.[116]

Yesterday's radioed appeal to the Soviet Union from the International Red Cross in Geneva to allow a truce in Budapest so that Red Cross workers can pick up the wounded still lying in the streets was heavily interfered with by Soviet jammers. As a consequence, few, if any, heard it in the Soviet Union. Nevertheless the International Red Cross says it has begun negotiations with Soviet authorities in Moscow to permit Red Cross efforts in Hungary.

A Danish Red Cross spokesman in Vienna claims that the Soviets have given permission for an international truck convoy (actually the Danish field hospital) to enter Hungary tomorrow.[117] At Schwechat, Vienna's airport, there are about five hundred tons of general supplies and about twenty tons of medical supplies ready to be flown to Hungary, with more arriving every hour.[118]

Very few refugees manage to cross the frontier through the icy drizzle alternating with snow today. Meanwhile, about thirty Communists who fled from the Revolution in Hungary have told Austrian authorities they wish to return. In Paris a coachload of forty-three mud-stained, weary Hungarian refugees arrive from Vienna tonight, welcomed by a cheering crowd of Parisians at the Hungarian Relief Center. The French Government today announces it will donate the three million francs it had set aside for the visit of members of the Supreme Soviet, scheduled to arrive here next week, to Hungarian Refugees. The Soviet authorities are informed that their visit has been cancelled. In Sweden, the government decides to take one thousand of the fifteen thousand Hungarian refugees now in Austria.[119]

At the United Nations in New York

The long-awaited special session on Hungary of the UN's General Assembly gets under way this morning. There are two resolutions, one by the Americans and one by the Italians. As the Italians have now been joined by Ireland and Cuba, the British have no difficulty in getting a copy and are able to persuade them to drop any reference to a UN observer team, as this would be a bad precedent for their situation in Cyprus. The Italian Resolution repeats the call for Soviet withdrawal but then "leads with its chin" in calling for free elections, absolute anathema for the Soviet Union. On the other hand, it does not even call for a UN police force for Hungary, something that would be acceptable to the British. The British find the Americans are simply not talking to them and thus they can have little influence on the American resolution. It concentrates entirely on the problem of humanitarian aid to Hungary and in its last three paragraphs the Hungarian refugee problem. There is nothing about Soviet troops withdrawing from Hungary, nothing about sending a team of observers as there had been in early draft resolutions, not even anything about sending a UN police force to Hungary. While it "urges the U.S.S.R. and Hungarian authorities to cooperate fully with the Secretary-General and his duly appointed representatives for carrying out the humanitarian tasks," there is nothing encouraging the Secretary General, who has been inactive for four days, to act with urgency even to get just humanitarian observers into Hungary.

In the opinion of many delegates who are prepared to rip into the Soviet Union and at last do something concrete instead of just mouth words, it is a strangely weak and passive resolution.

Before either resolution is introduced, however, it is learned that the U.S. delegation would like to adjourn the meeting until tomorrow so that it can "marry" the Italian resolution to their own. Despite many countries' vehement attacks on the Soviet Union and praise for Hungarian patriots—all of which gets extensive coverage on VOA and RFE—the first day's debate, in the opinion of Sir Pierson Dixon of the UK, is "on the whole, apathetic."

Secretary-General Dag Hammarskjold does two things tonight. He meets, in private for forty-five minutes, with Anna Kéthly, Socialist and sole member of the Nagy government who is in the free world. He sends a message to the Kádár Government in Budapest asking whether UN observers will be permitted to enter Hungary and, if so, when that might be.[120]

CHAPTER IX

The Revolution Goes On

Budapest

BY FRIDAY, NOVEMBER 9, *the sixth day of the Soviet blitzkrieg, Hungarian resistance was crumbling in all sectors of the city but Újpest, Kőbánya, Soroksar and Csepel—all working-class industrial districts, where proletarian solidarity and discipline were paying off. Elsewhere, the surviving Freedom Fighters—largely students, young workers and children, all of whom had been transformed into hardened killers—began to lose heart. It was not just a question of exhaustion and of running out of ammunition, though these were major factors. It was the gradual realization that they had been betrayed. Now, three days after the American election, and with nothing but talk in the United Nations, it was becoming clear that help from the West was not, in fact, coming. Or if it did, it would be too late.*

Some of these young fighters had been so sure help was coming that they had stood on the rooftops Wednesday and yesterday looking for the UN airplanes which would bring soldiers to relieve them. But the planes hadn't come. And now it was clear they were not coming. "We are victims of a giant hoax," they thought. "The West, which has encouraged us for years and which has even urged us to keep fighting just a bit longer, has betrayed us. Can it be that all we've endured—all this fighting, all this destruction, all our friends who have been killed—was in vain?" It was too hard a lesson to absorb. Many wept bitterly before saying goodbye to their comrades and heading home, vowing to keep up the struggle, somehow.

433

EXPLOSION

Others, who had never put their faith in the West but were determined that they would never again live under Soviet domination, decided to keep on. They regrouped, formed smaller bands, and went off to Csepel where some had originally come from or decided to flee into the countryside to join some partisan groups operating in the woods and mountains.

November 9–12, 1956

With fighting finished in all of central Budapest, people are back on the streets examining once again what the Russians have done to their city. Destruction is everywhere, but the worst is Rákóczi Avenue where not a building on either side, even if still standing, is habitable. Every one is shattered, burned-out or roofless. But equally destroyed is the Grand Boulevard (or outer ring), where practically every building is marked by shell holes and bullet holes, and not a window has any glass in it. The worst, of course, is where József and Ferenc Boulevard crosses Üllői Avenue, by the Kilián Barracks. Amidst the street rubble are the remains of the last few Stalin tanks utterly destroyed by nitroglycerine. Glass on the streets and underfoot is everywhere, for windows anywhere near the fighting were shattered. With temperatures hovering around zero centigrade, frigid nights are now added to hunger as a further goad to the population to submit to their conquerors. Many people, in fact, are carrying blankets, evidence of their having slept last night at some friend's apartment or cellar, lacking one of their own. One woman whose letter is smuggled out to Vienna and later published writes, "Never have there been so many suicides. It is like an epidemic."[1] Black smoke billows from buildings set afire days ago; no one has attempted to put out the fires.

Russian tanks are everywhere, with Russian soldiers in or standing by them. To the citizens of Budapest, neither tanks nor soldiers exist. Hungarians look through or past them. When Soviet soldiers, at bridges or checkpoints, cannot be ignored, they are cursed in Hungarian and spat upon by the older citizens, or taunted in school-learned Russian by the young people. If the soldiers try to reply that they are here as friends and by invitation to get rid of the fascists, they are scornfully laughed at. They feel uncomfortable and are sometimes puzzled, but they are soldiers who obey orders; they are not paid to think and argue—even the officers. They can easily see, however, that all the "fascists" are working-class like them.

There is, as yet, no regime press to speak of, but revolutionary papers, particularly *Igazság* [Truth], are distributed all over the city, even when the shortage of newsprint reduces them to only one sheet. These contain not only new resolutions calling for withdrawal of the Russians, the return of Nagy and a neutral Hungary, but also articles urging implementation of many of the decisions by the Nagy government. The regime radio, which no one listens to, is becoming more and more the mouthpiece of General Grebennyik, the Soviet commander of Budapest and hence the Gauleiter for the whole country. He issues decrees and orders directly to citizens of Budapest as though they were in the Soviet Army. The exception, of course, is that each order is followed by threats of what will happen if is not carried out. Grebennyik drops all pretense that there is a sovereign Hungarian government. The Kádár clique makes elaborate promises of amnesty and lenient treatment and in the next moment Grebennyik renders those promises meaningless by executions, arrests and, what is becoming clearer by the day, deportations. Grebennyik's decrees and proclamations are posted in Hungarian all over the city. Almost as soon as these posters appear, posters calling for the withdrawal of Soviet troops, return of Imre Nagy, and neutrality of Hungary are plastered over them. These are signed "The Workers of Budapest" or "The Hungarian Youth which goes on Fighting" or one of the dozens of workers or national councils which were set up as a result of the Revolution and still are operating.

There are many signs in Budapest that while defeated militarily, Hungarians remain uncowed. Among these is the fact that everywhere the national flag with the Communist symbol cut out of the middle is hanging from windowsills and flagstaffs, many with black flags next to them. The national flag is even still flying in place of the red star on top of the Soviet War memorial.

Since they are powerless to get rid of Kádár, people ridicule him with scathing wit.

Jokes

Handbills and posters are put up all over Budapest with the following notices:

WARNING! Ten million counter-revolutionaries are at large in the country.

LOST: The confidence of the people. Honest finder is asked to return it to János Kádár, Premier of Hungary, at 10,000 Soviet Tanks Street.

and

WANTED: A Premier for Hungary. Qualifications: no sincere conviction, no backbone; ability to read and write not required, but must be able to sign documents drawn up by others. Applications should be addressed to Messrs. Khrushchev and Bulganin.

Around this time the British Foreign Office announces to the public that its Legation in Budapest, which has been trying to make contact with the new government, "has no evidence that the Kádár government is even in Budapest," scarcely a source of pleasure to the Kádár clique cowering in the huge Parliament building for at least three days.

Now that most of the fighting is over, Western journalists, trapped in their hotels or national legations, want to escape from Budapest to be able to file their stories. They are about to learn from firsthand experience where real sovereignty lies. On Saturday the tenth they think they have permission to leave for Vienna in a convoy of some fifty cars, for the Soviets are happy to get rid of them. Thirteen kilometers outside of Budapest they are stopped by a Soviet roadblock. There are partisans fighting on the road to Győr. If any of the journalists were to be killed or wounded, they, the Russians, would be blamed for it. Please to return to Budapest and "try again tomorrow." Unfortunately, the cavalcade of cars all flying foreign flags, as it re-enters the city, is taken by Hungarians in the streets to be the arrival of the long expected UN. Cheers and applause go up until they are made aware of the truth. The correspondents, particularly the Americans, feel very small indeed.

"Tomorrow" finds the road now clear, but they have no Hungarian exit visas. Please to return to Budapest and obtain proper Hungarian exit visas. When later these visas are proudly shown to the Soviet officers at the roadblock they are instantly declared invalid. The only authority that can issue exit visas is the Soviet High Command. This takes another day of gratuitous insults and waiting. Finally on Monday, November 12, the convoy is allowed through and makes its way out to Vienna. Suddenly, through a raft of cables issuing from Vienna, the world learns about what has been taking place in Budapest for the past eight days. The following day Hungary is back on the front pages in the Free World's newspapers.[2]

One of the dispatches tells of what it was like as they finally left their rooms in the Hotel Duna. Swarms of Hungarian secret policemen protected by Russian soldiers with machine guns rushed into each room, turned bedding upside down, opened drawers, peered into cupboards and generally tore each room apart. The Duna, with over one hundred Western journalists, was on the Communists' blacklist. Many a Hungarian who clandestinely brought information to journalists during the fighting was observed by secret police informers, who make up much of the hotel staff. All of the rooms are said to be wired with microphones.[3]

Correspondents arriving in Vienna do not hold back the superlatives.

"It was the most heart-rending thing I ever saw in my life," says Dominique Auclaeres, correspondent for *Figaro*. "Never have I seen such brave and kindhearted people before!"

"Today I returned from a lost week amidst the horror of hunger, blasted buildings, gutted tanks and unburied bodies that is Budapest," writes William Krassner of Reuters.

"When I left yesterday evening the country was still fighting and the people still defiant," writes RFE's Fritz Hier, who has spent two weeks reporting from Győr and has been grilled by the Soviets before being freed. "I make no apology for having gone into Hungary as a news correspondent and having come out a missionary." Fritz Molden, editor of the Vienna's *Die Presse*, manages to get out with some colleagues in an eventful, seventeen-hour journey a day ahead of the press convoy. In one of his articles he writes of his thoughts on the way out. "I wonder," he writes, "whether it would be presumptuous to say that the thirty or more thousand Hungarians who have been killed in this first week of the war in Hungary have not died in vain. I honestly feel entitled to declare: by their unhesitating sacrifice they have proved to their own people, to the world and also to the Soviet dictators that, in the long run, it will be impossible to reduce the Hungarian people to slavery, and perhaps the other satellite countries also."[4]

The Russians are showing signs of preparing for a prolonged occupation. All four airports near Budapest are now especially heavily guarded and the suburban town of Budaörs, which contains one of them, is being taken over entirely by the Russian High Command.[5]

In most of the working-class districts of the city the food shortage is close to catastrophic. While the Soviets prevent shipments of food from coming into the capital, the fifteen-truck Red Cross convoy which had been held up at the Austrian border is allowed to come to Budapest and unload its sixty tons of food and medicine. Distribution is supposed to be exclusively by the

International Red Cross, but a remarkable number of items, still clearly marked, turn up in food stores or in the hands of the Red Army. Another convoy is supposed to be on the way. Much of the promised Soviet food, when it finally comes, will turn out to have East European, rather than Soviet, origins.

A few white-collar workers are going back to their offices, fearful that they will lose their jobs, but once there, they find there is nothing to do. Others go only to collect pay packets. The workers go only if it is their job to maintain machinery. Some, like one thousand MÁV (State Railway) workers, agree to report for work and then, after voting a series of new demands, one of which is that the Soviets stop deporting Hungarian youths, return to their homes.[6]

But the booming of artillery and the low bombing runs of Soviet aircraft can still be heard from Csepel, ten to fifteen kilometers to the south of the city's center, where the workers have dug in, not only in their factories and apartment buildings and houses, but in an elaborate trench system they dug in open fields to the south of the vast industrial complex. Using Kossuth Avenue as a guide to fly along, the Soviet bombers peel off to one side or another to drop their loads either over the forest of chimneys or over the network of trenches to the south. Though the workers have been under bombardment since early on November 4, the major Soviet offensive does not begin until the eighth.

Márk Molnár, General Pál Maléter's aide de camp, without uniform, decides to go where his Army training will do the most good. He bicycles down Soroksári Avenue between bombardments to the bridge over to Csepel and offers his services. He is astonished at the discipline and professionalism of the workers. The Hungarian trench works extend for over seven miles across the width of the island. It is split up into twelve sections facing an estimated twelve Soviet battalions. Molnár is immediately given charge of 450 men and assigned a half-mile section in the middle. His dugout headquarters has telephone contact with the other sectors and central headquarters to the rear. There are crisscross trenches for a quarter of a mile behind the main lines, and many key posts have been sandbagged.

Also to the rear is the Incandescent Lamp Factory, where production of light machine guns is in full progress. Hot meals are fed to men in the trenches three times a day, and the workers have already established a regular routine: eight hours in the trenches, eight hours in the factory, eight hours at home. There is an improvised field hospital to the rear and Molnár finds himself allotted volunteer medical students to take care of the wounded.

Following the Soviet command's ultimatum of surrender or annihilation, an unusually heavy bombardment opens up, and by days' end Molnár estimates at least three hundred men and women in his sector have been killed, though this includes persons not directly under him. The trenches are so filled with frost-stiffened bodies that the only way he can get anywhere is to get out and run. All phone lines but the one to headquarters are cut.

Soviet attacks go on for four days. For four days Molnár and his workers hold out, beating back each attack, though at great cost in men. Early on the morning of the eleventh, Molnár is told by headquarters that the Russians have broken through and occupied most of the factories behind him during the night. "The Revolutionary Committee has decided that further resistance is useless. Leave your weapons where they are. Do not get caught carrying a gun."

Elek Nagy, an Army officer who works in Csepel and who will later be elected Chairman of the Central Workers' Council of Csepel, is not so stupid as to be caught with a gun. Fluent in Russian, he feels he can talk his way through Soviet lines by saying he is concerned about his wife and children. He soon finds himself being searched by one soldier, then another, then another. It is almost a game as they pass him on, despite his protests in Russian, to the next "inspector." He undergoes at least five more searches before he reaches the bridge to the mainland. There he sees two youths also being searched. Suddenly there are two quick shots and both youths crumple to the ground. They had tried to conceal guns.

The workers who have been defending themselves in the Kőbánya beer factories in the tenth district also hold out until the eleventh when they run out of ammunition. It still takes hours of Soviet tear-gassing to rout them out of the brewery's cellars.

Even with the major centers of resistance now broken, gunfights and ambushes still take place in isolated parts of the city. On side streets and sections not dominated by Soviet tanks, young fighters, still armed and still proudly sporting their tricolor armbands, can be seen walking around.

Fighting in the Countryside

The battle of Dunapentele, the last city to remain in Hungarian hands, is over and the city in flames. Near Pécs there have been only skirmishes. The

Soviet Commander in the town rounds up many of the parents of soldiers who have fled to their cannons in the hills. Transporting these anxious parents by bus to the foot of the hills, he offers them loudspeakers to call to their children by name to come down and surrender—so far to very little effect.[7]

In the east, in Szolnok County, insurgents are resisting tenaciously at Mart, Tószeg, and Rákóczifalva, and partisans near Debrecen paralyze railroad traffic by blowing up installations and switches.

In the west, small groups of partisans launch surprise attacks on Hungarian Security police on the outskirts of Nagykanizsa, Kaposvár, Győr, and Székesfehérvár. There is also fighting in the Mátra and Bükk mountains in the north. In Bács County in the south, small guerilla bands blow up railroad installations.[8]

Major General Béla Király, now holding in his person the Supreme Hungarian Command, with his four hundred soldiers and eight tanks, attempts to organize guerilla resistance from his base on Szabadsághegy (Freedom Hill). He fights off Soviet attacks and harasses Soviet reinforcements coming into the city. But after four days with no news of the Nagy government reemerging, he decides to retreat to the old castle at Nagy-Kovács, ten miles west of the capital. After a few days, however, the Soviet High Command learns of his whereabouts and launches an attack supported by artillery and newly arrived infantry. After a bloody battle in which Király loses many men and all eight tanks, he withdraws with the remnants of his troops in the night and heads west. Bivouacking on ridges of the Vértes mountains, they are plagued by Soviet helicopters overhead, tracking their retreat. Somehow they manage to stay intact and avoid contact with the enemy, which they know would now be fatal. They have no need of scouts or spies, for the sparse local population keep them informed and the Soviets misinformed. Anxiously listening to foreign radio broadcasts in hopes of a change that will bring Nagy back onto the scene, Király decides after many days of disappointment that "If there is no place for Imre Nagy and for his political solution, there can be no place for us." He gives the order to split up into small groups and head for the Austrian border, which most of them, including Király, reach in early December.[9]

The Soviets are embarrassed to be still fighting a week after they launched their lightning attack, so their propaganda machine comes up with a solution. It is all because the West has sent in fighting men to help the Hungarians and has been parachuting in both men and military supplies into

Hungary. This will explain it adequately to their own and the satellite publics. They realize, of course, that when the West vehemently denies these charges, those denials will have a depressing psychological effect on the patriots who had hoped for just such help. The propaganda machine also has an explanation for why people in Budapest are beginning to starve: armed gangs of "fascists" are breaking into food trains from the Soviet Union and carting the food off in trucks. No matter how outrageous or just plain untrue, there are always people who believe something just because they hear it.[10]

Deportations

As early as November 5 and 6, people in Budapest reported Soviet soldiers, accompanied by ÁVO officers, rounding up young people and herding them off, often with hands tied behind their backs, to the West and East Railroad stations. The ferocity of the fighting in the first few days, however, tended to prevent corroboration of these initial reports. As the reports become more persistent, the word begins to spread quickly around the capital and even into the provinces. It is only a matter of hours before the reports are being broadcast back into Hungary by Radio Free Europe and other Western radios. By November 8, the reports are so upsetting to the populace that regime radios in Pécs, Szombathely, and Szolnok simultaneously broadcast at 4:00 p.m. an announcement that these rumors of deportations are not true. Yes, young people were being rounded up and yes, they are being taken to railroad stations, but no, they are not being deported to Russia. They are only being held for questioning and to prevent them from going to join partisan groups fighting in the countryside. Each case takes up to eight hours to hear and where there is no sign of guilt each youth is then let go.[11]

By the tenth, the British Legation in Vienna reports a refugee as having seen young men of military age rounded up on November 7 by Russian troops and loaded onto railroad boxcars.[12]

The man who is in charge of the deportations, KGB Chief Ivan A. Serov, in a secret report directly to Khrushchev on November 11 states, "By November 10,...3,773 people have been arrested and seven hundred of them have been dispatched to the railroad station in Csop [inside the Soviet Union] under heavy military cover."[13]

Confirmation that deportations are in progress comes to Sir Leslie Fry's attention on the twelfth with two reports. First, a report from a source believed to be reliable that workers in northeastern Hungary blew up a stretch of railway line, attacked the train and set the prisoners, all young men and boys, free. The other, a middle-aged woman who showed the Legation a pathetic piece of paper which had been brought to her by someone she did not know from the countryside. It bears the name and address of her son in his writing and a signed message reading, "Please let my parents know that I am being taken to Russia." On the same day Edward T. Wailes at the U.S. Legation speculates in his report to Washington that the Soviets "may be attempting to deport to the USSR any Hungarian, on a low or high level, who shows leadership qualities for continuation of the resistance movement. Persistence of reports reaching this Legation…indicate that the population is in the grip of this fear."[14]

The Red Cross Convoy

The Danish Red Cross Field Hospital, which has been turned into an International Red Cross convoy, has been waiting for permission to enter Hungary for four days. The original regime excuse for refusal is that aid from the West is simply not acceptable, but this is quickly superseded by Moscow, saying in a Tass report that the convoy is not acceptable because "the Red Cross cargoes of thirty planes which arrived on November 2 and of seventy planes which arrived on November 3 were found to contain arms in part, although they were designated as medical supplies." For this reason, "the government has to suspend for a time the reception of Red Cross parcels from Western countries.…"[15]

There are hints from Budapest that if the convoy were to come through Yugoslavia, this might be acceptable. The Yugoslavs have not yet admitted to their people that there is still fighting going on in Hungary. Yet on November 9, the first train to enter Hungary from Yugoslavia in two weeks crosses the border at Kelebia with a load of Red Cross supplies, coal and wood. And on November 10, Reuters reports from Belgrade that a Swiss Red Cross convoy of sixteen trucks is crossing the Yugoslav frontier into Hungary. At three o'clock on the afternoon of Sunday the eleventh, the International Red Cross Convoy consisting of ten trucks, three Volkswagen minibuses and two small Volkswagens undergoes a minute search by Soviet soldiers in the no-mans-land stretch of border between Klingensbach and Sopron. The search consists of dumping the carefully packed bundles on the ground and opening for inspection every small package and roll of bandage. After several hours of this, the convoy is allowed to proceed to Sopron and thence to Budapest. Even before it reaches its destination, the Red Cross announces in Vienna that a second convoy of forty vehicles is leaving Vienna for Budapest.[16]

Nagy/Kádár and Tito/Khrushchev

It is gradually becoming known that Imre Nagy and his friends took refuge in the Yugoslav Embassy early on November 4. There is now a tug-of-war going on between the Russians and the Yugoslavs over who in the end should get Nagy and his party. Meanwhile, Kádár, who is not unaware that the Soviets are all too aware of his impotence, is desperately trying to persuade Nagy to resign from his premiership, confess his "guilt" and join the Kádár government. Rumors say that Kádár is trying to do this through Nagy's colleague Géza Losonczy, who is also in the Yugoslav Embassy. These same rumors say that the "old man" will not budge and considers Kádár a traitor.[17]

A Kádár-Nagy government would be the best possible solution for Hungary, say high Government and Party sources in Belgrade.[18]

Now Khrushchev has Andrei Gromyko, a Soviet diplomat known to and trusted by Kádár, write a letter putting pressure on Kádár to come over to the Soviet line, for Kádár had earlier agreed that it would be alright if Nagy sought asylum in Yugoslavia.

> We fully support your response to the Yugoslav Ambassador to the effect that Imre Nagy…should not be transferred to Yugoslavia under any conditions because…you cannot allow two Hungarian governments to exist at the same time—one in Hungary, and one in Yugoslavia….
>
> We believe that the Yugoslav insistent demands regarding the transfer of Nagy and his group under their authority are unprecedented and violate Hungarian sovereignty….
>
> A. Gromyko[19]

Tito's Pula Speech

Tito, meanwhile, finds himself attacked on November 8 in the pages of *Pravda*. The attack is nasty and gets under Tito's skin. On November 11, Tito strikes back in a typically long Communist speech he gives on November 11 to the Yugoslav League of Communists at the small city of Pula. The speech is not released by Tanjug, the Yugoslav press agency, until four days later, but when its contents appear it causes a sensation in the West and waves in the East.

It appears to be a hard-hitting speech revealing things he had learned from Khrushchev during their talks at Brioni just prior to the Soviet second intervention. The talks brought to light a struggle raging in the Kremlin, he says. "Soviet leaders," he says, "have erroneous attitudes and defective views regarding relations towards Poland, Hungary, and other countries." He had not considered this fact tragic, because he had assumed that these attitudes were in the minority in the Presidium. But now he sees he was wrong and these erroneous views belong to the majority (i.e., Khrushchev, by implication).

Tito goes on to pick many bones with the Soviets; indeed, one of RFE's kremlinologists, Herbert Ritvo, goes so far as to call the speech "the most significant development in the Kremlin intraparty struggles since the Twentieth Party Congress." There will be many repercussions from the speech, which causes a major rift between Tito and Khrushchev. But basically it is a defensive speech, full of irrational arguments such as calling the first Soviet intervention in Hungary entirely uncalled for and the second fully justified and necessary. It is the speech of a cornered man lashing out.[20]

Kádár's Impotence

Ever since it announced its existence, the Kádár government has been spewing into the airwaves proclamations, threats, enticements, new decrees, and bogus news reports designed to convince people that things are getting back to normal. The main purpose of this is to break the nationwide general strike crippling the country. But since the only power the people can see is that which is coming from foreign occupation troops on the one hand and the still-operating revolutionary and workers councils on the other, few people pay any attention. Eight days after the Kádár "government" has made its existence known, Peter Strasser, the Austrian Socialist Deputy who had gone back to Budapest and been caught after leaving Anna Kéthly at the border, tells people in Vienna, "The passive resistance is unbelievable. People stand in front of Russian tanks and openly put the revolutionary red-white-green colors on their clothing and make anti-Russian remarks. The Russian solders seem very unhappy. Some told us, 'War no good.' There is practically no government power and I doubt whether the Kádár government really exists."[21]

The day before, Ivan Serov is one of several Soviet Presidium members to arrive in Budapest. While Serov is largely concerned with his deportations operation, he is also here to see what can be done to buck up their new puppet government and make an assessment as to whether Kádár needs to be replaced. He cables Khrushchev about Kádár's objection to the Soviets making such extensive use of Security Police members whom the Nagy government had fired. Kádár, he says, claims "it is not advantageous to us for the [former] employees of the security forces to participate in the arrests.... Further, Kádár says that in the Ministry of Internal Affairs...where a number of security agents are concentrated, an unhealthy situation is created, since among these employees are individuals who worked in the forces under Rákosi....These people should be immediately removed....He thinks it expedient to disband the guards since there are dishonest people [there]." Kádár also pointed out that "it is written in the declaration of [his] government that those who give up their weapons and stop resistance will not be punished. The Hungarian government should not take revenge...and display cruelty to them."

Since there have been dozens of instances where Soviet troops have simply executed on the spot those who surrender, and since Ferenc Münnich, Moscow's original choice to head the government, is in charge of the Ministry of Internal Affairs and is purposely using the former ÁVO agents, Kádár has little chance of having his wishes fulfilled.[22]

The regime's first stratagem for getting the workers to return to work is to announce, "All those who have deliberately not reported at their place of work will be considered as having resigned their jobs." Since nobody shows up following this announcement, something else must be tried. So next there are promises of bonuses and "advanced payments" of salaries, particularly if a worker shows up having brought another along with him. Then there are suggestions of just working four-hour shifts, but getting paid for eight hours' work. When this also is totally ignored, Kádár feels forced to join in the Soviet strategy of using hunger to get the workers back to their jobs. When promises of food being made available at the workplace are made, some workers begin to show up—to collect the food, not to go to work. And even when the regime manages to arrange this luxury for the few who do show up, they find themselves apologizing to the complaining workers and promising that next week the food will be hot.[23]

While TASS reports on all the food caravans which are piling up on the

Czechoslovak and Soviet borders, Kádár's Commissioner for Public Supplies, Rezső Nyers, decrees that he is "blocking all stocks of agricultural produce stored in the warehouses of agricultural purchasing and selling enterprises" and that "the use of these blocked stocks can be authorized only by the Commissary for Public Supplies...," that is, himself. The fact that young Freedom Fighters recently succeeded in replenishing their food stocks by breaking into (or, more probably, being allowed into) these warehouses may be the main cause for this announcement.[24]

Interior Minister Münnich makes a fool of himself by announcing that all prisoners who escaped from prison after October 23, but who had already served two-thirds of their term, should immediately report to the nearest prison. If they do so, they will be forgiven one-third of their term. He gets no takers; the ex-prisoners appear not to be so dumb as he.[25]

Kádár's utter inability to control events can be seen when a new decree signed, not by himself, but the figurehead President of the Nation, István Dobi, famous for staying inebriated for long periods of time, is promulgated. The decree is announced one day after Kádár's conversation with Serov. Kádár may not even have seen it; certainly it originated with the Russians, not him. The new "law" states that murder, manslaughter, arson, and plundering can now be punished by death within twenty-four hours of arrest. The radio explains that the new law is necessary because of the "extraordinary increase in the crime rate." In other words, from now on the Soviets and the Kádár government will treat the revolutionaries as common criminals, but under a law far more Stalinist than Hungarian.[26]

Lacking the cooperation of Imre Nagy, Kádár decides he must at least prove to the Hungarian people that the Revolution was not in vain and that he, in fact, will see that many of its demands are carried out. Thus on the same day of the decree on death sentences to be carried out within twenty-four hours of arrest, he makes it known that Soviet-style uniforms will be discarded in favor of the old Hungarian uniforms, the Kossuth coat of arms will be used in place of the former Communist insignia designed by Rákosi, March 15 (the anniversary of the Revolution of 1848) will again be a national holiday, and students will be allowed to choose which foreign language they wish to study.[27] A month ago, such concessions would have been considered sensational, but since Nagy had already granted them, this announcement causes no stir whatsoever.

In the Countryside

The revolution goes on in the countryside as well. In County Szolnok the Executive Committee of the County Council decides that those collective farms which do not prove firm, and where management is not satisfactory, will be liquidated and become individual farms. Every cooperative's final accounts have to be prepared, after which farmers can freely choose the form of farming they wish to follow.[28]

But it is the Soviet occupiers who are calling the tune. The Soviets have the regime issue instructions to the commands of all local police forces to hand over immediately all prisoners to local Soviet forces. No special list of the prisoners need be made. In the Hungarian Army hospitals, on the other hand, lists of all the wounded including all personal data are to be compiled and submitted to the local Soviet commanders.[29]

Washington, D. C.

William Jackson in the White House receives an urgent cable from his predecessor C. D. Jackson on November 8 complaining that:

> The UN has postponed three times any action to implement resolution and send inspection team to Hungary....Hardly anything more required than firm prod to Hammarskjold to get cracking on appointing and sending this commission to the Hungarian border. The argument...that they will be denied admission...misses the moral pressure point completely. The commission should be sent immediately and should remain knocking on the...border every day, every hour demanding admittance in the name of the United Nations, demanding the right to send in food and medical supplies.... Appropriate word from the President spelling out urgency and calling on Hammarskjold to get cracking is the only way to get this matter...off dead center.[30]

United Nations, New York

On Friday, November 9, the Special Session of the General Assembly on Hungary has three resolutions placed before it. Before the evening session begins, however, U.S. Ambassador Lodge complains in a telephone conversation with President Eisenhower, "there is a feeling at the UN that for ten years we have been exciting the Hungarians through our Radio Free Europe, and now that they are in trouble, we turn our backs on them."

The President insists that this is wrong—that we never excited anybody to rebel. He says that he can check with the State Department and the USIA.

Lodge thanks him and says he will call the State Department and get them to prepare something on RFE for him to say in the UN.

Two minutes later the President calls John Foster Dulles recuperating in Walter Reed Hospital and repeats what Lodge has told him. Dulles says, "We have always been against violent rebellion." The President says he told Lodge this, and was amazed that Lodge was ignorant of this fact. He then goes on to another topic, but Dulles, who has been mulling over what the President had said about RFE, cuts in and says he doubts that the feeling about our turning our backs on the Hungarians exists in any quarters but the French and British.[31]

The U.S. delegation has failed to get the Italians to meld their resolution with their own, though it does manage to water it down somewhat. Basically the Italian resolution calls on the Soviet Union to withdraw her forces completely from Hungary so that UN-supervised elections can be held. It passes by a vote of forty-eight to eleven with sixteen abstentions, largely from Asian countries. Next comes the U.S. resolution, which concerns only humanitarian aid to Hungary and aid for the Hungarian refugees. This passes with a majority of fifty-three to nine with thirteen abstentions. Last comes an Austrian resolution, also strictly on humanitarian aid. It manages not to mention the Soviet Union at all. Before the vote, however, the Austrians are persuaded to delete something that could be offensive to the Soviet Union. The resolution as submitted reads:

"Considering the extreme suffering to which the Hungarian people are subjected by the fighting which is still going on...."

The offending phrase, "by the fighting which is still going on," is removed and the resolution then put to a vote. It carries by sixty-seven votes to none opposed and eight abstentions.[32]

On the following day, over Soviet and Eastern Bloc objections, the unprecedented dual emergency sessions vote to carry both the Middle Eastern and Hungarian items over into the regularly scheduled General Assembly meeting which opens Monday, November 12.

Secretary General Dag Hammarskjold is at last beginning to act. On Thursday he requested permission for observers to enter Hungary. On Saturday he announces that the Hungarian government has informed him that it is "weighing" his request. On Sunday he says he has asked the Kádár regime to please speed up its answer, and on Monday he says he has asked the Soviet Union to "lend its assistance in having the new government of Hungary admit United Nations observers."[33]

While Hammarskjold was willing to receive Anna Kéthly in his office, he is reluctant, lacking pressure from the United States and other major powers, to allow her to address either the General Assembly or the Security Council, as many wish her to do. She receives a tumultuous, highly emotional welcome, however, by fifteen thousand people in New York City's Madison Square Garden on the eve of the UN debate on Hungary. Sponsored by the International Rescue Committee, a private organization, the meeting attracts New York's Governor Harriman, Senator Clifford Case of New Jersey and many dignitaries from Labor, the churches, and all the American Hungarian organizations. Other speakers, though not Ms. Kéthly, are constantly interrupted by cries of "Talk is cheap!" "Arms for Hungary!" "Down with Russia!" and "We want action!"[34]

On Monday Ambassador Lodge says, "If they do not permit observers in, then we shall have to have another meeting of the General Assembly and we shall have to exhaust every peaceful means. I do not know what the means will be." He adds that he expects "big developments within a very few days that could lead us to very big things indeed." In point of fact, unless there is a two-thirds vote in favor of an early debate, the Assembly's rules of procedure are so strict that it will be at least another week before any debate on Hungary can begin.[35]

Eisenhower, however, feels it is a time for action. On November 8 he calls in Acting Secretary of State Herbert Hoover, Jr. and proposes that the United States take advantage of the worldwide fright, which he is sure Bulganin and Khrushchev share, to make some progress on disarmament. How about offering to withdraw American ground troops from West Germany and pulling all other NATO forces behind the Rhine? Hoover doubts that Secretary Dulles would agree to such an offer. Well, says Eisenhower, he just wants the Secretary of State to have the thought, because "as long as we are before the world, just calling each other names, being horrified all the time by their brutality, then we get nowhere."

When Hoover reports this conversation to Dulles, the Secretary says absolutely not. Though he would not put it this way, he much prefers "getting nowhere" to the risk of engaging directly with the perfidious Soviet leaders. Eisenhower's grand idea is soon lost among the Black Angus cattle on his Gettysburg farm, to which he soon retreats.[36]

Refugees

In Austria, Hungarian refugees are once again flowing across the border, despite the fact that border guards are again shooting, killing and capturing many who try to escape. Up until nine p.m. on November 9, 1,828 had crossed the border in the previous twenty-four hours. The flow has kept at approximately two thousand per day since then.[37]

Countries as far away as Argentina, which is arranging to take in three thousand orphans, are pledging money and numbers they are willing to accept. Britain pledges up to ten thousand pounds sterling to cover the costs of transportation and resettlement of 2,500 refugees. In the United States, which has pledged to take five thousand, the administration is trying to get Congress to pass legislation making it possible for them to come in under the Austrian and German quotas, since the quota for Hungary is both tiny and already used up. It is being called "slashing of red tape," but it will take more than this to make it possible for these five thousand to get visas and emigrate to the U.S. before the end of the year when the current refugee act expires. As *The New York Times* puts it, the law will have to be stretched and "bent, if not broken to make it possible..."[38]

Each refugee has his or her own tale to tell, and many have fresh information about the fighting and Soviet troop deployments, of interest not only to journalists but to Western intelligence officials as well.

There is also the problem of spies among the refugees: these are Communists, particularly ÁVO, who fled from the Revolution and now are collecting information with the intention of taking or somehow sending it back to Hungary, and ÁVO spies who are deliberately planted among the refugees currently escaping. Most of the Hungarians are alert to this possibility, but the Austrians, seeking to be as hospitable as possible, are less so. They are soon prodded by Western intelligence agencies into being more vigilant.[39]

November 13–18, 1956

Budapest

The main fighting is over; now begins a long guerilla war. The miracle of heroism is transforming itself into the miracle of endurance in a mass rebellion of passive resistance. Now the entire nation is involved, not just the young people. Workers may be streaming back to their factories, but it is still just to pick up their October paychecks and socialize with their fellow workers. Even those who remain in the factories next to their machines are not working, but only discussing what to do next.

The Kádár puppet government, unable to get the workers to pay much attention to it—particularly its toothless threats—is producing more and more carrots while the Soviets provide the sticks. These carrots consist not only of inducements like food for workers in their workplaces, but also more and more concessions duplicating the rights already granted by the Nagy government. There is no talk, however, of either Soviet troop withdrawal or neutrality. Now Kádár even goes beyond the Nagy government pledges to specific promises of wage hikes for miners and others at liberal percentages, provided, of course, the miners are back at work by Monday, November 19.

But the workers and intellectuals of Hungary, many of them still Communist Party members, have their own agenda. On November 15, two manifestoes are printed and posted all over Budapest. One, a resolution passed by a group of Workers' Councils in Buda, meeting in the Hungarian Optical Works, offers to resume work connected with the city's reconstruction, communications, and the food supply, but all other work would not be resumed until their demands are met. These are: free elections with such parties as are ready to accept "our socialist achievements based on Socialist ownership of the means of production"; the release of Imre Nagy and his colleagues, including Pál Maléter and those arrested during negotiations with the Russians, and all patriots currently under arrest; the immediate withdrawal of Soviet troops from Budapest and negotiations for their later orderly withdrawal from the country; and full publicity for all of these demands in the press and on the radio.

The other manifesto, even more widely distributed, is a proclamation issued by the Writers Federation, the Petőfi Circle, the Hungarian Telegraph Agency and many other educational and intellectual organizations. It demands withdrawal of Soviet troops and neutral status for Hungary; retention of the 1945 land reform and state ownership of mines, big industrial enterprises, banks, etc; all obligations and rights of membership in the United Nations; and full observance of human rights. The manifesto says that because of the circumstances by which it came to power, the Kádár government is totally unacceptable. It proposes the formation of a provisional government drawn from various revolutionary committees and workers' councils under the leadership of some internationally recognized personality such as the musician Zoltán Kodály. The assembly should draft and pass an electoral law providing for secret parliamentary elections in which all parties who "recognize that Hungary is a socialist, democratic and independent people's republic should take part."[40]

Down in Csepel, where the fighting actually went on several days past the official capitulation on the eleventh, the workers yesterday held a mass meeting after putting down their arms. They demanded the dismissal of Kádár and the reinstatement of Imre Nagy, and vowed to continue their strike until Russian troops are out of Budapest. Welcoming foreign correspondents to their mass meeting, they repeatedly shouted, "We do not recognize Kádár and his so-called government!" Nor do they recognize the Communist-established trade unions. Labor competitions to raise production norms, they boast confidently, are a thing of the past. When one worker is told no wages will be paid to those on strike, he answers, "They won't defeat us through our stomachs. The peasants know that we are fighting for them, too."[41]

In the city workers and partisans take quick action when they feel someone is breaking the strike. Some number "20" buses were seen running early in the morning of the seventeenth in Újpest. Workers quickly boarded them and had the drivers stop and all passengers were forced off. Then, to make the lesson stick, they overturned the buses. Similar action is taken in other parts of the city when one tramline tries to start up.[42]

A massive demonstration of ten thousand angry workers gathers in Parliament Square on the fifteenth and is reported by phone to someone in Vienna before the line is suddenly cut. They are protesting not on their own behalf but on that of the boys and girls whom have been deported to the Soviet Union. They have proof of these deportations since thirty of the under-aged youngsters had just been returned to Budapest that morning and have told their story.[43]

The workers find other methods of maintaining the strike. When four hundred workers of the Divat Shoe Factory begin working, some other workers, unknown to them, come in and threaten them, whereupon they go home. When three hundred workers show up the next day, the same threatening workers arrive at the same time to send them on their way. When a number of workers show up at the Ganz Waggon Factory, nearby bakers hear of it, rush over and shout, "If you guys work, we don't." The Ganz factory workers take the hint and go home.[44]

The workers of Budapest know that to hold onto the gains of the revolution they have won they themselves have to unite. Thus, workers' councils from all over Budapest send over five hundred delegates on November 14 to the Egyesült Izzó factory to establish a Central Workers' Council of Greater Budapest. In the evening the new Council sends a delegation of nineteen to Parliament to present their demands to Kádár.[45]

Kádár is full of sweet talk, agreeing with many of the workers' demands, until it gets around to the withdrawal of Soviet troops and neutrality. Then he gets so exasperated with the workers that he threatens to have them all deported to Siberia. News of this outburst, of course, is all over Budapest in no time.

In the Countryside

Large areas of Eastern Hungary are still controlled by partisan forces. In the mining town of Ózd, which is northwest of Miskolc near the Slovak border, a daily newspaper is being published which openly attacks the "Kádár clique" and gives advice to workers as to how to carry on the general strike. Workers and miners of the Miskolc area are following instructions from the Ózd Revolutionary Council. Russian soldiers are said to be scared to go beyond Molnár Rock Pass in the Bükk Mountains.

Freedom Fighters from Budapest are said to have joined up with miners from Dorog and Tatabánya in the Pilisi Mountains region. Russian troops are employing flamethrowers in an effort to flush them out of these heavily wooded areas, but with little success; the partisans do all their attacking at night.

Hungarian railroad workers are sabotaging the entire railroad line between Szolnok and Záhony on the Soviet border in an effort to disrupt the flow of Soviet supplies and soldiers, as well as stop deportation trains headed east, but there are many Soviet troops and railroad employees in the area who hamper and repair their sabotage. Fresh Soviet infantry divisions are crossing into the country at Záhony. Officials in Budapest claim that a full twenty Soviet infantry divisions are on their way, comprising more than two hundred thousand men. Presumably these are to replace the fifteen mechanized divisions now in the country, but it may also be because of continuing Hungarian armed resistance in the countryside.[46]

One Soviet counterintelligence officer, Captain Zlygostev, reports to Deputy Minister of Internal Affairs M.N. Kholodkov that "in a number of villages he found himself in situations where anarchy reigned....It was impossible to find out from anybody who among these local residents participated in the counter-revolutionary demonstrations." KGB head Serov, meanwhile, complains to Khrushchev, "The data that we have testifies to the presence of even more weapons among the population. However, the voluntary surrender of these weapons is proceeding slowly. Weapons are given up only after the agency establishes the presence of weapons and a search is conducted."[47]

The Nagy government has already abolished compulsory agricultural deliveries, a staple of the Soviet Communist agricultural system. On November 15, the Kádár government bows to the inevitable and allows the new law to go into effect. To reverse the decision at this point, he realizes, would cause a fresh upheaval in the countryside.[48]

For the first time since November 4, telephone lines to the outside world are opened on November 13.

Deportations

Through an inadvertent slip, the regime radio in Szolnok reports on November 14 that railroad workers in the Debrecen area have again gone out on strike, this time because of reports that Hungarian young people are being deported to the Soviet Union. They do not say that the reports are true, but they make no effort to deny them. People who hear the broadcast cannot but wonder whether the slip may have been intentional. Radio Free Europe and Western news agencies pick it up and repeat the report as confirmation that deportations are going on.[49]

Notes giving their names and addresses dropped by the young people while the trains were passing through the Hungarian countryside have been turning up in Budapest for several days.

One deportation train that was halted in the station at Cegléd, a town southeast of Budapest, is captured in a surprise attack by partisans and close to one thousand young deportees are freed.[50]

Vacuum tactics for deportation have produced lots of young people from all over the country, but even with screening before the departure of the trains a great many people who took no part in the revolution or who are actually loyal to the new regime have been caught in the dragnet. Soviet

Deputy Minister Kholodkov writes indignantly to his superiors on November 15, "Among the people who have arrived are a significant number of members of the Hungarian Workers' [Communist] Party, soldiers in the Hungarian Army and students. Also [there are] sixty-eight people who are underage, born between 1939 and 1942, of which nine are little girls." By this time there are 846 people in the Uzhgorod (formerly Ungvár, Hungarian) prison "including twenty-three women."

Two Hungarian Army officers about this time write indignantly to the Soviet officer in overall charge of the prison: "[We] have been identified as guilty people, without any official investigation, and have been treated like fascists for four days now. The most terrible thing is that we—officers and Communists—are being held with this scum and forced to listen to their dirty stories about the counter-revolution.... We are convinced it doesn't make any difference to 'our Soviet Comrades' who, on what street, and when [people] are caught or whether or not a person participated in the...uprising."[51]

Refugees reaching Austria from such towns as Szolnok, Debrecen, Nyíregyháza, and Püspökladány say deportations in each of these towns began on November 10, and they seem to be carried out under a very well coordinated plan.[52]

In Budapest on November 16, Soviet soldiers, accompanied by ÁVO, enter the Sándor Péterfy Street Hospital in Pest and take away an unknown number of wounded youths. In the same operation they discover in a sub-cellar of the hospital the printing presses used by István Angyal and his Tűzoltó Street group to print up posters and manifestoes. Angyal is among those arrested.[53]

Many younger people are now fleeing to Austria to evade these deportations, particularly those who have been most active in the revolution.[54]

The General Strike

Just as the workers are saying they will not return to work until the Russians withdraw from the country, so Kádár is trying to convince the workers that the Soviet troops will not withdraw from the country until they go back to work. On the fifteenth, Kádár actually meets with several groups of workers and at least one group promises him that they will return to work on November 17, while retaining the right to go back on strike. Since the seventeenth is a Saturday, not a full workday, the workers' pledge would seem to be somewhat tentative.[55]

Radio Kossuth has since been stressing this decision with quotes from leaders of the workers' councils.

> János Fazekas, Chairman of the Workers' Council of the Újpest Mining Machine Tools Factory and a member of the provisional Central Workers' Council for Greater Budapest, says on the radio, "I am fond of my craft (he is a turner) and would again like to work eight hours a day for reasonable pay, in a free and independent country, not in the shadow of guns. But can we reach that goal by continuing the strike? Can anybody give us a valid guarantee of it....I do not think so.... Our people have won the praise of the whole of humanity because we have shown a strength without precedence. This national force can put aside, without use of guns, the leaders who do not carry out their duties with honor in all fields of our national life. Therefore, to work!"

The workers are becoming aware of how the strike is hurting their own families. If garbage is not removed from the streets, there will be the danger of epidemics. The city's standstill traffic is hampering people's search for food. The whole city needs heating and light, particularly in the hospitals. And then, there are eight hundred apartment buildings to be rebuilt.[56]

In spite of the call to return to work on Saturday, the forty thousand workers of Csepel continue their strike. Many of them show up at their place of work, but they do not even bother to change into their work clothes and just stand around talking.[57]

In the provinces there is no discernible movement to return to work.

The Regime's Impotence

"The demand for Nagy's return is so strong and the rejection of Kádár so widespread, it is considered unlikely the Premier can survive." So writes Endre Márton, the Associated Press's Budapest correspondent on November 16. Márton goes on to describe an "agreement" that Kádár had come to with the Central Budapest Council of Workers concerning a three-stage program of Russian troop withdrawal: first to barracks in Budapest, then to bases in the countryside, and third, negotiations with Moscow and the Warsaw Pact on withdrawal from Hungary. There is, in fact, no such agreement; it was simply Kádár extemporizing in response to a worker's question. He is happy to have this considered an "agreement" by the populace and people in the West if it will gain him time. He knows from the Soviet viewpoint, any thought of withdrawal is out of the question.

Kádár is so sensitive to accusations that the Rákosi-Gerő days are coming back that he has his "executive committee" strip eight former Government leaders of their party membership and former offices. This includes Gerő and Hegedűs, István Bata, and László Piros, Münnich's predecessor.

Kádár is also reported to have consulted with veteran Peasant Party leaders Ferenc Szabó and István Bibó and to have sent an emissary to Béla Kovács and Zoltán Tildy, Smallholder Party leaders and all former members of the Nagy government, in an attempt to broaden the base of his regime from its current six Communist leaders. The uproar over the deportations frightens Kádár; these are a Soviet idea and not his. The regime has little control over the media, even though purges are undertaken at the top. The radio, for instance, instead of following the Soviet line on the Tito speech made at Pula, spends a full hour delivering the full text word for word.[58] In an interview with the Minister of the Interior, Ferenc Münnich, the radio asks him whether it is true that the new police force contains members of the old ÁVO. Münnich lies by insisting that this is totally untrue. And when the radio reporter says that former ÁVO officers have somehow been able to "outwit the pertinent government decree" and are now operating in the new police force, he is told that "every case which becomes known will be investigated and that the disbanding decree of the government will be [not "has been"] carried out."[59] Short of staff, the radio depends on the BBC's Hungarian language broadcasts for seventy percent of its foreign news. This is not relished in Moscow.[60]

The Party newspaper *Népszabadság*, which is just the old *Szabad Nép* resurrected, quotes a radio address given by Sándor Gáspár, chairman of the Trade Unions. "It is our firm standpoint," says Gáspár, "that non-Party members, as well as workers having other party affiliations, must be given responsible positions both in the government and in the various fields of social and economic life, provided they are loyal to the people's democratic system and enjoy the confidence of the workers." Later in the address, he says that in the future the Trade Unions will be independent both of the government and all political parties.[61]

There are workers in every factory, if only to guard it or maintain the machinery; but in only three out of the 182 factories in Budapest are there as many as sixty percent of the workers in place. Only eight to ten percent of the workers staff the other 179 factories, and few of these men are working.[62]

Interior Minister Münnich is also the Minister of Defense. He must worry about a totally unreliable Army in addition to building up the police with ex-ÁVO officers while denying he is doing so. A questionnaire is devised for all Army officers to fill out, designed to weed out those who might prove disloyal to the new government. Not only must all officers write what they were doing during the revolution, they must pledge complete loyalty to the Kádár regime and agree that it was necessary to seek help from the Soviet Army. Those who refuse to sign the pledge—and very few so far have signed—are automatically dismissed and given half a month's pay. The price of this screening is that twenty-five percent of those who have not already quit refuse to sign, and they, of course, are all of the best officers.

Workers' Councils

Though students and intellectuals are still prominent in their opposition to the Kádár government, Kádár is beginning to realize that they no longer matter. The real powers opposing him are the workers and their workers' councils. As long as these councils exist they will be able to cripple the country with the general strike. But he realizes that he is far too weak to try to challenge them head on. They are a fact of Hungarian life and growing stronger every day. He must show that he realizes this, if he is going to get any respect from the workers. Thus, at the suggestion of the Trade Unions, he decides to issue a decree to codify their existence and rights while framing these in such a way as to wear the councils down. His decree, issued November 13, starts off saying, "Workers' Councils are the rightful units of workers' self-government. The scope of the council encompasses all activities within an enterprise." It goes on to list such activities conforming to the existing model. In the second paragraph, however, the decree states, quite correctly, "as not all workers' councils have been elected by a majority of their workers, they should be confirmed by re-election, with the participation of the entire work force. This should take place in all factories and workplaces not later than three weeks after the resumption of productive work." In fact, of course, most of the elections *have* been by clear majority of the entire work force. By this decree, Kádár is forcing all workers' councils to hold new elections, giving him time to infiltrate and sabotage, as only the Communists can, these new elections.

The founding of the Central Workers' Council of Greater Budapest on the day after the promulgation of this decree shows that the workers are aware that Kádár is trying to box them in and that they need to maximize their power.

They use that power the next day to urge their fellow workers to return to work, albeit on a Saturday, which is only a half workday. By now, however, there is so much in the media about Soviet deportations that many who had decided to go back now decide not to.[63]

Opposition to Kádár is not confined to workers, students and intellectuals, as four Western correspondents discover when they interview the manager of an important government institution. The manager keeps referring to "the Prime Minister," without mentioning his name. When Endre Márton asks him whom he is referring to, the man answers "Imre Nagy, of course."[64]

Red Cross Convoys

The first Red Cross convoy returned to Austria and reported that it had been searched repeatedly by the Soviet military forces both going to and coming back from Budapest and, in fact, had never actually reached Budapest. It was allowed only into the outskirts of the city, where it was forced to unload and hand all medical materials and food over to the Hungarian Red Cross. Because of these difficulties, M. Bovet, the local representative of the International Red Cross in Budapest, temporarily halts operations and has the next convoy on November 15, turn back to Vienna. Meanwhile he and Dr. György Killner, Chargé d'Affaires of the Hungarian Red Cross, journey to Vienna, where they negotiate an agreement whereby Swiss Red Cross nationals are to supervise the distribution in Budapest from now on.[65]

Refugees

So many people are fleeing across the border these days that the Austrians can scarcely keep count. On the same day that Austrian Vice Chancellor Adolf Schaerf tells the Japanese press in Tokyo that Austria has admitted twenty thousand Hungarian refugees, it is announced that nearly five thousand crossed today and the total is now twenty-seven thousand.[66] There are sections of the border where it is very dangerous to attempt a crossing, and others, like the area near Rábafüzes, where it is not. The guards at Rábafüzes say they have been given strict instructions to shoot to kill anyone attempting to escape; instead, they fire into the air and sometimes urge escapees to run. Near the Austrian town of Mogersdorf guards "complain" that their section of the tracer field (freshly plowed land) is full of footprints, but they cannot erase these because they have no rake. These guards say they have not shot at a refugee since the first day of the revolution and have no intention of beginning now.[67]

Private and State Austrian relief organizations are stretched to the limit and urgent appeals are being repeatedly broadcast to the nation for more assistance. The Austrian government declares that unless more financial and material aid is received from abroad, the refugee program may collapse.[68]

In Geneva, the United Nations is keeping track of all the offers from around the world of aid and asylum. Little Switzerland has offered to take four thousand, as has Belgium. West Germany will take three thousand and Great Britain 2,500. Australia has offered to take three thousand and New Zealand five hundred. All told, West European nations alone have so far offered to take a total of 17,500 refugees, and that does not count France, which has put no limit on the number she will take. Next to this the American figure of five thousand—provided legislation can be changed in time— seems almost paltry.[69]

United Nations

On the same day, Secretary General Dag Hammarskjold receives a cable from Acting Hungarian Foreign Minister, István Sebes, replying to Hammarskjold's inquiry about Hungary's needs. He sends a detailed list of medical supplies as well as foodstuffs, fats, cereals, flour, gasoline, coal, glass, wood, trucks, ambulances, and tires which are urgently needed in Hungary.[70] At the same time, Hammarskjold appeals to Sebes to "reconsider" the Hungarian government's decision turning down his request for Hungary to admit UN observers. The Hungarian reply stated that it was an internal affair and the Soviet forces were there by invitation. But in replying to the humanitarian offer, Sebes suggests that the representative appointed by the Secretary General could participate "on the spot." That gives Hammarskjold an idea. Sensitive to all the criticism that he has spent all his time on the Middle East and neglected Hungary, Hammarskjold is now trying to make up for this neglect.[71]

Since he is about to depart for Cairo on the thirteenth, he decides to put off his departure for twenty-four hours to be able to discuss the situation with the Kádár regime's Foreign Minister, Imre Horváth, who was arriving that afternoon. In his subsequent meeting with Horváth, Hammarskjold offers to stop over in Budapest on his way to Cairo. Horváth, being only a puppet, is unable to give Hammarskjold any reply but promises to get one the following day. The reply, which arrives after Hammarskjold's departure on the fourteenth, was that Sebes would be willing to meet him in Rome. This reply, which reaches Hammarskjold in Naples, is not satisfactory, and Hammarskjold tells him in a diplomatic way they should meet in Budapest, or not at all, pointing out he can stop off on his way back from Cairo. The Hungarians stick to Rome.

On his return to the UN he announces the composition of the three-man team he has selected—in response to the General Assembly request of November 4—to be the observers who will "investigate the situation caused by the foreign intervention in Hungary" and report back to the General Assembly. They are Arthur Lall of India, Judge Oscar Gundersen of Norway, a man with considerable UN experience, and Alberto Lleras of Columbia. They are to act as individuals, not as representatives of their respective countries.[72] Gundersen is so eager to go that he applies for and gets his Hungarian visa on the day he learns of his appointment.[73]

Aid

Aid for Hungary is accumulating in scores of Western countries.

But it is not just the free world which is responding. The Poles, who were the first to send blood and medical supplies in the first days of the revolution, are still collecting funds and clothes, as is the Yugoslav Red Cross. Elsewhere in the bloc it is a somewhat different story. The destruction of Budapest, which was not in the original Soviet war plan, is a great embarrassment to the Soviet Union. It is in their interest to get rid of the evidence of their brutality as soon as possible. Under the guise of humanitarian aid, a tremendous effort is now launched by the USSR to get Hungary back on her feet and erase all evidence of its butchery. This means putting tremendous pressure on the peoples' democracies of Eastern Europe to cough up as much aid and building materials as their overtaxed economies can manage. This takes place on a governmental level, but there are also efforts to get individual citizens to contribute. In countries like Czechoslovakia, where the regime is still Stalinist, workers "volunteer" one percent of their pay for a month or two. The collection of this "volunteered" money is simple; each worker's paycheck is docked one percent by the state. In Romania, where there are many ethnic Hungarians and there has been a particularly enthusiastic

461

response to the Revolution, the sacrifice of the workers, though strictly dictated by the state, is nonetheless genuine. As Agerpress (Romanian news agency) reports on November 14, "The workers of the industrial enterprises of the Oradea* region have sent so far to workers in enterprises and machine tractor stations of Debrecen, close to three hundred tons of gas oil, firewood, lignite, salt, and window glass."[74]

Tito is not without feelings of guilt about what has happened in Hungary and is eager to see Hungary rebuilt as soon as possible. Thus Tanjug (Yugoslav news agency) reports on November 17 that "the first quantity of one hundred tons of rice was sent today by train to Hungary as aid which the Yugoslav government has allotted to the Hungarian population.[75] And, of course, the mighty Soviet Union must lead the way in rebuilding Hungary. The Soviet news agency TASS, which has a tendency to report intentions as accomplished facts, lists the following on November 15:

> Archangelsk—Cars loaded with timber leave daily for Hungary....
>
> Novorossiisk—A big batch of cement has been sent to Hungary....
>
> Leningrad—Fifty flatcars of timber were shipped to the Hungarian Peoples' Republic and three hundred and fifty carloads more are to be sent within the next few days.
>
> Chelyabinsk—Workers at the Chelyabinsk Tractor Plant are speeding up the manufacture of tractors for Hungary....
>
> Gorky—Local sawmills have sent thirty-four carloads of timber and logs to Hungary. In the next few days three hundred carloads more of timber will go to the same destination....
>
> Poltava—Four hundred tons of meat and one thousand tons of high grade flour have been shipped to Hungary by the packers and millers of the Poltava region.
>
> Taganrog—One hundred and thirty tons of gas pipes were turned out two days ahead of schedule by workers of the Andryev Steel Mills for the restoration of buildings barbarously destroyed by the fascist bands in Hungarian towns.[76]

Repercussions and Comment among Communists

It is too early to discern what repercussions are occurring in the Soviet Union, but there are repercussions among the Soviet troops in Hungary.

---

* Romanian city very near to the Hungarian border.

The Revolution Goes On

Though his figures are too inflated to be credible, Dr. Tamás Pásztor, a leading member of the Hungarian Revolutionary Council, who recently escaped from Hungary, tells a press conference in Paris on November 16 that "some three thousand Soviet soldiers and about sixty tanks" have deserted and actually fought with the Hungarians against Soviet forces freshly arrived in Hungary.[77]

In the French, British, and American Communist parties, which differ greatly in size and influence, wholesale resignations are taking place. In France, which has the most influential Communist Party outside of the Soviet bloc, the Party bosses resemble a team of dike repairmen desperately fighting with their bare hands against a surging flood. Also in Paris, the head of the Communist-organized Peace Movement, M. Frederic Joliat-Curie, backs a resolution approved by fifteen leading members of the Peace Movement calling for a special congress of the organization to dismiss the movement's Communist members and denounce the Soviet action in Hungary. Joliat-Curie makes a special call on Communist Party Secretary Maurice Thorez to chastise him for taking a pro-Soviet stand on Hungary.[78]

But it is the single voice of one Yugoslav Communist which produces the biggest repercussion in the Communist world. Milovan Đilas, former Vice President of Yugoslavia and long-time aide and friend of Tito, though ousted from office in 1954 and briefly jailed for advocating more than one party in Yugoslavia, publishes an article on November 19 under the title "The Storm in Eastern Europe." He knows he can never publish it in Yugoslavia, so has it published in a small socialist journal in the United States, *The New Leader*. It takes a while for the contents of this article to become known, particularly in the Communist world where only smuggled copies are available. But soon the Communist propaganda machine is after Đilas, and when his book, *The New Class*, also appears in the West, he is at once jailed as a traitor. Here are some of the words Đilas wrote:

"The Hungarian uprising is…a new phenomenon, perhaps not less meaningful than the French or Russian Revolution…."

"In Hungary…the Communist system as such was repudiated…. Nagy could only install national communism with the assistance of Soviet bayonets, and this threatened the very end of Communism…."

"Had the Hungarian Revolution not only brought political democracy but also preserved social control of heavy industry and banking, it would have exercised enormous influence on all communist countries, including the

463

USSR. It would have demonstrated not only that totalitarianism is unnecessary as a means of protecting the workers from exploitation (i.e. in the 'building of socialism') but also that this is a mere excuse for the exploitation of the workers by bureaucracy and a new ruling class....

"Despite the Soviet repression in Hungary, Moscow can only slow down the processes of change; it cannot stop them in the long run. The crisis is not only between the USSR and its neighbors, but within the Communist system as such....

"As in all other great and decisive events, the Hungarians fighters for freedom...may not have foreseen what an epochal deed they had initiated. The world has rarely witnessed such unprecedented unity of the popular masses and such heroism....

"This event will probably not be repeated. But the Hungarian Revolution blazed a path which sooner or later other communist countries must follow. The wound which the Hungarian Revolution inflicted on Communism can never be completely healed..."

Worldwide Reactions

Though it is ten days since the second Soviet intervention in Hungary, world reaction is still growing, not subsiding. On November 14 the premiers of four Asian nations, whose total combined population is 473 million, meet in New Delhi and call on Soviet Russia to withdraw her forces "speedily" from battered Hungary. At the end of a three-day meeting, India's Jawaharlal Nehru, Indonesia's Ali Sastroamidjojo, Burma's U Ha Swe and Ceylon's S. Colomen Bandaranaike issue a communiqué saying, "The Hungarian people should be free to decide their own future and form of government that they will have without external intervention from any quarter."[79]

Also in Asia, the Japanese Free Men's Association in Tokyo cables the Congress of Cultural Freedom in Paris on the same day, "The Japanese people condemn the Soviet Union for colonialist acts [and] praise the Hungarian Freedom Fighters as the greatest twentieth-century contributors to the promotion of freedom and dignity of man."[80]

In Brussels, the executive of the free world's main trade union organization, the International Confederation of Free Trade Unions, representing fifty-six million organized workers, calls on its member union to boycott all Russian shipping and refuse to handle Soviet cargoes of any type as a gesture of solidarity with Hungarian workers.

On November 13, which was declared "Hungarian Day" in France, fifteen thousand wildly enthusiastic young people pack the city's biggest indoor sports stadium, the Velodrome d'Hivier, for an anti-Soviet rally, while another crowd of twenty-five thousand watches the famed Hungarian soccer team, Honvéd, defeat the team from the Racing Club of Paris by four to three. Premier Guy Mollet announces that next Sunday, November 18, is to be observed as a national day of mourning for "the martyrs of Hungary, of shattered Hungary which refuses slavery."[81]

Demonstrations of solidarity with Hungary are taking place in every parish in Italy, where major religious tributes have already been held in Rome, Naples, Turin, Florence, and Livorno. In Rome, the chairman of the Italian PEN Club, Ignazio Silone, answers the plea of the Hungarian PEN Club. "We hope that the heroic sacrifice of the Hungarian people," says Silone, "has not been made in vain and that this noble nation will soon enjoy peace, independence and all the democratic freedoms."[82]

It is learned in Montreal that the plan of Hungarian-Canadian émigrés to send five hundred willing volunteers to Hungary to fight alongside the patriots has had to be abandoned.[83]

Soviet Political Action on the World Scene and U.S. Reaction

The architects of Soviet foreign policy are having a field day. On the fifth of November, Bulganin made his outrageous proposal to Eisenhower that the U.S. and USSR join military forces to keep the peace in the Middle East, as though nothing had happened in the UN. On the next day, November 6, Bulganin threatened to dispatch rockets with atomic warheads to Paris and London. On the same day the Soviets offered to send 250,000 "volunteers" to Egypt to fight against the Anglo-French-Israeli forces. All this was done consciously against the brutal backdrop of what they were doing in Hungary. Few people knew there were no rockets targeted on Paris and London and that warheads to fit such rockets were some years away. Nor could anyone in the West—remembering all the Chinese "volunteers" in Korea only a few years earlier—be sure that those 250,000 Soviet volunteers were a figment of Khrushchev's imagination.

To use a boxing term, the West felt rocked back on its heels. Eisenhower and Dulles had already made it abundantly clear that they were not going to come to Hungary's rescue, that Hungary was in the Soviet sphere and they were not trying to detach it and bring it into NATO. They had also made something else abundantly clear, namely that they were more afraid of doing something which might touch off World War III than were the Soviets, who knew that they themselves were not ready, did not want war, and would always retreat in the end in order to avoid it.

Now, before a splintered West had time to recover and put the full spotlight on Hungary, came an even more audacious maneuver. On November 17, the Soviet Union proposed a summit conference of the Big Four plus India and China which would accept, in a limited way, President Eisenhower's "Open Skies" inspection plan offered at Geneva just fifteen months before. It also proposed a non-aggression pact between NATO and the Warsaw Pact countries. Both in the document, which was in the form of another letter from Bulganin, and in *Pravda*'s comments the next day, the fear of World War III was made much of. The implication being, of course, that if Soviet terms for peace were not accepted, war could very well break out. To put an exclamation mark behind the offer, that very day they conducted an atomic bomb test high in the atmosphere and announced it to the world, something they had never done before. Usually, those in the West who detected them announced Soviet atomic explosions. To ensure that fear of war was also instilled in their restless satellites, Soviet Representative Kuznetsov had earlier declared in the General Assembly that other nations should "draw appropriate lessons" from the Hungarian rebellion and the Soviet response to same, about as bald a threat as one could deliver in a diplomatic setting.[84]

The timing of this maneuver, from the Soviet viewpoint, could scarcely have been better. The Americans were barely speaking to the French and British, Eisenhower was missing his Secretary of State, though Hoover was a true and loyal substitute for Dulles, and America's famed "Liberation" policy was in shreds. Because there were many things in the Soviet offer which Khrushchev seriously believed in and later fought for, the Soviet move could not be dismissed as purely a propaganda maneuver. But until a better one came along, this would do handily. Many in the Third World were taken in by it, and those who feared war felt intimidated.

It happened that on the very day this last move was announced, Khrushchev was giving a reception for Polish Premier Gomułka, with whom he had just had satisfactory negotiations. He was in an ebullient and aggressive mood, and was not unlike the father in the parable of the prodigal son, Gomułka being the prodigal son and the Western diplomats being the slaughtered fatted calf. "Things stand bright for us," he bellowed in full voice. "If we believed in the existence of God, we would have every right to thank him."

He then gave such an offensive extemporaneous speech that the British and American, and then all of the NATO ambassadors, walked out in the middle of it. Khrushchev, never one to be upstaged, shouted after them, "If you don't like us don't accept our invitations and don't invite us as well!"

Most of the speech was about Poland and the new relationship it had with the Soviet Union. But he did not hesitate to speak of Hungary and complain about "a great clamor…now being raised in capitalist countries around the so-called Hungarian question." He followed this with the standard Soviet line on Hungary. He went on to assure his audience that "Normal life is now being restored in Hungary and there is no doubt that the Hungarian people, having overcome all the difficulties in its way, will successfully cope with the task of the consolidation of the Peoples' democratic order."[85]

Initial U.S. reaction to the new Soviet initiative was "no comment; we haven't even received the document yet"—a rather clear indication that the Soviets were more interested in its propaganda value than in a serious meeting. And yet, even when the document arrived and there was time to study it, the usual comment that the Department would make, that "there seemed to be nothing new in it, it was pure propaganda" could not be used, because there *was* something new in it. Just as Eisenhower had suggested to Hoover that NATO offer something to the other side, the Soviets appeared to be offering something, too. In the Department of State, the inertia of caution, fear of doing something which might trigger war, and a disinclination to deal directly with the Soviets, at least for a time, took over.

November 19 to December 8, 1956

Budapest

No buses or streetcars are running yet in the central part of the city. In those few sections where there is some public transportation, sheets of cardboard to keep out the cold have been stuffed into places where windows have been shot out. Trucks bearing signs saying "Food" or "Foodstuff" cross the Margaret Bridge in both directions stopping at either end to show drivers' identifications. Swarms of hitchhikers jump on or swing off when they do, like so many fleas off a dog, for these trucks provide much of the public transportation available. There are also Red Cross trucks, and Soviet fuel trucks bringing diesel for all the tanks parked around the city and at the bridgeheads. Pedestrian traffic is not stopped at the bridges, though the Kossuth footbridge, which today no longer exists, is blocked because of its direct access to the Parliament building where the "Kádár clique" are still protected from the people's wrath by Soviet tanks.

Most stores on Váci Street, Budapest's most fashionble street, are open for limited business, and Budapest is again connected with the outside world in that one can phone Vienna, though it may take a couple of hours to get a connection.

All Soviet memorials have been demolished save the one in the Kerepesi cemetery honoring the Soviet dead from the Second World War. On what the Russians still refer to as Stalin Avenue, the former Andrássy Avenue, not a single trace of Stalin's name can be found. People refer to it these days as "Avenue of Youth," referring to their recent dead, but also because it leads to what used to be called "Heroes' Square." That Square, known as "Stalin Square," was recently re-dubbed "Boot Square" by the people, in honor of Stalin's metal boots which still stood on their pedestal with a Soviet tank guarding them.[86] But overnight on November 15, the boots and the tank disappeared.[87] Still, hundreds of people have their souvenir chunks of the statue, which are now known as "Stalismans."[88]

People take their children to Calvin Square to see the damaged church and to Üllői Avenue where so many buildings have collapsed into the street. They must walk in the middle of the street, for tons of rubble cover the sidewalks. People walk great distances every day for a piece of soap or cup of flour or to lay fresh flowers on the graves of their loved ones. Along the way are scores of Soviet tanks, but they might just as well not be there for the notice anyone pays to them.

While some schools in the provinces have re-opened, no schools in Budapest are operating and the government has announced they will only begin again after January 1. Likewise, no high schools or universities have reopened, after the government decree closing them. Professors have told their students not to listen to any orders they may receive from the radio or press, but to adhere only to what they tell them by phone.[89]

Some public figures reappear, while others disappear. One who reappears is the Lutheran Bishop of Hungary, Lajos Ordass, who has just reassured friends in the West that he and his family are safe. The letter declares, "Our

Lutheran Church has now found its freedom," but he adds, "What is to happen to our country is at present an unsolved puzzle."[90]

Up until November 19, all of General Grebennyik's notices containing orders for the population are headed, "I demand...." From the nineteenth on, all his messages merely begin, "Hungarian Workers." These orders are generally printed on leaflets distributed by Soviet Army trucks. As many as are picked up are torn in two.[91]

The "WANTED" posters that Hungarians distribute or post are much more eagerly received. Two recent ones are:

WANTED: a Hungarian Prime Minister. Qualifications: a criminal record and a Russian Passport. Character and backbone unnecessary.

WANTED: Applications for admission to the Hungarian Communist Party. If more than ten are received, a mass rally will immediately be held.[92]

And there are dozens of jokes in circulation which never get written down. One that does get recorded concerns some little boys attacking Soviet tanks:

Two small boys are standing in a gateway on a boulevard when a Soviet tank comes by. They jump out, throw a Molotov cocktail on it and the tank blows up. They go back to their gateway until another Soviet tanks comes by. Again they run out, throw a Molotov cocktail and another tank goes up in flames. They return to their hiding place. Then one of the kids looks out again. He turns back to the other, his face all pale with fright. "Hey!" he says "We'd better beat it. Here comes Mom!"[93]

The unofficial press, though it is now largely reduced to mimeographed rather than printed copies, is still thriving. In addition to *Igazság* (*Truth*), there is *Élünk* (*We Live*) and *Hazánk* (*Our Homeland*). But the regime, which refuses to let the Central Workers' Council of Greater Budapest have even its own house organ, is determined to get rid of all of what it regards as subversive literature. On November 30, Kádár's police raid all suspected printing shops and seize all of the mimeograph machines they can lay their hands on.[94]

Tito and the Soviet Abduction of Imre Nagy & Company

Ever since Imre Nagy and his colleagues sought asylum in the Yugoslav Embassy on November 4, the Russians, through Kádár, have been trying to get Nagy to (1) resign from his premiership, (2) confess that he had let things get out of hand and it was right that a new government be formed under Kádár, and (3) join that government. This is done not by visitations and face-to-face confrontations, but by notes back and forth through the Yugoslav Ambassador, Dalibor Soldatic. The Yugoslavs know full well that they have given refuge to a head of state, but they argue that Nagy and company were admitted as private individuals, as if politics had nothing to do with it. Tito had thought it possible to persuade Nagy to join the Kádár government—the best solution for Yugoslavia. But Nagy adamantly refuses to resign his premiership, so that obviates the possibility of his confessing his sins and/or joining the Kádár government. The problem now is what to do with him. Sitting in the Yugoslav Embassy he remains a major threat to Kádár, and to Tito a time bomb waiting to go off, which might ruin his already shaky relations with the Soviet Union.

By November 16, there is agreement between the two sides that Nagy and his colleagues cannot remain in the Embassy. The Yugoslavs say there are two options: (1) be allowed to go home and remain in Hungary as private citizens with written guarantees that they will not be harmed, or (2) seek asylum in Yugoslavia. They add that they and Nagy prefer the former. The Russians, through Kádár, say there are two options, have him go home with oral guarantees for his safety, or have him seek asylum in another people's democracy, but not Yugoslavia.

On the eighteenth the Yugoslavs insist that the Hungarian side give written guarantees for Nagy and company's physical safety and guarantees of no future molestation. Kádár is reluctant to do this. At length he is "persuaded" by the Russians to provide such a written guarantee so as to break the impasse. On November 21 a written guarantee is provided to Ambassador Soldatic and arrangements are made for a bus to come and pick up Nagy, his family, Losonczy and others and their families around 6:30 p.m. the next day to take them all to their homes.

On November 22 the bus arrives on time, fills up with the designated Hungarians (twenty-three in all), and then is boarded by two Yugoslav Embassy officials. The bus then pulls out in the street and makes a turn; it goes a hundred yards but finds its way blocked by Soviet vehicles. Soviet soldiers surround the bus, the driver is forced out of the bus over the protests of the Yugoslav officials, a Soviet driver climbs aboard and the bus is driven off under heavy military escort.

The next day it is announced over the radio that Imre Nagy and his

470

friends have all voluntarily sought asylum in Romania. Since not one of them called home and all left with only the clothes on their backs, it is obvious that there was nothing voluntary about it. The Yugoslavs soon let it be known that while Nagy had been willing to seek asylum in Yugoslavia, he had expressly stated he would never agree to go to Romania.

When Tito makes his protest it is not to the Soviets who did the deed, but to the Hungarians who had provided the worthless written guarantee. Tito was well aware of what would probably happen. Without confronting those whom he knew to be responsible, he simply went through the charade of wiping off his responsibility for Nagy's fate and proving to the world that it was the Kádár regime that betrayed his trust. A day later Tito "protests energetically" to the Soviets for their role, but his protest is a great deal less "energetic" than the one he sent Kádár.

When he was still hopeful of getting Nagy into his government, Kádár said on November 11 that the blame for the recent events was on Rákosi and he absolved Nagy of any intention "to help the counterrevolution."

Three days after Nagy's removal from Budapest, and reminded by the people's reaction how popular Nagy still is, Kádár says on November 25, "We have no intention to call Nagy and his group to account for the events [of the revolution]." But on December 2 he is already saying, "I am convinced that the opposition group led by the comrades of Imre Nagy...went so far in their criticism as to become the ideological organizers of the armed revolt against state institutions and the Hungarian People's Republic as a whole."[95]

U.S Minister Wailes tells Washington that "with Nagy and associates gone, and because the Soviets are willing to take this step, the chances for any meaningful broadening of the Kádár regime seem slim."[96]

November 23 is the first monthly anniversary of the Revolution. Kádár and his cohorts are petrified of what may happen. They warn General Grebennyik to double the strength of his troops and armor in the city. On the twenty-second, leaflets are passed out in the streets. KGB General Serov reports to Moscow, "Leaflets appeared, in which it was written, 'All who are against the Kádár government must not come out on the street from 2:00 to 3:00 p.m. on November 23; the empty streets will show Kádár and our well-wishing friends—the Russians—that they are not wanted here.' As a result," Serov's report went on, "almost the entire population of Budapest deserted the streets, which were empty from 2 to 3 p. m. Inhabitants, who were in the streets at 2:00 p.m., suddenly went into buildings and the courtyards of buildings and stood there until 3:00 p.m."[97]

On this dark and snowy day from the two o'clock deadline until three those doubled Russian patrols careen eerily around the empty city. Lace curtains are pulled back by thousands of apartment dwellers to see whether they can spot a single Kádár supporter. None are reported.

The demonstration, which brings the city to a standstill, is entirely peaceful. It is an incredible manifestation of solidarity in opposition to Kádár, three weeks after he came onto the scene. A defenseless people have won a bloodless victory, and they know it. People flock noisily back onto the streets. Groups form and sing the national anthem in front of bewildered Russian troops. When a U.S Legation car tours the city, smiles break out and friendly waves come in response to the sight of the tiny Stars and Stripes flying from the aerial. It is a cheery moment for a dark and cheerless day.[98]

Kádár has yet to get any real control over his own media. In a commentary on the radio reviewing the events of October 23, the commentator stresses that the demands of the Revolution have not yet been fulfilled. The Hungarian Army newspaper, *Magyar Honvéd*, editorializes that it is necessary to continue to fight for the just claims of October 23.[99]

The Central Workers' Council of Greater Budapest acts as though it were a national organization representing the workers. Now the intellectuals, on November 21, form a central revolutionary committee under the chairmanship of the composer Zoltán Kodály, calling for unity in the country against all Stalinist forces. It issues a program that totally ignores the existence of the puppet government. Since the country does not have a government, says the Committee, it quickly needs to acquire one by electing a leadership from the national and workers' councils under the supervision of the United Nations. Troops from the UN should quickly replace the Soviet troops so that the latter will be able to exit the country as speedily as possible. No publicity is given this program, however, and it soon sinks into oblivion.[100]

Ten days later the Writers Association produces an eloquent document called "Concern and Creed." This, too, completely ignores the existence of the "Kádár clique" and stresses that had the Russians not intervened there would have been no doing away with Hungary's socialist achievements. "National independence and democratic social structure—these are the wish of the Hungarian people," says the document. "We must…find our national independence in the very interest of socialist progress. And by self-government through the people we must create a healthy society." The revolution, in other words, must go on in spite of the impediments of foreign occupation. No publicity is given this proclamation either and it never becomes imbedded into the public consciousness.[101]

But while intellectuals work to perfect the revolution which they had done so much to bring about, the Soviet vise is tightening on Hungary. Every day makes it plainer that regardless of anything intellectuals may plan or Kádár may say or promise, the Russians have decided to return Stalinism to Hungary. That decision appears to have been made on November 24, the day after they have seen the dramatic evidence of how totally the Hungarians reject their puppet regime.

One of the chief results of so many Soviet infantry divisions pouring into the country is that arrests of young people from the ages of fourteen to thirty are incessant, both in Budapest and the countryside. The mass roundups in the streets are becoming less common, but now raids are made on individual buildings, and toward the end of November even on schools. Proof of the deportations is gathered from the many notes dropped from trains and published in an underground "newspaper" called *October 23*. But much of the news reaches the West in the form of refugees, a few of whom have avoided deportation by escaping a roundup, escaping from a deportation train while still in Hungary, or even, in a few cases, having been returned to Hungary for being underage. The flow of refugees has not only increased by these round-ups, but the average age of those seeking to leave now plummets by the inclusion of many unaccompanied teenagers.

Three days earlier there is a near massacre on Lenin Avenue when hundreds of irate Hungarians menace some Russian soldiers whose fingers are on the triggers of their submachine guns, following an abduction of a young Hungarian in broad daylight. Derisive whistles and curses are not enough to panic the soldiers, but their discomfort is clear.

Having so many young Russian soldiers undertaking these unpleasant tasks among a population which is not shooting at them and occasionally is even friendly is taking its toll. The József Bem Barracks already contains a large number of disarmed Russian soldiers considered unreliable and being held under guard until they can be shipped back to Russia.[102]

A new development involving the deportations may indicate a reversal or stoppage is being contemplated. On December 3, a large number of people are rounded up by soldiers and taken to the Corvin warehouse. Here, in order

473

to avoid arrest, they are made to sign papers asking for political asylum in Russia. They are then released. The only conceivable use for such papers may be that when the Soviets are accused of deporting Hungarians, they can now show proof that many Hungarians were seeking asylum in Russia, and this is where the rumors of deportations came about.[103]

As noted earlier, Kádár still lacks control of the media even though it is all government supported. *Népakarat* (People's Will), the new daily newspaper of the National Federation of Free Trade Unions, is particularly outspoken. Under the headline "Bill of Indictment by the People," it speaks of the "thousands of crimes committed against the people by Rákosi, Gerő and 'other would-be Stalins.'" It was because of "this infamous clique that the people, from workers to university students, shouted 'no!' to the whole past." The article concludes by demanding a public trial of Rákosi and Gerő. There is a news item in the same edition stating that Workers' Councils have recently secured the release of innocent workers who had been arrested, and that there will be further talks with the "representatives of the Soviet City Kommandatura" on this topic this very afternoon.[104]

On November 29, the Central Workers' Council declares that people should boycott the regime press until the Kádár government agrees to allow the Council to have its own newspaper. Not only do people boycott the press the next day, they buy ten copies of *Népszabadság* at a time and then light bonfires in the street with them. When police see what is happening, they simply shrug their shoulders and walk away. The Soviets, on the other hand, order the people to disperse, particularly when the fire is at dusk and attracts a large crowd. People refuse, and this leads to abuse, insults, "Russkies go home!" and, not infrequently, blows and even shootings. The Hungarians take a macabre pleasure out of defying the Russians and flirting with death. The Russians feel furious and impotent.[105]

If it cannot win people over to its side, there is one thing the Kádár regime can do: it can divide and confuse people through deliberate deception. Noting how effective the notices of the Central Workers' Council of Greater Budapest are, the regime prints bogus announcements in the Council's name and even goes so far as to forge signatures of the Council's leaders. Thus in the first days of December, Budapest is plastered with posters closely resembling those of the Central Workers' Council; these announce another ten-day strike and urge mothers and children to quit Budapest before December 7. Other posters urge a second uprising on

December 8. The Central Council has to print its own handbills and put notices in its "Bulletin" exposing the bogus posters, but considerable anxiety and confusion is caused before they are able to convince people that these posters are not theirs. On the other hand, Budapest Radio does announce the Council's communique denying authorship of the posters in a 4:00 p.m. broadcast on December 1, much to the annoyance of the Kádár clique.[106]

As tension builds toward a showdown between the occupation forces and the workers' councils, sudden gunfire on December 2 reminds people that the guerilla war continues. In the afternoon, the capital is rattled by six artillery blasts, a sound not heard for two weeks now. It turns out that these rounds were fired after a burial ceremony in Kerepesi cemetery for Russian soldiers and officers killed during the recent fighting. Earlier in the day thousands of desperate Budapesters trudged through all of Budapest's cemeteries, in the midst of snow showers, looking for relatives and loved ones who disappeared during the revolution and the second Soviet invasion. Hundreds of simple black coffins, their lids open and thus gathering snow, are scattered in the yards of the big Rákoskeresztúr cemetery. Most of the frozen corpses are half naked, some still bloodstained, and do not seem three or more weeks dead. More than one thousand bodies have already been buried in this cemetery since it all began.

That night there are sharp skirmishes to the southeast of Pest, and intense small arms fire is heard in the Buda hills. Russian reinforcements are rushed there, and loud explosions follow.[107]

*   *   *   *

People are eating somewhat better, at least those who can afford to. Luxury items such as smoked goose and hams, which have not been on the market for years, suddenly appear. With exports blocked by the Soviet occupation, the regime has decided to continue with the Nagy government's original decision to open these stocks to the home market. In addition, many items that came in as aid from the West, even Red Cross items, somehow also end up in food stores with high prices on them. And citizens are surprised to see Soviet soldiers eating oranges—not seen in years—and chocolates, in the streets. People know they did not come from Russia.[108]

There is no senior diplomat at the Indian Mission in Budapest, thus Dr. Jagan Nath Khosla, India's Minister to Prague, arrives on November 25 to begin an investigation unobtrusively; he correctly calls on the right people in the Foreign Ministry (all Stalinists), then Kádár (lunch), and Münnich, the man in the Kádár group who holds most of the power. Khosla holds two long sessions with Sir Leslie Fry, so is well informed by the time his superior, Ambassador K.P.S. Menon, arrives from Moscow on December 2. Sir Leslie, who served in India for many years and knows all of the top Indian officials, is careful to see that Menon has a full tour of the devastated city and suburbs before sitting down with him to a three-hour dinner. It is Menon's intention to remain in Budapest for at least a week. While there is no official announcement, people seem to know where the Indian from Moscow will turn up next. When he visits Kispest, for instance, so great is the crowd cheering him that the Russians, not knowing he is the cause, shoot over the heads of the crowd to make them scatter.[109]

On the evening of December 3, handbills appear on the streets announcing that a demonstration of wives, mothers, and daughters of those killed in the fighting will take place the next day, and will all men please stay off the streets while this takes place. Their intention is to lay flowers on the grave of the unknown soldier in Hero's Square on the first month's anniversary of the second Soviet invasion. One keen observer who watches the demonstration from start to finish estimates that thirty thousand women are taking part; others put it at from three to five thousand. But, since at no time are they amassed in one place, it is difficult to judge.

The women, many leading children by the hand or pushing baby carriages, converge on the unknown soldier's monument on this cold and rainy day shortly before eleven o'clock. Some are early and are able to lay their flowers before the scores of Soviet armored cars arrive. Many of the women have black armbands and those few who can afford it black veils, but it is clear that most are working class wearing their everyday bandanas. After watching for a few minutes, soldiers suddenly jump out of the trucks brandishing tommy-guns and try to seal off the square. "Look at those Russians!" cries a grandmother, "they have guns and yet they are afraid. We are only women with children, but we are not afraid." The Russians have a difficult time, for instead of marching ten or twelve abreast, the women march in single files, one hand holding a candle and flowers, the other on the shoulder of the woman ahead of her. With so many access roads to the Square it takes a while for the soldiers to get it properly sealed, even though tanks are blocking portions of some streets. There is considerable yelling back and forth between the women and the soldiers. At one time the troops shoot over the women's heads. The effect is the reverse of what was intended; they stand their ground and refuse to be pushed back. Prevented from going forward to their goal, the women start to sing the national anthem and soon everyone watching them is singing with them.

In the midst of this impasse, Minister of Defense and Interior Ferenc Münnich arrives with two Soviet generals to survey the scene. After a short conference, it is decided to let the women through. They push forward, but in an orderly column, to the monument. Here they reverently place their wreaths and flowers, sprays of white, red and yellow chrysanthemums, on the white stone tomb. At this point the Indian diplomats, K.P.S. Menon and Dr. Jagan Khosla, drive slowly past the square in their diplomatic car taking it all in.

The demonstration, which has lasted two hours, now breaks up.

A militant group of about two hundred, however, march to Parliament, where Soviet personnel carriers and foot patrols block their entrance to the Square. They then turn back and go to the nearby U.S. Legation singing hymns and the national anthem. While they are shouting slogans in front of the legation, a Soviet tank attempts to run them down and disperse them. The crowd whistles, screams and shouts, "Russians Go Home!" and "Down with Kádár," but refuse to leave. Minister Wailes receives three of the leaders and promises to pass their messages on to Washington.[110]

In the Rest of the Country

Guerilla warfare in Budapest may have become sporadic, but in the countryside, where there are concentrations of thousands of partisans operating in the mountains and forests, it is now fairly constant. The area northeast of Budapest from Pesthidegkút to Piliscsaba and Pilisvörösvár is completely controlled by the Freedom Fighters as of November 16 and heavy fighting in the area is reported up to at least November 25. On the night of November 22, the Soviets began a major offensive to try to drive two to three thousand Freedom Fighters out of the Dabosi Forest north of Lake Balaton near Sümeg. There was shooting all night long and many tanks were in action, but the Soviet effort failed. The Freedom Fighters went into the town of Padragkút, where they took Communist officials off as hostages and then disappeared into the Bakony Forest.[111] Fighting in the Borsod/Mátra mountain area is also in progress on the twenty-seventh.

In fact, Soviet forces control only what is within range of their guns. They patrol all the main roads from Budapest to the Austrian border day and night, and they control the railroad line from Miskolc to the Soviet border; but from Budapest to Hatvan, thirty-six miles east of Budapest, only one train a day attempts the round trip. Between Hatvan and Miskolc, so many stretches of track have been torn up and destroyed that there is no traffic at all.

Meanwhile, at least a thousand partisans are still at large in the Mecsek Mountains near Pécs. This is the group that raided Pécs last week and killed the Soviet commander there in a firefight. The new Soviet Commandant is threatening to hang all those still holding out in the mountains "as traitors."[112] In the northeast, constant guerilla raids are being made in the Sátoraljaújhely and Nógrád areas.[113]

Fifteen hundred college students from Sárospatak in Eastern Hungary are waging guerilla warfare with small arms and two anti-tank guns they captured recently by getting Soviet soldiers drunk.[114]

Aside from the rarity of Soviet troops fighting against each other, morale of troops in the countryside is sagging. Not only are troops getting extra indoctrination, but also they are being separated as much as possible from the Hungarian people and confined to their winter barracks. Garrisons are much more widely spread than they were before October 23 and now exist in all of the major towns in Hungary, twenty-one not including Budapest.

No Soviet vehicles or troops are allowed any closer to the Austrian border than ten kilometers. The Soviets have let it be known that this is to insure that they do not mistakenly violate Austria's neutrality. The real reason appears to be fear of defections. No such regulation exists regarding the Yugoslav border and on November 20, the Yugoslavs announce that six Soviet soldiers, including an officer, "lost their way" and entered Yugoslavia. They were immediately disarmed and interned.[115]

There are almost as many troop trains going out of Hungary as coming in. Some of the mechanized divisions are returning to the USSR, as are some units that took heavy casualties. Some are also going home without their weapons; their future is uncertain. One such train is estimated to have carried between one and three thousand depressed and worried soldiers. Nearly all of this traffic through Záhony takes place between midnight and 4:00 a.m., for the Soviets are certain that spies are watching.[116]

Former members of the disbanded Workers' Council of Borsod County, still operating in the capital city of Miskolc, feel they have had it with the Kádár government. On November 30, some of them manage to wrest control of Radio Miskolc and announce to a surprised listening audience that they no longer recognize the Kádár government and are setting up their own "independent republic." Asked by locals what he is going to do about it, the Russian Commandant replies, "I do not care what happens, so long as my soldiers are left alone." No more announcements come from the radio and within a week most of the former Council members are under arrest.[117]

Following the example of worker's councils, peasant councils are now being set up all over the country. Once this has been completed, a Central Peasants' Council organization, similar to the Central Workers' Council of Greater Budapest, is to be established in the capital.

On the same day that the workers of Borsod County are declaring their lack of allegiance to Kádár, Kádár himself is making his first trip outside Budapest. He flies to the mining town of Tatabánya by Soviet helicopter and lands in the middle of a football field around which the miners, who, except for maintainance workers, haven't been in the mines for weeks, are already gathered. As a former ironworker, Kádár figures he can talk their language. But while they are pleased to see him in the flesh, they give him at best a lukewarm reception. The field is full of Russian soldiers and the Soviet helicopters that have accompanied him. In the four-hour session with leaders of the workers' councils in their headquarters, also surrounded by Soviet troops, Kádár finds more blunt opposition then he has expected.[118] While his move appears to be a dramatic one, it is actually one of desperation. The miners have a stranglehold on the country. Unless they produce coal, industry cannot operate, no matter how many workers want to go back to work and start earning money. The miners know this and feel that Kádár's coming to them is a clear indication of their power.

Most of the mines are still operational, and there is enough electricity to keep the pumps working and the water out. But in some mines, where it looked as though the Soviets were about to seize them, as in some of the uranium mines in Pécs, the miners deliberately flooded them. One mine in Pécs has water to the depth of twenty-five to thirty meters, and it may be six months before that mine will be able to produce again.[119]

Mimicking the citizens of Budapest, the people of Sopron have their own hour of empty streets on November 26; this bewilders and frightens the local Soviets, who have not heard of the Budapest demonstration. Workers in Sopron's various factories are going back to their factories, but no work is done; they discuss, play cards, and go home early. The local Commandant is furious and has issued his "Third Proclamation" which forbids workers to hold meetings among themselves when they are idle in the factories. More than ten thousand people from Sopron have already fled to the West.[120]

Factories in Győr are assigning workers only for guard duty and maintenance work. There is only enough coal for hospitals and power plants. Radio Pécs says that uranium mine workers refuse to work until they have a guarantee of a public accounting as to where the uranium is going. In Szolnok, workers have gone back to the mills but only for four-hour shifts. Radio Miskolc announces that the Workers' Council of the Hungarian Railroads says workers are to ship only goods approved by the Council, implying that government orders are to be ignored.[121]

The Central Workers' Council of Greater Budapest

The first Hungarian worker's council in Budapest was formed on October 26 at the United Izzó factory, so it is appropriate that the Central Workers' Council of Greater Budapest was formed in the same factory on November 14. By now, there are workers' councils not only throughout the metropolis of Budapest, but in industrial enterprises all over Hungary. As one of its founding members, Miklós Krassó, later observed, the Central Council was founded because of the two opposing forces in Hungary—the Red Army and the Hungarian people—only the Red Army was organized.

Since the Kádár government represents nobody and is not recognized by the workers, there needed to be a centralized body to represent the Hungarian people. That was the first decision. But the second decision, to send a delegation to negotiate with Kádár, whom they simultaneously did not recognize, was a foolish, possibly fatal mistake. As Krassó pointed out, Kádár was irrelevant; he was only the spokesperson for the power which was opposing them, the Soviet Union.[122]

The delegation that visited Kádár on the night of November 14 presented him with seven demands and one pledge, that they would return to work if he granted the seven demands. The first demand, that Imre Nagy be reappointed premier in place of Kádár, was a slap in the face, and none of the others were within Kádár's power to grant, so the meeting was unsatisfactory in that it produced no real results. Kádár pretended to accept the demands with restrictions, and at times was most beguiling. He even went so far as to say, "We will have to give up the Party's monopoly of power. We want a multiparty system and clean, honest elections. We know that this will not be an easy matter, because it is not only with bullets, but also with voting, that the power of the working class can be brought down. We have to take into account that we may be thoroughly beaten in the elections, but we shall take on the electoral struggle because the Communist party will have the strength that it takes to win once again the confidence of the working masses." This sounded genuine, but was, in fact, all lies.[123]

After reporting to the Central Council in the early morning, it was decided that another visit should be made to Kádár that night to inform him of the Council's reactions to his positions. It was thought wiser to send a smaller delegation, so only nine delegates were chosen to go along with the President of the Council, József Dévényi, who was from the Csepel Iron and Steel Works. Among the nine was a little-known young man, Sándor Rácz, a toolmaker, who was put forward because of his straightforward outspokenness. At 23, Rácz was by far the youngest member. The meeting in the Parliament building was scheduled for 8:00 p.m. To tire them out, Kádár deliberately kept them waiting for four hours. This meeting was even less satisfactory than the first. After the report to the Council the next morning by Dévényi, Rácz was allowed to give his opinion of the delegation's performance. His indictment of Dévényi was telling and he ended his remarks by requesting a vote of "no confidence" in Dévényi. His eloquence carried the day and he got his vote. Dévényi was voted out of office. Rácz assumed that there were many other senior men who might replace him, so when a secret ballot was taken he was genuinely surprised to find an overwhelming majority on the first ballot had chosen him. From that moment on, the Central Council provided strong leadership and initiative until the Soviets, through arrests, managed to destroy it.

One of the first things Rácz did was to recognize that the real center of power he faced was General Grebennyik. After the one-hour shutdown of Budapest on November 23, which had been largely organized by the Council, Grebennyik quickly acquired respect for the Council. He invited the President of the Council to dinner, and Rácz immediately accepted, not only because he did not want to offend the Russian's sense of hospitality, but because he preferred to have Grebennyik get his information from him rather than through Kádár. Grebennyik and his fellow officers, who, to Rácz's astonishment, all had the Kossuth emblems stitched to their dark uniforms, was good-natured toward Rácz and his companions. The meeting succeeded in reducing the deportations and getting two hours taken off the curfew. But a second meeting, which involved a huge Mongol or Tartar general and a man he took to be Serov, was not so friendly.[124]

The Council wanted everything to be aboveboard and always invited a regime person to attend their meetings. When they decided to convene delegates from all of the workers' councils around the country for the purpose of establishing a National Workers' Council, they duly informed the Kádár government. Getting no objection to this, they called the meeting for November 21 to be held in the Budapest Sports Stadium. In the words of President Rácz's report given later that day:

"We notified them that we wanted to hold this conference....We also argued...about the way in which so many of our fellow workers were being arrested. They said this was 'accidental.' We told them there had been 'too many such accidental incidents.'"

"We asked for permission to publish a paper. They said there were twenty papers and they 'didn't see the need for a twenty-first....'"

"When we notified them that we wanted to hold the national meeting, they didn't raise any particular objection. Indeed, we even invited the government. And yet then, to our great astonishment, when we went to the Sports Stadium, it was cordoned off. On top of that we weren't even allowed to hold it in the Ferenc Rózsa House of Culture...the place we'd agreed on if...we weren't able to hold it in the Sports Stadium—because we did not have police permission. So we were forced to straggle over here" (the Dózsa Street office) "and here, too, only with security forces present.

"So are the security forces needed here?

"Why do they have to be afraid of us?

"We are unarmed."[125]

For while Rácz was able to give his report, the national meeting could not be held. Most of the out-of-town delegates, not familiar with Budapest, had been unable to find the third meeting place and felt intimidated by all the helmeted soldiers and tanks.

The Central Council did not take this defeat lying down. It immediately ordered a forty-eight-hour general strike. As this strike was surprisingly thoroughly observed, the government found itself back on square one.[126]

With the Nagy issue quickly fading after his abduction by the Soviets on November 22, and the successful forty-eight-hour strike now over, the greatly dispirited workers felt a return to work, reserving the right to strike again, was best for the country. Yet their call to the country to return to work was not as effective as they had hoped, for deportations and particularly arrests of workers' council leaders led many to refuse. And Kádár's radio speech on November 26, viciously disparaging Nagy, did not help.[127] Kádár's speech also contained an attack on the Worker's Councils, saying, "they should draw in their horns, the sooner the better." The Council's reaction to this was to protest this "vicious" attack and restate that "We openly recognize the achievements of socialism. Our aim is the…strengthening of socialism…and the stepping up of productive work…."[128]

Sándor Rácz and his fellow Central Council members met with Kádár yet again on the night of November 29. By this time they had scaled down their demands considerably and were hoping for a breakthrough after nearly three weeks of fruitless negotiations. "We are the last legal body which can solve the situation peacefully," pointed out a Council spokesman. "If we fail, there will be a spontaneous strike throughout the country and we will not be able to control the workers. Total anarchy will follow."[129]

The following day the government, which had no intention of doing more than listen, had an article published in the government-controlled trade union publication, *Népakarat,* turning down the workers "requests"—for that is what asking for cessation of arrests, return of those arrested, and permission for a journal of their own now are—flatly, calling them "destructive."[130]

*   *   *   *

It is now December and tension between the government and workers is increasing. Arrests are usually carried out at the worker's home and at night. Fifty workers' council officers are arrested this way the night of December 5. Workers who fear arrest are now staying at their place of work. The Soviet solution to this is to surround a given factory with armored cars and tanks and have squads of heavily armed soldiers, Soviet or the new "Workers' Militia," made up entirely of ex-ÁVO thugs, go in to make the arrests. This morning, December 6, one factory in Budapest hears of this in time to react. Seven hundred workers put down their tools and go to block the roadway into the factory. Though encircled by tanks, they know that the roadway is the only means of access to the factory. They remain there for over half an hour until the Soviets and militia give up and go away.[131]

On the seventh, workers turn in to the government lists of those who have been arrested, protesting and demanding their release. Before riots break out, the government that night releases ninety-six of the arrested council members and the word spreads quickly. By the morning of the eighth the tension is reduced. The only trouble is that in the forty-eight hours before their release the government had arrested over two hundred council members. When this is discovered, the Central Council goes right back into session, which lasts all night. President Rácz, meanwhile, goes back to see Kádár. Rácz and his fellow delegates tell Kádár that he has until 8:00 p.m. today, Saturday, to give them a satisfactory reply. They suggest he do it over the radio. If he does not, the forty-eight-hour general strike will begin at 8:01 p.m. Saturday night.[132]

8:00 p.m. comes and Kádár gives no reply. The strike is still on, but the mass of workers do not yet know about it.

Deportations

Deportations began on November 5, the day after the second Soviet intervention. The man who had engineered the deportation of 170,000 citizens of the Baltic states in 1940 and been named Hero of the Soviet Union for this accomplishment knew his business well. Reports of roundups and groups being marched off to railroad stations came within days of the second intervention, but actual proof of deportations only came when the underage deportees began to return to Budapest. One seventeen-year-old girl, who was picked up on November 7, turned up with her mother at the British Legation on November 20. She had just been returned with fifty other underage young people from Uzhgorod (Hungarian: Ungvár), a city just inside the Ukrainian border. She had seen many other people loaded onto her train, including a number of Hungarian soldiers who had been quietly sitting in their barracks. All her captors were Russian.

In the prison in Uzhgorod everything had been taken from her, even her shoelaces, lest she attempt suicide. Badly fed, interrogated all night and not allowed to sleep, she was not let alone until she agreed to sign her "confession." She had the impression they had all been selected at random. On November 10 she and others were given ten lumps of sugar, four loaves of bread, and some canned meat and told they were going home. It was a two-day process, taking them through Debrecen and involving a "stupid" indoctrination lecture at Soviet Military headquarters after their return to Budapest. The Soviets had refused her mother any information. On the twenty-first, she and her mother visited the U.S. Legation to tell the same story. For a week fear of the authorities had prevented them from coming forward with the girl's story.[133]

As more and more evidence builds up and reports are broadcast by Western radios and carried in the Western press, strong pressure builds up to denounce the deportations publicly in the United Nations. The Cuban and Spanish delegates are among the first to point the finger, but soon the U.S. and British and others are denouncing the deportations.

On November 19, Ivan Serov reported in writing to Khrushchev that "during the military operations, 4,700 people were detained, 1,400 of them arrested and 860 people were transported to Uzhgorod and Striy where they are in custody." (This, of course, does not include all those who were returned to Hungary before this date, nor all those who were deported after November 19.)[134] Whatever plans Serov had for accomplishing deportations by subterfuge had to be abandoned. Whether Uzhgorod and Striy were just to be staging areas for Siberia was not clear. There were signs that the jailers were not prepared for them, which would indicate that the decision not to go to Siberia, but to stop in the border area was made en route. Certainly Serov was forced to make changes against his will. Publicity in the West and in the UN had a great deal to do with mitigating and then stopping the deportations, though they continued well into December.

It was not only the Western publicity,* however, but the Hungarian protests, particularly in the form of worker protests and worker strikes, that made the Soviets realize that the deportations were becoming counterproductive.

The General Strike

A general strike all over the country has been in effect since October 24; even though there was no original call for it, it occurred spontaneously. The formation of workers' councils only came later.

Now the only legitimate remnants of the Nagy government, the workers' councils, are the ones who call for continuation of the strike or give the signal to go back to work. The trade unions have reverted to their usual role as a tool of the Party, and since no Party to speak of exists, they have no role as yet.

The strike is self-enforcing; that is, certain industries like transportation

---

*The British Foreign Office slyly announced on November 22, "We have no evidence to support that deportations in Hungary have ceased."

and energy can effectively prevent production even when many workers are eager to return to work.

And for a while, those who do return to work are harassed not only by their fellow workers, but by the wives of their fellow workers as well.[135]

As hunger and cold and a lack of money begin to take their toll, more and more workers turn up at their factories and the regime radio is daily full of mounting percentages of workers reporting for work at this or that factory, in an effort to get a groundswell of workers to return. But as people can easily see, smoke is coming out of very few factory chimneys. There is companionship, sometimes food and some warmth in the factories, but little work to be done when there is so little coal and no raw materials to work with.[136]

Soviet railwaymen are running Soviet trains in Hungary, but they cannot run Hungarian trains without the help of Hungarian railwaymen and they, largely because of the deportations, are maintaining their strike. Major complaints are coming from outside the country as well, for no trains from Czechoslovakia and countries to the north have passed through to Romania, Yugoslavia, or Bulgaria, nor in the other direction for a month, and this is having a deleterious economic effect on the entire Eastern bloc.[137]

But it is in the coal mines that the strike is most effective. The miners, through the control of their workers' councils, are producing just enough for the needs of homes and hospitals. The country's daily needs are seventy thousand tons and not more than ten to twelve thousand tons are being produced.[138] When the Soviet Commandant informs the miners of Dorog that Soviet miners may come in to man the mines if they do not go down soon, one miner's loud reaction is "Good! We've been working for them for twelve years. Now they can come work for us for a change!"[139]

Kádár and His Regime

When János Kádár agreed to be a Russian puppet, he insisted that his should not be a puppet government, thereby trying to convince himself that it would not be. He was still in favor of most of the revolution's demands, including that the Russians should leave Hungary. He somehow convinced himself that he could save most of the Revolution and still stay on the good side of his backers, thus having the best of both worlds. But in his trials, Kádár has acquired a thick skull as well as a thick skin. To arrive in Budapest, four days after he is named the Premier of his country, in a Russian tank and then be holed up in the Parliament building with no Party, no levers of government, not even a full cabinet, and not realize that he is nothing more than a puppet takes some doing.

Only days before, with Soviet chicanery added to his own, he got rid of his greatest threat, Imre Nagy. He has been desperately trying to add Nagy and/or some of his followers to his own cabinet so that he may have the allegiance of at least some of his countrymen. Two weeks later, the Soviets complain in their own Presidium that they cannot get Kádár to approve a law they are trying to ram through because his "Presidential Council [cabinet] is [still] incomplete," and "if the new law is approved by Comrade István Dobi alone, it would be a serious violation of existing constitutional norms which could later be brought against both Comrade Dobi and the Presidential Council as a crime." The Soviets proceed to ignore Kádár and have Dobi sign the decree.[140]

While Kádár was put in the driver's seat of a revolutionary stagecoach pulled by eight galloping steeds, he was given no reins by which to steer or rein in the revolution. Thus, as much as two weeks into office, his Party newspaper, *Népszabadság*, in discussing the crimes of Rákosi, prints the statement, "The Hungarian people's desire for freedom has now become so great that no force can suppress it." Almost three weeks later, an article in *Népakarat* describes how on December 5 the committees set up by the government to investigate the activities of the ÁVO and its members are just beginning their work. There are twelve such committees in Budapest and one each for the country's twenty-two counties. To have such thorough investigations going on while all of the worst of the ex-ÁVO officers are becoming the backbone, under Münnich's guidance, of the new police and new militia is a contradiction of immense proportions. In the atmosphere of fear that is building up, it is not likely that many people will want to cooperate with these investigations. That they are going on at all is proof that so far as the Hungarian people are concerned, the Revolution's goal of disbanding the ÁVO must proceed.[141]

Another instance of Kádár's inability to stop the momentum of the Revolution is in education. Among the changes announced on November 30 are the abolition of all personnel (read Secret Police) departments in all universities, and the abolition of all Marxism-Leninism departments, along with the so-called "Internal Section."

A day earlier, John MacCormac of the *New York Times* writes from Vienna, "At a number of meetings of the Socialist Workers (Communist)

487

Party, not even a quorum can be assembled. The results appear to confirm a statement by Károly Kiss, a member of the Party's Executive Committee, that 'in many places the Communists are still on the defensive politically.'"[142]

The regime radio complains that there are not enough judges to handle all the Hungarians whom the Russians are arresting. In Moscow, Presidium members Malenkov, Suslov, and Aristov come up with a draconian solution. They tell Kádár it is necessary "to select from those arrested...five to seven people, and in the interests of deterring the counter-revolution...try them (Moscow style) and shoot them. Comrade Kádár," they conclude, "agrees with our suggestion."[143]

As Kádár finds himself having to agree to more and more of Moscow's "suggestions," the political line of his regime gets more and more rigid. Gone are all of the pro-revolutionary remarks of early November. Péter Veres and Gyula Hay are told that an independent literary gazette "is not needed in this country."[144] The United Press correspondent Russell Jones is told essentially the same thing, then given a three-day extension before being expelled. When Kádár learns how many academics and professional people in the intelligentsia have received passports to go abroad (i.e. flee legitimately to the West) he has the issuance of all passports suspended indefinitely.[145]

After a month there is some inclination to push back at the Soviets a little, so on November 30, Hungarian officials draw up a document containing "recommendations" for the "realization" of the Soviet Declaration of October 30. Among the seventeen "sore" points in Soviet-Hungarian relations to be discussed are: frequency of "accidents" (often resulting in deaths) caused by Soviet troops; the lack of any agreement about compensations (including pensions) to Hungarian citizens (i.e. spouses of the "accident" victims) for loss of income; and the need for a separate agreement defining the purpose, "distribution," "quantity," and length of stay of Soviet troops in Hungary, "as stipulated, for example, in the Soviet-Polish declaration."[146]

With Soviet might behind his threats and pronouncements, Kádár has now acquired some reins on which he can pull. On December 6, he pulls hard on them and starts to turn the stagecoach around. He does it with a decree published not even in the Party paper where all would be sure to notice it, but in a lesser regime paper. The decree "abolishes all revolutionary committees and other organs with similar names," on the grounds that their activities were "detrimental to the public interest." Now he is ready for a direct assault on the workers' councils.[147]

No man, newly come to power, can resist the first opportunity to project himself onto the wider world, as he sees himself, through a first interview. Kádár is no exception, and, from all the requests for interviews, he chooses a Swedish woman journalist, Mrs. Barbro Alving, of the Stockholm daily, *Dagens Nyheter*, as his most likely gullible prey.

He receives her and a female companion on November 26 in his "work-room" after they have been led by a machine-pistol-toting guard through the grand, dark hallways of the Parliament. He enters the waiting room where they are seated, shakes hands and says simply, "Kádár," and then escorts them to his large and pompous office with its magnificent furniture and red carpet. After a few moments' chitchat a servant enters. Kádár steps out from behind his table and takes a wine glass from the tray and with a nod bids them do the same.

"Drain your glasses in a toast for the Hungarian people and for our success in our endeavors," he says.

"Our," Barbro Alving takes to mean the tiny Kádár cabinet. She can scarcely believe he is serious in thinking they would join such a toast.

"A toast to the Hungarian people," she says demurely.

Having recently heard the figure of thirty-seven thousand deported Hungarians she asks him directly, "How many have been deported?"

"Nobody has been deported," replies Kádár courteously. "Nobody will be deported either."

"He will try to make a lot of this interview," thinks Mrs. Alving to herself. Only recently did he attend a diplomatic reception and the foreign press saw that he did, in fact, exist. It was his first public appearance.

She finds him a gray man. It is her first impression. Not only his gray suit and gray sweater under it, but his little gray eyes which do not flutter but seem "somehow dead, with an everlasting uneasiness in their bottom." He is of medium height and in his 40s; only his oblong face, with high frontal lobes and deep transverse furrows in his forehead, gives him any distinction from the man in the street. His manner of looking with great concentration at "the lady who interprets into German shows that he really cannot speak the language himself."

Mrs. Alving cannot believe that he believes all the lies he is telling her; either that or he lacks all contact with the Hungarian people. "The Nagy question is no longer important; Nagy is hated by so many in this country that we could not protect him from assassination, etc."

The workers' councils? The government is not opposed to the worker's councils. It sees in them a way of getting the people to support the government.

The stream of falsehoods is punctuated by small, puckered smiles, which broaden to the point of revealing a metal filling when he is trying to emphasize a point. Every straw that seems in his favor becomes, in his telling, a foundation rock on which his regime is based. Elections are not needed; every worker who returns to work is voting for the government.

He has talked to bourgeois (i.e. non-Communist) politicians who would be prepared to support the socialist aspects of his government, but if they apply the old terror methods, he will have the police arrest them at once. And as for the idea of using any of Rákosi's tactics, he would have the police come and arrest himself if that were ever to occur.

Nothing is said of the Russian occupiers. Mrs. Alving has learned precious little by the time she is reminded her time is up and the obsequious, puckered smile returns.[148]

*　*　*　*

The American and British diplomats read the Kádár government correctly. On November 30 Edward T. Wailes begins his telegram to Washington: "The Legation has so far focused little attention on the Hungarian Government headed by János Kádár, largely because this government has to date been only a shadow and a mouthpiece of the Soviet occupation power."

Sir Leslie Fry, concentrating on the upcoming December 3 debate in the UN, cables, "At today's meeting of the General Assembly every opportunity might be taken, I suggest, to expose the Kádár "Government" as sham. This would serve the dual purpose of:

1. (a) discrediting Kádár's representative in New York; and (b) bringing home to the Russians that reliance on Kádár cannot break the deadlock.

2. The questions might be put: what in fact is this "government" in whose name the Soviet Union is re-imposing an alien system on Hungary, violating every human right and disregarding all United Nations resolutions? Does its writ run in the countryside? Everyone, whether peasant or workman, completely ignores and despises Kádár."[149]

The United Nations and Nehru

From the early days of the Revolution, rather clear advice has come from both the U.S. and British legations in Budapest as to what their respective countries might do, especially in the UN. Unfortunately, this advice has usually gotten lost or badly diluted as it passes through Whitehall and Foggy Bottom.

By November 19, with no progress toward getting UN observers into Hungary, Sir Geoffrey Wallinger in Vienna tells his colleagues in Whitehall that a "visit to Budapest of the Secretary General...should have some restraining influence on the Russian Occupiers and would let the Hungarians know they have not been abandoned.... I therefore...suggest that the real objective of the UN General Assembly today should be to insist that Hammarskjold be received at Budapest as soon as possible...."[150]

The next day his colleague in Budapest, Sir Leslie Fry, complains that "the impotence of the United Nations in the face of undisguised and mounting Russian barbarism has submerged the Hungarian people in agonizing despair; and what, perhaps above all, disgusts them is that the United Nations should permit to appear before it, as Hungarian representative, the man who was Foreign Minister under the Stalinist Gerő, himself even condemned by the Kádár regime. The world...must surely know that Imre Horváth* represents only Kádár and a few other Muscovite Communists and the Russians themselves.... The time seems to me to have come at which his credentials should be challenged in some way or other, provided this would not jeopardize the existence here of our Western missions...."[151]

Instead of any challenge to the Kádár representative on this date, the Cuban UN delegate, whose resolution last night contained a charge of genocide against the Russians because of the deportations in Hungary, was forced to drop this paragraph from his resolution so as to increase the chances of obtaining the support of several countries, which, like the United States, have not yet ratified the United Nations genocide convention.[152]

While no resolution concerning Hungary was passed by the United Nations between October 23 and November 4, the long pending American resolution *was* finally passed on November 4. Three more were passed on November 9, two of which, including one American, concerned only humanitarian aid. Also passed was a fourth, by Italy, Cuba, and Ireland, calling for Soviet withdrawal and free elections under UN auspices. The new Cuban resolution on deportations was tabled on November 18 but passed on the twenty-first over strenuous objections by the Soviet Union and its satellites,

---

* Rákosi and Gerő's Foreign Minister, fired by Nagy, but rehired by Kádár

but with the Polish delegate abstaining. Another broadly based resolution on aid to Hungarian refugees passed overwhelmingly on November 21, and then one calling on Hungary to admit UN observers and "requesting a reply by December 7" is passed overwhelmingly on December 5.[153]

In all these debates, the Kádár representative takes full part, even though no action has been taken on accepting or rejecting his credentials. He makes long outlandish speeches, proposes amendments and slows up and confuses the process. Many from the Third World countries consider him a legitimate delegate just like themselves.

On the night of November 27, Sir Pierson Dixon tells the Foreign Office that "Pressure from the Latin American and other delegations for a decision to reject the credentials of the Hungarian representative has so far been held off. With the position of the United States Legation in Budapest in mind, the Americans think it best to continue postponing a decision. No meeting of the Credentials Committee has therefore yet taken place.... The present U.S plan is that it should like the Credentials Committee of Emergency Sessions to defer a decision 'pending further clarification.'"[154]

On Monday, December 3, the U.S. and ten other countries introduce a resolution urging the Kádár government to reconsider letting UN observers into the country and "requesting a reply by December 7." But there is no provision for punishing the Kádár regime if it remains adamant in its refusal. The Cuban delegate pledges to submit a resolution to expel them if they don't comply.

The day after that resolution is voted, the American conservative commentator Walter Lippmann writes in the *New York Herald Tribune*:

"In the spirit, if not the letter, the Kádár government's treatment of Mr. Hammarskjold amounts to saying that though Hungary has diplomatic rights in the General Assembly in New York, the United Nations Organization has no diplomatic rights in Hungary. This is not an acceptable doctrine, and if the Kádár government continues to stall, the least that the General Assembly can do is to suspend the right of Kádár's Representatives to participate in the General Assembly."

Hammarskjold has been treated shabbily, but being the world's top diplomat he can neither admit it nor do much about it. He feels himself the servant of the Security Council and General Assembly, obliged to do his best to carry out whatever they decide the UN should do. He dares not initiate anything on his own other than, say, decide to take advantage of a flight to Cairo to suggest stopping off in Budapest coming or going. He seems unaware that his mere appearance in Budapest would transform the scene dramatically.

Kádár knows what would happen and is petrified. Feeling he can reveal the real reasons why he is turning Hammarskjold's visit down—well, postponing it for now—at Soviet behest, he tells a *Pravda* reporter:

"All of the appeals of the counterrevolutionaries boiled down to one thing: 'hang on a bit, the American forces will be here—hang on a bit more, the United Nations forces will arrive.'

"In the minds of many people the difference between United Nations and American forces disappeared.'

"The very fact of the arrival of any United Nations representative in Hungary would have caused confusion in the minds of many people. Certain elements would not have laid down their arms." He adds that the decision to refuse the observers and Hammarskjold was "not easy for the Hungarian government or the Soviet government."[155]

There is a flurry of excitement at the UN when, in the process of again denying access to the UN observers, the Kádár government, in an effort to forestall having its representative expelled, notifies the Secretary General on December 3 that it regrets that no meeting took place in Rome and "is ready to welcome your Excellency in Budapest at a later date appropriate for both parties." Hammarskjold seizes this opportunity to inform the Hungarians that fine, he can come on December 16, almost two weeks later, and would intend to stay the sixteenth, seventeenth and eighteenth. He adds that he will be sending his aide, Undersecretary Philippe de Seynes, a week ahead of himself, but that if this arrangement is not made, he will arrive somewhat earlier than the sixteenth.[156]

This quick reaction causes panic in both Budapest and Moscow. But the Soviets simply are not prepared to let it happen. They tell Kádár to put Hammarskjold off, somehow. The best the regime can come up with is that "the United Nations sources did not officially ask for this visit of Hammarskjold to Budapest so we must consider this visit will not take place December 16." The Foreign Ministry spokesman adds that the Hungarian government declares that "both parties will agree on a date in the immediate future," meaning agreement in the immediate future, not the visit. "We will receive Hammarskjold," he concludes, "only after negotiations to set a date have been concluded with him."[157]

India is trying to play a constructive mediating role behind the scenes.

Ever since the vote of her UN delegate, V. K. Krishna Menon, shocked the world by siding with the Soviet Union against the first U.S resolution on Hungary, Nehru has been trying to mitigate the damage done to India's image of neutrality. *The Hindustan Times* attacked Nehru, saying that Menon was not "an acceptable channel of Indian diplomacy," and Menon himself later tries to make amends by urging the Hungarians to accept observers and urging the Soviets to withdraw. But inadvertently he is also playing a destructive role by persuading Hammarskjold to delay action and wait for a positive response from the Hungarians.

In Budapest, where the Indian Ambassadors visiting from Prague and Moscow are staying in the Grand Hotel on Margaret Island, Hungarian intellectuals are able to make contact with them, without, they feel, being unduly observed by Kádár spies. A three-man delegation from the Revolutionary Committee of Hungarian Intellectuals, Professors György Markos, Endre Nizsalovszky, and Pajzs, meet with Ambassador Jagan Nath Khosla from Prague on November 29 to discuss their plan, which involves UN occupation troops from neutral countries, or Poland and Yugoslavia, and the establishment of a democratically selected "little parliament" which would prepare the country for free elections—all of this to take place after Kádár has been removed. Ambassador Khosla sees merit in their plan and says he will pass it along to Nehru. Later he tells Sir Leslie Fry he sees "little prospect of useful mediation over Hungary by either Tito or Nehru."[158]

Refugees

UN Secretary General Dag Hammarskjold announces to the world on November 20 that some thirty-four thousand Hungarian refugees have crossed over into Austria, while no more than three hundred had entered Yugoslavia. He adds that they are coming in at a rate of at least two thousand per day. Six days later the Austrians tell the UN that the figure has shot up to eighty-two thousand refugees. Four days later Austrian officials announce that 95,700 Hungarians have registered with the authorities by November 30, and by December 2 the figure has reached 105,000.[159]

The numbers per day fluctuate wildly according to what is going on in Hungary and what is going on at and in the border areas. Most crossings occur at night and in places where mines have not yet been sown. Most Hungarian border guards are sympathetic to those fleeing. Instead of manning the forty-foot towers where it is windy and cold, they are warming themselves over outdoor fires. They receive an order to remove a footbridge one day, but when fleeing refugees put it back that night the guards, unless specifically ordered to remove it again the next day, leave it. In places where the main border guards are Soviet, wristwatches and bottles of liquor will sometimes do the trick.

But the impediments to flight grow daily as the Soviets realize that the Kádár regime is incapable of stemming the flow. Every refugee bears further testimony to what is going on; in addition, Hungary can ill afford to lose the labor and talent. Consequently, the ten-kilometers-from-the-border ruling is lifted, and Soviet soldiers sometimes pursue their prey right up to the border. In one case three Soviet soldiers mistakenly pursue too far and Austrian border guards open fire, killing one, wounding another, while the third escapes back to Hungary. The story might never have come out, but the Soviets feel they must make a big fuss over their man's "murder."[160]

Now Soviet planes act as spotters for vast hordes of refugees hiding in the marshes or woods waiting for nightfall. Soviet infantry move in quickly and round them up by the hundreds and transport them away in trucks. Sometimes these trucks have signs on them saying, "Hungarian Repatriation Committee" as though the people in them have actually been refugees and have fallen for the broadcasts of amnesty that the Hungarian radio broadcasts incessantly to the refugee camps in Austria.[161]

On November 27, fewer than four thousand refugees make it, the smallest number in over a week. The bodies of twenty murdered refugees are lying in a forest just over the border. Residents of the Hungarian village of Bucsu nearby are denied permission to bury the bodies which, in the fifty-degree weather, are now beginning to stink. They must be left there to intimidate other refugees fleeing in the area. Radio Budapest, in an attempt to slow and possibly even reverse the flow, promises a blanket amnesty to the nearly one hundred thousand citizens who have fled the country, provided they return by March 31, 1957.[162]

By the end of November the Soviets begin using tanks. But in an even more drastic move, the Soviets set up a false border several kilometers inside the real one to fool would-be refugees. They set up long lines of Austrian flags and illuminate them at night so that anyone might assume they are looking over the border into Austria. Many hundreds of Hungarians, mostly now from Eastern Hungary and unfamiliar with the landscape, fall down sobbing on what they think is Austrian soil only to be rounded up by Soviet soldiers with bayonets and herded into big Army trucks which take them to prison camps in Hungary. Inside the country, meanwhile, permanent travel and residence controls are introduced in Western Hungary. People found without these special permits are liable to automatic arrest.[163]

After the French, the West Germans are among the first to declare they will put no limit on the number of Hungarian refugees they will take. Britain and Canada quickly follow suit. The U.S. Consulate in Vienna, meanwhile, is struggling to stay on top of the growing mound of papers and documents required under the McCarran-Walter Immigration Act. In one week in late November, for instance, they approve the issuance of one thousand visas but are physically only able to stamp as "approved" 520. The Austrians, however, have the biggest problem. The overcrowded camps are becoming something of a scandal and a detailed report of the bad conditions reported in Moscow's *Izvestia* is not far off the mark, for there is so little supervision that recruiters for cheap labor gangs, dancers for nightclubs and intelligence agencies are able to operate at will.[164]

On November 29 the United Nations puts out an appeal to virtually every country in the world. Hungary, meanwhile, puts out its own appeal to the Austrians. It wants the Austrians to return several thousand young people "intimidated by fascist terrorists" who were abducted to Austria.[165]

By November 19, two thousand families in the United States have each agreed to take in a Hungarian, and the Deputy Administrator of the State Department's Refugee Program, Pierce J. Geretty, is confident three thousand more offers will come in to enable the U.S. to make good on its pledge to take five thousand refugees. Only fourteen candidates for America are fully processed as of November 18, and seventy are due to leave by plane on the nineteenth. They will be met by President Eisenhower at McGuire Air Force Base in New Jersey.[166]

On November 27, the *New York Times* notes editorially that several countries are taking unlimited numbers of Hungarian refugees. "Is this not the time for the United States to make a large-minded and generous gesture?... We are the wealthiest nation in the world. Money could be found to send many millions of dollars worth of goods and medicine out of the public funds of the United States to the refugees in Austria and to Hungary itself...." Two days later the announcement is made that the US figure is being raised from five to eight thousand refugees it will now take.[167] On the same day as this announcement Edwin L. Dale of the *New York Times* points out that there is a "strong streak of anti-immigration sentiment in the country" and that the White House has been getting a lot of mail from these people.

"Austrian newspapers have sharply criticized the United States for fixing a limit on the number of refugees it will accept," writes Larry Rue of the *Chicago Tribune* from Vienna on the twenty-eighth. "The major criticism here seems due to a misconception of American law. Many Europeans do not understand. They presume the President can waive the laws of the nation."

On December 1, the White House says it hopes to dramatize its change of policy by announcing that only minimal processing will be required and the processing of applicants and screening by law will take place in this country after the refugees arrive. In a few days there will be a massive airlift and sealift to bring not eight thousand but fifteen thousand refugees to America by the end of the year or soon after.[168]

Red Cross and Aid

The International Committee of the Red Cross announces on November 19 in Vienna that the third convoy of relief supplies will begin its journey from Vienna tomorrow. This is just five days after the second convoy has been recalled pending the solution of irregularities with the handling of the contents of the first convoy. The Communist-controlled Hungarian Red Cross carefully favored Hungarian Communists as well as Russian troops with much of the contents of the first convoy, which had been unloaded in the outskirts of Budapest. Nevertheless, the International Red Cross, knowing that it will soon have its own employees in Budapest handling the distribution under the newly signed agreement, does the diplomatic thing and loudly denies in Vienna that there has been any misappropriation of their gifts in Budapest. The fewer embarrassed Hungarian officials they have to deal with the better.[169]

The Hungarian Commissioner of Public Supply, Rezső Nyers, explains on the radio why foreign aid and food from the Socialist countries is not being given out free, as is the aid from the West. This aid is intended by contract for the Hungarian state. Thus it will not be distributed gratis, but sold at normal prices in the food shops.[170]

One Hungarian who spots a convoy of Russian trucks going through Kecskemét on November 21 notes that each truck has a large placard on the side of it reading in Hungarian, "A gift to Hungary from the Russian People." Curious to see what the gift is, he manages a peek while the convoy is stopped. Each truck is filled with cabbages.[171]

U.S. Minister Edward T. Wailes tells Washington on November 27, "the aid promised Hungary, or stated to have been promised, is of such magnitude that only problems of transportation, distribution and Soviet pilfering would seem to stand in the way of the people's getting enough food to pull them through the winter."[172]

Food is one problem, but adequately heated living quarters is another. A Portuguese Red Cross official who has spent some time in Budapest reports on December 6 on his return to Lisbon that fifty thousand people are homeless, eight hundred apartment buildings are destroyed, and thirty thousand homes are seriously damaged as a result of the Soviet onslaught.[173]

Some Western Press Reaction

Britain's *Manchester Guardian* continues to keep the spotlight on the Soviet empire through the front-page reports of Polish-born correspondent Victor Zorza. In early December, he reveals that "Soviet authorities have arrested a number of Moscow students on suspicion that they have formed an 'underground political organization.' The news of this, brought from Moscow by a traveler whose reliability is beyond doubt and who was in touch with some of the students concerned, sheds a more sinister light on recent Soviet press attacks on ideologically non-conforming students.

"The particular 'organization' which is now being liquidated by the police began innocently and openly enough as an informal literary discussion group. The students' discussions of the repressive policies of Stalin...led, naturally enough, to discussions of the government and to criticism of the present leadership for delaying 'genuine democratization'....

"Student discussion groups have grown greatly in number in recent months and criticism of various aspects of the Soviet system is being freely voiced. Much of this criticism is being deliberately encouraged by the Party, which uses it both as a safety valve and as a means of putting right the many wrongs which still persist from the Stalinist era."[174]

Soviet and American Policy

Bulganin's letter offering a summit conference of the big four plus India and China comes too close on the heels of the Soviet Union's butchery in Hungary for anyone in the West to regard it as more than a diversionary tactic to draw attention away from Hungary. It is dismissed as pure propaganda, even though, were the West to take up the invitation and call the Soviet's bluff, the chances of confusion, exposure, and retreat on the Soviet side might be great. But the Soviets know that the chances of the West's responding positively are so close to nil that they are risking very little. So while they are about it, they do everything they can to play upon the Eisenhower/Dulles fear of confrontation and war. They point out in the letter that the Soviet Union does not need atomic weapons to overrun Western Europe. Though the Soviet military naturally has plans for the invasion of Western Europe, the Soviet leadership has none. They know all too well that the day they invade Western Europe all of Eastern Europe will begin to blow up in their faces and it will be the beginning of the end of their empire. They also know, however, that NATO and the Pentagon do not know this and that they are, in fact, all too aware of Soviet superiority in numbers. Thus they play on the Western fears. They can easily tell how well their propaganda is working by reading the Western press and noting the statements coming from NATO and the Pentagon.

When one New York newspaper asks, "Can the Western world, including the United States, continue only to wring its hands, while the Soviets hide their crimes with propaganda about disarmament?"[175] the answer to that question can be found in a letter that President Eisenhower writes to his former Cold War adviser, C. D. Jackson, on the very day the above words appear in print. "I know your whole being cries out for 'action,' on the Hungarian problem," the President writes. "I assure you that the measures taken there by the Soviets are just as distressing to me as they are to you. But to annihilate Hungary, should it become the scene of a bitter conflict, is no way to help her...."

"One of my friends sent me a particularly moving document on the case of decency versus extinction. I quote from it two or three sentences:

"Partisanship has no place when such a vital question (as atomic self-destruction) confronts us. Mothers in Israel and Egypt, sons in England and France, fathers and husbands in the United States and Russia are all potential victims and sufferers. After the event, all of them, regardless of nationality, will be disinterested in the petty arguments as to who was responsible....That war (would be) so terrible that the human mind cannot comprehend it."[176]

Eisenhower the soldier appears to feel that any real action on the part of the United States will lead ultimately to atomic warfare, and therefore he must reluctantly choose the decency of no action over indecency of action leading to nuclear annihilation.

There are others in Washington, well versed in the devious ways of the Soviets, who argue persuasively that Moscow's greatest fear is not the United States and NATO or even instability and revolt in the satellites, but its own people. But these people are not in leading positions in the administration and have no say in policy making.

And, of course, the U.S. is doing everything it can to expose the ruthless savagery Russia is employing in Hungary, particularly in the Third World. But even in carrying out this publicity, there are those who caution that Moscow's too rapid drop in prestige could panic the Kremlin; that a bear at large is better than a bear at bay.

The Salgótarján Massacre and More Workers' Council Arrests

On Saturday, December 8, the miners and factory workers of Salgótarján, a mining town near the Slovakian border northeast of Budapest, drop their tools and pour into the town from all parts of the county. Word has spread by telephone that two leaders of their Workers' Council were arrested yesterday evening after reading out leaflets for strike calls. Over two thousand shouting workers assemble in front of the district administration (Party) building in the early afternoon, and a similar crowd gathers in front of the police station. Both groups are demanding the release of the two workers. There are Soviet tanks and Hungarian militia (all ex-ÁVO members) guarding both installations. At three p.m., without warning, both tanks and militia at the Party building open fire on the crowd. First reports say at least ten of the workers are killed and scores wounded. Later reports say no less than eighty people died, putting it in a class with Mosonmagyaróvár. Three days later the town is put under martial law, as is the surrounding area.[177]

Dead and wounded are also reported in disturbances in other Hungarian towns today—the mining towns of Pécs and Tatabánya and the railway junction town of Békéscsaba in the southeast. The crowds in Békéscsaba also demonstrate for the release of suddenly arrested workers' and peasants' council members and fight briefly with Soviet troops. In Pécs, where police broke up a demonstration of ten thousand women yesterday, the fight is against Hungarian militia.[178]

Budapest

News of the killings of these unarmed workers further embitters the populace of Budapest, particularly the workers. Rumors, meanwhile, abound of large units of partisans fighting in several mountain ranges. One of these even claims that whole Russian tank units have deserted and are fighting alongside Hungarians in Borsod County.[179] The morale of Soviet troops is going from bad to worse. So many and so diverse are the rumors of Soviet desertions being circulated that some are bound to be true.[180]

The pace of life in the capital has considerably slackened. Many shops are closed, and those that are open close at 2:00 p.m. By 4:00 the streets are almost deserted. The regime is doing its best to get the rubble cleaned up, in order to show foreign correspondents, or any UN officials who might appear, that life in Budapest is returning to normal. Meanwhile, many workers are privately urging their colleagues to slow down the clean-up so foreigners will see how bad it still is. Radio Budapest, in fact, actually reports on December 6 that Construction Enterprise No. 31 is advising people not to hurry with the clean-up lest there be nothing for the UN Secretary General to see. A huge but peaceful demonstration is being planned by the Central Worker's Council and affiliated revolutionary organizations, including peasants and women's organizations, to show the Secretary General when he arrives how solidly against the puppet regime the nation still is.[181]

Long lines are still in front of all food shops, though there is more food available now. The peasants no longer bring food to the general populace in central distribution centers, but deliver it directly to needy families of Freedom Fighters killed, missing, or wounded in the fighting.

Ever since the women's demonstration on Tuesday, December 4, Soviet tanks and helmeted infantry patrols have been out in force.

The new wave of arrests that began with students on December 6 is continuing with workers and intellectuals today, and the city is becoming tense with fear. Many arrests today take place in factories, most of them leaders of workers' councils.

The Central Workers' Council of Greater Budapest is reduced to demanding the cessation of arrests, release of those already arrested, and their own newspaper. They have given Kádár until 8:00 p.m. on Saturday, December 8 to give a satisfactory reply on the radio.

When Kádár fails to answer the workers by 8:00 p.m. on December 8, the revolution is over and "a new national tragedy" begins.

CHAPTER X

Suppression

THE "NEW NATIONAL TRAGEDY" *that appeared to the workers to have begun on December 9 actually began around November 24. It was then that the Soviets realized that Kádár was going nowhere, and that they had to do something drastic like take over the country completely and re-Stalinize it, using Kádár not so much as a puppet as a fig leaf. There would be time, once the strike was broken, to bring Kádár back to his puppet status, gradually giving him the means to take over the country and run it on his own with less and less direct assistance from them. But for now, the strike had to be broken. That meant breaking the back of the workers' councils and crushing them, then transforming them, just as they had long since transformed the trade unions, into instruments of their own control.*

So, too, Soviet suppression did not begin on December 9. Suppression had begun with the first round-ups, arrests and deportations after the second intervention. To call this chapter "Suppression" is only to note that with the outlawing of the Central Workers' Council of Greater Budapest, the Soviet repression began with a fury that had not existed before. While the revolution was not really over, part of it went underground, much of it continuing quite openly above ground as well. Waves of suppression and waves of revolution went through each other as sea swells rebounding off massive rocks go through the waves coming in behind them. This went on for some time before suppression got the upper hand.

So, while the accent of this chapter is on suppression, there were many other things going on, including the continually evolving revolution, at least for the remainder of 1956.

EXPLOSION

Budapest

The forty-eight-hour national strike, called by the Central Council of Greater Budapest, becomes automatic when Kádár fails to answer the workers by 8:00 p.m. on Saturday, December 8. But the strike itself is not to begin until one minute after midnight on Tuesday, December 11, and finish at midnight on Wednesday the twelfth. The Central Council, as it is denied access to the public media, needs time to get the word out to the nation's workers' councils. The Council also hopes to get the word out to workers around the world, for in its resolution calling for the strike it says, "We request all workers of trade unions in the world to support Hungarian workers simultaneously with solidarity strikes," something which tragically does not occur.[1]

The regime immediately cuts all telephone contact between Budapest and the rest of the country, as well as the outside world. In spite of this, word that the strike is on does get out—but only barely. United Press correspondent Ilona Nyilas persuades Ronald Farquhar of Reuters to take her in his Škoda with Czechoslovak license plates to the Beloiannisz factory. There she manages to talk her way through to Sándor Rácz. He hands her a copy of the strike order, saying, "Our phone lines have been cut, and Akácfa Street headquarters raided and everyone there arrested." She and Farquhar rush back to the Duna hotel, but all the phones there are dead as well. By chance a call from Reuters, London, comes through for Farquhar. First identifying it not as a Reuters, but a United Press story, he begins to dictate as Ilona translates the strike document into his ear. "Bulletin!" he begins, "a general strike was ordered today..." but before he can reach the end of his sentence the line goes dead. No matter. London realizes what has happened and in a matter of minutes the news is out on the wires. Within an hour Western radios are broadcasting it back into Hungary, spreading the news far faster and more thoroughly than could have been accomplished by phone.[2]

In an effort to pre-empt the strike, the Soviets, through Kádár, do what they were preparing to do eventually: they have Kádár outlaw the Central Council and all other county and city workers' councils on Sunday the ninth, in an attempt to make both the strike and the councils illegal. The statement says, however, that the government continues to recognize the individual factory workers' councils.[3]

No sooner is this decree announced than massive arrests begin, mostly of the leaders of the Workers' Councils, but including also a number of intel-

504

lectuals. By the end of three days an estimated three thousand people have been arrested. Sándor Rácz, the twenty-three-year-old President of the Central Council, avoids arrest by not going home and staying at his place of work, where he has scores of fellow workers to protect him. But he is lured out of his lair by a scenario he has grown used to, that of confronting Kádár, that and his own ego. He is invited to the Parliament to "negotiate," and cannot resist. When he goes he is arrested before he even has a chance to enter the building.[4]

On December 11, the first day of the strike, a clandestine radio station declares:

"We warn the government, the police and the Russians that we are determined to fight with all means at our disposal, because the democratic way of negotiations had been denied to us in our aim of achieving the ideals of the revolution of Hungarian workers and peasants."[5]

As U. S. Minister Wailes tells Washington, "The success of the two-day general strike and the continuance of total defiance of the population this week show…that the opposition's spirit has been hardly bent, much less broken, by the Soviets and that prospects for public capitulation in the near or medium future are poor, unless even more forceful and terrorist moves are used."[6]

Though coverage by the three English language reporters continues to be excellent, the impression most people have in the West is that the Revolution has long since been snuffed out and the Kádár government, backed by the Soviets, is now in complete control. From time to time, newspapers notice that the story is far from over and send a correspondent to investigate. One such is Britain's *Daily Express*, which sends back Richard Kilián.

Kilián notices to his astonishment that Budapesters, down to the smallest child, are defiantly wearing red, white and green. People do not wave to him, as they would when he was here during the Revolution, and there is a different bustle in the streets; workmen stringing overhead tram wires and relaying paving stones, while others sweep away the dust of rubble.

At Újpest he comes across a crowd surrounding a three-part yellow tram. The driver has only a squad of militia "protection" as his passengers. The crowd shouts, "We're striking. Why aren't you?" They stop the tram. More militiamen arrive and soon there is shooting, at least in the air. The Russian troops stay in the background, letting the militia handle the problem. This new militia, made up of ex-secret police, communists and ex-Army officers, seems to enjoy their work, however brutal, thinks Kilián. They should; they are very well paid. He notices there are still tanks at the end of every bridge and at every major corner. That is Budapest by day.

By night—the city is different. Only Russian patrols and secret police are in the streets. In his hotel room the only sound he hears is the rumble of tanks, all night. As he dictates over the phone to the *Daily Express*:

"The lights in this Hotel Duna are dim. Characters in leather coats flit around. Everybody speaks in whispers. Everybody is under watch. This report is probably being recorded as I phone it.

"I have dinner of paprika goulash. It is curfew time—9:00 p.m. Two Russian colonels come in. They see five of us sitting at a table. They give an order and the dim lights are switched off completely.

"We are five people, but that is almost big enough for a demonstration. And demonstrations in this city are banned."

So, soon, will Richard Kilián be banned. He is ordered to leave the country by midnight the next day, December 15, along with an Austrian reporter. But it is not for his dispatches to London, which the Hungarian secret police doubtless have recorded, that he is expelled. The next day he accompanies Ronald Farquhar of Reuters and Eric Waha, an Austrian representing the Associated Press, to Csepel to talk with the workers there. All three are arrested by Soviet troops. When a Soviet Army officer asks them in broken German why they are there and they tell him, his immediate reaction is, "I think that is forbidden." It turns out that yes, "that is forbidden," and all three are locked up for eight hours and questioned by Soviet officers who speak English. The Soviets can give them no reason for their arrest, but eventually discover that Kilián is not "registered with the Foreign Ministry," and there is a mistake in the date of Waha's accreditation document. Those, it turns out, are grounds for expulsion.[7]

Despite an atmosphere that grows grimmer every day, the people of Budapest continue to display their sense of humor with signs, posters and jokes which quickly circulate around the city. In the Ferencváros section of the city, where much of the fighting took place, someone has painted on a wall, "Tremble, Zhukov, here come the kindergarten children." Among the jokes in circulation are:

Q. What is the difference between an intervention and a miracle?
A. An intervention would be if the Archangel Michael and 20,000 angels

were to come and drive out the Russians. A miracle would be if the UN were to come with an army and drive out the Russians.

and

Q. Why does the Hungarian government consist of only five members?
A. Because that is all that can fit into a Russian tank.

One newsboy selling copies of the Party newspaper, *Népszabadság*, is heard yelling out on a street corner, "Here is *Népszabadság*, every word of it is a lie!" When someone calls out to him asking why it had more pages than usual, he calls back, "So it can print more lies!"[8]

While the Russian troops are hanging back and letting the growing Hungarian "militia" and a new unit of police, called the "R" police, handle crowds and make raids and arrests, the Russians in their frustration can no longer stay out of the factories. They are seen quite conspicuously in the giant MÁVAG and Ganz factories, which make buses and trucks and railroad rolling stock respectively, especially during the forty-eight-hour strike.[9]

The Forty-eight-hour Strike

On December 9, the Russians, panicked by the call for a forty-eight-hour nationwide strike and suspecting that this is a signal for a renewed uprising coordinated with the partisans fighting in the countryside, have Kádár declare martial law for the entire country. All telephone contact between Budapest and the outside world is cut; even the U.S. Legation's telex line is cut for forty-eight hours until, following strenuous protests on December 10, it is restored on the eleventh.

While the once daily Prague-to-Bucharest train goes through Budapest for the first time in six weeks, the few Hungarian trains still running are soon stopped by the strike. Before the strike begins, however, the once-a-day train to Vienna, which leaves Budapest on time Monday, is stopped by the Russians at Tatabánya where it must sit for at least a day to be carefully inspected. Austrians later cite this as one reason for the sudden drop in refugees crossing the border on the next day.

Following the declaration of martial law, a widespread search for weapons gets under way and Radio Budapest puts out a desperate call for all Hungarians who support the Kádár regime and are "capable of bearing arms" to report immediately "to repulse an open attack." The radio is also full of appeals to the workers not to heed the strike call, insisting that since the

Central Workers' Council has been abolished, the strike call is no longer valid. Workers, on the other hand, point out that since the Council was still legal when the call was made, so is the strike.

A clandestine radio heard in central Hungary transmits this message several times:

"We are not frightened of anyone. If freedom requires us to take up arms again, we shall do so, even though our struggle be without hope. At least we shall have served as an example to others. Long live the workers and peasants of Hungary!"[10]

Another clandestine radio broadcasting one day later says:

"The government has now shown that it does not respect, and never will, our work. The workers and peasants must remain united. The other side wants an open struggle. Despite our weakness we are continuing the struggle."

Later the same radio says:

"We workers are not counterrevolutionaries. We fought to gain liberty. We have created legal workers' councils to negotiate with the central Government. Now we are considered outlaws. Let everyone consider on which side justice lies and he will understand how we have been betrayed."[11]

Roadblocks are set up not just on the approaches to Budapest but throughout the city, particularly in the working-class districts, including Csepel. The police and militia carry bulky lists of names against which they check identity cards. Kádár militia paint in white letters on walls all over the city, "Death to those who hide arms!"

Members of the Central Workers' Council, who were not expecting such a drastic reaction on the part of the Soviets, are now uncertain how well the strike will be observed, for they have no way of communicating with their members and with councils outside of Budapest except by courier. One council member says that a Soviet colonel told him that if the strike takes place, all the council members will be held responsible.

All uncertainty is laid to rest on Tuesday when the strike, reinforced by angry workers stopping trams and buses, is an outstanding success. Those few workers who did not know of the strike call or had decided not to heed it soon change their minds and go home when they see how little company they have. Only utilities, bakeries, bread stores and markets are not shut down; all other stores are closed. The regime's newspaper, *Népszabadság,* writes the following day that the strike was one "the like of which has never before been seen in the history of the worker's movement."

Western wire service correspondents Ronald Farquhar and Endre Márton corroborate such praise from the opposition press, which had been urging its readers not to observe the strike. Farquhar writes that "the city has a 'Sunday look' with crowds strolling (in their best Sunday clothes) along the battered streets in bright, wintry sunshine. There are no reports of violence, but observers say there is an underlying tension throughout the city…. The vast majority of workers in factories in the capital appear to have stopped work. Only a handful of smoking chimneys can be seen." The reporters come upon a small group of strikers standing outside the main gates of their factory. A fifty-year-old man with flowing gray whiskers turns to the group of reporters and shouts, "Look at us! We are all fascists!" The group of workers behind him burst into laughter.

At the tram depot in Újpest, a few trams are dispatched; armed militiamen stand beside each driver while a truck full of the same follows behind. But as the morning wears on, these few trams return and the drivers go home, leaving their trams parked beside the hundreds of others that have been standing idle all morning.

Two explosions, like distant shell bursts, come from the hills of Buda, indicating the partisans are still active there, but otherwise the day is like a calm Sunday.[12]

A few more trams are running on Wednesday, the second day of the strike, and a few workers go back to their plants without hindrance from their fellow workers. Basically, the strike holds for the second day.

On Thursday December 13, the workers flock back to their factories. But some, such as those at the Beloiannisz Electrical plant where Sándor Rácz, the President of the Central Council, and his colleague Sándor Bali, who was arrested with him, both work, immediately vote to go out on strike until their leaders have been set free. Hours after the six thousand workers have left the Beloiannisz plant, hundreds of blue uniformed police and khaki-clad militiamen, guns at the ready, storm into the empty factory. Thus, while ninety percent of the work force returns to Budapest factories, possibly as many as twenty percent go right out on strike again. Those who are willingly back in the factories have little work to do, for there is little energy available to work the machinery, and raw materials are either in short supply or not available.

Bali will return in ten days, but Rácz is still being held and is headed for a sentence of life imprisonment from which he will eventually be paroled.[13]

Some Hungarians with sources in the government tell Endre Márton of the Associated Press that Ivan Serov is now running the country, in effect replacing, at least for now, the puppet government of János Kádár.[14]

For all the raids and arrests, which are continuing despite the end of the general strike, people are contemptuous of the new twenty-four-hour trial and execution law, feeling "What's the difference?" In most cases if a gun is found on someone, it is taken, an ex-security policeman gives him a shove to make it look as though he were trying to run away and the second shoots him down. And there are many stories of ÁVO planting pistols on those they want to arrest or do away with.[15]

With most workers back on the job there is increasing agitation in the factories for workers to join the new Socialist Workers' [Communist] Party. In many plants, agitators appear with printed membership forms which they distribute wholesale. There is no form to fill out; all that is needed is a signature. No references are needed nor, say the agitators, is any checking done. Rewards for membership are only hinted at.

The Budapest press is now beginning to carry notices of the new "kangaroo" courts and their sentences. Apparently murder and possession of weapons are not the only crimes drawing capital punishment; political action during the revolution is also such a crime. Two brothers in the village of Kesztölc near Dorog had organized a local guard consisting of twelve men. One brother gets twelve years, but the other a death sentence for high treason.[16]

In the Countryside

During the build-up to the forty-eight-hour national strike, the rest of the country is gripped in as much tension and conflict as is Budapest. There is fighting reported outside of Pécs, Szombathely and Komárom. But the greatest friction is in the northern city of Miskolc, where demonstrations break out because of the arrest of local workers' council leaders. The people actually succeed in forcing the Soviets to free three members from being deported, though one has already had his head shaved. But before this occurs, partisans under the leadership of a certain "Géza Bárány" invade the town and succeed in occupying the main Miskolc printing plant. Here they print up their twenty-one demands, similar to the original student demands, but only asking the Soviets to withdraw after negotiation, not immediately. When Soviet forces arrive to dislodge them, they are forced to give up the printing plant, which they attempt to destroy and burn. They then manage to take over the radio station, where they explain over the airwaves who they are and urge the population to remain calm. Streetcars are overturned in the urban fighting before the rebels are forced by Soviet troops to withdraw from the city, but fighting continues outside the town. By Saturday morning, five days after the first disturbance, there is still fighting going on.[17]

The Russians and Kádár can live with flare-ups like that in Miskolc. What they cannot live with is the continuing strike in the coal mines.

The note of satisfaction sounded by the Kádár regime after the forty-eight-hour total strike produced no uprising —"the industrial counterrevolution now is smashed"—is quickly superseded by government pleas for the miners to go back to the pits. The regime offers pay raises, even "prizes" for those who go back by December 15, and appeals to their pride as skilled professionals, even calling on them to "save the fatherland."[18]

The miners, however, know their strength and, in fact, take over from where the Budapest Central Workers' Council left off. They are reported to have a plan for a stage-by-stage armistice with the government. The plan is a virtual take-it-or-leave-it "peace offer." They will return to one-quarter output when all Soviet soldiers and Communist police have been withdrawn from the region of each coal mine. They will return to half output when certain wage and employment conditions are met and finally to full output when all those workers' council members who were arrested are freed. The real sting of the proposal is that it is addressed not to Kádár, but to the "successors of the Kádár government," thus rubbing it in that Kádár is a temporary imposter kept in office only by the cordon of fifty Soviet tanks surrounding Parliament.[19]

Once news of this proposition leaks out to the public, the regime radio is quick to deny it as a malicious rumor, thus confirming its veracity in people's minds. The plan, however, never becomes operational.

The regime now turns to replacing the miners, or at least supplementing them, with volunteers. One of the first offers at the Dorog mines is to have three thousand Czechoslovak miners go into the mines. The Hungarian miners' response to this is, "Fine. We have no objection whatsoever to the Czechoslovak miners going down into our pits. We simply won't guarantee that any of them will come up again." The subject is quickly and quietly dropped.[20] In Pécs, where one-third of the miners are either in the hills fighting or have left the country, and one-third have been discharged owing to a shortage of electricity, the remaining third are busy keeping those mines not flooded in working order. The government-sponsored trade union newspaper, *Népakarat*, estimates that only half of the country's eighty-four thousand miners are actually available and thus figures that at least twenty to thirty thousand volunteers are needed.[21]

The dissolution of farmers' cooperatives continues apace. In Zala, Vas, Szolnok, Baranya, Somogy, Csongrád and Győr counties, statistics show that of the 1,571 cooperatives which existed on October 23, 1956, by mid-December, 1,036, or 62.5 percent have been dissolved.[22]

Echoes of the women's demonstration in Budapest continue to reverberate around the country. Here is a verbatim internal police report of Police Major Miklós Antal, commander of the Central Duty of Zala County for December 14:

> By 15 o'clock [3:00 p.m.] on December 13 a demonstration was scheduled by some women in Zalaegerszeg, but due to a power cut the factories stopped working at 13 o'clock [1:00 p.m.] and the demonstration took place earlier than scheduled. The women, wearing black shawls and black mourning bands, were joined by some of the workers flocking out of the factories. According to the report of the County Police Department the crowd amounted to some four to five thousand women. The goal of the demonstration was to pay homage to the memory of those fallen, and its form was a silent procession. In order to dissolve the demonstrating crowd the Soviet military units fired several warning shots and used tear-gas grenades, too. As a result, the crowd first broke up into smaller units and then dispersed completely by 19 o'clock [7:00 pm]. There was no provocation. In the late evening hours the city was quiet.[23]

And from the town of Szekszárd in Tolna County Police Captain Pál László writes in his report of December 19:

> Yesterday a leaflet was discovered on the notice board of the elementary boy's school of Bonyhád with the following text: "Our father, Khrushchev, who art in Kremlin, cursed be thy name, in Moscow as it is in Hungary," etc. The text of the leaflet continues in accordance with the form and content of the Lord's Prayer in a very inciting manner and concludes like this: "But save us from thyself and lead us not to Siberia, for thine is the kingdom and power, but not forever." Investigations were started to find the writer of the

leaflet. Some seventh- or eighth-grade students of the school presumably wrote it.[24]

Regime vs. Continuing Revolution

While the Hungarian government remains incomplete and even admits that after more than four weeks in office it has not had time to put together a "positive government program" for the country, the Ministries are filling steadily with the worst Hungarian Stalinists, who are coming out of retirement or even back from the Soviet Union. This is mostly Münnich's doing. They need little direction, since basically they are given carte blanche to do the things they did before, and it is, in any case, the Soviets who give them orders.

But for every repressive action undertaken by the regime, there is an action not dictated by the regime but by the common humanity of people who still hold responsible positions. These actions either mitigate those of the regime or counteract them entirely, indicating that under the surface the revolution goes on.

After his decrees abolishing the revolutionary councils and then the workers councils, Kádár boasts on December 11 that "the counter-revolution will be broken up by early next week."[25] Yet early next week, over sixty percent of all the workers in Budapest are on strike again, protesting the arrests of workers' council members.

Sometimes Kádár's decrees end up, in effect, by canceling each other. His blanket amnesty for nearly all who have fled the country that all is forgiven and they can have their property back if they return by March 31, 1957 is completely negated by his decree only days later that the government is confiscating all the property of those who left the country after October 23.[26]

While he tells the Soviets that the recruitment for the new party is progressing, enrollment by early December is only 1,600 as against a Communist Party of over a quarter of a million on October 23. The Party paper, *Népszabadság*, on December 21 explains why recruitment is so slow. "The majority of former party members," it writes, "never again want to get into conflict with the people. They do not want to be forced to carry out an anti-democratic policy, decided upon without their consent, and to be the target of the rightful wrath of the people, instead of the leaders who discreetly disappear at the right moment."[27]

In late December the Hungarian Writers Association passes a resolution by a vote of 250 to eight with five abstentions, pledging no concessions to the Kádár government but only loyalty to "the flag that symbolizes that a nation was born again from the unity of the revolution." They condemn the arrest of six of their number, including Tibor Déry. Earlier, the writers had written in an article, "We are not counterrevolutionaries, no reasonable, decent Hungarian could be one. We refuse to write now.... We are deeply hurt by the slanders cast at us. We will write again when official forums will recognize that we are not Fascists but true Hungarians."[28]

But the new chief of police, Col. György Sós, says, "There are some Hungarian writers whose activities are more harmful than simple crime. Those against whom serious suspicions exist will be arrested and held in custody...."[29]

In Belgrade, to which he has fled, the young Hungarian Communist writer and onetime Stalin Prize winner, Tamás Aczél, publicly repudiates his work as a Communist. "I am not a Communist any more. Perhaps you could call me a Socialist."[30]

* * * *

Since the Soviets are openly running things, the workers come into contact with them frequently. Naturally, the workers, when asked to speak their minds, do so freely and give the Soviets a hard time. They usually begin with, "Why don't you people go home and leave us in peace?" To which the standard reply is, "we're here to protect you from the fascists and reactionaries." In the Cable Factory in the First District, a worker and a visiting Soviet official, who has made a speech urging everybody to take up work again, have the following conversation:

"What happens if we don't?"

"We will declare this factory as necessary for war production, and we can legally force you to work."

"And if we don't, what happens then?"

"Then the railroad wagons will come and take you away," says the truculent Soviet.

"And after you have taken us away in the railroad wagons, who will you get to work in this factory?"

"People will come back here in the wagons which took you away, and they will be happy to work where we tell them to."

The two belong to different worlds, so here the exchange ends.[31]

By December 19, *Népakarat*, under the headline, "In the Name of

Legality," attacks the excesses of certain judiciary organs toward arrested people, adding that only part of the arrests are justifiable. "Persons…are being detained in various prisons for days on end and no one interrogates them. They are not informed of the reason for their provisional arrest. Mothers are complaining they have no news of their sons for as much as two weeks.…Lawyers tell us of their difficulties in contacting their clients, since the authorities often do not, repeat not even know where they are being detained."[32]

Complaining that Western radios are distorting the summary justice decree, *Népszabadság* on December 16 says that "summary jurisdiction applies only when a culprit is caught in the act of committing a crime or when proof of his guilt can be produced at once."[33] By the sixteenth, a whole group in Budapest is given the death sentence, though they have asked for mercy and their applications are forwarded to the Presidential Council. Meanwhile, a decree which had been published in the official legal gazette, but not otherwise made public, is finally announced on December 20, saying that a public prosecutor must investigate a case within thirty days but can also "detain" persons (in prison, understood) for as much as six months without charges.[34]

Refugees

The days of five thousand refugees crossing into Austria in a single twelve-hour period are past. Thousands of would-be refugees are picked up in the border area and shipped back to holding camps or back to their homes. There is a small spike around Christmas, as Hungarians want to celebrate the holiday in the free world, but the flow drops to 391 two days later due to so few trains operating during the holidays in Hungary. Still, by Christmas, 150,424 have crossed into Austria and 81,122 of these have already left Austria for other countries. The United States by this date has finally taken the lead with 13,915 taken in, closely followed by Britain with 12,629.[35]

Included in the Christmas increase is Nikolai Rokanoff, a thirty-four-year-old defector from the Soviet Army. The total number of Soviet defectors successfully reaching Austria is now six. Also in the flow toward the end of the year are some North Korean exchange students who had fought at the side of their Hungarian counterparts and who report that some of their fellow Koreans gave their lives for Hungarian freedom. They came West rather than heed orders to return to North Korea for re-indoctrination and possible punishment. Also among those seeking refuge in the West are many Hungarians like General Béla Király and ex-Mayor József Kővágó, who, having only recently been released from jail, knew that they would certainly be arrested again. Both men will become active in the West for the Hungarian cause; Király will be sentenced to death in absentia, later commuted to life in prison.[36]

Because of the embarrassing initial performance of the United States in comparison to other countries, the White House sends Vice President Nixon to Austria on December 19 to see the refugee situation firsthand and then report back to the American people. Nixon is taken to the border town of Andau, where he literally sees refugees who have just come across, including a man with no legs. On asking how he did it, Nixon is told, "His friends carried him." In interviews in the camps, he is impressed with the people's pride and spirit. He sees that they do not want relief or charity, but an opportunity to do in the free world what was denied them in Hungary. Before leaving Austria he says, "I am convinced the United States must do more than it already has done in order to contribute adequately our share...."

On his return to the U.S. Nixon addresses the American people on Christmas Eve. After stating his hope that a much higher number of refugees be taken in and more money given, Nixon describes what he saw. "I saw volunteer workers of different nationalities speaking different languages, but all working tirelessly and unselfishly day and night to care for these escapees from Communist oppression.

"There were even gifts for the President and Mrs. Eisenhower and for my two children from people who have every reason to feel that they should be receiving, rather than giving...."[37]

On December 27 Walter Lippmann writes in the *New York Herald Tribune*:

"Mr. Nixon will have aroused great expectations and we must hope that it will not be said that the mountain labored and gave birth to a mouse.... We can provide for only a fraction of the refugees, and behind the refugees are the Hungarian people and Hungary itself. We have a duty to them if we can find a good effective way to do our duty.... It would seem that there is a stalemate between the people and the Soviet Army of occupation. The rebellion is not crushed, but for the time being it is quelled...."

Americans are finally getting a close-up view of these courageous Hungarians, for pictures of them arriving have been in the newsreels and on television. Members of Congress, on the other hand, get to see only hooded figures, for those who testify wear hoods to mask their identity from the regime's agents. Some of the young Freedom Fighters testify before Congressional Committees under assumed names. They have harrowing, almost unbelievable tales to tell and show their contempt for the Soviet Army, which they say is "vastly overestimated in the West." "The fight would still be going on," says one of them, "if we had had enough anti-tank weapons."[38]

At Camp Kilmer in New Jersey, the only processing center in the U.S., Hungarian refugees are arriving by sea and air at an accelerating rate. Unfortunately, the machinery for absorbing them into the country and offers to take them in cannot keep up with the influx. With anywhere from eight hundred to twelve hundred arriving daily, no more than 275 are going out, and at that rate the camp will soon be completely full.[39]

"The prospective increase in the American quota up to a possible thirty-five thousand or even fifty thousand Hungarians is a gratifying response to a desperate need," writes the *New York Times* on December 21. "But before we congratulate ourselves too enthusiastically over our own great generosity, let us remember that we are the largest and richest country of the Western world and we owe it to humanity as well as to ourselves to take the maximum possible number."

Back in Austria, the Austrians erect a long row of lighted Christmas trees just inside their side of the snow-covered border so that the nightly flood of refugees can clearly see their goal. As they emerge, often dripping wet from the marshes or small canals they must cross, the Austrians cry out "Fröliche Weinachten!" (Merry Christmas!) and step forward to give them a hand. Right there they are given hot, steaming grog and oranges and sent to the village of Andau several miles distant in carts pulled by a noisy tractor.

In the camps Christmas feasts are prepared for all. Many youths and girls under twenty are tasting oranges and figs for the first time. One man who comes to a refugee hostel in Vienna on Christmas Eve takes twenty children to "give them some cakes." When he returns "all twenty are dressed in brand new clothes from head to foot."[40]

Christmas in Budapest, Before and After

On December 17 the now outlawed Central Workers' Council of Greater Budapest officially ends the strike. The forty-eight-hour strike which brought the country to a standstill was over by the thirteenth, but nearly all workers across the country went out on strike again to protest the mass arrest of their leaders. Many workers, however, were drifting back to work with the idea of earning some money for the Christmas holidays, and who could blame them? It is obvious that it is better for the Central Council to call an end to the strike than have it appear that the regime, through attrition, is winning.

The regime is now assigning surplus labor from specific industrial plants to "volunteer" for work in specific mines. The coal shortage is not only affecting lighting around the city, Radio Budapest suddenly goes off the air for thirty-seven minutes on the nineteenth and blames it on a power outage when it comes back on.[41]

Someone has prevailed on the regime to let up. It may even have been the Russians, for there seems to be no interference from them as the regime decrees first that while December 22 will be an ordinary working day, December 23 will be a half day and December 24 a holiday, December 27 an ordinary working day, December 30 a half day and December 31 a holiday. This means that for the first time since the Communists took over there will be a three-and-a-half-day holiday at Christmas time and a two-and-a-half day holiday at New Year's. Second, the regime decrees that alcoholic beverages, banned since the beginning of the forty-eight-hour strike, will be purchasable from midnight on December 21 on. Third, the curfew will be lifted on Christmas Eve so citizens can attend midnight Mass. This last decree, announced only in the afternoon of the twenty-third, comes too late for most churches to notify their parishioners, so most "midnight" Masses will still be celebrated in the afternoon so that people can get home before dark.[42]

Before these decrees are announced, Budapest citizens are nonetheless thronging Budapest's drab, dimly lit stores two Sundays before Christmas searching for something to brighten up their families' Christmas. The theatres are all closed and only a few cinemas functioning, and with alcoholic drinks prohibited, the wine and beer bars are all closed.[43]

There is one bright spot in this cold and cheerless city: there is now an abundance of food in the shops. This is partially due to the fact that the International Red Cross began issuing food parcels in Budapest on the sixteenth, three days after a convoy of twenty-five trucks and a bus arrived in the free port of Csepel, and that numerous packages have been arriving from America through the private organization CARE.[44] People seem to have enough money to buy a turkey, goose or the traditional live carp, which must be wrestled home to a water-filled bathtub until its slaying on Christmas Eve. But pork and sausages are also in good supply. In fact, the radio announces on the night of December 21 that there is not enough cold storage room for all the meat that is coming into the city, and the government has therefore decided to export meat, livestock (namely pigs and cattle), poultry and turkeys to Austria, West Germany, and Italy.[45]

With Christmas almost here, Budapesters queue for hours under cold, rainy skies to buy dolls and teddy bears for their children, the customary shirts, ties and socks for the menfolk, and pullovers, undergarments and scarves for the women. Then on the twenty-third, Budapest is blanketed in snow, not light but heavy snow, adding a Christmas card touch to the first Western-style Christmas people have enjoyed since 1948. For the time being the bitterness of the past two months gives way to an atmosphere approaching pre-revolution normal. The government relaxes its appeals for more coal production, the police ease up on the search for weapons, and the Russians withdraw more and more of their tanks.

For weeks people have been getting out of Budapest, not to flee West, but just to get away from the tension. They go to relatives and friends in the countryside. Now, on Christmas Eve, comes the final rush of people who are going to celebrate with family in the country. Fur-hatted Soviet soldiers and airmen going on leave mingle with the crowds in the dimly lit station platforms which, with their shrapnel scars and broken windows, remind people of the recent fighting. Tall, green, brightly lit Christmas trees, draped with artificial snow, stand in the station waiting rooms and booking halls.

There are numerous spills and accidents this morning as bicycles and motorcycles, even occasionally trucks and buses, slide on the icy roads which froze over before the snowfall.[46]

An official forecast that two hundred thousand Hungarians will be out of work next year puts something of a pall on the holiday, for there has been no joblessness under the Communists. People realize that it would have been worse had not so many already fled the country. *Népszabadság* puts out a thirty-two-page "Christmas" issue containing many articles about the coming year, the lower coal production and need for more energy even with imports of electricity from Austria, and the need for foreign loans from capitalist countries. All three government newspapers have a Christmas atmosphere about them, though the holiday itself is never mentioned. *Népszabadság's* editorial is headed "A Festival of Peace."

Churches throughout the capital hold their midnight Masses in the late afternoon and some at midnight, and the sound of church bells, somewhat muffled by the snow, peal through the cold crisp air.

Church bells are also heard over Radio Budapest, as are carols and other Christmas music, folk music and Johann Sebastian Bach's "Christmas Oratorio." For the children there are tales by Hans Christian Anderson, a seventeenth-century nativity play, Negro spirituals and O'Henry's "Gift of the Magi."

Also on Christmas Eve there is a radio message from the "Hungarian Revolutionary Young Workers." They say in part:

"We Hungarians find ourselves this Christmas under the oppressive shadows of tragic events. But the homes of many, many Hungarian families are warmed by the faith, burning in their hearts, that our battles and our sacrifices for a true and more abundant life will not have been in vain and will not remain unsuccessful...."

"We Hungarian working youth wish with all our hearts this Christmas night that love, mutual respect, understanding, level-headed thinking and humaneness—the better feelings of mankind—may govern in our country the actions of those whose calling it is to lead our people and mold its future...."

"We Hungarian Young Workers wish...peace in our country as soon as possible, so that our desires and endeavors may soon be realized which, during the October days, forged into one our young workers, peasants, and intellectuals, the best sons of our people."[47]

On Christmas Day, Hungarians flock to their churches, both Protestant and Catholic, through the bright sunshine made brighter by all the snow. The churches, decorated with fir branches, are packed, and the congregations even overflow into the streets, while inside people are standing in the aisles. Old people and parents carrying children trudge through the snow and ice as early as 5:00 a.m., all wearing their Sunday best under heavy overcoats, fur hats and heavy scarves. Many of these are in black. At dawn and at dusk and into the night, candles flicker and glow on the snow-covered graves around the city and in the cemeteries, as people remember their fallen loved ones. Cardinal Mindszenty's eighty-two-year-old mother is allowed to come to the U.S. Legation to hear her son say and sing the Christmas Mass and receive communion with three others. She remains with him until tomorrow, the eighth anniversary of his arrest.[48]

On the day after Christmas, the city is quiet. The clacking wheels of the few running trams are muted by the snow. People stroll with their families and friends in both halves of the city, though in Pest the snow is beginning to turn to slush. Hardy citizens hike in the Buda hills. Cafes, though unheated, organize five o'clock teas and are filled to the last chair. They serve alcohol, still banned in the shops, but many people come to buy and take home full bottles of wine. The theatres play to packed houses. The loudest noise is the occasional roar of Soviet tank engines, no longer patrolling the streets, but pulling back from positions along the Danube and around the Parliament building.[49]

Though the industrial strike in Budapest and other cities is now ended, the miners continue their fine-tuned stranglehold. Production for Christmas week, in fact, has fallen still lower, and on the first working day after the holiday, December 27, 3,800 fewer miners go down into the pits as did on December 21.[50] On the twenty-eighth the radio says that the rumor that the uranium mines of Kővágószőlős will cease to operate and the workers will be dismissed is not true. In fact, the mine is only temporarily ceasing operation due to lack of power, and therefore one-third of the miners will be given a "long, unpaid holiday." They will, however, "be directed to the coal mines."[51] The radio also announces that area peasants, who are otherwise idle during the winter months, are being registered for work in the mines.[52]

Hungarian Athletes

Little Hungary, with fewer than ten million people, has been a powerhouse in the world of international athletics. In the 1952 Olympics in Helsinki, the first in which the Soviet Union competed, Hungary was third in the world after the United States and the Soviet Union in medals won. In 1954 it almost won the World Cup in a thrilling final match against West Germany. Before the Revolution much of the nation's attention was riveted on its athletes and on speculation as to how it might fare at the Olympic games at Melbourne. Most of the team left by train for Prague when the Soviets had the airport blocked just prior to the second intervention. Others had left before the Revolution. In Melbourne, they did well, winning nine gold medals, but they did not come close to being third in the world. Perhaps the gold medal which meant the most was earned in the final match of the

521

water polo team against the world-champion Soviet team. It came some days after the Soviet second intervention in Hungary. To say it was a well-fought game would have been a misnomer. It was the roughest, dirtiest water polo match anyone had ever seen, and by the time the Hungarians had triumphed, the pool had more blood in it than any water polo match before or since.

The closing ceremonies were a traumatic experience for these young athletes, for by then thirty-five of them, including some coaches, had decided not to go home to Hungary. There were many tearful partings.

Of the original team of 178 athletes, coaches and officials, fifty-one eventually defected. A few stayed in Australia, thirty-four were flown directly to the United States by the CIA, thus avoiding immigration and visa procedures, and three more defected just before the team, which had re-assembled in Milan after various airplane flights, boarded their special train.

Practically the entire team, laden with last-minute purchases in Milan, kissed and hugged tearful gymnast Alíz Kertész, who had decided not to go home. Her red-eyed teammate and gold medalist, Károlyné Gulyás, even though she had just received an Argentine visa, decided at the last minute to go back home to Hungary.[53]

Gyula Hegyi, the head of the Hungarian Olympic team, was instructed from Budapest to have the Italians re-route the train through Belgrade instead of Vienna, where it was suspected many more would defect, especially if they learned, from Hungarians who would be greeting the train in Vienna, that they had a relative or fiancée who had fled to Austria.[54]

In Belgrade the next day a busload of leather-coated political officials from Budapest met the train. The Yugoslavs offered to accommodate the team in their "Pioneer City," but the officials from Budapest declined the offer on the team's behalf. The team was moved to another special train on a nearby siding which was due to leave that night.[55]

At the battle-scarred West Station the next day, December 18, a cheering crowd of fans who had waited more than an hour and a half in the chilling winter fog to greet them brought some sweetness to their bitter homecoming. Athletes and officials leaned out of train windows waving and shouting to relatives and friends as klieg lights lit up the scene and movie cameras rolled.[56]

In Washington later the same day, U.S. Attorney General Herbert Brownell authorized the admission of forty Eastern European Olympic athletes who had defected at Melbourne, including thirty-five Hungarians, four

Romanians and one Czech.[57] On the day after Christmas, they all arrived in San Francisco from Australia. One Hungarian athlete, twenty-year-old Lidia Dömölky, former world foils fencing champion, broke from the ranks after the playing of the Hungarian national anthem, upon spotting her brother in the crowd. She had heard he had escaped to Austria, but seeing him in San Francisco was a delightful surprise.[58]

In Europe, Hungarian authorities worry not just about defections from the Olympic team; soccer teams playing in Western Europe also need watching. Already the national junior team broke up in Geneva in order to leave members free to return or defect as their conscience dictated. Now the star of Club Honvéd is given permission to remain abroad until next March 31 after the Chief of Hungarian Football (soccer), Gusztáv Sebes, who had flown to Brussels to persuade him to come home, failed in his mission.[59]

United Nations

Ambassador Henry Cabot Lodge, Jr. takes advantage of United Nations Human Rights Day to lambaste the Soviet Union, which "by its barbaric actions in Hungary today is showing its contempt of all individual rights and human freedom in very much the same way as was shown by Adolph Hitler."

"The people of Hungary—especially the young people," says Lodge, "are proving more than ever that Communism is not only sub-human, but is also out-of-date. They have demonstrated that no system not based on human freedom can succeed. They have shown that no man—regardless of difference of race or creed—will be forever enslaved."[60]

While the rhetoric continues, action in the UN on Hungary has been slowing down. Both the Czechoslovaks and the Yugoslavs have declined to allow the UN observers to enter their countries. Hungary's Foreign Minister has had the chutzpah to walk out of sessions which discuss Hungary and there has been no further movement on rejecting his credentials, due to the United States' fear that such a move might endanger the continued existence of its legation in Budapest. The Soviet Union, on the other hand, managed to get a resolution attacking the United States for interference (via RFE) in Eastern Europe accepted by the General Assembly steering committee on December 13 by a vote of twelve to one with two abstentions. U.S. Ambassador James Wadsworth tried to put a good face on it, saying the U.S., while it felt the charge "ludicrous," nevertheless "welcomed the cleansing power of free debate" and felt the USSR would regret having brought the subject up. Washington is assured that since it is the last item on the agenda, it is not likely to come up before February.[61]

The U.S. resolution reiterating all of the previous resolutions is co-sponsored by nineteen other countries but is getting bogged down with amendments. A revised draft now calls on the Secretary General to take "whatever initiative" he deems helpful in relation to the problem, thus giving Hammarskjold a virtually free hand and releasing him from any pressure to visit Moscow, as many had urged he do.

The Secretary General is not eager to go to Moscow, nor is he eager to send the observer team to Austria only to have it sit on the Austrian border. The three chosen observers feel likewise. As a result, they submit a report recommending that inasmuch as they can do nothing, their committee should go out of existence and a "watchdog" committee be set up to take over responsibility for Hungary from the Secretary General. It is an idea the U.S. is willing to "go along with."[62]

Both in and outside of the United Nations the Indians are trying to make themselves useful. The Indian Ambassador to Moscow, K. P. S. Menon, makes a second one-week visit to Budapest, arriving on Christmas Eve. In an interview with the Hungarian newspaper *Mai Hírlap* (*Journal of Today*), he says, "I sincerely hope that a satisfactory and peaceful solution can be found which is acceptable to both the Soviet Union and to Hungary." He says that during the week here he may meet with one or two members of the government. The facts that (1) he does not mention Kádár, (2) he sees the problem entirely as one between Hungary and Russia and (3) during the whole week he is here he will see at most two of the puppet government officials are not lost on the Hungarian reading public.[63]

Nehru, meanwhile, on a visit to Ottawa, Canada, says, "I have no doubt that this Hungarian episode has shown the way, and lights the path to greater national freedom of many countries.

"Hungary has shown by many things that you cannot impose—even a strong and great power cannot impose—its will and methods for long on a relatively weak country…." The Hungarian people's policy of passive resistance is a weapon of strength which "has really shown the strength of the movement both to the Soviet people and government and to the rest of the world." The Hungarian people have "suffered undoubtedly, but they have established something of great value."[64]

Costs to the Soviet Union and the Bloc

Quite apart from the loss of prestige, the physical costs to the Soviet Union and its satellite people's republics are enormous. All are now "voluntarily" giving raw and building materials to Hungary. Many of these gifts are made to match commitments made by the Soviets, not their own officials. The economies of all these countries are centrally planned and, like the Soviet Union, are based on five-year plans, some of which interlock. None of these plans have contingencies of any size built into them. After two months of revolution and suppression in Hungary, all of these plans are now in shreds. In addition to this, Gomułka and the "Polish October" have put Polish-Soviet economic relations on a new footing. The Soviets have been forced to give the Poles a one-hundred-million ruble loan as well as pay world prices for their coal, which for years they have been getting at dirt-cheap prices.[65]

The first order of business, of course, is to move as many building supplies into Hungary as possible to rebuild Budapest and repair other damaged buildings around the country. The world must never know how much damage there was, or at least must never be able to prove it. The next goal is to get the Hungarian economy back on its feet. With the coal miners tying up the Hungarian coal supply, coal, which is already allocated for other uses in the Soviet Union and the rest of the bloc, must now be shipped instead to Hungary. The Soviets are already delivering one hundred thousand tons before the end of the year, on an old contract, and have promised another six hundred thousand tons for the first quarter of 1957. Hungary is already dependent for some of its electricity on imports from Czechoslovakia, Poland, and East Germany.[66]

But the cost is not just in goods and energy. Hungary needs first to be forgiven debts it already has; then it needs new loans. It is already beginning to negotiate these in the form of credits with Bulgaria, Czechoslovakia, East Germany, and Romania and soon will turn to Poland and Yugoslavia.[67]

In a five-day end-of-year meeting of the Presidium of the Central Committee in Moscow, revising the current Soviet five-year plan takes up most of the discussion.[68]

The total costs are difficult to calculate, but there is no doubt they are enormous.

Soviet Policy

Soviet policy is undergoing changes. The Kremlin was unprepared for the upheaval in Hungary. Nearly everything it has tried in dealing with it—getting rid of Gerő, coming to an accommodation with Nagy, crushing the insurgents with tanks, trying to win Nagy over to the Kádár government, crushing the revolution and breaking the people's spirit with deportations, outlawing the workers' councils—has failed. It is now clear that Serov's deportation plan *did* involve Siberia, for a Japanese prisoner who returned from eleven years in Siberia, Tochimichi Nakagawa, said on December 26 that he was told by Soviet officers that the camp he was leaving was being prepared to receive Hungarians.[69] Now, much to Serov's disgust, it is decided to return the deported Hungarians as soon as possible and maintain that it never happened.

The international initiatives undertaken by Khrushchev with Bulganin as his mouthpiece have kept the Western powers on the defensive and given the Soviets breathing room, but they are largely a smokescreen. Real policy changes must be undertaken if the empire is not to fall apart under its present strains, so the Kremlin is doing everything it can to prevent what happened in Poland and Hungary from breaking out elsewhere—including the Soviet Union. Cracking down on intellectuals and students must go hand in hand with raising the living standards of workers and peasants. The October 30 Document still stands, but first comes loyalty to and stability within the bloc. At the five-day Central Committee meeting around Christmastime, Khrushchev does very little talking. Domestic and economic affairs—completely revamping the current five-year plan—dominate the discussions.

On the political front the conclusion is clearly reached that Khrushchev went too far in his denunciation of Stalin and it is time to try to put the demons back into Pandora's box. This includes cracking down on dissidents in the USSR, such as Assistant Philosophy Professor Erik Yudin, who speaks critically of Soviet action in Hungary. But Yudin, who is employed at a Siberian university, does not actually speak his criticism in public, he merely writes it in a letter to his sister. He is arrested when the KGB reads his mail, and given a long sentence.[70]

The Soviet media has become as strident in its condemnations of the U.S. as it is in its attacks on the "fascist counterrevolutionaries" in Hungary. The press and radio are beginning to sound very much the way they did in

Stalinist days, and the Russian people are pulling in their horns and hunkering down as they have so often in the past, praying that it does not mean war.

There are those who feel that not too much should be made of Khrushchev's remarks made at a New Year's Eve party where liquid refreshments have been flowing bountifully. He maintained loudly that Stalin was a great leader and that "all of us in the Soviet leadership are Stalinists." Others think, "in vino veritas."[71]

British and American Policy

As stated earlier, the observers whom Hammarskjold appointed and who have never left New York came up with the idea of a "watch-dog committee" to be established in the UN to take their place and relieve Hammarskjold of the responsibility. The idea did not come from the Americans, but they "went along" with it. The British, on the other hand, felt it extremely important that Hammarskjold be persuaded to go to Budapest, but they, because of their recent adversarial position with him on the Middle East, did not feel they were the ones to do the persuading. They were afraid that just appointing a "watch-dog" committee might prove as ineffectual as previous resolutions. They suggested instead that the UN make up an official report on Hungarian events based upon the many reports of chiefs of diplomatic missions in Budapest. Third, they suggested that, inasmuch as UN observers are being prevented from going to Hungary, the Secretary General simply appoint certain diplomats already based in Budapest, presumably those from neutral countries, as the observer team. All three of these reasonable initiatives found little resonance with the U.S. Department of State for fear of jeopardizing its mission in Budapest, where they have a Minister who has not yet presented his credentials. As a result, nothing was done about any of these sensible proposals.[72]

Frustrated by the extreme caution of U.S. policy on Hungary on the one hand and embarrassed by American self-righteousness on the other, the Alsop brothers let fly in their column on December 19:

"In this country, the Administration's activity about the refugee problem has been made to look like activity about the Hungarian problem. But in fact our total activity about the Hungarian problem has been to support high sounding but empty resolutions in the United Nations, which are voted with universal, cynical hypocrisy, in the clear knowledge that they will produce no result whatever."

EXPLOSION

John Foster Dulles, back in the saddle at the State Department after recovering from his cancer operation, attends the NATO meeting in Paris on December 11. There he hears the West German Foreign Minister, von Brentano, warn that there is serious danger of a third world war breaking out due to the prevailing tension in Eastern Europe. He is thinking particularly of East Germany, which had erupted three years earlier. He knows if something were to happen again it would be impossible this time for West Germans to stand by inactive while their brothers are rising for freedom.[73]

Secretary Dulles agrees that there is danger of a third world war, and he therefore suggests that West Germans keep their cool and keep their emotions in check, as people have not over the Hungarian situation. His solution to the problem is the same two-legged stool he has been repeating for years: (1) maintain strong moral pressure on the Soviet Union and its satellites; and (2) maintain NATO's own military strength and resolution.[74]

Columnist Walter Lippmann, who is following the NATO proceedings, writes on the same day in the *New York Herald Tribune*:

"It will be a case of inexcusable neglect if the NATO governments do not prepare themselves for what might at any time in the next months explode into a European crisis of the first magnitude. The way to prepare for this crisis is to anticipate it, and to avert it with negotiable proposals which are directed toward the unification of Europe. The Hungarian horror cannot really be ended, something like it elsewhere cannot surely be prevented, unless the NATO powers can work out with the Soviet Union an all-European security system.

"Merely to go on passing resolutions in the U.N. is not nearly good enough. These resolutions do not gather force and effectiveness by being repeated. They do not liberate anyone. Nor do they reduce the threat of a European explosion...."

On his return from Europe, Dulles holds a press conference on December 18 in which he goes out of his way to assure the Soviet Union that the United States will do nothing to aggravate Moscow's troubles in Eastern Europe. Thus he knocks out from under himself the first leg of his two-legged stool solution proclaimed a few days earlier at NATO. Informed sources tell the press that Dulles and his advisers at the State Department believe that the evolution of independent states in Eastern Europe will be accelerated if the Soviet Union is given room to make compromises. As for seeking all-European security measures, the time is not ripe for that.[75]

To this Walter Lippmann in his column on December 20 responds, "It may be right for Mr. Dulles to wait, but in big governments, waiting only too often means doing nothing until there is a crisis and then improvising in a hurry."

Columnist Roscoe Drumund, writing in the *Christian Science Monitor* a day earlier, quotes the view of the one American most knowledgeable about the Soviet Union, George F. Kennan, whom Dulles forced out of the State Department when he took over as Secretary of State. "The Soviet Union," says Kennan, "will never recover."

"The proletariat in Poland and in Hungary have defied the dictatorship of the proletariat.

"The Red Army, sent to Hungary, so they were told, to put down a revolt by a few capitalist malcontents, found themselves shooting down not enemies of the workers, but workers themselves.

"The two supposedly strongest arms of the Soviet dictatorship—youth and the Army—are proving vulnerable."

In answer to why this is happening Kennan says:

"The reason is the plain fact that the Soviet Communist system is deeply wrong—wrong about human nature, wrong about how the world really works, wrong about the importance of moral forces, wrong in its whole outlook.... I have always doubted whether the Soviet system would ultimately survive in full totalitarian form even in Russia itself. I think this thesis of mine has been proven...in Poland and Hungary...."

New Year's Eve in Budapest

The period between Christmas and New Year's Eve, with so few workdays, is a sort of truce period on both the passive resistance and the guerilla fronts. Where it is possible, real work is performed. The tram service in Budapest is extended from six in the evening until eight p.m. to accommodate holiday visiting. Little fighting is reported from the countryside, except for Miskolc. There the partisans have retreated from the town up into the Bükk mountains and Soviet troops are gathering in overwhelming force to pursue them.[76]

With Soviet tanks gone from all the bridgeheads on the Danube, the huge cluster of tanks still surrounding the Parliament building look all the more conspicuous. Now these, too, begin to thin out, and by New Year's Eve all but a very few are gone. People now discover the reason why. István Dobi, the President of the Hungarian People's Republic, has invited the entire diplomatic corps of Budapest to a New Year's reception in the Parliament. Neither the Soviets nor the Kádár regime wish to have reports going back to the capitals of the world that the reporting diplomats had to squeeze through rows of Soviet tanks to get to the Hungarian government's reception. This, it would appear, also accounts for the gradual weeklong removal of tanks from the river sites.[77]

It seems strange in a city with one hundred thousand families without fuel and half that many people homeless that fellow citizens would go out on the town to celebrate the coming of the New Year. But Hungarians love parties and people desperately need some relief from the tragedy, hardship, and bitter disappointment they have all been through. So celebrate they do. The celebration does not hold a candle to prior years when restaurants were open all night and one could party well past midnight into the dawn. The curfew of 10:00 p.m. is still in force and establishments must close at nine, so midnight is celebrated at home or in the home of a friend or relative. But comic hats and balloons are seen in dimly lit, snow-blown streets, and raucous laughter of the not entirely sober is heard in the bars, cafés, and theatres. There are also church services in most of the larger churches, both Protestant and Roman Catholic.[78]

But by well before midnight people and traffic are off the streets and Budapest returns to its deserted, occupied status, even without the Soviet tanks.

In far off America, where celebrations will only start after Budapesters are asleep, journalist Edmond Taylor writes, "the Hungarian Revolution, which a month ago seemed to be drowning in blood, has proved itself unconquerable, and that it will go on, probably through alternate phases of military 'pacification' and political negotiation...."[79]

Hungarians, who cannot view it from such a distant perspective, are less confident and more fearful of what the future will bring. Still, they are fortunate in their ignorance.

January 1, 1957 to March 31, 1957

Turning Back the Clock to Stalinism

It has taken nearly two months for the Soviets to be able to squelch the Revolution and give the Kádár clique time to convert back from fig-leaf to puppet government. The Russians are still calling the tune, but no longer are the pronouncements so obviously coming from Moscow and there are now others in the puppet government besides Kádár to make them. With continuing attacks on Rákosi and Gerő as a sort of badge of legitimacy, the regime proceeds to hire all the old Stalinists and do its best to turn the clock back to ruthless Stalinism.

One of the first places this is noted is at the Austrian frontier. The Iron Curtain, which was nearly dismantled during the liberalizing period prior to the Revolution, is now re-erected with a vengeance. New mines are planted, all the watchtowers are strengthened and manned with ex-ÁVO armed with machine guns. Even places where there had been no barbed wire in the coldest of the Cold War period—the shallow waters of the lake Neusiedlersee, forming a portion of the border—now are having barbed wire strung down to the bottom.

On January 8, the tone is set by *Népszabadság* when it declares:

"There is no truce with the Hungarian counterrevolution. Our fight against them will now be pressed on a political basis, and we will concentrate on isolating and destroying the anarchists, the petty bourgeois and all those with a false outlook."

"This fight will be pressed where these hostile elements try to disguise themselves as Marxists and proclaim slogans about democratization and de-Stalinization."[80]

Three days later Radio Budapest broadcasts a new government decree striking a blow at the dissolution of collective farms that has been going on since October and reached a climax in December. The decree states that the peasants who obtained farm machinery and other tools when the inventory of the collectives was divided up have fourteen days to return it all to the State or face fines, jail, or both. The decree further orders all collective farms which "were dissolved by force or by hostile elements" (i.e. everybody) must be reformed into their former collectives.[81] Now the regime unleashes what it hopes will be the final blow to the Revolutionaries. It threatens to use the death penalty against virtually all effective resistance. And since it is an official decree, it is no mere threat. The first section of the decree reads: "Those who deliberately disturb the functioning of public utility services...or obstruct the activities of organizations declared essential for the public by the government...as well as persons inciting others to commit such acts, or

531

those who enter the premises of the above-mentioned places without proper authorization...are punishable by death."[82]

Sounding almost as though he were Ivan Serov himself, Gyula Kállai, former Minister of Culture, says, "The present state of emergency will continue until we have finally crushed out the counterrevolution.... No concessions shall be made since concessions, however small, would result in greater demands and lead to a new October 23."[83]

In the midst of decrees against the "counterrevolutionaries" and attacks on Rákosi and Gerő, various regime spokesmen begin to insert attacks on people around Nagy and even Nagy himself as "a traitor to the people."[84]

What is perhaps unique in this drive to turn back the clock is the regime's unseemly assault on children. Three thousand children, according to Radio Budapest, have been caught since November trying to flee the country and have been returned to their parents. Now the Communist Party newspaper *Népszabadság* carries an article recommending that since relations between children and parents have greatly deteriorated, children should be separated from their parents and brought up in "children towns" where they "can grow up in a healthy [read Communist] way of thinking and be taught socialist patriotism in a disciplined and conformist atmosphere."[85] The writer, a good Communist, is probably thinking about his own children who rebelled against Communism as they saw it in practice.

Since this is not about to happen, other things must be tried. There is the problem of "children who refuse to learn Russian." From now on Russian is to be taught to all children between ten and twelve. No parents are consulted. One parent comments on hearing the news, "They will also have to find a lot of new textbooks. The kids burned all the old ones."[86]

All teachers in Budapest's secondary schools are ordered to attend police lectures on February 9 to learn "how to deal with the counterrevolutionary behavior of children."[87]

Perhaps the practice most hated by workers in all Communist countries is the system of "work norms," whereby workers are made to compete with one another and then held to the highest work norm they have achieved. It is a sweatshop system on the grand scale and the Communist-controlled trade unions, instead of guarding against it, help keep the system in place. It is one of the basic things which Hungarian workers have vowed they will never go back to. So the system is re-introduced, not by decree or all at once, but in those factories where the regime feels there is the least resistance.[88]

Then, just to heighten tension with and put more distance between Hungary and the outside world, the Soviets have the regime harass the Western legations.

People are surprised that Endre Márton and his wife, Ilona Nyilás, so recently out of prison, refuse to flee to the West after November 4, insisting on sticking to their jobs of reporting for the Associated Press and United Press, respectively. As the only Western correspondents with native Hungarian, they become invaluable to other reporters by observing what is actually going on. By early January, however, with the Revolution all but crushed, the Mártons realize that their arrest is only a matter of time, and this time the charges will not have to be trumped up. Yet they labor on until a phone call comes one night from a worker whose voice is well known to Endre. "We understand they plan to arrest you tonight. I would advise you and your wife not to stay in your apartment." The caller then abruptly hangs up.

Fortunately, the Mártons have become close friends with an American Legation family, the Rogers, living next door, who are prepared to take them in. Over the next few days hints are dropped that the regime would be happy to see the Mártons leave the country and might even make it possible. Passports are obtained with surprising ease and on January 16 Tom Rogers drives the Mártons and their two small daughters in his station wagon to the Austrian border, where they cross without difficulty.[89]

When in February the Americans decide to give the annual George Polk memorial award for "distinguished achievements in journalism" to the Márton husband and wife team, the regime announces the very next day a ruling which forbids Hungarians to represent any foreign news agency or publication.[90]

About this time someone reports hearing a newsboy yelling in the streets of Budapest, "Get your latest *Népszabadság*! It contains a complete list of all the people still in Hungary!"[91]

The only way the new Communist Party can attract membership is to drop all charges against former members who were kicked out of the old Party for being too Stalinist. After all, says Antal Apró, Minister for Industry, in a speech on February 11, they were not responsible for Rákosi's mistakes. They were only following orders.

Religion, too, must be attacked. The Nagy government agreed that religion could again be taught in the schools. This decree is now rescinded.

Protestant and Roman Catholic Church leaders are attacked by name in the press and called backers of the counterrevolutionaries. Mindszenty is called a "capitalist hireling." Protestant religious and lay members had formed themselves into a National Executive Committee, overriding the government body set up to control the Protestant Churches, and they had appointed Bishop László Ravasz as president. This committee is now declared to be null and void. The attack on Mindszenty happens partly because he issued orders dismissing the phony Communist "peace priests" after he was already in the American Legation. Thanks to the Kádár questionnaire, the officer corps is now disappointingly small. The Communist Party is to play a much greater role in the new army.[92]

The formation of an armed "Workers' Guard" is announced in the Government Trades Union newspaper *Népakarat* on February 15. The main purpose of the guard is to keep rebellious workers in order and prevent strikes. They are not expecting to be popular.[93]

There are a good many writers, particularly those who have been long-time Communists, who remained to fight it out with the regime, many of whose members they know personally. First comes the suspension of the Writers' Association on January 18, then come arrests, including some as famous as Tibor Déry, and on April 21 the Writers' Association is officially dissolved.

It is never announced, but the infamous death camp at Recsk, in the Miskolc area, is temporarily re-opened. This is the camp which Nagy had closed shortly after coming to power in 1953, and in which quite a few of the writers who have now fled the country spent many harrowing years. It is now taking in women prisoners as well. Its lesser-known sister concentration camps at Kistarcsa, a village just northeast of Budapest, and Tököl to the south have been filling up for some weeks.[94]

Raids and Arrests

Starting in February the regime undertakes daily raids and arrests around the country. The most conspicuous are in Budapest, but there are almost an equal number taking place in smaller cities and even villages.

Then there are the raids on student hostels just before the beginning of the new term, which yield more literature and arms. The raiding police always carry arms as "evidence" they can plant. Then there are the raids involving dozens of police and militia on whole factories. These also often yield arms even if they do not result in arrests. Arrests are better done at the workers' homes after midnight.

Trials, Sentences, and Executions

News that a few secret trials and summary executions took place in December reaches the West, but nothing is mentioned in the official media. There is great reluctance, however, for Hungary's supreme court judges to sit for trials which are brought under the new law and many judges simply resign rather than do so. By February 2, ten of those who have not resigned but refuse to try such cases are relieved of their posts. The regime is forced to bring judges in from the countryside to replace them, and naturally they are inferior, at least insofar as experience is concerned. And not all who are asked agree to come. It also gives the regime an opportunity to emplace politically reliable judges, whom they know will not flinch at giving out death sentences.[95]

On February 2 comes the shocking news that a twenty-year-old girl was sentenced to death and executed by hanging today in Békéscsaba. On December 17, writes the Budapest evening newspaper *Esti Hírlap*, she organized and led fighting groups in the village of Gyulavári. A former Hungarian Army officer was convicted and hanged with her on the same charge. Twelve others were sentenced to from five to fifteen years.[96]

Then on February 5, Radio Budapest announces the execution by hanging of one of the more celebrated heroes of the Revolution, "Uncle Szabó," leader of the Széna Square group of young workers which had held up so many tank columns and destroyed so many tanks in the process at that strategic juncture. Unwilling to let it be known that a common worker could have achieved what he did, the announcement resurrects his First World War military status, promoting him from his former low rank to "Lt. Col. János Szabó" and claims he "tortured and killed security policemen." Szabó, who for years has been just a truck driver, headed a band of some two hundred youngsters, most of them teenage workers. Ironically, the ex-ÁVO officer, Lt. Col. Béla Balázsi, who conducted the investigation, had escaped from the Secret Police Barracks on Maros Street with two others when "Uncle Szabó" and his youngsters captured it during the Revolution. Later, when the three ÁVO men were captured by villagers in the Pilisi Mountains and were at the point of being hanged, a law-abiding insurgent commander stayed the execution and brought the three back to Budapest for a proper trial. The Russians had freed them on November 4.[97]

On Feb 8, the first public trial in Budapest gets underway. In the dock are a couple who are accused of killing one of their group when it was discovered he was a spy for the Russians. But the biggest shock of the day comes when State Prosecutor Géza Szénási reveals that up to January 28, 148 persons have been tried by summary courts, twenty-nine have received sentences of death and fourteen of these have been carried out—far more than has been indicated in the media.[98]

Sensing that the announcements of death sentences have a restraining effect on the populace, the government now makes a practice of it and five more are announced on February 13, three of them already carried out.[99]

Five days later a second public trial opens before a crowd of three hundred spectators in a dimly lit courtroom. Ilona Tóth, a twenty-five-year-old medical student who acted as a volunteer nurse in the Sándor Péterfy Street Hospital, is accused, along with two other men, of killing a wounded ÁVO officer by injecting gasoline into his veins. Slim, blond, and pale, the small-featured Miss Tóth does not seem like a murderess, and that is probably why the Western press and photographers are invited to cover the trial. She is the only child of a factory worker, but in the end she does not deny that she did it on November 18, two weeks after the Russians intervened to crush the Revolution. During the day she tended the wounded, but at night she helped István Angyal print leaflets in the sub-cellar of the hospital.

There are eleven others standing trial for a variety of "crimes" in this trial, which will take another three days. Ilona and her colleagues will receive sentences of death and be executed shortly thereafter.[100]

The People's Opposition

The Revolution is crushed, but not yet people's spirit. The whole nation, but particularly the workers, still feel united in opposition to the Soviet occupation and the puppet Kádár. The opposition now, however, shows itself less in armed attacks, now increasingly infrequent, and strikes, which now flare up only briefly in individual shops or factories, than in the general slowdown of work itself and the attitude of non-cooperation.

And then there is the sustaining power of humor. During and shortly after the Revolution there were jokes like this:

Small boy with rifle to housewife: "Ma'am, may I come in and use your window to shoot from?"
Housewife: "Of course, you can, Sonny, but only if you first wipe your feet."

or

"How lucky we are that 'friends' have come. Imagine what it would be like if an enemy had."

And during those few days of freedom:

Hungary has now reached the ideal state of Communism taught by Lenin:
"The State has withered away, the Party disintegrated, people work only for a few hours every day, and everybody has enough of everything...."[101]

For many years Radio Budapest has had a brief nightly program for small children. It begins with a mellow-voiced woman saying: "Good evening, children, are you already in your beds?" The modified version during the fighting should have been, "Good evening, children, are you all back from the barricades?"

After the fighting ceased, jokes were more like the following:

Question: Which are the four powers which can resist the Soviet Union?
Answer: The United States, Britain, the Eighth District of Budapest, and the Ninth District of Budapest.

Somebody looking around the ruins of Budapest remarks: "You know, if I didn't know that we are building socialism, I would think that the city is destroyed."[102]

There are dozens of jokes and insults painted all over Budapest which are either unprintable, or because of the puns, untranslatable.

The last powerful workers' council, which, in a way, had been a rival of the Central Worker's Council of Greater Budapest—though it had been represented on it—is the Council of Csepel's Iron and Steel Works. The regime, through arrests of its leaders, wants to break but not destroy it, for they hope to take it over. On January 8, however, the Council meets and decides that inasmuch as these arrests have made it impossible for them to "fulfill our duties in the changed circumstances," they have come to the conclusion that they should "unanimously resign our mandate. We must not create," they say, "vain expectations among our workmates. Therefore we hand our mandate back to those who have charged us with it."[103]

The regime's reaction is ill-concealed anger: "Some workers' councils," says the Party newspaper, "have shown they merit the trust and confidence placed in them by the workers *and the state* (emphasis added—ed.) But others shy before the tasks facing them and announce their own dissolution in a provocative manner...."[104]

The regime, which has perhaps ten thousand hard-core Communists as its only adherents, most of them in the security police and militia, feels isolated by all the hostility and cannot refrain, from time to time, from complaining. Thus *Népszabadság* complains that former ÁVO members are being ill treated in their civilian jobs. It gives as an example the case of a former ÁVO man who, when he reported to the machine and tractor station where he had previously worked, was told there was no work for him and was dismissed without getting a penny. Another had been beaten up by "counter-revolutionaries" and had to spend over a month in a hospital.[105]

Népszabadság also complains about the treatment local workers' councils give to the Communist-organized "Factory committees" and the Trade Union organizations. At the workers' council of the RECS depot of the Municipal Electric Railway, they dismiss and persecute Communists, and practically force the local organization of the Hungarian Workers Party into illegality. The story of the Trade Union elections, at which...the trade union itself was liquidated, should also be made public. The whole thing was prepared beforehand by the workers' council, but in such a way that the earlier elected factory committee did not even know about it...."[106]

The newspaper's plaintive question in the cultural section, "Why do we never see a single Soviet film in the movies?" could be answered by any child of ten: "No theatre manager wants to have his theater burned down."[107]

There is much talk among the young Freedom Fighters of rising again, and the "Ides of March," which happens to be the day the Revolution of 1848 broke out, has a romantic ring to it. But it is only talk; the country is not ready for more bloodshed. Kádár, however, has no idea what the country is ready for and his spies pick up the talk. In a speech he makes at Salgótarján in the first week of February, he says, "There are rumors that a new armed uprising is planned for March. But we warn that anybody who lifts his hand against the People's Democracy will be mercilessly liquidated."[108]

Regime Consolidation

The regime is still struggling for international recognition. The visit by

Chou En Lai and Kádár's own visit to Moscow help within the Communist world, but it is still finds itself completely shut out by the West. At last it sees a way to force the West's hand. Four typically venturesome English students, one the nephew of Sir Stafford Cripps, another the nephew of the writer Robert Graves, have managed to get into Hungary and have been arrested by the police. Instead of just ejecting them from the country, the regime, coached by its Soviet masters, begins to make a big "Spy case" against the four. The British and Western press are up in arms over this new outrage. Sir Leslie Fry soon finds himself forced to deal directly with the Hungarian Foreign Ministry and the precedent is set. As soon as these dealings are sufficiently involved, the regime surprises everyone by dropping all charges.[109]

Physically, the regime re-opens air traffic with Yugoslavia, once weekly beginning February 7, and with Austria, three times weekly, beginning March 5.[110]

On February 28, the regime announces a major re-organization. The new government, still headed by Kádár, consists of a thirty-seven-man Central Committee (it was sixty-three on October 23) and a ten-man Executive Committee steered by a five-man secretariat, with Kádár heading all three. Münnich, however, who still heads the Ministry of the Interior, has been promoted to Deputy First Premier, Kádár's potential successor. The rest, even though Rákosi may have jailed some, like Kádár, are basically hard-core, old-style Communists. Sándor Rónai, who had been in the Nagy government and was in the Parliament building when he was named to the Kádár government, is relieved of his post as Minister of Trade. Though ultimately major decisions will continue to be made by the Soviets, the Kádár government now looks more like a collective leadership.[111]

Imre Nagy

There is still only one man whom all but Kádárite Hungarians would be willing to accept as the head of government, and he has been languishing in enforced exile at the village of Snagov, Romania, for the past three months. Still, his shadow looms large over the Kádár regime. It is essential for the Soviets and Kádár that Nagy's popularity, which sagged during the Revolution and then soared afterward, be undermined.

It begins when the Party Secretary, Károly Kiss, gives an interview, not for home consumption but for Prague Radio, in which he says, "More and more people are of the opinion today that Imre Nagy ought to be tried by a court, because he has caused great damage." Then, when a Western reporter in Budapest asks about the meaning of Kiss' statement recently published in a Czech newspaper, a spokesman for the Foreign Ministry states flatly that the Hungarian government has no intention of bringing former Prime Minister Nagy to trial. The outside world needs to be stroked and put off the scent, the Hungarian people need to be made ready for the inevitable.[112]

Damage, Costs and Aid

The physical damage to Budapest from the fighting last fall, says the Hungarian Press Agency, MTI, on February 1, amounts to 1,150,000,000 forints (roughly $150,000,000 in 1956 currency). Some twenty thousand apartments are uninhabitable and need to be repaired or completely rebuilt at an estimated cost of 260,000,000 forints (approximately $25,000,000 in 1956 currency).

Damage to stocks amounted to 600,000,000 forints (approximately $50,000,000 in 1956 currency) and damage to power stations 50,000,000 forints (about $6,000,000 in 1956 currency), and repairs to the Csepel Steel Works, where much of the later fighting took place, some 15,000,000 forints (around $1,900,000 in 1956 currency). The approximate total thus is $232,000,000 in 1956 currency. But these are just the basics. None of this includes any of the personal property that was destroyed or damaged, nor does it include any property destroyed or damaged in the rest of the country.[113]

On March 2, *Népszabadság* says that factories run by the Hungarian Industries Ministry report a deficit of more than $50,000,000 for the month of February. Costs in January were 20% more than they were in January 1956. This "unprecedented increase in production costs is partly justified" the paper says, because the government has raised wages. Another reason partially justifying it is that industrial production, heavy industry and chemical products, decreased because of the lack of coal.

But the main reason, the Ministry admits, is that output per worker has decreased considerably. The Ministry hints that the reason for this is that the Workers' Councils got rid of the piecework norm system and it plaintively requests that the Workers' Councils reconsider their having abolished this system. The real reason for the drop in labor productivity, that no one cares to work hard under the Kádár government, is not acknowledged.[114]

There is a tremendous increase in burglaries and petty crime and even teenage prostitution. *Népakarat*, the trade union newspaper, asserts that part of the blame rests with the press, which "for years loved to report about juvenile crime in Western countries but neglected to report our own problem."

Factors increasing Hungary's juvenile crime, the paper says, are "the declining living standard since 1949, the atmosphere of unrest and dissatisfaction and the breaking up of families...and the fact that during the October troubles automatic pistols and hand grenades were given to teenagers."[115]

The Soviet Union, too, is paying incalculable costs. All of the other satellites are quickly catching on to the fact that they can now petition Moscow for funds the way the Poles and Hungarians have. On the other hand, it is not possible to turn back the clock in one country and not in the others, with the result of increased tensions with the students and intellectuals, some of whom have to be jailed.

Refugees

The Soviets are bringing tremendous pressure on the regime to stem the flow of refugees fleeing the country. Trains are now checked before they depart from Budapest for Western sections of Hungary and at each station outside Budapest, to remove people thought to be potential refugees. One hundred and eighty so-called "defector candidates" are removed from a single train in early February, according to *Népszabadság*. Budapest Radio announces on February 1 that some two thousand people who tried to cross the Yugoslav border in January were arrested.[116]

The number of Hungarians now getting through the Iron Curtain into Austria is down to a trickle. But between November 7 and January 31, 105,000 refugees have been transported from Austria to other countries, with the United States having taken by far the most.[117]

Hungary's athletes are still defecting. On March 2 the Hungarian Football (Soccer) Association meets to decide what to do with its star club, Honvéd, which has been touring South America and Western Europe. Half of the team wants to return to Hungary, half does not. The next day in Vienna it is announced that the team captain, Ferenc Puskás, will definitely never return to Hungary. Within a short time Spain's top professional team, Real Madrid, will pick him up.[118]

Many of Hungary's most distinguished writers and poets are now in the West. Most will settle in Paris, Brussels or London, but not a few will find their way eventually to the U.S.A. József Kővágó, ex-mayor of Budapest, first tours European cities speaking on behalf of his native land and then moves on to New York.

Another famous veteran of the Revolution, Major General Béla Király, announces in New York on March 9 that he is appealing to Hungarian Freedom Fighters now scattered around the world to unite into a Federation. The purpose of the proposed Freedom Fighter Federation is "to continue the work on behalf of an independent and democratic Hungary."

"Our program," he says, "is to bring to bear upon the Soviet Union the moral weight of world opinion through the United Nations and other governments of the Free World. To keep the homeland accurately informed through all available means, to keep other people of the world informed of events in Hungary, and to undertake cultural, educational and vocational projects for the assistance of our people who were forced to flee their homeland."[119]

United Nations

The United Nations General Assembly establishes on January 10, 1957, a five-nation Special Committee on the Problem of Hungary to investigate what has and is happening and report back to the Assembly. The membership, in effect, represents five world areas: Europe (Denmark), Africa (Tunisia), Asia (Ceylon), Latin America (Uruguay) and Australia, with Mr. Alsing Andersen of Denmark acting as chairman.

The Committee takes most of January to get organized and collect written materials and then on January 28 hears it first witness, Mrs. Anna Kéthly. The sixty-seven-year-old Mrs. Kéthly uses the opportunity to plead that the UN expel the representative of the Kádár government and support the legitimate, though deposed, government of Hungary which she represents. She also asks that the UN send a police force to Hungary to supervise free elections.[120]

On February 15 by a vote of sixty to seven with three abstentions, the General Assembly votes to keep Hungary on its agenda.[121]

A week later, the Special Committee on the Problem of Hungary issues an interim report containing the testimony of Miss Kéthly, General Béla Király, Mayor József Kővágó and many others. The type of testimony given since the first well-known figures testified has changed considerably. These first witnesses had, in fact, begun to make a negative impression on the Committee members, several of whom felt no animus toward the Soviet

Union and found the "speeches" they were hearing from these leading Hungarian refugees longwinded and repetitious. One of the early witnesses, Dr. János Horváth, asks the advice of one of the staff members of the Committee, Paol Bang-Jensen, the Danish Deputy Secretary of the Committee from the UN Secretariat. Bang-Jensen advises him to keep his presentation short, factual and stick to just his own experiences. The whole tenor of the hearings change and all five of the committee members now find themselves overwhelmingly convinced by the candor and believability of the witnesses. The report is very detailed in its examination of the revolution, basing much of it on Hungarian government broadcasts of the time, in addition to the testimony of the witnesses.

The Committee says that the witnesses who have appeared before it so far are unanimous in testifying that:

—The events occurring in Hungary between October 24 and November 4 were a revolution, not a counterrevolution;
—The insurrection was not at the outset directed against the Soviet Union;
—It was not sponsored from outside;
—The uprising was not organized beforehand, but was spontaneous and that action taken by writers and students rapidly grew into a movement comprising all segments of the population;
—The conduct of the State Security Police (ÁVH), both in the years preceding the Revolution and during and after, contributed to the bloodshed and loss of life.

By March 23, the Special Committee arrives in Vienna and prepares to take massive amounts of testimony from Hungarian refugees all over Western Europe. The word has gone out from János Horváth in New York that "You can trust the Dane," and thus is born the precedent of promising anonymity to witnesses who do not want their names ever known to the public. Realizing that many good witnesses will not testify if they think it will endanger their families in Hungary, Bang-Jensen, who was in charge of scheduling the interviews, makes the promise on behalf of the UN. No instructions on this have been given him from the Secretary General; indeed, the Committee does not even have a security officer. While hearings are held in Rome, London and Geneva, the bulk of hearings take place in Vienna at 6A Wallnerstrasse, a short cobblestone street near the Graben in the city's center. Bang-Jensen notices that there are people (doubtless the ÁVO) taking pictures from the building across the street. There is little he can do about it except to warn witnesses to try to conceal their faces coming and going.[122]

Soviet Policy

Soviet policy on Hungary is set: crush the opposition and turn back the clock as far as possible. Part of its pressure on Kádár to heat up the border situation with Austria is designed to intimidate the Austrians just as they are about to play host to the UN Special Committee on the Problem of Hungary. And part is simply to turn off the flow of refugees.[123]

But the Soviet Union has many other things to worry about within its empire and it is engaged in a foreign policy offensive to keep the United States and its allies at bay. The Bulganin suggestion for a four-power summit plus India and China has fallen of its own weight when the Western powers reply that the United Nations already exists for just such high level diplomatic contacts.

The Soviet Union is not yet known as one of the world's two superpowers; indeed, Khrushchev feels it is quite inferior to the United States. Since the Soviet Union is a growing nuclear power, it wants to be thought of as the U.S.'s equal. Every time it can meet the U.S. at the summit it gains further status, not only in the world at large, but within its own empire and the larger Communist world. All Soviet strategy, therefore, is based upon using its power to force acceptance, and with acceptance the relaxation of tension so as to consolidate its hold on its empire, which includes the peoples it governs directly within the Soviet Union.

Right now the Soviets, for all their ruthlessness in Hungary and their bombast in the international arena, are feeling very much on the defensive and more and more isolated from the outside world they have been successfully breaking into over the past three years. Khrushchev and Bulganin's next visits to the West were scheduled for Scandinavia in the spring. But now, after the mess in Hungary, Norway, Sweden, and Denmark have all withdrawn their invitations. When, therefore, during a routine meeting in Moscow with the Finnish premier Karl August Faerholm, the Premier suggests a possible return visit, Khrushchev accepts with alacrity, saying, in effect, "How about this coming spring?"[124]

Within the Soviet Union itself, the best way to clamp down on dissention is to spread fear. Thus a raft of spy stories break out in the Soviet press, not all of them pointing to the USA. One big one involves a Swedish spy ring operating in Estonia. The Swedes label the story "absurd."[125]

U.S. Policy

It is difficult to discern much firm direction to U.S. policy as regards Hungary. In the United Nations the U.S. delegate is no longer making inflated statements about "big things to come." But the U.S. has not pushed for the acceptance of the UN observers nor pressed the Secretary General to visit Hungary; indeed, it has played an almost passive role in the UN, not even reacting positively to the sensible ideas of the British. The U.S. continues to prevent any action toward rejecting the credentials of the Kádár government's representative.

In Budapest, meanwhile, time has run out on the American policy of not having Minister Edward T. Wailes present his credentials. The insult to the Kádár regime has been keenly felt but there comes a time, February 22 to be exact, when the Hungarian Foreign Ministry presents the Legation with a note reading in part:

"This delay is untenable even from the point of view of international law.... The Hungarian Government...sincerely hopes that the American Government...will put an end to a situation which undoubtedly disturbs the relations between the two countries."[126]

Minister Wailes and the Department of State take the hint, and he is reluctantly withdrawn to Washington. Around the same time, the long-time Charge d'Affaires, Spencer Barnes, who had witnessed the long build-up to the Revolution and its tragic aftermath, is replaced by Garret G. Ackerman, Jr., a diplomat who has experienced none of the trauma of the past twelve months in Hungary and thus sees things from a somewhat different perspective.

On the wider international front, while the Bulganin proposals have been deflected, no serious counter-proposal has been offered. At the April disarmament talks in London in March, there is consideration of the possibility of discussing Bulganin's proposal for a five-hundred-mile pullback of troops on either side from the center of Europe. The proposal would, in effect, remove Soviet troops from most of the satellites, but also would appear to remove American troops from the continent.

John Foster Dulles is strongly opposed to this idea. Not only would it wreck NATO and his and Adenauer's plans for building up the Bundeswehr (new German army), but it would, he thinks, be totally unacceptable to the East Europeans who realize how quickly the Soviet Army could reoccupy Eastern Europe while the American Army would be stuck in the U.S. or, at best, in Britain.

In a word, American policy at this point is reacting to Soviet initiatives, but appears to have no clear purpose other than maximum exposure of Soviet ruthlessness in Hungary to the UN and around the world.

April 1, 1957 through 1958

Turning the clock back

The Writers' Association, which has been suspended in January, is now dissolved entirely on April 21. In the same announcement a long list of writers and journalists who have just been arrested, including Tibor Tardos and Gyula Hay, is read out.

Perhaps the cruelest decree issued in the first half of 1957 refers to "those who became disabled while taking part in counterrevolution." They "cannot claim a pension, nor can any pension be paid to any dependent of those who died while fighting on the side of the counterrevolution or who were executed because of counterrevolutionary actions."[127]

Reacting to charges that the U.S. instigated the "counterrevolution," the Department of State, in an unusually bitter pronouncement, accuses the regime of reverting to "Stalinist terror."[128] But no amount of Western publicity about the terror campaign appears to have the slightest effect in slowing down or mitigating it. Indeed, the arrests and trials increase, though they appear to come in waves, all through the spring of 1957.

There are now an estimated seventeen thousand people in prison or concentration camps,[129] and according to a new decree promulgated on July 18, those in camps may have to remain there up to a year and a half without being charged. Up to this point, six months was the longest a person could be held without being formally charged, but now those sent to camps are not covered by this regulation. In addition, the Public Prosecutor, in conjunction with the Minister of the Interior, can now prolong for an unlimited period any political prisoner with an initial sentence of at least six months if it is deemed that that person is still a danger to the State.[130]

István Bibó and Zoltán Tildy, both members of Nagy's government, are arrested about May 23, though the news of Tildy's arrest only comes two weeks later. Bibó will later be tried and given a life sentence. The two arrests are obviously connected with the coming trial of Imre Nagy, about which there have been rumors all spring.[131]

Many of the trials concern actions which have some basis in fact, but evidence is twisted and sometimes entirely fabricated, and confessions forced, though not many convincing confessions are obtained, nor do they stick, once the defendant is in court. But there are also cases where people are condemned to death and even executed when they had nothing to do with the "crime" supposedly perpetrated.[132]

The rumors about the Nagy trial have a strong basis in fact. On April 14 Nagy, in fact, is "arrested" at his villa in Snagov, where he had been in enforced exile, and brought back secretly to Budapest. Only ten days before, Kádár had assured a group of foreign journalists that in view of the delicacy of the situation there would be no trial of Nagy. The Soviets are not eager to stir up the West at this point, particularly with the Special Committee on Hungary now back in New York writing up its report. Also, the Soviet peace offensive is still in full gear. The Hungarians, too, do not wish to do anything which might possibly annoy Moscow, as they are still engaged in talks about the status of Soviet troops in Hungary. They are hoping to get an agreement much like the one Gomułka has just recently negotiated for Poland.

Hungarian-Soviet Talks

Talks between the Kádár regime and the Soviets, which had begun in December 1956, finally reach an agreement on April 26, defining the "legal status of Soviet troops in Hungary," as well as the quantity, composition and exact locations of the Soviet troops stationed "temporarily" in Hungary. In accordance with the Warsaw Pact and the Soviet-Hungarian friendship treaty of February 18, 1948, they are to remain in Hungary as long as the "aggressive North Atlantic bloc (NATO) exists."[133]

The UN's Special Committee on Hungary Issues Its Report

On June 30 the Special Committee on the Problem of Hungary issues its report to the world, a 148-page, 160,000-word document complete with annexes, indexes and maps. It is one of the most lucid, well written and hard-hitting documents ever put together by a committee and it causes headlines all over the world.

Not only headlines and front-page stories result from the report's distribution, but innumerable editorials and articles are based on it.

"This is a last service to Hungary from those who did her scarcely any other," writes the *Manchester Guardian* in England; "it was worth performing. People outside Europe will note that two of the signatories are a Tunisian and a Ceylonese, and that the report is unanimous."

"What the report does," writes the *Times*, "in every one of its carefully written pages is to fill in the details drawn from over a hundred witnesses.... New evidence emerges to give firmer emphasis or a slight twist to what was generally known before.

"For a start, it becomes far clearer than before that the Russians began taking military precautions some days prior to the students' meetings on October 22...."

Virulent attacks from the Communist press and radio come as expected. It is interesting to note, however, the difference between the Soviet and Hungarian responses. The Soviet attack was immediate and decisive: the report is flawed because it reports only one side. The Hungarian Foreign Ministry says no official comment can come until the document has been received. The next day, however, it mimics the Soviet line; this pattern of reiterating Moscow's position a day later continues for several days. At one point Radio Moscow literally criticizes the Hungarians for not reacting forcefully enough.

The broadcasts of RFE, BBC and VOA quoting large sections of the report day after day is too much for the regime. After a few weeks of this saturation broadcasting it cannot resist replying. One of its cleverest propagandists devotes a five-part series of long articles in *Népszabadság* on the last five days of August trying to refute the report's findings. These not only call more attention to the report, but by putting certain quotations and information in print, make it possible for astute readers to figure out quite easily what the report actually says.

Even so the five articles quote only portions of fifty-five sentences out of a report containing 2,492 sentences, or a total of 1,623 words out of the report's 160,000.[134]

Trouble in the Kremlin

The Soviet Union also attacks the report, but is too busy with its own agenda to give it much attention. Two days before the report is issued,

Khrushchev's opponents on the Presidium—and these are now a majority, since only Mikoyan, Suslov, and Ekaterina Furtseva are definitely on his side—plot to unseat him and demote him to Minister of Agriculture. They get a sudden meeting of the Presidium together on the pretext of deciding the order of speakers at an upcoming celebration of the 250th anniversary of the founding of Leningrad (St. Petersburg). Khrushchev, who loses the vote, cagily demands a vote of the entire Central Committee, which is within his rights. As the call goes out to Central Committee members to convene in Moscow, Khrushchev gets Marshal Zhukov, who is still in his corner, to fly Khrushchev's supporters secretly from the far-flung regions of the Soviet Union to Moscow via Army transport planes. By the time the plenum of the Central Committee opens on June 22, Khrushchev has a majority and the Presidium vote ousting him is overturned. He has already put together a case, threatening to release incriminating documents proving the complicity in Stalin's crimes of Molotov, Kaganovich, and Malenkov, whom he knows are behind the attempt to dump him, and whom he now labels "the anti-Party group." Khrushchev knows they have just as much incriminating evidence against him, so he realizes it is in his interest not to make good his threats of exposing their full complicity in Stalin's crimes. Instead he gets rid of all three of his archrivals by having Molotov appointed ambassador to Mongolia, Malenkov the director of a power station in Central Asia and Kaganovich the director of a cement factory in Sverdlovsk, Siberia.[135] Kremlin watchers in the West now figure that with re-Stalinization the Kremlin has a new Stalin, but with a major difference. Purge victims are now simply humiliated rather than being executed.

Publicizing the UN Report on Hungary

Back at the UN there is considerable controversy as to whether or not to re-convene the Eleventh General Assembly to discuss the Special Report or whether to wait until the fall and the next General Assembly. The Eleventh General Assembly *is* reconvened, but only just before the scheduled meeting of the Twelfth General Asembly so that all the heads of state and foreign ministers are present for both sessions.

The U.S. Delegation does its best in September to see that the African and Asian delegates not only get copies of the report to read, but see a film called "Hungary Aflame" which has been made by a Hungarian émigré in Munich from actual newsreel footage of the Revolution. It was cut and rendered into English by Free Europe Press.* The special session of the Eleventh General Assembly opens on September 10 and closes one day prior to the opening of the Twelfth General Assembly.[136]

Soviet/Kádár Reaction

As if in willful response to the UN Special Report on Hungary, the Soviets and their Hungarian puppets increase their campaign of terror in July to a much higher pitch than seen heretofore. Travelers from Hungary say as many as eight hundred have been arrested in two weeks, while Minister of State György Marosán admits that several hundred have been. They are said to be "stamping out the last traces" of the Revolution, but, in fact, as József Kővágó points out to a New York audience, "the whole nation" participated in the Revolution, therefore "everybody could be sent to prison."[137] In the end the regime detains close to thirteen percent of the population in one way or another, and twenty percent of these has to be let go for lack of evidence.[138]

The mood in Budapest is now one of sullen resignation. No one knows who will be arrested next or when the regime's bloodlust will be slaked. Rumors are rife and people are learning to be more and more careful about what they say to whom. Still, there are Budapesters who can still savor a good joke. The latest doing the rounds goes like this:

> Question: What is the difference between a democracy and a people's democracy? Answer: Why it's exactly the difference between a jacket and a straightjacket.

The *New York Times*, which has been running almost daily stories about the arrests, trials, and executions in Hungary this summer, comments under the heading "Kádár's War on Hungary": "Even with thousands of Soviet troops on Hungarian soil the puppets in Budapest still fear revolution and the end of the privileges they have bought at the price of betraying their own people. Could there be a better unintended testimony to the heroism of the Hungarian people and the fact that they have not yet reconciled themselves to the foreign yoke…?"[139]

Imre Nagy, Again

The jackals are after Imre Nagy again. This time it is József Révai, a lead-

---

*The author was privileged to have headed this enterprise.

ing Stalinist of the Rákosi era, who was last seen on the night of October 24 fleeing from the *Szabad Nép* building back to his villa on Rózsadomb. He demands that Imre Nagy "should be called to account. If smaller crimes can be sent to court," he says, "why should not proceedings be instituted against the chief criminal?"

The "chief criminal"'s name pops up in New York City in mid-August when it is announced that an essay of Nagy's entitled "In Defense of the Hungarian People" will be published by Praeger and Co. in the fall. It is the second book from Eastern Europe within a few days to make news in New York, for Ðilas' *The New Class*, for which he is now in a Belgrade jail, is published on August 12.[140]

The name of Nagy comes up in a meeting of Kádár's politburo on August 26, along with the names of his close associates Géza Losonczy and Ferenc Donáth. Also the names of Miklós Gimes, Pál Maléter, József Szilágyi, and Béla Király are mentioned. What these men all have in common is the Politburo's hatred of them and the decision as of that meeting that all should be tried and put to death.[141]

But much as Kádár would like to put Nagy and his friends in the dock, the Soviets are still calling the tune, and the special session of the Eleventh General Assembly to be devoted entirely to Hungary is coming up on September 10. The decision is made to put it off until the end of the year.

More Arrests and Mass Trials

Hungarian personnel working for the Western legations are no longer just being followed and persecuted, they are now being arrested. Several employees of the American Legation and six from the British Legation are now in jail.

Now people who actually were prominent in the revolution—not just those caught with guns or other incriminating evidence—are being tried in secret and executed. Two of these around December 10 are Col. Antal Pálinká-Pallavicini, commander of the tank unit which had "freed" Cardinal Mindszenty and brought him to Budapest, and László Iván-Kovács, chief organizer of the Corvin Passage Freedom Fighter group, which accounted for so many Soviet tanks.[142]

In the Markó Street Courthouse a large trial is under way in mid-December. It involves eighteen workers from the Csepel Iron and Steel Works accused of "counter-revolutionary activities and the murder of a mayor." Only thirteen are in the dock; the other five escaped from the country and are being tried in absentia.

A second trial is under way involving twenty persons, all members of the Transdanubian National Council based in Győr. Since its chairman and longtime Communist, Attila Szigethy, who became a flamboyant revolutionary leader, manages to commit suicide, and many of the others have already fled to the West, the trial is of little consequence.[143]

With so many trials and executions taking place, The *New York Times*, under the heading "Terror in Hungary," editorializes:

"While trying to create the impression of a gay holiday season in Budapest, the Communist regime in Hungary is staging a final drive to liquidate the last freedom fighters who led the national anti-Communist uprising last year. Most of the freedom fighters are either dead or are refugees abroad, but many of them are still in Communist hands and it is these who now face their doom."

Yet two days later in Budapest Prosecutor Géza Szénási differs sharply with the *Times* on the finality of the drive. Speaking at the year's last session of Parliament he says, "Pursuit of counter-revolutionaries who took part in the anti-Russian uprising will continue for years.... After martial law was repealed some people expected that there would be a lessening of rigor.... If the years disclose those who have committed counter-revolutionary crimes, we will strike at them the blows they deserve."[144]

The Special Committee on the Problem of Hungary did not go out of business once it produced its report last June. More than any other body it is keeping track of what is currently going on in Hungary. In connection with the three large trials now in progress in Budapest, the Committee Chairman, Alsing Andersen, addresses a letter on December 20 to the Hungarian Foreign Minister requesting more precise information on these trials, reminding him of the General Assembly resolution passed on September 14, 1957 calling upon Hungary "to desist from repressive measures against the Hungarian people."[145] While the UN Secretariat releases the letter to the press, very few newspapers bother to mention it. The Hungarian issue is once again fading from the public consciousness in the West.

Sputnik

On Friday, the fourth day of October, 1957, something occurs which has nothing whatsoever to do with Hungary, yet is to have a greater effect on

Hungary's future and the whole Cold War than anything else in 1957 and for many years thereafter. Soviet scientists launch *Sputnik*, the first man-made satellite ever to circle the earth. It is the opening act of the age of space exploration and a stunning achievement. No nation is more stunned than the United States, which has assumed that it is ahead of most countries in all scientific enterprises, and certainly well ahead of the Soviet Union. It causes consternation among the American people and in the U.S. Congress. To find that America is actually behind the Russians and that they are the first into space is a jolt for every American. It takes years for Americans to adjust to it. Before the year is out the National Defense Education Act is quickly enacted by Congress to beef up American education in the sciences. But money from the NDEA spills over into many other educational fields felt essential to winning the Cold War, including the learning of Russian.

Overnight, Soviet Russia achieves the status of superpower, able to do in space what the Americans have not yet done. No amount of Western information programs and propaganda about Soviet brutality in Hungary can overcome the fact that Russia has done something scientifically new that no one else has. And for backward countries emerging in Asia and Africa, modern technology, which is first on their shopping list, can now be obtained from another source besides the U.S. and the former colonial powers. The Soviets, for whom propaganda has always been a *sine qua non*, make the most of it, not just in the remaining months of 1957, but for years to come.

Talk about suspending Russia's membership in the UN was conceivable before *Sputnik*; after *Sputnik* it is unthinkable. Russia is still a pariah, but its prestige has risen dramatically overnight and the Soviets do everything possible to exploit this newly won respect. Hungary is fast becoming history and the Cold War is now operating on a different level.

1958

Budapest

Taking note of the new academic semester, *Népszabadság* says that Party-induced political discussions in all of the universities and secondary schools on the subject of the counter-revolution show that "the most dangerous, false ideology among students is nationalism." The paper divides students into three groups: (1) those who support the Party (hardly any); (2)

EXPLOSION

those who are hesitant to express themselves (the vast majority); and (3) those who still cling to the "false ideals of the counterrevolution."

"The possibility that power could slip from the hands of the workers and that capitalists and landowners could again sit on their necks sinks into insignificance beside the question whether Soviet troops called in to help would leave Hungary.... What is the cause," the paper muses, "of [students thinking] that belonging to a particular nation is more important than proletarian class interests?"

Perhaps the answer can be found in the announcement of László Gyáros, Press Chief for the Hungarian Foreign Ministry, who announces two days later that deportations from Hungary to the Soviet Union or even from Budapest to the countryside never took place. They are a complete "invention of the foreign press."

United Nations, New York

Népszabadság scathingly denounces a dramatic scene which took place the day before on the roof of the United Nations Secretariat building: the burning of the list of 81 out of 111 Hungarian witnesses who requested perpetual anonymity before they would testify before the Special Committee on the Problem of Hungary. It is the culmination of a dramatic battle between the Secretariat—and ultimately Dag Hammarskjold—and the Deputy Secretary of the Committee, Paol Bang-Jensen, who has since been suspended and is later fired from the Secretariat for his refusal to give up the list for the UN's "safekeeping." Bang-Jensen knows, as the chairman of the Committee Alsing Andersen puts it in a memo to Hammarskjold, "the communists would be willing to pay a high price for the documents of the Hungarian Committee." Indeed, they have already obtained some documents. A thirty-six-year-old Indonesian member of the Secretariat, Dhanala Samarasokara, was dismissed from the UN Secretariat on December 16, 1957 for having earlier given to a Soviet member of the Secretariat, Vladimir Grusha, documents he had obtained from the Ceylonese member of the Committee. The F.B.I. already had enough evidence of Grusha's spying to have him sent back to Russia on April 10, 1957, eight months prior to the UN's disciplinary action. Bang-Jensen's reputation for discretion as well as his repugnance for Communism had caused him to be approached by several potential Soviet defectors, at least one of whom offered to expose active Communist spies in the Secretariat. Nothing more had come of this approach, but he knew that handing the list back to his superiors at the UN might easily spell suffering if not death for hundreds of people in Hungary. For months there was a standoff between demands of the Secretariat that he hand the list over and his refusal to do so. Finally both parties accepted the sensible compromise suggested by Ambassador Alsing Andersen that the list be returned to the UN where, in the presence of all parties concerned, the UN security would burn them.

To the Hungarian refugees and to much of the American and even world public Bang-Jensen is a hero. To Hammarskjold and the UN bureaucracy he is an insubordinate troublemaker who makes them look both sinister and petty. He is fired with all the trappings of "due process," which are quickly exposed as anything but,[146] and subjected to a UN-conducted smear campaign which leads to unemployment, depression and his early death. Though a devoted family man with a wife and five children who writes his wife a memo at her request saying he will never commit suicide, nevertheless in a period of depression he will do just that on the day before Thanksgiving 1959. Many people refuse to accept that it is suicide, convinced that the KGB has performed many such "suicides" in the past, but the bulk of evidence runs against this.

A Trial of Imre Nagy in Budapest?

Since the West has not responded to its peace offensive in any satisfactory manner, the Kremlin finally gives Kádár the green light on January 28 to go ahead with the secret Imre Nagy trial. The public prosecutor now formally presents charges against Nagy and "his accomplices."[147] But even though the trial is to be held on camera, the regime feels the Hungarian public needs to be softened up with further attacks on Nagy. So the Editor-in-Chief of *Népszabadság*, Dezső Nemes, now obliges in two consecutive articles. He writes that Nagy followed a policy of betraying the dictatorship of the proletariat because, together with the renegade Yugoslav Communist Milovan Đilas, he was trying to establish an anti-Soviet federation to which Hungary, Yugoslavia, and Austria would belong. "Nagy and his friends wanted to bring the neutral, anti-Soviet bloc under the imperialists' power."[148] The four main prisoners, Nagy, Pál Maléter, Miklós Gimes and Géza Losonczy, are held in solitary confinement in the Fő Street prison in Buda, where they have been since late 1957. At first Nagy and his secretary József Szilágyi refuse all cooperation, declining to answer a single question. Eventually Nagy decides to communicate, if only to set the record straight. Along with Maléter, however, he consistently denies all charges, the main two of which are: "preparing and unleashing of the counter-revolutionary uprising" and "treason" against the Hungarian People's Republic.[149] The opening day of the trial is held on February 6, but abruptly on the seventh the trial is suspended. Moscow, it seems, is hoping for a rapprochement with Tito's Yugoslavia, which could include an improvement in Hungarian-Yugoslav relations.

Contrary to opinions in the West, Khrushchev at first is doubtful about the efficacy of an Imre Nagy trial and for a while resists Kádár's request that he be returned from Snagov, Romania to Budapest to stand trial, even pointing out that the Hungarians themselves promised in writing not to arrest Nagy. He agrees only reluctantly when Kádár points out that unless Nagy is tried and convicted, an un-criminalized Nagy remains a threat to his regime's legitimacy.[150]

Khrushchev makes a visit to Budapest in early April, ostensibly to celebrate the anniversary of Hungary's "liberation" by the Red Army. But he is also doing his best to bring about a summit meeting and relaxation of tension with the West, so he comes with thoughts of amnesty and relaxing the terror in Hungary, something Kádár strongly resists. Khrushchev has already used the inauguration of a new Ambassador to Budapest, Yevgenii I. Gromov, to try to instill the idea of relaxation and amnesty, so far to little avail. The talks, however, appear to go well. It is noted that Khrushchev omits any castigation of Nagy, at least in the official text of his speech. Unlike previous visits to Budapest, Khrushchev gives his speech out of doors, in Freedom Square, of all places, before a carefully screened and selected audience. He has read how American journalists wrote that he would not dare show his face in public while in Budapest, which may be the reason for the public meeting and the selection of Freedom Square. After the speech, Kádár points out the American Legation on the far side, saying, "Look over there to the left and you'll see the American Ambassador [it was only the Chargé d'Affaires] standing with his men. I can see Mindszenty, too."

At this point Khrushchev recalls saying, "Comrade Kádár, let's go down from the speaker's platform and walk straight into the crowd" (an "impromptu remark" which was doubtless stage-managed well ahead of time). Kádár, who, according to Khrushchev, is not enthusiastic about the idea, remarks, "There's a lot of people down there, you know." "All the better," responds the Russian. "This way we'll show the American journalists and the American ambassador and Mindszenty that Khrushchev is not afraid to stick his neck out." They are greeted warmly with smiles and handshakes as they pass through the handpicked crowd of Party faithful.[151]

Something else which Khrushchev manages to his satisfaction during his April visit is the quiet removal of Kádár himself from the position of Premier and Party Secretary, to just that of Party Secretary and the elevation of Ferenc Münnich, who had been his original choice for the Premiership, to that position. The switch is handled without fanfare in May.

A startling proposition, which is revealed only decades later, is Khrushchev's offer to Kádár to withdraw all Soviet troops from Hungary as the Soviets are about to do from Romania in June in accordance with the Declaration of October 30, 1956. Kádár's reaction is immediate. Knowing his regime would collapse overnight if the troops were to withdraw, he declines the offer. The excuse he gives Khrushchev, however, is that Hungary on its own would not be able to defend itself from external aggression.[152]

The Political Committee tries to convene the Hungarian Central Committee in May to settle the Nagy trial once and for all, but Kádár has them postpone it until June 6. Three days later the secret trial gets under way and runs until June 15. Neither Nagy nor Maléter give an inch. They decline pleas of mercy, declaring that the final verdict will be made by the Hungarian people and the international working class. The sentences are handed down the next day and carried out within hours.

On June 17, 1958, a year and three quarters after the outbreak of the Revolution, identical announcements come from Moscow and Budapest that Imre Nagy, Pál Maléter, and two colleagues have been tried, sentenced to death and executed. Because there was never any official announcement that Nagy and his colleagues had been returned to Budapest from Romania— where he was technically in Romanian custody—and the fact that the announcement came from Moscow as well as Budapest, people in the West at first assume the trial and execution has been held in Moscow. Even when it becomes clear that this is not the case, that it all took place in Budapest, the assumption continues that this is Khrushchev's vengeance on a Communist Party member who has given him more trouble than any other.

In fact, the trial, if not its exact timing, is totally in the hands of the Kádár regime. So much so, in fact, that Khrushchev is genuinely surprised and shocked that the death sentence is immediately carried out. He has advised Kádár in a telephone call to make the sentence "exile or imprisonment for life," or if he must have the death sentence, to have it immediately commuted to life imprisonment. Except for Beria, who was executed the same year Stalin died, no Communist leader has been executed since Stalin's day.

World Reaction

Neither Khrushchev nor Kádár could have anticipated the reaction, which now bursts forth from every quarter of the globe. After all, there has been *Sputnik*, and many other events that have occurred on the world scene since the fall of 1956, and Hungary and its fate have long since faded from the public consciousness. But it is as if the whole revolution were suddenly erupting all over again. As Prof. Paul Zinner of Columbia University puts it, "Imre Nagy was not a man whose death might have been expected to dramatize the suffering of an entire people. Only he, and at the last moment, could have made it so." By his refusal to bargain he "sealed the world's memory of the Revolution, a revolution he could never have inspired, could never have controlled, but, by his last action, sustained in the minds of men."[153]

In addition to headlines and front-page coverage of the executions, not to mention editorials in nearly every serious newspaper around the globe, statesmen issue statements deploring the action, and spontaneous demonstrations break out in front of Soviet Embassies and Hungarian Embassies and Legations wherever these are known to exist.

At the UN the Special Committee on the Problem of Hungary springs to life and publishes by June 21 a "special communiqué" on the subject. This in turn causes a new round of worldwide comment. The communiqué, says the *New York Times* editorially on June 23, speaks "for the overwhelming majority of civilized humanity." "Public opinion" writes the *Times*, "is a real force in the modern world" and the UN has helped to form the world's opinion of what transpires in Hungary.

In Moscow a number of Western embassies are picketed in retaliation for demonstrations in the West, but it is clear that the Komsomol (Soviet Youth) members are not quite sure why they are picketing and may even be curious enough to find out.

In Budapest the trials and rumors of trials go on as though there had been no world outcry at all. Dr. István Bibó, arrested on May 23, 1957, is only tried and sentenced to life imprisonment on August 2, 1958.[154]

East-West Sparring over a Summit and Eastern Europe

There is considerable turmoil among policy makers in the West over what to do about the situation in Eastern Europe and how to handle the Kremlin's overtures. Many hours of meetings are held in the State and Commerce Departments in Washington trying to figure out how to give aid to the Hungarian people without Congress labeling it aid to Kádár. In the end it is conceded that the only way to avoid objections at both ends, American and Hungarian, is to funnel all aid through the International Red Cross.[155] In England there are those in the House of Commons who resist any aid to Gomułka's Poland because Gomułka is a Communist and Poland is Communist. Edward Crankshaw, writing in the *Economist,* sees "a shining opportunity…to help the Poles to maintain their recklessly won, precarious, demi-semi-independence with goods and credits to shore up their tottering economy." Alas, what Britain did do was "too little and lukewarm."

"The impression made on [Khrushchev]," writes Crankshaw, "by our excessive fear and rigidity must be encouraging in the extreme. By treating the countries of Eastern Europe, with all their teeming variety, as part of a monolithic communist bloc, we play exactly his own game and show a lack of imagination and boldness, a total lack of conviction in the strength of our own cause which must be nectar to him—and to the people of Eastern Europe, slow, corrosive poison.

"They do their best to stand up to Moscow, working through the instruments that come to hand. We cannot fight for them: all right, that is understood. But what is not understood…is that we will not, where we can, move heaven and earth to help them moderate elements in their countries in an attempt to strengthen them."[156]

The American ex-diplomat Prof. George F. Kennan voices similar frustration. In the previous January at Oxford he gave a series of lectures known as the Reith Lectures, later to be published as a book. Newspaper reports had Kennan advocating that U.S. forces be pulled out of Germany and plans for a German Army, which is to become the European backbone of NATO, be scrapped in favor of a neutral, united Germany.

Like many cursory reports, this does not do Kennan justice. Kennan feels, much like the British diplomats in Eastern Europe, that by far the most important goal for Western policy is to get the Russian troops out of Eastern Europe. "It seems to me," he says, "far more desirable on principle to get the

Soviet forces out of Central and Eastern Europe than to cultivate a new German Army for the purpose of opposing them while they remain there…. NATO will not be weaker, as a political reality, just because it may be supplemented or replaced by other arrangements so far as Germany is concerned."

The only way to get the Soviet military out of Eastern Europe is if the "entire area can in some way be removed as an object in the military rivalry of the Great Powers." And the only way to do that is a *quid pro quo* of both sides pulling their troops back. He points out that Khrushchev himself keeps bringing this up, and he, Kennan, does not buy the idea that Soviet troops can move right back in overnight, while American troops would be in England or the U.S. Americans, he feels, see the whole conflict in strictly military terms, yet it is every bit as political as military. The Soviet Union is not like Nazi Germany; it moves in militarily only when an area is ripe for conquest. It was the Marshall Plan's resurrection of West European economies and societies that kept the Soviet Army from invading Western Europe in the late 1940s and early 50s, not our possession of the atom bomb.

The American military exaggerates "the value of the satellite armies as possible instruments of Soviet offensive policy" and underestimates "the advantage to Western security to be derived from a Soviet military withdrawal from Central and Eastern Europe."

Kennan does not advocate unilateral withdrawal, nor withdrawal any time in the immediate future. But he fears that unless advantage is taken of the present opportunity at least to discuss withdrawal, the division of Europe and Germany will settle into an indefinitely long period at great cost to the U.S. and a dangerous prolongation of insecurity to Europe.

Criticizing current American policy, he says, "Until we stop pushing the Kremlin against a closed door, we shall never learn whether it would be prepared to go through an open one."

It is as well that the venue of these lectures is Oxford, for no one in Washington is listening. While it is understandable that the U.S. policy of the day is marked by suspicion, the accompanying total opposition to any serious engagement with the Kremlin is neither reasonable nor practical.

Hungary

In Hungary the arrests, trials and inordinately severe sentences continue throughout the summer and fall of 1958.

That all of this is vengeful reprisal is obvious to all. But even those who have lived through the worst of the Rákosi regime and the worst of Kádár's reprisals are not prepared for the extreme cruelty which the regime metes out to the children it has condemned to death. In a pretense at humanitarian treatment and to stay within the law it pretends to wait until each one of these children has reached his or her eighteenth birthday before executing each by hanging. In reality, only one eighteenth birthday is reached. The rest are executed well before they reach that age.

Between December 1956 and the summer of 1961, when the last of these children is executed, a total of 341 people are hanged—as many as in the worst years of the Rákosi regime. Two hundred and twenty-nine of that total are killed simply for participating in the Revolution. Many more are given death sentences later commuted to life imprisonment. Most of those killed are young workers or soldiers in their twenties. During the first three years of the reprisals, that is, well into 1959, thirty-five thousand people face legal action for activities during the insurrection; twenty-six thousand of these go to full trial; and twenty-two thousand are sentenced. Almost half of these receive more than five years. Forty-five point eight percent of those held are industrial workers, and nearly twenty-five percent are agricultural workers.[157]

Between 1957 and 1960, approximately thirteen thousand people are incarcerated in camps. Tens of thousands are banned from their homes (i.e. deported, in most cases, to the countryside), dismissed from their jobs or placed under police supervision. The suppression involves over one hundred thousand persons and their families, which means, at a minimum, three hundred thousand people. But, of course, it really has an effect on the entire nation of almost ten million people.[158]

CHAPTER XI

Accepting the Suppression (East & West)

1958 to 1961

Budapest

BY THE EARLY SPRING OF 1958, Budapest, in its outward appearance, seems to have returned to normal. The life of the city goes on as usual, there is variety in the food and clothing shops, and the window displays are by far the most tasteful and imaginative of any in the Communist world.

The rebuilding of the exteriors of the buildings most damaged in the fighting is almost complete, particularly along Rákóczi Avenue, and the scaffolding has been removed, revealing a row of new facades. The interiors of these buildings are another matter, and there are still many other signs of damage that the regime has not yet managed to cover over. Damage from the Second World War, meanwhile, is carefully left in place, unrepaired, so people can later say, "No, that's not from the Revolution." Reconstruction on the Lenin Ring and the Üllői Avenue is far from complete. Üllői Avenue, in fact, was so totally destroyed that Hungarians now sarcastically refer to it as "The Soviet Road to Socialism."

There are plenty of traffic signs, but few signs of traffic. Motorists have few problems other than the paucity of octane in the gasoline and the occasional clots of pedestrians in the middle of the street engaged in lively conversation. Though there are plenty of trucks and not a few buses, Hungary today has only one car for every ten thousand people. Permits are required just to purchase a car. Last year 893 citizens were permitted to buy new cars and another eight hundred to buy used cars. This year's plans call for 1,500 new cars to be available.

Tanks in the streets have long since disappeared and Soviet soldiers are seldom seen, except being taken somewhere in a truck. They are confined to their installations near the Árpád Bridge, although most of their barracks are outside the city. Officers are occasionally seen in shops or at railroad stations. All of the Soviet military are new; none of those in the former occupation or who took part in the fighting are left. Discipline and behavior are exemplary, as is their spit-and-polish appearance. There is less hatred toward the Russians than there was a year ago, but that may simply be because they are less in evidence.

Despite two harsh winters since the Revolution, living conditions are actually better than before the Revolution, due to all the aid that poured into the country, mostly from the Soviet bloc, in the last year and a half. Shortages have ended and consumption of consumer goods is up. The people of Budapest have not lost their sense of style and penchant for good living. Although people's garments look drab during the week, a stroll down the Váci Street (Budapest's equivalent of Bond Street in London, or Fifth Avenue in New York) on Sunday, when all the shops except the cafés are closed, might make a Westerner wonder whether he is really behind the Iron Curtain. Fur coats, the mark of capitalist luxury, are making a comeback, even though few can afford them. But everyone can afford a cup of coffee and a piece of pastry, and the quality of these is as good as ever.

There are seventeen theatres, two opera companies, an operetta, an ice show and a circus giving performances at this time. *Tea House of the August Moon* is the current hit, but French comedies and three plays by George Bernard Shaw are also currently on the boards.

While the Corvin Cinema has been completely rebuilt, few people care to patronize it with the memory of so many patriots killed there. Now it is showing *Trapeze*, with Burt Lancaster and Gina Lollobrigida, in Cinemascope, and people are being drawn back to it, particularly those who are unaware of its bloody history.

A year ago people were still seething with anger, and arrests and terror were rampant. People could not resist talking of Kádár and politics. Today, because of the tremendous fear they have lived through, they find it judicious to talk about anything but politics.[1]

Regime propaganda harps on a number of themes, many of which involve RFE, whose daily broadcasts they must constantly counter. RFE planned and fomented the counter-revolution, RFE lured nearly two hundred thousand Hungarians through mendacious promises to leave the country to the West, and RFE is responsible for the discontent in Hungary today. But most Hungarians do not read their press nor listen to Radio Kossuth except to get the weather and sports.

The official media, however, is more critical about internal matters and less vacuous than it was in Rákosi's day. Close observers in the West can glean much about current moods and problems. There is no closer observer of Hungary than RFE's Audience Analysis Section. Combing the press and radio monitoring reports and interviews with the small but constant stream of refugees and now increasing number of foreign travelers to Hungary, the Section is able to reproduce accurate pictures of life in Hungary. The following sampling of quotations is taken from its Report No. Sixty, January 1958.

"Hungary has nothing to hope from the West." This theme is hammered hard in conjunction with the nearly ten percent of Hungarian refugees who have re-defected, returning to Hungary after a hard time in the refugee camps. The redefectors are a double-edged sword, for most have seen the opulence of the West, and this helps foster further discontent among those who hear second-hand about it. "Where people go to work with the slogan 'I am off for plunder' [factory thefts] there is something fatally wrong with honesty." "Terror, which...perpetuates the malaise resulting in the total indifference and numbness of the population: 'Who cares? Nothing matters!'—is the mood of the masses," and "moral laxity is everywhere." Indeed, the Police of Hajdú-Bihar County find this sentence the previous spring in a letter they have intercepted on its way out of the country: "Suicides, maniacs, neurotics, cowards, cynics, crooks, hypocrites and a few men of principle, that is the social composition here." An exaggeration, surely, but symptomatic of the mood of many who had participated in the Revolution.[2] "There is only one thing left for us to do: like the clever and patient prisoners...we have to try to make our lot tolerable and to keep on hoping that by our 'good conduct' the time of our sentence will be reduced, and perhaps one day we [i.e. Hungary] will be liberated." "To have been arrested in consequence of the Revolution still gives one the halo of glory."

"Hungarians have an unbroken faith, based on hope which has no foundation."

For the children of those who have been condemned to die it is an especially difficult time. Years later they will recall it in these words:

"He did not have a face. I could see only bars. We went through the bars and then I sat on his knee. I knew he was my Daddy, but I couldn't see his face because I was snuggled up close to him and he had a wonderful smell.... He taught me two lines of Greek, which I still remember today. It was amazing...since I was only a little girl, just three and a half years old. Later, if particular friends arrived, I had to repeat the lines to them. And those two Greek lines contain all my memories." (Margit Brusznyai)[3]

"My mother asked if she could bring her children....But my father said it was out of the question: 'I would rather remain in the children's memories as I was when I said goodbye to them when I was arrested....'" (Anikó Gulyás)[4]

"I remember that my mother came in and told us, and then she fainted.... I didn't go to school for three months. My heart.... I think I was angry with everyone. I think I loved him the most." (Margit Batonai)[5]

"We were always preparing, preparing so much, and I always left the prison with a sense of failure.... I prepared so hard, I wanted to tell everything so much, and then I was incapable of doing so. For some reason I couldn't.... I remember how Mum and Dad discussed so many things in a roundabout way. They understood each other very well." (Éva Z.)[6]

Changes in Western Policy Toward Hungary

The "Liberation" and "Rollback" policies are obviously in shreds, exposed for the sham that they have apparently been all along. American policy toward the satellites in general and Hungary in particular now returns to something much akin to Kennan's policy of "containment." Indeed, RFE was set up under a Democratic administration with Kennan as one of its progenitors, long before there was any talk of "rollback" and "liberation," which came in with John Foster Dulles. Its main purpose was to keep the subjugated people of Eastern Europe informed and feeling themselves part of Europe and to make it impossible for the Soviets to digest these once independent nations and absorb them into the Soviet Union, if not physically, as they had the Baltic States, at least then politically and economically. A Soviet Union with indigestion would be less likely to hunger for Western Europe.

This incredible gap between words and action on the part of the U.S. now means that major changes must take place at RFE if it is to continue broadcasting.

RFE has long been resented by many West Germans, who have been told they have full sovereignty, yet can do little about the "private" American broadcasting stations, "Radio Liberation" and "Radio Free Europe," which operate on their territory without any German control whatsoever. The Adenauer government in Bonn is highly embarrassed, particularly when an opposition party, the Free Democrats, attack RFE for having fomented the Hungarian Revolution and the Adenauer government for tolerating its presence on West German soil. The Bonn government feels obliged to investigate the charges.

The Role of RFE

To Hungarian refugees, particularly those who took part in the fighting, the charge that RFE provoked and led the revolt is a monumental insult to all the heroes who did lead it and martyrs who died for Hungary's freedom. "It is we, the Hungarian workers ourselves," says a member of the Workers' Council of Greater Budapest, in Vienna after his escape, "who are demanding justice and not any foreigners. For two days after the outbreak of the revolution, RFE was helpless. It was clear to us that they knew nothing about what was happening. Only in the later days of the Revolution did Radio Free Europe catch up with events and begin to help us with factual news." RFE did more than just "help with factual news"; it was careful not to spread rumors it could not verify. It rebroadcast many of the local "free" radios as they came on the air, careful to identify them as such, making clear to the listener that it was not RFE they were hearing. Also, as will be remembered in its securing an iron lung for the hospital in Debrecen, it performed many services for individuals, including, after the second Soviet intervention, sending thousands of messages back to Hungary from those who had escaped.

But thousands of Hungarian Refugees swore that RFE had said that help in the form of arms and armies was coming from the West if they would just hold on. Though few had actually heard this, many swore a friend had heard it and that the fighting had been unnecessarily prolonged for that reason. Two programs by a military commentator using the name "Colonel Bell" clearly implied that assistance from the West would be coming if the

Freedom Fighters succeeded in establishing "a central military command." The same commentator in another program implied that the United Nations would be more apt to give armed support if the Freedom Fighters, despite overwhelming odds, kept fighting.[7] The content of these three programs, magnified by the intense emotion all Hungarians were subject to at the time, spread instantly around the country by word of mouth.

RFE's grievous original mistake of assuming Nagy had called in the Soviet troops and then bashing him daily as the man with "Hungarian blood on his hands" and worse did more damage than any single script. RFE also called Nagy an "inveterate liar," a man who hid behind Soviet tanks, a puppet of Moscow, a traitor and in one commentary by the Head of the Hungarian Radio, Andor Gellért, Nagy is referred to as a man who has "Cain's stamp on his forehead" and was "one of the biggest traitors of Hungarian history who will be talked of for centuries to come."[8] These vitriolic broadcasts made Nagy's task of unifying the nation that much more difficult; some, like Leslie Bain, feel critically so. Bain will later write in his book *The Reluctant Satellites*, "the effect of this calumny was tremendous, and contributed most importantly to the inability of Nagy to control events and thus avert the major catastrophe of November 4."[9]

But to the charge that RFE had deliberately provoked and then deliberately prolonged the Revolution, no investigation of the tapes—and there were a number—ever found a shred of evidence. What RFE and VOA were guilty of was reporting factually, over a period of more than four years, the pronouncements by American leaders, particularly Eisenhower, Dulles, and Lodge, regarding America's policy of "liberating" the countries of Eastern Europe and "rolling back the Iron Curtain."

Perhaps the biggest discovery of the investigations is that Hungarian language programs were only read and translated into English *after* they had been broadcast. While Hungarian editors were supposed to review all scripts before broadcast to see that they conformed to policy guidelines, illness and overwork during the Revolution and after made this reviewing sporadic at best. There was only one American in the political advisor's office fluent in Hungarian.

Unlike the VOA and the BBC, both of which were felt by educated people to be more reliable and less polemical than RFE, there was a certain intimacy and trust that existed between certain Hungarians and RFE that did not exist with the other radios.

Nevertheless there were so many bitter complaints by Hungarian refugees about RFE's leading Hungarians astray that this was quickly picked up in the Austrian, German, French, eventually British and even American press. As early as November 9 the *Freies Wort*, official organ of the right-wing Free Democratic Party in West Germany, attacked RFE in a bitter editorial, saying, "We are convinced that...RFE's aggressive propaganda is responsible to a large extent for the bloodbath which has occurred in Hungary...." People felt so badly about not being able to do anything for Hungary, that having a scapegoat came as a welcome relief. And the negative attitude was fed by the views of prominent Hungarians, like Anna Kéthly and Béla Kovács, two members of the Nagy government. It took some months for RFE to get Kéthly to mitigate her criticism. Kovács, given "temporary shelter," though not asylum, in the U.S. Legation for one night (November 4–5, 1956), revealed his opinions that night to Legation staff members and U.S. reporter Leslie Bain, who had also sought refuge in the Legation. Kovács "expressed the opinion," the Legation later cabled Washington, "that the U.S. radios misled the Hungarian people into believing they could count on effective U.S. aid in the event of trouble with the Soviets.... Official pronouncements from the highest U.S. government level had also leant toward creating this illusion. He vehemently stated...that if U.S. policy toward the Soviet Union was purely a defensive one, the U.S. should have directed its anti-Communist propaganda activities at the USSR and should have left the East European states alone. Kovács left little doubt in his opinion that the U.S., for the attainment of its own selfish goals, had cynically and cold-bloodedly maneuvered the Hungarian people into action against the USSR."

In this same cable, Minister Wailes tells Washington, "There is no question that our past radio propaganda is at present a source of much embarrassment to us. Legation personnel who have lived through the entire period here since October 23 are keenly aware of the idealistic manner in which Hungarians behaved and of the high moral plane on which the Revolution was conducted. This makes it all the more difficult to explain or attempt to justify our radio propaganda programs and political pronouncements."[10]

Even after the crucial period, RFE's Hungarian Section was still making questionable broadcasts. On December 18, Minister Wailes complained to Washington that ever since December 16, RFE "has been emphasizing repeatedly the idea that in view of the enormous number of Hungarian refugees already in the West, Hungarians should not now try to leave their country."[11]

The hue and cry brought forth a plethora of investigations. The Bonn government, which was already being given tapes of all RFE broadcasts,* was the first to institute an investigation, but was quickly followed by the Council of Europe. Both cleared RFE of any evidence that it had helped to instigate the Revolution. The CIA and Free Europe Committee conducted their own internal investigations, and while one was called for in Congress, it never materialized. The most comprehensive review was carried out by RFE itself.

The RFE internal investigation revealed that there were twenty programs, over the critical period, which, in the words of the Political Advisor William E. Griffith, involved "distortions of policy or serious failure to employ constructive techniques of policy application." In plain English, some of RFE's Hungarian broadcasters were carried away by their emotions and neglected to follow, or were not even aware of, policy guidelines laid down by the American political advisor. In addition to programs already cited knocking Nagy, there were programs openly advocating Cardinal Mindszenty as the only logical national leader. This may not have followed a specific American guideline, but it was Hungarian Section head Andor Gellért's theme from the first day on and William Griffith and his staff, by raising no objections, went along with it, even incorporating it into their daily guidances.

RFE's predilection for Cardinal Mindszenty appears to have been picked up by both Allen Dulles and the *New York Times*.

Now, with chickens coming home to roost, drastic measures had to be taken. People in Washington wanted all Hungarian programs cleared by American management prior to broadcast. While a seemingly reasonable proposal, it proved to be a physical impossibility, so was never implemented. Nevertheless, the State Department rather than the CIA now assumed responsibility for major policy guidance. The guidances, however, were never country specific, but general in nature. At a time when the vast differences between the various East European countries were clearly making

---

*Tapes of the complete RFE broadcasts for October and November 1956, which for decades were thought to have been destroyed or stolen, were discovered recently in the Bundesarchiv in Koblenz. Full sets of these tapes are available for scholars to inspect not only in Koblenz, but also in the Szechény Library in Budapest and at the Hoover Institution on War, Revolution and Peace at Stanford University, California.

themselves manifest, the U.S. government went back to treating the countries of Eastern Europe as a homogenized bloc.[12]

The sick Hungarian Desk head, Andor Gellért, who had spent half of the Revolution in a Munich hospital, was soon replaced by a cautious diplomat, István Bede, whose last official post had been Ambassador to Great Britain. "The Voice of Free Hungary" now became "The Hungarian Broadcasting Department of Radio Free Europe." And a new Hungarian country policy paper was issued (through the Free Europe Committee) by the government's Committee on Radio Broadcasting Policy.

During the Revolution RFE's American management seemed unaware of much of what its Hungarian Desk editors and broadcasters were saying. Hungarians in Hungary, however, were fully aware of what was being said, and by whom. Béla Kovács, in that night he spent in the cellar of the U.S. Legation, said, "many of the exiles the Americans are backing are men who are marked because of their war crimes. Some of the voices that come to us over Radio Free Europe in particular are not welcome here. I understand the American eagerness to fight Communism, but this is not the way to do it."[13]

Policy Advisor William Griffith goes into great detail in his investigation couched as a long memorandum to his boss, Richard J. Condon, European Director of RFE. The memorandum, entitled "Policy Review of the Voice of Free Hungary Programming, October 23–November 23, 1956," analyzes what went wrong and advocates necessary changes, but also explains why he could not do a more comprehensive job. "The lack of a Hungarian language summarizer-analyst in the Program Department (this position was eliminated last June) has...been keenly felt." Thus his analysis is based only upon seventy percent of the programming in the period under review.

Nevertheless, Griffith's review turns up a number of grievous instances in which the Voice of Free Hungary had overstepped both policy and good sense, some twenty in all. What is interesting about the analysis, however, is what it reveals about the American management:

"We were not aware at the time that Gellért was not editing and approving scripts before broadcast. His [Borsányi's] attacks on Nagy are in themselves not out of keeping with the policy guidance in effect at the time.

"It was agreed that RFE should not take an irrevocably anti-Nagy position as long as no alternative figures capable of assuming leadership of the Revolution appeared. [And yet Griffith was looking right at Gellért in the Hungarian Desk meeting of October 24 when the latter declared: "There is now only one man in Hungary whom everyone respects...and that man is Cardinal Mindszenty."]

"In retrospect it can probably be said that both the commentary (Gellért's of October 25) and the guidance (Griffith's of October 24) went too far in taking a dim view of Nagy.

"Since this time [Bery's program of November 23, 1956] I have been requiring all commentaries dealing with Hungarian internal events of international reflections of them to be presented to me in English translation before broadcast."

The New York headquarters of RFE issued daily policy guidances as well, but no one in Munich paid much attention to them because they were mostly based on yesterday's news, and by the time they reached Munich, six hours ahead of New York, the situation had often changed. On October 24 New York had said, "Actions of the new Communist leaders in Budapest...are better not prejudged at this time." Yet New York made the same assumption that Munich had and in the next sentence said, "That Nagy called upon foreign troops to restore 'order' is a fact he will have to live down."[14]

Two of Griffith's basic conclusions were:

"The Voice of Free Hungary failed to measure up policy-wise to the challenge of the Hungarian Revolution primarily because of incompetent personnel in positions of major importance on the Desk.

"The Voice of Free Hungary told Hungarians things they either already knew or could not in any case have been taught at the last minute by radio. The mere fact that the Voice of Free Hungary broadcast so much advice, whether it was needed or not, puts RFE in the position of appearing to have wanted to direct or supervise the Revolution."

Among the recommendations for changes, including letting certain persons go, such as the then hospitalized Gellért, Griffith has this earth-shaking suggestion: In order not to be caught in such a bind again, he recommends that one more American, fluent in Hungarian, be hired, so that in the future there will be two.[15]

In March 1957, when the axe fell on the Hungarian Desk with the mass firing of eleven Hungarian editors and writers, an immediate uproar in the Hungarian émigré community ensued. The firings implied that these eleven people were entirely responsible for the poor performance during the

Revolution and no Americans bore any responsibility whatsoever. This remains the official viewpoint to this day.

Subdued by a strong sense of guilt and shame, American political leaders make no more such pronouncements and RFE does not have to worry about how to handle them.

Changes in Hungary

Kádár is becoming less and less a puppet and he is getting ever nearer to his long term goal of isolating those elements of the population whom he regards as hardcore opposition. There is no more harassment of those who merely showed anti-Russian, anti-regime attitudes, but played no part in the Revolution. He knows that people in general are not really interested in politics, only their own material well-being. So instead of holding back on consumer goods, once these reach their former level, he encourages higher consumption. While the government does not support the growth of private artisans, it does nothing to hinder their multiplying. Other changes which soften life somewhat: no more "social background" questionnaires for applicants to universities, no more having to listen to some Party hack reading the Party newspaper out loud while you are trying to get your factory job done. No more having to attend demonstrations in support of the Party or government. This is Kádár's new social contract.

There is another unwritten, possibly unspoken contract, which takes a few years to jell but is real nonetheless. That is the contract of understanding that evolves between Kádár and Khrushchev. Kádár, in his first few years in office, is genuinely worried at certain times of year that a revolution may break out again. The more confident he becomes that this is not going to happen, the more he transfers this fear to Khrushchev, particularly at times when he is trying to get something from him. It is almost as though they had had the following exchange: "Hungary erupted once, it could happen again if you do not let me handle things my way," says Kádár. "OK," would be Khrushchev's response in this imaginary discourse, "you can do some things socially and economically your way and not conform to the Soviet way or the rest of the bloc, so long as you follow Soviet foreign policy to the letter, becoming our trial balloon in foreign affairs whenever we ask it." Out of this bargain in a few years' time will come the phenomenon known as "Goulash Communism."

For now, Hungary takes little part in international events outside the bloc.

But 1959 also sees Khrushchev's visit to the U.S.A., his triumph as he rides on the tail of new Soviet achievements in space, making it a discouraging event for Hungarians at home and in the U.S.

Events Outside Hungary

By 1958, with John Foster Dulles no longer Secretary of State, Eisenhower's desire for friendly, peaceful contact with the Communist world finally reaches fruition in the Lacy-Zarubin Cultural and Scientific Exchange Treaty with Moscow. Similar cultural exchange treaties with the satellite countries soon follow, including one with Hungary. The year 1960 sees the shooting down of the American U-2 spy plane over Siberia, wrecking the Paris Peace talks and canceling Eisenhower's return visit to Russia. It also sees the Belgian Congo given its freedom about two decades ahead of the Belgian schedule, with the consequent turmoil which the Communist world is happy to mix in. Ever since *Sputnik*, the Soviets have opened a major drive into Africa in an attempt to spread the Communist doctrine, with enough success to alarm Washington. The Congo leader, Lumumba, while not a Communist, falls under Communist influence. Both he and, shortly afterwards, UN Secretary General Dag Hammarskjold die in the Congo: Lumumba the victim of assassination, Hammarskjold in a mysterious airplane accident. Meanwhile new hope is born in many people's hearts when John F. Kennedy becomes President in the U.S and launches such programs as the Peace Corps. His confrontation with Khrushchev in Vienna is quickly followed by the erection of the Berlin Wall to stem the hemorrhaging into West Berlin of professionals from East Germany and the rest of the bloc. Partial mobilization in the U.S. gives hope that America will not back down in the face of Soviet threats, but all of this is a long way from Hungary.

In Hungary

The period of arrests and trials is almost over. But in November 1959, István Szabó, one of the Ministers of State in Nagy's government, is released early (he had been sentenced to three years). Ferenc Jánosi, Nagy's son-in-law, who had been given eight years, is paroled on April 1, 1960, as is the journalist Miklós Vásárhelyi and Nagy's protégé Ferenc Donáth. From this date until 1963, when a general amnesty is announced, sentences are shortened and a few paroles are quietly announced. While the great majority of people in jail are freed by the general amnesty of 1963, discrimination against them continues for decades to come. The stigma is not only on them, but also on their families. This is hard on the children, particularly those who were too young to have remembered the Revolution or to have realized what their father or mother did or for what they were jailed. In families where religion and/or patriotism is strong, the stigma is bearable, even a secret source of pride, but for those families without faith or shared patriotism, the children continue to feel humiliation and shame that a parent has done time as a common criminal.

In order to legitimize its existence, the Kádár regime has to make the lie of "counter-revolution" stick. This means relentless and constant repetition in newspapers, journals and children's textbooks until "white" has been declared "black" so often that anyone who did not actually participate actively in the revolution (the vast majority), but merely went along with it, can become confused about what actually happened and prefer not to think about it any more. In order to do this consistently, nearly every fact about the Revolution needs to be falsified and those who have been paroled must still be regarded as "enemies," former "criminals" with no rights to participation in normal society.

Society, in fact, becomes atomized, the very reverse of that remarkable national unity which had existed during the days of the Revolution and some weeks after. People retreat into their private lives and concentrate on improving them or getting by as best they can. Church attendance takes a tremendous drop; for once again this can bring about harassment. Why bring about trouble with the authorities it if can be avoided?

While correspondence with friends who have fled continues for some time, envy of their good fortune and resentment that they have deserted their homeland in its time of need eat away at these ties. Communication with those in the West, still a cause for regime harassment, becomes less and less frequent.

The remembrance of personal history may remain strong in the home, but in the regime-controlled society it loses its validity and so must be kept private.

The machinery of falsification, which includes doctored films, "white books," and the re-writing of official history and school textbooks, includes the setting up of new memorial sites and the demolition of old ones. The regime tries mightily to obliterate all memory of the events of 1956 and the retribution that followed by substituting the Soviet version and repeating it endlessly. The participants are made non-existent except for those ÁVO members who were killed or lynched. They now become the new heroes.[16]

Over time the majority of people begin to accept the rules of the regime and erase from their minds former memories, feelings, and opinions, becoming silent. Such massive repression of a whole nation's memories is without precedent. Outside of their private lives they become silent observers, except, of course, at sports and entertainment and the arts, which now fill up their public lives. There is also much happening in the world at large that can be a fulfilling distraction from their circumscribed lives.

Of course society has to pay a price for these things. There are too many painful memories, nothing but sorrow came from it, it is best not to think about it.[17] In a few more years, young people, after years of hearing it referred to as a "counter-revolution" carried out by "fascists" and "criminals," will find it difficult to understand that that emaciated man who has just returned from years in prison is not an ex-convict, a common criminal as people treat him, but a patriot who did nothing but fight honorably for his country.

1962–1965

The World Outside Hungary

There is a great deal of coverage of the outside world in the Hungarian press, for this is the period of maximum Soviet international activity. Not only does Khrushchev bang his shoe on his desk in the UN and embrace Fidel Castro as a fellow Communist, he is aggressively championing "wars of liberation" in Africa and Latin America and feeding arms to these insurgents. America and the West appear to be fighting defensively as the Cold War moves from places like Hungary, Poland, and Berlin to the Third World. The "victories" are by no means all on the Communist side, but if you live within the Third World or within the Soviet bloc it is difficult not to believe so, so aggressive and triumphal is the Communist propaganda. The Soviets even set up a university in Moscow, Lumumba University, just for Third World students, whom they hope to make into good Communists to return and run their countries. It is a venture which has unintended consequences, but is by no means a complete failure.

All of this aggressive activity culminates in the Cuban Missile Crisis of 1962, that showdown between the world's two superpowers, which brought the world closer to the brink of a nuclear war than at any time before or since. The Soviet retreat is managed through the face-saving cover of the UN and some secret concessions from the Americans. Then the world, having realized it was not going to die of a heart attack, breaks out into a case of measles: a proliferation of little local wars, only one of which is to escalate into a major war: Vietnam. Here Hungary is involved only because the UN needed some non-Asians as observers in 1954 and the Soviet Union was quick to offer the services of Poland and Hungary. No sooner does the U.S become militarily involved in Vietnam than President Kennedy is assassinated.

There is one other major event in this period that has a long-term effect upon Hungary and the rest of the bloc. This was the ousting of Khrushchev and his enforced retirement in the early fall of 1964 by the Soviet Presidium, led by Leonid Brezhnev. The Comrades feel he has grown too big for his britches and has nearly taken the Soviet Union into a nuclear war with the U.S. They need a leader with a steadier hand. In Brezhnev, they get this in spades. His hand becomes so steady and unchanging that some think that rigor mortis has set in well before he actually is pronounced dead in 1982.

The years 1965 and 1966 are the years the Beatles take the world of pop music by storm, soon as popular in Eastern Europe as anywhere else. These are also the years in which the West German politician Willy Brandt launches his "Ostpolitik," bringing to an end the policy, forged by Adenauer and his Foreign Minister Hallstein, of refusing to grant recognition to any country that recognizes East Germany as a sovereign nation. Eventually, this policy of "Ostpolitik," which amounts to reconciliation with the East European countries, will have an enormous impact, not only on the Hungarian economy, but on the collapse of the Iron Curtain in the fall of 1989.

In Hungary

Kádár is still despised by many, but those who have had no run-ins with the police or whose economic lot has actually improved somewhat in the past several years are now willing to give him the benefit of the doubt. He has been in power now for almost a decade, has even been to the U.S. to attend the United Nations General Assembly, which, since 1961, no longer has Hungary on its annual agenda. He appears in public and many newsreels and even gets applause at the end of his speeches. People are aware that "Goulash Communism," if not invented by him, at least has come about under his regime.

Dr. István Bibó, who was sentenced to life in prison and then in 1962 had his sentenced commuted to fifteen years, suddenly is paroled on March 27, 1963. There are only a few people still serving their sentences; the bulk have been paroled, like Bibó, in the general amnesty of 1963.[18]

Kádár adopts a laissez faire policy encapsulated in the phrase, "he who is not against us, is with us,"[19] the exact reverse of what Stalin once said. This brings further relaxation of government restrictions and a spurt of entrepreneurs that Brezhnev's Kremlin looks askance at, but tolerates. Soon Hungary is gaining the reputation of being "the happiest Barracks in the whole Eastern bloc."

Those who have served long years in prison and are still ostracized do not share in the happiness. In many cases their homecoming is traumatic: children do not remember them or have never seen them; wives in some cases have become estranged, or have come to believe the regime propaganda and think of their husbands as ex-criminals who by their actions have ruined their lives and chance for happiness. In many homes the wife has spoken many times of the children's missing father, showing pictures and recalling good times they had as a family, so the child builds up eager anticipation for the reunion. But in other cases, where the wife resents the husband's actions that have led to this sorry state of affairs, the child, too, treats the father at first as an unwelcome stranger. And the fact that he is now out of prison has little effect on the fact that he and his family continue to be treated as pariahs by society at large.

In school, children learn that Lenin and Kádár are very nice men and write essays about them, which they bring home. This is too much for many parents. Zsuzsa Mérei recalls that her father stood up "and waved his arms about. He told me Kádár had come to power on the back of Russian tanks and that he was a scoundrel" and "was a very bad man. But this was enough to give me a direction in life."[20]

Children in school still hear teachers announce that "anyone who talks to the bastards of reactionary jailbirds in the future will be sent to the Headmaster, because such children are subversive."[21] (But in a few schools, it is just the reverse. "They made exceptions for me. I could get away with more than the others," says Katalin Litván.)[22] Others who come from religious families are lucky enough to be taken in by church schools, where they are made to feel protected against discrimination.[23] Out of school they have support systems, particularly grandparents. "My grandmother was a cheerful and very kind woman. We laughed a lot. I think she did everything she could to keep up [my mother's] strength, good humor and will to live," remembers Margit Brusznyai, and "My grandparents loved and respected him complete-ly. This was crucial, because they kept alive my image of my father and they must have played an important role in shaping it," adds Márta Regeczy-Nagy.[24]

1966–1970

The World Beyond Hungary

The United States is more and more involved with Vietnam and the arms race with the Soviet Union. The Soviet Union finds itself with another run-away satellite in the form of a fast reforming Czechoslovakia in 1968. It is soon dubbed the "Prague Spring," a play on that city's annual music festival. And, as usual, it is led entirely by Communists. The Party Secretary, Alexander Dubcek, who happens to be a Slovak, calls the movement "Socialism with a Human Face," and for the first six months of 1968 it flour-ishes to the point, in the Soviet view, of getting out of control. Dubcek is called to meet Brezhnev in the Ukraine; while he is there, the Soviets orches-trate a surprise attack, using Polish, East German, and token* Hungarian forces to supplement their own overwhelming numbers of tanks and other armor. There are a few deaths, but the Czechs, who have always been the most friendly in the bloc toward the Russians, put up little but passive resist-ance. The Russians become, however, their bitter enemies overnight. This new move on the part of the Soviets, though little different from their actions in East Germany and Hungary, is dubbed "The Brezhnev Doctrine": no fra-ternal (i.e. Communist) country is allowed to leave the Camp.

The invasion of Czechoslovakia, of course, puts a damper on the Soviet Union's campaign for "detente" with the West, to say nothing of catching the West completely off guard.

As the U.S. sinks deeper and deeper into the Vietnam quagmire, riots erupt in Gdańsk and Sopot on Poland's Baltic coast and are put down with

---

*Token because Kádár is sympathetic to the Czechoslovak reform.

extreme police brutality. Things are still bubbling in Eastern Europe, despite the enforced "normalization" in Czechoslovakia.

But in July 1969, the Americans go far ahead of the Soviets in the "space race" by putting a man on the moon and bringing him back. It is, as Neil Armstrong says, "one small step for a man, but one huge step for mankind," and it captures the wonder and awe of people everywhere. America is again the acknowledged leader in technology and scientific innovation. The invention of the microchip, which has made this feat possible, is soon used in commercial computers and makes its first major impact on daily living through transistor radios and handheld calculators.

In Hungary

It is now more than a decade since the Revolution. The opposition has long ceased to exist, and under the new doctrine of "he who is not against us is for us," life takes on a certain monotony. Everyone minds his own business, doing as little work as possible and getting away with as much as possible, without attracting the attention of the authorities. Tourists from within the bloc have become a big business, and now even Western money is being attracted to build Western hotels in anticipation of Western tourists. Joint business ventures with the Soviet Union, completely unlike the Joint Companies which existed before the Revolution, are springing up. Hungarian engineers and specialists are quite willing to go live in the Soviet Union, if that is where their careers take them. Hungarian specialists are also being called to Syria, Iraq, and Yemen for technical assistance projects, and not a few Hungarian specialists go abroad under the aegis of the United Nations. Austrian tourists are beginning to show up, though not yet West Germans. Hungary and its Lake Balaton, however, rivals the Black Sea for the most popular vacation spot for East Germans and many others in the Bloc.

For children born in Hungary these days, there are already ten years of textbook accounts of the "counterrevolution" and a compact web of lies about the "1956 events" embedded in the culture.

Starting in 1968, there is also a new "economic policy" experiment in Hungary with leanings toward a less centralized economy. After several years, however, the Soviet Union calls a halt to this, fearing where it might lead. Stagnation is beginning to take over in the USSR, so anything slightly different or unorthodox is seen as a threat.

1971–1976

The World Beyond Hungary

The U.S., now thoroughly enmeshed in Vietnam, erupts with the domestic government scandal known as "Watergate." Aside from the still escalating arms race with the Soviet Union, the Cold War for the U.S is really the hot war in Southeast Asia. Hungarian UN observers are still in Vietnam, so Hungarians hear more about Nixon's invasion of Cambodia than their European neighbors. They can sympathize when they hear that four innocent student bystanders have been shot and killed by their own National Guard troops at Kent State University in Ohio during a student protest of that move. The Watergate scandal ends with Nixon's resignation in disgrace. This, too, is a major topic of discussion in Budapest, for he has been a popular figure in Hungary.

His successor, Gerald Ford, is in office when the United States celebrates the bicentennial anniversary of the nation's founding.

The Soviets are still striving for "détente"; a keystone piece of this is a peace treaty which will end the Second World War in Europe and settle once and for all the boundaries of postwar Europe as they developed in 1945. They hope that the treaty will also solidify the division of Europe and help put an end to the restlessness of the satellites, just as the Berlin Wall has put an end to turmoil in East Germany and helped that entity toward becoming a bone fide nation with an esprit de corps all its own. Brezhnev gets his Helsinki Conference on Security in Europe signed in the late spring of 1976, but through his eagerness to sign he has to swallow what he feels to be an inconsequential section which has come to be called "Basket Three," the section on information and cultural exchange. "Basket One," the political settlement, and "Basket Two," economic agreements, are what he has had his eye on. The information and cultural exchange part of the Treaty will become, over time, a Trojan Horse for the Soviet bloc, for it will involve ever more exchange of persons and groups between the East and the West. The corrosive forces of freedom will work on the Easterners whether they are playing host to Western visitors or are themselves visiting the West. The numbers exchanged are tiny, but in almost every instance it is a win-win situation for the West.

Before there is much evidence of this, however, a small group of Czechoslovak intellectuals in Prague attempts to make use of this portion of the new treaty, which their country, along with all the other countries of Europe, has just signed. Because it is formed in January 1977, they name their group "Charter '77." They keep pointing out actions by the Czechoslovak government that do not conform to the treaty. The group will become a thorn in the side of the Czechoslovak Government; regardless of frequent arrests and persecution, it never goes away. Every document produced finds its way to the West and is broadcast many times over RFE and other Western radios.

In Hungary

On September 29, 1971, after nearly fifteen years of living in the U.S. Legation, Cardinal Mindszenty is allowed to leave Hungary and move to Vienna. The Vatican has finally cut a deal with the regime whereby the Cardinal, who still does not want to leave his native land, is removed from Hungary with certain restrictions as to what he can say and do; these will be strictly enforced by the Vatican. He has become an obstacle to their working out a deal with the Kádár government for appointments they wish to make in Hungary; so long as Mindszenty is still in Hungary and recognized as Primate, their hands are tied.*

Something of a malaise develops with the economic stagnation enforced by the Kremlin's refusal to sanction Hungary's New Economic Mechanism (NEM), but Kádár manages to persuade the Soviets to let them begin again, slowly, after a few years. Kádár has gone from fig leaf to puppet to a subordinate, and now he is beginning to feel like the head, not of an independent country, but of one with limited sovereignty. His Goulash Communism has definitely won over the masses, and other satellite leaders are actually jealous of his popularity. People even refer to the Kádárization of Hungary. It has been a remarkable metamorphosis of a very enigmatic man.

Kádárization, however, is a very pragmatic process. He has gained favors from the Kremlin incrementally. Without the chimera of the Revolution in his pocket it is doubtful he could have done any of it.

---

* The author happened to be in Hungary the day Mindszenty left and lunched with a university professor whom he believes to have been a Party member. When he remarked that this was "quite a day" the Professor begged to differ with him. He said he had asked his class that morning what they thought about Mindszenty's leaving and was surprised to find that a majority of his students had no idea who Mindszenty was, nor the significance of his removal.

1977–1980

The World Outside Hungary

With the Vietnam war now history, most of the wars of liberation are quiescent, if not over, and sports and entertainment are the major public diversions.

England will see its first woman prime minister elected, Margaret Thatcher, whom wags soon refer to as "Attila the Hen."

In Afghanistan, in order to prevent the loss of a country which the Kremlin thought was certainly going Communist, the Soviets pull a clumsy coup d'etat, flying in from Prague the puppet they will put in place of the leader they have just had assassinated. This, like the sudden invasion of Czechoslovakia eleven years earlier, comes as a shock to the West and sanctions against the Soviet Union are soon called for. The coup turns into a war between the Afghans and the Russians. President Jimmy Carter decides that the U.S. will not participate in the 1980 Olympic Games, set for Moscow, and most other Western countries follow suit, wounding Russian pride considerably. By the time the games are held, Ronald Reagan has been elected President, but he upholds the Olympic boycott.

No sooner are the truncated Games in Moscow finished than strikes break out in Poland, particularly at the shipyard at Gdańsk led by an electrician named Lech Wałęsa. Overnight labor discontent and a feeling of solidarity sweeps through Poland. In a matter of days a nationwide workers' movement, "Solidarity," is born which successfully defies the Warsaw Government. Within months, so many intellectuals and office workers, journalists, and shopkeepers have joined "Solidarity" that it claims ten million members in a country of thirty-eight million.

Inside Hungary

There is tremendous sympathy for Solidarity inside Hungary, but real support comes only from intellectuals, not the workers, who are not well informed about it.

But frankly, labor and living conditions are not bad enough for there to be much resentment in Hungary against the government. The workers are probably more in Kádár's corner than any other segment of society. The New Economic Policy has caused a definite spurt in the country's standard of living. Budapest already has several large Western hotels on the Danube.

Tourists from Western Europe are beginning to show up, as are even some Americans, including Hungarian Americans who fled in 1956. Only those who are known to have taken no part in the Revolution, however, are permitted visas and those who do get visas find their non-relative ex-compatriots cold, if not purposely rude to them.

Cultural and academic exchanges with the West have been going on since the mid-1960s. These include symphony orchestras, opera singers, dance troupes, exhibitions, and also scholars and graduate students. The American Academy of Sciences has an agreement for exchanges with the Hungarian Academy. American scholars in the humanities and social sciences visit Hungary through the private, but partially government-subsidized, International Research and Exchanges Board (IREX) in New York, which is partnered with the Institute for Cultural Relations (KKI) in Budapest.

Particularly active in the exchanges field is the American Ford Foundation, which first entered Eastern Europe when it set up a children's hospital near Cracow in 1957. It became very active in Yugoslavia in the 1960s and 1970s and began to share with the State Department expenses of some of the other exchanges, like those of IREX in the late 1960s.

Now the Foundation is dealing with the Karl Marx University of Economics, as well as many government ministries, in an effort to get specialists, particularly those involved in planning and carrying out the New Economic Mechanism, to United States institutions, especially the best U.S. business and law schools. These short visits, lavishly paid for, quickly become very popular with the Hungarian elite. They are one-way visits; the Hungarians are not required to reciprocate, as they are on all of the other government-supported exchanges.

The twenty-fifth anniversary of the Revolution passes virtually without incident in Hungary, though security precautions are taken as usual. Children born today are much more likely to have had grandparents who participated in the Revolution than parents. Everyone talks about the "1956 events" if they do not care to use the commonly accepted "counterrevolution."

1981–1984

The World outside Hungary

Afghanistan is turning out to be the Soviet Union's Vietnam. Not only are the Afghans tough mountain fighters who had defeated the British nearly a century ago, they now get help from the CIA in the form of "Stinger" missiles designed for shooting down aircraft; these are particularly effective on helicopters. Tanks, though they are employed, are too cumbersome and slow for the great distances in Afghanistan, and the Soviets are forced to use helicopters extensively.

The Soviet military was all prepared to invade Poland in December 1980, though it heeded the advice of President Ronald Reagan and did not. Now, in December 1981, the new Premier of the country, General Jaruzelski, makes war on the Polish people by declaring martial law in a sudden move. He rounds up all "Solidarity" leaders and literally plunges the country into darkness by cutting all internal and external telephone lines. A large underground opposition soon develops, and martial law eventually has to be lifted, but few problems are solved.

Brezhnev finally dies on November 10, 1982, and Andropov, the Soviet Ambassador to Hungary during the Revolution and head of the KGB from 1958 on, emerges as the new Soviet leader. Though he acquired the name of "Butcher of Budapest" at the time, Hungarians put a good face on it, reminding each other that "the man knows and likes Hungary, and is one of the few Ambassadors from anywhere who actually tried to learn and speak our language." "I saw the delight with which they responded," recalls Soviet Advisor to First Party Sectaries Fedor Burlatsky, "to the sound of their own language coming from his lips."[25]

Andropov's attention, however, is on Poland, which has just given the world its first non-Italian Pope in over four hundred years and which is still in the grip of Solidarity. The attempted assassination of the Polish Pope in Rome takes place while Andropov is in office, but the planning for it by the Bulgarian Secret Police, who use a wild, right-wing Turk to carry it out, appears to have taken place while Andropov was still head of the KGB. Even if he has not ordered it, he surely knew about and did not prevent it.

Andropov does not last long in his new job. He dies of cancer in November 1984. The Hungarians handle his death with finesse. Scheduled programs are cancelled. All day long, movies of Moscow, Mother Russia, and the Bolshoi Ballet are shown on the television; Tchaikovsky and Shostakovitch are played on Radio Kossuth and huge black flags replace in the early afternoon all of the Red ones (in celebration of the November 7 Revolution) which were hanging all around Parliament Square in the morning. But neither Kádár nor any other government official feels called upon to give a eulogy, as is happening in all of the other satellites.

The obvious man to succeed him is Mikhail Gorbachev, known to be his protégé. Konstantin U. Chernenko, however, was technically next in line and has been waiting for years to inherit the job. He, not Gorbachev, is given the job of First Party Secretary, but being sick himself, conveniently dies five months later.

In retaliation for the Americans boycotting the Olympic games in Moscow in 1980, the Russians—and, of course, all their East European satellites—boycott the 1984 Games being held in Los Angeles.

In Hungary

Budapest no longer bears any resemblance to a city behind the Iron Curtain. Modern, stylish hotels are sprouting up all over, business centers in Pest are being built, each every bit as posh as anything in Paris or London. Major Western companies and banks have offices in the center of town, and joint companies with Western firms are springing up all over the country. The tourist industry is booming, and includes no small number of Americans and Japanese.

Traffic, like that in Belgrade a decade earlier, is becoming impossible and many of the sidewalks impassable because of mini-cars parked on them. To make matters worse, Mercedes and Peugeots and Jaguars and Cadillacs are now seen in the traffic jams.

Unfortunately, the prosperity of the countryside, though produce is as bountiful as ever, is not keeping up with the prosperity in the capital. There are private lots and free markets, but the State still has too much control over the nation's farms and prices. Nor is the capital all that prosperous, for very little of the Western funds pouring into the country reaches the factory workers of Budapest or any other Hungarian towns. The same is true of the teachers and people in the professions. For all that, Hungary remains the happiest barracks in the Eastern bloc.

1985–1987

The World outside Hungary

Chernenko's unexpected death on March 11, 1985, brings Mikhail Gorbachev to the head of the Soviet Party and the Communist world in

Europe. Before the year is out, Gorbachev launches "glasnost" (openness in speech and media) and later "perestroika" (restructuring, reforming) to the consternation of old Communists, particularly those in East Germany, which has been resisting reforms for years.

The wreckage of the White Star steamship *Titanic*, sunk by an iceberg in 1912, is found in the North Atlantic, and a worrisome hole in the ozone layer over Antarctica, first discovered in 1977, is pronounced indisputable.

In April 1985, the Chernobyl nuclear plant in the Ukraine explodes and burns, spreading radioactive particles all over the Ukraine and northeastern Europe. For a short while, the Soviets try to hide the disaster, but Gorbachev insists on full disclosure and even accepts international help in capping the reactors and testing those affected by the radiation. It is the worst nuclear disaster on record.

In the U.S. the Reagan administration is doing its best to play down what is known as the Iran-Contra scandal, and in the Philippines a widow, Corazon Aquino, ousts the corrupt regime of Ferdinand Marcos to become the first woman President of the country.

In Russia there is consternation, and in the rest of the world delight, when a young German pilot flies a single engine plane all the way in from the Baltic and lands in Red Square without being intercepted by the Soviet Air Force, nor shot down by ground forces.

In Hungary

Hungarian Foreign Trading Organizations, banks and the Hungarian Chamber of Commerce are making decisions affecting the future economy of Hungary. These decisions are certainly not dictated by the central plan; in fact, they ignore it. The Party in many instances seems to be irrelevant.

While Kádár hangs on, most of his colleagues in the Politburo and Central Committee have either died or retired. He was only forty-four when the Russians installed him, while almost all the others were by ten to twenty years his elder. But there are many new members of the Central Committee, few of whom were around at the time of the Revolution.

Now, as the political atmosphere of the country grows more relaxed and there is more access to archives and information, to say nothing of all the information that is available from the West, a good many of them have their doubts about the "events of 1956" having been a "counterrevolution." They are all for the New Economic Mechanism, whereas Kádár's contemporaries tend to be against it, and they are frustrated by how out-of-date the party has become in the light of changes taking place in Hungary. While these mostly younger members of the Central Committee began to coalesce as a reforming wing of the Party in the late 1970s, they do not emerge as a major factor until the mid-1980s, when Gorbachev comes to power in Russia in 1985. They like "glasnost" and "perestroika," whereas their more conservative colleagues do not.

It soon becomes obvious that there is a growing split in the Party that has to be healed lest the crisis lead to chaos and collapse. The reform wing of the Party now lobbies for a special Party Congress to resolve the crisis. They succeed, and a Party Congress is then set for May 1988.

CHAPTER XII

Reemergence

BACK IN 1956, when tens of thousands of Hungarians were streaming into Austria and being placed into camps before moving on to other countries, the great majority of these refugees spoke only Hungarian. They were cut off from their native land and from publications in Hungarian; in addition to their sorry plight, the fact that they had no idea what was going on in the world or their homeland added to their depression. To alleviate this, Free Europe Press in Munich, which had ceased the launching of balloons with leaflets, began to publish a small, three-times-weekly newspaper, *Magyar Hírlap (Hungarian Journal)*, which it distributed free to the camp inmates. The paper soon became popular, for, as many readers attested, it was the most objective, non-partisan Hungarian newspaper they had ever read. As they moved on to Germany, France, Britain, Canada, Sweden, the U.S., and Australia they would write in, giving their new addresses and requesting that their subscriptions be continued. News of the world and their homeland rendered in Hungarian, even two weeks old, was more than worth it.

Many professional people, professors, writers, musicians and those in the arts—people who already knew at least one foreign language—were included among the 200,000. These people had less need for *Magyar Hírlap* and were able to adjust more quickly to their new lives, even if they were not at first able to find employment in their own profession. The writers and intellectuals among them soon established Hungarian journals, or resurrected ones which had existed in Hungary, in cultural centers like Paris and London such as *Irodalmi Újság (Literary Newspaper)*, *Új Látóhatár (New Horizon)*, *Nemzetőr (National Guardsman)*, and *Szemle (Review)*. *Szemle*, which was published in English and French as well as Hungarian, was the product of a new institution called the Imre Nagy Institute for Political Research founded in Brussels by György Heltai, who had been a close associate of Nagy.

These periodicals, and many others belonging to established Hungarian émigré organizations in the West, kept the memory of the Revolution alive by publishing articles, books, and memoirs. Many of the best of these were translated into Western languages and published by reputable British, French, German and American publishers.

All of this publishing meant that when Hungarian scholars, students, and tourists began to travel to the West in the 1970s and discovered Hungarian bookshops and other Hungarian émigré outlets in Europe and North America, they received books on 1956 as gifts (secretly underwritten by Free Europe). Hundreds of volumes were smuggled back into Hungary, where they received wide clandestine circulation among the liberal intelligentsia.[1]

Meanwhile, some brave student groups kept the memory of the Revolution alive by demonstrating each year on March 15, outside the official commemorations, and secretly observed the Revolution's anniversary each October 23.

Émigré organizations in the West, particularly new ones like the seven-thousand-member World Association of Hungarian Students, observed these anniversaries as well, and reports of these were broadcast into Hungary by the Western radios. Likewise, the memory of the Revolution was kept alive by whole institutions, like the Forestry College at Sopron which had moved en masse to Vancouver, Canada, and the Philharmonia Hungarica, basically Radio Kossuth's symphony orchestra which, with the help of the Ford Foundation, had established itself in Vienna, toured the U.S., and then found a permanent home in Darmstadt, West Germany. It soon acquired worldwide recognition under Hungarian conductors living abroad, particularly Antal Doráti.

All of this meant that the regime's attempt to wipe out the memory of the Revolution, while successful with much of the general public and the public record in Hungary, was a losing struggle. Too many participants and their descendants were still living in Hungary, and too much factual information still existed in the archives or filtered in from abroad.

A new generation was growing up curious about the so-called "counterrevolution," and when Kádár, in a toast, referred to "the October events" as a "national tragedy," it became possible for people to make reference to it in print and in public, though never to refer to it as a revolution. The writer/scholar Péter Kende, then living in Paris, observed at the time, "The double meaning of the notion of tragedy makes possible the apparent bridge-building.... Yet if the lament reads your fight was in vain, that does not mean the same as when it reads, our fight is lost."[2]

Meanwhile, the wives and loved ones of those who had been executed and buried in unmarked graves refused to accept not knowing where they had been buried. Out of sympathy or for a price, some of those who had been in some way involved in the burial process revealed to these women where, in fact, their husbands had been buried, often in a common grave. This was plot 301, an overgrown, untended plot in the Rákoskeresztúr public cemetery on the outskirts of Budapest. While it was forbidden, these modern-day Antigones began to visit plot 301 with their children and flowers on special days, and even the regime's attempts to intimidate and humiliate them did not keep them from exercising their basic human right to mourn; they kept on coming.[3]

In the early 1980s the underground press, *Beszélő (The Speaker)* and *Napló (Diary)*, began breaking the silence on the Revolution. They were joined by a new journal, *Új Forrás (New Source)*, which carried a poem cryptically capitalizing letters such as in the line "the grave Is Nowhere...," so that the reader at once sees the capitals stand for Imre Nagy. These journals, however, reached only a tiny portion of the educated population. Moreover, the regime did its best, through harassment, arrests, and confiscations, to contain them, if not wipe them out.

By the mid-1980s all the old Party stalwarts like Münnich and Marosán have died or retired. The Central Committee, except for the aging Kádár, now consists almost entirely of Party members who were not around when the "tragic events" of 1956 took place. They are as eager as are their non-Communist peers in the underground to know what really happened. They belong to the Party's "liberal wing," which seems to grow stronger every year.

By early 1988, the differences in the Hungarian Party are so great that the liberals, led by Imre Pozsgai, Rezső Nyers, Iván Berend, and many others, force Kádár and his Politburo to schedule an extraordinary Party Congress for May to resolve the crisis. Rather than resolve it, the liberals overwhelm Kádár and his Politburo and in the end, vote them out of office. Realizing they have humiliated the founder of their Party, the delegates quickly elect

Kádár President of the Party for Life, but it is a meaningless title which gives him no power whatsoever. The new Party Secretary, Károly Grósz, begins with popular reforms, the most important of which is the appointment of a fifteen-man committee headed by Imre Pozsgai to analyze the situation which has led to the crisis and come up with a new Party program. This large committee has five subcommittees.

By far the most important of these subcommittees is the historical subcommittee. The President of the Hungarian Academy of Sciences, Iván Berend, is selected to head this committee and he is joined by three other liberal members of the Party, Gyula Horn, later destined to become Party Secretary, Mária Ormos, and Ferenc Tőkei.

Berend is the very epitome of the young liberals. A brilliant scholar hired as an assistant professor of history by Karl Marx University of Economics back in 1953, he rose to the post of Rector in the early 1980s and then, in 1985, was elected President of the Hungarian Academy of Sciences, a post heretofore only occupied by white-haired professors near retirement. Berend, though just into his fifties, looks not a day over forty and sports the black whiskers and long hair with receding hairline of a young Dickens or Disraeli. What is more, he has the personality to match his looks, being something of a bon vivant, with numerous friends in the artistic and cultural world. Nevertheless, he is a serious scholar and loyal Party member who achieved Central Committee status at the special Party Congress in May.[4]

A few months before this historical subcommittee is established, the relatives of the executed leaders of the Revolution and those who have spent some time in prison before the general amnesty get together and found the Committee for Historical Justice. Unable to publicize their existence in Hungary, they have a statement printed in foreign newspapers on June 6; RFE and other radio stations simultaneously broadcast it into Hungary. They demand, among other things, "the complete moral, political and legal rehabilitation of the—living and dead—victims of the retributions, a decent burial for those executed, and the erection of a national memorial." Despite actions of the police to prevent them, memorial gatherings follow, involving several hundred people in cemeteries and public places on June 16, the thirtieth anniversary of the execution of Nagy and his fellow martyrs. On the same day in the Père Lachaise cemetery in Paris a large-scale commemorative ceremony takes place, with many Hungarian émigrés and French dignitaries taking part.

The new Károly Grósz government also selects this date to issue one of its first decrees. "Those imprisoned for criminal acts committed against the state between 23 October 1956, and 1 May 1957," says the decree, "or for other acts related to counterrevolutionary activities, and those whose death sentence was commuted to imprisonment by an act of mercy will be exempt from all disadvantages related to the possession of a criminal record." It is a halfway measure, since it says nothing about rehabilitation, but it is welcome nonetheless.[5]

Meanwhile, the government, after much procrastination, secretly gives permission on November 23 for the reburial of those who have been executed following Imre Nagy's trial and for the exhumation of other executed persons.

By December, the fifteen-member Pozsgai Committee is winding up its work. The historical subcommittee under Iván Berend comes up with a ninety-page report, and Pozsgai decides to attend the meeting in late December, during which the subcommittee discusses the finished report.

The report traces the history of the Party, not just since its "rebirth" under a new name in the midst of the Revolution of 1956, but from its entrance into the provisional government during 1944, the last year of World War II. It covers all of the disputes, purges, and policies carried out during the Rákosi era, the brief "new course," under Imre Nagy, the reimposition of the Stalinist Rákosi regime in 1955, and the changes that were engineered from Moscow. Though the committee has the timing slightly wrong, it tells the truth about Imre Nagy's decisions to declare neutrality and withdraw from the Warsaw Pact when it writes, "When the attack was launched, Imre Nagy—completely disregarding the geopolitical realities and basic international conditions—declared the resignation of Hungary from the Warsaw Treaty on purely moral motivations and turned to the UN for help...." (These actions actually occurred several days before the second Soviet attack, but if one regards the massive invasion of Soviet troops beginning on October 31 as the beginning of the actual attack and Nagy's actions being in response to this, the truth is borne out. Soviet action caused Nagy's action; Nagy's declaration of neutrality and withdrawal from the Warsaw Pact did not cause the Soviet invasion.)

The report tells the truth about Kádár, as well.

For the Soviets, "giving power back to the conservative Rákosi-Gerő group, which had been overthrown by popular anger in bloody fighting, would have made consolidation very difficult."

Hence the only solution was the Kádár puppet government. "The scope of action available to the [Kádár] government...[was] naturally determined by the way power had been restored" (i.e. by the Soviet Army).

"After November 4 Hungary still had to align its policy with the Soviet political line." Despite Khrushchev's attempts at liberalization, "laden with lots of contradictions, from the 1960s up to the middle of the 1980s a practically post-Stalinist policy gained the upper hand, so there was no chance for any radical transformation of the Stalinist model...."

"The uprising that was called a revolution...soon came to be called...the unfortunate October events, but later it was simply called, in a rather one-sided way, a counterrevolution.... The regime excluded significant groups of the reform wing of the Party and the intelligentsia....It had to resort to any forces that seemed available in its fight.... Even Rákosi and Gerő, then living in the Soviet Union, were admitted to the Hungarian Socialist Workers' Party."[6]

Most important, the report tells the truth about the Revolution itself.

"The extremely powerful mass demonstration of October 23 took place as a response to apparently ineffective old solutions and reactions, to be followed the same evening by the 'critique of arms' replacing the 'arms of critique,' which eventually led to an overall national uprising against the ruling regime.

"The University students...were soon joined by huge masses of workers in the last week of October. This was demonstrated by their participation in the fights as well as the organization of a united and long-lasting political strike. The national and democratic demands of the workers were clearly formulated by the mass movements of people in the capital and in the country.

"The only common platform that linked the various different groups of the uprising...was the endeavor to demolish and destroy the ruling Stalinist model of socialism....

"The geopolitical determination of the country...was accepted even by the United States, and of which the U.S. leaders...informed the Soviet leadership in due time....

"The Nagy government could not rise to the occasion...was unable to meet the needs of the man in the street...was more like drifting with the events rather than having control over them...."

The report even reveals the true role of Suslov and Mikoyan in their dealings with Imre Nagy, saying that they "did make an agreement with Imre Nagy under the pressure of necessity concerning the withdrawal of Soviet troops from Budapest and the transformation of the government into a coalition cabinet."

Discussion of this long report lasts several hours, but Pozsgai, listening intently, does not utter a word. He is concentrating on his next move. Unbeknownst to his fellow committee members, he has a date that afternoon at Radio Kossuth to be interviewed about the workings and aims of this all-important committee he heads. The overall report of his committee is not due to be discussed by the Central Committee until January 27 in the new year, so nobody expects him to reveal much. Every member of his committee is a member of the liberal wing of the Party. There is no way the remnants of the Kádár faction can prevent the new program which his report will call for being adopted. And yet, one can never be sure.

At some point Pozsgai decides to reveal to the Hungarian people the major finding in the Berend report: what has been referred to for thirty-two years as a counterrevolution has been found by experts to have been a true national uprising and revolution all along.

The news electrifies the nation. People realize that Pozsgai has been given no permission by the Party to reveal what has not yet been told to the Central Committee, and they admire his guts in doing so, knowing that many Party bigwigs in the past have had their careers ruined for much lesser offenses.

For those who have suffered in silence for more than three decades, the feeling of redemption is overwhelming. For those who have believed in, taught, and written about the "counterrevolution" for many years, there is shock and bewilderment, a feeling of double betrayal. But whatever the reaction, the name of Imre Pozsgai is now on the lips of nearly every Hungarian.

As the Károly Grósz government had secretly given permission on November 23 for the reburial of those who were executed after Imre Nagy and his compatriots and for the exhumation of other executed persons, the Ministry of Justice now begins negotiations with those relatives who have signed the statement of the Committee for Historical Justice. Just as in the case of Júlia Rajk thirty-two years earlier, it is the Ministry's intention that the reburials be private. The signatories of the Historical Justice statement, however, want it to be in accordance with the statement they signed in June.

EXPLOSION

The Central Committee's acceptance in January 1989 of the new Party program outlined by the Pozsgai Committee doubtless has some influence on the foot-dragging bureaucracy; on March 29, 1989, the bodies of Imre Nagy, Miklós Gimes, Géza Losonczy, József Szilágyi, and Pál Maléter are dug up out of Lot 301 in the Rákoskeresztúr public cemetery, in the presence of their families and the members of the Committee for Historical Justice. To everyone's horror it is discovered that they have all been buried face down, the ultimate mark of dishonor.

Historian János Rainer, secretly researching birth certificates in the municipal archives, has already come up in 1986 with a list of those who were executed. He and other scholars have also begun an oral history of the Revolution, secretly recording the accounts of known participants. Now in May 1989, an amended and updated list is published along with a request of the relatives that they indicate whether or not they wish their loved ones' bodies to be exhumed.[7]

There is no stopping the reemergence of the Revolution. Its heroes and martyrs will not be reburied in secret. The word goes out that the reburial will take place with full honors on June 16, the thirty-first anniversary of Nagy and his fellow victims' executions. On June 2, the families of the victims, and organizations such as the Historical Justice Committee, National Association for Political Prisoners, Alliance of Recsk Ex-prisoners, and many political opposition groups issue the following appeal to the Hungarian nation:

"We ask our fellow countrymen to respect the request of the relatives and the privacy of the funeral. During the next two days, Saturday and Sunday [meaning the days following the funeral on Friday, June 16], everyone will be able to place a flower or a candle on the graves. On the day of national mourning the various churches invite the believers to memorial services during the evening hours. After dark everyone should burn a candle or a night light in his or her window.

"We call upon the population of Hungary: let us pay our last respects to all the victims of 1956. Let us place national and black flags on the houses, let us wear mourning bands on our clothes. Places of amusement ought not to be visited, we are to refrain from any kind of entertainment or turbulence including political turmoil, demonstrations or conflicts which are contrary to the spirit of the day. No banners with political slogans are to be taken to the funeral service! Only national and black flags and signs indicating the names of towns and villages are allowed....

"This day shall be the funeral of an entire tragic period. With dignity and unity, let us express our faith in the Revolution of 1956, in the martyrs, and in our ability to start a new, more humane era."[8]

People who have been in seclusion for decades prepare to come out of the shadows. Freedom Fighters around the world, who have longed to come back to their native land but have been prevented by the government from doing so, now make frantic preparations to return. A whole jumbo jet is rented and flown in from Canada and the U.S. Its most famous occupant is General Béla Király, who, after heading the World Federation of Freedom Fighters, has taken a Ph.D. at Columbia University and settled into the life of an academic, albeit one devoted to publishing books related to the Revolution and Eastern Europe.

Ferihegy Municipal Airport is the scene of both tension and excitement as a giant Boeing jumbo jet, not on any airline schedule, circles the field in anticipation of landing. Neither the tower nor the pilot are certain that the field is long enough, but with smoking tires, the huge plane manages to stop several hundred feet short of the runway's end and wheel around to face the airport building. No plane that big, Soviet or Western, has ever landed at Ferihegy.

Less than twenty-four hours before the ceremony on June 16, the Historical Justice Committee holds its last press briefing before a packed room of four hundred journalists and photographers. Sitting at the head table with Historical Justice Committee members András Hegedűs* and chairman Miklós Vásárhelyi is the current Minister of Justice, Dr. Gyula Borics. But the attraction of the meeting, sitting one head taller than any of the others, is General Béla Király, who has just arrived on the jumbo jet.

"Although I live in America," he tells the journalists, "I feel Hungarian and follow the fate of this nation very faithfully and with excitement. I am ready to make sacrifices, too, for the well-being and better future of this nation." Király is donating the royalties of his latest book to the new Youth Party FIDESZ and proudly wears the badge of the Danube Circle, a Hungarian organization fighting the Communist-proposed dam on the Danube north of Budapest at Nagymaros. (He will later make good on his pledge by moving back to Hungary and running successfully for Parliament.)

The press conference is told that several hundred thousand people—the

*No relation to the András Hegedűs who had been premier at the time of the Revolution.

biggest crowd since the Rajk funeral in 1956—are expected to come to Heroes Square for the ceremonies tomorrow, and that the new political parties, like the Democratic Forum, the Smallholders, and the Free Democrats, have arranged for several thousand people to keep order.[9]

Friday, June 16, is a beautiful sunny day with just enough breeze to move the innumerable long flags—banners actually—hanging down around the rim of Heroes Square. There is just one abnormality; every one of these Hungarian flags has a jagged hole in the middle of it.

The architect László Rajk, Jr., and his associate, Gábor Bachman, have designed the funerary setting. Rajk, who was only seven when he and his mother stood in the cold wind at his father's reburial in 1956, is part of today's political underground and a member of the Committee on Historical Justice, but his passion is drawing and architecture, not politics. His design for the occasion is both striking and stark.

Five black catafalques shaped like upturned, seagoing dories and slanting down into the plaza between the six black columns hold the five black coffins containing the remains of Imre Nagy in the middle, flanked by Pál Maléter, Miklós Gimes, Géza Losonczy, and József Szilágyi. A sixth coffin, not easy to see, because it is on its own catafalque behind Nagy's and well under the portico, is draped in the national red-white-green flag with a hole in it. This coffin is empty and symbolizes all those who died fighting for their nation's freedom. The five men in front were all Communists. Not so those symbolized by the empty coffin, though many were, in fact, Communists. From early morning the square has begun to fill, and by just before nine a.m., when the six candelabras are lit, estimates are that some 250,000 to 300,000 people are present.

The families of the martyrs, government and foreign dignitaries take their seats in front of the catafalques soon after the candelabras are lit. Now, on the dot of nine, all are asked to rise and observe a minute of silence. Prime Minister Miklós Németh, Minister of State Imre Pozsgai, Speaker of the Parliament Mátyás Szűrös, and Deputy Prime Minister Péter Medgyessy are there representing the government. Cardinal and Archbishop László Paskai and Gyula Nagy, Bishop of the Hungarian Lutheran Church, are seen standing near the young American Ambassador Mark Palmer, sporting his non-conformist bow tie. The entire diplomatic corps, including representatives from four Communist countries, Albania, China, North Korea, and Romania, and many foreign guests, as well as Hungarians from abroad, are in the seated area.

Short tributes to the martyrs and prayers by the chief clerics follow, and then at ten o'clock, Kossuth Prize laureate and actor Imre Sinkovits, who had delivered the Petőfi national song in the first hours of the Revolution, steps up to the microphone. Age has made him almost unrecognizable, but his voice still has strength. He reads not a poem, but the June 2 Declaration of the Committee on Historical Justice quoted earlier.

Then begins the wreath-laying ceremony, a solemn procession of citizens from all over the country bearing beribboned wreaths with the name of the community from which it comes on each. The first is from Kaposvár, Imre Nagy's hometown. By the end of the day there are literally tons of flowers and wreaths heaped up on the steps of the Palace of Exhibitions.

At 12:30, the church bells throughout the city begin to chime. But not just in Budapest; church bells all over Hungary are ringing, and factory sirens are sounding at this hour. Traffic everywhere stops, and the whole nation observes a moment of silence; even radio and television are silent.

Now the national anthem is played in Heroes' Square, and someone switches on a tape. It is the voice of Imre Nagy delivering an impromptu speech from the Parliament balcony on October 30.

"My Hungarian brothers! Patriots! Loyal citizens of our homeland! Preserve the achievements of the Revolution, ensure law and order with every means possible, and restore confidence. Do not let the blood of brothers be shed in our country!"

Next Miklós Vásárhelyi, in his capacity as President of the Committee for Historical Justice, steps up to the microphone.

"The Hungarians' name never shone so brightly in the course of our history as in the days of the 1956 Revolution. The brutal outside interference crushed the Revolution and put an end to our endeavors and hopes, but it could not end the memory of 1956 and that of Imre Nagy, who has become a symbol of a historic turn."

He is followed by Sándor Rácz, the former President of the Central Workers' Council of Great Budapest, who had been sentenced to life in prison, but freed in the great amnesty of 1963. He is no longer the firebrand he was, but he is still provocative and calls a spade a spade. "Will Hungarian freedom burst forth from the blood of Hungarian heroes?" he asks, then startles everyone with a resounding "No!" There are still many obstacles before Hungarian society.

The number one and most difficult obstacle, he says, is "the presence of

Soviet troops on Hungarian territory." He calls on all honest people in the world to help the Soviet Union withdraw its troops from Hungary as soon as possible.

The number two obstacle is the Hungarian Communist Party, which rigidly clings to power. The third obstacle is the lack of cohesion in Hungarian society. He calls on the nation not to split up its strength into a hundred political parties, but to pull together.

At the graveside in plot 301 of the Rákoskeresztúr cemetery, which is now cleared, and where it has been decided the exhumed heroes will now lie in honor, the writer Tibor Méray pays his final tribute to Nagy on behalf of all the Hungarian exiles in the world. He calls Nagy not just a politician, but a true statesman who genuinely wanted peace with the Soviet Union and saw neutrality as the only way to have it. Hungary, he says, must never be a member of a military bloc.*

There are many young people for whom this day has no particular meaning. And there are many old Hungarians, Party faithful, for whom it is a sad and bitter day.

Whether or not Kádár watched any of it on the television, he certainly did not watch for long. For years he had been the most popular leader of a people's democracy in Eastern Europe, father of his people, creator of "the happiest barracks in the bloc." Now his whole life is being unraveled before his very eyes. And it soon becomes apparent that it is not just his life that is unraveling, but his mind.

During the late spring of 1989, he asks and is granted an opportunity to speak to the Central Committee. He is no Lear, but it is obvious to all that he has lost his mind. Although Nagy is to be reburied, so long as Károly Grósz was Party Secretary, he would not allow Nagy's full rehabilitation.

When, after the reburial, Kádár learns that Nagy is soon to be rehabilitated, he cracks up completely. He is reported to have packed his bag in anticipation of arrest. He then told his wife not to let anyone into the house and lie across the threshold of the door if necessary to keep them out. On July 6, 1989, the very day on which Nagy is rehabilitated, some say the very hour, János Kádár dies.[10]

---

*It still is, of course, a member of the Warsaw Pact as he pronounces this statement and today is a member of NATO.

CHAPTER XIII

Significance of the Revolution— Then and Today

Revolution versus Uprising

Some time went by before the Hungarian Revolution of 1956 was acknowledged as such. First it was thought of as an "uprising." Even the Hungarian Freedom Fighters themselves were referred to in Hungarian as the "Uprisers." As late as 1981, when the first full account in English was published, the book was called simply *Uprising*. The American organization Free Europe and many others referred to it as a "revolt." Indeed, the world's glimpse of it was so brief and its suppression so seemingly total, that when Andrew Wheatcraft published *The World Atlas of Revolutions* in 1983, the Hungarian Revolution was not even mentioned, having slipped completely under his radar.

Nevertheless, it is generally accepted today as a full-scale revolution, albeit an aborted one, for it completely overthrew the existing government throughout the entire country and set a new course that was both desired and accepted by more than ninety percent of the population. Had there been no outside interference, it would have completely transformed the country in a matter of months. As it was, the Revolution continued throughout the country for some time, despite the Soviet armed occupation. Only through sheer Soviet military power and brutal force on the part of the police was the Soviet-backed Kádár "government"—in a true display of counterrevolution—able to force Revolutionary Hungary back into a Stalinist cage.

Contrasting Views of Casualties, Then and Now

The Revolution happened fifty years ago. That's a long time, more than half a lifetime and time for several generations to have grown up without remembering anything about it. Moreover, in Hungary there were thirty-two years of deliberate misinformation about it which permanently damaged some Hungarians' remembrances of it, and which may well have an effect on how the Revolution is still regarded.

There is always a tendency to blur the past, to telescope events and to assume that, when all is said and done, the official record will tell the basic story. And there is a tendency today to depend overly much on what the bureaucrats and military officials over time have recorded.

The fact is, the Hungarian Revolution of 1956 resulted in a great amount of bloodshed, particularly during its suppression by the Soviet Army after November 4. A great many Hungarian lives were lost, but also quite a few Soviet soldiers were killed. How many will never be known, but the figures now being accepted by scholars who have combed the official records in no way correspond to the figures quoted at the time of the Revolution.

Granted, the figures cited at the time, with all the drama and excitement, were bound to be exaggerated, some grossly so. Some of the journalists were prone to exaggerate from the get-go; they were in the business of selling newspapers, and sensation was their trade. But there were others, responsible journalists on the ground, working day in and day out, who had reliable sources, and there were also responsible diplomats, doctors and Red Cross officials who had no reason to exaggerate and whose whole lives had been concerned with precision and accurate reporting. It is the contemporary reports of these people that put the figures accepted by scholars today into question.

What are these accepted figures?

Marshal Zhukov, who had predicted that it would all be over by November 6, reported that as of that day, November 6, 1956, 377 Soviet soldiers had been killed and 881 wounded. But, of course, major fighting went on for at least another three days, so this has been brought up-to-date by two Russian scholars, retired Soviet General Y.A. Malashenko, who was there, and Soviet military historian Alexander M. Kirov, who happens to have been born in 1956. They come up with the following figures in the book *Soviet*

Military Intervention in Hungary, published in 1996 (English language edition in 1999):

—Soviet soldiers and officers killed–640
—Soviet soldiers and officers wounded–1,251

Since the Hungarian editors of the book, Jenő Györkei and Miklós Horváth, do not question these figures, we must assume they accept them as accurate.

Further on in the same book Malashenko puts the killed figure at 670 and the wounded figure at 1,500 (page 273), but even the figure of sixty-seven "disappeared" (read "defected"), carried in the table on page 205, does not account for this discrepancy.

On October 28, 1956, KGB General Ivan Serov reported to Khrushchev that "our losses amount to six hundred dead," (quoted from page sixty-nine of the same book). Since fighting did not cease before the thirtieth and much more intense and extensive fighting took place after November 4, are we to believe that in all those days of fighting only seventy more of the Soviet military were killed?

On the Hungarian side, these two Russian scholars report:

—Hungarians killed amounted to "more than 2,000."
—Hungarians wounded amounted to 12,000

Again, the Hungarian editors of the book, while making such comments in their footnotes as "Malashenko and Kirov both overstate Dudás' role etc.," do not question or comment on these figures.

I must admit that in the thirty-two separate casualty estimates made by Hungarians and Westerners during and just after the Revolution that I have seen, there are wild differences. The highest can be dismissed out of hand. But as the fighting died down and there was more time for people to assess the human carnage, a certain uniformity, though always stated in rounded figures, begins to set in.

The question is: does one believe statistics which have filtered through any number of hands of Communist bureaucrats—persons who have every motive to keep the figures small—over a thirty-two year period, or do you believe persons speaking at the time? In the case of Soviet soldiers killed, staff members from both the British and American legations talked to the caretaker of the Kerepesi Cemetery on December 9, 1956. As Minister

Edward T. Wailes reported to Washington the next day, "The caretaker stated that approximately nine hundred Soviet dead from the recent freedom revolt were buried in this section of the cemetery. Of the nine hundred, sixty or seventy were officers."[1]

Sir Leslie Fry told the Foreign Office that the caretaker had told his man "over eight hundred," but this is a small difference. The point is that the Soviets were known to have taken some of their dead back to the Soviet Union along with their wounded following their pullout of Budapest, and some of these wounded may well have died. Kerepesi, though one of the largest, is only one cemetery of many in Budapest. Soviet soldiers, moreover, were killed in all parts of Hungary, not just in Budapest.

One can impute from this alone that well over one thousand Soviet soldiers, at a minimum, must have been killed.

To take current reporting of Hungarian losses in a single incident, the otherwise excellent book, *The 1956 Hungarian Revolution: A History in Documents*—without which this book could never have been written—writes of the October 25 massacre in Parliament Square, "all told, the massacre claimed the lives of one hundred and left three hundred wounded."[2]

None of the eyewitness accounts I have found put these figures so low. One even believes eight hundred were killed. The Special UN Committee on the Problem of Hungary interviewed about a dozen eyewitnesses only months after the massacre. Their report states on page eighty-three that "estimates of the number of killed vary from three hundred to eight hundred." Shortly after the massacre, the British Legation sent to the scene an employee who reported seeing twelve truckloads of bodies being removed. Since a Hungarian truck in those days could carry as many as fifty live bodies, twelve would have carried a lot more than one hundred dead ones. The trucks did not take them anywhere for burial; they were dumped into various tributaries of the Danube, from which twenty-five were later fished out of the Danube by Hungarian Naval units.

If the three to one ratio of killed to wounded held, there could easily have been as many as one thousand wounded in addition to the dead.

As to the overall casualty totals, the Hungarian scholar Péter Gosztonyi came up with figures for Hungarians up through January 1957; these figures seem be accepted both by the Freedom Fighter Gergely Pongrátz, who included them in his book, *Corvin Circle 1956*, and the editors of *Népszabadság*, which carried them on November 3, 1990. They are:

—Total Hungarians killed–2,502
—Total Hungarians wounded–19,226

This, of course, does not include those who were later executed or died in prison.

Against these figures gleaned from records, there are the estimates of casualties from people on the scene at the time:

Before the Second Soviet intervention:

"Doctors at University Clinic estimated there were between ten and fifteen thousand casualties in seven days of fighting." Endre Márton, AP, October 30.

"Casualties, estimated by Hungarian sources, are 2,500 Russian troops killed and five thousand wounded and thirteen thousand Hungarians dead and wounded, including three thousand armed nationalists." Ronald Farquhar, Reuters, October 31.

"The estimated number injured in the previous week's fighting in Budapest [is] between thirty and forty thousand." Red Cross Headquarters, Bonn, West Germany, which was in radio contact with its field hospital in Óbuda, November 5.

After the Second Soviet Intervention:

"On the first day of fighting the Russians lost sixteen tanks, twenty-five armored vehicles and four hundred soldiers, the French Military Attache told us." Herbert Stiff, *Neues Österreich*, November 5, 1956.

"The newest casualty figures for the fighting which began Sunday are seven thousand Hungarian and three thousand Soviet dead. Estimates of wounded range as high as forty thousand." Ronald Farquhar, Reuters, November 8, 1956.

"Up to November 13, over 13,400 bodies have been taken to the Central Cemetery. There are, of course, other cemeteries, in particular, that in Buda; and the hospital morgues are still full. My informant is therefore disposed to put the total number of Hungarians killed in the capital alone at twenty to twenty-two thousand. This may be on the high side but not, I fear, greatly so." Sir Leslie Fry, British Minister to Budapest, reporting to the Foreign Office, November 15, 1956.

"Indian Prime Minister Jawaharlal Nehru estimated earlier this week that twenty-five thousand Hungarians and seven thousand Russians had died. Jones said that every park in the city was covered with bodies like a giant outdoor morgue. He said the Russians dumped hundreds of bodies into the Danube. He said twelve thousand persons died in one day when the fighting was at its worst." Russell Jones, UP, upon his arrival in New York on December 14, after spending seven weeks in Budapest.

It should be noted that Nehru did not take his figures from journalists. He had his Ambassadors from Moscow and Prague spend the equivalent of several weeks in Budapest in November and December, talking with everyone they could.

The reader may take all of these figures with skepticism. My reason for quoting them is simply to demonstrate the wide discrepancy between perceptions of observers on the scene at the time and the perceptions of those years later who must depend entirely upon official records, the residue, as it were, in the crucible.

The Mood of America in 1956

Even before the second Soviet intervention one foreign delegate in the UN defined U.S. policy toward Hungary thus: "Since the United States has decided not to go to war over Hungary, it has decided to do nothing."

Few Americans at the time would not have taken offense at that remark, yet few could have said what, in fact, the U.S. was doing or could do short of going to war to help the Hungarians. When Americans in the U.S. Legation in Budapest were accosted by complaining Hungarians and asked them, in turn, what they would suggest America do that would not lead to the Third World War, the Americans took comfort in the fact that the Hungarians themselves usually "didn't know."

And yet, as Spencer Barnes said in his telegram of October 26—which was not read in the Department until October 30—"Legation does not have a clear view of the possible alternatives open to the U.S. Government between the extremes of a 'legalistic case' before the UN and material support [i.e., supplying arms]. But *alternatives between the two extremes must exist* [emphasis added], and for some the alternative risks might not be too great."[3]

Why is it, then, that no alternative actions were taken by the U.S.? People in Europe were surprised that the U.S., in effect, did nothing. Even a good many Americans, particularly those closest to the scene, like those working for RFE, could not believe that after five years of touting the "liberation" policy, officials in Washington would not do "everything short of war" for Hungary in its hour of need.

To understand why the U.S., in effect, did nothing, it is necessary to recall the mood of the country and the beliefs of its leaders after ten years of Cold War.

The countries of Eastern Europe, already occupied by the Red Army, soon began to slip behind what Churchill in 1946 had already referred to as the "Iron Curtain." Then came the Berlin Blockade and the allied Air Lift, the shock of learning that the Soviets had acquired the atom bomb a good five years before Western experts said they possibly could, and the shocking loss of six hundred million Chinese "to Communism," when that country fell to the Communists. And almost simultaneously Stalin, we thought, unleashed Kim Il Sung's North Korean Army to conquer South Korea in June 1950. We were sure Stalin did it to divert American attention away from West Berlin, which, to everyone's great relief, he did not grab. U.S. determination to stop the aggression in Korea may have given him pause. In any case, by 1951, when the Korean "police action" turned into a full-scale war, America, which eventually took over two hundred thousand casualties, was more aware than many other countries in the Free World of the Cold War's reality.

The American public had already been alerted to the fact that Communist spies had stolen atomic and other secrets, and by 1952 Senator Joseph McCarthy was able to spread fear and intimidation with thoroughly false "information" about alleged Communist influence in America.

Into this atmosphere of fear and uncertainty the man who had led the allied armies to victory over Nazi Germany and later led the Crusade in Europe which set up NATO rode to victory at the head of the Republican ticket in 1952. The first thing General Eisenhower did was to bring the stalemated war in Korea to a truce. He was not able, however, to choose his own Secretary of State. At the beginning of 1952 no one knew who would be at the head of the Republican ticket, though Senator Robert Taft was the frontrunner. There was, however, no doubt as to who would be Secretary of State if the Republicans won. John Foster Dulles had twice been the Secretary of State-designate and twice been disappointed. There was no question in the mind of any leading Republican that he would be the new Secretary of State.

So John Foster Dulles and Dwight D. Eisenhower were to form and carry out American foreign policy for the next seven years. Eisenhower, a soldier all his life, who had seen a lot of war, was a man of peace. But he knew little about Stalin or the methods of Communists and he was all too prone to assign the thinking of Hitler and the Nazis to them. Dulles, who had been involved in international affairs ever since attending the Paris Peace Treaty of 1919, and was the chief architect of the U.S. Peace Treaty with Japan, felt he knew about Communism and Communists, but his experience in dealing with them was slight and his actual knowledge of Communism quite shallow. He had once read what he took to be the Bible of Communism, Stalin's *Problems of Leninism*. He had memorized many passages of it, just as he had the Bible, and kept a heavily underlined, thumb-worn copy of it on his bedside table.[4] He felt, thereby, that he knew Communism to its core. Unfortunately, it was his only exposure to Communist thought and it caused him to view all Communists as being as ruthless and paranoid as Stalin.

His development of the "Liberation" and "Rollback" policies came less from criticism of Kennan's "containment" policy than a fear that mere containment, which had not stopped China from going Communist, was not enough. Unless the West undertook a moral crusade against godless international Communism, this entity, he feared, would gradually swallow up the rest of the undefended world.

More than any other American, Dulles had written, spoken and preached of the dangers of international Communism and the importance of challenging the Communists where they were weakest. In the process, he did much to educate Americans about the Communist menace. But with memorized paragraphs of Stalin's "Problems of Leninism" in his head, he tended to view Communists not as human beings but as devils in human form. As a good Christian he wanted as little to do with them as possible and was always averse to dealing with Communists directly.

As his proselytizing began well before he took office, by 1956 Americans were saturated with his view of Communism, government officials as well as the public at large, and a great many Americans had come to share his views.

At the same time Dulles had been championing a new nuclear posture, making it not the last line of defense, but potentially the first. Tactical atomic weapons were developed and deployed so that "massive retaliation" could be rained on the enemy almost as soon as he attacked. As one of his biographers put it, "Dulles…possessed a vast technical ignorance of nuclear weapons' effects…. He spoke of 'new and powerful weapons of precision which can utterly destroy military targets without endangering unrelated civilian centers.'"[5]

The policy of "massive retaliation," which seems to have scared West Europeans and Americans more than it did the Communists, coupled with a diplomatic posture which transformed every difference with the Soviet Union into a moral issue, tended to make every compromise look immoral and thus politically unacceptable. Any shading of gray quickly became black. Those who had not declared themselves with us, particularly those who claimed they were neutral, were suspect; for how can you be neutral on a moral issue?

This heavy reliance on atomic weapons and the threat of their use tended to put the U.S. in the straightjacket of "all or nothing." The policy did not apply to most international conflicts. It could never have been applied in the Suez crisis and Eisenhower himself wrote in a personal message to his former psychological warfare assistant, C.D. Jackson, on November 19, 1956, "…but to annihilate Hungary…is no way to help her." In his memoir he added, "The United States did the only thing it could: we readied ourselves…to help the refugees…and did everything possible to condemn the aggression."[6]

There was, of course, something else which Eisenhower himself had several times suggested, only to have it batted down by Dulles or his deputy, Hoover. "Now is the time," he told Dulles as early as October 29, "to talk [to the Russians] about reducing tensions in the world." Talking to the Russians was anathema to Dulles. He immediately pointed out that "we would have to be very careful not to do anything that would look to the satellite world as though we were selling them out." That remark was enough to kill the matter.[7]

Three days earlier Dulles, in a telephone conversation with Eisenhower, said that he "did not think we should get into talks with the Russians about it [Hungary] unless through the [UN] Security Council. We could have some backstage talks going on during the time the Council was in session, but…," as the White House transcript of the conversation records, Dulles did "not want to get into anything that looked as though backstage talks were going on."[8] There is no record of any talks, direct or "backstage," ever having taken place.

Three days after his election in the midst of the Hungarian crisis,

Eisenhower again felt it was time to engage the Soviets directly. He called in his Acting Secretary of State and proposed to take advantage of the world-wide fright to make some progress on reducing tension and making progress on disarmament. He said he would be willing to make a dramatic offer, such as pulling NATO forces behind the Rhine and withdrawing American ground forces in Germany. Hoover very much doubted that Dulles would agree, and indeed, the latter did not waste much time thinking about it before he poured cold water on it.[9]

Eisenhower, thinking as a military man, even had second thoughts about military aid to the Hungarians. In his memoirs he mused, "I still wonder what would have been my recommendation to Congress and the American people had Hungary been accessible by sea or through the territory[10] of allies who might have agreed to react positively to the tragic fate of the Hungarian people." This does not sound like a man fearful that any direct military contact with the Soviets would inevitably lead to World War III.

U.S. Policies and Weaknesses

When it came to a final decision in foreign policy it was usually Dulles who made it.

This should have worked out, and often did, but the two men were so different in temperament and outlook that there was bound to be confusion at times as to what exactly American policy was. Eisenhower's foreign policy goal was to make peace in the world and spread prosperity. If this frequently entailed having to oppose our wartime allies, the Russians, or fight international Communism, well and good, the world was made up of difficult choices. But his main goal was assuring and furthering world peace. Not so Mr. Dulles. While he paid lip service to that goal, Dulles's real goal was the ultimate defeat of Soviet Russia, the mainstay of international Communism. He felt great responsibility as the leader of the West in the Cold War against the source of international evil. He saw the Soviets as representatives of the devil, to be dealt with only at arm's length. Eisenhower saw them as misguided human beings, who had helped the Western allies to crush Nazi Germany, but whose ideology was every bit as dangerous as the Nazis, if not more so. Nonetheless they were human beings with human aspirations who could and must be dealt with.

To put it in simple Aesopian terms, Eisenhower felt that warm sunshine, in the form of disarmament treaties and troop pullbacks, increased trade, and cultural and other exchanges would work faster and better in removing the heavy cloak of Communism from the Russian and other peoples under the Soviet empire than would Dulles's cold north wind of hostile propaganda, threats of "massive retaliation" and ostracizing. But it was more of a gut feeling with him and only became established U.S. policy after death had removed Dulles from the scene.

The result of differing goals and differing approaches resulted in the U.S. National Security Council stating in its February 29, 1956 progress report: "It may be that the U.S. will have to undertake to follow simultaneously two policies with inconsistent courses of action, representing divergent approaches to the one objective." The problem, of course, was that this was as confusing to the Communists as to anyone else. They could feel the north wind but never felt the talked-about sunshine. Dulles's "increasing pressure" through threats and propaganda "to induce negotiation and modify Communist behavior," as the scholar James D. Marchio observed, "ultimately retarded rather advanced U.S. interests behind the Iron Curtain."[11]

While there were people in the State Department who much preferred the Eisenhower approach, there were people close to Eisenhower who were counseling a "full press" execution of the Cold War. Chief among these was Eisenhower's advisor on psychological warfare, C. D. Jackson. Jackson, the son of a wealthy importer of Italian marble, had been in the OSS during the Second World War and settled at Time Incorporated after the war as publisher of *LIFE* magazine. Just before coming to work in the White House, he had done a stint as President of the Free Europe Committee, so was a tremendous booster of RFE which, because of its supposed "private" status, could hit the Communists so much harder than the Voice of America (VOA). One might assume that the author of "Liberation" and "Rollback" might hit it off with the ex-president of Free Europe, but the cautious lawyer and the flamboyant propagandist had difficulty melding.

By 1956, C. D. Jackson was back at Time Inc., replaced by a William Jackson (no relation), who was far less flamboyant than his predecessor. Foster's brother, Allen, at the CIA quickly caught wind of Khrushchev's secret speech and its importance and managed to get the text four months later and publicize it to the world. The CIA reported more accurately than did the U.S. diplomatic posts on the ferment that was racing through Eastern Europe. But with the exception of Spencer Barnes in Budapest, neither U.S. diplomats in the area nor policy makers in Washington realized that something exceptional and different was going on. As late as mid-July 1956 the CIA senior research staff on Communism concluded, "The Eastern Bloc is politically, economically and militarily so tightly knit that major deviations could and would not be tolerated by Soviet leaders."[12] Shortly thereafter, Allen Dulles embarked on a grand world tour of CIA posts, a trip which CIA executive Ray Cline later called "one of the most highly publicized clandestine expeditions ever made."[13] Due to return to Washington only in late November, Dulles cut short his tour, alarmed by reports of what was going on in Poland and Hungary, and arrived back in Washington on October 8.

If he briefed his brother on the latest developments in these two countries, there is little indication that much of it took. Foster Dulles had fairly fixed ideas about the satellites, and like Ambassador Jacobs in Warsaw, he was inclined to think that anything resembling real change was likely to be a trick engineered in Moscow. When the revolution broke out in Hungary he was furious—just as he had been with the East Germans—that they had ignored his script for "peaceful" liberation, and he was inclined to think that whatever happened, they had brought it on themselves. Then, when the country appeared to have been liberated by, as Allen said, "in a sense…a miracle," he was delighted and took it as given fact.

When Harold Stassen argued on the twenty-sixth that it was important to make it clear as soon as possible to the Russians, who were apparently still undecided about what to do, that we had no designs on Hungary and would be happy to have it become an Austrian-type neutral and not able to join NATO, Dulles reacted not only negatively to the word "neutral" but to the idea of accepting half a loaf when a few more days might give them a whole one. The President rejected Stassen's idea on the ground that he did not think the Soviets feared an American attack, but later relented when Dulles agreed that it would be prudent to reassure the aroused bear that the U.S. was not going after any of his honey.

"This fundamentally modified version of Stassen's original proposal," wrote János Bak and Lyman Legters in their book on the Revolution, "did not achieve the original aim of pacifying the Soviets…. Whereas the original idea had been to try to induce concessions from the Soviet Union through explicit recognition of its security interests, [Dulles'] version was of a distinctly defensive tenor which the Soviets logically assumed to mean that the U.S. was not going to take any action whatsoever…."[14]

About this time Dulles appears to have conjured up his own view of what was going on in Hungary. He could not have been reading Barnes's dispatches from Budapest nor those of Sir Leslie Fry, as Bohlen had hinted he should, in the absences of delayed U.S. telegrams, for he assumed that time was on the side of the Freedom Fighters and the West, just the opposite of what all these messages were saying. He could not avoid seeing what was in the newspapers, yet he repeated in the UN and had Lodge repeat almost as a mantra that "the situation is unclear," "we lack specific information," etc. in order to delay and thereby get the whole loaf of Hungary at no price to the West. While Lodge knew this mantra of "the situation being unclear" was a ruse to gain time, his disbelief and fury at Sobelov, when the second Soviet intervention came on November 4, was genuine.

What was uppermost in Eisenhower's and Dulles's minds, during the twin crises of Suez and Hungary, was their fear of either crisis escalating into World War III. This American fear of war was somewhat self-engendered since the new policy of tactical atomic weapons and quick massive retaliation implied that matters could rapidly escalate, particularly if the other side feared first attack. And the Soviets, conscious of all those American bases surrounding them, constant peripheral overflights of Soviet territory by American military planes, and America's Strategic Air Command with atomic bomb-laden planes continuously in the air, feared first attack far more than did the United States. They might well panic and do something rash if things seemed to be falling apart.

Nonetheless, there was the danger of the U.S. becoming paralyzed by gross exaggeration of Soviet atomic power and delivery capabilities, exaggeration which Admiral Radford, then Chairman of the Joint Chiefs of Staff, said was leading to "defense hysteria."

In the early days of the Hungarian crisis the U.S. fleet was deployed to sea to avoid a repetition of Pearl Harbor. Such a responsible journalist as C. L. Sulzberger of the *New York Times* wrote on November 10:

"Quietly but efficiently we...have alerted our global striking forces and warned them to be prepared for immediate defense and immediate riposte....

"Moscow is not releasing conscripts and must be summoning reservists, for there are entirely too many Soviet divisions assembled in the Ukraine and Byelorussia and being moved into Romania and Hungary and, across Poland, into East Germany to calculate that these come only from available units....

"The USSR is building a massive force on one side of the Iron Curtain at the particular instant when NATO's counter-force approaches the condition of a vacuum...."

Sulzberger then followed this up with all sorts of speculations as to what Moscow may be up to, nearly all of them offensive and inspiring fear.

The fear went so deep that officials in the National Security Council and Department of State were determined to do nothing that could possibly increase the danger of anything leading to war.

Europeans did not share this fear. The Soviet Army's threat to Western Europe was a diminishing threat, particularly now that they had such troubles in Eastern Europe. Yes, East Germany was restless and it would be difficult to keep West Germans from volunteering to join them should they rise again, but East Germany had already experienced the total failure of the West to help them, and they now had witnessed the repetition of that failure in Hungary. East Germany was not the danger that Dulles and von Brentano would later make it out to be. And there were many young men in Western Europe and in Britain who would have volunteered, in fact, who *did* volunteer, to go fight in Hungary, had there been any way to get there.

It was in the context of this pervasive American fear that Eisenhower and Dulles' stand-in, Herbert Hoover, Jr., decided on the afternoon of November 4 that unlike Suez, "there should be no UN force for Hungary," lest it bring on a direct confrontation with Soviet troops.

That decision was never announced, but it was followed with such rigor by Lodge at the UN that it soon became apparent that America's primary role was still one of restraint and delay insofar as any positive action was concerned. Anything that smacked of direct confrontation, be it challenging the Kádár representative at the UN or counseling Hammarskjold to fly to Budapest without an "invitation" from the regime, was shied away from. "No UN force for Hungary" became no action by the U.S. which could "increase the danger" of anything which might possibly escalate into war. Even the decision to use U.S. military aircraft to pick up Hungarian refugees from neutral Austria was reversed in favor of using civilian planes, lest this be used by the Soviets as proof of American involvement in the Hungarian Revolution.[15]

Though it was being carried out by Hoover, this exaggerated interpretation of the November 4 White House decision is precisely what Dulles would have done, for Hoover knew his boss's thinking thoroughly. He may well have shared his boss's feelings of guilt at the U.S having done so much to cause the Hungarian tragedy. Thus he indulged in the overreaction of withdrawing anything and everything that might be interpreted as further U.S. provocative involvement in Hungary. This, of course, did not yet extend to RFE, even though that station's broadcasts were now greatly curtailed.

This policy did not go over well with the American public.

Whatever the majority of Americans felt, fear, fear of the unknown, fear of the unpredictable consequences of their actions, seems to have been the guiding motive of American leaders in the crisis. While this fear should not have prevented some potential actions, such as immediately recognizing Hungary's neutral status or proposing some major *quid pro quo* pullback of troops, it did eliminate the possibility of any covert or overt support of the Hungarian revolutionaries. If there was to be no UN police force, there would certainly be nothing comparable from the U.S. or NATO, and Eisenhower reportedly twice turned down requests from the CIA to airdrop military weapons and supplies to the rebels during the crisis. General Andrew J. Goodpaster later wrote in his memoirs that Eisenhower felt that "elements in our government—specifically the CIA—had gone beyond their authority and in fact had carried out a line of propaganda of their own which was not in accord with his policy."[16]

Fear, of course, comes from ignorance, ignorance of one's adversaries and one's adversary's intentions and capabilities. American policy-makers at the time were abysmally ignorant of the Soviet Union and even more so of the countries of East-Central Europe. Eisenhower and many others thought of the Soviet Army in terms of the Nazi Army launching blitzkriegs across foreign borders (i.e. Western Europe). Others thought in terms of the sneak attack at Pearl Harbor. George Kennan, who knew Russia and the history of Soviet behavior well, could have disabused the administration of all of these erroneous notions, but his counsel was no longer being sought.

The administration has a "tendency to shove off" problems onto the United Nations, complained Senator William Fulbright, calling it a "form of escapism" resulting from an inability "to think of anything to do ourselves." This, of course, was an oversimplification. But it does underscore the Eisenhower administration's over-dependence on an international organization that had never done anything of significance up to then without full American support and leadership. Suez worked out because of American leadership; in Hungary, the U.S. provided none.

The only move the U.S. made outside of the UN was to warn the Soviets that the U.S. would regard any violation of the "territorial integrity or international sovereignty" of Austria as "a grave threat to peace." Even this came at Austria's request.

The record shows that every suggestion of offering to pull back troops from Germany to induce a comparable Soviet troop withdrawal, whether made by Eisenhower, Stassen, the National Security Council or Soviet Premier Bulganin, was vetoed by Dulles virtually without discussion.

Changes in U.S Policy

As one American employee of Radio Free Europe told the writer Edmond Taylor at the time, "God knows we tried to be responsible toward our listeners. We were just caught by surprise in Hungary. We thought these people had been taken in by Soviet propaganda, that they were demoralized, apathetic. Hell, we've been whipping a dead horse [i.e. Communism] for months, maybe for years."[17]

"Whipping a dead horse" could no longer be RFE's mission after the Hungarian Revolution had revealed the true state of affairs in Eastern Europe. The policy of putting "pressure on the Communists" via the "Liberation" and "Rollback" policies was every bit as much a dead horse. The U.S. needed a new policy toward the area.

A hint of this came when Dulles gave his press conference on returning from the NATO meeting on December 18, 1956. Conceding that there was a change in his assessment of the area, that the East European states were not dependable allies of the Soviet Union, he nonetheless stated that "if East European states achieved genuine independence, that certainly would facilitate a general review of the whole European security system."[18] That is akin to saying "if the apple falls from the tree we will call a conference to decide whether or not to pick it up."

Such sangfroid was not shared by the Alsop brothers who, having discovered that resistance was still going on in Hungary, wrote a few days earlier that if the U.S. did not do something to help the Hungarians at this late date, the alternative was "to stand idly by while the Soviets grind the Hungarian resistance slowly into bits.... It may be as unpleasant as disregarding the cries of a small animal caught in a trap, while it is worried to death by a large one. At the very least, the Soviets should not be assured (as Secretary Dulles assured them...) that we will never in any circumstances do anything at all but talk."[19]

During Dulles' hospital convalescence, Assistant Secretary Hoover did show signs of trying to change U.S. policy from being "in irons" to taking a port or starboard tack. Relying on his two strongest Ambassadors in the area, Thompson in Vienna and Bohlen in Moscow, he engaged them in conversation via cable. He agreed with Thompson that "the cardinal objective should be to bring about Soviet troop withdrawal from Hungary." This was three weeks after Barnes and Wailes in Budapest had urged it, but it was the first time anyone in Washington had mentioned the idea as priority number one. He also agreed that Bulganin's statement to Nehru on the subject of Soviet troop withdrawal had not gone further than any previous statements, but that he would now bring to Nehru's notice the "importance of making troop withdrawal a key test of Soviet promises." As to the advisability of direct talks with the Soviets, he was afraid the Soviets might try to broaden these "into an attempt to privately negotiate with us on the Middle East." He thought it better for "some neutral West European state to act as our confidential surrogate in such talks. The appeal of this neutral surrogate should concentrate broadly on the need for plans of withdrawal of Soviet forces...perhaps in connection with the Hungarian declaration of neutrality." He then asked for their views.[20]

Nothing came of this flurry of cables and we do not know of Dulles' reaction when he re-took the helm of the Ship of State [Department], but Hoover resigned a month later and was replaced by Christian Herter, former Governor of Massachusetts.

The dual policies in Washington went on. Stassen pushed for disarmament without foolproof inspections and engagement with the Russians through exchanges, if nothing else; the cold warriors tried to fashion a policy of encouraging "national Communism" in Eastern Europe, oblivious of the fact that the events of 1956 had already made this concept obsolete, that only a Gomułka could walk the tightrope he was walking on in Poland and only a strong dictator like Tito could keep his anti-Communist populace at bay.

Eventually the U.S. had to adapt its policy to the realities of geopolitics. It recognized the Kádár regime, slowly introduced Eisenhower's sunshine approach and for some thirty years "let well enough alone," with the sole exception of the Helsinki Conference for Security in Europe, which was initiated not by the West, but the Russians.

Soviet Policies and Weaknesses

The year 1956 started out to be a watershed year for Soviet policy when Khrushchev delivered his secret speech denouncing Stalin at the close of the Twentieth Party Congress. It ended as a watershed year not only for Soviet policy, but also for the entire Cold War as the consequences of that speech played out within the Communist empire. The near upheaval in Poland and the explosion in Hungary exposed the dangerous fragility of the empire so completely that the two sides, in Europe at least, were content to support the status quo for the next thirty years.

Three years after Stalin's death, with ghostly figures returning to Moscow and Leningrad from Stalin's death camps, the leaders in the Kremlin agreed that Stalin's ghost had to be laid to rest if they were to get on with the reforms that would allow them to stay in power. Not the original choice to make the speech, Khrushchev, when forced to give it, put his own particular twist into the telling that gave it more explosive force than any had intended. Even had the speech remained within the Party, as it was supposed to, the repercussions would have been sensational. As it was, the speech soon leaked out and by June was all over the world.

While ferment swept through the empire, Khrushchev and Bulganin courted Britain during an April visit, quite unaware that they would be threatening Britain with atomic rockets in November. In June they welcomed Marshal Tito, champion of "other roads to socialism" which the Soviets had indicated were to be tolerated, only to circulate a nasty letter about him behind his back in September and denounce him vehemently in November. On October 30 the Kremlin issued a Declaration announcing a new relationship between the USSR and its East European neighbors, only to reverse this the next day and make war on Hungary a few days later. Yet the Declaration was never formally reversed, and indeed became the operative document governing these relations in the following years. Starting out the year by launching a massive campaign of de-Stalinization, Khrushchev ended the year by drunkenly shouting to Western diplomats at a New Year's Eve celebration, "We are all Stalinists!"

If there is a pattern to such erratic behavior it would have to be ascribed to Khrushchev. And yet the Soviet Union at this point did have a "collective leadership" and most of these zigs and zags were only undertaken after full deliberation in the Politburo, if not the full Central Committee.

The Soviets were feeling their way into the post-Stalin era, and it was only natural that they should discover the limiting barriers along this new pathway by stumbling into them.

One of Nikita Khrushchev's main goals at this time, though not realized sufficiently in the West, was a reduction of armies, both the Soviet and satellite, so that more money could be spent on raising the standard of living. He did not wait for reciprocity from the West, but plunged ahead, announcing on May 15 that the Soviet Union was preparing to withdraw large amounts of its troops from those East European countries which had them, but only specifying a number in one country, thirty thousand from East Germany. This was followed by announcements during the summer by Romania, Hungary and Poland of cuts in their armies of 20,000, 15,000 and 50,000 men, respectively.[21]

At the same time it was obvious to the reformers in the Kremlin that there would have to be some major changes in their relations with the countries of Eastern Europe if de-Stalinization was to take place there, as well as in the Soviet Union. The Communist parties in Eastern Europe took to de-Stalinization much more readily than did the Soviet Party, and Khrushchev sensed that it was progressing much too fast in Poland even before the explosion at Poznań. When he appeared at the hastily-called Polish Party plenum in March to make sure the Polish comrades picked his man to replace their deceased leader, Beirut (they didn't), he gave a second "secret speech" denouncing Stalin, but this time indicated it might be time to apply the brakes to de-Stalinization.[22]

Sometime during the summer, the more liberal members of the Politburo must have commissioned a committee to work out a long-range plan to put relations between Socialist states on a new footing. The draft of this document, long in preparation, but not fully discussed until the October 30 meeting of the Politburo, underwent a number of changes during that meeting to bring it up-to-date. Nonetheless, this far-reaching document reached its final form before the end of that meeting, was approved unanimously and broadcast in full on Radio Moscow that night as well as printed in full in *Pravda* the next morning. The fact that the Politburo voted to reverse it the next day, insofar as Hungary was concerned, in no way nullified the Declaration as official Soviet policy, for it was argued that Nagy had already left the confines of the "socialist countries" by the thirty-first by indicating that Hungary would be permitting other parties to join the government and was contemplating withdrawing from the Warsaw Pact and declaring neutrality. The Declaration was not just a trick to lull Hungary before the surprise attack, as Dulles and Eisenhower and most Americans thought at the time. Gomułka at once made use of the newly declared policy. Military and other advisors were later withdrawn, all Soviet troops left Romania in 1958 and trade relations were greatly altered in favor of the East European countries, including Hungary. All of this was carried out under the aegis of this October 30 Declaration.

Khrushchev was extraordinarily lucky in having the Suez fiasco fall into his lap just when he needed something to divert the world's attention away from Hungary.

But the series of events in Czechoslovakia, Poland and Hungary which led up to the showdown with Gomułka in Poland and the explosion in Hungary was already having repercussions in the Soviet Union. Just as it was not possible to have de-Stalinization in one country and not the others, so it was not possible to re-Stalinize Hungary without re-Stalinizing the others.

By the end of 1956, however, Soviet policy had come full circle. The empire had been shaken as it never had been before and only Stalinist use of force had kept it intact. Satellite armies were seen to be unreliable, NATO and the West were still a threat, all the bridges they had been trying to build to Third World countries were sagging if not in flames. The standard of living was not rising as planned, Hungary had thrown all economic planning out of kilter; there was great discontent among the populace and great dissention among the leadership.

As a result of their actions in the previous year, however, the Soviets now faced an array of problems far in excess of what they had faced a year before. From becoming an influence in the Third World and friend of neutralist leaders, the USSR was now a pariah on the world scene, condemned by the UN. From feeling in charge of at least the European portion of the Communist empire, it now saw several of its client states as unruly and not to be trusted. Communist Parties throughout the free world had shrunk significantly, diminishing their influence. Where only recently Soviet students were inspired to work as volunteer pioneers in the virgin lands, its students now questioned government authority, the Party and Soviet actions abroad, particularly in Hungary. There was more unrest in the republics than before. De-

Stalinization had revealed weaknesses in the Party, re-Stalinization had brought the worst elements of the Party to the fore and was eclipsing the better elements Khrushchev and the liberals had been encouraging. It was a bleak outlook.

Then, in the fall of 1957, the pressure of all of these problems found overnight relief with *Sputnik*. *Sputnik* solved few of the actual problems. The economic problems remained, the diminished Communist Parties did not recover their previous numbers, the client states in Eastern Europe were as troublesome as ever, but the United States was rocked back on its heels. Within two or three years the Soviet Union was no longer a pariah and was becoming a Mecca for the Third World. Its youth recovered its pride in the USSR and the Party was able to relax its re-Stalinization campaign. *Sputnik* transformed the scene and saved the day for world Communism as no other event could have.

With the Soviet Union now judged to be the world's second superpower, the Cold War in Europe settled into a mutually accepted status quo.

What Might Have Been

Historians are never supposed to speculate on what might have been, but as I am not a historian in the strict sense, I do not feel constrained by that dictum. In any case, all speculations contain so many "ifs" that the chance of all the right "ifs" being lined up properly to achieve the desired end will always remain remote.

But just suppose that the United States had had a policy behind the slogans "liberation" and "rollback" and had been prepared to do everything short of war to help Hungary achieve its independence. Volunteers might well have been in place, and the mechanisms to get them, or just military supplies, to Hungary might have been established. Hungary's neutrality would have been recognized immediately and warnings against any violation of that neutrality issued virtually simultaneously. Massive medical aid and food could have been sent in such quantities by land and air that the Soviets could not possibly have stopped it. And with a UN presence in Hungary the Soviets would have been forced to make the best of a bad situation by agreeing to Hungary's neutrality and to a date for the removal of their forces.

The point, of course, is that the United States did not have any "Liberation" policy. It was a policy designed to make trouble for the Soviet

621

Union in its backyard, but with little thought about the people of Eastern Europe themselves.

But even lacking any such policy, there were still many things that the United States might have done, short of war, which it did not.

There is a perception among many in the West, and in the United States in particular, that the United States had only two choices, denounce the Soviet Union in the UN or go to war with nuclear weapons. Spencer Barnes in our Budapest Legation did not know what they were, but he was sure there were alternative actions short of war between a legalistic case argued in the UN and action that might bring on atomic warfare.

Here are some of the alternative actions—all suggested at the time, that is, with no benefit of hindsight—which the United States might have undertaken and did not.

Alternative Actions by the U.S. alone after October 23 and before November 4:
- —Recognize Hungary's declaration of neutrality on the day it was declared and urge all other nations, particularly its NATO allies, to do so;
- —Call for the same treatment of the Hungarian situation as that in Egypt, which would have meant a UN police force for Hungary;
- —Follow the advice of its own Legation in Budapest, which included making the removal of Soviet troops from Hungary, rather than denouncing the Soviet Union in the UN, the number one priority.

Alternative Actions by the U.S & NATO:
- —Call for a meeting of Chiefs of Staff;
- —Call a general mobilization;
- —Call for a diplomatic meeting with the Warsaw Pact;
- —Initiate "camouflage" maneuvers.

Alternative Actions by the U.S. in the UN:
- —Lead a strong attack on the USSR by calling a spade a spade and using language at least as strong as that used against Britain and France;
- —Call on Hammarskjold's office, after the attack on Egypt, to assign someone under him full-time to Hungary.

Alternative Actions by the U.S. Alone after November 4:
- —Have President Eisenhower appear at the UN the day after his election to appeal for peace and mercy and offer to discuss matters with the Soviets;

—Offer to protect "neutral Austria" on the fourth or fifth of November, not two weeks later;

—Threaten to, or actually break off diplomatic, trade, technical and cultural relations with the USSR until they cease their action in Hungary and urge NATO countries to do the same;

—Use diplomatic contacts everywhere to divine what the Soviets might accept in return for modifying their actions in Hungary or actually pulling their troops out of Hungary.

Alternative Actions by the U.S. in the UN after November 4:

—Urge Hammarskjold to go to Budapest immediately, with the threat of expulsion of Hungary from the UN if they refused to receive him;

—Select an observer team without delay and simply send them to Budapest;

—If the Hungarians do not allow them in, appoint at once an alternative observer team from among the diplomats already in Budapest representing neutral nations, say India, Switzerland and Finland;

—If the Kádár regime and Russians make it difficult for this observer team to operate, make up a UN report from all of the diplomatic cables sent out of Budapest since November 4;

—Fly in Red Cross supplies in aircraft marked with UN insignia and if they are not allowed to land parachute the supplies into designated areas where the Soviet forces are not present;

—Introduce a resolution to expel the Soviet Union from the UN until such time as it conforms to the UN resolutions passed or agrees to withdraw its troops from Hungary.

Other Alternative Measures:

—Parachute in arms and volunteers at night from NATO or U.S. planes with no insignia piloted by volunteers;*

—Get the Bonn government to begin serious preparations for negotiations on German reunification;

---

*For years the U.S. had experimented with the idea of a Volunteer Freedom Corps made up of young East European exiles and managed by the CIA and Pentagon. Henry Cabot Lodge, Jr., when still a Senator, had drafted the legislation, and there actually were some units, later turned into labor battalions, secretly stationed in Bavaria. But they had been disbanded by the time of the Revolution, even though the CIA may have tried to re-activate them. Lodge, as late as 1958, was still trying to get the VFC launched.

—Propose a demilitarized area from the Rhine to the Soviet border.

These are only some of the alternative actions proposed at the time that might have been taken. Any one of these, such as Hammarskjold's early arrival in Budapest, might have considerably changed the way matters actually turned out.

If just a few of the above alternative actions had been taken, could not matters have turned out differently? Certainly there was a window of opportunity on October 29 and 30 when the Politburo, even Zhukov, had come to terms with the idea of having to pull their troops out of Hungary and learn to live with the situation. And even after the second intervention, if there had been a serious proposal from the West to discuss pulling back troops on both sides, would not the Soviet Union, which had much to gain from this, have modified its behavior in Hungary to take advantage of a larger settlement which might be to its lasting benefit?

Did the West miss an opportunity to bring the Communist empire down decades earlier than it did collapse? There can be no question that had Hungary somehow gained its independence in 1956, even at the cost to the West of pulling troops out of West Germany, the rest of the Soviet bloc would have crumbled within a few years. Was it really necessary to wait another three decades? Think of all the crises, from the Berlin Wall to the Cuban Missile Crisis to Vietnam to Nicaragua to Mozambique, we might never have had to go through had the Communist empire collapsed in the late 1950s and early 60s. Think of all the wasted lives, the delayed justice, and the delayed prosperity in all of these countries for hundreds of millions of people. It would certainly seem that an enormous opportunity was missed.

But could Hungary have been saved?

The answer, alas, is no. Given the circumstances of 1956, but particularly given the personalities who were in charge on both sides, there is no way that things could have turned out any differently than they did. The mindsets of Eisenhower, Dulles, Khrushchev and Zhukov and other key figures of the day were so deeply ingrained, their ignorance of the other side's motives, intentions and capabilities was so vast that gross misjudgments and miscalculations were inevitable. The past is messy, no matter how much those of us who attempt to record it may want to tidy it up. There are reasons for things turning out the way they do. We are lucky if we can identify just a few of them. And it is much easier to do so from the distance of fifty years.

So what is the significance of the Hungarian Revolution? One has to ask this question on two levels: what was it then, and what is it today?

The Significance of the Hungarian Revolution Then, in 1956

On the first night of the second Soviet intervention, Béla Kovács, still a legitimate Minister in Nagy's government, told the American journalist Leslie B. Bain as they crouched in the cellar of the U.S. Legation:

"It has brought modern history to a turning point. It has exposed totalitarian fallacies more sharply than any event before. Our people were beaten, cowed, and for years lived in abject surrender, yet when the hour struck they all streamed out of their homes, Communists and non-Communists alike, to regain their self-respect by defying their tormentors. And look what happened to the Communist Party! It disappeared overnight—not forced to dissolve, but by common consent! Have you ever heard of a ruling party voting itself out of existence? Once the Revolution touched them, all became Hungarians—all except those whose crimes were too many to be forgiven. These are the ones who now serve their Russian masters."[23]

Only days later the renegade Yugoslav Communist leader, Milovan Ðilas, unable to publish in Belgrade, wrote in the American magazine *The New Leader* that the Revolution was "a new phenomenon, perhaps no less meaningful than the French or Russian Revolution....

"Had the Hungarian Revolution not only brought political democracy but also preserved social control of heavy industry and banking [which, of course, is precisely what the Nagy government intended], it would have exercised enormous influence on all Communist countries, including the USSR. It would have demonstrated not only that totalitarianism is unnecessary as a means of protecting the workers from exploitation [i.e. in the 'building of Socialism'], but also that this is a mere excuse for the exploitation of the workers by bureaucracy and the new ruling class."[24]

Other comments at the time were more terse. The Polish-born journalist for the *Manchester Guardian*, Victor Zorza, wrote that Hungarians "paid with their lives not only for the freedom of Hungary, but for freeing the world of the fear that has hung over it for so long [i.e. the inevitable spread of Communism]." George Urban, the Hungarian exile then working for the BBC, later to become Director of all of RFE, recorded in his book what he had said in one broadcast: "Whatever grim and fearful things may still lie ahead, Hungary has shown beyond any shadow of a doubt that Communism is a broken reed."[25]

For Patrícia Kállay, interviewed decades later, the Revolution was important for other reasons.

"For me 1956 was so beautiful and important, because people from all walks of life acted like brothers and friends to one another. It didn't matter if a person was a gypsy, a Jewish doctor, the descendant of a baron or a worker, they simply said that that person was a human being. What really mattered was that after so many centuries the country should be free and independent, although we had no idea what would be the consequences.... They weren't afraid to make sacrifices for each other, to make a stand...and they put their personal interests to one side. I think that was beautiful."[26]

Most Americans felt overwhelmed by guilt. Recalling Ambassador Lodge's pledges in the UN that the United States would assist "the brave Hungarian people in their struggle for freedom," John MacCormac of the *New York Times* commented that:

"The Hungarian people could scarcely be blamed for regarding Lodge's words as a pledge of help, nor could the United States propaganda media be reprehended for recording them. If history should one day hold the United States guilty of having deluded a brave people with false hopes it would seem that the responsibility must be placed higher up."[27]

It was not just Americans who were made to feel guilty. The Spanish philosopher Salvador de Maderiega in the midst of the fighting asked, "How can the West ever live down the fact that the only people who volunteered to fight and die alongside the Hungarian Freedom Fighters were Russian soldiers?"

Hugh Seton-Watson, a British historian who specialized in East-Central Europe, pointed out in the November 9 issue of the *Spectator* that for "the first time in history a nation had overthrown a totalitarian regime. Unlike mere dictatorships, of which thousands have been overthrown before, totalitarianism aims not only to prevent its subjects from doing certain things, but to tell them what to do, say and think." A month or so later two French writer/philosophers, Raymond Aaron and Hannah Arendt, were to make the same point. The basic point about the Hungarian Revolution, they wrote, was that it was "anti-totalitarian," and unique, being the first of its kind.

After the Revolution was crushed, many in Hungary, seeing that their goals had not been reached and that their struggle, on the contrary, had caused nothing but misery and terrible consequences for their families, felt that it had all been in vain. As one person said in 1990, "Nothing was achieved, and if my old man was living today I'm sure he would say, 'Son, it wasn't worth it.'"[28] And for many Hungarians that seemed so.

But as Alexandre Mataxas, a scholar of Russia, wrote of the reaction of young Russians that November:

"We know beyond question that they have been deeply affected by what has happened in...Budapest. The Russians, like the British, like to feel certain that right is on their side. They were so perfectly convinced of this in the war against Hitler that they fought like demons."

"But the massacre of Budapest has made them think again. Both in Moscow and elsewhere there is a deep disquiet and grave heartsearchings at the news of Russian soldiers deserting in the streets, and Russian officers who have returned from Hungary are openly critical of what happened there...."

"News flies faster...than telegraph or radio can send it. What is done is done: the canker is at work in Russia itself...."[29]

And the Russian scholar Vladislav M. Zubok, speaking to an audience of scholars and former participants in the Revolution at a conference in Budapest on "New Archival Evidence," in September 1996 said that:

"Immediately after the restoration, the Soviet leadership took a very tolerant stand towards the puppet government of János Kádár: 'Kádárization' became a synonym for far-reaching economic reforms and rapprochement with Western Europe, a gradual abandonment of the Soviet model of 'socialism,' protected from Soviet wrath by a personalized authoritarian regime and by its unfailing support of Soviet foreign policy and Soviet security needs. During the stormy Plenum in June 1957 Mikoyan revealed that Khrushchev had consistently supported the course of 'buying out' Eastern European workers by giving them a higher living standard, even at the expense of Soviet living standards, in order to prevent a repetition of the Hungarian revolt."[30]

On the first anniversary of the Revolution Senator John F. Kennedy said in a speech, which today is engraved on the memorial to the 1956 Revolution in Boston, Massachusetts:

"October 23, 1956, is a day that will live forever in the annals of free men and nations. It was a day of courage, conscience and triumph. No other day, since history began, has shown more clearly the eternal unquenchability of man's desire to be free, whatever the odds against success, whatever the sacrifice required."[31]

The Significance of the Hungarian Revolution Today

"The 1956 uprising of the Hungarian people belongs to those rare, truly epochal events the importance of which does not fade with the passing of time." Thus wrote the Hungarian scholar Péter Kende at the beginning of his "Afterword" essay in György Litván's book *The Hungarian Revolution of 1956: Reform, Revolt and Repression* ten years ago. That statement is as true today as it was then and will stand for all time.

For not only did it reveal that the Soviet Empire had no clothes, it proved that Communism and all totalitarianisms are incompatible with the nobility of the human personality. It was the first complete overthrow of a totalitarian system and a shining example.

"The message from Poland," writes Kende, "was that society is alive, and from Budapest that Communism can be toppled."

"These messages were clearly received in Moscow, and the subsequent thirty-odd years of the Soviet system could be described as a series of measures aimed at avoiding a repetition of 1956. But the messages also touched the hearts and minds of people in the farthest corners of the countries under Moscow's rule. The disobedience of an entire people—however unbelievable it may have appeared before—became a cherished example in the collective memory of an oppressed people.... There are indications that the Hungarian uprising...had worried even Gorbachev, suggesting that the Hungarian question was still a 'question' in Moscow thirty years later."[32]

This is another way of saying that had it not been for the sacrifices of the Hungarians in 1956 and Moscow's memory of it, the countries of Eastern Europe would never have gained their independence so quickly and bloodlessly in 1989.

Like faint echoes of the Big Bang that astronomers can detect in the farthest reaches of the cosmos, the echo of that explosion in Hungary reverberated everywhere within the Communist empire. The mere mention of "Budapest 1956" or "Hungary 1956" brought it all back in a flash, and with it the thought "never again."

This in no way detracts from the erosion produced by many other uprisings, from Vorkuta to East Germany of 1953 and Poznań 1956 to Sopot and Gdynia 1970, nor the great national movements like the Prague Spring of

1968 or the Solidarity movement in Poland which began in 1980 and eventually prevailed in 1989 in such a way that it caused the whole house of cards in Eastern Europe to collapse in a matter of months.

All of these events are shining milestones in the long collapse of the twentieth century's greatest scourge. Đilas' prediction that "the Revolution in Hungary means the beginning of the end of Communism generally" held true, in spite of *Sputnik* and the fact that the geographical spread of Communism did not reach its high water mark until after Vietnam in the early 1970s.

The explosion at mid-century that was the Hungarian Revolution is now an important part of European and twentieth century history. But because it was, for those few days, so clear-cut, so clean and idealistic, and because it so completely overthrew a thoroughly totalitarian system—the first ever to do so—it is an important part of human history as well, something which having been accomplished once, may never have to be repeated.

That this was done not by Serbs or Russians, Romanians or Ukrainians, Croats or Bulgars, Czechs or Slovaks, Poles, Germans or Balts—all of whom suffered under the yoke of Communism at that time—but by Hungarians, does not seem to be a historical accident. Every Hungarian alive today, no matter where, and every Hungarian born between now and the end of European history, can rightfully take pride in that fact.

Notes

PROLOGUE

1. *Volunteers for the Gallows, Anatomy of a Show-Trial*, Béla Szaz, Chatto & Windus., London, 1971, p. 238

CHAPTER I DEMONSTRATIONS

1. U.S. Legation, Budapest tel. no. 151, October 23, 1956, National Archives, College Park, Maryland
2. Author's interview with Stephen Lakatos, Brentwood, New York December 8, 2004
3. 1956 Institute for 1956 Revolution interview no. 235 with Tibor Tankó by Gyula Nagy, 1990, translated by Judit Hajnal Ward
4. *Soviet Military Intervention in Hungary*, edited by Jenő Györkei & Miklós, Central European University Press, Budapest, 1999, p.7
5. "László Beke" is not his real name. This passage and all subsequent passages involving this individual are based on his book, *A Student's Diary*, Hutchinson of London, 1957, in which he used an alias in order to protect his relatives in Hungary.
6. *The Nineteen Days*, by George Urban, William Heinemann, London, 1957, p.16
7. *Report of the United Nations Special Committee on the Problem of Hungary, p. 5*
8. *Szabad Ifjúság*, October 21, 1956, p. 5
9. Ibid., October 19, 1956
10. This scene and other information from Szeged is based upon the author's interview with Dr. Stephen Lakatos, Brentwood, New York, December 8, 2004
11. *Szabad Ifjúság*, October 21, p. 3
12. *The 1956 Hungarian Revolution: A History in Documents*, Csaba Békés, Malcolm Byrne & János M. Rainer, Central European University Press, 2002, pp. 186–187
13. Hungarian Refugee Oral History Project of Columbia University, (HROHPCU) Interviewee M-37, p.III/4, and *East Europe*, July 1957, p. 17
14. *Szabad Nép*, October 22, 1956, p.2
15. *A Student's Diary*, p.23

16. *The First Domino*, Johanna Granville, Texas A&M University Press, College Station, Texas, 2004, p. 90
17. *Seven Days of Freedom*, Noel Barber, Stein & Day, New York, 1974, p. 39
18. *A Student's Diary*, p. 23–24
19. Urban, p. 15
20. Ibid., p. 47
21. Attila Szakolczai, Lecture at Rutgers University, October 23, 1996, p. 1
22. Ibid., p. 1
23. *Szabad Nép*, October 23, 1956, p.1
24. Györkei & Horváth, p. 8
25. Urban, p. 24
26. This passage and much of the following paragraphs are largely taken from *A Testament of Revolution* by Béla Lipták, Texas A & M University Press, College Station, Texas, 2001, pp 25—29)
27. *That Day in Budapest, October 23, 1956*, Tibor Méray, Funk & Wagnall's, New York, 1969, pp. 24–26
28. Urban, p. 24
29. Lipták, p. 30
30. Ibid., pp. 30,31
31. Méray, p.18
32. "Zoltán Horváth," not his real name, HROHPCU interviewee 21-M
33. Lipták, p.32
34. Urban, p. 25
35. Méray, p.28
36. Ibid., p. 34
37. *The First Domino*, p. 55
38. *The Revolt in Hungary,* Free Europe Committee, New York, 1957 p. 3
39. "Antal Nógrádi," not his real name, HROHPCU interviewee 13-M
40. Lipták, p. 39
41. Ibid., p. 40
42. *The First Domino*, p. 34
43. Barber, p. 36
44. "András Kiss," not his real name, HROHPCU interviewee 21-M, p. 4/III
45. "Tibor Kalombos," not his real name, HROHPCU interviewee no. 46-M p. III/6)
46. *Debrecen 1956, Revolution, National Resistance, Retaliation,* Tibor Filep, Csokonai Kiadó, 2000, p. 22, translated by András Bocz
47. Imre Garab, 1956 Institute interview no. 382 by Tibor Valuch, translated by Judit Hajnal Ward
48. *In the Name of the Working Class*, Sándor Kopácsi, Grove Press, New York, 1986, pp. 97–101
49. Ibid., pp. 101–102
50. Ibid., p.103
51. Méray, pp. 137–139
52. Lipták, p. 43
53. Méray, p. 143
54. Ibid., p.183
55. Lipták, p. 42 & 43
56. Kopácsi, pp. 103,104

57. Méray, p. 152
58. Ibid., pp. 184–5
59. Lakatos interview, "János Telegdy," not his real name, HROHPCU interviewee 23-M, p.5/III
60. *Debrecen 1956*, by Tibor Filep, Csokonai Kiadó, 2000, p. 29, translated by András Bocz, also "Tibor Kalombos," HROHPCU interviewee no 46-M, p.III/6
61. Not his real name, HROHPCU, interviewee 61-M
62. Méray, p. 151
63. Barber, p. 40–41
64. *A Student's Diary*, p. 27
65. "István Dobos," not his real name HROHPCU, interviewee 32-M, p. 5/III
66. Kopácsi p. 104
67. Györkei & Horváth, p. 16
68. Méray p. 156
69. "Hungary's Terrible Ordeal," Judith Listowel, *Saturday Evening Post*, Jan 1, 1957, p. 26
70. *The Revolt in Hungary, p. 4–5*
71. Tibor Méray p.199
72. *Documents*, p. 192
73. "János Kiss," not his real name, HROHPCU, interviewee no. 26-M, p. 5/III)
74. "László Beke," p. 29
75. Pál Madocsi," not his real name HROHPCU, interviewee 61-M, p. III 7
76. *Debrecen 1956*. p. 29, translated by András Bocz
77. "Pál Madocsi," not his real name, HROHPCU interviewee 61-M, pp. II 7,8, & 9
78. *Debrecen 1956* p. 29, translated by András Bocz
79. Interview with István Lakatos, December 8, 2004, "János Telegdy," not his real name, HROHPCU interviewee no.23-M, p. 5/III
80. *Szegedi Forradalom Kronológiája*, October 1999, given by Stephen Lakatos to author, March 2, 2005
81. *The First Domino, p. 62*
82. Kopácsi, p. 104–105
83. "László Szigeti," not his real name, HROHPCU, interviewee no. M-1, p. 5, Béla Lipták, p. 47)
84. Kopácsi, p. 106
85. Méray, p. 162
86. Ibid., p. 164
87. Ibid., p. 166,167
88. RFE monitoring from *Revolt in Hungary*, p. 5, Méray, p. 194, 195
89. "László Szigeti," HROHPCU interviewee no. M-1, p. III/4
90. Tamás Aczél in writing as recorded in Méray, pp. 167–169
91. U.S. Legation, Budapest tel. no. 154, Midnight, October 23, 1956, National Archives
92. András Molnár," not his real name, HROHPCU interviewee no. 21-M, p. 6/III
93. Méray, pp. 172,173
94. Méray, p. 30
95. *You Are All Alone*, József Kővágó, Frederick A. Praeger, New York, 1959, p. 141

CHAPTER II HUNGARY, ITS ORIGINS AND HISTORY

1. *Jewish Nobles and Geniuses in Modern Hungary*, William O. McCagg, Jr., *East European Quarterly*, Boulder, CO, 1972, pp. 114–5
2. Ibid., p. 118
3. Ibid., p. 119
4. Ibid., pp. 121,125–6
5. *The European Right*, Hans Rogger and Eugene Weber eds., *Hungary*, István Deák, University of California Press, 1962, pp. 267–8
6. Ibid., p. 372

CHAPTER III HUNGARY UNDER COMMUNISM

1. *Hungary and the Soviet Bloc*, Charles Gati, Duke University Press, Durham, 1965, p. 82
2. *Communism in Hungary: From Kun to Kádár*, Bennett Kovrig, Hoover Institution Press, Stanford University, Stanford, CA, 1979, p. 171
3. Kovrig, p. 121
4. Ibid., pp. 179–80, 183
5. Ibid., 195
6. Ibid., pp. 228, 289
7. Ibid., p. 261
8. Ibid., p. 257
9. *The Soviet Sea Around Us: A Message from Berlin, Graphische Gesellschaft Gruenewald, GmbH*, Berlin, Gruenewald, 1959, pp. 11–15
10. Kovrig, pp. 267–8
11. Ibid., p. 272
12. FEC Press release of December 20, 1954, Papers of C. D. Jackson, Box 54, Dwight D. Eisenhower Library, Abilene, Kansas
13. RFE Evaluation, Item no. 500/55, January 22, I-14021, p. 1, author's private archive (a.p.a.)
14. RFE Evaluation item no. 492/55, January 21, I/13889, p. 2. a.p.a.
15. RFE Evaluation item no. 3300, 21/55, April 25, XIV/699 p. 2, a.p.a.
16. RFE Evaluation item no. 11592/54, Dec, 29, 121.66, a.p.a.
17. RFE Evaluation item no. 904/ 55/, a.p.a.
18. RFE Evaluation item no. 1558/55, March 1, 164.91, p. 2, a.p.a.
19. RFE Evaluation item no. 1071/55, February 14, XIV/689, a.p.a.
20. RFE Evaluation item no. 878/55, February 5, IX/3071 a, a.p.a.
21. RFE Evaluation item no. 492/55, p. 6, a.p.a.
22. RFE Evaluation item no. 11610/54, a.p.a.
23. RFE Evaluation item no. 876/55. a.p.a.
24. RFE Evaluation item no. 1337/55 p. 3, a.p.a.
25. RFE Evaluation item no. 1365/55, a.p.a.
26. RFE Evaluation item no. 6379/55, a.p.a.
27. Papers of C. D. Jackson, Box 54, Dwight D. Eisenhower Library, Abilene, Kansas
28. Kovrig, p. 280
29. *Memoirs*, Mikhail Gorbachev, Doubleday, New York, 1996, p. 62
30. FRUS 1955–1957, p. 169.
31. London *Times*, Vienna, July 16, 1956
32. U.S. Legation, Budapest, Desp. No. 469, June 13, 1956, National Archives

33. Leslie B. Bain, *The Reporter*, October 2, 1956.
34. *Uprising,* p. 174
35. UP, Vienna, October 3, RFE's CNR item C-112, a.p.a.
36. Reuters, Vienna, Sept. 29, 1956, RFE's CNR item D-22, a.p.a.
37. UP, Budapest, Sept. 15, 1956, RFE's CNR item D-116, a.p.a., U.S Legation, Budapest, Desp. No. 95, September 14, 1956, National Archives
38. State Department Top Secret memorandum, 9.21/56, National Security Archive, Washington, D.C. Record Number 65235
39. Reuters, London, October 10, 1956, RFE's CNR item B-35, Reuters Vienna, October 15, 1956, RFE's CNR item D-18, a.p.a.
40. U.S. Legation, Budapest, tel. 137, October 15, 1956, National Archives
41. Urban, p. 210

CHAPTER IV EXPLOSION
1. Barber, p. 23
2. *Népszabadság*, January 22, 1957
3. Urban, p. 40
4. HROHPCU interviewee 5-F, p. 3
5. Méray, pp. 249, 250
6. Méray, p. 190, Kopácsi, p. 111, *Népszabadság,* January 22, 1957
7. *Népszabadság*, January 22, 1957, Barber, p. 31, Méray, p. 180
8. *Népszabadság*, January 22, 1957
9. Tibor Tankó, 1956 Institute interview no. 235 by Gyula Nagy, translated by Judit Hajnal Ward, p. 2
10. *Népszabadság*, January 22, 1957, Barber, p. 32
11. *Népszabadság*, January 23, 1957, Méray, p. 181, Barber, pp. 32, 33
12. *A Student's Diary*, p. 34
13. *Népszabadság,* January 23, 1957
14. Méray, p. 253
15. Kapocsi, p. 109, Méray, pp. 251, 252, 1956 Institute Interview # 274, József Nagyidai, by Adrienne Molnár, translated by Attila Kőszeghy
16. *Népszabadság*, January 23, 1957
17. "Károly Szabolcsi," not his real name, Hungarian Refugee Oral History Project of Columbia University (HROHPCU) interviewee 54/M, p. III/4
18. Barber, p. 21
19. *The Revolt in Hungary, p. 5*
20. Méray, pp. 238, 239, *Manchester Guardian,* October 25, 1956, Uprising, p. 243
21. Barber p. 37
22. Méray, pp. 283–285, Barber p. 37–38
23. Hungarian White book, *"The Counterrevolutionary Forces in the Events of October in Hungary,"* (a Kádár regime publication) Budapest, 1957, Vol. II, p. 23
24. Györkei & Horváth, p. 19
25. Györkei & Horváth, p.18, British Legation Dispatch # 521, Fry to Foreign Office, October 31, 1956, NH10110/204, Public Records Office, Kew Gardens, London
26. Barber, p. 22
27. "Beke," p. 34
28. Lipták, pp. 51, 52

29. *Daily Express,* October 24, 1956, *Uprising,* pp. 237, 238
30. *Cold War International History Project Bulletin*, Winter 1996/1997, Mark Kramer, p. 336, Györkei & Horváth, pp. 8, 10, 20, Szabó, pp. 6, 7
31. *Boy on a Rooftop*, by "Tamás Szabó," not his real name, Heinemann, London Melbourne Toronto, 1958, pp. 1–7
32. *Petőfi Circle: Forum of Reform in 1956*, András B. Hegedűs, *The Journal of Communist Studies and Transitional Politics*, vol. 13, 1987, #2, Frank Cass, London
33. Kopácsi, pp. 112, 113
34. Méray, p. 252–254
35. *The First Domino*, p. 57
36. Ibid., p. 238, endnote 104
37. Not his real name, HROHPCU interviewee 21-M, p. 7/III
38. Pál Kabelacs, 1956 Institute Interview 202 by László Örsi, Budapest, 1996, translated by Andrea Kicsák & Judit Hajnal Ward
39. Méray, pp. 286, 287, 290, 291, Litván, p. 59
40. Lipták, pp. 52, 53
41. "Szabó," pp. 8,9,10
42. Méray, p.18
43. HROHPCU interviewee no. 21-M, p. 8/III
44. *Népszabadság,* January 23, 1957
45. *The Revolt in Hungary, p. 7*
46. Lipták, pp. 53–55
47. Hungarian White Book, Vol. II, p. 20
48. *Nepszabadság*, January 23, 1957, Installment II, "The Siege of Radio Budapest."
49. Information on Gellért supplied by Ross Johnson, Hoover Institution on War, Revolution and Peace, Stanford University
50. Griffith Analysis, October 24, 1956, Central Newsroom item # C-90, a.p.a.

CHAPTER V REVOLUTION

1. Györkei & Horváth, p. 34
2. *Andropov,* Beichman and Bernstam, Stein & Day, New York, 1983, p. 149, Kopácsi, p. 121
3. Kopácsi, pp. 121,122
4. HROHPCU interviewee 33-M (clearly this is Ödön Pongrátz) p. 4
5. RFE Monitoring, October 24, 1956, a.p.a.
6. "Szabó," pp. 12–15
7. "Beke," p.38
8. "Szabó," p. 24
9. HROHPCU interviewee 33-M (clearly Ödön Pongrátz) p. 13
10. Méray, pp. 338, 339
11. RFE Monitoring, October 23, 1965, a.p.a.
12. *Neue Kurier,* Vienna, October 27, 1956 quoting Austrian businessman
13. *A History in Documents*, Document no. 26, p. 220
14. HROHPCU interviewee 25-M, p. III-4, Lomax, p. 94, Attila Szakolczai to author, February 2006
15. HROHPCU interviewee 23-M, p. 6/III
16. Györkei & Horváth, p. 41

17. Lomax, p. 98, HROHPCU interviewee 36-M, p. 4/III & 4-M, p. 2
18. Lomax, p. 83, HROHPCU interviewee 15-M, p. 5 III
19. HROHPCU Interviewee 8-M, pp. 5–7
20. Györkei & Horváth, p. 34
21. *A History in Documents*, Document no. 27, p. 225
22. István Rév, *Cold War Broadcasting*, Impact Report on a Conference organized by the Hoover Institution, Stanford University and the Cold War International History Project, October 13–14, 2004, p. 27
23. U.S. Legation, Budapest, Dispatch no. 157 to Department of State, October 24, 1956 764.00/10—2456, National Archives, College Park, Maryland
24. British Legation Budapest to Foreign Office, Confidential telegram no. 415, October 24, 1956 H 10110/83 Public Records Office, Key Gardens, London
25. U.S. Department of State Document 764.00/ 10-2456, National Archives
26. FRUS, 1955–1957, Vol. XXV, Eastern Europe, doc. 106, p. 176
27. Confidential Telegram no. 418, British Legation, Budapest to Foreign Office, H 10110/85, Public Records Office
28. *The Revolt in Hungary*, p. 11
29. *Die Presse*, Vienna, October 27, 1956, RFE's CNR item D-149
30. *The Revolt in Hungary, p. 12*
31. Ibid., p. 13
32. Györkei & Horváth, p. 35
33. *Pál Maléter*, Miklós Horváth, H & T Kiadó, Budapest, 2002, p. 64. translated by András Bocz
34. Györkei & Horváth p. 37
35. Méray, pp. 80–82
36. Kővágó, p. 152
37. 1956 Institute interview no. 294, Péter Bíró, by István Lugossy, translated by Ábel Mészáros
38. Méray, p. 83
39. Associated Press (AP), Vienna, October 25, 1956, CNR item D-194, a.p.a.
40. U.S. Legation, Budapest, Unnumbered telegram October 25, 1956, (Section FIVE) to Department of State, F760003—2184, National Archives
41. Györkei & Horváth, pp. 37–38
42. "Béla Kocsis," not his real name, HROHPCU interviewee 19-M, p. 7
43. Méray, pp. 81–83
44. 1956 Institute interview no. 294, Péter Bíró, by István Lugossy, translated by Ábel Mészáros, p. 7
45. *Hungary's Terrible Ordeal, conclusion* by Judith Listowel, *Saturday Evening Post,* January 12, 1957
46. HROHPCU interviewee 44-M, p. 9/III
47. "János Bartolmy," not his real name, HROHPCU interviewee 62-M
48. Barber, p. 90
49. Györkei & Horváth. p. 39
50. HROHPCU interviewee 62-M
51. Reuters, London, October 26, 1956, CNR, item C-172, a.p.a., Telegram 2283, U.S. Embassy, London to Department of State, October 26, 1956, National Archives
52. Györkei & Horváth, pp. 50 & 51
53. Ibid., pp. 40–41

54. Foreign Office Guidance for News Department by T. Grimshaw, October 25, 1956, NH10110/175, Public Records Office
55. Unnumbered telex (Section Four), U.S. Legation, Budapest to Department of State, October 25, 1956 F760003-2183, National Archives
56. HROHPCU interviewee 34-F, p. III/5
57. "Karoly Sabolcsi," not his real name, HROHPCU interviewee 54-M, pp. III/5 & 6
58. 1956 Institute Interview no. 225, Imre Vizi by László Eörsi translated by Abel Mészáros
59. "Beke", pp. 74 & 75
60. RFE Monitoring, Kossuth Radio. 18:44 hours, CNR item D-83, a.p.a.
61. Elek Nagy, Former Chairman of the Central Workers' Council for Csepel, 1956 Institute interview no. 22, by András Hegedűs, translated by Attila Koszeghy
62. Lomax, p. 88
63. "Kálmán Hajnal," not his real name, see 36-M below
64. HROHPCU interviewee, 36-M, p. 5/III
65. Ibid. pp. 5 7 6/III
66. HROHPCU interviewee 27-M p. III/6
67. Reuters, Vienna, October 26, 1956, CNR item B-106, a.p.a.. (Hungarian scholars today say that Herr Henne was telling complete lies)
68. United Press (UP), Vienna, October 25, 1956, CNR item D-37, a.p.a.
69. USIS October 25, 1956, CNR item D-86, a.p.a.
70. RFE Monitoring, October 25, 1956, CNR item no. D-180, U.P., Vienna, October 25, 1956 CNR item D-152, a.p.a.
71. FRUS 1955–1957, vol. XXV, Eastern Europe, doc. 104, p. 273
72. Outgoing confidential telegram Department of State to U.S. Embassy, London, 7:00 p.m. October 25, 1956, 764.00/10-2656, National Archives
73. *Moscow Diary*, Veljko Mićunović, Doubleday & Company, Garden City, N.Y., 1980, p. 127
74. Noel Barber, *Colliers* Magazine, December 15, 1956, CNR items C-25—30, a.p.a.
75. *The Revolt in Hungary p. 16*
76. Noel Barber, *Colliers* Magazine, December 15, 1956, CNR items C-30—32, a.p.a.
77. *The Revolt in Hungary, p. 16*
78. 1956 Institute interview no. 630, Gyula Taky, by László Eörsi, translated by Judit Hajnal Ward
79. *Corvin Circle 1956*, Gergely Pongrátz, 1992 (English language version provided by author's brother, András Pongrátz), p. 91
80. HROHOCU interviewee 33-M (Ödön Pongrátz), p. III/22
81. *Corvin Circle 1956*, p. 72
82. HROHPCU interviewee 33-M, p. III 7
83. Zsuzsanna Horváth (Móriné), 1956 Institute interview no. 465, by Zsuzsanna Nagy, p. 3, translated by Judit Hajnal Ward
84. 1956 Institute interview with Mrs. József Zsinka, nee Katalin Gieber, by Adrienne Molnár, translated by Judit Hajnal Ward; Ritchie McEwen, *Sunday Times*, October 27, 1956, *The Times* of London, October 29, 1956, Jeffrey Blyth, *Sunday Dispatch*, October 27, 1956, Urban p. 94–95, Bruno Tedeschi, *Il Giornale d'Italia*, Rome October 30, 1956, Noel Barber, *The Daily Mail*, October 28, 1956, Homer Bigert, *New York Times*, October 28, 1956
85. Reuters London, October 26, 1956, CNR items D-244 & D-245, a.p.a.
86. *FRUS*, 1955–1957, pp. 296–299

87. Marian Bielicki, *Po Prostu*, November 25, 1956, *The Hungarian Revolution, a White Book*, edited by Melvin Lasky, Martin Secker & Warburg, Ltd, 1957, pp. 87,88
88. Reuters, Strasbourg, October 26, 1956, CNR item C-244, a.p.a.
89. A. P., Paris, October 26, 1956, CNR item C-242, a.p.a.
90. Reuters, Rome October 26,1956, CNR item D-203, a.p.a.
91. Reuters, Madrid, October 26, 1956, CNR item D-247, a.p.a.
92. A.P., Vienna, October 26, 1956, CNR item C-168, a.p.a.
93. "Szabó," pp. 43 & 44
94. HROHPCU interviewee 33-M (Odon Pongrátz) p. 4, Barber, pp. 64 & 65
95. *Corvin Circle 1956*, pp. 92 & 191
96. Györkei & Horváth, pp. 49 & 50
97. U.S. Embassy, Moscow telegram no. 984 to Department of State, October 26, 1956, 764.00/10-2656, National Archives
98. U.S. Embassy, Paris, telegram no. 1992, October 26, 1956, 764.00/10-2656, National Archives
99. "Beke," pp. 29 & 30
100. Kopácsi, pp. 131, 132
101. Used with permission of the recipient, Éva Veress, to the author
102. Györkei & Horváth, pp. 51–54
103. *Revolt in Hungary* pp. 22 & 23
104. Ibid., p. 24, Urban pp. 102 & 103
105. Reuters, Budapest, October 27, 1956 CNR item C-23, a.p.a.
106. *Hungarian Tragedy* by Peter Fryer, Dennis Dobson, London, 1956, pp. 15—24
107. *Corvin Circle 1956*, p. 102–3
108. HROHPCU interviewee 27-M, pp. III/7–8
109. *The Revolt in Hungary*, p. 27
110. Györkei & Horváth, p. 21
111. Urban, p. 113
112. *New York Times,* October 27, 1956 p.1
113. U.S Legation, Budapest tel. no. 168 to Department of State, October 26, 1956, 764.00/10-2756, National Archives
114. FRUS, 1955–57, p. 310
115. British Legation, Budapest Confidential cypher telegram nos. 456, 462 and 464, to Foreign Office, October 27, 1956, NH10110 116, 118 & 120, Public Records Office
116. British Legation. Budapest, Secret cypher telegram no. 465 to F.O. October 27, 1956 NH10110/121, Public Records Office
117. Priority, Confidential telegram no. 2186 from F.O. to British Legation, Budapest, October 27, 1956 NH10110/128, Public Records Office
118. Urban p. 142
119. Immediate Secret telegram no. 180 from United Kingdom Permanent Delegation, Paris, to F.O. October 27, 1956, 122380 213909, Public Records Office
120. F.O. Draft Secret Paper, October 27, 1956, 122389 213909, Public Records Office
121. Department of State, Incoming Telegram no. 417, from New York, October 27, 1956, 764.00/102756 HBS, National Archives
122. Department of State, Incoming Telegram no. 421 from New York, October 27, 1956, National Archives
123. UK Mission confidential telegram no. 945, to Foreign Office, October 27, 1956, NH10110/110, Public Records Office

124. Reuters, Vienna, CNR items B-119, C-84 and C-160, a.p.a., Sir G. Wallinger, British Ambassador to Vienna priority confidential telegram no. 198 to Foreign Office, October 26, 1956, NH10110/124, Public Records Office
125. RFE Hungarian Analysis to 1330 hours, October 27, 1956, CNR items C-220 and C-221, a.p.a.
126. Györkei & Horváth, pp. 55 & 56
127. *The First Domino*, pp. 82 & 83, Györkei & Horváth pp. 65 & 65
128. *New York Times*, October 28, 1956
129. *Corvin Circle 1956*, pp. 124–126
130. Györkei & Horváth pp. 57–60
131. Béla Király, *LIFE* magazine, February 17, 1957, p. 119
132. Ibid., p. 31
133. FRUS, 1955–1957, Confidential U.S. telegram 916, Vienna to State, p. 319
134. Noel Barber, The London *Daily Mail*, October 29, 1956
135. *The Revolt in Hungary*, p. 33, Lasky p. 111, Györkei & Horváth, p. 68
136. Lasky, p. 117
137. *Corvin Circle 1956* pp. 114–116
138. HROHPCU, 33-M, (Ödön Pongrátz), p. III/12
139. *Corvin Circle 1956*, pp. 116–118
140. *Pál Maléter*, p. 100, translated by András Bocz
141. State Department Incoming telegram no. 423 from Rio de Janeiro, October 28, 1956, National Archives
142. A.P., Berlin, October 28, 1956, CNR item B-31, a.p.a.
143. *Corwin Circle 1956*, pp. 107–111
144. Incoming Telegram from Budapest no.171 to Department of State, October 28, 1956, National Archives
145. Confidential cypher telegram no. 472 from Budapest to Foreign Office, October 28, 1956, NH10110/1388, Public Records Office
146. RFE Special, Fritz Hier, Nickelsdorf, Austria, October 28, 1956, CNR items D-125 & D-126, a.p.a.
147. Dept. of State Incoming Telegram no. 979, U.S. Embassy, Moscow to Department, October 28, 1956, National Archives
148. Noel Barber, London *Daily Mail*, November 2, 1956, CNR items C-35-37, a.p.a., Sefton Delmer, *The Daily Express*, October 30, 1956, CNR item C-51, a.p.a.
149. Kramer p. 367, János Rainer, Rutgers U. lecture, November 1, 1996, pp. 5–7
150. *New York Times,* October 29, 1956, Alistair Cooke, *Manchester Guardian*, October 28, 1956, UN verbatim record, Security Council, October 28, 1956
151. USUN NY telegram no. 424 to State, October 28, 1956, National Archives

CHAPTER VI REVOLUTION TRIUMPHANT (PART 1)

1. U.S. Legation, Budapest, telegram no. 182, October 29, 1956, National Archives
2. U. S. Legation, Budapest, tel. no. 187, October 30, 1956, 764.00/10-3056, National Archives
3. HROHPCU interviewee, M-33, (Ödön Pongrátz), p. III/14
4. Gordon Shepherd, *The Daily Telegraph*, London, October 30, 1956, John MacCormac, *The New York Times*, October 30, 1956, U.S. Legation Budapest telegram No. 187 to

Department of State, October 30, 1957, National Archives, Peter Stephens, *The Daily Mirror*, London, October 30, 1956

5. RFE Monitoring, CNR item C-220, a.p.a.
6. Marian Bielicki, *Pro Prostu*, Warsaw December 9, 1956, Laski p. 118
7. Lasky, pp. 126–7
8. *The Revolt in Hungary*, pp. 36–37, RFE Monitoring, October 29, 1956, CNR item C-212, a.p.a.
9. *The Revolt in Hungary,* p. 37
10. A. J. Cavendish, United Press, October 29, 1956, Lasky, pp. 129–130
11. *Corvin Circle 1956*, pp. 152–156
12. Béla Király, *LIFE* magazine, February 18, 1957 pp. 120–3, Lasky p. 134
13. British Embassy, Moscow, Confidential cypher dispatch, no. 1502, October 29, 1956, H 10110/167, Public Records Office
14. Secret shared dispatch, U.S. Embassy, Moscow with F.O. October 30, 1956 FO 371/ 122386 213909, Public Records Office, T. Popovski, *Borba*, Belgrade, October 30, 1956
15. U.S. Legation, Budapest tel. No. 176, October 29, 1956, National Archives
16. U.S. Legation Budapest tel. No. 180, October 29, 1956, National Archives
17. U.S. Legation, Budapest, tel. No. 180, October 29, 1956, National Archives, FRUS, 1955–1957, pp. 321, 22
18. FRUS, 1955–1957, p. 328
19. Ibid., p. 328
20. United Kingdom Delegation to the United Nations tel. No. 957 to F.O., October 28, 1956, Public Records Office
21. F.O. memorandum on Budapest tel. 482 para. 1, H10110/245, Public Records Office
22. F.O. tel. No. 809 to British Legation, Budapest, October 29, 1956, Public Records Office
23. Debate and Questions in British Parliament, House of Commons, October 29, 1956, RFE's CNR item B-170, a.p.a.
24. U.S. Embassy, Belgrade tel. No. 553 to State, October 29, 1956, National Archives, Reuters, Belgrade October 29, 1956, RFE's CNR item D-148 & D-168, a.p.a.
25. PAP (Polish Press Agency) Warsaw, October 29, 1956, RFE's CNR item D-196, a.p.a.
26. From a Foreign Office translation, FO 371/122380 213909, Public Records Office
27. RFE special from Knaur, Stockholm, November 5, CNR item C-95, a.p.a.
28. RFE Special from Knaur, Stockholm, November 2, CNR item D-68, a.p.a.
29. Unclassified Despatch no. 80, U.S. Consulate General, Toronto, October 29, 1956, National Archives, Unclassified Despatch no. 34, U. S. Consulate Vancouver, October 29, 1956, National Archives
30. Department of State Memorandum of Conversation, "Situation in Hungary," October 29, 1956, National Archives
31. U.S. Consulate, Munich tel. No. 210, October 29, 1956, National Archives
32. RFE Monitoring, October 29, 1956, CNR items C-204, B-39 and B-40, a.p.a.
33. Reuter, Vienna, October 29, 1956, RFE's CNR items D-312, a.p.a., U.S, Legation, Budapest, tel. no. 182, October 29, 1956, National Archives
34. HROHPCU interviewee 29-M, p. 10
35. RFE Monitoring, October 29, 1956, CNR items D-299, D-300, a.p.a.
36. Reuter, Tel Aviv, October 29, 1956, RFE's CNR item D-23
37. Urban, p. 35
38. *The Reluctant Satellites*, Leslie B. Bain, MacMillan Company, New York, 1960, p. 158

39. Davis Davidson, *Daily Herald*, London, October 30, 1956
40. *The Revolt in Hungary*, p. 39, RFE Hungarian Monitoring, October 30, 1956, CNR item D-216, a.p.a.
41. Endre Márton, Associated Press, Budapest, October 30, 1956, RFE's CNR item D-252, a.p.a.
42. RFE Monitoring, October 30, 1956, CNR item D-91, a.p.a.
43. Per Olaf Csongovai, 1956 Institute interview no. 420, 1992 by László Eörsi, translated by Attila Kőszeghy
44. MTI (Hungarian Telegraph Agency), Győr, October 30, 1956, Laski, p.148
45. Urban, p. 168
46. RFE Monitoring, October 30, 1956, CNR item C-57, a.p.a.
47. RFE Monitoring, October 30, 1956, CNR item D-212, a.p.a.
48. *The Revolt in Hungary*, p. 44
49. Györkei & Horváth, p.71
50. RFE Monitoring, October 30, 1956, CNR item D-211, a.p.a.
51. Reuters, Vienna, October 30. 1956, CNR item D-185, a.p.a.
52. The London *Times*, editorial, October 30, 1956
53. *Corwin Circle 1956, pp. 189—192*
54. Mark Kramer, *Cold War International History Project Bulletin*, no. 8–9, 1997, p. 368, Györkei & Horváth, pp. 73–74
55. *Documents*, document no. 47, p. 292–3
56. Kopácsi, pp 151–2
57. *The Revolt in Hungary*, p. 47, Urban p. 166
58. Ibid., pp. 42, 43, RFE Monitoring, October 30 1956, CNR item B-99, a.p.a.
59. *The Revolt in Hungary*, p. 44
60. Ibid., pp. 42, 43
61. British Legation Budapest tel. No. 515, October 30, 1956 to F.O., H10110/197, Public Records Office
62. John MacCormac, *New York Times*, October 30, 1956, Urban pp. 198–200, *Corvin Circle 1956*, p. 167
63. John Sadovy, *LIFE* magazine's *Hungary's Fight for Freedom*, a special 96-page picture report , December 1956, pp. 27–28, József Nagyidai, 1956 Institute interview no. 247, 1989, pp. 14–15, by Adrienne Molnár, translated by Attila Kőszeghy
64. *The Jewish Chronicle*, London, December 7, 1956
65. RFE Monitoring, October 30, 1956, CNR item C-35, a.p.a.
66. Urban , p. 172
67. József Cardinal Mindzsenty, *Mindszenty Memoirs*, MacMillan, 1974, pp. 135–6, "The Mindszenty Story," *New York Herald Tribune*, December 16, 1956, *The Revolt in Hungary*, p. 46
68. Sydney Gruson, *New York Times*, Warsaw October 30, 1956, PAP (Polish Press Agency) Warsaw, October 30, 1956, CNR item D-221, a.p.a.
69. CETEKA, (Czechoslovak Telegraph Agency), Prague, October 30, 1956, CNR item C-120, a.p.a
70. London *Daily Telegraph*, Berlin, October 30, 1956, CNR item C-313, a.p.a.
71. RFE Monitoring, October 30, 1956 CNR item C-256, a.p.a., Welles Hangen, *New York Times*, Bucharest, Oct 31, 1956, British Legation, Budapest, October 30, tel. No. 869, FO 371/ 122398 213909, Public Records Office, Tibor Karcsó, 1956 Institute interview no. 487, 1993, by István Gagyi-Balla, translated by Judit Hajnal Ward

72. Confidential Letters from Ambassador Wallinger to F.O., October 30, 1956, H10110/239 F.O. 371/122380 213909, Public Records Office
73. British Legation, Budapest, cypher cable no. 498, delivered October 30, 1956, H100110/172, 122378, Public Records Office
74. F.O. Tel. No. 566 to UKDEL Paris, October 30, 1956, NH10110/195, Public Records Office
75. F.O. Cypher/OTP no. 1399 to UK UN Delegation in New York, October 30, 1956, F.O. 371/ 12383, Public Records Office
76. U.S. State Department Circular telegram 322, October 30, 1956, National Archives
77. British Embassy, Moscow restricted dispatch to F.O., June 4, 1956, FO 371/122068, Public Records Office, also see Confidential Minutes by G. G. Brown of F.O. meeting, June 5, 1956, Public Records Office
78. See also page 190 of *Nikita Khrushchev and the Creation of a Superpower*, Pennsylvania State University Press, University Park, Pa., 2000, where his son, Sergei Khrushchev, writes of his father's plans for troop reductions.
79. Kramer, p. 368
80. *Khrushchev, the Man and his Era*, William Taubman, W.W. Norton, New York, 2003, p. 358, note 122
81. British Embassy, Moscow cypher telegram no. 1519, October 31, 1956 FO 371/122/068, Public Records Office

CHAPTER VII REVOLUTION TRIUMPHANT (PART 2)

1. *Nikita Khrushchev and the Creation of a Superpower*. p. 191
2. *Khrushchev Remembers*, translated and edited by Strobe Talbott, Little, Brown & Co., Boston, 1970, p. 417
3. Ibid. p. 418
4. *Documents*, pp. 307–308
5. *Khrushchev Remembers*, pp. 418, 419, *Documents*, pp. 308, 309
6. *FRUS*, 1955–1957, pp. 348–9
7. *Khrushchev Remembers*, p. 419
8. British Legation, Budapest, tel. no. 516, Sir Leslie Fry to F.O. October 31, 1956, HI0II0/210, Public Records Office
9. FRUS, 1955–1957, p. 349, 350
10. British Legation, Budapest, telegrams nos. 517 & 524, Budapest to F.O. October 31, 1956, H10110/202 & 206, Public Records Office
11. HROHPCU interviewee 29-M, p. 11/111
12. RFE Monitoring, October 31, 1956, CNR item B-103, a.p.a.
13. *The First Domino*, p. 72, RFE Monitoring, 31, 1956 CNR item D-173, a.p.a.
14. RFE Special by phone, Koch/Palásthy, CNR item D-60, a.p.a.
15. RFE Special from Paris, CNR item D-78, a.p.a., Urban, p. 133, United Press, Berlin, October 31, 1956, CNR item C-77, a.p.a., Zoltán Tótfalvi, *Reactions to the 1956 Revolution in Transylvania, Romania* p. 4 of translated by András Bocz
16. RFE Special from Stockholm, October 31, 1956, CNR item D-152, a.p.a., F.O. minute 92, October 31, 1956, NHI0110/246, Public Records Office
17. FRUS, 1955–1957, pp. 356–7
18. RFE Griffith Analysis, October 31, 1956, CNR C-18. a.p.a.

19. U.P., Washington, D.C., October 31, 1956, text of President's speech, RFE's CNR items D-237-39, a.p.a

20. *Nikita Khrushchev and the Creation of a Superpower*, pp 195–197

21. Ibid., pp. 197–8

22. Reuter, Vienna November 1, 1956, RFE's CNR item B-51, a.p.a.

23. RFE Monitoring, November 1, 1956, CNR item C-86, a.p.a

24. Barrett McGurn, *New York Herald Tribune*, November 1, 1956, CNR items C29, C-153, C-188, a.p.a.

25. Reuter, Budapest, November 1, 1956, CNR, item D-77, a.p.a.

26. *Documents*, doc. No. 61, pp. 321–3

27. *Pál Maléter*, Miklós Horváth, H & J Kiadó, Budapest, 2002, p. 110, translated by András Bocz

28. RFE Monitoring, November 1, 1956. CNR item D-112. a.p.a.

29. RFE Monitoring, November 1, 1956, CNR item C-208, a.p.a., Laski, p. 168

30. Welles Hangen, *New York Times*, Bucharest, November 1, 1956, A.P., Vienna, November 1, 1956, CNR item D-75. a.p.a.

31. RFE Special, Eric Bourne, Belgrade, November 1, 1956, CNR item D-87, a.p.a.

32. RFE Yugoslav Evaluation and Research, November 1, 1956, CNR item C-108, a.p.a.

33. U.P. and Reuters, Berlin, November 1, 1956, CNR items B-108 and C-9, a.p.a.

34. Sydney Gruson, *New York Times*, Warsaw, November 1, 1956

35. *Documents*, doc. No. 62, p. 324

36. *Gentleman Spy, The Life of Allen Dulles*, Peter Grose, Houghton Mifflin Company, 1994, Boston, New York, p. 439

37. U.S. Legation, Budapest tel. No. 210, November 1, 1956, National Archives

38. *Documents*, doc. No. 64, p. 328

39. Laski p. 171, RFE Special, Vienna, November 1, 1956, CNR item C-169, a.p.a.

40. Györkei & Horváth, p.151

41. RFE Monitoring, November 1, 1956, CNR item D-182, a.p.a.

42. RFE Monitoring, November 1, 1956, CNR item D-100, a.p.a.

43. RFE Special, Sopron, November 1, 1956, CNR item C-25, a.p.a.

44. George Palaczi-Horvath, *Der Monat,* Berlin, March 1957, *The First Domino,* p. 128

45. Laski, p. 183

46. Much of the above and following draws heavily upon an article by Gordon Gaskill entitled "Time Table of a Failure," first carried in the *Virginia Quarterly* and reprinted in the December 1958 magazine *Best Articles and Stories*

47. Department Outgoing telegram 228 to USUN, October 31, 1956, F769001—0360, National Archives

48. Outgoing Telegram to USUN New York, NIACT 234, November 1, 1956, F769001-0375, National Archives

49. RFE's CNR November 1, 1956 items B-95 & C-248, a.p.a.

50. Laski, p. 187, RFE's CNR items B-93, C-283. D-157, a.p.a.

51. FE's CNR items C-160, 161, a.p.a.

52. Laski, p. 204

53. Gordon Shepherd, *Daily Telegraph*, Budapest, November 2, 1956, Katherine Clark, INS, Budapest, November 2, 1956, PAP Warsaw, November 2, 1956, CNR items B-26, B-74, C-31, C-111, a.p.a.

54. *The Hungarian Revolution of 1956,* Béla Kiraly, *Thought Patterns,* no. 7, Issue on East-

West Problems, St . John's University, N.Y. 1960., p.88, Princeton University Library's Rare Book Collection.
55. RFE Monitoring, CNR item C-259, a.p.a.
56. Laski, p. 198
57. RFE monitoring, CNR item C-252, a.p.a.
58. Henry Giniger, *New York Times*, Miskolc, November 2, 1956, CNR item C-205, a.p.a.
59. Geoffry Blyth, *Daily Mail,* Budapest, November 2, 1956, CNR items C-33, C-163, C-180, D-52, a.p.a.
60. John MacCormac, *New York Times*, November 3, 1956
61. RFE Special, Vienna November 2, 1956, CNR items C-71-83, a.p.a.
62. FE Special, Gedye, Vienna, November 2, 1956, CNR item C-157, a.p.a.
63. RFE Special, Gedye, Vienna, November 2, 1956, CNR item C-155, a.p.a.
64. Laski, p. 202
65. USUN to Department of State, tel. 471, November 2, 1951, National Archives
66. Ibid.
67. Col. László Zólomy, 1956 Institute Interview no. 194, 1989, by Gyula Nagy p. 221, translated by Andrea Kicsák
68. U.P., Budapest, November 1, 1956. RFE's CNR items C-94, C-120, a.p.a.
69. RFE Special, Gedye from Vienna, November 2, 1956, CNR items C -155-6. a.p.a.
70. Reuters, Prague, November 2, 1956, CNR item C-135, a.p.a.
71. Harry Gilroy, *New York Times*, Berlin, November 2, 1956
72. A.P., Vienna November 2, 1956, CNR item B-87. a.p.a
73. RFE Special, Paris, November 2, 1956, CNR items C-354-5, a.p.a.
74. *Spectator*, London, November 2, 1956
75. *New York Post,* November 2, 1956
76. RFE Griffith Analysis, November 2, 1956, CNR item D149, a.p.a.
77. *Documents*, Document 70, pp. 336–9
78. British Embassy, Moscow to F.O. telegrams 1533 & 1537, November 2, 1956, Public Records Office
79. *Documents*, Document 76, pp. 348–351
80. *Khrushchev Remembers*, pp. 420–22, *Nikita Khrushchev and the Creation of a Superpower*, pp. 198–201, Granville, p. 105
81. FRUS, 1955–1957, pp. 366–7
82. *New York Times*, November 2, 1956
83. Part of this paragraph and much of what follows is taken from Gordon Gaskill's "Timetable of a Failure," first carried in the *Virginia Quarterly* and reprinted in the December 1958 issue *of Best Articles and Stories*
84. A.P., UN, N.Y. November 2, 1956, CNR item B-86, a.p.a.
85. British Embassy, Vienna, tel. No, 240, November 2, 1956, to Foreign Office, 122380 213909, Public Records Office
86. FRUS, 1955–1957, p. 364
87. British UN delegation tel. No. 1027 to F.O., NH10110/292 Public Records Office
88. Based on a memorandum of telephone conversation, November 2, 1956,4:11 p.m., FRUS, 1955–1957, p. 365
89. Gaskill, pp. 36, 37, British UN Mission telegram no. 1027 to F.O. November 2, 1956, NH10110/292, Public Records Office
90. USUN Telegram to Dept. of State, 11:00 p.m., November 2, 1956, FRUS. p. 368, 369
91. Reuter, Ronald Farquhar, Budapest. November 3, 1956, CNR item D-56, a.p.a.

92. Excerpt from István Angyal's Confession, *Kortárs Krónika 1956,* Budapest 2001, pp. 156–7, translated by András Bocz
93. RFE Monitoring, November 3, 1956, CNR item B-166, a.p.a.
94. RFE Monitoring, CNR item D-361, a.p.a.
95. Fritz P. Molden, *Die Presse*, November 13, 1956
96. RFE Monitoring, November 3, 1956, CNR item D-187, a.p.a.
97. RFE Special, Leason, Vienna, November 3, 1956, CNR item D-180, a.p.a.
98. RFE Monitoring, November 3, 1956, CNR item C-6, a.p.a.
99. RFE Monitoring, November 3, 1956, CNR item D-188, a.p.a.
100. RFE Special Report, Vienna, November 3, 1956, CNR item C-125, a.p.a.
101. RFE Monitorinng, November 3, 1956, CNR item D-188, a.p.a.
102. Katherine Clark, INS, Mosonmagyaróvár, Hungary, UP, Vienna, London *Times*, November 3, 1956, CNR items D-273, A-99, C-3, a.p.a.
103. Noel Barber, *Daily Mail*, London, November 10, 1956, CNR items C-41-2, a.p.a.
104. Reuters, Geneva, November 3, 1956, CNR item C-124, a.p.a.
105. UP, Vienna, November 3, 1956, CNR item C-59, a.p.a.
106. TASS, Budapest, November 3, 1956, RFE's CNR item B-2; RFE Political Advisor's Office's "Soviet Propaganda on Hungary," CNR item C-142, a.p.a.
107. UP, Berlin, November 3, 1956, RFE's CNR item C-140, a.p.a., RFE Evaluation & Research. East German Reaction, CNR item D-214, a.p.a.
108. PAP, Warsaw, November 3, 1956, RFE's CNR item D-210, a.p.a., Sydney Gruson, *New York Times*, Warsaw, November 3, 1956
109. Welles Hangen, *New York Times*, Bucharest, November 2, 1956
110. RFE Special, Knauer from Stockholm, November 3, 1956, CNR item D-265, a.p.a.
111. INS, Washington, November 3, 1956, CNR item D-168, a.p.a.
112. RFE Monitoring, November 3, 1956, CNR items C-77-8, C-147, RFE Evaluation and Research November 3, D-121 and RFE Evaluation and Research November 16, C-17, a.p.a.
113. *The Revolt in Hungary*, pp.79, 80
114. Malin Notes as translated by Mark Kramer, *Cold War International History Project Bulletin*, no. 8–9, pp. 397–8
115. FRUS, 1955–1957, pp. 370–1
116. Judith Gyenes (Mrs. Pál Maléter), Kortárs *Krónika, 1956*. Budapest, 2001, p. 156, translated by András Bocz
117. Barber, p. 173
118. Ibid., pp. 173–5
119. Kopácsi, p. 179–83
120. British Legation, Budapest, tel. nos. 560 &562, November 3, 1956 NH10110/260 and 289, Public records Office
121. British Legation, Budapest, tel. nos. 554,556, 563 November 3, 1956 H10110/256/258/286, Public Records Office
122. U.S. Legation, Budapest cables nos. 219, 220, 221, 222, 224, 226, Budapest, November 3, 1956, National Archives
123. FRUS, 1955–1957, pp. 373–4
124. RFE Analysis, 6:00 p.m., November 3, 1956, CNR items D-78-9, a.p.a.
125. British Mission to UN to F.O. tel. 1038, November 3, 1956, NH10110/293, Public Records Office
126. Ibid, p. 2

127. This passage, and many following, is based on the article "Timetable of a Failure," by Gordon Gaskill (see endnote 46)

CHAPTER VIII THE SECOND INTERVENTION

1. Györkei & Horváth, p. 106
2. Kopácsi, pp. 183–4
3. Györkei & Horváth, pp. 106–109
4. József Cardinal Mindszenty, *Memoirs*, MacMillan, New York, 1974, pp. 211–12, Leslie B. Bain, *Daily Express*, London, December 7, 1956, Fr. József Vecsey, *N.Y. Herald Tribune* (Paris), December 10, 1956
5. Kopácsi, pp. 187–189
6. Ernst Halperin, *Münchner Merkur,* November 15, 1956, CNR item D-114, a.p.a.
7. British Legation tel. No. 567 Fry to F.O., November 4, 1956, NH10110/264, Public Records Office
8. Fritz Molden, "Seven Days on the Budapest Battlefield," *Die Presse*, November 13, 1956, Dr. Herbert Schiff, "Seven Days About Which the World Should Have Heard Nothing,." *Neues Österreich*, November 13, 1956
9. Györkei & Horváth, pp. 109–110
10. Barber, p. 184
11. Györkei & Horváth, pp. 112–113
12. Molden, *Die Presse*, November 13, 1956 p. 3
13. Unnumbered telex, U.S. Legation. Budapest, pp. 1–18, November 4, 1956, F760003-2211–2228, National Archives
14. British Legation, Budapest, November 4, 1956, tel. nos. 567,575, 577 & 578 NH10110/264,271,272, & tel. No. 346, November 5, 1956, NH10110/215[k] Public Records Office
15. Gordon Gaskill, p. 41, Urban, p. 257, USIS, RFE's CNR item D-138, UP and Reuters, United Nations, N.Y. November 4, 1956, CNR items B-8 and B-32, a.p.a.
16. UKUN delegation tel. No. 1139 to F.O., November 8, 1956 H10110/413, Public Records Office
17. Ernst Halperin, *Münchner Merkur*, November 4, 1956, CNR item D-113, a.p.a.
18. *Corvin Circle 1956*, Gergely Pongrátz, pp. 251–258, (English version), Barber, pp. 184–5. According to Dr. Attila Szakolczai, Gergely Pongrátz turned against Iván-Kóvács on November 4, held him prisoner as a "traitor," but was dissuaded from executing him. Instead he had him taken during the night under escort to the Kilian Barracks. On the way the Russians opened fire. One escort was killed, the other, Péter Renner, managed to return to Corvin, while Iván-Kóvács escaped. The Russians later caught him and both he and Renner were tried and executed by the Kádár government.
19. István Szigetvári, 1956 Institute interview no. 371, p. 73, by László Eörsi, translated by Judit Mészáros Ward
20. *Documents*, doc. 87, pp.389–90 translated by Judit Hajnal Ward
21. These texts are taken from *The Revolt in Hungary*, pp. 80–92
22. Secret Memorandum, Department of State, November 4, 1956, 764 00/11-456, National Archives
23. White House Press Release, November 4, 1956, 764 00/11-456, National Archives
24. Pongrátz, pp. 268–273

25. U.S. Legation, Budapest, "Messages received between November 5–11," Despatch no. 238, December 11, 1956, National Archives
26. U.S. Legation, Budapest, tel. No 235, November 5, 1956, National Archives
27. Reuters (delayed) Budapest, November 8, 1956, CNR item D-98, a.p.a.
28. U.S. Legation, Budapest, tel. nos. 234,235, 237, November 5, 1956, National Archives
29. Halperin, *Münchner Merkur,* November 15, 1956, CNR item D-113, a.p.a.
30. U.S. Legation, Budapest, tel. nos. 239, November 13, 1956, and no. 277, Nov 5, 1956, National Archives, Györkei & Horváth p. 103, Granville, p. 108
31. RFE Monitoring, November 5, 1956, CNR items B-103, C-18, D-95, a.p.a., RFE Special Vienna, C-138, Reuters, Vienna, November 5, 1956, CNR item B-38, USIS CNR item C-215, a.p.a.
32. RFE Monitoring, November 5, 1956, CNR item C-218, a.p.a.
33. RFE Monitoring as recorded in *The Revolt in Hungary,* pp.91, 92, 94
34. UP, Vienna, November 5, 1956, CNR item B-5, a.p.a.
35. Attis Jungstrom, *Svenske Dagbladet,* Stockholm, November 12, 1956, RFE item C-64, a.p.a.
36. INS, Paris, November, 5, 1956, RFE's CNR item C-261, a.p.a.
37. RFE Special, Paris, November 5, 1956, CNR item C-186, a.p.a.
38. RFE Special, Rome, November 5, 1956, CNR item A-75, a.p.a.
39. Reuters, Berlin, November 5, 1956, CNR item C-176, a.p.a.
40. UP, Amsterdam, November 5, 1956, CNR item C-223, a.p.a.
41. *Chicago Tribune,* AP, Reuters, Vienna, November 5, 1956, CNR items B-69, B-112, C-235, a.p.a.
42. RFE Special, Vienna, November 5, 1956, CNR item D-149, a.p.a.
43. RFE's Political Adviser's Office analysis, CNR item C-120, a.p.a.
44. TASS, Moscow, November 5, 1956, RFE's CNR item D-91 & D-144, AP, Washington, November 5, 1956, CNR item D-204, a.p.a.
45. British Legation, Budapest, Tel. No. 607, November 6, 1956, H10110/341, Public Records Office
46. RFE Analysis of Hungarian Developments, CNR item B-134, Reuters, London, November 7, 1956, CNR item C-108, *Revolt in Hungary,* p. 102
47. British Legation, tel. No. 609, November 6, 1956, NH10110/343, Public Records Office
48. Reuters, Prague, November 6, 1956, CNR item D-178, RFE Eval. & Research, CNR item D-166, a.p.a.
49. U.S. Legation, Budapest, unnumbered telegram, pp. 5 & 6, December 11, 1956, National Archives
50. Fritz Molden, *Die Presse,* Vienna, November 15, 1956, Herbert Schiff, *Neues Österreich,* Vienna November 14, 1956
51. Fritz Molden, *Die Presse,* Vienna, November 15, 1956, Reuters, Vienna, November 6, 1956, CNR item D-83, a.p.a.
52. USIS, Vienna, November 6, 1956, CNR item D-373. a.p.a
53. U.S. Legation, Budapest, Open tel. pp. 3–4, December 11, 1956, U.S Legation, Budapest, tel. No. 242, November 6, 1956, 764.00/11-656, National Archives
54. FRUS, 1955–1957, pp. 401–403
55. UP, Vienna, November 6, 1956, CNR item D-226, a.p.a.
56. RFE Special from Graz, November 8, 1956, CNR item D-203, a.p.a.
57. RFE Special, Koch/Palásthy, November 6, 1956, CNR item D-251, a.p.a.
58. RFE Monitoring, November 6, 1956, CNR items C-15, C-104, D-161, a.p.a.

59. *The Revolt in Hungary*, pp. 94, 95, 96
60. Reuters & AP, Luxembourg, November 6, 1956, CNR items D-291 & D-185, a.p.a., A.A.W. Landymere to British F.O. November 8, 1956, NH 10110/425 Public Records Office
61. UP, Amsterdam, INS, Madrid, RFE Special, Paris, all November 6, 1956, CNR items B-12, B-38, D-2, D-207, D-239, a.p.a.
62. UP, Buenos Aires, November 6, 1956, CNR items D-376, D-388, a.p.a.
63. RFE Special, Vienna, November 6, 1956, CNR item C-119, a.p.a.
64. RFE Special, Stockholm, November 6, 1956, CNR item D-115, a.p.a.
65. RFE Specials, New York, November 6, 1956, CNR items C-162, D-111, a.p.a.
66. RFE Special, London, November 6, 1956, CNR, item C-201, a.p.a.
67. TASS Moscow, November 6, 1956, CNR items A-1, A3, A-4, Reuters, London, November 6, 1956, CNR items D-119,D-127, a.p.a.
68. "Szabó," p. 84
69. Ibid., pp. 86–100
70. Halperin, *Münchner Merkur*, November 6, 1956, CNR item D-116, a.p.a.
71. Reuters, Belgrade, November 7, 1956, CNR item D-246, USIS, Vienna, November 7, 1956, CNR item D-203, a.p.a., U.S. Legation, Budapest, tel. 248, November 7, 1956, National Archives
72. British Legation, Budapest, tel. no. 618, November 7, 1956 NH10110/371, Public Records Office
73. Herbert Schiff, *Neues Österreich*, November 14, 1956, p. 10
74. RFE Daily Background, November 7, 1956, CNR item D-211, 212, a.p.a.
75. RFE Specials Koch/Palásthy, Hungarian Border, November 7, 1956, CNR items D-152,3,4, a.p.a.
76. RFE Special, Collins, Vienna, November 7, 1956, CNR item C-47, a.p.a.
77. TASS, Budapest, November 7, 1956, CNR item A-15, a.p.a.
78. RFE Monitoring, CNR items B-119, 120, a.p.a.
79. Reuters, Paris, November 7, 1956, CNR item D-185, RFE Special, Dreyfuss, November 7, 1956 CNR item D-185, a.p.a.
80. AP, New York, November 7, 1956, CNR item D-313. a.p.a.
81. *New York Herald Tribune*, November 7, 1956, CNR items C-151, 152, a.p.a.
82. *New York Times*, November 7, 1956
83. USIS, Vienna & *New York Times*, Vienna November 7, 1956, CNR items D-64 & C-107, a.p.a.
84. USIS, November 7, 1956, CNR items D-245 & D-122, a.p.a.
85. István Szigetvári, 1956 Institute Interview no. 371, pp. 7–8, 1991, by László Eörsi, translated by Judit Mészáros Ward
86. USIS November 7, 1956, CNR item D-122, a.p.a.
87. British Legation, Reykjavík, November 8, 1956, tel. no. 151, Public Records Office
88. Reuters, Bonn, November 7, 1956, CNR item D-252, a.p.a.
89. AP and Reuters, Moscow, November 7, 1956, CNR items B-23, B-236 & C-82, a.p.a., British Embassy, Moscow, tel. no. 1614 November 10, 1956, NH10110/485, Public Records Office
90. Reuters, Geneva, November 7, 1956, CNR item D-199, a.p.a.
91. RFE Special from Heiligenkreuz, Austria, November 7, 1956, CNR item D-162, a.p.a.
92. USIS, Washington, D.C., November 7, 1956, CNR item D-243, a.p.a.
93. RFE Specials, United Nations, N.Y., November 7, 1956, CNR items D-6, D-146, a.p.a.

94. *Neues Österreich*, Herbert Schiff, Vienna, November 14, 1956, p.10
95. U.S. Legation, Budapest, tel. no. 253, November 8, 1956, F760003-21790 National Archives
96. Poal Trier Petersen, Stockholm's *Dagens Nyheter*, Vienna, November 12, 1956, CNR item C-66, a.p.a.
97. British Legation, Budapest, tel. no. 628, November 8, 1956 NH10110/408, Public Records Office
98. U.S. Legation, Budapest, unnumbered tel., December 11, 1956, pp. 8–10
99. British Legation, Budapest, tel. no. 629, November 8, 1956, NH10110/409, Public Records Office
100. UP. Belgrade, RFE, Paris, Reuters Vienna, UP, Vienna, November 8, 1956, CNR items B-27, C-68, C-97 & D-79, a.p.a.
101. RFE Special, Leason, Klingendorf, Austria, November 8, 1956, CNR item C-7, a.p.a.
102. "Andropov's conversation with Kádár: Shall we let Imre Nagy and company leave the country or not?" *Missing Pages from the History of 1956, Documents from the former archives of the Central Committee of the Soviet Communist Party*, Zenit Books, pp. 143–145, translated by András Bocz
103. RFE Special, Vienna, November 15, 1956 C-174, a.p.a.
104. *Documents*, documents 90 & 91, pp. 395–400
105. Laski, p. 255
106. *The Revolt in Hungary*, p. 104
107. UP, Vienna, Nov 8, 1956, CNR item D-238, a.p.a.
108. Reuters & UP. Paris, November 8, 1956, CNR items D-185, D-88 & D-177, a.p.a.
109. Reuters, London, November 8, 1956, CNR items D-173, D-219 & D-135, a.p.a.
110. RFE Special, New York, November 8, 1956, CNR item D-285-6, a.p.a.
111. USIS, Geneva, November 8, 1956, CNR item C-191, a.p.a.
112. RFE Special from Stockholm, Knauer, by mail, CNR item D-25, a.p.a.
113. AP Montevideo, UP Djakarta, Nov, 8, 1956, CNR items C-111 & D-108, a.p.a.
114. AP, Washington, November 8, 1956, CNR item B-50, a.p.a., *New York Herald Tribune*, November 8, 1956
115. Reuters, Berlin, November 8, 1956, CNR item D-198, AP, Washington, November 8, 1956, CNR item B-130, a.p.a.
116. FRUS, 1955–1957, pp. 418–421
117. USIS, Munich & UP Vienna, November 8, 1956, CNR items D-90& D-80. a.p.a.
118. RFE Specials from Paris and Stockholm November 8, 1956, CNR items D-30, C-89, D-26, a.p.a.
119. UP, United Nations, N.Y., November 8, 1956, items B-72, D-216 & D-239, a.p.a., UK UN Mission to F.O. tel. no. 1148, November 8, 1956, NH10110/417, Public Records Office
120. United Nations, N.Y., Reuters & INS, November 8, 1956, CNR items D-180 & D-237, a.p.a.

CHAPTER IX THE REVOLUTION GOES ON

1. AP, Vienna, November 9, 1956, CNR item D-143, a.p.a.
2. Pooled Dispatch, Reuters, AP, UP, Budapest via Vienna, November 12, 1956, CNR items D-85-88, a.p.a., U.S. Legation Budapest, tel. no. 7311 [Army Message] November 10, 1956, National Archives

3. Boris Kidel, *News Chronicle*, London, November 12, 1956, CNR item C-76, a.p.a.
4. Reuters, Vienna, November 11, 1956, CNR items C-76 & D-11, RFE Spedial (Hier) Vienna, November 11, 1956, CNR item D-166, a.p.a.
5. British Legation tel. n. 685, November 12, 1956, NH10110/511, Public Records Office
6. U.S. Legation, tel. no. 273, November 12, 1956, 764.00/11-1256, National Archives
7. RFE Monitoring, November 10. 1956, CNR item C-16
8. RFE Monitoring Reports November 9 & 12, 1956, CNR items A-8, D-223, a.p.a.
9. UP, *New York Times,* December 30, 1956, Barber p. 221 AP & UP, Vienna, November 9, 1956, CNR items B-32 & C-62, a.p.a.
10. AP & UP, Vienna, November 9, CNR items B-32 & C-62, a.p.a.
11. RFE Monitoring, November 8, 1956, CNR item B-60, a.p.a.
12. British Legation, Vienna, tel. no. 299, November 10, 1956, NH10110/469, Public Records Office
13. *Missing Pages in the History of 1956*, Documents etc., Zenit Books, pp. 182–184, translated by András Bocz
14. British Legation tel. no. 684, November 12, 1956, NH10110/510, Public Records Office, U.S. Legation tel. no. 271, November 12, 1956, National Archives
15. TASS, Moscow, November 11, 1956, CNR item A-18, a.p.a.
16. Reuters, Vienna, November 9, Reuters, Belgrade, November 9 & 10, Reuters, Vienna, November 12, RFE Special Vienna, Michie/Leason, November 12, 1956 CNR items D-214, D-130, D-81, D-41, C-75, respectively, a.p.a.
17. Elie Abel, Vienna, *New York Times*, November 12, 1956
18. Reuters, Belgrade, November 12, 1956, CNR item C-5, a.p.a.
19. *Documents,* Document no. 93, pp. 404–5
20. AP London, November 15, 1956, CNR item D-31, Tanjug, Belgrade, November 15, 1956, CNR item C-150 & RFE, Ritvo Speech Assessment, November 17, 1956, CNR item A-1, a.p.a.
21. Reuters, Vienna, November 11, 1956, CNR item C-8, a.p.a.
22. *The First Domino*, p. 153
23. RFE Monitoring, November 10 & 11, 1956, CNR items B-64, D-71, D-72, a.p.a.
24. TASS, Budapest, November 11, 1956, CNR item D-102. RFE Monitoring, November 11, 1956, CNR item C-73, Reuters, Belgrade, November 9, 1956, CNR item D-257, a.p.a.
25. RFE Chronology of Events, November 10, 1956, CNR item B-86, a.p.a.
26. Reuters Vienna, November 11, 1956, CNR item D-95, a.p.a.
27. U. S. Legation, Budapest, tel. no. 264, November 11, 1956, 764.00/11-1156, National Archives
28. RFE Monitoring, November 11, 1956, CNR item D-70, a.p.a.
29. RFE Monitoring, November 10, 1956, CNR item D-9, a.p.a.
30. C. D. Jackson Papers, Box 52, Dwight D. Eisenhower Library, Abilene, Kansas
31. FRUS, 1955–1957, pp. 424–5
32. UP, Reuters, United Nations, New York, November 9, 1956, CNR items D-213 & D-255, a.p.a., FRUS, 1955–1957, p. 428
33. UP, United Nations, N.Y. November 12, 1956, CNR item D-130, a.p.a.
34. RFE Special, New York, November 9, 1956, CNR item B-23, a.p.a.
35. UP, Reuters & *New York Times*, United Nations, N.Y. November 12, 1956, CNR items D-130, B-32, C143 respectively, a.p.a.

36. *Eisenhower, Volume Two, The President,* Stephen E. Ambrose, Simon and Schuster, N.Y. 1998, p. 374, UP, Washington, November 12, 1956, CNR item D-15, a.p.a.
37. Reuters, Vienna, November 9, 1956, CNR item D-196, a.p.a.
38. UP, Buenos Aires, November 10, 1956, CNR item D-1, Geneva, Reuters November 10, 1956, CNR item D-73, a.p.a., *New York Times*, November 10, 1956
39. Confidential Report on Hungarian Security Police in Austria, Foreign Office memo by T. Brimelow, November 12, 1956, H10110/663, Public Records Office, RFE Special, Napier, Graz, Austria, November 9, 1956, CNR item D-161, a.p.a.
40. Frederick Brook, *Christian Science Monitor*, Vienna, November 14, 1956, Foreign Office Paper B.410, November, 1956, H10110/648, Public Records Office, Reuters, Budapest, November 15, 1956, CNR items C-89, C-90, a.p.a.
41. AP, Endre Márton, Budapest, November 14, 1956, CNR item D-48, a.p.a.
42. RFE Monitoring, CNR item B-88, a.p.a.
43. Reuters Vienna, November 15, 1956, CNR items C-177, C-201, a.p.a.
44. RFE Monitoring, CNR item C-127, Reuters, Vienna, November 15, 1956, CNR item D-192, a.p.a.
45. Lomax, p. 101
46. UP. Budapest, November 18, 1956, CNR item D-15, a.p.a.
47. *The First Domino*, p.148,
48. RFE Hungarian Daily Background, up to 1200 hours, Dec, 17, 1956, CNR item Distribution "E", a.p.a.
49. RFE Monitoring, CNR item D-50, a.p.a.
50. UP Vienna, November 16, 1956, CNR item D-75, a.p.a.
51. *The First Domino*, p. 149
52. AP, Vienna, November 14, 1956, CNR item D-13, a.p.a.
53. U.S. Legation, Budapest, tel. no. 311, November 17, 1956, 764.00/11-1756, National Archives
54. RFE Special, Leason, Vienna, November 14, 1956, CNR item D-152, RFE Monitoring, CNR item, C-101, a.p.a.
55. RFE's "Chronology of Events in Hungary." November 17, 1956, CNR item C-92, a.p.a.
56. RFE Hungarian Daily Background, CNR items D-71, D-72, a.p.a.
57. AP, Budapest, November 18, 1956, CNR item B-23, a.p.a.
58. UP, Vienna, November, 16, 1956, CNR item C-3, a.p.a.
59. RFE Monitoring, November 14, 1956, CNR item B-95, a.p.a.
60. RFE Chronology of Events in Hungary, November 14, 1956, CNR item C-167, a.p.a.
61. RFE Hungarian Daily Background, November 15, 1956, CNR item D-132, a.p.a., RFE Monitoring, November 13, 1956, CNR item B-146, a.p.a.
62. Reuters, Budapest, November 16, 1956, CNR item D-121, British Legation tel. no. 747, November 17, 1956, H10110/595, Public Records Office
63. RFE Monitoring, November 13, 1956, CNR, item D-26, a.p.a., Lomax pp. 97–110
64. *The Forbidden Sky*, Endre Márton, Little Brown, Boston, 1971, p. 246
65. RFE Special, Collins, Vienna, November 15, 1956, CNR item C-23, UP, Vienna, November 16, 1956, CNR item B-76, a.p.a.
66. Reuters, Tokyo, Vienna, November 14, 1956, CNR items C-225, D-148, a.p.a.
67. RFE Special, Napier, Graz, November 17, 1956, CNR item D-116, a.p.a.
68. AP, Vienna, November 15, 1956, CNR item C-159, a.p.a.
69. RFE Special United Nations, N.Y., November 13, 1956, CNR item D-66, Reuter, Geneva, November 13, 1956, CNR item D-100, a.p.a.

70. UP and INS, United Nations, N.Y. November 13, 1956, CNR items C-194 & D-220, a.p.a.
71. UP, United Nations, N.Y. November 13, 1956, CNR item D-205, a.p.a.
72. Reuters, New York, November 16, 1956, CNR item D-61, a.p.a.
73. Reuters, Oslo, November 13, 1956, CNR item B-29, a.p.a.
74. Agerpress (Romanian Press Agency), Bucharest, November 14, 1956, CNR item B-72, a.p.a.
75. Tanjug, Belgrade, November 17, 1956, CNR item D-10, a.p.a.
76. TASS Moscow, Nov 15, 1956, CNR item A-28, a.p.a.
77. Reuters, Paris, November 16, 1956, CNR item C-140, a.p.a.
78. RFE Special New York, November 14, CNR item D-45, a.p.a.,Walter Waggoner, *N.Y. Times*, London, November 14, 1956, RFE Special, Paris, November 16, 1956, CNR item D-119, a.p.a.
79. UP, New Delhi, November 14, 1956, CNR item C-78, a.p.a.
80. RFE Special, Paris, November 14, 1956, CNR item C-193, a.p.a.
81. RFE Special, Paris, Reuters, Paris, November 14, 1956, CNR items C-116, D-103, D-221, a.p.a.
82. RFE Specials, Rome, November 13 & 14, 1956, CNR items C-209, D117, a.p.a.
83. Reuters, Montreal, November 14, 1956, CNR item D162, a.p.a.
84. Reuters, Moscow, November 17, 1956, CNR item D-34, UP, United Nations, N.Y., November 13, 1956, CNR item C-183, a.p.a.
85. Reuters, AP, Moscow, November 17, 1956, CNR items C-70, D-11, D-153,4,5), *Süddeutsche Zeitung*, November 21, 1956, CNR item C-148, a.p.a.
86. RFE Special, Vienna, November 26, 1956, CNR item C-83, a.p.a.
87. U.S. Legation, Budapest, Desp. no. 205, November 20, 1956, National Archives
88. U.S. Legation, Budapest, Desp. no. 216, November 27, 1956, 764.00/11-2756, National Archives
89. RFE Evaluation and Research, November 22, 1956, CNR items 59–60, RFE Special, Graz, November 26, 1956, CNR item D-103, a.p.a.
90. National Lutheran Council News Service, New York, November 26, 1956, CNR item D-103, a.p.a.
91. RFE Special Graz, November 20, 1956, CNR item D-67, a.p.a.
92. Reuters, New York, November 18, 1956, CNR item D-93, a.p.a.
93. *Kortárs Krónika 1956*, p. 64, translated by András Bocz
94. Reuters, Budapest, November 28, 1956, CNR item D-161, UP, Budapest, December 1, 1956, CNR item D-18, a.p.a.
95. Tanjug, full text of exchange of letters between the Yugoslav and Hungarian governments, December 3, 1956, CNR items C-32 to C-41, a.p.a., U.S. Legation, Budapest, tel. no. 347, November 24, 1956, 764.00/11-2456 HBS, National Archives, INS, United Nations, N.Y., November 23, 1956, CNR item D-264, a.p.a.,Victor Zorza, *Manchester Guardian*, November 26, 1956
96. U.S. Legation, Budapest, tel. no. 348, November 25, 1956, 764.00/11-2556 HBS, National Archives
97. *The First Domino*, p. 140
98. U.S. Legation, Budapest, November 23, 1956, tel. no. 339, 764.00/11-2356, National Archives, British Legation, Budapest, Desp. nos. 394, 395, November 24, 1956, NH 10110/215(BP, BO), Public Records Office
99. RFE Chronology of Events, November 23 & 24, CNR item D-16, a.p.a

100. Reuters, Vienna, November 27, 1956, CNR item C-155, Reuters, Belgrade, November 30, 1956, CNR item A-11, a.p.a.
101. U.S. Legation Budapest, Desp. No. 267, December 2, 1956, National Archives
102. UP, Budapest, December 2, 1956, CNR item D-48-49, RFE Special, Paris, November 26, 1956, CNR item C-88, a.p.a.
103. British Legation, Budapest, tel. no. 913, December 4, 1956, FO 371/122398 213909, Public Records Office
104. British Legation, Budapest, tel. no. 773, November 20, 1956, NH10110/637, Public Records Office
105. Reuters, Budapest, November 2, 1956, CNR item D-19, RFE Special, Fehérvári/Koch, Vienna, Dec, 12, 1956, Distribution "E," a.p.a.
106. RFE Special, Vienna December 6, 1956, CNR item D-8, RFE Monitoring, December 1, 1956, CNR item D-26, a.p.a.
107. AP, Budapest, December 22, 1956, CNR item D-5, AP Vienna, December 2, 1956, CNR item D-7, Reuters Vienna, December 4, 1956, CNR item D-48, a.p.a., British Legation, Budapest, Desp. nos. Y 412 & 435, December 3 & 9, 1956 NH10110/215 (CD) & (CT), Public Records Office
108. RFE Special, Graz, November 26, 1956, CNR item D-101, Reuters, Vienna, November 28, 1956, CNR item B-69, a.p.a.
109. RFE Special, Vienna, December 2, CNR item C-155, a.p.a. British Legation, Budapest, Desp. Y 424, December 6, 1956, NH10110/215 (CL), Public Records Office
110. Reuters, Budapest, December 4, 1945, CNR items C-57, 58, 60, 61, 65, a.p.a., Zsuzsanna Pajzs, 1956 Institute Interview no. 512 by László Eörsi, translated by Andrea Kicsák, British Legation, Desp. No. Y 421, December 6, 1956, NH10110/215 (CI), Public Records Office, U.S. Legation, Budapest, tel. no. 388, December 4, 1956, 764.00/12-456, National Archives
111. RFE Special, Vienna, November 17, 1956, CNR item C-155, UP, Vienna, November 19, 1956, CNR item C-96, RFE Special, Graz, November 27, 1956, CNR item C-65, a.p.a.
112. John MacCormac, *New York Times*, Vienna, November 20, 1956, Ronald Farquhar, Reuters, Budapest, December 2, 1956, CNR item D-17, a.p.a.
113. UP, Budapest, December 2, 1956, CNR item D-48, a.p.a.
114. UP, Budapest, November 28, 1956, CNR item B-93, a.p.a.
115. UP, Belgrade, November 20, 1956, CNR item B-32, a.p.a.
116. British Legation, Budapest, tel. no. 850, November 30, 1956, NH10110/752, Public Records Office
117. Reuters, Vienna, November 30, 1956, CNR item D-70, a.p.a.
118. Lomax pp. 168–9, *Tatabánya 1956,* László Gyüszi, Tatabánya, 1986, p. 96, translated by András Bocz, British Legation, Budapest, tel. no. 411, December 2, 1956, NH10110/251 (CB), Public Records Office
119. RFE Special, Graz, November 26, 1956, CNR item D-104, a.p.a.
120. RFE Special Vienna, Tormay/Leason, November 28 & 29, 1956, CNR items D-46 & B-50, a.p.a.
121. RFE Monitoring, Vienna, November 25, 1956, CNR item C-126, a.p.a.
122. Lomax, p.307
123. Ibid., p. 102
124. Ibid., p. 421
125. Ibid., pp. 111 & 112

126. Reuters, Budapest, November 21, 1956, CNR item C-153, a.p.a.
127. Reuters, Budapest, November 26, 1956, CNR item C-113, UP, Budapest, November 29, 1956, CNR item D-96, a.p.a.
128. Lomax, p. 150
129. UP, Vienna, November 30, 1956, CNR items C109, 110, a.p.a.
130. UP, Vienna, November 30, 1956, CNR item C-109, UP, Budapest, December 1, 1956, CNR item A-84, a.p.a.
131. Reuters, Budapest, December 6, 1956, CNR item C-19, a.p.a.
132. Reuters, Vienna, December 7, 1956, CNR item B-63, Reuters, Budapest, December 8, 1956, CNR item C-83, UP, Budapest, December 8, 1956, CNR item D-33, AP, Budapest, 1956, CNR item C-54, a.p.a.
133. US Legation, Budapest, Desp. no. 210, November 23, 1956, 764.00/11-2356
134. Serov's report of November 19, 1956 to Khrushchev, *Missing Pages in the History of 1956*, Documents from the former archives of the Central Committee of the Soviet Communist Party, Zenit Books, pp. 143–145, translated by András Bocz
135. U.S. Legation, Budapest, Desp. no. 228, December 7, 1956, National Archives
136. Reuters, London, November 22, 1956, CNR item C-145, a.p.a.
137. AP, Budapest, November 20, 1956, CNR item D-156, a.p.a.
138. RFE Monitoring, November 19, 1956, CNR item C-123, a.p.a.
139. U.P., Budapest, November 19, 1956, CNR item C-34, a.p.a.
140. Barrett McGurn, *New York Herald Tribune*, Vienna, November 26, 1956
141. Reuters, Vienna, November 20, 1956, CNR item, B-99, a.p.a.
142. RFE Special, Vienna, November 27, 1956, CNR item D-52, a.p.a., John MacCormac, *New York Times*, November 26, 1956
143. "Report by Malenkov, Suslov, Aristov and Serov to Central Committee," November 30, 1956, *Missing Pages of History 1956*, Zenit Books, translated by András Bocz
144. RFE Chronology of Events, November 17–18, CNR item D-61, a.p.a. *Népakarat*, December 6, 1956, p. 3
145. RFE Monitoring, November 30, 1956, CNR item D-149, a.p.a.
146. UP, Budapest, November 30, 1956, CNR item D-77, Granville, p. 152
147. U.S. Legation, Budapest, tel. no. 366, November 29, 1956, National Archives
148. Barbro Alving, *Dagens Nyheter*, December 2, 1956, CNR items C-20 to C-24
149. U.S Legation, Budapest, Desp. 222, November 30, 1956, 764.00/11-056, National Archives, British Legation, Budapest, tel. no. 897, December 3, 1956, FO371/122398 213909, Public Records Office
150. British Embassy, Vienna, tel. no. 336, November 19, 1956, NH10110/606, Public Records Office
151. British Legation, Budapest, tel. no. 768, November 20, 1956, NH10110/633, Public Records Office
152. Reuters, United Nations, N.Y., Nov, 19, 1956, CNR item B-19, a.p.a.
153. RFE Special, United Nations, N.Y., November 21, 1956, CNR items D-23-30, a.p.a.
154. UKUN Mission, N.Y., tel. no. 1493, December 1, 1956, NH10110/760, Public Records Office
155. Reuters, New York, November 29, 1956, CNR items B-35 & 36, a.p.a.
156. Reuters, United Nations, N.Y., December 3, 1956, CNR item C-139, UP, United Nations, December 4, 1956, CNR item A-18, a.p.a.
157. UP, Budapest, December 5, 1956, CNR item D-79, a.p.a.
158. AP, New Delhi, November 24, 1956, CNR item D-172, AP, United Nations, N.Y.,

Nov 27, 1956, CNR item D-112, Reuters, New York, December 6, 1956, CNR item D-97, UP, United Nations, N.Y., Nov 30, 1956, CNR item A-8, RFE Special, Vienna, December 7, 1956, C-35-37, a.p.a., British Legation, Belgrade, tel. no. 804, November 27, 1956, FO 371/ 122396 213909. Public Records Office

159. UP, United Nations, N.Y., November 20, 1956, CNR item C-191, Reuters, New York, November 26, 1956, CNR item D-203, Reuters, Vienna, December 2, 1956, CNR item C-30, a.p.a.

160. INS, London, November 28, 1956, CNR item D-171, a.p.a.

161. RFE Special, Austrian Border, November 19, 1956, CNR item D-81, a.p.a.

162. Reuters, Vienna, December 8, 1956, CNR item B-115, AP, Vienna, November 30, 1956, CNR item C-68, Reuters, Vienna, December 8, 1956, CNR item D-38, a.p.a.

163. UP, Vienna, November 22, 1956, CNR item D-137, AP, Vienna, November 23, 1956, CNR item C-95, a.p.a., Max Frankl, *New York Times*, Vienna, November 25, 1956

164. *Izvestia*, via TASS, December 2, 1956, CNR item B-36, a.p.a.

165. Reuters, New York, November 29, 1956, CNR item D-92, AP, Vienna, November 28, 1956, CNR item D-109, a.p.a.

166. Max Frankl, *New York Times*, Vienna, November 19, 1956, AP, Vienna, November 19, 1956, CNR item D-69, Reuters, Washington, November 19, 1956, CNR item D-108, a.p.a.

167. UP, Washington, D.C., November 29, 1956, CNR item B-40, a.p.a.

168. Max Frankl, *New York Times*, Vienna, November 30, 1956, UP, Augusta, Georgia, December 6, 1956, CNR item C-140, a.p.a.

169. Reuters, Vienna, November 19, 1956, CNR item D-152, RFE Special, Vienna, Nov 26, 1956, CNR Item C-145, a.p.a., British Legation, Budapest, tel. no. 770, November 20, 1956, NH 10110/634, Public Records Office

170. RFE Monitoring, November 16, 1956, CNR item D-60, a.p.a.

171. RFE Special, Graz, November 26, 1956, CNR item D-101, a.p.a.

172. U.S. Legation Budapest, November 27, 1956, Desp. no. 215, 764.0011-2756

173. UP, Lisbon, December 6, 1956, CNR item C-71, a.p.a.

174. *Manchester Guardian*, December 8, 1956,

175. *New York World Telegram and Sun*, November 19, 1956

176. FRUS, 1955–1957, p. 463

177. Reuters, Budapest, December 10, 1956, CNR item D-62, a.p.a.

178. Reuters, Budapest, December 8, 1956, CNR item D-83, AP, Budapest, November 8, 1956, CNR item D-115, a.p.a., British Legation, Budapest Y Desp. No. 439, November 10, 1956, NH10110/215 (CX), Public Records Office, Reuters, Vienna, December 11, 1956, CNR item C-40, a.p.a., Lomax, p. 102

179. British Legation, Budapest, tel. no. 898, December 3, 1956, FO 371/122398 Public Records Office

180. British Legation, Budapest, tel. no. 905, December 3, 1956, FO 371/122398, Public Records Office

181. RFE Distribution "E," December 6, 1956, pp. 2 & 3, a.p.a.

CHAPTER X SUPPRESSION

1. Reuters, Budapest, December 9, 1956, CNR item B-45, a.p.a.

2. *The Forbidden Sky,* pp. 225, 226

3. *Népakarat*, December, 11, 1956

4. Reuters, Belgrade, December 12, 1956, CNR item C-39, U.S. Legation, Budapest, Des. no. 262, January 4, 1957, 764.00/1-457, National Archives, Reuters, Farquhar, Budapest, December 13, 1956, CNR item B-62. a.p.a.
5. Reuters, Belgrade, December 12, 1956, CNR item C-39, a.p.a.
6. U.S. Legation, tel. no. 430, December 12, 1956, National Archives
7. Richard Kilian, *Daily Express*, December 14, 1956, CNR item C-96
8. AP, Budapest, December 20, 1956, CNR item C-38, a.p.a., U.S. Legation, Budapest Des. no. 235, December 11, 1956, National Archives
9. USIS, Vienna, December 13, 1956, CNR item C-105, a.p.a.
10. Reuters, Budapest, December 10, 1956, CNR item C-163, a.p.a.
11. Reuters, Belgrade, December 11, 1956, CNR item C-122, a.p.a.
12. Reuters, London, December 10, 1956, CNR item D-53, Reuters, Prague, December 10, 1956, CNR item C-6, AP, Washington, December 10, 1956, CNR item D-148, Reuters, Vienna, Dec 10, 1956, CNR item C-49, Reuters, Budapest, December 11, 1956, CNR item C-46, 48 & 56, Reuters, Vienna, December 12, 1956, CNR item C-54, a.p.a., U.S. Legation, Budapest, tel. no. 427, December 11, 1956, National Archives
13. Reuters, Budapest, December 21, 1956, CNR item D-62, Reuters, Budapest, December 13, 1956, D-85, a.p.a.
14. AP, Budapest, December 13, 1956, CNR item C-34, a.p.a.
15. RFE Special, Fehérvári/Koch, Vienna, December 12, 1956, RFE Distribution "E", a.p.a.
16. RFE Special, Tormay/Ponikiewski, Vienna, December 20, 1956, CNR item D-25, a.p.a.
17. Reuters, Belgrade, December 10, 1956, CNR item C-79, Reuters, Vienna, December 14, 1956, CNR item C-6, Reuters, Vienna, December 14, 1956, CNR item C-1, RFE Special, Tormay/Koch, Vienna December 16, 1956, CNR items D-29–30, a.p.a.
18. TASS, Budapest, December 24, 1956, CNR item C-78, a.p.a.
19. Frederick Brook, *Christian Science Monitor*, Vienna, Dec, 18, 1956, CNR items C-132,3,4, a.p.a.
20. RFE Special, Koch, Vienna, December 14, 1956, "E" distributions, a.p.a.
21. Reuters, Vienna, December 18, 1956, CNR item B-52, Reuter, Budapest, December 22, 1956, CNR item D-28, Reuters, Vienna, December 30, 1956, CNR item D-28, a.p.a.
22. RFE Hungarian Daily Background, December 20, 1956, Distribution "E, a.p.a.
23. Budapest December 14, 1956, Summary report of the Central Duty (Police), Reference no.: 2-100-52, translated by András Bocz
24. From the Daily Report of the Tolna County Police Department, reference number: 2-100-57, translated by András Bocz
25. Reuters, Vienna, December 11, 1956, CNR item D-65, a.p.a.
26. Reuters, Vienna, December 11, 1956, CNR item D-7
27. USIS, Vienna, December 13, 1956, CNR item C-145, a.p.a., *Népszabadság*, December 21, 1956, p. 2
28. Reuters, Budapest, December 29, 1956, CNR items D-41,2, RFE Hungarian Daily Background, December 10, 1956, distribution "E", a.p.a.
29. *Mai Nap*, December 16, 1956, p. 3
30. Elie Abel, *New York Times*, Belgrade, December 20, 1956
31. RFE Special, Fehérvári/Koch, Vienna, December 12, 1956, "E" distribution, a.p.a.
32. RFE Monitoring, December 19, 1956, CNR item D-34, a.p.a.
33. USIS, Munich, December 17, 1956, CNR item B-57, a.p.a.
34. RFE Monitoring, MTI in French, December 17, 1956, CNR item C-54, Reuters,

Budapest, December 20, 1956, CNR item D-14, RFE Hungarian Daily Background, December 22, 1956, "E" distribution, a.p.a.

35. RFE Special, Tormay/Koch, Vienna, December 15, 1956, CNR item C-44, AP, Vienna, December 18, 1956, CNR item C-102, INS, Vienna, December 19, 1956, CNR item D-8, Reuters, Vienna 25 & 27, 1956, CNR items C-46 & B-46, a.p.a.

36. Reuters, Vienna, December 24, 1956, CNR item B-54, *New York Times*, Vienna, December 25, 1956, RFE Special, Koch, Vienna, December 21, 1956, CNR item D-27, USIS, Vienna, December 29, 1956, CNR item D-1, a.p.a.

37. Reuters, Vienna, Dec, 19, 1956, C item D-25, UP, Vienna, December 20, 1956, CNR item C-117, UP, Salzburg, December 22, 1956, 1956, CNR item B-63, INS, Washington, C.C., December 24, 1956, CNR item D-39, a.p.a.

38. *New York Herald Tribune*, Washington, D.C., December 18, 1956

39. Camp Kilmer, N. J., *New York World Telegram*, December 27, 1957, AP, New York, December 28, 1956, CNR item D-103, a.p.a. (For a less rosy and more realistic account of the underside of the Hungarian refugee situation see Leslie B. Bain's *The Reluctant Satellites*, pp. 187–195)

40. John MacCormac, *New York Times*, Vienna, December 17, 1956, Reuters, Vienna, December 19, 1956, CNR item D-45, a.p.a.

41. RFE Monitoring, December 18, 1956, CNR item C-135, AP, Vienna, Dec, 21, 1956, CNR item D-45, RFE Monitoring, December 23, 1956, CNR item D-9, a.p.a.

42. Reuters, Budapest, December 16 and 19, 1956, CNR items D-22 & C-3, a.p.a.

43. Reuters, London, December 13, 1956, CNR item D-152, Reuters, Budapest, December 16, 1956, CR item C-40, Reuters, Geneva, December 27, 1956, CNR item C-36, RFE Monitoring, December 23, 1956, CNR item A-17, a.p.a.

44. RFE Monitoring, December 21, 1956, CNR item D-104, a.p.a.

45. Reuters, Budapest, December, 22, 1956, CNR item C-17, UP, Budapest, December 23, 1956, CNR items D-7 & C-25, Reuters, Budapest, December 24, 1956, CNR items B-79,80, a.p.a.

46. Reuters, Budapest, December 24, 1956, CNR items D-55, C-79,80, RFE Monitoring, December 24–5, 1956, CNR item B-58, a.p.a.

47. RFE Monitoring, December 24, 1956, CNR item D-51, a.p.a.

48. Ronald Farquhar, Reuters, Budapest, December 25, 1956, CNR items C-8, C-9, a.p.a.

49. Reuters, Vienna, December 26, 1956, CNR item D-5, a.p.a.

50. AP, Budapest, December 29, 1956, CNR item C-81, a.p.a.

51. RFE Monitoring, December 28, 1956, CNR item D-118, a.p.a.

52. RFE Monitoring, December 27, 1956, CNR item D-97, a.p.a.

53. Reuters, Milan, December 16, 1956, CNR item C-3, a.p.a.

54. UP, Milan, December 15, 1956, CNR item D-36, a.p.a.

55. Reuters, Belgrade, December 17, 1956, CNR item C-32, a.p.a.

56. Reuters, Budapest, December 18, 1956, CNR item C-18, a.p.a.

57. AP, Washington, December 18, 1956, CNR item D-86, a.p.a.

58. UP, San Francisco, December 26, 1956, CNR item C-67, a.p.a.

59. Reuters, London, December 14, 1956, CNR item B-5, UP, Vienna, December 22, 1956, CNR item C-100, a.p.a.

60. UP, United Nations, N.Y., December 10, 1956, CNR item D-103, a.p.a.

61. Reuters, New York, December 11, 1956, C-item C-142, AP, United Nations, N.Y., December 9, 1956, CNR item D-136, a.p.a., UP, United Nations, N.Y., December 13, 1956, CNR item D-93, FRUS, 1955–1957, p. 531

62. Reuters, United Nations, N.Y., December 12, 1956, RFE Daily Guidance no. 1093, p. 2, FRUS, p. 543, a.p.a.
63. RFE Monitoring, MTI in French, December 27, 1956, CNR item D-106, a.p.a.
64. UP, Ottawa, December 23, 1956, CNR items D-84-5, a.p.a.
65. TASS, Budapest, December 22, 1956, CNR item A-27, a.p.a.
66. RFE Monitoring December 22, 1956, CNR item B-65, Reuters, Vienna, December 21, 1956, CNR item D-90, Reuters, Vienna, December 21, 1956, CNR item D-48, a.p.a.
67. Reuters, Vienna, December 30, 1956, CNR item B-27, a.p.a.
68. Harry Schwartz, *New York Times*, New York, December 26, 1956
69. Reuters, Tokyo, December 26, 1956, CNR item D-55, a.p.a.
70. *Khrushchev and the First Russian Spring*, Fedor Burlatsky, Weidenfeld and Nicolson, London 1991, pp. 95–6
71. *New York Times* editorial, January 3, 1957
72. FRUS, 1955–1957, p. 543
73. UP, Paris, December 13, 1956, CNR item C-15, a.p.a.
74. Reuters, Paris, December 11, 1956, CNR item C-143, a.p.a.
75. Reuters, Washington December 18, 1956, CNR item D-78, a.p.a.
76. Frederick Brook, *Christian Science Monitor*, December 29, 1956, CNR items C-87,89, a.p.a.
77. UP, Vienna, December 27, 1956, CNR item C-54, a.p.a.
78. Reuters, Budapest, December 31, 1956, CNR items C-87, D-23,4, a.p.a.
79. Edmond Taylor, *Reporter* Magazine, December 27, 1956
80. AP, Budapest, January 8, 1957, CNR item C-59, a.p.a.
81. AP, Budapest, January 12, 1957, CNR item D-14, a.p.a.
82. *Magyar Közlöny*, January 15, 1957, John MacCormac, *New York Times*, Vienna, Jan; 15, 1957
83. Reuters, Budapest, February 4, 1957, CNR item D-74, a.p.a.
84. Reuters, London, January 30, 1957, CNR item D-122, a.p.a.
85. Reuters, Vienna February 8, 1957, CNR item C-52, Reuters, Budapest, February 4, 1957, CNR item D-74, a.p.a.
86. AP, Budapest, January 31, 1957, CNR item C-97, a.p.a.
87. Reuters, Vienna, February 8, 1957, CR item D-78, a.p.a.
88. *Népszabadság*, July 21, 1957
89. *The Forbidden Sky*, Endre Márton, pp. 252–255
90. UP, New York, February 5, 1957, CNR item D-146, AP, Budapest, February 6, 1957, CNR item C-83, a.p.a.
91. AP, Budapest, January 9, 1957, CNR item C-67 ,a.p.a.
92. John MacCormac, *New York Times,* Vienna, February 11, 1957, a.p.a.
93. Ronald Farquhar, Reuters, Budapest, February 7 & 22 1957, CNR items C-67 & D-85-6, *Magyar Közlöny*, March 24, 1957, Reuters, Budapest, February 6, 1957, CNR item C-59, a.p.a.
94. AP, Budapest, February 19, 1957, CNR item C-28, Reuters Vienna, February 17, 1957, CNR item D-4, a.p.a.
95. RFE Special, Dreyfuss, Paris, February 18, 1957, CNR item B-102, AP, Budapest, March 10, 1957, CNR item C-125, a.p.a.
96. AP, Budapest, February 7, 1957, CNR item C-98, a.p.a.
97. Reuters, Vienna, February 22, 1957, C item D-136, AP, Budapest, February 26, 1957, CNR item D-71, AP, Vienna, February 17, 1957, CNR item D-54, a.p.a.

98. Reuters, Budapest, February 15, 1957, *New York Herald Tribune.*
99. Reuters, Budapest, February 2, 1957, CNR item D-15, a.p.a.
100. AP, Budapest, February 8, 1957, CNR item C-55, a.p.a.
101. AP, Budapest, February 13, 1957, CNR item C-87, a.p.a.
102. Ronald Farquhar, Reuters, Budapest, February 18, 20, 22 & 24, CNR items respectively, C-3,4, D-53, D-75,D-67, a.p.a.
103. AP, Budapest, January 9, 1957, CNR item C-66, a.p.a.
104. Reuters, Vienna, January 12, 1957, CNR items C-14 & D-46, a.p.a.
105. *Népszabadság*, January 24, 1957, p. 7
106. *Népszabadság*, January 25, 1957, p. 4
107. AP. Budapest, February 2, 1957, C item C-87, a.p.a.
108. Frederick Brook, *Christian Science Monitor,* Vienna, February 3, 1957, CNR item C-129, a.p.a.
109. Reuters, Budapest, February 28, 1957, CNR items C-24 & C-86, AP. Budapest, February 28, 1957, CNR item D-94, Gordon Shepherd, *Daily Telegraph*, Vienna, February 28, 1957, CNR item C-120, a.p.a.
110. Reuters, February 8, 1957, C item D-81, AP, London, February 9, 1957, CNR items C-64 & 87
111. Reuters, Budapest, February 26, 1957, CNR item D-54, a.p.a.
112. Reuters, London, February 1, 1957, CR item D-60, a.p.a.
113. AP, Endre Márton, Budapest, March 2, 1957, CNR item C-19, a.p.a.
114. AP, Vienna, February 19, 1957, CNR item D-44, a.p.a.
115. AP, Budapest, January 25, 1957, CNR item D-12, a.p.a.
116. Reuters, Vienna, February 1, 1957, CNR item C-50, a.p.a.
117. Reuters, Vienna, February 4, 10, & 11, 1957, CNR items B-77, C-28 & B-92, Reuters, New York, February 5, 1957, CNR item D-112
118. Reuters, Budapest, February 2, 1957, CNR item B-46, Reuters, Vienna, February 3, 1957m, CNR item C-37, a.p.a.
119. RFE Special, New York, March 9, 1957, CNR item B-92, a.p.a.
120. AP, United Nations, N.Y., January 28, 1957, CNR item D-23, a.p.a.
121. UP, United Nations, N.Y., February 15, 1957, CNR item D-164, a.p.a.
122. AP, United Nations, N.Y., February 21, 1957, CNR items D-130 & 131, a.p.a., *Betrayal at the UN, The Story of Paul Bang-Jensen*, by de Witt Copp and Marshall Peck, The Devin-Adair Company, New York, 1963, pp. 124,25
123. "Austrian Press on Hungarian Developments No. 1," UN Special Committee on Hungary Archives, Copp & Peck, pp 126, 134–5
124. John MacCormac, *New York Times,* Vienna, February 25, 1957
125. Reuters, Moscow, January 31, 1957, CNR item D-2, a.p.a.
126. "Test of the Hungarians' Note of 22 Feb, 1957," Annex to Bulletin no. 49, UN Special Committee on the Hungarian Problem Archives
127. "Compilation of Official Laws, Decrees and Pronouncements by the Kádár Regime," UN Special Committee on Hungary Archives
128. *New York Times*, Washington, April 3, 1957
129. John MacCormac, *New York Times*, Vienna, April 2, 1957
130. London *Times,* Vienna, July 17, 1957, Frederick Brook, *Christian Science Monitor*, Vienna, July 18, 1957
131. Reuters, Budapest, May 29, 1957, Special UN Committee on Hungary Archive, John MacCormac, *New York Times*, Vienna, June 16, 1957

132. Györkei & Horváth, p.85
133. *New York Times*, June 28, 1957
134. "On the Reactions of the Soviet Union and Hungary to United Nations Action in the Hungarian Question," Sept. 6, 1957, UN Special Committee on Hungary Archive
135. Granville, p. 139
136. FRUS, 1955–1957, p. 638–9
137. UP Vienna, July 26, 1957, Arch Parsons, Jr., *New York Herald Tribune*, July 22, 1957, UN Special Committee on Hungary Archives
138. *The System of Retaliation in the Kádár Regime,* Tibor Zinner, Béla Hamvas Research Institute, 2001, p. 224, translated by András Bocz
139. Elie Abel, *New York Times*, Budapest, July 6, 1957
140. *New York Times*, August 3, 1957
141. Mary Hornaday, *Christian Science Monitor*, United Nations, New York, August 12, 1957, UN Special Committee on Hungary Archive
142. *The First Domino,* p. 137
143. *Neue Zürcher Zeitung*, December 20, 1957
144. AP, Budapest, December 21, 1957, UN Special Committee on Hungary Archive
145. UN Press Release PM/3608, 23 December 1957, UN Committee on Hungary Archive
146. For a convincing argument for just how shoddy and illegal the case was see "The Bang-Jensen Tragedy, A Review of the Official Record," by Julius Epstein, *American Opinion*, May 1960
147. Granville, p. 142
148. *Neue Zürcher Zeitung*, February 4, 1958, UN Special Committee on Hungary Archive
149. *Documents*, pp. 373–4
150. Sergei Khrushchev, p. 204
151. *Khrushchev Remembers*, p. 426, and author's interview with Sergei Khrushchev, September 22, 2004
152. *Documents,* p. 411, footnote 116 (no source given)
153. *Columbia University Forum*, Fall 1958, p. 10
154. Tibor Zinner, p. 58 fn. 80, translated by András Bocz
155. *FRUS, 1955–1957*, pp 576–7
156. *Observer*, January 26, 1958
157. Tibor Zinner, p. 245, translated by András Bocz
158. *Documents*, p. 375

CHAPTER XI ACCEPTING SUPPRESSION (EAST & WEST)

1. Dan Karasik, former CBS correspondent in Vienna, *Overseas Press Club Bulletin*, March 12, 1958, CNR item F-171-174, a.p.a.
2. Political Investigation Department, "Strictly Confidential: Subj.: summary of Miklós Orz's case, Debrecen, March 29, 1957, János Kenedi, p. 123, translated by András Bocz
3. *Carrying a Secret in My Heart,* Zsuzsanna Kőrösi and Adrienne Molnár, Central European University Press, 2003, p. 31
4. Ibid, p. 32
5. Ibid, p. 43
6. Ibid, p. 40
7. *Voices through the Iron Curtain*, Allan A. Michie, Dodd, Mead & Co., New York, 1963, p. 256

8. *Broadcasting Freedom*, Arch Puddington, University Press of Kentucky, 2000, p. 107
9. Michie, p. 253
10. U.S. Legation, Budapest, tel. no. 324, November 19, 1956, National Archives
11. U.S. Legation, Budapest, Desp. no. 249, December 18, 1956, National Archives
12. Puddington, pp 118, 119
13. "Budapest: Interview in a Basement Hideaway," Leslie B. Bain, *The Reporter,* December 13, 1956, pp. 4 & 5
14. Puddington, p.107
15. *Documents*, document 105, pp. 464–484
16. Zsuzsanna Kőrösi and Adrienne Molnár, pp.1–2
17. *Documents,* "Hungary in the Aftermath," p. 376
18. Tibor Zinner, p. 58, fn. 80, translated by András Bocz
19. *Litván*, p. 147
20. *Carrying a Secret in My Heart*, p. 100
21. Patrícia Kállay, Kőrösi & Molnár, p. 83.
22. Ibid, p. 82
23. Ibid, p. 86
24. Ibid, pp. 75–6
25. *Khrushchev and the First Russian Spring*, Fedor Burlatsky, Weidenfeld and Nicolson, London, 1991, p. 105

CHAPTER XII REEMERGENCE

1. Litván, p. 162
2. Litván, p. 163
3. Kőrösi & Molnár, pp. 118–119
4. Much of this information and in paragraphs following comes from an interview with Iván Berend conducted by the author on September 20, 2005
5. Kőrösi & Molnár, p 120
6. Berend Committee Report, pp. 34–37, *Társadalmi Szemle*, special edition 1990, translated by András Bocz
7. Kőrösi & Molnár, p. 121
8. *Ravatal,* Bachman, Rajk, Peternák, META-R Ltd., p. 77
9. MTI *Daily News,* June 17, 1956, p. 1
10. Told to the author by Iván Berend, September 20, 2005, and Attila Szakolczai in February 2006

CHAPTER XIII SIGNIFICANCE OF THE REVOLUTION

1. U.S. Legation, Budapest, Desp. No. 231, December 10, 1956, 764.00/12.1056 HBS, National Archives
2. *The 1956 Hungarian Revolution: A History in Documents*, p. 197
3. U.S. Legation, Budapest tel. no. 168, October 26, 1956, 764.00/10-2756, National Archives
4. *The Devil and John Foster Dulles*, Townsend Hoopes, Atlantic-Little Brown & Co., Boston, 1965, p. 64
5. Ibid., p. 277
6. *Waging Peace*, Dwight D. Eisenhower, Doubleday & Co., New York, p. 89
7. FRUS, 1955–1957 p. 322

8. FRUS , 1955–1957 p. 306
9. *Eisenhower, Volume Two, The President*, Stephen E. Ambrose, Simon and Schuster, New York, 1983, p. 374
10. *Waging Peace,* p. 88
11. *Rhetoric and Reality: The Eisenhower Administration and Unrest in Eastern Europe, 1953–1959*, James David Marchio, Dissertation 1990, UMI Dissertation Services. p. 476. It is a mystery to the author why this excellent, meticulously researched and well-written dissertation was never published.
12. Marchio, p. 339
13. *Gentleman Spy,* p. 429
14. *The Hungarian Revolution of 1956*, edited by György Litván, Longman, 1996, p. 93
15. Marchio, p. 403
16. Ibid., p. 427
17. "The Lessons of Hungary," Edmond Taylor, *Reporter* Magazine, December 27, 1956
18. James Reston, *New York Times*, Washington D.C., December 18, 1956
19. *New York Herald Tribune*, Washington, D.C., December 14, 1956
20. Priority Cable 601, Department of State, November 15, 1956 to Embassies in Moscow, Vienna, Stockholm and Bern, 764.00/11-1156 CS F, National Archives
21. *Tinderbox*, pp.187, 189 & 192
22. Ibid., p. 91
23. *Budapest: Interview in a Basement Hideaway,* Leslie B. Bain, *Reporter,* December 13, 1956
24. Milovan Đilas, "The Storm in Eastern Europe," *The New Leader*, November 19, 1956
25. Urban, p. 138
26. Kőrösi & Molnár, pp. 134–5
27. John MacCormac, *New York Times*, November 25, 1956
28. Kőrösi & Molnár, p. 136
29. London *Sunday Times,* December 2, 1956
30. Vladislav M. Zubok, *The Kremlin Power Struggle and the Hungarian Crisis, Hungary and the World, 1956: The New Archival Evidence*, Budapest, September 26–29, 1996
31. Litván, p. 154
32. Ibid., p. 167

Bibliography

Aczél, Tamás, & Tibor Meray, *The Revolt of the Mind, A Case History of Intellectual Resistance Behind the Iron Curtain*, Frederick A. Praeger, New York, 1959

Ambrose, Stephen E., *Eisenhower, Volume Two, The President*, Simon and Schuster, New York, 1998

Andersen, Alsing, Chairman, UN Special Committee on the Problem of Hungary, *Report of the Special Committee on the Problem of Hungary*, United Nations, New York, 1957

Andrew, Christopher & Oleg Gordievsky, *KGB: the Inside Story of Its Foreign Operations from Lenin to Gorbachev*, Harper Collins, New York, 1990

Andrew, Christopher & Vasili Mitrokhin, *The Sword and the Shield: The Mitrokhin Archives and the Secret History of the KGB*. Basic Books, New York, 1999

Bain, Leslie Bálogh, *The Reluctant Satellites*, MacMillan Company, New York, 1960

Barber, Noel, *A Handful of Ashes,* Wingate, London, 1957

——*Seven Days of Freedom*, Stein and Day, New York, 1974

Beichman, Arnold & Mikail Bernstam, *Andropov*, Stein and Day, New York, 1983

"Beke, László," (real name unknown), *A Student's Diary*, Hutchinson of London, 1957

Békés, Csaba, Malcolm Byrne and János M. Rainer, *The 1956 Hungarian Revolution: A History in Documents*, Central European University Press, Budapest, 2002

——*The 1956 Hungarian Revolution and World Politics*, Working Paper no. 16, Cold War International History Project, Woodrow Wilson Center for Scholars, Washington, D.C., 1996

Bibliography

Berghahn, Volker R., *America and the Intellectual Cold Wars in Europe*, Princeton University Press, Princeton, N.J., 2001

Bibó, István, *Democracy, Revolution, Self-Determination: Selected Writings*, edited by Karoly Nagy, Atlantic Research and Publications, Highland Lakes, N.J., 1991

Bohlen, Charles E., *Witness to History, 1929–1969*, W.W. Norton & Co. Inc., New York, 1973

Botka, Ferenc, *Tibor Dery, Crucial, Historic Years in X, 1957–1964*, Petöfi Library Museum, Budapest, 2002

Brandt, Willy, *The Soviet Sea Around Us*, Graphische Gesellschaft Grunewald, GmbH, Grunewald, West Berlin, 1959

Brzezinski, Zbigniew K., *The Soviet Bloc: Unity and Conflict* (revised and enlarged edition), Harvard University Press, Cambridge, MA, 1967

Burlatsky, Fedor, *Khrushchev and the First Russian Spring*, Wiedenfeld and Nicolson, London, 1991

Burrows, William E., *By Any Means Necessary: America's Secret Air War in the Cold War*, Farrar, Straus & Geiroux, 2001

Cohen, Stephen F., *Rethinking the Soviet Experience: Politics and History Since 1917*, Oxford University Press, 1965

Copp, DeWitt & Marshall Peck, *Betrayal at the UN: The Story of Paul Bang-Jensen*, The Devin-Adair Company, New York, 1963

Cox, Terry, *Hungary 1956—Forty Years On*, Frank Cass Publishers, London, 1997

Eisenhower, Dwight D., *Waging Peace*, Doubleday and Company, New York, 1965

Epstein, Julius, *The Bang-Jensen Tragedy: A Review based on Official Records*, American Opinion, Belmont, MA, 1960

Djilas, Milovan, *The Fall of the New Class: A History of Communism's Self-Destruction*, Alfred A. Knopf, New York, 1998

Dorril, Stephen, *MI6: Inside the Covert World of Her Majesty's Secret Intelligence Service*, The Free Press, New York, 2000

Fryer, Peter, *Hungarian Tragedy*, Dennis Dobson, London, 1956

Filep, Tibor, *Debrecen 1956* (in Hungarian), Csokonai Kiado, 2000

Free Europe Press, *The Revolt in Hungary*, Free Europe Committee, New York, 1957

Gaddis, John Lewis, *We Now Know: Re-thinking Cold War History*, Clarendon Press, Oxford, 1997

Gati, Charles, *Hungary and the Soviet Bloc*, Duke University Press, Durham, NC, 1986

Bibliography

Glennon, John P., Editor-in-Chief, *Foreign Relations of the United States (FRUS)1955–1957 Volume XXI, Eastern Europe*, United States Printing Office, Washington, D.C., 1990

Gorbachev, Mikail, *Memoirs*, Doubleday, New York, 1996

Granville, Johanna, *The First Domino,* Texas A & M University Press, College Station, Texas, 2004

Gromyko, Andrei, *Memoirs*, Hutchinson, London, Sydney, Auckland Johannesburg, 1989

Grose, Peter, *Gentleman Spy: The Life of Allen Dulles*, Houghton Mifflin Company, Boston, New York, 1994

——Operation Rollback: *America's Secret War Behind the Iron Curtain*, Houghton Mifflin Company, Boston, New York, 2000

Györkei, Jenö and Miklós Horváth, *Soviet Military Intervention in Hungary*, Central European University Press, Budapest, 1999 (English edition)

Harászti, Miklós, *A Worker in a Worker's State*, Universe Books, New York, 1978

Hegedüs, András (the politician), *The Structure of Socialist Society*, Condille, London, 1977

Hegedüs, András B. (the scholar), "The Petöfi Circle, Forum for Reform in 1956," *The Journal of Communist Studies*, Frank Cass Publishers, London, 1987

Helms, Richard with William Hood, *A Look Over My Shoulder: A Life in the Central Intelligence Agency,* Random House, New York, 2003

Holt, Robert T., *Radio Free Europe*, University of Minnesota Press, Minneapolis, MN, 1958

Hoopes, Townsend, *The Devil and John Foster Dulles*, Atlantic-Little Brown and Co., Boston, 1965

Horváth, Miklós, *Pal Maleter*, H. & T. Kiado, Budapest, 2002

Immerman, Richard H., *John Foster Dulles and the Diplomacy of the Cold War*, Princeton University Press, Princeton, N.J., 1990

Irving, David, *Uprising: One Nation's Nightmare*, Veritas Publishing Company Pty., Ltd., Australia, 1981

Jonás, Pál and Béla K. Kiraly, "The Hungarian Revolution in Retrospect," *East European Quarterly,* Boulder, Colorado, (distributed by Columbia University Press), 1978

Kecskemeti, Paul, *The Unexpected Revolution: Social Forces in the Hungarian Uprising,* Stanford University Press, Stanford, CA, 1961

Kennan, George, *Russia, the Atom and the West*, Harper & Brothers, Publishers, New York, 1957

Bibliography

Kiraly, K. Béla, *The First War between Socialist States: The Hungarian Revolution of 1956 and Its Impact*, Social Science Monographs, Brooklyn College Press (distributed by Columbia University Press), 1984

——*From the Hungarian Army to the People's Army*, CO-Nexus, Pinty tér, Budapest, 1968

Knight, Amy, *Beria, Stalin's First Lieutenant*, Princeton University Press, Princeton, NJ, 1993

Kovács, Imre, *The Fight for Freedom, Facts about Hungary*, The Hungarian Committee, New York, 1966

Kovrig, Bennett, *Communism in Hungary, from Kun to Kádár*, Hoover Institution Press, Stanford Univrsity, CA, 1979

Körösi, Zsuzsanna & Adrienne Molnár, *Carrying a Secret in My Heart*, Central European University Press, Budapest, 2001

Kövágó, József, *You Are All Alone*, Praeger, New York, 1959

Khrushchev, Nikita S., *Khrushchev Remembers*, edited by Strobe Talbott, Little Brown & Co., Boston, 1970

Khrushchev, Sergei N., *Khrushchev on Khrushchev*, translated and edited by William Taubman, Little Brown & Co., Boston, Toronto, London, 1990

——*Nikita Khrushchev and the Creation of a Superpower*, Pennsylvania State University Press, University Park, PA, 2000

Kramer, Mark, "The Early Post-Stalin Succession Struggle and Upheavals in East-Central Europe," *Journal of Cold War Studies*, Vol. 1, No. 3, Fall 1999, Cambridge, MA

Laski, Melvin J., *The Hungarian Revolution: A White Book,* Martin Secker and Warburg, Ltd., London, 1957

Lashmar, Paul and James Oliver, *Britain's Secret Propaganda War, 1948–1977,* Sutton Publishing, Ltd., Stroud, Gloucestershire, UK, 1998

Laquer, Walter, *A World of Secrets: The Uses and Limits of Intelligence*, A Twentieth Century Fund Book, Basic Books, Inc. Publishers, New York, 1985

Litván, György, *The Hungarian Revolution of 1956, Reform, Revolt and Repression, 1953–1963,* English version edited and translated by Janos M. Bak and Lyman H. Legters, Longman, London and New York, 1996

Lomax, Bill (William), *Hungary, 1956,* Allen & Busby, London, 1976

——*Eyewitness in Hungary: The Soviet Invasion of 1956,* University of Nottingham Press, 1980

——"Hungarian Workers' Councils in 1956," *Social Science Monographs*, Boulder, Colorado, Atlantic Research and Publications, Highland Lakes, NJ, 1990 (distributed by Columbia University Press)

Bibliography

Lucas, Scott, *Freedom's War: The U.S. Crusade against the Soviet Union, 1945–1956,* Manchester University Press, UK, 1999

Macartney, C. A., *Hungary, a Short History,* Aldine Publishing Company, Chicago, 1962

Marchio, James David, *Rhetoric and Reality: The Eisenhower Administration and Unrest in Eastern Europe,* dissertation, 1990, UMI (University of Michigan) Dissertation Services

Márton, Endre, *The Forbidden Sky,* Little, Brown & Co., Boston, Toronto, 1971

Mastny, Vojtech, *The Cold War and Soviet Insecurity: The Stalin Years,* Oxford University Press, 1996

McCagg,William O., "Jewish Nobles and Geniuses in Modern Hungary," *East European Quarterly,* Boulder, Colorado, 1972 (distributed by Columbia University Press, New York)

Medvedev, Roy, *All Stalin's Men,* Anchor Press, Doubleday, Garden City, New York, 1984

Meyer, Cord, *Facing Reality: From World Federalism to the CIA,* Harper and Row, New York, 1980

Meray, Tibor, *Thirteen Days that Shook the Kremlin,* Praeger, New York, 1959

——*That Day in Budapest, October 23, 1956,* Funk and Wagnalls, New York, 1969

Michner, James A. *The Bridge at Andau: The Story of the Hungarian Revolution,* Secker & Warburg, London, 1957

Michie, Allan, *Voices Through the Iron Curtain: The Radio Free Europe Story,* Dodd, Mead & Company, New York, 1963

Micunovic, Vejlko, *Moscow Diary,* Doubleday & Company, Garden City, New York, 1980

Mikes, George, *The Hungarian Revolution,* André Deutsch, London, 1957

Mindszenty, Cardinal József, *Mindszenty Memoirs,* MacMillan Company, New York, 1974

Mosley, Leonard, *Dulles: A Biography of Eleanor, Allen and John Foster Dulles and Their Family Network,* The Dial Press/James Wade, New York, 1978

Nagy, Imre, *On Communism: In Defense of the New Course,* Praeger, New York, 1957

Nelson, Michael, *War of the Black Heavens: The Battles of Western Broadcasting in the Cold War,* Syracuse University Press, Syracuse, New York, 1997

Nóvé, Béla, *Kortárs Krónika 1956,* Krónika Nova Kiadó, Budapest, 2001

Palóczi-Horváth, George, *Khrushchev: The Making of a Dictator,* Atlantic Monthly Press Book, Little, Brown & Company, Boston 1960

Bibliography

Pongrátz, Gergely, *Corvin Circle 1956*, Framo, Chicago, 1982. English language edition published in 1992

Puddington, Arch, *Broadcasting Freedom, The Cold War Triumph of Radio Free Europe and Radio Liberty*, University Press of Kentucky, 2000

Radvány, János, *Hungary and the Superpowers*, Stanford University Press, Stanford CA, 1972

Sakharov, Andrei, *Memoirs*, Alfred A. Knopf, New York, 1990

Saunders, Frances Stonor, *The Cultural Cold War: The CIA and the World of Arts and Letters*, The New Press, New York, 1999

Shawcross, William, *Crime and Compromise: János Kádár and the Politics of Hungary Since the Revolution*, Dutton, New York, 1974

Shevchenko, Arkady N., *Breaking with Moscow*, Alfred A. Knopf, New York

Solovyov, Vladimir and Elena Klepikova, *Yuri Andropov: A Secret Passage into the Kremlin*, MacMillan Publishing Company, New York, 1983

Sosin, Gene, *Sparks of Liberty, An Insider's Memoir of Radio Liberty*, Pennsylvania State University Press, University Park, PA, 1999

"Szabó, Tamás" (not his real name), *Boy on a Rooftop*, Heineman, London, 1958

Száz, Béla, *Volunteers for the Gallows, Anatomy of a Show Trial*, Chatto & Windus, London, 1971

Szeged, City of, *Szegedi Forradalom Krónologiaja*, October 1999

Talbott, Strobe, *Khrushchev Remembers: The Glasnost Tapes*, Little Brown & Company, Boston, 1990

Taubman, William, *Khrushchev: The Man and his Era*, W.W. Norton & Company, New York and London, 2003

——*The View from Lenin Hills*, Coward McCann, Inc., New York, 1967

Taubman, William with Sergei N. Khrushchev and Abbott Gleason, *Nikita Khrushchev*, Yale University Press, New Haven and London, 2000

Urban, George, *The Nineteen Days*, William Heineman, London, 1957

——*Radio Free Europe and the Pursuit of Democracy*, Yale University Press, New Haven, 1997

Weaver, Howard S., *Balloon Leaflets: Operations of Free Europe Press, 1954–1956,* Free Europe Press, New York, April 1958

Zinner, Paul E., *National Communism and Popular Revolt in Eastern Europe*, Columbia University Press, New York, 1956

Zinner, Tibor, "System of Retaliation in the Kádár Regime," Bela Hamvas Research Institute, 2001

Index

Index

Index

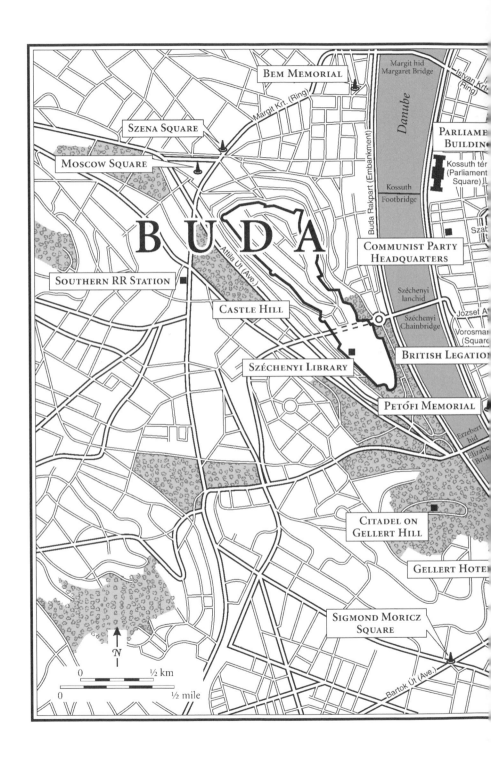

BEM MEMORIAL

Margit híd
Margaret Bridge

Istvan Krt.
(Ring)

Margit Krt. (Ring)

SZENA SQUARE

Danube

MOSCOW SQUARE

PARLIAME
BUILDIN

Kossuth tér
(Parliament
Square))L

B U D A

Buda Rakpart (Embankment)

Kossuth
Footbridge

Attila Út (Ave.)

COMMUNIST PARTY
HEADQUARTERS

SOUTHERN RR STATION

Szat

Széchenyi
lanchid

CASTLE HILL

Széchenyi
Chainbridge

Jozsef A

Vorosmar
(Square

SZÉCHENYI LIBRARY

BRITISH LEGATION

PETŐFI MEMORIAL

Erzebert
híd

Elizabe
Brid

CITADEL ON
GELLERT HILL

GELLERT HOTE

SIGMOND MORICZ
SQUARE

𝒩

0   ½ km

0   ½ mile

Bartok Út (Ave.)

Raves for the novels of *Inda:*

"The world creation and characterization within *Inda* have the complexity and depth and inventiveness that mark a first-rate fantasy novel . . . This is the mark of a major work of fiction . . . you owe it to yourself to read *Inda*."
—Orson Scott Card

"Intricate and real . . . Filled with magic and glamour . . . Characters spring to life with humor . . . Complex and compelling." —*San Jose Mercury News*

"Many fans of old-fashioned adventure will find this rousing mix of royal intrigue, academy shenanigans, and sea story worth the effort." —*Locus*

"In this lively, accessible follow-up to *Inda,* Smith dares to resolve several plot lines, in defiance of fantasy sequel conventions. Smith deftly stage-manages the wide-ranging plots with brisk pacing, spare yet complex characterizations and a narrative that balances sweeping action and uneasy intimacy." —*Publishers Weekly*

"The achievement of this writer is only getting more remarkable. In the past few months I've started reading more than a dozen fantasy novels or series; I haven't reviewed them here because they were, to put it kindly, a waste of my time, and I didn't bother finishing them. By contrast, I didn't want *The Fox* to end. I savored every paragraph and continued to live in the book for days afterward. I keep thinking that if I write a good enough review, the publisher or author will relent and let me read the next volume early. Like now. Please." —Orson Scott Card

"Pirates and plotters fill this swashbuckling sequel to *Inda*. This is a middle novel in this series, but it's full of action, adventure and delightful, larger than life characters, and manages a sneakily sudden, uplifting twist at the end that provides a satisfying conclusion despite looming diassters."
—*Locus*

KING'S SHIELD

SHERWOOD SMITH

DAW BOOKS, INC.

DONALD A. WOLLHEIM, FOUNDER

375 Hudson Street, New York, NY 10014

ELIZABETH R. WOLLHEIM

SHEILA E. GILBERT

PUBLISHERS

http://www.dawbooks.com

First Paperback Printing, July 2009
2 3 4 5 6 7 8 9

Acknowledgments

My thanks to Beth Bernobich, who trudged faithfully with me through early drafts, and to Donald Hardy, who read and encouraged me, and clued me in to hot zones.

Thanks to Tamara Meatzie, who generously donated her time to proofread *The Fox* for its paperback release, and came to my rescue with this one.

And a heartfelt thank you to the following, who gave me a crash read in the middle of holiday season: Twila Oxley Price, Julia Unigovski, Faye Bi, Maggie Brinkley, Jenna Waterford, Allison Bishop, Jennifer Shimada, Alexandra Morris, Stephanie Zuercher, Surya Lakhanpal, Su-Yee Lin, and Jarratt & Evie Gray.

Finally, my gratitude to three people who went above and beyond: Hallie O'Donovan, Eliana Scott-Thoennes, and Orson Scott Card.

For readers who like timelines and worldbuilding details, here's the webpage for this story, with all kinds of links: www.sherwoodsmith.net/inda.html

Sartoran Continent
southern hemisphere

N

Venn Empire

Geranda

Inglenook Islands

Fire Islands

Star Isles (Starborn)

Freedom Islands

Lands End

Chwahirsland

The Fangs

Dei Chael

Tchorchin

Everon

Khanerenth

Ymar

Colend

Port of Jaro

Drael

Duna

Sarendan

Fal

Mardgar

Sartor

SARTORAN SEA

Bren

Llyenthur

Anaeran-Adrani

The Nob

Idayago

Ghost Isles

Iasca Leror

Delphin Islands

LINDETH HARBOR

Choraed Elgaer

Stormborn Islands

Narrows

Toar

Pirate Island

Land Bridge

Freedom Main Isle
Freeport Harbor

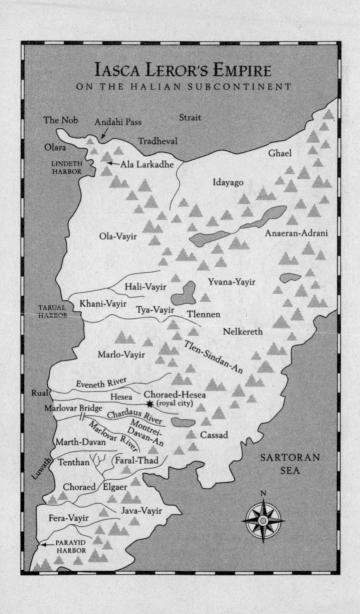

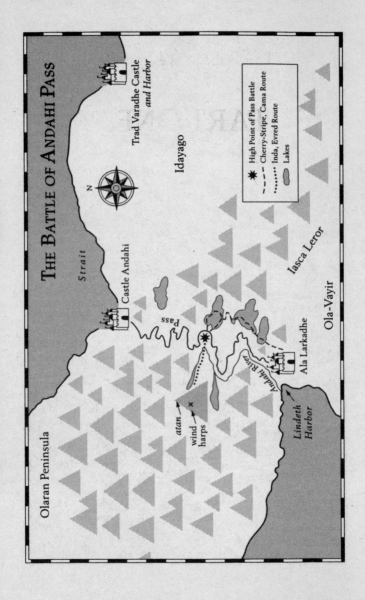

The Battle of Andahi Pass

- ✴ High Point of Pass Battle
- — — Cherry-Stripe, Cama Route
- ⋯⋯ Inda, Evred Route
- Lakes

Olaran Peninsula

Strait

Castle Andahi

N

Trad Varadhe Castle *and Harbor*

Idayago

Pass

atan

wind harps

Anddah River

Iasca Leror

Ala Larkadhe

Ola-Vayir

Lindeth Harbor

PART ONE

PART ONE

Chapter One

AFTER nine years of exile, Inda was going home.

The still-wintry wind sent the scout craft *Vixen* scudding down the coast of Iasca Leror. Four crew and four passengers crowded the small craft, the passengers on watch as they drifted past tall bluffs of sedimentary stone. Above the cliffs occasional conical roofs were visible but seldom any living thing other than wheeling, diving sea birds. At night signal fires twinkled with a ruddy, sinister glow along the highest bluffs, beacons tended day and night, kept ready for any sighting of Venn raiders.

Inda was not alone. Three of his companions would go with him.

Inda fretted over the way the Venn Dag Signi had taken to standing at the rail, staring up at those forbidding cliffs, her hands clasped tightly together. The only way he could think of to break that silent, white-knuckled tension was to attempt a joke. "How often does a fellow fall in love with the world's most wanted woman? Maybe we should help the balladeers along. Make up some good verses about us."

Signi shifted her gaze from the horizon to Inda's hopeful face. The gulf between twenty and thirty-two had never seemed wider. What could she say? *You are notorious throughout the world, but you are coming home. I am renegade only to my people, and nothing to the world. There is no home for me.* No. If he did not see the difference, why cause him pain?

He said, "Don't your people have a lot of songs about evil villains or great heroes? Mine do. In ours, you Venn are always the villains strewing blood and death everywhere—and I'm sure we Marlovans are the same in yours."

Inda flashed a smile aft at Tau, lounging at the taffrail next to Jeje, who had insisted on handling the tiller until they reached land. "Tau," Inda called into the wind. "This is more your skill. Make up a ballad? A heroic one." He smacked his chest, then indicated Signi with his thumb. "About us."

"You want a hero's song?" Taumad's manner was languid as he covertly studied the two forward: the small, spare Venn mage with her hands gripped together, and Inda, not much taller, broad and strong through the chest, golden hoops affixed with rubies glittering at his ears. His face had been scarred in battle, making him seem older than his twenty years. He was a sinister figure, except for his expression. His worry was as evident as her tension.

Tau flicked a glance between them again, and guessed with typical accuracy at Inda's motive. Tau had been trained to sing as well as to observe, and making up verses was an old game for him.

> *"Scar-faced Inda riding the wind,*
> *His fleet a scout craft. Surrounded closely*
> *By powerful mates, standing beside him,*
> *Oath-sworn and loyal, to guard Inda's ass—"*

"Hey," Inda protested. "It's supposed to be about *my* greatness."

"But there isn't any," Tau retorted.

The banter sparked chuckles from a pair of brothers crewing for Jeje, and a deep, husky laugh from her.

For a moment a smile eased Dag Signi's expression. She raised a hand, the gesture—like all her movements—stylized with trained poise. She said something in a low voice; Inda bent his head to touch hers as they talked privately.

Jeje muttered, "She's got to be scared now that we're close to land."

"I would be." Tau hitched himself up onto the rail. "A Venn, landing in a kingdom that's been under Venn attack—or Venn-directed pirate attack—for five or six years?" He shook his head. "Does anyone besides me appreciate the irony that she, an enemy, has more recent news about what's going on in our homeland than the three of us?"

Jeje scowled landward. "I suppose it's stupid to say that Inda will make everything all right when he doesn't know what kind of a welcome *he's* gonna get after all these years."

"His boyhood friend is now king," Tau reminded her.

But she just flipped up the back of her hand. "Kings," she uttered in disgust.

Tau and Jeje had been with Inda for the entirety of his exile. They'd met as deck rats on an old trader. During those nine years—as they'd followed him from the trader to the Freedom Islands to become marine defenders, been taken as pirates, and escaped just to turn around and take on the worst pirates of all—Inda had told them absolutely nothing about his past. When he announced a few days ago to his fleet that he was going to return to his homeland to warn them of imminent invasion by the Venn, everyone had assumed it an act of madness. He'd be killed! Thrown into a dungeon! Thrown into a dungeon *then* killed!

Jeje leaned into the tiller as the *Vixen* sped closer and closer to the coastline; Tau lounged forward to help the brother on day watch shift the tall, curved mainsail.

The contrast between the two secretly entertained Jeje, though she had long known better than to comment to Tau. He was astonishingly beautiful—well made, golden-eyed, with silver-touched hair the color of ripened wheat. Her young crewman, who towered over Tau, was gangly and knot-limbed, with a beaky nose exceeded only by that of his brother. Not that they were bad-looking fellows—it's just that everybody looked a little rough and unfinished next to Tau. *Especially me,* Jeje thought with an inward laugh.

Inda stayed at the rail, sea glass at his eye, his body leaning toward the shore as if doing so would get him there
faster.

They did not want to be seen by Venn spies up near the
peninsula, so they had sailed round the curve of land bulk-
ing out to the west that encompassed Khani-Vayir, then
dove in eastward toward one of the great rivers that flowed
seaward from the eastern border of the kingdom. Inda had
chosen this landing place after days of sailing past cliff-
lined shores that looked pretty much the same.

Earlier, Jeje, who had spent her childhood on the shore
they first passed, had said, "We ought to bring in some
catch as a peace-gift, so they don't shoot us from the shore.
People here know one another. If the Venn have been trying to land spies as well as invade, not to mention burning
their fishing boats whenever they catch 'em, they're going
to really hate strangers." Inda had agreed.

Now, as they loosened sail, Inda said, "Leave the talking
to me."

Jeje was surprised. After all, they didn't look the least
like Venn. Even Signi looked anonymous. And though they
were far south of Jeje's village, the people were pretty
much the same mixture of old Iascan and Marlovan that
she'd known from babyhood.

But as the sun slanted behind them toward the western
horizon and they drifted into a cove, suspicious villagers
lined the shore. The people did not hide their ready
weapons—even when they could clearly see the nets of fish
that the *Vixen* trailed behind. The villagers watched the
four climb down into the rowboat, attach the nets, and row
for shore. By the time they jumped out and brought the
boat ashore, Jeje was thoroughly intimidated and felt no
desire to speak.

Inda called out formal greetings in Iascan. His accent
seemed to calm the people enough for them not to kill the
newcomers outright, as the villagers came down to help
haul in the net of fish. But no one, they all noted, let go of
their grip on their spears and knives, despite the peace-gift.

The Fisher brothers and the wakened night crew sailed

the *Vixen* away, hoping they would be able to catch the rest of the fleet, now commanded by Inda's second, known to them only as Fox.

Jeje forced herself to watch the *Vixen* slant toward the setting sun, though it felt like her heart was pulled thinner with every surging wave. Then she turned her back. It was her choice to be here.

They were brought to the central house of the small coastal village, a round structure made of heavy, thick stone. The door was on the east, a custom inherited from their ancient Venn ancestors, who'd come from the north where wintry winds and storms blustered and howled in from the west, over the sea. The floor was covered by bright, thick rugs, woven in patterns of running animals: foxes, deer, wolves, horses. Later they would discover that the rugs covered trap doors, connecting tunnels built for escape against the Venn and pirate incursions of the past five or six years.

The people dressed like those in Jeje's village had when she was small: tunics sashed or belted at the waist, leggings or loose trousers, everything with some embroidery at the edges. The people themselves were the usual mix of Marlovan and Iascan—dark people like Jeje among blond heads, and all shades between. "It's a good day's catch you give us," said a man, entering the roundhouse.

"The fish are a gift," Inda said. "The boat is trade."

All deferred to the man, whose attention stayed on Inda. He was older, his blond hair gone gray. "What do you want in trade?"

"The loan of mounts for our journey, as far as we need until we can arrange for our own. Then we will send them back."

"Where do you go?"

A young man, strong of arm and gripping a knife, said, "How can you prove you are not Venn spies?"

Inda pointed eastward. "I am first going into Marlo-Vayir land, where I have allies. And then to the royal city, with news that will not wait."

Quick looks. "Who's your ally?" the headman asked, not hiding his suspicion.

Inda attributed that suspicion to the years of war. He
had no idea his accent was an anomaly: he sounded like an
aristocrat, but he looked like a brigand off the sea.

"Cherry-Stripe—uh, that is, Landred-Dal Marlo-Vayir,"
Inda said. "And if you are going to try to trick me with
questions about his personal life, you will find out quickly
that I haven't seen him in years."

"Your name being?" the headwoman asked, her suspicion far less hostile since the stumble over the private
name of Landred Marlo-Vayir.

But then Inda hesitated, and suspicion narrowed eyes
and tightened shoulders again as he wrestled with that old
memory, the orders from the King's Runner, Captain Sindan, when he was eleven years old: *You must find another
name, another life.*

So Tau spoke up from where he lounged against the
wall: "He is Indevan-Dal Algara-Vayir of Choraed Elgaer."

Tau's accent was a perfect mirror to Inda's. Eyes turned
his way, observing the long, hard body below the watchful
face that brought to mind the old goldstone carvings of ancient kings. They observed the presence of three visible
weapons near his hands. Those who knew about such
things saw instantly that from his position in the room, he
could take out the three most important adults before anyone could reach him.

Jeje bit her lip. Beside her Signi breathed softly, slowly,
but the older woman kept her gaze lowered, her hands
folded.

Jeje winced, remembering the danger Signi was in. No.
She was a mage—what the Venn called a sea dag. Supposedly, that meant she could gabble some spell or other and
transfer away in a poof of air. What Signi had to be feeling
was fear of discovery, and Jeje considered what it must
mean for her to be a renegade, wanted by both sides once
the Marlovans found out who she was. "Wanted" not in
welcome, but the opposite.

Jeje flicked a look Signi's way, unsettled by how the
woman made herself unobtrusive. Not by magic. It was the
way she moved, subtleties of posture that you couldn't

really put words to, but the overall effect was unmistakable: Signi was adept at vanishing in plain sight.

A coltish young girl announced, "I know *all* the Jarl families, including in Choraed Elgaer. My tutor made us learn them. There is no Indevan-Dal in Choraed Elgaer."

"Yes, there was," said the headwoman, finally. "I remember the stories from some ten years ago, though most of that was deemed mere rumor. I also heard other stories, from the Queen's Runners—so more believable—that Indevan-Dal had gone to sea under another name, a name associated with the defeat of the pirates belonging to the Brotherhood of Blood two years ago."

Jeje hooked her thumb in Inda's direction as she said proudly, "Elgar the Fox."

"Ah," said the headman, and smiled.

Later, as they sat in a circle and listened to local stories of pirate and Venn attacks and burnings, Jeje leaned over and whispered to Tau, "Why didn't Inda come out with his own name?"

Tau whispered, "Later. When we're alone."

Jeje quieted. These people unnerved her, and they were coast folk: Iascans, like her own family. The inlanders might well be much stranger because they would all be Marlovans.

Chapter Two

"**I** GAVE orders for a castle attack."

Tdor Marth-Davan stiffened at the sound of Branid Algara-Vayir's voice.

This was just about the time Inda and the *Vixen* parted with the Fox Banner fleet. Dawn had brought the first clear spring day to the beleaguered principality of Choraed Elgaer. The warmer breezes coming through the castle's open windows had carried the smells of loam and budding greenery. People rose with strengthened will, and laughed again. There was a pervasive, heart-lifting sense of renewal, and of possibility.

Tdor had gone with the castle folk to begin the spring planting in the rich fields lying east of the outer wall. She did not really need to be there, but it felt right to see them choose this year's soil and hook up the oxen to the plow.

Her good mood vanished the moment she heard Branid's voice. She closed her eyes and made certain her own voice was even. "A castle attack can wait. It's the first good day. We have to get the plowing and harrowing done."

"It's our *tradition* to have a war game on the first good day of spring," Branid retorted, as if Tdor hadn't spent most of her almost twenty-two years in this castle.

He was always going to remind her that she was "just" a

Marth-Davan because he wanted the authority she already had. She knew it. She'd grown up knowing it. But it was always a struggle to speak to him as if his words deserved consideration, to grant him the dignity he never granted her.

"The Iofre said we must get the plowing and harrowing finished first."

Here comes the insult, Tdor thought.

"That old woman!" Branid scoffed. "She squats in that tower of hers with her nose in her stupid scrolls. If she knew anything about defense, which my grandmother says she never did—"

A slight noise behind Tdor reminded her of the tall, solid woman standing there. Head of the fielders, she'd worked under Fareas-Iofre since she was a girl.

The field boss glared at Branid. His lack of respect for the princess infuriated her. Tdor sensed that fury in the woman's audible breathing, the way she shifted on the muddy ground. But she would not speak, so Tdor had to.

"Branid. All of us would love a game. We've been closed in the castle far too long."

His face tightened in the familiar frown of fretful anger. How could he not be aware of the mood of the people around him? They so needed a sense of hope, of control over one small aspect of life. The old prince, Jarend-Adaluin, was weakening by degrees; the long sorrow of the princess, Fareas-Iofre, whose elder son, Tanrid, had been murdered and whose younger, Inda, had been sent from home nine years ago; the fading of the magic spells that eased daily life because the distant Mage Council saw Iasca Leror as a kingdom of warmongers; the years of pirate raids on the Iascan harbors culminating in deliberate destruction by powerful Venn warships—all had steadily ground away spirit as well as strength and resource. So when Castle Tenthen's people woke with spring's clear light at last, they did not need any reminders of war.

Branid frowned down at her, uneasy because she seemed to be agreeing but hadn't actually acknowledged his order. His authority. Which he should have by right!

The two women watched him with practiced patience—

big, muscular Branid-Dal, so angry and anxious he wearied everyone within earshot, as if his steaming, boiling emotions drained everyone else's. He balled his hands into fists, then he swiped one hand over his fair hair, which was bound up in a warrior's horsetail.

"*Someone,*" Branid stated, "has to care for our defense while Whipstick Noth is doing the prince's border patrol. You've had your nose in the scrolls, too. We haven't had what *I* would call a full drill yet this year. We're soft from winter, and when the Venn come they aren't going to send a messenger to ask if we're ready."

Tdor breathed slowly. Out, in. His sarcasm flew wide of the mark; he always talked like that, like his words were arrows and she was a target.

"I know that," Tdor said, fighting to maintain her even tone. The years had taught her a hard lesson in dealing with Branid: he never tired of sneakery, sensing slights, escalating arguments. "We all know it. But we simply have to get the seeds in."

"And have them washed away by another rain? What if we get another three weeks of storm weather?"

"We don't know that we will. What we do know is that the growing season is on us. As soon as the planting is done, you and the Riders should be ready to attack us. We'll drill as long as you think. How's that?"

It sounded like a compromise, didn't it? She tried so hard, but she never knew how he'd hear her words.

Branid snaked a furtive glance to gauge the reaction of the field boss. Did she think Tdor could order him around?

But she was only watching the slow-plodding oxen in the fields. Probably just waiting for orders.

Tdor pitied Branid too strongly to sustain hatred. He had to live every day with his horrible grandmother, who never opened her mouth without complaining, demanding, deriding. As long as she lived, she would never cease trying to shame and vex Branid into forcing his way into the heirship.

Branid's gaze flickered to her face, then down her trim form. Some said she was too tall and plank-shaped to be attractive, but he liked long legs, and though she was only a Marth-Davan, he knew the castle folk all listened to her.

She wasn't the beauty Joret Dei was. By rights he should be married to Joret now, but she'd been whisked over the mountain to marry some prince. So here was Tdor, and if he married her, he'd have his hold on Castle Tenthen. His spies all reported she seldom went down to the town pleasure house, and everyone knew that no sex made you sour. Yes, he could sweeten that tongue! And if she were in his bed, she wouldn't be so quick to speak against him, would she?

Branid gave a small nod. Tdor was not to think he was subordinate. She was the subordinate, a Marth-Davan here on sufferance, and he was the Algara-Vayir. Out of kindness he wanted to have her to wife, not drive her away, and she did do a fine job seeing to house defense. But the Riders must belong to *him*. "Very well, then. Carry on. But when you go back upstairs to your archives, my grandmother says it is past time to find the heir's owl clasp and give it to me." He flicked his horsetail then marched away, chain mail jingling.

Tdor and her companion waited until he vanished around the stable wing of the castle. In the fields the oxen plodded steadily on, and those who tended the plows and harrows sang the old planting songs, in three part syncopations, the fast tripled grade notes rising like birdsong on the brisk air.

Then the field boss said in a low voice, "It's the young who listen to him, who want to be playing at war-gaming instead of real drill." She spoke in Iascan, the language of the people the Marlovans had conquered several generations before, and with whom they now lived. Iascan was the language of everyday life; Marlovan was for war. "And also those who fear threats from his granddam Marend-Edli." Marend-Edli made war in her own home, and all the servants and field workers knew it.

"Tell them this," Tdor said, in Iascan. "Whatever Branid-Dal says or does, it is the prince who pays them their ten flims a month, and his wife who runs the castle. The

princess wishes the planting done. And games *after* Shield
Arm Noth returns from patrol."

The speaker smiled, struck her hand over her heart, and
they parted, the field boss to oversee the people driving
the slow-moving oxen, and Tdor to tramp back to the castle through sludgy mud and fast-growing thistle-weeds. She
was glad of the cool wind, carrying the scents of sedge and
sweetgrass. Maybe the ground would dry out enough for a
good seeding.

Seeds. In front of her boot two lines of insects marched,
some going one way carrying seeds, the others bearing
nothing. She leaned her hands on her thighs and bent
down. *I have to look where I step,* she thought. *I almost
didn't see you. Do you see us? Are we great, terrible beasts?*
She touched her forefinger gently beside the stream of insects climbing over loam and new-sprouted grass; the insects scrambled round her finger and moved on.

She straightened up. Branid? There. Fresh prints—an
extra-long stride. He'd stepped over the insects.

She ran all the way back, and because there was time before her next chore, she sat down at her desk. There lay her
ongoing letter to Joret. Now that the weather had cleared,
she could send it over the mountains.

But should she? She skimmed it rapidly, frowning. What
a dreary thing to receive! Mostly descriptions of the long
winter, punctuated by reports of Venn attacks far in the
north. And at home the make-do inventions forced on
them by the gradual fading of the magic spells that were
such a part of daily life. Spells she grew up taking advantage of, and never thought much about—until they began
to fade.

That was the outside trouble. The inside turmoil was
caused by Marend-Edli, who wanted her grandson Branid
declared the heir so that she could become principal
woman. What a horrible thought.

Tdor frowned at her closely written pages. Paper was so
expensive, but she wondered if she should toss it all into
the fire. Strange, that her foster-sister, Joret, would someday be a queen like their other foster-sister, Hadand. Only

Hadand was a Marlovan queen. Tdor could write anything to Hadand because home business was also her business. Joret had been born and raised Marlovan, but she'd married an Adrani prince. Where was her first loyalty now?

Joret was now a princess in a land where apparently the women didn't do any defense whatsoever. Instead, they danced, and ordered new gowns when the fashions changed, and listened to music from foreign lands, and ate things like cream cakes and delicacies cooked in the Sartoran manner.

Tdor couldn't imagine what "fashion" meant. Oh, she knew that it had something to do with making new clothes, or having them made, and changing things on them. But why? What difference did it make if you wore sleeves with ribbons, or embroidery, or silk instead of velvet? Weren't you the same person underneath all that weaving and stitch-work?

She picked up her letter, her fingers poised to pitch it into the fire. She hated the idea of some Adrani servant nosing into Joret's papers and reading private Algara-Vayir family business. Yet, to destroy the letter and write cheerful, inconsequential natter was to cut off real communication from someone with whom she had shared her childhood—

A knock at the door interrupted this unpleasant inner debate. With some relief she said, "Enter."

Fareas-Iofre herself walked in, her wide-spaced brown eyes marked with exhaustion.

Tdor seldom spent much time in her own room. She was usually too busy. But today most of the castle inmates were employed out in the fields.

Fareas-Iofre sat in the only other chair, her hands in her sleeves. "Tdor, this is the time of the year when I can best spare you."

Tdor gazed in surprise. "Iofre?"

"Branid's claims are a problem we cannot solve. I know that many of the younger men listen to him because he promises them anything, in particular freedom from work if they play follower to his commander. But he is not a good commander, despite Whipstick Noth's attempts to teach him."

Tdor opened her hand in understanding, and the Iofre went on, "So we are now presented with a difficulty that is dividing our people. I would like you to ride to the royal city. Tell our problems to Hadand. And then, if she believes it to be a good idea, ask the king to officially appoint an heir."

Chill prickled the backs of Tdor's arms, the nape of her neck. "You mean you are giving up on Inda?"

Fareas-Iofre turned her face to the window. Tears gathered the light along her lower lids, but did not fall. She was a thin, strong woman, someone who had never seemed to age all the years Tdor was growing up. Until this last year, when her brown hair showed shocks of gray, and the lines in her face did not smooth out in the saving grace of candlelight.

"I never 'give up' on my children," she said to the window in a low voice. "But it will be ten years come summer, so I think it fair to assume he will not be home again. We must do what we can to ensure peace here because there is so little peace elsewhere in the kingdom."

Tdor bowed her head. "Very well," she said, the chill grown to a ball of ice behind her ribs. But she would not complain, or indeed show any emotion. She knew Inda's mother had to be feeling far worse. "I will leave today."

Chapter Three

JEJE encountered her first inland Marlovans after a long, hard, increasingly painful day of travel. At first, seeing the others on horses was funny. No, not horses—ponies. As if there were any difference, except maybe these beasts were hairier. Oh, they were also shorter.

Shorter was good. Before they'd lost sight of the village, Tau managed to slip off the skimpy quilted saddle twice, just by looking around when the beast shifted its weight. The boy who accompanied them to an inn shook with laughter, his face crimson as Tau picked himself up, cursing vilely, and climbed back on.

To Jeje's eyes Inda rode like a prince. He sat tall in the saddle, riding with an easy assurance that he previously had exhibited only in fighting practice.

Inda was scarcely aware of the muscle strain of riding again. The sounds, the smells, even the way the light fell across the stubby green grass shoots on the sloping plains all brought back his childhood with an intensity that made him answer the others' questions somewhat at random.

And at first Tau and Jeje asked lots of questions about birds, plants, hills that they passed. Inda sometimes answered, though when he gazed off at a hawk on the wing, his mind distant, the boy answered.

By midday no one spoke. Tau winced at every jolt of the

horse. At sundown, when the road brought them to an inn at the edge of a small riverside trade town, Tau dismounted and his knees nearly gave out. He clutched the stirrups of Jeje's saddle and whispered, "My balls are crushed. No wonder Marlovans fight all the time. They can't possibly have sex."

She snorted and scrambled down. They followed the others into a courtyard, where the village boy took over the ponies. There seemed to be more room for horses than for people, Jeje thought, looking around. Three sides were stables. The structure was built largely of a warm, honey-colored stone that she was to discover all over the interior of Iasca Leror, instead of the ubiquitous gray stone of most other castles.

A lookout, bow to hand, sat in a tiny window under the peak of the baked tile roof. They'd reached Marlovan land, all right.

Inda's party walked inside as the sun touched the horizon in the west. A land horizon, not the sea, Jeje thought, resisting the sense of being stifled. *I chose to be here.*

The inn was crowded inside. The people dressed pretty much alike, fitted tunics and riding trousers on the men, long robes over riding trousers on the women. The children dressed much like ship rats: shapeless smocks, few of them dyed, and baggy trousers gathered at the knee. They wore woolen stockings and flat-weave mocs, which reminded Jeje of her childhood on shore. The shoes would be kicked off on the first nice day and not worn again until the first day of frost when the sun had bent north again for winter.

The main difference was their speech, so quick with sharp consonants, very different from the northern slur. She'd always thought of this as "Inda's accent"—one of those personal quirks, like a twitching eye, as she'd never heard anyone else use it. She'd learned after meeting Fox and Barend on the pirate ship *Coco* that this was actually the Marlovan accent.

Inda's head jerked up, his eyes wide at the soft, sinister sound of hand drums. Jeje's neck prickled.

"You'll join us for Restday drum?" the innkeeper, an old woman, asked.

Inda's mouth had gone dry at the first *tap-tap-tap*. He opened his hand in assent and walked numbly into the common room, where the drummers gathered one another with little nods and shoulder shifts as they settled into a rhythm. Three established the beat, and the rest added a counterpoint. The galloping tempo resonated with Inda's childhood memories, shaking loose emotions he had worked so hard to shut away.

Over by the fireplace a group of young children sang songs that were familiar to Jeje; familiar, too, were the rye pan biscuits passed around by the women. Everyone sent uneasy looks at the three newcomers, as if evil intent was woven into their eastern-style long jacket-vests, wide-sleeved linen shirts, deck trousers, and mocs. Or maybe it was the bloodred glitter of rubies in their golden hoop earrings. *Pirate* earrings.

Would these people know that the rubies attached to their hoops signified pirate ship kills and not the destruction of traders? Jeje wondered, and then answered herself: of course they wouldn't. Marlovans had no fleet. They knew nothing about ships.

Tau took the rye biscuit handed to him by the innkeeper: the outer crust crispy, the inner bread heavy and nut-flavored. His memory shot back to his mother's house in Parayid Harbor and the elegant little cakes she always served on Restday as her senior worker poured the expensive Gyrnian wine. Restday had been an easy day on the Pim ships, which Tau joined in his mid-teens, before pirates destroyed that life. Pirates did not keep ritual days except at a captain's pleasure. Inda's fleet had gotten out of the habit.

Signi took the bread in her hands, closing herself inside her private grief.

A squirt of wine for each, brought by the innkeeper's son, and Jeje felt the wine burn pleasantly through her, assuaging some of the ache in her thighs and butt, the intensifying stiffness of muscles she had not known she had.

Inda had gone distant as he participated in the ritual; only Signi was aware of the trembling of his fingers.

Inda breathed in the scent of the rye bread, his eyes blurring with tears. He'd gotten used to those. He closed his eyes as he ate and drank, thinking over and over, *I am truly home.*

After a filling supper, accompanied by more of the drumming and chanted songs—mostly in Marlovan and thus unintelligible—Jeje began sliding toward sleep right where she sat. She rarely drank, but Tau had called for mulled wine. It was served in curiously shallow, flat round cups that required two hands to hold. The mulled wine here was more tart than sweet, mixed with hockleberry and spices rather than the cloves and the citrus common elsewhere. Jeje found it delicious, and lapped at it, her chin dipping toward the table, until her eyelids started drifting down.

She roused at the sound of Inda's voice. ". . . two beds? That will be fine."

Jeje sat up, her sleep-thick boredom banished by the question of who would be sharing with whom. Jeje had assumed she'd bunk with the dag, leaving Tau and Inda as bunkmates. Signi murmured something and Inda smiled at her, whispering back, then he slid his arm around her. Signi glanced back at the Restday singers with a look that seemed melancholy to Jeje.

They vanished in the direction of the rooms, leaving Jeje thoroughly awake and unready to consider the prospect of sharing a bed with Tau. She said, "Inda never took a lover all the years we knew him. I like her—don't think I don't— but I don't see how he ended up with her. Why not Gillor or someone our own age?"

Tau leaned toward her, his smile pensive. "He has been lost for nine years. She is now lost. I think it was inevitable they would find one another."

Jeje sighed. She liked Tau better than anyone alive— when she was younger she had struggled against an awful passion for him—but there were times he simply did not make sense. "Lost? Her, maybe. But he's going home!"

"Yes. Home. Think about that, Jeje." Tau ran his fingers

lightly around the rim of the shallow wine cup. "No, think about this. Until very recently, do you remember ever hearing Inda laugh?"

"Of course! Well—oh, I don't know." She sat upright on the bench, her entire body expressive of protest. "What are you getting at? That Inda's a stick?"

Tau flickered his fingers. "No. No. Let me try another way. Why are we along to protect him? No, think first. He's got a rep—earned as one of the most dangerous men in the entire southern half of the world. He may or may not be able to beat Fox, but you and me?"

"I know." Jeje snorted softly. "Dead in three heartbeats."

"Probably at the same time. And yet here we are, changing our lives yet again, because we felt he needed protection. Why?"

Jeje felt the urge to protest, argue, deny. But as she considered his words the instinct to protest weakened, then vanished. "It *is* odd," she admitted. "All right, so tell me why we did it. All I know is I thought he needed protection. Yes, his old friend is a king, but is that a good thing? The only thing I am certain about with kings is that they can order their killing done easy as a sneeze."

Tau laughed soundlessly, then sobered. "I think the reason we want to protect him is that until a few weeks ago Inda remained the boy we've known for nine years. I don't mean physically, but here." He touched his heart. "And in some ways, here, too." He touched his head. "That seems to have changed when he was a prisoner in Ymar, and changed again when he neared home, then decided the time had come to end his exile. But part of our impulse to come along is that we think he needs watching over."

Jeje pushed her cup between her fingers back and forth along the rough table. "All right. Maybe. But the other reason I'm here is because I don't trust these Marlovans. Or this king, old friend or not. What's your other reason?"

Tau thought, *Because of you.*

What if she took it the wrong way? Sentiment could be so sickening. So provoking of false expectations, which destroyed the clean, uncluttered bond of friendship.

But he couldn't lie to Jeje.

Jeje watched his profile, outlined against the roaring fire on the other side of the inn room. Gradually the sounds of other merrymakers intruded into her awareness: the clink of crockery, the soft tap of drums and chanting voices punctuated by laughter. The smells of spiced wine, of the peppered vinegar that the locals put on their fried fish, the sweetish scent of brown onion simmering somewhere to be mixed into the steamed cabbage and rice balls.

"I . . . I think we need to make certain his past hasn't turned lethal." Tau raised his voice as someone nearby began another of those galloping drumbeats, this time accompanied by a syncopated cymbal. "He believes this king is a friend."

A song began, sung by women—a jolly, rollicking tune.

"Aha! You don't trust him either."

Tau raised a hand. "I don't mistrust him because he's become a king. What I mistrust is how things might have changed in nine years. Inda says he knows everything might be different, but I don't think he believes it. Because in so many ways he hasn't changed in nine years. That clearer?"

Jeje nodded. "Bringing us to that past. Let's have that business about Inda using his right name."

"How much do you remember about Inda?" Tau tipped his head, ducking out of the way of a young woman's elbow as she danced by, her embroidered robe swaying.

"His name isn't Inda Elgar, it's Indavun Algraveer, or whatever it was you said back on the coast." Jeje jerked her thumb over her shoulder. "I remember that much. And I remember what you said about his father being a prince, and some scandal or other, hoola hoola hoola. But he's home, so why not speak up and use his name?"

The dancing women whirled near.

"Because." Tau leaned toward Jeje. "One thing that's fairly clear about Marlovans—besides their rep for conquering—is their notion of honor. That seems to include very long memories for old troubles."

He scooted up next to her, their thighs touching, as two

or three young women danced very close to their table, hands clapping to one side then the other, point and counterpoint, hips swaying. The top of one's hand brushed against the back of Tau's head, lingering on his silky hair.

Jeje scowled at the table, finger drawing the *Vixen's* long, elegant shape in the moisture ring from her mug as she tried not to be aware of the warm press of his leg against hers.

So she'd think about Inda. Old troubles, yes, like a thirty-year-old murder in the previous generation. Like Inda and Barend—an old shipmate and a Marlovan. Upon discovering that Barend's father had hired people to kill Inda's father's first family all of thirty years ago, Inda had acted like it happened three days ago.

At the sight of her straight black brows lowered in a line across her forehead, Tau said, "Whatever it was that Inda did as a boy to get him exiled, it might not make sense to us. But what happened matters to Inda."

"And so if he walks right into trouble, thinking he deserves it, we'll haul him out if we can." Jeje huffed. No use in complaining about the crazy ways of Marlovans. She'd forced herself on this quest of Inda's, which meant she had no right to complain.

So she turned her attention outward again; it sure had gotten noisy and crowded all of a sudden.

Then she laughed. It was mainly noisy right in their corner: the young women gathered for their Restday socializing seemed to be aiming their songs and dancing at Tau. They sang in his direction, as the boldest danced as close to him as they could get, despite the jumble of tables and shoved-back chairs they had to navigate around.

He smiled absently when one bumped her hip into his shoulder then leaned down to apologize. He opened his hand in polite salute, but no invitation. She withdrew, hips rolling, and glanced back once, but he wasn't watching. Jeje was. She met the woman's eyes and the woman gave her a rueful grin. Jeje grinned back.

Tau whispered to Jeje, "We're being crowded out. Let's get some sleep. You know Inda—we'll be riding before the sun rises."

They rose together; as the innkeeper handed Tau a candle in a ceramic holder Jeje looked back at the women to encounter several appreciative glances directed at Tau's backside and long legs, outlined as they were in the deck trousers—narrow at the hips, gradually widening down. The same woman as before gave Jeje a flick of fingers to heart in respect.

If only you knew he thinks of me as a sister, Jeje thought with an inward flutter of laughter as she followed Tau to the room the innkeeper had pointed out. *No, more like a little brother.*

The door shut and they were alone.

It was a small room, smaller than the one she'd had to live in for that long harbor stay in Bren, and no sound of the sea. The room smelled of wood, and faintly of mildew, and herb-laced leddas-wax candles; it had only a tiny table next to a bed. There were hooks on the wall for clothes. The air was sharply cold after the warmth of the inn's main room.

Tau set the candle on the table and moved to the window to look out. While his back was turned she flung off her tunic, kicked off her trousers, stockings, and shoes, then climbed hastily under the quilt and lay straight, and as close to the edge of the bed as possible. Tau sighed, "Ooh, I'm sore," as he yanked the laces free on his shirt and pulled it up over his head.

Jeje had conquered her old girlhood passion, thoroughly and competently. Yes, she had. What she struggled against now was a young woman's awareness of candlelit golden hair; a long, lean form with hard muscle moving under smooth, golden-brown skin; the smell of male—a compound with sea brine and sweat and a faint whiff of horse. Unexciting smells when considered separately, but combined, emanating from Tau's flesh, they evoked all the old passion and desire. And so she pulled the quilt to her nose, sniffing in its faint aroma of mildew, and resolutely shut her eyes. Though she was acutely aware of the soft sounds of shifting cloth as Tau finished undressing and neatly hung up his clothes.

Then he puffed, and the red light on her lids went out. The bed shifted, and she fell inward as Tau's weight settled beside her. The aged mattress—stuffed with old horse blankets—promptly slid her toward the middle. She arched away, hoping he wouldn't think she was encroaching.

The bed shifted, and Tau said, "My ass aches."

She dared the smallest peek. In the cool blue moonlight from the tiny window he was barely visible lying back, arms crossed behind his head. She caught herself wanting to sniff more deeply of his scent, and pressed the quilt firmly over her nose. "Ump."

Tau exhaled softly. "All right. Let's sleep."

And—she almost could have counted his breaths—he soon was. His breathing slowed to a light snore that she found amazingly endearing, until he turned to the side and his breathing quieted.

She lay there staring upward, her emotions midway between laughter and exasperation. Much deeper, her young self wailed over what might have been, and she wondered how many years this night would last. But tiredness conquered awareness at last, and she dropped gradually into a jumble of restless dreams.

When she woke, the blue light of impending dawn diffused the shadows in the dingy little room. The air on her face was chilly.

She was at once aware of a warm back pressed against her side. Tau! She eased away, her inner thighs sending white-hot lightning bolts of pain to prickle tears in her eyes.

"You awake?" came a drowsy, husky voice. "How do you feel?"

"Sore." She was not going to say where.

"Me, too. How can these people do that every day, all day? Though I guess they could say the same about us. I remember when I first came aboard the *Ryala,* and Fassun set me to the hardest ropes until my hands bled. Kodl thrashed him for it. Remember Fassun? How long ago that seems!"

Jeje said in a gruff voice, "I hope Testhy is all right."

"He would be. He's like me, always seeks comfort first."
Jeje snorted.

"You don't believe me?" Tau shifted to face her, raising
himself up on an elbow, hand supporting his head. His eyes
were clear and smiling, his hair loose and spilling across the
pillow; the end of a lock almost touched her.

Once—after they'd been captured by the pirate Gaffer
Walic—he'd cut his hair off with a sword and thrown it into
the sea, just because the pirate's woman Coco had loved
playing with it. It had nearly grown out to its old length
again.

Jeje gritted her teeth, her arms crossed across her middle, her hands balled into fists.

Tau's brows came together. "Are you in that much
pain?"

A way out of this impossible situation? "Yes."

"Oh, well, then, turn over. Let me work on you."

"Don't be ridiculous." And, because he not only looked
surprised but a little hurt, she added, somewhat desperately, "I know you hate being touched. That means you
must hate touching other people."

His long lashes lifted. "That's not true."

"I've seen you when people grab at you. Caresses. Fingering. Coco, and others. How disgusted you were. They
couldn't see it, but I did."

The curve of Tau's mouth thinned to a white line for a
moment. "That's not touch, that's possession. It's true, I
hated being regarded as someone's pet lapdog, and I have
always wondered if dogs feel the same. It's why I never
wanted a pet. But you've never done that to me, tried to
make me a possession. You've never made any move
toward me at all."

"Well, then, I'm glad to be of service."

Tau was puzzled by her flush. Anger? Her voice, so
deep—she'd had the deepest voice of all until the boys
crossed the threshold of puberty—was like the rough,
chesty growl of a big feline.

He laughed. "Jeje, you are impossible to understand at
times. Will you, or will you not, permit me to use some of

my trained trickery on you? Inda has asked me often enough, when his wounds trouble him. I believe we survived the encounters."

Jeje flumped over, her arms stiff at her sides. She knew her shift was awry, her drawers twisted, but she wouldn't fumble at her clothes. Wouldn't move.

Fingers traced lightly along her back muscles, leaving tiny trails of warm prickles. She shut her eyes and clenched her teeth harder. Tau's fingers expertly found the knots and kneaded deeply, a rhythmic, soothing sensation that really did ease the aches gathered all along her lower back—aches she hadn't even been aware of because of the worse ones down below.

Despite her control her breathing eased as the pain faded, leaving the warmth of . . . no. No! But when his fingers moved to her legs, and he worked his way along her pain-stiffened thigh muscles, the easement, and the attendant crescendo of building desire, made her unable to resist when he gently tugged at her to turn over. She kept her eyes shut, but her flesh and nerves tingled with expectancy.

"Ah," Tau breathed. "Ah." And his hands drifted up her body, so gently, so softly, she didn't even realize he'd lifted her shift until the cold morning air touched her charged flesh.

He chuckled, the sound sending another flare of insistence through her.

She opened her dark brown eyes. He gazed down, enjoying very much the confusion he saw in her usually capable, closed face. Jeje the wise, the considerate, the cool hand with bow and arrow who sailed through the worst firefights, and there were two, no, three, arrow scars to prove it. Not that she had ever complained, or even let anyone see them.

He saw them now, and bent to kiss each. Long, soft kisses, and he sniffed her warm, slightly salty scent, and then bent to kiss her brow, and when her breathing altered, the tip of her nose, and then her parted lips.

She growled, the jagged purr of a mountain cat.

Now thoroughly enchanted, Tau pressed soft kisses on

her collarbones, and she lay with her hands open, eyelashes fluttering on her cheeks as he, with infinite care, moved downward—

A thud on the door startled them.

"Sunup! You awake?" Inda yelled through the flimsy wood.

"No," Tau called, and grinned down at Jeje, a laughing grin that brought an even deeper flush to her cheeks, and her own rare, endearing grin in return. "We're busy."

"Well, hurry up!" And, diminishing down the hall, Inda's plaintive addition, "Why didn't they think of that last night?"

"Should we go?" Jeje asked.

Tau was delighted to see his own want reflected in her steady dark eyes. "Let them linger over their breakfast," he suggested, and she laughed.

Chapter Four

CHERRY-STRIPE Marlo-Vayir and his brother, Buck, watched from the dining chamber windows as their father limped across the courtyard below toward the stable. When old Hasta was out of sight, his thin gray-white horsetail flopping on his broad back, Cherry-Stripe elbowed Buck. "See that? He's like a boy again."

Their father had returned for a short time from the enormous horse stud the Marlo-Vayirs maintained in their plains, a day's ride to the north. He had begun this past winter brooding and quiet. Though no one referred to it, they could not forget that shortly after the previous New Year's Convocation, Hasta had been drawn into Mad Gallop Yvana-Vayir's conspiracy, which had led to a royal bloodbath.

When it came time to depart for the royal city for this winter's Convocation, as all Jarls had to do each New Year's in order to renew their oaths, Hasta had insisted on his elder son going to make his vows to the king as the new Jarl of Marlo-Vayir. "Young kings need young Jarls," he had said. His son obeyed—but he'd been afraid he'd return and find his father dead.

Instead, old Hasta had retired to the horse stud, where he seemed happier than he'd been for years. He came back only to consult with Buck about the crop rotation and arrange for some supplies, then he was off again.

Buck shook his head in silent amazement, then grabbed a last bread roll from the plate on the table. "Cama up yet?"

"I don't think so," Cherry-Stripe replied, rolling his eyes as he dropped down onto his seating mat before the long, low table his ancestors had had put in generations ago, when Marlovans had first taken over the Iascan castles.

Buck snickered. "Mran?"

Cherry-Stripe groaned. "Wailing like balladeers."

Who could have predicted that little buck-toothed Mran, Cherry-Stripe's practical, quiet, efficient twig of a wife, a daughter of the ancient and efficient Cassads, would conceive the grandest of passions for the handsome one-eyed Camarend Tya-Vayir? No, that was to be expected. All the females seemed to lust after Cama. What was strange was that he—the handsomest man in the kingdom and once the lover of the handsomest woman, Joret Dei—had fallen for Mran just as passionately.

Buck found the absurdity hugely entertaining. He laughed as he loped down the stairs to begin the day. But Cherry-Stripe lounged on his mat, one elbow on the table as he slurped down a last cup of steeped mountain-leaf. He scowled at the prospect of facing the icy air. Wasn't winter supposed to end *some* day?

His sour mood received an unexpected diversion, the quick step of his First Runner. The man ran in, amazement widening his eyes. "Word from the outer perimeter Riders."

"Attack?" Cherry-Stripe leaped to his feet.

"No. They encountered a party on the west road at sunset, about to camp. Two men, two women, all dressed in outlandish garb. Four horses from the south—river lending stock. One of the men says to tell you, and the words are these." His expression smoothed into the studied neutrality of formal mode, approximating the tone of the verbal message as close as was humanly possible, "Tell Cherry-Stripe Inda is here."

"Inda," Cherry-Stripe repeated, at first thinking of his old academy mate Noddy's newborn baby, and then he grabbed the Runner by the tunic laces and yelped, "*Inda*?"

The man's head rocked. "Yes," he wheezed, eyes bulging.

Cherry-Stripe let go, threw back his head, and yipped the ancient cry of Marlovans on the charge.

From far below came his brother's voice, *Yip! Yip! Yip!* And then from the guest rooms above came a faint answer: *Yip! Yip! Yip!*

All over the castle servants, Runners, armsmen, bakers, brewers, weavers stopped what they were doing and exchanged wondering glances.

It was inevitable the first one they noticed was Tau.

Buck, Cama, and Cherry-Stripe drew rein on a grassy bluff above the curve of the road. As the newcomers rode sedately around the bend below, accompanied by a pair of Marlo-Vayir perimeter riders, the three surveyed them: two men, two women, all in outlandish garb. One, a scar-faced fellow, medium height and broad through the chest and shoulders, the other fellow, tall, fair-haired, and striking.

Cherry-Stripe muttered in amazement, "Is *that* Inda?"

"Nooo," Cama drew the word out, expressive of disgust. His breath clouded in the cold air. "Inda wouldn't ride like an old sack of bran."

Buck smothered a crack of laughter, and they studied the party more closely, bypassing the short, solid woman with the chin-length, flyaway dark hair and a glittering ruby at one ear. The tall man wore one as well. The other woman was even more nondescript. No earring. The husky scar-faced fellow wore a long brown sailor braid down his back. Same outlandish attire—his long shirt-tunic was sashed with pirate purple, old and stained as it was. And he wore *two* rubies, one in each of the gold hoops in his ears. But at least—unlike the others—he knew how to sit a horse. He rode easily, his head bent as he listened to one of the others jabbering—and when he turned his thumb up, that gesture resonated down nine years of memory.

"Inda?" Cherry-Stripe said in disbelief, and then howled, "Inda!"

Who jerked his head up, hands snapping to the knives strapped to his forearms inside his loose sleeves. He peered up at the three silhouettes on the hill. The diffuse sunlight glared from behind them, but he could make out some details: two blonds and a black-haired young man with an eye patch.

Inda's heart drummed when he saw that eye patch. "Cama?" Then one of those blond men had to be— "Cherry-Stripe!"

Signi flinched as the three on the hill uttered high, harsh cries like some predatory beast on the run. Their horses seemed to leap down the hill, raising a spectacular cloud of dust. The rising wind sent it swirling as the three circled Inda, laughing and shouting questions that no one could listen to because they all spoke at once.

Then Cherry-Stripe yelled in a field-command voice, "Weather's on the way! Come on, let's ride for home!"

Buck yipped again, taking the lead. Cama and Cherry-Stripe were after him like arrows from a bow. Inda started to follow, then kneed his horse to a prancing, snorting stop as he called over his shoulder, "Come on, Tau, Jeje. Signi?"

Tau waved. "Ride on, we'll catch up."

Inda sent an inquiring look to Signi, who understood at once that he was torn by concern for her and longing to be with the friends he had not seen since childhood. She lifted her hand toward them; he smiled, wheeled the horse, and was gone in a cloud of dust.

Jeje cocked an eye at Tau. He lifted his chin. Jeje and he parted, and with some determined knee-nudging and tugs on the reins, got their horses to jounce forward to either side of the Venn dag.

The storm Cherry-Stripe had seen on the horizon was sending sleet pounding against the windows as the party sat on mats in the Marlo-Vayirs' dining room.

Since their arrival they'd been barking questions at one another. The servants coming and going stared at the exotic dress of the newcomers. None of the old academy mates noticed. Jeje stayed by Signi, who never made an unnecessary movement at any time; she seemed smaller, almost invisible again.

"I can't hear anyone. Let's ask questions in round," Buck said. "Me first. Inda! D'you really command a pirate fleet?"

Cherry-Stripe leaned over the table, ignoring his brother. "Barend said it really was you, scragging those soul-sucking pirates two winters back. How'd you come to fighting pirates?"

"Didn't Barend tell you?" Inda replied, turning from one to the other. "What's happened to Noddy? Flash?" And to Buck, "We were building a fleet in the east, when—"

"Flash is a great man now—Flash-Laef, no, what's his real name?"

"Tlennen." Cama snickered. "Now Tlennen-Laef. Imagine calling Flash Tlennen."

"His mother must." Cherry-Stripe whacked Cama. "Quiet. Inda, Flash is now Laef of Olara, his father being Jarl. Brother died leading an attack against the damned red sails on the Idayagan coast—"

"—and Noddy married a year back, because his cousin never did get an heir, and Noddy's dad being Randael before he died at—"

"—ho, Evred told us we all needed to marry early. On account of the war—"

Inda's head jerked back and forth as he tried to keep up his end of the question-answer cross-shoot. "—and took his raffee, then we netted us a couple of trysails—"

"What's a raffee?"

"—and Noddy's wife had a baby over winter. Did you know he named him after you?"

"Barend Montrei-Vayir stopped here before he went north, and he said you were goin' after the Venn up on the north coast—"

"What's a raffee?"

The voices got louder and louder until Buck smacked his hand flat on the table. "Quiet! All of you!"

The guests fell silent. Cherry-Stripe made a rude noise.

"I can't hear, and worse, no one can hear me." Buck scowled down the table.

Cama was laughing silently; Cherry-Stripe flipped up the back of his hand at his brother, at which Buck's wife Fnor made a scandalized hiss, tipping her head meaningfully toward the guests. Mran quietly made certain everyone got some hot cider to drink.

Buck hooked his thumbs toward his chest. "First me, since I'm the Jarl here." And over his brother's even louder rude noise, "What is a raffee?"

"It's a capital ship, named after its foresail, which—"

Buck smacked his palm on the table again. "What's a foresail?"

"On the foremast you have—"

"What's a foremast?"

Cama was laughing so hard his face was crimson, which made Buck and his wife begin to laugh. Even Mran chuckled, a sound not unlike boiling water.

Cherry-Stripe now smacked the table, making the dishes clatter. "That's enough with the boats. Nobody wants to hear about boats. Not until we see one, which we never will. Inda. Your turn to ask a question."

Inda said, "How did Sponge come to be king?"

Chapter Five

THE humor vanished as quick as the sun that morning, as all three of Inda's old academy mates reacted typically: Buck busied himself with unnecessary gestures to the servants now bringing in the meal, and waited for his brother to speak, Cherry-Stripe having been Inda's scrub mate. Cherry-Stripe grimaced at Cama, waiting for the others to broach the subject, knowing it was craven, but sometimes he just had to rabbit out of a nasty duty. He wasn't any good with words anyway, he told himself.

Cama, who was on the wrong side to see Cherry-Stripe's not-so-subtle glances and surreptitious jabs of the chin in Inda's direction, glowered down at the table through his one good eye while the food was served, thinking about how to word the bleak story.

A servant offered Inda the rice-and-cabbage balls that were so familiar from his childhood. That sight, and the long-missed aromas of the food and the fresh-baked rye biscuits made his eyes sting. He had to get used to that, how joy and pain together would fountain up inside him until it splashed out in tears. He dashed his sleeve impatiently across his eyes.

Cherry-Stripe gawked at the tear-stains gleaming on Inda's scarred cheek. "Something amiss with the spoon?" he asked in a tentative voice.

"It's good to eat with a spoon again." Inda held up the plain, carved-wood implement with its wide, shallow bowl. "A Marlovan spoon. No more forks."

Buck and Cherry-Stripe turned to the other for clues, just to find mirrored perplexity.

Cama said, "Forks are useless. You have to stab things. Imagine stabbing rice. Especially with one eye. I remember that from when I was a boy, and got taken to the healer down south. They eat Sartoran-style there. I thought I'd starve!"

Fnor had also noticed the spring of emotion in their scar-faced guest as he turned the spoon over and over in his hands. She, like Cherry-Stripe, was nonplussed at Inda's reaction, but she could try to be a good host. "I remember those forks, when we girls had to do duty up in the queen's room. Just think, the girls now get to eat with Hadand, and not sit there with those funny dishes, listening to the tootle and footle music."

Mran said, "Woodwinds and strings. Like in Sartor."

Fnor waved a hand in a circle. "Wheedle-deedle is what it sounded like. Nothing like a good strong beat, or a melody you can sing a ballad to. Well, no more!"

Buck moved impatiently, and sent a scornful glance at his brother and Cama for their cowardice, but one was busy studying his spoon, the other the walls. "Back of my hand to music! Inda, you should by rights talk to Evred-Harvaldar. Better, your sister—"

"Hadand-Gunvaer defended the throne herself," Fnor put in, and Mran signified agreement and approval with a flick of her thumb upward. They had been in the queen's training with Inda's sister, had liked her then, and respected her now as a proven fighting queen, young as she was.

Buck said, "Evred or Hadand, they can tell you the details. The gist is this: the king was killed. It was a conspiracy started by Hawkeye's dad. Only Hawkeye wasn't in on it. But the three of us were there at the end, see, on account of Mad Gallop Yvana-Vayir dragging our father into it blind."

Now that Buck had broached the subject, Cherry-Stripe leaned forward. "Noddy was there, too."

"King's room full of blood, all his Runners killed—" Cama put in grimly.

"But he died in the Sierlaef's room. Opened his arms to the blade," Buck put in.

"Yvana-Vayir killed him. King wasn't even armed!"

"Yvana-Vayir went down to try to take the throne, and your sister headed him off. And when he tried to ride her down and grab the throne—" Cherry-Stripe mimed a side-cut and thrust from a sword "—she took him down. Only wounded him, because his son was there. Later she said she should have finished him."

"—execution in the parade court, because he wouldn't take a knife and do it himself." Cama's husky voice was even rougher with disgust. "Of course they had to put all his captains against the wall. Even the ones who claimed not to know anything about the plans."

Inda turned his palm up, remembering talk from child-hood, exciting at the time: a commander who led his men into treasonous action took all his captains down with him. But they weren't flogged to death, being under orders. The thought of it actually happening made his gut tighten.

"The rest of the royal family was killed by some of the Jarl's men," Cherry-Stripe said. They had fallen back into Marlovan, the language of their ancestors. "Four more sent to kill Evred, but he escaped."

"What?" Inda exclaimed. "Evred—you mean Sponge, right? Wait, wait. The rest of the family, including the queen, and Barend's mother? Why? Surely they didn't blame her for the Harskialdna's plots?"

Fnor consciously switched back to Iascan, though she would have rather the guests had gone away. It didn't seem decent, to talk of these things in front of strangers. "Not the queen. She being an outsider, no one noticed her. As for Barend's mother, Hadand thinks that the Harskialdna knifed her, and not the Yvana-Vayir men."

The king's brother killed his own wife? "I don't know which is worse." Inda rubbed the scar on his jaw. "And Sponge? I mean, you said Yvana-Vayir sent—"

"—four of his riding captains north to assassinate him.

Evred was in command in the north, see, while his brother
was riding around in the south. But Evred dressed as a
Runner so they couldn't find him, and Captain Sindan
routed the assassins until backup could get there. Died in
the process," Cherry-Stripe said.

Inda whooshed out his breath. "This sounds worse than
us fighting pirates, if you ask me."

Buck turned his thumb up in agreement. He was about
to go on when he remembered the rest of that terrible day,
and sidled a glance at his brother.

Cherry-Stripe made surreptitious motions that Buck
couldn't make out, but when Inda glanced his way he
yanked his hands down, thumping the table. Fnor repressed a sigh as she righted a spilled pepper dish. Cama's
head turned sharply as he tried to keep everyone in the
view of his one eye.

"So Evred and Hadand had to marry. Did that on Mid-
summer Night, and Evred officially took everyone's oaths
as king." Buck hastily shifted to a description of the coronation, joined in relief by the other two. They spoke in Iascan, but they may as well have stayed with Marlovan. Their
words were so quick, their accent so strange, and their Iascan so full of Marlovan slang, that Tau, Jeje, and especially
Signi found it difficult to follow.

The Marlovans had all been trained by the same masters
in giving a report; Inda had given and received enough
since then to know when he was being bustled past details
the speakers did not want to address. That was all right.
Like Buck said, he could ask his sister or Sponge—now the
king. Even after a few weeks, he still couldn't get used to
that idea.

Inda listened, assimilating most of what they said, but his
attention was on his old friends and how they had changed.
Except for Buck being seven years senior, they all were
pretty much of an age. But in Inda's memory they had
drifted through the years as scrubs of eleven and twelve,
dressed in academy smocks as they played war games
through the eternal sunshine.

Cama's sudden, white-flashing grin, Cherry-Stripe's

waving hands, his laugh—the same laugh as in boyhood, only deeper—sparked recognition yet caused those cherished memory-images, sharp for so long, to blur and evanesce.

The account of the coronation and Evred's first Convocation fumbled to a close in a morass of mutual interruptions and half-finished gossip, until Buck cast a quick look around as if spies had crept into his own citadel. "Is it true you were really sailing with the Montredavan-An heir?"

Inda's first impulse was to laugh, but Buck's uneasiness reminded him of the historical context. Every Marlovan grew up knowing that the Montredavan-Ans had been exiled by Evred's own ancestors to their land for ten generations when the throne had changed hands. If they crossed their border except to go to and from the sea they would be killed as treaty-breakers. This was why Fox had gone to sea in the first place—not stepping over the border included not being permitted to train at the academy with the other Marlovan heirs.

"Yes, I did," Inda said. "He saved my life."

As soon as the words were out Inda regretted the impulse—which he couldn't really explain.

Sure enough, they all looked surprised, and Cherry-Stripe said, "What happened?"

Inda loathed any reminder of the days of torture at the hands of the Ymaran Count Wafri. Either he explained it all—which he had no intention of doing—or he skipped over the complicated story about how the Ymaran count had pretended to be a Venn ally but wasn't. His old friends wouldn't care anyway. Inda suspected that to them, Venn and Ymar and Everon were all alike. So he said, "Stupid plan went wrong. Fox Montredavan-An put it right. Here's the fun part. On our way out, we set fire to the enemy's castle."

Sure enough, that worked to divert them. Cherry-Stripe crowed, Buck laughed, Cama demanded the story.

"It was the biggest sting I've ever done," Inda said, and gave them a fast description, mostly of the chaotic aftermath—chickens squawking, people running around yelling and throwing buckets of water at one another, the furious hand-motions of some guards who each thought the others should try to storm the wall as he and Fox sat there alone, holding off the entire garrison with their bows and arrows.

Cherry-Stripe led the laughter, and launched into boyhood memories of stings—safe territory. Or so it seemed at first.

"Remember that first call over? We thought Gand was going to thump us right there!"

"The first flag run?"

"The first overnight? The horsetails stuck us with cook drudge!"

The cider, well laced with distilled rye, had caused their speech to slow, making it easier for Tau and Jeje, if not for Signi, to follow. For the first time in the nine years they had known Inda, they were hearing his boyhood memories—explored with the boys who had shared them.

Inda laughed, and laughed again to rediscover laughter. At the sight of Inda's shaking merriment, Cama and Cherry-Stripe batted reminiscence between them; by now all that was required were a few words.

"The horse piss in the bunks?"

"Th-the bread pills?"

"Spying out the pigtails when they tried to—"

"—shoeing at the Games—"

"Oh! Oh! When Basna took bets on beetle races?"

"How he howled when Gand measured his shoulder blades with King Willow," Cama exclaimed, flipping up his eye patch to mop his eyes with his sleeve; Jeje quickly looked away from the purple scarring round the bad one.

Inda whooped for breath. "Basna squawking *gambling? That's gambling? Nobody ever told me that!* None of the beaks believed him."

"That's Basna all over." Cherry-Stripe thumped the table again. "Invents gambling just to get himself dusted and gated."

"Remember when Flash—"

"—Fijirad and Tuft had that fight over—"

"—tried to get Noddy to laugh?"

As the memories slid past those first two years into the summers after Inda had gone, Fnor kept smothering yawn after yawn of boredom. But she was Jarlan now—Buck and Cherry-Stripe's mother had moved back to live with her own mother, and while Fnor knew little (and cared less) about the minutiae of the fellows' academy history, manners were manners. The Algara-Vayir name required that, as did the presence of outland guests—a rarity, after all these years of pirate and Venn-enforced embargo. Not that Tau and Jeje were strictly outlanders. Both said they had been born on the coast of Iasca Leror, one in the north and one in the south, but to the inland Marlovans they may as well as been as foreign as . . . where was the sandy-haired woman from? Fnor smothered another yawn, longing for bed. Her day always began well before sunup.

"Remember the shearing, when you got us a month's gag?" Inda leaned toward Cherry-Stripe.

"Ah, I'd forgotten. It was fun, wasn't it, until Lassad made it sour? D'ya know he's a hero now?"

"Smartlip Lassad? You set him and the rest onto us," Inda said, pointing at Buck. "We always thought the Sierlaef was behind it."

"Of course he was. We thought he wanted Sponge toughened up." Buck Marlo-Vayir scratched his nose. "It was fun, watching our little brothers busy shying rocks and scragging beds and the like, all of 'em dead serious. You scrubs were better than anything for laughs. We didn't think it really meant anything. Nothing did. Except winning."

Mran sat beside Cama, her hazel eyes wide, wondering when she could break into the old memories and ask Inda to go back to talking about the sea. She wanted to hear what it was like, being on the ocean that she'd glimpsed just once.

Jeje listened at first, but couldn't make sense of much. Her interest shifted, as did Tau's, to the astonishing change in Inda as he ranged freely among these old memories, to which he had never once referred during all their nine years together. He looked like a ship rat again, despite the scars—younger than his twenty years. *Do you remember ever hearing Inda laugh?* He laughed now, more than she had ever seen.

"—and our very first Restday, and Dogpiss' story about the Egg Dance?" Cherry-Stripe wiped his eyes, thinking *Dogpiss, everything was funnier with Dogpiss*—and then his thoughts galloped off the road. "Oh, shit. Oh, damn. Inda, that was what ditched you, wasn't it? What happened to Dogpiss?"

Tau's heartbeat quickened. In one conversation they were learning everything about Inda's past that they'd spent nine years speculating on; Jeje sat there, food forgotten, her lips parted as she tried to catch the quick words.

"Dogpiss," Inda repeated softly. The pirate commander was back with that narrow, direct gaze, the jut of his jaw and thinned lips. His words were slow and reluctant. "I tried to stop Dogpiss from running that sting in the prisoner-of-war camp."

Prisoner-of-war camp? Jeje sent a questioning look at Tau: *Weren't they just boys?* He flicked his hands outward in question.

Cama said, "All I remember is you reminding him of banner-game rules. No stings. So me 'n' Flash, we rolled up. Remember how tired we were, the horsetails running us all night long? Slept in a heartbeat."

"Night? Nights!" Cherry-Stripe protested.

"We talked about it for a long time, after," Cherry-Stripe said. "Tried to figure it out. What happened? What did Dogpiss do?"

"Argued. Then slipped out when I was half asleep, and I went after him. Hawkeye jumped up. Took us by surprise. Dogpiss slipped on that big rock, I tried to catch him—almost got his wrist. But he fell. You know the rest. Hit his head." Inda pressed the heels of his hands into his eyes. "I saw him like that in dreams. Still do. If that rock hadn't been there—if I'd gotten his wrist—"

Buck said in a low voice, "He also broke his neck."

Inda laid his hands on the table. "Noddy was on guard,

he saw the most, and I told him everything afterward. Why wouldn't the Harskialdna listen to him?"

"Partly Kepa's lies. Then Kepa's father called in old promises. Ruse to get rank out of the Harskialdna, and it worked." Cherry-Stripe spread his hands wide. "But we didn't find that out until a lot later."

"A Harskialdna is a Royal Shield Arm," Jeje whispered behind her hand to Signi. "It's the king's brother. I mean, if he has a brother."

Signi gave a sober nod—of politeness, not of sudden comprehension. Jeje suspected that the Venn mage probably knew more about the Marlovans than she did, and blushed. But Signi's grateful smile made her feel slightly less stupid.

The escape to the past was now over, they all sensed it. In the Marlovans' minds these past events connected directly with the threats of the present.

"We called that one the Summer Without a Banner," Cherry-Stripe said.

Chapter Six

"THE Summer Without a Banner," Cama repeated, his rough voice quarry-deep with regret.

"That summer changed a lot of things, though we didn't see it at the time. We were just boys." Buck gazed into the fire.

"And *we* were only Tveis," Cherry-Stripe said.

Later on Tau learned what that meant—second sons, defenders and spare heirs. Inda and his friends had been among the first class of brothers brought to the academy to be trained under the Harskialdna instead of by their families, as was traditional.

"What about Sponge?" Inda's expression was troubled. "Did he say nothing?"

"After you disappeared he cried himself to sleep every night," Cherry-Stripe said, grimacing as he scratched under his horsetail clasp. "Heyo, most of us blubbed. Dogpiss dead, you gone, and no one would say where. Ev— Sponge—we call him Evred now, y'see. He talked among *us*—Noddy, Flash, Rat—"

"Rat?" Inda interrupted. "Rattooth Cassad?"

"Yep. We call him Rat now. And Cama—" A gesture toward Cama, who turned his thumb up, firelight gleaming in his good eye.

"His Sier Danas." Cama swept one hand in a circle.

"May's well call ourselves that. No strut, not anymore. Not when Evred said it at his coronation."

Cherry-Stripe grinned. "We arranged a nine-times-nine drum corps. He was only going to have the second-son-inherits nine."

"We had so many volunteers, it was hard to keep 'em to just eighty-one." Cherry-Stripe rocked back on his mat, grinning with pride.

"Good." Inda radiated pleasure on behalf of Sponge, they all felt it.

It was so odd, having Inda back. Especially looking like he did, with nearly ten years of unimaginable experience evidenced on his face, and in his strange clothes.

"You should have seen Horsebutt when Evred called us the Sier Danas," Cherry-Stripe gloated. "Like he'd bit into a berry and found a worm."

Inda said, momentarily distracted, "What does being official mean? I remember that the Sier Danas in our day were just you horsetails with the Sierlaef." He indicated Buck. "I don't mean translating the words into Iascan. I know that: King's Companions. But the real meaning. At the academy, you were the heir's allies. You could strut around, break some academy rules even, and no one touched you."

Buck turned his palms up in silent agreement.

Cama said, "What it means for me is, I can leave Tya-Vayir on King's Business, even though I'm a Randael. But the king's order comes first. And since Horsebutt never lets me do anything at home anyway, I'm under what you could say is permanent order from Evred."

"And if there's war, we'd be his first choice for commanders." Cherry-Stripe thumped his chest, laughing. "Anyway, that summer he talked a lot about justice, but we all knew there wasn't going to be any. The strangest thing is, the Harskialdna wanted my Ain here—" He indicated his brother with a thumb. "—to be the Sierlaef's Harskialdna someday. Not Sponge. We never did know why."

"I know why," Buck said, and everyone turned his way.

"It was because Evred *thinks*. I never did. Not in those days, anyway. I believe the Harskialdna thought he'd be alive forever, commanding Aldren-Sierlaef when he became king instead of t'other way around."

"Isn't that—no, I guess it isn't treason." Inda's elbows thumped onto the table, hands pressed over his face as he tried to impose all these new notions onto his old understanding of his homeland.

"Not as the Harskialdna saw it," Buck said. "He saw it as protecting the kingdom, but it all had to be done his way. The Tveis had to be trained his way, so everyone would obey him if war came to us. I think Evred scared his uncle, so he had to be kept down, for everyone's good. 'Good' being everyone thinking like Anderle-Harskialdna."

Everyone considered the Harskialdna, the only sound the flutter and snap of the fire.

Buck shook his head, bright blond horsetail swinging. "I never said anything. No use. But I was beginning to see I didn't want that."

"As for us, we banded together, us against everyone." Cherry-Stripe wound his rough-palmed hand in a circle. "We used your plans, over and over, Evred building on 'em. And we won. All the time, though for years no one noticed. The Sierlaef was out of the academy, see, and started chasing your brother's Joret all over the kingdom, then there was war against the north—and, well, the short of it is, when the Harskialdna did finally notice we'd become real Sier Danas, he broke us up fast, sent us home, and Evred off to the war."

Cama said, "But it was too late. Evred saw us as his Sier Danas, and he never forgot you. He always brought your name up, wondered where you were."

Awash in rye-spiked reminiscence, Cherry-Stripe stumbled over the first hurdle he'd earlier scouted around. "Tanrid's man told us once that Evred was going to have someone search the ports for you, the word having spread you'd been put to sea."

"Tanrid? He promised Tanrid?"

Cama sent Cherry-Stripe a one-eyed glare.

"Your brother was sent north as his commander," Buck said reluctantly.

Inda straightened up. "He was? But Tanrid's good with command, isn't he? That brings me to my next question, may I borrow a Runner to send word to him—"

An indrawn breath from Cama caused Inda's gaze to snap to the three. He found shock, anger, dismay. "What? No, he can't be—"

Buck cast a look of distrust, almost of dislike, at Inda's visitors, wishing he could shove them out of the room. They were outsiders, not fit to hear personal tidings. But they sat there, uncomprehending, and he was honor-bound to show them hospitality. "You must first know that he died with honor. In an ambush. Took most of them first. As to who set it, well, he too is now dead."

"The Harskialdna," Inda whispered, all the old pain back again, strong as ever. "He always hated my brother. That much I could see. Though I couldn't see why."

"Actually, it was the Sierlaef," Cherry-Stripe said, and then the two exchanged glances. On his brother's slight nod, Cherry-Stripe added, "Look, you're here for what, better horses and some gear, right?"

Inda had his hands pressed to his eyes. His last memory of Tanrid was so vivid, there in the guard cells: Tanrid looking so old and tough, his fingers tousling Inda's hair behind his ears—

Strange, how grief hurt far more than a sword cut. But now was not the time to sit and bleed. He was here for—

The reminder of the Venn wrenched his mind to the immediate. "Yes. Yes! I came back because the Venn are coming. To take word to Sp—to Evred." He pressed the heels of his hands to his eyes again. *Tanrid is dead.*

Cherry-Stripe grimaced; Cama was the first to comprehend Inda's news. "Venn? When? And where?"

"Venn?" Buck and Cherry-Stripe said together.

Inda looked up. "Soon as the winds change. Maybe sooner, though I doubt it. But they have to suspect when I broke their line up north that I'd come here to warn the king."

Cherry-Stripe's mouth dropped open. "You mean they're really *coming?*"

Buck added, "After all these years?"

"The army's other side of the strait, the ships maneuvering. We slipped past the whole southern war fleet."

"Then we'll need to get you on your way," Buck said. "I'll send a Runner tonight to warn Evred. What should I say? Prepare for invasion?"

Inda raised a hand. "No. That is, tell him I'm coming, but not why. Better if I'm there to explain it. That way rumor doesn't start traveling around, getting crazier with every new person shoving their opinion in as fact."

"Right," Buck said, grinning. "Coming and news it is."

"And you better get some rest," Cherry-Stripe said.

"But first Baukid has to string you." Buck went to the door, and sent his Runner to summon the tailor to measure Inda. Trying to recapture their earlier good feeling, he added, "And I'll find you a hair clasp. You're going off to the royal city looking proper, not like something the Venn dug out of a pirate's port."

Inda glanced down impatiently at his shirt, vest, and the deck trousers below. They were terrible to ride in. "No," he admitted. "I guess you are right. There's been nothing proper in my life so long I've forgotten what proper *is.*"

"Don't ask me," Buck said, smiling faintly as he thought of the events of the previous year. "But you'll have a proper coat come morning." He appraised Inda. "Baukid can remake my old first-year horsetail coat. You're no taller than I was at seventeen. Shorter. But you're a whole lot broader here." He smacked his own chest. "Do you have a decent sash?"

Mran showed the guests their bedchambers, and the Marlovans parted as soon as the tailor had measured Inda.

Fnor, giving in to her yawns at last, said to her husband, "Who *is* that piece of art Inda brought? If I thought all pirates were that pretty I'd go to sea tomorrow."

"No you won't," Buck replied, kissing her on the neck.

Cherry-Stripe, Mran, and Cama wandered down the hall the other way. "That was bad, having to tell him about Tanrid," Cherry-Stripe said low-voiced across Mran to Cama. "And after we were so careful not to tell him that his father was there that day. Should we tell him the details?"

"You leave that to Evred," Cama replied. "Now, who's sleeping where?"

Mran slipped her hand into Cama's; Cama turned his eye to Cherry-Stripe, who returned a comical grimace. He considered going over to the pleasure house, where he had five current favorites. But no, he did not want to risk oversleeping and missing Inda before he left for the royal city. So he retired alone—for once.

"Did you understand any of that?" Jeje asked Tau when they stopped outside the row of rooms Mran had showed them.

"Some," Tau began.

"Was *that* Inda's big secret? Somebody slipped and died? At first I couldn't figure out if Dogpiss was a little boy or a horse," Jeje said.

"They were all little boys," Tau reminded her. "Sounds like the older people used them in their own games. Makes it worse, somehow. And explains a lot about Inda."

Jeje stretched. "You'll have to tell me how, but later. Who would ever call himself 'Cherry-stripe'? What can that possibly mean?"

Tau yawned. "No idea. I didn't really follow what the little one said just now. Do we get the same room, I hope?"

Jeje grinned. "I thought your balls were crushed?"

"Let's find out, shall we?"

"What are you thinking?" Inda asked Signi, as he closed the guest room door behind him.

She sorted through her impressions of the great, imposing castle, the short light-haired people with martial comportment, so like the Venn and yet so unlike, and shook her head. She had not comprehended much, except how they'd said the word *Venn* at the end with attitudes of hatred. She was worried what would happen when they found out who, and what, she was. Inda seemed too overwhelmed by emotion at being in his homeland again to have considered this. She would not disturb him now. "They are fine friends, these brothers," she said.

"And to think old Cherry-Stripe was once my worst enemy in the world," Inda said, laughing silently. "Oh, to have life that easy again."

"But it was not easy at the time."

"No. All our little matters were just that: little matters. Though we thought 'em life and—" He grimaced.

"Yes?"

"Mmm. I was going to say that at least they didn't touch others' lives, but even that turned out not to be true." They were silent as they climbed into bed, and then she heard him say softly, "Oh, Tanrid." Shortly followed by the compressed, shuddering breath of grief.

She slid her arms around him and held him until at last, at last, he slid into sleep.

Chapter Seven

INDA'S former fleet drifted into Parayid Harbor on the tidal flood, stripped to fighting sail, armed crew hidden along the rails.

Fox, at the helm of the middle ship, the knife-lean, black-sided trysail *Death,* knew very well how sinister they must look from the harbor. He did not order signal flags raised. No one would believe them anyway. They drifted in slowly.

Nobody wanted a fight, but the last time any of them had seen Parayid, just after they'd defeated Marshig's pirate federation, the Brotherhood of Blood, Inda's fleet had been mostly driven off by people fearful that the victors would be as merciless as the Brotherhood had been.

Fox Montredavan-An had begun his command by thrashing anyone who started a sentence with *But Inda always did it this way,* or *Inda always says.*

He had two claims to that command. First, Inda had handed the fleet off to him, before the eyes of all. Second, he could wipe the foredeck with anyone in the fleet in hand-to-hand fighting—including Inda.

Otherwise, instinct had prompted him to avoid having to explain himself over and over to a fleet made up of independents, privateers, and even outright pirates, most of whom had joined to follow Inda because he always won, and not because they shared Inda's ideal of dispensing rough justice against pirates.

So Fox had kept control, but that didn't mean they were his crew. At most they were Inda's crew, prudently (or sullenly) putting up with him until either Inda popped up again on Parayid's long dock or until someone organized a mutiny, whichever happened first.

What Fox needed, he knew, was a battle—and victory.

But not against these locals, he thought as he steered the trysail in under a lowering sky, flanked by his two capital ships, Dasta's *Cocodu* and Eflis' magnificent schooner *Sable* gliding on either side of the *Death*.

The harbormaster's tower, half rebuilt, sent up flags. Fox could just make out the yellow over black-and-red, meaning: *Warning! We regard you as pirates,* and below that, the green-striped flag for *Anchor in the road.*

Pilvig, fifteen, and on duty as flag mid, bounced lightly on her toes, anxiously watching Fox. She knew every single glass in the harbor was on them. On *her.*

"You can answer," Fox said lazily, hands loose on the helm. "Will comply. Parley and supplies."

He also knew every glass was trained on them, but that he, not the girl, was the focus.

He snapped out his glass and gave the harbor one quick sweep; the dozen or so big fishers upwind had people on them, but they were not about to launch out against the tide.

So he said, "Anchor."

Fibi the Delf, his sail captain, yelled in her unlovely squawk, "Flash!"

The sails thundered briefly, the wind spilled, then came smoothly to rest; the fight teams along the rail straightened up, still holding their weapons.

From the long dock a single small boat tacked bravely against the choppy sea, two lanky young men pulling hard, and what appeared to be a skinny lad leaning out, tending the sail one-handed.

As the boat fought its way toward the *Death,* the harbor's denizens slowly appeared, lining the dock and the

quay, even crowding into small boats. These stayed close to
shore, glasses leveled steadily on Fox's fleet.

A wash of rain on a strong offshore gust of wind
skimmed the boat closer, and the lad's awkwardness was
explained: he had only one arm, and further, he was not a
lad, but a lanky girl with a head full of unruly butter--
colored curls.

A high, shrill screech made him wince.

That was Pilvig, the flag mid. *"Nug-get!"*

"Pil-vig!" Nugget shrilled from the water, bouncing up
and down so hard she almost capsized the boat.

There were snorts of laughter, which caused Nugget,
once one of Inda's crew, to grin and preen a little. As the
boat thumped alongside on the choppy waves, she called
up to Fox, "Some of Marshig's pirates just left day before
yesterday. Are you here to chase them?"

The rain lifted briefly as a row of supply boats slid down
Parayid Harbor's ebb tide to the pirate ships alone at their
anchorage. Three times fishing smacks returning to shore
appeared on the horizon, took one look then sheered off,
vanishing beyond the land rise to the north. No one
wanted to risk the harbor, not with those infamous and sinister ships brooding in the middle of the bay.

Pilvig and Nugget sat side by side in the mids' bunk area
in the *Death*'s narrow forepeak, the hull slanting sharply in
overhead.

They had just finished a delicious hot meal, cooked by
Lorm, who'd been a chef in Sarendan before he was forced
aboard a pirate ship.

"I *missed* his cooking. Mmmm." Nugget licked her fingers.

"We haven't eaten that good for ages," Pilvig said. "We
didn't dare stop for any supplies. Venn were after us, and
then we were passing by the Marlovan land. Where they let
Inda off."

Nugget's thin face pinched up. "Inda gone? Where did
he go?"

Pilvig sat back on her elbows, the expression in her round, flat-cheeked Chwahir features difficult to make out in the guttering light of their swinging candle-stub. "Dunno, really." She jerked one shoulder up. "Something about the Venn attacking the Marlovans. When anyone mentions either Venn or Marlovans, tempers get hot and I stay out of the way."

The two girls brooded, Nugget remembering how much fun they'd had in the two weeks they'd sailed the Land Bridge before the Brotherhood attack. They'd talked all day and all night, Nugget showing Pilvig everything, introducing everyone. Offering to teach her Inda's fighting. *Those pirates won't have a chance,* she remembered saying right before the battle, when Pilvig's already pale face had gone chalky.

But it wasn't Pilvig who'd nearly died, and Pilvig had spent the two years since with Inda and the crew. Now Pilvig knew everybody better than Nugget did. Nugget didn't even know who captained that big schooner except that the captain was a tall, handsome woman with fair hair.

"I was stupid," Nugget admitted, and saw in Pilvig's black eyes no comforting denial, but a silent agreement.

Nugget flushed, but couldn't get mad. For months she'd had nightmares about the pirate who'd almost killed her, laughing the while. Stabbing her and then laughing while she shrieked and begged for her life as she tried to protect her half-severed arm. Torture had been sport to him.

She was only alive because the fighting had shifted, and somebody stabbed the pirate in the back. He fell dead across her, and she'd had just enough wit and awareness to lie still and pretend to also be dead.

"Did any of our other rats get it?" she asked.

Inda had been firm about the ship rats under sixteen staying out of the main fight, remaining under Jeje's command in the support boats. They'd had a real job—attacking pirate sail crew with arrows, so they'd have trouble guiding their ships—but Nugget had not thought that exciting and heroic enough.

She'd gone into the battle thinking it sport, but not because she liked killing. She'd just wanted to be a hero. She wanted people to admire her. She'd never believed that *she* was in any danger, because even if others got massacred, heroes never did.

"No," Pilvig said. "*We* all made it. Except you."

"Because I went with Tau, but we got separated. The Iascan fishers who saved me said he was alive. They said a golden-haired pirate threw money onto the beach and yelled something, as if gold coins could be traded anywhere. Anyway, the fellow they described had to be Tau."

"Jeje ordered us to stay on the scouts. So I did." Pilvig jerked her shoulder again. Her life on the sea had begun as a ship's girl aboard a merchant. Sharl the Brainsmasher took the ship, killed most of the crew, keeping her because he'd killed his last cabin rat in a fit of anger and he needed a new one. She'd had to learn fast that when he sat in *this* chair, he wanted food. If he sat in *that* one, he wanted his charts. If he smashed his fist on the table, he wanted a messenger. Or his latest favorite. If Pilvig wasn't right there, no matter what time of day or night, and fetching whatever he wanted, he beat her.

Then, when that mysterious Ramis of the *Knife* killed Sharl and his worst mates, the locals had killed most of the rest of the pirates but left her alone because she was young, and promised she'd not joined Sharl of her own will. They'd spared her life, but never trusted her.

Nugget's showing off had been a pleasure compared to life under Sharl, and the begrudged existence in the Pirate Island orphanage. Pilvig said, "It's past. You'll know better. Come with us."

"I don't know if I can fight," Nugget admitted, her voice going high, and hot tears burned down her cheeks.

Pilvig chewed her lip. "You don't mean with one arm. You mean at all."

Nugget ducked her head, gulping on a sob.

In Chwahirsland you never admitted to cowardice. Nugget's soft words, her muffled sobs made Pilvig's arms tingle with some complex emotion she could not define—something between pity and warning.

She set aside her wooden mess plate and put her arms around Nugget, hugging her tight. There weren't any words that seemed right.

Nugget sobbed, sniffed, then leaned against Pilvig. "They kept me alive, but they didn't want me. Didn't trust me. Called me Pirate Girl. Counted the spoons after I left a room, and wouldn't let me go ashore because they said I wanted to signal pirates! All I wanted was to light a candle and sing the 'Leahan Anaer.' For you, and Inda, and Jeje, and the rest. Because I thought you were lost, going to Ghost Island and you'd sail forever as ghosts."

Pilvig gnawed the inside of her cheek. Ship-to-ship battle could be bad. Well, she'd seen it. But everyone was afraid of sailing into the deeps and never being found. The old lament "Leahan Anaer"—"the ship without sails"—was reserved for mates who'd sailed away never to return.

Nugget gave a short sigh. "They said all I was good for was sheep tending." She gulped. "If Inda was here, I'd go. I think he'd understand. But that Fox?"

"Some—the ones who came on since we left the east—like him better than Inda," Pilvig said. "They say he looks like a commander. They thought Inda was crazy. Because he would yell in his nightmares."

"He did? Why?"

"Well, we don't know. But we do know he got caught by the Venn and Fox rescued him. Jug was on one of the schooners when it happened."

Jug was their age, so he was to be believed.

A quick rap outside the cabin, and Mutt stuck his face in. He looked taller and older than Nugget—seventeen or eighteen, almost grown up.

"How's that arm?" he asked, pointing to her empty sleeve tucked in her sash. She hated the thought of sewing the sleeve close to the stump; she wanted two sleeves, even if she couldn't have two arms.

"It's all right. But I feel it in cold."

"Was it disgusting, when they took it off?"

"Wasn't awake." Nugget made a face, and the others

twitched, Mutt rubbing his shoulder. "Just as glad," she
added, and no one gainsaid her.

"So, ye comin' back aboard us?" he asked, his ruby glinting against his bony jaw.

Oh, it was so good to hear Dock Talk again!

But the joy was followed by another wave of anguish.
Nugget sent a keep-silent look at Pilvig, who returned a I-
don't-blab chin lift, and Nugget sat up, wiping her nose on
her sleeve. Nugget had had to get rid of her own ruby when
she was among the lands-people, but they'd called her Pirate Girl anyway.

She fingered her ear, wondering if the hole had grown
shut; she'd tugged her curls down to hide her ears. "Can I
get another ruby?" she asked, feeling her way.

Mutt laughed. "Course! But right now, Fox is finally
done with them harbor folk, and he sent me to fetch you.
He wants to hear more about this pirate."

Nugget scrambled up. "Don't know much, only that she
comes from Khanerenth. Just like me. There's rumor she
was sister to the old king, before he got turfed."

Mutt whistled.

"They took the island where I was staying. The fisher
people got all of us young ones over here to the harbor last
year, but they took a lot of other people hostage. They'd
kill them one by one if they didn't get what they wanted.
The pirates stayed on the island a whole year—it was horrible—but they left as soon as a report came that the Land
Bridge ice broke. The rumor was, there's some Marlovan
Jarl, Fera-Vayir, who was raising a big army to come down
and attack them soon's the snow cleared."

Mutt said, "What have they got?"

"About sixteen schooners, a few capital ships. I never
saw them."

"That it?" Mutt asked.

Nugget nodded. "Fox's going after the pirate?"

Mutt grinned, his ruby sparking against his lean cheek.
"He says we need the practice." His smile faded. "Are you
coming with us?"

Pilvig scrambled over to sit next to her. Her black eyes were anxious under her broad, puckered brow.

Nugget glanced down at her arm, then up, uncertain.

"We've got two single-armers," Mutt said coaxingly. "Well, one's missing a hand, not an arm, but still. They fight good, and Sock isn't any bigger'n you." He added in a mumble, "Your brother misses you. *We* miss you."

Nugget drew in a deep breath. The salt water, the rocking of the ship, her old friends—so much older now—the two years on land, learning all about wool, seemed part of a long strange dream that had begun as a nightmare.

She glared at her damp palm and shaking fingers. Fear, well, that happened anywhere. Fighting? She could think about it later.

The feeling that she couldn't get over—didn't want to get over—that felt like wine inside, like the first time you hear a wonderful song, was *belonging*.

"Let's go talk to Fox," she said.

Chapter Eight

THE sounds and smells of home reached down into childhood habit and woke Inda before dawn. He had a slight headache, but carried his clothes down to the baths at the lowest level of the castle. He splashed about, enjoying a Marlovan bath again, though it seemed to smell more dank than he remembered his home being. Maybe it was just this castle.

When he emerged, the familiar cadenced sounds of drill drew him out to the enormous courtyard between the stable against the castle walls and the long line of the Marlo-Vayirs' castle.

There he found Buck and the other two in the front line as the Marlo-Vayir riders performed morning drill under the steady rain. Inda was stiff from the days of riding after so much time away from horses, and his head still ached from the combination of rye cider and powerful emotions.

Glad for a chance to stretch, he took a position at the back. As he worked through the drills, remembering old patterns from childhood, he wondered why they seemed so slow, the combinations clumsy. He recognized that the drills all benefited the man on horseback, slashing with the curve-tipped sword. The close-in work, he saw with experienced eyes, was intended mostly for finishing off an enemy, not for foot engagement.

At the end he followed Cherry-Stripe and Cama inside to the roaring fire, where hot steeped leaf was waiting.

The old arms master who'd led the drill stopped Buck. "That one in the vest. That's the Algara-Vayir laef?"

Buck opened his hand. "So?"

The arms master rubbed his jaw. "From the look o' him, he ought to be runnin' drill."

Buck whistled softly. "What, was he strutting back there?"

A shake of a grizzled head. "No. Held himself back, all proper. But the others move heavy, he moves like an arrow through the air, especially with the knife, and the other hand, too. You get him to run us once, if he stays, we all learn something."

Buck grunted, remembering what Inda had said about the Venn coming in summer. *We'd better learn everything we can.* Winter was barely over. Surely one day wouldn't make a difference. "I'll do that." He walked in, absently wringing the rain from his hair, mentally rehearsing what to say.

Upstairs, Signi woke at the sounds of steel clashing, and found herself alone. Alone in a huge room. She rose and performed a full *visan varec*—the strenuous set of stretches and exercises the hel dancers of the Venn performed each day. She'd not been able to do the complete routine for many days, confined as she'd been on the little scout ship *Vixen,* and then in the small chambers shared with Inda whom she might disturb. As yet she had never let anyone see her do the exercises, nor had she danced; now she could no longer bear to hide her first self away, and so, accompanied by the sound of the rain, she danced out the complicated emotions of the last weeks.

Her muscles were warm, smoothed of the knots of passion, anger, regret, and grief, her blood flowed with the quiet of contentment when she had finished, leaving her mind clear. She bathed and made her way to the dining room, where she was relieved to find that Tau and Jeje had arrived ahead of her. Despite the rain the windows were all wide open. Everything here smelled of horse, grass, and wildflowers.

When the yellow-haired Jarl appeared in the doorway to join them for breakfast, the man with him looked at first like another tough Marlovan rider. Then Tau, Jeje, and Signi saw the ruby earrings and recognized familiar brown eyes. It was with difficulty that their minds inscribed a palimpsest of their Inda over this strange warrior. His sun-streaked brown hair, usually escaping in curls from his neglected sailor's queue, had been pulled up tight into a horsetail, which emphasized the hard bones of his face.

He wore one of those fitted coats of severe lines that splendidly graced shoulders and chest, but it seemed to separate him into another identity—except for the sight of those earrings, which Tau and Jeje knew were emblems of the terrible cost he'd paid as a commander fighting pirates.

Then he trod into the room, wincing at each step. Reality, so often absurd and thereby curiously steadying, reasserted itself.

"No kicking the boots off," Cherry-Stripe warned as he followed Inda into the dining room. "Your feet'll get used to 'em in a day or two."

Buck sat down. "Eat. You may as well wait until tomorrow, unless you're all good at riding into a storm that smells like it's gonna drop some snow."

Cherry-Stripe rubbed his hands vigorously. "Roads are getting worse. Everyone's been west fighting pirates. Wait until the day after tomorrow unless you want to swim. You can leave before dawn next day. We'll send you with Runners, so you can take our post horses. Better, use the king's, because if you aren't on King's Business, then I'm a Venn." He grinned. "So this morning, you run the drill, pirate style."

Inda snorted. Then saw by the intensity of the brothers' gazes that they were serious. "All right."

"Good." Buck clapped his hands and rubbed them. "Now, first things first. Me an' the boys talked this morn. You can guess that becoming king didn't make all Evred's problems go away." Inda opened his hand, and Buck went on. "We think you should know some of what he's facing."

The brothers deferred to Cama, who said, "Besides the

embargo, the wreckage of the coast, the army spread too thin. Oh, and the lack of magic renewals."

Inda grimaced, not telling them that Iasca Leror's problems had been gloated over elsewhere in the world. "Go on."

"There's trouble at home. My brother Horsebutt at the head." Cama's voice sharpened with derision; Stalgrid Tya-Vayir was one of the few who hated his academy nickname, but everyone used it when not in his presence. Especially Cama, after enduring a lifetime of bullying. "He's using the excuse of lack of trade to pressure Evred into revoking the royal portion of guild taxes during wartime, since the guilds are already sending warriors."

Inda said, "But isn't the guild portion traditional?"

" 'Traditional' since we moved into castles and figured out what guilds were," Mran Cassad observed wryly.

Buck flicked up the back of his hand. "That's what Horsebutt gives for tradition—unless it serves him. He also knows the king can't take over paying warriors in the field, unless he gets money. But he thinks because Evred is young that he's weak, that he'll give in and the Jarls will get concessions that make them stronger. And Inda, there isn't a single jarl family that doesn't have a flight or more of riders out there somewhere, helping with the defense, so the question of who's going to pay for their food and fodder concerns everyone."

"But can't Barend belay that? Or Hawkeye, if he's doing some of the Harskialdna work?"

Belay? The Marlovans looked puzzled, but let it pass. "Barend doesn't command anyone's loyalty. They don't know him," Buck said.

Inda scratched his scalp. Binding his hair up hurt his scalp fiercely, though he wouldn't tell the others that. "Why is Horsebutt doing it? What can he think he's going to get?"

Cama said, "A future crown."

Inda understood at last: marriage negotiations over future daughters and Evred's firstborn son. Those were usually settled by treaty a generation or even two generations before birth. But if there had been so many attacks and deaths—like in his own family—

Tanrid. Inda remembered his brother's warm fingers ruffling his hair over his ear. *How* that memory hurt.

Cherry-Stripe said, "People are talking about future babies and alliances because Evred says with the war and everything so uncertain we Tveis ought to marry, and the Ains ought to get heirs born right away. Not to wait until we're forty like usual. Imagine being forty!"

"We might not make it to forty," Cama muttered.

Cherry-Stripe snorted. "That seems a real enough possibility. Especially after Inda's news."

Chapter Nine

HADAND gripped Tdor's shoulders. "What would you say, Tdor," she breathed, her eyes bright, glittery, full of tears. "What would you say if I told you that Inda is coming home?"

Tdor's nerves flared, then chilled to snowmelt. She had arrived in the royal city that day from the long ride north, having spent most of it rehearsing what she'd say.

And in the space of a single breath, the weight of painful choices was gone, flown like a caged bird tossed into the air.

Hadand laughed now, an unsteady laugh as the unheeded tears spilled over. She smeared them away with her palms, and then hugged Tdor. "He's coming home, he's coming *here*. He's probably a day or so to the north. Maybe less. Can you believe it? After all these years!"

Tdor gulped down a sob. "D'you know what brings him?" she managed, her voice high and squeaky. Not that she cared.

Hadand sniffed and wiped her eyes again. "The Marlo-Vayir Runner only said that Inda has news for the king. Oh, Tdor. I'll send one of my own Runners back to Choraed Elgaer, as soon as we actually see Inda, to tell my mother. You must stay here and greet him. Mother will be so happy!"

The two embraced again, laughing and crying.

Hadand had received Tdor alone in her own rooms, and now waited for Tdor—who looked about from window to door to table as if she had never seen such objects before— to recover.

Tdor could not yet believe she was being given back what she had wanted all her life. She felt light as a bird as they shared a quick meal, and then she accompanied Hadand up to the sentry walk, where the wind had died down, leaving a clear sky.

The early-spring slant of the sun was not nearly strong enough yet to be hot; it felt good on the backs of their shoulders as they sat easily on crenellations watching the girls of the queen's training at knife practice below, as Hadand caught Tdor up on kingdom news.

". . . and *guess* whose daughter Horsebutt is trying to force us to take as future wife to our son?"

Tdor shook her head. "Wasn't all that set out in treaty before any of *us* were born?"

Hadand looked grim. "Yes. But you don't realize how many of those careful marriage treaties have been disrupted by war deaths." She twiddled her fingers. "The next queen was supposed to be descended from the Ola-Vayir heir, but he died defending the coast. And his brother wasn't to have children. They want to change that, to get a connection to us, but Horsebutt wants to prevent the Ola-Vayirs from gaining any extra influence that he might gain himself."

Tdor pushed her palm away, a gesture of warding. "Who? Horsebutt can't possibly be trying to break his own family treaties, or he'd have trouble with the clans. So—oh, ugh, *not* Mudface?"

Dannor Tya-Vayir, Horsebutt's sister and wife to Hawk-eye Yvana-Vayir, had been the most unpopular girl in the queen's training, even more disliked than Cama's wife, Starand Ola-Vayir.

Tdor rested her chin on her hand. "But didn't Hawkeye's family have their generation's children all promised?"

"Yes, but some rescinded after the conspiracy. Mad

Gallop Yvana-Vayir died the death of treason, which can undo all his treaties if the other side wants. It's accepted custom."

Tdor's brow puckered. "Wait. You said the next generation. Wasn't your future son to marry outside the country, like Evred's father did?"

"Yes, but there's no treaty. Evred's father had approached the Idayagans, thinking it a peace gesture. That horse won't run, because we're evil conquerors, despite how the Cassads made a success of marrying our ancestors. So. What with all the other changes, it's I who must settle it all."

Tdor huffed a sort of laugh. "How strange! I was so involved in my own worries—wondering who you and Evred would pick for me to marry—I never considered that it would fall to you to choose for our children. Or is the treaty with the Montredavan-Ans to hold?"

Hadand smiled. "I promised Shen that she would still raise Inda's and your daughter. If Inda came home."

Tdor turned her palms up. She'd grown up knowing that Inda and she were supposed to have a daughter, who was promised to the Montredavan-Ans. A son would have been the future Algara-Vayir Rider captain. It was a prospect that had always seemed impossibly remote.

Hadand grinned wryly. "And now Inda *is* coming home! We must arrange the marriage as soon as possible."

Tdor's euphoria damped: Inda was yet to arrive, and what if he did not want to return to Choraed Elgaer after almost ten years?

Hadand went on. "Back to Horsebutt. He thinks he can get a Tya-Vayir in the royal family one day. He's using every political weapon he can contrive to force Evred into accepting Dannor's daughter." She mimed an exaggerated shiver. "Can you imagine how horrible it would be if Dannor's daughter is like her?"

Tdor turned her thumb up, stray impressions flitting through her tired mind, distracting moth-wing thoughts that she tried to banish: how strange it was to be back here, a grown woman, how careworn Hadand looked, how shabby the clean, much-mended tunics on the girls appeared. Even Hadand's fine-woven cotton-wool robe was not new, its yellow dye faded along the shoulders, the seams worn, and Tdor laughed inside, thinking of the mad scramble back at Castle Tenthen the night before she left, stitching her frayed cuffs and carefully turning the hem to her robe to wear in the royal city, so she wouldn't bring shame on Choraed Elgaer by looking threadbare.

She faced Hadand. "Surely Starand has to be fighting that. After all, she's an Ola-Vayir. I'm surprised she doesn't want to put forward her own future daughter and break whatever treaty they have."

"Starand." Hadand shuddered. "Why is it the two men Evred needed most as interim Harskialdnas have impossible wives? Poor Hawkeye! Poor Cama!"

"Starand would *hate* Dannor getting a daughter married to a future king. Why isn't she interfering in Horsebutt's plot?"

Hadand frowned. "I don't think she knows. Horsebutt is trying to keep it secret. Imand avoids Starand, and though she despises gossip, she thought I'd better know about Horsebutt's plan for the kingdom's sake. Starand really would hate that, wouldn't she?"

Tdor said, "Beyond anything."

"So . . . if Imand lets her know, then the trouble shifts between Starand and Dannor, each pulling Horsebutt's arms in opposite directions, so he's too busy to plot." Hadand whistled the chords of a cavalry lance charge. "I call that good for the kingdom!"

"The only things Starand and Dannor loathe more than not having precedence and power is one another. You can make a vow on it."

Hadand was still smiling when she brought Tdor to the dining room where she and Evred usually met. It was a room with pleasing proportions, windows down the west side, the balcony outside, the old raptor table and chairs, it all reminded Tdor of the nursery room that she'd seen once. She wondered briefly if one's notions of comfort and appeal arose from warm memories of childhood joy and safety.

"Sit down, we can begin. Evred will get here when he gets here," Hadand said.

Tdor dropped cross-legged onto her mat and took up the broad, flat wine cup in her hands. They'd drunk some of the good sweet wine when the door opened, and Tdor saw Evred for the first time since her single meeting with him in his mother's chamber, years ago. He had changed from the shy, skinny red-haired boy with the bobbing throat-knuckle; his high-pulled hair had darkened to a reddish-highlighted auburn. He was tall and well-built, with the austere, hawk-nosed look of his forebears.

He touched his hand to his heart and held it out to Hadand; they brushed their fingers together. Then Evred sat down, turning Tdor's way with an air of puzzled courtesy. He did not recognize her. That was obvious.

"Tdor is joining us," Hadand said, as Tdor saluted, hand flat to her heart.

Evred's brows lifted. "Tdor Marth-Davan?"

"Yes. My mother sent her to ask who the next heir should be." Hadand chuckled. "So I asked her to stay. Who better to be here to welcome Inda, after all these years?"

"Who better indeed?" Evred said, the faint aloofness gone. Now he seemed merely a quiet, rather reserved young man. "Welcome, Tdor. I confess I hadn't expected to see you here, but Hadand is right. I am sorry about your father," he added.

Tdor murmured her thanks, not saying that she'd never really known him, that her reaction, on hearing of his death the year before, had been sorrow on her mother's behalf, but not her own. Even on her yearly visits, which had stopped when she was in her mid-teens, her father had paid no attention to her whatsoever. She scarcely remembered his features except for a glaring frown. He had been too bitter that he had not had a son. "My mother writes that Cousin Ander, uh, Mouse, is a good Jarl," Tdor said.

Evred's polite smile broadened to real warmth. "Mouse

Marth-Davan was with me in the academy, did you know that?"

"Yes. Whipstick says that during his academy days he became proud of being called Mouse, though I confess I do not see why." Tdor laughed, a rich, soft chuckle, her smile transforming her plain face. "But then I've never understood how Whipstick could abide his own nickname. I didn't even find out he had a given name until he'd been living with us several years."

Hadand put her chin in her hands, pleased at her husband's relaxed face and Tdor's happiness, which seemed to radiate summer warmth in her smile, her eyes, even in her voice. "I never even thought of that. Like his father Horsepiss. Somehow those Noths wouldn't have ordinary names. What's Whipstick's?"

"Senrid."

"Oh, how boringly everyday. I'd hoped it was something more awe-inspiring, like Adamas—for Adamas Blacksword of the Deis—or Savarend, which has the mystery of former kings plus the appeal of the forbidden." Hadand laughed.

Evred gave Tdor a rueful smile.

Tdor smiled back, wondering if Evred knew that the Montredavan-An heir, using the name Fox, had been one of Inda's companions out on the sea. And would Fox be coming back with Inda? If so, his sister Shendan, so loyal all these years, would want to know. Should she bring it up?

Not knowing how Evred felt about his family's history with the Montredavan-Ans—which felt unsettlingly current, like the question of marriage treaties—Tdor shifted the subject. "Whipstick says if he hears 'Senrid' he thinks his mother is angry with him, and he insists she's even tougher than Captain Noth."

Hadand whooped and this time Evred chuckled as servants passed round dishes of spiced rice well laced with cabbage and slow-cooked chicken.

Then Tdor said, "Whipstick rode all the way to Marth-Davan to hear the details of that last pirate battle. You can imagine how many songs there are about it in the south."

"I shall have to hear some," Evred said. "What tidings of Jarend-Adaluin bring you? And Fareas-Iofre?"

Tdor made a business of helping herself to the rice while she considered what to say about Hadand and Inda's parents. She sent a quick glance at Hadand, who gestured palm up.

"Jarend-Adaluin does not do well in winters," Tdor said. "We think his mind wanders endlessly in the past. Fareas-Iofre is well, and bade me carry her best greetings. She cherishes those copies of Old Sartoran texts you made her when you were up north. They give her much—" she avoided the word "comfort" and settled on "—pleasure."

Evred lifted a hand in acknowledgment and the talk slid easily to her journey, and thence to defense preparations at Castle Tenthen against possible invasion.

Hadand watched the last of the too-habitual tension ease from Evred's brow, and smiled at Tdor in gratitude. She always knew what to say and do, she had a gift that way.

As for Evred, he did not remember having met Tdor, and had scarcely given her much thought, but he found this tall, thin, sober-browed young woman quiet, knowledgeable, and interesting. She had a low, pleasing voice, quiet yet brisk. She would make an excellent wife for Inda, now that he was coming home.

Inda was coming home.

The potential joy was like the feel of the summer sun after what had seemed an endless winter storm, and yet there was the instinctive question, the readiness to disbelieve. There had been too many disappointments in the past.

With the ease of practice he shut away his emotions and bent his attention on Tdor, but she sensed that the meal was over.

They parted amicably, promising to meet for breakfast, which Hadand assured her later was rare on Evred's part.

"He's worried about the north," she said. "He's received word from his Runner there that no Venn warships at all are in sight, and the people have been dancing victory dances. Should we call Barend and the forces on the north coast back home, as soon as the weather holds good? Especially with all this trouble over who pays to support them?"

"If he calls them back, who defends the north?"

"That's exactly the question. I hope Inda brings an answer, because we do not have one." Hadand sounded tired and tense. "Who defends the north?"

Chapter Ten

E VRED woke at a touch.

His room was dark. He smelled the mingled sweat of horse and man, heard a quick step. The guards would only let a Runner past—

Runner? His heart thumped.

"It is I, Evred-Harvaldar," came the familiar voice of Kened, the Runner he had been expecting. "I just arrived. Indevan-Laef is half a morning's ride west."

"Thank you." Evred's mouth was dry. "You met him?"

"Yes. As you instructed."

"Does he ride with banners flying?"

"No." Kened chuckled as he thought about the scar-faced young fellow, barely older than the academy horse-tails by the look of him, who rode barefoot, hair hanging down in a scruffy round braid. His gaze was keen for all that. "He wants to come in quiet. No noise, is what he said," Kened finished.

"Good. Then quiet it shall be. Go get some rest."

If Inda had wanted a formal welcome, Evred would have roused the city to give it, complete to an audience in the throne room, bone-chilly from the long winter. He felt his family owed that to Inda.

A short time later Evred, bathed and dressed, stood at his window gazing out into the night-black west. They would probably be up and riding by now. Evred had glimpsed Inda once, right after the defeat of the Brotherhood of Blood, though Inda did not know that. No one did. Inda had been dressed like a pirate, not like a Marlovan. Evred wondered if he still dressed like a pirate. Well, such things no longer mattered.

But Inda knew what was due to his old scrub mate.

At drill that morning they wore the old clothes they'd slept in, as usual. Then they retreated to the tents to change and pack for the last ride to the royal city.

Tau was surprised when Inda emerged with his hair bound up, and his new coat smooth and buttoned instead of hanging open, the green sash Mran Cassad had managed to find (the proper green of Algara-Vayir) neatly tied around his waist. The biggest surprise was those boots Inda had gotten from Cherry-Stripe Marlo-Vayir. They'd given him terrible blisters the second morning when at Buck's heavy-handed invitation Inda had commanded all the castle males, from Jarl to the youngest runner-in-training, in one of Fox's drills.

Inda had used a single knife. Marlovans thought of the left arm as the shield arm. Only women used two knives, their feet, and above all, balance and the power of motion. What little Inda showed them of Fox's style of fighting had puzzled most, and inspired some—Cama most of all. Drill had been protracted that day; halfway through the morning Inda had kicked off the boots and finished his routine barefoot, leaving pink smudges of blood on the courtyard flagstones from where the boots had rubbed him raw. His feet were not yet healed after their hard ride southeast to the royal city.

Inda minced with meticulous care. "I put two pairs of socks on," he complained. "Can't believe those blisters still hurt." He twitched his brows, then shook his head. "While I'm whining, may's well get it all out: it hurts my scalp, my hair tied up like this. I wonder if the horsetails ever noticed at seventeen."

"What, you're an old geezer at twenty?" Jeje laughed.

"He's only twenty?" One of the Marlo-Vayir Runners sent as guides said to the other, as they saddled the horses.

The second Runner pursed his lips. He was surprised too. It wasn't just the scars, it was the way Inda moved; he was too stiff in the early morning, and too powerful when he got warmed up. More like a man of experience.

Tau said, "At seventeen you'll do anything to look tough. Like pierce your ears and hang golden hoops through 'em."

Inda cracked a laugh, flicking his rubies with his fingers. "Still don't know if it was a good idea or a stupid one."

"Oh, it was a good one." Tau's mouth quirked with irony. "We stood out. It was swagger without us having to say a word. We're going to stand out here, too. Whether that is good or bad, you'll have to tell me."

"We're about to find out." Jeje waved a hand at their tent, which was still standing. "*If* you ever stop blabbing and help me pack that thing so we can go."

A low band of gray rain clouds wept a sleety mizzle, darkening stone and clothing and the wood of wagons, so that Tau's first view of Inda's royal city was dreary indeed. The city was surrounded by a vast high wall whose line was broken only by intimidating towers. In sunlight the stone of the walls and towers glowed a warm honey color, but in the gloom and wetness of rain it had darkened to a flat dun. The gate was massive, giving Tau and Jeje the sense that once it closed there was no possibility of escape.

Surmounting gate and walls were gray-coated armsmen, some standing, others moving, all with weapons at the ready, all alert. On the inner walls prowled gray-robed women, equally armed, equally alert. They had bows strapped across their backs, making Jeje wonder what the men did in times of trouble. Maybe they scrambled down to fight hand-to-hand, while the women shot anyone crazy enough to attack a Marlovan castle, from their vantage point. It figured the women would have the position that made the most sense.

All those Marlovan eyes watched Inda's small party join

the traffic at the gate, peaceably following carts and other riders. Jeje hated being stared at by so many people bristling with weapons, whatever their gender, and glowered at her horse's ears.

The interior of the city was equally unnerving to Tau, who marveled at how alike these people dressed and acted. But he did not see the fear nor the servile attitudes that he expected to find in such grim surroundings after years of hearing slander against the Marlovans.

Tau mocked himself, ending that thought trail. He knew better than to assume Marlovans were any more of an indistinguishable "they" than any other body of people. He met gazes, not hiding his interest anymore than others did theirs. The range of expressions was what one would expect anywhere: curiosity, wry glances at their exotic clothing, soberness, and glances of frank appreciation from some of the strong-looking robed women either standing guard on walls or driving wagons in the streets.

Tau turned his attention to his companions. Jeje scowled at her horse's head. Signi's brow and hands subtly betrayed her strain. Inda was oblivious to the mage's distress. He slewed back and forth in his saddle with an intensity Tau had rarely seen in him, his breathing audible as he tried to take everything in at once.

Inda was overwhelmed. There were two places he loved most in the world: the academy and his home in Choread Elgaer. After nine years of resisting the stubborn homing spirit, he was approaching one of those places: the royal city was home to the academy.

The Marlo-Vayir guides led them a short way into the broad street beyond the gate and then up a slightly narrower street to the left.

Just inside another set of gates, the courtyard traffic cleared, deferring to the three people who emerged from a tower archway, a tall man and a short woman in the lead.

Inda uttered an incoherent cry and vaulted from his

horse. His companions watched him hurl himself at the short woman, who closely resembled him. He picked her up into the air, kissed her smackingly, and then took in the tall red-haired young man just beyond her. "Sponge!"

Laughter rose from guards and armsmen around and above them, and a curious crowd gathered by ones and twos outside the gate.

Inda thumped Hadand onto her feet again; and faced Evred. He clapped his right fist over his heart, then opened his hand to indicate the other three. "Signi, Jeje, and Tau." Inda's voice was high, almost unrecognizable. "We stopped over a day at Marlo-Vayir, rain making the roads into rivers . . ."

While Inda gabbled a disjointed summary of their journey, all attention was focused on him, with two exceptions.

Tau was one. Tdor was the other.

She had walked out with Hadand, but on the approach of the newcomers, she had stepped deferentially aside so as not to hinder the royal pair. After her first glimpse of her childhood companion, Inda, now all grown up, and scarred, and dizzyingly alien and familiar at the same time, Tdor turned to Evred for her cue to step forward and be noticed.

So she and Tau were the only ones who caught Evred's intense gaze, and bloodless, compressed lips, the passion that for a long breath the guarded young king could not mask.

Two heartbeats only, then he regained his self-possession. Inda paused for breath, and everyone began talking at once.

As word spread outward (a passing carter having asked the Marlo-Vayir Runners who the foreigners were) that the one with the earrings was in truth Elgar the Fox, Tau stayed back, holding the reins of his and Inda's horses. He observed how with two swift gestures this king got everyone moving. In the midst of orderly chaos he separated Inda from the rest and they promptly vanished into the crowd.

After Signi and Jeje took their gear from the saddle straps, a couple of stable hands led the women's animals away. The short woman who looked like Inda made inviting gestures to Jeje and Signi; the tall one stood at her side, staring bemusedly into space.

A pair of stable hands approached Tau, their manner expectant. What was *he* supposed to do?

One held out his hand for the reins to Inda's horse, the other waited for Tau's reins. Tau relinquished the reins, but then the men just stood there. Waiting for? Was Tau supposed to remove his own and Inda's gear?

One of the stable hands made a motion toward the saddlebags, and the two helpfully steadied the animals. Ah. So he was now a servant. With a rueful smile, Tau unloaded the bags and hefted them over his shoulders. The animals were taken away, leaving him standing there alone.

Inda's sister was conducting Jeje and Signi toward the entrance to the tower looming over them. He decided to follow the women.

Hadand and Tdor stopped just inside the tower entrance. Tdor closed her eyes and took a deep breath. Her nerves tingled. Shock pooled inside her; her mind refused to work, senses walling off color, smells, noise, until Hadand stepped close beside her, giving a watery chuckle. "Can you believe that?"

"Believe?" Tdor tensed.

Hadand flicked her hand outward. "Evred and Inda slinking off like a pair of scrubs scamping wand-duty!" A quick look back at the two strange women who stared upward at the winding stone stairway of the tower, shafts of light angling down from the slit windows. "I don't know what to do with Inda's people. I guess take them upstairs and give them something to eat until Evred brings Inda back." And she gave quick orders to her personal Runner in a whisper.

As Tesar sped up the stairs ahead of them, Hadand gestured to the women. "Come with me," she said in Iascan, and to her relief, both signified agreement. Good. They spoke a language Hadand knew!

Tdor trailed after Hadand and the two strange women, peripherally aware of the tall young man with the golden hair falling in behind her, burdened with a double load of travel gear. Her insides now cramped, her knees had gone watery. She did not see the stairs or hear Hadand's determinedly polite questions. She could not reconcile her own reaction to seeing Inda again with the vivid memory of Evred's wide, hungry gaze. She found herself relieved that Evred took Inda away too fast for her to be noticed. She couldn't define any of her emotions—she needed time to think.

Deeply withdrawn, she walked uncomprehending past Vedrid, Evred's First Runner, who stood very still on the first landing.

Kened had reported to Evred only that Inda traveled with two women and a man he'd defined as a Runner. Evred had issued orders to Vedrid to get Inda's Runner situated once they arrived; he'd been on the guard-side, at the far end of the long castle, when the wall sentries had signaled the arrival.

So he'd come at a run, but when he looked past Hadand-Gunvaer and the other women to find a familiar golden-haired man, he froze, wit-flown.

Tau also stopped, surprised at this Marlovan blocking his path, whose face had blanched almost as pale as his hair.

"Angel," Vedrid whispered as the women vanished up the stairwell leading to the royal wing.

Tau's mild surprise sharpened. *Angel?* That's what they'd called him in Bren. A series of rapid memory images: a tall, thin man with pale hair almost kicked to death on the floor of an abandoned building, mistaken for a Venn spy. His whispered words a mumble because of a broken jaw.

"I remember you," Tau said. Yes, it was the same man, now buttoned into one of those blue Marlovan coats, his pale hair skinned back into a squirt at the nape of his neck "In Bren, was it not? Aren't you the Runner those sailors jumped?"

"Vedrid Basna. King's First Runner. You saved my life," Vedrid said slowly, his eyes wide and staring. "I thought I'd dreamed—" He made a visible effort to gather his wits. "If you are Indevan-Laef's First Runner, I am to show you the chamber set aside for him."

I did not know what a Runner was—or for which king, Tau thought, his perspective shifting. Now he comprehended the questioning looks, the hesitations. All these Marlovans, including Evred, were trying to define his relationship to Inda. In the Marlovan world, everyone had a specific place.

Well, why not go along? He was used to playing roles. And it was clear that the personal Runners—whatever those might be—had the inside line of communication. "Yes," he said. "I'm Inda's First Runner."

And Vedrid's brow cleared. "Please. I owe you my life. I was charged to assist you, but it would be my privilege."

Inside line indeed. Tau opened his hand for Vedrid to lead the way.

Inda and Evred had forgotten them all.

As they passed through the gates and into the street, Evred talked at random, even laughed, merry and free, body, mind, and heart afire with joy. Inda laughed as well, cast back in time to the happy days of boyhood: his welcome had extinguished in a heartbeat the last shadows of homesick betrayal.

It was inevitable that the random questions would settle first on the circumstances of their last meeting. ". . . and so Cherry-Stripe told me what little they knew," Inda was saying.

Was that anger or a wince tightening the corner of Inda's eye? Inda's voice was husky as the words tumbled out. "Why didn't the Harskialdna believe me? He had decided against me before I spoke a word. I figured that much out, sick as I was. Cherry-Stripe and Buck say it's because of a promise made to the Kepri-Davans, but that sounds too easy."

"Right. Underneath that was a lifelong jealousy," Evred said; the word *jealousy* taunting him with an image of that tall, golden-haired young man in the courtyard. Evred was sure he was the same one with Inda at Lindeth Harbor that terrible day.

Inda tipped his head in question, the same way he had as a boy of ten. The gesture, so well-remembered, was curiously painful.

"Lifelong jealousy?" Inda repeated. "Lifelong. Then you can't just mean at the academy. Over what, my father's first wife, Joret? I know she was as beautiful as the Joret we grew up with. Everyone seemed to want her. Did that include your uncle, then? Is that it?"

Inda grimaced again, almost a flinch. Evred frowned, disturbed that he could not interpret Inda's reaction.

"Wait." Inda flung out a hand, whirling to stand in the middle of the street, oblivious to traffic. "Your uncle was only a year older than my Uncle Indevan—ten. Aunt Joret would have been almost done with the queen's training, and my father had to have been nineteen or twenty, because their class started a couple years late on account of the war up north. So your uncle can't have wanted either Joret *or* my father. Not at ten. That dog won't run."

"Not the jealousy of thwarted desire, but of my father's notice."

"Huh." Inda's brows rose, as if such a concept was blindingly new. "Wait!" He patted the air with his hands, neither of them aware of wagons rolling past laden with sacks of rice, a young boy hawking fresh-baked pies, a trio of stone-layers trundling by some new-shaped honey-colored stone. "Wait," Inda said again.

Evred braced himself for the shock of Inda's wide brown gaze, still guileless in spite of the years and their unknown burdens.

Then Inda made an impatient movement, flipping his fingers up, another remembered gesture. "But you can't say 'Oh, everything he did was because he wanted his brother's attention.' Too easy. Nobody acts on a single cause except in the old heroic ballads."

They started walking again—neither aware of it, anymore than they were aware of the unconscious pull of very old habits—in the direction of the academy.

"Can we ever define exactly what shapes an individual's character and perception of events?" Evred answered. It was like the old days, their endless debates in the summer sunshine while pitching hay, or tending horses, or repairing tack, or drilling over and over; he shivered inside, then coughed to clear his throat, to force his voice to normal. "My uncle wanted two things. He wanted to be first to my father and he wanted to keep the kingdom safe. How he exerted himself to get these things is shaped by these other matters."

"But that doesn't explain why he blamed me for Dogpiss' death," Inda said. Then he cast a furtive look behind him, which surprised Evred. No one was following them— he'd made that order clear.

Evred was further surprised when Inda abruptly shifted the subject.

"This might seem an odd question, but was there any mention in all those records of a fellow . . . named Dun?"

"Do you mean Hened Dunrend?" Evred asked, surprised at this sudden, completely unrelated turn of subjects.

Inda whistled, long and low. So far, only Signi knew about the ghost riding at his shoulder. Inda couldn't see him, but he knew the ghost was real, because he'd felt a weird prod inside his head during battle, ever since Dun's death, when Inda woke up a prisoner of pirates. It—he— had saved his life repeatedly with those unmistakable internal warnings.

Should he tell Evred? No, better to wait; a lot of people didn't like talk of ghosts, and wasn't there something nasty about one of Evred's ancestors and a ghost? So he said, "I knew him as Dun the Carpenter's Mate. He signed on with me that first day, when Captain Sindan first brought me to Lindeth Harbor. Afterward, well, I noticed things. He talked like the northerners, except some of his words reminded me of Marlovan. And he was really, really good at staff fighting, far better than any sailor. But then it was too late to ask. He died when we were first taken by pirates."

Evred said, "He was one of the King's Runners; I don't know if you remember, but they have their own training. I discovered in my father's papers that he sent Dunrend to run shield for you, though you were never to know it. If you came back—and I think my father wanted you to, but events got in the way—you could thus never reveal that he'd interfered in my uncle's decisions. Sindan met with him, after your first journey, and that's how we found out that you were alive. Did you ever ask him any questions?"

"No. And he didn't ask me, either. Typical Marlovans, eh?" Inda laughed, the long white scar on his temple creasing. That scar hadn't been there when Evred saw Inda in Lindeth. "Hoo! Look where we are."

They stood directly across from Daggers Drawn, the tavern belonging exclusively to the academy boys. There was the weather-worn fox sign with its oddly raptorish face, the same face on Inda's fleet foresails: the academy fox banner.

"It's strange," Evred said, expelling his breath in a not-quite-laugh, "but I have never looked inside that place."

Inda acted on impulse. "Then you shall now."

Chapter Eleven

THE custom in those days was for boys new to the academy to be introduced to Daggers Drawn by their fathers. In the cases of boys invited as a result of superior service on their fathers' part, they were introduced by the nearest relative of the Jarl in whose territory they lived. When Inda came to the academy, it was the first year younger brothers were invited, so older brothers (or cousins) were expected to introduce the newcomers.

Aldren-Sierlaef, Evred's brother, had so resented this change in tradition he had refused to introduce his brother, and no one else had dared to bring Evred, or to prompt the king, who never thought of it, as he'd had no interest in the place when he was young.

Inda hadn't thought about Daggers Drawn since he was a homesick sea rat on the *Pim Ryala,* but now, as he looked at the worn sign with the fading fox face, all the emotions of those days crowded back into his mind.

"I'll introduce you." Inda took Evred's arm. The muscle tensed under his fingers. Puzzled, Inda said, "It's all right." Though he had been long away from the customs of home he didn't make the mistake of pointing out that Evred was king, that the entire city obeyed his will. "You haven't a father now, or a brother, except me, through marriage. Let's see if old Mun's still alive. I was only there once, as it happens. The day Tanrid introduced me."

"I know. I saw how you and the others never went."

"You did? But we were so careful not to say anything. Well, and it wasn't like a great vow or anything. We, that is, some of us didn't want to be all gone and you alone in the scrub pit. Did they all stay with it, then, after I was taken away?"

As if I hadn't noticed, Evred thought, and the memory of their innocence, their uncalculating good will, was a knife-strike of bittersweet anguish.

Aware of the stiffness of his hands, Evred clasped them tightly behind his back. "Oh, more or less," he said. "Kepa sneaked over whenever he thought the others didn't notice, usually taking Lassad. But the others, I think, never got into the habit. We made our own secret meeting places. And when we got older, I could always bring food. Nobody was going to punish us for that."

Inda plunged across the street, moving with a slight stiffness in his walk that made Evred wonder if he carried more severe wounds not visible to the eye.

Inda paused outside the Daggers door. "I don't hear boys."

"No, the scrubs would be in the stable picking hooves, the pigtails out with the scout dogs, now that the weather's finally broken—" Evred shook his head. "Never mind."

But Inda looked surprised and delighted. "*You* run 'em all now, right?" He sniffed the air. "And a very late spring. Those pits must be pret-ty chilly." He grinned in remembrance, using the old slang word, pit, for barracks.

"Winter was reluctant to let go this year. The boys have been shivering here for a month, and the last snow melted scarcely a week ago."

Inda gave one of those "Hah!" laughs of memory as he swung inside the tavern, his head barely clearing the low door. Evred ducked his head and followed.

"Mun! You here? Maybe you won't remember me—"

"I do. Indevan-Laef." Kethan Mundavan was the proprietor, a retired lancer the boys were privileged to address by his academy name, Mun. He was grayer, stiffer, but very much alive, his eyes alert as he and his grand-nephew polished glasses. "You've got a look of your brother."

Was every reminder of Tanrid going to hurt like stepping on glass? Inda opened his hand. "I'm here to present my brother-by-marriage, Evred-Harvaldar Montrei-Vayir."

Tau might have smiled; Jeje would have laughed, believing them to be participating in an elaborate joke, but to the Marlovans everything was as it should be. The city answered to the king, yet this little tavern within the city was Mun's kingdom, and they were there by his leave.

Mun indicated a table with his gnarled hand, and the two sat down by the fire, at the table reserved for the teenage horsetails, top of the academy ranks. Though neither had actually ridden as a horsetail, he made it plain that in his view they had earned that right.

"Tell me about Tanrid," Inda said, aware of Mun's presence; the man made no pretence of not listening as Evred unlocked the memory of Tanrid's death. He described everything he had seen, heard, thought. And what he had promised at the last.

Inda had thought he'd wept out his grief back at the Marlo-Vayir castle that first night. Elation and sorrow chased through him now, choking up in his throat. He could so clearly see Tanrid at the end, there, saying "Inda" with his last breath.

He rocked on his bench, deep in memory—regret—renewed grief, unaware of the lengthening silence, until the thump of two mugs of clear amber ale on the table startled him back to the present.

Evred had fallen into watchful silence.

Inda's first sip caused a sudden, indrawn breath—this time of pleasure. The grief began to recede.

"Bad ale?" Evred asked.

"No. Good." Inda closed his eyes, then opened them; the bright sheen of unshed tears reminded Evred of Hadand at rare, unexpected times.

Inda set the mug down with a sigh. "So good. But why is it tastes and smells and sounds gravel you harder than sight? My scrub memories are back, and kicking like a wild colt."

"All the ancient Sartoran records maintain that where you experienced the most pain, or joy, plants the deepest memories." Evred gripped his hands together under the table. He found the emotions that Inda expressed so easily impossible to ward, so that sounds were too distinct, the light sharp, his skin hurt.

Mun carried a tray of glasses into the back, and they had the room to themselves: an old, somewhat stuffy room, smelling of boys and old drink, with its knife-scarred tables and the atmosphere of boyish presence. Both their fathers had once sat here.

Inda said, "The last time I saw Tanrid, he came in his horsetail coat—all dressed for parade—and begged me to take that beating. I thought he was going to thrash me, sick as I was. For family honor, you see." Inda's gaze went diffuse as he stared into the past. "I didn't really know him. Too busy trying to avoid his discipline. Is it right, what we have brothers do to brothers?"

He glanced up, and Evred turned his own gaze to the fire. "I vowed to myself on my long ride home from the north that I would change everything. I would raise my own sons so they would not see me only as a distant figure to be saluted but never spoken to about things that matter. So they would not see one another as enemies." He smiled briefly. "Barend warned me that if I expected him to raise any boys I might have, he'll send them to sea."

"I was so glad to find out Barend's alive," Inda said. "He left us right after the pirate battle. We'd found out about his father hiring those pirates—well, you know all that, of course," Inda finished awkwardly, remembering the quiet determination in Evred's cousin Barend, who was usually easygoing. Barend had left Inda's fleet determined to confront his father about this treachery that cast dishonor on the family name: Inda found out only recently that Barend's quest touched off the Conspiracy at Hesea Springs and the deaths of nearly everyone in Barend's family.

"Barend nearly killed himself, trying to get back up to Lindeth to rejoin you. He'll be glad to find out you are back home. As for raising sons, when will I do it? I understand my father a lot better now: you can rise earlier than your cooks, and go to sleep with the night watch, but you never quite stay the pace of duty."

The Marlovan verb *understand* carried connotations of *forgive*. But there wasn't time to consider Evred's boyhood with the king. Kings were too far beyond Inda's experience. Brothers were not.

"We talked about it, Cherry-Stripe and Cama and I, before I left. They won't change anything, they said, much as we used to whine and moan. How else to get tough enough to face the constant wars?"

"Wars." Evred fingered his mug, frowning into its glinting amber depths. Then he glanced up. "So you did not know about Tanrid's or my father's deaths before you left your ships and the sea. What brought you back?"

Inda shook his head, his smile rueful. "Forgot, soon's I saw you again. Can you believe that? Got one thump too many. The Venn are coming, Sponge. I think they'll launch as soon as the winds make the summer change."

"The Venn," Evred breathed.

"Here's what's bad: they've been training in the plains of Ymar. I saw them a year ago. And they've had spies here for several years."

Before Inda's eyes his old friend hardened into someone else. Already taller than Inda, he now seemed even larger, his countenance as cold and remote as his brother's ever had been. He leaned forward. "Then I take it you did not defeat their fleet, as everyone in the north is claiming."

Inda snorted. "Defeat? There wasn't even a battle. If there had been, we would have been sunk. We were a handful against eighty-one big Venn warships."

"Eighty-one," Evred repeated.

"And that's only the primary warships. Each has seekers and raiders attached."

"You can explain what that means later. So what happened?"

Inda flicked his fingers out, palms up. "Nothing! We slipped between their lines. They sailed away, and I came south." Inda's mug clunked to the table, empty. "We didn't land at Lindeth—we picked an empty cove west of Marlo-Vayir. But I don't think that'll fool the Venn spies. They've got to figure I'd come to you."

"What do the Venn know about your past?"

"Everything," Inda admitted. "Got caught in Ymar. Under kinthus I yapped out everything I've done. I'd be there yet, or dead, if Fox Montredavan-An hadn't got me out."

Fox. Evred's lips shaped the word. Brown eyes met hazel; for Evred the sensation was like staring into the sun, and he shifted his gaze to his ale, scarcely touched.

Inda had been looking for a sign of invitation to speak further about Fox. Though he didn't see it, he spoke anyway. "Is there any chance of setting aside that damned treaty?" And he was about to add, *Let me tell you what really happened all those years ago,* but then he remembered that the villain of the real story was Evred's own ancestor.

And to Inda's dismay, Evred's features tightened in anger. Within a moment he'd schooled his face again, but Inda had seen that first reaction. And Evred saw to his undisguised shock that Inda had seen it.

Evred toyed with the glass in his hand, fighting to regain control. He despised himself for his weakness, for revealing the most loathsome and petty of all emotions: jealousy.

Long habit enabled him to regain an appearance of calm, of neutrality. "This is not the time to be revoking treaties—not when we're facing the war we've been bracing against for years. The only thing I have to rely on with everything else slowly disintegrating is the . . . expectation, let's call it. The expectation of tradition."

And Inda thought, *You were right, Fox. Though Sponge is right, too.* He regretted his first impulse—it was not only stupid but the worst sort of strut to expect his old scrub mate to wave away four generations of unfairness just because Inda asked him to.

Inda made a last effort, trying to be practical. "We could probably use their men."

"If the Venn make it this far south, the Montredavan-Ans will need their own men, who are limited in number by treaty. They will have to defend their own land, because again, by treaty we cannot do it." And, to get away from the subject altogether, "What does 'as soon as the winds change' mean? I understood you put up various sails to counter winds."

Inda drummed his fingers on the initial-carved tabletop, considering his words. "I take it Barend didn't explain currents and winds and points of sail to you?"

"He did, but I comprehended only a little, and don't remember any of it now. Though I do remember that the Venn have ships more seaworthy than everyone else's. Larger."

"All true, but they don't sail as close to the wind as we do. Anyway, my guess is we'll see them after summer shifts the winds into a steady stream, out of the north by northwest. Need it right on the beam." Evred looked blank; Inda smacked his outer thigh. "Beam. It'll give them the push they need with ships crammed to the captain's deck with men and horses."

"And then what?"

"All I have for that part is guesses. I never could get close enough to see much beyond maneuvering, but I do know Rajnir is throwing everything he has against us." The old gestures were there, the enthusiasm for a plan.

Evred forced his attention away from Inda himself and onto his words. "We had better leave now." He stood, felt his pockets. His face changed. "I don't carry coins. I'll have to send a Runner——"

Mun reappeared. "Your brothers left plenty on their shots."

Inda and Evred started, wondering what he'd heard. Probably everything, Inda thought, trying not to laugh.

Evred controlled his annoyance. Already he had accustomed himself to the privacy requisite to his royal rank. But he knew that Mun, an old dragoon lancer, would say nothing, and a wise king would therefore not breach his trust by commanding him to do so.

It was, in short, their own fault for discussing the king-dom's affairs in a tavern set aside for boys. But it had seemed right at the time.

"There is much to be done," Evred said only, and he saluted Mun, who saluted him back, fist to heart. And then, with equal deliberation, Mun saluted Inda. Inda returned the salute—a gesture he'd had to fight against using for nine years. It felt good down to his bones to have the right to use it again.

They left. Inda matched Evred's quick pace, but there was that wince again.

Evred's mind, given free rein, was galloping ahead: inva-sion, the magical communications locket, Nightingale in exactly the right position. Barend on the north coast to oversee defense of the harbors. Hawkeye Yvana-Vayir holding down the headquarters at Ala Larkadhe. All of them courageous and reliable within their limits, but not a one to defend the land against the Venn . . .

Unknown spies—information—map—Barend, who can-not lead an army—

—Mun's salute to Inda—to a commander—

—to a Harskialdna—

Harskialdna.

Which of them had shifted the subject away from Evred's uncle's actions nine years ago? Sustained through all these ideas skirmishing for precedence was guilt, inten-sified by the faint grimace that occasionally narrowed Inda's eyes as they walked: Evred attributed it to the nine years of his unkept promise of justice.

He said, speaking low and rapid, his heartbeat loud in his own ears, "You have the right to demand justice of me." The answer was clear, as clear and right as sun and wind and life. "My uncle ruined you because you were loyal. My brother killed yours. It is right, it is just, that you shall lead the army against the invaders."

Inda jerked round to face him.

There. The words were spoken, Evred could not call

them back. Not that he wished to. His sudden joy, the dizzying sense of rightness, was far too intense for that. A glance. There was no answering joy in Inda's face—

You have the right to demand justice . . . Inda stared back, stunned. That wasn't justice, it was something so different he could not define it, or even express his reaction. Yet Sponge stood there in the street, his hazel eyes wide, unblinking, awaiting an answer.

Inda tried to gauge him, why he'd done that, and discovered that he couldn't really gauge Sponge. He'd never been able to. He'd never had to, when they were boys. Sponge had talked so freely about everything, excepting only his family, and his feelings. Now "Sponge" was Evred-Harvaldar, and wasn't it treason to gainsay a king?

"It was your uncle, not you, who denied me justice," Inda began slowly. "And your brother who had Tanrid murdered."

Evred flushed. "But I was the one who made a vow."

Inda realized that Evred felt *guilty*. Why? He had done his best for Tanrid and Inda both, Inda could see that. If only Cherry-Stripe's damned boots didn't rub the damned blisters so!

"We will ride north together. You will command the defense. Who better to fight the Venn than one who has already fought them?"

Evred's voice took on authority in Inda's ears; Evred himself was only aware of the overwhelming sense of rightness that Inda ride at his side to defend their homeland.

Inda expelled his breath. "If Barend agrees."

"He will."

Evred spoke with conviction; Inda heard a royal order.

And so he struck his fist against his heart, and Evred laughed with pleasure, and said again, "There is much to be done." Adding, "We will do it together."

Chapter Twelve

THE yip-yip of boys echoed through the open windows of the tower the women ascended before entering the residence portion of the castle. To Signi it was a barbaric, horrible sound, like foxes on the hunt, only more horrible because of the intelligence and anticipation shaping those shrill voices.

She followed the Marlovan women upstairs and along a narrow hallway, her hands folded on her bag, eyes down-cast, her posture one of deference, though her muscles were tense as a humming string. Inda was gone, leaving her alone among enemies in this bewildering castle, and she could not understand more than occasional words or phrases of the quick, strange-accented Marlovan, their shared Venn roots notwithstanding.

She was not angry with Inda. She had seen in the tautness of his body as they approached this city, and in his joyful welcome of those he had loved longest, that at that moment there was no room in his mind for anyone, or anything, else.

Inda was like a river, sometimes slow and tranquil on the surface. When he fought he was fast and dangerous as river rapids. At all times he flowed toward the single goal: home. Like a river, there was no pretence, no hiding his nature.

She did feel anger, and fear, and her wrists would have trembled if she had not learned control.

She was angriest with herself. After all her years, all her hard-won experience and oft-repeated lessons, how had she—despite all her careful thought—succumbed like the most shallow youngster to the illogic of lust, wherein reason is reduced to making excuses for the actions of the beloved?

She closed her eyes, trusting to her senses to guide her as she sought the inward way to Ydrasal, the right and true road to honor. It was sometimes called the Golden Tree, because in the realm of the spirit, it shone with golden light, and the same luminosity shimmered around Inda when he was most intense.

Her path at this moment did cleave with his path. That her inner vision had insisted, even before she knew Inda except as the terrible murderer Elgar the Fox.

She must be here. She did not know why, not anymore than she knew why Inda, a war leader, should shine with the golden light—unless it was his ghost companion, who, though mostly a blur of light, was sometimes clear and distinct. No, that was a different aura.

What she did know was that the Golden Tree was not easy to perceive, and sometimes the way toward it was fraught with danger. But she must walk the path.

She opened her eyes, breathing the dancer's long breaths of calm and serenity.

While she concentrated on clearing her mind of conflicting emotions, down the hall in the area reserved for the Runners, Vedrid was talking quickly, half a dozen other Runners listening. From their attitudes, Tau suspected they'd heard Vedrid's version of their encounter in Bren.

"You'll need a blue coat," Vedrid explained, turning back to Tau. "If you dress as a Runner, then you have more access than if you wear what you have on now. And no one stops you because they expect Runners to be about their business. A foreigner in these times—" He turned his palms up, and Tau could easily imagine these ubiquitous armed sentries stopping him for questioning every single time he ventured out.

"I have no objection to adopting your dress," Tau said.

Vedrid looked relieved. "Then we'll get you a coat at once. And teach you the Runner signs and signals as well as our own accesses through the castle. What would you like first?"

He set his and Inda's gear bags down in the room assigned to Inda. "I'll admit the first thing I'd like is a tour of this castle. I lost all sense of where the stable was while just following you up the stairs."

While Tau was measured and then taken on his tour, Hadand finished the long walk to her public interview room.

The windows opened onto a view of the women's outer court. The voices of young women rose on the warm summer air as the guests entered, their manner uncertain. Behind them, Tdor glanced from object to object with the distraction of the seeker of a lost key. *She's been my sister in all but blood since we were small. Does she feel brotherlove for Inda, or am I seeing a different emotion? Surely not, after nine years apart!*

So said reason. *But who knows better than I that reason very seldom communicates with the heart?* Hadand thought with self-mockery. *Very well, leave Tdor to her thoughts.*

Hadand needed to find out, first of all, who these women were. Easy and polite questions—Hungry? Thirsty? How was the journey?—on the long walk had elicited equally polite, monosyllabic responses from the dark-haired one. Each woman carried her own bag, which argued for similar status. The dark one appeared wary and ill-at-ease. The sandy-haired one was as devoid of expression as a windworn statue.

Outside the cadenced voices rose and fell amid the clash of weapons, proof that Marlovan women really did fight, as rumor had it. Signi had glimpsed a boot sheath as they'd walked in, before the woman took up her station guarding the door. The woman outside the door wore a wrist sheath beneath those long-sleeved blue robes. Blue! The color mages wore in the Land of the Venn. But here there were no mages. Blue here apparently meant fighters, or fighting servants.

Hadand shut the door, leaving Tesar watching outside. She faced her exasperating guests, thinking, *You're a queen, you can ask questions. What can they do back?*

She turned her attention midway between the two women, and asked what for a Marlovan was a reasonable question: "So, why did you come with my brother?"

Jeje flicked a glance at Signi. As she expected, no help there. And Inda had gone off on his own with that king. So much for protecting him!

She said in her best Iascan, "I'm the captain of Inda's scout cutter—" Then paused. The two women waited, polite but blank.

Maybe she was supposed to say *Lord Indevan.* Or put *dal* in there somewhere? Neither of the Marlovans seemed angry, though. More puzzled. So she plunged on ahead. "And Signi over there is his lover." There, that was innocuous enough. Except why did the short one look so startled, and the other go stiff? "And you are?"

Hadand was indeed startled—it'd seemed impossible that her little brother could have a lover. Oh, he was no longer the small boy she'd seen in memory all these years, she had proof of that outside in the courtyard. He was twenty, so a lover wasn't surprising. What surprised her was that the lover was the old one rather than the young.

Of course he'd have a lover, Tdor thought. *And—* firmly—*I'm glad.*

"I am Hadand-Gunvaer. This is Tdor-Edli Marth-Davan, my foster-sister. Who is the blond man?"

How to define Tau? Jeje smothered a laugh and stated, "He's my lover. And we came along in case, well, Inda needed, um, help."

Hadand smiled, and Tdor raised her brows and rounded her lips in appreciation. Then, in a valiant effort to keep some sort of conversation limping along, "What is a scout cutter?"

Jeje suspected these women had exactly as much interest in ships as they had knowledge—which would be none—nevertheless, she resolutely picked up her cue and launched into a definition of types of ships and numbers of

masts, broadening (on their encouraging nods) into trade
ships versus pirate ships versus warships. She was slogging
grimly and bravely into the intricacies of fore-and-aft rigging (as opposed to the Venn's square) when a door
opened.

In came people in gray smocks and baggy trousers with
crimson piping. They carried platters of rye biscuits with
toasted cheese on top. Jeje hadn't eaten since long before
dawn. These were pan biscuits instead of the baked ones
she'd had in childhood but they smelled good. Her stomach rumbled as the platters were set on the low table.

Everyone settled on the mats. But before they could
begin to eat, an authoritative thump at the outer door
stopped the talk. A tall woman in a blue robe entered and
made a sign to Hadand and a heartbeat later a new woman
strode in.

The newcomer was dressed like other female Runners,
her blue robe splashed with mud up to her thighs and curls
the color of ripened wheat escaped from her braid. Her
manner was definitely not that of a Runner as her wide, intense brown eyes searched the room. Familiar eyes, though
Jeje had never seen her before.

"Shen!" Hadand exclaimed. Then, in a more cautious
voice, "How did *you* get here?"

"A Runner rode through Darchelde." Shendan
Montredavan-An thumped her fists on her hips. "Said Indevan Algara-Vayir was in Marlo-Vayir territory, coming
here. We know Foxy sails with him. I took my Runner's
robe, which got me across the border. Marend didn't come
only because we were afraid the border guards would balk
at two of us." She flung back her hair. "As for your Evred,
as long as he doesn't see me, he can pretend I'm not here."

Your Evred. Hadand let it go by. She'd come to realize
that nothing was going to mend the resentment between
the Montrei-Vayirs and the Montredavan-Ans, at least not
until something was done about that exile treaty. For the
rest, as usual, Shendan was right. Evred knew that she was
Hadand's friend, so although he had to know that she was
in the castle, he wouldn't interfere unless forced to.

Shen said, "And I'll be gone as soon as one of you gives me news of my brother."

Jeje had her placed now. That broad brow, the sardonic eyes, the sharp-cut bones: Fox's sister!

Jeje set down her untasted biscuit. "I think I can help you there."

Except for the brief roughness in the road when Fox's name was introduced, Inda's and Evred's minds galloped parallel, so free and effortless neither was prepared to hit the stone fence of divided boundary.

As they walked back, Inda talked fast, describing what he'd seen on the Ymaran plains. Evred's two years of hard-won experience in the north enabled him to follow the swift stream of Inda's thoughts and to ask questions. "What kind of horse bears those tall men? How fast? Have they changed to our swords, or do they rely on ax and straight sword? Do they use the composite bow now? They were known for their great longbows, with the tremendous reach."

Inda dipped his chin at each point. "I couldn't see much, only distant movement. I did see some horsemen, but there was always dust. Looked like they kept trying charges, but they always had to pull up short. From what we—I—saw, it looked like their favorite defense is these squares. Big men in front. Curving rectangle shields instead of the round ones. Longbows in back, and on flanks, and the old ax and straight sword at front."

"How did they handle their horses?"

Inda wriggled his shoulders, then tipped a hand as he searched for the right word. "Heavy." He stumbled over a loose stone in the street, making a face at the ground. "I will ride with you to the north, but I don't mind going as your Runner, or as a scout, or as anything, really. Don't you have *any* commanders?"

"The best of the older commanders are dead, except for the Jarl of Cassad, and he can no longer sit a horse. And he never faced the Venn. None of us have, young or old. Don't you remember the speculation when we were boys?"

"But what about Gand?" Inda exclaimed. "I can't believe Master—*Captain* Gand—couldn't lead them. Ho, Sponge, everything I ever did right was because I had a memory of Gand's voice in my head. *You'll learn as much as we can teach you because the more you know, the fewer signals needed.* Didn't *that* turn out to be true! 'Course I don't know if signals can foul as easily on land as on sea—oh, listen to me yap. Don't tell me Gand is dead?"

"No, I called him in, almost my first command once I got back here. He runs the academy. Told me he can't command, which was why he never made it above captain. He said—and you tell me how this makes sense, I just accepted it because I didn't dare not—he said that he only sees the shape of individuals, not the shape of battle."

Inda tipped his head back. "Oh, yes. I see. Tau's that way, too. Funny, how you remember someone being all-knowing. Gand! He sure was good with us!"

"He's good with the academy now."

"Hoo, that was well thought. So what about everyone our age? They've all seen action against pirates, haven't they? Your cousin Hawkeye—that's who I was trying to remember! Didn't he run command at the front under you in the north? He was your Harskialdna, wasn't he?"

"He can't command," Evred said slowly. "Oh, he's dashing at the lead in skirmishes. No one would question his courage. But his idea of command is to lead whoever's around him straight at the biggest mass of enemies. That worked fairly well against pirates, but will it against Venn?"

"No," Inda said, remembering those big men and the heavy rectangular shields held edge to edge. "They'll hold. Then use those shields to shove, and the swords between 'em to spike our horses or us if we're on foot. I could see that much."

"Then we lose lives to no purpose, except added verses to the tragic ballads. Hawkeye will take orders from you if I make it clear that is my will. He certainly understands chain of command. We've all been raised to it."

Inda said slowly, "One thing I've learned since I left is that chain of command might look like a ladder on paper, but you really get twists and bends. I could make the plans, but won't the rest of the Vayirs expect to see him riding beside you, right behind your banner?"

"You forget his father's disgrace."

"Oh." Inda's eyes were so candid and earnest—and so painful to meet. "Don't misunderstand." Inda opened his hands, palm up. "I want to ride as your Royal Shield Arm for this battle. Very much! But it seems wrong somehow. Frost. Like there's no one else in all Iasca Leror."

Frost in the old academy slang of boyhood meant arrogance, the assumed superiority of rank. Evred said, "Inda, you have forgotten my uncle, and what he did to those who showed command ability."

Inda drew in a sharp breath. "Then I wasn't the only one?"

"You were the only academy boy exiled, and I do believe that was actually my father's idea, or maybe Sindan's. I saw my uncle's papers after he died. Most of those he found a way to shift out of the possibility of command accepted disgrace, or their families accepted for them. You were the only one who stuck it out—and your father apparently was willing to back you."

"I never knew that," Inda said, and sighed. "How could I?"

"I would not say it before anyone else, because we must seem united, but it comes so clear in my uncle's writings. He had a reason for everything he did because he trusted no one but himself and my father. The shadow of the assassin's knife haunted him all his life, worsening when my grandfather died. Some said under suspicious circumstances, others believed it was a riding accident."

"Your uncle thought it was conspiracy?"

"Oh, yes. Then he really did believe, or talk himself into believing, that any Vayir with the gift of command who didn't fall right in behind him was a future danger to my father, to my brother. And so the best left the academy early—heaped with praise—to go home to guard, or if they were not Vayirs they were promoted—heaped with praise and promises—and sent to the borders. And to the coast."

"Against the Brotherhood?"

"Yes. A few died in action, because his orders were always clear: we ride like our ancestors, commanders in the lead. Others died under circumstances that their personal Runners could not explain—the Runners who survived, and too often they all died too. Mysteries we might have solved if my uncle's personal Runner, Retren Waldan, had lived, because apparently Waldan's orders were never written. But he himself was assassinated after Yvana-Vayir's Conspiracy. I don't know by whom. Another mystery."

"No one knows any of what you're telling me?" Inda asked, grimacing.

"Only Hadand. And Barend, somewhat. He didn't want to know the details, as his own father was behind them. Here's what I am sure of. The only one who really understood command in the strategic sense, I believe, was Captain Sindan. When I look back, his suggestions to me were not just sensible, but far-reaching. And it was his grasp of Idayagan territory and tactics that turned the Battle of Ghael Hills from a terrible massacre into victory. But he is dead."

Inda pressed the heels of his palms into his eyes in the old, remembered gesture, then came the snort of decision, the outward flick of his hands. "All right. I'm just going to have to learn on the run. Well, I've done that all along."

Tension released its grip on Evred's skull.

Inda thumped his fist on a barrel top as they turned the corner outside a tavern. "Here's what I'm thinking. I haven't seen Marlovans drill for battle since I was a boy, and I've never seen them fight. You know I barely started training to fight on horseback, and isn't that what we do?"

"We will drill on the march north. Every day."

"Yes. Yes." Inda turned his thumb up. "That to start. But Sponge," a sudden turn, sidestepping a pack of tail-waving dogs being chased by laughing children, "what kind of battleground are we looking at? What can you tell me about the Idayagan terrain?"

"I know it well."

"And you saw *our* limitations, which is a place to start." Inda took a wider step to avoid another loose stone—where was all the road guild? Off defending the coast, probably. He grimaced. "Damn these boots anyway."

"Boots?" Evred was bewildered.

"Cherry-Stripe's old ones. He said they were soft as butter, but when you go barefoot most of the year—" A shrug. "What I need to know first is the exact terrain of the pass."

"I'll give you that. But we in turn need to know more about the Venn. If only you had gotten more detail from your source!"

"Well, we can ask," Inda stated, and that was when they hit the stone wall.

"What? A Venn? Here?"

"Dag Signi. With the women." Inda opened his hand toward the castle towering over them.

Evred's face blanched. "You brought a Venn spy into my castle?"

"She's not a spy, she's a mage."

"She's a *what?*"

Inda stopped, looking up at the castle tower without seeing it. They were surrounded by haywains being brought from the storage sheds to the great stable yard, amid shouts and clopping hooves, and the smells of summer and horse and sweat, but Inda had gone blind and deaf.

Evred stilled, his rage visible to the men and women on the walls, who watched uneasily, some reaching for weapons.

Inda brought his chin down, his expression perplexed. "A mage, but on parole," he said as he rubbed his eyes. "She can't go back, they'd kill her."

"All that could be a ruse. How do you know it's true?"

Evred's sharp voice caused Inda to swing around and crash head-on into the wall of Evred's white anger. "I—I trust her." He groped with one hand, a gesture of appeal. "I *love* her." As if that explained everything.

Evred's face had hardened, reminding Inda of Evred's older brother, the Sierlaef: angry hazel eyes, the rigid stillness that threatened violence. "So pirates think with their prick?"

Inda stepped back abruptly, his earrings winking bloodred.

But Inda's reaction was not nearly as intense as Evred's own self-loathing: thinking with his own prick, wasn't he, with all that agonizing over the angel-faced fellow he'd dismissed with the women? Who mounted the wrong horse first?

"As do Marlovans," Evred said, breathing out hard. All the tension went out of his manner; he forced his voice to neutrality. "And probably Venn as well. Tell me about this woman. Why you brought her."

Inda groped for words. "Signi can't be a spy—her life is forfeit if she ever goes back. You know about their deep water navigation, right?"

"I remember Barend speaking of it." Evred's heart was beating fast.

"Well, she was on her way to Sartor to offer that knowledge to the Sartoran Mage Council, who in turn could give it to the world. Level things up on the sea. And circumvent Prince Rajnir's plans. He's the Venn heir, you know. He doesn't just want us, he wants our entire continent."

"So your mage is a traitor to her own people?"

Inda shook his head. "It's not betrayal, don't you see? It's a greater cause. She was chosen, by one of their own, and lost everything in trying to see it through. Because I caught her. And then, well, by the time I learned all that, events brought us here."

Evred now stood with his hands clasped behind his back, as he studied the weatherworn stones of the street. Reassured that the king was not in danger, the wall sentries turned their attention away and resumed their pacing.

Evred's thoughts, accustomed now to the never-ending pressure of kingship, picked up the race yet again. He scouted ahead of Inda, because he must, but the first unreasoning rush of joy had been muted. "I see that there is far more here than I assumed, but we will have the time to explain. And your other woman? Is she also a mage?"

Inda laughed. "Jeje! No, Jeje came along to protect me

against the wiles of kings." Inda's delight was the old transparent Inda—he expected his academy mate to share the jest.

Evred forced a smile. "I see! Behold me rabbiting with fear. Listen, Inda. I need to give some orders. Rearrange the day's events so that we can discuss our plans, and you must watch the horsetail drills. You must also," he added, "speak to Tdor."

They had reached the great gate, where the next watch's perimeter patrol riders reined in at the unexpected sight of the king, some stroking the tossing heads of their impatient horses.

Inda stopped to let them ride past, but they waited. Evred walked past, head bent and expression absorbed— another reminder that Inda was back among Marlovans, where everyone had a rank and a place.

"Tdor," Inda repeated as he followed. "Is she here?"

"You did not see her? She was there with Hadand and me."

Inda's smile was rueful. "I saw Hadand, and you, and next thing I knew we were at Daggers."

"You will see her anon," Evred said, his plans now made. "Come, let's go through to the academy. I have business that cannot wait, but I will give you an escort, and rejoin you the moment I can."

Chapter Thirteen

SIGNI had begun to compose herself for the inevitable. Jeje answered Shendan's rapid questions, which switched to Marlovan and back again like stormy wind shifts at sea. Jeje had picked up a lot of Marlovan on the ride from Cherry-Stripe's. While she talked, she watched Signi, who seemed more and more still and silent.

Jeje finished with, "Finally there was the mystery rescue. Inda got captured when scouting the Venn in Ymar, and Fox went in alone and got him out. By the time the news got to Bren, before the Venn cut off anyone leaving Ymar, the gossip was that the two of 'em set fire to half the kingdom."

"Good," Shen stated, and then gave a fierce laugh. "I hope they burned it all down."

Signi pressed her hands together; Tdor felt a wave of compassion when she saw tension in Signi's fingers.

Jeje shrugged. "Dunno. All we know is the Venn are coming."

"Coming after Inda and Fox?" Shen asked.

"More like after all of us. Marlovans, too. Invasion."

"What exactly happened in Ymar? Before they torched it, I mean?"

"Inda won't say." Jeje's voice was unexpectedly deep. "Anyone who dares ask Fox gets a nasty 'Convince me it's your business first' for their pains."

Shen laughed again. "That's my brother! So what is Foxy doing now? Why didn't he come home?"

Jeje turned a helpless look Signi's way, struggling to find diplomatic words.

Shen flung up a hand to forestall her. "Never mind. I can see the shuffle coming. Save your breath for your soup. I will ask Inda himself."

Dread tightened Signi's neck at the casual reference to impending war. Her own chief Dag, Brit Valda, had said years ago, *It is a shame when we must regard a people as an enemy. It is a shame and a regret when the two peoples share so much. And it is a shame, a regret, and a tragedy when those peoples meet as individuals and find much to admire.* Signi knew that if Inda were to meet Fulla Durasnir, the commander of the Southern Fleet, they would probably become fast friends. If they could meet anywhere but in battle, that is, when they would do their best to kill one another because duty to king and country and honor required it.

Signi no longer regarded the Marlovans as enemies. So she cherished the spring-green glow around Hadand when she observed her with the *Yaga Ydrasal*, the Inward Eye of the Golden Tree. Green was good, it was the new life of the bud; so too was the rich tree-bark brown of Tdor's spirit. These were good women, Signi could see it in their spirits, even if she could not yet understand many of their words to one another.

Shendan had just asked where Inda was when another of the women in blue entered. She spoke softly to Hadand, with a fast, revealing peek Signi's way.

Comes my trial, Signi thought. Here was the first hard rock in her road, as inevitable as rain.

Tdor watched uneasily as Signi rose in a swift, dignified manner, put her palms together, and followed Tesar out.

Hadand observed Signi's resignation, and wondered how much she'd understood, despite Jeje's assurance that Signi did not comprehend Marlovan. Was it possible she was a spy?

As soon as the door shut behind Tesar and Signi,

Hadand took a deep breath. "It seems that she is a Venn." And turned a questioning look Jeje's way.

Jeje said, "Inda trusts her. Well, she's the one who got us free o' the Venn, there, when we fumbled into the whole soul-sucking fleet. She's a renegade. Inda can tell you more. Or I guess she's going to tell you herself, right? Is there some kind of trouble here?"

Hadand's hands vanished into her sleeves. "Trouble, not necessarily, but questions, yes. I will attend. If Inda trusts her, then I owe it to him." She turned to Tdor. "First, Evred requests you to finish showing Inda around. Give him news of home. He's at the academy now. He might want to see . . . other things. Jeje, Shen, please feel free to rest here before we all meet at dinner." She left.

He might want to see other things—but not Evred questioning his mage, Jeje thought.

Shen put out a hand to stop Tdor, saying in Marlovan, "I will not be stabled here like an old mare. You and I are going to find Inda together."

Tdor signified agreement, and they left.

Jeje turned to the untouched food. Over her years of sea-roaming she'd learned that, just as you could not command the wind, you never pass up a good meal, much less a chance to catch a nap. You never know what the next watch will bring.

Evred met Vedrid on his way inside. Vedrid reported that Inda's Runner was getting a tour. Evred spared a heartbeat to mock himself for his earlier heart-gnawings. The golden-haired fellow was Inda's First Runner, not his lover. Proof again that emotions were not only useless, but dangerous.

He sent Vedrid to show Inda the academy.

He sent another Runner to summon the mage.

He chose his study over his more formal (and formidable) rooms in an attempt to mitigate the circumstances, which Signi took as a well-meant gesture, though it failed its purpose. He might as well have summoned her to the throne room amid armed guards, for she saw in the great raptor furnishings, the crimson-as-blood rug worked with golden-winged predator birds, the silence and shut door, mute testimony to kingly supremacy.

But she was not powerless. She had her brains and her magic.

Evred studied the small, sandy-haired older woman walking with smooth grace between two of his most trusted armsmen, Hadand just catching up. This was Inda's lover? His inward vision of a tall, pale-haired version of the staggeringly beautiful Joret Dei vanished, leaving him puzzled indeed. The mage had to be ten years older than Evred himself, who had two years on Inda. She was ordinary in all ways, except in the manner she moved, neat and curiously compelling as she stepped forward, hands pressing together then opening. She bowed her head gravely.

He beckoned to Hadand, then dismissed the men.

"I would like the benefit of your eyes and ears," he murmured to his wife. "She's not just Venn, but a mage."

Hadand hid her consternation. A *mage?* So that's what Jeje meant!

Evred sat down in the great carved raptor chair one of his ancestors had taken from the Montredavan-Ans after their defeat. "Who are you?" he asked in slow, clear Iascan.

Signi stood before him, outwardly composed. Evred, whose keen gaze missed little, noted the fast pulse at the side of her temple. The cause of tension could be anything from simple human fear to deviousness, but it meant that her mind would run fast.

Well, so could his.

"My name doth be Jazsha Signi Sofar, second daughter of Jazsha Fafna Sofar, Hel Dancer to the Venn. My life-place doth be Sea Dag of the third rank, though outward be that place."

Outward be ... She was using, with great care, the outdated verb forms of Iascan that related most closely to Sartoran. Evred switched languages to Sartoran—"Does that mean you have a public rank and a secret rank?"—and saw her eyelids lift in surprise.

So Marlovan kings spoke Sartoran! Rumor persisted in the far north that they did not even know how to read. Prince Rajnir had been told by the well-traveled Dag Erkric that they were ignorant in all things except war.

This king's accent was the elegant court accent of two generations ago; she had no idea it was the Sartoran the Adrani king had brought home after his service in Sartor and taught to his daughter Wisthia, who brought it west when she married Evred's father. In Signi's world Sartoran was the language of magic and scholarship. This king spoke like a scholar. He was subtle, the shimmer around him was the deep blue of midnight that blends with and hides the presence of other colors. A blue deep and vast enough to house the distant stars. Blue was the color of knowledge, magic, the eternity of sea and sky. Deep blue was blue made dangerous: the red of anger and malice was easy to comprehend because its motive was so single-minded, it did not take you by surprise. The motivations of midnight blue could not be predicted.

"I do," she replied.

"Is this doubling of ranks customary?"

"No."

"Tell me," he said, "how came you to meet Inda."

The questions were strange. She had expected a military interrogation, or demands for magic spells: again she saw the shimmer of midnight all around him.

A young man sat in a corner, writing fast. He was a herald, surely. The Venn had been taught that Marlovans had no written records, only the boasting war songs of warriors.

A brief spurt of humor prompted her to begin at the very beginning. "I was born in the Land of the Venn, in service to the family Durasnir. When a child I was trained to be a . . . a hel-dancer. It translates as hall dancer, but you could say a court dancer. It is the ritual of the King's Hall . . ." She frowned; the Sartoran and Venn courts were such very different concepts. And she was not at all certain that Marlovans had a court at all.

The king returned to what interested him. "How did you become a mage?"

Signi gazed down the years, flickers of emotion-laden images running rapidly through her mind, evoking all the hopes, anxious competitions, determined training. All for that one goal. To be told at the last level of training but one, when she'd reached an age where most had already begun their life's work, *You will never attain the Hel-Dance.* "I was not good enough to be a hel-dancer," she admitted.

Not for her the far easier life of the play or pleasure house performer. Dance was art, art was truth, truth was dance, the triune concept so drilled into her that it was impossible to adapt to the notion of dance as mere entertainment or enticement. So she had stopped using the name Jazsha that she shared with her furious mother. She became Signi, and faced the necessity of learning an entirely different way of life, memories not relevant to this moment, definitely irrelevant to these people.

"I was adept with what we call the small magics as part of the dance. I professed an interest in magic knowledge. And so the Skalt—the person in charge of our training— took me to the House of Blue, where dags are trained, and I learned very rapidly."

Rapidly indeed, but that was to be expected when one is surrounded by children half one's age who think that two bells' time is a strenuous workday, and she had come from a life wherein two bells of warm-up exercise was the daily regimen before one even had breakfast.

Evred leaned forward. "Learned what, exactly?" He gave her a near smile. "Do not be afraid that too much detail will bore me."

Chapter Fourteen

IT amazed Vedrid to be pacing side-by-side at last with
the infamous Elgar the Fox. His reputation was not as
real to Vedrid as the memories of the small, scruffy boy
who vanished in disgrace from the academy years ago, or
as the terrible memory of the more recent long, difficult,
and nearly mortal search in Bren.

But he must no longer think of him with the foreign
name. Elgar the Fox was gone. No, he had come home. He
was once again Indevan-Dal Algara-Vayir, Laef of
Choraed Elgaer.

Indevan-Laef chose the pace—slow—and paused often,
sometimes staring into empty courts or at jumbles of worn
willow-swords and old gear, sometimes listening to the
childish voices through the open windows of the barracks.
Once or twice he stopped without looking at anything; he
shut his eyes and breathed deeply. Clearly Vedrid would
not have to exert himself to keep this exile-returned-home
occupied. Indevan-Laef's own memories did that.

The first court with activity contained pigtails at staff
practice. Inda halted outside the narrow archway, watching
from an angle that kept the thirteen- and fourteen-year-old
boys from noticing him.

The preliminary drills were the same, right down to the
remembered drum cadences. But the boys looked slow,

their movements sloppy. Without focus. The sights, the smells, brought back memories of slouching through drill, especially when it was raining and cold after a night of short sleep.

The boys paired off. Again, as in Cherry-Stripe's castle drill, they were so slow, so clumsy, not at all like Inda had remembered the older boys looking to his ten-year-old eyes. During training sessions on Freedom Island—first with Dun and then later with Fox—he'd exhorted the crew to speed up, to think ahead, to refine skills and measure up to remembered standards.

He had to laugh at himself. His recollection of the older boys' skills had obviously receded like a mirage. No matter how good he got, he always saw them as far better. That was before Fox Montredavan-An took over the training. Fox really was superlative. His boys and girls of similar age back on the deck of the *Death* were much faster, stronger, and more skilled than these pigtails. But then they also had been seeing action.

"What are the horsetails doing?" Inda asked Vedrid.

"Lance practice."

"Take me there."

They crossed to the side of the academy Inda had only glimpsed as a boy: the senior riding field, where the horse-tails were doing lance evolutions.

Inda peered under his hand, blocking the sun, and trying to see past the clods of mud kicked up by the horses' hooves. The lances were warlike, but seemed worthless except for a charge. Or did you use them like a boom? From horseback?

The boys' riding was as good as he remembered. Inda had adapted his early training in riding and shooting to riding the upper masts and shooting at sea. Could he readapt fast enough? More to the point, could he adapt his ship-board tactics to horse?

A familiar voice broke his thoughts. It was a man's voice, but he recognized the intonations.

A lean fellow his own age, wearing the academy masters' plain coat over riding trousers and boots, led boys toward the stable. Inda's gaze scarcely touched on the boys, who shoved and poked and scuffled like groups of boys the world over. The man turned his head to see who they were. A narrow, snub-nosed, fire-scarred face and familiar eyes.

"Lassad?"

It was! It was Smartlip Lassad! A master? Oh, hadn't Cherry-Stripe said something—

"Olin is waiting," Lassad said to his charges. "Run."

They ran.

Lassad said slowly, "Algara-Vayir?"

Inda opened his hands. Lassad's gaze flickered over him: earrings, scruffy old boots, weapons, back to Inda's face, searching, searching. Waiting. Though he no longer hunched his shoulders, or slunk, Inda saw the apprehensive Lassad of old who had lived for others' approval.

"You saw some action," Inda observed.

Lassad flushed. "Pirates. Fire arrows, here and here." He indicated his jaw and the top of one shoulder. His constantly moving gaze flickered toward Vedrid again. "They said you'd become one. A pirate, I mean. Went up against the Brotherhood."

"I never thought of myself as a pirate, but I took some pirate ships. Rest is true enough as well," Inda said. "You're a master."

Lassad's shoulders hitched tighter. He was defensive, though Inda couldn't imagine why. He assented with an open hand, then whipped the hand behind his back.

"Sponge sent me to observe. He wants me to relearn the old ways," Inda said.

Lassad's expression changed. Eased. "This is my first year. Most of the old masters had to go back in the saddle. For defense."

Inda turned his palm up. Lassad began talking fast, describing the academy's changes over nine years, his tone of pride gradually becoming more strident. And when Inda did not answer, he shifted to his experiences on the coast.

At first the details were precise and vivid. Inda listened, envisioning with the ease of experience the shoreline battles, as he and Lassad paced through the academy.

Just as they reached the senior barracks, Inda, deluged

by memory, found the pieces of Lassad's stories increasingly difficult to put together.

The bells rang for the midday meal. Beyond high walls rose the gull-shrill voices of stampeding boys. Inda was surprised to discover the old wariness and hunger back in Lassad's gaze.

Inda had wanted to see the senior barracks, but now he just wanted to get away. "I'd better go. Sponge will be looking for me."

Lassad mouthed the word *Sponge*, then flicked his fingers to his tunic, an inadvertent gesture.

Inda returned it and started back. The details did not fit. Just as in the old days, Lassad had been strutting, maybe outright lying. Perhaps not at the beginning, but certainly toward the end.

When he and Vedrid reached the archway connecting the academy to the castle, two women emerged.

Inda looked up.

"Tdor?" He jolted to a stop. She was taller, older, but he knew that face better than he knew his own.

"Tdor-Edli," Vedrid said, saluting. The other one in Runner blue he did not introduce, though he was aware of her sardonic smile.

"I'll take him," Tdor said, and Vedrid ran off to report to the king.

"You're . . . tall," Inda managed, and then his face heated. What a stupid thing to say!

Tdor chuckled, that same wonderful sound, like the whuff of a pup, that he'd cherished in memory through all his years at sea. "You're not tall."

They laughed; seeing one another again made them both feel giddy and awkward, their minds filled with nine years of questions and nowhere to begin.

Then Inda put together the clues at last. Midway between amusement and irritation, he said, "I suppose Sponge is grilling Signi."

"She's a Venn," Tdor answered with a sober look. "You brought her here. We've been at war for years, and the Venn have been behind it."

Her voice, it was just the same, but lower. His scalp itched, his clothes pulled at him; a flicker of memory, of Tdor's hands smoothing out his unruly hair and pulling his shirt laces right. He shook his head, trying to gather his wits. Signi was in trouble—with Sponge. "I wouldn't bring an enemy."

Tdor turned a palm up. Her hand was still square, but bigger than he remembered, hard from years of bow and knife work. "I suspect he knows. But he cannot afford to be wrong." Her hand swept to one side. Inda finally perceived Tdor's companion.

"Inda," the blonde woman exclaimed. Inda had only peripherally been aware of the short blonde in mud-splashed Runner blue next to Tdor. He flicked a questioning glance her way. The sardonic quirk to her dark, wide-set eyes was familiar. "Remember me?"

"Sh—Shendan?" Inda asked, amazed. He laughed. "Last time I saw you, I was ten."

"Yes." She crossed her arms the same way Fox did when he was in his nastiest mood. "I rode all the way here, and you are to tell me where Fox is, and why he did not come home."

"He is with the fleet. He's my—the commander now," Inda said. "As for why he didn't come—"

"Don't feed me any bran mash," Shen cut in. "I'm not sick. Or old. Or weak. I want the truth."

As Inda squinted up at the sky, Tdor's emotions swooped. Despite the years, and the scars on his face, she still knew what he was thinking: he wished he were anywhere else.

But instead of slouching off as he might have as a boy, he said very quietly, "He doesn't want to come home."

Shen drew in a breath. "All right. Tell me this. Is it us? Mother and me, and Marend? Or . . ."

"No. It's the treaty. Mostly. And I think your father as well." Inda considered, then added with a tentative air, "He hasn't said. But, well, you travel a lot with someone, you learn to hear the words they ride around. If he comes home, it'll be later. After your father—"

"Drinks himself to death," Shen stated in a hard voice.
"Yes." She swiped at her eyes. "Thank you for the truth."
Without a word she swung around and vanished after
Vedrid up the short tunnel.

Inda whistled. Then shook his head. "I could have done
that better. Though I don't know how, with no warning."

"That's why she waylaid you. So there wouldn't be any
well-considered speeches." Tdor thought back to the single
visit from the Sartoran mage all those years ago, and how
she'd used diplomacy to deny them magic. Because they
were Marlovans, that had been the real reason for all the
compliments and diplomatic assurances, making her refusal much worse to bear—as if they were dangerous animals to be coaxed and praised back into their loose-boxes.
She turned his way, wondering how to explain when she
saw by his expression that he'd guessed.

Her chest went cold, her skin rough. *Inda* was *here*.

The world around her had gone awry, like the pieces of
a dropped cup fitted badly together. She was the splattered
drink. She couldn't fit the world back together until she understood why she felt this way. But there wasn't time to
think.

As always, duty funneled her back into motion. Tdor
withdrew her hands from her sleeves and held out a heavy
silver owl hair ornament. Once Tanrid's. "Your mother desired me to bring this along. So that Branid would not rampage through the castle to find it and start wearing it,
calling himself the heir." She studied the mossy stones
arching overhead, the dusty, scuffed toes of Cherry-Stripe's
boots on Inda's feet. "I had come to ask the king to decide
who will be heir to Choraed Elgaer."

Inda pressed his heels to his eyes.

"Inda?" she asked, concerned.

"Too much, too hard, too soon." His face burned again.
"Well. Nine years. I guess I'm to catch it all up in a month."

She held out the clasp, and when he extended his palm
she dropped the heavy ornament onto it. Her fingers trembled slightly before vanishing back into her sleeves.

He searched her face. "Tdor?"

"It's good that you are back." She swung around and started up the tunnel with long strides. "You are needed at home."

"I'm glad to see you," he said, walking sideways. Still with that searching gaze. She could feel it. "Tell me of home."

"Let's go inside." She indicated the flagged path ahead. For once she was relieved that the castle was enormous. She needed the time. "Hadand will let us use her rooms."

Inda fingered the heavy ornament that he had last seen in his brother's hair, right before Captain Sindan took Inda to the coast. He tried to think—he needed to think—but he was distracted by the long corridors, the guarded stairwells, the occasional Runners of both sexes who stared at him with expectant faces, but most of all by Tdor striding next to him, her head a little bent, her brow tense.

Tdor led him into a small room with a Fire Stick burning low on the grate, and Marlovan furnishings, so familiar from childhood.

Tdor shut the door and stood with her back to it. "Your father has aged terribly. Your mother has been waiting so long in hopes of seeing you." She shook her head. "Did you know about Tanrid?"

Inda's grimace was almost a flinch. "Evred told me."

Tdor lifted a hand, dropped it to her side. "Will you be coming home?"

"Don't know. I hadn't thought ahead, except to warn Sp—Evred about the Venn. I hadn't even known he was king, at first. The embargo has kept news from getting out, d'you see? All I could think of was, would the Harskialdna put me against the wall for breaking exile. But it was my duty to bring the news even so." He felt he was making excuses, that he needed to apologize, yet there was no accusation at all in her face, voice, or manner. "Sponge. Evred, that is—he wants me to command the defense." Now that they'd started to talk, the impulse to speak was almost overwhelming. It had always been this way. He could tell Tdor everything, and she would make sense of the world.

Her eyes widened. "And you agreed?"

Inda held his hands out. "I'm used to command. And Evred seems to want me to do it."

"Yes," she said. "I can see why."

"Can you? I can't. Is Hawkeye really so bad? Or is his father's conspiracy held against him? I have never even seen a land battle. I haven't shot from horseback since I was eleven. I have no idea what they do with those damned lances once they charge. The idea seemed right and true when we were sitting in Daggers, and Evred seems convinced, but when I'm away from him it seems crazy."

"Doesn't most of your life seem crazy?" Tdor asked. "I mean, *pirates?*"

He sent her a startled look, saw her wry smile, and laughed. "Last time I saw you," she said, "I called you a haywit. And wished for nine years that you could get home just so I could unsay it. All right. Choraed Elgaer can wait." Tdor made an attempt at a smile; Inda could feel her effort. "Hadand is so very glad to have you safely back—"

A tap at the door caused her to whirl. She opened the door, spoke to someone outside, then shut it again and faced Inda. "Your—Mage Signi is with Evred in the map room right now. We're to join them."

Inda was relieved and annoyed. Relieved because he could not define why this conversation with Tdor did not feel right: it had started fine, but then blew off course somehow. And he was annoyed at having been deflected from whatever had happened between Evred and Signi.

But he dismissed that reaction. He'd been his own master too long, he had not thought ahead of the rights and wrongs of bringing Signi into Evred's kingdom. Of course Evred had to interrogate her, and Inda could not be there.

But Tdor knew all that.

He studied her, truly uneasy now.

She said quickly, reaching toward him, "It's all right, Inda. It's all right. They found common ground, there is nothing to fear."

"Then why are we here?"

Her cheeks colored, and she turned toward the window as though the answer lay there. The hand she had stretched

out to him withdrew into her sleeve. "It was Evred's idea.
To give us time alone," she said to the window, and then
she faced him resolutely. He could feel her effort. She did
not want to be here having this conversation Why? "You
have to remember that tradition is important here. More
so now than ever. It gives a sense of stability that we really
don't have."

He still did not understand.

She fingered her cuff, brushed a total absence of lint
from her robe, then yanked the door open and walked out
in her characteristic long stride.

Inda followed, disagreeably aware that he had missed an
important cue, or clue. He had that sickening sense that he
was entering action blind. Except he was surrounded by
people he loved, so the danger couldn't be here—and yet,
so far, not a single encounter had been even remotely like
he had expected.

The map room was a relatively short walk. Armed
guards parted, and they entered a room with a huge carved
table, covered by an exquisitely drawn map.

All three were there, the women back by the windows:
Evred watchful, Hadand quiet, Signi tired but composed.
Inda was relieved, not that he'd expected his old friend to
fling Signi up against the wall for execution just because
she was Venn. The Harskialdna, Evred's uncle, wouldn't
have hesitated, but Inda would never have brought her if
he were still here.

At a subtle gesture from Evred, Hadand invited Signi to
accompany her to get some refreshment, and they left.
With a questioning look at Inda before she soundlessly
shut the door, Tdor moved to the window, out of the way
but within view of the map.

What? Inda asked her silently, but their childhood understanding seemed to have vanished.

So he shifted to his own questions. "Lassad," Inda said to
Evred, jerking his thumb toward the west window, overlooking the academy. "A master?"

"You have an objection to his promotion?" Evred asked,
his voice neutral.

Inda opened his hand. "How would I know? He told me about his action." He did not want to say: *He lied to me. How much has he lied to you?*

Evred said even more neutrally, "Dag Signi has told me a little about Prince Rajnir of the Venn. We will have to find out more."

Inda flicked his hand toward the door through which Hadand had taken Signi. "We can do that on the road, can't we? We've got weeks ahead of us."

She'll be locked in a windowless cell where she cannot harm us with magic or messages to her masters, Evred thought, but said only, "She says that there is no family continuity as we define it, in their kings."

Inda rubbed his jaw. "All I know is that they are coming." He studied the map. "I see the mountains dividing us from Idayago. The only land route to Idayago is through this pass, right?"

"Andahi Pass, yes."

"Whose are these castles at the north and south ends of the pass?"

Evred said, "Ala Larkadhe is this one, at the south end. It's an easy watch's ride from Lindeth Harbor. The castle guarding the north end was called Sala Varadhe by the Idayagans. We've taken to calling it Castle Andahi, after the pass. The middle harbor's castle is Trad Varadhe, and the eastern one, its harbor too small for capital ships, is at Ghael."

Inda said, "Flash's dad is the Jarl at Castle Andahi, isn't he? Has he changed his name to Andahi-Vayir? I remember that except for us, names had to match land."

"He's been resisting." Evred smiled briefly. "Says he should be Idayago-Tradheval-Andahi-Vayir, which sounds ridiculous, so that point has not been settled."

Inda studied the map, whispering the names to himself to get them firmly in mind.

Evred went remote again, assuming what Inda was beginning to think of as his king face. "If Prince Rajnir has spies living among us, he has to know where most of our forces are. What do you see as his plan of attack?"

Inda remembered what he'd said to Fox so casually, what seemed a hundred years ago, when he lay under an Ymaran oak recovering from Wafri's torture. "Raids along the north coast first stage, to bring our defenses there."

"Which is where Barend is now. And the Venn have been raiding, according to his report. Our people have been fighting them off, with sporadic cooperation from the Idayagans," Evred added with a wry smile. He thought of Nightingale, his Runner in the north, and his hand twitched toward the locket hanging inside his shirt.

He yanked his fingers away again, though the Venn mage was no longer present. A surge of hatred tightened his muscles: a *mage*. A Venn! How could Inda be so simple? She was old—at least thirty—and as plain as a corn husk. She must have ensnared Inda by some magical trickery, at least to preserve her life. At most to spy.

He dropped his hand to his side. She was probably far more dangerous left behind—could even his walls guard against the wiles of a mage?—than going along as a prisoner under his own eye. In which case he didn't have to figure out some ruse to get her locked up when he took Inda north.

Inda went right on, fingers tracing over the map. "Since we have no navy, they know we're forced to go through the Andahi Pass to defend the north. But they have to come down through the pass if they want to attack by land. They have to figure we'll be on the watch for an attack through the pass, so they'll also come round by sea."

Evred looked at the long coast of Halia, now held by Iasca Leror. "They have enough men and ships to attack the entire coast?" he asked, sick with horror.

Inda smacked his hand on the map. "No. That is, I don't know what they might have next year, but this year they have eighty-one warships and their attached raiders and scouts. Say thirty-five hundred men per, all told. Eighty-one times over, give or take because they'll have to find room for horses, and because some stay on board to handle the ships."

Evred's eyes narrowed as he calculated, then he opened his hand. "Go on."

"The big Venn warships can't get in close enough to land a lot of horses, even if they had them trained like ours. A big force needs the draft of a deep harbor in order to off-load animals and heavy equipment. They'd have that at the Nob, of course, but then they'd be forced to march all the way down the peninsula. Is that practical?"

"No," Evred said with the conviction of experience. "You can ride in pairs at best. It would take them a month or more. But they can land men on a beach?"

"Well, only just south of Lindeth. Boats, through the breakers. The coast of Ola-Vayir is rotten landing. Saw that when I was coming home. From near Lindeth on down it's pretty much steep palisade above rocky beaches. Good defense, bad offense. So if they want to land in force anywhere along the coast from Ola-Vayir down to Parayid, it'll have to be through a deep-water harbor."

"Harbors we can cover. We may have no navy," Evred said grimly, "but we did learn how to defend harbors after all those pirate attacks."

"Which they have to know." Inda thumped his fist down. "Where was I? Right. I think they'll land a second force here at Lindeth Harbor, soon's they know we're up the pass, and bottle us up from behind." He jerked his head up. "Didn't Cherry-Stripe say the Arveases are doing well at the north end of the pass?"

Evred said, "Yes. What cooperation there is has been best at that end of Idayago. I will be dispatching certain orders to Barend before we take horse. We do have a last, somewhat desperate defense if needed. It wouldn't stop the Venn, but it might slow them."

Inda rapped his knuckles lightly on the map. "It might come to desperate defenses, if we don't have those kinds of numbers."

Evred shook his head. "No. We never have. Our people live spread out. This is our only large city, and my mother once told me there are much larger ones. The Venn have twenty times the population we have. Maybe more."

Inda said, "So we've never depended on numbers."

"No. Speed and skill. Sudden strikes, hard, so the

Idayagans find it easier to surrender and walk away with their lives."

Inda thought of pirate fighting, and thumped his fist on the table, *bump, bump, bump.* "That many men squeezed down into a trail in the pass, that won't be any hit and ride."

"I know. What do we do?"

Inda scowled at the map. "We've got to throw everyone we can at the north, because we have got to hold that pass."

Evred stared down at the map, hardly seeming to breathe. Then, "Tell me what you expect."

"They have to get a hold on the north coast. That means take Idayago, then they have all the resources of Idayago at hand."

"I perceive that much."

"Well, that's the first stage. They grab the north, push as far south as they can, then dig in over winter. Their king sends more men. They land fresh occupation forces along the north coast over fall and winter, ready themselves for next spring's big launch into the Marlovan homeland. Then they not only come down the pass like thunder, they can send the entire fleet against our coast. They hammer the harbors in force, land, and march up from the south and the west. Three fronts, not just two."

Evred said slowly, "I am already near the end of the oath-levies. My father called four times for a decade's one out of nine, and last year I called for one from all the northern Jarls. We used second decade men in rotation to the harbors when the pirate attacks were the worst."

Inda reached back into childhood, remembered the decade system: each Jarl, when called, owed the king one of nine Riders between the ages of twenty-five and thirty-five. Second decade was for men between thirty-five and forty-five. A Jarl could choose to send men, or ride himself. When a Jarl had been called four times, it meant four out of every nine of his younger men was away serving the king.

"Though the treasury is nearly empty, I will do what must be done. But Inda, when you say 'everyone,' I can only realistically raise all men once."

Inda felt like someone had gripped his skull in a vise. For the first time, he considered what raising an army meant in human terms. Out on the ocean, he'd always had more volunteers than he needed or wanted, for whatever reason. They were usually pirates, or independents who sailed mighty close to outright piracy. They weren't Marlovans with homes, families, and land to take care of.

He'd always thought of a newly hired sailor killed on board as a sailor replaced at the next hiring. A Marlovan killed left a hole in the work of home, to say nothing of the hole in his family. He could be replaced only with the gradual reweaving of time.

Evred spoke to the map. "We cannot get the south up there fast enough, not for the start of summer. It's going to be difficult enough to raise the north."

Inda said, "I thought our people were supposed to be fast? Cherry-Stripe mentioned something about your Runner making it all the way to the north in a couple of weeks? Said the fellow's become a legend."

Evred smiled. "Vedrid nearly killed himself doing it. But he was one Runner, with access to fresh horses along his route, and the ability—and determination—to sleep in the saddle. He slept for a week after that ride. You cannot raise and race an army like that. Even if the roads were good, which they won't be, how can you expect them to fight at the end of such a journey?"

Inda whistled, and Evred's smile vanished. "I will have to call for a double decade out of the north. Heretofore I've avoided pressing Ola-Vayir, which is by far the largest jarlate. He had dispensation due to some leftover treaty business with my grandfather, and I said nothing last year. He thinks this is because I'm weak, but I've been holding them in reserve. I can raise his entire land if I must. Nine for nine."

Inda rubbed his scar. "But that still won't give us numbers to match theirs?"

"No, but it's as close as we can come short of raising the entire kingdom. That must be only a final resort."

A bleak image: fields and castles abandoned except for

women, the old, children, left to defend if the enemy smashed through the men. "Right," Inda said, his throat constricted.

"Will that suffice?"

"We'll make it suffice."

"Done," Evred said.

An almost sickening thrill buzzed through Inda's nerves. *Done,* just like that. Evred was the king, he said *Done* and people's lives changed. Inda struggled against the instinct to shout, *Wait! Wait! What if I am wrong?*

Evred straightened up and crossed his arms. "I'd first planned to make you my commander at the celebration. Mark the transfer of power for the coming battle to every Jarl we could draw within a month. Let the word spread. But when I consider the distances, and what you say, we don't have time. I'm going to strip this city of warriors, a double decade. I'll handle the other levies in person on the way north. We'll ride out at dawn."

" 'Celebration'?" Inda asked. There it was again, that sense that he'd missed something obvious and important.

Evred opened his hand toward Tdor, standing so straight at the opposite wall as he said gently, "Taking your place formally as heir to Choraed Elgaer—and getting married."

Chapter Fifteen

TINY flakes of snow stippled the little scene in the middle of Five Points Parade, the broad flagged expanse below Pirate Island's chalky cliffs where the isle's only five roads came together.

"I've had a very bad couple of years," Captain Scarf said to the three islanders kneeling before her, as a circle of pirates waited for the fun to begin. "Very bad," she repeated, though no one had moved or spoken.

A rising wind fretted with clothing, hair, and the long silken fringes of Scarf's beautiful embroidered kerchief. Pirates did not have gray hair, but she dared not land where there was a healer-mage who changed hair color, so she'd become Captain Scarf.

Pirates circled the three, some with weapons readied.

The harbormaster, who'd been a privateer before one wound too many kept him off ships, stared forward with an air of stolid stupidity. It had been his best weapon when the island was taken by surprise almost fifteen years ago, by the previous set of pirates.

At his right, Captain Swift, another grizzled middle-aged privateer, tried to hide the lancing pain in his knees that kept him from hearing much of what the pirate was saying.

"If any of you were with that soul-sucker Elgar the Fox two winters ago," she added, "you are going to wish you weren't." Scarf'd been past forty when Khanerenth had lost its former king, and she'd lost land and rank and power with her royal brother. She'd been taking revenge on the world ever since.

"Why are people so impossible?" Scarf mourned, turning toward the third victim, the only woman.

Mistress Svanith was the youngest, at forty. She owned one of Pirate Island's two chief inns, and a great deal of the waterfront besides. She did not make the mistake of thinking that Scarf actually wanted her question answered—she just waited patiently.

Scarf waved a negligent hand toward the small scout craft moored along the dock. Several of her crew were busy cleaning blood off the sides and deck. "I hate rules," she said. "Never obeyed 'em when I was growing up. Princesses make rules for others to obey."

She frowned down at three impassive faces. "You're probably thinking that I'm no longer a princess."

Her pirates laughed appreciatively. None of them had ever been within a month's journey of any royal court, but they'd managed to learn the primary survival skill of the successful courtier: laugh at the royal jokes.

"I know I'm no longer a princess," she said, with another of her languid, courtly gestures. She felt a speech coming on: why not educate them about power? She had a good quote ready, from none other than Elian Dei of Sartor, who (if you read closely) had apparently been a bit of a pirate herself.

But first: "I'm reasonable, so I try to give out as few rules as possible. My single rule was that you people give us what we want. We just want a modicum of comfort after a long, starving year on that damn coast off that damned Iascan land. So why are you sending messengers?"

The harbormaster couldn't resist. He knew he was in trouble anyway, so he said, "Wasn't against your rule."

She sighed, half turned, then lashed out with her iron-shod boot, kicking him in the face. He fell back, hands over his mashed, bleeding nose. "Now, that's just common sense. I guess I have to teach you common sense. You don't like to see your girls and boys dead? Then—"

Scarf was just settling in for her lecture when the sound of laughter echoed from the old warehouses on the quay.

Annoyed, she peered at the rowdy crew on the dock. Leading them was her only remaining nephew, young Falthum. She smiled at the sight of him—tall, strong, mean, handsome, and none too smart. Her sister's smart ones were all dead. She'd kindly taken and raised them after her sister died in that damned revolution. The result? The smart, educated one tried to lead a mutiny. The stupid, educated one had tried earnestly to talk her pirates into going back and turning themselves over to the law. She hadn't made the mistake of educating the youngest one. The result? He loved his work. She contemplated that sometimes, mourning that no one around her had the wit to discourse on the irony.

"Ho, Auntie," he called. "Running battle comin' in on the wind. Betting is already up in the hundreds. Come see!"

She lifted her gaze to the skyline behind the warehouses and shops along the strand. Indeed, smoke billowed and tumbled on the wintry wind; the current through the Bridge was still a southward flow. Which was good. Let her get a tight hold on this damn island before the seasonal shift in current. No one besides her (and she'd taken three weeks) was crazy enough to come south with the ice still breaking up. And it had been a bad journey, damaging several of her fleet.

So where did these ships come from?

She vaulted over the harbormaster, leaving behind Mistress Svanith and Captain Swift, who bent to help him.

Despite her years, and the bulk she'd put on since her abduction of a royal chef during a raid on a Damondaen prince's yacht, she was in good shape; she ran to the dock where she could see past the warehouses, grabbed her glass from her coat pocket, snapped it out, and pressed it to her eye.

The wind had tangled the smoke into an uneven white bar across the green and choppy seas, but just above it she could make out the tiny pinpoints of fire arrows arcing back and forth. A heavy gust of wind cleared the smoke just long enough for her to descry two schooners running side-by-side. Behind, ghostly and tenuous, the predator: a bigger, beautifully lean and elegant schooner—

She laughed. So someone was behind the times. How fun! Both hunter and quarry obviously thought Pirate Island open. Well, she could use all three ships.

Another brief flaw in the wind revealed more detail, but smoke billowed from one of the smaller schooners, hiding them again. That must be some fight! "The big schooner has a hand on the foresail—no, I think it was a leaf." She turned to her crew in question. "Anyone familiar with that?"

Falthum just shrugged, but she expected nothing out of him. She sifted the crowd for the balding head of her efficient first mate, remembered he was on watch aboard the flag. "Damn."

"Oh, I know who that is," exclaimed one of the younger pirates, new crew just before they'd sailed east to join Marshig for the disastrous Brotherhood of Blood battle. "That's the *Sable,* once out of Khanerenth."

Another refugee-turned-pirate from home! Scarf gave a snort of amusement. Then—quick to suspect a trick—"Not part of Elgar the Fox's rabble?"

"No." Shake of the head. "Captain Eflis wanted to join the Brotherhood, but she never pulled off any raids good enough."

"Won't now, either," Scarf said, and the others laughed, some of them resuming the betting.

The embattled ships were coming in fast, both predator and prey. Her own fleet lined the narrow harbor. Old habit made Scarf wary, but what could one ship do? Even two, supposing the little schooners started fighting everybody? Damn the smoke anyway, couldn't those idiots even put out their own—

Pause, and her heart quickened its beat.

"Fires?" she said aloud, and the anomaly resolved: all three ships afire, but no pumps going? "Signal the fleet, fighting stations."

Falthum gaped, then ran, the others stampeding after him. Her signal boy pounded down the dock to the harbor-

master's to use the flagpole there. She held her breath as
the ships came on, faster and faster—she cursed the snow—

A bigger gust of wind thinned the smoke into swirling
ribbons of mist just long enough for her to make out the
three fighting ships.

And they were followed by launches full of—

"Blood and death! It's an attack!" she screamed, leaping
down into her gig. "Row, row! I'll flay the backs off every
one of you soul-eating . . ."

Her voice was the faintest screech, no louder than the
raucous cry of a seabird to those crouched along the rail of
the *Skimit* and the *Rippler,* weapons to hand.

"Fox is cutting it close," one muttered to another, gripping his cutlass tightly.

His mate returned with mordant humor, "Guess he
wants to sail us right up the dock—"

A screamer arrow whirtled weirdly overhead, and
teenage Mutt, commanding the first schooner, howled,
"Hard over!" His voice cracked into a squeak. He flushed,
but nothing could long diminish the excitement of his first
command in battle. Gripping the wheel, he hopped on his
toes, his brown sailor braid thumping his bony back as he
trembled with anticipation and fierce joy.

Drift, drift, and then they were in the middle of the pirates, and what had begun as a brisk, entertaining ruse
through the quiet, snow-stippled seas turned into a fast,
hard battle against far too many ships—but they had taken
the pirates utterly by surprise.

Arrows hissed across Mutt's deck. A pirate schooner
slanted round, boarding crew ready to leap over. Mutt
swept his glass across those faces, the ready weapons, the
puffs of breath as the pirates laughed in anticipation.

"Fox? Where are you?" he breathed through clenched
teeth.

The plan was simple. Gillor and Dasta said they'd used it
when Fox and Inda were in Ymar.

Fox hated whatever-it-was that kept him from seeing battle on a large scale the way Inda could. This plan was already more complicated than he liked, and the attack had yet to begin.

Smoke swirled, some of it damped down by the snow turning to sleet on the rising wind.

Ahead of him, Eflis brought her big schooner hard over, aiming straight between two raffees—the entire bay was converging on the schooners, just as they'd hoped.

Time for the surprise.

"Signal fleet attack," Fox called. Adding to his motionless crew, "Fighting sail. Let's not miss the fun."

Scarf smashed one of her own small craft in her determination to get clear of the smoke and the battle—only three ships, but they were fierce, driving skillfully between hers, maneuvering brilliantly as they shot from both sides. She had to get upwind of the schooner so she could—

"Arrrrrrah!" the wail rose to a pitch that caused her neck to prickle.

"What? What?"

That was her first mate, the toughest man on her crew, pointing, his eyes distended.

She whirled, peering through the dissipating smoke, scarcely aware of the numbing sting of sleet as—impossible, *impossible*. From the ghostly gray vapors emerged a sinister black trysail, masts raked back, sails flashing in thrilling precision. That knife-lean predator was famous the world over as the flagship of Boruin Death-Hand.

Who was burned to death by Elgar the Fox.

Scarf's crew erupted into a frenzy of anger, accusation, shouts screamed at one another—demands that no one heard, all of it the result of gut-gnawing fear.

She pounded down the length of her deck, whacking people with her sword. Her first mate pulled himself together to follow and deal out similar blows, as she screamed for their attention. But even while screaming, she watched—they all watched—the trysail begin its running attack.

Impossible, her brain wailed, but there it was, Elgar's flagship, last seen two years ago, riding in the middle of the sea of burning wreckage of Marshig's fleet. Though she outnumbered Elgar, she knew her crew was already falling apart. The single thing all pirates agreed on was that no one could beat Elgar the Fox on the sea. Even Norsunder obeyed his command—they'd all seen that rip between sky and sea at the end of the battle just as the sun was coming up, a sky-high rift opening onto an eternal night into which Marshig and his favorites had sailed, and vanished.

All right, when battle doesn't work, treachery does.

"Signal for a parley," she bellowed. "Every ship—truce and parley flags. *Now!*"

Chapter Sixteen

AFTER his castle tour, Tau decided to explore the city. He had to ask directions to get out of the castle. Every person he approached regarded him with puzzlement until he added, "I am Indevan Algara-Vayir's First Runner, and I'm lost." Inda's real name cleared their faces like sunshine through clouds, and their manner was invariably interested, often friendly, as they offered detailed directions.

When the sunset watch change bells tolled in all the towers, the massive, brassy bongs echoing along the stone streets and off the heavy walls, he fumbled his way back to the guest chambers.

His shipmates were gathered in Inda's room, Jeje at one end staring out the window at one of the many courtyards, and Inda and Signi huddled together near the fire, intent on a low-voiced conversation.

Biscuits, wine, and ale had been set out in shallow ceramic bowls. Tau poured wine into the strange flat cup that one had to use with two hands, then Jeje summoned Tau with a jerk of her chin. "We're waiting for the king to finish kinging, then we're to have dinner with them."

"What happened?" Tau asked, watching Signi shake her head and raise a hand as if warding something. Inda twined his fingers through hers, and Tau heard a brief, "Evred

would never hurt you. Try not to see them as enemies."
Then Inda's voice dropped to an indistinct rumble.

"She got grilled by the king. Then Fox's sister showed up.
She grilled everybody she could catch—including Signi—
then rode off into the sunset."

"Fox has a sister?"

Jeje snorted. "From all he's ever told us about his family,
I thought he'd hatched out of the ground."

"Hatched? From the ground?" Tau repeated, brows
aslant.

Jeje waved a hand dismissively. "Last, the king booted
everyone out. When I woke up from my nap, someone
brought me here, and I found these two. I think Signi wants
to renew spells. I guess they haven't had mages here in
ages. But that king of Inda's made it real clear he doesn't
trust her far's he can spit into the wind."

"Who's the tall woman who was standing with the queen
on our arrival?"

Jeje made sure Inda and Signi were busy with their low
talk, and turned her back on them. "Tdor. Inda's future
wife. I got that out of Inda's sister. They've been promised
since she was two and he was born. That's the way they do
marriage here. With the rankers, anyway. You don't choose
someone to share your hearth and home and children, it is
done for you, by treaty, before you're born."

Tau whistled soundlessly.

"Tau! You're back!" Inda reached for an ale cup.
"Where'd you go?"

"I am now your personal Runner. Whatever that
means." Tau raised a hand toward the window. "So I went
exploring in order to learn where to run. As much as I
could in a city that seems to have yet to discover the ben-
efits of street signs. Do the streets actually have names?"

Inda grinned. "Yes, but they change around. When we
took over the royal city from the Iascans, the king had all
the old names changed, which meant taking down their
markers. But then he decided it was better for defense
never to put any up. So there aren't any. It's not like a lot
of foreigners come visiting."

We, Jeje thought. *Nine years away, and he says "we."*

"All right. So there's a reason, even if it seems slightly demented. Second question: why are the bells so loud here? Is it that the entire city is made of stone with those extra high walls?"

Inda looked tense, though he was obviously trying for lightness. "The bells have to be audible on the plains below the city. When ringing alarms, not just watch changes. What else did you find?"

Tau observed Signi's strained expression, the smudges under her eyes as he said, "That there are no fan-makers or ribbon-makers, that musical instruments other than drums and reed-pipes seem yet to be discovered, that most of the business one sees relates to horses in some way. Horses, food, and war gear."

"Well, in a harbor, everything relates to the sea." Jeje shrugged. "Outside of trade goods going inland."

"Anyone who wants instant wealth has only to draw the meanest set of traveling players over the mountains and set up a theater. There is no such thing here, can you imagine?"

Inda sat back, one arm round Signi's shoulders. She leaned into him, her eyes closed. Tau's gaze shifted to the flush along Inda's cheeks that indicated he'd been drinking. A rarity; the last time Tau remembered seeing Inda downing anything potent was the night before the Brotherhood battle at The Narrows.

"We read ancient Sartoran plays when we're tutored," Inda mused. "I didn't know people did other things than read 'em."

"Plays," Tau struck a pose, "are meant to be performed."

"Maybe they wouldn't like that here." Jeje yawned, not because she was tired, but because she was restless. It had been a stupid idea to come here. "Unless you've got some about battles and horses."

Tau wondering why Inda was drinking, why his free hand traced round and round the top of his cup. He was home at last, where he'd wanted to be for almost ten years, and the trouble that had kept him away appeared to have been summarily banished by his friend, the king.

Ah, yes, the king. Had Inda understood that look of hunger? Did he even see it? More to the point, what was the responsibility of the friend who had definitely seen it?

But the subject was plays. "Anyplace you can walk into the meanest inn and hear people singing twenty verse ballads, unerring, with carters and hay-pitchers correcting the slightest omission, sneering at the tiniest fumble in cadence, you've an audience waiting to discover the joys of the stage."

"You can stay and try it, or ride with us tomorrow," Inda said.

"Ah. Am I to hear the reason why we have to renew our just-healing butt blisters? I confess I assumed we were to stay in this royal castle more than a day. Unless they decided we're pirates after all, and are about to come in force to toss us out?"

A distant bell rang, and Inda got to his feet. He looked strange with his hair pulled up high. Binding his hair up was something new, a heavy, ornate silver hair clasp fashioned in the shape of an owl in flight.

"I'll explain on the way to supper," Inda said, and did.

Dinner was in a room down the hall, with low tables and more of those flat wine cups. The same three people who had come to greet them were there. During the interim Hadand and Evred had worked feverishly hard to set in motion the enormous chore of equipping an army overnight; Tdor had shown Inda and Signi the way to Inda's room.

There she had endured an uncomfortable stretch as they all made painstaking conversation in Iascan, which Signi barely understood. Tdor's heart had wrung at how hard all three of them tried to find something of interest to the others.

Tdor did not know how long that excruciatingly boring conversation about horses would have limped along until Inda muttered something that caught Signi by surprise. The dag turned her head, her trembling fingers just touched his, and his hand tightened round hers as they leaned into one another. It was only a moment, but it was so profound a withdrawal from the world, a cleaving to one another that left Tdor out at the same moment she had been wondering if she could sniff his hair—did he still smell like a puppy?—she wanted to touch the scar by his eyes—

No, she wanted to kiss it.

Just then the two caught themselves up—they remembered her—and consciously pulled away from one another. Signi asked a polite question while Inda poured out three cups of wine that no one wanted. All well-meaning, all consciously including her. But she had found herself business elsewhere as soon as she decently could, and went to walk in the cool air until she heard the bell for dinner.

Tau lingered at the back as everyone filed into the dining room. He wondered what the role of Runner was supposed to be.

He watched Evred-Harvaldar for clues. The king's hazel gaze brushed past Tau with no invitation, but no rejection, so he followed Jeje in. And on impulse Tau threaded himself expertly through the where-should-I-sit shuffle to a place next to the tall, brown-haired Tdor, Inda's affianced wife, who had effaced herself so quietly that morning.

"We can all speak Sartoran, I trust?" Evred-Harvaldar opened a hand toward Signi.

His reward for making it clear she was not to be shut out was Inda's sudden, wholehearted smile.

Servants brought the food in, setting it out for everyone to help themselves. Evred spoke to one; the servants touched hand to heart, but there was no bowing, and at no time did Tau ever hear the customary honorifics such as "Your Majesty" that were common elsewhere. The servants then left.

Conversation skimmed the surface with scarcely a splash: the ride from Marlo-Vayir—food—harvest—food in port cities—worst food ever eaten. Jeje sparked the first laugh with her scathing portrayal of the terrible food at Freedom Harbor's pretentious Colendi eatery.

Everyone laughed but Signi, whose head ached from the demands of this exceedingly long day. For now she would listen. These Marlovans all spoke the quaint Sartoran of generations ago, soothing to the ear.

Evred laughed, but absently, and gradually withdrew into watchful silence; the weight of enormous preparation for riding out pressed on him and he longed to take Inda and be about it. But his mother was an Adrani, she had raised him to be aware of outland expectations due to guests. He would not be perceived as a barbarian.

"... I'm chief mate of *Vixen*, like I said. Scout crafts don't have captains. And Tau didn't want to be a captain," Jeje was saying to Hadand.

Jeje's Sartoran was difficult for the Marlovans, a blend of Inda's accent and something flat and odd—Chwahir, in fact, though the Marlovans did not know it. Jeje had learned the language from a former crewmate who had sailed back to Chwahirsland after the pirate defeat.

Sensitive to the subtlest motion of hand or eye, Tau became aware of a furtive but persistent scrutiny. He glanced up once to meet the steady brown eyes of the queen.

Hadand flushed and concentrated on Jeje talking about Inda's fleet, leaving Tau to study her with interest. Hadand's wide brown gaze was unexpectedly like Inda's. He was intrigued by the slight tension in her shoulders, the nearly imperceptible flare of her nostrils that revealed her awareness of his attention. She appeared to be about his own age.

"... and that's the last of 'em now," Jeje finished.

Evred forced himself to speak. "You say they have sailed to the south, then? Away from us?"

"That was the plan," Jeje said warily.

Inda said, "Even if we hadn't lost most of Eflis' tail of small craft in the sail west—they were worthless anyway—we couldn't take on the Venn's southeastern fleet."

Evred said, "I understand that. Your former ships won't turn on us, then? That's my only concern."

"No," Inda said.

"No," Jeje stated, now glaring a challenge.

Inda sent her a mild look of reproach. She flushed, her black eyebrows an unbroken scowl-line across her forehead, and busied herself with her food. At Tdor's prompt, Inda described Freedom Islands.

Of the Marlovans, only Hadand had been beyond the borders, and she remained silent. Tau shifted smoothly to the royal city, and his appreciation of the local music. Tdor showed her good nature by talking determinedly about old ballads, as if anyone cared. With Tdor the center of attention, Tau sat back, turned his head—and there were Hadand's light brown eyes again. This time he sustained her gaze.

Tdor was thinking: *Is it beauty creating a universal resemblance, a high art of human structure, or does he really resemble Joret?*

Hadand was thinking: *those eyes really are gold . . . yellow-flecked light brown that blends into gold, surrounded by long, curling lashes . . .* perhaps she should stop drinking wine. She was staring. And the room seemed far too warm.

Then he raised his cup in salute. He had beautiful hands. Strong and graceful, slender wrists emerging from the cuffs of a fine linen shirt that, though he'd worn it all day, was not rumpled like Inda's clothes. It fitted in a smooth line over his well-shaped shoulders and the contours of strong arms—

Warmth rushed through her veins, leaving the tingle of possibility as she raised her own cup. And she braced herself to meet again those amazing eyes, touched with gleams of light reflected from the candles.

"Ah, it's good to eat home food again," Inda said into the protracted silence that he hadn't even noticed. He reached over to help himself to more rice-and-cabbage balls.

"What do you eat on your ships?" Tdor asked, exasperated. *No one cares about songs. Let's do food again.*

Inda grinned at her. "Don't be imagining shipboard food is bad. Not on the *Death*. Lorm is a great cook. Trained in Sarendan. They use a lot more spices, and cream in a lot of things."

"Like the Adranis," Hadand said.

"Lorm—our cook—couldn't often get cream, but the spices he had in bunches all over the galley, and even growing right on the ship, in pots, during the warmer seasons. Since nobody but me likes our food—they think it too plain—" He waggled a hand. "The spices were popular. Especially on long cruises when there isn't much of a change."

"What's the best food you ever had?" Hadand asked, turning politely to Jeje.

"Colendi. The real stuff." Jeje jerked a thumb at Tau. "He showed me where to get it, when we were grounded in Bren."

Hadand turned Tau's way again, and he enjoyed the tingle of anticipation that burned along his nerves at the impact of her gaze. Laughter flared behind his ribs at the unexpected: he never thought to sit at a table flirting with a queen under her king's nose. But marriage was different for the likes of kings, not just here but in most places. Royal marriage was often a dynastic or diplomatic requirement—you needed heirs, you needed one of each of the two sexes as symbolic heads—it seldom had much to do with the heart.

"Tell me about Colendi cooking," Hadand said.

"Typical of Colendi life. The senses must all be in harmony, including sight. You could therefore say that in Colend, food is an art . . ." He brought his discourse to a smooth close, with reference to the Colendi penchant for music and illusory art in their plays.

"They have Colendi plays in Anaeran-Adrani," Hadand said, elbows on the table, chin on her laced fingers. "Even though I couldn't hope to catch all the references, I came to enjoy them very much. Once I learned how to watch a play."

Tau savored the curve of her lips, the hint of rueful humor there. Inda's sister! How much of his attraction stemmed from his long friendship with Inda? She did not have any of the grace, style, or perfection of feature of the Comet, his lover in Bren, but he found her far more compelling just

from one day's acquaintance. Comet was too artful, too
much like Tau himself. This Hadand seemed to have Inda's
total lack of guile, though she was not as open.

". . . what I want to know is, what are magic's limitations?" Evred asked, rapping his knuckles gently against
his still-full wine cup.

Tau and Hadand forced their attention away from each
another.

"Is your context that of battle?" Signi spoke for the first
time. "Magic is not a weapon." She said the words, yet
knew them for a lie. Because the Dag Erkric, once the head
of the Venn mages in the south, had been courting Norsunder in search of exactly such magic: that to be used as a
weapon. This was in part why Signi sat here now, an anomalous prisoner.

The path of Ydrasal had led her steps here. She met the
young king's watchful gaze and said, "Magic moves, mends,
heals. It serves, it does not conquer."

Inda flicked his fingers. "Magic isn't used for the military. I know you can't make swords fight on their own or
enemies burst into flame." Then he turned to her, struck by
a thought he'd never followed before—never had time to
follow. "How about art? Do mages live in fabulous palaces
and whenever they want a change, they do a spell?"

"No. It takes as much labor to make a thing by magic as
it does by hand, it is just a different kind of labor."

"Can you make art?" Hadand asked, resisting the impulse to ogle Tau. She felt his presence like the warmth of
the summer sun: even when not looking up at the sky, her
body always knows precisely where it is. "Artists talk so
about their own limitations, about vision being greater
than execution."

Signi smiled. "There is no spell for beauty, not outside of
illusion. You can create illusion, but it changes nothing material."

"Is art illusion?" Tau asked.

Signi's serious face turned his way. "How do you mean?"

"It can't be," Inda said. Now he was rocking back and
forth on his mat. "I don't remember exactly, but I think my

mother once read me something about art being truth." He
laughed. "And you talked me out of it, Sponge, remember?
Oh, the yapping we did while wanding out the stables. We
took ourselves so seriously. And the masters must have
laughed themselves hoarse."

The red-haired king smiled, the tension momentarily
gone from his face. Tau heard a short intake of breath from
Tdor.

Evred's nerves tingled. Inda's enthusiasm was exactly
the same, despite the scars, despite the years. He cleared
his throat, long habit controlling his voice. "I remember
now. I asked you something my father had recently had
read to me. Is art truth, or beauty? I do not see a mirror, or
art which reproduces the effect of a mirror, as art. Just so
truth is not art."

"Then it *is* illusion," Tau said, to keep the conversation
going. "Hah."

"Contrary." Evred's smile was easy, even friendly in a
detached way. It was not the sudden, unthinking beam of
inward elation that he gave Inda, and Inda only.

Hadand, in her determination not to be staring at Tau at
table, turned her attention to her husband to discover the
merry, free smile of their days in the schoolroom together,
when the Sierlaef was safely far away. Surprised, delighted,
she thought: *Inda's return has brought his boyhood back
again.*

Evred said, "It was Adamas Dei of the Black Sword who
wrote that art is harmony of all things perceivable, our finite attempt to express the sublime—the infinite. True art
strives to break the bonds of the finite, and the effect of art
makes us part of that harmony, for a time."

Signi pressed her hands together then opened them outward, a stylized gesture of grace. "Art transcends."

Tau waved a hand to and fro. One of his conversational
skills was the ability to pose as antagonist to bring the others together, if only to argue with him. "Most art demands
wealth. Art separates the leaders of style from those who
want to be perceived as stylish; it enhances prestige. Or the
pretence of prestige." *Is Hadand impressed with my*

pomposity? "I can't think of towering pastries that look like castles and cost a gold coin apiece as art but merely as ostentation."

"It's art to the pastry-maker," Tdor observed. "There is beauty in all things to those who perceive it."

Signi's lips moved as she translated, then she smiled, lips parted.

Tau made a gesture of deference. "But then you are saying that art is beauty. Is beauty therefore art?"

Inda rose to his feet, surprising them all. "What I want to know is, is art necessary to magic?" Without waiting for an answer, he loped out, wincing at every step.

Chapter Seventeen

HADAND frowned. *We will not come back to war, we are not barbarians.* "Magic is necessary to life. We have been learning again what our ancestors knew, as our magics begin to fade."

Signi said, "I know. I have seen. I will do what I can."

Hadand's expression eased. Her husband's remained inscrutable.

Inda reappeared then, and set on the table eight slim golden cases. Six of them were paired, each pair covered with matching images in very fine scrollwork: leaves, ribbons, poppies. One had roses—Jeje recognized that as the mate to the one she had in her gear—and one, the mate to the box he'd given Fox, was carved with stylized flames.

"Tau there knows what they are; he got 'em for me. Only one is missing—staying aboard my flagship." He avoided Fox's name. "T'other missing one Jeje has. They're made as art, but my use was intended to be military. Your Rajnir must use 'em, right?" He turned to Signi, who bowed her head in assent. "Well, my first question is, must they be in gold with all the artwork, and second, how does he manage with eighty-one pairs in order to talk to his captains?"

Signi said, "Eighty-one pairs? I do not comprehend."

Inda turned on Tau. "You said they only came in pairs."

"So the mage told me."

"Ah." Signi's brow cleared. "It is a misapprehension. You do not have to have them in pairs. Perhaps your mage thought that was what you required?"

As Tau assented, Signi observed tension in both men. She remembered the rueful conversation by the Marlo-Vayir people about the lack of mages for spell renewal. Here was yet another fraught question: magic. Would they accept the magic renewal so badly needed if offered by a Venn?

She forced her thoughts back to the subject at hand. "You can make them talk with as many others as you wish, but the cost is greater because each must be spelled to match each of the others in turn. Every possible exchange requires another layer of spells."

"So that's how it works." Inda dropped the one he'd been holding. "Too bad they're worthless on the sea." He turned Evred's way. "I'd thought we could put together a semblance of the Venn communication, but you need line of sight. There are no landmarks beyond the horizon to give your position in reference to anyone else." He turned back to Signi. "Your navigation is like a net laid over the world, right? And only your captains know the system of knots."

"True." She inclined her head. "As for your first question, gold is merely the conduit. Those in power have always preferred gold. My chief dag said it was the way of the powerful—whether in governing or in trade—to secure this tool to themselves, for who else can afford so much gold?"

Tau added, "So there's truth in the assertion about ostentation. The paired ones are called lovers' golds in Sartor. When I bought these I told the mage they were for a popular player in Bren. For her dalliances and as gifts to favored admirers. It was the only thing I could think of to deflect any interest in why I wanted 'em. In case mages duplicate messages for some political reason."

"You cannot do that." Signi leaned forward. "You cannot make two sheets of paper out of one, except like this." She mimed tearing. "But you can divert a message, often without the correspondents knowing. And then restore it."

Evred's brow puckered in doubt, then he walked out. He was gone only a very short time, returning with a golden locket suspended from a chain. Everyone except Hadand looked at it in surprise.

"Have you ever diverted anyone's messages without them knowing?" Inda asked, turning back to Signi.

"Not I," Signi said, scrupulous as always. "But my . . . my mistress had begun to try, yes. To Dag Erkric. To do so is very, very dangerous," she added.

Evred had been toying with the locket, his ambivalence obvious to Hadand and to the observant Tau. With a sudden movement he cast the locket onto the table before Signi. "Can messages sent inside of these be diverted?"

Signi touched it with a tentative finger. It was warm, as if it had been just taken off; she was startled, but hid her reaction. "This is old-fashioned," she said. "It is a court love locket, from Sartor, very common the generation before us. They usually come in pairs."

Evred said, "It is not a single artifact. Can its messages be diverted and read?"

"No. No one would think to divert them: the magic transfers love tokens from one locket to the other, and it would take the presence of both before they could be respelled to cause a third party to receive their tokens first."

Evred retrieved his locket, ran his fingers through the chain as if to lift it, then he dropped the whole into his pocket.

Signi was astonished. That old-fashioned, quaint ornament—intended for the idle times of wealthy Sartoran city dwellers—functioned as a communications device for this king. Were they truly so devoid of magical aid here? She wondered if she should have told young Shendan, who had taken her by surprise after the king had sent her and Hadand away from the map room, what she had about basic magery and how to find books on learning. Yet knowledge was to be shared—that was what her own secret order had sworn.

As the meal ended and talk became general again, Signi came to a decision. She whispered it to Inda.

Evred's head turned sharply at the sound of her soft
voice, but he said only, "Inda. We must get you equipped,
and see to the last of the preparations."

He leaned down to speak to Hadand. She rose, and together they went out, talking rapidly in low voices.

"Do it," Inda said to Signi, pointing with his chin in the
direction Evred and Hadand had gone. "From the sound of
it, we'll be busy a watch, maybe more. And you're right, it
will be a while before he trusts you. Go ask Hadand. I
think she'd welcome your help."

Evred was going to keep Inda busy most of the night
with preparations to ride. Signi would have the night to
herself in this vast, martial castle. She would use it to do
some good for those whose patient faces turned their
king's way—and Inda's—with such hope.

Chapter Eighteen

MARLOVAN women had been required to defend their camps back in the plains riding days.

Their defenses had been adapted to castles ever since the Marlovans had taken Iasca Leror. And so Hadand and Evred swiftly arranged the shift of certain of his duties from him to her on the walk to their royal suites across the hall from each other. Each was matter of fact, terse in speech because each understood the other so well. There would not be another chance to speak; Evred's mind was clearly racing ahead to the north.

He left her after this short colloquy and she summoned her captains, issuing orders for new patrol patterns to be given out. Among their new duties the women would take to horse, defending the city's perimeter. The girls here for training would combine with the men over fifty and the boys in the academy under eighteen for sentry and gate duty.

When the women left she discovered that she had a headache. And so she retired to her inner room, because she would rise early indeed. The men would not depart in silence.

*　　*　　*

Tau retreated to the high sentry walk between the towers, and strolled along in the cold, rye-scented evening air, studying everything and everyone. The entire city smelled of baking bread.

He stopped at the east tower. Below, the vast stable yards were lit by torchlight, smaller hand torches being carried in and out of side buildings so that the whole resembled a great beehive filled with orderly activity picked out in golden pinpoints of light. Once or twice he caught sight of Evred striding hither and yon, always with Inda by his side. There was no indication Inda needed Tau, so he was content to observe.

A quiet step behind brought Tau round, one hand brushing over his wrist, touching the handle of the knife strapped to the inside of his forearm. Tdor recognized the gesture. It was strange to see a man mirror what she was used to in women on guard.

She stopped, hands out. "May I talk to you?" she asked, her manner hesitant, even contrite. As if she expected rebuff.

He was intrigued at once. "Please do."

"I am here on behalf of Hadand," Tdor said, without any coy preamble. "She doesn't know I'm here. I thought perhaps you were interested in her."

"Mmmm." Tau gave the sound an interrogative rise at the end.

"Well, if you could see your way to visiting her," Tdor gestured downward. "She's alone now. She shouldn't be."

Her profile, lit by the ruddy light from below, was troubled. Kind, and Tau sensed that rarity, the generous nature that expects no gain. "No one should be," he said. "Unless they prefer to sleep alone."

His tone was ambiguous. Tdor sent him a quick look, then stepped back, and gave a half laugh, awkward, troubled, sad, and Tau, on impulse, said, "Your king is . . . enamored of Inda, did you see that?"

"Yes." She breathed the word, looking away. "I didn't know anyone else saw it. Hadand didn't." Tdor gripped her elbows. "She only saw her brother. Back again." Then, quickly, "Only how could he be in love with Inda, after only a day? Is that love?" Her tone made Tau wonder how many shadows that question cast.

"From the little I've heard today, it sounds like all his brother love went to Inda when they were boys. And remained steadfast all these nine years." Tau remembered his mother's discourses on love, scarcely understood when he was small. But remembered, as she had intended. "At some point that changed to something else. Despite the poets' praise for such steadfast love, it's not always good. That is, if it's unreturned, it can become . . . consuming."

"You mean a craze." Tdor's gaze was unwavering. "Those are common in his family. His father, Tlennen-Harvaldar, had one for Captain Sindan. That one was good because it was two ways. They were mates. Evred's brother had one for Joret Dei, who was to marry Inda's brother. That one was bad, because she didn't want him. So it brought about many deaths, beginning with Inda's brother Tanrid, and ending with the Sierlaef himself."

Tau grimaced. "Princely passions can be dangerous."

Tdor said soberly, "I don't know what to think, except to be afraid for them."

"If your king doesn't act on it, Inda may never see it." Tau stepped closer, lowering his voice. "You knew Inda when he was a boy. I've known him since. My guess is he was surrounded by love back then."

"Yes." Tdor sighed. "His mother, Hadand, Joret. Me. The castle children—" *Except Branid. No, even he in a twisted way, but then everything in his life is twisted.* "—the servants, they all loved him, hugged him, kissed him, wrestled with him, laughed with him, retied his sash when he forgot. His father, from a distance. I once thought his brother didn't love him, but since then I have changed my mind. Tanrid loved Inda the way he knew best—the way he loved the castle dogs. Who adored him." Her eyes lifted skyward, her voice dropping to a whisper with the depth of long-suppressed feeling. "And it seems to have been the same when Inda went to the academy."

"So love was Inda's natural state. Love—loyalty—was

like air to him. And though I believe his ability to love was
frozen up with his memories of his home for nine years, his
loyalty wasn't. He is loyal to us all. That's part of his appeal
as a captain."

Tdor let her breath out. What an extraordinary conversation, with an extraordinary person. He resembled a
painting of an impossible hero in one of the ancient scrolls,
haloed as he was by the torches beating with ruddy light
above and around them as they cast a glow onto the courts
busy with the preparations for war. But she had grown up
with a girl whose beauty had brought her more grief than
pleasure and in a sense Tdor was inured to the effect. What
intrigued her was the shape of his features and the subtlety
of his mind.

Still. The conversation had turned intimate of a sudden,
and that made her uneasy. Life this day had taken so very
many peculiar turns. She would expose no one's secrets
any further.

She struck her hand over her heart, and said, "I thank
you."

She left without saying what for.

Tau lingered, thinking, thinking, and at last made his way
back down, and to the room where Jeje had retreated. "I
shall probably not be back tonight," he said, in apology. His
expression, not his tone, asked a question.

Jeje understood the question. She regarded him for a
long breath, half lit through the reflected glow in the open
window, tall, graceful. Truth was, she was disappointed, but
then she had never expected to hold him to her anymore
than one holds the sun that warms you and then leaves at
night.

But the sun always returns. Instinct said he was telling
her because he would always come back, if she would have
him, like the sun greets the world each day.

"It's the queen, isn't it?" she asked, her husky voice low.
"I saw the way she looked at you at supper. Though she
was trying not to."

"Are you displeased?"

"No," Jeje said, looking inward and finding it was so. "I

like her. She's a good person, like Inda. Well, she's Inda's sister." She snorted a laugh. "Go on, give her a night to remember."

He blew her an airy kiss and slipped out, running downstairs to one of the old parlors where he'd seen a lute, set aside after the former queen left and forgotten since. He stopped long enough to tune it, and then trod down the hall to Hadand's rooms.

Two women guards stopped him. He brandished the lute. "I came to offer some foreign tunes for the queen's amusement."

The female guards exchanged glances; one smiled at him with grim approval as the other slipped inside.

The queen came herself and opened the door, looking up at Tau in mute question.

The guard stepped out and took up her stance, facing out.

Tau walked into an austere room that smelled of summer grasses and wildflowers and baking bread; all the windows stood open, despite the cold air. Candles burned at the far end of the room, where they would not worry her eyes.

"Shall I play?" Tau asked, studying Hadand's wide brown gaze. "I'm deemed very good. Or," he said, not quite touching her brow, "I can get rid of that headache. I'm very good at that, too."

"Please," she said, too distressed to ask how he knew she had a headache.

At his gesture she lay down right before the fire, and he knelt beside her. And as heels clattered and horses clopped and steel rang in the courtyards below, he hummed softly, his strong fingers polishing one by one all the knots and splinters of her neck and shoulders and back into smoothly cambered silk.

At the last she exhaled deeply. "You *are* good."

He laughed, and bent and kissed the lovely curve of her neck. She sighed again—a deep, pain-free breath—and turned over, stretching out on her back.

The invitation was there in her smile, her welcoming

posture. But—he bent and sniffed again, identifying the distinctive, slightly bitter herbal smell of—

"Are you using birth-herb?" he asked.

"My moon-cycle ended not two days ago," she responded, and, her lower eyelids crinkling just the way Inda's did at inward pain, she added, "I won't be drinking it tomorrow. Or the day after."

Of course not, with her king riding off to war. Tau sat back on his heels for a long moment, appreciating those wide eyes so like Inda's, and yet so unlike, and then with a deliberation that caused her to tingle he admired the enticing curves that her parting night-robe did not hide. "You are beautiful," he whispered, as passion radiated up through him, echoed back in her breathing, blazing into incandescence.

She made a sound midway between a laugh and a sob, but then his lips met hers, and the only sounds were those of love, and the music of the night birds outside, and beyond them the noise of preparation for war.

Jeje, left alone, prowled around the room once, twice, and then gave up. She'd napped all afternoon when the others had been whisked away. It had seemed a good idea at the time. But now she couldn't sleep.

So she decided to take a walk from one end of the castle to the other. She'd see if she could make it without getting lost, and maybe it would tire her body enough to catch some rest before yet another horrible all-day ride.

She slipped out. No one in sight. Not surprising. It was late. But when she reached the tower with the spiral stairway there was a bright glow in the slit windows. She stood on tiptoe. Below lay an enormous court full of men in gray tunics and long-skirted coats checking horses' feet, adjusting saddles and gear, carrying loads this way and that.

The rhythmic hiss of slippered feet coming up the stairs caught her attention. It was Tdor. She probably had a room on the same hall.

She gave Jeje a tentative smile, and Jeje blurted, "Are you really going to marry Inda?"

Tdor halted midway on the stair, and then resumed her climb. One, two, three steps, and then she reached the landing. "I don't know," she said finally. Her accent in Iascan was exactly like Inda's. Until recently, only Fox and Barend had Inda's accent. Now Jeje heard it all around her. "That is, I expect so, once he returns from the north." She raised a hand to tuck a loose strand of hair back behind her ear. Her sleeve fell back, and there was the glint of a polished black knife hilt. Her smile was bleak. "If. If he returns from the north."

She doesn't just mean if he's dead.

Tdor opened the door to her own chamber, and made an inviting gesture. "Do you want to come inside? Or am I keeping you from something else?"

Jeje stepped into the room. "I was wandering around trying to get tired enough to sleep."

Tdor's chamber was furnished exactly like all the others. Jeje plopped down onto a mat.

Tdor sat more slowly. "Tell me about Taumad. Where does he come from? His accent is not northern Iascan, like yours. It's more like ours in the south."

"That's because he grew up in Parayid Harbor. His mother runs—*ran* a pleasure house. He didn't want to work there, so he went to sea. He pretended he was fourteen, which is the oldest most traders will take on new ship rats. But he was older. Though at that time he was short and skinny. He started getting his growth as soon as he got on board."

"Do you know his family background?"

"No. His mother changes their name every few years."

"He seems very well-spoken. More so than any pleasure house person I've ever met."

"Oh, he is. Inda told me once he thinks Tau probably got more learning than he did, he just hides it. Except when he needs it. Maybe a different education. He doesn't know Old Sartoran—you know, the ancient script where they write up and down, not sideways. But he sure knows the modern kind. His mother made him read lots of poems and plays so he'd learn to speak properly." Jeje added with a quick grin, "If you're warm for him, well—"

Tdor laughed, raising her hands. "Not the least. Oh, he's a handsome fellow. Very. And kindly spoken as well. He reminds me of someone I grew up with. I wondered if the resemblance was merely in their, oh, their refined looks. If that kind of beauty creates similarity in features? Does that sound foolish?"

Another surprise. Midnight was nigh—how many more surprises lay ahead to hit her broadside on before the day-change bell? Jeje pulled her knees up under her chin and wrapped her arms around her legs. "Tell me more," she said.

Chapter Nineteen

EVRED-HARVALDAR'S people took heart from the sight of their king moving tirelessly through the chaos of preparation. There was a lift to his chin, a sense of assurance in his manner, even joy: he did not seem to believe defeat was possible.

The news spreading outward that Evred-Harvaldar would ride himself to the kingdom's greatest threat surprised no one. After all he had no real Harskialdna, though everyone hastened to give Barend-Dal credit for his valiant attempt to learn what he should have been taught over a lifetime. So he would ride, and beside him would be the infamous pirate-fighter Elgar the Fox, who really was a Marlovan after all.

When dawn bleached the torchlight, after a night of almost overwhelming effort, the great parade court was filled with ridings of men and horses, talking, shifting, checking and rechecking gear, their breath and the horses' clouding and mingling.

In the adjacent academy parade court, the boys lined up, their high voices shrill, shivering with excitement more than the bitter cold to witness history in the making.

*　　　*　　　*

The window was a square of weak blue light when Hadand woke Tau. "Inda is riding out at sunup." She gave him a lingering kiss. "Thank you." Another. "Watch out for him, will you?"

"Inda? Or your Evred?" Tau asked. For between the tides of passion there had been the intense talk that sometimes happens at the prospect of imminent parting. Tau understood a lot more about the royal pair's complicated relationship, which was built on love and respect. But the flame of ardency only burned in one.

"Watch out for them both," Hadand said.

"I'll do my best."

He stopped in the men's baths briefly, then returned to the guest chamber to discover Jeje waiting at the window, her gear bag over her shoulder. She gave him a searching gaze. "The king wasn't in with her, was he?" She did not make it a question.

"No." He packed in a few brief moves.

Now I've got it, she thought. *Tau, who can have anyone he wants, likes to be needed. So he becomes what they need. I want him but I don't need him like the others do, so with me he can just be Tau.*

He straightened up, his head canted in question. She gave a short nod of satisfaction, his expression cleared, and they walked out together.

Halfway down the stairs they met Vedrid. "Indevan-Laef sent me to fetch you," he said.

Fugue shrouded Evred's mind during the predawn scramble as an endless stream of Runners converged on him, all with emergencies to be instantly resolved. He spoke automatically then randomly as his feet carried him steadily home.

Not the castle. Home—though never consciously defined as such—was the academy.

When his conscious mind brought him back to his surroundings he found himself facing rows of boys lined up, elbowing one another surreptitiously. Memory: the first day he'd come down from the castle to take his place among his fellow scrubs, all nudging, wriggling, staring around. Where he'd first seen Inda, looking lost.

". . . before the signal to mount up?" Headmaster Gand was saying.

Gand. Waiting. For what?

The sudden return to consciousness struck Evred with a sickening conviction unlike anything he'd ever felt before. Not before battle, not after. Not when he came home to a crown after assassination and murder.

They were waiting for him to make a speech.

Speeches were traditional before important occasions. This departure was desperately important. Good speeches had been turned into songs, and sometimes even written down in the records, because they had successfully lifted men's hearts, inspired their minds to courage and duty. But great speeches were made by great heroes. Not by ordinary second sons who found themselves yoked to kingship, before a battle that—

He snapped his attention away before so terrible, so treasonous a thought could finish itself, and swept his gaze round the court full of waiting faces.

Disoriented, unsettled, Evred hesitated, his manner appearing cold and remote to all who watched him so expectantly. The boys, thinking the king displeased, stopped fidgeting, and stood as straight as fence posts.

He loathed the idea of himself uttering pompous words about courage and duty.

But he had to speak.

And so he cleared his throat. The exhaustion he'd escaped all night pressed on his skull. He forced his voice to parade-ground pitch. "You know the orders. Boys under eighteen to remain, and men over fifty. This is traditional. If we do not hold the north against the Venn, it is your task to hold the royal city. And to carry on. Because if we lose the north, it means not one of us is coming back." He drew a cold breath deep into his lungs, and his heart drummed. *Don't end with defeat.* "We intend to come back in victory, knowing that you will make certain we have homes to come back to."

Master Gand struck his fist to his chest, and the boys cried out, "Evred-Harvaldar!"

And, from behind, the men's deeper voices shouted so loud the echoes bounced back from the high walls of the castle.

"Evred-Harvaldar Sigun!"

Evred drew breath. The nausea had transformed into giddiness; his nerves tingled with ice, then as abruptly flared sun-bright. He had nearly forgotten the oldest of traditions.

But Gand hadn't. Here were two boys, appointed ahead of time, who blushingly brought forward two swords. And the senior boys now stepped forward with their hand drums at the ready.

Evred took the swords and swung them while restlessly scanning the crowd for Vedrid. It wasn't right. He should not be alone. They had to see—

But here was Vedrid, and right behind him Inda, his coat brushed and neat, his hair smoothed up on his head, the silver owl clasp glinting. His jaw tightened at every step, but when he spied Evred he grinned.

Evred snapped his fingers for two more swords. The joy was back, at steel-forging heat. This time he did not have to make an effort to be heard. "And at my left will ride Indevan-Laef Algara-Vayir, who will command this battle, while my cousin Barend-Harskialdna conducts the defense of the shore."

A susurrus of whispers rustled outward, and Gand himself came forward, offering two more swords, his own and another master's, hilts out.

Inda gripped them, swung them once, twice, then he stilled, facing Evred.

"Hep!"

Their swords clashed together overhead, right hand against right, sending blue sparks arcing out. And thirty-six boys who would talk for the rest of their lives about this moment pounded the rolling, rumbling tattoo of the war dance on hand drums, as Inda and Evred spun, clashed left against left. Whirled and clashed again and again. And then—together—threw the swords ringing onto the stones, north-south, east-west.

They stomped, whirled, and hopped, hands high, as the big boys drummed, the small boys clapped. Perfectly in sync, they danced through the complicated patterns that Inda had last performed two years ago on the deck of his flagship, with Fox Montredavan-An.

Then, as the boys shrilled the high, savage fox yip, the king and his commander walked side-by-side to the parade court, where the men waited, each by his horse.

Gand silenced the boys with a gesture.

"Mount up," Evred said, turning his gaze upward at the castle—and yes, there was Hadand high on the highest tower. Tdor at her side, he was glad to see. All as it should be.

A great clattering of hooves, the jingling of chain mail and weapons, brought his attention back.

Exhilarated to almost an unbearable degree Evred indicated Inda ride by his side, and not behind and to the left in Shield Arm position. Every man who saw Evred's smile, the rare, bright-eyed smile of unshadowed joy, took heart in his lack of fear, his assurance. Here was a young king who believed in victory!

Together they led the long columns through the old archway between the throne room and the great hall, where horses had not been ridden since the city had been conquered. They crossed the royal stable yard, and thence to the main street. On all the walls the old men had their hand drums out, and played the war charge. Evred gave the signal to gallop as the women lining the castle walls shouted, over and over, "Evred-Harvaldar! Evred-Harvaldar Sigun!"

The horses had been prancing, tails lifted, ears flicking. They plunged into the gallop, their riders easy on their backs, tear-shaped shields held aslant.

Tau rode behind Inda, Jeje and Signi at either side as Marlovan warriors closed around them. He saw at once the impulse behind the rumor of Marlovans on their flying horses: the dust-blurred line of galloping horsemen were like raptors with folded wings stooping to the kill.

So what does that make me? A duck? As he bounced and jounced in Inda's wake, he was glad that he'd learned to stay on his beast's back.

Civilians crowded along the city walls, drumming on family hand drums, clashing together pot lids and metal implements of every variety as children screeched and jumped. To them the day was exciting, and they danced about, some singing old war ballads, others fighting with sticks, Marlovan against the evil Venn.

Their elders cheered and drummed, but the faces of the oldest were grim.

On the highest castle tower, Hadand held a locket gripped tightly in one hand. At her side stood Tdor.

Neither looked away from that dust-obscured line fast diminishing over the open ground as Hadand said, "You know where they went right after Inda arrived?"

"No. Somewhere in the castle, surely. No, wait, didn't they go out into the street?"

Hadand compressed her lips. Then, "They went to the academy."

Tdor did not answer; she dared not answer.

Gradually she became aware that Hadand did not expect an answer, though her free hand sought Tdor's, and gripped hard. Hadand shouted until she was hoarse, her women shouting with her. Tdor gazed westward until Inda had long vanished into the dust-shrouded mass on the plain.

Chapter Twenty

BETWEEN the weather and the distrust on both sides, the parley at Pirate Island took a very long time to arrange. The actual conversation, however, was absurdly short, screamed across railings into the howling, sleeting wind: the two leaders would meet, alone, on the dock at midday the next day.

The midday sun peeked between racing clouds at the sleet-washed harbor where, according to the agreement, Scarf stood alone in the middle of Five Points Parade.

Directly against the agreement (she had dispatched them even before her boat met Elgar the Fox's midway between the two fleets) her people lay on the rooftops surrounding the parade.

They were all watching when a last gust of sleet from the departing storm briefly blew back the smoke from the burning remains of the last of the docked trade ships. She'd set these locals on fire partly out of revenge, but mostly to make certain her cheat force was screened from the northern side of the harbor where Elgar the Fox's ships gathered. Two could play at that game. The damned thing was, the murk also screened Elgar's approach.

A whisper ran round the hidden attack teams as a single silhouette strolled out of the smoke.

Another gust of wind, and there was Elgar the Fox, a tall,

knife-lean figure dressed all in black sauntering through the thinning haze. The only color picked out by the chill slants of early spring light was the smoldering glint of the ruby hanging at one ear, the ruby worn by those who'd defeated the Brotherhood of Blood. His sword was strapped across his back and knife hilts gleamed faintly at the tops of his boots. Even to pirates he radiated menace.

Fox was only aware of his own sick sense of events moving beyond his control. He hated this plan. But he had agreed to it.

With his heartbeat drumming in his ears he lifted his voice slightly and said, "Well?"

And braced inwardly for arrows. Counting on others' fear is not much of a shield. He hoped Mutt and the other young ones would learn that as his much-pierced corpse hit the boardwalk.

Fear stayed some hands, each pirate hoping someone else would shoot first, just in case Elgar had that Norsunder rift ready for anyone who attacked him. Curiosity stayed others'. It would mean something in the pirate world to sail under Elgar the Fox, who couldn't be beaten. If he killed Scarf, well, it happens!

Falthum was crouched behind one of the barrels stacked in front of a cooperage. His aunt gave a jerk of her chin. He rose, and together they walked out. Already breaking the accord—but Elgar didn't retreat, or protest, or even react. Unsettling.

He stopped just a few paces short of the edge of the dock, empty wagons parked at either side. Scarf had searched them herself.

She advanced slowly, drawing strength from her trusty crew lying on roofs all around the parade.

All right, then. "Elgar. Can you really command Norsunder?" she asked, when they were maybe twenty-five paces apart. She could see him clearly now: maybe mid-twenties, lean, stance easy but ready for action. Intelligent, that narrow, slant-eyed gaze, the sarcastic mouth.

Command Norsunder? he was thinking. *Only two winters, and already the truth has warped.*

So use it.

He lifted a shoulder. "As sure as my name is Elgar the Fox."

"I think we take him now, just the two of us," Falthum said, ready to lunge forward.

Scarf saw the Fox's smile thin and warning prickled through her. He *couldn't* have gotten anyone onto the docks to back him. She'd had her own watchers posted along the dock and shoreline before the two ships even met for the parley—a long-used plan. But.

She caught the back of Falthum's coat. "Just a moment. Maybe we can work something out, here. No use in spilling more blood." The idea was to make it clear that two on one put her in the command position.

Elgar, the shit, smiled just wide enough for her to see the edges of white teeth. "I don't mind spilling blood."

Falthum looked back at his aunt: what do we do now?

She didn't like showing her strength so early, but it didn't seem this Fox was going to cooperate. So . . . "Maybe spilling some of your own will change your mind."

She drew her sword.

Fox had glanced up only once when approaching the dock. He knew he was being watched, and while one sweep of the area for enemies was to be expected, another would make the pirates suspect he was looking for something specific.

Over to you, Dasta, Gillor, he thought, flinging up one hand.

Scarf and Falthum charged him.

He had about a heartbeat to wonder if he was going to die stupidly with one arm in the air, then Dasta's fight teams surged over the rooftops to take the pirates from behind, and Gillor led hers down from the back two streets just below the white chalk cliffs over which they'd spent two days trudging, out of sight of the pirates.

Scarf stared, as shocked as her crew. She had not expected anyone to come over the west side of the island, climbing mountains in the brunt of the storm.

That was her second mistake.

"Shoot!" Scarf yelled.

Fox whirled, sword blocking Falthum's downward stroke. He grabbed Falthum's thick wrist with his other hand, and pulled him round in front of him just as the hissing arrows struck.

Falthum cried out, stiffening. Fox dragged him backward the precious few steps he needed to vault behind the wagon he'd positioned himself near as another wave of arrows thudded into the old wood.

That would be the last wave of arrows from the rooftop pirates who were now busy fighting Dasta's team.

Fox lunged out, knife and sword raised, as pirates came at him from all directions—Scarf, enraged past caring, in the lead.

Fox spared them a glance. The pirates still outnumbered his people. He whistled sharply. Those who'd reached the parade snapped into the threesomes he'd drilled into them and took on the overwhelming numbers, backs forming triangles.

That was when the locals stampeded from three of the side streets, waving either real or improvised weapons, and flung themselves at the pirates. The press intensified, sharpened steel cutting almost as much inadvertently as by directed blows, until Scarf and Fox emerged from the crowd and stood face-to-face.

Fox whipped up his sword's point, then lowered it, stepped back, and smiled.

Scarf started a scornful question that was never asked because the consequences of her first mistake caught her squarely from behind: a hard wooden chair, swung with all her strength by Mistress Svanith.

The younger crew danced on the deck of the *Death*, surrounded by lamps and torches, as some clapped and sang. Mutt twirled on a barrelhead at the center, a bottle of wine in either hand as he kicked his legs up high to the tweetle of a flute and the shouts of his friends. Just below him Pilvig and Nugget sat side-by-side, Pilvig clapping and Nugget thumping a mug on the deck to mark out the beat.

Fox had snagged his own bottle of wine. His usual custom after an action was to get thoroughly drunk. It masked the pain of cuts and bruises he hadn't been aware of getting, and it also masked the howling, wintry gusts of laughter through his skull, reminding him that no matter what he did, no matter how many fights he won, there would never be justice for him to go home to.

Or for Inda. He was probably dead. Inda certainly had not been at Parayid. The golden magical transfer case was empty.

And there it lay on the side table. Fox checked the impulse to fling it into the sea—as usual. Visual reminder of the stupidity of hope, wasn't it? Or was there still some stubborn kernel of hope down inside him somewhere, bitter as aloe, dry as dust? Well, leave it.

He thrust open the stern windows to let out the cold stuffy air. Rain hissed on the sea just beyond, numbingly cold, but he smelled a difference in the air: spring was reaching the south at last.

He slammed the wine bottle down onto the table, dropped into his chair, and stared at the lamp. For a time after the fight he too had enjoyed the sweetness of successful command. But even at the height of enjoyment there had been moments of doubt, or something stronger than doubt. Moments too quick to identify during the swift flow of events.

He shut his eyes, trying to sort the images. Falthum, Scarf's nephew—Mutt, dancing and singing in his triumph—Scarf lying dead on the stones.

Her cabin had surprised him. Not just the neatness, but it was full of old and expensive books, carefully preserved in glass-fronted shelves. The nephew—

That was it. He leaned over and fingered the books he'd taken from Scarf's flagship, as Gillor (as the newest captain to earn her command) did not want them. There was not a book anywhere in his own fleet, that he'd swear.

The—call it anomaly—had begun during that parley,

short as it was. The nephew and the aunt speaking so differently. Their accents—no, it wasn't the accents. He knew smart people who spoke in dockside idiom. He knew stupid people who had been tutored to emulate the Colendi cadences of the upper ranks. Scarf had spoken like one tutored to the upper ranks, but she hadn't taught her nephew to speak so. More to the point, she hadn't taught him the *vocabulary* to speak well.

That was it. Had she deliberately kept him ignorant? Intent was now past question, thanks to Mistress Svanith's summary justice. The fact remained the nephew had been ignorant. And ...

Fox tipped his head back, listening to the rise and fall of young voices on deck. Mutt, the oldest of their young ones, celebrating his first command of one of the small schooners. He loved being a privateer. Fox wondered if he'd turn pirate if given a chance. What other life did he know? What was he, eleven or twelve when Inda first hired him, a hungry castaway off the docks at Freeport Harbor?

Fox took a long pull from the bottle, wrenched open the cabin door and yelled, "Mutt!"

The song on deck faltered for a moment, then resumed. Mutt's bare feet slapped down the hatchway a moment later, and he dashed into the cabin, his strong-boned face emerging from the roundness of childhood, his gangly limbs beginning to take on the shape of the man he would be. If he weren't killed. During the past two years they'd lost three of the young ones in battle (one recently returned); the others had cried fiercely at the time, but then recovered, eternally optimistic about the future and their place as future commanders.

"Do you know how to read?" Fox asked.

Mutt's mouth dropped open. His eyes shifted to the bottle—

"No. I'm not drunk. Yet. Do you know how to read?"

Mutt looked affronted. "Inda never made us—"

Fox's hand snapped out, quicker than a whip. He didn't use a knife, or even much force, but the Marlovan women's fighting style, called Odni, illegally taught to Fox by his own mother, enhanced Fox's speed so he caught Mutt off balance. He fell on his butt.

"I thought you stopped that." Mutt scrambled to his feet, rubbing one butt cheek. "Anytime anyone mentions Inda. It's not like we'll ever forget him—"

"If you want a life of violence," Fox cut in, "you have to be ready at all times. Now answer my question."

"A little," Mutt said reluctantly, glowering through his tangled hair at the pile of books. Then away, as if they were more a threat than Fox's ready fist.

A little. Fox knew that Inda, at age twelve, had taught his fellow ship rats how to read the winter they were all imprisoned in Khanerenth when it was undergoing its political upheavals. But he had apparently stopped teaching when they lost the Pim ships, and any hope of a legal existence. After that, all his energy had gone into building his defense marines. Mutt had been hired during that time.

"From now on, your duties will include reading to me at night."

"Me? *Why?*" Mutt glanced at Fox's long hands lying there so lightly on the one knee he'd cocked over the other as he leaned back in his chair. Then his wary brown eyes turned upward to Fox's ironic gaze.

"Quiet," Fox said. "And before you continue whining questions about why you're singled out for this torture, and what did you do, you may pass the word among the rest of the rats that you will be rotating this duty. You will all continue until you've all read these books. Even the ones in Sartoran."

"But I don't know any Sartoran!"

"You had better find the time to learn it, hadn't you? Go away. Finish your dancing and drinking. I'm certainly going to finish mine." Fox picked up his bottle. "Tomorrow, you start."

Mutt ran out. His young honk was audible from the deck as he reported Fox's newest outrage, his tone the distinctive teenage mix of belligerence and injury.

Fox turned back to the books, sliding them aside one by one until he reached one bound in finest blackweave edged with gold. His colors.

Over his life so far he had sustained many temptations, not the least of which was to kill Inda and take the secret treasure of the Brotherhood of Blood, now known to only five people in the world. Six, if you counted Ramis of the *Knife*—wherever he was.

And now a new temptation . . .

He dropped the black-and-gold bound book, uncorked the bottle, took a swig, stepped to the open windows. Then smashed the bottle against the stern timbers. And at the sudden silence abovedecks, he laughed.

Chapter Twenty-one

TAU and Jeje were given a tent to themselves. They set up next to Inda and Signi, who were next to the king in the center of camp.

Everyone rose before dawn for warm-up drills before they took to horse.

Evred asked Inda to run the morning drills for the warriors. After some talk with Tau and Jeje, Inda decided to stay with single knife drills. He would attempt to train them in Fox's and his refinements on fighting techniques they knew. He would not attempt to train them in the two-knife style. The Venn would not wait for them to gain expertise.

So Inda did his double-knife drills on his own, then drilled the men while breakfast was made and packed up camp.

Tau and Jeje did not join the warriors out on the nearest grassy field, but worked between their tent and Inda's. They were used to lack of space. They had trained on shipboard, and then, for almost two years, they had practiced on a narrow rooftop with no rail.

Early one morning a few days outside out of the royal city, Tau finished warm-ups with Jeje in the dim predawn light, then wandered toward the cook tent for something to drink to find Vedrid waiting for him.

Vedrid was outlined in the glow from the cook fires, fine pale hairs drifting down on either side of his face as they were not really long enough for even the back of the neck tuft that confined the rest of his hair.

Tau felt a pang of sympathy. He'd once cut off his hair on a whim he still could not entirely explain. Consequently he'd endured the tickle and annoyance of short hair for a couple of years until, at last, it was long enough to bind back again. It had surprised him at first that Vedrid, the only one of the Runners with this absurd tuft sticking out over his collar, endured no teasing. After several nights at the Runners' camp, he recognized that Vedrid's short hair was a badge of honor.

• Vedrid extended an armload of cloth.

Tau held it up to the ruddy light and discovered a newly made Runner's blue coat. "Thanks," he said.

Inda popped out of the tent beyond Tau's, his bare feet slapping through a rain puddle. Tau laughed inwardly at Inda's obliviousness to the bemused looks that followed his rolling sailor's walk as he crossed to the field where the men were gathering for morning drill, his sailor-braid flapping against the Marlovan coat Buck had given him.

"No bandages today," Tau observed. "He must be getting used to being shod."

The planes of Vedrid's face shifted as he smiled. "We fixed the uppers of Landred-Randael's boots with cotton-wool."

Landred-Randael? Oh, yes. Cherry-Stripe. *Why don't these Marlovans get rid of their titles entirely, and just use their academy names?*

Tau signified agreement in the Marlovan manner—hand opening—which seemed to satisfy Vedrid, for he departed, vanishing in the gloom to go about his morning's tasks.

Tau smoothed his hand down his new Runner's coat. Someone had been stitching that by firelight every night since their departure. Of course he must wear it.

He had always believed that identity is mutable, at least group identity, if not individual. You dress like others, mimic their manner of speech and their interests and the way they move, and you become one of Us, and cease to be Them.

He'd played at roles ever since he was small, and been aware of himself playing at roles. Pulling on the long-skirted blue coat for the very first time changed the way he stood, the way he moved. It was tight through chest and shoulders, yet cut for a range of motion in using sword or bow; the high collars kept out wind as one rode, the long skirts warded the worst splashing from streams and puddles. For part of the day his spine seemed spiked, but by late afternoon, when they customarily halted, he felt as if he'd been wearing the coat all his life; only his muscles pulled from the alteration in his bearing, forcing shoulders back and down.

By sundown the Marlovans' attitudes toward him had altered. He'd made the transformation from stranger to Runner.

The day they expected to cross the Eveneth River into the southeast corner of Marlo-Vayir land, where they would be resupplied, they rose to a thin, chill rain. To Tau's surprise Jeje did not step between Inda's tent and theirs to begin warm-up drill.

In the faint ruddy glow from the cook fires fifty paces away, Jeje glanced around furtively, then motioned for him to follow. They passed Inda's tent and were crossing behind the king's before Jeje spoke. "Let's go somewhere these Marlovan nosers can't hear us."

They paced through the tough green grass to the other side of the enormous horse picket, swinging their arms in the old warm-up pattern.

Tau matched his rhythm to hers as they snapped into strike-block, whirl, lunge, strike-block, kick, whirl, strike-block-strike. So they had worked every day during their time in Bren harbor. They had talked freely about everything while running through these mock fights.

Jeje threw Tau. He rolled to his feet and lunged.

She whirled away, circling, then said abruptly, "Inda spent two years with that Evred. With these others like Cherry-Stripe. He lived with us for *nine* years. Or most of that. And he thinks of them as home."

"They *were* home." Tau feinted, blocked, sidestepped, and slammed her over his hip. "You seem to forget—" *Smack*! Block. Whirl, kick. "—we all chose the sea. He was forced aboard the *Pim Ryala*."

"I thought he liked it with us."

"He liked us, not the sea life. Though he got used to it. You seem to be mixing the idea of home with friendship."

Snap, feint. Block, *wham-wham-wham*. "What do you mean?"

She dropped, snapped a hook kick round his ankle, caught him just before he could shift his weight, and flipped away as he fell trying to take her down.

He laughed as they rolled to their feet. "I think I mean that there is no single definition of home. For you and me, home is wherever we are comfortable. You on *Vixen*, me anywhere I have . . . interests. For Inda, home is here. This flat land that smells like horse and rye and wind-borne weed."

She ducked her head in acknowledgment and began again: strike-block, feint-block-lunge. "Which is one of the reasons why I'm gonna leave."

"What?"

Her palm smacked against the side of his nose, splashing shards of pain-lights across his vision.

"Ow!"

"Augh!" She hooted. "You should have warded that!"

Tau clapped a hand to his nose, blinking away the stinging tears. He pulled his hand free—no blood. He repeated, far less forcefully "What?"

"I'm leaving." Her voice was a growl. "And don't even try to argue. I was awake all last night arguing with you in my mind, and I won. I'm not going through it again."

Tau wheezed a laugh as he carefully fingered his nose. "Why?" He winced, trying to think past the pain reverberating through his eyeballs. "Is it this ride? The Marlovans themselves?"

"I could stand the ride, the smells, the boring food, the war gabble—I could even bear being treated like I am as invisible as a ghost. Did you see it on Restday, how they acted as if Signi and I didn't even exist? I mean, I guess I can see why they wouldn't ask Signi to pass round the bread, her being a Venn. But what's wrong with me?"

Tau said, "You weren't left out of the wine, were you?"

"No."

"They aren't used to bread while on ride, you could see that. Bread and wine are for home, with their families."

"I know, I know." Jeje waved her knife back and forth. "See, none of that would matter if Inda really needed me. But he doesn't. I'm about as useful as a rug in water."

"It's not—"

"I know what it's not. Marlovan women don't ride to war, so these fellows don't know what to do with me. I don't fit anywhere, not even on Restday—they pretended I was another fellow. I wouldn't care about any of that if Inda needed me. I've been thinking about what you said, our first night at that inn. Inda *didn't* get a knife in the back when these people saw him again. He didn't even get a bad welcome. He doesn't need me to protect him, not with that king sticking to him like a barnacle on a hull. Anyway, he's got you. And Signi."

Tau rubbed his hand over his head. "But what will you do? Fox and the fleet are long gone. Maybe as far's the Land Bridge by now, if not farther."

To Tau's surprise she gave him an evasive glance and a tight shrug. "I have my plans. All thought out. I have a–a thing to do," she said to the tumbled gray clouds, then faced him. "So don't try to stop me, because you can't. I've got my dunnage packed, and I'm just going to wait until I can catch Inda alone, then I'm off."

Tau stood there with cold rain tapping his scalp and trickling down into his collar, scouring his mind for any possible secret.

Regret sharpened to ache when he remembered that Jeje had a home. A family. People she cared about, from whom she had not parted in anger, unless the war had struck them down. But Jeje had maintained stoutly that they were too smart to be caught short.

Jeje knew that Tau's own mother had been caught

short—that is, she'd been taken aboard a pirate ship, her
house burned down, and he had wasted much time and
money in Bren trying to find word of pirate ships that
might have carried a golden-haired pleasure-house owner
of astonishing beauty from Parayid Harbor in Iasca Leror.

Of course Jeje wouldn't want to say anything about
going home!

Jeje glared at him. How he loved that face, a love that he
had defined as wholehearted and free of restraint or expectation. So how would he endure this great hollow behind his ribs?

"I thought you'd stay," he said finally, and laughed somewhat shakily, a sound that came out a nasal honk through
his throbbing nose. *I came here because of you,* he thought,
but he knew it had been a whim, not a purpose. *I don't have
a purpose.*

Her cheeks reddened. "Look, Inda gave me the gold
case back, after Signi did whatever it was she did to them.
You can get one from him, too. He did say you should have
one. And I remember Inda's writing lessons just fine."

"Yes." Relief flooded through Tau. "Good."

He held out his arms, and Jeje flung herself into them.
They hugged, hard, a bone-cracking grip of wordless fervor,
then she gave a strangled laugh that was half sob, and pushed
away. "Oh, Norsunder take drill. I'm off. Sun's up anyway."

It was true. Muted by the heavy mist came the cadenced
clashes of others working somewhere on the far side of the
tent city. The horses were being fed and saddled by the
young Runners on duty, horses and gangling boys now
clearly visible in the strengthening gray light.

They walked back in silence, heads bent, and when she
slipped around the other side of Inda's tent, he forced himself to walk on.

Jeje stopped behind Inda's tent, eyes squeezed shut. The
worst was over, she repeated inside her head. Worst was
over, worst was over—now to find Inda, if she could just
get him away from that—

"Shall we," someone said in Sartoran, "go somewhere
the Marlovan nosers cannot overhear?"

Jeje started violently, then whirled round. There was that red-haired king not two paces away, and much taller than he seemed when glimpsed across the camp, his attention on someone else.

She sidled furtive glances left and right. Sure enough, he was—for the first time—speaking to *her*. Anger burned away the numbness of shock. But since she was leaving, why not answer? "You're the king," she retorted. "Seems to me you can go right ahead and order people out of hearing any time you want to."

He opened a hand—invitation or command, she wasn't sure which. Maybe both. She followed him back in the direction she'd gone with Tau, his long-legged stride rapid enough to require her to hop a couple of times to keep up.

When they were well beyond the horse picket she demanded, "What do you want?"

"Right now, to understand your place in Inda's life," the king replied, without heat.

Jeje did not consider herself the acute observer of the silent language of the body, as Tau put it, but she could see that Evred was trying to put her at ease without being embarrassingly (or condescendingly) vocal about it. After all, he could have summoned those muscular Runner fellows to haul her into that big tent of his, with all those commanders and their swords clanking around inside.

And *she* had started wrong, with her comment just outside that same tent. She grimaced, knowing she'd never remember that even if you can't see into these blasted tents, or see who's just outside, you can hear everything, unlike on a ship, where with the scuttles, hatches, and windows closed, there is a semblance of privacy, if you keep your voice low.

So she said far less trenchantly than she might have, "I came along as a bodyguard."

His brows lifted. In the gray light of dawn, the fine mist heightened his coloring. He really did remind her unsettlingly of Fox. It was not just how tall he was. Fox was taller, though more lean. Fox's hair was a much brighter red, his eyes the color of spring grass, whereas the ones

regarding her so steadily now were more grayish than
green. Their faces were wholly different—it was their manner that sent echoes through memory. Even though Fox, at
his most mordant, also reminded Jeje of Tau in his most
withdrawn, artificial mood.

Meanwhile, Evred observed the change of emotion in
Jeje's face. He had been far too busy to spend time or
thought on this woman who'd come along in Inda's party,
who did not fit in anyplace he could conceive.

Then she made that remark about Marlovan nosers right
outside his tent. Not deliberately—she hadn't used the
tone for that and had spoken in the odd sort of Sartoran
that Barend had called Dock Talk. But it was intriguing
enough for Evred to set aside his ongoing tasks and wait
for her return.

"Inda did not tell you we were friends when we were
young?" he asked.

She shrugged rather sharply, her lips compressed into a
line. He leaned forward, trying to divine the emotion behind that glowering brow. She did not betray the manner of
a spurned lover. Then there was what Inda had said shortly
after his arrival: Jeje was here to protect him from the wiles
of kings.

Wiles. Inda had meant it as a joke, but there was some
kind of truth behind it. Yet she just stood there, arms
crossed, fists hidden down by her sides.

"Speak freely," he said, and with a smile, "Inda does. And
there is no risk of retribution."

She snorted her breath out. "For how long?"

Evred rocked back on his heels. "What?"

Jeje clenched her fists more tightly, determined not to
reach into her sleeves and grip her knife handles. "You said
to speak freely. Well, then, I'm going to, but I warn you, you
won't like what you're going to hear."

"Which is?" He crossed his arms, but in an attitude of relaxed waiting, of listening.

She was briefly distracted, noticing he had fine hands.
And they were no more revealing than his face.

Another snort, and she let it all out. "I hate kings," she

stated. "I hate the very idea that one person can wake up in a foul mood and launch an army against people he's never seen. Or she's never seen. Near as I can tell, there's plenty of queens just as bad."

"You seem to assume that kings escape the consequences of their actions. I assure you it is not true."

"It's not the same. I wake in a foul temper and my mates joke me out of it, or give me a trimming. Or Fox gives me extra watches of drill. Your father wakes up one day, and maybe he didn't like his dinner the night before, but the next thing Idayago knows, they are under his yoke—and he can't possibly know all the consequences. I don't mean just on land, though from everything I heard in Bren Harbor, those were bad enough. But our captain, as good a man as ever lived, at one far away stroke, ended up deprived of his whole life." Her voice trembled. "Don't tell me you ever even heard of Captain Peadal Beagar."

"He was the captain of Inda's first ship," Evred said. "A merchant trader, one of a fleet of three."

She was momentarily checked, then shook her head. "Oh, yes. You could send spies, or whatever, to find out what happened to Inda, once you gained power. Bad example."

Evred suppressed the heat of irritation. "Never mind examples. To your original point. If you assume that my father's decision to take action against Idayago was a whim borne of mood, then you assume wrong. Nor did he escape the consequences of that action."

She jerked her head, then wiped impatiently at the beads of mist along her lashes. "Never mind, never mind, I know what's coming next, and no, I don't know anything about your politics. Don't care to. Here's what I'm worried about. You could wake up one day and not like something Inda says, and next thing he knows, he's on the death list."

Evred's eyes narrowed, and a betraying flush edged his cheekbones. "You really think I'd do that?"

"Of course!" she said. "Because you can! You're one person. That is, you've got one man's temper, but because you're a king you have a kingdom's worth of warriors to

throw at someone when you're crossed. And no one can
stop you."

Evred gripped hard on his temper. Not that he was
about to sic the guard on her. The idea was absurd! He,
who had spent his lifetime laboring to control—to disen-
gage from—the danger of emotions, did not want to betray
how annoyed he was with her assumptions. Power! She did
not know how very powerless he'd been most of his life.
But yes, he did have power now.

And so. To the real issue. "You are here," he said, "not to
protect Inda from the Venn, or even from my people, but
to protect him from me."

And she said, "Yes."

Another wave of anger, this time a deep stirring of rage.
But again he controlled it. She did not know him. She
made assumptions about kings. And most of them were re-
grettably true.

She let out an unsteady breath, and he understood that
she was as upset as he. She said, "That is, that was my purpose. I can see that everything is fine. May stay fine. I don't
know. What I do know is that Inda doesn't need me right
now. He won't need me in this battle, either. I'm best in sea
battles, carrying him about the line, and while you could
probably use my bow, it seems to me you'll have plenty of
bows on hand. So I'm going to see to another matter."

Evred did not smile, but a hint of humor was there in the
deepened corners of his mouth. "In fact you have decided
to entrust him to me—for now?"

Jeje blushed. "Inda can take care of himself. And I know
I'm being a busybody. Just, we didn't know what he'd find,
coming to land," she admitted. "And I can't help worrying."

"Then how about this?" Evred lifted his hand, that same
gesture Inda had used, which they could never quite figure
out. "All I can offer is my word. Not as a king, but as a person. If I ever get angry enough with Inda to want to throw
a kingdom at him, I promise I will halt long enough to summon you from wherever you are to defend him first. How
is that?"

She scrutinized him in suspicion, suspecting facetiousness. But he'd never spoken facetiously, and there was no smirk now. Then she wanted to reject his words as the useless words of a king, except wasn't that a kind of reverse swagger? She could just hear Tau! *Oh, you say kings are just people who happen to have power, but when they speak as just people, you won't believe them because they are kings?*

She gave a curt nod. "All right. I'll take you at your word."

Evred opened a hand in agreement, then started back. Once again Jeje tramped through the mud past the row of smelly horses, this time not in companionship but next to a stranger she thought of as a waiting thunderstorm in human form.

But she'd been given the sign for clear sailing. She'd already readied her gear. The king walked out beyond the tents to where his captains and the rest were doing their best to follow one of Inda's and Fox's knife drills, and she had to admit they were doing really well.

She watched Inda striding back and forth, and listened to the sound of his voice. His countenance was so different from what they'd thought normal. This lifted face, the easy laughter, the quick, broad smile that brought out long dimples in his cheeks—this was his normal face. This observation left her with a heartsick sense that she didn't really know him.

Well, Tau would say whatever needed to be said.

She reclaimed the horse that had been assigned to her, and during the rush to break camp and get breakfast she rode away, unnoticed except by Tau, who did not trouble her with any unnecessary words, and by the vigilant sentries on their perimeter patrols, and finally by Evred, who felt a strong sense of relief that one of his many minor problems had so neatly solved itself.

Chapter Twenty-two

TAU sat on his mat near Inda and Signi, across from Evred. They had their own campfire, pleasant under a sky full of stars. The golden haze of the men's campfires outlined the jutting skyline of tents surrounding them. The air smelled of the supper Runners brought in wooden bowls, cheese-sprinkled rice-and-cabbage balls cooked in pressed olives.

Before Inda and the king could begin another of the endless iterations of past battles, often blow-by-blow, Tau said, "Jeje's gone."

"She's gone?" Inda asked, slewing around as if searching for her. "I thought she just rode off exploring."

Signi sustained one of those painful heart constrictions: she felt she had failed Jeje. Two women alone, and one had inadvertently so shut the other out that she departed unnoticed. She pressed her hands over her face, her head bowed forward. Sitting there in Inda's shadow, she was unnoticed by everyone except Evred.

Tau said, "I think she went home. There wasn't really a place for her here." *Or for me either.* He would have gone with Jeje if she'd asked, but she'd been very clear about going alone.

Evred said nothing, which Tau found interesting as he'd glimpsed him talking with Jeje shortly before she rode off.

Inda rubbed his jaw. "Well, then, we'll know where to find her. And she'll know where to find us."

"Where was her home? Do you know?" Signi asked, raising her head.

"Just below Lindeth," Tau replied. "Though she had relations in Parayid."

The fire snapped, whirling sparks into the air; a shout of laughter rose from a campfire fifty paces away. Neither Evred nor Inda noticed. They'd withdrawn into reverie.

The day Inda arrived Evred found himself in another condition of being. Words like *happiness* or *desire* or *pain* lost their meaning the same way *red* or *blue* or *green* weakened in hue in the midday summer sun.

Pain and enchantment whipsawed Evred. The moments of enchantment were brief, and deeply concealed: he cherished Inda's manner of eating, unchanged from his ten-year-old self. Either Inda bent over and ate fast, laughing, talking, or listening, or he sat motionless—as now—spoon suspended above his dish, gazing beyond the world.

Pain . . . was more complicated, the sharper because Inda had not returned alone, but with this woman at his side, hands so gracefully composed as she listened, or talked inanities with Taumad. There was nothing offensive in her voice, her presence, or her manner. It had taken Evred only a day to observe how hard she worked to keep it so. Not that her effort showed. It was the opposite. Only someone who has learned habitual wariness can recognize another who never ceases vigilance.

She was as plain as a woman could be; what figure she had was entirely hidden by the old smocks she'd apparently gotten from the Marlo-Vayir women, the worn riding trousers and riding boots cast off by one of the castle girls. From a distance Dag Signi resembled one of the half-grown runners-in-training whom Vedrid had as part of his staff, only she was shorter than those boys, her shoulders rounder. When she wore the old hooded cloak one of the Runners had given her, she was indistinguishable from the boys. What could Inda see in her?

Inda had said that he was in love with her, but what

exactly did "in love" mean? The definition changed from person to person. Inda did not follow her with his eyes the way her eyes followed him, but he sat close to her, some part of them touching, when at rest. And during the first night on the road, when Inda had cried out in some kind of nightmare, it had been her voice that soothed him into sleep. Evred had waited through the night for another cry, and in the morning for explanation, but Inda appeared to have forgotten, and the mage moved about in her courteous way as if nothing had happened.

The matter remained: she was a Venn. One who was aware that men had been detailed to guard her. She never strayed far, and sometimes even paused for them to keep her in sight. As if she knew they would be flogged if even once they lost sight of her.

Evred had seen how his Runners and staff walked around her as if she did not exist, not knowing how else to react to so puzzling an anomaly in their midst.

She is not just a Venn, but a mage. So far she had done no spells that he was aware of, and more important, had not asked for paper or pen, so she could not have sent off spy reports.

Perhaps it was time to examine the subject further. "I have some questions," he said.

No response. Inda's brown eyes did not even blink as they reflected the fires he stared beyond.

"Inda! Wake up." Tau leaned forward.

Clack! The spoon dropped. Inda looked around with an air of surprise. "It's the smells," he said, as if continuing a conversation—one that had never taken place.

Puzzled, Evred sniffed the air. "Smells?"

"Home smells. Horse. Grass. Rye—"

"Rye? What do they eat, elsewhere in the world?"

"Seldom rye. Someone is burning rye biscuits." He waved in the direction of one of the distant campfires, and everyone sniffed the breeze, now aware of the distinct aroma of singed bread. "Like they did on our last night all together, that spring, on the ride to the royal city. When I was eleven." He shook himself. "Never mind. Did I miss something?"

"The Venn," Evred said. "We postponed discussion of them. Now perhaps is the time. I want to know more about Prince Rajnir. And his commanders." He turned to Signi, his manner polite, formal. "I do not ask you to betray any military information that you possess. I would like to understand the individuals—especially this Dag Erkric, whose intention to use magic to ensorcel my will is part of what brought you here."

Her face did not change, but her shoulder tensed against Inda's arm. "You must understand that I am a sea dag. I know nothing about land war."

Inda flashed a grin. "She was right there in the sea battle off Chwahirsland. Remember when we were small, and heard about it? But the sea dags navigate, and do some ship repair, and healer spells. They don't fight."

"Understood," Evred said.

Inda was sensitive to voices; a subtle flatness to Evred's tone indicated some kind of conflict, or ambivalence. Yet he'd started this conversation.

Make it easy for them, talk about what she's told you, Inda thought. And, to Signi, "You said that Rajnir's commanders are a lot older than he is." On her nod, "I noticed when I was in Ymar that the army was war-gaming far from the coast. If I was planning an invasion in the next year, I would have army and navy together, practicing landing and launching an attack over and over on a coast with as similar a terrain as possible. Why didn't Rajnir order them to drill together?"

"He cannot." Signi laid her palms together, fingertips pointing outward. Evred had seen her do that before, and again wondered at its significance. "That is, he could. He is the prince, though his position as deposed heir is anomalous. But then the heirship itself, for the first time in centuries, is anomalous."

Evred drew a slow breath. Signi regarded him in mute question, her manner tranquil.

"Go on." Inda smiled encouragingly. She sensed his concern, and tried not to let it magnify her own as he went on, "You told me there's rough weather between sea and land forces."

She spread her hands, then closed them again. "Hilda—that is the land warriors. Hilda Commander Talkar is well-respected by the Oneli Commander, Hyarl Durasnir."

"The Oneli are the sea lords," Evred said. "Correct?"

Signi bowed her head over her steepled fingers. "Hyarl Durasnir and Hilda Commander Talkar respect one another, all attest to it. Yet all Venn grow up knowing that in the lost times, when Venn came to this world, they sailed through the sky-between-worlds aboard a *drakan,* the first Venn warship. The Oneli are the First Venn, the sea lords. They have the precedence. The kings are chosen from Oneli families. There are Hilda families, but they have precedence only over commons. Anyone may join the Hilda."

"So they don't work together," Inda prompted. "Outside of orders."

Signi considered, then bowed her head in agreement. "They will do what they are ordered to do, for that is the oath of Drenskar. The—the military oaths lie alongside our own—"

Drenskar. Evred heard a twisted version of the Marlovan word for *honor* and knew it for the origin of their own word. "I am familiar with it. Back to the commanders, if you will."

Signi's fingertips touched gracefully in peace mode. "They respect one another. But each makes his own plans in order to carry out orders from the prince."

"The prince won't command by himself?" Evred asked. "I was told that he led the ship battle Inda just mentioned, when your people took Ymar."

Inda flicked his hand out. "He lost. And that was after Ymar's queen made some kind of deal with Durasnir to hand over the kingdom."

"The Ymaran queen is believed to have died by treachery," Signi said. "Not by our people. She was killed by one of her own relations, the young Count of Wafri."

Inda's hand jerked; Signi started, fingertips pressed to her mouth. Evred's tension sharpened in question as Inda murmured under his breath to her, the tone comforting, as she shook her head, her manner remorseful.

Signi said to Evred, "Prince Rajnir means to take your kingdom for the good of the Venn, and to prove himself. The king has desired that the Marolo-Venn, the lost ones, be brought back to us, and their lands, too."

Evred's mouth tightened but he only inclined his head.

"Hyarl Durasnir will do his best to implement the plan from the sea and Commander Talkar the land, with the sea-trained Drenga, marines, joining the Hilda for the landing." Signi leaned forward. "Dag Erkric serves the prince, but his own plans are different, and that is part of what brought me away from my people."

Was it mention of this Prince Rajnir that had made Inda recoil? It wasn't Durasnir, Evred had watched closely. He leaned forward, the firelight reflected in his eyes. "Erkric's your chief magician, is he not? Yet you assured me that magicians are not concerned with war, that magic is confined to making and mending."

Inda said, "Erkric is trying to get around that by dealing directly with Norsunder."

Signi pressed her hands together again. "It is so."

Inda pointed at Evred. "Everything is to benefit the Venn. He wants our land to feed the Venn, wants our army to fight their enemies—and he wants you as his puppet to see to it all, so that he can help Rajnir reclaim his position back in Land of the Venn."

"Me as puppet," Evred repeated. So it was true, then.

"Magic spells from Norsunder, to ensnare your mind."

Now it was Evred's turn to recoil. He snapped a gaze of cold fury at Signi. "Is that possible?"

"It is not for me." She touched the front of her smock. "Or for anyone I know. But this is what he seeks from Norsunder. We do not know if such spells actually exist."

The fire crackled. From outside their camp circle came normal sounds: the racket of spoons against travel dishes, the fart of a horse on the picket, followed by the snickers and chortles of young runners-in-training working their way down the line with feed bags. From another direction, the crunch of footsteps in the gravel. Men's voices, talking quietly, an occasional laugh, and in the distance the muted thump of hand drums as voices rose in an old war ballad. Normal, familiar sounds, but not comforting.

Evred said, "There is a question about Prince Rajnir inheriting his father's throne?"

"The king is not his father," Signi corrected gently.

Evred opened his hand, a quick gesture. "Thank you, I remember now. They cannot choose their own sons as heirs."

"Kings do not have children at all," Signi said. "It is part of the agreement. The Houses choose the heir. Or have. When the sons of the Great Houses born in a Breseng year—a king year—reach fifteen, the most promising of the youths is chosen by the Houses after examination. He who is chosen trains for fifteen years. When he is thirty, and the king is sixty, he becomes the new king, the old king retires honorably to head the Council of Elders. Queens are chosen separately: the marriages are entirely symbolic."

Inda thumped his bowl down and played absently with the edge of Signi's scarf. "So the Oneli Houses all try to have their babies born that specific year, is that it?"

"If they wish a son to be a possible king. But the Breseng youths cannot inherit at home," Signi said.

"So what happens to the ones not chosen?"

"They go into service, usually to the sea. They are Oneli, and the honor of a captaincy is much sought."

"Is Durasnir one of those?" Inda asked.

Signi's face took on a ruddy hue, but her voice was even. "He was. He became the heir on his brother's death. But the king required him to remain at sea to guard the prince. Some say for his military prowess, some say for his loyalty—and some say so that the king could keep him at a distance during the troubles. All would be equally true," Signi said.

Evred's gaze was intent. "Bringing us to the present situation. Rajnir was chosen, right? And disinherited a year afterward?"

"Well, you might say two years. You must remember, in the south you all use the Sartoran calendar. In the north we do not. That is, our year is the same 441 days, but when you have the dark time, we have light, and so our new year begins at a different time." She paused.

Inda said, "Go on."

"So Rajnir was chosen in what you call your year two."

"Two years before we started at the academy." Inda grinned, causing Evred to smile briefly back.

Signi studied the pair before her, back and forth, back and forth. "There was trouble the year he was chosen. There was another chosen first, you see, but he died that week. No one knew how it happened. The second went mad and attacked someone, who killed him in self defense. There were witnesses, but no one understood the cause of the madness. When Rajnir was chosen, the king sent him to the south to acquire more land for the empire's needs, and to learn governing at a safe distance, while the troubles at home were investigated."

"So Rajnir ran the defense against the Chwahir and Everon, lost, and was disinherited." Evred held up three fingers. "And there is a new heir?"

"No." Signi's voice was so soft it was difficult to hear her over the crackle of the fire. She was silent for a long moment, as if inwardly struggling, her brow tense, eyes somber. "That is, there was. But he drowned—no one knows why he sought to swim during winter. There has been no heir since. The king feels the old ways can be set aside until it is discovered why these boys did not survive heirship for even a year, and it is whispered he would like to rule past sixty."

There was another, longer silence. Inda, who knew these things, was recalling the war games he'd viewed on the Ymaran fields; Evred contemplated kingship, and how difficult it was for kingdoms to guarantee continuity, whatever rules they imposed. There were the Venn, with a chosen king changing their ancient tradition. Ymar's long-lived queen was killed by her own kin—as Evred's father was by one of his own Jarls. Idayago and Olara conquered. Their kingships abolished by his own family . . . "So your kingship is supposed to change in three years, according to our calendar."

"It is true."

"Thank you for explaining." Evred rose and gestured for Inda to follow.

The two walked beyond the firelight, and when Evred felt he was safely beyond earshot, he said, "I've sent orders to Barend." His hand slid within his coat to clench on the locket; again he fought distrust and hatred of mages. A Venn mage, yet!

He did not want Inda mentioning the locket to Signi, which Evred had made the mistake of showing her. If she knew he was using it now for military communication, would she somehow magically extricate his latest note to Nightingale? She'd said that both lockets had to be present for their messages to be tampered with. Was that true, or a spoken convenience because he wanted it to be true?

"The north end of the pass is a narrow river valley spanned by a formidable castle, very old. The North Road runs directly underneath the outer walls. Flash discovered that the locals know how to destroy the road by bringing the mountain down on it."

Inda jerked around. "Collapse a *mountain*? I take it you'll need to get a couple thousand men digging?"

"No. Magic will supposedly bring the cliffside down so thoroughly nothing can get through, except through the castle. Some long-ago mage designed it."

Inda whistled softly.

"If we don't get to the north coast before the Venn do, we can at least destroy the road leading southward. It won't stop them, Flash told Barend, but it might slow them up."

"Why didn't the Idayagans use it against us when your brother and uncle went up there?"

"Flash found out that the Idayagans were arguing with the Olarans about who had to pay for restoring the road. Before they knew it, my brother and uncle were already through."

"So the pass road won't be usable at all?" Inda asked.

"It will be blocked only at the north end, with access through a narrow tunnel that opens a short way farther up the pass. That goes through the castle, like I said, which is why the castle *must* be held."

Though Inda could calculate rough estimates of sea journeys with only a glance at a map, he still had trouble figuring out how long a ride would take, especially through the mountains. On the map, the pass seemed the size of a footpath, its length an afternoon's stroll. No doubt that would be different when he reached it. "Flash and his dad hold this castle?"

"Yes."

"If he's as fast as he was when we were boys, that's good."

"Fast, trustworthy, and popular. The Idayagans still hate us, but they seem to exempt Flash and his family from that hatred." Evred flexed his fingers once, then clasped them behind his back again. "This is not for any ears but yours. Barend and Flash have arranged a beacon system over the mountains. When the Venn land on the north coast, Flash will light the beacons, and we'll know within a night at the southern end."

Inda was about to say, "How did you find that out?" But he remembered the talk about magic at their dinner in the royal city, specifically that little locket. He guessed that one of Evred's Runners, if not Barend, had another locket. But it was also clear why Evred wouldn't say: he still didn't trust Signi.

Inda looked away, grimacing. He knew you can't just trust someone on command. Trust isn't something you order, or not in his experience. It only comes over time.

Inda let out his breath in a hiss between his teeth. So far, the winds were yet in Marlovan favor, though the weather had been against them.

Evred waited, but Inda's gaze had gone distant.

"Inda."

Inda started.

"I require you to keep knowledge of the beacons to yourself. It is only for you, and eventually the Sier Danas, to know. Not even the riding captains will be told."

Evred clenched his hands behind his back. Insects

chirred and buzzed. Far in the distance a fox barked, causing the scout hounds to whimper and fret.

Inda said at last, "I understand."

While they were gone, Signi stared into the fire, wishing
she had not brought up Wafri's name. Inda had not cried
out in his sleep since that first night of travel; she hoped the
stirred memories would not bring another nightmare.

She dared a glance at the two figures silhouetted against
the glitter of the night sky. Even obscured by darkness
their bodies spoke with intensity, Evred at war with his
own emotions, Inda seeing in Evred's intensity only boyhood loyalty and the stress of impending battle.

Tau sat just outside the circle of firelight in order to observe the others. He had less interest in the Venn—especially in a bald recitation from which motivation had been
stripped—than in his companions' reactions.

Not that Signi the Venn revealed much. Her training was
a magnitude above what his mother had taught him about
masking emotion. *Most intelligent people can control the
expressions of their mouths,* Sarias Elend had taught Tau. *It
is the skin around their eyes, and their hands, that betray
them. If you cannot see their faces or hands, watch the entire
body.* Signi didn't move so much as flow—and she was
about as outwardly expressive as water.

Evred and Inda returned, the king beckoning to his Runners on duty, and Inda rolling toward his tent in his distinctive sailor's gait. Signi followed, her step composed, her head
slightly bowed, her hands together in the mode of peace.

Inda flung open his and Signi's tent, letting the stuffy air
change for fresh as he unfastened the carved-wood buttons
of his coat. He folded it, laid it on the mat, then brushed his
fingers over the smooth, cool golden case lying half out of
his saddlebag, the campfire light twenty paces away reflected in a ruddy gleam along the edge. He felt an unexpected tingle.

The end of that first day's ride away from the royal city,

he'd sat here on his mat, his feet bound up to protect the new blisters he'd given himself after dancing so wildly with Evred, and had written:

> *Fox: I'm staying. Evred is now the king, and he needs me to run defense against the Venn.*

There was no immediate answer, or even one the next day. Inda hadn't expected one. It was possible that Fox had chucked his gold case overboard as soon as Inda sailed from the fleet, but Inda didn't think so. During their long journey together across Ymar, Inda had learned a lot about Fox. He could so clearly see how angry Fox could be—angry, then cynical. But he would answer, it was just a matter of when.

And so it seemed he had.

Inda picked up the case, aware of the little rustling noises Signi made as she readied the bedding. "Fox wrote back to me."

"Ah."

He clicked the case open and took out the folded paper. He had never seen Fox's writing before. His letters were a long, slanting dash.

> *You will no doubt be delighted to discover that you just retook Pirate Island. Oh, yes, and you're also responsible for the rift to Norsunder that rid the world of Marshig the Murderer.*

Inda smothered a laugh, looking out of the tent for someone to share the news with. Evred had remained at the campfire, a tall silhouette surrounded by Runners, giving them their orders from the look of things. Inda remembered Evred's sudden reaction to mention of Fox, as quickly hidden, that day at Daggers Drawn. No, maybe best not to share this joke with Evred.

"Inda?" Signi asked gently. "Something bad?"

"Nah. Fox just retook Pirate Island. Has to be from some of Marshig's gang who slithered away when the fighting got hot. Says that rumors are going that I made Ramis' rift. How could they think *I* did it?"

The firelight reflected in Signi's wide eyes. The rest of her face was in shadow. "What did they see?"

"Everyone at that battle saw the rift. It reached right up to the clouds."

"But did everyone see who made it?"

Inda closed his eyes, trying to recall the jumble of images from that night. "I don't know." He sighed. "I think only those of us in the northern part of the battle actually saw Ramis and the *Knife.* He sailed in from the northwest. Made the rift. From the south, all they probably saw was the rift, because there were burning ships surrounding the *Death,* there at the center of things."

Signi dipped her head. "They attacked the *Death* thinking that you were upon it, is that not right?"

"Yes. And that was our plan. Anyway, Ramis hauled round, came directly to me before sailing away again, like I told you before. Tau told me that people in Bren didn't even believe Ramis had been there, but I thought that was the usual garble of distance."

Signi bowed her head. She suspected who had set it about that Elgar the Fox was dealing with Norsunder, and why. But because she had no proof, she said nothing.

Inda bent over the rest of the letter.

> *As for you. Before you get yourself killed in useless causes, you really ought to marry your Marth-Davan and have a daughter to marry my hypothetical son. I've decided that the best revenge against the Montrei-Vayirs is for your blood to mingle with ours.*

Tdor, Inda thought. Saying her name in his mind used to evoke her childhood face: during his long exile he used to talk to that image in his mind. He pictured the steady gaze of the Tdor who had met him in the tunnel to the academy, her eyes brown with little flecks of green, her face long and clean-boned, tiny wisps of hair around her ears. Her smile, though, it was just the same.

"What is it?" Signi asked as he snuggled in next to her warmth.

"Tdor. If—when—we return, I'm supposed to marry her."

"Was it not always arranged so?"

"Yes. Tanrid was the heir, Joret would be Iofre. I . . ." He lay back, his breath slowly easing out. "Until a few weeks ago I'd gotten used to the idea that I'd never see Tdor again. That I had no home. No future but what I made."

No you hadn't, Signi thought, pulling him to her. *Nor, I believe, had she.*

Chapter Twenty-three

FIFTY years of rising before dawn for meditational sword drill had brought the Venn's southern Fleet Commander Hyarl Fulla Durasnir to this realization: his ancestors had been aware of the moral advantage of meeting the day alert, dressed, muscles warm when everyone else was stiff and half asleep.

On land, his breakfast time would be given over to his wife and small son. This was time that he cherished because it had become so rare. But now that he was asail he sat alone, sipping steamed milk with honey as he scanned sky, sea, and sails, and contemplated this particular vagary of human nature.

Conclusions so far: people felt comforted at the notion that the commander was at watch while they slept. Second, people were orderly and efficient if they knew the commander was up and about before they were.

And finally—this would be the unspoken advantage—one really needed that quiet watch, because it was far too seldom that the rest of the day would permit the luxury of uninterrupted thought.

His aide had left fleet communications at his table. Durasnir did not touch his scroll-case until he'd eaten the last bite of vinegar-soaked cabbage. The first message—as well as the fifth and eighth—were from Erkric. The last also had Prince Rajnir's sigil scrawled below it: a royal summons.

This was why Durasnir never opened his scroll-case until he had eaten his breakfast. If there was enough of a crisis, Erkric would come to him.

He acknowledged the order and sent it. He checked sky, wind, sea, then moved to the tiny Destination alcove off the outer cabin. He picked up the transfer token, braced himself, said the spell, and transferred.

As always, the spell nearly wrenched his breakfast away. Pain and nausea wrung through him in waves, then vanished with about the same speed, leaving him in the Destination square in the high tower at the Port of Jaro in Ymar. Here, the sun was nearly overhead, half the day gone.

When the blur cleared from Durasnir's vision he found Prince Rajnir and Dag Erkric waiting.

Durasnir showed his palms to the white-dressed Erama Krona, the prince's personal bodyguards, surveying the round tower room as they surveyed him. As always the room was almost bare, only one chair on the tile floor, and the prince was not in it. The only other furniture was a small table carved like ivy vines. On it rested a very old Ydrasal candle-tree.

The Erama Krona moved away, permitting the fleet commander to step off the Destination tile.

All three saw in the other two their own tensions. Rajnir always had to fight the urge to exclaim, "Uncle Fulla!" He had fostered with the Durasnirs when he was a Breseng candidate; of all the Houses he had stayed at, he had liked theirs best and had been often invited back. His best friend had been Vatta, Fulla's son who had died in that damned useless sea battle against the Everoneth and the Chwahir.

Rajnir flushed, looking younger than his late twenties. He hated any reminder of that battle. Not just because he'd lost it, but because Lord Annold Limros, Count of Wafri, had so easily tricked both him and the Everoneth into that stupid clash that got so many of his own age-mates killed. Including Vatta.

"My prince," Durasnir said, on a note of question.

"I am still angry with Wafri," Rajnir admitted, in part to try to provoke a response from his mage.

Has he been talking about that again? Durasnir thought.

But Erkric just smiled from his place by the window, the light haloing around his silver hair. "We have greater concerns than a petty Ymaran traitor," he said in a mild voice, and then turned to Durasnir. "Hyarl Commander."

The dag was older than Durasnir by ten years, but until last summer he had seemed ageless.

"We have received news from our people in the western seas," Dag Erkric said.

Durasnir remained silent, asking his question with gestures rather than words. He learned more if he did not provide the response that Erkric wished.

"Pirate Island's scout reports that Elgar the Fox just retook that island from some of the pirates leftover from the Brotherhood."

"I hope he got rid of them," Durasnir replied, an indirect arrow at Erkric. Durasnir believed it had been dishonorable to ally with pirates, though tactically it had been masterly. Such a decision—practical but immoral—seemed only to lead to Rainorec, Venn-doom. Yet not just Rajnir but the king had approved, so nothing could be said. Directly.

"Yes," Erkric responded. "He did, or someone did. This was an eyewitness report. The one everyone claimed was Elgar the Fox was not Wafri's prisoner, Indevan Algara-Vayir, but the one we think came to rescue him: tall, red-haired. Green eyes, not brown. Wears black clothing."

Durasnir had sent out his own scouts since that summer and was fairly certain he'd discovered the identity of the mystery redhead who sometimes shared the name Elgar the Fox but he did not yet know for certain.

So he just bowed. "Did you issue assassination orders?"

"Our scout could not get near him. He slept onboard his flagship and they sailed as soon as they had sorted the pirates, their ships, and their supplies, leaving the surviving pirates to the justice of the locals." His lip lifted in distaste.

Prince Rajnir's sky-blue eyes flicked between them, his broad brow tense. "Then he will attack us on the sea?"

Erkric said soothingly, "He sailed west, toward Toar, my prince. He will not interfere with our invasion. He is farther away every day. And even with the new ships he took on, his fleet is a mere handful against ours, and undisciplined at that."

"So where is the real Elgar?" Rajnir asked.

"We think he might have landed along the coast of Iasca Leror," Erkric replied. "But—"

"—someone is killing our observers, yes." Rajnir gripped the windowsill. "If Elgar did land, he will soon be marching northward at the head of an army. Why haven't we gotten word of it by magic?"

Erkric fought against an angry reaction. He had to remind himself that Rajnir and Durasnir were doing their duty. Still, Durasnir's duty concerned the seaborne military, not the magical.

It's tension, he thought, slowing his breathing in an effort to restore calm. Durasnir was unswervingly true to his Drenskar oath, which he saw as the trunk of the Golden Tree. That must be remembered.

But Erkric knew that the true trunk was magic. The military, like all the other guilds, formed branches. He was going to change the traditional limitations of magic. Such change would only make the Venn stronger.

So what could he say?

"You must remember that many of our scouts have been murdered," he said.

Rajnir's brows lifted in an "Oh, that's right!" expression, and Erkric was just drawing a breath of relief when Durasnir said, "But what about your dag scouts? Have they been murdered, too?"

Rajnir snapped round, eyes widening with surprise. "*Dags?* Murdered? Why did no one tell me?"

"Because we have found no bodies," Erkric said. "I will make a full report as soon as I know where my dag scouts are. When the military scouts were murdered, the bodies were left for us to find, as you know."

"Yes, I remember that." Rajnir's fretful tone subsided. *He did need further soothing,* Erkric thought. A king needs his mind serene and clear, and not cluttered with worry over what he cannot help.

Durasnir said, "Your dags have vanished in the way of our scouts, but you have found no evidence of their being killed?"

Anger flared in Erkric, to be fought against. Anger clouded the mind. This was not the time to reveal any weaknesses on the dags' part, which would be so misconstrued.

This was not the first time dags had just vanished. No one had been able to discover yet if Dag Jazsha Signi Sofar, captured by none other than this Elgar the Fox, was alive or dead. Even worse, no one knew why Brit Valda, Chief of the Sea Dags, had vanished, as well as the dag scouts they'd had to replace with army scouts.

Finally, and most important of all: were these questions connected to his recent, shocking discovery that the warding magic over his own scroll-case had been compromised?

These matters, he reasoned, were magical affairs. And the strain was great enough for each in his own realm.

So he said only, "That is true. As yet we do not know why. Our magical communications need to be limited for the same reasons we have to be careful landing observers. It was your own wish, my prince, that the invasion remain a secret. It requires as much effort from us as from the military to keep the plans from becoming known. This was before we discovered our long-established scouts were being murdered."

Durasnir signified agreement. "Someone definitely knew who and where they were, and permitted them to operate undisturbed for years before this sudden sweep. This long wait before action argues against that 'someone' being the Marlovans, handing us yet another line of inquiry to pursue."

Again Erkric felt control of the conversation shifting. Since Rajnir had not yet asked the question that Erkric had encouraged him to summon Durasnir here to ask, he gave in to temptation and asked it himself: "When will you be ready to launch?"

"The plans have not altered since last year. As soon as the winds change."

Rajnir flicked his gaze between them. "But the Dag just told us that secrecy is hard to maintain. The secret of the invasion might even be broken."

"If you discover that there is a large army marching north across Iasca Leror," Durasnir said, "then you will know that the truth got out. But I never planned on surprise anyway. Only a fool counts on a major invasion being secret."

Rajnir's brow cleared. "So you planned on them knowing."

Durasnir compressed his lips against saying, *I told you that before.* Rajnir either did not remember or more likely, needed reassurance. Or . . . he frowned, remembering something Signi had hinted at, very obliquely, some time ago—

Later, later.

"The plan is unchanged. Whether or not the Marlovans find out, we must have the steady summer winds. We don't need entire ships swamping, killing our people before we even sight an enemy."

Erkric said, "I will leave you to review the details and return to my own investigations, then, my prince."

Rajnir saluted Erkric, again addressing him as Dag. Very close to the title he so coveted: *The* Dag, or The Dag of the Venn. The King's Dag.

Durasnir bowed. "Dag Erkric." He gave the proper formal title.

The mage's return bow was polite, his smile faint. "Hyarl Commander." He vanished, not needing a Destination tile.

The window overlooking the harbor was open, so they did not feel the displacement of air. Rajnir breathed deeply.

Durasnir had not expected to be left alone with the prince. He had far too much to do on the other side of the strait; two long transfers in a day would leave him with a headache so he would be slower at accomplishing his work.

Yet, yet. Dag Signi had once hinted—unless he misunderstood—that some of the dags were trying to discover spells to guide minds. It was so hard to believe! Yet it had once happened, if the records were correct, and that magic had been forbidden for a long time.

He wished he could talk to her now, or to Valda. Only after months of thought had he recognized that her hint, given when it was, where it was, had not been a general comment, but was directed toward one person: the prince.

If that is true, how will I know for certain?

Rajnir whirled around. "It's been two weeks since the Dag has come to see me."

He whirled again and pressed his hands on the windowsill, leaning dangerously over the spectacular drop as he gazed down at the ships in the harbor. Durasnir was aware of the Erama Krona stiffening.

"Other than that all I get are couriers from you both, saying everything is fine, everything is fine. Fine, fine, fine. And yet someone is killing our scouts in Iasca Leror, just before our invasion. Elgar the Fox turns up in the south, and they are claiming he knows Norsunder magic, can rift time and place to thrust his enemies through. And now dags are popping away like bubbles. Yet everything is fine, fine, fine." He leaned farther out of the window, glaring southwestward in the direction of Iasca Leror.

Durasnir knew what would happen to the Erama Krona if the prince came to harm. Yet they could not speak unless spoken to and had no authority over the prince.

"Please do not lean out like that," Durasnir said, to spare them anxiousness. "I only know what Dag Erkric reports on."

Prince Rajnir pulled his head in. He appeared sane enough. Surely that argued against some mysterious spell guiding his thoughts, if such a thing even existed.

Durasnir said with care, "He seems to be as limited as we are in gathering information. You will have to address him directly to find out why."

"I do." Rajnir breathed deeply of the cold wind. "He says I won't understand, but it's couched in words meant to comfort me. Uncle Fulla, I am not comforted. I *must* win this battle before the Breseng Menn." He touched his neck, where the golden torc of kingship should rest, though he did not wear the silver torc of the heir. "Everything has gone wrong since I came here to Ymar."

"We now know that a great deal of that was due to Count Wafri's treachery," Durasnir said.

"He was my friend." Once again Rajnir sounded oddly young, and he prowled around the room, stopping at the table. "How could he turn on me? I gave him *everything*."

"You gave him everything in his own kingdom," Durasnir corrected gently. "And we all share the blame equally for not discovering that he was an enemy all along. I dismissed him as a fool to my regret. So, it appears, did Dag Erkric."

"He won't tell me what he did with Wafri." Rajnir had lifted the ancient, gold-inlaid candle-tree. He turned it slowly around in his hands, frowning at the whorled wood-grain highlighted with threads of gold, the twined leaves around each holder, and each of the nine unlit candles, as he spoke. "Wafri was my friend. I told him every thought, and he smiled, and praised me. Shared his wine with me, his cymbal dancers." He set the candle-tree back on the little table. "Some days I want him dead, others, I remember the fun we had—" He shook his head. "The Dag won't tell me."

"Maybe he deems it better for you not to know. But you must ask him, my prince. I know nothing either. You'll remember I was dispatched to sea soon after that wretched business."

Rajnir sighed. "And you have much to do, yes, I hear it in your voice. Just tell me this. Am I a coward to be so concerned? I find my mind full of questions during the day, and confusing dreams at night."

Durasnir said, "In my experience, the only people who use such words as cowardice are those who do not understand the weight of time, and anticipation, before battle. It is like the advent of thunder, only in the soul. We all feel it, from commander to the smallest horse boy. Yet we will all be in our place, though our heartbeats drum in our ears, when the time comes to face the enemy. I believe that the most fearful man is the bravest because his struggle to be faithful to his Drenskar oaths is the hardest. On him shines the golden light of the Tree."

"The golden light of the Tree," Rajnir repeated, his eyes wide as he rested his hand on the candle-tree. "Ydrasal. I must remember Ydrasal," he whispered, and Durasnir's neck prickled. These words were not for him, they carried the undertone of a private oath. But then Rajnir looked his way, and his gaze was sane. He smiled and gestured in peace mode. "Go prepare, then, Uncle Fulla. Bring us victory. The Venn need it. I need it."

Durasnir stared into Rajnir's young, troubled face. Was this young man he had loved like a son what good kings were made of? The thought made Durasnir uneasy. The question it seemed to be leading to was far too close to treason.

So he would not give it time to form. He had sworn his own oath. Behind all the sonorous words was a simple idea: you are trusted to be where you are ordered to be, doing what you are ordered to do. That was Drenskar. To disobey that oath was to betray the trust of the king, and therefore the trust of the entire kingdom. The good of the kingdom was Ydrasal.

Someday—if he lived—if he were to be called home at last—as a Hyarl he would be choosing a king. That would be the proper time to contemplate the question of what makes a good king.

He saluted, stepped onto the Destination tile, and vanished.

Chapter Twenty-four

IN Lindeth Harbor, five people cursed the sudden spring downpour as they eased along the otherwise mostly empty early morning streets.

Lindeth Harbor was in the process of being rebuilt. Sheets of rain rumbled over raw-planed boards and plinkled against new glass as two of the five splashed from opposite ends up the narrow alley between the dark shells of River's Edge, the part of town that dealt with the inland river trade.

In many parts of Lindeth people lived crammed in what once were their basements, or stables, or storage sheds as their houses went back up, stone by stone, and then room by room inside. River's Edge had twice been the entry point for pirate attack (its unofficial name was Pirates' Bunghole, which the locals, who wanted their new streets and buildings to be stylish, unsuccessfully tried to stamp out) so no one lived there until it was finished, lit, and patrolled.

Occasionally lights were seen, mostly at the old cartographer's. As the wind sheered, moaning along new roof poles and under bare eaves and around corners of fine stone, one of the two figures surged through the puddles with angry determination, her gaunt body bent into the wind, arms pressed close.

She looked around only twice, each time getting a face full of cold rain. She cursed the rain, cold, her old bones, and the necessity that forced her out into this weather.

She edged closer to the stone wall of what would be the cartographer's drawing chamber, with its bank of high arched west windows. This cartographer was the best sky-liner—that is, mapmaker who drew in skylines for the traveler to recognize—on the northwest coast.

She slipped into the newly built stable behind the cartographer's. Justly famed as well as rich, the cartographer had made certain that his house was going up first. Well, she was earning extra money, too. And her house (though small and unpretentious) was done. Meetings had been held there when they did not want the harbormaster interfering in guild business.

But this meeting was no one's business.

The stable was just boards inside with a tile roof over-head. No new wood had come for two seasons, so a lot of building had come to a halt.

She shook herself off, staring through the open stable door at the back wall of the house, complete to Sartoran sun-circles under the gabled roof-trees. All Lindeth was going to have Sartoran-style architecture—and at the expense of those damn Marlovans.

The doorway darkened. "Guild mistress," came a familiar voice from inside a shrouding cloak.

The young man she only knew as Rider shook out his cloak, laid it over a beam, then lowered his lanky form to the edge of the new trough, fists on his knees, elbows out.

She did not like him. He reminded her of a human stork with mud-splashed legs and a nest on its head. Even soaked with rain, his short pale hair stuck out in shocks. But there was nothing comical about his steady blue gaze nor, for that matter, was there anything comical about her own tall, meager form, her thin braid of gray hair wound tightly on her head, the grooves in her face worn by decades of pursing her lips.

She had preferred her old contact, a very young woman whose understanding and sympathy had been beyond her years. Rider despised this spy duty, forced on the army since the mage spies had begun vanishing, and he despised this miserly old woman who sold out her own people for a handful of gold pieces. He did little to hide his contempt.

But they needed each other, so they got right to business. "What have you for me?" he asked.

"Two pieces of news," she said, thinking of her new parlor floor and the fine etched glass she would have upstairs in her own Sartoran sun-circle. "Brought yesterday with a caravan out of the south. One, that Elgar the Fox is a Marlovan, and two, that he not only landed in Iasca Leror, but was seen at one of their Jarl castles. It was called *Marlo-Vayir*. I remember that because it sounds so much like *Marlovan*."

"How many mouths from the truth?" he asked, not moving.

She said, "Three, including me."

"For that I need to know exactly who spoke to whom," he said. He much preferred news that she overheard herself.

"I was told yesterday in conversation with the caravan guide who accompanied the millwheel maker just arrived to help set up our new mill." She added stiffly, "He's my sister's boy's mate, been running caravans for ten years. He dropped off the millwheeler up at Dockside Circle, to begin working on the kingpin today. The millwheeler saw Elgar himself. He described him clearly enough for me to be certain that he's the same one who was here two years ago: short, scarred face, brown hair. Rubies in hoops through his earlobes, pirate style. The Jarl family all used his real name, not Elgar. He's a Marlovan, all right. Probably a murderer, just like they all said years ago."

She let her voice show her affront. Selling information she might be doing, but it was for the greater cause, and so what if it also netted her money? After the last few years, a person had a right to tuck some extra behind a brick for the next time either Marlovans or pirates burned the harbor down to the ground, and this Elgar fellow was both.

Rider said nothing, just handed her the amount for thirdhand news. Then he picked up his cloak, shook it out, and swirled it around him as he stepped out into the rain.

Her shoulders twitched with ill-humor as she tucked her coins into her belt purse. She began counting to one hundred. They must never be seen walking together, and there was plenty of time yet before the Marlovan patrollers would be this way.

A thump and a thud against the outer wall startled the guild mistress out of her count, but she shrugged, figuring Rider had slipped on the stones and caught himself against the wall. After all, there had never been the slightest problem in the eight years she'd been meeting these . . . riders.

She stamped her shoes well to rid them of mud before she started toward the door, beyond which rain sheeted steadily.

She started violently as three tall figures loomed in the doorway.

She backed inside the stable. The foremost figure strolled in at a languid pace, removed his cloak with an elegant air, and tossed it, dripping, over the bare frame of a loose box.

"Mardric." Fear gave way to exasperation. She loathed Skandar Mardric, head of the Idayagan and Olaran Resistance. "What are *you* doing here?"

With him was a tall, massive Olaran ironmonger, who rarely spoke but often attended Mardric when he met with harbor leaders. The other was a young rope maker, big ears standing out from his tangled curly hair. She knew he ran messages. Together they seemed oddly . . . purposeful.

Mardric lounged against a roof support.

"Well?" she demanded, perching primly on the edge of the trough where Rider had sat, her rigid posture expressive of indignation. "I am very busy. By the first bell I am expected to meet with the harbormaster."

Mardric said, "You have been complaining about me." His heavy-lidded eyes, usually so mocking and sleepy-looking, were wide and direct.

"Yes," she retorted, determined to maintain her authority. Mardric and his "resistance," what a joke! She sat even more upright, voice tart with righteous anger. "You go behind everyone's backs. You sleep with anyone, man or woman, in order to winnow out their secrets. But do you do anything *useful* with that information? No. We are still under the rule of the Marlovans, and you've accomplished precisely nothing, except collect large sums from who knows how many cities, for your 'expenses.' Which you have never justified, anymore than you have your actions."

She stopped. He made a wide gesture, almost a courtly bow. "Go on."

"Two of my neighbors *saw* you row out to talk to those pirates the winter the old Marlovan king was killed." She squared her shoulders. "Why, to tell the truth, we all thought you were spying for the Marlovans. After all, you never did manage to kill that Prince Evred, despite everyone telling you the Ala Larkadhe castle is honeycombed with secret ways, and two people I personally spoke with said they showed your people ways in."

"Ye-es," Mardric drawled. "And every one of them was caught. The Marlovan prince, in his arrogance, let my own brother go free. They, it seems, don't take us any more seriously than you do. Go on."

"Go on? I have work to do, even if you don't."

"Your work right now is to defend your life," Mardric drawled, then feigned surprise. "Oh, I didn't say? My mistake. I thought you heard your Venn friend get his final judgment."

He turned a hand outward in a lazy gesture. The ironmonger tromped out the stable door, then dragged someone in by his mud-covered heels. Fear flowed cold and terrible along the guild mistress' nerves as the rest of Rider's lanky form bumped lifelessly in, sodden cape last. The front of his tunic was dark, soaked with blood where he'd been knifed in the heart.

Mardric said, "Leave him there."

The ironmonger dropped Rider's heels.

Mardric laced his fingers together as he regarded the

guild mistress. "It's true that the Marlovan prince—now
their king, despite all our efforts—yet lives. But that's
only because no one can get into his citadel in Choraed
Hesea. If the word you yourself just sold to the Venn, or
tried to—Zek, get the money, would you?—is true, no
doubt he'll soon be back up here at the head of an army.
The question is, *why* did you sell that information to the
Venn?"

"Isn't it obvious?" She ignored Zek's outstretched hand
and batted mud off her cape, outrage and fear evident in
the twitches of her shoulders, the jiggles of the flesh at her
jawline. "The only ones strong enough to fight the
Marlovans are the Venn."

Zek turned to Mardric, who made another lazy gesture
as he said, "Yes. And if they win, what do we get? Yet another overlord."

She extended her finger, saw it tremble, and tucked her
hand into her armpit. "He promised that the Venn only
want to defend against the Marlovans before they get
strong enough to launch northward and attack across the
sea. We've all experienced how no one can stop them. It
takes military people to stop military people. The Venn live
far away, so once they've made sure their borders are safe,
they will go home again. I was *promised.*"

Mardric sighed. "Are you really that stupid, or is it just
greed? Did you really believe that any great power comes
to your home soil just to defend you? Without a price?"

The rain had lifted abruptly, leaving the sound of drips
and splashes outside. At a gesture from Mardric, Zek left
to do a perimeter prowl—something Rider and the guild
mistress had neglected, he thinking she had, and she having relaxed her vigilance years ago.

The guild mistress, authority for so many years—an authority she had worked hard for, and gloried in to the extent that she hadn't used her own name for twenty-five of
those years—turned increasingly horrified eyes from
Mardric to the ironmonger. The latter would not meet her
gaze.

Mardric smiled. "You have been selling information to

the Venn for years now. I finally tracked you down. Thought it was a pirate spy at first, or a Marlovan, or a thief or dockside rat, but it was *you*. I didn't believe it. Had to hear it myself. Not thirdhand, not even secondhand. You, an Olaran. With pride of rank." His teeth showed on the last word.

"I told you why. It's so they can fight the Marlovans." Her voice shook.

"They are going to fight the Marlovans anyway." Mardric waved a hand to and fro. "If you had told us about your spy contact five years ago—two years ago—we could have included you in the plans."

"You talked of big plans, but no one ever saw anything actually happen," she retorted. "I'm not the only one who thought you were just a cheat, taking good money as an excuse to seduce those foreign boys and girls if they were young and pretty enough. I remember *quite* well, your going on about how pretty those pirates were!" She made a spitting motion to the side.

"Spying," Mardric said softly, "means idle listening, waiting, talking in order to provoke more talk. It means smiling. It means flattering. The fun part is the seducing. My sister," he said gently, "has a very important one by the prick right now." He waited, and when she didn't answer, he went on, "And then, all at once, when they are relaxed, you strike." He dusted his fingertips together. "Gone!" And dropped his hands. "Your information is correct. We had an eyewitness see Elgar on the royal road. He followed him to their city and stayed long enough to see their mighty garrison preparing for imminent departure. My witness just reached us yesterday."

Zek came back in, stamping mud off his feet. Mardric looked a question. Zek waggled his hands.

The guild mistress tried to find a response—disbelief—attack—anything to fend off the sense of menace exuding from these men she'd considered fools.

"Elgar the Fox is, no doubt, on his way with an army," Mardric said. "He will fight the Venn, and who knows, maybe he'll even win, because the Venn are not going to

get any help from Olarans or Idayagans. We're here to
make sure of that."

"I don't understand," she whispered.

"Because you decided what was best for everyone."
Mardric's voice sharpened. "You worked against us as well
as against the Marlovans. Well, just so you know. The
Marlovans can win, but it won't do them much good because their king will be dead. He has no heir, which means
that if they beat the Venn they'll be fighting each other for
their throne. And they'll leave us alone. If they don't win,
they'll fight the Venn to the last man, and still leave us
alone."

She said poisonously, "Who is going to kill their king?
You?"

"I've had plenty of practice of late, dispatching all the
Venn spies I just mentioned. Spies we spent years locating.
And watching. Talking to. Seducing, even, until one day—
one night, actually—on the pillow, one let something slip:
the invasion everyone has talked about for years is happening right now."

She licked her dry lips. "But—"

Mardric lifted a hand, turned over. "Strange. We say 'he
has blood on his hands' but mine are clean. That is, blood
washes off. Blood causes guilt only when you feel guilty. I
have to confess I really enjoyed killing those spies. Most
put up a good fight. I like that in a relationship." His teeth
showed. "Even one as brief as these must be."

"I did everything I did to protect Lindeth," she stated,
now trembling all over, and no longer trying to hide it.

Zek and the ironmonger had stepped closer, both with
closed faces, neither letting his gaze touch hers.

"No, you did everything you did to make money, and
gain secret authority, and oh, yes, to strike at the
Marlovans, but your strike wasn't an important enough
reason for you to share information with us. Well, despite
you, the Venn are no longer getting help. From anyone."
He glanced away, grimacing. "And while I enjoy fighting
tough young men who've been trained to kill people like

me—" His hand flicked out in a gesture that she didn't understand until the garrote had whipped round her skinny old neck.

The ironmonger's muscles bunched.

"—I take no pleasure in killing old women," Mardric finished on a sigh. "Thanks, Retham. I hated her, she hated me, a good cordial hate can make these things bearable. But—"

He shook his head as the ironmonger laid the old woman's lifeless body down. She was unexpectedly light, little more than skin and bone.

"Leave them for the Marlovans to find," Mardric said, grimacing again. Despite his words, the impact was a gut churning with remorse, and even a little thrill of fear.

You lived your daily life, you even fought for it occasionally, while managing to forget the fact that you could not Disappear anyone whose death you participated in.

You could go away. You could lie about it. But you could only Disappear someone you had not killed and even then, you could not do it alone, but would be compelled to talk about it unless the Disappearance was before witnesses. Rules so inescapable that some lands formed rituals around them.

That argued for . . . *someone* watching, did it not? Except who? And why those rules, though those three could leave, and— "No one will believe she could stab him, so let's spread the word the Marlovans did it."

Zek rubbed his jaw. That was his specialty: rumors. "But the Marlovans always account for one another," he said. "I mean, they always know where they are. Patrols and the like."

"True. But we don't care what they think. People believe what they want to believe. Spread the rumor. Get the Marlovans tied up in a useless investigation of their own people, and by the time they sort it out, everyone in Lindeth will believe that the Marlovans killed an old woman for her money. Got her belt pouch? Good. Same with this fellow."

Mardric picked up his cloak, holding it by a finger, where it gently swung. "Meanwhile, I have an army to find." He smiled. "The nice thing about armies is, they can't hide."

Mardric tossed the bag of coins on his hand, then pulled his cloak on and they departed. The dead were left to the sound of slowing drips, and the widening light from the sun reappearing between parting clouds.

Chapter Twenty-five

Jeje: here's a puzzle for you. Elsewhere in the world servants are invisible. Runners here are not. Nor are they the same as servants. They serve but they do a lot of things. More things than I could have imagined. For example, there are two whose entire job is to see to it that all orders are written in an order book, and then copied in the book for the watch commander. One night, one day. So you could say that at least two Runners know as much about what's going on as the king and all his captains.

Yet I am invisible to Evred. He has never spoken to me, and if I cross his field of vision, he looks through me. Strange, how people look at one and see . . . what they want to see. Fox hated me on sight. Evred—some sort of cousin to Fox, if I am untangling these ballads and old stories right—finds me invisible. Odd, that.

Enough about me, are you saying? (I can almost hear your voice. Maybe if I throw myself onto the ground and put a knife to my neck, I will be able to imagine you here.) I guess I can say these things to you because I can't to Inda. I like practicing with him in the mornings. It's like a bout with Fox, but without the extra bruises. And I have been welcomed among the Runners, which means they give me things to do if I join

*them at their fire: fletching arrows, making the
"smacker" arrows they use in practice. Sewing.*

*Here is my life: up at dawn, fight with Inda with two
knives behind our tents. (I've a tent to myself. Respect
or rejection? You tell me, Jeje.) Then he goes to drill the
men while the Runners and the boys training to be
Runners get tents down, loaded, and the animals ready.
The wagons leave first. A day of riding—me with the
Runners, or behind Inda in case he wants something,
which he never does. You know how he is: never notices
what he's wearing until I muscle him into something
new, and he eats what's put in front of him.*

*When we stop, it's time for the horse drills while Inda
watches and the wagons catch up and make camp. Then
campfire. Inda inevitably sits with Evred, and they talk
history, or about their boyhood days. Signi (who is
under guard, though they keep a respectful distance)
sits in silence during the latter, but converses politely on
the former. My only use is to knead Inda's shoulder and
arm when it gives him trouble. I said I am invisible to
Evred. Signi gets cold looks if she's not aware, though
if he has to speak to her, he's very formal, distant, courteous.*

*She and I don't speak. Inda and I only talk when we
practice. Inda frets about how slow we are, about the
muddy roads. (Need I mention it rains every night?
Thought not.)*

The first balmy night of the journey, the Marlovans'
drums rattled and tumbled in the familiar galloping
rhythms as voices rose, fell, shouted in strict cadence, then
broke into laughter.

Tau was still ambivalent about staying with this army in
which he had no real place. The reason for the ambivalence
was not only unspoken but unacknowledged. Tau sensed
danger—and unfortunately, he had discovered a taste for
danger these past few years.

Maybe it was time to find out if he had a place with Inda.

His chance arrived unexpectedly when the halt signal sounded while the sun was relatively high in the sky.

The usual orderly commotion followed, orders shouted up and down the disintegrating lines for horses to be led to the river. Evred rode back to talk to the lower-ranking captains.

Tau edged his mount up to Inda's. The horses lipped each another, snorting and tossing their heads.

"What's wrong?" Tau asked. "Why did we stop?"

Inda turned his way, brown eyes wide. "It's not a stop, it's a halt. We're going to break out the battle flags and ride properly into Cherry-Stripe's."

"Properly? What does that mean?"

Inda rubbed the old scar on his jaw, long gone white. "When we flashed sails, what did it mean?"

"To whom? To Kodl, it meant showing off. Strut," Tau said.

"Did *you* think it was just strut?"

"Not when we did it. We were making a gesture."

"Right." Inda snorted a laugh. "So riding in at the gallop, banners flying, is kind of like we flash sails all at once, instead of sensibly handling 'em as needed. Every man here—though they won't say it out loud—wants to be seen riding in like in the ballads, banners snapping, horns blaring. And if—" His smile thinned. "Whether we win or lose, in the local songs, anyway, that ride will be a whole verse." He tipped his chin eastward. "Lay you any wager someone will be on the walls, paper in hand, to scribble down who was where in line, how many banners, and what color horse the king rode."

Tau laughed.

Inda turned his palms up. "Everybody likes to strut. Just depends on how they do it."

"We" flash sails. So Inda had not completely turned his back on his years at sea.

Tau did a quick scan. Evred was still talking to a group of captains. Signi had taken her mount to the riverside, thoughtfully keeping within view of her discreet guards as always. He was alone with Inda, with as much privacy as they were ever going to get. "Inda, do you need me along on this endeavor of yours?"

Inda slewed around, shading his eyes from the sun resting just above the hazy western hills at the edge of the vast plain. "Tau," he said, exasperated. "I never could figure out what you were thinking. Do you want to stay, or not?"

"All things considered, I do. But I could as well do something else. Anything else. If you don't see a purpose for me being here." That wasn't getting him anywhere. "What do you want from me, Inda?"

Inda's eyes were honey-colored in the strong late afternoon light. His body shifted as his horse thrust her weight from one hip to the other, but his gaze stayed steady, his smile fading. "What I want . . . I got what I want. I think I got what I want. I got my name back," Inda said, low as a breath. "Seemed easy as that. But right after it, Evred hands me this war to command. To him it makes sense—he never expected to be king. Didn't train for it. But it happened, so he got to work. So I come home and he gives me a command I didn't train for. But he expects me to get right to work, just like he did."

"As a trade for your name?"

Inda flapped a hand as though shooing a troublesome insect. "No, no, I said it wrong. It's a *part* of my name, see? With my name comes all the duties. D'you see it?"

"I think I do." Indeed, Tau felt that a window had opened where he'd once perceived a wall.

"Good. Because I just don't understand people and their reasons for doing things, not the way you do. I can sometimes hear things in their voices . . ." Inda made a quick, warding motion. "Here they come. Something's happening. Look, Tau, I don't blame Jeje for scouting off. I wouldn't blame you if you did. But if you will, stay. I need you to help me see . . . what I might miss."

Like your king's passion for you? His hatred for your mage, and his inability to see me?

Evred and the others stopped just a few paces away, all peering toward the east.

If I tell you any of those things, all I can see as a result is life becoming far more uncomfortable for all four of us. Because Jeje is right, the only one who has the power to change things is your king. And he cannot change the Venn coming, or how vexed you are at traveling only during daylight, or how ill-trained you think these men compared to our independents on the sea.

Tau then asked a question he hadn't meant to: "Do you think you can win?"

Inda snorted his breath out again. "I don't know." He flicked a glance at the others, still busy. "Tau, we're too slow. That is, not just the travel. We should be in the field every day, dawn to dusk, training. Like the Venn were last year. Not doing it just at dawn and sundown, while in between mud, rain, and bad wagons slow us down." He snapped his fingers against his thigh, then said, "We *have* to get to the pass." He lifted his hand, rough-palmed, scarred on top.

"I don't suppose they will be surprised that we found out about their surprise attack," Tau said, watching as Evred laid his horse's rein against its neck. The animal turned; all the horses turned.

Inda's expression was rarely sardonic, which made it the more startling when he lifted a brow and quirked the corners of his mouth. "Durasnir isn't that stupid." He swiped his hand over his head. "He'll expect us to be as surprised as we expected Marshig to be."

He spoke low-voiced; Tau had a heartbeat's time to see the king's hazel gaze flick between Inda and himself before they were surrounded by the group, including a scout, everyone talking at once. Inda and Tau picked out the words "east road . . . riders . . . horns."

"Here they come," Evred said.

In the distance a horn blared a single triplet, over and over.

"Riders!" a scout bellowed. And, "Khani-Vayir pennons!"

Everyone relaxed, joking and hoots rising on all sides as a neat column of riders trotted into the outskirts of the camp, the men dividing off toward the riverside, and only the leader and his banner-carrier and First Runner proceeding down the center divide toward the crimson-and-gold Montrei-Vayir banners behind the command group.

Signi and Tau gazed in curiosity at the young man in command. He was tall, his sloping shoulders powerfully built. His face was jowly, making him look much older than he was, his long horsetail was a thick, wiry mud-brown, his expression dour.

Inda flung himself off his mount, laughing hoarsely. He stumbled to a halt at the man's stirrup, sending pebbles skittering as he yelled "Noddy! It's *you!*"

"What brings you?" Evred's concern made him sharp.

Noddy's voice was chest-deep, and even less expressive than his face. "Got a message from Cherry-Stripe that Inda was back. My cousin thought you might need a few extra mouths to feed." A thumb hooked over his shoulder indicated his column—a wing of eighty-one men, with Noddy—busy dismounting and expanding the horse picket. "We're here to make sure you don't get lost on your way up north, where he's drawing more in."

Noddy Toraca slipped off his horse. His heavy face split in a white-toothed grin as he pounded Inda on the shoulder, and for a moment he looked like his twenty-one years. "Welcome back," he added.

"I didn't think I'd get to see you for weeks," Inda exclaimed in delight. "All we need is Cassad and Cama—"

Noddy said, "They were half a day off, last Galloper I got. We might catch them at the gates if we bustle. I think Cherry-Stripe wrote to every Jarl, threatening, begging, and pleading for us to be detached to ride as your Sier Danas commanders." He turned his chin toward Evred. "With a suitable force. Said you had to move fast."

Inda yipped, and tired as he was, executed a few steps of the war sword dance, to general laughter.

He didn't even hear it. "Come! We ride as soon as they finish watering the horses. You must need something to wet your throat. I know I do." He turned his head, still laughing. "Signi! This here's Noddy Turtle. I told you about him . . ."

The cook wagon's Runners had set up ensorcelled buckets of clean water for anyone who wanted it, and better drink for those of high command. Tau started toward the cook wagon. He'd decided he could, for once, do a Runner's job, and fetch the refreshments, only to discover Vedrid's pale head in the crowd, ten paces in front of him.

Chapter Twenty-six

THEY began their heroic gallop well enough, riding at a trot down the last winding part of the road, harnesses and mail jingling. In the distance they could just make out the tops of the castle towers through the mizzle, dense gray squares against the solid gray sky.

Evred was about to signal the change in formation for a gallop when the unseen outriders sent up a whirtler. A heartbeat later came the long, thrilling falls of a war charge from the direction of the eastern road just beyond a low hill covered with wandering sheep.

Evred's force halted, hearing the rumbling thud of horse hooves; it was too wet for dust to rise.

Noddy said to Evred, "War charge?"

"That has to be Rat Cassad." Evred was trying not to laugh. It was strictly against all the traditions, the rules they'd been brought up to respect: you did not blow a war charge until your cavalry was about to change from the trot to the gallop into battle.

Around the hill, as the sheep retreated sending up baas of reproach, bounced the snapping pennons of yellow and white.

"He wants to leave us eating his mud," Noddy observed mournfully.

"He can eat ours," Inda said, and kicked his horse into a trot.

Still laughing silently, Evred put up a gauntleted hand, held up two fingers, and pointed. The column picked up the pace, with a bit of frisky bunching and sidling here and there, summarily reined in hard.

They heard a faint cry on the wind and Cassad's force sprang to the gallop.

As did Inda. Evred and the others were a heartbeat behind.

So the triumphant ride turned into a mad dash to see who got to the main gates first, while Marlo-Vayir Riders crowded the walls, whooping and yipping as they watched the race, and laying bets on who'd get in first.

Everyone reached the gate at about the same time, the sodden, mud-splashed war banners almost indistinguishable from one another. For a time there was a confusion of horses, mud-imprinted coats, swinging horsetails (animal and human) as everyone laughed and yelled at once.

Inda's mood soared. "Rat? That you?" he shouted, catching sight of a sharp-chinned face with a buck-toothed grin and a high brow.

"My brother said better to fight Venn up here than at home!"

"Cama! There can't be another one-eyed Tvei!"

"Only one I know of," Noddy said, his flat tone implying "just as well."

Tall, martial Cama grinned, looking more piratical than the pirates with that black eye patch, boot knives, and two swords—one across his back and one in the saddle sheath.

Rat Cassad leaned around Cama to peer at Signi as he whispered, "*That* the Venn mage? Thought she'd be bigger'n we are."

Cama made motions to shut up, but Inda said, "Dag Signi."

Obvious to them all was the pride in his voice, the lift to his chin; Rat couldn't think of anything to say to a Venn, much less a mage.

Evred said, "Let's go."

They wheeled their horses and rode in side-by-side, shooting questions back and forth.

Inside the court waited yet another huge force, which was Cherry-Stripe's own surprise. The consequence was a tight-packed, milling crowd of men and horses, as Cherry-Stripe gripped Inda, yelling into his face, "I've got Riders from us, and from Tlennen, and some dragoons from the Sindans!"

They dismounted, all talking at once. From his post at Evred's shoulder, Vedrid swept his gaze over the crowd, his fine pale hair, almost all escaped from its inadequate clasp, flying about his face. He lifted his eyes. Ah, there in the window above was Fnor, making a hand signal to her women on guard duty.

She scanned the court and spotted him at once. They smiled the quick, inadvertent grin of lovers who'd parted amicably. Their teenage passion had entertained three clans while it lasted.

Inda shouldered past his friends and dodged around the horses to Signi's side, drawing her protectively against him.

The kindness of the gesture and the scintillation of Inda's ghost—brighter than Signi had ever seen him—caused her throat to tighten. How could Inda not see? Yet he was oblivious as he exchanged jokes with his friends. They talked over her head, or around her, or across her, always with that loud, raucous laughter that hurt Signi's ears. They all looked alike, these strong young men, their sun-brown skin flushed, mouths wide in toothy grins, their voices like the bark of hounds on fox-scent. How happy they were! *On the other side of the strait, if the long march west is over, the men of the Hilda are without doubt just as happy, just as wild.*

Even with her shoulder tucked under Inda's and her hip jammed against his, she was isolated, in spirit and in time, if not in the physical sense. The pitiable ghost was even more isolated, and yet shone so brightly.

But Mran and Fnor had not forgotten Signi, and Mran soon appeared, her childishly small form deftly slipping between the men.

"Dag Signi." She touched Signi's offered hands. "Fnor sent me to fetch you, if you'd like to join us."

"Very much. I thank you."

Relieved, Inda relinquished her into Mran's care, his attention promptly claimed by his old friends, who strove to outtalk one another. Rat glimpsed his sister, gave her a lazy wave, but went right back to trying to shout down Cherry-Stripe.

"Fnor's getting a good meal together," Mran began, then stopped, halted by none other than the king himself.

It was adroitly done. Already her brother, her beloved Cama, Inda, and the others were lost in a gathering crowd of captains and Runners, all full of questions. The last thing visible was Cherry-Stripe's right hand gesticulating, and then he too was gone behind a wall of broad gray-covered backs bisected by sun-bleached horsetails.

That left a space just long enough for Mran to realize that the King's Runners at four points around them were there by intent.

She gazed up into Evred-Harvaldar's face, wondering what could possibly have happened between the time Signi and Inda left and now to make Dag Signi into a prisoner.

"She will be with us," Mran said quickly, in Marlovan, which Signi hadn't understood on her previous visit.

Evred regarded Mran Cassad, who was exactly as small and thin as she'd been when he met her years ago. She had the triangular face of most Cassads, sharper than most, her upper lip short and catlike, her eyes wide-spaced and enormous as one hand slipped protectively around the Venn mage's arm.

The women had obviously taken to Dag Signi, despite her Venn origins. Part of the women's secret quest to learn magic? Mran was Hadand's friend, and had once thanked him for civilizing Cherry-Stripe . . .

He held out his hand: over to you.

Mran twitched a faint smile, then bore Signi away.

The two women left the noisy courtyard behind. The hubbub gradually diminished to the sound of their own footsteps in the cool stone hallway, as they climbed the east tower stairs to the women's side of the castle.

Mran stopped on the landing. Watery sunlight slanted

through the old arched arrow slit, highlighting the texture of the honeycomb weave in the undyed linen of her robe. "Why are you a prisoner?" she asked. "What happened?"

Signi let out her breath slowly. What thread of truth could she offer Mran without creating more knots than skein? "Your king has treated me honorably." Which was true. When Evred could not avoid speaking to her, he was scrupulously polite, and his Runners, surely hand-picked, kept a respectful distance in guarding her. "But he cannot forget I am Venn, and mage." *And he does not know that I could leave at any time. Nor will he know, unless I choose to leave—but then I could never come back.*

"Inda hasn't said anything?" Mran asked, doubt creasing her broad forehead.

"He either does not notice, or pretends not to notice. I think . . ." Signi considered. "I think the guards' presence is a compromise between Inda and Evred. Neither of them has to say anything to the other, one not trusting me, the other demanding trust. Because, you must see, they trust one another to the last degree."

"Signi, you are a good woman," Mran stated, echoing what Fnor had said after the previous visit. Mran did not add Fnor's subsequent comment, *Too good for that ill-mannered pirate boy they're all drooling over so disgustingly.* Fnor had been irritated to discover that Inda had not offered Baukid, the house's tailor, so much as a copper in vails for sitting up all night remaking Buck's old coat. Even after Cherry-Stripe had said reasonably, *Remember Inda's been overseas the last ten years. Everybody knows, no foreigner's got the least idea of proper custom.*

"It is my turn for a question," Signi said, making a gesture of appeal.

Mran had forgotten the strange way Signi moved. It was beautiful: she didn't walk, she glided. Even when she sat on a mat to eat it was like a dance, the way she arranged her clothes, the way she sat, even the way she arranged her feet. "Ask," she said.

Signi touched her fingertips in thanks. "Your family, the Cassads. You were here before the Marlovans came. It is said that they were seers, the old Cassadas. Seers of the world outside of that of humankind."

Mran leaned against the stones, arms crossed. Laughter ran through her body, made her fluting voice breathy as she said, "Way long ago. Then they got lazy. And so?" An ironic gesture toward the arrow slit. "And so we became Marlovans. Why do you ask?"

"Do you see ghosts?"

Mran pursed her lips. "I don't. But some in my family do. My grandfather, yes. And my poor third-cousin Kialen, who was supposed to marry Evred-Harvaldar. Hadand thinks she ended up living more in the ghost world than in ours. You can't really say she took her life, but more like took off her body the same way we take off a robe." She brushed her hands over her sleeves. "And you asked because?"

"Inda carries a ghost," Signi said softly. "And I think he might be from here. Or knows someone here: Dunrend? Hened Dunrend?"

Mran straightened up, her eyes wide, pupils enormous. "Yes. The Dunrends are connected to the Sindans. Hened was mated with the old Jarlan's niece. A Runner. She's here now, so she can take word back to the Jarlan about this gathering." She shook her head. "Never mind that. What are you asking, whether we should tell anyone?"

Signi touched her palms together. "Among the Venn, the seers are much honored. But among you?"

"There aren't what we call seers," Mran said. "In fact, you won't hear much about ghosts at all, thought a few do see them. Hadand's father does, by her account. Anyway we just don't talk about them. My grandmother thinks this is because Evred-Harvaldar's first ancestor, Anderle Montrei-Vayir, killed old Savarend Montredavan-An, who'd conquered us." She thumped her flat chest in a gesture of ironic humor. "And after that Anderle slowly went mad, because he couldn't sleep without seeing Savarend's ghost come into his room. Knife sticking out of its back and everything. Since then, people tend to think ghosts go with treachery, but they don't say it." Her brows snapped together. "Did Inda kill Hened?"

"No, no, Inda says Hened Dunrend died most honorably, defending him. Inda still grieves over his death."

Mran whistled softly, a fall of notes Signi recognized as the Marlovan Hymn to the Fallen. "I wouldn't tell anyone," she said finally. "It can't do anyone any good at all that I can see."

Signi bowed. "It shall be so."

"Well, come in and eat and drink and rest," Mran said practically, glad to move away. Silly as it was—she knew very well the mind took its burdens right along with the body's—she also knew that from now on, that landing was going to feel haunted.

The combined forces set out an orderly camp city on the hills beyond the castle gates and the captains squeezed into the Rider barracks inside. Anonymous in his blue coat, Tau walked among the hundreds of men—some barely eighteen, others closer to forty—who all seemed excited as boys though the word had spread they would be on the ride again come dawn.

With the added forces from the powerful eastern clans came wagonloads of supplies, which were sent on ahead. The remainder of the day was given over to repairing horseshoes, gear, and weapons that hadn't been completed during the hasty night's preparation in the royal city. The Marlo-Vayir forges would glow all night as the old Jarl's grizzled Randael, known to everyone as Uncle Scrapper, whisked tirelessly about the stables, overseeing everything.

The old Jarl, Hasta, stumped for a while beside his brother, both feeling the high glee absent since youth. Hasta reminded the older inhabitants of Cherry-Stripe, the way he kept chuckling at the honing of weapons, shoeing of horses descended from his magnificent studs, the loading of wagons with household supplies that would leave the castle scrambling.

Buck and Fnor also moved about ceaselessly, she overseeing the division of supplies and the preparation of food, he beyond the gates, aiding in the massive task of organizing vast numbers of people for the long push northward. The castle's resources were stripped pretty much right down to stone, but no one cared. They all felt the bright sun of history outlining themselves and their castle.

Evred moved like a ship through the roiling currents, people flowing around him, aware of his presence and trying not to show it as they worked. With him was Inda. The Sier Danas came and went, seeing to logistical details of their own.

When they'd seen everything, Evred signed to Vedrid, who in turn gathered his own staff with minute tilts of the head. Runners smoothly isolated Evred and Inda as they paced back toward the hall where the king was expected to preside at the meal being prepared.

"Well?" Evred said, stopping at the foot of the wide, shallow stairs before the Marlo-Vayir great hall.

"It's not enough," Inda admitted. "Not if we're going to split in order to cover both ends of the pass. The Venn had easily twice this number out on the Ymaran plain. Probably more."

Evred lifted his chin. "I'm going to send my orders to Ola-Vayir from here, now that I have an idea of what we need. I will command him to raise a full decade."

Inda whistled. He still had to get used to the idea that Sponge could send out a Runner to raise half the fighting men in the largest jarlate.

Evred said, "I don't trust him, which is why I waited. He tried his tricks on my grandfather, who was forced to grant him all of southern Olara, but it's only made him more greedy. I shall not give him more land."

"How will you get around that?" Inda asked.

"Two ways. First, I am sending one of my father's old Runners, someone Ola-Vayir cannot misunderstand or make demands of. Second, I'm going to reinforce him with Buck, who's known to be loyal to me. Under Buck's eye, he will not be so likely to look for ways to linger, or bargain for more concessions if he thinks I cannot do without his men."

Inda rocked gently back and forth, heel to toe. "So we'll have a force going up the coast, then, to Lindeth?"

"That's my idea. By the time we get our men up through the middle of the kingdom and bear west, he'll have had time to raise his force and travel, though a much shorter distance. It's actually Buck who's going to have to scramble." Evred gave a brief, somewhat bleak smile. "But I know he'll do it."

Evred glanced at a group of men hammering and sawing fifty paces away, making new wagons out of wood that had been set aside for something else. "I also decided we cannot risk leaving the harbors below Lindeth open, after what you told me. So I'm going to require the southern Jarls—including your father—to cover them."

That night they celebrated, drums rumbling inside and outside the castle. Tau wandered through the busy courts, the lamplit stables, and up onto the walls. From the sentry walks he gazed over the dark plains on which a starfield of fires glowed, most with silhouettes dancing around them, occasional shards of ruddy light glinting off swords in quick-flash beams. Clangs and clashes marked the galloping drum beats, and voices rose and fell, the cadenced words adding yet another counterpoint.

Bright as the courtyards were, the great hall was far brighter, lit not only by torches all along the walls, giving off stupefying heat, but by carefully hoarded glowglobes brought out with increasing rarity as the magic spells faded. The massive iron-reinforced doors stood open, light and heat spilling out. Tau breathed in the warm, thick air, smelling of the pine pitch used for the torches, spiced wine, food, and too many people. In the cleared space the same songs and dances as he'd seen outside were performed, the same kind of food eaten. He found it interesting that though here, as everywhere, humans divided into hierarchies, the concept of the courtier was unknown.

As in many of the castles Marlovans had taken from the

Iascans generations before, the Marlo-Vayirs had adopted tables and benches in the formal halls. Chairs were set at the high table. Like castles, tables, benches, and chairs seemed more civilized than the mats and small, folding tables of their plains-roaming days; there was a jumble of tables and chairs and stools of various sizes extending down the long walls of the room, leaving the open space in the middle for the dancers.

The old Jarl liked tables because his bad hip made sitting on the floor more difficult by the season. He sat at the head of the table now, relieved to rest his old bones on a cushioned chair.

Evred sat at the place of honor midway along the high table. At his right was Inda, watching the dancing, at his left big, blond Cherry-Stripe, and next to him sat lean Rat Cassad, cousin to Evred and Barend. Across from them sat Noddy, and at his left Cama of the eye patch and curling black hair.

They were in the middle of their meal as the harassed servants ran about.

Tau had refined his skills at serving courtiers when spying for Inda in Bren. As the companion of the most popular female entertainer, he'd overseen expensive parties every night for most of a year, and had discovered that people forgot your presence if you held a tray in your hand or poured drinks.

Tau joined the other Runners who, on the command of Vedrid, Captain of the Runners, reinforced the overburdened Marlo-Vayir servants. Vedrid himself was seeing to the preparations for the King's Runners being sent out that night.

Tau indicated with a gesture that he would take over serving wine to the high table, got a brief, grateful raised palm from the old Jarl's equally old runner, and so he kept the oddly-shaped Marlovan wine cups filled.

A song finished, three or four young Riders began a drum tattoo.

". . . the Gallop Dance, Cama!" a woman cried.

Came peered up at the gallery, flashed a rakish grin, ran

lightly down to pick a sword from the rack against the far
wall, then took his place among the young men gathering.
Tau enjoyed Cama's heedlessness as most of the females in
the room, at the floor tables and up above, tracked him as
unerringly as flowers follow the sun.

"What's that?" Inda bent forward, frowning at the new
sash round Cama's narrow waist, a sash made of white and
yellow silk.

Cassad colors, Inda thought, remembering his childhood
days when he'd had all the Jarl colors by heart. Cama was
a Tya-Vayir, but commanding a force of Cassad men, so he
wore their yellow. Inda was surprised that the sash had
been hastily embroidered over in the pale blue and dark
green of the Marlo-Vayirs.

Inda reached across Evred and poked Cherry-Stripe.
"Why's Cama got your colors on that Cassad sash?"

"Mran made that for him. Lover's token. Haugh!
Sometimes I wish we could marry who we wanted to
marry. It would make the bedroom arrangements ever so
much easier."

Noddy snorted. "But how could you afford a wedding
every half year? Or would it be four times a year?"

The laugh lines at the corners of Cherry-Stripe's eyes
were a young version of the same pattern in his father's
sun-browned face. "Can I help it if I fall in love a lot?" He
hooted. "Isn't it a laugh that the first one o' us to get ourselves a son is ugly ol' Noddy?"

The Sier Danas grinned at stolid Noddy. "You'd think,"
Cherry-Stripe went on, "that Flash would have fifty by
now. Buck would have a couple—he and Fnor are disgusting. But *Noddy*?"

A snort from Noddy. "You fools don't even know what
good sex is."

A howl of laughter.

Noddy sat back. "My boy'll be a great commander. As
well as handsome. See it already in him, the way he drools
in my face when I toss him."

Another howl, and everyone tried to talk the others
down with insults. Inda shut them out, trying to accustom

himself to the idea of Noddy tossing a baby in the air.
Noddy having a son. *Any* of them having a son. "What does
your boy look like?"

"Me." Noddy's deep voice warmed as he added, "Got
hair like a duck's butt, sticks up all over." He snorted a
laugh.

"—a wife you *could* bed," Cherry-Stripe bawled, and
everyone gave up trying to talk over him. Cherry-Stripe
waved his wine goblet outward toward the dancers. "Take
Cama, now. He's too good a man, doesn't deserve
Starand."

"He doesn't deserve that shit of a brother," Noddy
stated. "Didn't get Horsebutt by marriage."

"Horsebutt," Cherry-Stripe repeated, making a spitting
motion over his shoulder, as Tau leaned down and refilled
his wine cup. "He and his coward's excuses for not sending
any men! That's why Cama had to join up under Cassad."

"Coward's excuses?" Evred repeated.

His tone was one of neutral inquiry, but the others
straightened up, or rubbed jaws, or showed in little ways
that for just a moment they'd forgotten that their old
friend was the king. Cherry-Stripe sidled a look at Cama,
whirling on the dance floor, oblivious to the conversation.

"Better ask Buck," Cherry-Stripe said uneasily.

"I will." Evred understood their hesitation—though they
all hated Horsebutt, nobody wanted to be a snitch.

Evred turned his attention to the dancers, tapping out
the rhythm on the table, and gradually the others loosened
up, the talk and laughter becoming more natural, as Cassad
began pestering Inda for stories about pirate battles, and
every single time Inda mentioned some aspect of sailing,
Cherry-Stripe would howl, "What's that?" or cup his ear,
never tiring of the joke.

Eventually, Evred eased his chair back and sat with his
elbows on the rests, the wine cup between his hands. But he
did not drink from it, just observed his boyhood friends
over its broad brim, his face more relaxed than Tau had
ever seen it. For the first time he looked like the very
young man he was.

Would such things ever appear in the ballads? Of course they wouldn't. No one would remember the grizzled old Jarl, the firelight making his silver hair glint like barley beards at sunset, muttering as he pushed his plate away at last that he wished he could ride with them, but his hip wouldn't even let him sit a horse. "And it's not like I ever saw battle anyway, outside of that disgrace of Yvana-Vayir's winter before last. When the *old* king died, I was just out of the academy, doing my rounds on the royal castle walls."

The old king being the present king's grandfather.

Evred said, "You will be needed here."

The old Jarl was now alert. "What's that?"

Evred made a motion toward the room. "When the plates are cleared."

"Heh." The Jarl grinned. "A royal order, is it? And in my house. Heh." Wheezing with laughter, he lifted his wine cup in both hands, downing what remained there.

Tau silently refilled it, then stood behind the Jarl, where he could observe the king. Evred lounged in his wingback chair, profile against the dark wood, watching Inda talk and laugh as his long fingers toyed with the wide, shallow Marlovan wine cup.

Evred had not just been watching Inda, though his face was turned that way as his academy mates caught up on one another's news amid much joking and laughter. He watched the captains at the adjacent tables, he watched the interactions between the men dancing, and he chose exactly the right moment—just after the dishes were cleared away, as everyone began to chat. His father had left an unfinished testament to Evred's brother (who would never have read it, which was perhaps why it was unfinished), with many observations about kingship. One had been: *You, as king, will end the banquets. If you have news, get their attention as soon as their stomachs are full. Never when they're hungry, and never later, when they are too drunk to stand. If you don't have news, but have to make speeches full of praise for the reasons I've already discussed, wait until they're drunk. Whatever you say, they'll remember only their emotions and call your effort brilliant.*

And always, always, keep it short.

He stood up, lifted his cup in his hands, and gestured a salute toward the old Jarl of Marlo-Vayir as Buck was still outside supervising.

As soon as he lifted the cup the hubbub of voices was replaced by the *graunch* of wooden benches on the stone floor as all stood.

"At dawn we ride away to war," Evred said, and paused, because he knew the word *war* would raise a shout, and a full-throated, enthusiastic shout it was. Stone rang; some shoved fists into the air, others laughed.

"I call to defend the kingdom those whose trust and courage is the most proven. Taking his place with my Sier Danas at the lead of my army is your Randael, Landred-Dal Marlo-Vayir."

Cherry-Stripe flushed down to the collarbones at having his family name said out loud so unexpectedly. He grinned around in obvious pride.

Evred took in the drink-ruddy, triumphant faces, grins of anticipation, laughter, pleasure. "But I am also calling upon the Jarl of Marlo-Vayir, Aldren-Dal, to ride to the coast to reinforce our men there, in case the Venn bring ships to our shores." *Let any Venn spies assume that means he'll ride up and down the coast.*

Buck was still outside, monitoring his people and resources, both taxed to capacity by this enormous gathering. Everyone in the hall shouted, some drumming with spoon and knife handles on the tables.

Laughing, Cherry-Stripe knocked his chair over and ran from the hall to tell his brother the news. Cama leaped on the table, saluted Evred with his wine cup with such enthusiasm the wine sloshed to the table, bright as blood. "Evred-Harvaldar Sigun!" he shouted.

"Evred-Harvaldar Sigun!" the crowd roared as one.

Cama then turned with a flourish, his coat skirts flaring. "Indevan-Harskialdna Sigun!"

"Indevan-Harskialdna Sigun! Sier Danas Sigun!"

The shouts rang up the stones. Evred, smiling at last, saluted the room full of people, fist to heart.

Thump! Fists to hearts, which beat for joy, exhilaration, triumph.

Everyone then turned to his or her neighbor to exclaim, laugh, ask questions no one listened to. All except the old Jarl who sat back looking after his second son, his face grim—almost grief-stricken. He was proud, yes, but the prospect before him was not glory, not with both sons going off to war. The prospect was duty—and death.

Chapter Twenty-seven

Hadand: I arrived home last night. How strange it is that you shall read this the very day I write it. Assuming, that is, you find it right away—that you have time to go to your trunk and check the gold case, or wherever you will keep yours.

Whipstick's voice echoed up the walls outside Tdor's open windows, the men's responsive shout reverberating from the stone. Tdor leaned out to look down at Whipstick in the court. He wasn't smiling—he never did running drill—but she could see pleased anticipation in the way he strode back and forth, and she heard it in the men's enthusiastic responses to his shouts. They were happy, because they'd been ordered to the harbor to reinforce the dragoons already guarding it.

Happiness. She considered that, absently running the quill through her fingers. Should she write about how strange that was, happiness at the idea of being hacked to death, at hacking apart other men? But that was duty, so why shouldn't they enjoy it? Maybe she should write about how happy she was to be home. She liked the royal city, and seeing Hadand as queen, how well everything seemed to be going, how much the women admired her. But oh, small as her room was, worn as the castle furnishings were, it was so, so good to be *home*. But would Hadand misunderstand?

Of course the weather stayed cold and sodden the entire ride down, holding me up at bridges over swollen rivers, forcing us to ride around puddles the size of ponds. When did the skies clear? Yesterday. But it was only a day after I got your message about Evred's orders.

Another shout, followed by a confused clatter of horse hooves.

Fareas-Iofre was full of questions about Inda, but as soon as I told her about the orders, she said her questions could wait.

Tdor ran the feather over her ear. How long had it been since she'd thought Fareas-Iofre so cool, so calm, so free of the tangle of emotions that seemed to be confined to the young? Tdor poked the pen at a glob of dried ink (time to make some more) as she thought back to her childhood, and her comfortable conviction that adults didn't feel love when they got old. Only what, really, was "old"? Until just a couple of years ago, Tdor had never considered the fact that Fareas-Iofre had been younger than Tdor was now when she was taken away from the people she'd grown up with and told that she was going to marry a man twenty-five years her senior. And everyone had expected her to be pleased because that would make her a princess.

Your mother and Whipstick decided that the Adaluin will not be told about the Venn possibly attacking the western harbors. You must know by now—your mother said a Runner went north while I was coming south— that your father had one of those brain-spasms, and his right arm and leg don't work. They say he is not in pain, he dreams like in winter. So Whipstick will take the riders to our harbor to reinforce Captain Noth's dragoons.

Everyone in the castle is full of jokes about how Horsepiss Noth can deal single-handed with ten, twenty, thirty mere Venn.

She hesitated, the quill in the air. Should she add how uneasy it made her, thinking that the Venn were probably making the very same sorts of jokes, away up there somewhere to the north? A droplet formed at the end and she hastily tapped the quill against the side of the inkwell.

Before she could write more, Tdor's Runner entered. "The Iofre," Noren said, and Inda's mother walked in, looking thin and worn. But she'd been smiling since she heard that Inda had returned to his native soil at last.

I was stupid to think she never had feelings, Tdor thought. *I just never saw them. Because when she was sixteen and came here to marry the Adaluin, she hid her feelings behind duty.*

But she couldn't hide her yearning now.

"Willing hands everywhere," Fareas-Iofre said. "The men will be ready to ride out long before they can possibly be needed."

"Even Branid's hands are willing?" Tdor asked.

Fareas opened her palms. "Whipstick thinks your message from Inda acted on him as a threat."

Tdor protested, "It wasn't a threat. Inda just said, 'Tell him I'll talk to him when I get home.' Just like that. I didn't intend to misrepresent Inda's words." She smiled ruefully, more of a slight grimace than a smile. "I guess I'd make a bad Runner."

Fareas leaned her elbows on the broad stone windowsill, the diffuse light on her profile softening the lines in her face. "You know that what we say and what Branid hears have always been askew." Her mouth curled up at one corner, a rare expression. "He certainly heard a threat, even if neither you nor Inda intended him to. But then hasn't his life with his grandmother always been understood in terms of threat, bribery, and guilt?"

Tdor laid her pen over the inkwell. "I don't know how this will sound, but I feel bad now for how happy I was last night when you told me his grandmother was dead." *Finally*. She wouldn't say that word, even if they were both thinking it.

"There was no grief visible at her funeral fire, though we scrupulously saw to all the forms." No emotion in Fareas' voice either, but her entire body was expressive of relief. Inda's mother then glanced over her shoulder. "I see you are busy. I will wait to indulge my motherly questions."

"I only saw him the one day," Tdor said. "Half a day."

Fareas' pupils contracted as she breathed, "I have not seen him in nine years." Tdor had gained just enough life experience to perceive the almost frightening intensity of a mother's enduring hunger for her missing child. "Any little thing you tell me will be news."

Tdor obediently described Inda, what he'd said and done before riding out. Fareas listened, still with that unhidden hunger. This was a different sort of hunger than what Tdor had seen so briefly in Evred, but just as frightening, because it was so intense, expressed by a person who had always been as calm and cool as the lake.

Different kinds of love, different kinds of hunger? Tdor felt she was riding over a rickety bridge. "And then they rode off. But here, I am writing to Hadand. Would you like to add a letter? I can let her know Evred's order is being carried out, and you could ask her about Inda."

Fareas-Iofre rose, frowning at the gold case lying there on Tdor's plain wooden table, the intent focus of her brown eyes bringing Inda vividly to mind. "Are you very certain no one else will see what we write?"

"Dag Signi promised it would be so."

There was a brief pause, broken only by the flutter of birds nesting under the sentry-walk crenellation just overhead. "Do you trust her?" Inda's mother asked.

Do you trust someone who—no. Stupid ballads—"stole your beloved's heart" meant nothing but a claim to victimhood. Tdor's inward struggle was short; she'd fought the battle and won, and won it again during her long ride home. Lust, she could honestly attest to—the thought of Inda's splendid shoulders, his big, expressive hands. The way he laughed, a burr deep inside his chest: the Sartorans (as always) had a word for it, *fremitus.* Everything about Inda made her want to laugh, to cry, to sing, to hold him close enough to breathe his breath and feel his heart beat against hers.

That sudden fire inside—that was lust. *Hunger.*

Tdor said slowly, "I think I must trust her. Inda does, though Venn she be. If she is full of guile, it is the deepest guile ever known, deeper than any of us can see. And she will be living among us, I suspect, so it's better to assume good will." She burst out, "I don't know why we have marriage treaties anyway. Wouldn't it be better if we were like the Anaerani, where Joret is, where they can pick the person they marry?"

Fareas-Iofre had not moved from the window. She laid her hands flat on the sill. "The girls are finished with knife practice. Chelis tells me the streams and the river are down enough to send the girls out to collect feathers from the high-water debris."

Tdor was about to say, "And so?" when she realized the Iofre meant for *her* to give the order. She felt hot all over.

Fareas-Iofre regarded Tdor's red face, and interpreted her expression successfully. "Yes, your first order as future Iofre. And your next act should be to go downstairs and use the measuring string on the Rider who seems closest to Inda's size, because you need to begin on his wedding shirt. And so you should tell the men, because it will cheer them enormously to think about that during the weeks to come, when these high spirits fade away. As they must."

Tdor—always so capable—stood up, sat down, and picked up her quill, playing with it absently as she frowned.

Fareas said, "As for your question. I never told you girls why we make wedding treaties—or why, for that matter, we make wedding shirts. Events being what they were, I always felt the subject could wait."

In other words, while the heir to the throne was trampling treaties and tradition by chasing Joret all around the kingdom.

"True," Tdor said soberly.

"Easiest first. In the plains days, we know from songs that men used to weave bands in clan colors for the wife, and the wife for her husband. Those bands were treaty markers: no war between the clan, and to seal it they sent a daughter to the other family to be raised with the son, and eventually married to him."

"I knew that much," Tdor said.

"Well, just before we made the change to living in castles, one of Evred's foremothers made a shirt for her intended, who was also her lover. She made a shirt for love—she embroidered it all over with his house symbol, and various ballad images and so forth. Thus the shirt was better than a mere band for a treaty-wedding. So then it became a matter of derision for the men who didn't have wedding shirts, the implication being no one would have picked them if there hadn't been a treaty."

"I think I get it now," Tdor said. "Jealousy? Lovers and spouses competing? Because of the wedding-treaty system?"

Fareas opened her hands. "No matter what kind of system you have, there are inevitably going to be lovers and spouses competing. Meanwhile, the move to the castles changed almost everything. The bands went out of use. Men, living in castles now, lost their skills at campfire weaving. The bands in clan colors were also considered barbarian. Everyone wanted *written* clan-treaties. So on."

Tdor was ruining her pen. She laid it carefully down again.

"As for treaty marriages, surely you know by now that there is no way to put rules to love or attraction. Because nothing successfully controls it."

"No," Tdor breathed.

"So we try to lessen enmity between clans with the treaties, the promise that *your* children and *my* children will produce *our* children. And we hope that a boy and girl who grow up together will know one another well enough to have family love."

Tdor's lips parted. Then her eyes blanked: she was thinking of how Signi had observed her, as if for a sign of what her place might be in Inda's household. Just as there were stories about favorites who entered a house and began changing the furniture, as the saying went, there were others who (there were sayings for every situation, Tdor realized) who found snakes in their bed.

Tdor remembered Inda's and Signi's self-conscious care around her. How that hurt!

"I'll give the order," Tdor said, going to the door. As if that would leave those memories behind.

"And I shall write to Hadand. Thank you, my dear," Fareas-Iofre said.

Tdor fingered the neatly hemmed length of Castle Tenthen's best, fine-hackled, double-bucked linen, nearly smooth as silk and finer in substance: warp and weft both the same size yarn, made not into the formal tablet that they used for the house robes and tunics, but the honeycomb, only used for the best sheets and shirts.

She ran her hands along the fabric, wondering what she herself really knew of love. She thought: *To say that I am "in love" with Inda would make everyone laugh, for I had not seen him since we were small, and when we did meet again, it was for only a day.*

The ache in her throat had nothing to do with her lack of skill at embroidery. She knew her Runner, Noren, who was skilled with a needle, would show her how to embroider, and she knew that Inda would not complain if the result was not exactly deft.

No, she thought, glaring at the needle, at the basket of silken threads in their neat twists. *I have nothing to regret. Inda will never refuse to come to my bed. His dag will not make trouble in my home. That much I could see by the end of that shared meal. Everyone will be thoughtful of the others. Everyone will be kind. If Inda loves her forever, then . . . then there is more love in the world.*

She threaded the needle with the brightest red she could find, and shoved a few stitches through with such violence she pricked her thumb. She popped it into her mouth lest she stain the shirt no more than thirty heartbeats from beginning her task.

What hurts the most is that I do not know if he will come back. So I am going to make this shirt and believe he will return, she thought firmly, and set a straighter stitch. *I will carry it with me everywhere I go, and every person in Castle Tenthen will see Inda's wedding shirt, and they will know I expect him to come back. So here will be a sun, and then I'll make the Algara-Vayir owl, and then maybe a ship, if I can get someone to draw me a model of one . . . and every stitch is going to bring him closer to home.*

Chapter Twenty-eight

ABOUT the time that Tdor arrived home in Choraed Elgaer at the beginning of spring's first stretch of warm weather, far to the north Evred-Harvaldar's army slogged their way across the mired countryside under band after band of rain.

Jeje: I notice you did not answer. Did I put you to sleep? Would you rather have less of Taumad's inner tempests, and more of the ones he is traveling through? We have been crossing an ocean of grass. The road usually runs alongside rivers, except when it winds around low hills. People working in fields straighten up, down tools, watch us pass, some looking with longing, others wary. I wonder if there are some who, despite the snapping flags and these magnificent horses, go back to their hoeing thinking: better you than me!

Tau also rode past the old men who'd been seeing dashing cross-country riders all their lives, or had been among the dashers themselves.

Two old dragoon scouts sat in a boat on a placid lake, trying to fish, until the rumble of hooves sent the marsh birds flapping skyward, scolding raucously. The two eyed the ordered ranks who galloped up the road and splashed their way across the shallow end of the lake, enabling the horses to cool off and drink before they surged up the bank on the other side and vanished over the ridge.

"Montrei-Vayir pennons." One gnarled thumb hooked over a shoulder. "Tlennen's pup going north again. Think the Venn're coming at last?"

"I don't know about that, but what I do know is they're a damned nuisance," came the sour reply. "First good day we've had in two weeks, and what happens? Look at the lake, all gone to mud. It'll be tomorrow afore it settles, and the fish all hiding down at the bottom. We may's well give it up and paddle ashore."

There was one other watching them ride.

After leaving Lindeth Harbor, Skandar Mardric had traveled hard and fast in search of the Marlovan army. From a hilltop opposite the lake where the two old men were rowing to shore, he scanned the long line until he spied the snapping pennons behind the king.

He felt no triumph. That would come when he had ensured Idayago's freedom by ramming a knife between the red-haired king's ribs.

He studied the endless columns, tear-shaped shields hanging at saddles, bows slung, lances, staves, and spears in loose hands, steel blades winking when the sun did peep out.

Mardric rode along the hilltop, hidden by the trees, until he caught up with the leaders again. The king was easy to spot, just in front of two huge crimson flags. They did not hide him, for who would dare to attack now?

Not me, Mardric thought wryly. He laid rein to his horse's neck and trotted back to the town he'd just left.

He had even less chance of sneaking into a Marlovan camp than into one of their castles. But he'd learned while listening for news of the approaching army that the Marlovans sometimes broke ranks for supply runs.

During the next three weeks, as he rode an easy parallel course to the army, he watched Runners arrive early to arrange for fresh grain for the animals (despite their vigilance, they couldn't always keep theirs dry) and fresh food

for people. They were welcomed, smiling, because word
had spread that they always paid.

The ghost at Inda's shoulder was strongest when Inda
drilled, though nowhere as bright as it had been the night
they stopped at the Marlo-Vayir castle. Signi continued to
be amazed that Inda could not perceive it, but so it was.

The morning routine had changed. The Sier Danas were
invited to join Inda's and Tau's predawn practice. Cama
and Noddy were there every day, the latter pairing off in
turn with Evred, who had begun to join them.

As they crossed into Khani-Vayir, Cama began conducting the early morning training for the men. He also worked
evenings with Tau, who was always willing and had no
other duties. Cama had been practicing in secret since
Inda's first drill in the courtyard of the Marlo-Vayir castle
before he went to the royal city; Cama had expected Inda
to be impressed with Marlovan skill after his years among
pirates, and instead had been shocked to discover the reverse.

Cherry-Stripe had started out in racing spirits. The parts
he loved were riding daily up and down the columns, sitting at the king's campfire at night, and he especially loved
commanding attack forces in the evening war games.

He would have loved the prospect of war, had not Buck
taken him aside for a private talk the cold, rainy morning
they departed. They'd gone up to the wall in the old part of
the castle and, stolidly ignoring the cold rain, Buck had
said, "Don't think war is fun, despite all the songs and the
drum beating. I told you about the Ghael Hills."

"I know, I know," Cherry-Stripe had said. "Your first
thought is you need to pee, and your second is what's going
on? But don't you see, we've got Inda!"

Buck had glared eastward toward the faint grayish blur
in the clouds where the rising sun hid behind the horizon.
Then he grunted. "Yes. Take a squint at that face of his.
He's all over scars."

"Aw, that was just pirates."

"Maybe. Here's what I do know. Ghael Hills was near to being a massacre. None of us knew what we were doing. If Inda really does, you do what he tells you. Come home alive."

Cherry-Stripe felt the cold grip of doubt when he remembered that his brother had to ride to back up Ola-Vayir. "You too," he'd said.

The doubt did not stay away. His belief that Inda could do anything—including lead them brilliantly to victory—wavered hard their second day out. The men warmed up by fast ride-and-shoot lines back and forth past a target, but instead of the commands being called by Evred through the captains, Inda took over himself. Right out loud he asked the stupidest questions, like he didn't care who heard. And didn't the men within earshot smirk!

But Inda just rode around, Evred giving answers the boys had known by the time they were fifteen-year-old ponytails: yes, light cavalry was for harassing attacks, mostly arrows; no, they didn't carry lances or staffs; yes the heavies still used the snap-staff, but only against enemies with no shield. How long could a horse go on charge? How about charges uphill? Did horses hold a line when under a rain of real arrows?

Evred just answered the questions as if they were the smartest ones ever aired, but then Evred had always been that way: wooden-faced, serious—you never knew what he was thinking.

Once or twice Cherry-Stripe overheard mutters go through his own men—just too low for him to take notice of, they knew it and he knew it. But he also knew that tone, and if he hadn't, the muffled snickers would have made it clear it was a wisecrack.

After the second time he whispered to Noddy, "Why's Inda acting like a scrub?"

Noddy leaned forward to brush a hovering insect from his mount's twitching ear. "Because he is one," he said. *Idiot,* his flat tone implied.

Cherry-Stripe had known him too long to care about insults. "Scrub?"

"Just in our ways of doing things." He gestured impatiently. "Limits of horse, of men on ground. *Where* was he these past ten years, Cherry-Stripe? At the academy?"

The sarcasm was easy to shrug off. Cherry-Stripe pondered the fact that despite those scars and how tough Inda looked out there behind the tents, whirling around with no shield and steel in both hands, he wasn't a one-man army. Could he actually run a battle against anything but pirates? Cherry-Stripe kept himself busy, and when he couldn't ride or drill himself to exhaustion he drank to escape that question, which made it easier to sleep.

During these same long days of travel and practice, Evred had begun confining himself to answering questions. After a time, when Inda seemed not to be watching the sunset evolutions he'd expressly ordered, Evred could not resist asking, "What do you see?"

Sometimes Inda started, other times he'd turn his head and out would come a rapid stream of observations, often scarcely coherent. Following these headlong thoughts was like trying to swim down a rushing river.

At first, Inda's observations were not much different than those Evred and his academy mates had expressed when they began lance training.

"I get it," Inda exclaimed, one bright day a week northward, as the men rode wearily around and around in their own dust, their hands drenched with sweat inside their gauntlets, tendons in their right legs quivering after long practices pressing the lower end of the lance holster against the mount's side.

Cama and Rat were the opposing captains. They galloped up and down the line, shouting orders to bring the evolution to a close.

"I see why you train in circles with the damn lances," Inda said to Evred as Rat and Cama looked their way. Evred raised his fingers, and Cama signaled yet another evolution, riding with seeming tirelessness at the fore, lance steady, which kept mouths determinedly shut in the ranks behind him.

"You build strength." Inda watched Cama's skilled lead, his powerful arcs with the lance. "He can put that thing wherever he wants to." When the evolution ended, he lifted his voice. "Now I want to see a charge."

Cama raised his fist, divided them into lines with himself in the center.

"So . . . one of us might even have to lead the front lines of a charge, especially if we don't have dragoon lancers. If any of us can find ourselves in the front lines, then we all have to know what lancers can do."

Cama gave a curt nod to his signal man, the charge was blown. The horses knew that sound: they began to walk in line, then to trot, and on the next signal they galloped hard at Noddy's men two hundred paces away. The lancers locked down their heels, couched the lances with the back end in the holster, and tigged the shields held out by Noddy's men as they rode past. Then they play-fought as the second and third lines charged and joined the melee.

Inda almost fell off his horse, he leaned so far out, as if leaning would clear the dust.

"What do you see?" Evred asked again.

"The weakest part is just after the charge," Inda said, scowling at the ragged line of horses milling about. "Do they ever finish in line?"

"No. Oh, in demonstrations on the parade ground, sure. But not in battle, when enemies are shooting at you," Evred said. "It's why we have the second and third lines so tight after the first. Our horses hate strange, untrained horses. The Idayagans don't train their horses any better than they do their men. Our horses also hate dead bodies. In the real records, not in the herald reports meant for archives, I've found time after time that they always break and run. And the men, losing their order, lose sight of one another. It's why we never use anyone but experienced dragoons in the first and second lines, but third can be mixed dragoons and riders. If the first two hold the line during the fighting, the third does as well."

"The Venn use their heaviest men in front." Inda's eyes narrowed as he tried to see past the dust. "They make a wall, standing shield to shield."

But all he could make out were silhouettes: he had to listen for, and try to make sense of, the hoofbeats on the ground. Something you didn't worry about on the ocean.

"They had few horses, but those were big. The men wore full, heavy armor," Inda said. "The men on the ground get into these square formations, shield held to shield, spears out if they are flanked."

"As long as they don't have the spears out in front for the horses to run onto, our dragoons can break one of those," Evred predicted.

"Can we armor our chargers?"

"Yes. It slows them, but it works."

Inda rocked in the saddle. "So we can break those shield walls."

"In the records we could. We sweep around them, attack from two sides or more. There's nowhere for a square to march, so they break up and then it's every man for himself. That's why our ancestors stopped using that formation."

Inda exhaled, short and sharp. "I used fire ships like dragoons. No one else did," Inda added. "It seemed so obvious."

Evred said wryly, "Well, pirates are free that way."

Inda snapped his head around. "What do you mean? You said something like that before, once, I think, when we were talking about the Brotherhood battle, but we got sidetracked."

"We always get sidetracked," Evred retorted, laughing for a moment. "You were *pirates,* Inda. You took ships, you did not build them. So you never had to deal with the Sartoran Wood Guild, who—I assure you—has the power of the Magic Council behind them. We have to deal with them, lacking as we are in forests. And even if you have them, the Mage Council comes down hard on anyone who cuts down a forest—"

Inda looked amazed. "I knew that. Or, I once did. I even

remember where I sat when Mother told Tdor and me about the old days, when humans were nearly exterminated and magical balance and all that. But I don't know, I didn't think of it when on the seas."

"You were happily burning up some smaller country's entire year's allotment of wood," Evred explained, and then lifted his brows. "No one reminded you?"

Inda spread his hands. "Dhalshev of Freeport Harbor made a comment about Khanerenth's fleet growth once. How limited it was, I mean. But I thought it referred to the empty treasury after the war. Because the old king and his sisters didn't just run, they ran with a good deal of the kingdom's gold. I do know that they used to burn everyone's ship who'd fought on the other side as revenge." As he said it, Inda considered his time on the sea. He'd never thought about the building of ships. He'd been put in one, and when it was taken, he took whatever he needed from his enemies.

It was a hard realization, because beneath the temporizing of necessity, worthy goals, and the rest was the truth: he really had been a pirate in others' eyes.

Evred, watching carefully, sensed the direction of Inda's mood shift. "The biggest problem in the north has been this." He gestured toward the circling men. "Once the dragoons smash through the enemy front line, they give chase, which has drawn our second and third lines behind them, and the lines usually break. That hasn't mattered much because the Idayagans always gave way, and then our men went into a frenzy of chase-and-strike before we got them back under command. I don't think the same will happen with the Venn."

"Right." Inda's head jerked up. "So let's put the captains in the second line, then."

"What?" Evred's horse shied. "But we've never—"

Inda jerked impatiently. "Tradition that can't be changed, or that won't be changed?"

Evred did not answer. Instead, he beckoned Cherry-Stripe and Cama over. Then opened his hand to Inda.

Inda said, "Try commanding from the second line. Most

experienced dragoons in the first line. See if you can keep
'em tight that way. I want all the smackers shot at the first
and second lines, and the 'Venn' are to ride wild."

Cherry-Stripe waited for someone else to say it was a
crazy idea—captains didn't hide in the second row—but
Cama fingered his bad eye under his patch, looked around,
at the horses, the ground, and then grunted. "Good notions.
Let's do it."

They pushed northward into Khani-Vayir, where true to
his word, Nadran Khani-Vayir, Noddy's cousin, sent them
men as reinforcements, wagons of dry grain, and sacks of
spring vegetables. Not long after they were grounded for
three days under pounding rain, and Evred had them out
riding evolutions signaled by a single dripping pennant.

The men were furious, but silently so, because all the
Sier Danas were right there among them, the king and his
temporary Harskialdna as well, everyone equally sodden,
mud-smeared, and cold.

A last line of reinforcements and supplies caught up
with them, having encountered each other on the road and
combined. They were sent by the Jarl of Hali-Vayir and by
Horsebutt Tya-Vayir; Evred met the latter's Runner in silence, listening expressionlessly to Horsebutt's message of
flattery and loyalty. At the end, he said only, "Inform the
Jarl that I appreciate the spirit of his message. So much so
that he is chosen for the honor of hosting the triumph
when we return."

Inda listened to that in mild amazement. Return? Appreciation? *Horsebutt?* But from the Runner's attitude, he
recognized that a lot more had been conveyed—and understood—than Inda had perceived.

Well, asking about that could wait till after the battle.
Assuming they survived, triumphant or not.

> *Jeje: I wish you would send me just a single line
> telling me why you will not answer. Is the silence my*

answer? We did not part in anger. Have you lost your golden case, and I am sending these thoughts of mine into the wind between worlds? Well, as there is no one else to say many of these things to, I might as well keep writing. It's comforting (even if only my imagination) to think of you reading my words, rather than hearing them rattling around in my head.

So, I forget how many days it's been. Each is so much like the last. We've pushed northward toward Ola-Vayir, once the southern reach of Olara. Your ancestors lived here, did they not? The afternoon games have improved. Inda sets us different battle-situations, more interesting ones. The men thought themselves tough before, but now they are beginning to shape like our pirate fighters under Fox's eye. And they game with the same enthusiasm as we did. Inda told me this morning (as he threw me over his shoulder into a patch of nettles) that he thinks he's finally learning to evaluate despite the dust. We never had dust problems on ships. Sun, yes. And smoke. Then there are the horses to consider—they are more like men. Limited stamina, have to eat. You will be surprised to discover that horses are not like ships.

The limitations of vision are different. At sea, you do not have dust, mud, grass, bushes, and milling men and animals to make evaluating movement difficult unless one can climb a convenient hill. Climbing a mast gives perspective in ship battles, unless there's fire or bad weather.

Evred watches the games, but he also watches the men. He seems to know how much he's asking of them, to drill before and after long rides every day. He announced today that when we reach the border of Ola-Vayir, where the great trade towns are built at road and river crossings, a night's liberty would go to the winners of Inda's mock battles.

Inda also told me (while sitting on my back with my arm bent behind me as he urged me to throw him off) that Evred handed down orders to the captains about giving no information beyond "We're going north to reinforce Idayago against the Venn." He obviously expects spies to be planted along our route. Certainly nothing is said to the men about the actual plans once we do reach the north, but then I don't think even Inda is sure about those. Not from the way he keeps looking at that map in Evred's tent, rocking back and forth, or else roaming around the camp, round and round. Rather like those questions in my head, beginning with, are you all right?

Far to the west, just past the jut of Toar called Land's End, a last hissing of rain departed quickly, the drops leaping back up from the deck of the *Sable*. The strengthening spring sun, regaining its southern height, shone under the fleeing clouds, lighting up the drops with crystal fire.

Eflis and her crew ignored this moment of beauty. They were too busy cleaning the deck and repairing the damage after this last fight.

Eflis swept the deck, pleased with the speed of repairs. They wouldn't have to slosh down the forecastle where the pirates had tried to board, as the rain was scouring away the last of the blood, a rose-colored flow down the sides and into the sea.

She stepped into the cabin, where Sparrow was about to turn in, having stayed awake through a day and a night.

"It worked again," she crowed. "Weren't we fast? Think Fox was impressed?"

"Nothing impresses that soul-ripper," Sparrow muttered, flinging her wet clothes to the deck and climbing into the hammock. "He expected us to be there, and we were there. End of conversation."

But Eflis' mood was not to be doused. "Quick as a fiddle, right down the middle." She chortled. "Naughty pirates, too greedy to have sense. That's a beautiful trysail, too, if on the narrow side. Hold'll be small. But Tcholan will love it, just like you always love your first ship. Seems right it was his and Dasta's plan, ha ha!"

Dasta had created that wounded ship ruse not long after

Eflis and her fleet of schooners had joined the supposed Elgar the Fox. In those days, he, Tcholan, and Gillor had been trading off wearing black clothing like Fox. Eflis still found it hilarious, that one woman and two men as different as Dasta and Tcholan could have fooled everyone— and still there was another layer to the ruse, because in those days Elgar the Fox wasn't Fox at all, but Inda.

Who was now gone. Her smile turned pensive.

Sparrow, watching through heavy eyelids, misinterpreted and said, "You going to do it this time?"

It. Eflis made a comical face. "I'd better."

Sparrow said, "It's none too soon. Before she affects the rest of the crew."

Eflis turned on her. "I don't suppose you would—"

Sparrow gave a hoarse chuckle. More of a gloat. "You're the captain, my dear."

"And you're a stinker for laughing," Eflis said, bent, kissed the tip of Sparrow's nose, then left her to her well-earned slumber.

She walked through the ship to the forward crew quarters, where the mids and lower mates bunked. Mostly empty, except for one wounded young fellow, and two from Sparrow's watch who'd been dismissed from cleanup, as they'd served four watches in a row. And then fought.

Eflis handed out praise where deserved, helped shift a barrel here, held a hammer for a moment there. But she kept moving until she reached the hatch to the aft portion of the hold—and then backed up as a furtive face topped by wild (and dry) honey-colored curls peered round. Then up. The eyes rounding in dismay.

Nugget was caught flat. No excuses this time of being somewhere else, covered for by her sympathetic mates. Nugget had definitely abandoned her battle station, had gone down to hide, and there'd been no chance yet to concoct a story.

"Right," Eflis said. "It's time for a talk, Nugget."

The captain did not lower her voice. Forward in the hold, above, there were quiet rustles and slaps of feet on deck as crewmates dropped what they were doing and listened.

Nugget hooked her arm more firmly round the rung of the ladder she'd been sneaking up, and said wistfully, "Right here?"

Eflis crossed her arms. She was tall, fair-haired and blue-eyed, good-natured—not the sort you'd expect to find a-pirating, but that was where circumstance had placed her. She had found a way to become a privateer. And she was going to keep that place.

"Why not right here, among the crew who protected you while you didn't do your share to protect them?"

Nugget's large, pretty, wide-spaced eyes lowered. Eflis fought the instinct to feel pity, suspecting that if Nugget had been born plain as a walnut, there wouldn't be nearly the impulse to sympathy on everyone else's part. "I can't," she said, lips pale and drawn. "I just can't."

"Right," Eflis said again, not wanting to argue with poor Nugget, who it seemed was fast becoming better at being poor Nugget than being a crew member. But she'd apparently been a kind of mascot to Inda, whose rep among the older crew members was still so strong it was more like legend.

So Eflis just said, "Unfortunately, after this fight, I have to shift my watch bill about. You've got to go back to the *Death*. I just don't have room on *Sable* for everybody who wants to be here."

"But Fox hates me," Nugget protested. And, in a lower voice, "I hate *him*."

Eflis felt that burst of sympathy again, but did not give it voice. Fox did absolutely nothing to make himself liked by the crew, but she had to admit that within his clearly stated rules, he was fair.

He would be fair to Nugget—within those rules.

"You can ask someone on free watch to row you over," she said.

Chapter Twenty-nine

INDA bent over his food, deaf to the fireside talk. He had been staring at Evred's map so often he could pretty much draw it himself, but there was something he knew he wasn't seeing. He hated that uneasy sense of meaning just out of reach. Maybe if he thought about something else, he could catch it . . .

To his friends, it was like boyhood again, Inda hunched at the plank tables in the academy mess hall, his body present, his mind galloping off somewhere distant. They never paid him any heed when he did that.

But during a pause, just as Cherry-Stripe tossed back some wine, Inda jerked his chin up, looked vaguely around, and asked, "What's a claphair?"

Cherry-Stripe spewed wine into the fire, which hissed and steamed. Rat uttered a coarse "Hah!" Cama thumped Cherry-Stripe, who was now coughing and laughing. Evred did not react.

Noddy handed his empty plate to his young Runner, who bore it off to dunk it in the magic buckets at the cook tent. "Horsetail slang," he said matter-of-factly. "Original meaning: in the baths, when your hair gets caught between your butt cheeks as you're getting out."

Inda smacked his hands on his knees. "But why didn't I ever hear it? Tanrid never said it at home. I'd remember.

Don't *you* remember, how we'd strut around using horse-tails' slang? And anything about butts had us laughing our-selves sick."

Cherry-Stripe snickered. His sense of humor hadn't changed much since those days. Rat flashed the sharp-edged Cassad grin.

Noddy gave a faint, one-shoulder shrug. "Has several meanings."

Cama muttered roughly, "You can look to my brother for that. Before Horsebutt got there, it also meant sporting in the baths. Which's why your brother didn't say it in front of you at home—we were all still in smocks before you left."

Inda had been frowning, but now his brow cleared. "In the *academy* baths? When did you have time?" He remembered being hustled in and out of the stone pools, the splash fights, shoving, soap flung around, towel-cracking at your butt if you weren't wary, scrambling into your clothes (and having to unknot your socks, and finding out who did it so you could get suitable revenge later), then running to the barracks for callover, your short hair wet and dripping nastily down inside your collar. You wouldn't think anyone would feel the least urge for sex *there*.

"When you're seventeen and you wake up with saddle-wood, you find the time. And anyplace is good. Especially for Flash," Cama added, and they all chuckled.

"Flash?" Inda asked, remembering the grubby boy with wild brown hair, a lopsided grin, and a taste for scrapping out behind the barracks. Flash never walked, always ran.

The others laughed. "Flash liked everybody," Rat explained. "And he always seemed to be able to find a place. He was first for most of the girls over in the queen's train-ing, we kept hearing. I don't know how he even got near them, rules being what they were."

"Nobody ever said no to Flash," Cherry-Stripe said. "He had you laughing too hard."

"He was the first for most of us, too," Rat said, hands open. "So it followed we'd practice on one another until they finally gave us liberty and we could get to the Heat Street girls."

"I didn't," Noddy commented. "You lot were too ugly."

Crows of scorn and guffaws rose.

"Ugly?" Cherry-Stripe hooked an arm round Cama's neck and jerked him close for a smacking kiss but his pooched lips met Cama's hairy, muscular forearm, snapped up in a block.

"Ech." Cama shoved him away and adjusted his eye patch as everyone hooted at Cherry-Stripe.

Who turned his palm Cama's way. "The girls insist Cama's the prettiest of us boys. Even one-eyed. Almost as handsome as me—"

When the pungent commentary died down Inda said, "So, what, Horsebutt went after people? They didn't go after *him.*"

"Nah." Cherry-Stripe flicked up the back of his hand toward the general direction of Tya-Vayir. "He changed the meaning again. Called anyone who got promotion a claphair. Came to mean a lick. Worse. Sort who'd spread 'em in order to get something."

"It was mostly aimed at my brother's Sier Danas after they got to go north without having to put in their two years of guard duty, and when they returned there was still no duty, just riding around the kingdom with my brother," Evred said.

"Buck says they would rather have had guard duty." Cherry-Stripe chortled. "Even stall-wanding."

"True," Rat put in. "Very true. My brother told me they were bored sodden and had to put up with his temper. Two *years.*"

Cherry-Stripe went on, "By the time the Harskialdna pulled us out of the horsetails and sent us home, that word was in everyone's mouths down to the littlest boys. They didn't have any idea what it meant."

"My brother," Cama's voice was rough with old anger, "can step out of the baths into clean clothes and boots, walk onto a clean floor, and still track shit prints all over before he leaves."

"Someone called you a claphair, eh?" Noddy asked Inda, who turned his palms up.

"Doesn't matter. They can say whatever they want. Long as they obey orders when it counts. Anyway I don't think I was supposed to overhear," Inda added, then tipped his head, considering. "Though I could be underestimating 'em." He grinned. "I don't blame 'em. I know what it had to look like, spending those first weeks doing academy exercises again and again while I was just watching." He flicked his fingers out, and the conversation turned to other things.

While the camp settled in to enjoy itself for the night, far to the northeast, on the extreme western end of the strait on Drael, Fleet Commander Hyarl Durasnir stood on the captain's deck of *Cormorant,* Prince Rajnir's royal flagship, in his most formal battle dress, the polished copper torc of a Hyarl at his neck—a very rare sight. Another rare sight was the three beaten-gold bands around his right arm that signified the Stalna, the Commander. The gold winked and gleamed as he swept his glass over his fleet, all as close in as they dared, anchored down as steady as possible.

Contrasted against the white beach, lines of men were silhouetted, each with his dunnage at his side. Weapons polished, helms glinting in the moonlight as the strong northern wind rippled hair and tunics. Men of the Hilda, the army, and men of the Drenga, the armed sea warriors, their rivalry buried in common cause. It would inevitably surface later but Durasnir had found that they fought harder, each trying to outdo the other. Good.

The tide had just turned. The anchor cables no longer strained to keep the ships from crashing on the shore but had eased to a vertical line. The ships were already loaded with supplies. The flat-bottomed troop boats were neatly lined on the sand, awaiting men and horses.

All was ready. Restday wine and bread had been shared before the call to line up, as always on the eve of battle. Even the wind was ready, blowing steadily from their homeland, warm from the sun climbing toward its highest arc of the year here in the south.

They waited only the prince's word.

Under powerful glowglobes hung from the mastheads— so the army could see him—Rajnir stood just before the whipstaff, his armor glinting silvery-blue, except for the rich gold of the Tree of Ydrasal gilding his chest plate. He wore his winged helm, which he hadn't touched since that appalling sea battle ten years ago. His neck was bare of the silver torc of heirship, the more noticeable for its absence.

Everyone who saw that bare throat wanted to be the one to win it back for him: his success was their success, and theirs was his.

Flanking him were the ubiquitous Erama Krona, fully armed as they always were when away from the prince's quarters, though Rajnir would never be within a day's journey of any fighting.

Rajnir breathed deeply, his countenance proud and joyous as he surveyed his invasion force, ready at last.

Their readiness was somewhat of a fiction, but it was one they all participated in. Durasnir's long experience had taught him that last-moment scramblings and surreptitious tidyings were inevitable, no matter how long the plans, or how carefully executed. But each knew his unfinished tasks, and would see to them on board.

It was a necessary fiction, and not just for the king's ears far away, or for the prince's sight. They all needed it. They were going to war; many were going to death. They would be kept busy in the tight quarters on board the transport ships as they crossed the strait.

At the prince's shoulder Dag Erkric waited, the wind tangling his silver hair, the grooves in his face deepened by the harsh light of the glowglobe hanging just above him.

"Hyarl my commander." Rajnir lifted his voice. "Let us depart."

The horns gave long, weird blats, reminding Durasnir of the cry of some of the bigger sea creatures up in northern waters, to be drowned out by a roar rose from shore:

"Victory to the Venn!
Victory to the prince!
Honor to Ydrasal, nine times nine!"

They began to move, men to boats, boats to ships.

Chapter Thirty

TAU and Inda had been watching the sky, sniffing the air, frowning at the quality of the light for several days.

It seemed remarkable to them that none of the Marlovans noticed anything, but then they themselves weren't certain that they'd felt that shift of the wind from one side of the world to the other. Neither said anything, wanting independent corroboration.

Everyone knew that air currents played over land from every direction, sometimes coming from all directions during a single storm. In some places, and seasons, there would be breezes from one direction in the mornings, then the air stilled in the heat of the day to flow in from over the water at sundown.

But the big, steady winds that drove cloud bands over the oceans, those were unmistakable to those used to the ways of the sea.

What Inda could not determine was whether the strait lay under the summer winds as well. Mindful of Evred's order to keep silent about the beacons, he scanned the mountaintops as soon as they appeared, hazy and indistinct, on the horizon.

The third morning when they met for practice, as Inda was working his right arm to loosen the stiffness that he couldn't seem to avoid, Tau said, "Do you feel the wind change?"

And instead of a mild yes or no while they continued on down to a good, flat, grassy spot away from the command tents, Inda stilled and drew in a long breath that Tau heard in the quiet summer air. "Third day I've been sure of it." He shook his head, and to Tau's surprise, loped back, stopping outside Evred's tent.

"Sponge," Inda said softly.

"Inda?" came an immediate answer, with no trace of sleep.

"I think—that is, we're pretty sure. The wind's changed."

Evred was silent so long Tau wondered if the king had been asleep after all, except that Inda stood so still, his head slightly bowed. And what Evred finally said was, "I understand. Thank you."

Understand what? The quality of the silence had changed, though Tau could not define how. But Inda's manner, Evred's long pause before speaking, it was as if some great, invisible burden had passed from one to the other.

Keeping his questions to himself by now had become habitual, so Tau paced beside Inda until they reached the riverbank. They were alone. The Sier Danas had gone back to leading their own men in morning drill. It was too late to learn a new form, better to hone the old, they'd decided. All except Cama, who practiced both forms when he could get someone to partner him. But mornings he drilled his men, his single eye merciless. The Cassads had given Cama their dragoons, and Cama was determined to shape them to Horsepiss Noth's standards. Better, if he could.

Inda and Tau began the swings and twists of warm-up. Dawn was just beginning to color the east blue. Inda felt Tau's question more than he saw it. Tau seldom spoke in front of the others anymore, and even when he did, Evred never noticed. It was strange, but Inda hadn't pursued it. Evred was too much like Fox that way, in his reactions to people. Those two weren't just silent, they seemed to wear their silence like clothing.

Inda considered this particular one of Evred's military secrets. Surely he could tell Tau. Signi was also discreet—

Inda suspected she knew secrets far deeper and more world-important than anything he could even think of—but he wouldn't burden her with things that would affect this coming battle against her countrymen. He sometimes wondered why she was still here. He knew she could do a spell and vanish any time she wished. When she spoke, she always made him see and think far outside himself, and outside of war. He was grateful for her presence, though the thought of her being by when they and the Venn met made him uneasy.

Later, later.

"Tau." He already had Tau's attention as they moved, struck, tumbled on the long summer grass, whirled, struck again. But saying his name somehow made the subject more important without his having to say so. "Tau. There is a back-up plan. Was. Is. I think he's going to have to signal it, because we're just not fast enough. We can't risk being too late."

"Back-up plan? Signal? I take it you do not mean the flags. Or even Runners," Tau added, indicating his own blue coat lying neatly on the bank—then striking a double blow toward jaw and gut.

Inda's hands blurred as he blocked, feinted, grappled Tau, and threw him to the grass. "Remember that locket thing Evred showed us at dinner in the royal city?" A puff, a grunt, and they rolled to their feet and began circling. "Evred told me recently he wears one. Barend's up at the north end of the pass, with Flash Arveas, and he has another one, Nightingale—Noddy's brother—the third."

Tau found it amazing, almost absurd that these powerful Marlovans were confined to tiny love lockets for communication. If the stakes hadn't been so terrible, he would have laughed.

Unaware of his reaction, Inda tried a couple of feints, then went on. "Evred is probably writing orders to Barend right now. With the winds changed here, we have to figure maybe the winds are changing up in the strait as well. I wish we knew how widespread the wind changes were."

Tau shrugged, though Inda's comment had been to the

air, and not to him. He whirled and swept Inda's feet, but as Inda fell he twisted, snaked an arm around Tau's ankle, and yanked.

"So anyway—" A fast exchange of light blows, Tau pinned Inda, but Inda heaved with enormous strength and Tau somersaulted away before Inda could catch him. "—anyway, the Venn could be launching any time. To stop them in case they get to the pass before we do, well, Flash is going to bring down a mountain onto the road."

"A *mountain*?" Tau repeated, and Inda dropped on him.

When Tau slapped the grass, Inda let him up. "The side of one, anyway. The Venn won't be able to come over the pass until they take this castle squatting across the entrance. Evred says the castle is almost as big as his in the royal city."

Tau whistled. Then ducked and caught Inda's wrist. Inda shifted his grip and pulled, which Tau anticipated. He was as quick as Fox that way. He matched Inda's moves until Inda shifted his feet, then twisted, whirling Inda off balance. Whomp! Inda hit the dust flat on his back, breathing hard. Tau dropped on him, knees holding Inda's arms down, thumbs at Inda's windpipe.

Tau leaned over him, his golden hair hanging down as he panted lightly. "That's good. Isn't it?"

Inda tapped out, and Tau dropped his hands. "For us," Inda said, a little hoarsely. "But with the road gone, there's no way from Idayago to here except through this ancient waterway tunnel somewhere under the castle. Our people have to hold the castle. Alone. Until we get there."

Tau's lips parted. "Shit." He pulled Inda to his feet.

Barend woke sticky and hot. His head ached. They'd drunk too much iced birch beer the night before, sitting on the battlements of Castle Andahi in hopes of a breeze, chattering as they drank. Barend had brought the recipe for birch beer from the east. There was plenty of black birch up here along the north. Add yeast to the distilled sap, some of the

precious sugar left from the days when Idayago still had
trade with the islands, and it had become more popular
than cranberry punch with the castle folk.

Especially with ice. That was the one good thing about
those blasted high mountains. The few trusted men who
traded off beacon-watch always brought down ice from the
heights, packed inside a number of closeweave bags. Since
there were traders who made a living doing that, it was
easy enough to lie and say they'd bought it, and thus they
could have iced punch almost every night.

Every night of this hot weather, because for ten days—
Barend had been counting—they'd woken up to a bright
blue sky and still, warm air. Was this the summer shift in
winds? What he needed was a good storm, straight out of
the northwest, then he could be certain. But no thunder
had wakened him.

What had? He scratched his head vigorously as he sat
up, and when the locket slid over his bare chest, he started.
The locket!

He thumbed the catch, and sure enough, there was a tiny
rolled piece of paper inside. First thing in the morning?
That could not be good.

He grimaced, fingering the paper open. The tiny letters
twinkled and danced. Reading had never come easy even
when he was young. He'd had some sympathy for his
cousin Aldren-Sierlaef, who couldn't make sense of letters
at all. That is, he'd had sympathy until the Sierlaef began
taking out his frustrations on Barend and Evred with his
fists.

Barend scowled at the tiny print, then reluctantly rolled
out of bed. He pulled on his pants and shirt and ran down
the hall, the stone cool on his bare feet, bursting into Flash's
bedroom directly downstairs from the old Jarl's suite.

There seemed to be two shapes under the tumbled
sheets. Of course Flash was in bed with someone—he always was in bed with someone. Even if he went to bed
alone, lovers came looking for him, Barend had learned.

He found Flash's dark hair on the pillow, and peered

past. With relief he recognized the pale yellow hair of Flash's wife, Ndand. She knew all the kingdom business.

"Flash," Barend said.

The two started, Ndand yawning as she pushed a braid out of her face. "Oooh, Barend. Why did you—" She yawned again, more fiercely. "—wake us up?"

"Don't you ever knock?" Flash added with mild injury.

"No. You'd not answer, and I'd have to come in anyway." Barend sat down on the bed. "Since it's just you two here, I can get you to read that."

Flash sat up abruptly when he saw the tiny paper in Barend's hand. His expression tightened as he angled it toward the weather-smoothed arched window, the shutters open wide to the balmy predawn air. "Evred says they've got summer over the mountain, and he's still a couple weeks outside of Ala Larkadhe. We've orders to smash the road, and Barend, you have to ride south to join him." He balled up the paper. "Last, Dad is to abandon the harbors and pull everyone back to defend this castle."

The three had spent far too much time speculating and calculating distances, especially in the past few days. The truth was, if the Venn came first, with or without the road collapsed, they would be the only ones defending the entire north shore of Idayago.

Ndand was the first to move, jumping out of bed and whirling her cotton robe round her slight, hard body. "I'll order the horses and supplies for your Runners, Flash."

Flash dropped his hands to his knees. "Dad and the others should have been here by now."

"Well, they aren't." Barend flung out his empty hands. "So let's send the rest of our Runners to every castle. All at the same time. Faster than just one fellow stopping everywhere along the way."

"Good." Flash grinned. "Past time to bustle Dad along." Flash reassured himself with laughter. His wily old father was probably presiding over the destruction of every dock and siege weapon used to fling stones at pirate ships. And he'd want to do it at all three harbors, then maybe even set up some traps and pitfalls. He'd love that, but such things did take time.

Ndand whisked herself through the narrow door on the other side of the room that led directly down to the baths.

Flash flung a towel round his hips without bothering with any clothing. The smell of old, wet stone and the caress of relatively cool air touched their moist flesh as they followed Ndand into the bath passage. They could hear her light voice calling to her Runners in the women's baths as they took the turn to the men's side.

"Timing could be better," Flash said.

Barend had been thinking the same thing. He'd thought it a good idea at the time to let Dewlap Arveas take Barend's men—who had been assigned to patrol and defend the pass—in addition to his own castle guard. Many hands made work go faster, and the hostile Idayagans at Ghael always cooperated more when presented with a show of strength.

Dewlap Arveas might just be just a day or two away, delayed by the weather. The spring rains had been intense this year, and some of the bridges, destroyed in a fruitless effort to halt the Marlovans years ago, had yet to be replaced. Men would be needed to help lash boats together to make floating bridges.

If so, the Runners would turn around and come back.

Barend, Flash, and Ndand bathed fast, dressed, and grabbed biscuits to eat on the way to the day's tasks. Despite the steadily increasing heat, Flash's dark hair was still hanging down his back in damp tangles when he went to seek his mother.

She was in the office she and the Jarl shared, poring over sketched-on pieces of paper. He leaned down to get a look at what appeared to be design drawings of the castle itself and its jumble of outbuildings before his mother said crossly, "Don't get your crumbs on the—"

The door banged open, and nine-year-old Kethadrend raced in, sun-touched brown hair lifting, his pale eyes—typical for the Arveases—wide in his flushed brown face.

"Everyone is running around like a stick in a hive! Are

the Venn coming?" He hopped from one foot to the other, his dusty toes leaving prints on his mother's prize woven carpet. "Are they, Flash? Are they? Shall I get my bow?"

To Keth's surprise, his brother, who always laughed, knuckled the top of his head lightly, then he knelt down so they were face-to-face. Keth didn't remember ever seeing Flash so owl-eyed, and his skinny shoulders hunched up.

"Look, Keth." Flash's mouth smiled, but his eyes didn't.

Keth's shoulders hunched tighter to his ears.

"I know how tough you are. And how ready you are for the academy come next spring."

"Yeah." Keth eyed his brother warily, knowing that when grown-ups looked serious and said nice things, something bad was sure to be snapping right on the heels of all that sweet talk.

"Would you . . . like to ride with Barend over the mountain and help the king? I'll wager anything you'd be the youngest boy there."

Keth's eyes widened with joy, then narrowed into wariness. "You don't want me here."

Flash turned to his mother, who took the boy's twitching shoulders in her strong, rough hands. "Keth," she said calmly. "We're about to let you in on a secret. Everyone will know by nightfall, or maybe tomorrow—we're not sure—but in the meantime, we're going about it quiet. We have to smash the road. The Venn are coming, and the king might not be able to get here before they do."

"What about Dad?" Keth looked from one face to the other as he put together the clues. "You mean we'll face the Venn *alone*?"

"Maybe," Flash admitted. Then at the distress in his brother's face, he added, "But Dad might very well get back in time."

Keth swelled with joy. "Let me get my bow. I'll fight 'em. You'll see."

"Wouldn't you like to go help the king?"

The boy wavered, then scowled. "Is Gdir going?" Naming his ten-year-old betrothed.

Flash looked unhappily at the Jarlan, who said, "I'm

talking to all the mothers, including your aunt. Anyone
under twelve might be going."

"I'm not if they aren't," Keth pronounced. "I think you
want to get rid of me, cause you don't think I can fight!"

"I know you can fight," the Jarlan said gruffly, the last
word wavering. Then she cleared her throat. "I *know* you
can fight. But I would rather you get a chance to grow before you have to."

Keth's upper lip lengthened, then trembled. "You don't
think we can win, is that it?"

"Even a castle as tough as this won't withstand the entire Venn army, Keth." Flash tried to speak easily, but the
words were not easy ones. "Though we'll do our best. And
we know the king is coming as fast as he can."

Keth jerked free of his mother's grasp. "You think we're
cowards. I'll show you. And so will Gdir and Hal and Han,
you'll see!" He dashed out, his voice breaking on the last
word.

"I'm sorry, Mother." Flash got to his feet, looking shame-
faced. "I made a mess of that."

She swept her palm downward, her gray braids falling
forward. "Don't you see? He doesn't want to show us he's
scared. So he gets mad. Not at the Venn yet, they're too distant. So he has to get mad at us."

"I hope you're right." Flash sent his breath out in a rush.
"Should we force the young ones to go over the pass?"

Liet-Jarlan brushed her hands over her papers, thinking
hard.

Her life had been like a gallop over mountains. At first,
everything was laid out straight before them. Liet was the
second daughter of the Tlens' primary family, unexpected
in the sense that there'd been no treaty plans for a second
daughter. But she'd been born a girl instead of a boy so the
family had sent her to the Arveases, as they were the premier Rider family, the boys being consistently picked for
king's dragoons. Liet had grown up with Dewlap, had been
sent to the queen's training in case she was the head wife
of any future garrison. That had worked so well that she'd
made a treaty with one of her own guardswomen to take

any daughter she had if Liet had a boy. And so it had come to pass, and Ndand came to them at two. And when Dewlap got promoted, she brought along several girl-cousins and their families, all guards except for little Gdir, daughter of the primary Tlen family.

A big family, tight-bonded. All fighters. The Arveases and their Tlen kin were tough! Tougher than Vayirs . . . except now they *were* Vayirs in all but name, and now they might actually be fighting right down to the last child, just like they'd bragged . . .

She shook her head hard. "I'll talk to the others, but I don't think so. I don't think a woman here—or a man— would fight the better knowing their children left 'em angry. And we don't know if the king will win even if he does come."

"He could send them all to the royal city."

"True. I would like that. Knowing they were safe." The Jarlan's voice roughened on the last word. She swallowed—he heard it—and compressed her lips. Then said, "Though that would mean the king would have to be sending them south with people he needs here. I don't know . . . maybe it was a mistake to train them young to think tough. They're all going to insist on staying."

"There's tough and there's crazy. Our ancestors only took the boys on raids after thirteen or fourteen or so." Flash grinned. "Rat Cassad used to comb every ballad he could find, trying to discover an excuse for us to get out of the academy early and come north here to fight pirates."

The Jarlan's smile faded. "And here we all are."

"Here we all are." Flash felt inexplicably sad. Despite all the talk about glory and honor and duty, he loved his life without the threat of war.

She sensed it in his sober downward glance, and said in her training voice, "In those old days, there were raids on the camps. That meant the defenders were the women and children. We all had to be tough, or we wouldn't have survived."

Flash lifted his hand, his palm up, fingers expressive of a regret he couldn't put into words.

The Jarlan snorted. "I know what I'll do. I'll send the smallest ones up into some of the cliff caves. Maybe that's a good compromise. But one thing's for certain—we'd better get to it." She smacked her hand on the papers. "And if things come to the worst possible, we'll have plenty to do here."

Flash finally realized the papers at hand weren't just a random stack of reports. "What have you got there, Mother?"

"Sabotage," she said grimly. "Ndand and I have been working on these plans for weeks. Ever since Barend brought the news the Venn were coming, and the king thought they'd land here first. We've never had enough people here to defend the north, and it's plain we're not going to, even when your father gets back with Barend's men."

Flash breathed, "You're going to sabotage the castle?"

"And the entrance to the tunnel. If the Venn reach us first, we want to make certain it takes them as long as possible to get through us and find the tunnel to the pass."

As long as possible. Flash's regret tightened his throat.

The Jarlan studied her son. "You go collapse your mountain. We'll start as soon as the dust clears. No one will have time to worry because we'll be too busy."

Flash's personal courage was unquestioned—proven—but she could see how disturbed he was. Yet he could not deny the necessity.

She made herself laugh, and was surprised at how convincing it sounded, though her heartbeat drummed in her ears. "While you're playing with your mountain, keep your eye on the blue horizon for those sails. If you see 'em, you get that beacon lit. I intend to have some fine gifts waiting for any Venn who show up before the king."

Chapter Thirty-one

ON Restday, Evred-Harvaldar and his army passed the last town before their road would begin the long curve along the base of the highland. Another week would find them joining the Great Northern Road, which zigged its way up the deceptively gentle slope toward the distant, hazy mountains, and Ala Larkadhe.

Another week if the punishing heat let up. Despite the threats awaiting them, they could not gallop in this still, heated air.

Before dawn the runners-in-training were up, leading the animals to water. The air was already hot by the time they rode out.

By midmorning the horses were foam-flecked and drooping, and some of the men leaned on their animals' necks, dizzy from the heat. After three separate requests for water breaks for the mounts, Evred called an early halt within a short distance of the market town.

"We will make up the time with a night march as soon as the weather breaks," he said, and the Sier Danas agreed with unhidden relief.

When the signal to camp reverberated off the gentle hills just beyond the bend in the river, Evred said, "Since it's Restday, and we've camped early, we'll have contact fighting competition. The winner gets a night's liberty. After you fight the winner," he added, palm toward Inda.

Cherry-Stripe yipped, echoed by Rat. Those within hearing passed the word outward.

"With weapons," Evred added. "Both knives."

"I only do that with Tau," Inda protested.

Evred dismounted. He smiled. "I think the time has come for everyone to see what your style of fighting can do."

The subvocal commentary of those listening made a low, intense hubbub. Everyone had been hearing about Inda's fighting style with two knives—like the women's Odni— and a few had seen it from a distance while patrolling the inner perimeter at dawn.

Odni was defense, not offense. Women did not ride into battle, did not wield swords, so what use was there in fighting a war with two knives, except to look tough? You'd look stupid, dropping your shield! Well, maybe it made sense for pirates—maybe they didn't have shields on boats, but one knife had always been good enough for Father and Grandfather, hoola-hoola-hoola . . .

Cama thumped Inda's shoulder. "Time to show 'em." His husky voice rasped. "Time to show 'em."

Ripples of interest ran through the ranks, and then word splashed back that this market town had not one but two pleasure houses. Liberty, everyone knew, extended until riding time the next morning. If you wanted to be in the saddle all day after being up (with all the various meanings of up) all night, that was your business.

"I tell you what I want, and that's to see what a Marlovan pirate offers by way of a fight—one knife or two," a man said as he led his mount to the horse picket, to general agreement.

Tau overheard that as he rode by on his way to the Runners' area. He got brief looks, some disinterested, one or two speculative. By now everyone knew that, though the would-be Harskialdna's Runner would willingly tell how Indevan-Laef had gotten those gold hoops with rubies in his ears, would describe pirate fights and pleasures in as much detail as you wanted—he'd even tell you what a theater was if you asked—he was even more closed mouthed about the person of Indevan-Laef than was the king.

Tau reached Inda's tent first to discover a small gathering of the runners-in-training. These boys would one day be the King's Runners, who would serve the king in dealing with important affairs. The youngest in the army, they did not go to the academy. They were all from jarl or King's Rider families, mostly cousins or third sons, and were trained separately.

"Let us give him his gear," begged a young Khani-Vayir cousin.

"We need the practice," declared husky young Goatkick Noth, who hoped to be Runner to the king's dragoon commander one day. Younger brother of Flatfoot Noth, he was the oldest of the runners-in-training, and the others had been teasing him over the past week or two after he'd begun sprouting a beard. He'd had to ride into a market town with the supply run so he could find a healer to do the beard spell. His face still tingled faintly, which caused him to rub his jaw—a gesture the others regarded as pure swagger.

On Tau's wave of permission, the youngest boy, a weedy fourteen-year-old, plunged his hand into Inda's seabag and pulled out Inda's war gear, all wrapped in cloth. First was a fighting sword, disappointingly like the ones everyone carried, and not the expected pirate blade all crusted over with blood and jewels. Then there was Inda's second set of knives in wrist sheaths, and last, two bulky packages.

"Here, what's that?" asked a Tlennen cousin, impatiently shaking free the much-patched cloth around one heavy object. "Ow!" He dropped the thing, and stuck a bleeding finger into his mouth. "What *is* that?"

"It's a wrist guard," the fourth said, poking at the article in question.

They gazed in doubtful silence. Wrist guards were customarily only given to horsetails, or those who had attained full growth—wearing them too young, said current wisdom, made your wrists depend on them too soon and thus not strengthen. Wrist guards were usually worked

with house devices or martial designs. This worn object
with its dark stains (that *must* be pirate blood!) was not or-
namented whatsoever, instead had a crosspiece as a palm
guard (maybe pirates didn't wear gauntlets?), and worked
into the back of it were slightly hooked sharp blades.
Barbs.

A shadow at the tent flap caused them all to look up
guiltily.

"What are you doing?" Inda asked, suppressing the urge
to laugh. There were times he felt downright *old,* though
these boys were only three, maybe five years his junior. A
few years in age, and two or three lifetimes, it sometimes
seemed, in experience.

"We wanted to get your weapons for you," said the Tlennen boy. "Runner Taumad gave us permission."

Inda sent Tau a wry look, to be answered with a rueful
shrug.

"But what is that?" asked Goatkick, knuckling his chin
with one hand, and pointing with the other.

"Wrist guard," Inda stated, looking surprised.

"But it's *barbed.* Do you, well, use it as a weapon?" one
of the boys asked. "Isn't it for bracing your wrist in lance
work?"

"And why only one like it?" asked another, as he care-
lessly rewrapped it in the patched cloth. "This other one is
more like ours."

"Here, be careful with that," Inda warned, and the boys
all looked in confusion at the ragged cloth. "That's my
fighting shirt," Inda explained, amused at their various attempts to hide disgust and revulsion.

That worn, patched old thing?

"There are no laces," Tlennen pointed out.

"No. Why get someone's point tangled in 'em and stran-
gle me?"

"No chain mail?" the youngest asked. All of them were
now somewhat subdued.

Inda had untied his stained green sash and dropped it to
the bedroll, then began unbuttoning his coat. "You don't
want to fall overboard in mail. You'd sink and drown."

"So you don't use any shielding at *all*?"

"Some do. I never did. Slows me up." He indicated the wrist guard. "As for that, when I was on my first ship, my wrist broke." He flexed his right hand. "I don't think it ever healed right. It hurts in battle, always the first thing to go. I lose my grip with that hand, after a time. So I better be able to use the back, see? But it's also stiff, and shortens my range of movement, which is why I wear a regular one on the left."

Tlennen pointed toward the barbed one. "Are those bloodstains on it?"

"Of course." Inda shrugged out of his coat, which was instantly caught by one of the boys and laid carefully aside.

Inda ripped off his shirt.

Scars all over! The boys stared, semaphoring questions with grimaces and rolls of eyes: How many pirates do you think he's killed? And that fighting shirt! Those patched tears had to have been made by real weapons; the brown splatters, bloodstains that hadn't gotten to the cleaning bucket in time and had set.

Inda had stripped off his regular wrist sheaths, the ones he'd carried for years. "I'll take those." He pointed to the longer ones lying on the ground. "Need to practice with them. Longer blades, d'ya see?"

They respectfully handed him the wrist sheaths. There was a short, intense, and covert struggle to be the one to buckle them on for him. He was used to doing his own, but mindful of the fact that these boys were part of Evred's army, and would be in as much danger as the grown men, he let them do it.

Then the old shirt last, the billowing sleeves falling over the wrist guards. As he ducked out they followed, silent until they could reach their fellows and render themselves intolerable by bragging about what they'd seen and heard.

Supper was eaten and Restday wine more hastily distributed than ever before. Then two fires were built up with about twenty long paces between them. They served as illumination and as borders for the matches; the air had cooled only slightly with the slow slide of the sun into the west. The fires were not set as high as they would be in winter, just enough for light, though the heat they threw off in the still air made it feel like midday.

But everyone ignored the heat. The camp crowded round, captains on sitting mats along either side with the best view and the best position from which to judge in case of a difficult call. The king had the central place, Indevan-Laef next to him, the Sier Danas at either side of them.

Tau found a spot just behind and to Inda's left, out of the king's line of sight.

Men crowded behind them, some on their knees, others in back having to stand. Those who'd drawn this watch for perimeter guards were justly pitied as the captains conferred, then began calling out their best men from each riding to compete in the first matches.

Bottles and bets passed back and forth as favorites emerged. Inda watched intently to gauge what they'd learned.

Finally a shout of approval rose skyward, contrasting with a groan of disappointment from those who had lost bets, after a big front-line lancer flattened a skirmisher bowman.

The martial ardor intensified as the lancer faced one of the dragoons' own riding captains—one of those for whom the privilege of declining to fight without loss of honor was reserved. Captains were expected to be good, but they were also expected to rise fresh and ready to command at dawn.

The dragoon captain checked to see if Indevan-Laef was watching, then charged his opponent. Evred divided his attention between the two men—in the prime of life, strong, fast, courageous, fighting to win—and Inda.

Though around them shouts and cheers of approval rose, Inda's profile was troubled.

"What's the problem?" Evred asked, low-voiced.

"Two things. They use the safety rules by habit." Inda spoke without shifting his gaze from the men, who were now straining for the captain's dropped knife in the dust a pace away. The lancer had already lost his. "And not one of them has used any of the moves I've been teaching them for weeks."

Evred's brows rose. "So is it not time to demonstrate what your drills are for, Captain Claphair?"

Inda flicked back the loose, frayed cuffs of his sleeves, revealed polished darkwood knife hilts nestled against his inner wrist. "I'm ready."

Evred smiled. It was a quiet smile, one he meant to be encouraging, but the anticipatory triumph expressed in every line of his taut body, the compressed breathing of denied hunger, made Signi fade quietly beyond the tents, where she could sit on a rock and study the stars, her long-suffering guards trying to position themselves where they could keep her, one another, and the fighting space all in view.

Matches were not with wooden or blunted blades, but your own weapons. You were expected to have the skill to stop short of death. Minor cuts and slices were a matter of course.

Three matches later, a muscular scout, faster than the dragoon captain and stronger than a bowman, was declared winner.

Inda stood up, knives already gripped in his hands. The entire camp had gone quiet. He noted then shut it out, and tipped his head toward the winner. "He's tired. Not a fair match."

Evred turned up his hand. "Then take them both on." He pointed to his dragoon captain, who was standing nearby with his men; the bowman had strained his arm in losing.

A howl of approval met that, and then someone brought out a hand drum. Several laughed. Inda heard the challenge in their laughter, and as usual, shrugged it off.

The two former combatants, recovering their breath as they recovered their weapons, exchanged glances, circled the fires, and then came at Inda from either side.

Inda knew within a heartbeat that neither had fought with the other. Worse, they'd let their gazes get drawn to the fire. Fighting on shipboard at night had taught Inda never to turn his eyes directly into fire because for a few crucial heartbeats it blinded your night vision. All it took to be killed was a single blind or unwary moment.

The captain wanted to recover his lost prestige and the scout to earn a win that would be remembered by everyone who witnessed it, and so they converged determinedly, using well-learned ploys from years of drill.

Inda gave his head a shake of disappointment. His strategy here was so obvious—get them into each other's way—it wouldn't be much of a challenge.

Still, it was practice, and practice was always good.

To the silent watchers, he moved with catlike speed and power, and when he struck, it was so fast, so unnervingly predictive of the others' moves, it was difficult to follow with any clarity. They saw only that he didn't pull out his weapons until the very end. Hands, feet even, and then the flash and glitter of steel, and one lay on the ground with Inda's knifepoint at his neck, while the other had to kneel as a kill, hands to his throat where Inda's knife had pricked a neat line from side to side above the collarbones—no more than a pink scratch. That, the earlier scoffers agreed, having changed their minds about the commander in a heartbeat, *that* was control.

"Three, this time," said Evred-Harvaldar.

Inda cast him a look of comical dismay, but in truth it felt good to practice against others again, though he did not feel the mortal challenge of a fight with Fox.

The spectators watched him turn his wrist with the ease of long familiarity and, still gripping his knife, wipe his hair back, the sharp-edged blade passing a finger's breadth from his ear. His scarred flesh moved over rib and muscle in the open neck of the old shirt; he looked tougher than the toughest dragoon, and his total lack of self-consciousness reinforced the impression.

The next match lasted longer. Again, Inda was a continuous whirl of movement, steel fire-limned, horsetail describing arcs in opposition to the flow of complicated circles and curves his hands, feet, body made. Then *thump! Thump! Thump!* Down they went in defeat.

"A riding." Evred gripped his knees, the fires gleaming in his night-black pupils. "They've seen what two knives can do. Inda, lay aside your weapons. Let's see what just hands, feet, and balance achieve." For Evred, too, had studied the women's Odni, taught by Hadand herself at Inda's boyhood request. But he'd had to try to adjust to moves designed for women's different centers of balance.

This new fighting of Inda's had been adapted to men.

Inda flung his unruly hair back, drops of sweat splatting on the beaten dirt of the fight circle. "Sponge!" he protested.

Whispers, quickly silenced. More drums appeared. The drummers changed the beat to the rolling syncopation called *the gallop*.

Evred-Harvaldar opened his hand toward a big riding captain out of the forest of fists raised. The man motioned his riding out onto the ground, smacking two of the fellows who'd begun to crow at being chosen. "Pay attention, you turds. Yip when you win."

"Either weapons or aid, then," the king said to Inda through the laughter and insults from the ringsiders.

"Tau!" Inda called over his shoulder.

Tau got up from his mat, carefully removed his sash and blue Runner's coat, and when Vedrid appeared, surrendered them to his care. Dressed in shirt and breeches and riding boots, Tau stepped into the fire ring. He flicked his knives from his sleeves and angled them, blade out, up his forearms, ignoring the susurrus of whispers that ran back through the crowd: so Inda's Runner also carried two knives.

Tau took Shield Arm position behind Inda, slightly to the left and back, as they had drilled so many times: on the deck of a ship you are confined in space. Whether facing two or many, they had discovered, a trained pair guarding each other's backs could do mortal damage to a dozen fighting as individuals. A riding is only nine.

One moment Tau stood between the tremendous fires, feeling the drumbeat in blood and bones, the heat of anticipation burning down through his belly and below; not for the first time he considered how close, how very close, were the pleasures of sex and fighting.

Just before the opponents attacked he risked a look toward the king. He saw what he expected to see: Evred's inscrutability was gone, his gaze unwavering and intense. What surprised Tau was how strong Evred's personal boundaries were to make just one fast glance feel like trespass.

Then the attackers reached them, and the world was reduced to instinctive movement, the exhilarating joy of strength overcoming strength. Together he and Inda divided and took out the entire riding, then Inda, laughing, gave his winner's liberty to the nine, muttering privately to Tau as the talking, yelling, singing camp broke up, "Can you get your fingers into my shoulder? I think I landed on it wrong."

"I'll get some linseed oil." Tau knew Inda hadn't landed wrong. There was something really amiss with the bones or tendons or muscles—probably all three—in that shoulder. He could feel Inda favoring it in drill, and after a prolonged fight he could see him favoring it.

Inda said nothing. He knew he needed a mage-healer, but there weren't any available to Marlovans in the entire subcontinent.

The night was warm, the stars dim—a pleasant evening, with insects chirping and stridulating in the thick green grasses surrounding his tent. Over that was the screel of birds in the distance, just discernable over the steady rumble of men's voices as the army prepared to enjoy itself before the horns announced the watch change.

Inda eyed the breaking crowd, wondering where Evred was—probably issuing orders for the next day's travel. And where was Tau? Not in that impatient line of liberty men who'd reported to the paywagon beyond the cook tents for a portion of their pay, duly noted down by Kened, the Runner in charge. The first of them tore off to fetch horses for a couple of his mates so they could ride posthaste to the town, whose lights twinkled cheerily to the west. They did not intend to be robbed of a moment of their fun.

Inda pawed ineffectually at his right shoulder, which throbbed in painful tingles down to his fingers. Liberty was good, but a speedy night march would be far better.

Well, Evred had said they would have one when the weather broke. Maybe that was better for the horses, who might be expected to be running up a mountain pass within a week or so. He'd ask Signi to work on his shoulder until Tau got back with his oil.

Chapter Thirty-two

HIGH on the cliff marked by wind-twisted conifers, Flash and his last and most trusted men gathered. Filthy to their scalps with the dirt they had been digging almost nonstop, they peered down at the bottom of the pass. This was where it began, a broad expanse just behind the castle, rising and narrowing toward the first ridge turning.

Kethadrend stood close to his brother. He'd kept the secret, though he'd longed to tell the children his age.

Keth's reward was Flash saying, "Would you like to do the spell to start the landslide?"

Would he! Just wait until Gdir and the others heard *that*—would *they* turn sour!

So Keth did his best to possess himself with what patience he could by jiggling up and down as the last digging team struggled up the treacherously steep footpath above the cliff that had been marked on the secret map somebody had made ages and ages ago, like fifty years. If they weren't just making some kind of joke. Except that metal thing that felt like one of the magic buckets when you touched it, well, that made everything seem real. And the trees the map said would mark off the unsafe space were all there, huge and wind-twisted.

"See that rise on the west side?" Flash pointed across the wide mouth of the pass behind the castle. "That's where Cousin Shend put the magic thing for the stone to shift to. She said there's a clearing, and we ought to be able to see it from here," Flash said to his little brother. "So if the magic spell still works, well, then, the big stone supposedly hidden somewhere in that cliff down below us will transfer there. And so we'll see if the rest happens. As soon as Den and his team get up here, we'll do it. Now, let's practice a few more times, to make sure you have the words and the sign right. I don't know if doing magic wrong spoils the spell or does something really terrible, and we don't want to find out, do we?"

Keth crowed with joy. What a thing to tell the boys at the academy next spring!

Below in the castle while he and Flash practiced the magical spell, Ndand finally found her quarry—the last person not accounted for.

Ndand had insisted on being the one to search the entire castle to make certain no one was in any of the rooms, just in case. The inhabitants were all gathering on the western wall.

She had begun below and worked her way up toward the jarl's suites at the top, giving out onto the sentry walk facing the harbor. She dashed through room after room, all empty, and slowed as she approached the family suites.

Estral the Poet must have gone back home after all, despite being rejected by her own people for her friendship for the Arveases. Ndand was not sure whether to be relieved or worried when she came unexpectedly on a familiar short, round figure with dark curls, just inside the Jarl's office.

Estral whirled around, her mouth opening, her arms stiff at her sides, fingers spread.

"There you are," Ndand exclaimed. "I couldn't find you! Looking for Flash? That's what I came to tell you. I'm afraid there isn't much time, but I could signal if you like, and they'll wait."

"What will wait? Is there a drill?" Estral's hands wrenched together. Poor thing, she was taut as an overdrawn bowstring!

"Didn't you get the message to go up to the west wall?" Ndand studied her in pity, and took Estral's small hands in her own, sliding her thumbs gently over the tops to press away the stiffness.

"Yes." Estral's hands trembled in Ndand's warm, strong grip. "I thought it was another of those drills. Against the invaders. Since I don't fight—" She shook her head, her mouth working, then lowered her gaze. "I'm an enemy," she whispered.

"Estral." Ndand spoke gently. "You are a poet. Doesn't being a poet rise above things like borders and different kings? Anyway, we don't think of you as an enemy. How could we, when you were the first friend we made?"

Estral closed her eyes, but tears leaked from her lids.

Ndand kissed the blue-veined eyelids, tasting the salt of Estral's tears. "Neither Flash nor I will ever forget how brave you were, that first week we arrived. Coming to us with that armful of lilies when everyone else was so hateful. Not that I blame your people," Ndand amended quickly. "When I heard just some of the stories about the Kepri-Davans! Well. I just wanted to say, it's not a drill. That's why I'm here, to make sure everyone is out, and that you got the message, because I know sometimes you're absent, both person and mind." Ndand smiled, and kissed her again. "So like a songwriter! But Estral, we're going to collapse the mountain onto the road. Flash is up on the mountain right now—"

Estral's eyes widened in horror, and her lips shaped the word beacon.

Ndand did not mistake the word. So Flash had indeed told Estral the secret! Ndand didn't know whether to laugh or get annoyed. Better just to laugh, because that was so typical of Flash! As serious as he was about this whole matter, it was inevitable he still managed to make it fun. Like taking a lover along. Estral, being an Idayagan poet, would appreciate the quiet mountain heights, and she had fallen so desperately for Flash. Ndand and Flash had both seen it—not just a short passion, but she seemed to live in a state of anxious desperation unless she was with him.

Ah well, Ndand thought, looking down into Estral's huge pupils. Even now she seemed to be so afraid! She'd kept the secret of the beacons, the main concern.

"No beacons yet," Ndand whispered, though no one was in the empty Jarl's office, or anywhere within earshot. "We haven't sighted any ships on the horizon. But somebody seems to be sure they are coming. What's happening is this. The king ordered us to crash the road. Now, here's why I wanted to speak to you alone."

Estral stiffened, not even breathing, her eyes wide with dread.

"You said you couldn't go home into Tradheval because you made friends with us, but, see, if the Venn are really coming, well, I'm afraid things will get . . . busy here," Ndand breathed out in a rush. "So if you'd like to ride over the pass to safety, well, I know that Flash would be glad to know you're all right. Whatever happens. And no one would know you over there. Didn't you say both your brothers are on that side? Anyway, Barend already rode out. I know you didn't like him, though I still can't think why. But he's galloping as fast as he can to the southern end of the pass, on the king's orders. So you wouldn't encounter him if you took a nice easy ride."

Estral shivered. "Thank you, Ndand," she whispered. "Thank you. But I'll stay." She swallowed, closed her eyes. Ndand was dismayed to see fresh tears fill her eyes and overflow down her distraught face.

Then Estral reversed Ndand's hands with a jerky, convulsive movement, bent—almost a bow—and kissed her palms. One, then the other. Kisses too fervent, her forehead too tense, for the gesture to be easily interpreted.

Then she let go, and sped from the room before Ndand could say another word.

Ndand plunged through the last set of rooms, all empty. Then she dashed up the stairs and through the sentry walk doors, pressing through the crowd on the western wall until she reached the Jarlan.

"All clear." She turned her thumb downward. "Only one I found was Estral, but she ran off."

The Jarlan lifted a hand. "One of the women spotted her just now, scurrying up one of the inner footpaths." She nicked her head toward the eastern side of the pass, where Flash and his diggers were gathered above Twisted Pine Path.

"She might want to watch the landslide from above," Ndand said. "Maybe that kind of thing appeals to poets. We—"

She paused, aware of the oddest sensation. The other women stilled, chins lifting bird-quick, some of their arms rising instinctively outward as if they were balancing on something narrow and rickety.

The solid stone shuddered under their feet. They whirled, faces toward the eastern cliff, the striations in the rock barely visible as the last of the sun sank behind the headland.

On the crag above, Keth had just finished the spell, his fingers still rigid, forming the magical sign.

In a puff of moldy dust a huge rock appeared on the opposite cliff, causing a faint clap of an echo as the displaced air smacked out and then back again from the rocks on their side of the pass. Everyone laughed, exclaimed, and watched expectantly.

But nothing happened for a count of five, then ten. Keth had just turned his head up to his brother in disappointment when the ground twitched beneath his toes, like a horse dislodging an insect.

Everyone on cliff and castle wall stilled.

Below Keth, the clitter-clatter of small rocks gradually quickened to a rock-thocking, thumping rush, and then a low, constant rumble. The ground shivered and shook as the mountainside beneath them cracked, sending waterfalls of brown dirt and dust tumbling down.

And then the entire lower cliff crumbled with a vast roar as the falls expanded into cataracts of rushing brown dirt, clogged with stone and the roots of long-dead trees. The cataracts joined into a wild torrent, its power so terrifying and exhilarating that not just the boy but most of the men shouted in a wordless mix of terror and glee. The mountainside, unstoppable now, folded in on itself, slumping into the broad road beside the castle. The spillage piled higher and higher, heaping upward toward the solid stone curtain wall of the castle. Higher, rimming the crenellations, and spilling between the battlements in thin brown streams until the main mass poured over the top of the wall. And buried it.

"It'll smother the castle," Keth screamed.

No one heard him. He could not hear himself over the tumult.

The flood of dirt coursed over the jumble of houses, causing the wooden additions to shiver then twist, and finally shatter, sending splinters the length of a man spinning into the eddying mass.

The slide rolled across what was once the castle's shared truck garden, burying all the spring planting beneath tumbling boulders, and yet the dirt still spilled outward, reaching the inner wall, then mounding up toward the battlements. And over again, filling the shorter gap between wall and the castle itself with frightening speed.

But despite the rising pall of long-buried dust, in the fading light the men could just barely make out a gradual slowing.

The skull-ringing roar diminished to a low, thundering rumble, and the sliding ground thinned to a rubble of tumbling stones, slowed, slowed, leaving at last a clacketing of pebbles.

One or two last boulders thumped and jumped crazily down. And came to rest.

Keth let out a whoop of sheer joy.

Flash exchanged looks with his men, seeing his own amazement mirrored in their faces.

From the inner walls, the women stared down at the slope of dirt halfway up the two east towers. Then aching shoulders were loosened, locked knees worked until trembling legs would hold up, tightened jaws released gritted teeth.

The Jarlan tried to swallow, but her mouth was too dry.

"All right," she croaked, her thoughts as bleak as the

sight below. She cleared her throat, coughed out some dust, and lifted her voice. "Time to get ready for our guests."

In the town farther downriver from Evred-Harvaldar's enormous camp, people were out for their Restday stroll, enjoying the mellow weather. Many turned their attention east, toward the golden glow of the army's campfires, and speculated about the warriors they planned to watch galloping by on the morrow.

From the eastern road the sound of laughter accompanied the beat of horse hooves, as a small party of gray-coated warriors rode townward, looking to spend their money and have a good time.

From the main street inn's balcony Skandar Mardric glared, his mood murderous.

Dead. His brother—the little boy who used to eat flowers and try to catch pollywogs as pets—*dead*. Along with eight others, and all as a result of his order.

It had seemed a whim, after seeing one of those damned blue-coated Marlovan Runners trotting arrogantly by. One saw them everywhere, reminding everyone just who held the whip in this land. *Kill the Runners,* he'd said. A whim, but one that swiftly gained meaning and rightness. What better way to harass the enemy than by interrupting their communications? Intercepting them and using them? Who knew that they went armed, that they were trained to fight?

Eight of his good men dead. Eight dead, and only one Marlovan killed. One could say he was old, yet it took five of them to bring him down.

Time for a drink. Mardric's foot scraped, his hand—aching to close around a Marlovan throat—lifted from the rail. He'd just begun to turn away when a lone rider trotted into view, at first only a silhouette.

A familiar silhouette. Or was that just his desire to see the one he wanted most to kill?

Mardric stared into thickening darkness. He had seen

that rider before, always from a distance, hadn't he? Only was this some Montrei-Vayir cousin made one of their Runners? Because he was unaccompanied and wore one of those blue coats.

Still, Mardric's heartbeat quickened as he leaned out so far he was almost in danger of falling, until the Runner reached the nimbus of the inn's glowglobe.

And Mardric laughed. The impossible had happened. That dark red hair, the bony face, the kingly shoulders, trim waist, splendid legs: unmistakably Evred Montrei-Vayir himself.

And all alone.

Chapter Thirty-three

"VEDRID, I can't find any linseed oil." Tau stuck his head inside the king's tent.

When the king was present, one or more of his Runners stood guard outside. But no one was on guard, and inside Vedrid and a couple of his staff were busy brushing the king's gray riding coat and readying his bedroll. Tau noticed the coat; despite the warmth of the evening, Evred did not seem one to wander about in only shirt and trousers.

"I think the farrier got the last of the oil," Vedrid said over his shoulder. "Shall I send someone to the town?"

"Yes." Tau spared a glance through the open flap of Inda's tent, where, in the hanging lamplight, he could make out Cherry-Stripe, Noddy, and Rat with Inda. Signi knelt behind Inda, her fists pounding on his right shoulder; she said something and the others all laughed. Inda would be fine for a while. "On second thought, I'll go myself."

Yes. An evening away from academy reminiscences, old battles refought, and king-avoidance would be pleasant. The town was not far. He could ride in, find linseed oil, maybe find a pleasure house, drink a glass of local brew and look at other people besides warriors. Like women. Tau missed the sight of women. Signi did not count, shrouded as she was in those rumpled clothes that underage boys and girls wore, her manner so unobtrusive it was like she was invisible before your eyes.

He could be back about the time Cherry-Stripe and the others—talked out for the night—would be wandering to their own tents to sleep. Didn't matter if Inda was awake or asleep; more often than not he ended up snoring halfway through one of Tau's kneadings.

Tau retreated to his own tent to get some coins and drop off his knives, as there were stringent rules against bearing weapons inside a pleasure house. People needed to feel safe to enjoy intimacy—unless you went to one of the houses that made sex games of risk and pain. He undid the wrist sheaths and dropped them into his bag, followed by his Runner's coat and plain linen shirt. Out came one of his fine civilian shirts and tunic-vests.

He shrugged back into his coat, claimed one of the mounts designated for Runners to use at night, and trotted through the camp, amazed again at its immensity. It seemed there would be no end to the campfires and neat half-circle tent villages, the streaming and bobbing torches of men visiting one another's camps, the drums rolling and tapping, songs, shouts, and laughter, but he finally reached the outskirts and then the outer perimeter. His blue coat got him past with a wave of a hand in salute, which he returned. After he'd crossed a feeder stream and passed a ridge of ancient, tangled vines that had marked someone's border long ago, he halted long enough to unclasp his hair, tie it back, and fold his coat into the saddle pouch. He pulled his long vest over his shirt, retied his sash, and finished the ride at a trot.

Like most western towns, he discovered, this one was not built in a walled, Marlovan castle-square or in a wheel shape, as was common in the east, but in a line alongside the river. The main street, with the best shops and wealthier houses, bordered the river.

The entire population seemed to be out on the stroll along the haphazardly-lit street. There were stone posts with big glowglobe glass casings atop them, all but one dark. Until the mages returned, the glowglobes were only

used in emergencies. Lanterns, lamps, and torches proliferated up and down both sides, smelling heavily of the ubiquitous leddas oil and giving the place an agreeable party air.
The equally pungent aromas of Restday mulled wine and
pastries and special dinners made Tau's mouth water after
weeks of smelling nothing but horse, man, dust, and the
camp food whose main constituents were rye and cabbage.

Ah. There, upriver a way, the sign of a horse's head. Stables with tack shops were where most people bought linseed oil, as it was used for horse as well as human. Tau had
been raised in a pleasure house, where they often used fine
oils. Many patrons liked a rubdown before or after sex and
some houses boasted people so good with their hands that
patrons came just for their muscle aches to be kneaded.

Tau peered over the strollers' heads. Most pleasure
houses were named for pleasing images—flowers, birds,
songs, stars, sunset, dawn—except for those that catered to
the stranger side of human desires.

He found a sign with a painted sun, a moon surmounted
by stars next door. The crowd thickened up as he neared.
These two houses were clearly at the party end of town. By
the time he'd threaded through groups of talking, laughing
people, many holding mugs of local brew in their hands,
he'd figured out that the Sun was where all the younger
people went, the Moon-and-Stars preferred by the older.
Music poured out from the Sun, and all the downstairs
windows were open. Inside the crowd was even bigger,
clapping for the dancers in the center, talk and laughter almost drowning out the musicians.

His mother's influence had gradually traveled up the
coast from Parayid: the pleasure houses were decorated to
please all the senses, the way they were in the older kingdoms on the eastern side of the continent. Murals, fine
porcelain, the best scents and music, everyone dressed as
artfully as imagination and the range of local fabrics could
make them. Everywhere he saw signs of what he was certain was his mother's influence.

The music gave way to throbbing drum beats, followed
by a delightful Sartoran ballad sung antiphonally by male

and female voices—only reversed, men doing women's verses and women men, which gave the song an unexpectedly bawdy layer of meaning. Auditors (those who could hear over the street noise) bellowed with laughter.

He stopped to listen, and to thoroughly appreciate the spectacle of young women wearing soft summer robes. After weeks of nothing but men, women seemed exceptionally entrancing: tall, short, young, old, plump, scrawny—it didn't matter. They were all delightful.

Everyone was loose, free, bent on pleasure, so the sight of a tense body slipping between celebrants drew Tau's eye. His attention sharpened when the man seemed familiar. Who? When? Where? Dark, glossy long hair, well kept as any noble's, though the man wore ordinary travel clothes: the short tunic common here in the west, dun riding trousers, mocs. A fine profile, well-shaped mouth, now compressed—

Tau chirped softly, and his mount, ears twitching, moved forward a couple of steps just as the man glanced to the right and then to the left.

A dark, sardonic gaze brushed past Tau indifferently, obviously seeking someone, or something, else. *Where have I seen that face?* Tau recalled a reaction of annoyance, but not why the man had annoyed him.

Tau leaped down and tossed a coin to one of the hopeful children lurking around, who led his mount around to the hitching post between the two houses.

Tau had learned about stalking quarry when spying for Inda in Bren. He eased through the crowd, keeping three people between the dark-haired man and himself as he sorted memories, trying to fit the man into them.

Skandar Mardric did not expect any interference as he patiently followed Evred, but he kept searching the crowd for those blue or gray Marlovan coats.

The king himself wearing a plain blue coat had surprised him. So that was how Evred-Harvaldar had vanished so easily from the Nob that first time! Who'd think a king would lay aside the trappings that boosted him above everyone else?

Mardric's heart thumped with the thrill of danger, of anticipated triumph.

Estral, we're about to change history, he thought to his sister, far away in the north. Unfortunately, he could no longer dash notes off to her: the gold cases they'd so laboriously obtained had ceased transferring. Either the magic spells had faded, or—more likely—the Venn had interfered.

Considering what Mardric and his inner circle had done to their spies, it seemed a fair trade. The thought made him smile. Besides, there was no more planning to be done. Estral had her orders, and Mardric's long-sought target had just walked with typical Marlovan arrogance right into easy reach. *Two deaths and a vast empire falls. Then three kingdoms regain their freedom. All accomplished by you and me, Estral, a victory that will be the sweeter as our brother is now another of their many victims. Have you thought about what you'll ask for your reward?*

Evred-Harvaldar moved up in the waiting line on the men's stairs, twin to the stairs on the other side of the main room for those who wanted a female partner.

He spotted a couple of the Marlovans on liberty on the far side of the room, and turned his shoulder before any of them could look up and catch his eye. He didn't care if they saw him from the back; what he didn't want was to talk, to smile or laugh with them anymore than he wanted to choose a partner from among the dancers circling so smilingly among the townsfolk, for that meant chatter, a decent pretence of interest, of friendship. Evred did not want any of that, nor did he want to give it: it was sensible, it was sane, to rid the body of unwanted passion; it was not an act of celebration.

I love the beloved that loves not me—the triune heart, symbolized by clover. Evred had discovered that in the ancient white tower of the castle of Ala Larkadhe where they were heading, in an archive so old its origin was impossible even for the Morvende caretakers to know. He'd found the saying written in Old Sartoran. After seeing that, he'd recognized the clover symbol when it showed up in poetry and verse histories, one of many symbols of hidden motivations and consequences. He'd once found it comforting to see in old texts that all the range of human variation had been experienced. *Shared*—

"Your turn."

He started. Discovered a pair of young women standing behind him, one laughing, the other's impatience becoming a slow head-to-toe of speculation.

He turned up his palm in polite thanks, and left them giggling and whispering behind him as he trod up to the landing where the plump, balding proprietor waited, a broad smile on his ruddy face.

Tau, just squeezing inside the front door behind a large, loud party of merrymakers, spotted the dark-haired man on the lower stair on the men's side. The fellow was in the act of extending a hand to push past two young women who were arguing with the proprietor. "If we're *sharrrr-ing* a fellow, we should *onnn-ly* pay for *onnne*," a woman declared with the earnest exaggeration of the tipsy as the dark-haired fellow attempted to slip behind her. But he was prevented by the woman swaying backward a step as she raised a dramatic hand, pointing a finger toward the ceiling. "One!"

Tau peered past her at the fellow, who tried again to get past her, his entire body tense with impatience.

His reaching hand tweaked harder at Tau's memory— that hand, where had he seen it? Close, close, yes . . . *gripping his arm*. Lindeth harbor, the guild mistress's house. That same hand stopping him from following Inda, just after the pirate battle, when they'd gone to pay for supplies at Lindeth. He recalled those sardonic dark eyes, the drawling voice that did not hide hostility, *Is he really Elgar the Fox?*

So who was the fellow chasing after now? Puzzled, Tau flicked a glance to the top of the stairs, a heartbeat before another familiar figure vanished down the hall. An instantly recognizable figure despite the blue Runner's coat: that height, those shoulders, and above all the long, dark red horsetail Tau'd been riding behind for weeks.

Evred? In a blue coat?

Alone?

Tau pinched the skin between his brows. Could this possibly be some assignation? He watched the dark-haired man squeeze past the women at last as they leaned forward, both arguing with the proprietor. Tau's interest sharpened when the man pressed past the second woman, a hand going revealingly to his side the way one did to steady a hidden weapon.

Assignation—or assassination?

The sharp inward goad of danger propelled Tau through the last of the crowd and up the stairs. Tau grimaced at how very angry Evred would be if Tau thrust his way in on a privately planned encounter, but instinct was against anything planned on Evred's part, especially with this Lindeth fellow.

Tau tried to slip past the women—but his own looks worked against him. One of the women gasped, lips parted, and Tau nearly tripped when the proprietor stuck out a foot. "Who are you?"

"I'm . . . meeting that fellow who just went up. Dark hair? Dark eyes?"

The proprietor's jolly face puckered into wariness. "Last one in was one of them Marlovan fellows. Red hair. What are you trying to pull here, pretty boy?"

The women were eyeing him speculatively. In desperation he bent toward the surprised proprietor and whispered into his grizzled ear, "I was trained by Saris Eland of Parayid." He added the insider code, and as the man's jaw dropped, Tau straightened up and forced a smile at the women. "If you'll excuse me a few moments, why don't I entertain you both? You can pay for the price of one, and I'll donate the second price." He indicated the proprietor, whose surprise altered to the smile of a good bargain made.

As the woman whispered, pooling their last coins, Tau murmured, "Where'd you send the redhead?"

The proprietor said in a whisper, "Four suns on the door."

Tau galloped past them and up the stairs, grimacing. There was no possible way he was going to avoid either farce or tragedy as soon as he opened that door. He just hoped it would not be both.

The doors were differentiated by painted suns, stars, and moons, arranged in charming groups. This was another of his mother's touches. He raced past the triangle of three suns and was just pulling up to listen at the next door when from within came thuds and a choked cry.

He knew the difference between cries of passion and cries of pain. He shouldered the door open into the small room furnished only with a low bed and a chair. Those within froze for the single heartbeat it took him to take in:

The naked young man lying on the bed, a widening pool of crimson sinking into the mattress, the knobs down his thin back pale and vulnerable as he curled round his slashed gut.

Evred, hair loose over his bare chest, one arm and his ribs slashed and bleeding, a deliberate nick dripping down into one of his wide, hazel eyes.

And the dark-haired man standing over him with a bloody dagger, intending to play with his prey before killing it.

Skandar Mardric jerked a glance Tau's way.

He had not expected the king to defend himself, which just added to the fun. Now, carried on the tide of triumph, he recognized that beautiful face, golden hair, golden eyes. "Elgar's lover?" he gasped in amazement.

Evred's mouth whitened.

Tau crossed the room in three steps.

Mardric grinned and slashed at Tau with the knife.

Two steps, snap-kick to the downward slashing knife hand, whirling palm-heel strike, and Mardric fell to his knees with an *oof*. Tau glanced once more at the young man lying there in shock, blood leaking between his fingers, and kicked again, this time straight at Mardric's head. "Wrong," he said.

Mardric seemed to hear, or maybe his plans had never included the possibility of his own death; his brows crimped in pained question just before Tau's heel snapped his head back, and he was dead before he hit the floor.

Leaving Tau alone with one wounded pleasure-house worker, and a very shocked, angry, spectacularly bloody king who'd rolled up into a fighting crouch.

Tau had grown up learning all about the symbolic boundaries of clothing. If you pretended it was there even if it wasn't, then you handed back the invisible wall of reserve to those who required it. He also knew better than to castigate this self-isolated, volatile-as-fire king. Evred's entire life was bound up with military necessity: the fact that he'd come away without a guard evidenced how desperate he was. The crushing weight of impending war day and night would distort the thoughts of the sanest man.

Tau's mind raced. *You will not grant me the authority to speak of your duty to your Marlovans, but I can speak within my own realm.*

"I grew up in a bawdy house. I can arrange these things with a lot less risk." He nodded toward the bed. Then, without waiting for an answer, he bent, slid his arms under the knees and shoulders of the wounded young man, and picked him up. "There will be a private exit out that way," he added, pointing with his chin toward the other end of the hall. "Kick the door shut behind me."

He hurried out with his moaning burden.

Twenty fast steps—he counted each—then he just had to get down the stairs. "Quick, help."

The proprietor gasped, casting an anguished look at the young man's face and the blood dripping down his bare flesh.

Then the screams and shouts began.

Chapter Thirty-four

THE sun was just lifting the eastern darkness when the Venn longboat, its sail lowered, the oars silent, drifted on the tide toward the headland above Castle Andahi's bay.

Nine Drenga, the Oneli's sea marines, all dressed in black, slid noiselessly overboard into the shallow water, gripped the black-pointed boat's sides, and ran it up onto the sand without a splash.

The tenth person leaped out, a tall, strong woman of middle years, wearing the blue robe of a dag. She stood aside as the nine swiftly used sea wrack to cover the boat.

There were no sentries in sight. The Drenga had landed themselves well west of the patrol line.

Motioning quietly, the leader dispersed his men in teams of three. As they progressed over the headland, in the strengthening light they spied a peculiar pall over the inner part of the bay, reaching as far as they could see between the enormous, sheer cliff walls. They moved belly flat in the brush so that they did not create a silhouette along the top of the headland, stopping when they could look down into the bay.

Squatting squarely between the bay's long, naturally terraced shingle beach and the narrowing gorge forming the Pass of Andahi sat a massive castle. From under the rocky ridge below the precipice the Venn crouched on, the northern branch of the Andahi River poured into the bay. The dull granite of the outer curtain wall was warm lit in the rising sun but the eastern side of the castle, still in shadow, did not look at all like their carefully drawn map. The whole east side was distorted in an enormous tear-shaped mass.

They puzzled over that as the sun crested over the eastern headland, bringing the shadows past them, down, down into the bay, then vanishing, and at last they made sense of the startling change. Gone was the great road that they were supposed to find curving round the base of the cliffs at the east side of the castle. Instead, a sharply slanted fall of loose dirt angled up the mountain from the castle, revealing a raw wound in the mountainside.

The Marlovans had collapsed an entire slope in order to block access to the pass.

The dag motioned peremptorily to the leader of the nine-man team and pointed with meaning at the lower paths along the headland as she started up toward the mountain heights. This sort of thing was exactly what Dag Erkric had planned for.

The ships of the invasion were right behind them, soon to be visible. Until then, no word must go up the pass and over the mountains to Ala Larkadhe.

As soon as Dag Mekki was well out of sight, the Drenga leader cursed. Dags had no business interfering with a military exercise. But the Marlovans had just invited them in, with their damned mountain foolery.

The Drenga continued along the headland single file, where they surprised their first outer perimeter sentry, who was admiring the hanging dust pall instead of doing his job. It was the last thing he saw.

DAWN'S bleak blue light had harshened the contours of the old wooden building in the riverside market town, rendering bright paintings garish, and cozy cushions and mats into trampled, dirty wads of cloth that would not just require cleaning but restitching, the floor strewn with empty mugs and plates. Tau slowly picked his way across them to take leave of the proprietor.

"I know there's something missing in your story," the owner said hoarsely. "A murderer just picks out a random Marlovan for assassination? But the knife was there, and the murderer was there, and my sister's son with his gut slashed. I don't know what was worse, the sight of him like that, or the panic after. So bad for business. So bad."

Tau gave a tired nod. He'd helped the proprietor turn fear into excitement—his mother had trained him for that, too—by organizing the panic-stricken patrons in a search. When they discovered the dead man, the panic ended. Criminal found, end of threat, Tau there to congratulate everyone on the satisfying end to the mystery and to help along the spreading word.

Then everyone had to offer their version of what had happened—no one knew the dead man—not one of *us*— and the proprietor offered a free round of drinks for all. Tau went up to the prettiest woman there and began an Iascan hand dance, in which one or both hands have to be touching the partner at all times. The musicians picked up their instruments and hastily assembled themselves, weaving round them a merry tune. With her willing participation they'd made their dance so lascivious everyone soon was laughing, dancing, or going upstairs to carry on.

The proprietor, also thinking back over the surprising night, gave a short nod, his jowls jiggling. "But you earned your right to a secret or two, I'm thinking."

He cast a meaningful glance over his shoulder toward one of the larger suites across the main parlor, where parties with more than one partner usually disported.

After the dance, the waiting pair of women had appeared, and Tau enthusiastically kept his promise. After months of enforced celibacy (though plenty of offers had come his way, he did not think a dalliance with anyone in Evred's army a wise idea) it had not exactly been a trial.

The two women were just leaving, a garland dropping from one's hair, the other softly singing, their arms around each other's waists.

Tau and the proprietor fell quiet as they walked past. The taller woman, dark-haired, some of her ribbons still untied, reached up to lay her hand against Tau's cheekbone. "I'm always going to think I dreamed you." She laughed soundlessly.

He caught her hand, kissed it, ran his fingers along her palm as he let her go. She laughed again, and walked out of the house, and out of his life.

The proprietor said, "You saved Ulec. The healer said he would have bled to death not two glass-turns more. And the way you got 'em all singing instead of yelling—" He groped forward, then shook his head. "If you come back this way, know we'll give you a place, a night, a meal. Whatever you ask. Even half the business," he added shrewdly.

Tau smiled and moved to the door. The proprietor sighed, then turned wearily back to his disaster of a parlor.

Tau stepped outside, breathing in fresh, pure air. It was going to be sunny, maybe even hot. Not good if he had to walk; by now his horse would be long gone from the hitching post. At least armies were not subtle about leaving trails.

He almost stumbled into the boy sitting on the porch, arms folded over his knees, supporting his brow. At Tau's step he raised a weary head, squinted, then said, "You know a Marlovan called Sponge?"

"Yes," Tau said.

"I was to tell you that the horse is at the stable." The boy added importantly, "He gave me a *whole golder* to make sure you found it."

And so Tau rode back, discovering that the army had not departed after all. From the dust and noise coming from the hills above the river bend, they were engaged in a war game; yes, there was Inda riding along the riverbank, watching intently.

Tau left the horse with the Runners on stable detail, and walked through the mostly packed camp to his tent, still standing. Inside were two ensorcelled buckets.

When he emerged, feeling cleaner if no less tired, there were several of Vedrid's staff waiting to collapse the tent.

But what surprised him was Signi waiting with them, her ubiquitous guards just out of earshot.

She had never precisely ignored him, she just did not speak often, and never when Evred was present, unless he addressed her first. And she was so far Tau's superior in the art of self-effacement, he'd rarely noticed her unless he sought her out.

Yet here she was before him, her sandy hair untidy, her rumpled old clothes sun-faded, having sought him out for the first time. "The king returned last night bleeding over his eye." She touched her brow. "I think he was hurt elsewhere, for he moved as if in pain. And he was very angry." Her Marlovan had improved; the only reminder of her origin was her accent. She made one of her little gestures, tipped her head and smiled faintly. "No one asks a king questions—except Inda, and sometimes his friends. But you know Inda."

Tau huffed a tired laugh, beyond surprise. "I know Inda. I'm sure he didn't ask."

"Oh, he did. *Where were you,* he said. *You can't vanish on us like that.* And Evred-Harvaldar said back, *I fell down the stairs. But I won't trip again.* And they all laughed. Is that a metaphor that I have missed, or perhaps more of their private language?"

"Private language is my guess," Tau said.

"Ah. The king added these words: *Your Runner caught the reins.* He went into his tent, the others dispersed, and that was all. What happened?"

Tau said, "Evred went to get laid. Why he didn't take a couple of guards, I don't know—he doesn't usually seem stupid. Sure enough he was attacked, I think by an assassin. I recognized the fellow just before I killed him."

Ahhhh. Her mouth opened, shaping the word, but no sound emerged. Then she said with care, "If I understand right, the king used to assume the guise of a Runner when he wished to move about unnoticed. I overheard Vedrid making reference to that being the way he escaped the assassins two years ago."

"Maybe." Tau was too tired to hide sarcasm. "But even

he should see that there's a difference between a prince roaming around anonymously and a king leading an army to defend his borders."

"Privacy appears to be very important to Evred-Harvaldar."

"More than that." It was a relief to talk, tired as Tau was. He needed to sound his ideas, to determine if his insight was only misunderstanding. "He sometimes gets even more lost inside his head than Inda does. But he's a king, so no one can force him back."

"I hope you tried." Signi touched her fingertips together. "For his own sake."

"I did."

They turned away from one another and toward the hills, where mounted shapes hurtled in and out of the considerable dust. Evred was just visible beyond Inda, no more than a silhouette himself.

"I hope he won't resent it," Tau commented.

Signi's green-brown eyes were wide in the strengthening morning sunlight. "You think he will? Why? Did you lay a debt upon him?"

Tau snorted. On the hill Cherry-Stripe emerged from the dust, yipping at the head of a tight flying wedge of young men on the chase of a scattering of Rat's dragoons. "Gratitude wins great renown in ballads, not in real life." Tau lifted a shoulder. "In real life as often as not people hate you for doing them a good turn."

She did not deny it. "When the doer of the deed assumes moral superiority, but you have not done so. Do you think Evred-Harvaldar so small-minded?"

Tau shook his head. "The camp is here. And I found a horse waiting, when he could have taken it back." He drew in a deep breath, feeling the first pangs of a headache as the sunlight glinted off metal and glared on the light-colored dirt. "Small-minded, no. Complicated, yes."

A whoop went up from the other side of the hill and a moment later the war gamers galloped back. Tau gestured toward the Runners carrying his rolled tent to the wagon. "And certainly not rancorous."

Signi opened her hands as the arriving warriors abandoned their mounts to be watered and strung with the remounts. Fresh horses were readied, and some waiting slices of stale nut-bread handed around; the supply wagons had already rumbled ahead. Signi walked toward the picket line to meet Inda, leaving Tau to follow.

They were on the move before noon, everything exactly as it had always been, as if the night before had never happened. Or as if Tau had dreamed it, but he had not dreamed the crunch of the assassin's chin and the snap of his neck under his heel—nor had he dreamed the fire-charged beauty of blood-smeared, naked Evred, all muscle over long bones, and hard hazel eyes.

Tau's own walls had nothing to do with physical privacy, but everything to do with the danger-fraught haunts of the heart.

He suspected Evred would not say anything to him or about him, that things would go exactly as before. So he would not question it, or even think about it. Because every step brought them closer to battle, where the summary cut of a Venn blade could resolve all questions.

But for now . . . he sank his chin down onto his collarbone and dozed as his horse plodded behind Inda's.

Chapter Thirty-five

LIET-RANDVIAR Arveas assumed a stern look. She knew very well how bitterly the children had been complaining, which was why she'd been firm. Girls of fifteen—old enough for the queen's training—could stay to defend the castle. There was a single fourteen-year-old boy, the cook's prentice, who had begged to stay, saying he'd be fifteen in two weeks. The other boys his age were down south at the academy.

All the parents had backed her up, some so intensely they'd frightened their children, who stood before the Jarlan now. The littlest ones were very small and bewildered, clutching the hands of older sisters or cousins. She was grateful there were no babes in arms. Sending three-year-olds to hide out for who knows how long was heart-wrenching enough.

"Your orders," the Jarlan began, studying the oldest three girls in turn—expectant Gdir, stone-grim Han, chin-lifted Lnand. The latter furtively watched the others for their reactions. "Your orders are as follows. Hadand, you are in charge."

Han straightened up, her spine rigid. When anyone used her full name, they were serious.

Gdir flushed with anger.

The Jarlan saw that and sighed inwardly. She'd tried so

hard to raise a tough future Jarlan, maybe too hard. Or maybe Gdir would have been . . .

I am out of time. "My choice is not a judgment on any of you. You're too young for anyone to be certain how good you'll be in the future as leaders," the Jarlan said, not looking at Gdir. "I picked Han for this mission because she's closest kin to me. That happens in command. It's not fair but it's a clear, easy chain of command. Get used to this. When there's an emergency, people will make things as easy for themselves as they can, and sometimes that means ignoring all the expectations of rank."

The girls listened, each face giving tolerable clues to the thoughts behind it. Gdir's resentment did not abate. Lnand stood in a chin-raised pose she thought heroic, spoiled by the lizard-flicker of her eyelids as she watched the others for reaction. Only Han seemed to comprehend how serious the situation was as she glanced doubtfully at the three-year-olds.

"Second order. You are to hide out until the king comes. Hiding out means you will not attack the Venn. I don't care what happens here, and I know you'll probably hear sounds of battle, since the robbers' cave is just beyond the first ridge. Sounds might carry that far. You will ignore them. Understand?"

She waited until childish fists struck skinny chests all along the row, right down to the five- and six-year-olds. The half a dozen younger than that were bewildered, and would remain so, the Jarlan thought with another spike of dread.

"Your third order. If the king hasn't arrived yet and the enemy finds you, use the goat trails and run to the south. And report to Tdiran-Randviar. *No. Raids.* You fight back only if you've been discovered. This is not a war game. Understand? I want to see those salutes, which means you understand your orders."

Thump! Fists hit ribs, Gdir and Han at the same time, Lnand with dramatic reluctance, her lips tightening to deliver some heroic speech she was surely formulating.

The Jarlan forestalled it. "Now line up at the tunnel.

You're going to go up that way and cross the pass under cover of dark. Then use the goat trails to get up to the old robbers' cave." She thought of the report of sails on the horizon, so many the fisher had said they looked like the teeth of a comb. They were as yet not visible from the castle. But everyone knew they were there.

The Venn are here.

"Now!" she barked.

Ndand began to follow, but the Jarlan stuck out her hand. "Something is wrong, I feel it." Her gut seized and she sucked in a breath. "I mean more than the obvious. I didn't expect to see Flash back. His orders were to go straight to the beacon as soon as the ships were sighted. But why haven't we seen any of his men come down? And where is my husband and the Riders? Where are Barend's men?"

Ndand's skin roughened with an inner chill. She worked to sound practical, unemotional. "You want me to light the beacon, if . . ." Her throat tightened on that last word, and she forced the words out: "He didn't reach the beacon."

"Yes. Then go out onto the viewpoint. If I'm running the red-black flag, you are not to come back here. You are to go to Tdiran in Ala Larkadhe." Liet's gut tightened again and she took her daughter-by-marriage's arm, and squeezed with all her strength. "Ndand. I don't care what you see or hear in this castle. If I run that signal and see *you,* I'll break your marriage myself. Throw you back to Tlen. Stable wanding. Rest of your life." She ended on a trembling whisper; the Jarlan let go of her arm and hugged Ndand so hard her lungs labored for air, and Ndand felt the tremor of a hard-suppressed sob go through the woman she thought of as a second mother.

But she knew better than to say anything except, "Orders received." She summoned Keth with a jerk of her thumb, picked up her gear, and left.

The Jarlan then picked up the knapsack she'd packed and searched through the castle, until she found Radran, the cook's prentice. She looked at that frail body, the knobby neck knuckle, and met those anxious eyes. *It would take just one strike to kill you,* she thought. *The Venn would forget you before he'd stepped over your body.* But of course she couldn't say that. Nor could she say that what she and the other adults faced could be borne if they believed their children might live. "No Runners have returned. I have a mission of desperate importance. Only you can do it."

Radran's eyes widened.

She handed him the knapsack.

"You are to sneak up Lookout Mountain. Right now. Under cover of darkness. Hide out in Spyglass Cave, where you can see the bay and the road to the east. You have to count all the Venn you see—I put a slate and chalk in the pack. The Jarl will need those numbers. Or the king. Whoever comes first. But don't move until our banner rises over the castle."

The boy struck his chest and was gone.

"Barend-Harskialdna!"

The triangular face in the Ala Larkadhe forecourt lifted, squinting against the sunlight. To Nightingale Toraca, standing in the tower just off Hawkeye's office, Barend Montrei-Vayir always looked as if he'd been put together by someone with a strange sense of humor: a triangular, squint-eyed Cassad face framed by thin dark hair pulled back into a sailor braid instead of a horsetail. A golden hoop with a ruby dangled against his blade-sharp jawbone, his body covered by the Marlovan gray coat and riding trousers, but instead of boots he wore field mocs. Barend was thin, hard as wire-reinforced rope, tougher than anyone on the practice mats—but he rode like a drunk who'd never seen a horse.

Nightingale grinned as Barend flipped up a hand in greeting. Barend slipped from the horse, whooshing a sigh loud enough for the sound to echo up the granite walls to the weird white tower at Nightingale's back.

Nightingale leaped down the stairs four at a time. Everyone

gave way for the King's Runner, though he seldom demanded precedence. But word had flitted through the castle that Barend-Harskialdna was back.

Nightingale made it all the way to the court before Barend had finished rubbing his scrawny butt.

Barend was secretly amused by Nightingale, who looked like a shorter and thinner edition of his brother Noddy, but he moved with exactly the same slope-shouldered slouch. His hound-dog face was split by a gap-toothed grin as they exclaimed at the same time, "Any news?"

A laugh, then Nightingale said, "I just got in last night from the Nob. Biggest news out there was another murder. I thought we'd seen the last of that."

"Shit," Barend exclaimed. "We can't be rousting all the men out again—"

"No, no." Nightingale patted the air. "This time not a secret murder. A gang of Olarans 'fessed right up. Said the fellow was a Venn spy. Caught him with reports written on the new defense plan. It was all there on paper."

"You mean we didn't get blamed?"

"Naw. It's only down in Lindeth, and over the hills into Idayago, that they hate us. Up on the Nob they like us. We can fight, and they've been overrun and burned out too many times to squawk about who thinks they're ruling 'em. In fact, worst complaining I heard's been about the Idayagan Resistance. Talk, trouble-making, money-gathering, and no results." Nightingale turned his hand up.

"We seem to get double the trouble down at this end." Barend made a spitting motion. They'd had to waste time at Hawkeye's request investigating a double murder in Lindeth Harbor just before summer. One body was supposedly a Venn spy, but the other was the well-respected guild mistress. Lindeth was still blaming the Marlovans for that, even though every single man had been accounted for. They may as well have saved their effort— the polite and noncommittal responses of the harbormaster and his council had made it clear that no one had believed them.

Nightingale said, "No news at the north end, I take it?"

He flapped a hand that took in the entire north side of the castle as he glanced ever so casually upward.

No one visible at the windows.

Barend slewed around, peering skyward past the strange white tower that looked so much like a block of ice. Beyond it soared the mountains that created the Andahi River, rank on rank.

"Nothing—" He lowered his voice, so that the watching sentries could not hear his words. "Unless the beacons lit over my head on the mountaintops. You can't see 'em from below in the Pass." Barend touched his coat over his locket, his brows rising in question.

Nightingale flattened his hand, palm down.

Barend went on quietly, "Last thing I saw was the dust way up over the cliffs after they collapsed the road."

"Good." Nightingale also kept his voice low. "As for the beacons, Hawkeye says there's been no fires. And doesn't he have a special duty rotation just watching the mountains?"

"Hand-picked, between him'n me and Flash." Barend lifted his hands. "Venn sure are taking their time. Maybe the wind hasn't changed up northside of the strait."

They turned their eyes upward again, making sure that no one was within earshot.

Barend and Nightingale each carried a locket matched to the king's. Until just a couple weeks ago they knew more than anyone else did, including most of each other's news, but they'd had to go through the forms. It was Evred's will that no one, ever, find out about the magical communications.

Now, at a glance, they discovered that neither locket worked. Both of them had been cut off from magical communication. That meant they were equally cut off from the king.

Well, what was good enough for our ancestors, Barend thought as he yanked his sash free.

Nightingale hoped uneasily that the midday sun wouldn't conceal the beacon fires when they did come, and Barend wondered uneasily where the king's army was. "Ola-Vayir or Buck Marlo-Vayir reached Lindeth yet?"

"No sign of anyone," Nightingale said.

Barend paused in the act of unbuttoning his coat, then continued. Nightingale had to bite back a protest as Barend shrugged out of the sturdy cloth and slung it across the saddle just before the stable hands took the horse away, leaving him there not in a proper linen shirt, but one of those cotton tunic-shirts he'd brought from the other side of the continent. It was all rumpled and sweaty, but Barend did not seem to notice as he retied his crimson sash.

Crimson. The reminder that this was Barend, the king's cousin, who'd had no training except for that pirate-style contact fighting that reminded them of the women's Odni. No fault of his own, being thrown away to sea where nobody learned anything else of use. So the men reassured one another when he broke yet another unspoken rule.

A sharp-chinned face appeared in the window above: Hawkeye, summoned by a Runner who'd heard the familiar voices below.

He waved them to come upstairs. They vanished from below, through the entrance to the newer, granite-built part of Ala Larkadhe castle, and Hawkeye turned away to await them, staring down at the desk.

The poets maintain that the most vivid memories are happiness and sorrow, but there are others who will insist that guilt and humiliation reach far deeper, so deep that they are not just vivid memories, but have the strength to motivate across decades, even centuries in a clan or kingdom. Who seeks revenge for happiness?

Hawkeye Yvana-Vayir had had almost a month to think about the news from Evred-Harvaldar, spoken from Runner to galloping Runner: *The army is on the march, and at its head the king with Indevan-Laef Algara-Vayir at his side, to command the war as Harskialdna.*

Algara-Vayir. The first mention of that name threw Hawkeye back in memory to the Summer Without a Banner, the night a careless slap of his own hand struck a shivering, exhausted scrub to his death. Hawkeye hadn't meant to hit him hard, but he'd been drunk on smuggled wine given to him by the Sierlaef himself, as consolation for being stuck on night guard duty. His companions had not blamed him afterward, and united in hiding the forbidden wine from the masters. They knew he hadn't intended but a slap. There hadn't even been a mark on the boy's face, but he had died all the same.

Now, riding back to take Hawkeye's place as commander (because no one regarded Barend as Harskialdna in anything but name) after all these years of jolting memories and terrible dreams was the boy who witnessed that. Who, for some unaccountable reason, had been given the blame for that death. Then exiled, young as he was.

By the time Barend and Nightingale arrived outside his office, Hawkeye had had time to consider what he'd say. He was technically under Cousin Barend's command, but they had agreed on how they'd handle that fiction during their very first interview. Barend had been disarmingly forthcoming, which won Hawkeye over immediately: he devised the orders that Barend either spoke or endorsed.

Barend said, "No news north of the pass when I left."

Hawkeye returned, "Nothing from our beacon watchers. And nothing from Ola-Vayir."

Barend whistled under his breath. Nightingale said shrewdly, "What do you wager he's dawdling along the road somewhere?"

"That family made no secret of wanting the north as part of Ola-Vayir." Hawkeye tipped his head back. "Probably think because Evred's young, they can shoulder him into it."

His cousin Evred had been a quiet, scholarly sort of boy, but kingship had changed him. The older generation all said—in private—he was every day becoming more like the grandfather Evred and Hawkeye and Barend shared. Hawkeye's mother had said once, *My father inherited all the trouble the Montredavan-Ans willed us, along with their crown. The only way he could see to unite the Jarls was to ride off to war, give 'em more land. But our generation is paying for that war. And that land.* He'd always thought that meant old monetary debts of some sort, but since he'd come to live here in the north he wasn't so sure.

Barend's thoughts were obviously running parallel.

"Hope I get to be there to watch Ola-Vayir try to squeeze Evred for more land before the old wolf brings his boys in."

Hawkeye said, "Why don't we save 'em the trouble? Nightingale, I'm thinking you'd better go yourself down the coast road out of Lindeth until you find Ola-Vayir. Ride alongside him. Offer to be helpful. He's not going to lag under your eyes."

Nightingale's grunt was midway between agreement and a laugh.

Barend rubbed his backside again. "Wasn't that supposed to be Buck's job?"

"Right." Hawkeye grinned. "And Buck would cut out his own heart with a spoon before he'd risk missing the action, but there's no sign of him, either. So that's why Nightingale better go, just in case they got mired somewhere."

Nightingale said, "I'll ride out soon's we're done here."

"Barend." Hawkeye tipped his chin toward the east. "I got a Runner this morning. Evred's just a couple days from us, and wants you to ride down and meet 'em."

Barend chuckled under his breath. "You mean hand off command to Inda, then. And not a heartbeat too soon."

His lack of strut made even Hawkeye grin.

Barend cocked his head. "Wonder if I'll have to fight for it. Don't Harskialdnas fight? I mean, in the old days, if someone wanted to challenge them for the position?"

Nightingale gave his turtle shrug.

"Challenges happened, yes. Usually at Convocation," Hawkeye said. "Come to think of it, some of the old ballads have it happening in the field, too." A corner of his mouth curled. "Did in the old ballad my father's family sings, 'Yvana Ride Thunder.' We lost to the Montrei-Haucs, but we lost heroically."

They all laughed, then Barend ran a hand over his broad forehead. "But isn't that for Harskialdna as permanent rank, not for one battle? Or does he want Inda for life? Either way is all right with me. I never wanted it. Everyone knows that. Oh. It's not me, it's Inda, is that it? There can't possibly be problems accepting him. I can't believe people are that stupid."

Nightingale tipped his hand back and forth, like a trader's weight scale evenly balanced. "Some of 'em— coastal men, mostly—remember the pirate fights. No problem there. It's the inland men. A lot of 'em from Horsebutt Tya-Vayir's connections. Mostly think he's the king's claphair."

Barend raised his brows. "Claphair?"

"Academy slur." Hawkeye snorted. "Sex for favors."

Barend looked vaguely surprised. "Not Inda. He hardly sees it when a *woman* wants him, unless she grabs him by the balls." *And after he'd been living around that Taumad with absentminded indifference for years, it was safe to say that Inda hadn't any interest at all in the fellows*, Barend thought, laughing inwardly. As for Evred, Barend remembered him having occasionally sent for fellows from Hadand's pleasure house the winter before, but instead of loading any of them with privileges, he hadn't even kept them for the night. "Naw, that can't be right."

"It's just Horsebutt," Hawkeye said impatiently, already through with the subject. He'd been remembering the men's faces, their talk, before the battle at the Nob. "You might have to fight Inda to get the men behind him. Right before a battle, they have to believe he's the best."

Barend, veteran of many ship battles, recognized Hawkeye's low, intense tone. *Just like a pirate duel on the captain's deck.* He flicked his hand up in agreement. "I'll rest my aching ass. Be off in the morning."

Chapter Thirty-six

"HEY, you men!" The high voice off to Tau's left sounded thin as a gull's cry, as he rode a way back along the column.

Tau turned his head. A skinny, barefoot boy had darted from the hedgerow lining one side of the North Road and shouted through cupped hands.

Heads turned, then back again. An embarrassed mother marched out and grabbed the urchin by the scruff of his smock.

The boy spread arms and legs, fighting to stay. "When's the battle?" he cried. "When's the battle? We wanna waaaatch!"

The mother thrust her son back through the ancient hedgerow, leaving behind the sound of her scolding and his rising wail of protest.

"Ye might tell us," an old man wheezed from a rocky outcropping above a slight bend in the road. "Where it's gonna be, so we can hide ourselves." And he cackled, as if at a very good joke.

From his clothing and the crook he was a shepherd. Sheep grazed over the slow incline rising toward those sky-touching mountains, evidence of a catastrophic landslide ages ago. The long flat slope had long been tamed by old trees and complicated long-grass communities, patchworked on the eastern slope with farms. In the center, guarding the narrowing entry into the mountains, sat Ala Larkadhe, shaped like a crown with its mysterious remnant of Old Sartor in the weird white tower soaring above the newer granite castellated city.

Tau turned back to the crowd of people alongside the road. Some sat in the trees planted by some long ago noble, or peered over the far older hedgerow; most stood out in the open, faces upturned. Many hostile, most awed, though they hadn't meant to be. But the sight of the long, long columns of warriors on their beautiful horses with the tear-shaped shields and gleaming helms hanging at their sides, the warriors' hair pulled up into those martial tails just like the horses', the tight gray coats with the long skirts, the composite bows, and above all the long swords with the wickedly curved tips in the saddle sheaths—it all impressed them. The Marlovans rode so well—they made it look so easy—they seemed easy, talking quietly, or looking at the countryside, but not answering back because (though the watchers did not know it) the captains had issued orders that the men were to remain aloof, no matter what. No comments, no questions. If they didn't look they wouldn't see the backs of hands, or spitting. Most important of all, they were not to answer questions.

It had been easy to ignore the first gawkers, but they had been coming out in greater numbers over the past couple of days. Now, within two days' ride of the city up there on the slope, the warriors had other things to think about.

Tau clucked to his mount, passing a pair of dragoons, one saying, "What's that tall one with the long leaves?"

"Corn," his riding companion replied. "Don't you southern boys know anything? That's corn. Just you wait until you taste cornbread."

Tau was past, and did not hear the answer. A commotion ahead caught his attention: a signal from the outriders.

Everyone's attention snapped forward as dust rose around a pair galloping toward the great war banners at the front of the column. When the dust settled, the word passed back that Barend-Harskialdna Montrei-Vayir was with them.

Two Harskialdnas!

Inda hadn't any such thought in his head. Alight with joy, he was about to yell "Barend!"

Barend saw him, but his mouth stayed tight. His posture stiff.

Inda's joy cooled to question as Barend leaned back, clumsily halting the horse, who snorted, ears flat, whuffing in protest at the heavy hand on the reins. Barend snapped his fist to his chest, the salute returned thoughtfully by his cousin Evred-Harvaldar.

Inda turned his gaze between the two, and as Evred gave the signal to ride on at a company trot, Barend slid a glance Inda's way, one thin brow ever so slightly raised, a corner of his mouth curling up.

Intrigued, Inda pulled back, ceding the Shield Arm position next to the king. For the first time, he dropped behind to ride with Signi and Tau.

Tau took in the alert glances of the men behind them, the furtive whispers. Everyone expected something to happen.

The king's army camped directly south of the city of Ala Larkadhe within a hard day's ride up the slope. Tau and Signi were taken by surprise when, in place of the usual drill, Evred gave the orders for two fires and then summoned the pair of Harskialdnas to his tent. Surprise was followed by apprehension when they witnessed the hand signal that Evred made when he wanted privacy, and the Runners formed an inside perimeter, not even Signi's guards within earshot of the royal tent.

In the privacy of his tent, Evred flicked a considering glance from one to the other, saw the unguarded grins, and his brow cleared. "Barend?"

"We have to make it good, see." Barend laughed. "Hawkeye agreed. Men have to see a tight win, commander against commander. Like pirates, Inda." And when

Inda made a noise of disgust. "If I rode in friendly, well, then they don't expect a tight win."

Since his return home, Inda had come to the conclusion that his boyhood knowledge of history, once seemingly so complete, was far too sketchy. He smothered a laugh. "I'm to challenge you? I guess I can see it. But we really don't want a pirate duel, do we? Guts on the deck?"

Evred breathed in relief. He had not expected any trouble from his cousin, so the possibility had caught him up hard; and he had not even considered what Hawkeye had clearly foreseen. He said, "It has to look that way, they're right."

"Why?" Inda sighed. "What does a fight, any kind of fight, have to do with *us*—" He smacked his gray coat. "—taking on the Venn invaders?"

Barend jerked his chin outward, toward the camp. "It has to do with you looking so tough you'll lead them into victory. That means they might actually survive." Seeing Inda's grimace of misgiving, he added, "Worked for our fleet, too. You never saw it on the ships, but they saw *you*. You were good with leading, good hand-to-hand. See?"

"No. I don't. Because a ship fight is so different from a battle this size, when maybe a hundred of them might see me. No one else will."

Barend waved him off. "Never mind what's true. They have to see you win against me, and it has to be a fight better than anything *they* could win. Like one of our whoop-ups at Freedom. Even better. Then they'll blab it to everyone else."

"Oh." Inda grimaced down at his sleeve, which covered the scars on his arm. "Not with blood?"

Barend's eyes widened briefly, almost enough for one to see their color. "Of course with blood. But you'll be airing more of mine." He turned to Evred, and brushed his fingers against the front of his coat.

Evred said, "He knows about the lockets, Barend. I have not been able to send anything for a couple of weeks."

"Us either. Weird, that," Barend said, without much interest. He'd never expected magical things to work long, and now he no longer had to try to make out words from those tiny letters. "Here's my report. Nightingale rode off to join up with Ola-Vayir."

"They're at Lindeth already?"

"No. No sign of 'em yet. So Hawkeye sent Nightingale south to find 'em."

"Nightingale's presence will no doubt smooth the road with miraculous ease." Evred's voice had gone dry.

"Just what Hawkeye said." Barend gave his wheezy laugh, smacked the tent flap aside, and strode out.

Evred said, "Whoop-up?"

Amazing how often Fox's name came near to mention. Inda gave his head a shake, one hand on the tent flap. "Display fights at Freeport Harbor, to attract captains to hire us. Later, to gain crew."

"Inda," Evred said, his voice low, almost inaudible.

Inda stiffened at the shift in Evred's tone. He could not have defined it in words, but it burned warning along his nerves like a shower of wood sparks. Wafri's voice had been like that at times.

But this was Evred—and the subject was imminent war.

Inda let the flap fall, cutting the flow of light. The two of them stood there in the hot, stuffy tent, each seeing the other mostly as shadow. Evred clasped his hands behind his back. "This fight. They'll expect . . . Barend never wanted . . . will you consider making the change of commander permanent? I cannot think of any better benefit to the kingdom."

Inda stared. "You mean become your Harskialdna for *life*?"

"Yes. Does that seem so impossible?"

"Impossible? No. Yes!" Inda laughed, tossed dizzyingly between joy and astonishment. He'd spent his entire exile schooling himself to face the fact that he would never get what he wanted. People didn't, sometimes. So you made a life as best you could.

But since his return, what he'd wanted not only fell into his lap without his having to grasp for it, but more. Honor, rank—far more than he'd imagined even in the craziest homesick dream. "I . . . well. I. Ah, look. I'll do whatever needs doing. You know that. And, well, if we survive this battle . . . well. I'd be honored." His voice was no more than a gruff whisper, but it resonated with conviction.

That resonance was so intense it was akin to pain. Evred unclasped his hands, one palm toward the tent flap.

Inda almost leaped out, then jolted to a stop. He was not supposed to grin, or laugh, or give any sign of the fact that he'd just been offered the highest rank in the land after king. Not just for this battle, but for *life*.

All right, a show fight was what the men needed? He'd see that they got one.

Schooling his face as best he could, he settled on a mat opposite Barend. Cherry-Stripe and Cama sat with him. Despite his attempt to remain impassive, everyone could see that Inda was tense, but they all mistook his uplifted chin, his compressed lips, his stillness, as challenge.

Whispers rustled and hissed back through the men crowding forward.

Evred emerged from his tent and sat between Barend and Rat Cassad, inscrutable as always.

When the supper was over (cooked and eaten with un-precedented speed), Evred walked out between the two fires, something he'd never done before. By the time he'd taken half a dozen steps every man within sight stopped talking.

Evred turned in a slow circle. "Barend-Dal Montrei-Vayir, my Harskialdna, has accepted a challenge from Indevan-Laef Algara-Vayir."

The men were so quiet (except for a furtive curse or two as the men in the back tried to shove their way forward enough to see) the crackling of the fires was clear in the balmy air.

The duelists took off sashes and coats, handing them to Runners to hold. Barend loosened the top of his shirt laces to ease his breathing, but Inda ripped his free with an ab-sent movement and tossed them aside; on the pirate ship he'd never fought with laces. Tau, on the watch, caught the silken cord from the air.

Inda and Barend took their cavalry swords from waiting Runners, and at Evred's silent gesture saluted him and then faced off, standing only in shirt and breeches and boots, knife in left hand and sword in right.

"Begin," Evred said, settling back onto his mat.

They hurled themselves at one another, commencing a duel so wild, so unpredictable that the men crowded in on one another even more, leaning on those in front in an effort to follow the flurry of moves.

Clash! Clang! One, then the other, was sent rolling, to leap up and whirl straight into a complexity of fast moves nearly impossible to follow. Balance, speed, precision raised fierce joy in fighters as well as watchers; unknown to the Marlovans, it was just the sort of showy mock-duel that Kodl used to choreograph back in the Freedom Island days to draw ship captains to hire marine defenders before their reputation had rendered such displays unnecessary. But they had always been great fun, especially when Fox designed them.

At just the right moment Barend whirled, his sword hissing over Inda's head—nearly slicing off his flapping horsetail—then scything toward his knees. Inda tumbled over the sword, landed kneeling, arm straight out, sword point toward the sky, hilt toward the ground, the other hand bringing his knife into guard.

A single heartbeat later the square toes of Barend's boots (he'd stopped his horse and put them on when he saw the army's dust on the horizon) thunked smack under the hilt, sending the sword arcing over and over into the air. A small laugh escaped him, a brief flash of teeth, but by now the spectators were so intent that those few who caught it assumed it was the triumph of a man about to go in for the kill.

His foot continued its arc, snapping a sidekick toward Inda's head; he sheathed his knife, both moves beautifully coordinated. Inda tumbled away from the kick and rolled to his feet as Barend caught Inda's sword hilt in his free hand, to a roar from the watchers.

Inda pulled his second knife from the wrist sheath. Another susurrus whispered back.

Barend stepped toward Inda, swinging both swords with bloodthirsty zeal. Inda whirled in, caught one blade on his crossed knives, kicked up backward to block the second blade, whipped the first arm down, twisted, and slammed his elbow into Barend's gut.

Barend doubled over, the swords flying—one nearly landing in the fire, the other skittering across the dirt. Barend kneed Inda, who flipped backward. Barend threw a knife, light glittering in runnels off the slowly spinning steel until Inda nipped it out of the air, causing a shout from the crowd. He threw it back.

Barend kicked it whirling into the air, and caught it by the blade.

Roar!

They rolled to their feet and each gripped two knives as they circled, circled, then Barend attacked.

Zing! Inda's cross block ripped along the edge of Barend's knife, sending sparks showering down, causing another shout.

Now the fight was even faster, a blur of complicated moves: all the men could see were places the knife points had been, marked by gleaming crimson lines of blood on the combatants' flesh. Forehead, shoulder, wrist, above a knee, cheekbone, arm bloomed with cherry spots of blood. Barend showed more cuts than Inda.

Barend took three hard blows in a row, ending with Inda whirling to deliver a crushing sidekick in the gut. Barend folded, letting out a yell. Inda brought a knife hilt down against the back of his neck. Barend slammed to the ground and stayed there.

Inda walked to the edge of the circle while Barend took his time rising to a sitting position, then standing; Vedrid and the Runners surrounded him with strips of cloth to bind up the cuts, which they discovered were extremely superficial. Precise. Inda shook blood off his arm and wiped the nick on his temple, smearing it as he turned in a slow circle. "Are there anymore challenges?"

Silence. Profound silence.

"I ask again, anymore challenges?"

No one moved.

Inda faithfully repeated what he'd remembered from the old ballad, surprised at how serious he sounded even to himself. "For the third and last time I ask, are there any challenges?"

Cherry-Stripe discovered he'd grabbed Cama's arm when the latter, with a faint smile, peeled his fingers off one by one. Noddy whistled silently under his breath. He had an idea that that fight had something odd about it, but only because Barend had fallen directly in front of him. Surely a man whose stomach had just been flattened against his spine wouldn't be grinning as he went down.

Inda turned slowly, meeting wide gazes in which the fires twinned. *Listen to me,* he thought. *Whatever it takes to believe you can win.*

The Sier Danas had watched intently, Cherry-Stripe trying to figure out whether it had been serious or not. Cama had figured it out from the first move, so he'd watched in silent appreciation, wondering if he was ever going to meet Fox Montredavan-An. Probably not.

What surprised Noddy was the intensity in Inda; he just did not seem the same person they rode with every day, even the same one who scrapped so deftly with Taumad-Runner each morning behind the command tents.

An impulse caused Noddy to flick a glance Evred's way, to catch an avidity in his old mate who was usually the model of reserve. He realized the impulse had come from hearing Evred's breathing; and that explained why Evred and Hadand, who so noticeably admired each other, behaved like brother and sister. Noddy was surprised at the sense of rightness he felt at the idea of Inda and Evred heart-bound.

Then Inda spun about, smacking the knife blade against his heart in a gesture more extravagant than anything Tau had ever seen on the stage—but it worked. "Evred-Harvaldar, I present myself to be sworn as your Harskialdna."

Evred stood, remote again. "Bring me your sword."

Noddy, leaning forward, observed little signs that his

first impression was wrong. Or almost wrong. Evred was ardent, his speech only to Inda. They all could have vanished right then, would he have noticed? But Inda spoke to everyone in hearing, not just to Evred.

Evred's vowing to Inda, and Inda to the Marlovan king. Noddy sat back, grimacing. Was that good, or not? He usually didn't think about such things. And he wouldn't now, either, he decided, reaching for the wine being passed from hand to hand.

Signi alone had not enjoyed the mock duel, nor did she like the intensity in these young, determined faces. She and Tau were the only ones who saw the tremor in Evred's hand as Inda dropped to one knee before him and held up the sword.

In those days Marlovans knelt when making their first vows at Convocation, at promotion on the field, or at public judgment.

"I, Evred-Harvaldar, call you, Indevan Algara-Vayir, to become my Harskialdna, Royal Shield Arm."

Then—assailed by hoarse, fervent cries of approval from all around them—he offered the hilt of his own sword to Inda.

Inda rose, flushing, and took the sword as Harskialdna, and raised it.

"Do you swear," Evred said in his throne room voice, "to defend me, and by defending me, defend Iasca Leror, with your body and your blood, your heart and your mind, as long as you shall live?"

Inda spoke the words, his halting voice sounding to his own ears like it came from someone else. Tau, blocked by the shoulder-to-shoulder crowd of Marlovans, heard Inda's voice for the first time just as a voice—unexpectedly deep and resonant when he pitched it just so.

Tau clasped his hands together, thinking, *For six years you called no one master. I hope you know what you are doing.*

Signi kept Inda in her gaze, even though her eyes blurred. This was the time of life when the young, so new to adulthood, gave structure and meaning to their lives with vows. Sometimes so blithely spoken, so heartfully meant—sometimes so very hard to keep.

"... then you shall be my eyes and my ears, and my right arm. And you shall speak with the King's Voice at all corners of the kingdom."

Signi laid her palms together, breathing *May the Stars above the Tree light the path for the both of you*—and then the two clashed the blades together, sending sparks arcing skyward.

Inda and Evred returned together to the mats as the solid-packed crowd stirred and slowly broke up. Some brought out hand drums, and the ballads began, this time not in groups here and there, but everyone singing together, voices ringing with conviction.

Inda sat at Evred's left again. He sang all the songs he knew, his voice clear and unexpectedly melodic. He thumped time on his knee to the ones he didn't know, but joined the chorus as soon as he had some of the words. Tau had never before heard Inda sing. On Evred's other side, Barend-Dal Montrei-Vayir also sang, tuneless as a crow, but just as full of conviction. He was still the king's cousin, and still would command as Evred directed, but he was no longer Harskialdna.

He would no longer speak, and act, with the King's Voice.

That was now Inda's responsibility—and his life.

PART TWO

Chapter One

NDAND Arveas and the children of Castle Andahi made a long, weary trek up the side of the rocky mountainside, sleeping under the stars when the sun vanished. Ndand walked with them, leading her horse by the reins. She left the children with the older girls in the old robbers' cave that the youngsters used as their main headquarters when they camped out and played scout and stalk games.

From Twisted Pine Path upward horses were useless; the trail was too steep and narrow. Ndand retreated back over the ridge that divided the cave from the castle, and trudged straight upward, Keth with her. He kept looking back down at the avalanche, admiring it anew.

When they reached Twisted Pine, they came to the fork. One way led into deep old forest, eventually winding down into Idayago. The narrower path led straight upward. They began to climb that path. The landslide, then the castle, dropped away from view.

Upward for the steepest portion of their climb they toiled, through three drenching lightning storms followed by the blaze of the summer sun. Down below that meant stifling heat unless a breeze came directly off the harbor, chasing up the canyons of the pass. Up on the mountains, the sun was bright but the air more mild, summer defining itself in a rainbow splash of wildflowers. The higher they reached the colder the night air, and they huddled together in the same bedroll, Keth dropping off within half a dozen breaths, Ndand lying back quietly to think, the horse on a long line nearby.

The three oldest girls had begun the trek in silent cooperation, but by the end Ndand had seen the little signs that there was going to be trouble between them. Inevitable, she'd discovered during her teens. Some girls were natural leaders, some just had to be leaders whether they were good at it or not, and some would do anything for attention. You could make do if you had only two of these types in any group, but all three always meant trouble, and they had all three.

Before she left the children in the robbers' cave, Ndand assembled them so that no one would feel singled out. She looked at each face as she repeated the Jarlan's orders. If good sense didn't prevail, the threat of the consequences of not following orders would.

She had no fears for them otherwise. The castle children had been all over the mountains since their arrival at Castle Andahi almost four years ago. They knew all the local trails and caves; they had sometimes camped out for days at a time. The Jarl and Jarlan had thought such ventures good for developing responsibility as well as hardiness.

Good sense will keep you alive better than ambition, she thought as she got to her feet and helped Keth up.

After another long trek, she and Keth reached the last fork. The left-hand trail wound around the mountain to the lookout point, which was lower than the beacon crag, but from which the entire bay and the castle were visible. The right-hand trail climbed all the way to the heights. There at the very top of the mountain someone long ago had built a one-room house out of stone. Flash and Barend and their chosen men had built the beacon there, after tests with lanterns. The burning beacon (or its smoke during the glare of day) would be visible from the crags up the pass, though the bulk of the mountain blocked it from the view of the harbor and castle below.

She wiped her brow. Even if the air was cool, the bright sun was warm. Keth had begun stoutly determined to do his share, but for most of the afternoon she'd taken his little bag of clothes and he'd been holding her hand. Her shoulder ached from the constant pull.

She eyed the two trails, then dropped the packs on a nearby rock and swung her arm. "Let's have something to eat, then push on," she suggested, and watched the boy sink down with silent but expressive relief.

They wolfed down a portion of their journey bread, then got to their feet. She forced her voice to cheery briskness. "Come on, then. We can reach them before nightfall if we really push. Horse'll wait here."

Keth's neck knuckle bobbed. "Right," he said sturdily.

And so they ran and walked by turns, stopping only to drink. As the sky clouded for the almost inevitable afternoon storm, Ndand sang songs. When the storm struck, with lightning flickering all around, she switched to heroic stories as they huddled under a tree. As soon as the sun peeped out, shining through the crystal drips all around them, they splashed on, a rainbow reflected in the puddles.

She was busy enough with her stories to keep her own mind from gnawing itself raw with the now-familiar questions. So she was not aware just when the atmosphere changed.

Maybe it was the emptiness. Instinctively she slowed, relieved to reach the last narrow trail bordering the rocky cliff on which the little hut was built. No one knew who had built it, or why, but it was there, the stone walls so old they were mossy. The roof had long since fallen in, but Flash and his men had made a new one, laddering scavenged branches from wind-twisted trees and covering that with cut turf.

Ndand sniffed, her shoulder stiffening. The air smelled like it always did: pine, mud, a trace of wildflowers. So why did she feel like a scout dog, hackles up, ears twitchy?

"Behind me," she said to Keth.

Her uncharacteristically sharp tone made him fall in obediently, tired as he was.

She began the stalk, treading on the outsides of the foot so that one moved in silence. The children learned it young; she didn't need to look at Keth to know that he'd begun stalking. His steps were soundless.

They circled the house in a wide perimeter first, scouting in all directions.

Nothing in the makeshift stable, which was nothing more than a roof on poles for the horses of Barend's or Flash's Runners. None of whom were here.

She eyed the house. Nothing. She looked skyward. No threat of a new storm, and the old one was now just a dark line in the east.

"Hello?" she called. The single small window was open, which is what you'd expect on a sunny day, but Ndand's neck hairs stood up and her scalp prickled with a sense of danger.

"Flash?"

A small foot splooshed the muddy ground next to her and Keth crept close, face blanched with question and fear.

She was scaring him. So she forced herself to walk briskly, her rain-soaked linen robe squeaking. Pitching her voice to heartiness, she marched straight to the warped wood-slat door. A faint smell made her throat close. She whirled and gazed toward the beacon farther up at the pinnacle of the mountain. It sat there unlit.

Unlit? Not only unlit but sodden from how many storms? Its leddas-weave, rainproof cover lay abandoned on the muddy ground, caught against a boulder where the wind had flung it.

She whirled back, sprang to the door and flung it open.

The faint stench intensified to the lour of death.

"Wait." She flung out a hand, then gagged.

Keth backed away rapidly, eyes enormous.

She thrust her nose into the crook of her elbow and forced herself to look again at the two corpses seated at the table, covered with a mess of wet leaves chased through the little window by the storms. There were no signs of violence.

Flash sat with his head cradled on his arms as if he were

taking a light nap. Across from him, Estral the Poet leaned on the table as well, one arm pillowing her head, the other rigid next to a pen and paper.

Ndand dashed in, took up the paper, and ran out.

Despite the weather the ink was clear. Estral had used the expensive heralds' ink, made to withstand sweaty fingers, years of seasonal change, decades of sitting on dusty shelves.

My dear brother Skandar:

If your plans work—and why shouldn't they in the south as well as they have right here? You will be the first to find this letter, and I want you to understand that I do not blame you.

Skandar? Ndand knew that name. Wasn't there a Skandar leading the Resistance? Skandar Mardric. *Brother?*

Sick with fear, anger, and grief, Ndand forced herself to read on.

The spell on my magical case abruptly ceased to function, as I am sure you are aware: I do not know if it was only mine, or all of ours wore out the magic. That is why the silence of these past days.

I shall keep my hands to the paper so that these words will be the third thing to catch your eye.

Not your fault, so I say again. You know I never desired to trade my old, silk-broidered words for the knotted ravels of current passions. You always mocked me with your smile and your "Oh, Estral, when will you face up to the truth, that the poems of olden times just decorated the same old betrayals, greed, and ambition." I still believe if it is so, the greater cause was better than the meanness of our present choices—either "our" king (our loyalty far stronger after he fell than it ever was before!) or the carefully planned and impartial overlordship of the Marlovans. You say the Marlovans must die because we did not choose them. I say, but we did not choose our king, either.

Despite the kinthus my thoughts scamper in fright down this tangled path toward the gathering shadows. Is that because I know what lies ahead? If only I could see! Though pain there is none and the fear is gradually fading. My fingers slowly grow cold, see how carefully shaped my letters are? I have to state my point: I chose to follow you. But here, at the end, I can say it is not out of conviction, nor out of a wish for fame. I did what I did to see your smile of pride.

I will not see it now.

In horror Ndand read the rest of Estral's confession: how she'd gone with Flash to the beacon. How she'd offered him a glass of wine while they waited for the storm to pass, so they could drag off the cover and light the beacon together. How she'd put a double dose of white kinthus into the wine, adding spices to hide it. The instant effect, Flash's last words—words of love, not of war.

How she held him until he was dead. Then she dragged the cover off the beacon so it would be ineradicably ruined, just as Skandar had made her promise to do.

Everything done as she'd promised.

How she had judged herself for what she had done.

So instead of your pride, give me your promise: that you send this letter to Ndand Arveas, Flash's wife. Yes, I am asking you to give information to a Marlovan. I beg you to try, just once, to see past the high fence of your political assumptions and extend a hand, human to human. Of all of them, she will understand most, and I would have her know that though I took his life away from him, away from her, away from his brother and father and mother and from the world, I gave mine in return. Not an equal bargain. Or a fair one. But it's all I have to give.

Ndand crushed the letter into her robe, unable to read farther. She had to get control of herself, for there was much to be done.

Keth watched, white-lipped. "Did she kill him?"

"Yes."

"Why?"

"She was part of the Resistance. We didn't know she was sister to the leader."

Keth's voice trembled. "Let's leave her here to rot."

Ndand closed her eyes against a lightning-bolt of anger. She'd shared her home, her heart, her husband with this woman, who had taken away the last. Estral had enabled the Venn to make it easier to take away the first.

But she had never wanted to hurt the second. Ndand knew it as true.

"No," she said, opening her eyes. "We will sing for her as well as him as we Disappear them. We will treat her with respect. We will—" No, they could not set the cabin afire to serve as beacon, for the furniture was as sodden as the beacon, and stone walls and a storm-soaked turf roof would not burn. Instinct urged her to move fast, not spend days here hoping to coax a fire out of sodden wood.

"We will leave this cabin clean and open to the air. And then we'll go back down the trail to the lookout fork . . ." She let out a slow, shuddering breath as she caressed Keth's face. "And if we see the red-black flag, and I am afraid we will, there won't be time to visit the girls, and leave you with them. You and I are going to ride like thunder over the pass to warn Ala Larkadhe. Because it doesn't look like there's anybody else to do the job."

Chapter Two

HYARL Fulla Durasnir, Commander of Prince Rajnir's invasion fleet, looked around the ruins of Castle Trad Varadhe.

The Marlovans had destroyed the castle and the harbor; it was no surprise that they had been ready for the invasion. The carefully timed simultaneous attack on all three of Idayago's castle-guarded harbors had thus been mostly a failed surprise; except for catching the Jarl of Arveas and his force leaving Trad Varadhe on their way to Castle Andahi.

Durasnir was here on inspection because his Drenga were a part of the invasion. Even though they came under the Hilda chain of command, Durasnir liked seeing whatever would be described in reports if he could. Hilda Commander Talkar had requested Prince Rajnir invite Durasnir as a courtesy.

The Drenga, as first in, had joined with the Hilda in attacking the Jarl's force. Once the Marlovans had been destroyed, Talkar had been shifted to the most important castle, the gateway to the pass.

Durasnir paced over the battleground where the Marlovans had been defeated, then he inspected the harbor, finally shaking his head.

"The docks will all have to be rebuilt," he said.

"The Idayagans can do it," Dag Erkric replied, and then turned to the prince.

The way he did it burned warning through Durasnir. He'd turned too soon, not with the manner of seeing if the prince had anything to say, but as if giving him a prompt.

Sure enough. Prince Rajnir said, "Oneli Commander Talkar sent a dispatch just before you came, Hyarl my Commander." He flickered his fingers, indicating a dispatch box. "He says they still do not have the castle gates down, even though he's been there since yesterday! If Talkar's men can't get the gates down, I desire the Yaga Krona to help them. Since you are going to inspect there next, you may carry my will to Talkar."

Behind the prince, Dag Erkric smiled.

"As you wish, my prince." Durasnir made his obeisance.

Erkric said smoothly, "I would be glad to send you directly to the *Cormorant* by transfer magic."

Prince Rajnir smiled. "It is a good idea. It will be so much faster."

The dag might have meant it for a courtesy, though he rarely did anything for a single reason.

"I thank you both, my prince, Dag Erkric. But I wish to finish inspecting the harbor so that we may begin rebuilding the sooner. We will need it."

Prince Rajnir exclaimed, "Yes. Yes! You always know what is right, Hyarl my Commander."

Durasnir saluted in peace mode, wondering if the prince really understood why "Hyarl my Commander" was insisting on traditional travel: because despite all the talk about expedience, and quick-thinking aid, and adaptation being equivalent of the bending Tree against harsh winds, *magic is not used in war.*

A direct order from the prince must be obeyed. And the method of delivery made Durasnir a messenger-ensign. He must take the order to Talkar, which would signal to everyone that Durasnir was part of this shift away from tradition to using magic in war.

Therefore, Durasnir refused the offering of magic transfer. He took his time in finishing his inspection of Trad

Varadhe's harbor, and then had himself rowed back to the *Cormorant,* his flagship. He signaled for his raiders to assume fleet battle stations as they sailed west from Trad Varadhe to Sala Varadhe, or Castle Andahi.

The Marlovans were there, defending it with life and blood, so he may as well adapt to their name for it.

The trip itself was all too short a distance, the shore winds having shifted to speed them along.

They reached the bay on the morning tide. He signaled for the fleet to anchor outside in the roads, as the bay itself was filled with the advance force's ships. As his crew went about their duty, he raised his glass to scan the horizon, where the bulk of the fleet tacked and tacked again, polishing the coast as they waited for orders to land the army. They were a fine sight, on strict station all across the horizon.

By the time Durasnir had finished breakfast and inspected his ship, no messengers awaited him with the hoped-for news. The gates to Castle Andahi remained closed.

So Commander Durasnir set out to deliberately waste time.

He summoned his personal ensigns to get him into his heavy formal battle tunic again, and to have himself clasped back into his armor.

He brushed his hair out, rebraided it, and settled his winged helm on his head to his satisfaction.

He toured his ship on inspection again, pretending not to see covert looks of annoyance from his men interrupted in their duty rhythm.

He ate a biscuit while reading the newest dispatches—all three of them. He read them twice.

Finally he sent a polite message to Falk Ulaffa, the dag in charge of the prince's Yaga Krona, sequestered in study down in the dags' cabins, in case he wanted a ride instead of using transfer magic like the dags usually did. He issued orders for the boats, adding that the Drenga must find some mounts so that he could proceed by horse up the newly-secured road to the castle, after an inspection of the aftermath of the landings.

That ought to take up plenty of time, he reasoned, since the local tides did not cooperate, being mild. Maybe by then Talkar would have those gates opened.

He was surprised when Dag Ulaffa accepted his invitation. Getting the old dag over the side and into the boat on a brisk sea wasted more time.

He climbed down, taking care that the frisky breeze just kicking up did not disturb the wings on his helm. He settled himself, asked the dag if he was comfortable. Ulaffa gave him an absent smile, and responded in the affirmative.

The men picked up the oars and pulled for shore.

Durasnir remained in the longboat until the marines had beached it, their usual smooth, swift competence more speedy than ever, directly under the eye of their commander. When you're at war, there's no way to tell your men to slack off, he thought wryly.

He stepped out of the command longboat. Ulaffa fumbled his way out of the boat with the painstaking care of the elderly who seldom are put to physical exertion.

Ulaffa bunched his robe up, extending a sandaled foot and setting it cautiously in the water. Then he trod with uncertain steps on the tide-washed beach shingle. He was so slow and deliberate one would almost think he was in secret sympathy with Durasnir and the army. But reading one's own emotions into others, especially the prince's own dags, was at best dangerous, at worst deliberately blinding to true motives. The Oneli and Hilda were forbidden to interact with the Erama Krona, the royal bodyguards. Durasnir did not know the strict wording of rules governing the mixing of the Yaga Krona and the Sea Dags, but he assumed they had a similar custom.

His efficient Drenga had somehow managed to secure a mount from the Hilda.

Durasnir turned away, scanning the shoreline road marked by darkened bloodstains. Here the last of the Marlovan jarl's defenders trying to reach the castle had been cut off and stood their ground to the end.

It had been a tough fight, the silent party discovered as they proceeded, weapons and mail jingling, at a stately pace. Bloodstains splashed all the way up the shingle to the rising land below the castle, stains soon to be diminished by rain, wind, and hooves and boots when the army landed to march up the pass.

Shortly before noon they arrived at the outer walls of Castle Andahi. The sweep of the great road to the mountains had been bisected by a massive landslide—not for the first time in history—which meant the only access to the road was directly through the castle. It was a crude defense, but it had been successful many centuries before.

Not against the Venn.

He paused a way from the outer curtain wall, studying the castle, an impressive structure nearly a thousand years old, much reinforced since then by ring within ring of massive walls and iron-reinforced gates made of the whole trunks of trees. What had been the cost of *that?* Or had the ancestors of these Idayagans ignored the wood guilds and mage councils, so far away on the other side of the continent . . . and was their decline a direct result of that?

Perhaps only Ulaffa could answer such a question. The old dag was studying the mountain heights under a shading hand, his blue robe blowing about his sandaled feet.

Time to get to business, distasteful as it was.

Approaching hoofbeats caused another halt as three riders traversed the scrubby land. The neat rows of tents belonging to the advance force lined the lower slope a short distance behind them.

The two snapping banners behind the riders sharpened into detail: one, the Owl-in-Hunt of Talkar's House, the other, the Great Tree Ydrasal. Talkar's jowly face resolved out of the dust as he and his banner-bearers drew near, the three golden rings of the Hilda Stalna, the army commander, embroidered on the upper right arm of his battle tunic gleaming softly: no one wore torcs into battle. Durasnir wore his torcs as a subtle reminder that he was here not to interfere with command but as courier only.

Talkar's gaze flicked from Durasnir's arm to his face. His

expression was grimmer than usual under his gleaming winged helm.

He can't get the gates down, Durasnir thought, as Talkar slowed and saluted, hands together then opened out. *Damnation.* "Your report?"

Talkar stated, "The gate is stronger than we had estimated."

"It is the prince's will that we use the aid of the dags," Durasnir said.

The man's face tightened as he saluted, palms together.

Durasnir turned Ulaffa's way.

The dag said, "It will take until sundown to prepare. If you will pardon me, Commanders, I will summon the mages appointed by Dag Erkric, and we will begin the preparations."

So Talkar has until sundown, Durasnir thought. *And now I would take any oath that Ulaffa is also dragging a sail.*

Ulaffa climbed with difficulty from his mount. His sandals crunched on the sandy gravel as he paced slowly away, the soft breeze carrying whispered fragments of his magic spells.

Talkar raised his gauntleted hand, and the banner-bearers halted. He and Durasnir rode down a short, rocky slope toward the long beach of shingle, ostensibly to give the dag plenty of room for his spell casting, but in truth well out of earshot.

"This order was spoken directly to you?" Talkar asked finally, after another tight-lipped, nostril-flaring silence.

The great siege engines the army had counted on taking from the other two northern castles had been so thoroughly destroyed there was no patching them together. And on Dag Erkric's orders, they had not brought over the implements for making their own, full as the ships had been with men, horses, and their own supplies. *We will use their own weapons against the two or three castles they have on this coast,* Erkric had said to the prince, who agreed with enthusiasm. *Next year, when we must penetrate to the formidable Marlovan castles inland, that is the time to fill*

*holds with the big siege weapons, if we cannot build our own
out of materials we find in Idayago.*

Dag Erkric's reasoning sounded sensible, and it certainly
solved the immediate problem: use the dags to loosen the
bindings in the gates to bring them down. It wasn't fighting, it was merely the opposite of repair.

Magic is not used in war.

But they were using it. And if it was successful now, what
would the next step be? Mages riding at their shoulders,
perhaps whispering spells to ensorcel their brains, make
their arms swing the sword harder and their feet march
faster, without any thought on the part of the warrior?

"It is Prince Rajnir's will," Durasnir said finally. "Spoken
in my presence."

Talkar touched his fingers in acceptance, but turned his
head to hide his loathing. He suspected that Erkric wasn't
sending these orders over the prince's name, he was getting
the prince to issue them himself. And forcing Durasnir to
do it before the men's eyes made it look like the Oneli felt
the Hilda could not carry out their orders on their own. It
was yet another tactic meant to cause ill will between
Oneli and Hilda.

Talkar faced eastward, away from the castle where his
men strained with chains and horses, and brooded.

At least he'd personally overseen the dispatch of the Jarl
of Arveas. A clean death, Talkar had made certain of that,
despite Erkric's hints he would like a Marlovan commander or two to experiment with, if any were captured.
Since the prince had said nothing about the disposition of
enemies, Talkar and his Battle Chiefs had agreed that an
honorable enemy—especially one who'd put up such a
brave fight—did not deserve mind-torture by magic, the
way Erkric had done with that Wafri fellow, before he went
mad and hurled himself directly off a castle wall to smash
on the rocks below. The very idea of taking prisoners was
dishonorable in the eyes of the Venn warriors, because
they were asking their enemy to dishonor himself by
throwing down his weapon. Talkar suspected the
Marlovans felt the same.

Durasnir broke into these degrading thoughts with a question marching uncomfortably parallel. "Any sign of the Jarl's heir?"

"No." Talkar removed his helm, careful not to poke himself with one of the stiff upswept white wings, the lacquered white feathers wired into place. He wiped his damp forehead, then resettled the helm carefully over his meager knot of hair. "He might be in the castle." He glanced back at where Ulaffa was carefully tramping out a square—probably a transfer square. Talkar hated the way the old man mumbled under his breath, like whispering secrets under your very ears. He hated the way magic made his arm hairs bristle in a kind of warning, like lightning about to strike. "What surprises me more is that there has been no recent message from the mage scout Erkric had promised was stationed on the highest pinnacle, overlooking the narrowest portion of the pass. I was given a scroll case into which she was to send me reports of anyone she saw and killed."

"Dag Erkric has dags killing people?" Durasnir asked sharply.

Talkar turned his fingers skyward in assent, his expression grim. "And I did get a report, right after we landed. She spotted and killed two messengers sent up the pass. But since then no word."

Durasnir did not ask why Talkar had sent no query. To do so would indicate a want, or a need, for dag interference in military matters. So the Hilda Commander would keep silent.

Talkar blew out his cheeks, then added, "Any news since our landing?" A wave of his hand indicated the northern shore of Idayago.

"Yes. You remember the murder of our observers here."

It wasn't a question, it was a context. Talkar touched his fingers together.

"Dag Erkric was in the process of replacing our military scouts with dags to be used as scouts. Like your dag on the pinnacle."

"Right, I understand."

"You apparently did not know that they all vanished overnight?"

"No, I did not." Talkar glanced at the mountain heights above the pass. Maybe that explained the sudden lack of reports from Dag Mekki. "Vanished, or dead?"

"Gone. No trace, and that means no bodies left for us to find. Unlike what happened with the observers in spring."

Talkar let his breath trickle out, glanced at the busy Ulaffa, then said uneasily, "No trace?"

"Dag Erkric himself went to the south. Found and destroyed the Marlovan and Idayagan communication scroll cases, once he located them."

Talkar grimaced. "How does he do that? Magic eyes watching everywhere?" He grimaced again.

"I'm told that magic leaves a trace in the air, like scent, and the dags are like dogs who sniff out what we humans cannot. He doesn't even have to touch their devices, which are much more simple than ours. He just casts a ward around them."

Talkar raised a hand. "I don't know what that means, and I don't want to."

"Very well. After he broke our enemy's means of magical communication, he searched for traces of our dag scouts. This was while we launched the invasion. There he had no success. He returned to the flagship before we rowed to Trad Varadhe for the prince's inspection. He reported to the prince in my hearing that all the locals south of the pass are talking about the great Marlovan army no more than a day or so outside of the city of Ala Larkadhe."

Talkar's granite-solid jaw tightened. "Then we have to get to the top of the pass first. An army two days' ride from the city at that end? That leaves us a day to take this castle. Because the reports put the climb from either end at roughly equal. That's tight."

These words caused a pang of regret in Durasnir for his deliberate procrastination. But he dismissed it. A day could not make that much difference, judging from the poor defense they'd encountered so far. Of primary importance was resistance to Dag Erkric's insidious plan to insert his mages into the conduct of war.

"Dag Erkric has readied a plan for that, too," Durasnir said.

"A plan to get us to the top of the pass faster?" Talkar asked, lifting his helm again to rub his sweat-soaked, metal-baked head.

"No, it's some sort of ruse."

Talkar pursed his lips. His innate distrust of the interference of dags appeared to be warring with his desire to get up that pass as swiftly as possible.

Ulaffa finished making his square, laid a series of transfer tokens down, then turned an inquiring face their way. They rejoined him, standing well outside of the square. A short time later, half a dozen blue-robed dags appeared.

At Talkar's somewhat ironic gesture a party of warriors, all of them rigid with unexpressed resentment, conducted the dags to the walls. There they began examining the massive hinges and conferring with one another, while the invasion force watched.

Durasnir had no more excuse to be present. Ulaffa would transfer back to the ship whenever he wished, using one of those instantaneous transfer spells. One heartbeat here, the next there. The warriors hated that, too.

Durasnir and Talkar exchanged salutes. Durasnir signaled to his waiting marines and was rowed back to the flagship.

Once again on the *Cormorant,* he retreated to his cabin to wait. Now he was left with nothing but the familiar, internal struggle with the concept—unexamined all his young life, now haunting him in his aging years—of one very young man embodying, in his person, the will of an entire people.

Especially when one was not certain how much of his will was truly his.

Chapter Three

"SIGNI!" Inda's voice broke into her sleep, light as it was.

She opened her eyes. It was dark, though she sensed the proximity of the sun somewhere below the eastern horizon. She sat up, brushing her tousled hair out of her face. "What is amiss?"

"Messenger. From the Venn," he said, setting a candle down on the single camp stool. "I mean, from Ala Larkadhe, with a message from the Venn. They came in by magic." Inda frowned. "Can they do that with whole armies?"

"No," she said, poking her elbow out of the bedroll and leaning her cheek on her hand. "That is why Dag Erkric desperately wants Norsunder's rift magic. You need such great spells to transfer great numbers. More then three together, and the three feel the wrench at triple strength."

Inda whistled. "Glad you told me that. All right. Evred needs you to tell us what their message means. I'll be with you," he added, and he couldn't resist leaning down to kiss her, so sweetly she lay curled up in their bedding, drowsy, her sandy hair wisping about her face. His hands reached for the softness of her curves, though he knew that Evred was waiting.

Her lips, so giving, her smell like summer grass and blossoms on a cool wind, arrowed straight into his brain. No, it arrowed straight to his arrow. He backed away, trying not to laugh, and saw her smiling, her eyes reflecting golden flames of the candlelight.

It was like that at night too. She wondered as she rose and hastily pulled on her travel-worn smock and riding trousers how long his ardor would last, and why such things were so mysterious, so wholly uncontrollable. She loved lying in his arms at night, at peace. She would have been happy just doing that on this long, terrible ride surrounded by Marlovan warriors, and curtained only by a leddas-and-canvas tent that did not really muffle sounds. But for him proximity ignited the fires of desire, and those, once quenched (as quickly as they could, as silently) caused him to drop into slumber, leaving her lying awake, body content, mind anxiously seeking answers to questions she could not ask, except of herself.

They emerged from the tent into the lantern light. Evred-Harvaldar looked past Inda's foolish little grin of sexual desire temporarily thwarted; there was no corresponding smirk in the woman's face. Her eyes focused inward, her expression the blind one that either meant mental turmoil or she was doing magic. No, he had to assume goodwill. Honor required it, and her self-effacing behavior during this long journey—she under guard—had been exemplary.

Evred handed Signi the letter.

Signi bent to the nearest lantern and read fast, her brow lined and tense. "Can you not read it? This is written in your own Iascan. It is from Prince Rajnir. He wishes his dag to parley under truce, on Restday, three days hence."

"There was a thing with it," the Runner explained. And on Evred's motion, the runner held out a metal disk with Old Sartoran glyphs on it.

Signi only had to glance once. "Ah. That is a Destination token. Did he give you phrases to say when you place it upon the ground?"

The Runner repeated what the Venn messenger with the truce flag had told him, there at the city gate: simple words in Old Sartoran, freighted with a transfer spell.

"It will transfer Dag Erkric to wherever you place this token," Signi said.

"Or one of us to their arms?" Evred asked, tone dry. "And I use that term in the fullest possible sense."

"No. The disks are different for that kind of transfer."

Inda said, "That's true. I used one once at Ghost Island." Evred's head snapped his way, his eyes narrow and remote, and Inda knew what question would come next. He quickly explained what Signi had said about transfers and rifts, and they all saw Evred relax.

"Very well," Evred said. "But we will prepare an appropriate reception first." He gestured for Hawkeye's Runner to take charge of letter and disk again. Motioning to Inda and Noddy, "We will ride ahead. The rest can follow us into the city." He raised his voice to the Sier Danas, now straggling from their tents, buttoning coats or tying sashes. "Rat! Cherry-Stripe! You two and Cama bring them in. Barend. You ride with us."

We did not mean just the commanders, but their personal entourages as well. Tau, as Inda's Runner, was left to sweep together his and Inda's belongings and give commands to the waiting runners-in-training for mounts.

The sun was still well below the hills to the east when they raced by streaming torchlight out of the camp, leaving the warriors cleaning weapons and talking among themselves. No morning drill for the first time—but there would probably be no more liberty.

Evred rode at the front with his Harskialdna and his cousin at either side, Noddy behind them, and from the sound of occasional hoots and crows of laughter, it was clear that no resentment had been harbored in the upper ranks at the permanent shift in command.

Tau and Signi rode side-by-side—Signi for the first time without her guards.

Stars twinkled overhead as they cantered behind torch-bearing Runners up the smooth, well-tended road. The setting moon still gave faint light. As they rounded a rocky outcropping, pungent with the scent of dry needle-grass and goldenrod, and spotted the glistening white tower projecting above the city, Signi swayed once in her saddle. As Tau urged his horse to close with hers, one hand reaching out, she shook her head and straightened up.

Tau dropped his hand. She'd slipped; Tau had made many riding errors before learning how to sit these scanty saddles.

Tau glanced ahead. The old academy friends rode together, talking back and forth in low, laughter-punctuated voices. Noddy was saying, ". . . so I'll raise my Inda to scrag your boys on sight. You better raise 'em to fear my name—"

"Noddy Turtle?" Inda asked, to shouts of laughter.

Did they not feel the tension? On the surface, no. Under the surface? Ah. The laughter sounded too loud, too bright, the voices too forced. There was just enough of some quality to them that caused Tau's heart to thump with warning.

Tau hated battle, and knew he was going to hate a war even worse. What truly bound him here? *Why am I here?*

Because—

His gaze strayed to the two figures ahead, the long tails of hair swinging against their backs just barely picked out in the smear of predawn light: one sun-streaked brown, the other red.

It has always been people. Not places, certainly not ideals. People.

He did not define *people* any further than that, but his hand clenched on the golden case he'd worn near his skin ever since Jeje left, in case she were to write back to him.

The sunrise lightened to pearlescent, the molten fire just rimming the eastern skyline sending spear-shafts of brilliantly pure, peachy-gold light to highlight the sides of trees, a rock here, and tuft of grass there. Signi observed Tau's profile against the dawn of a new day. Though Tau's proximity would never bring her the glory Inda's did, she had always loved beauty in all things, whether alive or not, natural or made. Tau was beautiful, riding easily now on his dashing young horse—both so alive, so capable of joy—the sight caused her heart to spasm in poignancy.

How different he was from Inda, and yet they had been

raised with love, she could tell in all the little muscle moves, the warmth of glance and voice: Tau, perhaps, had been raised surrounded by love, but had come to regard love as an object, or an objective. For Inda love was sun and air.

Signi's thoughts broke at the prickle of magic. Venn magic. It was very clear and distinct, as one might expect in this land where no dags dwelled. She could not test the trace, but suspected Erkric. Who else would be arrogant enough to transfer somewhere within the city to watch the Marlovans ride in under his nose?

So she pulled the old, weatherworn cloak about her shoulders, the hood hiding her face, and altered her posture to give the impression of someone either elderly or infirm. And she slowed her horse gradually, so that Evred's party drew ahead. As she had the previous time she'd felt that same trace, she rode just behind Tau, trusting that he would draw attention away from her.

Tau had noticed her doing the same thing once before, a week or two previous. He'd assumed she had a headache from the dust and warm air, and wanted to leave the loud voices of the Sier Danas behind. Because they were out of earshot, Tau met her eyes, which quirked in question. He asked, "Is this hood some kind of disguise?"

"In a way." She considered, then decided it was right to speak. "One of my people is spying on your army."

"Will you tell Inda?"

"If he asks. But I will not offer the information." She shook her head. "What can be done?"

"Nothing," Tau agreed. "So you refuse to fight against the Marlovans, but you're not fighting against your people either, is that it?"

How to answer that? Truth for Taumad, but also deflection. "I'm—I was—a ship dag. We had nothing to do with war, except at a remove. My job was to navigate, to assist in repair."

Tau shrugged ruefully. "I guess I hoped you might do some kind of spell and make the enemies go away."

Her nerves stung with cold. "You do not look forward to the coming battle?"

"Not," he said, "at all."

She closed her eyes. And though—maybe because—she had been so careful for so long, so watchful, the pent-up words tumbled out, almost too fast to comprehend. "Why do not we see animal bones left in the wild as reminders of what can happen to us? Why not leave ours? But would they not be reminders of life smashed away, of what war means, if we saw them every day?" She lifted her hands, her fingers expressing the anguish of the unanswerables. "How to remind humans, as we sing so bravely and dress so artfully riding to war that when we make war we are no more than predators?"

Tau had absolutely no answer for that. His fund of pleasant chat—taught to him by his mother to cover every possible social situation—had eased him through a variety of experiences all over the southern continent through the past ten years. Even with a pair of vicious pirates whose weakness was a wish to appear aristocratic. His chatter was inadequate now.

A quick indrawn breath from Signi ended the uncomfortable silence. She stiffened, staring downward, turning almost all the way around to gaze behind her as they passed by.

When she straightened again, her face was pale, making her light freckles stand out, her expression peculiar.

"Are you all right?" Tau asked her. "Do you need to stop?"

"No." Signi drew in another unsteady breath. "No, actually, I am quite well." She studied his concerned expression, and wondered if she ought to explain what she had seen, not once, but twice, now. On this otherwise unremarkable little hillock at the roadside, covered with summer wildflowers: placed amid the goldenrod a single blossom of milkweed.

"Are you worried about this mage fellow of Rajnir's?" Tau asked. "This Venn dag?"

The morning sunlight struck gold in his light eyes. How acute he was!

"Dag Erkric," she said gently. "He is not yet, I trust, The

Dag of the Venn. And I am not as worried as I was," she added, after some thought, within the shadow of her hood.

"Ah."

Was that an expression of comprehension, or of distrust? There were so many pitfalls here! But Inda trusted Tau. He had said so over and over, *I trust Tau with my life. Tau, Jeje. Barend—and Fox. I would have been dead many times over without them.*

"Do you know what wards are?" she asked, after more thought.

They could see the outer city wall now, and make out the sentries on the gates.

"No."

"Think of them as . . . walls," she said, gesturing toward the city just ahead, glimpsed through the overhang of flowering trees. "Walls of magic that can permit spells, or keep them out. There are none here, so those who know magic can come and go without your knowing. Yet I sense a very great ward near, a most powerful one, and very, very old, so it has nothing to do with this coming battle. But I do not know if I should tell your king."

Tau did not mistake the inquiry in her voice. "Don't," he said firmly. "If there's magic of any kind that is a danger he can't do anything about, then either fix it yourself or let it lie. Unless you want to deal with all the questions it will raise." And then, in a pleasant voice, "Is dag related to the Marlovan *daka,* meaning *maker*?"

"Yes," she said, grateful for the respite, and they talked of similar words shared between Venn and Marlovan for the rest of the ride.

She spied one more milkweed, faithfully planted at another juncture in the road to Ala Larkadhe. One could have been accident. Two made coincidence less likely, but three were a message. For her.

Inda and his companions raced up the road and into the castle. Signi never once raised her eyes to the castle prominences; Dag Erkric probably was hidden, and she must do nothing to draw his attention, which would be on Evred and those surrounding him. She and Tau followed more slowly.

Inda, Evred, Noddy, and Barend reined up in the fore-court, horses' hooves noisy on the stones. Hawkeye himself awaited them, flanked by his Runners. He and Evred saluted one another, aware of the watching sentries on the walls, and others in windows. There must be no sign of frantic hurry or fear. Everything must be deliberate.

Hawkeye watched Evred speak orders that sent the Runners off in various directions, each with a specific logistical task. *You have come a long way in two years,* he thought. *I hope far enough to see us through this battle.*

At last only Hawkeye, Evred, and his companions were left. Evred checked; Tau and Dag Signi were just riding through the inner gate to the stable court. A motion to the head stable hand, and the two were surrounded by helpful minions—and kept out of earshot.

Inda flicked a question at Barend, who just tipped his head toward Evred. Inda said, "Sponge. I don't think any of us trust this dag parley business. Too convenient a way to get at you. We're all going to be on hand."

"Then if he has the sense of a rock he'll take us all out," Evred retorted.

"You're a target anyway. That can't be helped." Barend turned his hands up.

Hawkeye cracked a guffaw, sounding just like he had as a horsetail. He'd always loved the prospect of danger. "But if the rest of us, say, wear coats from the armsmen, and one of our boys wears your House battle tunic, maybe we won't be obvious targets. Everyone seems to say that we Marlovans all look alike."

"Very well." To Inda: "I want you to set up the room we shall receive them in. Go through the castle, pick the best defensible place. Plan for every kind of treachery." To his cousin and Noddy: "Hawkeye, show Inda around. Noddy, get the watch captain to assign you Runners. You had better inspect the barracks, make certain we've got enough room for everyone."

They left, Inda hesitant, a backward glance toward where Tau and Signi stood on the other side of the courtyard, watchful Runners flanking them.

"She will be safe," Evred said, and Inda could not answer that; as soon as he was gone, Evred's gaze slid past Tau after the usual momentary hitch and he turned to Signi. "Please come with me." He turned away, and Signi followed with her graceful tread.

Leaving Tau alone. Tau cast an inward sigh, remembering what Vedrid had said privately after all the celebrating the night Inda was made Harskialdna. *Now that he's the new Harskialdna, when the time comes for battle, they'll expect a crimson-and-gold House tunic to be ready and waiting.*

Tau had seen the one they'd made for Inda during the early part of the journey, the green of the Algara-Vayirs, edged with silver. A one-time Harskialdna apparently wore his own colors. That tunic was neatly packed at the bottom of Inda's dunnage, along with a fine coat of chain mail; until they rode into battle, the Marlovan warriors traveled in their gray coats, now grimy at cuffs and hems, despite careful brushings and the occasional dunk into the ensorcelled buckets.

Tau hitched his and Inda's gear over his shoulder. Back to servant status, with a sidestep into tailoring. Well, it would keep him busy. Busy before battle was good.

Signi followed the king in silence. His head was bent, his expression thoughtful as they progressed from the granite part of the castle into the tower made of faintly luminous white stone. This stone was not marble, but something different and far more rare. It was called disirad. She had only seen it once before, in the magic-blasted remains of Roth Drael far to the north on the continent of Goerael, where humans had not lived for at least a thousand years.

The steps she trod now had ovals worn into them, testifying to the extreme age of this tower, possibly one of the oldest human structures on the world.

Her heart quickened its beat.

They paused on a landing and he touched a door whose wards and bindings she had sensed from the road outside the city. Powerful and *ancient* wards.

The door swung open, revealing the tall shelves,

arranged like spokes, of a very old archive filled with treasures, precious beyond price: scrolls and handmade books that had to range over the centuries since humans had begun keeping records.

"You may stay here," he said, and she turned to him, eyes burning with the prickle of tears.

He saw her emotion without comprehending it. "You will be safe from any magic treachery they might try," he said, struggling past the press of worries, the proximity of battle, attempting to be kind. "I promise there will be food and drink brought. It's interesting," he added, looking around with open longing, one of his rare unguarded expressions. His gaze lingered on the case of ribbon-tied old scrolls. "I have spent time here myself. Not as much as I should wish."

So he would not misunderstand, she said, "I would willingly stay here a year, if permitted. I shall begin reading at once."

His smile was quick, inadvertent, the first genuine sign of pleasure she had seen since that dinner long ago in the royal city. He lingered in the doorway, obviously reluctant to leave, but when his slow gaze met hers his expression shuttered. He stiffened subtly as he took on again the weight of that invisible crown and withdrew.

He could so easily have consigned her to a stone cell. It didn't matter that she could escape from one as easily as the other, what mattered is that he'd given a thought to her comfort.

And so she would not burden him with the facts that this place was so protected by powerful, ancient magic that she could not be detected by any mage—including Dag Erkric.

For the first time since she had been captured, she sent a magical summons to her Dag Chief, Valda, whose milkweed she had seen thrice outside on the road.

At Castle Andahi close to thirty dags were finally brought in, one to each massive gate hinge, others responsible for the heating and reshaping, thus loosening, the enormous nails in the outer curtain gates.

The Venn waited in patient ranks just out of arrow range, so the defenders, glimpsed on their arrival, had withdrawn. Talkar did not assume that the empty sentry walls meant an easy surrender.

Dag Erkric would have sent a hundred dags, had they been needed. The dags had been working hard, and so, just before dawn the next day, the great gates rumbled and cracked. With the aid of chain-reinforced cable pulleys supervised by Durasnir's own flagship Drenga captain, several teams of big warhorses pulled the gates enough off balance to fall to the ground with a thump felt at the distant camp.

The advance force—wearing armor, warhorses also armored, winged helms on the captains, great tree banners in the lead—trotted at a deliberate pace through the cloud of hanging dust in the motionless air. They halted at the castle's first inner gate, finding it closed and locked.

This time someone appeared on the battlements.

Arrows nocked and raised rattled behind Talkar, ninety-nine men across in the front line. Behind them a Battle Group of mounted heavy cavalry, drilled for two years, rode up in line, lances upright but ready to be lowered at command. Behind and to either side of the mounted warriors bowmen took their places, and finally rank on rank of marching warriors formed up in rapid order, disembarked on the tidal flow the night before.

To Talkar's extreme left the dags waited in an untidy group, a faint morning breeze just beginning to rise, worrying at long hair and bright blue robes.

He raised his hand, and the longbows creaked as arms drew back, arrows steady.

The person atop the gate could be just barely made out against the rising summer sun: a woman, gray-haired, her own bow drawn and arrow nocked.

Talkar called up in heavily accented Marlovan (having asked one of the mages for the words so he could practice them), "Open the gates, or we shall bring them down. And then my orders are to put everyone to the sword, regardless of age, sex, or degree. But if you permit us entry, and passage to the road beyond, I promise your lives will be spared."

The woman stared down, her face too shadowed to see, the sunlight crowning her grizzled hair with silver. But her answer was unequivocal. She held up her hand, and from the front tower two young girls appeared, pulling up the crimson-and-gold banner. They tossed it down to where the woman stood.

Venn and Marlovan gazes followed that slow, undulating length of fabric until it draped over two older women, who held it outstretched.

The gray-haired women took a knife and scored down the fabric, ripping it asunder. Destroying her own banner? Was that a surrender?

The summer air was so quiet Talkar heard Ulaffa's rusty whisper, "They will not dishonor their banner by leaving it to be taken."

And in a motion as swift as the any of Talkar's front-line archers could have achieved the woman raised her bow and shot her arrow directly at Talkar.

He had only to lift his shield with the helmed owl, and the arrow clattered harmlessly against the metal, and spun away into the dusty court.

The woman was gone.

"Mages," Talkar lifted his voice. "Take down the inner gates."

Chapter Four

LIET-JARLAN stood at the edge of the half-smothered truck garden. All of the castle women stood around her, each wearing her best robes, neat and clean. Honor required them to go into battle with dignity. But their knives were no longer hidden.

As soon as the first boatloads of Venn had landed, every single man in the castle had ridden to the defense. These were not the still-missing Guard. They were led by an old dragoon whose great-grandchild was up in the robbers' cave with the children. He was aided by the cook, the cooper, the old brewer, the woodworkers, two Marlovan merchants who'd come over the pass and lingered, wanting to spare their horses the hot weather. A cluster of boys considered too young for patrol, who had stable duty until they gained some seasoning.

They had barely lasted a watch. Liet had forced herself to witness it from the tower. It was what she owed them.

"What we are doing," she said, looking at each face, "is not defending. There must be a hundred ships out there. More. Crammed full of Venn." She waved at the horizon, where the Venn ships had spread in a line outside the bay. She knew her people had been sneaking peeks through the spyglasses. That was all right. She had too, but they were not a nightmare, to fade away like smoke in the morning light.

It hurt so much to look in the young, tense faces of the fifteen-year-old girls. But they had voted not to hide with the children. *If the boys were here, they would be fighting,* their leader had said.

There was no answer to that. But the Jarlan's heart ached unbearably. Her mouth dried. Now the men of the defense would have no witness, and there would be no witness here, either.

"So keep that in mind as you take all the safeguards off the traps. Get the cauldrons on the boil. Pull those stones and flood the basement." She groped in the direction of the emergency access to the tunnel. The main access had been thoroughly bricked up, hidden, and all the corridors leading to it sabotaged. When eventually they found the basement entrance, they would only be able to fit through two at a time.

"What we are going to do." Her voice scratched. She cleared her throat hard. "Until the last one of us stands, is buy the king time."

Chapter Five

VALDA appeared not long after Signi sent her message, stumbling forward as the magic released her, face exalted as she gazed at her surroundings.

"Oh, it is! It is!" she exclaimed, clasping her hands. "It is a Morvende archive! I had hoped, when I discovered Mekki and the *atan* platform—"

Signi waited through this tumble of words.

Valda made a visible effort and halted. Then, laughing and crying, she embraced Signi, her voice trembling. "I have never ceased to worry about you, my dear. But I dare not linger for long. I will return later, and we will talk."

"Wait, only tell me this: does Rajnir send Erkric to parley with the Marlovans?"

Valda regained some of her accustomed severity. "I never heard about that," she stated. "Are you certain?"

"I saw the letter myself. And a transfer token."

"I will find out," Valda promised. "You have to realize I have stayed out of contact with the Yaga Krona—I *must*. So I no longer know—never mind. Ah, Signi, things have come to a terrible crisis for us! No, I cannot explain even that. The Hilda and the Yaga Krona are pulling at the gates at the other end of the pass at this very moment. Hisht! I *shall* return."

The Yaga Krona? Battering gates? But she was gone.

When Evred came back some time later, he found Signi

absorbed in an ancient scroll, busily making notes in Venn writing.

He glanced in and around. He was looking for someone, probably the Morvende archivist whose hand she'd seen noting many scrolls in the collection. From the evidence she was a copyist, replacing with laborious exactitude any scroll deemed too aged to be safely unrolled and read.

"The Runners are bringing you a meal." Evred beckoned in a blushing youth carrying a laden tray. "I beg you will stay occupied until our conflict with your countrymen is past. Inda understands, and though reluctantly, he agrees. It seems the simplest solution."

"I understand," she said.

He closed the door. From the other side came the thump of guards taking up their stance.

Inda lurked on the stairway at the other end of the landing. "You can see, she is happily occupied," Evred said to Inda. "We can't risk having the truce party spot her, and force her to go along with them. You know that they would wring from her everything she saw in our camp, every word she heard spoken. I'd do the same, in their shoes," he added, with a faint smile. "Can you see that it is better not to put her between hard choices?"

"Yes." Inda rubbed his jaw. "But. Her there—Venn parley—mages. I don't know, it makes me feel I'm sailing into an unknown harbor without a chart. So different from planning an attack."

Evred was surprised at the spurt of annoyance these innocent words caused. *You've been home a full season, yet you have not abandoned your sea talk.* But he dismissed that thought as unworthy. "We will carry on with our plans as if their parley had never been offered."

Inda stopped at one of the arched windows, his fist pounding lightly on the rounded, smooth lip of the sill as he gazed sightlessly out at the army now riding into the big stable yard below. Cama was still mounted, overseeing the orderly division of the wings. "That's it," Inda finally said, unaware of the long silence. "That's it. I need to look at the map."

Evred did not ask what "it" might be. He led the way to
the office, which overlooked the barracks court where the
first two wings to ride in were milling about, gear slung
over their shoulders or resting before the squared toes of
their boots, as Runners dashed about. The low hubbub of
male voices rose on the warm summer air.

Inda ignored them, too, his knuckles rapping a cup-
board, the wall, Evred's desk (partitioned by Hawkeye's
neat piles), a wingback chair, and the doorway again as
they walked through to the map room, a chamber in one of
the granite towers. The only piece of furniture was a heavy
blackwood table, legs and supports beautifully carved in a
style that called to Inda's mind—to be instantly forgotten—the elongated lyre motif of faraway Freeport Harbor
on the other side of the world, in the Eastern Sea.

"Ah." He exhaled at the sight of the huge map.

Evred had promised him that the best map of the pass
lay here at Ala Larkadhe; his uncle had captured it before
it could be burned, when he first took Ala Larkadhe. Apparently, once a generation young Idayagans and Olarans
had been chosen to remap every curve and cliff of the pass,
as weather and wear changed them, an expedition that
could take the better part of two years.

But the result was a map of chartlike clarity—

Chart. Inda's thoughts forked between two trails, and
regained neither. Too many things demanding his next
moment.

*All right. Look at the map. You wanted this map, talked
about it. There are all the details humanly possible.*

He closed his eyes and struggled to shut down the chatter of his inner voice. Now he would just look. There was
the snaking long lake on the eastern side of the pass. And
on the west, directly opposite, the small lakes between the
circle of highest peaks that fed into the great Andahi River
carving its way down to empty into Lindeth Bay, and giving the pass its name. Above Ala Larkadhe the pass
roughly paralleled the river, reaching its narrowest point
between enormous cliffs at its highest reach. After that it
started its way down toward the north, following an an-

cient river bed that had once emptied into the bay below what was now called Castle Andahi.

"That pass has to be like the Land Bridge in the south," Inda muttered, looking down. "Says 'narrow as a neck' in your uncle's writing, here, but what does that *mean*? No wider than a man can touch fingertip to fingertip, or wide enough to sail a capital ship through? And what kind of 'enormous cliffs'—sheer ones, or ones you can climb?"

Evred said, "Sheer. Rising directly to either side. Some of them are broken by old animal trails. The trails usable by humans are mostly marked—you can see the small green dots—but it would take a year or more to get an army up or down those trails. They are mostly goat paths, and even the goats are slow. A man carrying a pack would have to rest frequently, and the footing would be dangerous."

"Width of the pass?"

"At the high point, you can probably get fifty mounted men in a tight line."

"That sounds—" Inda grimaced. It sounded wide if you thought about a couple of people ambling along. That was 'narrow as a neck' for an army—and narrow as a finger if you considered trying to negotiate it with a ship. "Not good for a charge, then."

"In desperation, maybe. The sheer walls are perhaps twice the height of the white tower here. Some are higher. The tops can be obscured by rain or snow clouds. This is before the pass ices over in early winter, and small thunderstorms might strike one side but the other will be clear and blue. Lightning hits the rocks far above."

Inda rocked back and forth, eyes closed. "No flank attacks, then."

"I assure you, there is no more formidable barrier than those walls. The only advantage is to whoever takes the top of the pass itself. Anyone coming up from the other end will have to fight uphill."

Inda still rocked. "Horses don't charge uphill, right?"

"A short distance is possible. Very short. I would say they could break lines of disorganized Idayagans, but those walls of shields you described would be best charged with the incline in our favor."

"How long to the top?"

"The fastest Runners take a week and a half or so to reach the top, and the same down to Castle Andahi," Evred answered. "In good weather. The road is steep, and there's no place to keep remounts, so you have to take them with you. Since we have not seen any beacon fires, we can assume we have two weeks' warning, three at the very outside."

Inda had opened his fist and was drumming with that hand, as his right traced over the mountain peaks where Hawkeye had labelled each of the beacon sites, with a notation on who was on duty at each, and when. "We'll call it two weeks. That's not much of a margin."

"Better than nothing." A couple of quiet footfalls, and Barend joined them at the table. "My beacons give us that two weeks." His tone was of mild approval.

Inda turned on him. "How many know about the beacons?"

"No one, I'll swear. Outside of us. Hawkeye and I picked the south end crews ourselves. Not a man with a family among 'em. No one to blab to. They report directly to us before and after rotation. Flash and I picked the ones at the north end."

"How often do they rotate?"

"One coming, one going, one staying every week." Barend added, "Flash does the same at his end. Reports weekly—"

"Reports that could take three weeks to get here, once they get down the mountain, and then sent south."

"Well, say, fifteen days, if they really bustle. It's the upward ride that's—"

"I know. So, when did you last get a report?"

Barend lifted his head. "I brought it myself, when I reported in."

"So when is the next due?" Inda asked.

Barend spread his hands. "Three days, maybe four, even five if there's bad weather."

Evred added, "If anything at all went wrong with the beacons at that end, we can trust Flash to have sent us word some way. And if there's real news, even bad weather won't hold them up."

"Right." Barend's broad forehead creased. "What's wrong, Inda? The beacons will be as near as sending a letter by magic as we can make it."

Inda did not hear him. He was staring at the map, feeling that almost-vertigo again, just the same as the first day he'd looked at Evred's far less detailed map back in the royal city. "This thing's as good as a chart, all the details. Wait. I almost had it, something to do with charts—"

"I don't mind saying—" Hawkeye clattered in through the door behind them. "—I don't trust this parley any farther than I can throw these soul-ripping mages. I'll wager anything you like it's an excuse to nose around here and report in by magic."

"They're mages. They can nose by magic without a parley, and no one can stop them—" Inda stared fixedly at his hands.

"Inda?" Evred asked. "You were saying?"

"I forgot." Inda's hands smacked down. "I think I was saying two things. Neither of 'em any use, or they'd stick. Let's go look at the rooms we've got available."

The first day or so in the old robbers' caves were mostly fun for the Castle Andahi children.

The three ten-year-old girls had been on plenty of overnight expeditions before, though usually with one of the older girls in charge, and they'd never take any of the ones everyone called the smalls—the children under six. Six was the age castle children got their first jobs, carrying dishes to dunk in the magic buckets, running messages, delivering small tools or packets of food out to those working in the gardens or outside the walls, and of course wanding horse stalls.

Hiding out felt at first a lot like an extra-exciting

overnight. One the adults had ordered them to be on. It wasn't until yesterday that things began to change.

Han rose before dawn and climbed out of her bedroll. For the first time since their arrival, the air was chilly. She crept past all the sleeping figures to the mouth of the cave, then she crouched down, grinding her chin on her knees as she glared out at the swirling drifts of fog.

At first, it had been wonderful not to have to brush her hair or bother with bathing. She hated going wet and chilled to breakfast. While she didn't mind going without a bath—that was part of the fun of overnights—her scalp felt gritty. She'd already had a small argument with Gdir about the fact that Han hadn't brought a hairbrush, and Gdir had said that meant she was a bad leader.

Han crunched up her toes, considering how she could get the hairbrush without having to admit she was a bad leader. She knew Gdir would make her say it before she'd let her use hers.

Somebody whimpered in the back of the cave where they'd made their camp. Had to be one of the three-year-olds. Han held her breath, hoping the small would go back to sleep. At first, the smalls had all just run around, laughing and splashing in the little stream that ran across the very back of the cave to vanish down a mossy crack. But yesterday they'd been more fretful than happy, whining a lot. What a relief when they finally got to sleep!

The seven- and eight-year-olds had gotten bored with staying inside the cave. They wanted games outside. No, not on the floor of the pass. That was orders, they couldn't go there, but they could be on the mountainside, couldn't they? Why not? Just to *there*? Han had gotten tired of the questions long before the sevens and eights got tired of pestering her.

A dusty rustle from behind made her half turn, as nine-year-old Freckles shuffled out, her toes grimy. Freckles shoved her bristly braids back, the reddish-blond hair imprinted with brown blotches of dried mud. "Babies are waking up," she whispered. Then she made a face. "Why'd we have to have babies on the overnight? Three isn't a

small, it's a *baby*. They don't talk good, and twice Rosebud's forgotten the Waste Spell and we've had to dunk her
drawers in the bucket."

"We can't blame her for that. Some don't learn it right
away. The Jarlan told us Flash didn't."

Freckles giggled at the idea of a grown-up learning the
Waste Spell, but it was more habit than humor, then she
made a face. "I never got an overnight until I was six. It's
no *fun* with them."

"Jarlan's orders," Han said.

Freckles sighed. For both girls, that was the end of the
matter. Lnand wore you out demanding to know why, and
Gdir complained about Han's orders (and about the Jarlan
putting her in charge), but Freckles didn't care why. The
grown-ups never made sense anyway.

Lnand came out, briskly dusting her smock and knee-
trousers. "I don't think Rosebud feels good. Her face is hot,
and her cheeks are even redder than her hair."

Han ground her toes harder into the cool, silken dust.
"Then she should sleep. That's what the healer told me, the
time I got fever. You sleep, and drink some listerblossom
steep."

"I'll use the Fire Stick." Lnand flung a braid back with a
self-important air. "I know how to make steep. First thing
they teach us in the kitchen."

Like I haven't known that since we were eight! "In the
way back. Remember Ndand's orders," Han cautioned.

Lnand rolled her eyes. "I've been baking since I was
smaller than Rosebud!" she retorted, and marched away,
shoulders twitching with righteous indignation.

Han clamped her jaw on a retort. She loathed the way
Lnand told you things you knew, except exaggerating
them, making her younger, or the work harder, and hinting
that you were stupid. But Lnand had been the best with the
babies. When they'd started to whine for their parents,
Rosebud starting the other pair of three-year-olds off,
Lnand had sidetracked them by telling stories and making
pretend people out of rocks. When they got bored with
that, she built a pebble castle for them to smash.

Gdir appeared. She looked like she'd just come from the baths, her smock and trousers neat, her braids shiny and straight. "Sun is nearly up. It's time for warm-ups," she said in that if you-were-a-good-leader-you-would-have-remembered voice.

Han dug her toes so hard that one foot cramped.

"After that, what're we going to do?" Freckles asked, turning to Han.

Gdir flushed, crossing her arms. She hated it when the others turned to Han.

"I have a new game," Han said, though she really hadn't yet. But she would by the end of breakfast, she vowed to herself. She could make up a new sort of training game, and—

A sharp boom cracked between the canyon walls. Han scrambled back, followed by Freckles. Gdir recoiled, then lunged forward, peering out.

"Get back," Han snapped.

Gdir ducked, then straightened up in affront. "It's just thunder," she snapped back.

But she knew it wasn't. They all knew it wasn't.

Everyone stayed in the cave that day.

Gdir was even quiet about the brush, so Han reinforced Gdir's insistence on everyone getting clean and changing into fresh clothes. They had to renew the water in the bucket between each child, dragging it from the stream. The older girls scrubbed the smalls down, then dunked their old clothes, and spread them on the lip of the cave in the brief sun, which shone hot and still. The smalls ran around happily in their skin, even Rosebud, who seemed better after drinking listerblossom laced with big dollops of honey, and sleeping during the long session of warm-ups and knife drills.

Just before sunset, when they were eating thick slabs of bread with cheese toasted on it, another of those loud booms echoed up the pass, quicker than the flight of a hawk.

The smalls ignored it this time, but the older girls exchanged looks. They went on with their games, just as usual. But that night, no one spread bedrolls out to be away from others, they laid their bedrolls side by side, in a clump. All three big girls made certain the smalls were in the middle.

The smalls had dropped to sleep and the older girls were each drifting on different thoughts when, faint but distinct on the strong wind from the sea, the screams began.

Chapter Six

JUST before dawn, Valda reappeared in the archive. This time she held a token flat on her palm. Signi recognized a tracer-token, warded against certain spells that Erkric might perform.

Valda took in the bookshelves extending in at an angle toward the center, the rolled up bedding on the floor, the shallow dishes neatly stacked on a tiny table by the door. Early as it was, the Marlovans had been up earlier and Signi had already eaten. "If Erkric moves, so will I," she said, angling one of the chairs so she could see the door as well as the token resting now on her knee.

"You left me with many mysteries," Signi said.

"I hardly know where to begin." Valda scrubbed her hand over her frowzled gray hair. She had not combed it in days. Her insides ached from too many transfers: the human body was not made to be wrenched in and out of physical space like that.

But needs must be met. And needs had never been greater. She leaned forward, forearms on her thighs, which eased her cramping stomach. "Erkric is searching for me again. I had almost had him convinced I was dead. He believes you are dead. You were very clever to avoid the major magics while you were gone. Anyway, he's put up formidable wards and tracers all over Ala Larkadhe and the pass, most of which I've spent the night removing or compromising. He's had a very easy time with his tracers, as these people have almost no access to magic. Ulaffa says days ago Erkric was scorning your Marlovan king for using old-fashioned courting lockets for military communications. Is that true?"

"It is," Signi said. *And I know how to restore that magic— the work of a few moments. But I dare not do magic, unless . . .* "Go on."

"There is nothing I can do when our king is determined to send our people against these Marlovans, and they are equally determined to resist." Valda touched her fingertips together. "But I am busy extirpating in any way I can magical interference in their battle."

"Ah," Signi said.

"Erkric has forced Ulaffa and the dags into it by getting Prince Rajnir to issue the orders." Valda's smile was thin. "I have not heard these orders. As our first oath is to the greater good of Ydrasal, my conviction that the intent of such orders owes more to Venn aspirations of power than to Ydrasal's harmony gives me leave, in good conscience, to act as if I never heard *of* them." She glanced down at her token. "I do not know how long I have, so to specifics. But first. Before I go on, why are you here? With these Marlovans? Are you helping them against us?"

"No. I am doing nothing. I am asked to do nothing." Signi flattened her hand and extended her fingers in neutral intent. "The war I cannot stop, not when our people and theirs are so determined upon it. You do not stand in the way of the river's flood, even when you know it will sweep away the seedlings." A pause, as Valda's steady gaze did not waver. "Valda, the truth is, the enchantment I labor under is that of the heart, and yes, I examine my reasons every moment, not just waking but in dreams. Aside from my connection to this young man, I know that somehow I yet see the Golden Tree, the greater cause. After all, you yourself removed me from this war to devote myself to that greater cause."

Valda leaned back, exhaling slowly. "It's good you did

not make it to Sartor. I think they know about Erkric and Norsunder, for they have adamantly refused to treat with us. And Erkric has his trusted followers watching as many of our movements as they can."

"Then our plan is abandoned?"

"No, postponed only." Valda's arms tensed slightly, cuing Signi to brace for the technique of emotional provocation. Valda loathed using emotional provocation, Signi knew, but it was often the only way to surprise the truth out of their formidably masked colleagues. "Why did you permit yourself to form a tenderness for Indevan Algara-Vayir? You know that, apart from Durasnir, whose opinions are necessarily shaped by someone's fitness for war, everyone believes he is the epitome of evil. He betrayed young Wafri and destroyed his home, causing terrible turmoil in Ymar. That's aside from all his bloody ship battles, burning people to death, and so on."

"He was Wafri's prisoner. Wafri was torturing him, did you know that?" Signi said.

"No." Valda's brows rose. "I did not. There were odd rumors. But that incident was so far removed from our concerns, I did not investigate further. Did Indevan tell you that?"

"No. He's never talked about it at all. But he wakes up in dreams shouting Wafri's name, or arguing with him and his— his—" She tried to find a term outside of the specifics of Hel dancing, which was so acutely observant of muscle expression. "His body," she said finally. "The scars of torture are evident not just in the pain he feels in his joints, but in the way he moves, sometimes in his voice. That is not what forced me from the old path onto a new. He shines, so." She flickered her fingers upward, miming the swirling rise of sparks.

"Ah." Valda looked skeptical. "A blood-handed battle leader shines with the light of the Golden Tree? I had not known the tree bloomed crimson for you as well as for Erkric."

Signi lifted her expressive hands, as if taking a precious gift. "I know I deserve this rebuke." Her fingers opened, like petals. "Yet that is not how I perceive him."

Valda sat back. Jazsha Signi Sofar was a woman of complexity, one who had trained at all the levels but one of one of the highest disciplines known to the Venn, the Hel dancing. And then she had become a mage, mastering in years what most took a couple of decades to even perceive. She was no child to mistake the sentiments of desire for anything but that.

"I think, desperate as I am for time I don't have, I must ask. Ydrasal has brought us here, you and me. Flows the crimson river of Rainorec between us? Or is it possible we perceive different branches of the Great Tree? You must know that what I see is a lover of the very enemy about to lead his people against us, because I have seen your Inda riding next to the Marlovan king." Valda rocked again, forearms against her middle, the token winking on her knee. "He is so young," she said in a casual voice. "As I have grown older I find myself enchanted by the way the young have only to catch one's eye, to smile, to offer smooth limbs with the unconscious beauty of youth, and they are instantly ready for the happiness of love, however tired, or worried, or stressed." She smiled. "It is most precious of all forms of wealth, youth."

Signi was far better trained in observation even than Valda. She could hear Valda's physical effort just to speak, much less to sound casual, as if she were merely testing the depth of Signi's infatuation.

You have been watching me, she thought, as from below the open window rose the faint but distinct stamp and clash of drilling warriors. *What do you hold back?* She would not know until this part of the conversation was finished. "Life is the most precious gift," she said, a reminder of the inner circle's vows that transcended Venn, Marlovan, Ymaran, or any mere political or cultural polity. "Youth is—youth. If I had met Inda at sixteen, I would have scorned him for his scars. Had I met him at his own age, I would have scorned him for the lack of grace that we Hel dancers believed, in our arrogant simplemindedness, divided artists from mere barbarians. He would have been ugly to me, compared to the male dancers."

"So define your enchantment," Valda commanded. "Are you telling me this is a life love, root and branch?"

Signi knew the answer to that, but hesitated before saying it. To some it was not given to find that kind of love, that lasted from acorn to the last bloom, through all the seasons and storms of life. But there were other loves, and age taught one to appreciate each kind.

"No," Signi said, reluctant because she knew that her love for Inda had rooted, while his (though he did not seem to know it) was still the green shoot of the young. "He's like the golden fish in the river," she said at last. "I can watch all day with pleasure, but he darts here and there, his movements as much a mystery to me as the currents of his river's waters."

Valda made the gesture of peace, as the rumble, zing, and clack rang up the stones from below, followed by full-throated roars in cadence.

"Then here's what you must know now. The king lies in a strange sleep, somewhere between dream and death. He has not wakened for days."

Signi pressed her fingers to her lips.

"The last command he made about us in the south was to bring the Marlovans back to the homeland. Those were his words, *Bring back the Marolo*—he used the old word—*into the embrace of the homeland.*"

"Which Erkric comprehends as spells to take their wills away, if we win?"

"The wit and will of their leaders. Yes." Valda bowed her head. "His present ruse is to further delay the Marlovans from marching up the pass so that the Hilda may gain an advantageous position. I know little about such details, but Signi, here is also what you need to know: he is forcing the Yaga Krona to use magic in aid of this invasion."

Signi's breath hissed. "Dags—"

"Do not belong in battle lines. Everyone knows it. But the prince commanded it, calling them 'aid,' not 'warriors.' So they must obey." She tipped her hand toward the castle. "Prince Rajnir is eager, no, desperate to win the coming battle. The Breseng is nigh, and he must return with a triumph for the Venn."

Signi had felt the problems of the Venn homeland as a looming storm beyond the horizon. Always there, but far away. Now once again she was in the midst of the thunder.

Valda said, "The Yaga Krona is not just divided, we are fractured. Erkric knows how to shape his words to reach the deepest roots of ambition, so that each of the most untenable of these orders is given to the dag who would most find a way to see them as reasonable. There are two of his spies in this city right now." And she named them. "There was also Mekki, up on the heights. She was not just watching for Erkric, she was killing messengers. There were two bodies directly below, one of them a Runner sent by the Jarl's heir, and the other a girl hardly over sixteen, sent through the tunnel under the northern castle, which is hard-pressed now by our invasion force. Mekki killed messengers, not warriors, probably dispatched to apprise the Marlovans of the our invaders landing along the Idayagan coast, and attacking the castles."

"Killed? With magic?" Signi cried softly, rocking back in horror.

"Yes." The soft folds of Valda's face trembled with the intensity of her emotions.

"How is it even possible? No, I don't wish to know—"

"This atrocity will revisit your dreams, as it has mine. I want that to happen," Valda said, low and intense. "I want every one of us to see that young man and the girl in dreams, the transfer of a stone directly into their hearts. And don't remind me that our transfer spells make that impossible, because Dag Erkric has been given by Norsunder some spell to remove those protective wards."

Signi hissed as if a stone had erupted into her own heart.

Valda breathed deeply in equal pain. "That was an act of war, not of magical necessity. Just as it was when our dags ruined the hinges of the castle gates. Though everyone called it aid, because no weapons were involved. Mekki did not deny it when I confronted her. And so she has been given the time these young messengers might have lived, twice eighty years, in which to meditate upon her actions in betrayal of our oaths," Valda added in the mode of *it-shall-be*.

Signi understood by these words that Brit Valda, Chief of the Sea Dags, had placed Mekki under a stone spell. To all evidence the body is so frozen that it takes in physical time half a year to move a finger. But the mind is free. One hundred sixty years as stone—a merciful sentence only because Mekki had been ordered to do what she had done.

Signi's temples panged. She knew she might not be granted that much mercy if Erkric caught up with her.

"What do you see as my duty, Valda?" Signi asked, as the sounds shifted to drums and chanted ballads from a balcony somewhat closer to the tower's prominence.

Valda sat up, fingers clasping around her token. "I will remove the last of Erkric's wards, freeing your magic. You can do nothing, I can do nothing, Falk Ulaffa can do nothing, to stop the war. With our own path so fouled by the dust of ambition, I must leave your actions to your conscience. Afterward, your purpose is still to find a way to get to Sartor."

Noise outside: the brave, syncopated rolling rhythm of drums broke of a sudden into patter, and laughter.

Valda whispered, and vanished.

Halfway through the night, the heat broke over embattled Castle Andahi. The mountain-reinforced echo of thunder, the crack of bluish-violet lightning did not diminish the occasional screams from inside.

Hilda Commander Talkar, in charge of the land portion of the invasion, knew those screams mostly came from the throats of his own men.

Talkar had set up a command post directly inside the outer curtain wall, his advance force one command from march-readiness around him.

He wrote in his scroll-case twice, asking for a report of

the Drenga captain inside. To his surprise, and increasing displeasure, there was no response. Did they shirk duty? No, he must not cloud his mind with distrust of the Oneli, with anger. The noise, the sudden, red-glowing gouts of fire in windows, the intermittent cries, indicated strenuous effort of some kind inside.

Once again he suppressed the instinct to send in his own men. A fight in an unknown space, especially in the dark, could easily end up with his force and the Drenga already inside thinking one another targets. A signal for reinforcements would be different. But no signal came.

At dawn the Drenga captain himself emerged from the inner castle wall to report, covered by two men, shields high. Arrows rained down, rattling on the shields. Talkar peered up at the walls, making out vague shapes that appeared just long enough to shoot, then vanished.

Talkar waited at his camp table, having signed for an orderly to bring steamed milk with honey, which Captain Henga downed gratefully at a sign. His eyes were red-rimmed with exhaustion.

"Captain Henga. You do not have the castle yet?" Talkar asked.

"No. But we believe we have one more section to go, and that most of them are dead." Henga's voice was a husky croak. "Unless there are more waiting for a last stand. Everything is dark in there . . . sabotaged," he finally said, because he couldn't think of a word strong enough to encompass such thorough, single-minded ferocity. "Every passage, stair, room was blocked or diverted. Most with traps. All the stairwells have brought down rains of burning matter, oil, even furniture flung on us in the dark." He waved a gauntleted hand vaguely. "Diverted over to the side where the mountain came down. Into traps. Burying my men alive." He threw back his head, staring blindly through the opening of the tent to the massive castle looming against the sky. "In pairs," he added in a low, tired voice.

Talkar said, "Then it's not a matter of doors to batter down?"

"If there is a direct way through to gain access to the

road beyond, we have not found it." He hesitated, reviewing the nightmare since the dags had broken down the last door: all the glowglobes had been smashed. Their reserve torches extinguished with tipped barrels of dirty water, leaving them floundering in the dark, to serve as targets for yet more arrows, knives, boiling liquids poured down onto their heads. Fire traps. Arrows shot from openings impossible to descry. Ugly traps, like sharpened spikes in walls and floors.

The worst, though, the worst had been entire floors sawn through in the two western towers. In both cases young girls had darted past his men, each of them carrying pieces of paper. Of course the men gave chase, one party under Henga's direction.

He'd just reached the door himself when the girl stopped in the middle of one of the round tower rooms, with its bare wooden floor. She looking back over her shoulder at them, and time seemed to halt for one rush and thump of his heart: this girl was just the age of his daughter, about fifteen, freckles across her nose, her hair light, her braids tousled. Her pulse beating in her skinny neck above the rumpled tunic much like Venn children wear during their brief summer.

Thump. His men moved in slowly, surrounding her, she stuck out her tongue. Then she tensed, glanced down—an abrupt, instinctive reaction.

And the floor dropped.

The entire floor, taking them all three floors down to death.

The second one he heard, not a hundred heartbeats afterward, across the length of the castle. That is, he heard the same *crack!* of sawn wood giving way, the smashing long fall, the screams and shouts of terror, and then that awful silence.

He swallowed, knowing that if he survived this battle, he would always remember that girl, how she stood poised, not letting herself look down at that sabotaged floor until it was too late for them all.

He blinked, forcing his attention back to Talkar, and reported how many they'd lost—dead, burned, punctured, wounded with shattered limbs who would no more march through the pass than they could fly.

It was absurd in the face of the thousands waiting, a desperately absurd defense. In another circumstance one could say a gallant one.

Now? Right now they could not afford the time.

"Get control of that castle. We know there is a tunnel, leading up around the headland onto the pass. They have to have bricked it up, or buried it. Do whatever you have to do to find it."

The man swallowed again, summoned his men, and the three ran heavily back inside, armor jingling, arrows clattering on the shields.

Chapter Seven

Jeje: My current domicile is a pantry closet between the kitchen and what was once the main banqueting hall or whatever they called those vast rooms. Now a barracks full of straw sleeping mats, smelling of wet wool and old socks. I was sitting in here sewing Inda's battle tunic when a message came that Inda was seeking me. He dashed in looking like he hasn't slept in a week, and it was just like the bad old days. With no warning, he blurts, "I might have to divide 'em, Tau. But I don't know who to send where. As commanders, I mean."

"You are not having this conversation with Evred why?"

He was ramming back and forth as if in front of a field of a thousand men and not in a room about four paces by five. "He knows 'em all too well. They don't— I don't—oh, I just want to know what you see. When Evred and I aren't there, or talking."

"You mean from your Sier Danas?"

"It has to be them." Then he stopped and glared at me. "Have you seen anyone else who could command?"

"No. They all expect to be commanded," is what I said.

"Who can I send to the top of the pass to charge the enemy and bring 'em all behind him?"

"Cama," I said, surprised he even asked.

But then I was more surprised when he waved me off for making a foolish error. "Hawkeye has to be one, and even I can see he doesn't like Cama. It seems to have to do with the past. He wouldn't—it's not enough to—oh, what about Cherry-Stripe?"

"He doesn't think you can do it," I said, trying to be offhand. Also, trying not to show how very strange it was to be included even at a remove in what in any other history would be called the Council of the Great, and Jeje, if that doesn't provoke you to answer me, even if it's a long curse against the pretences of kings if not my own pretensions, I don't know what will.

So Inda looks up, and snorts, just like the old days, and drums (we never knew his finger tapping was drumming, did we?) and says, "I saw that."

"The one you can probably rely on is Noddy. He's like a rock, that one. I keep forgetting he's only a year or two older than you, he seems like he's your uncle."

"He was always that way, even when he was twelve. Main thing is, I think Hawkeye likes him, so they'll work together. Good."

And out he shot. Will my advice net me a reward or a knife in the back? Not a dukedom, sadly, for they have no dukes here.

Having finished dispatching a meal to the dag imprisoned up in the archive and orders for new quarters in the city, Evred went hunting for Inda.

He strictly controlled his impatience at the crowds everywhere: they all had things to do but not enough space to do them in.

After a thoughtful glance at his face, Kened shoved unceremoniously ahead, elbowing aside Runners, Runners' aides, stable hands, horses and men moving this way and that, a few boys dashing between them, most laughing.

The startled glances sent Evred's way would have

amused him at any other time, especially one without the prospect of a battle pressing against his skull in the form of constant headache.

A brown, unruly horsetail was surrounded by taller heads, mostly blond. Was that Inda? Yes. Inda bounced on his toes, his eyes briefly appearing above the press in the court as far too many people tried to shoulder their way to their particular task.

"It's as ready as it ever will be," Inda called to Evred as they worked their way toward one another, and when Evred cupped his hand to his ear, repeated it louder.

Exasperated beyond endurance, Evred made a rare, flat-handed swipe, and Kened signaled to the duty guards to clear enough space for them to go inside.

"What did you say?"

"Remind me about the rings." Inda poked his finger under the owl clasp and rubbed his scalp vigorously, making a face. "The parley room is ready for tomorrow. We've got the ruse all laid along. But Sponge, I need another look at that map—"

Inda's big, scarred hands rubbed over his face, his eyes blanked as once again his thoughts turned inward, and Evred said shortly, "Let's go upstairs."

They ran up the stairs to the top floor of the east tower. Now the clamor was just a low, steady rumble far below.

Then Inda whirled around, his coat skirt flaring, and dropped onto the top step at the landing, head in his hands.

Below the open window an entire wing of men shouted in cadence; from behind them the rumble of laden wagons smothered the clatter of iron-shod horse hooves against stone. Evred moved across the landing and pulled the heavy shutters closed.

Inda rocked back and forth, his unruly hair as always escaping from his horsetail in wild curling strands. Evred stared down at a lock caught in the glittering ruby dangling against Inda's scar-slashed cheek, was overwhelmed by a skin-prickling onslaught of affection. So intense and so unfamiliar an emotion had an unsettling, vertiginous effect on his perceptions; the inexorable pressure of imminent battle fractured his habitual control. Words were so difficult, and usually so was gesture—even proximity, but now—

Inda. Loyal Inda. Everything Evred asked Inda granted, with the unthinking generosity of the ten-year-old he'd once been.

Evred stretched out his hand, fingers open, and just touched the sweat-damp, tousled top of Inda's head.

The gesture partook more of the warmth of affection than the heat of desire, but desire there was, there always was.

Affection and desire snuffed when Inda jerked upright, his face hardened into a killing glare all the more shocking because Evred had, as yet, never seen him in battle.

Just for a moment, then it was gone, but the deep, uncontrollable recoil forced Inda to his feet, color flooding his face.

He said to the ceiling, "Chart."

Then he whirled and sprinted to the office, trying to outrun that stomach-churning nausea, a visceral reaction from the days he lay under Wafri's stroking hands after torture.

Inda thumped against the map table, and threw his arms wide, as though flinging away the sensation brought by memory. *Wafri is not here. It was probably a spider, or the edge of his coat.*

He fought to shed the unwanted memory of Wafri's twisted passions, and to reclaim the insight that had eluded him for weeks. "That's it. That's *it*. I knew it would come to me, I just had to have quiet. Sponge! Look!"

He pointed down at the map. Inda slapped the back of his fingers against the carefully detailed top of the pass. "What do you see?"

They'd mulled over the map at least twice since their arrival, but Evred said in a voice devoid of any emotion, "Sheer cliffs at either side. Above the cliffs, the lakes on one side, and on the other, the source of the Andahi River."

"Exactly." Inda breathed hard. "Evred, that's the mistake we've all been making, and I knew better. I knew better, which was why I was thinking of charts: on land, water's a barrier. In the sea, it's your access. It's *land* that's the barrier."

"And so?"

"Don't you see? Talkar, their Hilda commander, is a land warrior. He's going to think the same thing!"

"But the sea commander won't."

"But he's not in their plans! They operate separately. Oh, Sponge. That's it. People move faster on water than on land, it's a conduit. We can use the lake on this side, at least, to get people to the top of the pass. That gives us a chance to attack from an angle and take them by surprise. If only we could get to the river on the other side, we could come at 'em from three sides, but no use in even thinking about it. From the looks of these drawings, it would take half a year to get men up those mountains. But this side? The lakes are long enough . . . looks like a few days of hard travel, and . . . Let's get the others." And he sprang to the door, yelling, "Vedrid!"

The Runner appeared at the other end of the office, pale head highlighted against the gray wall.

Inda said, "Grab Barend and the Tveis. Tau, too," he added, whirled back and danced about the room. "That's it, that's it, that's it!"

Inda thumped his fist on the map, spun around again, thumping the walls, the door, the windowsill, the table, the chair backs, walking and talking and striking and looking anywhere but at Evred's face. "I wish I could ask Signi, but it's one thing to ask about the people, and another to ask her about war plans. She has to know some of them, doesn't she? No, can't make her do that—not fair—and anyway I will wager anything Talkar would never think to send a force up and across the lake. I know it."

Whirl, pound. "Is she liking it up there in that library of yours? I didn't get a chance to go up there last night, and this morning Vedrid woke me up for the—you did see her, didn't you?" And inwardly, *It was a spider. Wafri is gone.*

"I had breakfast sent up to Dag Signi," Evred said neutrally. Was the introduction of Dag Signi calculating or instinctive? But Inda had never been calculating in human relations.

· Inda thumped a chair back with both fists, staring at the map, but sightlessly this time, and then he smiled, but for the very first time it was not the old unselfconscious wide brown-eyed gaze, the candid smile of childhood. It was the quick, slightly anxious smile that people gave Evred because he was the king. Sometimes anxious, sometimes cunning.

No, he must not permit himself to think like that. It was too much like his uncle, this immediate fear of conspiracy, so immediate that it would be far too easy for fears to take on a semblance of reality, the conviction driven by just how much he would hate it. *Face the truth. Inda did not react with calculation, it was disgust. No, it was revulsion.*

Inda was away again, prowling the room. "Truth is, I don't want Signi to find out how ignorant I am."

Evred snorted. "You were never ignorant."

"No," Inda agreed. "I wasn't. When I was eleven. But—I thought about this yesterday morning—I don't think I've read a book since. I think I've forgotten all the Old Sartoran letters, except the ones in my name."

Whirl, thump thump thump.

"The forbidden language." Evred looked away from Inda's scarred hands resting on the map to the latent strength in his arms straining against the coat sleeves. And away to the window. "I saw the note you wrote to Ryala Pim when you repaid her for her fleet: the Old Sartoran was quite clear." He did not add that he had recovered that note from the Pims, and had it still, kept in a box on the mantelpiece in his bedchamber at home.

Inda flung his hands wide. "Alphabet, yes. I can do my name, like I said. I can even sound out a few words. What I missed the most when they first put me to sea—besides home—was reading. But then I got over the habit."

Voices echoed up the stairwell. The moment of privacy was nearly gone, maybe lost forever. Touch was denied Evred; he had to make certain he had not lost the little of Inda he did have. "I've been reading the private records of

kings, when I can," he said, hearing the falsity, the calculation, in his own attempt at lightness. "I'll show you one day.
You would never believe why my revered ancestor Anderle Montrei-Vayir never wore a crown, though we took
everything else from Iascan custom."

Inda looked up, and there was the old wide-open curiosity, the grin of anticipated humor. No revulsion, better, no
awkward consciousness.

"He had one made, but it kept slipping over his ears,
bending them. Once someone laughed."

Inda snorted. "He didn't have the wit to have it fixed?"

"They're metal. You either make it so tight it won't fall,
then it hurts, he said, or it's so loose your ears dog down.
You can't line it, like armor, it looked ridiculous. So it was
either kill everyone or chuck the crown."

Inda was laughing as Cherry-Stripe charged through the
door. The others almost trod on his heels, and the room
filled with the smell of damp wool as Cama growled,
"Damn rain!"

Cherry-Stripe demanded, "What's the joke?" He didn't
wait for an answer, but flipped up the back of his hand
toward the sky. "Rain holds off all summer while we're
sweating up the road, and now the horses are penned up
eating their heads off. They'll be bellyaching just in time
for us to ride to war."

"Muck our way chest-deep through mud to war, more
like," Rat said as he flung the casement wide. "Phew, it's
like a sweat-box in here."

A gust of wind returned a hissing spray of rain; papers
circled like mad white bats and the map rattled on the
table. Everyone cursed Rat, who hastily slammed the casement shut again.

Hawkeye, coming in last, contemplated Vedrid's
Runner-exact rendering of Inda's order: *Grab Barend and
the Tveis* . . . There had been no sign of collusion to take
away his command, just the unthinking comradeship of the
academy—the way Hawkeye had felt about Jasid Tlen and
Cassad Ain and Buck Marlo-Vayir, and about Manther
Jaya-Vayir and Tanrid Algara-Vayir before they died.

Sure enough, Inda's gaze slid right past him. He had not been excluded, he'd been forgotten. Inda, after all, did not know Hawkeye, had never known him.

Hawkeye backed up against the wall as the others closed up around the table, and at a sign from Evred, Inda said, "Hawkeye and Noddy, you'll be in command going up the pass. But we're going to split our force."

Relief washed through Hawkeye. His cousin had been more than fair. He would command the lead force, as was right. And though one of the Sier Danas was also being sent, at least it was Noddy Turtle Toraca, who wasn't on the strut like Buck's and Horsebutt's scrubby brothers.

"Split?" Cama repeated. "You sure that's wise?"

"Look. You tell me," Inda replied, and explained his observation again, gesturing along the pass.

All of them comprehended the shift in perspective from land to sea once it was explained. It was simple enough, but you had to see water as a conduit, and not a barrier.

"So here's the basic plan. Charging is our strength, with speed and fast maneuvers. Speed and maneuvering is going to be about as useful as shit in shoes." Inda thumped the pass on the map. "With these cliffs on either side, what we need is heavy and steady. Dragoon lancers in front. As heavy and solid as you can get, instead of fast, because I think it's going to be their heaviest foot against you."

"You changed your mind about them being mounted?" Cama asked in surprise.

"Don't know." Inda thumped the map. "I still think a lot depends on how many horses they brought. And on how good they feel about their fighting skills on horseback. But now, after seeing the map, and those mountains, I'm thinking they're going to hate those sheer walls as much as we do. When I saw them drilling with horses, it was out on the plains of Ymar."

"Why don't they have enough horses?" Cherry-Stripe asked. "I thought they had everything."

"Everything you can pack into ships," Barend reminded him. This was not a new topic, but it was the first time Cherry-Stripe was paying attention. "Can't bring enough horses *and* enough men. If every man needs one horse and at least one remount, where do you put 'em in the ship?"

"On the pole things, of course." Cherry-Stripe cackled at his own wit. Then sighed when no one else laughed.

Inda said, "Next year will probably be different because they'll expect to face us on our plains. So back to the pass. They might have some chargers in front, but I'll bet Talkar will trust his heavy marchers, the ones I watched in Ymar." And to Cherry-Stripe, with faint emphasis, "Their shields are these big, heavy curved rectangles, much heavier than their round ones. They can either aim 'em forward or lift 'em high on command. But they can't aim 'em in both directions at once."

Cherry-Stripe was careless, but not stupid. He grimaced. "I did hear you say that much, when we were sweating on the road north."

Inda turned his gaze on the rest. "That's why I want archers up on the heights. So you, Cama, and you, Cherry-Stripe, are going to take your sharpest archers up there."

"No horses? Just bows?" Cama asked doubtfully. "What if we can't get up there in time? Then we're useless."

"That's why you leave now. Cross that string of lakes, which puts you almost at the top of the pass. Sit tight until we come, because that's our first line of defense. If we can push on down the pass toward Idayago without meeting the Venn, then you get back to the lake and go north—see, there's an old mountain path more or less parallel to the pass—and meet us again at Castle Andahi. You're our secondary force, our surprise. If we could only get at 'em from this side, we'd have a great plan: attack from the front, flanking support from the heights at either side. As it is, we'll have one side."

Cama's jaw tightened. "I'll copy the map soon's we're done talking. We'll be out of here tonight. But how much of our arrow cache do we take?"

"As much as you can carry. Don't worry about us. This morning the Randviar showed me the cache she's had the women making ever since Evred sent the word north to get ready for the invasion. She says every Marlovan family donated wooden furniture to be cut up for arrow shafts. So we've got that in addition to everything we brought."

He paused as the others made appreciative noises.

Noddy rubbed his ear. "Since you won't be able to ride up those trails, that means no saddlebags."

"We'll wear our fighting clothes." Cama shrugged. "More space in the packs for arrows."

"They're gonna smell us clear up the pass." Cherry-Stripe cackled again.

"No they won't," Noddy said, wooden-faced as always. "There's thousands of 'em bringing their own stink."

"Knocking the trees flat." Cherry-Stripe hooted.

"We'll pick up scatter-wood and feathers on the way." Cama squinted down at the stylized forest symbols on the map. "Make more when we camp."

Cherry-Stripe had also been studying the map. "I see how we're reinforcing Noddy, but all these wiggly lines mean canyons, right? With mountains between." He jerked his thumb downward. "How can we possibly coordinate an attack like that, when we'll be sweating up some mountain top and they'll be in the pass? I can't believe whirtlers or signal flags are going to work."

Inda faced Evred across the table. "Sponge?"

Evred endured another inward struggle. This subject of the magic cases was not new. He'd decided against trusting them, a decision reinforced when the lockets had abruptly ceased to function.

Inda waited. They all waited.

Evred knew he was going to give in, though he distrusted magic, Venn, and golden cases whose origins were obscure. The truth was, until the Marlovans had their own mage, he would never know if what appeared to be a distinct military advantage was just a magical trap. And even a Venn mage could have his own goals.

Just like Dag Erkric was closing his grip on Prince Rajnir of the Venn, by using magic.

Hatred burned through Evred. He loathed depending on something he could not control. "If we agree on a code."

Inda's smile was his quick, unguarded, real one. He

snapped his fingers. "Good idea." He remembered Fox saying just before they'd faced Marshig, *Codes are fun, but the first thing you forget in action, unless it's drilled into second nature.* "But it's got to be simple." He dug into his inner coat pocket, pulled out a golden case, and dropped it onto the table, where it gleamed with rich highlights. "You're each going to have one of these."

The others all stared in amazement as he explained the golden cases, how they transferred notes instantly. He taught them the transfer spell, which they grasped easily, then finished, "And I have enough for each of you, if I double up with Evred. Since I'm with him—that's my place as Royal Shield Arm—we only need one. You can practice as you move into position."

"What about the rest of us?" Rat said, pointing to himself and Barend.

"Let's get the parley over." Inda flipped up the back of his hand toward the window. "Find out what the Venn want. Anyway, we can't pull out of here until we have Ola-Vayir and Buck covering Lindeth and the road here—" Inda stopped, throwing back his head. One hand drummed absently on the map, then he jerked his chin down. "—what did I—yes. We have to have Buck and Ola-Vayir here, guarding our backs, because I just know the Venn are going to try to pinch us between two forces in the pass. That's what anyone'd do."

He sighed sharply, and flung out his hands. "Cherry-Stripe. Cama. I just—I want you in place."

"Watch," Cherry-Stripe vowed. "We'll be in place when you need us."

Strut, Hawkeye thought in disgust.

"Then it's starting now," Cama said slowly, turning his head so he could take them all in. "It's not in a season. Or a month. Or even a week."

The Sier Danas exchanged looks, as if something more was needed, some great speech, but Evred hated speeches, they all knew that, and none of them wanted to sing a ballad. Even the sword dance had been done.

"It's us," Cherry-Stripe marveled, his blue eyes wide and

earnest. "The Tveis. Not, you know, everyone we expected to lead the battle against the Venn. It's *us*. How did that happen?"

"Because things have changed, and we're different," Rat Cassad said unexpectedly. Ranged alongside his cousin Barend, one could see the differences between them, though they shared the Cassad features: broad brow, narrow chin, short upper lip, but Rat's front teeth were as bucked as when he was ten. He had the Cassad fair hair and slight build. Barend was thin but tall, as well as dark-haired: Montrei-Vayir traits. "Remember the Battle of Marlovar Bridge? In the old days the fathers would have used that to test us. Instead we were bundled away, because our fathers wanted to protect the inheritance."

He jerked a thumb toward the boys training to be future Runners, who were down in the courtyard now, yelling and playing, now that the squall was past. "They're the same age we were then," he said, opening the casement again. "Things have changed again."

The boys' voices rose as they played with the scout dogs. Everyone except Inda lifted their heads, listening. Inda had turned his face to the wall. It was that weird mental absence they'd all gotten used to. He thumped his forehead gently against the stone, his sun-ruined hair jolting against the back of his stained, dust-printed coat on every thump.

Rat jerked his thumb toward the window. "They'll be holding our weapons, right there in battle. The little girls up on the walls with Hawkeye's great-aunt want to defend the castle. Now the young'uns are raised up to war."

Noddy said, "Ten years of Idayagans, pirates, and Venn will do that."

"Something our fathers found unthinkable ten years ago," Rat said wryly. "Is it good or bad?"

Inda rolled his forehead against the stone, back and forth, back and forth.

Evred said, "Everything that happened was unthinkable. But it happened. We're done here. Pick your men, get them ready—"

"Wait," Inda said, a hand thrust out.

Hawkeye watched Evred-Harvaldar defer without any sign of affront. Defer to a command by this scrub mate who'd been fooling around with boats for years, learning fighting from pirates instead of properly at the academy. The academy bond seemed so strong it was unperceivable, like air.

Hawkeye remembered to breathe.

Your first loyalty was always to the king, and second to your family lands, but everyone knew that those were duty, that the strongest loyalty was the one that took no effort: to your academy mates. It was unprecedented for second brothers to ride to war like these had, yet they all appeared to accept it as an unquestioned right. And so had the king, because he was one of them. Though he'd scrupulously given Hawkeye this post, he'd relied most on Horsebutt's brother Cama for investigation, advice, all the other functions of a Harskialdna. Until Inda came.

"They're coming," Inda said. Grind, grind. "I've been feeling it for days, ever since the winds changed. If we didn't have the beacons, and people on the coast watching, I'd swear they were already here. I would be."

"But we don't have people watching the coast." Evred frowned, turning toward his cousin. "Aren't our patrols confined to the outer perimeter of the harbor?"

Barend said, "I tried to get a coastal watch but Lindeth fought me too hard. They scarcely tolerated the perimeter guard—except when pirates appeared, then they wanted us there to fight." He flushed. "I guess I should have put someone out a month ago, but I was up north—"

Inda snapped a hand out, palm down, and the two Montrei-Vayirs shut up.

"Tau." Inda's face was still to the wall, as he ground his forehead back and forth.

Tau had been lounging unnoticed against the wall opposite Hawkeye. "Present," Tau said after a protracted pause.

Inda said to the wall, "*I* should have asked if there was a coastal watch posted, instead of expecting—I thought Ola-Vayir would arrive when we did—yeah. Huh. Tau."

"Still here."

Inda turned around, dug his heel palms into his eyes,
then slapped his palms on the table.

"Go to Lindeth Harbor. You can get there by sunset if
you ride. Scout the horizon. If there's nothing there, talk to
the fisherfolk, but wear sailor duds. Don't look like one of
us. Find out who is watching the coast, and what they've
seen." Inda tapped his golden case. "Report back."

Tau was gone in half a dozen quick steps.

Inda jerked his thumb in the direction of the inner castle, and the room they'd picked for the Venn parley. "Let's
get that set up. Nothing in view, nothing to see out the windows, nothing they can learn about us, is what I'm thinking . . ."

Chapter Eight

EVERYONE expected trouble. No one expected boring.
The four men who appeared in a huddle around the transfer token were tall, two dressed like warriors—battle tunics, chain mail glinting at the side-slits, straight swords in baldrics—the other two in blue robes that hung down to the tops of their sandaled feet.

The Marlovans smacked hands to knives, ready to spring—then settled back to vigilance when they saw the strain magical transfer caused in the newcomers. One of the Venn staggered, another gulped in air, sweat beading his brow. The two in the blue robes plopped abruptly into the waiting chairs opposite a grand wingback chair.

The pair of warriors seemed to be an honor guard. As soon as they got control of the transfer-reaction they laid hands to their weapons.

The guards were herded behind the chairs by these muscular young Marlovans who had no intention of letting them anywhere near the red-haired young fellow in the crimson silk battle-tunic who sat in the wingback chair.

Since the guards' range of vision had thus been limited to shoulders, ponytails, and the backs of their two charges, they settled themselves into endurance mode.

The five Marlovan guards in the gray coats took up the remaining wall space around two seated Marlovans. The blue-coated messenger (also red haired) at the table leaned forward. His brows rose in question over steady hazel eyes as his inky fingers dipped a freshly sharpened quill in the inkpot and poised the pen over a paper.

The Marlovans studied the Venn truce party.

The ill-famed Dag Erkric introduced himself and his companions in slow, sonorous words. The mage was a long-nosed, heavily-built man with light-colored eyes that never stopped moving, and smooth butter-yellow hair. He stood with his arms crossed, a self-important pose. But he was the Dag of all the Venn, kind of like a king of mages, wasn't he?

The second mage was short, round, young, and fussed nervously with papers that he never read, just held or twiddled.

Inda had chosen a room with the only two windows firmly shuttered. If the dags asked for air, the windows opened onto the back court and the outer wall. No sentry walked there. The perimeter guards, out of sight, made certain that no person, horse, dog, or even cat—and the castle was full of mousers, though they were nearly all hiding from the unaccustomed onslaught of humans—strayed into view.

Inda, Barend, and the Sier Danas had insisted that yes, someone had to be king, but not Evred. So Barend had plucked out a tall young man with bright red hair who sweltered in Evred-Harvaldar's heavy silk House battle-tunic, best linen shirt, sturdy new riding trousers, and his good pair of boots. The hapless scout was trying not to sweat into the royal garments—unsuccessfully.

"King Evred," the shorter mage said, bowing to the red-haired scout. "I am here to translate. The Dag shall speak the words of our prince in our tongue. Then I can translate his words into your tongue. If you please."

Evred caught himself before he could say, "Why not speak in Sartoran?" He resigned himself to tedium.

The mages observed the king's gaze stray toward the messenger with the quill, then go diffuse. "Ah. Go on." The supposed king plucked at the stiff gold embroidery on the high neck of his tunic, then hastily lowered his hand.

Dag Erkric unloosed a long, droning speech in his own language, as the short mage nodded his head every few words, his eyes half-closed, his fingers running up and down the edge of his papers. Every so often he covertly watched the room.

The speech went on and on. Evred had tried to study some Venn, not that they'd had many examples of the language in the royal archive, the last communication between Marlovan and Venn having mainly been confined to the Montredavan-An family. He comprehended maybe one word in twenty.

Hawkeye's attention stayed on the two armsmen, but Rat's drifted. Inda, stationed by one shuttered window as far from the dags' line of sight as he could get, at first fought against the itch in his ears. He clenched one hand around his earrings in his pocket, fighting the urge to scratch and tug at his earlobes. But when the feeling finally subsided, he found himself lulled by the buzzing of an insect outside the shutter. He studied the scuffed toes of Cherry-Stripe's old boots. Though the uppers had long ago reshaped to his feet, he still didn't think of the boots as his.

He summoned the map to mind, and mentally evaluated the dotted path just outside the northern wall of the city, trying to estimate how far Cama and Cherry-Stripe had gotten. He wondered if the beacon was up there . . . maybe he should tell Cama to watch for it . . . *Oh, Cama'd think of that, wouldn't he?* Gradually his chin sank down onto his chest. *Evred . . . ask him . . . keeping beacons a secret, too late now, surely* . . . the thoughts turned into dreams . . .

A businesslike elbow thumped him in the ribs, and he jolted upright with a snort. Oh, it was a *snore.*

Embarrassment burned through him. He discovered that the corner of his mouth was wet. Fine Harskialdna, falling asleep against a wall, snoring and just about to start drooling!

Quick glance. Barend shaking as he tried not to laugh. Rat smothering a yawn so hard his eyes watered. Inda could see the tears from across the room. Even Noddy looked more brow-furrowed and jowly than ever. Only

Evred sat upright, writing away. What was he writing? Probably lists of what to do, in one of his codes . . . didn't his uncle used to do that? . . . maybe it's a good thing over-all, codes . . . stop that!

It was time for the tricks he'd used to stay awake on watch during long nights aboard ship, beginning with standing on his toes just enough to force his body to balance. Then he counted the flags in the stone floor.

Time wore on as the dag spoke, and the other man translated this long, complicated speech, full of compliments and diplomatic but empty phrases: . . . *mutual desire for honorable peace . . . assumed goodwill in negotiating a satisfactory compromise . . . with respect to all concerned parties . . . cognizance . . .* No words that meant anything, that you could get hold of.

Everyone shifted in relief when at last the Dag made a gesture of peace and nodded regally at the little mage, who said, "Dag Erkric wishes me to inform you that there have been petitions sent to the north side of the strait, from all three harbor towns along the Idayagan shore."

"What kind of petitions?" the fake king asked, after encountering several surreptitious glances, nods, and thumb-twitches to remind him of his role.

"What? Kind? Of petitions?" the interpreter repeated, hands out.

Evred's feet shifted. He repressed the urge to start tapping his fingers. This was the first Venn parley, ever, and he must not be the one to break it.

"You mentioned petitions," the scout repeated, forgetting whose tabard he wore for just long enough to draw the rich silken sleeve across his brow.

His face lengthened in dismay; Rat turned his attention ferociously to the sharply squared toes of his boots. New boots, those. His father and brother had insisted he'd go to war in style.

The negotiator placed his palms together and bowed, then he addressed the mage in a long speech, to which the Dag responded in slow, rolling Venn.

Then the interpreter turned, his air apologetic. "These

petitions, they request us to come to this land. To protect them. We demand nothing of the landmen, you see. Nothing. Only toll from ships, our just due for keeping pirates away from the trade ships."

Dag Erkric uncorked another long, sonorous flow.

Evred's gaze strayed to Inda, who stood against the opposite wall, his jaw locked as he repressed a yawn.

In the distance the bells rang. It was later than Evred thought. He stirred, picking up the quill and brushing it against his ear in the signal they'd arranged.

The scout was stiff and miserable—and bored. Yawn after yawn tried to pry his jaws apart, so he kept his teeth gritted until his eyes watered into the drips already running down his face. A dry cough and a scrape of a heel from Rat (who was now studying the ceiling) snapped him back to the present. He shot a look at the king, saw the signal for End It.

How long had he been doing that?

Thoroughly miserable, he waited until the talking magic fellow drew a breath, then said in his most polite voice, "It's getting late—"

The short one said, "We just have two questions. If you will permit, that you Marlovans withdraw from the lands in the north, as we identify it: the lands just above the mountains."

"And?"

"Our honored Prince Rajnir requires, you must comprehend, the, ah, how to term, the body of the pirate Inda Elgar, who stands accused of attacking and burning civilian ships in our waters, and must be tried and punished. To surrender a criminal, it is to be hoped, would serve as a gesture of honor, of peaceful intention."

The pretend king sat up straight, looking startled, and then uneasy.

Laying down the quill, Evred mouthed the word, "Who?"

The scout took the hint, and repeated, "Who?"

The Dag betrayed a flicker of expression, quickly replaced by the bland goodwill they'd all seen so far.

The scout remembered his coaching and added, "And what are you offering us?"

The negotiator sounded smooth and well-rehearsed. "Prince Rajnir offers a peaceful negotiation satisfactory to all parties if you demonstrate your goodwill with the two gestures we just mentioned." And, seeing the scout stir, "Shall we retire to permit you to consider? And meet again? Say, tomorrow, when the bells ring at midday? Or do you need more time?"

The scout waved a hand. "Tomorrow is agreed."

The two mages placed their hands together in the way Evred and Inda had seen Signi do, only with far less grace. In fact, it seemed that the short one, who had begun nervous and trembling, was now smiling with a faint smugness. But as soon as the two men-at-arms closed in behind them, they all vanished, the air briefly stirring.

Rat Cassad nearly cracked his jaws on a yawn. "So that's a diplomatic parley! If it was a meeting between battle grounds I'd call it stalling."

The scout stood up and, using great care, pulled the heavy Montrei-Vayir House tabard up over his head.

"Tau said diplomats can spin talks out forever when they have to," Inda said doubtfully as he rubbed his ears vigorously, then began to affix the earrings again. "But you'd think they'd want peace right away."

"Unless—" Evred frowned as he extended his arm for the scout to lay the tabard over it. So much of what he'd seen struck him as odd, though he couldn't define why.

The scout thought the frown was for him. "I tried not to, but I sweated these up something fierce," he said in a low, apologetic voice, indicating the damp, wrinkled linen shirt.

Distracted, Evred dealt with the easiest thing first. "It's hot enough to boil broth in here." He indicated the sodden shirt. "Just give the clothes over to Kened after you change. Thank you. You did well."

The others echoed the praise as the blushing scout hustled out to go bore his mates, in strictest confidence, about his day as king.

"Unless they're stalling for time," Rat finished Evred's

comment, and stretched his hands over his head. His back cracked as he kicked the door shut behind the scout.

"Thought the mage would know more of our language," Noddy said from his place in the corner. "Heh. Why not Sartoran? Isn't that supposed to be the court language for everyone who has courts?"

"If he's the right mage." Rat rubbed at his neck.

Evred turned. "Why do you say that?"

Rat waved a lazy hand. "Said the magic words mighty slow and stiff. Reminded me of a pigtail with the lances, instead of a dragoon."

Evred so hated the idea of magical powers that could, at a mysterious word or two, spy, transform, even kill, he had not considered that aspect. *I want magic to be difficult to perform.*

Inda smacked his hand against the table. "We better find out. I'm going to ask Signi."

"Vedrid?" Evred opened the door. "Please request the dag to join us here."

Signi's color was high, as though she'd been out in the summer sun when Vedrid brought her into the hot, stuffy room. Her cast-off child's smock and worn riding trousers were neat and fresh: she'd clearly had access to some kind of magic while in that archive. Well, they all knew the tower was full of some sort of Morvende magic.

Signi's earnest gaze sought Inda's first, then moved swiftly to the king's. Seeing no threat there, she glanced at the tabard hanging over his arm. Her sandy brows lifted, then met, puckering her brow.

"What is it?" Inda asked.

She stretched out a forefinger, but did not quite touch the crimson cloth so beautifully woven. "The tablet-pattern," she whispered. "In the weave. It is the same as our formal house robes."

Inda's indifference was mirrored in all the others' faces. "Signi, if anything I ask trespasses on the truce we've had between us, you have only to say."

Evred's muscles tightened against the now familiar resentment. Inda's words were entirely just.

"You have a question for me, then?" Signi asked, and made that peace sign—without the smugness of that young mage.

"You know Dag Erkric, right?"

"I do."

"Is he big and tall, maybe forty? Hair as yellow as Rat's there? Carrot nose?"

"No." She pressed her hands together tightly, then dropped them to her sides. "He is very tall. Very lean. His hair is thin, but silver. He is old."

Evred turned to Rat. "You were right. It's a ruse." His mouth thinned. "Do we look like fools?"

Signi made the peace gesture again. "You are all very young. And you know nothing of magic."

Evred said, "So the dag knows who we are."

She opened her hands. "I believe so."

"That means he's been here spying on us."

Her color faded. "Yes. So I believe. I felt his traces on our arrival."

Evred's gaze was unwavering. "Is he spying on us right now?"

"No." She gave him a rueful smile. "Because I just finished completing wards."

"To aid us?"

"That was not my intent."

To the surprise of some there, Evred's expression eased. "Because he has broken his vows not to interfere in military matters?"

"Yes."

Evred turned away at last, his slow outward breath a hiss between his teeth. Then, "Hawkeye. Give that magic token to someone. Tell him to chuck it down the nearest steam vent." He pointed out the window, toward the great square between the castle and the city, underneath which lay the massive cavern that served as the baths for everyone in Ala Larkadhe.

Hawkeye, who as the castle commander had taken charge of the token, said, "I'll do it." Like his cousin, he hated magic and would take great pleasure in seeing to this order himself.

There was a quiet double knock at the door. When Kened appeared, Evred handed off the tunic.

"So what now?" Rat asked, shutting the door again.

Inda said, "If they are stalling for time, there is a reason." He thumped his fist on the table. "It's those winds. I keep feeling we're late. I don't know if it's—"

His thoughts splintered, like they so often did, two and three separate ideas skittering away. The others looked at him. Waiting.

He smacked his hands down, the sting in his palms oddly steadying. For two heartbeats. "Hawkeye. Noddy. Take your dragoons, start up the pass as soon as you can. Yes! We've got Cherry-Stripe and Cama heading for the cliffs above the top, that's good. You go too, and between the four of you, hold it until the rest of us can get there."

Hawkeye twitched his brows up as Noddy held up three fingers. "We've got six wings. Against *how* many?"

"Doesn't matter," Inda said impatiently. "I need fast, not numbers, and six wings will move uphill faster than sixty wings. If we had 'em. You get there first is all I ask. Hold it. The moment we know we've got Buck and Ola-Vayir to guard our backs, the rest of us will be right on your heels."

Everyone began talking at once.

Signi touched Inda's hand. Distracted by too much going on at once, he cast her a quick, impatient glance—and her expression caught his attention entirely.

"I must speak to you," she murmured.

Without a thought Inda opened the door, followed her out, and shut it, leaving the others all talking. Except for Evred, who watched after them in tight-lipped silence.

The pair of would-be dags arrived at the Destination aboard the *Cormorant*. They looked hot, tired, weary as they surrendered their transfer tokens into Erkric's out-held hand, and then shed the heavy blue robes gratefully into the arms of orderlies. Durasnir had ordered steamed milk for them, but a glance at those shiny crimson faces and he beckoned for the stone jug. They drank down the cold water in greedy gasps as an orderly ran to apprise the prince.

While they'd waited for the parley to end, Dag Erkric had twice vanished from the ship, each time returning tense and curt. Whether from anger or worry, Durasnir could not tell, and Erkric did not give him a report. Instead, he restlessly studied the dispatches as they arrived and were brought in by the ensigns on duty.

The prince's quick step approached down the companionway. He flung the door open into the command cabin. "How went the ruse?"

The two scouts made their royal obeisance.

"We kept them there through the day. There were two redheads," the shorter one reported. "Judging from the motions of the others, the one posing as scribe was the king, and the one dressed as king a lackey."

Rajnir spread his hands. "You were right," he said to Erkric, whose smile held no vestige of humor. "He was stupid enough to fall for the ruse!" Back to the scouts, "Why didn't you kill him?"

Despite the balmy summer air, Durasnir sustained an inward chill as cold as the water in the stone jugs that were suspended on chains to drag deep in the low ocean currents.

Erkric tutted. "The parley was made under a truce flag, my prince. They believed Coast Scout Greba to be me, remember. Consider how the Marlovans would react to their king being killed under truce by Prince Rajnir's chief dag." And when Rajnir scowled, Erkric said in a low, soothing voice, "Then consider this, my prince. How it would be if they came here under truce and killed *you*? Do you think Fleet Commander Durasnir here would ever stop until he had exacted retribution? Are we not enjoined to pacify their kingdom once we take it?"

Rajnir's lips parted, his light eyes widened. "Oh." He whirled, walked to the open scuttle, and breathed deeply of the warm salt air. "Oh. I didn't think! So much to think about—I can't remember—"

"So much depends upon our plans," Erkric interjected smoothly, in the voice of a beloved tutor. "Scouts. Was Indevan Algara-Vayir among those at the parley?"

The two turned to one another for a moment, and read uncertainty in each other's countenance. "They denied him, of course," Greba said. "But that room was so dark. They had the windows blocked. And everyone but the scribe and the false king wore those gray coats."

The taller scout spoke up. "We were told that the pirate is short, scar-faced, and wears golden hoops with rubies on them. I couldn't see the face on the shortest one, but I heard him snoring on his feet. No earrings visible. It was too dark to see if his ears were pierced."

Rajnir waved his hands. "No matter, no matter. The snorer had to be a lackey, no commander would fall asleep in a parley. This is good, isn't it?" His anxious blue eyes turned to Durasnir. "Is it not?"

"It seems we have gained a day for Hilda Commander Talkar," Durasnir replied.

"Good! I like good news. So far we haven't had any. Are they *still* fighting those women in the castle?" Rajnir smacked the door open. "When he's back, send Henga directly to me before you put him in the prison ship." He slammed the cabin door behind him.

Erkric stared after the prince, exasperated. But then no one knew, must not find out, that Ala Larkadhe had in a single night been warded. No dag could transfer in, and the tracers were deflected by what appeared to be Morvende magic.

It was possible that he had inadvertently tripped an ancient protection ward. He hoped so. But the burden of not being able to see the enemy, of not knowing whose magic forced him out of the shaping battle, was thinning his hold on his temper. He could not lose his temper; a weary, sour glint of humor accompanied the thought, *I cannot lose my temper because I am not a prince.*

Unworthy, unworthy.

Erkric was irritated afresh at the narrow-eyed suspicion in Durasnir's face. It must be because Durasnir's favored

Drenga captain, Byoren Henga, had been assigned to the invasion, which placed him under the Hilda chain of command, outside of the reach of the Oneli. "I will investigate the attack on the castle," he said. "Since I must return to the camp to supervise the dags."

Durasnir signed acknowledgment.

Erkric turned to the coast scouts. "You are restored to your regular duties until tomorrow. With the Fleet Commander's permission, we will meet before you are to transfer to Ala Larkadhe, and we will discuss the details of tomorrow's plan."

The scouts made their obeisances. Dag Erkric performed a respectful salute to Durasnir, who returned it with the particular care of a deeply angry man—a detail that escaped the customarily perceptive Erkric, who picked up his own papers, and walked out.

Durasnir turned to his scouts. The rank Coast Scout had changed in meaning over the centuries. Once the title had been used by charters, but charting had developed into its own branch of service. Coast Scout was now a neutral rank meaning spy. Coast Scouts wore whatever costume would permit them to pass unnoticed, and they scouted people as well as places.

Durasnir said, "You will have liberty for the remainder of the day. In addition to whatever orders Dag Erkric sees fit to give you tomorrow, I would like you to observe closely. I want to know if Indevan Algara-Vayir is there," Durasnir said.

Chapter Nine

INDA shut the door and followed Signi into the office. Vedrid sat on a chair against the inner wall, sewing silver piping to the edge of rich crimson fabric. Inda paused, distracted. "Isn't that the one I saw Tau working on?"

Vedrid's needle flashed. "Since he is under orders, I'm finishing it."

Awkwardly, Inda asked, "Is that for me?"

Vedrid smiled. "As Harskialdna, you'll wear Montrei-Vayir colors."

Inda waved impatiently. "I know that. I guess I thought I'd be making it myself."

"When?" Vedrid laughed soundlessly.

Inda gave a rueful snort. "Don't know. Don't seem to have a masthead watch anymore." He followed Signi from the office out onto the landing. She shut the office door with both hands, leaned over the stone balcony, touching the bunch of grapes carved into the edge before the rail started down the spiral stairway. No one below: the Runners had partitioned this area off from the crowded castle, reserving it for the commanders.

She turned around. "I am going to leave, Inda. But there are things I must tell you first."

Inda's eyes widened with dismay. His quick sorrow and hurt, so true, so unhidden, made her eyes sting. She leaned into him, bringing the scent of the fresh mountain herbs among which she'd been recently walking. He was damp from being overheated; his own scent was dear to her.

"What have I done?" he mumbled into her hair. And drew back, his voice a low, unhappy rumble deep in his chest. "Or is it the war? Sure it is. I'm stupid."

"I will return to you when it is over. So lies my duty. Yours lies elsewhere," she reminded him, and his unhappiness intensified. "Now, listen. I have been exploring, not just the archive, but it opens through an atan, from which I have been able to trace and dismantle those wards Erkric made that go directly against our oaths."

"Wards mean magic warfare?" Inda asked.

"In part. Erkric also interfered with your king's courting lockets. His wards were clumsy, necessarily because performed from a distance. That is why they ceased to transfer."

Inda wiped his hand across his brow, then fingered his scar. "Should I tell Evred?"

"You must do what you believe best about that." She made one of her hand gestures, slow and graceful, though her fingers trembled.

Inda flicked his thumb up, and then the sense of what she had previously said penetrated. He knew she loved to share knowledge. "Atan?"

"The archive in the white tower is a Morvende construct, as I believe you know."

Inda turned his palm up.

"Well, what few know, unless they have studied old magic texts, is that long, long ago, the Morvende made what they called 'atans'—you know this word in Sartoran?"

"Sun," Inda said, wondering. "Atan means sun."

"Atan was just a part of the whole term, but we've lost the rest. We call them platforms or terraces or any number of other terms. The important thing is, these were places of meditation and observation, made high on mountaintops, where the Morvende could watch the progress of sun and stars unhindered. You touch the sun symbol in the archive, carved there beside the door. Say the word *atan*. That door will open a magic gate to the atan platform in the mountains above the source of the Andahi River."

Inda was stunned. "The river—but that goes right by the top of the pass!"

"The source of the river is far higher than the pass, and the atan is even above that. You would have to go down the young river to get to the ancient trail leading down into the highpoint of the pass. You will find an old plinth marking the trail head." She paused, observing the change in his expression.

"Can we—could someone come back the same way?"

"Ordinarily, yes. One steps on the sun carvings on the platform. One pronounces the word *atan* and steps through the archway. I tell you this for the sake of learning, not because I believe you will be able to use it."

"What? I don't understand."

"But I believe your king will," Signi said gently. "Forgive me if I mistake, but if you think to use this for military purposes . . . Inda, this is important. The Morvende have nothing to do with war. There is a risk, if you use this door. No, no, nothing will happen to you. As I said, they have nothing to do with war. The risk is that, if you use it, you will never be able to enter this archive again."

"But this entire war is the fault of the V—it's not us attacking anybody! We're defending—"

She shook her head. "I have no communication with the Morvende, and so cannot for certain speak for them. They might be aware of the circumstances or they might just not be paying attention to the archive now. How they view time is very different from how we do, who are so bound to the sun's cycle. But when that archive door is opened, they know it. And if you move armed men through—for whatever reason—they will know." She lifted her hand toward the white tower, just visible through the open window on the landing. "It will be closed to you, probably forever."

Inda felt a brief spurt of regret, but far greater was his eagerness to tell Evred: the impossible had happened, and now they had a means to come down on the Venn from both sides.

Signi cupped his dear, scarred face with her hands, a gesture of such tenderness that his galloping thoughts stumbled to a halt.

He gazed into her green-brown eyes, distracted by his own tiny reflection twinned in the great black circles of her pupils; time stopped, or seemed to for a measure of ten breaths, as he groped for understanding of her emotions.

To Inda, Signi was like the great birds drifting so effortlessly overhead, who with one snap of their wings lift to speed and power far beyond his reach. Magic was just that kind of power. Her emotions were as subtle as those flicks and shivers of wide wings, but so far she had drifted alongside him as he galloped toward this war: her ardor matched his ardor, compassion enfolded his grief when he first arrived in his homeland and discovered who had lived and who had died. His laughter sparked her smile. There were other times he sensed emotional shifts in her, but could not define them, and as he looked into her eyes and felt the tremble in her fingers, he thought, *I need Tdor to tell me what I'm seeing.*

That was it, he was ten years behind, because he hadn't had Tdor to comb out the tangles of his thoughts, make them smooth again. Signi made sense of history, the world, and magic for him, but even when she did he always felt that divide between Marlovan and Venn, and he knew she did too, because of the way she would frame questions. Tau could make sense of other people, but Tdor had always made sense of *him.*

"Fare well, Inda," Signi said, and kissed him.

And was gone before he could answer.

When the weird, howling horns began blowing in terrifying echoes up the pass from Castle Andahi, most of the three- and four-year-olds still hiding in the robbers' cave jerked awake. Most of them puckered up and began to whimper.

"Shut it!" Han hissed. The cave mouth, now half blocked by stone, glowed faint blue. Not quite dawn. Why was it horrible things always started before sunup?

Small bodies pressed up against Lnand. She twitched, wanting so badly to shove them all away. She kept the fret inside. Everyone would just call her a pug if she admitted the truth. The smalls climbing on her and demanding kissies and huggies were gratifying when Han and Gdir noticed, because everybody could see that Lnand was the favorite. But when the other two ten-year-olds were doing something else, Lnand wanted to smack the brats away. Those three-year-olds were *always* whining, and she was sick of snotty noses and pee in drawers that *she* had to dunk and spread to dry.

You'd think Queen Han would help, since the Jarlan called her such a great leader, but oh, no. Not *her*. She was too *important* for drawer dunking.

"Some kind of new noise," Han whispered, hopping back inside the cave.

The children huddled together, everyone uncertain whether fun or bad things were coming next.

"I'll be lookout," Gdir stated.

"No. We'll do it just like yesterday." Han smacked the dust off her clothes with impatient whacks.

Lnand had no desire whatsoever to go out there and see whatever horrors made those noises. All that screaming, and the crashes. Now those terrible moaning howls, like monsters out of an old story. How could Han stand it? She was probably pretending to be brave. *Everyone is pretending*, Lnand thought. *It's the only way people admire you, if you act like a hero.*

So she made herself say, "I'll stand watch. You two did it yesterday."

Gdir wrinkled her nose like someone farted, making Lnand want to yank her hair out by the roots.

Han sighed. "I *said,* we'll do it like yesterday."

"You think I'm a coward." Lnand knew she really was a coward, but she was angry enough to bite and kick and scratch if Han *said* it.

"No." Han whacked dust off her trousers.

"Why don't you change into your other outfit. Those clothes are disgusting," Gdir said.

Han ignored her. "Lnand. Your job is the smalls. Keep them quiet. That means keep them happy. Hal and I can watch the pass, it's just boring sitting there. Gdir and Dvar on next swap."

"Haldred's only nine." Lnand put her hands on her hips. It was working, everyone thought she wanted to be out there.

"So's Dvar." Han turned a dirt-mottled hand over. "So? None of us will be alone, and I know Hal and Dvar can be quiet as mice, because they are on the games. I never knew anyone as still and quiet. Keth, too," she added with extra meaning: even the Jarl's son had to follow orders. "If he were here."

Hal had been glaring at Lnand, but now he flushed with pride. Dvar was too tired to care; she wasn't going to whine, but she was sure she'd heard her mother screaming during the night.

"But what about *us? We're* good at games!"

Han turned on the seven- and eight-year-old boys and girls who made up the most of the children. She didn't care which of them had spoken. "Ndand never put anyone under nine on tower watch, so you don't even think it."

Some of the eights muttered. The sevens stayed quiet, and Tlennen, Gdir's six-year-old brother, slid his thumb toward his mouth. It tasted like grit, but everything inside his skin felt better when he sucked it. He stepped behind Gdir, so she wouldn't see. He hated it when she slapped his hand down and said that warriors didn't suck their thumbs. Maybe they didn't. But nobody had let him be a warrior yet.

Satisfied that everyone thought she was brave and eager to be out in the danger, Lnand turned away from Han, and there were all those waiting eyes. Rosebud's lips were starting to pucker, and Lnand said in a hurry, "Who's really big, and wants to help with breakfast?"

"No fire," Han called.

Lnand heaved a loud, shuddering sigh. "D'you think I'm *stupid*?" She said it all the more fiercely because she'd just been looking for the natural shelf where they'd put the Fire Stick high out of reach of the smalls.

But of course they couldn't have a fire. Even in daylight, they'd discovered, you could see flickers on the roof of the cave from below. They'd wasted most of yesterday trying to build a wall to block the cave from view but the cave entrance was too big and they couldn't shift big stones. And Gdir had reminded them that a stone wall visible from below would look like someone was inside, unless it was mossy and old looking.

As Lnand set about unwrapping and dividing up one loaf and one wedge of cheese, Gdir prowled around the cave entrance to examine the wall they'd made. It was only knee height, and out of view from below. She'd checked before sunset the day before, though it had meant climbing down all the way to the pass. The horrible noises had somehow been louder there, she did not know why. She'd only taken a fast look then scrambled right back up the cliff.

She paced to where they kept their food stash, ignoring Han. Even the sound of her breathing was irritating. Han was just the daughter of a guardswoman. Why was she made leader?

Gdir accepted her share of the bread and cheese, looking down to make sure Tlennen had his. When she saw his clean thumb on an otherwise dirty hand, she arced her hand up to slap him, then stopped. He might drop his food, and they couldn't spare extra. She wouldn't let him pick it up dirty.

"As soon as you eat, wash up," she muttered, glowering. "And if I see that thumb in your mouth again, I'm going to thrash you. *No* Tlen sucks their thumb."

Tlennen's resentment burned like a ball of hate in his middle. He knew she was wrong. She always said they were Tlens of the primary family, not just Rider-cousins, and they were better than anybody, but Tlennen remembered Keth used to suck his thumb. He'd decided he would stop thumb sucking when he was eight. Sometimes you're just not ready for things, like riding a horse over fences. Thumbs were like riding in that way.

Gdir glared at Han, who sat with Hal just inside their wall, where they'd found the best vantage down to the pass, at least as far as the last great curve, just where the tunnel opened. Out of sight was the long downward slope of the pass, gradually widening—an ancient landslide, Flash had told them. Really ancient. Even more ancient than the tunnel, which had been where the river went after the slide, until that, too, changed, going deeper underground somehow. She wasn't sure why she found that comforting, but she did.

Thinking about that was better than thinking about Han's bad leading, and how unfair it was of the Jarlan to pick her. Gdir was betrothed to Keth! She was future Randviar! She was primary-family Tlen! Of course, you couldn't keep rank if you were terrible at training, but Gdir could shoot as well as Han, could beat her with right-hand knife, and almost with left. They ran and climbed about the same. So why wasn't Gdir leader?

Gdir looked around irritably. The cave was filthy again, and they all looked like little pigs rooting for vegetable parings. She turned on a wrestling pile of eights—all boys, of course. "Why aren't you clean so we can start warm-ups?" she asked, loud enough for "leader" Han to remember her duty.

Scowls and mutters were the only answer, but at least the boys broke apart and headed for the stream.

Everyone else began doing their chores, even the fives taking each end of a bedroll and shaking it the way she'd showed them, though far too listlessly to actually dislodge dirt.

She nipped one end and gave the bedroll a snap. A cloud of dust rolled off. The child at the other end pouted at having her arms wrung; the one she'd replaced laughed at the cloud.

"Do it that way," she said, and satisfied that she had just cause, she marched across the cave to Han. "Why won't you do your duty?"

"Go away, Gdir."

"You're supposed to be leader. I seem to be doing the real work, like cleaning up and seeing that the brats don't just fight all day, while you just squat there pretending to be a warrior. Why aren't *you* giving those orders?"

Han snorted. "Because you're doing it. That means I don't have to argue about those orders like I do all the others."

"Who's arguing with orders?"

"You're doing it right now. I said go away, and you started to argue."

"Shut it, Gdir," Hal whispered, his pale eyes sidelit in the strengthening light. "I think something's happening."

All three ducked down and peered across the pass and down at the far end, where a massive crevasse opened into the tunnel. They saw nothing.

"I am not arguing," Gdir stated, turning back to Han. "I am quite reasonably pointing out the duty that you should be doing."

"You wouldn't point out the Jarlan's duty."

"That's because she always does everything right."

"This." Han flung her hands out. "Is an argument."

Gdir wanted to say Lnand argued, but she didn't want Lnand hearing her name and rushing over to pretend to be hurt so everyone would pet her.

Han looked in the same direction, and snorted again. "You know she's the worst pug in the world. But at least she's doing her job."

Gdir couldn't express the depth of her loathing. Lnand was the worst pug of all the castle children, always wanting to be petted and cooed over for just doing her duty. Duty was to be done because everyone trusted you to do it. They shouldn't have to praise you for it.

Han grinned. "Giving her orders is like trying to swim in mud."

"Then you should fight her," Gdir stated, though she knew Han wasn't a coward. In fact she so much wasn't a coward she didn't see the hint about cowardice.

Han made a face. "Waste of time, and it hurts. Hurts twice."

Gdir had to concede that, though not out loud. In a scrap, the idea was to get your enemy pinned, so they gave in and behaved. Most stuck with it, but some needed to be scrapped over and over. Lnand was one of those.

Lnand also didn't scrap fairly—she bit and pulled hair

and scratched, getting you in tender places that didn't show. And if you got her down, she always fake cried and sometimes even snitched. Then you got the thrashing for scrapping—and you still had the bite marks and throbbing scalp. But at least everyone knew you weren't a snitch. Though why that was any good when she got away with it, nobody could say.

"Seems better if she thinks she thought of it." Han wound her hand in a circle, including Lnand and the smalls. "If I'd told her to, you think she'd be crawling around with them right now, being foals? No, because she'd still be arguing. Just like you."

"Maybe. If the sevens and eights were watching," Gdir said, though she felt unmoored, as if the discussion had drifted like a little boat in a pool. Gdir frowned, trying to find her way back to the point.

Start from Lnand, who just always had to be the center of attention. *Her father's the same way,* Gdir's mother had said once, when Gdir complained about her. *Why he's never kept a mate longer than two years, in spite of him being as good a baker as any at the royal palace.*

Gdir knew what *that* meant. When she was exactly Tlennen's age, and they'd just arrived to live at Castle Andahi, she'd immediately gone exploring. She'd been curled up in what would become her favorite spot, a tiny jutting ledge where one of the towers joined the wall, where somebody small who didn't look down could sit and look at the mountains folding away toward the sea. She'd heard voices coming—the Jarlan and Ndand.

Ndand had said, ". . . and Star Indran wants to go back to Tlen-Sindan-An on the next caravan. She's parting with Cousin Dodger." And then—her exact words—"Star says she might not be a ranker's daughter, but she can take a hint when she's become just another duty to dodge."

The Jarlan had laughed, and her words started to fade away as the two passed along the sentry walk. "Second woman this season, and we're already short-handed. But who can blame them for not wanting to come up here? We'll have to reorganize the watch slates again, and . . ."

Duty, that was the point. You couldn't get promoted if you didn't do your duty, and apparently you couldn't even have a mate if you didn't do your duty. Duty was the purpose of life! Duty and everything clean and in order, it was so *important,* and Han wasn't *seeing* it.

Gdir sucked in her breath to tell Han exactly how stupid she was, when Hal knocked Han with his elbow. "Told ya."

As the three watched, tall men with horned helms emerged from the tunnel, their silvery armor glinting in the sunlight just topping the mountains behind the children's cave.

"Those are Venn," Hal whispered.

"Shut it," Gdir and Han both said.

The first ones were on horseback. As the children watched, the one with white wings instead of horns on his helm made a motion with a gloved hand toward another who carried a long oddly shaped brass tube. Like a trumpet, but not straight. This man put his lips to it, and his face turned crimson as he blew out a long, weird note, like the lowing of cattle when thunder is near, followed by a couple of loud owl-hoots and then a low bra-a-a-p.

"Sounds like a mountain farting," Hal whispered, snickering.

Han didn't hear. She held her arms tight against her, rocking back and forth, her mouth pulled awry, lower lip trembling.

Gdir stared at her, about to accuse her of cowardice when the enemy couldn't even see them, way up here. But then she realized what it meant, why Han looked like someone had slapped her.

If the Venn were here, it meant the castle had fallen into enemy hands.

Inda wished even more strongly for Tdor—or Tau—when he finally got Evred alone just after dawn. Inda had risen early, bolting down breakfast over a last talk with Hawkeye and Noddy in the officers' mess they shared with the other Sier Danas. When the two left to mount up, Inda discovered Evred up in the map room, reading the day's logistical reports gathered by the captain of the watch.

They were alone, everyone else either gone or busy, so Inda told Evred Signi's good news. He'd expected to see his own elation mirrored back, but instead Evred had reacted like someone struck blind and deaf. Half a riding of men old enough to know better were coming back from liberty drunk. They wove their way, singing loudly, directly under the open window, but Evred did not move.

Inda ducked out and snapped his fingers at Kened, who was on Runner duty. After making motions of grabbing the idiots by the hair and dunking them head first into the horse troughs (to prevent a far worse punishment; Evred was strict about drunkenness and sloth), he jerked a thumb toward the courtyard. Kened comprehended at once, and leaped down the stairs five at a time.

When Inda got back into the map room, Evred still stood motionless, one hand on the map, the other holding the papers. Through the open window the drunks' caroling abruptly ended. That was followed by some thuds, a muffled "Ow!" and the rackety-clack of heels on the stones: the sounds of a hasty withdrawal as Kened and the door guards muscled the delinquents away.

Evred didn't hear that either.

He faced, alone, a terrible struggle. Should he not be accustomed to bitter choices by now? At first, his anger had burned ineffectively round the image of Signi, but he knew she was only the messenger. The Morvende had made the real choice explicitly clear on his very first visit. They had permitted him access to the archive because he'd come to make peace. He was here to defend his kingdom now. Perhaps they knew, perhaps they did not; they lived deep in the mountains somewhere in the great range.

One thing was for certain, though: if he opened the archive to its platform and moved warriors through, the Morvende would know right away, and they would see it as an act of war.

But Inda said they needed to do it.

Inda watched Evred's blind gaze, his tense profile. What to do now?

Unexpected relief arrived with the guard Runner sent to let them know that Hawkeye and Noddy were ready to ride out.

Evred blinked. He recovered the room, Inda waiting, the Runner in the doorway. This was the deceptive relief of postponement, not a release from choice.

But he would accept what little he was given. "We must see them off."

The entire city agreed.

The night before, once Hawkeye had flung the damn magic token down the deepest steam vent at the back of the baths, he had been afire to depart despite darkness and rain, so determined was he to reach the top of the pass before Cama. But Noddy had said with his usual stolidity, "Inda's gonna send the main body after us at the gallop, like as not. Let's be the ones to remember remounts. Grain for the animals. Supplies. They won't."

Hawkeye flicked an interrogative look his way, and Noddy said, "Inda's learned about ten years worth of academy gaming in a couple of months, but he still thinks horses are ships."

Noddy was right. Hawkeye bit back his impatience and they went to the stable to issue the orders to have everything ready for dawn. The reward was an evening of relative quiet, which Hawkeye spent with Fala, his beloved. His wife, Dannor, had only stayed a couple of months in Ala Larkadhe. She'd made enemies so rapidly Hawkeye had had to constantly stop his work to negotiate, remonstrate, reestablish peace. Then came Evred's wish that their generation begin the next generation, and Dannor had been enraged that the king would interfere in their private lives. She had no intention of being burdened with supervising squalling brats ten years before she should reasonably be expected to do so.

Hawkeye had pointed out that if she were at Yvana-Vayir, she could hardly be expected to have his heir. She'd thought that over. Hawkeye's parents were dead, his brothers in their last year of the academy, those bratty girls they were going to marry in their first year of the queen's training. Dull as Yvana-Vayir was, at least there would be no one to get tiresome about what they considered to be her duty.

So Dannor moved out of Hawkeye's rooms to go back to Yvana-Vayir, and Fala moved in. Fala was a potter. She'd opened a local business so that she could be close to Hawkeye. She made familiar dishes for the Marlovans; the Idayagans and Olarans preferred the tulip goblets and flat plates of the east.

Fala had also volunteered to serve with the new Randviar's women on castle defense duty. So she was there this morning, standing next to the Randviar on the sentry walk adjacent to the white tower as thunder rumbled warningly in the northwest.

Below, Hawkeye and Noddy rode at the head of their six wings plus attendant Runners and stable hands, leading an impressive train of riderless horses and tarped wagons carrying supplies for a much larger force: horse armoring, bags of grain, and freshly scythed summer hay. They also carried a single wagon full of rusty old helms from the castle, leftovers bought as surplus by the Idayagan king the generation before. Many riders had none; most hated helms, especially these full-head ones with their narrow visored view, but Evred had insisted they take them. And wear them.

To the echoing sound of drums, and voices chanting the oldest and most stirring of Marlovan ballads, Hawkeye's and Noddy's men passed through the back gates of the castle into the city streets below. Inda, Evred, the Randviar, and the male and female sentries watched them wind through the old streets to the northern gates of Ala Larkadhe, under the shadow of the ancient tower. The northern gates stood open and beyond them lay the first great curve of the pass.

After a generation of Marlovan rule, the city was a mixture of adaptable Idayagans, Olarans, and Marlovans who had moved in as families of warriors and to carry on subsidiary business. Those who could not abide the conquerors had moved away or been forced out.

The atmosphere was tense and moody, with pockets of cheering, under the first heavy wet splatters of another storm. To civilian eyes, these gray-coated men with their shields and helms and jingling chain mail seemed a great army.

The women on the walls watched soberly. Their men were mostly in the castle guard, impatient to be riding after the dragoons. Fala stood next to the Randviar, motionless despite the rain streaming down her face, through her hair, dripping on her clothes. Her fingers gripped her bow tightly.

When the last of the wagons rumbled out of sight, Tdiran-Randviar and Fala turned away, the older woman scowling deeply.

The Randviar, Tdiran Vranid, was Hawkeye's great-aunt, who had come to run the defense of the castle when Dannor left the spring before. She glanced back just once as the last of the strings of remounts walked through the northern gates and vanished around that first curve.

She turned away and dealt Fala a well-meaning buffet. Fala lifted her head. She tried to smile, failed, and walked away silently to the women's guardhouse to keep herself busy making arrows until her next duty rotation.

Inda and Evred ducked under the awning outside the upper level sentry guard station; while splats of rain felt pleasant on the face, the prospect of having to wear a soggy coat through the rest of the day wasn't.

"Better get used to it," Tdiran-Randviar said to Evred and Inda, cackling as rain hissed in gray arrows against the stone walk and towers, the overhangs pouring sheets of water. "The locals are all saying this here is a little breeze. To let us know the winds are bringing a big one."

Blue flickered above the mountain peaks, mostly obscured by clouds. Inda wondered how far up Cherry-Stripe and Cama had gotten, hoped they wouldn't be struck by lightning. Then he swung around to face the Randviar.

"So. Now that it's just us," she began.

Inda had learned by now that when people said the obvious, they usually had something else on their minds. Something that might be problematical. So he said to the Randviar, "What kind of defense—"

"Inda!"

The shout echoed up the tower stairwell.

"Tau?" Inda said doubtfully.

"Inside," Evred said.

They entered the round room, bare stone except for the battered table of the guard captain on watch, the duty roster, and an ensorcelled jug of water.

Tau leaped up the stairs and dashed through the door. "There you are," he croaked, and bent over, hands on knees, to catch his breath.

He was almost unrecognizable in his sodden civilian garb, his hair hanging loose over his long tunic, wheat-colored even when wet; his linen deck trousers flapped like loose sails at his ankles. There were blood splotches down his right side, but they did not appear to be his.

"Tau?" Inda prompted.

"Inda . . . the Venn," Tau wheezed.

"They're coming?" Evred's voice was sharp.

Rain dribbled down Tau's forehead and dripped off his nose to the floor. "No." He sucked in air. "They are *here.*"

Chapter Ten

THE air above the Destination on the captain's deck flickered darkly. A moment later Erkric appeared, groped with one hand, sat down on the waiting chair so that the residue of transfer sickness could pass.

Durasnir signed to his Battle Group Captain to retreat; the crew of the *Cormorant* flowed around them, attentive to their duties. Captain Gairad, long accustomed to serving under the fleet commander, saw to that.

Erkric turned up his hand. "The Marlovans in Ala Larkadhe figured out the ruse." He did not add—they wouldn't understand anyway—that the transfer token that they'd sent to the Marlovans had had a secret ward on it that would permit Erkric to send an assassination team of Erama Krona if his ruse failed. But that ward had been blocked and he could not trace the token, despite a tracer spell he'd put on it himself.

So he shifted to the good news. "Hilda Commander Talkar's advance force has taken Castle Andahi, and found access to the tunnel. The army is now making its way through the tunnel to march up the pass."

Durasnir said to the waiting scouts, "You are dismissed," and they left.

Rajnir paid them no attention. He smiled over the rail toward the land, his fair hair blowing in the wind. The gold in the tree embroidered across his breast glinted with each breath. "We are on the march at last!" he repeated, but then his brow furrowed. "Why were you gone so long, Dag Erkric? Was it necessary for you to come to the aid of the army again?"

"No, no. The army has done well," Dag Erkric said, motioning to an orderly for something to drink. "But I had to make several transfers, including investigating the failure of the ruse."

"Well, now that all is as it should be, take me there," Rajnir commanded. "So that I may at last see them on the march. That is what we have been awaiting, is it not?" He brushed his hand down his silver and gold armor, the fine battle-tunic beneath.

Dag Erkric raised a hand. "I do not deem it safe even so," he said. "Remember, this is no longer drill. It is an invasion of a people desperate for bloodletting."

Rajnir stared at him in dismay, then whirled around. "Tell him, Hyarl my Commander. Tell him to take me there, so I may see my warriors march to victory."

Durasnir resented so strongly the position this statement put him in that he could not trust himself to speak for a long, tense moment.

It was long enough, and tense enough, for Rajnir to abandon his own worries to turn around, question overcoming his desperation. "Uncle Fulla?" It slipped out without his awareness.

The mage only smiled.

Durasnir said, "You know the oaths we make, my prince. I can only advise you in matters of the sea."

The mage made the bow and gesture of pacific acceptance, and Rajnir sighed, and once more relinquished decision making into the mage's hands.

Durasnir lifted his glass and swept the distant line of rough mountains. He could see nothing of import, but it gave his hands something to do, and his face a semblance of cover as he considered what lay behind the mage's sudden worry about the prince's safety. Was there a chance he did not, after all, have control over the magical part of this invasion?

The more Durasnir considered it, the more it seemed possible. That would explain Erkric's protracted absence. Otherwise, it would have been far more characteristic of Erkric to sweep Rajnir to a pinnacle somewhere so the prince could look down in triumph as his will was translated into the action of thousands of tramping feet. So he could revel in the power of a prince.

So he could revel in the power of a king.

Inda led the way through the sentry walk arch onto the top floor of the tower, where the guard station was. Everyone crowded in behind him, Tau standing in the middle, water pooling at his feet. Rain roared on the awning outside the door, running off it in hissing sheets. Vedrid shut the door, diminishing the noise.

"How many Venn?" Inda asked.

"Looked like an advance force, a raider group." Tau shaped a wedge with his hand. "Hull up in the west, probably a dozen warships. I'd guess with their attendant Battle Groups, but it was too hazy to see."

"Raider group?" the watch captain asked.

"Raiders are bigger, have say a hundred men. Scouts have about thirty," Inda quickly translated for the Marlovans. "Think of 'em as cutters, or tenders." And when those two terms earned him blank looks, "Nine scouts serve each raider. Nine raiders serve a warship. They make up all their Battle Groups in nines, like we do. Call it somewhat over a thousand men."

"Where?" Tdiran-Randviar asked.

"Standing off to the southwest."

"Ships?"

"Landed, or—"

"Tried a landing. Buck Marlo-Vayir fought 'em off."

Inda had always admired the way Tau seemed to effortlessly handle any situation with people. Now, as everyone (except Evred) shot questions at him he not only seemed to hear them all and answer in the order of importance, he also answered intent instead of just words. This was until Inda said, "So what about Ola-Vayir?"

"Ola-Vayir is not here."

"What?" Evred snapped.

Everyone had seen Evred express irritation, though it was rare. No one had ever seen him in a cold rage. Vedrid's neck tightened. That pale face, with the hectic color high on the cheekbones, most of all the wide, angry stare—Evred had never looked more like his brother, the Sierlaef.

"Lindeth knew the Venn were there?" His voice had dropped to a whisper. But they heard it.

"Had to." Tau sucked in breath, and threw back his wet hair with a loud smack against his back. "The first night, I hired a boat. Saw them hull down on the horizon, straight west. The Lindeth fisherfolk all knew they were there, and knew those masts did not belong to any fishing fleet. Came back. Started checking around."

"So Lindeth wants these Venn to attack us?"

Noise on the stairway brought Nightingale Toraca, one hand clutched tightly to the opposite shoulder. Blood darkened one arm, spreading in a dark purple smear down the side of his coat. Rat and Barend followed behind him, ready to spring to his support.

Nightingale wiggled his fingers interrogatively, and Tau said, "I'm getting there." To the others, "I spent the rest of the night doing some talking. To make certain. Here's what I don't think you know. There were a couple of murders earlier in spring—"

"The old guild mistress, and some fellow they said was a Venn spy," Barend said from behind Nightingale. "We've already been through that, including the blame being assigned to us."

"Well, he *was* a Venn spy. And she was in the pay of the Venn."

"What?" three voices exclaimed.

Nightingale grimaced, swaying on his feet. "That old hypocrite," he murmured, hoarse and breathless. "*How* she used to go on about our evilness."

"She was killed by the Resistance. One of 'em couldn't

keep his mouth shut, especially after their leader, er, died."
Tau tripped over that one. Maybe now was not the time to
reveal that the vaguely familiar man he'd killed in the market town pleasure house had been none other than Skandar Mardric, head of the Resistance.

"Lindeth has been divided since," Tau went on. "Half
think the Venn preferable to Marlovan rule. The rest think
that's crazy. Those people are divided between putting up
with the familiar, and pursuing the Resistance goal of getting rid of all overlords."

He coughed.

Vedrid, always thoughtful, brought water. Tau gulped
it down, briefly amused at the irony of being soaked to
the skin yet thirsty. It was a familiar sensation from life
on the sea.

"Go on," Evred said.

"That's it. With a strong application of sympathy and
flattery, I got them to accept me as an ignorant easterner,
and last night they opened up. Several rounds of the local
barley wine helped." Tau saw Inda shift impatiently. Evred
hadn't moved. Tau sensed his wrath; his nerves coruscated.
"They were stalled during what I gathered to be some very
heated arguments about whether or not to let you know
that the fishers had sighted the Venn on the horizon.
Standing on and off for just under a week."

"A week," Inda breathed. "Waiting on a signal?"

"I don't know. Whatever cause, the Venn raiders sent
that advance attack toward land before dawn today. I was
taking a last sighting before returning to report my talk
with the fishers. Spied shaded lights bobbing about, the
same way lights move when someone else in the fleet is
climbing down into boats. Had to mean a landing, so I took
to horse southward." He made a quick, self-deprecating
gesture. "I—" He shook his head.

Inda's eyes widened. "You were going to attack them
yourself?"

"I don't know what I was going to do," Tau confessed.
"I'd been up how many nights? All I could think of was,
you wanted me to scout, so I'd better go see for myself.

Which is how I met him." He gestured toward Nightingale, who leaned shakily against the wall. Crimson drips from his limp hand pooled beside his foot.

Evred made a flat gesture, quick and sharp. "You said Buck."

"There," Nightingale whispered. He was just barely hanging onto consciousness.

"Right. Buck first." Tau jerked his head up, his fine brow furrowed. "I need to go back a bit in Nightingale's report, which he told me on our ride here. The Jarl of Ola-Vayir never received his orders."

Pause for exclamations; Evred made another of those quick, flat moves of his hand, and everyone shut up.

"And we can corroborate that because one of the brags the rope maker in Lindeth made was of the Resistance having killed a Runner."

The reaction this time was no more than a whispered curse.

"Some time back, the Lindeth people were arguing with this Mardric fellow about how little the Resistance had accomplished. Mardric claimed he'd killed all the Venn spies, and got stung by their lack of belief. Double stung by their lack of gratitude." Tau paused to drink again. "Anyway, Mardric decided to make a grand gesture and issued an order to attack any Marlovan Runners they saw, after squeezing their orders out of them. They tried. All but one Runner killed their attackers instead. The one who died was an older man, they said. But as tough as any of the younger ones. Sifting through the brag, I figured the only reason they brought him down was because they were traveling as a gang. He took out half of them before they brought him down. The rest, ah, didn't bother with kinthus when they tried to pry his orders out of him." Tau grimaced.

Evred's fury intensified, mirrored in them all. "Go on."

"The man died without speaking. When they cooled off, some of them were fairly sick about what they'd done. When word got around, most of the Resistance decided not to go after Runners anymore. Too costly, and for no

benefit that they could see. Mardric got angry, and they
were shaping up for some in-fighting when he turned up
dead in a market-town pleasure house." He glanced
Evred's way.

Evred's mouth opened on a soundless *Ah*.

"Which seems to have ended the Resistance, as envisioned by Skandar Mardric. Back to Buck. He arrived in
Ola-Vayir, thinking to ride through his city, collect any
messages or things left behind, and follow up the north
road after the Jarl and his men. Get in a dig about how
much faster Buck was, if he did catch up."

A smothered laugh from Rat; Evred hadn't moved, but
they felt the gradual lessening of his wrath.

Tau coughed again, and continued. "But to his surprise
he found the Jarl and his people busy planting, training
horses, so forth. The Jarl was astonished, according to
Nightingale. Let's see if I can get this right, being as I am
employed (*does* this job come with pay?) as a Runner.
Here's how Nightingale gave me the Jarl's words." Tau shut
his eyes, dropped his voice to a gravel-rough intensity underlined by a high note of fear: *"I will swear on my knees
before the Convocation no such orders arrived."*

Tau had been trained in dramatic reading; his rendering
of the Jarl's words were probably truer than Nightingale's
had been.

This time Evred's "Go on" was almost in the normal
range of extreme tension, a storm cloud instead of cataclysm.

"So they consulted on what to do. Decided Buck would
ride north to Lindeth, as ordered. They wouldn't send a
Runner since one had already vanished, and nobody knew
why. Instead, Buck and his men would make the fastest run
they could. Ola-Vayir was going to strong-arm everyone in
his land to ride on their heels, though it would take time to
send the word out. But no one would be permitted to rest
until they had." He rubbed his exhaustion-marked eyes.
"Nightingale reached Buck's people about four days south
of Lindeth, turned around, rode back with them. Said his
locket wouldn't send his report."

Barend shuffled his feet at this out-loud mention of the secret lockets, but Evred did not move.

"When Buck heard about the mystery of orders not received, he figured the only answer was someone targeting Runners. Buck insisted Nightingale not try to ride ahead, that they were about as fast as Runners, or as near as damnation."

A brief flicker of humor; all of them could hear Buck's voice.

"So Buck saw this advance attack?"

"Correct. They'd gotten up before dawn to ride, thinking to reach Ala Larkadhe by sundown. Saw just enough winks from imperfectly covered lanterns out on the sea to raise suspicions. Buck told Nightingale if the lanterns had been swinging free, they would have assumed these were fishers, and ridden on. But a wink or two? They decided to lie up in ambush, did, and though the boats were obviously going to outnumber them, Buck remembered something Inda had said on his first visit, during spring, about how the worst possible moment of a landing was when the breakers take the boat and the men start leaping out into shallow water. So he commanded the men to hold up until then, arrows nocked and ready. They shot as each boat reached the breakers. Dropped three boats full before the others back-oared, and hung off the coast, by now shooting too."

"Me," Nightingale muttered, clearly fading fast. "Buck."

Tau held up a hand. "Buck decided to send Nightingale north to report. Unfortunately, the light was up enough by then for the Venn to make out his blue coat, and Nightingale became the target. His horse caught one in the flank, and he caught two, one along the ribs, and the worst one went through his arm into his side. He, ah, insisted we cut it out."

Tau's color faded for a moment, and everyone there twitched or grimaced.

"We left the animal with the Lindeth Harbor outer perimeter guard—we chanced to catch them—and I brought Nightingale here."

"Buck—" Nightingale lifted his one working hand.

Mistake. His mouth opened, and his body, rigidly held until his messages were discharged, failed him at last. He began to crumple, but Barend and Rat caught him as he fainted.

"Rat," Evred said, and Barend as well as Rattooth looked up, sharp Cassad faces wearing identical expressions.

Barend had been called Rat for years aboard a pirate ship before Inda's mutiny freed him. He grimaced, and his cousin cast him a rueful look as Evred went on, "You and Vedrid get Nightingale down to the lazaretto." To Tau, "Is there anything else?"

"Only this. Buck told Nightingale to tell you that if the Venn kept hanging off the coast, he was going to stay put, and maybe try to look like a force twice the size of what he actually had. He'd had the foresight to get his Runners to keep the horses in the gully alongside a stream adjacent to the road, so there were no silhouettes on the horizon for the Venn to count. But if they land anyway, it's going to be roughly two hundred to one."

After the commanders breakfasted with the prince, Dag Erkric departed from the Venn flagship on unnamed duties, as had become his habit. Durasnir was about to make his morning ship inspection when an orderly summoned him to the after cabin, where the dispatches came in.

"Hyarl my Commander." He put his hands together in the mode of orders given. "You said to come to you at any time if we receive anything from warship *Petrel.*"

Durasnir sat down. News from Captain Seigmad, the Battle Group Captain he had placed in charge of the transport to Lindeth Harbor, could not be good. Seigmad was even older than Durasnir, sixty years of wind, weather, and sea in the king's service. He would report only problems.

We were forced to abort the landing. What at first we took to be a sizable force was lying in ambush awaiting

*us. The night scouts now believe this force is little more
than skirmishers, perhaps detached from the army at
Ala Larkadhe. Without definite numbers, and because
we have lost the advantage of surprise, Hilda Battle
Chief Hrad demands we abandon this site and move in
all haste to the north side of Lindeth, despite the rocky
shore and adverse winds.*

Durasnir wrote a hasty note saying that they should
comply, but that they must wait for the most advantageous
wind and tide, and sent it off.

Then he continued his inspection, which was in part a
search. The prince had shown no interest in the latest dispatches, which alarmed Durasnir. It was so uncharacteris-
tic. Where had the prince gone? He was not in his cabin,
nor prowling around the mages' portion of the ship. Nor
was he below.

When Durasnir climbed back to the weather deck, his eye
was drawn upward by the glint of white and silver of the
Erama Yaga. They stood guard on the masthead. That meant
the prince had clambered all the way to the topgallants. He
had gone even higher than he'd loved to perch as a small boy.

Tradition said that anyone captain or above did not risk
his dignity by climbing to the tops unless under direct
threat of attack. Durasnir climbed past the strictly
schooled faces of the Erama Yaga and squeezed between
the shrouds on the narrow planking that pitched slowly on
the sleepy summer sea.

Rajnir sat on the narrower topgallant masthead. He
leaned back against the spar, eyes closed, so relaxed
Durasnir could see the veins in the prince's eyelids. Durasnir recognized how gradually he had become accustomed
to extreme tension in the prince.

"My prince," he said.

Rajnir opened his eyes. "Don't say anything, Uncle
Fulla." He gave a soft sigh. "I know it's not seemly to climb
up. But I can breathe here. I . . . the wind clears my head."

Durasnir touched his fingertips together in acknowledgment, then said as gently as he could, "If you truly

regard me as Uncle Fulla then you will permit me an uncle's trespass?"

Rajnir sighed again. "What have I done? What must I hear?"

"Only this. That Captain Henga is a good man. One of the best Drenga captains we have. This is why he was chosen for the honor of leading the advance guard on Castle Andahi. What—" *Dag Erkric might not have told you,* "—you might not know is that the defense of the castle was ferocious. Courageous, too. That must be acknowledged."

Rajnir leaned back, his eyes closing.

Durasnir went on. "Those women were armed and trained warriors. They sabotaged the castle, and killed almost half of Henga's entire force before his men finally gained control. And not a single defender, young or old, was left alive, because they kept on the attack to the very last. I will not be surprised if taking that castle does not end up being one of the harshest battles of this invasion."

And if not, we are marching straight into more grief than we've endured in centuries.

"So I beg you to reconsider your view of Henga's execution."

Rajnir opened his eyes and said, "Who?"

Durasnir stared into those blue eyes, so wide, so incurious. The skin over the backs of his hands tingled painfully.

"Thank you, my prince," he said.

Rajnir did not ask for what, so uninterested was he. One corner of his mouth lifted, then he closed his eyes again. The wind tousled a strand of his fair hair that had escaped its clip, and he breathed softly and steadily.

Durasnir climbed down. He finished his round of the flagship, and then sat down at the dispatch desk. Waving the duty ensigns off, he sorted the Oneli commands, scrupulously written and dispatched by magic, and then he turned to the Hilda commands. From the beginning, Rajnir had granted Dag Erkric and Oneli Commander Durasnir permission to read them, which Erkric did regularly. Durasnir read them seldom. He had tried to maintain that distance between the services that protected parity.

Had protected parity. He read them all thoroughly now.

The only recent order for Captain Henga of the advance guard at Castle Andahi was a commendation, written out in Erkric's hand, above the prince's name.

There were many of these orders written by Dag Erkric above the prince's name. And a few above other names, including Durasnir's; the prince often gave them orders to write for him.

So no hard evidence there.

Durasnir closed off the well-trod mental path about the dangers of mages. Here was a new path, as yet shadowed and perilous: for the first time Fulla Durasnir comprehended that he was not just set opposite Erkric in an adversarial position. That would be all right. It was part of the balance of power, of compromise, of parity. They spoke the truth expecting to hear other points of view, so that the king or his heir could determine the right path.

Did Erkric speak the truth, or shape it in secret?

Specifically, why had Prince Rajnir, who had debated the niceties of diplomatic usage with Durasnir's own son Vatta when they were about twelve years old, think that a truce was an opportunity for treachery? Every day it seemed the prince sounded less like a man nearing thirty, and more like a boy of ten. And now he was up on the masthead, higher than he'd sat as a boy, because it made his head clear . . .

And I cannot ask because I regard Erkric as an enemy. A dag—with all that magical power that none could gainsay— as an enemy.

Evred waited for Inda to speak. They all regarded Inda with the "what now" expression.

Inda beckoned to Tdiran-Randviar, standing there grim and silent the entire time. "You said something about a defense plan?"

The old woman said tersely, "Dewlap Arveas' Jarlan, Liet Tlen, is an old friend from queen's training days. Had a plan for making a castle into a trap. We talked about it once. When the word first reached us those shits were coming over in their boats."

Inda's lips parted. "Can you extend your plan to this city?"

"I can try."

Inda turned his head. "Barend. Take everyone you've got. Every arrow you've got. Split 'em up. Reinforce Buck with one group, get someone north of Lindeth to intercept that landing."

"That's all rock." Tau chopped his hands up and down. "I scanned it myself with the scout. Deadly landing."

"Exactly. So if you wanted to take us by surprise, and we were lying in wait right where you were going to land in the best spot, where would you go next? I'd go to the worst lonely spot beyond the harbor spyglasses."

"North shore," three voices said.

Rat had quietly returned. "But if they've got an advance force of a thousand just to clear the landing space, and we've got maybe that for each group, and no reinforcements—"

"The idea is, you don't let 'em land. They can't sneak ships in—" Inda's voice hitched when he remembered Dag Erkric and magic. Then he remembered what Signi had said, and continued firmly, "You'll see the landing boats coming in. Don't let 'em land. Eventually they will anyway, especially if they figure out how few of us there are, but for now—until Ola-Vayir gets here—that's going to have to do."

Evred said to the Randviar, "If they do land, and break through, your orders are to mire them as long as you can in city fighting."

Before Tau first appeared, Tdiran-Randviar had been thinking about what it meant if the Venn reached the pass. It meant that Liet Tlen and the Arveas guardswomen would be dead, because Liet would never let a Venn past her threshold while she lived.

"You leave them to me," she said fiercely.

Chapter Eleven

A T first, all the Castle Andahi children had to see the
Venn. They scrambled to the entrance to the robbers'
cave.

Han ordered them back in a voiceless whisper, making
terrible faces and violent hand motions instead of yelling
like she so badly wanted to. All she got was mutinous
looks, nasty hand signs back, and pokes from the eight-
year-olds to "go anyway"—a mutiny. At least it was a quiet
one. They were trained enough not to make noise with an
enemy nigh.

Gdir's sour expression made Han think of order—and
then she got an idea.

She left Hal on watch at the cavern entrance and beckoned for everyone to surround her as she retreated all the
way to the stream, where she hoped the rush of water
would smother whispers.

"Whoever is standing straight and quiet," she said low-
voiced, quoting her first arms mistress back at Tlen. "Any
noise, you lose your turn."

A hissing scrabble and all the children, right down to the
smallest, got into line. They all knew that command.

"Not the smalls," Han muttered to Lnand. "You'll get a
turn. I'll watch them when the sixes are done."

Lnand sighed loudly, then cut out the smalls, promising

them a fingerful of honey to lick if they sat down like
creep-mice.

At first it was interesting, watching the Venn march by,
so tall, so many of them yellow-haired, just like most of
their own people. They carried a different kind of sword,
and most of them had these odd round shields that Hal insisted in a whisper (that still earned a stinging swat on the
top of his head from Han) were really rain covers.

Two of the eights started a whispered contest about what
kind of turds they were made of and Han thrust them out
of line to wait at the back. No one talked after that.

The first time through, Han counted to a hundred for
each pair. The second time, the children were less eager, so
she let each pair stay longer. By the third time they got
bored fast, especially when they couldn't talk. So everyone
retreated all the way to the back of the cave, to where the
stream came out of a fissure in the rock. They got the pent-
up words out of their systems.

The younger ones wanted to ask questions: where were
their horses? Why did they have brass horn things on their
helms? Did they have an academy for their jarls? The
eights all wanted to offer disgusting ideas about how to
fight them, variations on not using the Waste Spell and
throwing their own droppings at the enemy, only could
they do it and not get chased?

Han told them exactly what Liet-Jarlan would do if they
tried it, and no, that was not snitching, because she'd be required to give a field report on all action, and turd-hurling
was action. The eights couldn't argue with that.

As the steady march of footsteps echoed up the stone,
more and more Venn emerging from the tunnel without
any end in sight, the children returned to their old games,
but quietly. Except when Billykid, the leader of the eight-
year-olds, who was always acting the goat he resembled,
tried to sneak to the cavern entrance and mount their low
wall in order to shy just one rock.

Han slapped him down so hard he went tumbling. But
when he sucked in a breath to yell, Gdir reached him first,
and stuffed the hem of her smock into his mouth so hard

he began to choke, legs kicking, hands clawing desperately though ineffectively, as they were pinned by her knees.

Into his purpling face and frightened eyes she hissed, "Shut it! Shut it! One noise and I'll kill you myself."

Billykid turned up both thumbs as best he could with his scrawny wrists pinned to the cavern floor. He looked more like a goat than ever when she turned him loose and he sloped to the back to pout and make vile gestures at Han and Gdir.

Somehow Billykid changed everything, even though he never got to throw a stone at the Venn. Maybe it was going to happen anyway, maybe it was the result of Billykid's muttered threats and insults, but once the last of the Venn had vanished up the pass in the other direction, and even their marching *thrump, thrump, thrump* had stopped echoing down the pass from above, arguments burst out.

As always, Lnand was the loudest and most persistent, shouting everyone down until she had their attention. "We *have* to go check the castle. We just *have* to," she began in a tragic tone, and went in an anguished, quivering voice: surely someone was there. Her father was smart, so was the Jarlan. Maybe they'd decided there were too many Venn, and they were hiding.

In Lnand's mind, it was all over. She had an intense, bright vision of all the grown-ups crowding around, proclaiming the children to be heroes for staying put while the Venn . . . did whatever they were doing. She very badly wanted to get home, get praise, and maybe her father would make honey-topped cornbread for everyone.

But there was no agreement in either Han's or Gdir's faces. She stamped her foot. "You with *two* parents might not care, but *I* only have a *father,* and I might even be an *orphan*!"

Han's mind had been wandering, the way it always did when Lnand acted the pug. So she was as surprised as anyone when one moment Lnand was standing in the center of all the children, her palm to her heart, and then she was tussling in the dust with Gdir, kicking, gouging, grunting and yowling in a horrible struggle that looked and sounded like the castle cats during mating season.

The children all gave voice, the older boys shrieking with laughter, shouting insults and encouragements, the smalls wailing and sobbing.

Han screamed, "Stop! Stop!" until her throat hurt.

No one was listening.

She looked around. No, she couldn't use a weapon, though she wanted to. Ah! The ensorcelled bucket.

Five steps. Splash! Cold water hit squarely in the fighting girls' faces. They rolled apart, Lnand's fingers clutching tufts of Gdir's pale hair. Gdir stood still, too shocked to make a noise. Her scalp felt like it had been ripped off her skull and her hair was filthy with mud, as were her clothes. Her front was sodden.

But everyone turned to Lnand, who was *bleeding*.

Beads of blood had welled where Gdir had scratched her face, running together in the splash. In the shadowy cave, to the excited children, the trickles looked like gouts of blood. Lnand commenced wailing and sobbing as she staggered toward her bedroll, pulling everyone after her.

When Han couldn't see her face, she could hear the falsity in her voice. Oh, sure, that scratch had to hurt, but they'd gotten worse slipping on rocks during their stalking games when camping, and no one had peeped (including Lnand) because tears meant instant dismissal back to the castle and the lazaretto.

Han turned her back. Gdir stood where she was, trembling all over. She hadn't even pushed her muddy hair, tangled as it was, out of her eyes. This was the girl who braided her hair twice a day—at dawn and before bed—because she couldn't stand mess.

Gdir said brokenly, between half-suppressed sobs deep in her chest, "She's even a pug about–about—! *Orphan.* L-l-like she's the only—my father. W-w–with the Jarl. *Your* father, day watch captain of the outer gate. My m-m—" She shut her mouth so hard that Han heard her teeth click.

Han rubbed her itchy scalp. She hated to think about her mother up on the west tower. Gdir's mother, as next arms mistress, in charge of the alter watch bow teams. Nobody knew if Gdir's father, Captain of the Riders, had made it back with the Jarl and the rest of the Riders in time to defend the castle. After watching all those Venn march up the pass, Han didn't know whether to wish they had or they hadn't. Since she didn't know what to think, she'd tried to think only about her orders, and what she would have to report. She didn't let herself consider to whom she'd be making that report.

Gdir said in a fierce, low voice, "I have to know. I have to go see. If they're alive. What if they need help?"

Han's body flared with warning. "That's against orders! We were told to wait until the king comes."

"The king isn't coming, Hadand," Gdir whispered. "He's too late. The Venn will get to him first, and they'll be fighting forever. You saw how many there are! If no one comes for us in a day, I think we should go see ourselves." Her voice changed, pleading. "Not right out in the open. At night, on the stalk."

"No."

"You can lead us. You're good on the stalk."

Han wavered, then crossed her arms tight. "No. The Jarlan's orders were to wait. Ndand's orders were to wait. We have enough food back there for weeks. So Ndand thought we might have to wait weeks."

"You don't care," Gdir began.

Han gave way to her own temper. "If you start pugging like Lnand—"

She never got a chance to finish the threat. Gdir's hand came round so fast Han only registered it just before it hit her face.

Gdir backed up, staring at her hand, and at Han, who had staggered back, her face buzzing like it had been stung by a thousand bees.

Gdir whirled around and ran to the back, where the water trickled down the wall from a crack way up in the shadows.

Han ignored Gdir for the rest of the day. Her cheek throbbed as she got everyone to clean up and organize the cavern. Then she conducted warm-ups for the first time, and the snap of her voice got them all in line and working their best.

All except Gdir.

Lnand abandoned her languishing pose when everyone else was intent on warm-ups, and with a tragic air of sacrifice, she drifted to the front. She made what looked like the supreme effort as she took up the rhythm, favoring one knee and one wrist, and making faces of silent suffering. The younger girls and all the smalls moved closer to her. A few of the boys called the gruff, joking encouragement they got from their older brothers, now away at the academy.

When Han, who watched narrowly, saw the familiar small smile Lnand couldn't quite hide, she picked up the pace, ignoring Lnand's limping and posturing. She also ignored Gdir, who remained a silent hunched ball of misery at the far end of the cavern.

The rest of the day they played blind-stalk, the one with the blindfold having to use other senses to catch people sneaking slantwise across the cavern and back. It was a great training game, one of the favorites, and the winners got a lick of honey.

At supper time Han ordered no lighting of the Fire Stick, and no one protested.

Gdir did not speak to Han or to Lnand. In fact, they did not see Gdir speak to anyone, but suddenly the eights and Hal, the nine-year-old, swarmed around Han, asking variations on "When can we check the castle?" adding, "We're cowards if we don't go. They might need help!"

Han was tired, worried, and unsure about everything. She said angrily, "No castle! If you even bring it up again, then I'll tell Liet-Jarlan that you broke orders! Now, lights out!"

Though everyone moaned and a few of the eights flipped up the back of their hand at Han (when she couldn't see), Lnand was relieved. Even then it seemed to take forever to get the smalls settled, especially as they had no more milk and didn't dare make a fire, so they couldn't even make warm steep.

But at last the younger children were settled, and Han climbed wearily into her bedroll. The last thing she saw was Gdir lying in her bedroll, Tlennen just beyond. Gdir had moved them away from everyone. Her profile was a pale blotch against the dark stone. From somewhere the faintest gleam reflected in her wide-open eyes.

Han was just as glad not to have her nearby and curled up gratefully. But as disjointed images from the day mixed with memory and as her mind chattered imagined conversations with everybody—all the things she should have said—something bothered her. She kept remembering Gdir's eyes open and staring in the dark. Was that it?

The creeping sleepies withdrew, and Han too glared upward at the shadow-hidden cavern roof. She didn't want Gdir to see her checking on her, if she was still awake.

Besides, it wasn't Gdir that bothered her. It was Tlennen, his bedroll on Gdir's other side. They'd never done that before. Tlennen had always had his bedroll next to Young Tana, Rosebud's six-year-old brother.

Slowly, so she wouldn't be obvious, Han turned over. She eased her head up . . . to see two flat bedrolls.

Han went cold all over. She scrambled out of her bedroll and groped her way to the back where Ndand had set their roll of weapons, with a whole list of terrible threats invisibly attached if they used them in any but dire need.

She unrolled the weave-reinforced canvas with its rows of wave slots holding weapons so they wouldn't clatter together and nick. She felt her way down with shaking fingers and yes, two bows were missing from their hooks, and one pair of knives.

But Tlennen didn't have a bow. None of the boys had their own bow until they were older.

Han's chill turned to sickness. The knives were Gdir's, of course, but who else was gone? Oh. Yes. Had to be Gdir's first cousins, seven and eight. The girl cousin, just turned eight, would have her bow.

Han grabbed her own bow, and her knives, but they felt heavy and clumsy, and she knew she couldn't fight a grown-up with them. But she strapped them on anyway, her hands shaking.

Then she turned away—and tripped over the lantern, set out ready to be lit. It jangled loud as thunder.

Lnand started up. "Who's there?"

"Me," Han said.

"Who?" Lnand crawled out of bed.

Han closed the distance, and drew Lnand away, toward the mouth of the cave. After the profound dark of the back, the cavern entrance seemed almost bright in the light of the stars and the rising moon. "Gdir left. Took Tlennen and her cousins. I have to go get them."

"I'll go," Lnand whispered promptly.

Han had figured Lnand would love a night sneak—and a chance to fight Gdir again. "No. You stay here. If something happens to me and Gdir, then you're in charge."

Maybe Lnand thought it was dark, but the starlight lit her teeth when she grinned. Han saw that grin, and her annoyance hardened to hate.

She hitched her loose-strung bow over one shoulder and her quiver over the other. She hopped over the low wall and walked out. Lnand called a soft question, words too low to make out. Han ignored her, feeling her way to the trail that led up over the ridge.

The air was soft and warm. Somewhere high up, wings flapped, and a wheeling shape crossed the low half moon. After the cave dark, Han's eyes had adjusted enough for her to pick out the animal-made ridge trail. Not the one that led down to the pass, but the one that ran parallel to the cliffs. From below you'd be outlined against the sky— the children had discovered that on their campout night sneaks—so they only used that one to travel fast, but never on the sneak. But now, at night, with the Venn gone and no teams of children out roaming, she hoped no one was around to see her.

Still, she remembered Lnand's pale face, and when she crossed a small stream winding down the mountain from the thunderstorm just after sunset, she stopped and scooped up the soft, silty mud, rubbing it over her face and the tops of her hands. She took off her brown sash and tied it around her head, tucking her braids into it. Then she smeared mud down the bleached muslin of her summer smock. That felt cold and nasty, but she was used to that from their stalking games.

She bent to the trail and stalked over the big ridge that jutted into the pass, forming the first big bend. When she topped that, she caught her first glimpse of Castle Andahi down at the bottom of the pass. It was reassuring to find it just the way it always looked, except for the familiar landslide slanting down to the inner wall on the east side. Relief welled inside her until she realized the ruddy glint of the night torches was missing.

A vague sense of motion caused her to squint at the base of the landslide. Four ghostly blobs were just beginning to climb the long dirt spill.

Had to be Gdir. So she wasn't marching right up to the castle at least. Looked like she was going to scout by going up the landslide to peer down inside. Han began to scramble down the ridge, her bow bumping on her back. Twice she tripped over unseen roots and fell flat.

She moved faster then the four. Gdir was treading cautiously. Her brother and cousins weren't very good at night moves yet. Gdir had Tlennen by the hand.

Gdir was a good scout. She spotted Han just as Han reached the landslide, which was disappointing: Han wanted badly to scare Gdir as she deserved.

At least Gdir halted the others about a hundred paces up the steep incline. Little rocks pocketty-pocked down the slope toward the castle, making Han wince as she bent lower and lower, almost crawling.

As soon as she reached Gdir, she put her mouth up to her ear. "I don't like it. No torches, and I can't see any sentries."

Gdir's wide eyes reflected the moon. "I saw that. Something happened. We need to check."

Han shivered, though the air was warm. Everything

felt wrong now, and not just because they were breaking orders.

"Let's get just a little closer." Han crouched low, instinct tightening the back of her neck. "Maybe the torches aren't visible from this part of the landslide. We never had a chance to check before they sent us away."

Gdir flicked her hand open. The three younger children crouched down. *They're following her orders now,* Han thought.

"I think you need to mud up," Han whispered.

Gdir shuddered. But she'd stalked long enough to know that pale faces showed up if you knew how to look. "If we see anyone."

"But that might be too—"

Late. At that moment a tall, horn-helmed sentry walked slowly out from the west tower arch on the castle wall and made his way northward.

He was on the other side of the castle from the children, moving away. The children stared in horror at the castle.

The moon shone down from overhead, just enough light for them to comprehend that the Venn had taken control of the castle. The children could make out sentries on the north wall of the castle, where the gates were.

"Did they take our parents prisoner?" Han whispered.

Gdir said, "Where would they put them? The garrison lockup only has two beds in each cell—"

"Four cells—"

"—then they must be down in the old dungeon, but they'd have to move everything around—"

"But remember, they already moved things, when we helped make those mazes."

Tlennen pointed his wet thumb. "Why are all the guards at the front?"

"They must expect attack from the sea," Han said slowly. "They must think nobody will come from the pass. Because they have all those marchers."

Han looked Gdir's way for corroboration, but Gdir was staring intently up at the top of the landslide. She pointed with her bow, and the others saw the line of pale faces all the way up at Twisted Pine Path, adjacent to where Flash and Keth had stood to start the avalanche.

The line spotted Gdir's pale face. They halted.

"They're sneaking up on the castle," Gdir said, sucking in a happy breath. "It's got to be *our* people!"

Han got a single heartbeat of joy before she had to say, "No. Ours'd be in mud. They wouldn't be standing up like that, making targets."

"They're attacking the castle." Gdir shivered with excitement. Everything was going to be all right! "We can help them! We can tell them how we'd do it!"

"I think we better hide," Han ordered, still crouched low.

But Gdir was already running. Her brother and cousins launched after her.

Gdir waved her bow, which she hadn't strung yet. "We can help," she called in Marlovan, and then in Iascan, "We can help—"

The attackers talked in Idayagan, too fast for Han to catch the words, or maybe it was the words themselves she didn't know.

The voices were angry. One carried on the summer air all the way to Han: "No, they won't," and then in the children's own language, accented but clear, "Little Marlovan shits!"

Twang! None of the four children saw the arrow until it smacked Gdir's chest, not twenty-five paces from the speaker.

Han's eyes swam with weird spots. But she could see—would forever see—Gdir's body twist around, her hands going to the arrow, just before she crumpled up.

Tlennen began to screech, high, breathless, shrill.

Hiss! Zip! More arrows, at least a dozen, and before Han's horrified eyes the other three children jerked then fell, Tlennen with four or five arrows in him.

Some of the Idayagans missed—one arrow landed within arm's reach of Han. She tensed, not sure whether to yell, to fight, to freeze.

From inside the castle a horn blatted. It was answered by another. Mounted Venn emerged from the back of the castle, carrying torches, and rode toward the landslide. The Idayagans had scattered, some running straight back up to Twisted Pine, others toward the far side of the landslide and out of sight.

Han backed all the way down the southernmost edge of the landslide as the Venn horses plunged in pursuit of the Idayagans, perhaps five hundred long paces away, racing at an angle away from her.

She remembered orders. She remembered the cave. She kept backing away, low as a turtle, until she reached the gulley between the avalanche and the ridge. Shivering with fear, terror, shock, she darted from bush to bush, pausing just once to look back.

There were the four small bodies, just barely visible on this side of the landslide, hidden from the castle. Memory was cruel, forcing her to see them fall—the small things—Gdir's jerk, Tlennen's little fingers scrabbling, and she bent over a bush and vomited.

She collapsed onto the trail next to the bush. The smell of the vomit forced her away, clawing at the back of her throat. And though her head throbbed, she got to her hands and knees, crawling until she could get her feet under her.

Somehow she got back to the cavern. Lnand had lit a lantern, shading it on the side where the children lay sleeping.

"Oogh, what is that stink?" Lnand whispered.

Han did not answer. She found the bucket and dunked her whole head. The water was merciful on her hot, smeared, itchy face, but memory granted no mercy.

She sucked in water then spewed it back out, and the magic fluoresced a brief blue as it snapped away the vile taste in her mouth. She raised her head, breathing hard.

Lnand waited, so still the lantern's orange tongue of flame reflected in her eyes.

Han had left hating Lnand. There was no room inside her for that now. She fell to her hands and knees, and Lnand stared in shock at the tears tumbling down Han's face, her contorted mouth.

"She's dead. Gdir is dead." Han keened, trying to keep her voice down. But a sob sucked in her chest, and she bent double, rocking as she fought to contain it. "All. Dead."

"Who did it? Venn?"

"Idayagans."

Lnand whispered, "Did they see you?"

"No." Han squeezed her eyes shut. What to do? They'd already broken orders once. And Gdir was dead! No, maybe she was alive. Han caught herself up. Yes, maybe she was alive—she saw a lot of bad shots—she might be hurt—

"I've got to go back," Han said.

Lnand hissed her breath in. She looked back toward the children, and Han knew she was scared. Lnand was far too frightened to hide it.

"You're coming with me," Han stated.

"But you said before if something happens—"

"It's all changed. The Idayagans know about us now. Maybe even the Venn. If Gdir is alive, any of them, the Idayagans might even try to find out where we are." Han breathed hard, the ideas coming faster. "Yes. If they're dead, we'll Disappear them. We won't just leave them there. I can't do that."

"No." Lnand hunched up. "But I don't see why I have to go. You're making me go to be mean."

"You have to help me against those Idayagans. They are talking right now, I bet anything. I mean the ones who ran away. They're talking right now, just like we are. 'Where did those brats come from?' They called us little shits. 'Where did the little shits come from? We better find out. Maybe the little shits we filled with arrows are alive. We can drag the bodies away so they can't Disappear them, and throw them off a cliff.' "

Lnand was too shocked to act shocked.

"They might think the Venn saw us, but I don't think they did. They might be afraid the Venn will find out about the Idayagans from Gdir, if she's alive. They might think grown-ups of *ours* will come and find out, and come after them."

Lnand's mouth turned down. "I wish we had grown-ups."

"We don't. It's us. So wake up . . . oh, Freckles and Dvar. I'll wake Hal. He'll have to be in charge here, since he's not very good with the bow yet."

Even Hal would agree. There was no insult in that. Boys started with sword when girls started with bow. Usually, they didn't get bow until they were eight or so. Hal had only been shooting a year—and that maybe twice a week, when the girls shot every single day.

Han and Lnand shook the three nine-year-olds awake and told them what had happened. Freckles and Dvar reacted with disbelief, and then angry determination, catching their mood from Han. Haldred shivered, all bony knots, but turned his thumb up when Han gave him his orders.

Under Han's sharp order, the girls bound up their hair and covered themselves with mud.

Then in low-running single file they stalked from cave up over the ridge, down to the landspill, and up.

They'd almost reached the four small death-sprawled figures when Lnand poked Han with her bow and pointed upward at Twisted Pine Path.

Han had been right! Figures slunk out from behind the wind-shaped conifer that clung to the broad ledge, and began picking their way down.

The Idayagans were terrible at the stalk. They didn't wear any helms. A few had mudded their faces, but most hadn't. They all wore dark clothes, but they faced the moon, and were clear as could be. Marlovans wouldn't be that stupid.

Han wondered if the Venn saw them, too. She glanced back at the castle, but saw nothing, not even any sentries.

"We have to wait for them to get into range," Lnand said, which was the second rule on drills.

Han said, "Right." Gdir would have gotten mad at Lnand for saying something they'd all known since they were six, but Lnand's shoulders relaxed as soon as Han said *right*.

Lnand's expression was hard to make out because of the mud, but Han could tell she was worried. "Will they come at us in that line? We can't shoot the first one, all the others will just run away."

She wants to know if everything we practice is going to work. Han said, "No. If they're looking for Gdir and them, they'll have to spread out. I bet they don't remember just where they were. They can't know the landslide like we do."

Lnand turned her thumb up: that made sense.

"So let's get into position—first rule—just like in practice." Han tried to say it the way the arms mistress had. The way Gdir's mother had. "And when I shoot, and you hear it, everybody shoot as fast as you can. Get square between your targets, lay out your arrows. Just like we were taught." Han paused, and the two little girls turned up their thumbs. "Lnand, you and me do odds, me left of the line, you right. Freckles, you the left, and Dvar, you the right on evens. Chest, no fancy shots. Now."

Dvar let a single whimper escape, but when Freckles poked her, she stopped. "Just like practice," Freckles whispered, and again, no more than a breath, "Just like practice."

The four girls blended with the dirt- and rock-tumbled slide as they wriggled across the landslide in a line roughly parallel to the spreading Idayagans. They positioned themselves between the enemy and the fallen children, their instinct to guard the latter.

As Han had guessed, the Idayagans had not remembered where they'd left those squalling Marlovan brats. They crossed the landslide, well spread, but moving at the wrong angle. They might even have missed their victims, at least on a first sweep.

Han's sweaty hands were tightly gripped on her bow, her arrow nocked. She had fixed on a certain rock as the perfect range, and counted the outermost Idayagan's steps as he moved toward it. He was scarcely visible as an individual, just a looming man-shape, eye sockets black. When he scuffed past her rock, she shot.

Spang! The noise sounded as loud as the thunderclap days ago. She hesitated a moment, then nocked another arrow as he fell. Lnand's shot hissed through the air a heartbeat later, and truer than Han's. *Thump.* Square in the chest.

"Augh!" the man howled.

The rest of the Idayagans stilled into perfect targets, standing upright to look around for danger. Four bows twanged, the nine-year-olds at the same moment, and Lnand and Han with their second shots.

Six down, though the girls did not know if they were dead or just wounded. Several Idayagans returned arrows, though they could not see their targets. When four more arrows zipped back at them from unseen shooters, each hitting at least a limb, the Idayagans began to scatter. The girls were good shots but had little power; the Idayagans were very soon out of range.

And then the Venn horn blew. The girls and Idayagans alike jerked round. From the castle's back gates rode a war party, a much bigger one this time. They galloped straight for the landslide.

Han waited only long enough to see what angle they came at, then worked her dry mouth. She was terrified she wouldn't be able to do the cricket chirp that the children used in games for *Center on me!*

But it worked—it worked—the other girls, anxious for orders, began crawling toward Han the moment they heard the familiar tongue clicks. When the ground trembled under the horses' hooves, Han gave the *kek-kek* hawk cry for *lie doggo!* Her voice was too high, she didn't sound like a hawk at all, but the enemies were making too much noise to pay attention to a faint mewling bird cry. The Venn galloped past at extreme bow shot, chasing the Idayagans, who were scrambling away as fast as they could over the hump of the landslide in an effort to get out of sight. Two or three fell, and slid, causing more dirt and rocks to cascade; a couple of horses floundered in the fresh, unsteady dirt flow.

Venn and Idayagans vanished over the landslide. There

was nothing the girls could see, but they all lay flat to the dirt until a horn howled from up high and another horn answered from the castle. The faint tinkle of harness and armor echoed back from the castle's inner walls as the Venn rode back down and into the castle.

Han and the girls waited until the moon had passed the top of the sky and was beginning its slide down the other way before Han gave a single cricket chirp. Then she counted to fifty, and gave another, and the girls homed on her. They arrived swiftly, Lnand pressing so close her breath was hot on Han's cheek.

"I thought it all out," Han said in as forceful a whisper as she could contrive. Now was not the time for Lnand to start pugging! "Those Venn will be back looking around as soon as sunup comes. Maybe the Idayagans, too, if any got away. So we have to go to Gdir and the others and Disappear them. We'll sing them as soon as we get back to the cave. They won't care, or if their spirits are still here, they'll understand."

She was relieved when Lnand stayed silent.

"Right now?" Freckles said.

"I don't want to see them dead." Dvar's whisper was softer than a sigh.

Han's whole body twitched, followed by a flare of anger, but she had just enough sense to recognize that she was mad because she didn't want to, either.

"We owe them. Gdir would have for us. You know that. And you've seen dead people before."

"Not our age," Lnand said somberly.

"So we're going to sing extra. But let's go. You each pick one, and straighten them out proper. Just like the Jarlan does. Then we'll all Disappear them at the same time."

Nobody had anything to say, so they elbow-wriggled back down the slope to where the children's bodies still lay.

Han wished one would still be alive. The Disappearance spell wouldn't work if one was alive.

Lnand avoided Gdir and went to little Tlennen, so Han crawled to Gdir, whose fingers curled around the arrow. The children's limbs were cold, loose, unexpectedly heavy,

life-abandoned; Lnand and Freckles were too shocked yet
for anguish, but that would come later. Dvar wept silently,
not just over the cold, open-mouthed face lying at her
knees, but because she *knew* that the same had happened
inside the castle. Everyone was dead.

Han had hesitated. The grown-ups always pulled arrows
out, but she didn't think she could, and anyway, she had to
stay dog-flat, or as low as she could crouch. Pulling an
arrow out was a standing up job.

So she unstrapped Gdir's knives and gently laid them
aside. She took Gdir's cold hands and put right hand over
the heart, like a salute, and left hand crossed over that. The
arrow stuck up nastily in the middle of her chest, but Han
tried not to look at it.

She straightened Gdir's legs, then moved up to her face.
Her eyelids were a little open, the sinking moon causing a
faint, gelid gleam. Somehow that was worse than anything,
even that arrow, because it reminded Han of Gdir staring
at the cave ceiling just a little while ago. Alive.

Han pressed dirty, shaking fingers over Gdir's eyelids.
And then, she did not know why, she pulled Gdir's filthy
hair out from under her head, and parted it with hurried
motions, and then braided it as neatly as she could. Finally, because her own mother had always kissed Han
before bedtime, and Gdir's mother wasn't here to kiss
her own daughter, Han pressed her lips to Gdir's cold
forehead.

Her mouth shook—she could feel a big cry coming, but
she *couldn't,* she had to keep the others alive, that was orders. She stretched out her hand the way the Jarl and Jarlan had when they Disappeared someone, palm up as
though holding a torch. The magical words whispered in
her mind, and she said them.

Gdir vanished in a soft puff of air.

Han looked up. The other girls had been watching. They
performed their spells. The three little bodies vanished.
The killing arrow tumbled onto the dirt. Even the blood
was gone. Han looked closely, then scowled. "These are our
arrows. They stole them." She closed her hand on the one

that had killed Gdir. "They're ours now. I'm going to use these to shoot them back."

The girls gathered up the arrows, the two bows, and Gdir's knives. They crawled down the landslide, and sneaked back to the cave.

Chapter Twelve

JUST after midnight, after a long day of planning sessions with everybody, Inda ran downstairs with Barend and Rat, who talked across him as they divided up the castle guard and the remainder of the force they'd brought.

When they paused for breath, he said, "Barend, I want your best wing of bowmen."

Barend stopped on the landing, his usually squinty eyes wide in the torchlight. "Inda, we've already stripped the castle of everything but the clothes we're standing in."

Inda lifted a hand. "I know. But if Ola-Vayir does get here, it's your bare asses that'll get drawers first."

Rat snickered.

Barend knew Inda better. He sent a "shut up" look at his cousin and crossed his arms. "What do you intend to do with them?"

Inda said, "If Venn are landing here, what does that mean?"

Rat turned a puzzled look from one to the other, then to the arrow slit, through which they could see a slice of mountain.

It hit the cousins at the same time: the unlit beacons.

Barend's mouth thinned. "Shit. You think they're already in Castle Andahi." He jerked his thumb in the direction of the pass.

"Yep. Why else would these ones on the ocean choose now to land? The signal just has to have been the northern force either attacking or getting past the Arveases. Let's figure on the worst."

Rat slanted up a brow. "So what can you do with eighty-one archers? Not thinking of trying on your Runner's idiot plan, one against ten thousand?"

"I'm going to take them to the heights."

Barend flexed his hands, then dropped them. "Damn. I just don't see—" He shook his head. "Damn. All right, Inda, I'll pick 'em out and leave 'em here for your orders. And as many arrows as I can squeeze from everyone else." He shoved past, talking to his cousin. "Come on, Rattooth. Let's roust our boys . . ."

They splashed across the courtyard in the direction of the barracks as rain hissed down, Rat sharing an idea about fire arrows, only would they work in rain? Barend would tell him about the fire arrows they'd used in their pirate fighting days, Inda thought as he vaulted back up the stairs three at a time.

He found Evred alone in the map room, surrounded by lanterns as he gazed down at the map. Evred's fingers traced up the pass, tapped lightly on the heights next to the lake. Then tapped rapidly thrice in succession: north of Lindeth, Lindeth itself, south of Lindeth.

He glanced up, a sharp movement. "Inda. Are you aware that you've got our army split five ways, and we cannot count on Ola-Vayir's reinforcement? Six, if you keep any here."

"Five. We're leaving the city to the Randviar and the women. They'll be better at getting civ cooperation than we would be. Especially if they make it clear the Venn are going to take the city else." He hesitated, fidgeting with his knife hilts. "No. Six, actually. What we were talking about before. If you give me leave to take a wing of archers through the archive magic door to the heights opposite Cama."

For a long time Evred stood with one hand resting on the map, as all around the tower rain sheeted down with a roar.

Here it was, no respite this time.

He said to the map, "This was not part of your original plan. Why do you think it necessary?"

"My plan depended on us getting to the top of the Pass before we faced the Venn. I think they've already landed. They might be marching up the Pass right now, and their numbers have to be far larger than ours. If we can reinforce Noddy from one side and Cherry-Stripe from the other, maybe from three directions we can hold the Venn at the top long enough for Ola-Vayir to back us up."

"If Ola-Vayir doesn't come, we're defending the north with a tenth of what they have. If that much." Evred breathed the words. He shut his eyes. "They all look at me. Expecting the problems I inherited to end. If I cannot—" He stopped, though his jaw ached. It sounded like whining to say, *People blame the king for failure, and so does history.* "How do you do it?"

Inda flinched inwardly at the pain shaping Evred's whisper. He said to the map, "I just don't stop. I won't be a prisoner again. I'm going to keep running if I have to. Until I die. Everything's easier that way."

"Run until we die. It does sound simpler, doesn't it? Makes death sound like rest." Evred made a great effort, and Inda sensed that too, in his forced laugh, the sharp twist of his head. "So where is their Commander Talkar? Sitting out in the ocean here, waiting to land?"

"Where he's at the mercy of the Oneli, and can't see anything? Naw." Inda was definite about that. "He's in the pass. So that's where I have to be," he added.

Evred straightened up. "Then the top of the pass is where I should be as well. We will go together," he said.

Inda heard the flat affect of his voice. Evred had not used old kingly so-shall-it-be verb mode, but it was there in his tone.

Inda brushed his hand against his chest, then ran out, clutching his head as he clattered downstairs. It seemed like his brains were leaking out his ears, leaving behind a hammer that kept whanging him somewhere around his eyes. It had been the same before the battle against the Brotherhood of Blood. *Run or die.*

So he ran, formulating his orders on his way to the barracks, where he found Barend's archers awaiting him, all dressed despite the midnight watch being well advanced.

"All right," he greeted them as he dropped down onto someone's bunk, hands on his knees. "We're going to need nine canoes. Anyone know where to get some? Good. You're in charge. Now. You have two days to get 'em and ready your gear, including as many arrows as you can get. First in, five pairs of socks, because where we're going, there won't be horses. Ever smelled your own feet after an all-day hike?" He paused for the laughter, fought off memory of running about war-gaming on the hills behind Freeport Harbor, and issued the rest of his orders.

In the robbers' cave above the northernmost end of the Andahi Pass, Han looked around at the other children. Babies! How was she supposed to run with babies?

She and Lnand had been arguing ever since they crossed the ridge. "We have to hide," Lnand insisted. "We're good at hiding."

"We can't hide if they have scout dogs."

"They don't. My father says they're too stupid to know anything about anything important. Or they wouldn't have given up when the old Harskialdna just rode up the pass."

"They might have them now. Look, Lnand, I don't think the Venn got all those Idayagans. I think some got away. And if they did, that means they're blabbing to everybody about us. And that means they're going to come searching in order to slaughter us."

"Why would they do that?" Freckles asked, her fists pressed together under her chin.

"Why did they shoot Gdir, and then come back? We're the enemy," Han snapped, goaded into sarcasm because once again, she wanted to howl.

She looked at the babies. The urge to cry changed to anger. That was good. That meant she could think. "We're not going to let them get us. That means we have to go, and that means we have to tell the smalls something so they won't get scared."

"What could *that* be?" Lnand demanded.

Han knew Lnand was scared, she'd seen it on the mountain. What's more, Lnand hadn't wanted to *be* leader. She just wanted to be *called* leader.

It felt like a window opening. Han drew a deep breath. "We're making up a story," she said to Lnand. "And you have to be the leader in that part. I can't make up stories like you do. The smalls have to think it's a game. And they'll get a big reward."

"What reward?" Freckles asked doubtfully.

Dvar hadn't spoken since they'd Disappeared the four fallen children. Her eyes were huge, her face streaky with mud and tears.

Well, all their faces were streaky.

Han groaned. "I don't know! But if we're going to wait for the king, like Ndand told us, then *he* can give them a reward. That's what kings *do*!"

That made sense to everyone. They roused the smalls, who were sleep-soggy and fretful. At the prospect of a game, and a reward, they soon were as bouncy and cheerful as ever. Lnand went around and in a bright voice renamed them after various animals. They wouldn't run as smalls, they would be ponies, scout dogs, cats, hawks. That made the little ones bounce with joy, as Haldred, Han, and Freckles faced the stores.

"How can we carry all that?" Freckles said it aloud after a protracted silence.

Ndand had brought the food on the horse to add to the bags of dried beans and rice they usually kept here for overnights. There was the huge, heavy basket of cabbages and carrots, untouched since the time they'd abandoned the Fire Sticks and Lnand couldn't cook food.

"We can't take anything we can't carry," Lnand said over

her shoulder, in a sugary voice so the smalls would think it part of the game.

"And we have to carry theirs," Freckles said, pointing to the little ones.

"Five and up, you all carry your clothes pack, and we'll put food in each," Han declared, aware of the passage of time. She wanted to be well away by sunup. "You eights? The more you carry, the bigger your reward from the king."

That caused a mad scramble. By the time the older children had rolled up the bedrolls, all the eight-year-olds had overstuffed their packs with food supplies.

Han, Lnand, and Hal divided up as much of the rest of the food as they could carry. Freckles and Dvar loaded themselves with four bedrolls, or they tried. Dvar's knees buckled when she tried to stand up, and she knelt there on the stone, tears spilling down her cheeks and her skinny chest heaving on silent sobs.

Han yanked the top three rolls off her pack sticks. "We're going to share these," she said.

"Warmer that way," Lnand added. "Aren't we going up higher? We can't go into the pass." On the word *can't* some of her drama came back.

"No pass," Han said shortly, and, seeing them more or less ready, "Let's go."

"Leaving this stuff?"

"Aren't we going to sing?"

"What if they find it?"

"We're leaving the stuff we can't carry. It's not like a blind goat wouldn't know we were here, with all the footprints around, and the smell of pee from you-know-who."

Round-cheeked Rosebud sucked her thumb, her ruddy curls sticky with honey and grime.

Han sighed. "As for the sing, yes. But not here. I keep feeling like the Idayagan spies are sneaking up right now. As soon as the sun is up, we'll sing 'em." She remembered Gdir's face, so still. Her voice broke. "We'll sing 'em good."

Chapter Thirteen

THE locals had been right.

For three days a howling storm battered its way down the peninsula, prowling along the mountains before it wandered east.

The Venn fleet, having seen the signs of trouble, had sailed out to win sea room; the north shore above Lindeth was a pleasant morning's ride in good weather, but it took two days for Barend to get his men there and into place.

The storm was a disaster for crops.

As Evred wrestled with angry merchants, pledging credit far beyond what he could hope to pay in his determination to keep his army supplied, Inda ended up spending watch after watch in sodden clothing, helping the people of Ala Larkadhe plan a lethal welcome for the Venn, under Tdiran-Randviar's general orders, but Inda added some piratical touches that pleased the grim citizens.

Everyone left in the garrison as well as in the city worked; Inda was seen everywhere, which (Tdiran-Randviar thought) either heartened people or shut up the slackers. They helped close off streets and create blind alleys, showing people how to set up traps. They also created a maze that would lead the Venn in a continuous loop, once they hammered together then dragged a false stable front across a narrow street.

Up in the castle the Randviar strode about, her ferocious determination wearing out much younger women as some parties worked to sabotage everything and other parties, mostly castle and city children, were put on duty to guard the few remaining warriors from impaling themselves or tripping traps and breaking limbs.

The storm reached all the way to the north shore.

In the pass, Hawkeye's and Noddy's force plodded grimly day after day, night after night, in occasionally horizontal rain, gaining a little relief only when the winds were baffled by the soaring cliffs. Because they had all the remounts they could keep going by the dim, flickering light of torches. Their pace was slow but steady.

Hawkeye liked Noddy Toraca, he realized that fourth morning, when at last they gained a brief glimpse of sky.

Noddy didn't talk much. Before his father's accursed conspiracy, Hawkeye had no memory of Noddy, though he knew he'd had been part of Evred's litter of scrubs during their academy days.

Hawkeye did remember the horror after his father tried to take the throne. The Marlo-Vayir men hauled his father off to the garrison prison, but no one had seemed to know what to do with him. Some thought he should be bound, others that he should be escorted.

Noddy said something to Hadand, and when she agreed with evident relief he appeared next to Hawkeye. "I'll walk with him."

And he accompanied Hawkeye to the garrison, even though he had been riding all day and was about to depart again. Not that Hawkeye knew that at the time. He was just aware of a slope-shouldered, scowly-faced fellow Evred's age who said, "I'll walk with him," and fell in step beside him as if they were boys on the stroll to Daggers Drawn for a root brew.

Hawkeye had a sketchy memory of that walk. At some point he said, "They'll flog me to death as a traitor."

"No, they won't," Noddy said, with about as much expression as someone else would say, "I prefer light ale to dark."

"My father—"

"Yes." Noddy made a vague hand motion. "No way around that. He took a sword to the king. But you didn't. We all saw that."

"But I disobeyed my father's orders."

"Evred will hear you out. Cherry-Stripe, Buck, and me, we'll tell him everything. You'll see."

"I'll stand against the wall. That I accept. Because I disobeyed orders. No, I don't accept it, because he betrayed his oath when he gave me that command. I–I–just not the traitor's death—"

"You have witnesses. We saw you disobey orders from an oath breaker. That's as much law as oaths are. We just don't hear about that one ... well ... because there's some dancing around the way Evred's family came to power in the first place. Never mind that now. Here's the thing. None of that will happen to you. Might have, had the Sierlaef lived. Or the Harskialdna. Bad business, all around."

Inside the garrison they paced side-by-side, past all the watching eyes. Some men muttered, some flipped up the backs of their hands. Two spat, one uttered "Traitor" and gripped his sword hilt. Hawkeye's blood ran from hot to cold to numb, but Noddy just walked by his side, past the eyes, and the whispers, and the weapons.

"But what if Evred's dead? Didn't my father say he did something?"

Noddy said, "That's what I'm going to find out. He's got Captain Sindan and an entire garrison up there in Ala Larkadhe, against four. If for some reason he didn't make it, then I guess they'll have to see if his cousin Barend is really alive. Didn't someone say something about him? Anyway—" They arrived at the door of one of the cells, and Noddy walked right in first, and sat down on the bed, propping his elbows on his knees, hands dangling between. "—anyway, you let Hadand-Edli and the Adaluin sort it all out. They've got rank on anyone else. They won't let anyone do anything more stupid than what we've already seen today."

Anything more stupid. That's when Hawkeye knew he

liked this fellow. Trusted him. And so he sat down at the other end of the bed and dropped his head into his hands.

Noddy got up and left. Quiet. Easy. Whereas (Hawkeye experienced during many cold-sweat nightmares afterward) if any of those sneering men with the spitting and the backs of their hands and their whispered "Traitor!" had tried to grab him there in the throne room or along that walk, and drag him to prison, he would have fought with all his strength. Killing if he could, to make certain they killed him, because life had ended anyway, or the meaning of the life, and he wasn't a traitor and would not die at the post flayed as a traitor.

He'd never told anyone about that afterward, not until much later, after Noddy kept his word, and Evred listened, and restored his lands, took his oath at the coronation, and then appointed him interim Harskialdna in charge of the north until Barend was ready to take on the work. Gave him back not just his own personal honor, but the family's.

Then to Ala Larkadhe came Noddy's brother, called Nightingale for the gap between his front teeth and the astonishing ability he had with whistling. This was before Fala came to live with Hawkeye, when he was drinking too much distilled rye. One night, after Dannor had been particularly irritating, he downed a bottle or two and blabbed the entire story to Nightingale.

And Nightingale just said, "Heh. Didn't know how dusted up Noddy got over that."

"He was the calmest man there."

Nightingale grinned, showing that gap between his front teeth. "No he wasn't, or he wouldn't've been that gabby."

"That was gabby?"

Hawkeye had laughed a long time, and after that, the nightmares ceased. And though Hawkeye had seen Nightingale and Noddy since, neither had ever referred to those events.

Hawkeye was thinking about that as the weather finally eased a little. You didn't really notice, but Noddy was capable. People trusted him. Evred, for example, had saddled them with those yapping half-grown runners-in-training, no use to man or beast. At fourteen, fifteen, and one sixteen, they were academy pigtail-age, not even old enough for lance training. Now they were expected to be running messages and holding weapons in the heat of battle, which was where commanders were?

If Evred had thought it a good idea when he departed the royal city, he'd changed his mind, because just before they left Ala Larkadhe he'd caught Noddy and turned them over to him, with strict orders to keep them at the back of the battle once the main force joined up with them.

Noddy had promptly assigned them to keep the wagons dry under the greenweave tarps, and to wand-and-feed duty on the remounts.

Hawkeye could hear them whooping and crowing in the back. He debated between riding back there and whacking heads to get them to settle down and ignoring them.

Noddy just rode along, apparently oblivious as he squinted up the steep cliffs rising to either side. Birds wheeled and darted about the craggy heights, so high up they were like fingernail dents against the sky. The pass had gotten more winding, narrower, and steeper, just over the last day. It smelled like wet rock, moss, and occasionally—strangely—brine.

They had slowed to a walk to protect the horses, while the scouts and the dogs made short forays ahead.

Another loud, braying teen laugh echoed from behind. The swirling fog that had descended after the storm deadened sound, but not quite enough. Hawkeye's patience gave out. His knee tightened against his horse's side and he laid the rein to his neck when the animal's ears twitched forward. Then flattened.

Noddy straightened up. He and Hawkeye peered into the gently falling mist over the rain-sodden green grasses. Neither could see anything, but their horses' ears flicked forward. Not long after the tall grass rustled crazily and a swarm of scout dogs raced down from the curve ahead. They pranced around the horses, quivering with excitement, ears flat, but quiet, as trained; behind came two riders, a scout and a young woman with a child riding behind her, leading a string of three horses that looked as droopy as the one being ridden.

Dripping flaxen braids flapped on the woman's back as she slid down. She leaned against the animal's shoulder, her face shockingly drawn. As Hawkeye and Noddy approached she lifted her arms to a brown-haired boy of perhaps nine, a boy with the distinctive pale eyes in a brown face and the generous, curving mouth characteristic of the Arveases. He too looked drawn, beyond exhaustion.

"I am Ndand Arveas. M-married to Flash," she said to Hawkeye, her voice high and breathy on the *married*. "Liet-Jarlan ordered me to ride up the pass in warning if. I. Saw the red-black signal flag." Her throat worked, then she went on in the hard, flat voice of tight control, "I checked the beacon. Since the men had not returned. I found Flash dead. At least several days."

Her hand slid into her robe, half-pulling out what looked like a folded piece of paper, but she slid it back again.

"The little girls I left in the old robbers' cave. With food. Like we arranged. I brought Keth—"

She indicated the boy, who lifted his chin as he said in a voice thin as a gull's cry, "Flash is dead."

The boy's chest heaved on a sob. Then he sucked in his breath, teeth gritted.

"The beacon couldn't be lit. My orders were to ride, no matter what. So I did. Me and Keth." Her lips twisted in a spasm of grief. "Found these horses without riders. In the pass. Took them. I knew you'd need a scout report. There's a place. On the pass. Where if you go up the path behind the Elm Cliff you can see down the pass. I counted at least twice ten wings of Venn marching. More coming, many more, judging from the noise all the way down the canyons."

A wing was eighty-one men. Hawkeye and Noddy had six wings.

"Riding or foot?" Noddy asked.

"Both. Mostly foot."

"In the lead will be the heavies for the front lines and the longbow men for just behind," Hawkeye said, remembering Inda's prediction.

Noddy tucked his chin into the collar of his coat. Then turned to the boy. "You're Flash's brother?"

The child straightened his back. "I am Kethadrend Arveas. I will be Flash's Shield Arm." His brows puckered. "Was. He was dead. We saw him—" He turned his face into the woman's arm.

"Is there anyone who needs aid?" Ndand asked, face tight with misery.

Noddy said, "Tdiran-Randviar in Ala Larkadhe will probably welcome another woman on the castle walls. Why don't you ride down to the city, talk to her?"

She touched fingers to heart, tossed the boy up into the saddle, remounted and rode past.

Hawkeye said, "We know they're there, then, and approximately the numbers."

Noddy gave his turtle shrug. "Time for Inda's trickery." He pulled out the gold case Inda had given him back in Ala Larkadhe, thumbed some damp paper from his inner pocket and a herald's field quill-and-ink tube, then cocked his head. "D'you think the Runners will rise up against us when these things take over communications?"

"They won't." Hawkeye was definite. "Take over, I mean. First, we don't have mages, and second, you'll never be able to use 'em in battle, unless you can convince your enemy to stand by, sword lowered, until you finish writing your note before you commence your fight." He forced a laugh at the notion. "Third, who'd trust 'em? You saw Evred when he insisted on all that code stuff."

Noddy whistled between his teeth as he wrote carefully on the paper, using Evred's simple code nouns. Then he put the paper in the case and said the words of transfer.

That done, Hawkeye summoned the Runners to pass the word down the line that the enemy had been sighted. "Tell 'em we're going to push on as fast as we can ride. Our orders are to reach the top first. Hold it until the Harskialdna gets here with the reinforcements."

Leaving everyone to wonder how long that would be. But no one said it as they changed horses and saddled up for a hard ride.

Rain began to fall shortly after.

Chapter Fourteen

ON the day the weather cleared, Inda found himself at loose ends for the first time. For a short time he caromed around the castle, but he was in the way of working women, and he couldn't sit still enough to listen to the various guild and merchant representatives all yawping at Evred, either demanding or begging or asking questions no one could answer.

The wind had shifted. The Venn had to be coming in for their second landing try. It was time to see the enemy.

He rousted the harassed stable hands to go through the diminished stock for the fastest, freshest horse they had left.

The Randviar had given them an impressive cache of arrows, but Inda had learned during his days dealing with pirates that you never had too many. So he loaded both saddlebags with wood to be planed and sharpened and fletched, and added a bag of feathers just brought in the day before by some of the Randviar's girls.

He found Evred surrounded by a committee of city merchants; he made riding motions from behind one's shoulders, saw Evred's eyes flick his way and register the fact. He was surprised by the many salutes—fist to heart—he received, and further surprised by how the salute created a ball of warmth inside his chest. He still felt like he was pretending to be a Harskialdna, like it was a war game, except for the hammer inside his skull, the nightmares. His body knew a fight was coming.

The horse was frisky and wanted a good gallop. Inda's ride was not particularly refreshing as they splashed through a brief hailstorm followed by steaming heat, but the intense green of the sloping countryside dotted with enormous elms, clusters of oak, and bisected by farm plots, it all looked so fresh and green and . . . *normal*. Was that it? He'd lost any sense of what normal meant, except as something akin to *home*.

The quiet of the countryside wasn't familiar. And the countryside wasn't normal either, he thought as the horse slowed just as they topped a rise. He stared down at the bay, with the harbor city scattered like square blocks along the inner curve. It was too empty. No one worked in those fields up on the slope, no one was on the road, the puddles left from the big storm reflecting the sky as they steamed gently in the sun.

The haze off the coast was too strong to spot any masts on the sea, which was still a thin strip of silver just visible from the hillocks the road climbed and descended.

Each descent dipped lower, until the patchwork of farm plots below the mountains on the far side of the Andahi River ended abruptly in rocky ground. Beyond, white cliffs dropped toward the shore. The mountains continued onward into the distance, forming the southern base of the Olaran peninsula. Below the white cliffs the shoreline extended thin fingers of treacherous rock into the sea.

The horseshoe of Lindeth lay far to Inda's left. Straight ahead was the north shore. Barend would have taken up position below the cliffs.

Inda turned off the road before it curved away left to the harbor. The horse took him to the cliffs. He stopped under the sheltering branches of some gnarled old firs so he wouldn't create a silhouette, dismounted, and loosed the horse to crop at grass while he snapped out his glass and swept it over the harbor, then beyond to the sea.

And there were the Venn, tacking in at a slant. From a

distance the ships were extraordinarily beautiful with their
arched prows, the pyramid of wind-curved square sails.
Inda's heartbeat drummed as, with deceptive slowness,
they shifted sail with skilled precision, came about and
began to beat in toward land. He shifted his glass directly
below him, at the rocky coast. There as he expected were
Barend's people, all crouched behind rocks, spread as far
as he could see.

Inda snapped his glass to the breakers. The tide was
nearly out. The waves were choppy, but was that all storm
wrack? No, the water surged over hidden and not-so-
hidden rocks. A deadly beach for a landing.

Now, where was Barend? No crimson flag planted, not
for an ambush. Inda remembered his gold case, slapped his
pocket—and then remembered that he'd taken it out of his
pocket to check it—

—and then put it down somewhere. Damn.

Well, if he could find Barend, he could write to Evred,
make certain there were no messages, right? He walked
the horse down the chalky cliffs to an old stream bed
below the rocky beach. Then he rode along the streambed.
He could not see the ocean, but no one with a powerful
glass would see a lone horseman, either.

The outer perimeter guard had already spotted him: a
Runner met him, and before long he was sitting with
Barend behind a jumble of glittering granite stones, his
bags of arrows at hand. His men were all hidden behind
rocks, effectively invisible unless you came directly up behind them, so uneven was the shore.

"Rotten ground for fighting, but equally rotten wind for
them, eh?" Barend said, grinning.

"Might work for us." Inda hunkered down. "Ground will
be rotten for them, too. Give me your gold case."

Barend tossed it to Inda, and the untouched paper and
traveler pen he'd packed with it. Inda wrote to Evred, who
promptly wrote back on a thin strip of paper saying only
that he hadn't received any messages from anyone.

Barend snorted when Inda read it before he ripped it
to bits and buried it under rubble. "They won't write to

him, they know he hates these magic things. They'll write to you."

Inda glowered at the golden case. "Should I write to everyone to report in, or would that seem like I was breathing down their collars? We should have practiced with 'em, maybe. Set up some kind of protocol—"

He stopped, and Barend finished wryly, "Except Sponge wouldn't have liked that, either."

Inda was surprised and then displeased at his spurt of impatience. It was disloyal. If Evred distrusted magic, he probably had a reason to. He'd been reading about it while Inda was out at sea and hadn't touched a book in years.

"Hai! Some kind of signal went out. They're shifting sail again—"

Barend had been sailing master for Inda's fleet. He peered through his glass, and though Inda watched as well, he couldn't predict movements with square sail like he could with fore-and-aft rigged craft.

Barend had no problem. "Advance landing, only one. They must have seen those rocks. That and the wind freshening, they'd be crazy to come in."

"Or they'd have some land commander above the navy in chain-of-command, doesn't know bow from stern." Inda spewed out his breath. "Give 'em a nice welcome. I'd better ride back."

Barend grinned. "You don't want to stay for the fun?"

Inda rubbed his scarred jaw. "I'm blind, here. I didn't think about that until I reached the cliffs. I'm blind without that case. I thought I could come while my archers are getting the canoes—"

"Canoes?" Barend repeated.

"We have to ride down the river."

"What river? No, don't bother wasting your breath." Barend shook his head. "This is even stranger than taking on Marshig and the Brotherhood. Here. An extra twenty or so." He brandished the arrows he'd finished. "We won't need 'em here. You take 'em wherever you're going."

"You'll need 'em tomorrow." Inda waved the arrows off. "Those rocks are going to do your business as well as your archers, but that's just today. I don't see any more storms coming. They're going to land down south if they can't here."

"Soon's we see 'em haul wind, we'll be off to reinforce Rat and Buck." Barend tipped his head.

"They probably sat out there during the storm making shields for their landing boats."

Barend's grin had vanished. "I know. I was thinking that last night. We bought ourselves a couple of days. Maybe that'll make a difference."

There was nothing useful to say to that. So Inda just picked up his arrows, backed downhill, and left.

There was no new flag over the gate, just the crimson-and-gold eagle banner indicating the king in residence, so Inda was surprised to find the castle swarming with men, a lot of them gray-haired or balding, mixed with loud, shoving young fellows who looked a year or so younger than Inda's own age.

He didn't waste time talking to any of them. They didn't know who he was. So he just turned the horse over to a harassed stable hand and used his considerable strength to muscle his way inside, leaving behind a trail of "Who's that?" "Hey, Scarface, who's burning your butt?" and "Stop shoving, there are enough Venn for all of us!" protests. He finally emerged into free space when the duty guards spotted him and summarily cleared the way.

This time the commentary was more specific: "Who's the strut with the earrings?" "Didya see the scars?" "Damn! That's not the pirate boy they were talking about . . . ?"

He left the answers, if any, to the guards to make, vaulted up the stairs, and reached the office to find a flushed, grinning Evred talking rapidly to a big-shouldered fellow of Inda's height, with butter-colored hair even more unruly than his own.

He knew that face, didn't he? "Tuft?"

"Inda!" Tuft Sindan-An roared, bounding around the

table and pounding Inda on the back with such enthusiasm
that Inda coughed, eyes watering.

Inda spotted his case, untouched, where he had left it.
He half listened to Tuft's exclamations and questions as he
grabbed the golden box and flipped it open. A paper lay inside. For how long? "It's from Noddy."

"What's that?" Tuft asked, shoving his horsetail over one
ear as he scratched vigorously at his sweat-salty scalp.

Inda didn't hear him. He read Noddy's short, succinct
message, the relief at the prospect of reinforcement con-
gealing to that sickening sense of being too late, of missing
something.

"How many did you bring?" he asked Tuft, whose eyes
narrowed, all the humor gone.

"Ten wings. All I could raise, after Dad gave in." Tuft
studied the floor.

Evred said reassuringly, "Your father and his clan allies
have already given me two nines. No one has forgotten his
great response to my father's call for men."

Tuft's broad cheeks colored under the sun-brown, but
his manner eased from the scout hound expecting the scold
to one eager for the run.

Evred said to Inda, "Tuft seems to have done his best to
bring his father to son-murder in his campaign to be released to join us."

Tuft grinned. "Drunk every night. Let the colts out.
Poured distilled rye into the watch's water bucket. Every
day, I did something new. My brother told Dad to either
kill me or send me after Cherry-Stripe, and Dad said to go,
but only with volunteers. I raised them in two days," he said
proudly, a thumb toward the window. "I kinda had my fellow spread the word, sort of, beforehand. And some are
old, and some a bit on the young side, but after that ride
north, they're tough enough!"

Inda said, "How soon can you mount up again?"

Evred leaned forward. "Noddy sighted Venn?" He
glanced toward the window, and the mountaintop, where
no beacon burned.

Inda tossed Noddy's note to the table. It fluttered

through the air, and landed on the map like a crumpled butterfly. "They're on the way, as we guessed. Ndand-Randviar rode over the pass. The castle fell, Flash was killed at the beacon site." Evred's wince hurt Inda on his behalf. His own memories of Flash were good ones; how much worse would it be for those who knew him well?

He turned to Tuft. "We meant Noddy and Hawkeye to be the advance scout, make sure we grabbed the top of the pass first. But they're alone until Ola-Vayir gets here. Flash's Randviar saw the Venn on the march. How fast can you get your men up to reinforce them?"

"We'll get there," Tuft said grimly. "We've gotten real good at the fast ride. And that gives us just the kind of odds I like."

Evred touched hand to heart, Tuft thumped his fist to his chest. Another clump to Inda's shoulder. "Good you're back," he said, and was gone in two steps, his strong voice roaring for his Runners.

Inda said, "Sponge, I rode down to see the Venn myself. Looks like an advance force. Listen. The important thing is, I forgot my case. I should have taken it with me. I lost Noddy a whole day by not reading that note until now."

Evred made a vague, negating motion. "If he'd sent a Galloper, it would have taken two or three days. I hear what you say about your Venn dag, but Inda, a part of me is afraid that we're supposed to rely on these things, find them so convenient we depend on them. And at the last moment, they cease to function. Like the lockets."

Inda felt words piling up behind his tongue, but he kept his jaw shut. It was only in the last day or so that Evred would even discuss these things. "I think I've failed Noddy," he said, reverting back to sure ground.

"Tuft just arrived. You didn't even lose half a watch."

"Well, then, that's all right." Inda shoved the case into his pocket. "Here's the thing, we're done here. Barend and Rat are set. If they aren't busy sabotaging that beach as soon as the sun goes down, and Barend knows plenty of pi-rate tricks for that, then, well—" He halted, not wanting to finish that thought. Reality was bad enough. "There's nothing more to be done except to get to the top and put our bows to work until the last arrow. I'm going to write a note to Noddy right now. Let him known what's happened."

"When should we go?" Evred asked.

"Dawn watch."

"It will be cold." Evred half lifted a hand, then dropped it. "Give the orders," he said.

Hawkeye handed Inda's paper back to Noddy.

The light was fading fast as it did in the mountains, the sun having disappeared beyond the western crags long ago. The horses had slowed on a steep switchback below a looming cliff. Water from the big storm sheeted down from the cliff, running across the road, and vanishing between rocks on the other side. Somewhere below the outcropping of rocks they could hear a gulley rushing, the sound thrown back by the dripping walls of rock.

When night fell, they would break out the lanterns and change mounts but keep going. Secrecy was no longer a possibility, if it ever had been. Each side knew the other was there, and approximately where. Speed was now the imperative. They galloped on the few declines and flat curves.

Noddy Toraca gave a long, low whistle. "Looks like we're the practice dummies."

Hawkeye's heart had begun to drum. They knew what the news really meant: instead of being an advance force, it was far too likely they were it, unless Tuft Sindan-An's ten wings could reach them in time. This was unlikely, unless they learned how to race. They were several days' ride behind. The Venn might be a week ahead, but could be less.

"But the Venn are marching," Noddy said, his thoughts paralleling Hawkeye's. "That gives us some time, because we haven't halted. We have to get us more time."

"By?"

"Looking like more than we are."

Hawkeye grimaced. He had never been good at ruses. His fighting style had always been to fly into direct attack.

Looked like he'd be doing that, all right—against the entire Venn army.

But the less that army knew, the better.

Noddy said, "What the Venn have to see when we meet is a mighty force."

"Right." Hawkeye glanced back at their six wings and all the remounts. "If they know we're this few they'll run right over us."

Noddy had slewed round in the saddle. "Yes. We want them to halt. Plan. Rest up, even. Meanwhile. Every arrow that is aimed at something other than us doesn't hit us."

"I won't argue with that," Hawkeye said, cracking a laugh despite the drumbeat of his heart. Strange, how he hated getting ready for a fight, but when the time came, well—

Noddy whistled between his teeth, thumb hooked into his sash as the other held the relaxed reins. Then he grunted. "How's this? We're the ones with all the extra horse gear. We'll armor all the horses. Not just those forward. Get all the remounts behind, say, the first five lines of lancers. That's half of us. Scatter the rest of our men through the rest, to shoot, yell, move around. The boys give us their fighting tunics, we stuff 'em with straw. We brought plenty of it. We'll wear our grays over our chain mail. We put the extra helms on the straw riders, helms on the ones in back."

"You mean, you and me're gonna lead ten or fifteen wings of straw men?" Hawkeye cracked another laugh.

"Twenty wings of lancers," Noddy corrected, blank as always in tone, expression. "More, if we've got enough clothes to stuff. They only have to look convincing in the front."

"We'll be sure to insist we go into the songs as Captain Hay and Commander Grass. Hah!" The echo ricocheted back like a clap.

"But first, I'm going to write me some letters," Noddy said and to Hawkeye's amazement, he fumbled in his pack, produced pen and paper, swung a leg up and crooked his knee over the horse's shoulder to make a rough-and-ready desk, then got right to it.

Chapter Fifteen

IN the officers' mess, Evred found Inda seated at the table, hands busy fletching an arrow. As soon as Evred dropped onto a seating mat, there was a movement in the shadows beyond the single lamp's circle, and Taumad appeared, a tray balanced on each hand.

"Everyone is at other tasks, and Nightingale is sleeping," Tau said to Inda. "So I took dinner duty." He swung the trays to the table with an elegant air.

Inda gave him an abstracted glance. Why did Tau have a red mark on his cheek, or was that the lamplight? "Good. Listen, Tau, what about that battle-tunic? The red one? Is it done, or should I finish it up tonight?"

"I finished it this afternoon." Tau set bowls and spoons out for two. "Before we Runners had a meeting. Vedrid scarcely left me anything to do but some edging work."

"Two places? Aren't you eating?" Inda asked, rummaging through the canvas bag on his lap for another feather.

"Ate with the day watch," Tau responded, unloading last the shallow cups and setting them down.

He served smoothly and quietly, the way Evred's mother's Adrani servants had. Evred had never particularly liked Adrani custom, but having grown up with it, he had discovered that he didn't care for food to be thumped down onto the table the way most Marlovan Runners did it. This night he found Tau's skilled efficiency oddly soothing, though ordinarily Tau's presence was distracting, sometimes disturbing. Even in his blue coat, with his hair queued back exactly like the other Runners, he seemed to be playing at being a Runner. Nothing could hide the way he spoke and moved so at variance with the others. Though it seemed disgustingly fanciful, and Evred would never have said the words aloud, Taumad's presence among the other Runners was like a golden Nelkereth charger among the sturdy workhorses of the north.

Evred had known better than to watch him fighting with Inda.

Inda finished the arrow, added it to the pile on the table, then stared sightlessly at the food.

"We don't have enough arrows?" Evred asked him.

Inda grunted, blinked. "Yes. No. I don't know. It gives me something to do with my hands, d'you see? Though I thought after we eat, I'd write letters." He said it somewhat shamefacedly, as though he'd committed an error in referring even obliquely to the possibility of his own death.

Evred sustained the usual grip of fear at the idea of Inda's death, but he'd gotten used to that by now. "It's a good idea," he said. "However, do you—" He wished they were alone, but knew the wish unworthy. Taumad had proved his trust: not just by saving Evred's life, but by the fact that no one seemed to have heard about it afterward. Not even Inda, who was worse at dissembling than the academy boys they once were. So he squared to the question. "This matter of the restored magic on the lockets. Do you know what Dag Signi is doing right now?"

Inda had begun eating in his absent way. He dropped his biscuit onto the plate and thumped his elbow on the table so he could regard Evred with that direct, searching gaze Evred had to brace inwardly to meet.

"Why don't you trust her?" Inda asked. "Is it magic, or is it her being a Venn?"

Tau poured out the light ale that was scarcely more potent than the root brew Inda had drunk as a boy. Inda seldom drank more than half a glass of wine, but many of the

Runners had not noticed. Evred had become aware of that himself only toward the end of their cross-country ride. Inda never said anything at all about food or drink. He just ate and drank what was put in front of him, or went without if he didn't like it.

Inda scarcely waited until Tau had finished pouring. Evred noticed Tau's long, beautiful hands were marked with red, and one bore a thin, puckered red line across the back.

From hands to face. Tau's profile was absorbed, as though his thoughts were at a far remove, though Evred suspected that was part of his role-playing.

The distraction had become a silence. Evred forced himself back to the irritating question that Inda had a right to ask.

Still, he waited until Tau picked up the empty bowl of cabbage slurry and bore it away. Then Evred said, "It's both." And, unwillingly forced the words out, "At night. Alone. It's so easy to see the worst. Over and over." In a low rush, "The older I get the better I understand my uncle. Not condone, but comprehend. You cannot be taken by surprise, you must imagine every contingency, and conspiracy is so very easy to envision. And then to believe. Because it does happen."

Under Inda's unwavering regard he busied himself with a biscuit he didn't want to eat. His stomach had closed.

"You're not like your uncle," Inda said after a pause. And when Evred half raised a hand, as if pushing the words away, Inda dropped that subject. "Signi won't do anything against us. Against her own people either. Against that damned Erkric, maybe." He waited, and when Evred didn't answer, Inda did not consider why. He grabbed up his spoon and shoveled slurry in as though he'd just discovered he was hungry.

"You too?"

Runner-in-training Goatkick Noth sat back in the saddle, surprised to discover two of his mates at the cook wagon, which creaked and rolled along.

"Here. You as well? What's going on up front?" asked the runner driving the cook wagon.

"It's *Toraca*," one of the boys snarled so ferociously his voice broke into a squeak. "He's gone mad."

"Probably gone rabbit," Goatkick sneered.

"Yeee-aaaa-hhhh," the third drew the word out. "Rabbit. So now he has to write Armband letters to everybody and his uncle, and we don't wait for the battle to end, we have to take them *now.*"

"I don't believe it!" Here came the fourth. He threw his arms out wide, one hand clutching a rolled paper. "He has to write to his old mother *now*?"

"He's getting rid of us," said Goatkick.

No one argued, but they all fumed, thinking variations on, *What'd we do? . . . He couldn't be holding a grudge about that little sting . . . He must've found out about me catching a nap behind the oats that night on midnight watch . . .*

The cook wagon driver, a man with two children back in Yvana-Vayir, said with unsubtle irony, "Don't you boys have duty? Or are you all promoted to commander? Move only when in the mood?"

Accused thus of the worst possible thing besides cowardice—frost—the boys flushed, hunched up defensively, and muttered among themselves.

"All this way, and we're not going to get within a sniff of battle," the first one stated in disgust, shoving his journey bread down into his pack, and twitching his reins.

The last of them appeared soon after, and on hearing that the others were already riding down the pass he snatched his travel loaf and took off, not even stopping to curse.

Ride on, boys, the driver thought, his armpits prickling. *Ride on and stay alive. Maybe someday you'll look down at your newborn sons and hope, if they get sent young off to battle, they'll be under a Noddy-Turtle Toraca. Because maybe then they'll live to complain about it.*

After supper Inda packed everything he'd need and set it below his hammock. He'd shared a hastily converted weapons storage closet off the officers' mess with Rat and Noddy: they'd put a bunk bed in for the two, and swung a hammock in the tiny remaining space. Even though Noddy and Rat were gone, Inda had found it unexpectedly comforting to sleep in a hammock again.

He picked up his gold case and ran up to the command tower. He found Evred in the office, his pen scratching swiftly and evenly over the page. Inda marveled at the speed with which Evred wrote. Another reminder of his own ignorance. He plopped down at the side desk, where ordinarily a Runner sat to copy or take down dictated orders.

Evred glanced up briefly. "Do you wish me to add any message for Hadand?"

Inda twisted around, and noticed the two closely-written sheets lying at Evred's left hand. "I'll write to her myself. But how are you going to get all that into the case? Cut it into pieces and number 'em?"

Evred made a negating move with the quill. "Runner."

Inda opened his mouth, but Evred smiled bleakly and forestalled him. "No, this has nothing to do with my distrust of magic. Don't you see? If I do not survive, there has to be a record, carried the way everyone expects." His brows slanted derisively, as usual bringing Fox to mind. "If she doesn't carry a child—and I would have heard by now if she does—this is probably a waste of time, and there will be a civil war. I can name who will start it, and probably who will win. Yet I must go through the forms and set out my wishes for the kingdom's future in case she's able to hold the kingdom long enough to see them through."

Inda was back a step, uneasily contemplating the alien idea of his sister getting pregnant. "Hadand is chewing gerda?"

"She drinks it, actually. Says the taste is less abom-

inable." Evred grimaced slightly, remembering the first day
she tried it, how she choked and gagged. He'd tried it too,
choked, and they'd laughed together. Laughing helped, she
said afterward. "For a year now."

"Oh." Shift again. "If anyone can hold the kingdom, it's
Hadand."

"I think so, too. And so will most. But inevitably not all.
Not if there isn't any heir." Evred flicked the quill, indicating the barracks-side of the castle. "Also, the only way I can
think to keep Nightingale nailed down instead of having
him try to drag himself after us is to appoint him the Armband."

Inda vaguely remembered his old history lessons. How, at
the bloodthirsty age of nine, he'd thought the notion of acting as King's Armband exciting. When you carry a dead
Jarl's or king's last wishes, you have all their power until
you deliver it to the heir or the heir's mother, if the heir was
underage. Nightingale's duty now was to stay out of battle,
for he must live and protect those papers. Inda perceived
the benevolence in that. Otherwise, Nightingale would
surely force himself to follow them up the mountain.

Inda turned to his own task. He pulled out one of his
knives and sliced one of the waiting papers into strips, then
picked up the Runners' quill, kept sharp and ready, and
opened the ink bottle, always kept full.

His first was easiest:

> Fox: We found the Venn. They found us. In a couple
> of days it will begin.

Now his family. Inda's nerves tingled. Hadand first.

> When you were training me, you kept stopping your-
> self. Saying you couldn't talk about things. Well, now
> you can. Evred made me his Harskialdna. Barend and
> I gave the men a smashing good duel beforehand. Well,
> it's time to prove myself. If I come back, I'll tell you all
> about it.

For the first time he signed himself *Indevan-Harskialdna*, knowing how much she'd enjoy that. But it felt very strange to write it.

Tdor's letter seemed impossible to start, a problem he'd been wrestling with all along.

> *Tdor: I'm at Ala Larkadhe. By dawn I'll be somewhere else far away. Evred doesn't want us saying where, just in case the Dag gets this somehow. But it won't be for long. The Venn are a few days away at most.*

That didn't feel like enough. He rocked back and forth, hunched over his little paper.

Once—not long after they'd left the royal city—Inda had thought about writing to Tdor. But when he'd had paper and pen to hand, he had had no idea where to begin. Everything he wanted to say had a "But wait!" behind it, and another behind that, and another behind that, going all the way back to the last time they'd seen one another at eleven and thirteen.

Signi, always near, had said gently, "Inda? What is amiss?"

"I was going to write a letter to Tdor. How do I start?"

Signi's profile lifted toward the west as the sun dropped beyond the city of tents. "If she were here and you had the space of a hundred beats of your heart to say anything to her, but then she'd be gone, what would you say?"

Someone had come to the tent, interrupting him, and he'd put it away for later . . . a later that had stretched out until now. Seemed reasonable at the time.

Inda shifted uncomfortably, forcing himself to the truth: he didn't know how to write a letter, not to Tdor. Strange. What to do had always come easy. Not what *was*. She'd always been the one to tell him what was.

Tell the truth, fool! So what's the truth? I miss her. I miss Tenthen. I want to be home. All three of those sound so obvious they're stupid.

Inda whooshed his breath out again. Stupid, but maybe

a place to begin? Yes. And if he didn't live, it wouldn't matter about being Harskialdna, and maybe living in the royal city, and all that.

Inda ducked his head down, and printed neatly:

I love you, and everyone at home. I want to be home. I want to dance at our wedding. I hope this is the last battle in my life, and that it doesn't end my life. But the battle's going to start.

Then he signed it just *Inda,* and stuffed it into the golden box, hating how tight his throat felt. The tap, the words, and it was gone.

Chapter Sixteen

GRADUALLY, dawn's blue lightened to the peachy clarity of a rain-fresh summer day. The molten gold of the new sun limned the reedy edges of grass tufting the sand dunes. It glinted off the minerals in the heavy rocks lugged to the shore all through the night when the tide was lowest. There they squatted as sea water hissed and foamed all about them, edges pointed seaward, ready to tear apart boats trying to land.

Sunfire glinted in the loose pale hair drifting below the cold, muted gleam of helms, along the cruel edge of drawn weapons, the tips of fish skewers, and in the grain of newly sharpened bits of wood planted all along the shore south of Lindeth. The same sunlight glinted in similar pale hair under similar helms out in the boats waiting for the signal.

A tangle of sea wrack pulled up during the recent storm had been artfully draped over holes dug in the wet sand, all evidence of a very busy night as Buck's, Barend's, and Rat's combined forces labored to make that shore as lethal a landing place as possible.

The last of the ebb tide hissed and flowed out, and then the surges gained strength as tidal flood began. The inrushing sea brought boats filled with warriors, all with shields angled upward, complicated arrow-fouling nets draped from the single masts to the boats' blunted prows.

A weird, moaning note from a horn and sails jerked up those single masts. The boats launched together, a hundred across. Then another hundred, fifty boat lengths behind them. The snap of the single sails as the air filled them, the lift of prows, caused hands to tighten on weapons, fingers to check the tension on snapvine bowstrings, whispered exchanges and shiftings of crouched positions.

The chief of each boat swept the shoreline through field glasses. The slowly strengthening light pricked the bristling of spikes, skewers, sharpened posts. Huge rocks. Nothing they hadn't expected. They knew the landing was going to be rough, they knew men crouched behind every boulder and shrub on that desolate stretch of beach where not a single seabird pattered or rooted.

They were the advance force, the Drenga. They had been honored with the task of making it possible for the Hilda coming in behind them to break through the enemy lines, even if they didn't. Hearts began to drum, bellies to tighten, mouths to go dry.

Breakers formed, surged under the boats and rolled beneath them. The breakers crested, rushed up the beach in creaming foam. The boats picked up speed as the rising waves pushed them forward; a command and the sails were loosed, brought down, the masts stowed under the benches.

On a second command, the men snapped out oars and rammed them into the pintles for the last ride toward the shore.

A strange sight wound its way up the glistening white stairs of the white tower. Three men per upside-down narrow-hulled canoe went first, followed by others carrying paddles as well as bows, and packs with helms attached to loops. The last of the line of men carried rolls of weapons.

Evred halted on the landing outside the archive doors, head bent.

Inda could not see his face, but the stiffness of his

shoulders, the audible breathing, brought back the memory of the other morning, when Evred had taken Inda's good news about the archive like a blow to the heart.

Inda was distracted by Tau's face, half lit in the torchlight. "Those marks *are* bruises. You been fighting?"

Tau grinned. Vedrid, behind him, smiled. "No, no, everything's fine."

"What?" Inda demanded.

Evred turned around, his face and voice neutral. "My father was not yet Harvaldar when you left, and so you did not know. The Captain of the King's Runners protects the king, but there was usually a competition to determine who protects the Harskialdna." Evred gave a brief, bleak smile. "Do you think my uncle would have tolerated Captain Sindan else, jealous as he was? But no Runner could best Sindan in those days."

Inda met Tau's eyes, got a rueful shrug of one shoulder.

And here is where Sindan met his death, right where we stand. He believed he was defending me—and I was standing there in Lindeth—

Evred thrust away the memory. "Shall we go?" He indicated the open doors.

Inda jerked his thumb toward the shelves, slanted in from the round walls. The men in front shuffled inside, looking around warily at the tall shelves, the ancient books and scrolls. When they got inside they turned around again, the ones carrying canoes wedging in uncomfortably, and doing their best to keep the canoes from whacking the bookcases. This was only possible because of the tower's high ceiling, enabling them to turn the canoes upright.

Nobody wanted to touch anything. Nearly ninety people were crammed into that tower room, along with packs and nine canoes, as Inda inspected the wooden carving around the door, with words in some ancient language worked into the images of green and growing things.

Not knowing what to expect—afraid he might not get any response at all—Inda touched the round figure of a sun with its stylized rays, said the word *atan*—

—and jumped violently back when the door to the landing flickered and vanished, leaving them staring not at the landing, but a flagstoned terrace with snowy mountain crags in the distance under a weepy gray sky.

"Damn!" someone exclaimed behind him.

Inda smiled. This would be about as far from damnation as one could possibly get.

He braced for the remembered transfer wrench and plunged through into the shock of almost-frozen thin air that smelled of wet rock and pine. "Hey!" he exclaimed. "It didn't hurt!"

The men hustled through, crowding on one another as if that magical door might flicker away again and cut one of them in half.

Inda backed out of the way and stared at that door, which was even stranger than the way the doorway had looked from within the tower: in the middle of the air a rectangular door-shaped hole existed, beyond which was the archive with its glistening white walls, the light slanting down from the unseen high windows, shelves visible behind the men, seemingly extending into nowhere.

When the last man was through, Inda spotted weather-blurred carvings in the carefully fitted, rainwashed stone flagging. The carving matched that around the door in the archive. He stepped on the carved sun and the weird door vanished in a blink.

"I wish you'd waited." Tau sighed. "I would have loved to go around behind it, and see what it looked like from there."

"It's magic," one of the men exclaimed. "Like as not your nose would fall off."

"Or your nob," one of the younger men cracked, and though some laughed, many made a surreptitious check to make sure they still had all their parts.

The change in air had clogged everyone's ears and noses. For a few moments they sneezed, sniffed, shook heads and stuck fingers in their ears in order to get them to pop. It was cold enough that their breath puffed brief clouds of vapor in the chilly drizzle.

Inda said, "The path seems to begin right here." He

pointed to a broad, flagged path cut in switchbacks down the rocky incline. The path was edged with small stones.

As the men filed past, Inda said, "Sp—Evred. I meant to remember, and I'd better do it now."

Evred half turned. "What's wrong?"

"Nothing. Just, if we get separated. These rings. I, ah, got 'em in Ymar. They *find* one another. All you do is touch it, turn around, go in the direction the ring, ah, buzzes at you. I don't know what else to call it. Feels like a bee caught in your skin. No sting."

"More magical surprises?" Evred asked, with a slight smile.

"Just rings," Inda said, sliding one onto his little finger; his other knuckles were too large for the plain golden band to fit comfortably over. "Don't do anything else. But now I don't have to worry about losing track of you in case something happens."

Evred took his in silence. Vedrid started ahead; Tau was the only one who observed the slow deliberation that was almost ritualistic as Evred slid his onto his left forefinger.

"Let's go." Inda plunged down the path.

Evred followed. Tau fell in last.

On board the flagship, Commander Durasnir finished his morning drill ritual, stepped from his inner cabin to the outer cabin. He drank a spice milk while he read the night's dispatches. Then he walked his accustomed morning tour of the ship, finding everything efficient and orderly as always under the watchful eye of Battle Group Captain Gairad.

He proceeded at an unhurried pace down one deck to the cabins for the leaders. Erkric was gone. The wardroom assigned to the mages was empty except for a young mage attending the communication device that eventually furnished the dispatches up in the cabin, and except for Dag Ulaffa, who was eating some berries and drinking a spice milk.

Ulaffa regarded Durasnir for a few moments, then said, "Alfrac, please bring me another spice milk. Would you like one, Commander?"

Durasnir made a brief sign, the dag whisked himself out, and Durasnir said, "Can you transfer me to some vantage so that I may see the battle in progress?"

Ulaffa's gaze went diffuse. His old hands gently caressed the sides of his glass, then he said, "I will see what I can do."

Durasnir put his hands together in peace mode and departed.

Inda and Evred followed the bobbing canoes down the slanting switchbacks. Stones clattered over the edge and down into an abyss as Inda's toes kicked them up. He scarcely noticed, he was too busy peering down into the enormous canyons to the east as the rising sun slowly lowered the shadows. He hoped they'd be able to spot the pass—or rather anyone in the pass—from these heights.

Evred's attention was drawn in the opposite direction. He rounded a wind-twisted pine and gazed upward, until at last the bends in the path led to a place where—however briefly—the cliffs and the ancient firs all parted. The drizzle had lifted in the west, promising respite later; the clouds were underlit like silver streamers, an arrowhead of ocean sparkled in the distance to the south. Green hills, fields, flower-dotted meadows all demonstrated the healing power of rain after the previous month's drought.

It was beautiful, and deceptively peaceful.

Aware of the irony, he rounded another cliff, which gave out onto an open vista, rank on rank of climbing crags. His eye was caught midway up by a rocky structure never made by nature. Ah, there they were at last! Tall stones curved, dimpled with wind- and weather-smoothed carving made by hands an unimaginably long time ago.

"What?" Inda asked over his shoulder, alarmed at Evred's intent stare upward. "Venn?"

"Wind harps." Evred's face was cold-reddened like everyone else's but his voiced burred with deep pleasure.

"What?" Inda asked, curious at that rare note of elation.

"The Morvende archivist told me about them," Evred said. "I did not explain them already? No, though I started half a dozen times. But we were always interrupted. Anyway, the harps were apparently meant to evoke the resonance of some old Sartoran stone called disirad. Supposedly, the tower is made of it, though all the magical virtue has long gone out."

Inda had a vague recollection of hearing something similar, though not about wind harps. Tdor? Fox? He couldn't remember anymore.

"They consider them a failure," Evred continued as the next switchback carried the wind harps out of view. He wished the wind would rise and sound them, but the soft rain remained vertical. "How could such a thing be a failure? I used to listen to them when I was alone in the tower, my first winter at Ala Larkadhe."

"What did they expect?" Inda asked over his shoulder, hopping over a tiny stream cutting slantways across the path to drip down the cliff on its way to some distantly booming waterfall. "What's disirad supposed to sound like?"

"It resonated in the spirit, the Morvende archivist said. It sang."

"Wonder what *that* means?"

And as they clambered down the path, feet sometimes sliding on mossy patches that were always in the shadow of a rocky outcropping, they speculated, drawing on old readings and half-remembered stories. It was for a brief, exhilarating time just like childhood.

Inda felt it as well. He'd had such conversations with Fox, and sometimes with Tau. Meaning—people bring meaning to things—Fox's thoughts on meaning—is there any meaning, and if not, why do human beings see meaning in so many things? Inda stumbled cheerfully over a tangle of questions and observations, wishing he'd made an effort to get books and read more as he fumbled for the words to express his conviction that there is meaning beyond the meanings.

Evred laughed. "Now I suspect we're chasing our own backs. Though Hadand says the same as you do. Is your mother's mind shaping the way you two see the universe? Fareas-Iofre once said to me that age has given her the ability to perceive just some of the patterns behind the patterns."

Inda was about to observe that Fox did not want there to be any patterns, because patterns suggested order outside of human creation, and order implied justice, but where was the justice for the Montredavan-Ans?

But that would shift the talk from questions of being to politics. "Is politics just another word for injustice?" he mused.

Evred was wondering how Inda's mind had jumped from his mother's patterns to injustice at the same time the archer just in front was telling Tau in a low voice that his father, a herald, had a good quote from Adamas of the Black Sword on the subject of politics—

"Hep," Inda exclaimed, and everyone stopped.

Inda dug a hand into his belt pouch. He pulled out his gold case, gleaming richly in the soft light. He grabbed the damp bit of paper inside, his face intense in a way Evred remembered from the old days, just before a game. "First report: Cherry-Stripe is just below the lake, but they split up to find boats and haven't seen Cama's men anywhere. They can write to each other, but since neither knows the terrain, the landmarks they describe are useless, and they're wasting time trying to find one another."

"Shall we pause and write to Cama?"

"And then what?" Inda asked, his good mood vanishing. "This is just as bad as on the sea, damn it. How do the Venn make it work on land? We get speed—no Gallopers taking days—but what's that mean when we don't have location to orient on?"

The men with the canoes shifted uncomfortably.

Inda sighed sharply. "They'll just have to find some mountain they recognize. If they can. Orient from there."

He sat down on the muddy trail, turned the paper over, held a hand out for the Runner quill-and-tube Tau carried, and scribbled quick words.

Durasnir was reading Captain Seigmad's report on the launch of the southern half of the invasion when the dag on dispatch duty stepped up. He laid a folded piece of paper down in front of Durasnir and then retreated.

Durasnir finished Seigmad's report. Even stated in short, succinct words, the horror of the dawn launch punched him with images: bodies tossed by the crimson breakers, swamped boats, men bleeding to death on the rocky shore.

He threw the paper aside. But the images remained.

He opened the dag's paper. A token slid out, ringing on the table. There was only a single rune inscribed on the paper, representing "U."

U had to signify Ulaffa. This was one of his personal transfer tokens.

Durasnir summoned his servant to help him into his armor. He slipped his baldric over his shoulder, hung his sword from the rings, and fitted his helm on.

Holding the token, he pronounced the rune and was wrenched out of time and space then shoved back in before his anguished heart could attempt to pump. Pain made him gasp and fall forward a few steps, but when he discovered who stood just outside the drawn square on a muddy hillside, he ignored the reaction. "Brit?" he said, forgetting honorifics, salutes, all the protocol he was usually scrupulous to observe.

"Greetings, Fulla," said Brit Valda, Chief of the Sea Dags—who had been missing for weeks.

Her old face was blotchy from cold; he could see her breath. And his own when he exclaimed, "Where are we?" He did not recognize the terrace of flagstones surrounded by thick, gnarled pine.

"Mountains. Erkric is nowhere to be found. But more

important, he is prevented from transfer anywhere here, and so are his dags. Ulaffa knows I am here. He and I made contact yesterday." Simple words for the terrible risk they both dared, out of growing desperation. "There is much to discuss, if you will hear it."

"May we talk while observing the battle?"

Valda dipped her head once, hands together. "The one at the landing waged all morning. Oh, Fulla, the waters of the shoreline carry blood all the way along the coast—" She pressed her fingers against her eyes, then said, "Our people broke through the Marlovan lines a short time ago, and are heading north to Ala Larkadhe, which blocks southern access to the pass."

"I know, he said. "Take me there."

As Inda and his party raced down the slope, they became aware of a stream tumbling beside them, sometimes on one side, sometimes another. Waterfalls that had been trickles now roared into white water, widening into a racing river.

The middle of the afternoon brought them to the point at which the river was flat enough to navigate—for a time. Most had wanted to risk it earlier, because they'd discovered that walking downhill was only easy for a while. Not one of them had escaped aching legs, or toes throbbing with pain after being jammed against the rigid squared toes of their high-heeled riding boots.

Inda stopped them at last, but stood there looking doubtfully at the fast-moving water as many of the men eased their boots off and dabbled their feet in the river, grimacing with pain.

Inda ignored his aching feet. This seemed to be the right place. Farther down would be one mighty fall, but the stone plinth marking the old trail to the pass was supposed to be well before it. That had seemed easy enough when Inda was standing in the office looking down at the neatly drawn map, but when he looked from that rushing river to the wild tangle of trees and outcroppings at either side, he hoped they'd be able to spot the plinth.

If not, they'd find themselves airborne over the big fall.

Above the sun rimmed the departing clouds through the cotton-batting of fog. Inda said, "This is it." And, eyeing the many barefoot men, "May's well stow your boots, you won't need 'em in the water. Wash out your socks, too, and wear three pairs when we move again, or stuff a pair in the toes of your riding boots. At least we won't be carrying canoes."

They lined the canoes along the edge of the fast-moving river, some of the men uneasily watching the water rilling the bank. What had sounded so easy before now looked daunting, and they paid attention as Tau showed them how to pack the canoes to balance them.

They had found five men who knew something of boats, and two who'd volunteered to steer. Ranging the steersmen in rows, Tau and Inda stood in front of them and demonstrated the stiff-armed stroke, and then the steering stroke.

Tau and Inda would steer the lead canoes of the first two groups. Inda went over the stroke with the lead steersman of the third group until he could sense resentment under the man's impatience. It was just water, after all; Inda gave up when he knew the fellow had ceased to listen.

They picked likely-looking strong men who seemed to have mastered the stroke for the bows of the canoes.

"All right." Inda demonstrated once more, moving his paddle slowly through the air. "Remember, keep to the middle of the wake of your leaders, and you should be fine. Take your places!"

Everybody clambered into the canoes, paddles in hand. The guide for the third boat watched Tau launch his and leap into the rear, every muscle straining as he steered; now they saw why the steersman was at the back.

The second and third canoes swiftly followed.

Inda went next, with Evred seated in the middle of his canoe, Vedrid taking the forward position. Evred took a paddle, too, listening for the call of the stroke. Seeing the king bend arms and back to the work, the men were more assiduous than they might have been.

Inda and Tau had learned how to paddle on Freedom Island, racing down the mountain streams for fun after a long day of training. Balance and rhythm came back within a stroke or two, opening them to the exhilaration of speed. The men whooped and yelled as they sailed in a fast line over a submerged rock, dove into foam, then came up again, whooshing between more rocks as the steersmen planted their feet and put their entire bodies into controlling their paddles, which functioned as tillers.

One group, two, three, they shot down the river, a snake line of nine, the cliffs passing with glorious speed.

It was fun until the lead boat in the third group came too close to a submerged rock. Their second boat, bobbing in their wake, hit the rock, hurling men and gear to smash against jagged granite teeth. The third boat nearly missed them, bucketed: the steersman turned purple in the face as he wrenched them straight. Three bodies floated past the line, one in a pinkish cloud, arrows from their packs spinning and bobbing crazily on the surface.

The rest of the line managed to pull four men out by catching their arms or legs as they tumbled past. One swept by the entire line too far out of reach, yelling incoherently.

"Swim to the side!" Inda roared.

White water ahead—this time they rode the foam in grim silence.

Chapter Seventeen

AT the same time that the Venn landed just to the south of Lindeth Harbor, the people of Lindeth woke early to the smell of smoke.

Uneasy gazes went to unlit fireplaces. No flames in sight, and anyway Fire Sticks gave off a faint smell, not this acrid, nose- and eye-burning reek. People popped tousled heads out of doors, checking the streets and then one another, all mirroring the same question: Where?

Finally, someone spotted the smoke billowing lazily up from the direction of the water, ghostly against the fading night as it rose above the jumble of new-laid tile rooftops.

A few ran to the harbormaster's house on the central square (still unfinished), to discover a crowd of his neighbors already there, all clamoring for him to Do Something.

He stood in his front door, tall, gaunt, his sparse hair nearly white. He was drinking the coffee he'd just scorched, ground, and brewed. Those who had enough wit left to notice the coffee realized he'd been awake a long time as he said, "Well, we didn't want 'em, did we?"

"What? What?" newcomers asked.

Someone in front turned around. "Marlovan patrols are gone."

"But first they set the docks on fire," the harbormaster said.

"Why? As revenge against us?" a woman demanded shrilly.

The harbormaster snorted. "I don't pretend to know much about running a war, but it seems to me, this is what you do when you have fewer men than the other side. And no stake in protecting people who've been causing you trouble ever since you came. But a big stake in keeping the enemy from landing."

"So they started a fire to keep the Venn from landing those warships," said the new guild master, a tall, gaunt fellow who'd been a merchant captain until sea trade was ruined. "Right. What do we do?"

The harbormaster said, "You go back to your house, shut the door and shutters, and sit. If the Venn do land, they won't stop and ask for your partisanship. Angry men with pointy things sent to secure a foreign city are pretty much alike anywhere. That's what I've heard. So far nothing's convinced me different."

So the word spread from house to house: sit tight.

That kept everyone indoors until early afternoon when the wind freshened, blowing off the sea and sending sparks showering over rooftops, walls, shutters. Sparks kindled to flames, joined, and spread.

The Lindeth people emerged once more. Whatever was going on elsewhere, they had a new war on their hands: people against fire.

"Kill the man, take his horse."

That was the strategy given the Venn chosen for the first wave of the invasion. They had drilled on the plains of Ymar, two men per horseman, the target being not chests or heads but joints. *A smashed knee and elbow gets him off the horse, then he's yours.* Everyone knew the mounted man had the advantage. But though they'd done their best to emulate the fighting style of the horsemen, no one had foreseen the killing effectiveness of those slightly curved blades when swung down from on high.

Many Venn died before a few of Durasnir's superbly trained Drenga figured out an adaptation: one feinted for the sword, the other went after the shield, and just when the horseman turned, the all-important third came up from behind and struck knee, elbow, shoulder, even wrist. Whatever was within reach.

It didn't always work. The Marlovans were good at sticking on their horses. But the Drenga discovered if they were fast and strong, they could get just that glimpse of an elbow, or a knee if the chain mail ruched up, or the shield angled another way—a smashed joint could be as effective as a stab wound. Best of all was a chance to cut the tendons at the back of the Marlovans' knees, and there was soon a plunging, wild-eyed horse with no rider.

The breakthrough occurred at the west end of the landing site, when a chief, having seen too many of his men die, pulled the remainder back long enough to regroup them into threes.

He had plenty of men to do it with because they outnumbered the Marlovans. Outnumbered them even with men still waiting for launches, so they could take the time to move down their own forces, regroup them, and put the tactic to work.

As soon as the other Venn saw ten, then twenty, Marlovans topple from their horses, the word spread, followed by the deep and fierce joy of battle lust and soon there were five hundred dead or dying on the crimson beach, limbs hacked up.

The first to recognize the shift in tactics was Rat. He then forced his way to Buck, who fought madly in the thick of the Venn who had flocked round the Marlo-Vayir banner, each thirsting to be the one to bring down a commander.

"They're killing us for the horses," Rat shouted.

Buck couldn't hear anything but the clang and ring of metal, grunts, and shouts, couldn't see anything beyond the lunging, stinking press of men, all blood, steel, wild eyes, teeth.

He flexed his calves and his horse reared, striking out,

driving three Venn back. A plunge, two hard strikes, and he was out of the melee, breathing hard. "What's that?"

"We're outnumbered. And they're killing us to get horses," Rat shouted.

One sweat-blinded glance toward the shore made it clear that they'd failed to halt the landing. Yet another massive line of boats was surging over the breakers toward the gore-splattered shore.

Buck whacked his blood-crusted sword against the shield of his trumpeter. "Fall back."

The trumpeter, scarcely out of boyhood, looked incredulous. Fall back before these shits who weren't even mounted?

"I'll be damned and soul-eaten before I let them use our animals against us," Buck yelled, yanking the trumpet from the fellow's fingers, and he played the charge in reverse, loud, hard, and flat.

The Marlovans lifted heads, some circling, others riding away in relief, clutching bleeding wounds. Many, infuriated by the piles of hacked Marlovans tumbled into the bloody water, gave chase and tried to get the animals to trample the running Venn. They struck from behind, *see how you like it,* before veering off.

The new Venn commander saw the retreat, and gestured to his ensign. He shouted orders.

The horn blatted once more, marshaling those with horses to ride toward the tall white tower sticking up like a ghostly finger against the dark mountains: the city of Ala Larkadhe.

Dag Signi watched from the top of the white tower as the Venn horseman gradually became a distant line on the southern horizon.

Tdiran-Randviar had placed a girl at that prominence, but as soon as the advance guard was spotted cresting one of the hills above Lindeth, she abandoned the white tower, useless as anything but a lookout vantage. They now knew the enemy was coming, and from where. The Randviar shifted her lookouts to the lower, granite towers, where they could watch and shoot. Dag Signi slipped into the lookout's place, unseen from below, then sent word to Valda.

So Commander Durasnir was wrenched in and out of time and space again. He found himself on another prominence, this one circled by a raised rail carved with the patterned overlap of acorn shapes, many of them worn to vague bumps by weather and time. The rail and the stone beneath his feet were made of the strange, glistening white metallic stone that he'd seen only once before. This had to be the famous white tower of Ala Larkadhe, and he and Valda shared it with a small figure in a youngster's smock and riding trousers, bare feet below.

Then the person turned, and he stared in astonishment at the familiar face of Jazsha Signi Sofar. "They told us you were dead," he exclaimed.

Her eyes were red and puffy, her nose glowing. The surge of compassion was acute enough to make him forget the war: so had she looked all those years ago when she discovered that she was not in the final choice for Hel Dancer. He opened his arms, she walked into them, her small, strong arms wrapping around his waist, her chin knocking against his armor, which made her chuckle tearily. He pressed her against him, one hand cupping the back of her head the way he'd done so many years ago.

The hug, brief as it was, restored warmth, reassurance. Sanity.

But sanity brings one back to question.

"You came to witness the fighting?" she asked, wiping her eyes with a freckled wrist as she backed away.

"Yes." The grooves in his face deepened.

He snapped out his field glass as he walked to the rail and peered down the road toward the harbor. The swarm on the distant hill, the tiny glints and winks of sunlight, became a galloping force shockingly besplattered with gore, the shards reflecting the new sun off naked weapons, helms, armor.

Signi sensed in the tightness of his grip on the glass, the rigidity to his shoulders that he was deeply disturbed.

Valda gripped her elbows, her inward senses blinded by auroral glare around the Golden Tree. She had not planned this meeting, yet now it seemed important for the three of them to be there.

Erkric had worked hard to isolate dags from the military, and the military branches from one another just as he'd isolated the sea dags from the Yaga Krona.

"You must watch," she said to Durasnir. "But we must talk as well. Did Erkric leave word of his whereabouts with any of your military people?"

Durasnir's brow contracted. "No. I thought all dags were enjoined to make their whereabouts known to one another, if not to us."

"We have to." Signi emphasized the "we" but with a faint irony that underscored the fact that she had been missing since winter as far as her own people knew.

"He ordered us to submit to tracers, in fact," said Valda. "He claimed it was for our own safety, after Signi vanished. That's why I had to vanish."

In the distance, a signal horn bawled, a hoarse, mournful note, followed by a couple of short blats. The Venn reformed into rough columns; some had not mastered the horses. On one of the lower hills in the distance, the glint and wink of sun on armor was just visible to the unaided eye.

"So you believe he uses the homeland as an excuse to cover his movements?" Signi asked.

"I did." Valda watched the Venn riders lurch toward the city gates below. The Marlovan women crouched behind the battlements on the walls below the tower, bows taut, cut-down barrels of arrows ready. Unaware of the three Venn above them. "Now I am afraid if he does go back."

"Afraid?" Durasnir repeated.

Another blat from the long, curled brass horn caused the mounted troop to rein to a ragged halt. Many of the horses jigged and backed, ears flat, heads plunging to protest riders who smelled like human blood, who sat wrong, held the reins wrong, moved wrong.

"So you too suspect something . . ." Too many years of careful silence made the words almost impossible to say to anyone outside her circle. "Something to do with the king?"

At the command, a Venn war party rode through the gates below, weapons gripped at the ready. The horses had bunched together, their ears forward: they smelled home.

Outside the gates the main advance guard milled in bad formation as they struggled with the horses and waited for the warriors on foot to catch up. Looked like there'd be no more horses. To Signi their jerky gestures and sharp-angled postures signified murderous tempers.

The commander made a gesture. One of the horsemen raised a fire arrow, aimed it at the crimson-and-gold banner over the gate. A shout went up from the men.

The city streets were empty, the shops closed, doors locked, windows shuttered despite the heat. It seemed no Marlovans were present to see their banner burn, but everyone knew that was false.

As the banner was consumed by pale flames, the men of the foray party moved slowly into the first courtyard of the castle, and finding it empty, to the second.

The women on the castle walls waited, still as death.

At the gate, the Montrei-Vayir banner dropped to the stones, smoldering. This time the Marlovans could hear the word their enemy shouted: "Ydrasal!"

The foray party passed directly beneath the tower, helms bobbing with the rhythm of the horse hooves' sharp, distinct clop. Mail jingled as the first foray party passed through the stable yard, out of sight.

A second foray party was motioned inside. They rode up the main street into the city.

Durasnir endured the wind-twist of inner conflict. Honor required he state one truth, the most fundamental. "You and Signi have betrayed our vows to the prince."

Signi stiffened. Valda half raised a hand. "Is he the prince we swore to?"

"Can you prove otherwise?" Durasnir retorted. "I can't."

"Neither can I," Valda said. "But if you had not doubts you would not be here. Yes?"

The hissing, humming zip of arrows echoed up from the interlocked stone canyons somewhere below. In two strides Durasnir reached the opposite rail, glass to his eye. Valda backed away, hands upraised, palms out, an instinctive gesture.

Signi herself had backed away from a horror she could not prevent.

Trained to locate and assess such noises, Durasnir could do nothing here, but old habit guides the nerves and muscles faster than the brain. He turned away from the rail almost as swiftly as he'd reached it.

A third party and then a fourth were sent in, each to scout a different quadrant.

Bone-deep pain wrenched Signi.

The work of war went on. Gently guided by their silent surroundings, the cautious Venn forays rode straight into traps. On signal each hidden shooter took aim and killed a chosen target. The horses found themselves taken by new humans, but these ones had the right hand-talk, the right smell. The animals went peaceably to the nearly empty castle stable.

Above, the three watchers struggled with the question that threatened to bring down the Venn way of life. Was it right to swear unquestioning obedience to another human being? *Could* any one person truly embody Ydrasal?

A short series of blats from the army at the gate pulled the waiting Venn riders back into a rough line, heads turned toward their chief, who stayed apart as he dictated a message to his ensign.

The ensign sent his message.

In the pass just days from the highest point, Hilda Commander Talkar read the message his signal ensign had just handed him.

He read it again, then gestured to his nearest captain. He held out a tiny strip of paper, already damp from the dreary weather, the letters running into a smear. "From Acting Battle Chief Vringir. Battle Chief Hrad died at the landing. They're at the gates of Ala Larkadhe. Four scouting forays went in, have not come out. No signals. The city looks empty from the outside."

"That city doesn't completely block the pass at that end." The captain had known Talkar for years. He stated the obvious to focus their thinking. "We could narrow up, ride along the river into the pass. Circle around the city completely."

That's what Talkar had been considering. But what about the scant numbers of Marlovans reported at the landing? "The enemy's entire army must be in there, waiting to strike us in the back," Talkar said.

The captain gave a short nod of conviction. "Soon as Vringir starts up the pass."

Talkar's rage was cold as the rain, deep as the abyss. Hrad had fought beside him for years. Talkar had trained those men killed at dawn, he knew most of their names. *I hope you are hiding in that city, Indevan Flame-Ship,* he thought. *See how you like your famous pirate tactics.*

He waved to his message ensign and said, "Tell Battle Chief Vringir to burn Ala-Larkadhe to the ground."

Chapter Eighteen

INDA shifted his gaze ceaselessly from the river water to either bank. He was in the lead now, Tau having hauled over when they spotted their missing man clinging in a blue-handed death grip to a low-growing tree branch. Tau's canoe group had swerved with him, the white-knuckled steersmen determined not to vary from what Tau did by a finger's breadth.

Inda had thrown his entire body into the stroke, shooting them past Tau's canoes no more than an arm's reach away. He feared they'd come too far, and strained to hear the boom of a waterfall over the roar and rush of the river. The canoe shot over water-smoothed stones, plunging down into rushing foam. Then they raced around a massive upthrust of striated rock—and straight ahead a tall carved stone stood up above the river's bank.

"Marker!" Five of the men raised their paddles.

"*Stroke!*" Inda bellowed, wrenching the boat over as it began to drift.

Hastily the men resumed paddling, using such vigor they veered sharply and plowed up onto the steep riverbank. Rocks ripped holes in the wood-and-canvas sides and the nose came to rest in a holly shrub, but no one cared.

They picked the gear out, shaking and wringing out the

excess water. The men they'd rescued stripped, shivering violently, and wrung out their clothes.

"Spread 'em on the rocks," Inda said. "We'll eat and then start down." He jerked a thumb at the plinth, which Evred was climbing up to inspect more closely.

The rescued men warmed up in the sun and their clothes baked dry on the rocks. A short time later Tau's boat appeared. Leaning into the paddle from the hip, he brought the canoe smartly up onto the riverbank.

The men leaped out, sorting gear and themselves. By then someone had started a campfire, prompting men from each riding to plunge into the water and hand catch swimming trout. Others broke apart the canoes so they could use the wood and canvas; trout were sizzling on former canoe ribs as Evred skidded down the hillock from the plinth.

"The carving on that thing is worn but readable," he said. "I don't recognize two of the alphabets. The third is Sartoran."

"Ancient or modern?" Inda asked, swinging and stretching his legs.

"Modern. I don't think the marker is that old." Evred accepted his share of the food.

"Might have been replaced." Inda waved his bread in a circle. "I'm going to take a look around."

Behind the plinth lay a clearing circled by mossy boulders that looked like they'd been set before Iasca Leror was named. The trail began at the far end, lined by melon-sized stones.

Inda wandered barefoot a way down the trail, wincing when he stepped on small rocks. Only a few months wearing boots and the bottoms of his feet were already losing their toughness from the years of shipboard life. He grimaced, bending to examine the trail. It was packed hard, scoured low along the center in the way of trails used for centuries.

He straightened up, unlimbering his glass, and swept it over the mountains. No sign of villages, but they had to be out there.

When he reached the riverbank again, everyone was dressed and the gear had been redivided, accompanied by some not-so-soft muttering about having to share arrows with idiots who lost their packs. Most of the men had shoved a sock into each toe of their boots.

Inda dropped onto a boulder and fingered some damp paper from his pocket. He uncapped the travel pen from the ink nub, wrote, *Where are you and Cama?*, put it into the gold leaf-etched case, and sent it to Cherry-Stripe.

The answer came back before Inda had counted nine nines.

We're on the way down. We found each other on opposite sides of the lake. Cama's boys are forcemarching on the north side of the lake, us on the south. Villagers say we'll come out on either side of the high point of the pass.

Evred said, "How long would you guess they are from the pass?"

Inda shut his eyes, mentally considering the map, and its drawings of the pass and the lakes relative to Ala Larkadhe. He still did not really have a sense of land travel, especially in mountains. "Three days?" He slapped his side and exclaimed, "Another!"

He opened the case, took out a badly crumpled paper. Evred recognized Barend's large, backhand scrawl, and his breath tightened in his chest.

"Venn outnumbered us too bad, and broke through." Inda's voice roughened as he gave Evred the details. "They started killing us to take horses, but Buck pulled our people out. Venn're on the way to Ala Larkadhe."

Evred's heart hammered against his ribs. "Send Buck to harry their back."

"Later. Not enough of us to make a difference, so let's protect Lindeth. Venn're going to want to bring those ships in, soon as they hold Ala Larkadhe. We might have a chance there. Barend knows some good pirate tricks."

Evred's throat was tight; he was too angry about the defeat to speak. He turned his thumb up.

Inda wrote and sent the command.

When the last of the Venn invasion reached their advance force outside of Ala Larkadhe's city gates, the horns moaned and blared, bringing the Hilda's southern invasion force into squares. They sat in place to eat and drink. Ensigns and their own orderlies passed around water from the stream alongside the road, and then waybread stuffed with dried and salted fish.

As they wolfed down their meal, Acting Battle Chief Vringir's ensigns walked among them speaking orders.

Signi, Valda, and Durasnir watched from the tower.

Durasnir observed the issuing of small bundles that surely were sticks and leddas oil soaked hemp: torches. Valda watched the commander gesturing toward various parts of the city as he talked to a group of armor chiefs. The way his hand chopped the air, he seemed to be dividing the city.

Signi went cold when she observed the subtle signs of battle-experienced men reacting in surprise, even shock.

Then a long blat brought the men to their feet and into line. War bands were ordered to mount up and trot into position outside the city walls. Others took up a stance blocking the city gates.

The rest formed up into offensive squares—helms on, shields up edge to edge, swords at the ready—and marched inside the city, each to a specific area.

One man per party passed by the armor chief's fire keeper to light his torch; the rest of fire teams carried the entire army's supply of leddas oil until the ships could offload the barrels down in the hold.

Valda exclaimed, "They are going to fire the city!"

Signi turned on Durasnir. "There is nothing but women and children and old people in this city."

From each square's torch man thin drifts of smoke reaching lazily skyward on the heavy summer air.

"If there is nothing in this city but women and children, it was women and children who killed the scouting parties," he returned. At the rejection in her face he said quickly, "I hate it as much as you do. But I cannot interfere. This is Talkar's battle to command. Vringir down there has his orders."

Valda pressed her hands to her face. "He must think the city is full of warriors."

"It is," Durasnir said.

"No it is not," Signi exclaimed. "I have been here several days. I spent all of yesterday down in the caverns where the water flows from beneath the mountains. They have the baths there for city and castle. I was renewing the spells, and saw everyone who came to bathe. The men are all gone, except for a few wounded, leaving boys ten and under, or men over sixty." She opened her hands in supplication as she faced Durasnir. "Can you not tell Hilda Commander Talkar?"

"No." His voice was gentle, but decisive.

"No," Valda said at the same time. Her eyes were full of tears, her face distraught as she added, "Fulla is not supposed to be here, do you not remember? Or you, or I."

"It wouldn't matter even so," Durasnir said. "In his eyes, the killing of our scouts means the inhabitants are warriors."

Signi remembered the armed women in the Marlovan royal city. Hadand and Tdor, so quiet and reasonable and kind—and every time they moved, there was the glint of polished hilts inside the gap in their sleeves, the glimpses of knife hilts in their boot tops when their voluminous trousers swung at their long strides.

It was true. The Marlovan women were warriors. Maybe two or three hundred of them, and easily ten times that slowly assembling around the city in a circle, so that no one would escape alive, but the fact was inescapable.

As if someone below had heard her thoughts, an eerie noise whirtled through the air. Heads snapped skyward.

The Marlovan women on the walls knelt on the sentry walks between the battlements, testing bow strings, pulling arrows close. The woman almost directly below Signi had an untidy gray braid. Her gnarled first and second fingers trembled as she expertly nipped the feathers of her arrows between them.

When the war parties had marched within arrow shot of the defenders on the walls, two more screamer arrows arced over the city.

Drilled and smooth, the women jumped up and took aim. *Zzzzip! Sssst!* With smooth, rapid, and deliberate skill they began shooting at the invaders.

Arrows clacked against upraised shields.

The Venn angled their shields high as they walked in cadence down the street toward the old, carving-decorated guild house on the opposite side of a broad square from the western castle entrance. The Venn crossed the square at a run, and spread efficiently out. The ones on the outside shielded the ones who smashed windows with rocks. The next two slung dippers of oil through the jagged gaps, followed by twists of straw touched to torches. On to the next window.

The shields could not ward efficiently against trained archers when the men were in violent motion: arrows hit two men as they reared back to fling the oil. They crumpled, and were promptly replaced.

A short blat from the Venn signal man and the back rows of each square raised bows, took aim at the bobbing figures on the walls. Arrows hissed and clattered in both directions now.

An arrow thunked into the woman directly below Signi, twisting her around like a cloth doll. She fell onto the safety walk, where she writhed at the feet of a young woman loosing arrow after arrow. The shooter glanced down once, face white and blanched, then she bared her teeth and kept shooting as fast as she could.

Presently, the wounded one stopped pawing at the arrow in her chest and lay unmoving, fainted or dead, Signi could not tell. Two younger women emerged onto the sentry walk and ran, bent and low. One lifted the fallen woman under the arms and dragged her off. The other strung her own bow and shot.

Signi sneezed. Smoke! She whirled back to face the guild house square. Now more than half of the windows belched flames and smoke. A flicker from a doorway: a young woman carrying a bundle ducked out and ran.

She made it ten steps before she dropped dead with at least a dozen Venn arrows in her. The bundle fell, and out rolled a baby too young to walk. The child opened its mouth wide, sucking in its breath for a long, agonized moment before the fist-clenching, body-shaking scream. An attack party crossed the court from another direction, their path intersecting the fallen woman and the squalling baby. Most ran past. The man at the end closest cocked his wrist back, sword high, but he faltered midway in his stroke, leaped over the baby and ran on, leaving the child sitting by the dead woman, screaming and screaming.

Signi smeared the blurring of hot tears from her eyes and coughed from the thickening smoke. More figures dotted the smoke-shrouded street, many of them absurdly small—children separated from families in the smoke, most wailing in fright. Some were shot or struck down by the swords of the Venn, others were hidden by the thickening smoke.

"I can't bear it," Signi whispered.

"Is it any more right when young men have life and light struck from their eyes?" Valda asked, gripping the stone rail.

"No. But most chose such a calling. Those children did not. My Dag Chief, I cannot stand by as witness." Yes. Yes. The words hummed through her, diminishing the pain, the screams, the smell of burning. The world below glimmered in a haze of light. "Yes, I will act."

Valda took hold of Signi's shoulders. "You *cannot.*" And when Signi did not answer, she shook her hard. "You. Must. Not. Act."

Signi's head rocked, but her gaze lifted beyond Valda's shoulder. She brushed at the fingers dug into her shoulders. "Go, Valda," she whispered. "Take Fulla. Go."

"I will not be able to ward you," Valda warned. A shake. "Do you hear me?"

"I know." Signi trembled with effort. Valda felt it under her fingers. "The consequence is mine. And if I am discovered, perhaps it is time to let Erkric know that I live. Because I am going to take a stand against him."

Valda shook Signi a last time in a frustrated attempt to hold her to the now, to her own plans, so desperately important. But Signi was gone, gazing beyond the rim of the world at Ydrasal, the Realm of the Tree; to Valda's magical vision Signi shimmered in pale fire.

So Valda let her go, and backed away a step as Signi began the deep breathing of a mage gathering all her inner resources. Valda gripped Durasnir's thick, bony wrist and without leave transferred him back to his ship. Then she left herself.

Signi did not see them go. Her ears rushed and thundered, closing out the screams of the baby far below, the shouts and cries and hissing arrows, the sickening thuds of falling bodies as she reached down and down, to the strong flow of water below the ground.

She began to whisper a chain of spells held together by strength of will.

If you knew it was there, and you were strong enough to form the conduit, then the water would drive itself upward. First a trickle, then a stream, moving in and out of space so that every pot, every bucket, every pond and pool and fountain in the city bubbled up to the brim, quivered, spilled over in a thin trickle that rapidly swelled to overflowing.

Small animals put ears up, twitched whiskers and noses, then scrambled, skittered, swarmed for higher ground. Water spilled onto shelves, tables, puddled onto floors, rilling out of doorways. Water rushed down stairs, through broken windows, seeping, dripping, gouting down into flames that sent up hisses of steam.

Thin sheets of overflow strengthened to cascades, the fountains jetted huge sprays that arced high enough in the air to glimmer with rainbows between roiling columns of smoke.

Spouts and falls lifted charred furnishings, papers, books,

clothing, carrying them out of windows and doors to wash down streets in ever-widening rivers. Black ash streaked the whitewashed walls of buildings as the jumble of furniture, curtains, pots, cups, plates, and corpses bobbed and spun in eddies across the courts.

Warriors and defenders alike ran from the deluge, or tried to run until they found themselves caught waist-deep in the swirling waters. Though no one signaled, the women on the walls began in ones and twos, and then in a mass, to run down to the aid of the old and the small, all struggling not to get swept away in the terrifying flood; Venn warriors dropped shields and weapons as they slogged heavily, weighted by their armor, through the climbing torrent. There would be no fires set now. They had to get out with their lives alongside city dwellers, some clutching bits of belongings gathered up witlessly. A Venn sloshed out of nowhere, thrust a squalling baby into the arms of an old woman guiding a frail old man, and surged on. Nightingale Toraca appeared with a string of the horses recaptured earlier, his arm in a sling. His wounds had reopened, and he half leaned on the lead mare. If the Venn even noticed his blue coat, they paid no attention to him or to the horses—who snapped at anyone unfamiliar who tried to touch them.

Screamer arrows and blats repeated frantically; everyone headed toward the gates, thrust forward by surging water.

When all living things had cleared the city's central square directly above the underground caverns, a rumbling boom punched through. A geyser shot skyward, tossing up massive flagstones like leaves in the wind. Water and stone rained down, dousing all the fires, the white-foaming crest near the height of the ancient tower where, unseen from below, a small woman stood, arms upraised, fingers trembling, until her spells collapsed around her and she fell to the white stone in a faint.

The geyser bumped lower. Then again. Gradually it subsided. Water roared through the southern gate, carrying most of the city's first-floor furnishings out into a spreading

tangle of wreckage. The torrent diminished into running
gutters, and then even those lessened to a thin trickle, leaving the city tinkling unmusically with drips.

The amazed defenders gradually perceived that they
were surrounded by uncountable enemies. The amazed enemies took in the defenders standing in small clumps
within easy reach. They looked around for weapons,
shields—most of them gone—and then sought out their
captains, their faces expressing variations of "What now?"

Nightingale was the first to recover. He knew the Venn
wanted horses; he hoped if he got the animals out of sight
they'd stay out of mind.

The last of the horses vanished inside when Hilda Acting Battle Chief Vringir broke through his dazed ensigns
and slogged toward the gates, eyeing the defenders in the
fading light. The army he'd envisioned did not exist. What
did were a few nine-nines of Marlovan women defenders,
most of them now as unarmed as his men. No one looked
ready to carry on a fight, and though he'd been ready to
slaughter them all at noon, he had no stomach for cutting
them down in cold blood now.

"Let them go," he said to his signal ensign.

Instead of blowing the permit passage toots, the ensign
said, "Who *did* that?"

Such a breach of discipline would have netted him summary punishment under ordinary circumstances—as ordinary as war ever was. Vringir ignored the persistent
longing to sit right down and empty the water out of his
boots as he said, "Dag Erkric's business if anyone's."
Adding wryly, but only to himself, *For a change.*

"Signal," he said, more sharply, for some of the people
were starting to stir and eye one another warily.

This time his order was promptly carried out. The
Marlovans reacted as if shot—it was almost funny, the way
they backed together, looking around for weapons that
were not there, some of them slipping in the mud or tripping over cushions and jugs and broken chairs. But when
his men backed up obediently, reforming into rough lines,

the Marlovans trudged back into their ruined city, some stooping to pick things out of the mess.

Ruined city, ruined camp. The flood had also carried away all their neatly lined up and guarded supplies.

More supplies would be on the ships, but first they must land.

Vringir contemplated the west in the fading light. A thin brown pall hung over the harbor city. It looked from this distance like the fires set early that morning were under control.

He beckoned to the signal ensign. Talkar would need an immediate report, but it was easy to guess the new orders: "We'll find dry ground and camp. At dawn we'll march on Lindeth Harbor and secure it." He thought of the men's bellies pinched with hunger by morning, and how hard they would fight. He smiled sourly. "If our ships can't get into the harbor to bring our supplies, then the city can re-supply us for our march up the pass."

Chapter Nineteen

THE children of Andahi Castle began their sing as soon as dawn lit up the summery grasses and tangled wild-flowers around them. As the light strengthened, turning blobby shadows of trees to bright green, glinting in the rocks, their high voices took on the cadence of ritual, the eights staggering under the weight of their packs.

They sang the "Hymn to the Fallen" four times for each of the four fallen children. It didn't seem enough some-how; when a grown-up died, the sing had always been fine, it was over, life got back to normal. But Han still hurt in-side when she thought about Gdir lying there so still in the pale moonlight, poor little Tlennen curled in a ball. The memory made her eyes burn and her middle shaky, so when Lnand suggested in her tragedy voice that they sing for everybody in the castle, no one argued, or said "But they're alive!" They just sang as they wound upward and upward, toward the second set of high cliffs, just below where the abandoned beacons lay. When the Venn marched through the pass, the beacon men figured out what had happened and scattered, some toward Ala Larkadhe, others over the mountains into Idayago to find other Marlovans in order to fight back.

By mid morning the children were too hot and thirsty to keep singing. They slunk wearily along a narrow path. The three-year-olds ran along willingly enough until the morning sun had lifted above the mountains, but when they came to a narrow bridge suspended high over a rumbling, rushing waterfall, everyone came to a halt.

They stared. There weren't any bridges in the territory the children had been permitted to roam. They eyed the rope and slat affair swinging gently in the tumbling air currents made by the wild frothing waters. To the children it looked like it was about to fall down.

"Let's go one by one," Han said.

"I'll go first. Test it." Hal stepped on the first slat, then hopped back uncertainly when it wiggled.

One of the smalls began to cry. Rosebud promptly puckered up, and when Lnand tugged impatiently at her hand, she started to howl.

"Come on, Rosebud. Just a quick run."

"No."

"We have to! The bad people will get us if we don't!"

Rosebud's answer was to shriek.

Lnand's hand clapped over Rosebud's mouth, and the brat twisted against her, scratching at Lnand's fingers. Lnand tightened her grip, her stomach burning with fury. She yearned to slap the brat. Not just slap her, but shove her right off the bridge into the cascade. How *good* it would feel to be rid of her!

Lnand was sick of whining, dirt, pee. When would it end? It would never end, they'd be lost in the mountains until wolves ate them, or the snows came and froze them, or Idayagans caught up and shot them all. Just because of these *brats*.

She opened her eyes. The sevens and eights had dropped their packs, and all their slogginess was gone, as if somebody had done magic on them. They ran back down the path a little way, to a grassy dell they'd passed, and happily scrambled around in a wrestling game. Young Tana had taken his sister's hand.

"Go on," Lnand told him, her whisper shaky. "Take the other two. Watch the big boys play."

Young Tana looked back once—she was watching as she

clutched the struggling brat against her—as he led away the other two babies, both sucking their thumbs.

Hal tested the slats once more, then jutted his jaw and ran over. At the other side, he broke into a wide grin, and Freckles and Dvar followed. They vanished over a pile of ivy-covered rock, exploring.

Lnand and Han were left standing alone. Lnand whipped a fast glance Han's way. Han was glaring—at Rosebud! *She wants to throw them over the cliff, too!*

A weird thrill sang along Lnand's nerves. Her mind jigged through possible plans—no witnesses, get the others away, not quite push Rosebud, just get her on the bridge and pretend she got loose, and just . . . *do it.*

Han shook with resentment and fury. The morning had just started, and the brats were worse than ever. They would only get even *more* worse. And the others couldn't move unless the brats did. Her head ached as if someone pounded it with a rock.

She hated those snot-smeared, filthy brats, Rosebud squealing so loud her voice was like glass splinters in her ears. She stank like an old dog. At least an old dog had done good service and deserved a place by the fire and frequent wandings. Rosebud hadn't done anything of use, she just whined, and squalled, and had to be picked up, and she wasn't even *trying* to use the Waste Spell any more.

Han jerked her gaze away from the brat as if not seeing her would make her disappear—and shock pooled inside her belly. In her experience, Lnand either sneaked looks at you quick as a lizard's tongue, or else she made one of her oh-poor-me faces, her eyes round and big but that little smile curling the corners of her mouth. This face was unlike any Han had ever seen, a steady look, a weird one, her pupils big and round as night.

Pin-jabs prickled along Han's arms. Lnand was thinking the same thing! The cold sensation in Han's middle formed into a clod of ice. She knew that ice. A small ice ball hid behind her ribs the day she'd been sent on an errand to the pantry, and when she passed through the empty bake room, there was a tray of honey corn muffins. She'd stuffed

them into her smock, then lied when Lnand's father, the
castle baker, questioned everyone. Lnand and the two
older kitchen helpers ended up getting a double thrashing,
one for theft, and one for lying.

Han had gotten away with it, and it had even felt good,
especially when she ate them and thought about Lnand's
wailing. The snitch! But when she saw Lnand's cousin, Radran, with his eyes all red, the ice ball came back, even bigger. Everybody liked Radran—he was fun and never
mean—and Han had gotten him a beating for something
he hadn't done.

The ice ball was big now. Could Gdir see ice balls? Han
knew that sometimes ghosts walked in the world, and some
people said they could see inside your head. Gdir would
never throw brats down a cascade. Gdir had said Han was
a bad leader because she didn't make everyone wash and
do warm-ups like when life was normal. Gdir said that a
good leader keeps everyone in order, and clean.

But the Jarlan wanted us to be kept safe. The ice ball was
taking over Han's body, turning her into ice.

I promised to keep Rosebud safe. That was it. It didn't
matter that Rosebud peed herself. It wouldn't matter if she
threw everyone's bedroll down a chasm, or screamed all
day and all night. The Jarlan trusted Han to keep them all
safe.

Han's breath slowly leaked out.

And Lnand slowly relaxed her grip on the squirming,
angry child. She could have done "it" when she was mad,
but to *plan* it? And with everyone there? What would they
say? Could she get Han to make up a lie? But Han never
lied.

"Blindfolds," Han stated. *Keep them safe. That's my job.
As long as I can.* The ice melted away. "We'll play the scout
game."

Lnand heaved a loud sigh. She would pretend that nothing had happened, that she was annoyed at more work, but
she was secretly relieved. Han wouldn't do it, and Lnand
couldn't. *Now,* her secret inner voice whispered, and
Lnand shivered. "We'll tell the smalls they're now sixes,

they get to have big people jobs. If we lead them around in a circle, and tell them they have to balance on wood that's on the ground, they won't know."

Neither was going to make any mention of what might have happened. Instead, energy infused them, Lnand worrying about what Han might say about Lnand when Lnand wasn't there, and Han whispering to Gdir in spirit. *Help me be strong, Gdir. I'll be a better leader.*

They gathered everyone again, blindfolded the smalls, started the scouting game, led them over the bridge, pulled the blindfolds off when they were out of sight of the cascade, then gave everyone a honey lick for doing a good scouting job.

Two more bridges, and everyone over five had figured out the ruse. Since they'd all survived, they found the bridges fun, and only the smalls needed the blindfolds, but it had become habit by now. Rosebud liked the game because she'd get a honey lick.

By noon, though, the smalls had had enough walking up steep trails. Even honey licks wouldn't get them along. "We're going to have to carry them," Lnand pronounced.

Han sighed. "Then let's arrange the packs again. Anyone who carries a three gets some of their pack taken away."

The eights hunched and sidled. That was when Han realized that they hadn't been staggering nearly as much, though from all the uphill climbing they should have been as tired as she was.

The flickering, sneaky looks exchanged confirmed her guess. They'd somehow been chucking away some of their burdens. "First, what are we going to eat in a week?" She was so angry she wanted to knock them all down.

"But we have plenty—"

"Too much—"

"We never get to cook anyway—"

"*Second,* when you threw away our food you left a trail even a stupid Idayagan can find!"

That shut them up.

The remaining food got redistributed. Lnand moved briskly, feeling like she'd escaped something horrible, that

Han might say something horrible when they saw grown-ups again. She dunked all Rosebud's clothes, then said sternly, "If you don't use the Spell, then you have to have diapers again. Drawers are only for *big* people."

She ignored Rosebud's wailing, and hoisted her onto her back, Han and Hal taking the other threes.

Han hoisted her child, rearranged the little arms trying to squeeze her throat, and told Lnand to walk in front. "I'll walk in back," she said, glaring at Billykid. And, before he could make up some excuse, she said, "Let's sing."

They sang through most of the day as they climbed up and up, over trails so old that they had been worn before the Marolo Venn had appeared on this continent. They began with the "Hymn to the Fallen," then went to the "Hymn to the Beginning." The drumming cadences of that one cheered everyone, just a little, even the smalls, who took comfort in the familiar sound, so from then on it was war ballads, which everyone liked.

They made their way up a steep slope to the goat trails that Han and Hal thought might be too small for grown-ups to see or to travel along. Thunder and lightning roiled, bellowed, and struck all around them, but they were too frightened to stop until lightning shivered weirdly just across a field, torching an old tree.

They stopped under another tree, seeing it only as shelter. They passed out pieces of cheese and journey bread, eating silently until the rumble of hail had passed, and the sun peeped bleakly out.

They were moving again as steam rose off puddles. They stopped at a brook, and Lnand made certain that all the babies drank whether they wanted to or not.

They'd nearly finished when, faint but distinct, the belling of hounds echoed from the direction they'd come.

"They're after us." Hal gripped his hand on his knife, which he'd stuck through his sash like the big boys.

"We'll get up this canyon. Then camp," Han said.

The children looked around. They stood on a grassy ledge between high, brooding rocky spires, with even higher crags above. When they set out again, some of the middle children began to fret at the dreary uphill climb. Han ordered the older children to each take a small by the hand, and on they marched.

Shortly before sunset they stopped, not because they couldn't see, but because they had gone cold all of a sudden, especially wearing still damp clothes.

They found an old cave that smelled of some long-gone animal. Hal explored to the back, but reported it wasn't very deep, or that it might have been, but only a cat could get beyond the place the crack narrowed.

"No fire," Han said.

Lnand straightened up and put her hands on her hips. "Then we're going to eat sodden food? Look! It's all *r-r-r-oooo-ined*! She pointed an accusatory finger at the pile of packs dropped by the drooping eight-year-olds.

"Nooooo," Han moaned.

She pounced on the packs, pulling out the canvas sacks and discovered that the rain had gotten into most of them. What had been fine in the relatively dry air of the cave of course had been spoiled by rain.

She pressed her hands against her face. "I should have thought of that."

Lnand was quite ready to remind Han of her mistakes if she strutted, but a Han standing there looking sad and anxious made her sad and anxious.

"No one else thought of it." Lnand lifted a pack that had contained the flour for their pan biscuits, and dropped it with a squelch. "So we learned something. We better separate out anything that will rot, and pack up the rest extra tight."

"Yes."

They tried squeezing into the bedrolls. That didn't work because people got tangled up, and shoving fights started. So Lnand said they'd be cheese-breads, that is, open a bedroll and have several people lie in a row, like cheese on a bread slice, and then pull another bedroll like a blanket over them.

That worked much better, especially as everyone drew inward into a puppy pile for warmth when the cold turned bitter.

The next day they set out again, but a terrible storm

boiled up overhead, this one much worse than the last. Hail and then sleet began to fall. When lightning struck not a hundred paces away, not just the smalls began wailing.

Hal ran ahead, but shortly came running back. "I found a cave!"

This was more of a crevice than a cave. They crammed in. It was narrow, and had a very smelly nest in it. They wrapped up tight, and as soon as they were fed cold, damp journey bread slathered with honey and crumbly cheese, the smalls all fell asleep where they dropped.

The others sat shoulder to shoulder, too weary to move. Han fell asleep without meaning to. She woke suddenly to a thunderbolt that sounded directly overhead. She wondered wearily where she was. White needle sleet hissed just past the cave opening. Her toes and fingers ached.

Lnand blocked the watery weak light, nothing more than a silhouette in the gloom. "Rain's gotten into everything." She held up a sack. "All the journey bread except the ones in the closeweave packs are moldy."

"How many breads do we have?" Han asked.

"Just those two. The eights all unwrapped theirs, I think to pinch pieces while they were walking. They shoved the food in with their dirty clothes, it all smells bad."

Lnand sounded so tired she wasn't even strutting.

Han knew she should have caught the boys at it, but at the end of the hike she'd just been putting one foot in front of another as she carried a small on her back, and she'd only watched the ground.

So she didn't even look at the guilty boys. "This crack is narrow, and there's all that rain. How about this. We'll post a watch, and squeeze in beyond the nest thing, and light the Fire Stick. We'll boil the rice and beans together. I don't care if they're soggy, they have to cook in water, right? We'll set the bucket—"

"Billykid says they lost it. On one of the bridges."

This time Han jerked around to glare at the eights all clumped together. She was about to ask who'd been careless, but she could tell from their faces no one was going to snitch. And anyway, what could she do?

"Do we have a pan?"

"*I* brought one."

Han decided Lnand's braggy tone was a relief—it meant maybe things would someday go back to normal. "Make the beans and rice. We'll have to figure out some way to carry it. We'll be careful with the food. When we have to, we'll do half rations and promise them rewards. And if we have to, half of that. But as soon as the lightning stops, we're going on."

"Where? It's just going to get colder up here."

"I know. We'll just have to go back down. Here's an idea. Let's leave a whole lot of the bad stuff in this place. So if the Idayagans find it, they'll think we went up even higher. Who wants to plant clues leading up the path farther?"

"I will." Hal hugged his skinny knees against him. "I know how to make a false trail."

Han thumped him on the shoulder, and he smiled a little. "We'll get hot food made while you do that. We'll eat and sleep. And if the lightning isn't hitting the ground tomorrow, we'll go back down toward the pass, but zigzag."

"And move every time it rains?"

"And move every time it rains."

Night fell suddenly in the mountains.

Nowhere were fires lit. The Venn sat in their rows, on signal, as they had been doing. Talkar's scouts returned at midnight to report that the top of the pass lay two days' march ahead, no sign of any enemy.

Just before sunset Noddy's and Hawkeye's scouts returned with the news that the top of the pass lay two bends ahead.

For the first time, the Marlovans camped instead of rolling drearily upward, changing horses four times a night. They had saddle-slept, others creeping into the wagons until the animals slowed, to be summarily turfed out. Many had put on a grim burst of speed, just to drop onto a rock and snore until the rest caught up.

Food was passed out, horses unhitched and cared for, then exhausted men and animals slept, the wagons with six and eight crammed in.

Up on the mountain above the pass, Inda and his party stopped on the trail as soon as the last of the light vanished. No one wanted to fall down the side of a cliff, so they settled with their backs to a broad stretch of rock, looking out at the jagged mountaintops blocking the lower reaches of the canopy of stars.

Tau sat above the others on a rock, paper aimed westward to catch the last faint gleams of twilight, and wrote:

> *Jeje. If I survive, will I remember anything of this dash down the mountains, my skull rocking on my neck, my leg muscles long bands of pain? Maybe I'll remember silly things: the slap of bare feet on a trail probably two thousand years old, the occasional yelp or curse when a barefoot man treads on a rock. The sight of drying socks flapping gently from the backs of packs at each step—every stop, the ones with boots change out their socks. Some of them have bloody toenails. If they live, will they bore their grandchildren with stories about those bloody toenails? At least the stars are out, which means no rain. It gets cold very fast this high.*

On the other side of the pass, Cama's men, filthy and stinking despite regular dousings of rain, marched across a plateau under starlight; most of them had long since resorted to bare feet. They were beyond exhaustion and into exhilaration. Cama strode at their head, seemingly tireless, singing one war ballad after another in his low, raspy voice. On the south side of the lake, Cherry-Stripe's men were scrambling as fast as they could force themselves. Cherry-Stripe no longer thought about Inda, the plans, or the future. His entire life was focused on one thing: making sure Cama didn't beat him to the pass.

By midnight, with one last snow-pale peak between them and the pass, Cama's men were too tired to sing, but they could hum, and hum they did, until teeth and bones resonated. Over and over the "Hymn to the Beginning," a beat on each step, a hum that only ceased when Cama held up a fist and the Runners took out their meal and passed it down hand-to-hand.

Both armies chewed the heavy, sweet-stale journey bread whose recipes shared the same origin, generations before; the only material differences were the Marlovan addition of rye and raisins as opposed to the Venn tradition of honey and nuts.

Signi stirred, waking to a dry mouth, her head pounding. It took her a long time to sit up. Grateful for the soft summer air, she contemplated the stairs on the other side of the tower. *Come, Signi, come. Twelve steps at most.*

She tried to stand, fell to her knees, crawled forward, then rested her damp forehead against her trembling wrists. Then again. Rest. Again.

The stars had wheeled halfway across the sky before she reached the stairs leading down to the first landing. Then it was easier to descend on hands and knees, seeking each step out with her toes, resting, then easing herself down. Step. By. Step.

But she made it. The door to the top room was open as it had been left. Though her knees had begun to bruise and her palms to ache, she crawled inside. The room was plain, empty but for a narrow bed: here, they said, the young king had slept so that he might have nearer access to the archive below.

She reached the bunk, fell in, and sank into slumber.

Tdor, have you heard from Inda or Evred since yesterday?

Hadand, you were in my mind all day. I just got in from perimeter ride. All I could think about was what is happening in the north. I confess I half wish we did not have these magical cases. Is it cowardice to admit that I hate knowing the battle is happening now? I hate it more because it is so quiet here that I can hear the robins scolding. It's like a mockery of peace. I don't feel peace, it's just the hush before lightning. Only would months' wait be any better?

Fareas-Iofre says to not look at records—they are all written later—but to letters sent during important times, they all speak of the agony of the wait. But I have had no time for the archive. We're making certain we have defense coordinated between the harbor and here, which means a lot of riding between Castle Tenthen and the Noths for me. On my return I have to undo all Branid's worst orders, because he's trying so hard to drill the men and be ready, he's become nearly impossible. Yet he tries so hard! I can't be angry!

O Tdor, if you are a coward, than I am one too. We are trying to do everything that must be done, but today was the very worst Fourthday of the games in my life. Not once, not twice, but three times I saw that everyone was watching me for a sign. My eyes took in those boys and girls competing down there, but all my mind could think about was—just to you I will confess it wasn't Evred I kept seeing. And I didn't see Inda, either. He's so blurred in my mind, sometimes old but mostly a young boy, despite his day here.

What I saw was Tanrid, and me, that day so long ago. How happy we were! Then I lost the siege, and he rode away to be killed by my betrothed—

No. I'm done. I gave the boys and girls the accolade out of guilt, and the watchers shouted out of duty. Everyone felt it, I feel sure. They cheered but did not smile. Even the boys and girls looked as if punishment awaited them, not praise.

Hadand, here is my idea. If we are being foolish, let us be foolish together. I will do my rounds, and you do

*your rounds, and then we will sit here with these magic
boxes all night if need be, and we will do nothing but
reminisce. We will not talk about what if, we will not
plan a campaign for next year. We will look back, not
forward, until we get news.*

**Tdor, that's a promise. I'm yours as soon as they
ring Lastwatch and I oversee the shift change. Everyone seems to like it when I do the Harskialdna's sentry watch station rounds, just as Evred had begun
doing before he left.**

Rain slanted down from mast-scraping clouds when the
lookout shouted, "Sail hai!"

Gillor rode the northernmost station closest to the island of Geranda, a very faint line on the horizon just off
the beam. She waved to the flag hand to let the rest of the
fleet know they'd spotted someone, then climbed up the
foremast herself.

She'd just snapped her glass out when someone yelled,
"Them walleyed masts . . . It's gotta be *Blue*!"

A wash of rain blew on, leaving sharp and clear the slightly
forward-leaning foremast and straight mainmast. Gillor
smacked the glass to. "That's *Blue Star*," she said. "We must
be clearing the rain now. They have to be able to see us."

Sails frantically jerked up on the distant ship.

"Thinks we're Scarf's *Princess*," Gillor said, sneering on
the word *princess.* Some of the crew laughed—the sneer
had become habit.

"Wait! Wait, wait, they're haulin' round."

"Heh." Imagine calling a pirate ship *Princess*! Gillor
liked the fancy work all over her new command just fine,
but she'd gotten rid of that ridiculous figurehead with the
crown, leaving just the rail scrollwork and nice, clean hull
planking. *Death* and *Cocodu* and *Sable* didn't have figure-
heads, so she wouldn't have one either, though she would
have liked something with crossed swords.

"He's raising a signal," the flag hand yelled. "Free
traders' flag below the parley."

"Run the same," Gillor yelled as she lowered herself to the masthead. "Signal the rest of the fleet. See if Fox wants to talk to 'em himself or what." And she slid down to the deck.

The *Death* signaled back for her to close with the newcomer, so she did, smiling when she recognized Captain Fangras, grayer but otherwise much the same as she remembered from the old days in Freeport Harbor, as he clambered aboard.

"Captain Fangras," she said in welcome as he flicked his fingers in salute to the captain's deck. He was an independent-turned-privateer who'd given Inda's marine band a cruise when they were just starting out. "I've got something to drink in the cabin."

Fangras' lips pursed appreciatively. "I take it Elgar got rid of Scarf, and a better job I never heard of, save Marshig being shoved back to Nightland with the soul-eaters, where he belonged." He jerked his thumb aft, where the new name was painted on the stern, and said in a lower voice, "*Rapier*? Are you by chance a Fal?"

She crossed her arms. "What makes you say that?"

Fangras turned a laugh into a cough. "Pirate fighting, dueling weapon, Fal, it seemed to fit together."

It fit together if you knew that rapiers were the required weapon for duels in Fal. "You from there?" she asked, ready for that sense of kinship that comes of unexpected encounters with countrymen, even far from the home you will never see again.

"No! That is to say, yes, but I don't think of myself as any Fal, not for thirty years!" His hands went out. "I left to get away from them and their everlasting quarrels. Now, was that the *Wind's Kiss* out there beyond Elgar's *Death*? We'd heard that that sorry crew'd turned outright pirate after Sarendan revoked the letters of marque 'gainst Khaner-enth. Mistake, if you ask me."

Despite Fangras' obvious attempt to smooth over the insult and shift the talk to sea gossip, she ground her teeth hard against a retort. And then had to laugh at herself. She'd left Fal because of those very same everlasting quarrels, yet here she was, arm already reaching for her side, the ritual words almost shaping her lips to call him out for an insult that wasn't even an insult. Because it was true.

So she said, "Yes, that's *Wind's Kiss*. We took them just off the tip of Toar, which we cleaned up for five years' berth privilege at Pirate Island. That was right after we got rid o' Scarf."

"Wish you'd do for that crew that took the Windward Islands. Moved right in, sitting on the west-end trade routes—"

"We did. Just came from there. That is, last action. We stopped out here to preddy up. Listen, before you give me the news about Sarendan and Khanerenth and Scarf, let's talk in comfort, what say?" She indicated her cabin. And when the door was shut, and the scuttles closed, "First, were you layin' for us?"

Fangras signed agreement. "Dhalshev paid me'n a couple others to polish the roads where you might come in. Here, south o' Sartor, he even sent someone up to the strait. Word is, now't Khanerenth has made peace with Sarendan, they're going to launch the navy against Freedom Islands. They may be on the way right now."

"Shit," she exclaimed. "And we're being called in to help defend?"

Fangras spread his hands. "That's the sved."

Gillor eyed him. "And so what's in it for you? I can't believe you are running Dhalshev's errands—oh. Yes. Right. If Sarendan revoked the letters of marque . . ."

". . . That's right," Fangras said. "Rest of us privateers either have to turn pirate or find someone else. There's no trade, not with the Venn threatening every harbor with fire and sword if they stick a toe out into the sea. So we're looking to join your fleet."

"All right, we gotta talk to Fox."

Fangras started to rise, then sank back down. "Fox? What Fox? Elgar the Fox, or that redheaded, green-eyed icicle Fox?"

"That would be Fox, yes," Gillor said, laughing.

Fangras rubbed his face. "Oh, damn."

"You got something against Fox's fighting skills?"

"Oh, not his fighting skills. Everyone on Freedom knows no one stands up to him. Some said even he can beat Inda Elgar. But . . . he's not Inda Elgar, who never loses a battle. Can Fox command one?"

Gillor thought of Fox sitting on the flagship the way he'd been the last day or so, drinking steadily, so angry you felt it like a blow just walking past his cabin. Never mind why—he wouldn't tell anyone—but how did he *do* that?

"Inda left him in command, and we haven't lost yet. As you noticed comin' in." She pointed through the stern windows at *Wind's Kiss,* and then down at the deck under her feet. "Come on, we'll row ourselves over. You talk to him."

Chapter Twenty

LONG before dawn, Hawkeye and Noddy woke. They were cold and exhausted from bad sleep, but they had reached the top of the pass first.

Now to hold it.

They must hold it with five hundred men and an army of straw.

The intermittent, rumbling din and faint clashes echoing up the stone canyons made it clear the Venn were somewhere near, maybe a day or two away at most. As soon as the light was up, Hawkeye took a couple of scouts and dogs to explore the downward slope and see how much time they had.

Noddy strolled back, watched by men who'd been straining forward, peering at the cliffs on the downward slope. A glance showed that most were still stupid with sleep, others peered back looking squalid in the way of men who had, under cover of night, taken comfort or consolation in various ways, one of which Noddy could smell. Five years ago a whiff of stale distilled rye would have caused the Harskialdna to assemble the men for a flogging, even on the eve of battle. Noddy pretended he didn't smell it, though his unsmiling glance as he passed by the dry-tongued culprits with pounding heads was judgment enough.

Noddy had grown up thinking human beings absurd, though he liked some of them as individuals. He loved few people—his family, his old mates—and few things, one of which was the idea of trust. He loathed war and tended to despise anyone who admired or craved it. But since that admiration or craving seemed to be a part of most of his friends, well, one came back to human absurdity.

When in doubt, you speak to the absurd, but act up to the ideal.

He kicked the wheel of the nearest wagon. "Still in the rack. Are you made of straw?"

A guffaw crashed in echo between the cliffs.

"Roust up. Drill time! Anyone slacking in the hay gets ninety-nine lashes."

More laughter, the high, sharp laughter of people who know through tightened muscles and tense jaws that it's here, it's soon, this muddy, mossy canyon is where they would make their stand.

"Army! To your mounts!" Noddy shouted, flicking straw in the nearest wagon.

He was answered with a roar as men leaped to the wagons and began making straw men. Noddy continued on down the line so everyone could see him, hear him.

"Where are your guts?" Noddy slammed a hand against another wagon, making the entire contents jump. "You got grass for brains? Grass prick, for certain. I've never seen anything so limp this side of the Venn."

More of the harsh laughter of emotional release as everyone got busy stuffing their good shirts and House battle-tunics. Then their secondary clothes, and when they ran out of those, they fashioned man-shaped forms out of bits of rope and blankets. Amid the laughter, people shouted increasingly coarse jokes as everyone tried to make up a name for the straw army that the others would heed. Breath froze and dropped, then clouded, and then vanished as sunlight slowly warmed the high cliffs above with color. The men had woken with numb fingers, but they were sweating by the time they got all the remounts armored with the link-reinforced leddasweave horse covers and the straw men firmly affixed to them, the hems of the battle-tunics sewn to ropes and tied to the armor belly-bands.

Ribald comments put a wall of mirth between them and what tomorrow or the day after might bring as the men personalized the straw figures wearing their clothing. Noddy watched from the driving bench of the cook wagon, where he'd hopped up to grab something to eat. As soon as the men became restless he'd have them run some mounted drills in order to get used to a charge between walls. But no fighting drills. He wanted them rested and ready. They were as trained as they were ever going to be.

The shadows on the western cliffs had sunk to the ground and the sun peeked at last over the eastern cliffs, boiling down onto their heads. Noddy climbed down, strolling among the straw men, addressing them as if they were alive.

The jokes were stupid—accusations of drunkenness, of impossible sexual feats, and he promised them insane punishments to be dealt out the moment the fighting was over. Men howled with laughter at a sentence of a thousand lashes for a crooked hair clasp, their hilarity just a little breathless, just a little loud. Noddy could smell the sharpness of fear in the air—they all could. But everyone worked hard to hide it.

Last, they shoved bent arrows and sticks wrenched from the wagons down the backs of the straw men in order to hold up helms. And when it was done, and they led the re-mounts back behind the animals selected for the actual charges, the effect was surprisingly lifelike.

The straw army was light enough to leave on the horses' backs. Buckets of water from one of the many trickle-downs, carried from horse to horse, became the main job, as they waited for Hawkeye to tell them *when*.

Jeje: we caught our first glimpse of the pass midafter-noon. The unreal is becoming real—a thought yet un-

*real. Does that makes sense? Don't answer that—weak
joke—I know you won't answer. Why?*

Tau sent the note and straightened as the others lined up
along the extreme edge of the cliff edge, trusting to the
screening effect of a tangle of firs. They ate journey bread
and peered down into the distant canyon in the pass. Steep
cliffs, yes, and narrow access. There were the Venn, marching in perfect order, winged helms on the commanders, the
men with steel or brass horns the breadth of a palm at either side of their helms. Inda wondered what the symbol-
ism of wings and horns were. Maybe the horns were
practical, to catch downward striking blades?

The question fled when he got a glimpse of the commander's chest just before he rode out of sight. Was that an
owl? This owl flew in the opposite direction of the silver
owl of Inda's own family, the Algara-Vayirs, but was that
device green? The sun dazzle muted color.

Is he some sort of relative from centuries ago? Inda felt as
if he stood in some strange place outside of time hearing owl
hooting to owl across the grassy plains of their ancestors.

"We've got a long way to go," Evred said.

And they were in motion once again.

Rattooth Cassad slammed the rough stable door open.
"Venn're coming back. Should be here midafternoon. Harbormaster's following me," he added, jerking his thumb
over his shoulder.

Buck and Barend sat in the converted tack room that
had served the Marlovans as their garrison headquarters,
just outside Lindeth Harbor. The patrols had rotated in
and out of Ala Larkadhe, half a day's ride away, so—with
wood a precious and increasingly rare commodity after
years of pirate incursions—the "garrison" had never been
more than a barn made into a stable, the tack room doubling as a rudimentary office, with a few beds for injured
men or for sleeping over during blizzards.

Now the converted barn was the command post for Barend's and Buck's combined forces. The animals were all outside on guarded pickets, the stalls full of wounded men from the failed defense of the coast.

They'd posted four rings of guards on the animals. Galloping horses could not be chased by men on foot, so they'd managed to get away clear, returning only after the Venn had all marched off to Ala Larkadhe.

They'd faced the grim chore of crossing that wrecked, blood-blackened beach to gather their hacked-up wounded after the commanders Disappeared their dead. They sang the "Hymn to the Fallen" until their throats were raw, the men around them singing or humming with them.

As the sun dropped below the sea they rode to the outskirts of Lindeth, the exhausted men and horses drinking from the streams swollen from the runoff up the mountain. Everyone was too tired to ask why the streams ran so high when there had been no rain for two days.

They bedded down around the garrison outpost.

At dawn, Rat had insisted on scouting himself. The other two agreed on the condition that he take a tough runner from each wing as backup.

Now they were back, and Rat waved an ironic hand toward the open door, through which they could see a gaunt old man picking his way soberly through the lines of wounded stretched out on the hastily-swept floor. The worst hurt were inside, the ones who could manage to sit or move about had been put on the grassy hills with the rest of the camp.

The harbormaster's furrowed face seemed to age as he took in the number of wounded. He stopped just outside the tack room door, and the three commanders watched him run a knobby hand over his sparse hair.

Then he drew in a deep breath. His scrawny chest expanded beneath the linen tunic that, like his dark robe, was part of his clothes of office.

It took courage to face these martial young men in their blood-spattered gray coats. But he was desperate. "Don't fight in my city," he said in the slurred Iascan of the north. "Please," he added, though more than half the angry people waiting back at his house had insisted he not beg the evil Marlovans.

"Your? City?" Buck repeated, powerful arms crossed.

Barend waved him off. "You're in trouble whichever way you turn, Harbormaster." He'd had several meetings with the man over the past year. The former guild mistress had been the Marlovans' most determined enemy, but the harbormaster had deferred time and again to her in his attempts to find a middle ground between conquerors and the older inhabitants.

Rat propped a foot up on a barrel and leaned his forearms on his knee, wriggling his shoulder blades to ease the pull of a long cut over his ribs on his back. "You really think they'll leave you alone if you let 'em in?"

The harbormaster said, "Do you think they'll go on a killing spree, then, Marlovan?"

Rat was indifferent to the sarcasm. "No. What they'll do is boot you out of the few standing houses you've got, because they're going to need space to bring in men and supplies for the second invasion next year. Though they might keep a few of you to work for 'em, but you'll be living in your own barns."

"Invasion? *Next* year?" the man said, appalled.

Buck snorted. "This here is just a welcome party. Next year they're coming back. And not just with these fellows. They'll bring more of 'em from the north. They need food, they need cloth, they need wood and steel, above all, they need workers and warriors. You'll be the workers." He jabbed his finger within a hair's breadth of the old man's chest. Then jerked his thumb at his own chest. "We're supposed to be the warriors. The word is, they have some kind o' magical spells that make your mind go blank, so they can run us clear to Sartor, and it's you people who'll be busy making the supplies."

The harbormaster stared, eyes distended. Then they narrowed, and his face flushed to the tips of his ears. "You're lying, Marlovan."

"So you think we're here watching our brethren die for the fun of it?"

"That's exactly what we thought," the man said, though without the conviction he might have used before treading through that room outside. That and hearing at dawn a private report of the horror of the south shore. His breath hissed in and he rubbed his hands over his head again. "You're protecting what you've already taken. And I suppose it's understandable, and you've not used us unfairly. But no one wants you fighting in our streets, or worse, setting fire to the entire city just to keep 'em out. As it is, you've destroyed the docks."

"And who will have to pay for rebuilding it?" Barend retorted.

Rat straightened up, wincing. Terrible fight yesterday, fast gallop this morning, the bandage was leaking. His coat was already ruined.

But he grinned, his prominent front teeth making him look fierce. "What if we only seem to set fire to your city?"

"What?"

"What?"

"Hah?"

He lifted a hand toward the shore, trying not to pull the open wound on his back. "Still haven't got all the fires out. Right? I saw smoke when riding in to report."

"That's so," the harbormaster said, adding dryly, "When you people set fire to something, you're as thorough as the pirates ever were."

"Hey—" Buck began.

Barend waggled a hand. "Never mind. What are you thinking, Cousin?"

"That we keep those fires going," Rat said. "From the ocean it's got to look like the entire city's aflame. Inda told us they have magic communications. That Venn mage o' his said so."

"Venn mage?" the harbormaster repeated, wondering if that shocking rumor could be true after all.

No one paid him any attention. Rat said, "Which means the fellows coming here got to see a burning city from this end, see?"

"You mean, make it look like all of Lindeth's gone up in flames?" Buck said, and whistled.

"That's it." Rat turned to the harbormaster. "We'd need your cooperation. We have maybe a watch or so before they reach us. So it has to be now if we're to do it."

Barend chuckled. "Oh, a watch ought to do it easily." He did not say that he knew some pirate ruses for making fires look far worse than they were.

The harbormaster huffed. "You won't be setting fire to the city?"

Barend raised his hand, palm out, in a gesture of promise. "You tend the fires yourselves. Just keep them going, lots of smoke, like I show you, and they won't set foot in Lindeth."

"Ourselves?" the harbormaster said, bushy white brows raised. "What will you be doing?"

"Riding over the white cliffs the back way. So when they turn around again to go upriver to the pass, well, they'll get their own welcome party."

"You don't have nearly enough men," the harbormaster protested.

Barend's grin faded. Rat looked sardonic. Buck widened his eyes. "We don't?"

The harbormaster kept shaking his head all the way back to his house, now crowded with frightened faces.

"We've got a plan," he said.

A thick cloud mass moved in on a strengthening wind. Just as the afternoon shadows began to lengthen the Venn smelled fire on the wind, and when they topped the highest hill before the gradual descent toward Lindeth Harbor, there was no harbor to be seen. Just a thunderhead of smoke over the entire city, glowing with flame.

Chapter Twenty-one

SIGNI woke before dawn. The headache was just a shade less murderous. She managed to rise and force her shaky legs to bear her out of the room and down the stairs. She stopped on the landing outside the archive, and felt the door. It was closed: she bowed her head, accepting judgment.

She made her way slowly downstairs, trusting in the dim light and her rumpled, anonymous clothing to draw little attention. The few awake paid her no heed. They were too shocked, too weary, and wondering where to begin cleaning up the sodden remains of the city. Not one of the few people moving about the castle that morning noticed a small, sandy-haired woman of indeterminate origin.

She drifted to the kitchen. In the light of a single lamp, she found less devastation than she'd feared. Certainly everything on ground level or below was ruined, but the water had left the bags, jars, and jugs on shelves above table height untouched, and tightly-made barrels had also survived.

She helped herself to some heels of the day before's bread and a hunk of cheese. She felt much better, enough to set to work. She was a sea dag. Most of her spells pertained to water in some way.

The morning sun had crowned the distant hills and the summer air was hot enough to spoil wet things when her spells began to take effect. In a reversal of the calling spell she evaporated pools and puddles, compressed water out of wood and cloth, sending it all back to the underground river. The dank smell diminished, leaving dry detritus for the citizens to clean up.

Signi found her way to the lazaretto. Her second set of skills was in healing. She knew she would be needed that day.

Hilda Battle Chief (newly promoted) Vringir's mood was vile when the sun came up. Overhead a blanket of low clouds promised stifling air later; it already smelled of smoke drifting from the still-burning city.

The thud of horse hooves caused his head to pang. All night long horsemen had attacked his camp: a flurry of galloping hooves and arrows, then they dashed away into the darkness. The Marlovans were far too fast to chase even if he'd had enough horses.

He issued the command to rouse the camp. The second half of the landing party had been ordered to share out their journey bread, which had been meant to get them through the first day. Instead, half rations would have to suffice until his scouting parties could gather food from the countryside and meet up with them.

They would have to march hungry, but march they must. He glared in the direction of Ala Larkadhe's white tower, hazily outlined against the rising sun, the battlements of the walls just visible. If anyone came riding out of the gates of Ala Larkadhe, there'd be no mercy this time.

He nodded at the signal ensign, who blatted the horn. The men rose and prepared to march alongside the river to the mouth of the pass.

When it was just barely light enough to make out figures, Evred woke with a snort. An Inda-shaped shadow stood in the middle of the trail, head slightly bent.

"Inda?"

The shadow straightened up. "Can you see me?"

"Barely."

The sound of their voices roused the others.

"Then I can see the trail. I've been wondering if I can or I just think I can."

Evred did not try to make sense of this. He got to his feet. "Let's go."

They emerged through a mossy natural archway onto an outcropping where the stone foundation of a tiny house sat looking over what once had been a spectacular panorama.

Thump. Thump. Thump. The tramp of many feet echoed up the stone canyons. Evred had thought the thumping was just the ever-present headache; he became aware that it was external.

They couldn't see the pass, only a wider gap in the rocky cliffs and crags. But they certainly could hear the army marching up the last leg of the pass toward the top.

They stopped at one of the many little waterfalls and drank, then shared out one of their travel loaves. Finally, with a luxurious whispering of cloth, Evred pulled out his heavy silken battle-tunic, golden light running along the embroidery, the silk itself glowing like the heart of a fire. "I think we'd better get ready," he said.

Inda grinned, sat down, pulled on socks and boots. Then stood up, wiggling his toes and rocking back and forth to get used to footgear again. "Tau?"

"Right here." Tau pulled from his pack the neatly folded battle-tunic that he and Vedrid had made.

Inda hadn't thought about clothing for so long, he felt strange as he took off his coat. Tau lifted the battle-tunic over Inda's upraised arms. His chain mail bunched at the shoulders, then lay flat again, jingling as the cool silk rustled down around him. He looked down, his rubies winking at his cheeks, then up. "I look like a hothouse fan dancer." And he swung his narrow hips from side to side.

The men nearby laughed heartily, for there could not possibly be any vaster a difference between a daintily and alluringly dressed pleasure house performer and this powerful, hard-bodied, scar-faced fellow with the king's eagle spread so splendidly across his chest, piratical earrings glinting. His total lack of strut won favor in their eyes— even if it did not in his king's.

But only Tau observed the quick contraction of Evred's features. Once again Evred had been moving with that ritual deliberation, signifying an internal scale of meaning of which Inda was unaware. But his expression shuttered again. "Let's run."

When Durasnir emerged from his cabin ready to begin the day, he found Dag Ulaffa waiting, eyes closed, hands together.

No one else was in the little breakfast alcove. Durasnir looked from his message case to Ulaffa, who gave a single shake of the head. "Erkric is not here," he said. "The prince sleeps. In the south, they are marching toward the pass." And then, "The clash will be in the north this day. Valda found a place if you wish to observe our people and the Marlovans meeting in the pass."

Durasnir did not wish to, but once again he felt the conviction that he *must* be there. Through the roots, the trunk, the mighty branches—people, culture, kingship—came meaning. Though roots were uplifted, the great tree twisted and cracked, and the branches shed leaves into the fires of ambition so that everything around him burned, he had to see.

Why? Perhaps his real motivation was only the military hatred of being taken by surprise. Simple curiosity.

Immaterial. He was not going to question anymore. "Please take me there," he said.

Chapter Twenty-two

HAWKEYE'S and Noddy's men heard the Venn approaching long before they saw them. The sound was intermittent because of the thick, swirling fog. But the animals knew they were there; ears twitched, heads tossed, forefeet plunged.

Noddy and Hawkeye waited side by side in the middle of the second row of lancers. The fifty in front were the biggest, toughest dragoons on the toughest horses. The wings of the second line were the next toughest. The honor of riding to either side of the commanders had been hotly contested, though a couple of them had not been able to hide little signs of relief when they were not picked. Maybe only Noddy noticed because he was paying attention: though all protested, some vehemently, there was just that lightening of the voice, the easing of tense faces, that betrayed the stubborn body that wanted to live.

Wanted to *live*.

In the realm of the spirit few can hide thoughts. As the Venn marched up the last distance, Noddy and Hawkeye fell silent, but their inner voices were clear to any who had the ability, and the interest, to listen.

Hawkeye had never told anyone that the urge to fight made him hot. All the others saw was smiling, fierce alertness, as he checked the placement of archers behind two lines of straw men, then more straw men and the stronger archers. His lust for battle being real lust, well, it sometimes bothered him—felt wrong, somehow, except wasn't he a fighting man? If he knew the fight was honorable, then it couldn't be wrong, could it?

Back in the academy days, he'd loved fights until Gand pulled him aside one day after lance practice and pointed out that broken bones and teeth on our side was doing the enemy's work for them, right? So Hawkeye had ceased scrapping, saving his martial ardor for a real enemy.

He'd got that when he faced pirates on the Nob. Battle was far better than scrapping, he'd discovered. But it had been over far too fast.

Now, at last, here were the Venn.

"Fog! Came down to help us, eh?" Hawkeye laughed, clapping a man on the shoulder as he rode down the lines in inspection, then he passed through the last line of lancers and reached the first line of the fake army. "Hey, straw man, where's your prick? Who built this one? Tlennen, get over here, give him yours. Who'li notice the difference?"

A shout of laughter amid hoots and jibes at the grinning Tlennen. Hawkeye rode back and forth, horsetail swinging, handing out insults mostly, but the tone was one of comradeship, and the laughter felt good.

Men took courage at the sight of his flashing smile, the ring of anticipation in his voice, the strut in his moves. He was not yet thirty, tall and tough and handsome, looking like he was riding off to Heat Street and not to a battle where he was outnumbered a hundred to one.

The men scattered among the straw army were under orders to yell and wave weapons, to look like more than one man. "We couldn't have asked for a better day," he said to another who kept chewing his lips, which were revealingly chapped and red.

Yes we could, Noddy thought. *A good day would be me at home, eating breakfast with my wife and cousin before we plan the day's work. Watching my boy drool. Chasing the colts around the paddock before the watch changes.* He had done his best, but he couldn't resign himself to certain death. He couldn't fight off the sickening conviction that Inda's plan was a shambles, that no one was where he was supposed to be—except for himself, Hawkeye, five hundred men, and how many thousand Venn?

Oh, yes. Five hundred men and a whole lot of horses and men of straw.

The *whisht!* of arrows was the first sign of battle. *Damn the wait,* Noddy thought, and was surprised at a small spurt of relief. The inevitable was here at last. He'd soon be too busy for regret.

"Helms!" Hawkeye shouted, one hand winding up his horsetail, the other thumping his helm over his head.

The men unhooked their helms, shoved their hair up inside to further cushion their heads, settled the helms down tightly over their ears. Though they'd all complained about their heaviness, the heat, no one complained now.

"Shields up!"

Conk! Plink! Clang!

Indistinct movement in the gray murk resolved slowly into tall figures, square shields, spears. Swords. Horned helms. Rank on rank of them, more shadows than shapes: a hundred men across, for Talkar had never liked how messily charges ended on the plains, and here they were in a terrain that couldn't be more different.

When in doubt, fight the way you know how.

A horn winded weirdly, and a rustling hum became the hissing rush of arrows. Noddy jerked up his shield. Four, five clunks jolted his arm.

The straw men jerked as arrows pierced them.

Cold fear washed through Noddy, followed by wordless rage when a shot, either better aimed than most, or carried by errant wind, struck his own Runner, who'd begged and pleaded to ride at his left. The boy clutched at his neck, then toppled away from Noddy's reaching hand and vanished.

"Lances!" Hawkeye shouted. "Archers high!"

Right arms brought up lances, heels locked down hard

behind the stirrups. Horses, trained, began the deliberate walk forward, muscles bunched for the expected command to leap to the gallop. Archers brought back arms, points high, a straight line from arrow tip to back elbow.

"Archers: loose! Second line: lances!"

From the Marlovans arced a lethal hissing of arrows. The front ranks of the Venn serried under the impact, but kept moving forward. Noddy's heartbeat thundered in his ears.

The second line fell in step, slow at first, then more rapidly; the horses' ears pricked, tails flicked, one whinnied as the third line formed up behind them.

The Venn blatted horns, the sound echoing like wailing ghosts. *Thump, clatch!* The men shifted, standing square, the big square shields braced and tight one against the other in a wall. They used round shields in the back ranks, but the front had extra heavy metal shields, locked edge to edge by big men with powerful arms, the only difference being no swords spiking between each shield for they wanted horses, they were ordered to just kill the riders. Their second row formed up on their heels.

"Hold," Hawkeye warned, eyes forward now, gauging. "Hold . . . hold . . ."

And when the enemy was a hundred strides off he shouted, "Charge!"

The front row's horses sprang to the gallop. "Yiyiyiyi yip yip yip!" Hawkeye shrieked, a high, harrowing cry, the sound picked up by the men in a shrill and savage echo.

The front of the Venn lines faltered as those behind shoved forward; the ranks shifted just before the thudding crack and smash of fifty lances striking shields, helms, chest plates.

"Charge!"

And it worked the way Inda had drilled them: the first line was still even, fighting furiously as the second line galloped up and neatly as a comb passed the first line and smashed into the Venn front lines, driving them back some twenty paces.

Many of the lances splintered. Hawkeye's did not, and

he wielded it with enormous strength, screeching, "Yip! Yip! Yip!"

"Yip! Yip! Yip!" the terrible shriek was taken up behind, the canyons echoing it back.

Venn front liners lost balance and fell, to be trampled under the feet of their own forces, far too tightly packed. The lancers used their spear-tipped weapons until they broke, and then out came the curve-tipped swords and the powerful downward strokes.

The captain of the third line shouted, "Charge!"

They hit with a thundering smash, driving the Venn ten more paces back: the Venn at the rear had stood fast, making a press as lethal an enemy as the Marlovan warriors. Men fought to stay upright, fought just for air.

The mass shoved against Talkar's struggling mount. He peered through the arrows, the weapons, the swirls of vapor: he had vastly underestimated the power of a charge. You couldn't really charge your own men in drill—

"Kill the horses!" Talkar shouted, but not even his ensign, separated by fifty shouting men, could hear him over the din.

There was no more thinking, just the whirl and judder of sword and shield, the plunging of horses, the flying of mud, while the slowly emerging rays of sun beat down on steel helms.

For longer than they believed they could, the Marlovans shoved the Venn down the incline, perhaps a hundred paces in all. For that length of time the Venn did not see anything beyond the high point but horses' heads and waiting men, shadowy and ill-defined, some shooting, some waiting for attack.

But then the lancers began to fall. Talkar grinned in satisfaction as Marlovans with hacked joints toppled from horses to disappear under the melee. Waiting hands gripped the riderless horses and muscled them inside the Venn lines. Just as well no one heard the order, Talkar decided, and did not reissue it. *Now just bring us a few thousand more—*

Another massive surge: the yellow-haired Marlovan

commander, his teeth flashing as he laughed, had rallied the remainder of his front lines into one, this time joining it himself and together, stirrup to stirrup, the horses reared and threw the Venn front line back into more chaos.

Talkar shot his arm up in the signal for "form attack circles."

Venn horns blatted with angry insistence, and Talkar urged his horse forward as he whacked the flat of his blade against helms to get the men into bands to surround each rider.

Noddy yelled something, lost in the noise, but his tip of the chin alerted his trumpeter, who sounded the retreat. The horses plunged, kicking out, biting, smashing with forefeet, forcing the humans back so the animals could go with their fellows.

The surviving lancers backed out of the surge to reform their lines and the Venn—directed by the mournful howl of horns in a new pattern—stamped, locked shields together, and charged uphill.

Hawkeye stopped his chargers at the top of the slope.

Runners brought fresh lances from the back. When the Venn were twenty paces off, the horses charged. They were tired, but a short charge downhill still packed power.

Again the lances smashed hard into the Venn shield wall. The Venn horns bleated. The men in the center of the shield wall performed a rapid retreat before those lances and the wing men scrambled along the canyon walls to flank the Marlovan horsemen.

Hawkeye and Noddy made their horses rear, followed by the others. The animals struck out with hooves. When the horses came down, their riders' slashing blades hummed through the air, cutting and hacking at the press of Venn.

Unbidden, the men from the back abandoned their ruse with the wagons and formed into a rough and ready line, sighting on Hawkeye and Noddy.

Noddy glanced back, saw them, and jabbed his sword skyward in the command to charge.

The line serried as the flanking Venn surged out of the way, exposing the Marlovan lancers, who had lost all semblance of order. The new chargers turned to one another for clues and then it was every man for himself as Venn pressed on them, trying to surround each mounted man.

Hawkeye laughed, kicking shields, striking down with maddening speed and force at the forest of swords around him. "Yip! Yip! Yip!"

"Yip! Yip! Yip!"

For a time he held the front by force of will and speed of blade, surrounded by his personal Runners tight on either flank. No one got past those three.

But on one wing five horseman went down under a concerted attack, and the Venn, running over the top of the high point, discovered the straw army.

The cry shrilled back through the ranks, "Ruse! Ruse!"

Talkar grunted in surprise. The straw men had probably taken most of the covering arrows. Smart move. But—

A series of images followed by a new idea: were they as lamentably shorthanded as their brethren on the far side of the pass? If so, would a spearhead attack be more effective?

Talkar scowled impatiently up at the cliffs. On the east side they were impossibly high, rugged at the top. But no one could scale those heights. And behind the cliffs, bodies of water made army access even more impossible. There was no getting an army up there, not without a year to prepare.

He peered more closely at the Andahi River side, which was rockier, full of chasms and cracks. Maybe there was some kind of—

He motioned to his Scout Chief. "Take a look along the western face here. If there's a way up, I want you to get high. Count the Marlovans."

Another charge, another roar, this one bright with howls of laughter as the Venn knocked down the straw men, grappling for the plunging horses. The real Marlovans abandoned the straw men and formed up for a desperate last charge—

"Yip! Yip! Yip!" Hawkeye screamed.

"Yip! Yip! Yip!" Horsemen erupted through the middle of the straw army, the last of Noddy's and Inda's dragoons, striking hard into the Venn warriors. But the Venn were over the top now, and it was the Marlovans' turn to be forced backward, step by step, downhill.

Hawkeye was closed in by the forest of steel.

"Yip! Yip! Yip!" His fox cry rose to a nerve-ripping shriek, and screeches answered him—primal cries like the terrifying shrills of predator birds—

From the heights.

"Yip! Yip! Yip!"

Arrows whirred down and smacked with liquid thuds into Venn. Eyes on both sides lifted skyward at the impassable stone walls to discover men lining the tops of the cliffs. One of them carried a huge pennon, just visible in the swirling mist: a crimson-and-gold eagle.

"Inda!" Hawkeye yelled, teeth flashing—

And dropped his guard, just for that moment. A sword smashed the back of his elbow; as he lunged up in his saddle, another blade cut viciously behind the knee. He fell back onto the saddle as the swords struck again and again.

Noddy was breathing through his mouth, which cut down the stink of fear-sweat, blood, and death-voided bowels. Sorrow had flared into hatred and rage, directed at the horn-helmed men trying to kill him: beneath was rage at the senselessness of it all, the meaty crackings and thunks no one should ever have to hear as men he knew were smashed out of life one by one.

A flurry at his left—he lifted his head, arm poised to block—and a Venn longbowman took aim just under his upraised arm, shooting at the shadowy gap in the chain-mail sleeve under his tunic.

Noddy recoiled as white fire bloomed behind his eyes. He clutched at the arrow in his armpit, fighting for consciousness, bitter and furious that there was no hope after all. He swayed, fighting against his fading strength. Two Runners slashed and hacked in a frenzy to get near and catch him; one pulled him over the shoulders of his horse.

Rage pumped through Hawkeye, the hot glorious rage of intent. He took shield position behind the Runners, fighting off a circle of Venn, as arrows struck all around him. He'd lost use of his left arm and right leg, but he stayed in the saddle even so, laying about him at a crazed pitch.

Five, six, ten closed in; crimson blooms of pain blossomed once, again. He willed them all away, but his body no longer obeyed, and he slowed. Again and again he lifted the blade, and then once more. The roaring, rushing sound in his ears grew—

As he fell the sweet, brassy ripple of horns echoed down from the heights. Cama's men appeared on the eastern cliffs and began a furious barrage of arrows, each aimed with deadly precision.

And from behind.

Muddy to the eyebrows after four days of running, horses flecked with foam, Tuft and his men had arrived, the trumpeter blowing wildly.

"They're here," Hawkeye said, as his own Runner caught him, sobbing. "Evred. *Here.*"

"Charge!" Tuft roared, and horses thundered by, wild-eyed and sweating.

Blood ran from Hawkeye's mouth, but he didn't feel it, he only heard the horns, the horns of triumph. Evred was here—the Sier Danas were here, he was not alone . . . the bond of brethren . . .

With the words "Sing me" on his bloody lips, Hawkeye lost grip on his broken body, his mind winging through ethereal streamers of honor and glory until it winked out beyond the world.

"What?" Talkar shouted, trying to peer round the shields his own men raised to protect him against the deadly arrows.

"There! Is! A! Path! Up! The! Cliff!" one of his skirmish

chiefs shouted through cupped hands, pointing at the cliffs they'd recently gained. "It looks like their king is up there!"

Talkar waved his sword up at the men near that insolent eagle banner. "Take a Battlegroup—take two, or three— but kill him!"

The skirmish chief grinned, for here was eternal glory indeed. He waved out a Battlegroup of the best men to follow him, and they surged through their fellows toward the trail.

"See that?" Tau asked, pointing down at them with a fresh arrow, which he slapped to the bow and shot. It flew straight and true—and clattered against a helm before spinning away. Damn. "They're coming up to dance."

"Right." Inda swung his sword from hand to hand, loosening his arms. "You and me at the front. They can't come at us more than three across if we get to that turn in the trail right there and hold it. Rest of you keep the cover shots, one arrow one man." He turned to Evred. "You better stay up the path."

"No." Evred gestured toward a spot directly above the high point of the pass, and the clashing, roiling forces below. "I have to see."

Of course he did—he was the king. Even if he'd pitched hay by your side when you were ten years old.

Talkar watched from below as the pirate (identified by his ruby earrings) and his golden-haired companion in blue moved to a broad bend in the trail. This position kept a good fifty paces between them and the redhead in crimson, who had to be their king. The latter stood partially shielded by a large boulder from below. The king could obviously see in all directions from that vantage.

Talkar cursed, wishing he'd arrived just half a day earlier. He would have been able to get his men on those heights instead. He waited for his skirmishers to make

their way up, impatient with the lingering drifts of vapor
revealing and obscuring those crimson-clad figures.

His signal ensign came forward at that moment. "Battle
Chief Vringir is a watch's march from the pass." He held up
a slip of paper.

Talkar smiled for the first time in days.

Chapter Twenty-three

TUFT and his men formed an arrowhead wedge and charged over the lip straight into the Venn, a tight-packed, fury-driven attack that shoved the Venn back again, even as it scattered the remainder of Hawkeye's and Noddy's lancers, far too few of whom remained in the saddle, and not a single one unwounded.

Hay drifted through the air as straw men were flung aside and Tuft's men leaped into the saddles of the fresh remounts, ready on signal to launch with murderous force into the foot warriors. They'd seen their own dead. They saw Noddy, bleeding from the mouth, lifted to a cart.

The fog had almost burned off.

Men intent on killing one another were just barely aware that it was easier to see who you were striking.

Inda's band of archers loosed arrows down through the swirling vapors, guided by faint silver glimmers off metal helms and chest armor when the fog thinned.

Inda stood at the turning he'd chosen in the trail, amazed at the extraordinary sharpness and clarity of rock, water, sky. Those Venn pounding up the trail toward him seemed to move so slowly, the dust kicking up from their footsteps limned in pearlescent light. Each sound—the steady lump of his heart, the soft paff of the crimson banner that Vedrid was draping over a rock, the crunch of

Tau's heels in the dirt to Inda's left, his own breathing as he waited for those figures toiling so slowly up the trail—each sound so clear, so distinct. So purposeful.

He sucked in another breath, feeling his lungs fill and then empty. Each indrawn breath a pleasure, each exhalation a sigh of bliss.

Purpose.

The scintillation, the purity of sound, the elation of a sacred vow, it was his and yet not his. And when the coruscation glowed into brilliance around the silhouette of Evred, embodiment of the Marlovan kings, Inda thought, *Dun? Is that you?*

For Inda knew that no one else saw that aura around Evred, that it was a vision from the world of the spirit. For the first time Inda was aware of Dun looking through his own eyes, feeling with his hands, breathing with Inda's lungs. Now Dun would fulfill his vow, a double vow, for he protected not just Inda, but the king himself.

What Inda could not see was how Dun's own presence in the spirit realm fluoresced like a comet, drawing unseen watchers: one mirrored the light over and over again, creating an aurora of complicated luminosity until the watchers drifted away, leaving only that one with intent.

Strength flowed through Inda's veins, like liquid sun.

Then the skirmish chief, foremost of the eager Venn, reached Inda at last, and thrust his sword in a downward stroke. The two big men flanking the skirmish chief twisted to take powerful side cuts at Inda. All three had narrowed their purpose to one intent, to earn glory by striking down the Marlovan pirate Elgar the Fox.

Time jolted abruptly back into remorseless speed. Inda's sword ripped the air with a hissing moan. Impossibly fast, impossibly strong, three strokes killed the three leading Venn.

Hiss, clang—Tau dealt with numbers four and five.

Inda planted himself in the center of the trail's turning, his eyes wide and strange. He slowly whisked the sword back and forth, back and forth, as he waited for the next group of attackers. Inda that day was two men, one stand-

ing at the gate between the worlds of flesh and the spirit as
Inda and Dun both fought to protect the king.

Evred intended to watch the battle, but he could not
look away from Inda, who had captivated him once before
in the contest between the two fires. Now Evred saw what
only pirates had seen, the vicious concentration of deck
warfare, as Inda and Tau as his Shield Arm carved tirelessly
through flesh, sinew, and bone, Inda always knowing just
where to turn, where to strike.

Evred was not the only one who could not look away. As
the last of the mist vanished in a faint, glaring haze, Talkar
and his chiefs watched from underneath their upheld
shields, their intent focus drawing the interest of more men
in the back rows as they waited for give in the mass struggling uphill.

From across the canyon, Cama could just make out Inda,
faster than a darting serpent as he faced down a line of
Venn. "Inda!" he howled, a hunting wolf's howl, hoarse and
low, the sound instantly taken up by his dragoons as they
shot tirelessly, one arrow to a man.

"Inda!" Cherry-Stripe heard the cry just as he rounded
the last rocky spire. He slipped and tripped down the
arrow-length trail, crowded by his men.

Cherry-Stripe nearly fell in his effort to scan and run at
the same time. "We're right here," he yelled at Inda, who
was directly across the pass, just like the villagers had told
them. But too far away to hear. All right, then, let Inda *see*
that he was here! "Shoot," he bellowed over his shoulder.
He pulled his own bow. "Arrow to man, on that cliff!"

An arc of arrows hissed across the distance, and the
Venn line wavered as a dozen or so dropped on the trail
leading up to where Inda fought. Two Venn fell from the
sheer rocky cliff, dead before they tumbled into the air.

"In-DA!" Cherry-Stripe bellowed.

"In-DA!" His men took up the cry.

"In-DA!"

The rhythmic roar echoed around the pass. The sound,
the rhythm, heartened the Marlovans. With equal strength
and speed the shouted name disheartened the Venn. The

word "Trap!" followed it down the ranks: the Marlovans
had scaled the heights everyone had believed impossible,
and were shooting down from both sides of the pass as well
as charging from ahead. Despite the ceiling of shields, their
archers were finding chinks for their lethal rain.

Obviously they'd planned it, which suggested they had
entire armies of reinforcements hidden on the heights. The
Venn commanders exchanged questioning looks across the
sea of bobbing heads. If they had marched straight into a
trap, the only hope of the speedy resolution they had been
told to expect now lay with killing this king, and with
Vringir's flank attack up the pass from Ala Larkadhe.

Talkar beckoned to his ensign, but wrote the report himself in three scrawled sentences.

He sent it off then beckoned to another chief, pointing
toward the cliff as he shouted, "Get up there and take the
king!"

Shafts of sunlight widened between the departing
clouds, striking blood-bright glints in Inda's dancing rubies.
Sun glowed on the crimson battle tunic and in the splashes
of blood that gouted up as Inda and his blond shadow
scythed their way through men who tried to rush them, but
who fell lifeless from that cliff. Venn tried to shoot them,
but more Marlovans had edged themselves just below that
trail's bend, shields angled out to keep any arrows from
reaching Inda or Tau.

From his towering crag Fulla Durasnir witnessed it all,
how slowly, inexorably the attention of all but the mass of
Marlovans and Venn shoving back and forth at the lip of
the pass shifted toward those two in crimson and blue on
the trail turning, the one fighting glimmering faintly in reflected sunlight as if he had a sun-shadow at his shoulder.

"Inda! Inda! Inda!"

Vringir noted with sour relief that the foolish Marlovans
had withdrawn with dawn's light. As well. Though they

could not possibly make any material difference, they'd done more damage than he'd expected.

Let them have their fun now. They'd pay for it once the pass was cleared.

He kept the men at a steady pace up the river valley alongside the wide Andahi River rushing its way toward the sea. Not ideal ground for defense, but this was not a battlefield, and the city of Ala Larkadhe, just visible beyond the sloping riverbank, was no threat.

He rode down the columns, his men in perfect formation. As soon as they gained the foot of the pass, they'd break for another even scantier meal and then begin the march up the heights at double-pace.

A rustle of voices whispering caused him to turn. The men faced right. Up.

He faced right. Up.

All along the top of the hills above the sloping riverbank horsemen appeared as it they had risen out of the ground, a thousand or more silhouettes against the westering sun.

Then another row behind them. And as the first two started riding slowly downhill, the beautiful horses dainty as dancers, yet more silhouettes appeared.

Shock made Vringir's horse sidle, head tossing. Vringir reined in hard.

The brassy fall of trumpet notes carried down the hills, and the Marlovans charged, flanked by flying archers—and smacked straight into the middle of the Venn column.

Ola-Vayir had arrived.

Durasnir was unaware that Dag Valda had left him alone. His focus was on Indevan Algara-Vayir, who swooped down to cut under a chopping blade to his left then lunged up and arched the blade behind him to block a strike from the right—a strike he could not possibly have seen. There was no breaking past his extraordinary guard. And the men on the trail below him knew it. Their faces had changed from battle lust and rage to fury and determination.

"Fulla."

Durasnir's head snapped around. Valda stumbled, almost falling, Dag Ulaffa at her side. Ulaffa blinked rapidly, gray-faced and haggard until he caught his breath. His skin was blotchy.

Durasnir gripped Valda's elbow. Under those blue robes she was no more than skin and bones held together by force of will. "I come to you first. The king is dead," she whispered, her eyes stark. "The king is dead."

"Dag Erkric says the prince has demanded a cessation. We are to return to Venn so that he may claim the golden torc as king." Ulaffa spoke in the reedy, trembling voice of a very old man.

The king is dead.

This is not a coincidence.

Durasnir pinched his fingers to the skin between his brows. "A cessation?" The Venn didn't lose—they had no drills for this situation.

Ulaffa said, "Hilda Commander Talkar just moments ago sent a message that we have walked into a trap. The prince declared that this news joined with our king's death means we must lay aside our endeavors here for another day. We are to go home at once."

Durasnir's hand dropped. "If the prince has spoken, then there is nothing more to be done."

Ulaffa made a brief sign to Valda and then transferred below to Talkar.

Valda said to Durasnir, "Erkric does not know I am here. Is it really a trap?"

"It looks that way," Durasnir said again, and this time she gave a minute nod, lips parted. "We were not going to win in days, or even weeks. But everyone knew that. Valda, what has happened?"

She whispered, "This war no longer serves Dag Erkric."

She knows the king's death is not a coincidence.

And that could only mean that Dag Erkric's hand lay behind the death of the king.

The truth was as powerful a strike as any dealt by a weapon, though the pain was all in mind and spirit.

Durasnir closed his eyes as he fought to comprehend just how vastly he had been blindsided. They all had. He opened his eyes. "Then the invasion was nothing more than a ruse."

"Oh, I think it was more than that: an experiment to blend war with magic and to get us to accept it. And a fast win would have done all that the king wished, as well as added greatly to Dag Erkric's and the prince's praise."

Durasnir shook his head slowly. The money for ships and supplies, the time for training, all of it a ruse? The men dying below—a mere decoy to keep the eyes of the homeland on the war in the south?

Valda's shocked gaze acknowledged his thoughts. "I traced Erkric's movements through his scroll-case. He was returning to the king in Twelve Towers. When I was certain, I told Ulaffa. He went to investigate and discovered yesterday that the Erama Krona's supply of white kinthus was missing the equivalent of five doses."

"The king's strange sleep?"

Valda made the sign of assent.

Durasnir said, feeling his way along this new pathway into darkness, "And now the prince has a well-drilled, well-supplied, powerful army to sail home and secure the throne."

"Yes." Valda tipped her head from side to side to ease her aching neck.

They had to talk fast. "If Erkric killed the king—why? Why now? He couldn't think we could lose?"

"No. There is the matter of magic."

Darkness—Rainorec. Venn-Doom. Which is not monsters, or war against well-trained warriors. Venn-Doom is when we turn on one another. "Signi's geyser?"

"Yes. Erkric is badly frightened. He thinks the Morvende aided her because their magical signature was blended with her own. She must have used spells she found in the archive to bind hers."

The magical talk meant little to Durasnir. "Our oaths, our cooperation, for *nothing*."

"Our purpose was superseded." Valda's face was bleak.

The word *supersede*—not just to replace but to replace something outmoded—struck Durasnir another blow.

He had to think. Magic was Valda's and Ulaffa's concern, but he knew the military. "If we cease fighting now, the Marlovans will go into a slaughter frenzy. We had better save what lives we can," Durasnir said, decision affording him a modicum of relief. "Can you take me below? Not to Talkar. To the Marlovans. There, on that bend in the trail on that cliff, the crimson tunics."

Valda glanced down at the blood-soaked cliff trail, and then away.

The transfer was short and wrenching, then came another wrench when the cloying, thick smell of blood scoured the back of Durasnir's throat. He flung up his open hand and said, "Truce!" He repeated the word in Sartoran.

The Venn on the trail fell back, more shocked than the Marlovans at the sight of their Oneli Commander there in his silver armor and winged helm. Valda stayed well back, so that the Venn could not see her.

The Marlovans surrounding their king slapped arrows to bows and aimed, but Evred held up his hand, palm forward. They stilled, arms taut.

As the Venn on the trail lowered their swords and backed out of range, Inda gave one sweat-burning, weary glance at the tall man in the winged helm and exhaustion hit him like a wave of seawater. His right arm tingled painfully all the way to his shoulder. Unnoticed his sword dropped from his fingers; he sank down onto a low rock, whooping for breath.

"We would call a halt." Durasnir also spoke Sartoran, hands spread, empty palms up. "Our king is dead. Prince Rajnir returns home. We are finished here."

Evred's first response was disbelief. It had to be some kind of trick, but even as he thought it, Durasnir walked to the edge of the trail head, Inda's face turning to track him.

Tau slithered in the gory mud, keeping himself and his sword between Durasnir and the other two. Vedrid took up a stance beside him.

Below, Talkar was with Ulaffa, of necessity shouting. Durasnir saw the Hilda commander gesture violently behind him, and he saw Talkar's lips shape certain words: rear-guard action . . . massacre. Then Ulaffa indicated the cliff and Talkar stiffened, the light glimmering on his armor, his horse backing, ears flat, when he recognized Durasnir on the cliff.

Talkar raised his arm, reluctance and anger evident in the set of his shoulders, but he too would do what needed to be done to protect the lives of his men. Rigidly he made the hand signal ceding Durasnir the right to parley.

"Wind the halt," Evred said sharply.

Vedrid had brought a trumpet in case they needed aid; he lifted it and blew a fair version of the "Halt Battle," to be picked up from below and then from above.

Cama's men straightened up from their cover, bows lifted high. "Yip! Yip! Yip!"

Cherry-Stripe's men joined, and then Tuft's down in the pass as they reformed into lines, Runners bringing lances forward as they lined up, watching for a signal.

Talkar gestured, hand flat down, and then a sideswipe. *Cease and retreat!*

The signal men stared, but one was quicker than the others. Two toots and a blat, two toots and a blat, hastily joined by all the other horns, and with more rapidity than either side would have thought men disengaged, backing up a step, then another and another, some cursing, some spitting, others wary, shields up, weapons out as gradually the distance widened a few paces between Venn and Marlovan, revealing a horror of mud and bloody, hacked figures sprawled together in the mindless intimacy of death.

Ulaffa transferred to the cliff. He tottered, but this time he did not splat into the gore-thickened mud because Tau and Vedrid caught him, one on either side, guiding him in silence to a flattish rock. Ulaffa was scarcely aware of them. He drew in a shaky breath, his heart laboring. *One more transfer,* he thought. *One more.*

He hoisted himself to his feet and reached for Durasnir for the last transfer.

"Wait." Evred stumbled forward. "Are you coming back against us next year?" Then hated himself for so stupid a question. As if he would hear the truth—as if he could believe anything they said!

Durasnir paused, studying the troubled young face before him. "I go where I am ordered. That decision is not mine to make." And then, because Evred Montrei-Vayir reminded him with unexpected pain of Vatta, his own son, he added, "Had your defense been less effective, we might have been ordered to stay and see the objective through."

No reaction.

How to convey meaning within the requirements of honor . . . He transferred his gaze to Indevan Algara-Vayir. That peculiar glow from the sun-shafts was gone, of course, leaving an ordinary young man sitting there, filthy and sweating. There was no wit whatever in that face right now, just the scars, the earrings, all testament to his surprising career.

Durasnir addressed him. "Did you meet Ramis of the *Knife*?"

Indevan the Pirate's Sartoran turned out to be the same curiously old-fashioned accent of his king. "Yes. He commanded me to meet him at Ghost Island." A brief smile. "I thought you sent a fleet to chase me."

"I chased you myself. Can you tell me what Ramis said?" *By the Tree, let it be pertinent . . .*

Indevan's eyes narrowed: there was the wit, or maybe just wariness. "Yes. That the three greatest dangers to me were your Prince Rajnir, Dag Erkric, and you."

And there was his chance. "Two of us," Durasnir said, "must obey." He nodded to the waiting dag.

Ulaffa closed his hand around Durasnir's wrist. They wrenched in and out of the world, then Durasnir stumbled forward, breathing hard. But now he was on his own captain's deck.

Ulaffa fainted with a quiet thump, ensigns rushing to his aid.

"Ah," Erkric said, standing behind Prince Rajnir. He flicked a glance at Ulaffa, who was being lifted up. Then turned his attention back to Durasnir. "Your report?"

"Talkar has ordered the cease and retreat, as commanded."

Erkric smiled, then turned his head to the prince. "Quite correct," he said in a smooth, calm voice. "Though this is not a retreat, it's a regrouping for the greater cause. We are called to escort a king."

"Hyarl my Commander," Rajnir said eagerly. "We must sail for home."

Durasnir stared into those blue eyes, empty of curiosity. Empty even of concern. Rajnir smiled, the sweet smile of youth. "Do you hear?" Rajnir opened his hands, holding them palm up in the sign of good tidings. "The king is dead, and the Breseng will be nigh when we reach home. You will walk at my right hand as I take the golden torc and bring us peace."

He turned around, hands out, including Ulaffa in his smile. The old Yaga Krona had roused and insisted on remaining on deck, though the two young ensigns remained by his side. As Rajnir turned his way, Ulaffa made a low obeisance, and Rajnir said again, "Home. At long last."

And went to his cabin. The Dag—*The* Dag of all Venn—followed him.

Durasnir's men, high rank to low, showed some of the same shock he felt. There was shock in Ulaffa's long mouth, his haggard face and distracted gaze.

There had been no shock in Rajnir's incurious blue gaze. There had been no shock in Dag Erkric's calm, serene assurance. Only the affect of sorrow.

Durasnir walked into the command cabin, where on the desk lay lists of the dead, all written out in red and gold. One of the signal ensigns opened a case and brought out three more lists, the ink fresh as blood.

Durasnir forced himself to look at the dispatches, and the initials that indicated what was sent to whom. The churning inside indicated his body knew what he would find, even if his mind insisted on evidence: and there they were, the reports on the attack.

The last one was Talkar's scrawled report on the trap. The neat initials in the corner indicating a copy sent to Erkric—which meant he was not waiting on the *Cormorant.*

So Erkric was in Twelve Towers, the king's city . . . and then the king died.

Durasnir looked at those pages and pages of dead. He remembered the pass below the cliff, the mounds of Venn and Marlovan lying together heedlessly. Young and old, the Venn faithful to the Tree unto death.

All for nothing.

He slid his hands over his face and wept.

Chapter Twenty-four

INDA never remembered descending the last part of the trail to the floor of the pass, once a riverbed.

He remembered pain. Not just the physical pain, though it bothered him that his right arm had gone from needle stabs to so numb that he couldn't pick anything up. But that had been happening every so often of late. He'd just tucked his hand into his sash and waited for the sensation to go away. Now it wasn't going away.

The pain he remembered consisted of sharp, distinct jabs to the heart. Like the ragged voices singing Hawkeye Yvana-Vayir's favorite ballad, "Yvana Ride Thunder," after Hawkeye was discovered under a pile of dead who Inda was helping to straighten the limbs of and then Disappear, one by one. Hawkeye, as a Jarl and Commander, would be Disappeared in front of as many of his men as could be found by nightfall. For now his body was hoisted to shoulders, followed by more men bearing his personal Runners, friends from childhood, who had died trying to protect him. The battered helm fell off, leaving his loosened long yellow hair hanging down in brown-streaked clots, his lifeless hands dangling as men sang in grief-roughened voices.

Inda did not remember the Venn pulling their own wounded out of the heaps and piles, Disappearing their

dead. Many looking at him strangely, some backing away
as he passed. Men of both sides avoided meeting anyone
else's gaze as they loaded their wounded over the backs of
their horses, and then onto hastily emptied carts brought
forward from farther back in their lines.

"Inda. You have to come now."

As Inda stared witlessly, motion beyond his shoulder distracted Evred. Most of the departing Venn glanced back at
Inda one last time before they vanished down the other
side of the pass whence they had come. Later he would
think about that. Now grief was too acute, need too immediate.

"Inda." As Inda's blank gaze slowly focused, and Evred
knew Inda heard him, he said slowly, "Noddy. You have to
come. He—" *Is dying? Won't believe me?* "—has to see
you."

He turned his back on the scattering of Venn mages who
recorded and then Disappeared the last of their dead, one
by one.

"Noddy?" Inda exclaimed. "Where?"

He launched toward the wagons being filled with
wounded. Men cleared space to the wagon where Noddy
lay, bluish white in the lips, except where an obscene pink
froth bubbled. One of his hands being clasped by Tuft, who
was almost unrecognizable with one ear almost cut off, the
other side of his face bandaged where a Venn blade had
sliced just below his helm, nearly spitting his eye. Crusted
cuts on his powerful arms and on one leg marked him beyond the edges of his chain mail. He leaned over the
wagon, breathing compressed as he labored to keep tears
back.

Noddy's free hand twitched, and Inda tried to reach, but
his right arm still wouldn't work, so he took Noddy's hand
with his left.

"See, Noddy?" Evred said, at Inda's shoulder. "We won."

Noddy tugged faintly.

Inda climbed up onto the wheel spokes and leaned next
to Tuft, a spring of burning tears dripping onto Noddy's
chest.

"You. Were. There. Like. You. Said." A quirk at the corner of Noddy's mouth might have been a smile, but the horrible froth bubbled there, and Inda caught his breath. "No. More," Noddy whispered. "Promise."

No more what? "What can I get you?" Inda asked, his voice unsteady as he thought of water—wine—food—*life*. But Inda couldn't give life. "C'mon, Noddy. Hold to us. You've got to lead the sing for Hawkeye." His plea broke on a sob.

"Promise. No. More. No war."

Noddy's voice had sunk to a whisper; was that *no more* or *no war*?

"Yes," Inda said. *Yes, if it will help him hold on.* "Yes, I promise."

Noddy relaxed; his fingers gripped Inda's with all the strength he had left. Inda had come, just as he said he would. They'd heard the Venn horns. Retreat, Evred said. The Venn were defeated because he and Hawkeye had held the pass. And now the Venn were going. *No war.*

Noddy floated, the thought winging away. He made a brief mental effort to catch it, then decided it could wait. Everything could wait. It was good right now, right here, to drift . . . like being on the lake behind Cousin Nadran's castle on a sunny day, light splashing and winking on the deep blue waters . . . His friends had come home with him. He could float here in the sun and listen to their voices. The sun was so bright. Shut his eyes . . . contentment . . . just listen to their voices on the other rafts. Inda. Evred. Tuft. Cama . . . Cherry-Stripe . . . as he floated closer and closer to the warm, bright sun . . .

Inda stayed beside the wagon, holding Noddy's hand until there was no return grip, and the hand went cold.

He looked across the wagon straight into Evred's eyes, taken aback at the hard glare of the Sierlaef, of Fox at his most infuriated. Evred shifted his gaze to Noddy, and in the compressed, downward turn to his mouth Inda saw that he'd mistaken wretchedness for rage: unmasked and bare was the severity of Evred's pain.

Evred reached, and with a gentle gesture closed Noddy's

eyes. Then sobs crashed through Inda's chest with relentless strength. He wept in gulps, and men wept around him.

There were more shards. The dying men, known and unknown. The uncovered faces of the dead, hands stiff and empty. Strewn mementos from packs. Fallen hair clasps. Inda had to sit down, sick and trembling and dizzy.

When he shut his eyes, there was the blurred image of Tdor's face. The blur was perplexing, not quite a blend of Tdor as she used to be and as she was now. He remembered his promise to write. But his hand could not grip anything well, sending more shards of pain up his arm. He got up and found his pack. Pen. Paper. He scrawled, *We're alive.* What else could he say?

Tuft's voice in his ear. "Inda. There's more of 'em over the top there."

Inda looked around, bewildered. The stars had gone and it was morning. He crumpled the note into the box and sent it. Then he forced himself into motion.

He must help see to the dead before they Disappeared them. He and Tuft and Evred all worked alongside their captains, taking care to smooth hair, to tug clothing into place, to straighten limbs not obscenely hacked. One by one, because each deserved to be restored to dignity, and then to be Disappeared by the hand of a captain or a commander. This was right and true in the eyes of all the men, who might so easily have lain there.

More shards. Blood squelching underfoot. Riderless horses leaping lightly over the unbreathing human obstacles and racing about wild-eyed, heads tossing. Carts, once loaded with horse armor, now loaded with wounded, Runners jumping up and down to and from the carts, putting cups to lips as others bandaged and sometimes sewed. And sometimes sawed.

Vedrid easing off Inda's crimson Harskialdna tunic so that his own cuts could be sewn—he had two, and a lot of nicks—and bandaged. Someone put his right arm in a sling, and he tried to protest—he wasn't wounded—but it was so much easier on his shoulder to let his arm rest in the cloth.

He remembered daylight fading as Signi walked out

from behind a group of men bearing one of the few wounded left untended, a bag of cloth for bandages over one of her shoulders, her trousers mud-and blood-splattered, her arms held out, fingers distended. She stared into the air, or something beyond the air.

Ghosts? Inda thought. Tired as he was, his heart pinched hard in his chest.

"I'm sorry," he said, meaning her countrymen who had died that day, and she said something in a tear-choked voice over and over, something in Venn, but it was all right because he couldn't hear her anyway, he just sought her mouth and lips met trembling lips in a sticky, salt-tear tasting kiss.

Chapter Twenty-five

OLA-VAYIR, Buck, Rat, and Barend sat on their horses atop the highest sand dune. Buck was supported by his Runner; they'd wrapped his half-severed arm tight against his body, the opposite knee stump was stiff with bandages, and his usually trim middle was bulky. Pain came and went in waves, but he insisted on being there. He said (once they got a heavy dose of green kinthus into him and he could talk at all) that he owed it to the king, but internally he vowed he'd be damned before he'd leave that strutting old man to scarfle up all the credit.

Ranged directly behind them, in lines nearly a thousand men across, their riders outlined the shape of the dunes down the beach, bows ready, swords loose in the saddle sheaths, their rich silken House tunics glowing with a splendid array of colors as they talked quietly back and forth. A closer look would reveal bandaged heads under helms, arms in slings, bulky lines under trousers indicating various sorts of bindings, hastily mended tears in the tunics, others stained badly.

No one moved, except horse ears twitching, tails flicking, the occasional cock of a equine hip. No one put arrow to bow, though everyone had bows strung and ready.

That battered impression was reflected in the mostly silent Venn on the beach as they waded out to the launches in orderly lines, climbed in, raised the single sails, and thumped back over a running sea driven by the brisk off-shore breeze.

The Marlovans watched, passing water jugs down the line and sharing out travel bread—except for Buck, who gently dozed, leaning against the shoulder of his Runner, who'd eased up on his side and shifted to the extreme edge of his saddle. The sun had begun its downward drop toward the west before the last of the Venn boats reached the tall ships out on the horizon.

When the last boat was taken up, the sails on the big ships dropped down, tightened, and filled. The ships slowly turned about and then began to rock away, slanting as they gathered speed.

Ola-Vayir finally sat back in his saddle, smiling. "They're gone, boys," he said genially.

Life was good. He'd made it in time, he'd won a smash-ing battle, only losing a hundred men. True there were ten or twenty times that in wounded, but most of those would be able to ride in a few days or weeks at most. He cast a glance of mild scorn at Buck. Young fool, who'd be im-pressed with his strut? Look at that green face. Ah well, live and let live, the point being, they were all alive. The number of wounded, he gloated inwardly, gave him the best reason in the world to linger. He looked forward to riding up to that white tower, there, where the others said young Evred would return: by the time Ola-Vayir reached his own home again, the old Jarl would have convinced himself that his wild ride had won the war.

"Let's go see what the king wants us doing next, eh?"

Buck jerked awake, and wiped drool off his chin with his good hand. Then he rolled his eyes, prompting a muffled snort from Barend. Rat just sat, face tight with pain. He hadn't drunk green kinthus, and wished he hadn't been so quick to turn it down so it would go to the worse wounded fellows; he was nearly fainting in the saddle, and just longed to lie down.

"I'll go find out," Barend said, and because he had the rank as former Harskialdna and no one could stop him, he

wheeled his horse and galloped along the beach, cursing
Ola-Vayir as he rode.

As the sunlight vanished in the Andahi Pass, Cama and his
men had just reached the bottom of a cliff after a solid day
of picking their way down, sometimes feeling like spiders
on a wall. Only they hadn't eight legs to help them; half a
dozen had lost grip and slid, one man had fallen to his
death.

"Where's Inda?" Cama demanded, striding forward.

Everyone gave way before the tall, one-eyed Sier Danas.
There was Inda in the center of things, his arm in a sling,
but otherwise apparently unhurt.

Cama walked up to him. "What needs doing?"

Inda did not see the exhaustion in their filthy faces because they were all equally exhausted and filthy. He looked
past Cama. None of his men seemed to be wounded, so
Inda said, "Follow the Venn back. Make sure they leave."

Evred stepped up and added, "If there are no defenders
left, and I suspect that to be the case, hold Castle Andahi.
I will send you more men in case the Venn leave anyone on
the northern shore."

Cama's lip lifted—not a smile, but a semblance of one.
He struck his fist against his chest, then strode on, seemingly tireless, to choose mounts from the former straw
army. His men hefted their gear and followed his straight
back and martial saunter.

Cherry-Stripe said under his breath to Inda, "Good
thinking, sending Cama north. Now he doesn't have to go
to Horsebutt's for that damn celebration. Because you
know Sponge hasn't forgotten."

Inda heard about half of that, and comprehended less.
He found a free corner of a wagon, climbed up, and
dropped down to rest, just for a moment—and sleep took
him so fast he did not even remember putting down his
head.

Just as the last of the day vanished, one of the sudden

summer storms piled clouds high above the mountain peaks. Evred set himself up in a half-empty hay wagon next to Inda's to begin the task of clearing the wreckage of a kingdom.

Around him, Runners and volunteer Riders joked and laughed. They were done here. The last of the dead had been Disappeared, the wounded were all loaded. The king gave the expected signal to start back down the pass.

The horse teams began to move, the drivers now with one hand on the wooden brakes of carts and wagons rattling and bumping over small stones. Evred grimaced as his wagon jerked and swayed; his report to Hadand would be illegible.

He settled his lap desk on his knees as Runners rigged a horse armor tent over him. Lightning flickered pale blue and thunder rumbled over the distant peaks. He could not see those who chatted and laughed, which somehow made their voices clearer. The undertone of hilarity, of relief, was extraordinarily different than the tight, hard barks and cackles of laughter after the rough jokes they'd traded back and forth on the long hike down the mountain.

For them the battle was over. They'd won. They anticipated songs, celebrations, a return to life. Admiration.

Normal life.

What was going to be normal in a kingdom with an empty treasury, most of its men scattered up here, far too many dead? He leaned forward, peering around the edge of the makeshift shelter at Inda in the next wagon, who lay like one of those dead—

Image: midnight last night. Hawkeye and Noddy, stretched out together on a wagon, surrounded by men with torches. Light beating on faces, most with the clean tracks of tears cutting through the grime on their faces as they sang the "Hymn to the Fallen," and Evred waved the torch over them.

Then he had to touch them and make their bodies go away. Noddy—flat-voiced, jug-faced Noddy—was no longer just around the corner with a comment, his components were in the ground, his spirit—where? It was not here, that was what mattered. It was not here, nor was Hawkeye, his dashing cousin, loyal to the last.

Evred pressed his hands against his face. When would he master the pain?

Not when. How? By keeping busy, not sitting around feeling sorry for himself. He permitted himself one more glance at Inda, and could not prevent the harrowing intensity of his relief. To no human being would he admit the vile helplessness he had experienced during that long battle, watching Inda—unable to not watch Inda out of a nightmarish mix of terror and desire.

Inda lay snoring where he'd dropped, one arm dangling over the side of the wagon. The Venn dag was, like Taumad, busy tending the wounded at the back in the slower wagons, so none of Inda's followers were here. He could sleep as long as he needed. Snoring, filthy from his tangled mat of hair to his muddy, blood-splashed boots, there was no sight in the world more dear.

Inda. Evred drew in a deep breath, and pulled out a sheet of paper. First duty: this report to Hadand. He would begin with the fact that her brother lived.

Inda did not stir for the rest of that day or night. He woke to the glow of light under one of the horse-armor tents, his mouth dry, his head hammering. He lifted his head—mistake. He lay back and shoved his grimy hair off his face. Turning his head slightly, he could just make out Evred framed by the space gapping between a makeshift tent of piled horse armor resting over lashed lances. Evred was writing steadily, his pack open beside him.

Tau appeared, seemingly by magic, and pushed a lukewarm cup into Inda's left hand, lifting his head with the other. Inda coughed at the bitter taste, but swallowed the rest, and then with more eagerness drank the cup of water Tau silently held out next. Inda sat up, wincing against the hammer inside his skull; it lost strength with rapid speed, leaving lessened aches and a yawning belly.

Inda looked around, this time with more awareness. They were moving briskly, the wagon brakes smelling slightly of singed metal. Somewhere ahead the cooks had jury-rigged a makeshift stove aboard one of the carts, for the delicious smell of toasted grain drifted back on a thin white stream of smoke.

"Oatmeal," Tau said, his mouth smiling, though no humor reached his eyes. "Got somewhat burned, but it doesn't taste bad."

"I'll eat it even if it's burned solid." Inda frowned. "Tau, you look terrible. You fought as hard as I did on that cliff. Why aren't you asleep?"

"No one fought as hard as you did." Tau looked away. *How do you bear the guilt?* he thought. But he would not speak. Maybe the Marlovan way of bearing guilt was to not think about it. Tau kept hearing his own voice over and over, so careless, so superior when he said he thought Noddy Toraca would be suitable to command with Hawk-eye. *I recommended a man to his death.*

He would not say it. It was his burden, and he would not add to Inda's. "I don't think you realize just how dismaying a sight that was. I just stood there and caught the occasional wild strike. And I did sleep, though probably not enough. But if we're comparing our deficits in slumber, yours would far exceed mine." He waved his hand. "We'll have plenty of catch-up time to rest when we reach Ala Larkadhe."

"No, we will not."

They turned. Evred had emerged from his horse-armor tent. He appeared to be even more tired than Tau, his eyes circled with dark flesh, his skin taut as he held up his gold case. "I just discovered that Ala Larkadhe seems to have been destroyed by a mysterious flood."

"That had to have been Erkric," Inda exclaimed.

A faint trumpet call from the advance riders interrupted them. Soon came the sound of a horse cantering uphill.

A Runner rounded the craggy cliff just ahead. "Outriders report it's Barend-Dal," the Runner said to Evred.

"Send him directly here."

They did not have long to wait. Through the middle of the lines rode Barend, rolling in his saddle as usual, reins in his fist. He'd made excellent time, finding plenty of horses to commandeer from the roaming patrols stretched between the coast and the southern end of the pass. His new mount, swapped with the outriders' remounts at dawn, was unaccustomed to so clumsy a rider, and jobbed scoldingly against his hand but he didn't notice. "There you are!" Barend called, relieved. "I didn't trust those gold things—"

"Never mind that," Evred cut in, too tired for amenities. "Report. First what you saw, then what you've heard."

Barend gave Evred a succinct report that was mostly good news: the Venn had departed in a fast, orderly manner from the south shore. Lindeth prudently kept their fires burning, though by then the smoke was a suspiciously thin combination of olive and leddas oils with a seasoning of grass and old blankets and broken wooden gear. The long beach (which would take the name Venn's End in Olaran for several generations, eroding to Visegn by the turn of the millennium) was stained with brown and crimson patches, though the bands of storms had done much to wash them away. He ended with what everyone was already calling Ola-Vayir's Charge (with the Jarl's and his men's enthusiastic encouragement), ". . . though it was actually Buck's idea, it being his scouts who spotted 'em and brought 'em to the right place. And Buck said we should form up in lines over the hills above the river road and charge together. Anyway. As soon as Ola-Vayir said he was going to wait for you, I figured I'd better come up here. Better than trying to find something to eat back in Ala Larkadhe," he added with faint humor. Then he squinted at his cousin. "He's going to be expecting some kind o' reward."

Evred turned his palms up. "I won't give him the north, and what else is there? We have an empty treasury, all the harbors to rebuild, and it sounds like Ala Larkadhe as well."

Inda rubbed his jaw with his good hand. "Treasury? Empty?"

Evred turned his way, but Barend rode over him. "Ala Larkadhe isn't destroyed. Just washed out. Except for the central square. You know, over the baths? That's gone. But the rest, the houses and the castle, those stand. There just isn't much in the ground floors as yet. When I rode past people were still picking stuff out of the mess."

"But there cannot be food for thousands of men."

"No. That's why I'm here. You better come fast, because everyone's a hero right now. A whole lot are flat on their backs recovering from Venn sword and bow work. They went after arms and legs—"

"Did here, too," Tuft put in.

"—but there's going to be trouble if we don't get 'em under orders. We ran out of barracks space, and we can't billet 'em on civs when the ground floors of every house lack furniture. Not a lot of extra food, and though the fun houses have all thrown open their doors, they'll run out of supplies about the time they run out of patience. Long before they run out of liberty men, is what Tdiran-Randviar said."

"We'll give them something to do." Evred's smile was rare, the tips of his teeth showing. It was a singularly unpleasant smile. "Packing to march. Because I promised there would be a triumph."

Barend gasped, "Who's paying for that?"

"Horsebutt," Evred said, the nasty smile even wider.

Inda had completely forgotten that strange moment during the long ride north, but he remembered it now, and gasped as the implications hit him. "You mean, he has to entertain us all?"

"That's what a triumph is. It's also an honor," Evred said. "It's an honor kings rarely confer, and that's only when they want to ruin someone without lifting a hand in anger. We have the moral force of our victory, and he the honor of being chosen as host."

Inda laughed, then shook his head. "That's . . . that's piratical. Especially since we didn't have a victory."

"Yes, we did."

Inda looked startled, and Barend lifted his brows. Evred had never flatly contradicted Inda before.

Inda rubbed his hand over his eyes. "Sponge, that wasn't any victory, they just retreated. You heard Durasnir, and even if he lied about everything else—"

"Inda." Evred looked into Inda's startled face. A stream of insights flickered through his mind, most images, scraps of past conversations. Inda's understanding of victory was purely military—you won when you either left your enemies in smoking ruin or ran them off the map. Inda was profoundly ignorant of the political side of war.

How to explain swiftly? Education could come later. It would, as Inda was now Harskialdna, and he would be the instrument of Evred's will. *Be immediate.* "Would you deny these men their triumph? Deny Noddy's family?"

Inda grimaced. "But—"

"Inda. The men saw you on the cliff, they shouted your name. That heartened them. You were unbeatable, and the Venn retreated. They are gone. You gave the men the victory. Do not take it away from them."

Inda smacked his hands over his face. "It's Boruin all over again," he mumbled.

Evred pointed at Tuft, who was gingerly fingering the stitches on his blood-crusted ear. "Vedrid?" The Runner appeared from the other side of the makeshift tent, wet clothes over his arm. "Horses for us all. Tuft, you are in command. The wounded must go to Ala Larkadhe, but all the rest of these men will ride for Tya-Vayir. We'll spend one night in Ala Larkadhe, then we will join you on the road."

Chapter Twenty-six

NIGHTINGALE Toraca cautiously leaned against the window of the tiny stable hand's room the Runners had taken as their watch station. The room smelled faintly of wet wood; through the open window came the heavy summer air, scented with the adjacent stables.

The Runners who had galloped ahead of the king all greeted Nightingale, scrupulously careful not to say anything, and went out about their duties. But the very care with which they greeted him—the lack of mention of Andahi Pass—prepared him for Evred-Harvaldar to come seeking him almost as soon as he rode through the gates.

Nightingale was shocked by the lines of tension and exhaustion in the king's face. He saluted, though the movement hurt, and whispered, "You're wounded?"

Nightingale was almost unrecognizable. His lips were bluish, and he had trouble breathing.

To few would Evred have answered that question, but Nightingale was already as far inside his personal boundaries as he let anyone, and now Evred felt he was owed more than evasion. "I never lifted a sword. No weapon was near me," he said, and ill as he was, Nightingale could not comprehend Evred's low, flat tone. Then Evred said in a very different voice, "Noddy and Hawkeye died defending the top of the pass. They held it in the teeth of half the entire Venn army."

Nightingale had thought he was prepared, but the words made it real. At least the king had come right out with it, not shuffling about, or speechifying about honor and glory.

He wasn't aware of reacting, but suddenly there was a chair underneath him, and Evred's hand on his good shoulder, keeping him from falling.

Nightingale held his breath, glaring at the table with its neat papers, a hastily scrawled duty roster on top. The big slate with messages from one Runner to another. Pens. Chalk. Papers, a couple of extra weapons, a sewing kit. He concentrated fiercely on each thing. His chest hurt too much to breathe.

Evred's voice went on, husky with grief: unexpectedly he sounded like Hawkeye. "Noddy died knowing we won. He asked Inda to promise him something. I could not hear what it was, but no doubt Inda will be speaking to you about it. Now, I have decided—and will tell your Cousin Nadran so—that you will choose whether you will take Noddy's place as Randael to Khani-Vayir. Noddy's son will inherit, all as before. But if you wish to become Randael, then you must marry. Unfortunately, there will be far too many unmarried women whose treaties cannot be kept, so you will probably be able to choose. Or you may stay my Second Runner, and name your preference in a Randael for your cousin, and then little Inda."

Nightingale could not speak.

"Do not decide now. There is time. Nothing will happen before Convocation, and that is half a year away. Recover first. Think about it."

The hand lifted, and Evred turned to leave.

Nightingale forced words out. "You'll sing them?"

"Yes. There will be a triumph at Tya-Vayir."

"Then. I'm going."

"We will arrange it."

"Here they are," came Inda's voice from the Runner barracks outside. And then, to Vedrid on duty outside the door to the Runner watch station, "Is he being private?"

Evred lifted his voice. "Enter, Inda."

He was at first annoyed to see that Inda was not alone. He'd hoped the Venn mage would vanish altogether, though he knew it an unreasonable wish. She'd stayed with the wounded, transferring by magic back to rejoin them just before they reached Ala Larkadhe. He did not hate her—that had vanished long ago—but he hated the magical power and freedom she used so easily.

Inda said, "We went straight to the lazaretto, but Signi says it's too late for Buck's arm. There isn't any magic for when it's gotten that bad. His leg above the amputation will probably heal. They won't have to cut all the way at the hip. And they sewed up his parts." Inda grimaced, brushing his hand over his crotch. "They said Nightingale was up here."

Signi's gaze scarcely touched Evred, going straight to Nightingale. "Ah," she exclaimed. "It *is* the lung. You are breathing blood. We must take him down to Hatha-Runner."

Nightingale had his face turned away; he made a vague motion to leave him be, and Signi faltered, uncertain. Then Inda snapped his fingers. "Message, Sponge. Tdiran-Randviar stopped me on the way in. Said to tell you that no one died in the mystery flood, it was the battle before that gave us a stiff list, mostly of women and a handful of civs. Also, they got the horses out. And this fellow here re-opened his wound doing it." Inda pointed at Nightingale.

Evred had been watching the Venn dag, who, tired, stressed, was far less masked than he'd ever seen her: on the first mention of the flood her hands stiffened. And then, on Inda's report *No one died,* her eyes closed in unmistakable relief.

"*You* did that," Evred said, advancing on her. Not that he had far to go in the tiny room. "The flood. Not the Venn Erkric. You."

"What?" Inda exclaimed.

Signi's eyes fluttered open, wide and frightened, then she straightened, her face smoothing with that inward control. "Yes."

"You did that against your countrymen? In aid of us? Why?"

"I did not mean for people to be killed, for then I would count myself among those who murdered others. Venn, Marlovan, Idayagan, Olaran—the inhabitants, they were all killing. Children, the old. Everyone. Not just your warriors, men and women. And so my people were going to burn the city."

Nightingale had shoved aside papers and dropped his head onto his folded arms. He turned his head and croaked, "True. Had us ringed. No one could get out. We half choked on the smoke."

"Do you not see," Signi said, her gaze wide and intent. "How terrible it is, when all fight? War is terrible, it turns everyone into murderers."

"But you yourself told us that your Dag Erkric was going to ensorcel us all, to take our minds and make us fight to his will."

"Not everyone," she said. "Even Norsunder has not such magic, or you can be sure it would have long been used. Just you, the king."

"So you believe it is wrong for people to defend the king?" Evred's voice flattened. "Would that include your king, your prince, who ordered you against us in the first place?"

"The people in the city would not have been put to death had your people surrendered. Life would have gone on much as it does under you. Perhaps with a greater wargild, I do not know and cannot answer. The warriors would then have gone up the pass, and yes, probably more men would have died there. I don't have easy answers, I only ask a question that I believe must be asked. Asked again and again. Is it right for everyone to make war without rules? What happens when war is something everyone expects, from baby to grandmother?" She turned away, hands toward Nightingale. "I have been helping Hatha-Runner, I have been teaching him some healer magics, since the Magic Council will not let healers come here."

Evred said, "I thought you could not do magic. They would find you."

Signi's smile was painful. "I have done magic all along. Restoring your lockets' magic most recently, and longer ago your castle spells. I did the same at the Marlo-Vayir castle. But no, those are not the major magics that would have drawn Erkric's eye. When I washed this city clean, I drew his eye. He now knows I am here, that I stand against him. This does not increase your danger from Erkric. Only mine."

Nightingale had gotten to his feet. Signi helped him out.

Inda fell in step beside Evred. "Tdiran-Randviar's putting on a dinner for all the captains and the city guild chiefs," he said. "Here's a surprise. The new guild master from Lindeth Harbor is coming, as well as the harbormaster. She says that's something new."

"It's more likely something prudent," Evred said, in the flat, soft voice he'd used ever since the battle. There had always been a small space of personal reserve between Sponge and the world, back when they were first year scrubs at the academy. Gradually—except for that one moment, just after Noddy died—that space had become a gulf.

"Prudent?" Inda asked, sliding his right arm out of his grimy sling and flexing his hand.

Evred gestured, palm up. "I'm certain the impulse is less a truce with us than making certain that they aren't overlooked when it comes time to rebuild. And I'm morally certain we will be hearing, underneath stirring speeches about heroism, that that time should be as soon as possible."

Inda grimaced. He'd thought the news of Lindeth's harbormaster coming, a first, would be a good sign. "We can deal with that later. Thing is, Tdiran-Randviar says that hoarded stuff is coming out right and left, now that they're beginning to believe they aren't in for a summer's siege. So we'll have a hot meal, our first in what? I don't remember, do you?" He didn't pause for Evred to answer, but ran right on. "I set the loose Runners to work on putting together a report on what supplies we've got, what the city's got. Told them to prepare for the ride."

"I'd like to leave at dawn," Evred said.

You'd do better with a night's sleep, Inda thought, but he didn't say it. Evred had not asked for personal advice, and even when he was small he'd hated to get it. Inda sighed, wondering how to broach the subject without offense. He didn't think Evred had slept more than half a night, if that, since the battle. Maybe work it in with the last bit of good news? One he'd been saving for the right moment.

Evred led the way along the back end of the castle, which was full of a jumble of furnishings rescued from below during the flood. Runners, women, servants dashed about, most distracted, some catching themselves short to let them pass, hands snapping to chests.

Evred, usually so observant, did not appear to see any of them; he walked with his head bent, hands clasped behind him. Inda recognized where they were heading, and grimaced again when they reached the white tower. So he filled the silence with a running list of the logistical chores he foresaw needing attention once they were on the road again, in hopes Evred would himself suggest a day's wait. Better, a week. They could scrounge food from somewhere.

No response. They mounted the last round of stairs in silence. The reserve had become a gulf vast as a sea, isolating Evred on an island of his own making.

"...and Rat gave me permission to send the rest of those Cassad dragoons north over the pass for Cama to use, as soon as they've gotten a watch or two of rest. Cama had the training of 'em, and Rat admits they're devoted to Cama. But I was thinking it would be right, wouldn't it, to send the Khani-Vayir men home? Or do we take them along with Hawkeye's people to the triumph, so they can hear their leaders sung?"

"We can give them the choice," Evred said. "I'd like to keep a few of them as an honor guard for Nightingale. After the triumph they can take him back home."

They stepped onto the tower landing. After the days of

summer storms and the constant jingle and creak and rumble of men on horses and in wagons, they had reached so still a place all Inda heard was Evred's breathing.

Evred walked to the closed archive door and laid his hand against the latch, which was immoveable as stone. His hand slid up the door, then he rested his forehead on his arm.

Just for a moment. He straightened up, turned, dropped his hand. "We were warned."

Inda tried to bridge the gulf. He'd saved what he'd thought the best news, but now he wasn't sure even this would make a difference. Feeling oddly diffident, he said, "Evred, Kened told me those tunics of ours made it into the bucket in time, and the rips are all sewed. And he has a section of the baths set aside for us. Right now! We can go soak! I don't know about you, but I really, really want to get rid of this stink. I'm surprised people don't run out of a room soon's I walk into it."

Evred opened his mouth, his gaze lifting to the smooth white stone ceiling, then to the stairs. He started toward Hawkeye's old office, saying over his shoulder, "You go along. As you said, there's much to do. I'll be there as soon as I see to things here."

Inda gave up, and galloped downstairs. He had a plan formulating in his mind. He was so involved with his own thoughts it was his turn not to notice others. He was not aware that his path was clear despite the crowds of people wandering about, either packing, unpacking, rebuilding, carrying, or just recovering. He never saw the stares in his wake.

He was Indevan-Harskialdna, winner of the battle of Andahi Pass—some said he'd even fought the wing-helmed commander of the Venn into surrender, there on the cliff. He'd hand-picked Hawkeye Yvana-Vayir and Noddy Toraca, who held the Pass with six wings against the entire Venn army, though only two out of each riding survived. But they'd held it for Inda-Harskialdna, who brought them triumph, and glory. Who couldn't be beaten.

As yet, only Signi was aware that Hened Dunrend, Inda's faithful ghost, was gone.

*   *   *

The children of Castle Andahi were settling into a new cave when Hal and Dvar arrived at the same time from different directions. Over the days after they'd spent coming down off the heights toward the pass in a zigzag, Hal and Dvar had devolved into the forward scouts, as both were fast and observant.

Han had been sending Dvar out because Dvar hadn't spoken since that terrible day on the landslide. Instinct prompted Han to give Dvar responsibility, but also something to keep her away from the little ones' crying. Most of the threes cried a lot now, they wanted their parents, they pushed away Lnand and Han when they tried to hug and kiss them. Everybody had snot noses, and there weren't any ensorcelled handkerchiefs. There was listerblossom—Lnand had kept that wrapped in closeweave cloth—but most days they did not dare light fires. Once again they'd heard dogs.

Dvar and Hal arrived, panting, and Hal said, "The Venn are coming back!"

And they were. Like before, what looked like a full wing in every line, too many lines to count. Their marching feet sent *thrump thrump thrump* echoes up the cliff walls.

The children huddled in their latest cave, the smalls asleep, the older ones silent until at long last the enemy vanished once again.

That meant one thing: the king had won, just like the Jarlan promised.

Hal said, "What now?"

Han smiled for the first time in days. Her lips cracked, but that was all right. She took her forefinger away from her teeth, which had been worrying at the nail. Strange, how she kind of liked crunching grit, when it used to make her shudder.

"Now," she said, "we wait for the king."

Chapter Twenty-seven

Evred, do you not see? You've already put everyone in place for the perfect solution. If you keep Cama in the north, create another jarlate and if you hold Castle Andahi for Flash's brother, then the problem is solved. And it seems to me, looking at your map here, that there is easily enough work for two Jarls in that area. In addition, if the Jarl of Ola-Vayir presses you to rescind the exile order I passed on Starand, well, if she is elevated to Jarlan far in the north, she thus regains her honor, yet she cannot possibly make trouble down here. If we give Cama a good pair as Randael and Randviar, they can be trusted for castle guardianship and good relations with the north, and to overrule Starand when necessary.

Hadand, once again I thank you for your wisdom. It shall be as you say. Now I can go to this dinner with a quiet mind. And tomorrow early we will begin the ride home.

Evred smiled as he slid the folded note inside the gold case. He'd had far too much business for the locket, and perforce had to trust the golden case. So far there had been no evidence of tampering or of untoward effects.

"There you are!" Barend entered, scratching his scalp

vigorously. "Come on, they've been holding one of the hot baths for us. None o' the Runners've had any, and it's empty, which makes it really unfair to the others waiting."

"I did not realize. I will come at once," Evred said.

"I did the round of the wounded with Ola-Vayir like you asked," Barend reported as they rapidly descended the stairs to the basement level.

"Who needs my attention?"

"I think those who lasted this long are going to make it. Hatha says the dag gave him some of the healer spells. Nothing is going to put a limb back—Buck's lost an arm as well as a leg, and he's not the only one. But she taught him how to seal internal wounds. Those are the worst." He whistled on a low note. "Like Nightingale's lung. We didn't know how bad it was. Hatha said he was a day or so from falling down into a coma. You know what happens then."

Evred swore under his breath. He'd not lose another Toraca, that he vowed.

They reached the enormous natural caverns that formed the baths, a hot spring having long ago been diverted to mix with the water of the underground river. Here they discovered that "complete ruin" meant a spectacular hole in the ceiling, and the men's side was pretty much unusable, enormous slabs of solid rock having been tossed • around like toys. Evred contemplated the power behind such an act.

The women's side was nearly intact, the rubble shoved to one side, neat curtains marking off a couple of private bath chambers. The open baths had once accommodated several hundred at either side, now reduced to maybe a hundred. One of the private, curtained alcoves was vigilantly guarded for the Marlovan high command.

The clean scent of running water caused Barend to suck in a deep breath. "Ah," he exclaimed, flinging aside the curtain then tearing at his clothes. He hopped and writhed toward the bubbling, steaming pool, throwing coat, shirt, pants, socks, drawers in every direction.

The Runners had done their best for them all during the descent down the pass. Evred had endured the lack of amenities in silence because his men did, because Barend, Inda, and Cherry-Stripe had appeared to be cheerfully indifferent to grime and smell. But now, with the prospect of being clean at last, his body seemed to protest in every pore, becoming one vast itch. Evred was right behind his cousin, impatiently flinging off his clothes until he sank into stinging hot water.

His body relaxed into the ruffling motion of the hot spring bubbles. He used the herb-soap from scalp to heels, and then lay back—

—and the burn of water in his nose caused him to surge up, coughing and sneezing.

Barend splashed over, eyes wide. "You all right?"

"Fine. I almost fell asleep," Evred admitted, scooping a handful of soap and applying it vigorously.

Barend snorted, ducking down until just his face was above water, his hair floating like weed around him. "How much have you slept in the last week? One watch all told?"

Evred ducked his head under one more time to make sure the soap had rinsed from his scalp, and then forced himself to rise, though his body felt as heavy as stone.

Sleep. Sometime he would have to sleep. He dreaded it, for every single attempt had brought those images back—

"You getting out already?" Barend said, surprised.

"As you point out, the Runners have not bathed yet. And we've a dinner to get ready for."

"Not this moment." Barend floated, torpid with bliss.

Evred waved a hand to keep him there, and stepped out to where his Runners had laid out fresh clothes, including his House tunic. The sight of that crimson tunic with its gleaming embroidered eagle brought back the images of the battle, more powerful than ever.

He held his breath, wrenching his mind to his immediate surroundings. He stared at Vedrid, waiting patiently for orders, and noticed the darn in his sleeve, and another along the bottom of his coat. When did that happen? Kened walked toward the curtain with an armload of dirty clothes, a bandage just visible at his wrist and a nick in his ear. Which battle was that? The sound of voices rising and falling: a local song in women's voices echoing off the stone, and on the other side of the baths, perhaps a hundred paces distant, male voices joined in the slow cadences of "Yvana Ride Thunder."

"Valiant, loyal men, ride the five hundred
Ancestors watching them, cheering the charge
Hawkeye Yvana-Vayir. Noddy Toraca
Lead the five hundred . . ."

The voices broke up, one protesting, "No, no, the next verse has to name the captains!"

"Try this—wait—listen! *Lancers united, three lines to charge*—"

"What about the second charge, eh?"

"I'll get to them, but Houndface, he was *there*, said the first charge was three lines, and—"

"Here, stop yapping, *listen* to me! Before the battle part, you have to say things about Hawkeye. And Toraca, too. Garid says it should sound like the same hero deeds in the first verses of the old ballad, when Fleetfoot Yvana issues the challenge to Nickblade Montrei-Hauc—"

"Yes! Yes! Like this." A cleared throat, and a young man began to chant,

"Surrounded at Ghael Hills, vastly outnumbered;
Fire and pirates, Prick Point defending—"

"Not bad, not bad. Only you can't say prick in a war poem—"

"Evred?" That was Barend. Close by.

"Why not? We say it in life—"

"But in the songs you use the right name, see!"

"In that case, why are we saying Hawkeye? I don't even know what his real name is. Wasn't he named for one of the kings?"

Evred met a searching gaze, then Barend's eyes narrowed to their customary squint. "You just stopped, like one of those mages froze you. Something wrong?"

"They're adding verses to 'Yvana Ride Thunder.' " Evred jerked a thumb toward the distant baths on the other side of their privacy curtain. "Was it always this way, arguing about what to put in those old ballads? I always thought bards stood up and spun those songs from the air, the glory of the event somehow turning into gold. Glory." He breathed the word out like an obscenity, then straightened up. "I thought you were going to stay in the baths."

"I did. Quite a while, while you took root there like some tree. I thought the Venn snuck in and put a spell on you. Sponge, you really need some sleep."

"Do you think any songs we make up will take?"

Barend flicked out a hand. "If people like 'em they'll sing 'em. Let's go. Sooner we eat, sooner you hit your hammock."

They fixed up their wet hair, checked to see that their clothes were straight (Barend's newly-assigned Runners had seen to it that he was in proper clothes, not a haphazard collection of old pirate wear under his House tunic), then walked together to the main hall, which hitherto had been converted to an extra barracks.

Evred did not know where the men were housed now. It did not really matter, since he intended Ola-Vayir's as well as his army to be on the march by morning.

Tables had been brought from all over the castle—probably from all over the city. Certainly dishes had been donated. Evred noticed sets of fine old porcelain mixed in with good Marlovan dishes. The Marlovan dishes were plain, shallow bowls, the Olaran and Idayagan varying shapes that the Marlovans eyed with misgiving.

A dais had been erected at one end, with a tapestry-covered table set on it. Inda was already there, laughing at something Cherry-Stripe was saying, Buck next to his brother, head bandaged, one arm in a sling, his face pale with long-endured pain. He blinked slowly: he was full of green kinthus. Inda was using his right hand more, Evred saw; Taumad had been working on it earlier, as he had from time to time during the journey back down the pass. There actually seemed to be some utility in whatever it was he did.

The Jarl of Ola-Vayir had claimed the seat of honor,

which irritated Evred. But if Inda had already ceded it, then it was better not to take notice. A glow of angry triumph warmed him briefly when he recalled that Ola-Vayir was not likely to get his way in much beyond that.

Evred stepped up, and as the old man turned his way, making the usual disclaimers about honor, glory, and the like in too loud a voice, Evred reminded himself that it was not the Jarl's fault that he'd almost been too late. He'd also lost his heir leading a defense against pirates.

Barend elbowed Cherry-Stripe to get him to scoot over, and swung a chair next to Ndand, Flash's wife, who sat at Tdiran-Randviar's left, looking thin and somber. She'd arrived after everything was over, but had been of enormous help in reorganizing the castle.

At Barend's appearance she smiled a welcome, and they fell into low-voiced conversation.

The room was full of civilians in bright dress, as well as all the captains. These latter rose when they saw Evred, and saluted. The merchants and guild chiefs surreptitiously eyed one another; when the tall, gaunt old man who'd been harbormaster of Lindeth for almost half a century gave a slight bow the rest followed suit.

Evred struck his fist to his chest. The civilians could take the gesture how they wished: his salute was for the men.

Everyone sat down. Kitchen people, male and female Runners, and some volunteer city people—mostly youngsters—came out bearing trays of food. Vedrid and Tau served the high table themselves, Tau so quietly and skillfully that the king was not, at first, aware of his presence.

Evred frowned down at the fine bowl set before him, its edges fluted. He hated porcelain. It was impossibly fragile, the pieces often too small to fit comfortably to the hand. It broke almost willfully. His mother, an Adrani, had had porcelain dishes. But the herb-spiced tomato soup in it smelled good, waking the appetite that had slumbered for uncounted days. The soup bowl reminded him of Hawkeye's mate, the potter.

He caught the grim gaze of Tdiran-Randael. He tapped the bowl, and was not surprised when she lifted her chin in comprehension, and then gave her head a shake. Fala was not here, probably by choice.

Another thing to make note of: that Hawkeye's beloved Fala would have a home to go to if she no longer wanted to remain in Ala Larkadhe. And if Hawkeye's twin brothers did not have a place for her—*twins*. Which one was to inherit? Was he to force a division between them by making one of them Jarl?

Evred's headache hammered harder.

He fought off the blanketing shroud of fugue and discovered that Ola-Vayir was talking. To *him*. He forced his attention to the food, and to the talk, which was the expected blunder-footed hinting about royal generosity for loyalty and courage.

Another flare of warmth at Buck's snort, which he turned into a cough.

Evred raised his glass to Buck and drank, then to Ola-Vayir and drank again, until his veins warmed. It was his duty to eat, to be seen enjoying the food, and to be seen smiling over their victory: there must be no reaction that Ola-Vayir, or his friends, could later name resentment, reluctance, or most of all, weakness. Then he must speak, and the praise must be as unstinting as the men's loyal efforts had been.

Inda kept patience until the food had been eaten, and the songs sung (many drumming on the tables with their knives, which plainly horrified the Idayagans)—old songs, mostly, though there were one or two new ones, hastily put together, but cheered with enthusiasm, especially the one that mentioned most of the captains' names.

Then Evred stood up and made a brief speech, naming every person at the high table and what he or she had done, to great cheering. "It has always been our tradition to award the loyal and the brave with further responsibility. I will have more to say between now and Convocation, but my first act shall be to create a new jarlate from the Niolay River in Idayago east to Ghael." Pause for cheers. "And the Jarl shall be Camarend Tya-Vayir, his Jarlan Starand Ola-Vayir." Pause for cheers, and a pensive smile from the Jarl of Ola-Vayir, a smile that hitched, his brows twitching, when he began to suspect the truth: that *this* was going to constitute the extent of family honors.

He cheered with the rest, but inwardly cursed his daughter for insisting he raise that dust over her exile when it really had been her own fault. Everyone would say their family honor was restored, but their gain was all just words.

"My cousin, Barend-Dal, will ride north to carry my wishes to the new Jarl, and to help design the defense of the northern shores. For we must look to the future—and guard against the Venn coming back."

Oh yes, Inda thought, amazed at how Evred had just handed him a good part of his own plan for Barend.

The stone walls rang with cheers, the tables rumbled with such enthusiastic pounding that the dishes jumped, liquids sloshing.

Evred said, "The Tradheval and Andahi regions of Idayago shall be held in promise to Kethadrend Arveas, in honor of his father, mother, and brother. We still do not know what happened at the north end, but what evidence we have is that they sacrificed their lives to hold off the invaders. We do know from the timing of our encounter that however long they held out made all the difference."

A full-throated, heartfelt shout: "Arveas Sigun! Ola-Vayir Sigun!"

And: "*Evred-Harvaldar Sigun!*"

"*Indevan-Harskialdna Sigun!*"

From his seat, Inda waved his empty wine cup in his left hand—his right was still giving him twinges, though a good soak in the baths had helped, and Tau's strong hands had helped even more.

Ola-Vayir's smile thinned, but the Arveases had been popular long before the rumors about their tragic bravery. Evred brought both hands under the wide, shallow wine cup and lifted it high in salute as the men shouted approval, then he recklessly drank the wine off. Hah! There was nothing the Ola-Vayirs could say to that.

Come, finish up, Inda thought, tapping the table. Cherry-Stripe, flushed with wine, glanced his way, question in his lifted brows. Inda stopped drumming and reached for the wine he didn't want to drink, hiding his impatience in movement.

"And so, except for those given specific patrol orders, we shall withdraw, and further announcements will be made at the Triumph to be held by the Jarl of Tya-Vayir."

Evred sat down amid rhythmic shouts of "Evred-Harvaldar! Evred-Harvaldar Sigun!"

Relieved at having brought that off well enough, Evred drained his wine again. Warmth streamed through his veins, rendering voices, sounds, the outer world a pleasant blur. For a time he let it all wash past, caught by the rhythmic crash and surge of his own heartbeat in his ears.

"You've got a headache?" Inda's voice was startlingly near.

Evred's eyes flew open. Ola-Vayir had left. Cherry-Stripe leaned back in his chair, laughing loudly at something Barend said to Ndand.

Inda knelt on Ola-Vayir's vacant chair, his eyes wide and expectant.

Evred turned his own attention to the empty glass in his hands. "Yes," he said, because it seemed simpler.

"I thought so." Inda grinned. His next words broke Evred's rigid but increasingly tenuous grip and flung him into cold air. "Tau? Would you take Evred off and do your magic on him? He's got a headache."

Evred's eyes closed. "No, don't bestir yourselves. I'm fine."

"No you're not," Inda retorted, surprising Cherry-Stripe and Barend, because they never would have dared. They knew how prickly ol' Sponge could be, and becoming king hadn't exactly blunted those thorns. "You've been walking around like a corpse who forgot to fall down. Go on. Tau's good at it, I tell you. I don't know why it is, but whatever he does to my shoulder makes it work. And I can't tell you how many headaches of mine he's killed off."

Evred turned slightly, and there was Taumad standing right behind him, tall, smiling, only a healing cut on his neck indicating he'd been anywhere near a battle. "I do not want to take you from your duties," he said, though he knew it was weak—and could see in the smile narrowing Tau's eyes that he knew Evred knew it.

Tau gestured toward Inda, a courtly gesture, though none of the Marlovans recognized it as such except for Evred. "I believe I was just given an order."

Evred closed his eyes, listened to the rapid wash-wash of his blood through his head, and felt the beginning of the stabbing prong through the eyeballs that was inevitable, especially after he was careless enough to drink more than three glasses of wine. And what had he drunk? Five.

"Very well," he said, and Tau was surprised. He'd made his comment about orders as a mild joke, but the Marlovans all seemed to be reacting as if he was the only one who considered being given an order and choosing to obey it two separate acts.

"Thank you," Evred said. "But not here."

Tau turned a thumb sideways. "The servants' old banquet station is through there. No one's using it."

Evred rose, taking up his wine cup and the bottle. Not because he wanted more wine, but it gave him something to do with his hands. He followed Tau through the back entrance where the servants had brought trays from the kitchens back when the castle served as dwelling for a single family and not as a garrison. To the immediate right was a small room where there had once been tables and shelves for ease of service during banquets, and a handy place to stack dishes afterward. Now it, like so many odd places around the castle, had been fitted haphazardly with sleep mats; the tables were gone, the stone shelves held people's gear. On the far wall the neatness of the folded clothes, the exotic colors and materials, seemed characteristic of Taumad.

Evred turned around. Tau was watching, his expression mild. "Yes, it's also our quarters. The other three are all on duty. You can sit here." He placed the single chair in the middle of the room, between the mats.

Tau shut the door, latched it and then, with a thoughtful

air, removed his Runner's coat, folded it, and set it neatly aside.

Inda watched the door shut from across the room, then turned away. "Keep him busy as long as you can," he'd told Tau.

Without any politeness whatsoever, he grabbed the front of Barend's House tunic and all but yanked Evred's surprised, protesting cousin from his chair. "Come on, you and me are going to have a talk," he said. To Cherry-Stripe, "It's something good. But I don't know if it'll work." To Ndand, "Were you and Keth going to ride back to Castle Andahi right away?"

She was surprised to find herself so abruptly addressed by Inda. "Once I talk to the king about Keth and the academy. Like, how we'll get his dispositions, when there probably isn't a stick of furniture or a stitch of cloth left."

"Leave that to me." Inda brushed his hand down the front of his crimson tunic: he was Harskialdna. "Evred and I know what the family did. You just get Keth down by spring, the rest will be fine."

"All right, then. I can leave anytime." Ndand flushed.

"Saddle up. Tell 'em the order is from me, say it's for at once, if not sooner—and pass the word for the rest of Cama's dragoons over at the Cassad barracks. Those fellows are going north with you." Inda grinned. "The sooner you are there covering our butts, the better everyone will feel."

Ndand found herself grinning back.

"I'll get the horses seen to, and ask my niece to fetch young Keth from the castle children," Tdiran-Randviar said, having listened to all this. "You go pack, Ndand. Including a full pouch of arrows," she added with scowling distrust. "You never know if them Venn'll come back on the sneak. Wouldn't put it past 'em."

Chapter Twenty-eight

EVRED set the wine bottle carefully by the chair leg, sat back, and braced himself to endure.

He trusted his lethal mood to keep the necessary distance between his will and his physical self.

Taumad said nothing about removing clothing, which would have been summarily rejected. Tau did not even try to disarrange Evred's heavy crimson tunic, stiff with golden embroidery. He just placed his hands over the top of Evred's shoulders, fingers either side of his collarbones, and thumbs on the rock-knotted muscle at the base of his neck at either side of his spine.

And then began to knead. At first gently, so gently Evred experienced a brief—and promptly dismissed—wish that there were not two layers of clothing intervening.

"As it happens I really can get rid of headaches," Taumad said, his tone light, impersonal. Evred was wary, all angles and tension over and above the rigid muscle structure caused by a lifetime of slowly tightening stress. "But it takes a few moments to discover the likely physical cause."

He said nothing about mental or temperamental causes.

Evred's shoulders dropped a fraction.

That was the right approach, then: easy, professional. The body seen as a vessel, only distantly connected to will or identity. He must talk to Evred-Harvaldar, and not to

Sponge. That citadel permitted access to few, and two of them had recently died.

Inda stopped on the stairway to what he considered the captains' wardroom. ". . . No, we hadn't bedded down," someone was saying. "We nipped at the Venn all night. Come dawn we'd just pulled back to plan another run when one of the Marlo-Vayir outriders reported Ola-Vayir on the way. Buck said we should bring them up to the hills above the river. What fun that was! We charged like thunder, all in a line, and half them vinegar-stinking shits pissed their pants."

Raucous laughter rose. Inda sent Barend a glance, brows raised in question.

Barend turned his thumb down. "Fought just as hard as we did." Inda shrugged; he'd learned after overhearing tavern talk following some of his pirate battles that they'd killed ten or twenty or fifty times more pirates than had been in both fleets.

They passed down the rest of the narrow stone hallway, and stopped. Barend checked to make certain they were alone. They were, though voices echoed up the stairways at both ends of the hall. "Here's what I didn't tell you and Evred in front of the others. Buck said he'd ride to Norsunder before he'd let Ola-Vayir lead the charge." He opened a hand. "His heir was the academy bully when Buck was a scrub."

Inda said, "So leading the charge shows the son up? I thought the son was dead!"

"Is."

"So Buck nearly gets himself killed?" Inda threw his arms out wide, then resumed his fast walk. "Maybe that will make sense someday. Here." They'd reached one of the cubbyholes that, from the looks of the contents, had been a wood repair station. A couple of sleeping mats lay on the floor, a reminder of how cramped space was. "Barend, I want you to go north with Ndand and the men, because I think I have a way to fill that treasury. Like, with treasure. Pirate treasure. What could be better?"

"*Pirate* treasure?" Barend's eyes widened for a moment, reflecting the light of the candle Inda lit from the torch in the sconce outside. As Inda shoved the candle into a lamp hanging on a wall hook, Barend demanded, "Inda, what exactly happened at Ghost Island?"

"We found the treasure." Inda spread his hands. "There really was one. More like fifty treasures. Well, not that I know how big a treasure is supposed to be. It lies in a cavern bigger than that feasting hall. Mounds as tall as a man, and that's just the stuff above the waterline. I read the Brotherhood Book—it really was written in blood, and remind me to tell you what Ramis said about that—but it was *generations* of treasure."

"Ramis," Barend repeated. "The one who made the rift to Norsunder and shoved Marshig through?"

"Along with five other capital ships. Yes, that Ramis. And yes, I know what you're going to say about believing, so belay it. I was there, the treasure is there."

"Right."

"So here's what I want you to do. Go to Bren, talk to Fleet Master Chim. He can tell you who's trustworthy. Take a fleet of ships. Bring the treasure to the north shore here, where we can rely on Cama to take charge and— what?" This last word Inda barked when he saw Barend's expression of skepticism.

"Inda, do you have any idea what problems a bunch of jewels and so forth will cause?"

"It's also Sartoran coinage, the big twelve-siders as well as six, all gold. But what problems? Evred says the treasury is empty. Won't that fill it?"

Barend rubbed his nose. "Treasury isn't treasure," he said finally. "Oh, I thought it was. Evred did too when we were in the schoolroom, he told me. Said he used to slide his finger past all mentions of money in search of more battles, when he was reading. I don't know how much of that is true and how much was him trying to keep me from feeling stupid. Because I know Uncle Tlennen was a master hand with the ins and outs of trade and so forth, and taught Sponge some." Another vigorous rub.

Inda said, "Evred said we have no treasury. I want to bring that treasure in as a surprise for Sponge. That's why this secrecy. I don't want him worrying about that, too, d'you see it?"

Barend held out his hands. "No, no, I agree. You're right. Less to worry him, the better. Things are bad enough. But . . . Inda, as for the rest . . . I don't know where to start."

Laughing voices neared.

"Start with what's in the treasury, if it's not treasure." Inda kicked the door shut and crossed his arms.

The tingle in Evred's muscles intensified to an itch. It was the strangest sensation—not exactly unpleasant, very faint but distinct. It bothered him enough to force him to stand, pull off his tunic, and set it neatly behind him over the back of the chair.

Tau said nothing. When Evred sat down again, he increased the pressure incrementally, following the contour of Evred's muscles under the fine linen shirt.

Tau controlled the impulse to let his fingers drift over those contours, and shifted to using his knuckles for a slow increase in pressure at certain points, then releasing. Much less personal—less dangerous for a person so taut.

Evred was only aware that the itch was almost . . . not scratched, what would you call it? Pressed? He had no words, no one had ever done that to him before. He hadn't wanted anyone to do that. But the opportunity to kill that persistent drum behind his eyes was so persuasive. The prospect of clear thought again . . . Except that his mind, gradually freed of pain, refused to ride to harness. Tomorrow's tasks, the next day's, next week's, what he must accomplish before he faced the Jarls at Convocation, he could not focus on any of it. His mind stayed stubbornly on his limbs warming to that itch-that-was-not-an-itch, even though Tau's hands had not strayed from his shoulders.

He cast down the golden wine cup onto one of the sleeping mats, grabbed up the bottle, and took a swig out of it. The wine chased away the tickle or tingle or whatever it was. That he did not want.

Tau's hands had lifted when he moved, but when he stilled, the wine bottle gripped in his fingers, back they came. Knuckles again, pressing down into the ache. Evred shut his eyes, leaning into them so the pressure would increase. He wished those hands could press the rocks away, right down to his bones; Tau was using his full strength now, and had loosened the top layer, but felt stubborn muscle beneath.

After a time, Tau said, "That's enough there. You don't need bruises. Instead, I'll shift to the sides. This is one of the places that kills Inda's headaches the fastest."

That was the first mention of the name between them. Evred had never wanted to talk about Inda with anyone, Tau least of all.

But now it seemed safe, for the matter was headaches. Nothing personal. Yet the questions in Evred's mind were nothing but personal.

He took another swig, like many who lock themselves from communication, permitting the liquor to turn the key.

"I'm surprised," he said, "that such methods work on Inda. I'd gathered he does not like to be touched."

Inda? What happened? Tau thought.

Tau dug into the sides of Evred's neck. The muscles were like knobs of bone. He said carefully, "Inda likes me to use my skills on that right shoulder of his. You know he's taken damage there. I think that actually happened when he first took ship, or not long after."

And Evred said, "Tell me." He bowed his head, resting it against his thumbs, fingers laced loosely around the wine bottle.

Tau kept his voice light and detached as he related the story of Inda's first days at sea, the fight with Norsh and its results. Events so very long ago, another lifetime entirely. Yet, judging from the subtle reactions Tau felt under his hands, still immediate for Evred.

He finished, "And we are fairly certain he was tortured while in Ymar. He never minded people's proximity before then, but afterward, we all saw him recoil if he did not expect to be touched. Especially around his head. His hair was drying on a mild day last winter, and we were on deck eating and planning a raid. Against the Venn raider at Ghael, as it happens. The wind blew a lock of Inda's hair into Dasta's slurry. He lifted it out. Inda whipped around and for a heartbeat or two we thought he would deck Dasta." Tau chuckled at the memory.

Evred had gone tense again at the word *tortured*, and did not relax during the quick shift to the funny story. Tau cursed himself for undoing all the good work he'd done, and added, "In any case, Inda never talks about it, so we know nothing of the details. But we never touch his head and keep our food out of reach of his hair."

A pause, another drink of the wine, then Evred took him by surprise, holding the bottle up over his shoulder. He did so without speech, without looking at Tau, but the offer was clear.

Sharing wine. A human gesture—a *personal* gesture. After having traveled in Evred's proximity for a season, Tau knew how very rare those were.

And though Tau never drank when he was working, he broke that rule now, and helped himself to a long, sweet pull. Fire burned along veins and nerves as he handed the bottle back, and Evred set it down. "I did not know," Evred said finally.

"Like I mentioned, he doesn't talk about it. He didn't talk about any of you, either, for nine years."

Tau shifted to thumbs, pressing outward in slow strokes, working up the side of Evred's neck to the muscles at the base of his skull, then at last the sides of his jaw.

A sharp indrawn breath. "That hurts."

"Let your mouth hang open. No one can see. It's the way you'll get rid of the headache. I press some of the knotwork out of the hinges of your jaw."

A soft laugh, a slight tightening, then an act of will to relax again. "If we used torture, this would be a sure one."

Tau said, "It works. But no one likes it."

Evred contemplated a sharp retort, except he didn't feel angry. The rushing in his ears was gone, leaving a pleasant lassitude. He said, "Do something that works but doesn't feel like a hot knife through the skull."

Tau hesitated, then shifted his grip, working the tightness out of the muscles below Evred's collarbones, back over to the shoulder blades, and then front again, slow and easy.

Evred's surface tension was nearly gone. Lingering in the deeper muscle layers was the iron-cable tension of years. Tau waited until Evred's breathing had lost the last of the self-conscious control then said mildly, "This goes better if you are lying flat."

The muscles under his hands jumped: back to surface tension, wariness, distrust.

But then Evred bent forward, almost pulling Tau off balance, grabbed up his wine. Passed it back, again without looking. And again Tau took a drink, a long one meant to mute his own responses.

Evred cast himself face down onto the nearest mat.

Tau set the bottle carefully under the chair, knelt down, and spread his fingers over Evred's back, testing the stresses there, and the pulse under the muscles.

Someone banged on the door to the woodworking alcove. Inda and Barend ignored the noise.

"I'm trying to think of a short way to explain," Barend said, after a scowling pause. "Heh. Remember when you paid off the Pims' debt? The guild didn't send money, did they?"

"No, they wrote up what they called a letter of credit. I signed it, and they put on a sved with magic."

"Well, when the Pims got that letter, like as not they didn't demand gold. Nobody in all Lindeth has that much gold anymore. So they used the letter in place of gold. She gives the letter to her own guild, and then writes letters of credit against that letter, until it's all used up."

"What's to stop her from writing letters for twice the amount, if everyone is just sending letters around?"

"That's what the sveds are for. Guild scribes are very specific. You're used to the cheap sved new hands carry on board new hires. All that promises is that someone accepted as a witness spoke for you, said you are who you said you are. Scribes write what they hear. Money scribes write what they count. Their standing depends on never being so much as a copper-flim off. In some places, their lives depend on it."

Inda remembered watching Kodl deal with dock officials—something he'd never had to do. "Letters of credit, right. I think I have it. So there's money somewhere, then, right?"

"Right. That's half of it. The other half is made up of time and the what they call 'kind.' Kind is trade of things for other things, and time is what the Jarls pay taxes in, along with kind: you owe the king a certain number of men per year. That means trained men with their horses and gear. In times of war, the king can ask for more, but there's another kind of cost to that, and he has to pay most of it. And then there are things like deathgild if a man dies while under orders, costs of animals, costs for training, costs for patrols and defense and so forth. It's mostly measured in time, and translated out into established charges for food and garrison and stable and who pays for boots and steel and the rest. The guilds all do that accounting."

"Got it. So Evred's used most of the crown's share up?"

"It was already being used up before Hawkeye's dad went after my uncle with a sword. If Yvana-Vayir had won, he would have discovered an empty treasury and no oath-sworn dues coming in, either. Not to *him*. Unless he had more allies than we knew." Barend snorted. "Always possible."

Inda waved a hand, as if waving away Barend's words. "So tell me why jewels and gold are bad. I didn't have any problems with them. Nor did any of the rest of us."

Barend shook his head. "Have you seen any Stringers in this country?"

Inda was going to point out that he hadn't been in it but a few months, and never in any harbor—then he realized what Barend meant. Even if he rode straight over to Lindeth, he was not likely to find any of the people in the brown clothes of their guild, silken counting strings at their belts. "No money changers because there's no trade. Right."

"People here deal with their guilds. There might be some willing to turn jewels into time or kind, but none of 'em could do a kingdom-sized job. So your jewels will just be a lot of bright stones. Good for plugging holes."

Inda sagged against a rack of woodworking tools. "Damn."

It was Barend's turn to wave a hand. "I didn't say it was impossible. Just that there needs to be a step between getting your treasure and turning it into anything Evred can use."

Someone banged on the door again.

"Tell me how," Inda said.

Tau kneaded his way down Evred's spine, trying not to think too much about the strength he felt in those slowly uncoiling muscles, the clean, strong lines of his body. Most of all the amazingly . . . human aspect to Evred, lying there in a rumpled shirt and trousers, no weapons or banners or throngs of attentive Runners to assist him in keeping the world at a distance.

No man is made of stone.

One can try to be, but like any other effort to wrest change from one nature to another, there is a cost.

Evred drifted. He could attribute the euphoria to wine haze, but that just muted the intensity of desire and well-being mixed that resulted from the touch of those strong, knowing hands. How could one know just where to press, where to stroke so slowly with the thumb, how scratching lightly down the outsides of the arms left trails of invisible fire?

Evred had not moved, save to fling his arms out in a loose curve round his head, which lay on one side, face to the wall.

He could not know that Tau heard his mood in his breathing, and smiled crookedly as he dug with the heels of his palms deep into the muscles supporting the trunk, knowing full well the effect it had. Tau laughed inwardly, aware of the danger he was playing with, but that was exactly the attraction. He could sympathize with the heart-wounded, be kind to the hopelessly devoted, hold off with cool reserve the hungrily possessive, but complexity and danger, yes, and power, were a constant allure.

He also knew that prolonged isolation did not make one sane.

And so, not knowing what to expect, he finished working to the extremity of hands and feet. And when Evred slowly, reluctantly propped himself on his elbows, head down, face hidden, Tau leaned down and placed on the back of that pale, exposed neck a loud, mocking kiss.

Evred's violent recoil surprised a laugh out of Tau. Who sat back on his heels and watched those angry, wary green eyes take in the locked door, the room, Tau. Who matched him in size, and strength, and mood.

Tau smiled, a rare smile: mocking, his upper lip curled just enough to show his white canines, unexpectedly sharp. "I think you're afraid of me," he drawled. "Prove that you're not."

Evred doubled up his fist and slugged Tau.

"So you're saying you won't do it?"

"No, that's not what I'm saying." Barend kicked the toe of his moc against a cabinet.

The banging on the door redoubled into thunder. "Go somewhere else! This is our room!" someone roared.

Inda turned his head. "Go away! This is important state business!"

Barend snorted, and as voices mumbled outside the

door—the only distinct one saying, "It is? No it's not, why would he lock himself in our closet?"—he said, "You shouldn't have done that. You know they'll be waiting when we open the door."

Inda turned his palm up. "Why not? There's no privacy anywhere else, why not an important conference here?"

"Because no one will believe it's a conference," Barend said with a wheezy laugh.

Inda's brows shot up, then he grinned like a scrub. "Good. Far fewer questions that way. Want to make some noises, help them along?"

"I do not." Barend straightened up. "All right. It'll take some time, mind you, because I'm going to be turning that treasure of yours into ships. Trade. I'll see if I can find wood anywhere, though we're bound to be paying triple the price."

"Whatever it takes. That treasure is just sitting there. Someone has to use it, may as well be us. Rescue a kingdom."

"I'm gonna laugh if we arrive and it's not there. Meantime, what do we tell Evred?"

"Nothing about the treasure," Inda said firmly. "If we actually get it, then let it be a surprise. He could use a good surprise. As for why you're going east, well, let's tell him you're going to contact Chim's fleet to negotiate the possibility of trade. Which has the advantage of being true."

"We'll tell him in the morning, right before I leave with Ndand for the pass. He's sure to like the idea of trade negotiations, not to mention a possible fleet."

"That's what I had in mind." Inda smacked the bar up and yanked the door open.

Three identical expressions of amazement greeted him and Barend as they walked out. Inda made it about five steps before he succumbed to snickers.

Chapter Twenty-nine

"INDA."

The whisper was more insistent, woven into the sound of the wind through snapping sails; when it repeated next to Inda's ear, the dream washed over and past him, leaving him lying in bed. He started up, hands flailing.

Signi sat up as well, a stray beam of departing moonlight shining in her wide eyes.

"Sorry to wake you, Dag Signi." It was Tau. "I need Inda for just a moment."

"In the middle of the night?" Inda protested. "I just shut my eyes."

"It's a couple of glass-turns before the dawn watch. Come outside?"

Inda muttered curses as he fumbled around for his trousers. He stuck his feet in, hopping as he pulled them on and followed Tau out of the room. Inda had been given an actual room, one with a real bed. Too bad he'd only gotten this half watch to sleep in it, he thought irritably as Tau shut the door behind them.

Then he recognized Tau's blue coat and his gear slung over one shoulder. Inda sniffed. There was the faint, distinct trace of herbs in the soap that Tau had bought at great expense from Colend, and had hoarded ever since he'd left

Bren. Tau was not only bathed, dressed, and ready for the day, he was leaving.

"Where are you going?" Inda asked in dismay. "Why? What happened?"

"To answer the first question is why I'm here. As for the second—" Tau checked the silent hall. The doors were all closed, behind which the remaining Sier Danas slept. "Come out on the wall," he said abruptly.

They walked through the empty stairwell to the sentry walk. The only posted guards were women as lookouts on the four towers: with an entire army cramming the city, Evred had declared the walls did not require sentries, and had issued general liberty.

Faint blue smeared the eastern horizon. The air was soft. It would be a very hot day for a ride. But they were no longer in a hurry.

Inda shook his head to get the fog out of it. The woman at the top of the east tower recognized him, touched fingers to chest, then turned away.

Tau said, "I need you to send me on an errand. Something a Runner would do."

Inda thumped his fist on a stone battlement. "What's going on, Tau?"

"I had a tangle with your Evred."

"You what?" Inda rubbed his thumbs across his eyelids. When he peered more closely at Tau in the torchlight, there was a mark on one cheekbone, and dark roughness across his knuckles. "You didn't get into a fight with him," he exclaimed in dismay.

"It was fun," Tau retorted, with a quick grin. "It was fun for us both. I don't think he's permitted himself to just have fun for far too long," he added reflectively, his tone odd enough to send warning prickles through Inda's nerves. Inda shook his head violently, trying to wake up as Tau went on, "He's had storm sail set too long. I gave him an eye in the storm. I'd better be gone before the winds hit from the other direction."

Inda leaned his arms on the battlement. "Tau," he said, exasperated. "That doesn't make any sense."

"Let me try it this way. One reason Evred's so taut is that he doesn't trust people easily. He doesn't trust emotions at all."

Inda said, "He's been—" He rubbed his eyes again. "Don't know how to describe it. Shut away, sometimes. All the time since Noddy died."

It started when he first laid eyes on you, is my guess. Or maybe it started when he was born. But Tau only said, "I used scrapping to seduce him. And he enjoyed it as much as I did, I made sure of that."

Maybe even more, because Evred so very rarely permitted anyone to breach the ringed ice-walls of his reserve. But the powerful effect of that breach had gone both ways. Tau had always known that sex and fighting were dangerously parallel desires in some people; he was drawn that way himself. But that did not explain the compelling, almost overwhelming lucency of Evred lying there wrist-lax and utterly undone.

Tau knew two things: that no one had ever seen Evred so exposed, and that Evred would waken to equivalent suspicion-impelled anger.

Tau became aware of Inda's confusion. "By the time Evred comes to breakfast he'll most likely have talked himself into thinking I'm as vile as Coco. People like Coco happen too often to those in power. It'll be better for everyone if I'm not there."

"Right. I get it now." Inda almost rubbed his eyes again, but dropped his hand. "If you're gone, and there isn't any bragging or any demands like Coco made, then everything goes back to normal. Huh. Since we already sent the Runners with the personal letters to Khani-Vayir and Yvana-Vayir, how's this? You go all the way south to Choraed Elgaer. Remember Tdor? See, after this triumph in Tya-Vayir, I'm to go home, get married. I did write Tdor a quick note, but I haven't had time for a letter about everything. That way, it's understandable orders."

"Perfect." Tau grinned. "I'll see you at your wedding, then." He gave Inda an ironic salute and vanished into the tower stairwell.

Wedding. What a strange sound that had. Inda had expected all his early life to marry Tdor, and had longed for a return to that life all the years he was at sea. And now it was time to do it. But it felt strange. No stranger than being a Harskialdna, though. He laughed inwardly as he let himself back into the room.

Signi had kindled a light, and dressed. She sat neatly, hands folded. "Is there trouble?"

"No. Tau needed an errand, and I gave him one. Sent him to tell Tdor to get ready for my wedding."

Signi smiled. "She will be glad of good news."

Inda dropped down and squashed her in a tight hug. "I wish I could marry you, too," he said huskily, his face pressed into her hair. "You hardly got to talk to her, but I know you'd like her. Everyone likes Tdor. I think she'd like you, too."

Signi held him away and looked earnestly into his face. "Ah. I was going to say, there are places where you can marry whom you like, and there is no limit in number. It's just a matter of degree—"

"Don't tell me: Colend."

She chuckled. "Yes. Among other places. I am honored, dear Inda. But you know, even if Tdor was not waiting, and no family expecting you to take your place, I could never marry in this country."

Inda's joy faded. "I guess I see that."

It was her turn to hug him. "I beg your pardon, dear Inda. You give love with both hands, without calculation. I take the joy of that, and we will not worry ourselves about what marriage means."

He played with her fingers absently, his brow puckered. "I never thought about *that* at all. I just knew, oh, I liked the idea of being married to Tdor. You too," he added uncomfortably, then grinned. "Just supposing we could marry anyone we wanted? If she's got a favorite, would that mean four people get married? I hope it's Whipstick. Not Branid." Inda remembered what Tau had told him, and laughed. "Whipstick. Huh. He was fourteen when I left. We thought him so old and tough! All he thought about were fart jokes and stings and winning scraps. Do you have to sleep with everybody you marry, in those other lands? I just can't see hopping under the covers with his skinny, hairy arms and legs, and then he cracks some joke about bran gas."

Signi chuckled, a quiet sound.

Inda said, "Though he probably wouldn't want me, either." His sudden grin reminded her how young he was.

She wiped her eyes, tenderness hollowing all around her heart. "Marriage and love have so many meanings." Her voice softened to huskiness. "Marriage cannot build walls to keep love inside. Marriage can give a structure to the family."

"To the castle." Inda jerked his thumb toward the walls. "The people of the castle."

"You Marlovans marry your place and your duty as well as a person." She made one of her complicated hand gestures. "Oh, it is the same with us: the meaning of marriage lies mostly in our place among our fellows. But love is free as air."

Inda swung his arm round, thinking that over. She caressed his cheek and then left to go down to the baths.

She's going to leave me, he thought, sobered. Then rubbed his shoulder absently. *But not now.*

He got up and sat at the little table, shoved aside the royal order book that he'd taken to look at before sleeping, pulled out one of the scraps of paper he'd sliced before, and wrote:

> *Fox. We're done with the Venn, and I'm alive. If you want details, let me know. I'm sending Barend to get the treasure. The kingdom is in worse shape than our fleet after the Brotherhood battle, and I mean to fix it.*

On the other side of the world, as the sun began to set, Mutt vented his sour mood by uttering a stream of curse-punctuated, unfair observations of Fox. If he and his mates had been stupid enough to think that the wind dying to calm would mean an easy day or two, Fox must have stayed up for nights figuring out so many ways to prove them wrong.

They'd begun by replacing winter-worn rope and changing to summer sail. As for free time before the afternoon drill? No! They boomed planks over the sides so they could sand and repaint the sleek, low hull of the *Death*. True, its fine black paint had worn streaky over the winter. But why paint it now, when there was every chance they were sailing straight into battle? Why not *after* the battle, when they weren't already drilling for two solid watches, making arrows with the wood and feathers they'd scrounged off the Fog Islands, and resharpening all their steel weapons?

They wanted to ask. Well, they each wanted the others to ask. Nobody wanted to risk getting flayed by Fox's sarcasm. He'd been in a nasty mood for days, either lurking in his cabin, or prowling around when least expected—or wanted.

The entire fleet knew Fox was in a temper.

All the other captains had remained prudently on their stations, their activities matching the flagship's. "Cowards," Mutt snarled, whacking his paintbrush against the sternpost. Naturally the ship gave a lurch, he nearly fell backward, and the paintbrush splattered back into his face.

And just as naturally, everybody was watching.

Out of the howls and comments came Pilvig's voice, "He's on the move!"

At once they fell silent, everybody sedulously painting, except those at the booms, attentive to the ropes.

Mutt peered over the rail. Fox looked exactly as wicked as always. Except—was that squint a laugh, or just an eye-tightening against the brightness of the sun?

"Who's on flags? I want all captains. Fangras as well." He paused, leaning down. "Less chatter and more work might get that done today," he added as several glares were shot at Mutt.

A short time later Fox faced the captains, with Fangras attending silently, as spokesperson for the loose confederation of former Sarendan privateers.

"We're not far from Freedom Islands." Fox held up his position chart so that all the captains gathered in his cabin could see the islands and their fleet a finger's width apart. "There's been no message since Fangras joined us, so Khanerenth is probably coming to attack Freeport Harbor. Now, we know Dhalshev. Once the king's friend, as well as former high admiral. He won't let us take any Khanerenth ships, despite this attack, which may only be a test foray. There's no reward in risking our lives boarding and carrying any of 'em."

The captains all signified agreement.

"So we want to damage them enough to make them feel their test has failed for a generation or more. How? Sail right through their midst, and let 'em chase us. Then we shoot 'em up. If they board, we'll board them, make as much damage as we can, then leave."

Eflis chortled, and Gillor sat back in her chair, arms crossed. "Schooner ruse, I'm guessing?"

"Right." Fox drummed his fingers on the chart. "Fangras, if you or one of your fastest craft want to be our chase, that's fine. Be aware they might not let you through unscathed."

Fangras grinned. "I'll take that position meself, then there's no arguing."

Fox lifted a hand in acknowledgment. "Here's the twist. Those of us on the chase are going to be running the red sails."

"Red sails?"

"*Brotherhood* sails?"

"But those are *pirate* sails!"

Fox waited for the noise to die down. When no one got an answer, they shut up. "I hope most of you have your red sails in storage."

"We turned the red storm sails into hammocks," Dasta said.

"Then unstitch them and make them sails again. The rest of you, dye some of your older summer sails with red paint. They just have to get through this one ruse. Now, we're all going to be trailing smoke, hunters as well as prey. The red sails behind me. What I want Khanerenth to see as they start their battle line is this ship, the *Death,* at the head of the chase, and behind that a gray cloud full of fire and red sails."

Gillor hooted. "I see where you're going." She hooked her thumb out at the weather deck. "We've got a bad enough rep on this tub to look like ten sails all by ourselves, especially in smoke."

Fox grinned. "Right. They won't know if this is a separate attack or a defense by Freedom's confederation. Throw them into confusion and fear. Above all fear."

Eflis chortled. "Red sails. No wonder we been prinking and prettying!"

"But if we're all smoking, how do we maneuver?" Tcholan asked. "We don't want to risk ramming one another."

"We'll sail straight through them, fire arrows both sides only at targets you can see. Then continue on straight north. Dhalshev and the Federation can deal with the mess."

Thoughtful looks, then Eflis said, "Why are we going north?"

"Thought it was time to investigate the strait. See if the Venn are back, or gone, or who thinks they rule the waters."

Eflis whistled on her way out.

Dasta, Tcholan, and Gillor waited until everyone else was gone. Then Dasta shut the door. "That's an Inda kind of plan," he observed. "The strait, I mean."

Fox tipped his chair back on two legs. "So no one else would think of sailing up the strait but Inda?"

Gillor and Dasta turned questioning gazes to each other. Tcholan just scowled down at the deck. No one knew who was in control of the strait anymore. No one had thought Fox would care one way or another.

"Sounds all right to me," Dasta said, and the other two signified agreement.

Chapter Thirty

CAMA and his front riders reined up.

None of them had believed the war was over, just like that. But following the Venn through the silent canyons day after day gradually brought them to think of it as true.

The pass was a long, narrow, twisting canyon of ever-changing shadow. Over the echoing rumble of a departing army rose the closer rustlings of brush as some unseen animal passed, the distant scream of the gliding raptors, and all around them the steady hiss, drip, and trickle of water after the frequent, short thunderstorms.

The Venn did not dispatch skirmishers to cover their retreat, though they guarded their tail. Venn occasionally caught glimpses of Cama's force and the other way around. As long as the Venn kept moving, the Marlovans would remain at a respectful distance.

The Venn fires at night beat with a ruddy reflected glow all the way up the cliffs. Prudently the dragoons made no campfires except once, when one of Cama's scouts discovered a curiously scooped-looking cave as if a gigantic hand had reached down and poked into the stone with a knuckle.

Morning poured warm light on water-smoothed walls, highlighting stripes in the stone. Once, unimaginably long ago, this pass had been the bed of a river. Cama frequently eyed the enormous cliffs overhead, aware of the silent power of stone, and water, and time. He tried to guess at the scale of the cataclysm that had caused a river to change its pattern of flow.

When the gradually widening bluffs gave a glimpse of the sea, the Marlovans ranged up. They'd been told that the castle lay two or three bends below that prospect.

There had been no letters from Inda in the magical gold case since the one informing Cama that he was now a Jarl—with his new orders—so Cama knew the Venn hadn't come back for a second try in the south.

"We'll wait here," he said in a low voice.

It was going to take a long time for the Venn to get through the tunnel. Cama surveyed the scene, then said to his dragoon captain, "We'll camp. Cold. Send scouts to watch 'em go."

Fists thumped scruffy travel-worn coats. They wheeled the horses and started a slow walk back, looking for a good spot to camp. The pair starting a perimeter inspection reacted, and Cama heard why a moment later: distant, faint cries.

Those were not birds.

One of the men said, "Up there."

The sun was dipping toward the western side of the pass, which lit up the eastern side with rare clarity. The seemingly solid cliffs had more cracks and crags than one assumed; just visible in an old crevasse a little figure waved.

Cama's dragoon captain exclaimed, "It's a girl."

A thin, filthy child of ten or so slid carefully around a water-carved rocky spire on a crag about castle-tower height. "You're Marlovans?" she called down.

Her voice was so thin and high Cama decided against a joking, "No, we're Venn." Despite the distance the sinking sun shone clearly on her filthy face and clothes, her thin limbs. So he lifted his voice. "I'm Camarend Tya-Vayir, sent by the king." And waited while she took in the riding coats, the Nelkereth horses, the tear-shaped shields. Runners in blue. The horsetails, the curved swords. Not Venn.

The time it took her to check everything, her head jerking birdlike, wiped every smile away.

She vanished behind the spire.

That released the men to action, amid the rough jokes that had become habitual as they followed the enemy along the pass, camping when they did.

The Runners carried around journey bread and jugs of water filled at the last waterfall. The men were just beginning their meal when the perimeter guard gave a shout. Everyone set aside their bowls to fetch weapons, lowering their hands when a line of dirty, gaunt children emerged from a barely discernable trail beyond a rockfall. The two tallest girls bore on their shoulders small children barely out of babyhood. Two other children carried a small one in a makeshift sling made of two packs tied together.

Cama said, "We've got food."

"Food." The word whispered along the line. The men offered their journey bread. Most of the children grabbed it and stuffed their faces. Two or three just stood, staring downward, and a couple of very small ones sucked in air and sobbed, a quiet, helpless, broken crying as if they'd been doing it for a very long time.

Every father and brother there ached to comfort them. But one look at the distraught faces, and they waited, distraught themselves, for the children to make the first move.

One girl silently surrendered the smallest to offered hands. Two of the babies—they really were scarcely more than babies—went willingly to strong arms, quiet voices. The third clutched a girl's trousers with one hand, thumb in mouth.

"I'm Han—that is, I'm really Hadand Tlen," the first girl said. "Rider-family, cousin to Liet-Jarlan. They call me Han." She wiped her nose on her dirt-gritty sleeve. Her face was smeared with snot and mud and moss stains. Cama realized the dirt was purposeful—camouflaging—as the child said, "Liet-Jarlan put me in charge. We were to wait for—" She clamped her mouth shut.

"Sit down." Cama made a sign to his Runner in charge of meals. "Find a cave that will smother most of the light.

Start a fire." To Han, in a calm voice, "Eat. You drink coffee? We have just a few beans left in the bag. We were saving it for—well." He didn't usually yap, but the silent struggle this girl made to keep control rattled him.

She stared down at the bread in her hands, her mouth working, for what seemed a long time. Then Cama said, "You can report after you eat."

She crammed the bread into her mouth with both hands.

Cama went around and spoke a little to each child. Most of the very smallest were frightened by him, and shrank near the one with the baby clutching her. "I'm Lnand," she said, and made a little business of fussing and petting them.

The two nine-year-old girls were too exhausted to speak, but the freckle-faced one smiled at the men, her relief at rescue clear to them all.

Cama paused when he came to Hal, whose thin face was familiar. Cama ruffled his hair. "Name?"

"Hal." Hal did not know why he was whispering. He was safe now. Maybe it was just being hungry. "Haldred. Mondavar." He cleared his throat and said in a stronger voice, "I ran as scout. Me and Dvar." Pointing at one of the girls.

"He was a good scout. He was the best scout I ever saw," Han said thickly, around a bite of bread.

Cama smiled down at Hal. "I know your brother. He was just a scrub when I was a horsetail. He fought in my army a couple of times, on banner games. Name's Moon, right?" And then, "Know what I think? I think you should join him next year."

Hal blushed furiously at having someone say right out the thing he'd wanted most, and had been told (with sympathy and understanding, but firmly) that he couldn't have. "But da's just a Rider captain. They said only one son could go."

Cama laughed. "You'll see. Now eat that journey bread. If you get any skinnier your trousers will fall off, and they'll all be calling you Moon Two."

Hal grinned, dizzy with happiness.

When the children were done eating, many took a child or two into their tents and tucked them up into their bedrolls. The smallest ones were slumbering within a couple of heartbeats. The older ones sat up, listening through the open flaps of the tents as Cama said, "Han. Are you ready to give me a report?"

"Yes." Han squared her shoulders.

Her report was disjointed at first, as she jumped back and forth in time. When she got to the name Gdir she hunched up, face distorted in a rictus of pain.

Cama's Runner scorched the last of his precious coffee beans—all the way from Sartor—then pressed them into powder with a spoon. He poured boiling water over them and handed her the fresh coffee before Han spoke again.

She held the mug in her hands, her light eyes glimmering with firelight from the low fire in the cave fifty paces away as she said in a dull monotone, "We—some—thought we were cowards if we didn't go back and check. But there were our orders to stay put, fight only if they discovered us. Gdir got mad." She turned her head, sent a long look at the other girl, who sat with a slumbering three-year-old on her lap, firelight glinting in the little one's red curls.

Cama sensed dire significance in that long look.

Han turned around again. "Gdir went anyway. With her brother and cousins. I went to bring them back. We saw Venn on the walls. Then a line of Idayagans came down the landslide. Gdir yelled to let her help, let her help. Then some Idayagan yelled little Marlovan shits! And shot Gdir dead. Her brother ran. To help. And her cousins. They killed them all. Left them lying right there." Han's skinny chest heaved. She took a big swallow of the coffee, and choked, then swigged down some more. "I didn't–I couldn't—"

"Hold hard." Cama leaned forward, his one eye steady in the distant firelight. "The Idayagans shot those children out of hand? Were your friends armed?"

"Gdir had her bow. So did I. But hers wasn't even strung, and mine was loose-strung, and I was doggo. I mudded up, see."

"Good," Cama said. "They didn't?"

"No. I don't think Gdir thought there would be anyone.

Her brother didn't have anything—he's six. Was." A hiss of indrawn breath. Her lips trembled, her knuckles whitened.

Cama rubbed his jaw, trying to get control of the rage her words caused. Rage made one issue stupid orders.

But he was aware of the listeners behind him, so he said, "You gave Gdir orders—the same orders you were given—and she disobeyed?"

The child shaped a protest, clearly intending to loyally defend her dead friends, but obedience to orders was the first concept drilled into them all.

She hesitated, then finally flicked her thumb up. "Yes."

"So the Idayagans began searching for you?"

"Yes." Han opened her dirty, rock-scratched palm. "The Idayagans came back. They spread out. Searching. They came down to the landslide from higher on the Twisted Pine Path. It was night, see. But we kept watch. Venn didn't patrol the landslide. So me'n Lnand and Freckles and Dvar, we went out and shot 'em. Outside in. So they wouldn't get Gdir and the others. I wanted revenge, too."

"We *both* did," said the girl with the baby on her lap.

Cama turned back to Han. "That was part of your orders?"

"Yes." Her shoulders hunched up to her ears. A grimy hand drifted near her mouth, exposing nails bitten down to the quick. "If they found us we could fight. They knew we were somewhere."

"Good work."

Her voice lifted faintly. "The Venn came. Chased them over the slide. We were doggo. All mudded. They didn't see us. When they were gone, we Disappeared them. We did it right. Except the sing. Then we had to move, because they knew we were there. They'd search. We took what we could carry, and we sang them when it was light. We heard scout dogs once. We moved during storms. We kept moving until there was big noise in the pass. The Venn were coming back."

"So you hid again?"

"Orders were no fighting Venn. We were running out of food. We've been doing halfies, then halfies of halfies. We were going to start halfies once a day while Hal and I did a sneak back to raid our cave, Dvar and Freckles covering us with their bows in case." She finished the coffee, then grimaced, her eyes watering. But her voice was a little stronger as she said, "Lnand saw to the smalls. Hal and Dvar were our scouts. Hal saw you. I came down to make sure you were us."

Cama had spent his life making and hearing field reports. He knew when details were bustled by—and he could gauge fairly accurately why.

He lifted his voice, aware of half a dozen children listening. "You did well. You did so well that I'm going to do what the Jarlan would have done. I'm giving you a nickname. So when you go to the queen's training—and I'm going to see that you do—they're to call you *Captain* Han. You tell 'em that comes from Cama Tya-Vayir."

"You're Cama One-Eye," the new Captain Han marveled. Keth told stories about him and the other Sier Danas, gleaned from Flash-Randael.

"Listen, Captain Han. New orders. I was sent by the king to secure Castle Andahi, so I can speak with his voice. You're all going to sleep, you right in my tent. Commander's tent, see? You can have my bedroll, because I'm taking a couple of my Riders down to grab a squint at the Venn and the castle under cover of dark."

He grinned, and she smiled. He was a Marlovan, sent by the king. He knew what to do, and she had orders. Tension leaked out of her, leaving her leaden with weariness. "Watch out for those horse-apple Idayagans," she mumbled.

This time his grin was even wider as he said in a voice rough as a rockfall, "Oh, I hope we meet them."

Chapter Thirty-one

CAMA was back the next evening, just as the sun was setting.

"All right, we're on our way. The Venn did not camp. They kept moving through the night. The last of them are getting into their boats in the bay. I think we need to take possession now. Those Idayagans are sure to be coming back."

"We *got* to help!" the other older girl shrilled, coming to stand at Cama's stirrup. She looked exactly like the rest to him, a scrawny pup of a girl with braids the color of flax and light-colored eyes, but her voice irritated him as she piped, "You *have* to let us. You *can't* shut us away like the little ones. I can't *bear* it! Not after what we've *been through*!" He shifted the irritation to himself, knowing she had endured a rougher time than many adults ever did. And it was not her fault she reminded him of the way his wife, Starand, used to talk in their schoolroom days.

"Mount up," Cama said.

The girl marched away, chin elevated. The children were all thin and dirty, but their cheeks showed color after a night of sleep and a couple of meals. The older girls all wore their bows tucked over their childish shoulder blades, and quivers full of arrows. The Runners packed the older children three to a remount and carried the smaller ones themselves.

As soon as they began the short ride toward the last bend, Cama said, "I've got a defense roughed out. The Idayagans have to be watching from the heights somewhere. I'm hoping we can get in before they see us, which is why we're riding down now under cover of dark. The Jarlan probably told you girls and boys that when attacking a castle, whatever the numbers, whoever has the inside has an advantage."

"Not enough," Han whispered.

And that other older girl shook her bow. "*We're* going to guard the walls."

She repeated it with a self-conscious flick of her braids that caused the rest of the big girls to give her a revealing, narrow-eyed glare.

"I'll just *die* if you leave *us* out. You *can't*!" she declared.

"Lnand," Han said. "Mount up."

If Lnand really was like Starand, she would keep that up until she got a response. "Wasn't going to," Cama said. "You girls can take the towers and walls, just like you've practiced. That's your best position, and it also leaves any hand-to-hand to us. Yes, I know you're training with knives. Odni is best when you've got some hips to balance with. None of you are anywhere near that."

Lnand tossed her head. "Just so you don't think we're *babies*. You don't know *half* of what we had to do—"

"Lnand," Captain Han said again.

"What?" Fists on hips—just like Starand.

"Shut it."

Lnand opened her mouth and began a long defense— she was just defending the girls' honor—but a freckle-faced girl and Haldred Mondavar made "Yeah," noises.

Captain Han said, "We'll all take care of our own honor."

After another odd look exchanged between the two, Lnand sniffed, but subsided.

Presently, they spied the castle at the bottom of the pass, a distinct pale shape, one side buried in a mighty landslide, the whole bathed in starlight.

"All right, into the tunnel," Cama said, leading the way.

The last stretch of the pass broadened out, except for a jut of rock at the left, the west side. What looked like a crevasse was actually access to the tunnel, carved by the river that had once flowed there. The pass itself was broad, stone-floored part of the way, the upper portion trampled down over centuries.

As soon as they were inside the tunnel they lit readied torches and rode single file downward, surrounded by stone walls worn smooth by water. The cold, motionless tunnel air smelled faintly of horse, wool, and sweat, and a tinge of vinegar from the exhalations of thousands who had breakfasted on vinegar-soaked cabbage the day before.

The tunnel ended at the castle, opening into one of the basement levels. It smelled dank, and mournful drips here and there were evidence that it had been flooded, then emptied out.

Cama motioned ridings of men to explore, torches held high, weapons out. The silence seemed thick and heavy, oppressive with the weight of old stone and the rusty tang of spilled blood.

The ridings returned looking bleak.

In brief words they all reported, giving Cama a dismal picture. But no enemy remained.

Cama said, "We'll set a close perimeter, everyone within earshot. Here's how we'll set up watches . . ."

Dawn brought a rise in the summer winds, kicking up dust whirls in the air over the enormous landslide looming over one side of the castle. From time to time tiny bits of rubble clicketty-clattered down the slide. At first, Cama's sentries stiffened. There were four sentries posted on the landslide portion of the back wall, with overlapping fields of vision. But nothing moved on the long, rock-strewn sweep all the way up to the mountain. Though they never ceased their visual sweeps, they stopped pulling weapons at every rattle.

The rest of the sentries patrolled near the front gates, which gapped open, the mighty hinges destroyed. From the walls, scouts watched the last of the Venn boats launching onto the turned tide.

The Venn had restored the baths on one side at least, patching up the hole that had let water into the basement to drown the tunnel entrance.

Once the children had been sent to bathe and eat, Cama rotated his dragoons through the baths in small parties. Since there was not so much as an oat left in the pantry rooms, the dragoons' Runners brought in the remainder of their stores. Their cook was exercising his imagination when midday made the shadows vanish under their feet.

The noon watch change was rung by a Runner. That had been chosen as the signal by Idayagans who figured the Venn would be gone by then.

A swarm of Idayagans raced out of what had seemed in the darkness to be shrubs growing below the level of the outer wall. These were actually the front entrance to some old tunnels, known to the Idayagans but not to Cama and his group.

It was an enormous force of Idayagans. Weapons raised, yelling wildly, they attacked in a mass.

A sentry shot a whirtler up over the castle. Cama abandoned his grim inspection and shouted for everyone to get to battle posts.

Captain Han and the bigger girls had been gathered in the kitchen, Han trying not to lose her temper at Lnand's loud grief at the destruction of the bakery.

Sure enough, Lnand's tears winked away the moment they heard Cama's shout. She was right behind Han as they raced to the top of the east tower.

The girls were just beginning to pick their positions when the slope of the landslide erupted as if by magic. Idayagans shook dirt off taut bows, nocked arrows, and let loose at the sentries.

Most of the first volley missed, but not all. Two of the sentries running for cover recoiled and fell dead. The rest dove behind battlements, though this was only partial cover as the enemy was shooting down almost on top of

them. One sentry took an arrow in the arm, the other in a
bent knee sticking out from cover.

The archers had copied what they assumed was the tactic used by the Marlovan children. Under cover of night,
while the Marlovans were in the tunnel, they'd crept down
the landslide and burrowed down, covering themselves
lightly with the loose rubble to wait for the signal: the noon
bells.

They loosed arrows as fast as they could, concentrating
on the hidden targets.

One of the eight-year-old girls started shrieking. Captain
Han yelled over her, "*Line!*"

The well-drilled girls scrambled into a line.

"Arrow!" Han's own first arrow was the one that had
killed Gdir. She'd dug her nail into the shafts of those arrows to mark them off. "Lnand, this one killed Tlennen.
Freckles, Dvar, here are yours."

Fingers had been hastily tightening strings; arrows were
clapped to.

"Loose!"

Spang! The girls shot together.

The front five Idayagans staggered, and one dropped:
each of the girls' arrows hit something. One girl squealed
in triumph and two brangled over whose arrow had gotten
the kill until Captain Han yelled, voice desperate, "LINE!
Arrow! Loose!"

Long-drilled habit snapped the girls back into a wavering line.

The girls spread behind the battlements. Han pretended
not to hear Dvar's keening breathing. Dvar was shooting
with everyone else.

The Idayagans scrambled for cover, then began shooting
back from behind rocks, unsure of what else to do. The
more decent ones did not want to shoot at children. Others
longed to shoot down the brats who had better aim than
they did.

The best Idayagan archers had been in front, the rest
were to provide a lethal rain to keep the Marlovans pinned
down. Consequently, at first the girls hit more targets than

the Idayagans, as shouts and clashes of steel echoed from the castle gates.

The Idayagans began shifting, spreading out, so that they could get a better angle on the tower and walls. Meanwhile, the underfed girls, inexorably tired, found their shots falling short and going wild.

One Idayagan arrow grazed Freckles' scalp just as she bobbed out too forcefully. She fell to her knees, bleeding spectacularly. Some of the eights began shrieking; Captain Han and her older girls, driven by anger, renewed the conflict, and this time, *Zip! Zip! Zip! Zip!* four Idayagans—lulled from cover by the increasing wildness of the girls' shots—fell, arrows square in their chests.

Then more arrows, fast and deadly accurate, began picking off the Idayagans from a new angle.

Barend, his reinforcements, Ndand and Keth Arveas had arrived, galloping wildly down the pass when they reached the ridge and heard the unmistakable sounds of battle.

As Barend and the dragoons raced to the aid of the men fighting at the gates, Ndand sent Keth inside with the horses. She sped up onto the tower opposite the girls' and took up position without being noticed.

"Lnand! Get her downstairs," Captain Han ordered, pointing to Freckles rocking back and forth on the tower floor, fingers pressed to her oozing scalp.

"Why does it have to be *me*? *I'm* as good a shot as *you*," Lnand announced.

Goaded at last beyond endurance, Captain Han said in a low, fierce voice, "Just wait till I tell Ndand-Randviar—"

"I didn't do it! And you're a snitch!"

"*I'll* tell her," Dvar said, stung out of her fugue.

Lnand went still. Han scowled.

Dvar flung her braids back. "I'll tell her you *always* argued."

Han said, "C'mon, let's get Freckles down before she bleeds to death."

Freckles squinted up through blood-sticky eyelids. "Not that you care about me, Lnand. You just want Cama One-

Eye to give you a nickname. But I'll give you one first: Frostface!"

Lnand veered between fury and relief that Dvar didn't know about . . . *it*. That meant Han hadn't told anyone. Did Han know, or didn't she? Lnand did not dare ask.

She's afraid I'll tell about Rosebud at the bridge, Han thought. The ice ball formed behind her ribs—the same ribs that splintered in Gdir when the Idayagans shot her. She sensed Lnand wanting it secret—maybe even demanding something as the price of secrecy. But Han knew that secrets are weapons. Her parents were gone. So was the Jarlan. She would tell Ndand. And if Ndand told her she wasn't good enough for queen's training, well, it meant she wasn't worthy.

The ball of ice was gone. Discipline was as well, that was all right. The sight of the reinforcements caused most of the Idayagans to panic and throw down their arms.

When the cease-fighting trumpet blew, the girls understood that the battle was over. Yes, here came warriors to take charge of the men on the landslide, who looked around uncertainly, not sure if their own people had surrendered, not sure what to do next.

Captain Han flung her bow over her back and bent to help the angrily sobbing Freckles to her feet. The other girls followed, half of them whimpering too, though they didn't know why.

Cama stood in front of the prisoners, who clumped together sullenly, fearfully, miserably in the middle of the rubble-strewn parade ground just inside the second gate.

There were twice and half again as many Idayagans as Marlovans. The former were dismayed, then angry, to discover that. It had seemed to them a full army swept out of nowhere onto them, and many couldn't throw down their weapons fast enough. Most had had little or no training. Cama strongly suspected the leader had been at the front gate. The ruse with the landslide had been clever, but there had been no one to follow up their advantage. If the leader had known how to command his two fronts, the battle would have gone a lot worse for the Marlovans.

And it would keep being like that, unless Cama could force them into peace through fear.

He walked back and forth, glaring at them with his one good eye. Then he said in Marlovan, which Ndand translated into Idayagan, "I want to know who killed those unarmed children the other night."

No one answered.

Cama lifted a hand, rigid with disgust. "Fine. You're under our law. That's specific about the consequences of cowardice."

"They were shooting at us!" came a voice from the back, which Ndand translated in a whisper.

Hissings and violent language issued from the Idayagans, but the same voice shouted, "Those soul-rotted brats *shot* at us!"

Cama said, "I am not talking about your attempt to take this castle. That comes under rules of war. I mean four children just after the Venn came. Unarmed. You killed them in cold blood, and I'm going to exact a price for that. From every one of you if I have to—"

"They were yelling!" the same voice protested. "They would've called the Venn on us!"

Cama waited until Ndand translated.

"So none of you were capable of saying 'Shut up, the Venn will hear you?' But apparently you *were* capable of calling them 'little Marlovan shits'—in their own language—before you killed them."

"*Murdering* shits. *All* of you—"

Ndand did not have to translate that. The man shouted it in Marlovan, which he'd learned in order to sell flour to Castle Andahi.

The Idayagans sidled and shuffled away from the speaker, as if contact with him would make them targets. Cama now had a clear view of a tall, plump man in a miller's heavy green apron over a jacket and old breeches. His face was red, distorted with a mix of fury and fear.

"Who else?" Cama asked.

No answer.

Cama said, "Then we'll flog the backs off every one of you cowards. Beginning with you." He pointed at the one he was fairly certain was in command.

"Your shit-stinking murderers pretend you have civilized laws—" He too had learned some Marlovan.

"You," Cama rode over him in a field voice, "don't even have the guts to speak up for the men under your orders. So you can watch us kill every one before we get to you."

Green Apron shouted in his own language, "So we'll have an easy win, eh, Djallac? And when I'm dead, your cousin—with his oh so convenient twisted ankle, he can't go on this stupid suicide run of yours—he gets my mill?"

Ndand caught up rapidly.

Djallac was the leader. A man of about forty, short and spare, he'd once done a stint of duty in the Ghael Hills before the Marlovans came. Like many, he'd melted back into civilian life, waiting and watching for a moment to strike back.

He turned an ugly glare from Cama to Green Apron, then back again. He licked his lips. "We want our land free. Last week those Venn soul-suckers sent out people to divide us up into land parcels. Telling us what we were going to plant for them. What we would make!"

"You thought you could stop that by taking the castle?" Cama asked, amazed at this combination of bravery and ignorance.

"We thought they were all gone up over the mountain. We didn't know they had left some here. As for the brats, you can blame that on me since you want to lay blame on someone. I killed the last of 'em before they could betray us to the Venn."

Cama made a grim face, then lifted his voice. "I am the new Jarl for Idayago. The new Jarl for Andahi, Olara, and Tradheval is nine-years-old Keth Arveas." The children standing in a line against the wall turned to look at Keth, as he stared down at the ground.

"Our job will be to keep the Venn from coming back.

Keep pirates away. Keep the law. And we do have law. You can grow what you want, you can make what you want. You can sell what you want, once you give us our share— the share you'd be giving your king, who used it to build palaces. If you attack us, we fight back. Hard. As hard as we fight pirates. If you kill our children you die as murderers. Understand?"

One of the younger men said in accented Marlovan, "So are you going to kill us all?"

"Not if you go home and get back to your usual life. You'll never even see me if you do that." And as Ndand translated, Cama turned to Djallac and Green Apron. "But you two? I meant what I said about those children. I'll offer you a chance to fight for your lives. Right now. You a sword, me my knife. You'll never get a fairer offer."

Djallac died without speaking, fighting viciously but wild; Green Apron protested and threatened and finally pled in a sobbing, gibbering whine, mixing up demands that his mill be left to anyone but Djallac's cousin with offers to do anything if his life would be spared. Even the Idayagans were relieved when Cama cut that short.

"All right, out of here. You can take these two with you and give them to their families, or we'll Disappear 'em, but with no ceremony."

Men exchanged looks uncertainly, then a mob of them turned to the bodies, the rest slinking away in haste, not believing they were still alive.

Before those carrying the dead vanished through the gate, one turned back to Cama, who stood watching, fists on hips.

"What about his mill?"

"You settle that." Cama peeled off his gauntlets, and jammed his knife into the dusty ground to clean it. He looked up. "But if you fight over it, you'll be dealing with me."

As soon as they were out of sight, Cama issued new orders for trackers to watch the Idayagans, new routes of patrol, a party to find wherever it was the Idayagans had been hiding. The wounded were taken inside the bare castle and the few dead gathered. At sunset they would sing them.

Then he started on the self-appointed inspection, but this time he had company. Ndand Arveas insisted on going with him.

Together Cama and Ndand walked through the ruined castle, room after room with scorch-marks, collapsed floors, sharp barbs worked into doors, floors, walls. Blood-stains, as yet unscrubbed, everywhere: the Venn had not had time to get more than the lower floor cleaned up.

"Damn," Cama kept saying, over and over. "What a fight. What a defense." And then, when they stood in a tower archway and gazed down at the blood-blackened splinters crashed below, "How many women were here?"

"I couldn't say exactly. Some might have been sent otherwhere. But including the girls fifteen and over, not quite two hundred."

"Of course including the girls," Cama said, his voice as rough as stone. He looked up, around, and down again, and shook his head. "Of course including the girls. Do you realize what they did? Two hundred women held off thousands and thousands of Venn. For how long? However long it was, they bought us that time at the other end. Fifteen-year-old girls." He shook his head again.

Ndand couldn't speak. Her throat had tightened and she held her breath. She would grieve later, but right now she was needed to restore the castle, to mother those poor children. She owed the women of Castle Andahi that.

Presently, Cama moved away. She squared her chin. "The way to the walls is through here."

In silence they toured what remained of the sentry walk, and gradually Ndand got hold of that cloud of threatening grief. A steadying list of immediate tasks formed itself in her mind.

She knew the grief would be back. The pain of Flash's death had stabbed her over and over, sharp as knife cuts, and no matter how hard she cried, she could not cry out the pain. But in Cama's astonishment as he looked around, in his evident respect, she found the small consolation of pride, and held onto it.

At length they stood alone in the Jarl's old office,

which had been stripped of all furniture by the Venn. The sun was setting. It was nearly time for the ceremony of Disappearance.

Cama was scarcely more than a silhouette, tall and strong, one dark-fringed eye gleaming with reflected torch-light, the other patched. When that eye met Ndand's, she was taken by surprise: there was, just for a moment, the spark she never expected to feel again. Other feelings promptly overwhelmed it with a cascade of the tears that must fall first, in spirit and in life. But the idea that she could feel something besides pain, regret, and grief again was another small comfort, next to the pride.

Cama regarded the slim young woman standing there, bow over her shoulder. Her robes were filthy from her long ride, the fight, the grim inspection of her home. Her face, like his, was grimy. Straight-shouldered, capable, she had a kind voice for those chattery girls downstairs. He smiled, without knowing why he smiled, for he, too, was tired, and overwhelmed by the destruction he'd witnessed in detail for his report to Evred.

"Cama!" a Runner dashed in, eyes wide. "A boy just showed up. Says he's Radran, used to be the cook's helper. Says he was holed up on the mountain counting enemies. Says he saw *everything*."

"Radran!" Ndand exclaimed happily. "Wait till I tell Keth."

Ndand took off, and Cama followed on her heels. This new responsibility seemed just a little easier now that he'd met her. He had an ally. Maybe a friend.

Chapter Thirty-two

DANNOR Tya-Vayir threw Evred's official tribute letter to the floor and kicked the nearest object.

It was a tall vase with herons standing in arch-necked poses, the colors blue and silver. One of those Colendi things Tdiran-Jarlan had droned on about so tiresomely all the years Dannor was growing up. You'd think if they were going to draw herons they would draw them with power and grace, lifting in flight. Otherwise, they were spindle-legged birds.

The vase was heavier than Dannor expected. The impact sent a shock of pain up her foot, but that was worth the spectacular smash, and the tinkle of pieces in the empty fireplace.

Her door burst open—something that had never happened before—and the twins dashed in, looking around wildly.

Dannor gave a hoot of angry laughter.

Badger Yvana-Vayir's voice was thick with dislike. "Did you read it?"

"I didn't read past the news about Hawkeye." *What would be the point?* She wanted to say, but the words stayed unuttered.

The boys were standing too close. For the very first time she was aware of having to tip up her head to look into their faces, which she seldom bothered to do. They were annoying, sulky boys, tedious as all boys are. But now they loomed over her, their faces tight with anger and grief, emphasizing the strong bones they shared with their older brother.

Now dead, *damn* him.

Badger dashed a muscular forearm over his eyes. "Y-you don't even care," he began, but Beaver sent him a quick look, and Badger gritted his teeth.

Beaver said, "So what are you going to do?"

Yes. That was the question that made her kick that stupid vase to pieces. From the stances of the two, their scowls, they were just waiting to turf her out of Yvana-Vayir.

She wouldn't give them the pleasure. Kicking some of the shards into the fireplace, she said, "Go home, of course." A wave of fury burned through her. *Stupid* Hawkeye, to run at the front of that battle. If only she'd taken the war talk seriously. But she'd heard it all her life—*When the Venn come*—and they never had. So now there was no heir, which would have cemented her for life as senior Jarlan.

But Hawkeye was history. Her business was living. She had to find a new life, preferably somewhere better than Yvana-Vayir. Definitely not back at Tya-Vayir, smallest jarlate of them all, and crammed with the worst people. So where to go? Wasn't Evred Montrei-Vayir going to her brother's? She bent to pick up the letter, but Badger was quicker.

"That's ours." And his eyes teared.

Dannor sighed. "It says that the king is going to Tya-Vayir for the triumph, am I correct?"

"Yes," Beaver said as his brother carefully rolled the letter, picked up the black ribbon from the floor, and tenderly retied the scroll. "We have to go. On account of the title."

I wish you joy of deciding who's Jarl and who's not, she thought, but she swallowed that. She smiled at them under her lashes, as if they weren't just tiresome boys. "Then please honor me with your escort home," she said sweetly.

She was a widow, they didn't want her here, she had to go home. And she'd used *that* word.

She watched them realize each fact, one by one. Idiots.

They were also handsome and popular. She'd look good arriving with them as escorts, and Hawkeye's death in battle would bring some glory to his widow. So . . . how much was glory worth?

Dannor was standing beside her brother in fine new robes, her hair brushed to a burnished gold and braided in a complicated pattern when the king's party rode up the curving road to Tya-Vayir Castle. The long columns of the Marlo-Vayir, Sindan-An, Khani-Vayir, and Cassad warriors snaked behind, led by what was left of the Riders who'd accompanied Hawkeye when he took the command at Ala Larkadhe.

The road was bordered with a low stone wall, and behind that tall, beautiful silver-leaved argan trees from somewhere east, planted by the first Jarlan's hands. It was the most impressive of all the Vayir castle roads, leading to the castle built along the highest of the gentle hills surrounding a small lake.

As soon as word had reached the Tya-Vayirs that the war was over, Imand-Jarlan had ordered the entire castle into a frenzy of cleaning. Stalgrid had sent a couple ridings of Runners out to his own allies, requesting them to come back with him. He did not say what for.

When a second Runner arrived with the news that Cama had gone north as the new Jarl of Idayago, Starand had wandered about wailing and moaning, "I caaaaan't live in Idayago! There's nothing up there! Nobody! Just horrible people, they all haaaate us!"

Inured to her eternal whining, no one paid her the least heed. That is, until Dannor arrived a day later—having been abandoned at the border by the twins, who said they'd been invited to Tlennen.

So she'd come home alone after all. After enduring half a morning of Starand's wailing and whining, she'd shoved past Imand, caught Starand by the shoulder, and swung her around. "Why don't you end the marriage, then, and go home to Ola-Vayir?"

Stupid Starand! She just stood there with her mouth open. Dannor could have come up with three return jabs by the time she'd drawn a breath, and one would even have been true.

Then it was her turn to be whirled around. Imand was much smaller and lighter in build than Dannor, but she was strong from daily drill, and from handling a castle full of difficult personalities.

"That was fair." She dipped her chin. "But don't think that makes you welcome to stay here making trouble. If you're moving back in, you're going to work, and I am going to ride you every watch to see that you do it."

Dannor flushed. She'd loathed Imand ever since they were girls. How she missed the days when she was ten and Imand only seven, and Dannor could sit on her and slap her silly—as long as Imand's shadow Hibern wasn't around. "Don't worry, Imand. I'll be out of here as soon as I can. So you just do your own work."

"See that you are." Imand pushed on by.

So here she stood at Stalgrid's side, where she had been since the king's outriders arrived to give them advance notice of imminent arrival.

Stalgrid's temper, always bad, had been foul all day. His only ally present was Hali-Vayir, who everyone knew licked whoever's boots were nearest. Marth-Davan was dead, probably out of spite, and Stalgrid's other allies had all sent excuses—harvest, shortage of men or money for travel. He knew they were all wary of the king who'd driven off the Venn, and they were afraid to cross the pirate Harskialdna who couldn't be beaten on land or sea.

Dannor peered at the lead riders. She was infuriated to see Badger and Beaver riding with a clump of Sindan-An, Tlen, and Tlennen men who'd joined Tuft Sindan-An's warriors. They must have ridden cross-country to join the returning warriors as soon as they abandoned her.

Everyone in the king's party wore their House colors, no helms or chain mail. Their shields were slung at the saddles.

The new Harskialdna (only medium height, and look at those disgusting scars) wore the green-and-silver of the Algara-Vayirs instead of the royal colors. There were two spaces for riders in the middle of the Sier Danas to honor the two fallen captains.

Everything done exactly right, to honor their host. There was no hint of a kingly mailed fist coming down hard on Stalgrid, which would have been obvious if they'd ridden in war gear, weapons clanking. The two Tya-Vayirs felt the fist anyhow. As did old Hali-Vayir, standing slightly behind Stalgrid, fingering his sash.

The unsmiling king dismounted, inclined his head so that the host could speak first.

Stalgrid said stiffly, "You honor our House, Evred-Harvaldar."

"Your House," Evred stated softly with just the faintest emphasis, "honors me."

Dannor watched him from under her lashes as he turned to formally name everyone. Again, everything according to form—the old way of making promotions known.

She ignored the male jabber. During her days in the queen's city, what little had been said about Evred, then just a second son, was that he was awkward, preferring old poetry to war games. That had clearly changed. There was no use in intriguing him—they said he was like his father in preferring men. Hmm, could that possibly mean he'd mated up with that scar-faced Harskialdna? Time for a bit of investigation.

She smiled, knowing that she had the same dimpled smile as her younger brother, Cama. As the Runners took away the horses, she fell in step beside Indevan-Harskialdna. His eyes were just below the level of her own. "I hope you will have the time to sit with me and tell me about Hawkeye." She did her best to appear sad, when—it was strange—she couldn't recall ever feeling sad in her life. Angry, yes, but sad, no.

Indevan's eyes were wide set, an unremarkable brown, his expression hard to interpret past all those scars. Was he simpleminded?

"You were his wife?" he asked.

"I am Dannor Tya-Vayir," she said gravely. "And yes, I was married to Hawkeye."

"I did not see exactly what happened to him." Indevan had one of those deep, resonant voices you get with chesty men. It was unexpectedly attractive. "Not many with him survived, but there are a few. I can point them out to you." And he actually craned his neck around, the fool.

Dannor looked past him at the small woman walking on his other side. She wore a plain linen robe, with a blue cotton under-robe beneath. "Did I miss hearing who you are?"

Evred turned away from Stalgrid and the cluster of Sindan-Ans and Tlennens. He regarded her out of cold hazel eyes, reminding her unexpectedly and unpleasantly of her older brother. "This is Dag Signi. She aided us as a healer."

The woman was plain as a potato, and old. Dannor relaxed, dismissing Dag Signi as no threat. "Come along inside," she said to Indevan-Harskialdna. "I'll show you to your room. I know Imand is busy—"

"No, she is not," came Imand's calm voice from behind, tall blue-eyed Hibern, her mate, at her shoulder.

Inda turned around, relieved. Dannor was standing too close to him—she made him uncomfortable. This new woman was shorter than he, with the pale blond hair of most of the Tlennen family, wide-spaced eyes with a Sartoran tilt to them.

"I am Imand-Jarlan," she said to Inda, and smiled past him to Signi. "Welcome to Tya-Vayir." Then, lifting her voice, "Welcome to you all. Stalgrid-Jarl will see that the men are properly settled. Evred-Harvaldar, if you and your Sier Danas will come inside with me, I will show you around."

It was pretty much the same as other castles: public and workrooms downstairs, living space upstairs, and an enormous stable with a barracks over it.

The room Imand opened for Inda was plain, clean, with a comfortable bed big enough for two. "Here you are."

Imand's smile included Signi as well as Inda. "We'll have biscuits and ale laid out just off the kitchens. Follow your nose if you're lost." She shut the door.

Vedrid had already gotten a Runner to bring Inda's gear up. Signi had carried her own small bag, which contained just a change of clothing and a comb. She set this down on the bedside table, one of those peculiar ones with the raptor feet as legs and thin, horizontal stylized wings curving from armrests up to the back.

Signi regarded Inda, who stood in the middle of the room staring at his bag. She waited in patience until he regained the present world, and his place in it. "I hope Evred doesn't make us stay here long." He ran his hand over his hair, a sure sign he was disturbed about something. "Though I like Imand."

Signi considered. While Hawkeye's wife had been talking to Inda, Stalgrid-Jarl had said with a strange, enforced sort of heartiness, "And so we stand ready to give you a triumph tonight. Say the word, Evred-Harvaldar."

"The word can wait until we have rested," Evred had said.

Signi knew she missed significance here, some kind of silent, private struggle between Evred and this tall, strongly built, ferocious-looking Jarl. Stalgrid's Venn ancestry was very much obvious in his stature and frost-pale hair.

Inda said abruptly, "I feel like I'm in one of Tau's plays. I wish he was here."

He sank onto the bed, elbows on his knees. Signi sat next to him, stretching an arm across his broad back. She hugged him to her. "Can you tell me?"

"Oh, it's more Marlovan thinking. Barend told me just before he left that I was going to have to get used to politics. What *is* that? I'm still trying to get used to there being no threat. Not just the Venn, but pirates." He gave her that slightly guilty, mostly uneasy look that he always did when he mentioned the Venn. "I feel like I'm becalmed. No wind, no sail. I'm here in Cama's house, but he's not here, and there's Horsebutt—Stalgrid, that is—with that pinched face, he's probably thirty but he looks old. Jowls. Then I think of Noddy." Inda shook his head slowly. A tear slid along the scar on one cheek as he stared at his hands. "I sent Noddy to that death, Signi. Don't say I didn't because I did. I sent a lot of people to their deaths. I killed a lot of people with my own hands. But a friend . . . oh, I wish I knew what I promised him."

"Did he die comforted?"

Inda closed his eyes and dropped his head back. A couple more tears escaped from under his lashes. Finally he drew in a deep breath, opened his eyes and swiped them with his sleeve. "Yes. Yes he did."

"And he went to the light. I saw them go."

"You saw Noddy?"

"No. There were too many." It was her turn for the throat-tightening, eye-burning pain of memory, and its spring of grief. "But they are all gone."

He took her hands. "All? Including Dun?"

"Yes."

"I thought so," he whispered. "Why can't the rest of us see that?"

"I don't know. But I did. Please take comfort in that."

"Noddy—and Dun." Inda kissed her hand again, and stood up. "Noddy left behind a son. He has my name. And I'm going to be teaching him in the academy as part of my duties. Isn't that strange? But I'm going to do it right, oh, such a good job, I promise Noddy that. Even though he can't hear it." He wiped his eyes again, and held out his hand. "May as well go find the others and do whatever a Harskialdna is supposed to be doing. Want to come?"

"No. You go be with your friends. Laugh, and give them comfort. Nightingale needs cheering. And Buck. As for me, this castle, the magics are fading, like in so many others. I think I will attend to that."

Chapter Thirty-three

STALGRID was worried about the magic as well. The baths under the castle drew water off the lake, but since winter it had begun to smell slightly dank under there, and the water had been gradually getting more and more chill. During the hottest part of summer they had not minded. They'd begun using the ensorcelled buckets to wash first, and the baths for a cooling soak once their bodies were clean. Less magic was used that way.

Now he was worried about what would happen to the last of the water magic with all these people using the baths. Even worse was the thought of that damned Evred forcing one more day's stay on them, with all those mouths champing at his harvest stores.

Stalgrid had risen early, determined to do his absolute best to bootlick Evred into making an end to this nightmare—lick until he choked on the words.

But. He would be on the watch for Evred's weakness while the fellow was camped in Stalgrid's best room, eating all his food. Only justice.

The first test would be this surprising Harskialdna. Dannor had sat next to him at dinner the night before. From what Stalgrid could see, the fellow just leaned over his food and shoveled it in, never saying more than a word or two.

After dinner, Stalgrid had asked Dannor what he was like, to get a furious whisper, "He's an idiot."

"You say that about everyone," he grumped.

Her lip curled. "I'm wrong?"

He snorted. "No."

So . . . was the pirate just a claphair? That would be prime, if so! Challenge him and you've got the king by the short hairs.

It was with the king's short hairs in mind he'd gotten up as soon as the man placed on watch reported the Harskialdna going down to the baths.

Stalgrid hurried down the stairs, and was distracted by steam. What had happened? The hot end was hot again? He sniffed—no dankness!

Relief—gratitude—then suspicion. Magic did not just happen. Was this some kind of oblique threat? Just what kind of stuff had that damned Evred been reading in those old archives, anyway?

". . . but Janden saw it, I tell you! Go ask him!"

"I heard the same thing."

The voices echoing up the access stair distracted Stalgrid. The latter one was one of his own Rider captains.

"They said it was plain as plain could be. Everyone was yelling IN-DA! IN-DA! The Venn commander was right up on the mountain with the Pirate—tall as a house, wings on his helm—and threw down his weapons, just like the old days! Right at the Pirate's feet!"

"And they just ran? Like that?"

"Gone quicker'n you could spit."

Stalgrid entered then, and his own two captains instantly moved down to the cooler end of the water, leaving the hot end for him. The other captains gave him an uneasy look—they knew who he was.

He did not invite them to stay, so they moved, too, and by the time he had taken off his robe and eased into the hottest end of the water—no bucket, not if the magic was back!—they were all gone. Good.

A moment later, there was the one they were calling the

Pirate. No pretending it was an insult, not in that admiring, possessive tone of voice reserved for heroes. Stalgrid had no use whatever for heroes—unless they could serve him.

"Good morning, Indevan-Harskialdna," he called, eyeing the fellow. He was medium in height, good shoulders and chest. He wore only a shirt; there were two white scars on one leg, and a long purple slash on the other. His feet were the same shade of brown as his face and hands, unlike everybody else's.

Did he go barefoot, then, like the farm laborers? *This* fellow was a Harskialdna? If he was as stupid as Dannor said, then who really made his plans?

Inda was surprised to find Horsebutt alone in the baths, which he'd expected to be crammed full of captains, leaving the lake for the men. When Horsebutt spoke he sounded just like he had in the old days, like he was accusing you of something, even when he was pretending to be friendly.

"Good morning, Jarl," Inda said, and set his towel down, hoping the fellow was leaving.

Stalgrid splashed out into the water. Not leaving then, just arrived, apparently. Inda sighed inwardly.

"Going to teach us fighting today?" Stalgrid asked, swimming all the way across his bath and then back, using wide strokes. There was definitely strut in the way he took up the whole bath. Was the man challenging him, or was this some kind of a sex lure?

Inda dropped onto one of the benches along the stone walls. "If Evred asks me to."

Voices in the stairwell: the Marlo-Vayir brothers, sounded like. Stalgrid retreated to the other side of the bath, annoyed. He considered how to issue a challenge without sounding too insulting. He didn't want Evred finding out and staying another week with his entire army. "I hope you will. I offer myself as a partner. I'm sure it will be most instructive," he added, cleverly not defining what he meant by "it."

Cherry-Stripe and Tuft were easing Buck down the stairs one at a time, Rat Cassad behind them. When Buck had been lowered slowly to a bench, his forehead dotted with sweat, he waved off Tuft and Rat, who threw off their robes and dove into the bath, causing a mighty surge. Cherry-Stripe began to help his brother get his shirt and bandages off.

Inda jumped up to help, which Buck permitted. They lifted the shirt off without it catching on Buck's stump, which still hurt enough to make him weak in his one knee if it only brushed against something.

Too bad the Venn weren't better fighters, Stalgrid thought viciously. If there was one thing he hated, it was favorites. Buck Marlo-Vayir had been on the strut ever since the academy, when he was one of the Sierlaef's favorites. Then, after the Sierlaef was killed (good riddance!) what does Buck do? Become one of Evred's favorites.

He looks bad now, Stalgrid thought as Cherry-Stripe loosened the bandage around his knee-stump and then bent to the one round Buck's hips. When Stalgrid saw the red flesh around Buck's groin, he looked away uneasily.

Cherry-Stripe threw off his robe and splashed down to help his brother. Inda pulled off his shirt and dropped down to the other side, presenting Stalgrid with an astonishing view of scars. Long ones, short ones, most of them gone white, but several pinkish and recent. Beneath those scars he was all rippling muscle.

Stalgrid grunted, for the first time regretting the last five years' lack of real drill. He was a busy man, and his Rider Captain tended to the tedium. Maybe he should swing a sword again . . .

Inda and Cherry-Stripe eased Buck into the water. Buck hissed, head arched back. At a glance from Cherry-Stripe, Inda waded out into the water.

Stalgrid muttered to Rat, "What happened to him?"

"Venn went after joints, mostly," Rat answered, low-voiced, as Inda ducked underwater and swam in a few powerful strokes. "One tried to tendon-slice Buck. Another got his other knee when he lifted his leg to avoid the first, a third mostly took off his arm, and he fell onto a fourth fellow's sword. Nearly lost his parts."

Stalgrid's own parts constricted. He shifted his gaze to the water.

Buck leaned his sweaty forehead against his brother's as Cherry-Stripe held him steady. "Let me die, Landred," he breathed. "Let me die."

They held the triumph the next night.

As many captains as they could fit into the hall were entertained sumptuously, with the very best Tya-Vayir's kitchens (as well as those of their surrounding liege-houses) could offer. Braised fish fresh from the lake, braised potatoes (rice being rare, with Idayago's lowland rice plantations all trampled up), buttered cabbage, perfectly crisped rye rolls, and after that, honey-and-nut cakes.

Imand's First Runner, Hibern, had noticed that Inda only drank the ale, so they served the locally brewed dark ale as well as wine. Maybe that explained Inda's mood, or maybe it was just the rise and fall of ballads, both the old ones—joined in by everyone—and the new.

Someone had added verses to Hawkeye's old favorite, "Yvana Ride Thunder," an ancient and somewhat self-serving song justifying Yvana ambitions, though it had a good, table-thumping rhythm and a chorus like a trumpet charge. The new verses vividly celebrated the five hundred men, most of whom had died at the top of the pass in order to hold the Venn back. Badger and Beaver (who had convinced Evred in their private conversation that they could swap half years as Jarl just as easily as they had intended to as Randaels) wept openly, hardly able to sing. The sight of those lifted faces and exalted voices from the Sindan-An, Tlen, and Tlennen clans choked Inda up. He was not the only one.

Noddy was given tribute with his share of songs as well. They weren't great as songs—one was too plainly an obscure old ballad with new names inserted—but the singing was resolute and heart-deep. Nightingale and the Khani-

Vayir captains listened to every word, drinking them straight into the spirit.

Evred did not relax until the speeches were done.

He'd said to Inda just before sitting down, "You'll need to speak, you know."

And Inda's jaw dropped open. "Me? I've never made any speeches!"

"It doesn't have to be long. My uncle scarcely said more than a couple of words, I'm told. But it's traditional. Before you lead the 'Hymn to the Fallen.' "

And so, after Stalgrid offered a toast to the Harvaldar and Harskialdna, Inda stood up and studied the rows of expectant faces. Emotion tightened his throat. He cleared it. "When the call went out. The king—" A hand toward Evred, sitting so still, his hands gripping his wine cup, his gaze in its depths. "—Evred-Harvaldar needed the Sier Danas. And they came." He lifted his gaze toward the ceiling, one big hand groping, then turning palm up. "They came."

It was the way he said those last two words, so simply, with the gruffness of undisguised grief, that caused many throats to tighten, and eyes to burn with tears of sorrow. And of pride.

Then he began the "Hymn to the Fallen," at first a lone voice: everyone had expected more of a speech.

But Imand joined in a sweet, high, clear soprano, and Badger and Beaver joined, tuneless and loud, and by the tenth word they were all singing full-throated, the emotion all the more intense for being shared.

Then it was Evred's turn.

He stood up. The room quieted. "You all have been hearing details about the two battles we fought. There was a third battle, far rougher than anything we saw."

Some of the men looked up in surprise. Stalgrid scowled, uncertain; he hated surprises. Imand, Hibern, and the few other women all lifted their faces. They knew, as the women always knew.

And so should it be. "The first Jarl I ever made was

Dewlap Arveas. His first son was lost fighting pirates. He
and his second son were lost when the Venn first arrived in
their boats. That left Liet-Jarlan and two hundred women
and girls to face nearly three hundred ships full of men."

The silence had been comfortable, but the small noises
of shifting fabric, whispers, quiet steps as Runners and servants moved about, had ceased.

"Two hundred women and girls. Against thousands.
Thousands. Of enemies. When surrender was offered
them, the Jarlan struck our banner herself, so that the Venn
could not take it. And then they fought to the last. Because
they fought to the last, we are able to celebrate today. They
held off the invasion for what seems to have been two, almost three days. Long enough for Hawkeye Yvana-Vayir
and Noddy-Turtle Toraca to reach that pinnacle."

He paused. From across the room he could see the
gleam of tears in Imand's eyes, but her face was exalted.

"There are no songs yet, because most of us did not find
out until we were already on the road to come home. But
there will be songs."

This time, he led the "Hymn to the Fallen" himself.

The volume of sound made glassware ring faintly, and
Evred himself found his throat closing. But he must speak
on; when the adulation that bound them into one inevitably faded, restoring them to individual ambitions, regrets, angers, and curiosity, they would be comparing
memories of what he'd said. Whom he'd ignored. Such was
human life.

So he said much the same as he had in Ala Larkadhe,
knowing that those old words *glory, bravery, heroism* forever remembered, forever sung, weighted with fresh grief,
and pride, and affection, carried meaning to those who
sought meaning.

Then he shifted from the dead to the living, as it must be.

He praised Ola-Vayir, now gone home.

He praised Buck, so badly wounded in leading the
charge at the river, and the ringing shout that went up—the
men standing and raising their glasses—had its effect on

Buck, who never should have been there. His glittering eyes, the flush in his thin face, all eased as Buck took in the tribute, and Evred waited, giving the men time to express their admiration. Giving Buck the time to look around the room at those shouting men, their fists held against their chests.

Then Evred praised Cherry-Stripe, whose ferocious covering flights of arrows from the heights kept the Venn from sweeping forward to a victory based on sheer mass.

He praised Tuft, who arrived so spectacularly, and he described Tuft's thundering arrowhead charge that threw the Venn back over the top of the pass, which caused cheers and drumming on the table, Imand's dishes rattling dangerously.

He ended by praising Cama, who was entrusted with following the Venn retreat. Cama was now a Jarl, which brought even more cheering.

Imand wiped away tears. Stalgrid showed his teeth in that false grin Evred had loathed since he was ten years old and watched the bigger boys at the academy games. Dannor's mouth was twisted, and she tossed back more wine, longing for this tedium to end; Starand sent her a triumphant smirk. One of the captains had told Starand that Idayago was at least four times the size of Tya-Vayir.

Now the ritual was done.

Evred ended with formal thanks and dismissal to his Sier Danas, giving them leave to return home.

The Marlo-Vayirs were never subtle. They rose together, Buck aided by the ready Runners. Together with Cherry-Stripe their Runners carried Buck out and straight to the wagon already prepared and waiting. The brothers would not spend a moment more in Tya-Vayir than they had to; Buck was very soon insensible to the constant, searing pain, having drunk from his Runner's anxious hand a mixture of green kinthus and liquor that probably would have killed a lighter man.

Rat and Tuft did their best to make conversation with their hosts as benches scraped and people began rising, talking in low voices, some repeating stories, or singing snatches of song, others discussing logistics of the long rides ahead.

Evred beckoned to Inda.

They walked out into the open air of the lakeshore. Evred didn't trust Stalgrid not to have spy holes riddling the castle, so he waited until they were down by the rippling, plashing water. "If you are ready," he said, "I want you to go home tomorrow. You have a long journey ahead, and I would like to have you and Tdor back in the royal city to make your oath at Convocation. Hadand will welcome Tdor as Harandviar. There is much work ahead for us all."

Inda turned around to search Evred's countenance in the golden light from the castle windows, but Evred gazed over the dark waters of the lake at the glimmering reflections of the stars.

"I will." Inda touched hand to heart. "But about my marriage. If I'm your Harskialdna, does that mean Branid is going to be Adaluin?"

"Yes, of course." Evred flung his hands behind him, clasping them tightly. "I wish there was a way to hand that rank off to Whipstick Noth. But Branid is Algara-Vayir. Reports state he's been trying to cooperate, and is in fact eager about defense. He can have the title, it will probably keep him to duty. But I want your children to inherit, not his."

Inda hit his fist to his chest, and Evred walked along the water's edge under a clump of willow, and past a row of late-blooming queensblossom, the pale petals just opening.

Inda followed. Tau had been right: Evred's mood had been terrible that first day they rode out, but not for long. He'd been quiet since, but not the tense, terrible quiet of those days right after the battle. Calmer. But not happy. Not the way you'd think a king would be after a terrible enemy ups and goes away, even if you didn't really defeat him.

Hurry, Barend, Inda thought. *He needs that treasure, in whatever form you bring it.*

Evred said in a low, tired voice, "And when you get to the royal city we can discuss Durasnir's words. I can't see them returning next spring, not unless they have another invasion force waiting, and their kingship problems are all resolved. But it seemed he was trying to tell us something without actually telling us—"

"Ah, there you are. Enjoying the stars from the walls?"

They turned, Evred sharply, as Dannor walked up, hips a-swing. With supreme confidence she walked right between them, but her attention was fully on Inda. "It is beautiful here, is it not?" She plucked up some queensblossom, sending a sharp fragrance through the summer air. "Though damp, soooo damp in winter. Is Choraed Elgaer damp?"

"I don't really remember," Inda said. "It seemed fine to me, or at least I remember it that way."

"I'll say good night," Evred put in, and turned away.

Inda wanted to call him back, but for what? They wouldn't talk about anything important now.

I don't want to be alone with her. Why not? Dannor was not about to pull a knife on him! "What a joy, to return in triumph to your homeland! Hadand and Tdor have said so many wonderful things about it," she said, shredding the petals and dropping them.

Inda grimaced after Evred. "Uh, yes. It's beautiful. From what I remember."

"And you're leaving? To go home?"

"Yes, tomorrow," he said, relieved.

"My life is totally free." She turned her back on the lake. The rising moon reflected in her wide eyes, off her golden braids. In her teeth. Funny, how her mouth was shaped like Cama's, but her grin was just like Stalgrid's. "I can go anywhere I want. Do anything I want." She stretched her arms out. The sharp-sweet scent of bruised blossoms filled the air as the petals fluttered to the lake water.

"Great," Inda said, looking around for an excuse to decamp. "So you should."

"Should what?" she asked sweetly.

Inda said, puzzled, "Go anywhere you want."

"Oh, I know what I want! To visit my old friend Tdor. What could be better? Thank you, thank you—your last kindness tonight is to make a widow happy. You honor me with your generosity," she crooned, emphasizing the magic word, *honor*. How stupid men were if you just tapped that word into whatever you said! "I will be waiting whenever you want to ride." She leaned forward, grabbed him by the ears and kissed him.

Chapter Thirty-four

"SIGNI, will you tell her to go away?"

They lay in their bedroll in their tent, Inda whispering into Signi's ear.

She shook with laughter. "Inda. You fight fleets of bloodthirsty pirates, yet cannot find a way to rid yourself of one woman?" But then she heard the hiss of his breathing: he really was in distress. "I beg pardon. I did not understand."

"It's how she turns words inside out. Like a sock," he whispered. "I feel like I'm falling. She says 'Oh, I am a widow' and I know how I'm supposed to act toward a widow. But she's not acting like one. Do you see?" He breathed out, "It's like being with Wafri, all but the beatings."

"I see." Now she felt sick.

"Whenever you go off to do your dancing drills she talks at me." His breath hissed again. "She wants to *marry* me! For me to set aside Tdor—she thinks Evred will do anything for me, even that. I'm pretending I don't understand what she wants, but now *my* words are starting to turn inside out. Here."

Inda sat up, snapped one of Signi's glowglobes on. The light would be visible to the other tents, but at least no one could see what he was doing.

He fetched a scrap of paper out of his bag, and dug out

the golden case that he'd half forgotten, then, as Signi watched, scrawled:

>   *Tdor: Dannor is with us, trying to trick me into mar-*
>   *riage. Can you have the wedding ready as soon as we*
>   *arrive?*

He tucked that into the case, carefully activated the spell, and lay back, dousing the light. "Don't leave her alone with me."

Signi had her chin tucked on Inda's shoulder, her lips to his ear. "I won't."

Tdor got to her feet, then sank back down as black spots swam before her eyes. Two deep breaths and they were gone, and she rubbed her eyes.

This time she got up more cautiously, but as the dizziness and disbelief washed away in the rushing heat of happiness, she ran out of her room yelling, "He's coming home! Inda's coming home!"

Fareas-Iofre heard the sound of her voice, and the tone, not the words. She left the preserving shed, wiping her hands, then stopped in the practice court when Tdor came dashing down the north tower stairs, her brown braids flapping on her back just the way they had when she was ten years old.

"Inda's coming home," Tdor cried, flushed and smiling. She really did look just like a girl again. "He's coming *home.*"

"Oh." Fareas sat down suddenly on a barrel, and drew in a deep breath. Joy chased fear, braiding like starlings in flight. She did not know if she dared to believe the news: she would see Inda again.

"What's that?" Whipstick called from above. He leaned out his office window, which was in the tower between the guard barracks and the house proper.

Whipstick and the men had arrived back in Choraed El-

gaer from their coastal watch days ago, on receipt of orders
from one of the King's Runners sent down the coast. He
and Fareas-Iofre and Tdor had been debating whether or
not it was too late in the season to do a full border ride.

"Inda's coming home!" Tdor laughed. Then wrinkled her
nose. "Mudface—er, Dannor Tya-Vayir is with him, which
is why he wants the wedding right away."

Looks like that settles that question, Whipstick thought,
laughing to himself as he turned back to his summer's
worth of reports to catch up on.

"Right away?" Fareas-Iofre repeated, looking around.
"At harvest time? There is so much work to do . . ." She
whisked herself off. "We'll talk tonight!" she called over
her shoulder.

Tdor went about the rest of her daily chores, buoyant
with happiness. Even Branid appearing from one of his
war games out in the stubble fields couldn't irritate her.
She smiled at the castle children, she smiled at the Riders,
at the women, even at Branid. The thought of Dannor Tya-
Vayir was irritating, but only mildly so. Tdor could put up
with her for a few days.

As for Signi . . . Tdor told herself firmly that she was welcome.

Late that night, after the castle people had separated off
to night duty or to their own chambers, Whipstick and Tau
entered the archive room together. They found Fareas-
Iofre reading an old history aloud to Tdor, who was busy
finishing up Inda's wedding shirt.

The princess laid aside the book. "We had better discuss
our plans," she said.

Noren, Tdor's Runner, went to the door, looked out,
then shut it and put her back to it.

"Branid's gone down to the pleasure house at Cedars,"
Tau said. "Vrad promised to keep him there."

"We'll have to let all the kin know, of course," Fareas-
Iofre said. "I wonder if we can get Branid to ride around
with the Riders as honor guard to do that?"

"Oh, what a good idea." Tdor poked her needle through
the cloth. "He can strut all he likes, and he'll be out of the

way. Let me try to figure out how to get him to think of it himself, since you know he'll complain and whine if we just ask him. What I wonder is, what will we do with Dannor?"

Tau grinned. "Shall I do my best to distract her?"

Whipstick snorted a laugh. He'd gotten a lot of secret entertainment from watching how the sober, hard-working Tenthen guardswomen almost fell off their sentry walks if Tau bent over to pick up a practice blade in the drill yard. "I'd say that would be a good plan."

"Here's another thing I can do." Tau turned his hand down toward the great hall. "I'll take over the wedding organization. I enjoy putting together parties."

"Thank you." Fareas-Iofre smiled with relief. "That would be a help, since we'll have to be rearranging furnishings for Inda and—"

She stopped herself when Whipstick shook his head, his smile gone.

"What is it?" Tdor asked, needle in the air. "Do you know something we don't? Dannor can't have—"

"No." Whipstick leaned forward. "There's something I think you have all forgotten. Inda's the Harskialdna now. That means he won't be living here. He can't. He'll have to go straight to the royal city, soon's the wedding is over."

"Then so will I," Tdor said in disbelief.

They were all looking at her. "It is a great honor, to be Harandviar. The highest honor a woman can have besides being queen," Fareas-Iofre said, her eyes anxious.

"You'll be with Hadand-Gunvaer," Whipstick pointed out, but his tone was tentative.

Tau did not say anything, but he was thinking, *Inda will miss his home as much as you will. And as much as these people are already missing you.*

"I look forward to it," Tdor said, because of course she must.

Chapter Thirty-five

AUTUMN had come and harvest was over by the time the little party reached the outer boundary of Choraed Elgaer.

Inda began saying, "That's familiar." Or, "I know I remember that stretch." At the end he rode in silence, studying their surroundings with a fervor Dannor mistook for stupidity. Signi watched in silent empathy, the more poignant because she knew she could never go home again.

As Inda's silence grew protracted Dannor was subdued, watching for clues that she could use. She had to find a home, and she was afraid this was her last opportunity. Too many men their age had died; there were far too many women who would end up without rank or establishment, who would be forced to go home as an unwanted extra pair of hands. She was not going to be one of them.

When a long line of tall trees rose like the teeth of a comb on the southern horizon, at last Inda spoke. "We'll get there soon. This is part of the castle's outer perimeter, and all that way are the farm fields. The lake is down that way. We used to have riding practice out here."

He would have gone silent after that, sunk into the memories that he had struggled so hard to forget for so long, but Signi kept gently making comments, asking about why this castle had a name when most didn't, asking about the Tenthen family, or were they all Algara-Vayirs now? — easy questions all. Dannor did not listen to the answers. She had no interest in the fact that the Algara-Vayirs had married into an Iascan family instead of taking the castle, like her own ancestors.

And then they rounded the line of trees at the far side of the lake, and there were the golden walls and towers of Tenthen. Inda thought, *How small it is,* but his eyes blurred. At first he didn't see the people on the walls, or hear the cheering. Or rather, the cheering blended with the memory of the day he left, for they'd cheered then too, and blew the trumpets, Tanrid riding there, Joret over there . . .

Dannor gasped as the most beautiful man she had ever seen walked alone through the gate. He was dressed in some outlander fashion—a long tunic that fitted his lovely body, trousers tight across the hips and widening down toward the feet, a style she'd never seen before but liked instantly.

And he walked right up to her, and raised dark-fringed golden eyes. "Are you Dannor-Jarlan?" he asked, his smile entrancing. "Let me show you inside."

Dannor followed him without a backward glance.

Inda snapped back into the present when he saw his mother. How small she was, how old!

She held out her hands, weeping and smiling both, and he closed his arms around her. He tried not to crush the life out of her as she buried her blurring eyes in his shoulder.

Tdor stood transfixed by the sight of a ring on Inda's finger. Didn't rings mean heart-bonds in Sartor and other countries? *Do not assume anything,* she scolded herself.

"Father?" Inda asked, looking around.

"Asleep." Fareas-Iofre wiped her eyes across her forearm in the exact gesture Inda used. "He's best in the mornings, generally."

"All right, then I'll wait and see him tomorrow."

Tdor was right behind the Iofre, gaze searching his face. Inda met that regard with a sense of relief that he couldn't explain. They didn't speak at all, but it felt like they had.

Then there was everyone else to greet: Branid, towering over everyone and anxious to be noticed before anyone with lesser rank, and there were all the castle children grown up. Inda recognized each instantly.

Finally, there was Whipstick, looking like a tougher, leaner version of Horsepiss Noth. "Inda." Whipstick smacked his hand to his chest. "Welcome home."

That was all, but memory came back in another wave, bringing Dogpiss' laughing face. Inda wiped his eyes, then pounded Whipstick's lean, strong shoulder.

Then they were inside, and there was food. Everyone talked at once, but Inda couldn't follow any of them because he was distracted by yet another half-familiar face, or by the way the light fell, and there was memory again. This time he was running through the house, a stolen rye biscuit in his mouth, as he raced up to the archive . . .

"Inda." Tdor's voice broke through, and he discovered he was standing in the children's old dining room. Here was the battered old table where they'd eaten. From the look of the worn mats, they still did. "We'll have the wedding tomorrow," she said from the doorway. "It's all ready. You can thank Tau for that. He knew exactly what to do. I've been busy with harvest, and we had to get everyone re-settled since Whipstick and the Riders were released from harbor duty, and it was too late to do a border ride—"

"Sorry, Tdor." Inda backed out of the room. "I'm hearing one word in five. Walk with me? I just want to look around."

Tdor glanced at that ring, and braced herself to hear what it would mean in their lives.

As they walked through the work rooms, the Iofre led Signi upstairs. "This is the heir's suite," she said, pointing. "And here is Inda's old room. I don't know where he will want to stay. For now you can have Joret's old room, which is here."

She opened the door onto a small, pleasant room whose stone walls were rendered more peach than honey-colored in the morning light. The furnishings were plain, carved with rough horse heads. Signi liked the room, and this kindly-faced older woman with Inda's eyes. She set her little bag down, and the Iofre took her down the back stairs and out on a castle tour.

By the time Tdor and Inda reached the front stairs, three Runners had nearly blundered into them, all seeking Tdor. And Inda hadn't even spoken. He was lost inside his head, just like in the old days. She turned away, issuing rapid orders.

When his reverie ended he found himself alone, unaware of the castle people ushering everyone else away on Tdor's quiet order; at least, Tdor thought with relief, Branid wasn't complaining about something.

Branid was busy with the pretty one who'd come with Inda. Dannor Tya-Vayir, a Jarl's daughter and a Jarlan in her own right, whose husband had died in the war. Pretty? She was *better* than that cold icicle Joret! Inda was obviously too stupid to notice, because everyone whispered the old one was his favorite.

Dannor had been disgusted to discover that the gorgeous Taumad had no rank, no name, nothing but his looks. She'd stayed with him just long enough to find out who was what in this family, and before the dinner bells, she'd found a chance to single Branid out.

Inda was now alone in his house.

He set his foot on the lowest step of the main stairway. Why wasn't he happier? He had everything he could possibly want. Impatient with himself, he ran up to the first landing, then halted. Should he just go to his old room? He was the heir now—except he wasn't, really. He was the Harskialdna, and Branid was the heir. Inda would have to tell him that.

He opened the door to the heir's suite, Tanrid's rooms. The outer chamber was exactly the same as it always had been: the fine wingback chairs with the claw feet that he'd thought real when he was little; the beautiful owl rug on the floor, kept away from the windows so it would not fade, and never walked on. Inda sustained a brief memory of Tanrid scrupulously stepping around it in his stable-dirty riding boots.

Inda paced the room, listening to the silence. Strange, how silences differed. Sometimes they were heavy with threat, like the silence on the sea before battle, before a storm. This silence was one of time suspended, and of absence. Tanrid wasn't here, there was no sense of him. The furniture was too old, he'd never used it.

Inda continued toward the inner chambers, wondering if the sadness sitting in his stomach like a hard knot was grief for Tanrid. There were no signs of him. Had everyone forgotten him? Inda peered into the bedroom. It was clean-swept, empty, the covered bed just a bed. Tanrid's things were gone, and he'd never had any books or papers. He'd been impatient with anything that kept him out of the stable or the practice court, or from riding the perimeter when their father permitted.

His clothes had surely gone to Branid, who was much of a size. All traditional, but Inda walked out again, head bowed.

Chapter Thirty-six

THE next morning, Tdor woke to her wedding day.

She hurried down to the baths, startled at the difference in the quality of the water and the heat. She was too busy to think about it, and ran back upstairs swiftly braiding her damp, cold hair. It was just before sunrise.

She pulled her robe around her and paused outside Inda's old room, her heart thudding. Inda himself had whispered to her before they'd parted just after midnight, "If I don't sleep soon I'll drop. Meet me in my room at breakfast."

She scratched softly, just once, then jumped when the door opened.

The smell of steeped silverleaf wafted out, bringing back a hint of summer, though here in the hall it was so cold her toes hurt on the stone, and she could faintly see her breath.

"Tdor? Come in."

He held the door wide, and she entered, seeing that he was alone, also in his night robe. The mage was nowhere in sight.

Because she would not live with any hint of deception or secrecy, she asked, "Where is Signi?"

"She went down with Mother to renew the house magic. Said it's not quite worn out, but near enough. I want to see Father, but he's apparently still asleep."

"He wakens after the sun comes up. We shifted him to an east room." Tdor forbore saying that, these days, he seldom woke even in mornings, other than to sip a little soup, a little healing brew, and then subside again into his dreams. "You said last night that you wanted to see me?"

Inda turned his thumb up. "You were so quiet during dinner. Is there—do we understand one another?" He shook his head. "I guess I wanted to talk to you. Just you. Before everyone expects us out there." He waved at the walls.

Tdor turned her gaze away from that ring on his finger to his searching brown eyes. There was pain in them; his lower lid was narrowed just as it had been in the old days, after Tanrid had thrashed him. "You wrote to me the once. After the battle. Then not again, until that note about the wedding."

"Yes," Inda said.

Tdor thought of those long weeks after that very first note, the letters ill-formed as if written by a numb hand by campfire, which reported so briefly and so baldly that Inda and the king lived. She'd had to find out from Hadand that they had won. Then nothing for long, tense weeks as they waited in the south for retaliation to come over the sea.

She said, "I wasn't sure if you didn't write because . . . there was a problem. That things had changed. Again. So much has changed! But I didn't write because of your responsibilities. I didn't want to trouble you unnecessarily."

Inda sank down onto the bed where once they had lain together so innocently. His hair was loose, falling down his back below his waist, his night robe unlaced; it did not hide the white puckers of long scars on his chest.

"Is that some kind of accusation?" he asked. "I couldn't write. You do not know what it was like." His voice cracked on the last word, ragged, husky.

She gripped her forearms, her blood cold in her veins. "Tell me."

"I hope one day to forget what it was like. It took us all night and then all day—an entire day, Tdor—to get the wounded away, and then to Disappear the dead. Everyone working. I helped as best I could, though my right hand had gone numb after the battle, and I didn't get feeling back for days."

He hesitated out of habit. With Signi he did not talk about war.

Tdor said, "Go on."

"Do you want to hear it?"

"If you want to talk about it."

He sighed. Yes. Everything had changed. Except Tdor. "I don't. But maybe if you know, the past will stay just a memory, and not come at me at night. When we came down from the cliffs, most of Noddy's and Hawkeye's men were already dead. Most! The only ones who made it through were Cama's and Cherry-Stripe's, because I had them up on the mountains."

"But it worked, right?"

"Only because the Venn left. We'd be up there now if they hadn't, Tdor, each side chewing the other to death day by day. They're hard fighters, a match for us. I keep having nightmares about two armies marching together without stopping and the bodies piling higher and higher." He shook his head and groped, his fingers opening and closing vaguely.

She hugged her arms against her.

"You were so right when you said it's not a game, Haywit."

"I was a pompous snot," she retorted.

"So you said in the royal city, but I thought about what you said all the years. It—it helped me. When I made a plan, it was because I thought you'd like it. That I was making a net. Not tearing it." He looked into her face for understanding. She looked back, a little puzzled, but waiting to hear more. "Well. The thing is, the Venn are gone north again. Evred is worried about the future. I think he can't let himself believe they're gone, though we don't think they'll be back next year." He looked inquiringly at her.

"Go on," she said.

"When I was coming down south, I got notes. In that gold box thing. Cama's in the north, d'you see? He had some trouble at first. The Idayagans thought they could attack us after the Venn left."

Tdor winced. "Will the war ever end?"

"He thrashed them hard, and they slunk off to their homes. Cama will ride around with his men on inspection, show off their numbers. Evred says we cannot let the Idayagans know just how weakened we were, or the war won't end. Now they're frightened, they think we're invincible. They seem to think I am invincible. Cama wrote that all he has to do is threaten to bring me north, and they settle down. Isn't that funny?" Inda made a peculiar grimace.

"No," Tdor said. "If it works."

"That's what I think, too. If it works. But after the battle, I just couldn't write."

"It must have been terrible for Signi," Tdor said, obliquely approaching the ring. And what marriage would mean: legally they knew their duties, and what they didn't know they'd learn. But the law said nothing about how a Jarl and Jarlan, or Randael and Randviar, or even a Harskialdna and Harandviar defined marriage in personal terms.

Inda's expression made it clear his mind was back at the battle, despite the mention of the Venn mage. "Signi won't talk about the battle. All I know is that she saw ghosts leave."

"Ghosts?"

"That's what she said. But she doesn't talk about those, either."

Tdor accepted that, and remembered her promise to herself. "You are wearing a ring."

Inda stared down at his hand as if surprised to discover it still there. "Magic rings." He lifted his hand. "Fox gave 'em to me. Evred wants me to wear it. He wears his. We can find one another. When I take up my duties in the royal city, it'll mean we can always—"

Evred's ring. I'm such a fool, she thought. There was a lot more to be defined than just Signi's place in their marriage.

A soft tap interrupted before she could think about how to begin.

Inda sprang to the door. Fareas-Iofre entered, with Signi behind her, wearing one of the women's blue robes. "Your father is breakfasting. Get dressed. Now is the time to see him."

Shortly thereafter, they walked quietly into the Adaluin's chamber. Signi effaced herself, a gesture of grace noticed only by Tdor.

Inda's father lay on his bed, white-haired, lined, and frail. His robe was clean, his hair freshly combed and tied back simply: all the signs of care by his wife and servants, though he was not always present enough to recognize them.

"Papa." Inda knelt down and took the thin hand lying loosely on the coverlet.

Jarend-Adaluin breathed deeply, but his eyes stayed closed.

"Papa, it is Inda. I am home."

No reaction, only the slow, steady breathing. Inda gently squeezed the gnarled, weathered hand lying in his so passive and childlike, remembering how it used to grip the hilt of a sword in practice early each morning, before his father went on the endless rounds of riding to protect Choraed Elgar. How strong he'd seemed. Strong, ageless, like the rocks and hills.

Inda wiped his eyes on his shoulder, then glanced at his mother, who said, "Jarend. Inda is back. The Venn are defeated."

Jarend's lips worked. He muttered something, too soft to hear. Fareas dropped down on the other side of the bed, bending close. When he muttered again, she faced them, her eyes stricken. "Pirates," she said. "And Joret."

"The pirates are gone, Father," Inda stated in a strong voice. "What Whipstick told you was true. They are gone. I defeated them."

Jarend's breathing came faster. His fingers twitched.

"They are gone," Inda repeated. "And I am here."

Jarend-Adaluin opened his eyes then. His gaze wandered vaguely until he found Inda's face. Then he focused, and his hand tightened. "Inda. You are home again. To stay?"

Inda looked to the women for clues, but they stood quietly, hands in sleeves. "I will always protect you, Father. But Evred Harvaldar made me his Harskialdna. I can ask—"

"The king honors our House." Jarend-Adaluin smiled faintly and lay back, his breathing slowing, his free hand moving restlessly over the coverlet to his side, where a sword would hang if he wore the baldric. "The king chose . . . Honor." He sighed, closing his eyes again. His breathing deepened into slumber.

"That's the most he's talked since last summer," Fareas Iofre said when they had filed outside. "He is glad you're back, my son."

"Maybe now he will regain some strength." Tdor gently closed the door.

Fareas-Iofre raised her head, listening. The sound of voices rose from the courtyard outside the window. "The people are arriving. It's time to get ready for the wedding."

They parted, the women in one direction. Inda took the long way, passing outside his brother's chamber again. The same strange sense of loss assailed him, and he stood outside the door, trying to resolve it.

But a flicker at the edge of his vision snapped him round, knives out and ready.

Branid gasped and nearly stumbled back down the stairs. His eyes widened. As Inda resheathed the knives, Branid said, "Hoo, you're fast." He glowered. "Why are you wearing weapons in your own house?"

"I wear weapons everywhere," Inda said. "Why are you lurking around like a thief?"

Branid's gaze shifted, and then the tips of his ears reddened. He couldn't believe that the beautiful Dannor Tya-Vayir, daughter of a Jarl, chose *him* to sleep with the night before. Maybe Dannor didn't want Inda because of all those scars? Or maybe that old one wouldn't share?

Branid had never gotten all the female attention first. Ever. And what a night! But—

It was strange to Inda, seeing so big a man hunch and sidle. Branid said, "I just wanted to know . . . what it was like. The battle, I mean."

Branid used the longing tone of a boy, not that of a man
who had witnessed violent death. "Bad." Inda gestured,
hand flat. "Very bad."

"We didn't see a sniff of any pirates. Or Venn. Or anything else." Branid's regret was odd. Defensive. "I've
worked hard. Learned all Whipstick's drills. I drill the men
myself, now. Just the way you learned it in the academy."

Inda's irritation vanished. For the very first time he wondered what it had been like to watch Tanrid and him go off
to the academy, especially when Inda, originally, was supposed to stay home. After Tanrid was killed, Branid was
too old and the Harskialdna had not wanted three Algara-
Vayirs, anyway.

Would Branid have turned out different if he'd gone to
the academy? It hadn't improved Horsebutt. Or Kepa.

Inda couldn't answer that, but he could do this: "Since
we're alone, let me ask you. Is your promise good?"

"What?" Branid looked affronted, his voice echoing
down the stairs to the alcove he'd shown Dannor the night
before—the place you could hear everything said in the
hall upstairs. Branid had just been showing off, but Dannor
always remembered useful information like that.

She was there now, mostly out of idle interest. She had
been debating whether she could tolerate being second
woman to a pompous duty-stick like Tdor Marth-Davan, if
she got this fool Branid to marry her, since he seemed to
be free to choose. By the end of dinner the previous
evening Dannor had figured out why the local women
avoided Branid, who had only two subjects: bragging about
himself, and whining about everyone else.

"When we were boys, you never kept promises," Inda
said. "But people change. I've changed. Have you?"

"I should hope so! Why, if it wasn't for me—"

"Then listen. Evred-Harvaldar has given me orders to
take my place as Harskialdna in the royal city."

Below, Dannor was beginning to turn away in disgust—
her weight actually shifted—when she heard Inda say, "He
agreed that when my father dies, you are to become
Adaluin."

Dannor stilled. Oh, this was far better than she could have imagined. Far, *far.*

On the landing, Branid's eyes widened with shock, then pleasure. Then narrowedwariness. "But? I can't believe you're just going to give me the title. Just like that."

"It's the king's order. Like it's his order that my children will inherit. But I'm happy with the title going to you if you promise me two things. One, you will honor my father as yours until he dies. Second, when he does, you will permit my mother to stay as senior woman. That means if you marry, my mother has to approve. And if someday my mother chooses to leave, you will see that she is able to travel wherever she wants to go."

"I promise," Branid breathed, his face so painful to see—so much longing, fear, greed, even shame.

Inda pulled the owl clasp from his hair, which fell down his back. He held out the clasp, and Branid's hand closed around it. "Then it's done."

Inda walked away before Branid could say anything. He thought about the things he'd say to Whipstick before he left, then forgot everything when he entered his room and saw the wedding shirt lying on his bed.

Tdor had made it; Inda knew it was customary for the wife to make the man's wedding shirt, to embroider it with his House device, or with things from his life, whatever her skill and patience permitted.

This shirt was covered front and back with intricate designs: ships and suns and owls and the House symbols of all Inda's Tvei friends, the lines somewhat crooked—Tdor was no needlewoman—the ships like nothing that had ever floated, but he knew as he ran his fingers over the bright lines and colors that every stitch was lovingly made.

An icy rain began to fall by midmorning.

Inda's shoulder ached, as if often did when the weather changed. He found Tau downstairs in the kitchen, which was filled with good smells. "I need your hands."

They went up to Inda's room, where he plopped into a chair and leaned his head on his hands. Tau kneaded his bad shoulder.

"Thanks for everything you did," Inda mumbled as little zings and shoots of pain, and then not-quite-pain, lessened the constant ache in his bones and shoulder socket. Maybe now he wouldn't have to wear that stupid sling at his own wedding.

"I had fun here," Tau said. "I was amazed to discover that the new cook has never made a feast for a family wedding. I find that sad."

"As sad as everything being worn out?" Inda asked. "I didn't see it yesterday. Then I was just glad that nothing had changed. But this morning, well, everything is worn through. The mats at the children's table have to be the ones my father used. I'd thought I would get me some new boots, but mine are in better shape than anyone's here. Mother's have patched toes."

"Signi has been renewing your magical spells. I came across her doing the buckets out behind the kitchen. It's like she's surrounded with the sun-glitter you see on water."

Inda sighed as Tau's strong hands moved to the muscles between his shoulder blades. "Thank you for taking on Dannor. Keeping her out of the way. She invited herself along, and I couldn't figure out how to say no. Soon's we were inside the gate, I could see that Tdor didn't want her here."

"I did my best, though it wasn't long. You should have seen how fast she dropped me when she discovered I had no rank or relation to anyone with rank." Tau shook his head. Dannor was the closest he'd ever met to the terrible Coco on Gaffer Walic's pirate ship—not the taste for blood, but the utter lack of conscience. Well, at least Branid seemed to like her, which kept her out of Inda's way.

"Tau. Are you coming to the royal city with me? You don't have to be a Runner if you don't want to. I can keep those two King's Runners Vedrid assigned me. Turns out Fiam, who was supposed to be my Runner, didn't like the knife training, and he's going to be the house steward."

"Yes, I taught him something about scent packets, and a few tricks for protecting old linens, like ribbon hems to make them last. It amuses me how many of my mother's lessons—all deeply resented as worthless, you understand—I've been teaching people hither and yon." Tau worked the muscle at the base of Inda's skull as he considered what to say about the royal city.

"I think—I think you did Evred some good. Back in Ala Larkadhe. You're right about him being taut as a bowstring." Inda breathed deeply, half ready to fall asleep.

Tau smiled at the thought of Evred taut as a bowstring. Tau knew his response to Evred was complicated, and could be dangerous—but oh, the temptation to . . . civilize a king was devastatingly seductive.

He thumped Inda lightly. "There goes the summons bell."

The wedding was held in the great hall, as rain was falling hard by noon. Below the family banners hung garlands made of ribbon-tied blossoms, all bound with ivy. Tau's contribution was bunches of fragrant herbs.

The best beeswax candles—also dipped with herbs—glowed warmly over everyone's House robes and tunics, hiding threadbare patches and striking highlights in silver embroidery. In that warm, golden, faintly glistening light everyone and everything looked its best.

Inda and Tdor stood side-by-side and made their vows before all their dependents, the chief men and women of the closest trade towns, and as many Fera-Vayir cousins as could make it in time. Standing just behind her supposed old friend Tdor was Dannor Tya-Vayir. It so happened that her place as guest put her next to Branid Algara-Vayir in his green-and-silver House tunic, the silver owl clasp binding up his hair. She smiled at him every time he happened to glance sideways.

He glanced a lot.

The vows were the solemn part. Tdor dug her nails into

her palm once, trying to make a memory. She was afraid the entire day would vanish like a dream, it seemed so unreal.

That was until she reminded herself she had to leave. She would be taking up duties as defender of the royal castle. It was good work . . .

But it was not Castle Tenthen. It was not home.

She closed that acknowledgment away, keeping the hurt private. No one must ever know—to all, including Fareas-Iofre, she was full of pride and expectation. Any other woman would trade places with her in a heartbeat. She would now be the most important woman in the kingdom next to the queen, beside whom she'd been raised as a sister.

Inda also felt unreal. The last Marlovan wedding he'd attended had been when he was eleven, when their academy tutor, Master Gand, married and moved away as Randael to a northern castle. He remembered being aghast that a master would marry. He had known even less about politics than he had about sex in those days.

As the Runners carried the trays in, and the hand drums came out, Inda remembered himself and the other children running round the perimeter of the room, trying to pinch extra lemon cakes. Just as at that wedding, the adults passed from hand to hand the flat open-flower wine cups full of hot spiced wine. One after another they called out toasts and drank, most speaking the ancient witticisms that were pointless to children but carried double meaning so funny to the teens.

Then: "Dance, dance!"

Flushing—almost unrecognizable—Tdor moved out in her new green-and-silver over-robe, flowers bound on her head, and took her place in the center of the inner ring of married women, the outer ring of single girls and women.

Drums and cymbals started the thump and ching in counterpoint, and people sang "Green Grows the Ivy" as the women wound round and round, Tdor leading.

Then it was the men's turn. Inda grinned stupidly, wondering why he'd forgotten to practice, but then the men's

circle dances were so easy, variations on the sword dance:
Stamp stamp, whirl, kick, whirl, clap clap, leap. High smack
of the opposite man's hand against yours. And then onward, as the drums raced through the gallop, gradually
picking up the tempo until men began to stumble, trip, or
just bow out. Incomprehensible until just a few years ago
was the old saying, "Married man who lasts out the Ivy
Dance lasts out the night!" It was silly—everyone knew
that—but Inda did his best, until only he and Tau and two
of the younger Riders from the outer ring were dancing,
and when Inda stumbled, Tau pretended to trip, and sat
down with Inda, laughing.

Inda could see how popular Tau had become, but he
could also see from Tau's smile, his flow of witty jokes, that
once again, Tau was playing a part. Tenthen wasn't his
home. It was another stage for his life's play.

The unmarried girls danced a ring dance next, many eyeing the young fellows speculatively. And vice versa when
the unmarried fellows took their turn.

The men brought out the swords next, to general acclaim, and this time the drums rumbled in the 5/4 rhythm
as men leaped, clashed, posed, whirled. Leaped, and clash,
clash, ring!

Signi watched it all from a corner seat. Fareas-Iofre had
meant to look out for her, but she was far too busy acting
as hostess, and because no one knew Signi, she was left to
herself.

It was Tdor who noticed her sitting alone at the very end
table where the children had been. At the other end of the
room, Inda was deep in conversation with Whipstick and
Branid. *I thought Inda's ring was something he shared with
her, and so I made myself jealous. The most unworthy, useless, and painful emotion there is. And totally unnecessary,*
Tdor thought, and crossed the room to join Signi.

"I remember you were trained in dance," Tdor said. "Are
our dances pleasing to the eye, or just strange?"

"Ah, all dance is good." Signi smiled up at her.

Tdor dropped down on the mat beside Signi and pulled
off her flower garland, which had begun to itch her scalp

mercilessly. She turned it around and around in her hands.
"But Venn court dance is very different, is it not? Hadand
looked it up and wrote to me about it. It's a lot like a play,
she said. Each gesture holds meaning. Levels of meaning,
even. I'm afraid ours must seem fairly simple."

"No, all dance tells a story." Signi extended a hand
toward the young girls. "See? They tell the story of
courtship, of hope. They may not have great skill, but their
youth gives them beauty."

Tdor leaned back with her elbows on the low table,
watching robes swirling against shapely young bodies,
laughing looks cast backward, neatly booted feet tapping,
flower-tucked braids swinging. "And the men?"

"Ah, theirs is so different. Some is courtship and desire,
some—" She pursed her lips.

"The sword dances aren't."

"They are challenges, to one another. They play war.
Sometimes they play sex and war."

"And they don't up north?"

"Yes, they do there too, though perhaps in different
ways." Signi looked troubled.

Across the room, Inda—flushed and laughing the way
they saw so rarely—said, "Come on, Tau!"

"Not here—"

"Someone has to uphold sailors' honor. Can't be me. I
always fumble the steps!"

Tdor had it on her lips to ask about the battlefield—if
Signi truly saw ghosts—but the melancholy quirk to the
woman's eyes, her pensive almost smile, made her hesitant.

The men shouted approval, and most of the women took
it up. The drums tapped a new rhythm, and Signi smiled.
"Ah! You must watch. Tau will dance a sailor dance. He is
quite good. His dance story is to seduce every watcher by
making them feel beautiful and desirable."

Taumad moved out to the center, laughing back at Inda,
and put one hand up, one at his waist, to begin an old Sartoran step-dance that had become popular on the decks of
ships all over the south, mostly because you could do it in
a small space. Many of the girls grabbed up drums and

rumbled up a stirring counterpoint, trying to catch his eye. He managed to flirt with every single one of them before he twirled to a graceful finish amid laughter and clapping.

Signi chuckled. "He will not sleep alone tonight, that one."

Tdor did not hear. Her ear, always sensitive to the atmosphere, caught Dannor's light, cruel laugh. Liet—who could be bossy—and a couple of newly married Riders' wives were flushed and uncertain, Dannor smirking in the way Tdor had hated ever since she was fifteen.

Tdor said, of a sudden, "Will you dance for me?"

Signi turned her head, searching Tdor's face, and Tdor waited, holding her breath, afraid she had trespassed.

But whatever the mage saw did not affront her, and she said, "I will."

Tdor got to her feet. "Silence," she said, turning around, but her gaze rested on Dannor. "Our guest from foreign lands is going to dance for us. Dag Signi, do you need a beat?"

"No drums." Signi moved to the center of the room.

For a short time she just stood in the center of the room, a small, compact figure with flyaway sandy hair, humming beneath her breath, and swaying gently, so that the hem of her blue robe brushed the tops of feet they saw were bare, her slippers placed neatly beside her mat.

Then she turned in a slow circle, her hands rising, palms up. The robe flared, revealing the plain linen gown beneath.

She danced in silence, at least most thought so, but the front spectators heard her humming in a soft voice that wasn't particularly musical. It was her movements, so fluid, so flowing, like water down a mountain or widening in a pool, that became conduits to vision. You were not seeing a small, plain woman dancing alone on the great stone flags, but youth, and summer days, and the long bonds of friendship and faithfulness.

But she was not done. She whirled and leaped across the floor in a startling change, evoking the horse and rider on the charge: the dash and valor of battle. The dread and clash of wills as well as swords and lances, and then, and then, she stood in the center again, arms raised, muscles articulating an agony of grief so expressive that throats tightened as muscles remembered private griefs. She threw back her head, mouth open as if uttering a long, wrenching howl.

Many wept, and Tdor, wiping her eyes, thought, *Oh, what have I done?*

But Signi had not finished.

She raised her arms again, and this time leaped, light as a drifting leaf, her wrists arched and airy as she scudded in a circle with the freedom of a childhood dance. Hearts lifted with remembered joy as Signi mimed the bonds of childhood. Her arms circled, her head canted, and there was a mother holding her baby; her shoulder led as she bent, and there was a young father teaching his son to walk. And then the child grew, and with a flirt of hip and a curling of fingers she danced the entrancing magic of attraction, miming the young who look on one another with the gleaming smile of spring.

Tau's dance had been unabashedly sexy, but this dance celebrated love—all the forms of love, transcending the physical and emotional into the upward-yearning realm of the spirit.

When Signi finished she bowed her head and folded her hands into peace mode, and people laughed, talked, exclaimed. Dannor smiled at Branid, who turned anxiously Inda's way as if to get a cue to how he should be feeling. The mulling rods were then brought out, and the sweet, heady scent of warmed spiced wine filled the air as everyone shared the wedding cups.

And at last the midnight bells rang, and Signi wasn't there. Inda, befuddled with wine and tiredness, met Tdor's gaze. He saw the invitation there, the faint pucker of question in her straight brow, and the profound tenderness that had overwhelmed him at the first sight of his wedding shirt seized him anew.

"Will you come to my bed?" she asked, holding out her hand.

Inda took her hand, and it was not the slim child's hand he had remembered from childhood, capable and square. Her hand was nearly the size of his—not as broad, but her fingers were long, her palm rough as all Marlovan women's were, her clasp steady.

Her room was unchanged from what he remembered in childhood. It confused him. He looked around at the familiar objects as if all were new, and then back at Tdor, who let go of his fingers and gripped her forearms.

He smiled and took a turn around the room. "All those years. I saw you as I left you. I even talked to you in my head. You were my guide. But you didn't change."

"I grew up." Her smile was crooked. "Same as you did."

"I know." He made a helpless gesture.

"Inda. Once before we tried to lie together. Do you remember? I think you were nine, and I was ten, almost eleven, and thought myself so wise."

"You were always wise," he said, laughter smoothing his face beneath those terrible scars.

"I was always curious. And far too bossy." Her fingers trembled, but she stilled them as she shed her robe, and then loosened her shirt laces. "I think we might try again. And if nothing happens, well, then we'll have a pleasant nap, just like we did that time."

Inda grinned. It was not the grin of a ten-year-old boy.

The warmth of his grin tingled through her, intensifying at the sight of those broad, powerful shoulders as he carefully lifted his wedding shirt over his head.

Sex had always been a duty for her. A sensible person saw to the needs of the body, so she had been raised. But though she had earnestly sought enlightenment in the matter of sex, she'd never felt what the songs had talked about, and she'd concluded that she wouldn't. It was the way she was made.

Then Inda had come back, both alien and dear, grown yet still so much like the boy she'd known from babyhood. For the first time, the fires within had lit for her. But he'd had to go off to war.

He stood naked before she did. He unclasped his hair,

braiding it swiftly; her heartbeat quickened as his gaze drifted down her length, a slow gaze of appreciation.

He held out his hands.

"You're grown up." His fingers caressed her cheek, and then stroked lightly down the contours of her body, his hands warm and lingering.

Her heartbeat thundered in her ears.

"You look so strong." He buried his face in her neck.

"I am strong." She gave in to impulse at last, pressing a light kiss over the scar just below the hollow of his throat. "I am very strong." And she was. For the very first time, the strength of need and promise and desire beat power through her veins, and she laughed, and reached for him. "Come see how strong I am," she whispered, pulling him down beside her.

Signi was wrong about Tau. He stood up on the tower under the sentry roof, watching the torchlight gleam through the sleeting rain, and then he tried one more time with his golden case:

> *Jeje: I am alive. Inda is alive—and married. I suspect his great day is over, and he will settle into the royal city, training boys for the possibility of glory, and that it is time for me to invent another amusement besides watching greatness in action.*
>
> *But because I'm drunk, I keep thinking. Does anyone, outside of madmen and kings, ever perceive his own greatness? What defines greatness, anyway, other than being the one who forces people and events to change whether they will or no? Inda does not see himself as a figure of history, but neither does he see himself as others see him: Fox who wishes to be him, Evred who wishes to possess him, and Signi who wishes to change him.*
>
> *Once, never mind when, I realized I have no driving purpose. Now that I am suffering under the so-called*

wisdom of wine fumes, I wonder if this is why I seem to be drawn to those who do have driving purposes.

Enough, enough. You have never answered me, and I believe this shall be my last time shouting into the wind. If you are well, stay well, and smile when you think of me.

He shoved it into the case without reading it over. He suspected that if he were sober, he'd throw it into the fire. But he was drunk, and so he tapped out the pattern that had become so familiar, and off his fool letter went into the void.

Then he trod downstairs to fall into bed.

But halfway down the stairs he felt, at last, the tap of an answer. His heart thumped with joy as he sat on a stair under a sconced torch and opened the case.

And there were the rounded, careful letters that Inda had taught Jeje to use so long ago, when they were in prison during Khanerenth's civil war:

I didn't write before because I didn't know if my plan would work. Or even if it was a good plan. But you'll have to decide, because I've found your mother.

Coming in August 2009
A DAW Books Hardcover

The Final Novel of Inda's Epic Story:

TREASON'S SHORE

Sherwood Smith

Read on for a sneak preview.

THE docks in Bren Harbor were deserted except for the roaming patrols of guards, all fully armed. On every single rooftop along the quay—warehouses, stores, taverns—guards roosted in the cold, snowy weather, bows to hand, and a cache of arrows apiece.

Behind windows, people watched. They speculated to no purpose, worried, cursed, laughed, laid bets. Others threw up their hands and went on with their lives, some with a pirate-thumping weapon ready to hand, just in case.

The sinister black pirate trysail floated in the middle of the harbor, its consorts at either side, crews (at least a hundred spyglasses made certain) ready to flash sail at word or sign from the lone red-haired figure, dressed all in black, lounging on the captain's deck.

Through an entire day the spyglasses stayed trained on that ship. Not long after nightfall, a stir at the main dock brought word relayed up to the watch commander: "Woman wants to hire a boat to take her out to the pirate."

"What? This I have to witness."

Jeje never saw Barend. As soon as she returned from her interview, she skinned out of the fancy clothes, rolled them up into a ball (with some regret treating silk with so little respect) and shoved them into her bag. She got into her sailor gear, pulled on the shapeless wool hat hanging by the door for everyone to use when going into the small truck garden. Always scrupulous (according to her lights) Jeje left her old knit sock cap in its place—too obviously a sailor's cap. Then she hefted her new gear bag and under cover of darkness slipped through the garden, over the back fence, through another garden, and into the street, walking anonymously past the patrolling guards.

She had spent the night at Chim's, as the weather had turned too rough for rowing out into the harbor. Then there was the matter of the King's Guard having the entire harbor locked down. Chim sent word to a couple of his more trusty watermen to be standing by when Jeje reached the first perimeter.

"Who are you? Where are you going?" the sentry captain asked.

"I want to hire a boat." Jeje poked a thumb toward the hire craft floating at the dock. "Get back on board."

"On board what?"

"My ship."

"Which would be?"

She hesitated. By now she was surrounded. In the lantern light, naked swords gleamed. Not the time to be mouthy. "My ship's out there on the water—"

"Look at this," one interrupted, pointing under the terrible hat, where her ruby glittered in the lantern light. "She's gotta be the pirate Jeje. I think you better get the Commander."

"I'm not a pirate." At the various shufflings, shiftings, and snortings of disbelief, Jeje sighed. "Look, no one wants any trouble. I just want to get back on deck. Princess Kliessin already interviewed me yesterday," she added.

The mention of the princess caused more looks and shuffles, then someone sent someone else loping off into the darkness as the warriors closed in around her, standing within sword length.

They stood like that, no one talking (Jeje wondering if

she'd start a war if she asked the one who'd been eating fried onions not to stand on her toes), until the approach of running feet broke the circle. A tall, strong man with grizzled hair marched up. This just had to be the watch commander.

"You belong to yon pirate?" he asked.

"Yes." That was simplest. "I've been acting as envoy," Jeje said. "Saw the princess yesterday. Now I'm supposed to report back." She jerked her mittened thumb toward the *Death*.

Heads snapped seaward, then back. Another day she'd remember that and laugh. Now she just stood there, jaw jutted, feet planted, arms crossed, mittened hands gripping her knife hilts.

"Send her." The commander waved, his attitude adding *good riddance*.

Chim's watermen appeared as if by magic, and Jeje, recognizing them, said loudly, "Got a boat I can hire?"

"Right at the dock," was the answer, hint hint, wink wink.

The commander rolled his eyes at this lumbering attempt at covert communication. If these people were sophisticated international spies, he was a Venn. "Row her out, and *you*'ll report back to me before you run off to Chim," he added grimly, causing the would-be secret emissaries to deflate a little.

On board the *Death*, Fox had posted sharp eyes at the mastheads, watching the coast as steadily as it watched him. He'd expected someone to row out and demand his business; the long wait made him wonder what was going on inside the city. He was considering whom to send when, at last, a boat set out from the main dock, lanterns aswing at every heave of the oars.

"I think that's Jeje," Mutt yelled, his voice cracking. He was acting as lookout, and as captain of the foremast bow team. And then a triumphant aside to one of his cronies on the mizzen-mast, "Nugget's gonna be *fried* she wasn't here t'see her first."

"She's too busy showing off for Cap'n Eflis," came the hoarse reply.

Mutt scowled into the darkness.

Below, Fox was quite able to hear the sotto voce conversation going on over his head, but the time for absolute silence had passed. And Mutt of course had known that very well.

So Fox snapped out his glass, satisfied himself that this was indeed Jeje on her way through the night-black, icy waters. He said, "Signal the captains of *Cocodu* and *Rapier.*"

Then he returned to his cabin for the first time since dawn, and sat down at the desk. Two movements were habitual: with one hand he reached for the desk drawer containing the gilt-edged black book, and with the other he touched the golden case. When his fingers tingled on contact with the gold, he shoved the drawer shut again. After months without any message, it seemed Inda had remembered someone besides his damned Montrei-Vayirs.

Fox, what are you doing in Bren?

Fox eyed the large, scrawling letters. Of course it could be Inda's fingers were almost as numb as Fox's were now, but Fox read anger in those sloppy letters, and laughed. "I don't yet know, but you're not going to find that out," he said aloud.

Inda deserved to sweat. How stupid he was, to even consider throwing away ten generations of pirate treasure on those fool Montrei-Vayirs, whose own stupidity had run the kingdom aground in the first place.

Fox warmed his fingers over a candle, dashed off an answer, and tossed the golden case back onto the desk as Jeje's boat thumped up against the hull. On deck he discovered the older crewmates surrounding Jeje, some pounding her on the back, everyone talking at once.

Well aware of the spyglasses trained on them from the shore, Fox flicked a drifting snowflake from his arm and said, "Come into the cabin." And as soon as the door was shut, "Why did you leave Inda?"

"To find Tau's mother." Jeje glared around the cabin.

Looking for signs of Inda, perhaps? No, Inda had never left any signs of habitation anywhere he'd lived, and she'd know that. Disapproving of the row of books on the carved shelf? The golden Colendi gondola-lamps, or the astonishing silk wall hanging of raptors taking flight in the pale shades of dawn? All legitimate pirate loot.

Jeje eyed Fox's smile as he dropped onto his chair and propped a booted foot on the edge of the table. A knife hilt gleamed in the boot top, winking with golden highlights as the beautiful lamp swung forward, back.

"Well?" she said finally. "I'm waiting for your usual nasty remark about Tau. Or his mother."

"Don't tell me," he said derisively. "She's a long-lost princess."

Jeje almost laughed out loud. Fox was interested. Despite himself. She thought about what she'd discovered, and decided he'd have to ask. "No. That is, long-lost yes, princess, no. So where's *Vixen*, and who's in charge?"

"Right now, Nugget—"

"She's alive?"

"Showed up in Parayid. All but one arm. Instead, you might say, she'd armed herself with the conviction she was now everyone's responsibility to protect and defend." His smile turned nasty. "I've been thrashing that out of her since summer. Now she's teaching herself to move around the rigging, either to impress Eflis, or to show me up. Maybe both."

From outside boat calls:

"Boats, hai!"

"*Cocodu!*"

"*Rapier!*"

Dasta and Gillor had arrived from their ships.

Jeje turned her attention back to Fox. "She's playing in the rigging on *Vixen?*"

"No. Maybe. After she and two loudmouths rerig the scout, and finish with some sail shifting practice." A snort of laughter. "She'll be back in time for dawn drill. It's for backchat on deck. We had a little brush with some of Boruin's former friends just off her old lair east of Danai, and Nugget acquitted herself so well she's got lippy." Fox shook with silent laughter as he glanced over his shoulder.

Jeje grinned. *Good for you, Nugget.* She hopped to the stern window and peered through the drifts of fog. The *Vixen* was only a faint silhouette, just emerging from the island's lee side, sails shifting with commendable speed. It would be a while before it tacked across the harbor.

Jeje fought off the strong surge of longing to see her scout again, and drew in a grateful breath of brine air, loving even the tangs of wood-mold and slushy ice and a trace of hemp. No better smell in all the world.

The cabin door banged open and there were Dasta and Gillor, looking tough and weathered. *I wonder if I look land-soft to them*, she thought, then leaped up, laughing, to find herself squeezed in a rib-creaking hug by Dasta, and then by Gillor. Laughing questions—half-answers—a sudden, sharp, "Where's Tcholan?" to be reassured by, "He's in command of the blockade—guarding one end, and Eflis at the other. Even a floating plank won't get past those two."

Fox cut through the chatter. "Jeje was in the middle of her report when you interrupted. Do continue, whenever they will let you."

Gillor snorted and dropped onto the bench, Dasta preferring to lean against a bulkhead where he could see everyone.

Jeje smacked her hands together. "So good to be back! I hate land."

Dasta ducked his head, making a sympathetic gesture. "But you went to help Inda."

"She went," Fox drawled, "to discover Taumad's mysterious heritage. And seems to have found his mother. Behold my curiosity."

Gillor snorted even louder, though Dasta thought, *I'll wager anything that for once he's telling the truth.*

Gillor said to Jeje, "Was it true pirates got her?"

"One of Marshig's gang was holding Parayid. Got bored waiting for battle. Wanted to burn the town down for fun. She offered to trade herself for leaving the town be. Which is why Parayid was only partially destroyed, unlike some of the other harbors."

Dasta looked disgusted. "So she's now a Coco?"

Fox's brows rose in satirical question.

"Not her! That is, she agreed to be the captain's favorite, but just for a while. She hated the captain's habits of carving up crewmembers who'd made him mad. She asked him not to. When he wouldn't stop, she organized a mutiny. Wasn't hard, she said."

Gillor whooped for joy. "So she's a pirate captain? Why didn't we hear about her?"

"Because she isn't any more."